Lecture Notes in Computer Science 10542

Commenced Publication in 1973
Founding and Former Series Editors:
Gerhard Goos, Juris Hartmanis, and Jan van Leeuwen

More information about this series at http://www.springer.com/series/7411

Essaid Sabir · Ana García Armada
Mounir Ghogho · Mérouane Debbah (Eds.)

Ubiquitous Networking

Third International Symposium, UNet 2017
Casablanca, Morocco, May 9–12, 2017
Revised Selected Papers

Springer

Editors
Essaid Sabir
ENSEM, Hassan II University of Casablanca
Casablanca
Morocco

Ana García Armada
Universidad Carlos III de Madrid
Madrid
Spain

Mounir Ghogho
International University of Rabat, Morocco, and University of Leeds, UK
Leeds
UK

Mérouane Debbah
CentraleSupélec LANEAS
Gif-sur-Yvette
France

ISSN 0302-9743 ISSN 1611-3349 (electronic)
Lecture Notes in Computer Science
ISBN 978-3-319-68178-8 ISBN 978-3-319-68179-5 (eBook)
https://doi.org/10.1007/978-3-319-68179-5

Library of Congress Control Number: 2017958827

LNCS Sublibrary: SL5 – Computer Communication Networks and Telecommunications

Printed on acid-free paper

This Springer imprint is published by Springer Nature
The registered company is Springer International Publishing AG
The registered company address is: Gewerbestrasse 11, 6330 Cham, Switzerland

About the UNet Conference Series

The International Conference on Ubiquitous Networking (UNet) is an international scientific event that highlights new trends and findings in hot topics related to ubiquitous computing/networking. Ubiquitous networks sustain the development of numerous paradigms/technologies such as distributed ambient intelligence, context-awareness, cloud computing, wearable devices, and future mobile networking (e.g., B4G and 5G). Various domains are then impacted by such a system, for example, security and monitoring, energy efficiency and environment protection, e-health, precision agriculture, intelligent transportation, home-care (e.g., for elderly and disabled people), etc. Communication in such a system has to cope with many constraints (e.g., limited capacity resources, energy depletion strong fluctuations of traffic, real-time paradigm, dynamic network topology, radio link breakage, interferences, etc.) and has to meet the new application requirements. Ubiquitous systems bring many promising paradigms aiming to deliver significantly higher capacity to meet the huge growth of mobile data traffic and to accommodate efficiently dense and ultra-dense systems. A crucial challenge is that ubiquitous networks should be engineered to better support existing and emerging applications including broadband multimedia, machine-to-machine applications, Internet of Things, sensor networks, and RFID technologies. Many of these systems require stringent quality-of-service (QoS) including better latency, reliability, higher spectral and energy efficiency, but also some quality-of-experience and quality-of-context constraints.

The main purpose of this conference is to serve as a forum that brings together researchers and practitioners from academia and industry to discuss recent developments in pervasive and ubiquitous networks. This conference will provide a forum to exchange ideas, discuss solutions, debate identified challenges, and share experiences among researchers and professionals. UNet also aims to promote the adoption of new methodologies and to provide the participants with advanced and innovative tools able to catch the fundamental dynamics of the underlying complex interactions (e.g., game theory, mechanism design theory, learning theory, SDR platforms, etc.). Papers describing original research on both theoretical and practical aspects of pervasive computing and future mobile computing (e.g., LTE-A, LTE-B, 5G, IoT) were invited for submission to UNet 2017.

Welcome Message from the UNet 2017 Chairs

It is our pleasure to welcome you to the proceedings of the 2017 edition of the International Symposium on Ubiquitous Networking, UNet 2017. The conference was held in the city of Casablanca, Morocco, during May 9–12, following up on the success of past editions. Morocco boasts a growing and active community of networking researchers and the choice of Casablanca for UNet 2017 allowed its attendees, coming from all parts of the globe, to interact in a fascinating environment.

The growth of pervasive and ubiquitous networking in the past few years has been unprecedented. Today, a significant portion of the world's population is connected to the Internet most of the time through smart phones, while the Internet of Things promises to broaden the impact of the Internet to encompass devices ranging from electric appliances and medical devices to unmanned vehicles. The goal of UNet is to be a premier forum for discussing technical challenges and solutions related to such a widespread adoption of networking technologies, including broadband multimedia, machine-to-machine applications, Internet of Things, sensor networks, and RFID technologies. Toward this aim, we organize four main technical tracks of papers covering all the aspects of ubiquitous networks.

The UNet 2017 program featured four special talks addressed by distinguished keynote speakers: Prof. George K. Karagiannidis from the University of Thessaloniki (Greece), Prof. Sofie Pollin from KU Leuven/ESAT/TELEMIC (Belgium), Prof. Liuqing Yang from Colorado State University (USA), and Prof. Halim Yanikomeroglu from Carleton University (Canada). Three tutorials on Backhaul/Fronthaul for 5G heterogeneous networks, on IoT for smart cities and on the most recent efforts in 5G area were also scheduled; they were delivered by Prof. Mohamed-Slim Alouini from KAUST (Saudi Arabia), Prof. Muhammad Zeeshan Shakir from the University of West Scotland (UK), Prof. Antonio J. Jara from the University of Applied Sciences (Western Switzerland), and Prof. Mehdi Bennis from Oulu University (Finland). This year, UNet was co-located with the IEEE 5G Summit Casablanca led by Prof. Latif Ladid (founder and chair of the IPv6 Forum and the 5G World Alliance, University of Luxembourg), Prof. Essaid Sabir (ENSEM, Hassan II University of Casablanca), and Prof. Mounir Ghogho (UIR Rabat-Morocco; University of Leeds, UK) exhibiting the new trends and research efforts, as well as the latest industrial innovations in 5G networks.

This new edition of the UNet conference series boasted a rich program that reflects the most recent advances in ubiquitous computing, involving a broad range of theoretical tools (e.g., game theory, mechanism design theory, learning theory, etc.) and practical methodologies (e.g., SDR/SDN platforms, Embedded systems, etc.) to study modern technologies (e.g., LTE-A, LTE-B, 5G, IoT).

We are very grateful to our technical sponsors, without whom UNet 2017 would not have been viable. We would like to thank Springer, IPv6 Forum, 5G World Alliance, IEEE Internet of Things, and IEEE Big Data. Among our Moroccan collaborators, we are especially thankful to the Hassan II University of Casablanca, ENSEM, FSTM, and ESTC for hosting and co-organizing this exciting event. We are also very thankful to all our sponsors and patrons (ANRT, CNRST, CN&S, National Instruments, MasterTec, SERDILAB, VOCALCOM, etc.)

May 2017

M. Ghogho
M. Debbah
M. Sadik
A. Badri

Welcome Message from the TPC Chairs

It is with great pleasure that we welcome you to the proceedings of the 2017 International Symposium on Ubiquitous Networking (UNet 2017) held in Casablanca, Morocco. The symposium comprised an interesting technical program of four technical tracks reporting on recent advances in context-awareness, autonomy paradigms, mobile edge networking, virtualization, ubiquitous Internet of Things and discussing the enablers, the challenges, and the applications of ubiquitous communications and networking in today's contexts as well as those of the future. UNet 2017 also featured: four keynote speeches by world-class experts; three tutorials covering the new trends and the research and industrial efforts in 5G, Internet of Things, next-generation fronthauling/backhauling, and software-defined networking; and two invited papers sessions.

We have received 127 paper submissions from 18 countries and four continents. From these, 51 were accepted as main track papers and five additional papers were accepted as invited session papers after a careful review process to be included in the UNet 2017 proceedings. The overall acceptance rate for UNet 2017 was 40%.

The preparation of this excellent program would not have been possible without the dedication and the hard work of the different Chairs, the Keynote speakers, the Tutorial speakers, and all THE Technical Program Committee members and reviewers. We take this opportunity to acknowledge their valuable work and sincerely thank them for their help in ensuring that UNet 2017 will be remembered as a high-quality event.

We hope that you will enjoy this edition's proceedings.

May 2017

E. Sabir
A. Armada
R. El-Azouzi
M. Benjillali
S. Lasaulce
F. De Pellegrini

Organization

Technical Program Committee

Mojtaba Aajami	Yonsei University, Korea
Taufik Abrão	State University of Londrina, Brazil
Mohamed-Slim Alouini	KAUST, Saudi Arabia
Tansu Alpcan	The University of Melbourne, Australia
Eitan Altman	Inria Sophia Antipolis, France
Said Andaloussi	Hassan II University of Casablanca, Morocco
Angelos Antonopoulos	Telecommunications Technological Centre of Catalonia, Spain
Yacine Atif	College of Information Technology, UAE University, Al-Ain, United Arab Emirates
Elarbi Badidi	College of Information Technology, UAE University, Al-Ain, United Arab Emirates
Abdelmajid Badri	FSTM, Hassan II University of Casablanca, Morocco
Gaurav Bansal	Toyota InfoTechnology Center, USA
Haythem Bany Salameh	Yarmouk University, Irbid, Jordan
Stylianos Basagiannis	United Technologies Research Centre, Cork, Ireland
Paolo Bellavista	University of Bologna, Italy
Yann Ben Maissa	INPT, Rabat, Morocco
Jalel Ben Othmane	University of Paris 13, France
Yahya Benkaouz	FSR, Mohammed V University of Rabat, Morocco
Mehdi Bennis	Centre of Wireless Communications, University of Oulu, Finland
Ana Bernardos	Universidad Politecnica de Madrid, Spain
Nik Bessis	Edge Hill University, UK
Md Zakirul Alam Bhuiyan	Fordham University, New York, USA
Andrew Blaich	Lookout Security, USA
Gennaro Boggia	Politecnico di Bari, Italy
Eleonora Borgia	IIT-CNR, Italy
Noureddine Boudriga	Sup'COM, Cartage University, Tunisia
Olivier Brun	Laboratoire d'Analyse et d'Architecture des Systemes, Toulouse, France
Bin Cao	Harbin Institute of Technology Shenzhen, P.R. China
Chung Shue Chen	Bell Labs, Nokia, Nozay, France
Yan Chen	University of Electronic Science and Technology of China, Chengdu, P.R. China
Satish Chikkagoudar	Pacific Northwest National Laboratory, USA
Raphael Couturier	University of Franche-Comte, France

Samson Lasaulce	CNRS - Supelec, Gif-sur-Yvette, France
Yee Wei Law	University of South Australia, Mawson Lakes, Australia
Gyu Myoung Lee	Liverpool John Moores University, UK
Jeremie Leguay Huawei	Technologies, France Research Center, Paris, France
Xinrong Li	University of North Texas, Denton, USA
Zihuai Lin	University of Sydney, Australia
Marco Listanti	University of Rome La Sapienza, Italy
Francesco Longo	Università di Messina, Italy
Valeria Loscrí	Inria Lille-Nord Europe, France
Abdallah Makhoul	University of Franche-Comté, France
Taras Maksymyuk	Korea University, Korea
Mohammad Matin	Universiti Teknologi Brunei, Brunei Darussalam
Rick McGeer	US Ignite, Orinda, USA
Daniel Sadoc Menasché	Federal University of Rio de Janeiro, Brazil
Lynda Mokdad	University of Paris-Est, France
Mort Naraghi-Pour	Louisiana State University, Baton Rouge, USA
Husnu Narman	Clemson University, USA
Septimiu Nechifor	Siemens SRL, Romania
Alexis Olivereau	CEA, LIST, Gif-sur-Yvette, France
Al-Sakib Khan Pathan	Southeast University, Bangladesh
Shashikant Patil	SVKMs NMiMS Mumbai, India Amalner Maharashtra, India
Marcin Piotr Pawłowski	Jagiellonian University, Poland
Thinagaran Perumal	University Putra Malaysia, Serdang, Malaysia
Khalid Rahhali	Mohamed V University, Rabat, Morocco
Imane Rahmouni	LIMS, FSDM, Sidi Mohamed Ben Abdallah University, Fez, Morocco
Fernando Ramirez-Mireles	Instituto Tecnologico Autonomo, Mexico City, Mexico
Shahid Raza	SICS Swedish ICT, Kista, Sweden
Mounir Rifi	ESTC, Hassan II University of Casablanca, Morocco
Joel Rodrigues	National Institute of Telecommunications, Santa Rita do Sapucaí, Brazil
Carlos Rolim	Federal University of Rio Grande do Sul, Brazil
Yassine Rouichek	University of Technology of Belfort Montbelliard, France
Giuseppe Ruggeri	University of Reggio Calabria, Italy
Rachid Saadane	Ecole Hassania des Travaux Publiques, Casablanca, Morocco
Essaid Sabir	ENSEM, Hassan II University of Casablanca, Morocco
Sergio Saponara	University of Pisa, Italy
Alonso Silva Bell Labs	Nozay, France
Dhananjay Singh	Hankuk University of Foreign Studies, Korea
Houbing Song	West Virginia University, Montgomery, USA
Susanna Spinsante	Università Politecnica delle Marche, Ancona, Italy
Razvan Stanica	INSA Lyon, Villeurbanne, France
Theodoros Tsiftsis	Nazarbayev University, Astana, Kazakhstan

Bruno Tuffin	Inria Rennes - Bretagne Atlantique, France
Félix Villanueva	University of Castilla-La Mancha, Ciudad Real, Spain
Yunsheng Wang	Kettering University, Flint, USA
Yiran Xu	Utah State University, McLean, USA
Zakaria Ye	University of Avignon, France
Huiyue Yi	Shanghai Research Center for Wireless Communications, P.R. China
Jie Zeng	Tsinghua University, Beijing, P.R. China
Haijun Zhang	University of Science and Technology Beijing, P.R. China
Adel Al-Hezmi	Fraunhofer Institute Fokus, Germany
Gholamreza Alirezaei	RWTH Aachen University, Germany
Abdelhamid Belmekki	National Institute of Posts and Telecommunications, Morocco
Nabil Benamar	Moulay Ismail University, Morocco
Mustapha Benjillali	National Institute of Posts and Telecommunications, Morocco
Igor Bisio	University of Genoa, Italy
Leila Boulahia	University of Technology of Troyes, France
Lin X. Cai	Illinois Institute of Technology, USA
Zhuo Chen	Rutgers University, USA
Stefano Chessa	Università di Pisa, Italy
Mohamed El Kamili	Sidi Mohammed Ben Abdellah University, Fez, Morocco
Ahmed El Maliani Drissi	Sidi Mohammed Ben Abdellah University, Fez, Morocco
Mourad El Yadari	Moulay Ismail University, Morocco
Alexandros Fragkiadakis	Institute of Computer Science, FORTH, Greece
Sye Loong Keoh	University of Glasgow, UK
Mohammed-Amine Koulali	Hassan I University of Oujda, Morocco
Franck Le Gall	Easy Global Market, France
Zoubir Mammeri	Paul Sabatier University, France
Tom Pfeifer	IoT Consult Europe, Germany
Mustafa Rafique	IBM Research, Ireland
Vasanthan Raghavan	Qualcomm, Inc., USA
Slim Rekhis	SUP'COM, University of Carthage, Tunisia
Carlos Rolim	Federal University of Rio Grande do Sul, Brazil
Jorge Sá Silva	University of Coimbra, Portugal
Mohamed Nabil Saidi	INSEA, Rabat, Morocco
Omid Taghizadeh	RWTH Aachen University, Germany
Fernando Terroso-Saenz	University of Murcia, Spain
Ali Saman Tosun	University of Texas at San Antonio, USA
Tzu-Chieh Tsai	National Chengchi University, Taiwan
Yang Xiao	The University of Alabama, USA
Zbigniew Zielinski	Military University of Technology, Poland

Abstracts of Keynote Talks

5G is Just Around the Corner; So What is Next?

Halim Yanikomeroglu

Abstract. Since the completion of the first 4G LTE standard in the late 2000s, the research community has been conceiving 5G, mainly from two tangled angles, the novel use cases and the enabling technologies. At the time of the writing of this book, the 5G standardization process has already started; the first 5G standards are scheduled to be finalized in the late 2010s. The 5G is expected to evolve throughout the 2020s; and, probably sometime in the latter part of the 2020s, the 6G standardization process will start, with possible deployments in the early 2030s. It is rather early at this point to over-speculate on 6G. Nevertheless, it is possible to highlight a number of important points in light of the experience gained from the first four or five generations.

The big promise of 5G is that the use cases in this generation will not be confined to the smart phone environment. Therefore, the success of 5G is closely tied to how quickly and to what extent these novel use cases will have market acceptance. Although the maturity of the 5G technologies for enabling the new use cases is essential, this is not the only factor for the success of 5G; arguably, market-readiness of these use cases will play an even more important role. One of the reasons for the great success of 4G LTE has been that the standard involved a number of technologies which were highly successful in enabling a primary use case, namely, video delivery on smart phones. At the same time, there was a great market/demand for this use case – the right synergy for success. 5G is coming with many powerful enabling technologies, many of which are highlighted in this book. However, anticipating the market adoption timeline of the 5G use cases is more difficult, as this timeline depends on factors beyond engineering. For example, the fully autonomous and connected vehicle paradigm cannot become a reality in a short time frame. A number of new use cases, such as this one, require policy and legislation chances which are inherently long processes. Therefore, during the latter part of the 2020s, when the 6G standardization is likely to occur, the discussions around many of the use cases attributed to 5G will likely to continue in the 6G context as well.

5G marks the start of a new era in wireless. The road towards 5G has been very exciting. The road towards 6G will be even more exciting…

Massive MIMO: From Channel, Antennas and SDR Towards User Fairness

Sofie Pollin

Abstract. Massive MIMO is widely seen a s promising kandidate for 5G as it promises high throughput, long range, low cost or power consumption, and perfect fairness among users. We will introduce the key principles behind Massive MIMO, and highlight the main assumptions that underly it's world record performance. Then, implementation aspects will be discussed going from the signal processing algorithms to the antennas. By looking at the real measured performance as function of various implementation choices, such as the antenna elements, we will shed some new light on Massive MIMO.

Simultaneous Lightwave Information and Power Transfer (SLIPT) for Indoor IoT Applications

George K. Karagiannidis

Abstract. The era of Internet-of-Things (IoT) opens up the opportunity for a number of promising applications in smart buildings, health monitoring, and predictive maintenance. It is remarkable that most of the data consumption/generation, which are related to IoT applications, occurs in indoor environments. Motivated by this, optical wireless communication (OWC), such as visible light communications (VLC) or infrared (IR), have been recognized as promising alternative/complimentary technologies to RF, in order to give access to IoT devices in indoor applications. However, due to the strong dependence of the IoT on wireless access, their applications are constrained by the finite battery capacity of the involved devices.

In this talk, for first time will be presented a framework for simultaneous optical wireless information and power transfer, which we call Simultaneous Lightwave Information and Power Transfer (SLIPT), and can be used for indoor IoT applications through VLC or IR systems.

Vehicular Communications and Networking: The Gateway to Connected Mobility

Liuqing Yang

Abstract. Vehicular communications and networking is an area of significant importance in our increasingly connected and mobile world. In the past decade, this area has gained significant attention from both industry and academia for its potential of ensuring road safety, improving transportation efficiency and of enhancing travel quality. Vehicular environments are inherently challenging with doubly selective physical channels, constrained radio spectrum bandwidth resources, and constantly changing network connectivity and topology. As such, research in this area is essential for bringing to reality the many demanding vehicular applications that consist of the gateway towards the ultimate connected mobility. In this talk, I will introduce fundamentals of vehicular channels, and various practical communications and networking techniques that we particularly developed for such channels. Challenges and opportunities in this field will also be discussed to stimulate future research and development.

Contents

Context-Awareness and Autonomy Paradigms

Studying Node Cooperation in Reputation Based Packet Forwarding Within Mobile Ad Hoc Networks 3
Sara Berri, Vineeth Varma, Samson Lasaulce, Mohammed Said Radjef, and Jamal Daafouz

Routing Game on the Line: The Case of Multi-players 14
Abdelillah Karouit, Majed Haddad, Eitan Altman, and Moulay Abdellatif Lmater

QoS-Aware Tactical Power Control for 5G Networks 25
Hajar El Hammouti, Essaid Sabir, and Hamidou Tembine

A Game Theoretic Approach Against the Greedy Behavior in MAC IEEE 802.11 38
Mohammed-Alamine El Houssaini, Abdessadek Aaroud, Ali El Hore, and Jalel Ben-Othman

Leveraging User Intuition to Predict Item Popularity in Social Networks 48
Nada Sbihi, Ihsane Gryech, and Mounir Ghogho

Quality of Experience in HTTP Adaptive Video Streaming Systems 56
Zakaria Ye, Rachid Elazouzi, and Tania Jiménez

Community Detection Through Topic Modeling in Social Networks 70
Imane Tamimi, El Khadir Lamrani, and Mohamed El Kamili

A Formal Framework for Adaptation 81
Anne Marie Amja, Abdel Obaid, Hafedh Mili, and Zahi Jarir

A Comprehensive Study of Intelligent Transportation System Architectures for Road Congestion Avoidance 95
Sara El Hamdani and Nabil Benamar

Enhancing Security in Optimized Link State Routing Protocol for Mobile Ad Hoc Networks 107
Houda Moudni, Mohamed Er-rouidi, Hassan Faouzi, Hicham Mouncif, and Benachir El Hadadi

A New Data Forwarding Scheme for DTNs Based on Coalition Game 117
Youness Larabi, Khalil Ibrahimi, and Nabil Benamar

Impact of Link Lifetime on QoS in Mobile Ad-Hoc Networks 127
Nabil Mesbahi and Hamza Dahmouni

Mobile Edge Networking and Virtualization

A Multi-broker Cloud Architecture for the Purpose of Large Scale Sensing Applications Development 141
Soumaya Bel Hadj Youssef, Slim Rekhis, and Noureddine Boudriga

A Simulation Framework for IT Governance in the Context of Corporate Relocation 154
Rabii El Ghorfi, Mohamed El Aroussi, Mohamed Ouadou, and Driss Aboutajdine

NGN Management with NGOSS Framework-Based IMS Use Case 166
B. Raouyane, S. Khairi, I. Haddar, and M. Bellafkih

Migration from Web Services to Cloud Services 179
Hassina Nacer, Kada Beghdad Bey, and Nabil Djebari

Improving Attack Graph Scalability for the Cloud Through SDN-Based Decomposition and Parallel Processing 193
Oussama Mjihil, Dijiang Huang, and Abdelkrim Haqiq

Performance Analysis of Intrusion Detection Systems in Cloud-Based Systems 206
Rachid Cherkaoui, Mostapha Zbakh, An Braeken, and Abdellah Touhafi

Towards Optimizing the Usability of Homomorphic Encryption in Cloud-Based Medical Image Processing 214
Mbarek Marwan, Ali Kartit, and Hassan Ouahmane

A Verifiable Secret Sharing Approach for Secure MultiCloud Storage 225
Kamal Benzekki, Abdeslam El Fergougui, and Abdelbaki Elbelrhiti Elalaoui

A Priority Based Task Scheduling in Cloud Computing Using a Hybrid MCDM Model 235
Hicham Ben Alla, Said Ben Alla, and Abdellah Ezzati

A Novel Approach for Security in Cloud-Based Medical Image Storage Using Segmentation. 247
Mbarek Marwan, Ali Kartit, and Hassan Ouahmane

Ubiquitous Internet of Things: Emerging Technologies and Breakthroughs

Toward Reliable Maritime Communication for a Safe Operation of Autonomous Ship 261
Abdelmoula Ait Allal, Khalifa Mansouri, Mohamed Youssfi, and Mohammed Qbadou

A Secure Machine-to-Machine Wireless Communication Using DNP3 Protocol for Feeder Automation in Smart Grid. 275
Anass Lekbich, Abdelaziz Belfqih, Cherkaoui Nazha, Faissal Elmariami, Jamal Boukherouaa, Omar Sabri, and Mohamed Nouh Dazahra

L-CAHASH: A Novel Lightweight Hash Function Based on Cellular Automata for RFID 287
Charifa Hanin, Bouchra Echandouri, Fouzia Omary, and Souad El Bernoussi

Group Authentication with Fault Tolerance for Internet of Things. 299
Otmane Elmouaatamid, Mohamed Lahmer, and Mostafa Belkasmi

Fully Distributed Indexing over a Distributed Hash Table 308
Simon Désaulniers, Adrien Béraud, Alexandre Blondin Massé, and Nicolas Reynaud

IoT-Empowered Smart Agriculture: A Real-Time Light-Weight Embedded Segmentation System. 319
Saad Abouzahir, Mohamed Sadik, and Essaid Sabir

Random Access Procedure Based on an Adaptive Prioritization Method for Integration of MTC in Mobile Networks. 333
Alejandro Borrajo Romero, Raquel Pérez Leal, and Ana García Armada

Adopting Fuzzy Technique to Save Energy in Smart Home Control System. 345
Sergio Henrique Monte Santo Andrade, Edvar da Luz Oliveira, Rodrigo Dias Alfaia, Anderson Vinicius de Freitas Souto, Nandamudi Lankalapalli Vijaykumar, and Carlos Renato Lisboa Francês

Multi-hop Clustering Solution Based on Beacon Delay for Vehicular Ad-Hoc Networks. 357
Soufiane Ouahou, Slimane Bah, Zohra Bakkoury, and Abdelhakim Hafid

F2CDM: Internet of Things for Healthcare Network Based Fog-to-Cloud and Data-in-Motion Using MQTT Protocol 368
Istabraq M. Al-Joboury and Emad H. Al-Hemiary

Compact Dual-Band CPW-Fed Patch Antenna for 2.45/5.80 GHz RFID Applications 380
Mohamed Tarbouch, Abdelkebir El Amri, and Hanae Terchoune

MRA*: Parallel and Distributed Path in Large-Scale Graph Using MapReduce-A* Based Approach 390
Wilfried Yves Hamilton Adoni, Tarik Nahhal, Brahim Aghezzaf, and Abdeltif Elbyed

Study of Energy Consumption in Wireless Sensor Networks Using S-Rhombus, S-Square and S-Circle Deployment 402
Saleh Bouarafa, Rachid Saadane, Moulay Driss Rahmani, and Driss Aboutajdine

Toward a New Extension of IPv6 Addressing to Connect Non IP Objects 411
Ali El Ksimi, Cherkaoui Leghris, and Faddoul Khoukhi

Enablers, Challenges and Applications

Channel Coherence Classification with Frame-Shifting in Massive MIMO Systems 425
Ahmad Abboud, Oussama Habachi, Ali Jaber, Jean-Pierre Cances, and Vahid Meghdadi

Spectral Efficiency Analysis of Two-Way Massive MIMO Full-Duplex Relay Systems with Direct Link 438
Houda Chafnaji

Robust Trajectory Planning for Robotic Communications Under Fading Channels 450
Daniel Bonilla Licea, Vineeth S. Varma, Samson Lasaulce, Jamal Daafouz, Mounir Ghogho, and Des McLernon

Performance of Enhanced LTE OTDOA Positioning Approach Through Nakagami-*m* Fading Channel 461
Ilham El Mourabit, Abdelmajid Badri, Aicha Sahel, and Abdennaceur Baghdad

Chaotic ZKP Based Authentication and Key Distribution Scheme in Environmental Monitoring CPS 472
Wided Boubakri, Walid Abdallah, and Noureddine Boudriga

Implementation and Performance Evaluation of Network Intrusion Detection Systems 484
Mohammed Saber, Mohammed Ghaouth Belkasmi, Sara Chadli, and Mohamed Emharraf

An Efficient Authentication Protocol for 5G Heterogeneous Networks 496
Younes El Hajjaji El Idrissi, Noureddine Zahid, and Mohamed Jedra

An Agreement Graph-Based-Authentication Scheme for 5G Networks 509
Maroua Gharam and Noureddine Boudriga

Green Base Station Placement for Microwave Backhaul Links 521
Alonso Silva and Antonia Maria Masucci

Joint Frame Detection and Channel Estimation for DCO-OFDM
LiFi Systems 532
Yufei Jiang, Majid Safari, and Harald Haas

SIR Based Performance Analysis of Dual-Branch SC Over Correlated
$\kappa - \mu$ Fading Channels 542
Stefan Panic, Caslav Stefanovic, and Hranislav Milosevic

Performance Analysis of Asynchronous and Non Linear FBMC Systems 550
Brahim Elmaroud, Ahmed Faqihi, and Driss Aboutajdine

An Improved Bernoulli Sensing Matrix for Compressive Sensing 562
Hamid Nouasria and Mohamed Et-tolba

Contribution to the Study of Beamforming at 2.4 GHz of a Smart Antenna
Alimented by a 4 × 4 Butler Matrix for Wireless Applications 572
Mohamed Hanaoui and Mounir Rifi

Adaptive Mapping for Multiple Applications on Parallel Architectures 584
Ismail Assayad and Alain Girault

Verification of SystemC Components Using the Method of Deduction 596
Elbouanani Soumia, Assayad Ismail, and Sadik Mohammed

Image Segmentation by Deep Community Detection Approach 607
Youssef Mourchid, Mohammed El Hassouni, and Hocine Cherifi

Data Mining Approaches for Alzheimer's Disease Diagnosis 619
El Mehdi Benyoussef, Abdeltif Elbyed, and Hind El Hadiri

Image Search Engine Based on Color Histogram and Zernike Moment 632
Nawal Chifa, Abdelmajid Badri, Yassine Ruichek, and Aicha Sahel

Risk Assessment and Alert Prioritization for Intrusion Detection Systems. . . . 641
El Mostapha Chakir, Mohamed Moughit, and Youness Idrissi Khamlichi

Author Index 657

Context-Awareness and Autonomy Paradigms

Studying Node Cooperation in Reputation Based Packet Forwarding Within Mobile Ad Hoc Networks

Sara Berri[1,2(✉)], Vineeth Varma[3], Samson Lasaulce[2], Mohammed Said Radjef[1], and Jamal Daafouz[3]

[1] Research Unit LaMOS (Modeling and Optimization of Systems), Faculty of Exact Sciences, University of Bejaia, 06000 Bejaia, Algeria
radjefms@gmail.com

[2] L2S (CNRS-CentraleSupelec-Univ. Paris Sud), Gif-sur-Yvette, France
{sara.berri,samson.lasaulce}@l2s.centralesupelec.fr

[3] CNRS and Université de Lorraine, CRAN UMR 7039, Nancy, France
{vineeth.satheeskumar-varma,Jamal.Daafouz}@univ-lorraine.fr

Abstract. In the paradigm of mobile Ad hoc networks (MANET), forwarding packets originating from other nodes requires cooperation among nodes. However, as each node may not want to waste its energy, cooperative behavior can not be guaranteed. Therefore, it is necessary to implement some mechanism to avoid selfish behavior and to promote cooperation. In this paper, we propose a simple quid pro quo based reputation system, i.e., nodes that forward gain reputation, but lose more reputation if they do not forward packets from cooperative users (determined based on reputation), and lose less reputation when they chose to not forward packets from non-cooperative users. Under this framework, we model the behavior of users as an evolutionary game and provide conditions that result in cooperative behavior by studying the evolutionary stable states of the proposed game. Numerical analysis is provided to study the resulting equilibria and to illustrate how the proposed model performs compared to traditional models.

Keywords: Mobile ad hoc networks · Packet forwarding · Cooperation · Evolutionary game theory · ESS · Replicator dynamics

1 Introduction

A mobile ad hoc network (MANET) is a wireless multi-hop network formed by a set of mobile independent nodes. A key feature about MANETs is that they are self organizing and are without any established infrastructure. The absence of infrastructure implies that all networking functions, such as packet forwarding, must be performed by the nodes themselves [1]. Thus, multi-hop communications

---

J. Daafouz—The present work is supported by the LIA project between CRAN, Lorea and the International University of Rabat.

E. Sabir et al. (Eds.): UNet 2017, LNCS 10542, pp. 3–13, 2017.
https://doi.org/10.1007/978-3-319-68179-5_1

rely on mutual cooperation among network's nodes. As the nodes of an ad hoc network have limited energy, the nodes may not want to waste their energy by forwarding packets from other nodes. If all the nodes are controlled by a central entity, this will not be a major issue as cooperation can be a part of the design, but in applications where each node corresponds to an individual user, it is crucial to develop mechanisms that promote cooperation among the nodes.

Several works in the literature provide solutions based on incentive mechanisms, such as those based on a credit concept [2–4] etc., whose idea being that nodes pay for using some service and they are remunerated when they provide some service (like packet forwarding). Others like [5,6] use reputation-based mechanisms to promote cooperation. Game theory has been a vital tool in literature to study the behavior of self-serving individuals in serval domains including MANETs. In [7–9], etc. the interaction among nodes in packet forwarding is modeled as a one shot game based on prison's dilemma model, extended then to repeated game. Furthermore, evolutionary game theory is introduced in [10–12], to study the dynamic evolution of system composed of nodes and to analyze how cooperation can be ensured in a natural manner. In [10] the evolutionary game theory is applied to study cooperation in packet forwarding in mobile ad hoc networks. Here, the authors used the prison's dilemma-based model [7] and the aim was to implement several strategies in the game and to evaluate performance, by observing their evolution over time.

The aforementioned works rely on incentive mechanisms, which has been proved to improve nodes cooperation. However, implementing such solutions often result in a large computational complexity during the game. We would like to find an answer to the following question, "Is it possible to achieve global cooperation in packet forwarding by a simple and natural way?". In this paper, we model the nodes interaction in a MANET as an evolutionary game by proposing a new formulation of the packet forwarding and reputation model. We introduce a simple reputation system with a quid pro quo basis, wherein, reputation is gained by forwarding packets and is lost when refusing to forward. However, a key feature is that the reputation loss depends on the packet source. If the packet is from a node with low reputation, less reputation is lost by not forwarding that packet. This simply means that selfish users will naturally have low reputation, while users are encouraged to help other cooperative users, resulting in a significantly different model from the likes of [10,12] etc. With this model, we study two node classes, one which try to maintain a certain high reputation, and another class which disregard their reputation. We show that nodes are likely to cooperating by means of evolutionary game theory concepts and provide numerical results showing how the proposed model improves network performance. The novel reputation model we propose will naturally result in the cooperative users cooperating among each other and refusing to forward packets from selfish users, thereby eliminating the need for a third party to punish selfish behavior.

The remainder of the paper is structured as follows. In Sect. 2 we formulate the reputation and game models. We propose to analyze the evolutionary game in Sect. 3, by providing the associated equilibrium, and studying strategies evolution. This allows us to determine condition ensuring global cooperative behavior. The numerical results are presented in Sect. 4; it has to be noted that the results are the same for any game settings satisfying the provided conditions and not only for the given examples. Finally, Sect. 5 presents the conclusion.

2 Problem Formulation and Proposed Game Model

In this section, we provide a game model to study the packet forwarding interaction. We consider a packet forwarding game, where the players are the nodes, each of them can be cooperative, by forwarding other nodes' packets, or non-cooperative, by dropping other nodes' packets. Thus, the players have to choose a strategy s_i from the strategy set $\mathcal{S}=\{\text{C, NC}\}$. The actions C and NC mean cooperative and non-cooperative, respectively. The two player packet forwarding game can be defined in its strategic-form as following.

$$\mathcal{G}^{(2)} = <\{1,2\},\ \{\mathcal{S}_i\}_{i\in\mathcal{I}},\ \{u_i\}_{i\in\mathcal{I}}>, \tag{1}$$

where:

- $\mathcal{I}=\{1,2\}$ is the set of players (two players), that are the network nodes;
- $\mathcal{S}_i$ is the set of pure strategies of player $i \in \mathcal{I}$, which is the same for all the players, corresponding to $\mathcal{S}=\{\text{C, NC}\}$;
- u_i is the utility of player $i \in \mathcal{I}$, that depends on its behavior and that of its opponent. To demonstrate the utility formulation, we consider the case of a pair of nodes from the network, within which a node may act as a sender and a relay (and vice versa). Thus, the players' utility can be represented by a payoff matrix as given by (2).

$$A = \begin{matrix} & \begin{matrix}\text{C} & \text{NC}\end{matrix} \\ \begin{matrix}\text{C}\\ \text{NC}\end{matrix} & \begin{pmatrix} \lambda-1 & -1 \\ \lambda & 0 \end{pmatrix} \end{matrix}, \tag{2}$$

where: $\lambda > 0$ is a coefficient representing the benefit associated to successfully sending a packet while spending a unit of energy. The first player actions are along the rows and the second players along the columns. Naturally, when $\lambda < 1$ no nodes are motivated to cooperate as the energy cost relative to the gain from having packets relayed is too high. In the interesting case (the case where a MANET framework is feasible) of $\lambda > 1$, the outcome of the proposed game can be characterized by the well-known Nash Equilibrium (NE), which is the strategy profile from which no player has interest in changing unilaterally its strategy. The resulting strategy profile is beneficial for players when they act individually. However, the NE of the packet forwarding game is inefficient, corresponding to drop all the time, and provides for players 0 as utility. Thus, to overcome this problem we propose to add to the game (1) a reputation model, that defines the reward and the cost in terms of reputation according to the node decision, cooperative or non-cooperative. On the other hand, it would be better to model the interactions among all the N nodes and not just the two-player case. To deal with this, we propose to introduce evolutionary game theory, where the dynamical evolution of game strategies is studied through pairwise interactions.

In the following section, we provide the reputation model we propose, and construct the new packet forwarding game including the reputation mechanism as an integrated system. That means the game is played taking into account the reputation, which we show can be interpreted as a constraint on the strategy space, while the nodes aim to maximize their utility function.

2.1 Reputation Model

We assume that there is a reputation system introduced in order to discourage selfish behavior and reward cooperative behavior by separating these two classes of nodes. The reputation system is represented as a function depending on the own action and the opponent's action. The reputation increases by a certain margin δ_r whenever a node relays the packet from another node, chooses C as action. Reputation is lost whenever a node refuses to relay a packet, by choosing NC as action. However, the loss of reputation from refusing to relay the packet from a node with low reputation δ_b is smaller than the loss incurred by refusing to relay the packet from a well reputed node δ_g. For ease of notation the reputation of a user $i \in \mathcal{I}$ is given by $R_i(t)$, and if $R_i(t) > 0$ the node has a good reputation and otherwise bad reputation. The change in reputation is given by:

$$R_i(t+1) = R_i(t) + d_i(t)\delta_r - (1 - d_i(t))(\delta_g \mathbf{1}(R_j > 0) + \delta_b \mathbf{1}(R_j \leq 0)), \quad (3)$$

where: $d_i(t) \in \{0, 1\}$ is the decision to relay or not at time t. 0 corresponds to the action NC, and 1 to C. j is a random variable indicating the sender requesting i to relay. $\mathbf{1}$ is the indicator function, it is one when the condition inside the brackets is satisfied and 0 otherwise.

We consider two primary classes of nodes based on their reputation value. The set H of "Hawks" who are selfish (non-cooperative) and don't care about reputation. As a result these nodes never relay packets, i.e., $s_i =$NC $\forall i \in H$, but use the network and try to make the other nodes relay their packets, and so we have $R_i(t) < 0\ \forall i \in H$. These nodes will always have $d_i(t) = 0$ for all t and therefore will also have a low reputation.

The other class of nodes are the set D of "Doves", who try to maintain a positive reputation. These nodes will have a strategy s such that on average their reputation gain is positive. Let us denote the dove population share (fraction of users who are in the dove class) by p. The population share of hawks will simply be given by $1 - p$.

2.2 Utility Maximization

In this subsection, we present how reputation system is integrated in the packet forwarding game in order to improve game outcomes and avoiding the non-cooperative situation. As even the doves do not want to waste energy, they will not attempt to transmit ever single packet, but only such that their average reputation gain is at least 0 (reputation must be an increasing function). We assume that even a cooperative node, i.e., the Dove class, does not relay packets all the time. The doves have a mixed strategy to relay messages, and it relays messages from other doves with probability s_d, and from hawks with a probability s_h, i.e., the action C is chosen with different probabilities depending on the opponent's class.

As a result, the net utility is given by the number of times their packets get forward subtracted by the energy cost paid is given by them. The expected payoff of doves is given by the formula (4).

$$U(D,p) = (\lambda - 1)ps_d - s_h(1-p). \tag{4}$$

This must be maximized over s_d, s_h while maintaining a positive reputation, i.e., $\mathbb{E}[R_i(t+1) - R_i(t)] \geq 0$ or

$$p(s_d\delta_r - (1-s_d)\delta_g) + (1-p)(s_h\delta_r - (1-s_h)\delta_b) \geq 0. \tag{5}$$

Therefore for a given population share of doves p, we can find the strategy of doves by solving the following optimization problem.

$$\max_{s_d,s_h} U(D,p)$$

$$\begin{array}{l} p(s_d\delta_r - (1-s_d)\delta_g) + (1-p)(s_h\delta_r - (1-s_h)\delta_b) \geq 0 \\ 0 \leq s_d \leq 1,\ 0 \leq s_h \leq 1. \end{array} \tag{6}$$

Hawks have the same utility function, but don't have a reputation constraint, therefore, the corresponding expected payoff is given by the formula (7).

$$U(H,p) = \lambda p s_h. \tag{7}$$

Thus, the expected payoff of any individual is given by (8):

$$U(p,p) = pU(D,p) + (1-p)U(H,p), \tag{8}$$

where p is the population profile.

If $\lambda > 1$, $U(D,p)$ is maximized trivially by choosing $s_d = 1$. Therefore, s_h will be the smallest such that constraint (5) holds.

$$\begin{aligned} p(s_d\delta_r - (1-s_d)\delta_g) + (1-p)(s_h\delta_r - (1-s_h)\delta_b) &\geq 0 \\ \Rightarrow p\delta_r + (1-p)(s_h\delta_r - (1-s_h)\delta_b) &\geq 0 \\ \Rightarrow p\delta_r + (1-p)(s_h(\delta_r+\delta_b) - \delta_b) &\geq 0 \\ \Rightarrow s_h &\geq \tfrac{(1-p)\delta_b - p\delta_r}{(\delta_b+\delta_r)(1-p)}. \end{aligned}$$

Thus, we have:

$$s_h^{\star} = \max\left\{\frac{(1-p)\delta_b - p\delta_r}{(\delta_b+\delta_r)(1-p)}, 0\right\}. \tag{9}$$

Note that the introduction of $s_h < 1$ is one of the main novelties of this paper, which can be different from $s_h = 1$ as defined in the traditional forwarding game payoff [7–10, 12], etc. where the cooperative nodes forward packet all the time without making distinction among the opponent nodes that can be cooperative, belonging to D, or non-cooperative, belonging to H. Furthermore, the proposed reputation system is simpler and can be defined as a constraint when nodes take decision purely based on the reputation class of the packet source node.

2.3 Evolutionary Game Formulation

We can formally define the resulting evolutionary game with the strategic form

$$\mathcal{G} =< \{D, H\}, \{(s_d, s_h)\} \times \{0\}, p \in [0, 1], \{u_c\}_{c \in \{D,H\}} >, \tag{10}$$

where:

- $\{D, H\}$ are the reputation classes (or population types);
- $\{(s_d, s_h)\}$ is the set of strategies playable by D, with H always playing 0 or NC strategy;
- p is the population share of class D;
- u_c is the utility of class D or H as defined in (4) and (7).

Our objective in the following section is to study the evolution of strategies in this game, and analyze possible equilibrium points.

3 Evolutionary Game Analysis

Evolutionary game theory study the dynamic evolution of a given population based on two main concepts: evolutionary stable strategy (ESS) and replicator dynamics. Let p the initial population profile. We assume that a proportion ε of this population plays according to another profile q (population of mutants), while the other individuals keep their initial behavior p. Thus, the new population profile is $(1-\varepsilon)p+\varepsilon q$. The expected payoff of a player that plays according to p is $U(p, (1-\varepsilon)p+\varepsilon q)$, and it is equal to $U(q, (1-\varepsilon)p+\varepsilon q)$ for the one playing according to q.

Definition 1 [13]. *A strategy $p \in \Delta$ is an evolutionary stable strategy* (ESS), *if* $: \forall q \in \Delta, \exists\ \bar{\varepsilon} = \bar{\varepsilon}(q) \in (0, 1), \forall \varepsilon \in (0, \bar{\varepsilon})$

$$U(p, (1-\varepsilon)p + \varepsilon q) > U(q, (1-\varepsilon)p + \varepsilon q), \tag{11}$$

$\bar{\varepsilon}$ is called invasion barrier *of the strategy p, which may depend on q.*

The replicator dynamics is the process that specifies how a population is distributed over the pure strategies set in a game evolving in time.

Definition 2 (Replicator dynamics). *The replicator dynamics is given by (12) [14]:*

$$\dot{p}_i = p_i[U(i,p) - \sum_{j=1}^{|S|} p_j U(j,p)], \qquad i \in \{1,\ldots,|S|\}. \tag{12}$$

The system (12) describes the replication process in continuous time. It gives the percentage of individuals newly playing strategy s_i in the next period, it depends on the initial value $p_i(t_0)$. Using the relation (12), the replicator dynamics of the proposed game is:

$$\dot{p} = p(1-p)(p(\lambda-1)(1-s_h^\star) - s_h^\star). \tag{13}$$

For the evolutionary game $\mathcal{G}$, we have the following results.

Theorem 1 *When $\lambda > 1$, the evolutionary game $\mathcal{G}$ admits exactly two ESS at $p^\star = 0$ with an invasion barrier $\bar{\varepsilon} = \min\left\{\frac{\delta_b}{\delta_r q(\lambda-1)}, 1\right\}$, and $p^\star = 1$ with an invasion barrier $\bar{\varepsilon} = 1$. When the initial configuration is such that $p < p_T$, the replicator dynamics takes the system to $p^\star = 0$ and when $p > p_T$, the replicator dynamics takes the system to $p^\star = 1$ with*

$$p_T = \frac{\delta_b}{\delta_b + \lambda\delta_r}$$

corresponding to the mixed NE.

Proof. First, we can easily verify that p_T corresponds to a mixed NE by noticing that the utilities of H and D classes are identical at this point. Next, we use the Definition 1, to prove the results stated in Theorem 1 corresponding to the invasion barrier. Let $x = (1-\varepsilon)p + \varepsilon q$, and $\bar{U} = U(p,x) - U(q,x)$. $U(p,x)$ and $U(q,x)$ are defined using the relation (8).

$$\begin{aligned}\bar{U} &= p(x(\lambda-1) - s_h^\star(1-x)) + (1-p)(\lambda x s_h^\star) - q(x(\lambda-1) - s_h^\star(1-x)) - (1-q)(\lambda x s_h^\star)\\ &= (p-q)(x(\lambda-1) - s_h^\star(1-x)) - (p-q)(\lambda x s_h^\star)\\ &= (p-q)(x(\lambda-1)(1-s_h^\star) - s_h^\star).\end{aligned} \tag{14}$$

1. In the first case, $p^\star = 0$, this gives $s_h^\star = \frac{\delta_b}{\delta_b+\delta_r}$. We can solve for the condition when

$$\begin{aligned}\bar{U} &> 0\\ \Rightarrow -q(\varepsilon q(\lambda-1)(1-s_h^\star) - s_h^\star) &> 0\\ \Rightarrow (-\varepsilon q(\lambda-1)(1-s_h^\star) + s_h^\star) &> 0\\ \Rightarrow (-\varepsilon q(\lambda-1)\delta_r + \delta_b) &> 0\\ \Rightarrow \varepsilon &< \frac{\delta_b}{\delta_r q(\lambda-1)}.\end{aligned} \tag{15}$$

Thus, from the Definition 1 we conclude that $p^\star = 0$ is an ESS with $\bar{\varepsilon} = \min\left\{\frac{\delta_b}{\delta_r q(\lambda-1)}, 1\right\}$ as an invasion barrier. Note that $p^\star = 0$ is an ESS only if the population share of D decreases, and that of H increases, i.e., the replicator dynamics is negative or $\dot{p}_i < 0$. If $s_h = s_h^\star$, $\dot{p} < 0$ gives the following result:

$$\begin{aligned} &\dot{p} < 0 \\ \Rightarrow p(1-p)(p(\lambda-1) - \frac{(1-p)\delta_b - p\delta_r}{(\delta_b+\delta_r)(1-p)}(p(\lambda-1)+1)) &< 0 \\ \Rightarrow \frac{p((\delta_b+\delta_r\lambda)p-\delta_b)}{\delta_b+\delta_r} &< 0 \\ \Rightarrow p &< p_T \end{aligned} \tag{16}$$

2. Now we prove that $p^\star = 1$ is an ESS. In this case $s_h^\star = 0$. Thus, the following result:

$$\bar{U} = (1-\varepsilon(1-q))(\lambda-1),$$

we have $\lambda > 1 \Rightarrow \bar{U} > 0$. This implies, according to Definition 1, that $p^\star = 1$ is an ESS $\bar{\varepsilon} = 1$ as an invasion barrier. This occurs if $\dot{p} > 0$, i.e., when:

$$\frac{p((\delta_b+\delta_r\lambda)p-\delta_b)}{\delta_b+\delta_r} > 0 \Rightarrow p > \frac{\delta_b}{\delta_b+\delta_r\lambda} = p_T \tag{17}$$

□

4 Numerical Analysis

In this section, we present numerical application of the proposed evolutionary game including a reputation system. All the results are based on the replicator dynamics which describes how the population evolves, and allows one to determine others performance metrics such as expected utility of players and the number of forwarded packets.

We study the effect of the proposed reputation model on the evolutionary stable strategy of the game. Figure 1 presents the results, we consider two scenarios: (1) The curve in solid line corresponds to results provided by the proposed game model including a reputation system, and assuming that the cooperative nodes forward packets of non-cooperative nodes with some probability $s_h^\star$. (2) The curve in dashed line corresponds to results provided by putting $s_h = 1$, meaning that cooperative nodes forward all the time, which corresponds to the previous packet forwarding game introduced in [7–10], etc. It is seen that using our new formulation, which integrates a reputation mechanism as a constraint, the system could converge towards a cooperative state, by carefully choosing the game settings. Thus, global cooperation could be guaranteed after a given time. Whereas, when the game does not include the reputation constraint, the population converges to the strategy non-cooperation, which is the unique evolutionary stable strategy of the game, regardless of the initial condition and game settings.

The results given by the Fig. 1 can be used to characterize the expected utility of players. Figure 2 presents the results of both cases $s_h = s_h^\star$ and $s_h = 1$. From

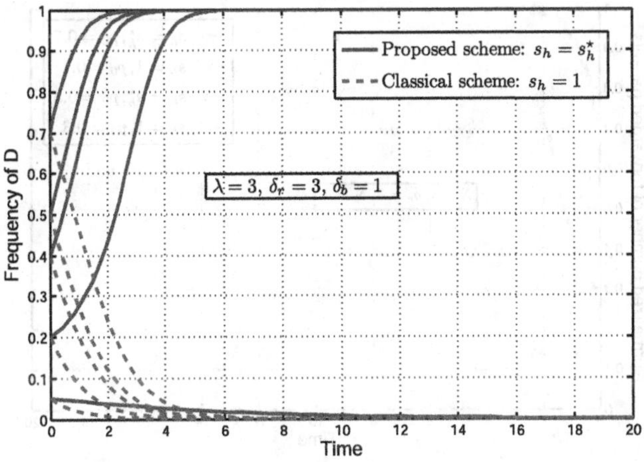

Fig. 1. Evolutionary dynamics of the Doves, nodes that play the strategy 'Cooperation' with a proability s_h^* in the proposed game model, and previous packet forwarding game model where $s_h = 1$. We plot for several initial frequency values.

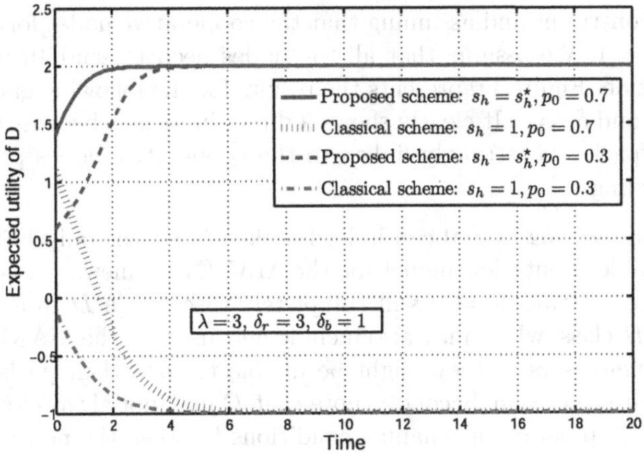

Fig. 2. The expected utility of D in the proposed game model and previous packet forwarding game model, where $s_h = 1$. We plot for several initial frequency values 0.7 and 0.3.

these figures, we observe that the utilities evolve over time in the same way that the proportion of the considered population, corresponding to D in that case. Thus, the proposed model provides better results, it promotes cooperation among nodes.

Indeed, in order to show the influence level of these results on network performance, we consider a network composed of 50 nodes, randomly placed in surface of 1000 m × 1000 m, with a transmission range equals to 150 m, and plot normalized number of forwarded packets within a network, using the proposed game model with constraint, and that introduced in previous works [7–10], etc. defined

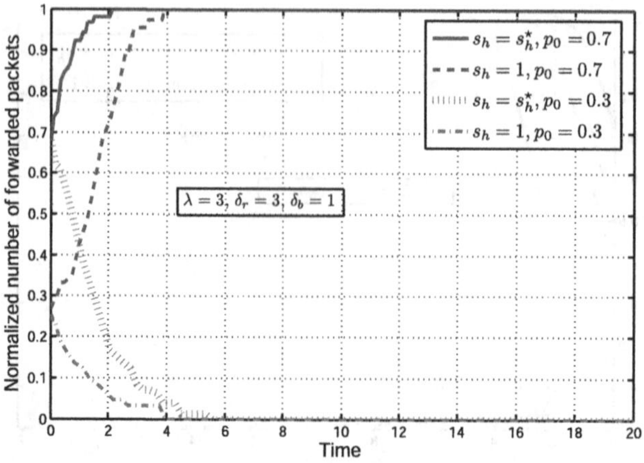

Fig. 3. Normalized number of forwarded packets for an Ad hoc network of 50 nodes, in the proposed game model and previous packet forwarding game model, where $s_h = 1$. We plot for two initial frequency values 0.7 and 0.3.

without any constraint and assuming that the cooperative nodes forward all the time, i.e., $s_h = 1$. We assume that all the nodes need to send 10 packets to a given destination. Figure 3 represents the results for the following game settings: $\lambda = 3$, $\delta_r = 3$ and $\delta_b = 1$. It clearly shows a direct influence, because the number of forwarded packets is strongly linked to the cooperative nodes proportion in packet forwarding.

Remark: While setting $\delta_b = 0$ can indeed make $p^\star = 1$ the only ESS, this may not be a suitable reputation model for the MANET framework due to several reasons. Firstly, setting $\delta_b = 0$ will completely discourage D from forwarding packets from H class, which may also include new users to the MANET, thereby discouraging new users as they might be unable to send their packets without increasing their reputation. Secondly, note that D may not always forward packets from D as in practice the channel conditions between the nodes also play a big role in determining the resource cost and therefore the utility gained by forwarding (which we have not accounted for in this work). Accounting for channel fading due to path loss or small-scale fading will therefore, be a relevant extension of this work. These considerations show that reputation model parameters must be carefully designed in practice.

5 Conclusion

The contribution of this paper is to propose a new formulation of the packet forwarding game [7], introducing a reputation system, which modifies reputation based on the reputation class of the packet source, i.e., cooperative or non-cooperative. The aim is to motivate node cooperation using a simple and efficient mechanism. As a smaller reputation is lost by not forwarding packets from selfish users (classified by the reputation system), cooperative users will effectively forward the packets from other cooperative users and may avoid forwarding packets from selfish users. Effectively, we have demonstrated using evolutionary game theory concepts that, global cooperation in the network can be achieved under some conditions we stated related to the game settings with a low computational complexity. Finally, through simulations, we have shown that in terms of the number of forwarded packets in the MANET, the proposed game model provides significant gains over the game model where the cooperative nodes forward packet regardless of the opponent's behavior. As an extension of the present work, we propose to study the multi-hop case, where the interaction involves more than two players. Another relevant extension would be to account for channel fluctuations and the resulting utility function which might result in the cooperative class users forwarding packets from selfish users and not another cooperative user despite the reputation losses, due the channel conditions being favorable.

References

1. Basagni, S., Conti, M., Giordano, S., Stojmenovic, I.: Mobile Ad Hoc Networking. Wiley, Hoboken (2004)
2. Buttyán, L., Hubaux, J.P.: Enforcing service availability in mobile Ad-Hoc WANs. In: Proceedings of the 1st IEEE/ACM Workshop on Mobile Ad Hoc Networking and Computing (MobiHOC), Boston, August 2000
3. Buttyán, L., Hubaux, J.P.: Stimulating cooperation in self-organizing mobile ad hoc networks. Mob. Netw. Appl. **8**(5), 579–592 (2003)
4. Krzesinski, A.: Promoting cooperation in mobile ad hoc networks. Int. J. Inf. Commun. Technol. Appl. **2**(1), 24–46 (2016)
5. Jianl, G., Hongwei, L., Jian, D., Xiaozong, Y.: HEAD: a hybrid mechanism to enforce node cooperation in mobile ad hoc networks. Elsevier Tsinghua Sci. Technol. **12**, 202–207 (2007)
6. Li, Z., Shen, H.: Game-theoretic analysis of cooperation incentive strategies in mobile ad hoc networks. IEEE Trans. Mob. Comput. **11**(8), 1287–1303 (2012)
7. Félegyházi, M., Hubaux, J.P.: Game theory in wireless networks: a tutorial. EPFL technical report, LCA-REPORT-2006-002, February 2006
8. Félegyházi, M., Hubaux, J.P., Buttyán, L.: Nash equilibria of packet forwarding strategies in wireless ad hoc networks. IEEE Trans. Mob. Comput. **5**(5), 463–476 (2006)
9. Jaramillo, J.J., Srikant, R.: A game theory based reputation mechanism to incentivize cooperation in wireless ad hoc networks. Ad Hoc Netw. **8**, 416–429 (2010)
10. Seredynski, M., Bouvry, P.: evolutionary game theoretical analysis of reputation-based packet forwarding in civilian mobile ad hoc networks. In: Proceedings of Parallel and Distributed Processing, Rome, pp. 1–8 (2009)
11. Seredynski, M., Bouvry, P.: Analysing the development of cooperation in MANETs using evolutionary game theory. J. Supercomput. **63**(3), 854–870 (2013)
12. Tang, C., Li, A., Li, X.: When reputation enforces evolutionary cooperation in unreliable MANETs. IEEE Trans. Cybern. **45**(10), 2190–2201 (2015)
13. Smith, J.M., Price, G.R.: The logic of animal conflict. Nature **246**(5427), 15–18 (1973)
14. Jonker, L.B., Taylor, P.D.: Evolutionary stable strategies and game dynamics. Math. Biosci. **40**, 145–156 (1978). Elsevier

Routing Game on the Line: The Case of Multi-players

Abdelillah Karouit[1(✉)], Majed Haddad[1], Eitan Altman[2], and Moulay Abdellatif Lmater[3]

[1] LIA/CERI, University of Avignon, Agroparc, BP 1228, 84911 Avignon, France
akarouit@gmail.com, majed.haddad@univ-avignon.fr
[2] INRIA Sophia Antipolis, 10 route des Lucioles, 06902 Sophia Antipolis, France
eitan.altman@inria.fr
[3] L-IR2M, Faculty of Sciences and Techniques, Hassan 1st University, Settat, Morocco
moulay.elmater@gmail.com

Abstract. In this paper, we tackle the problem of a sequential routing game where multiple users coexist and competitively send their traffic to a destination over a line. The users arrive at time epoch with a given capacity. Then, they ship their demands over time on a shared resource. The state of players evolve according to whether they decide to transmit or not. The decision of each user is thus spatio-temporal control. We provide an explicit expression of the equilibrium of such systems and compare it to the global optimum case. In particular, we determine the expression of price of anarchy of such scheme and identify a Braess-type paradox in the context of sequential routing game.

Keywords: Sequential routing game · Nash equilibrium · Price of anarchy · Braess-type paradox

1 Introduction

We consider in this paper a spatio-temporal competitive routing game where the network is shared by several users in which each one having a non negligible cost while routes are chosen by the players so as to minimize the delay. Routing game is characterized by source-destination pair and demand function. It can be analyzed using the non-cooperative game theory. An appropriate solution concept in non-cooperative game theory is Nash equilibrium.

This concept has been long studied in the framework telecommunication networks. Such framework is used to model the flow configuration that results in networks where the routing decisions are made in a non-cooperative and distributed manner between the users.

The number of users can be infinite or finite. In the case of an infinite players each player is assumed to be atomless. Atomless means that the impact of routing choices of a single player on the utilities of other players is negligible.

E. Sabir et al. (Eds.): UNet 2017, LNCS 10542, pp. 14–24, 2017.
https://doi.org/10.1007/978-3-319-68179-5_2

The resulting flow configuration corresponds to the Wardrop equilibrium [1]. This concept, has long been studied in the context of road traffic where there is an infinite of players (drivers) [2]. In the telecommunication community, Orda et al. [3] consider that the number of players is finite, where a player (typically corresponding to a service provider) takes the routing decisions for the whole class of users that it controls. It then decides on how to split the demand it controls between different possible routes. They establish existence and uniqueness of Nash equilibrium over large class of general cost functions. This approach also appeared in the road traffic literature (e.g. [4]), but was not much used there. Such a routing game may be handled by models similar to [5] in the special case of a topology of parallel links. An alternative class of routing games is the one in which a player has to route all the demand it controls through the same path. A special case of such framework is the "congestion games" introduced by Rosenthal in [6]. In [10], a load balancing network and Kameda type paradox has been studied, where losses occur on links in a way that may depend on the congestion, which by adding capacity, all players suffer larger loss rates. All the above works have been well studied in time-invariant networks in the last few years.

Our focus here is a spatio-temporal competitive routing where the network is shared by several users in which each one having a non negligible cost. The demand has to be split not only over space but also over time (see Fig. 1). As an example, assume that M players have each its own demand which should be shipped within a T days from a given source to a destination. Thus each player has to split its demand into that corresponding to each of the days of the week. At each day, the route corresponding to the daily demand of each player should be determined. Examples of such games in road traffic appear in [12].

An important property for an equilibrium is efficiency, (social optimality). It is well known that Nash equilibria in routing games are not efficient. Which can lead to the well known phenomena of Braess paradox where adding a link to the network, the cost to all users increases. For specific examples see [8,11].

Our starting point here is the work [7] in which the authors have already studied a routing game on a line where the decision of a user is spatio-temporal control. They addressed the case where only a single user arrives at time epoch. The game considered in [7] assumes that a single user ships its own traffic over a line. However, this assumption may be not always true. Indeed, several users can coexist and competitively need to ship their own resource over a line.

Without loss of generality, we extend their game problem into a general problem, where multiple users arrives on line. In particular, we consider an extreme scenario in which all traffic that arrives at a node could be shipped at the next node over a line. We show that even with this simple demand matrix, which is clearly biased in favor of choosing the direct path, we establish the counter-intuitive fact: "It is possible that not all players send their traffic through the direct path at equilibrium". Examples of such games in road traffic can be found in [8–11].

In the rest of the paper, we assume that M players have their own demands which should be shipped within a week from a given source to a destination. Thus each player has to split competitively its demand into that corresponding to each of the days of the week. At each day, the route corresponding to the daily demand of each player should be determined.

The paper is structured as follow: We present the system model with the assumptions considered in the next Section. Next we give the explicit expressions of the Nash equilibrium and the global optimum, respectively in Sects. 3 and 4. Section 5 presents some performance results including price of anarchy and Braess-type paradox. Finally we conclude the paper in Sect. 6.

2 The Model

Let $G = (\mathcal{N}, \mathcal{L}, \mathcal{I}, \mathcal{P})$ be a network routing game with $\mathcal{N}$ the set of nodes and $\mathcal{L}$ the set of links, $\mathcal{I}$ is the set of classes (e.g. players), and $P = (s_i, d^i, \phi_i)$ is a set that characterizes class i: s^i is the source, d^i is the destination and ϕ_i is the demand related to player i.

We describe the system with respect to the variables x_l^i which are restricted by the non-negativity constraints for each link l and player i: $x_l^i \geq 0$ and by the conservation constraints for each player i and each node v:

$$r_v^i + \sum_{j \in In(v)} x_j^i = \sum_{j \in Out(v)} x_j^i \tag{1}$$

where $r_v^i = \phi_i$ if v is the source node for player $i, r_v^i = \phi_i$ if v is its destination node, and $r_v^i = 0$ otherwise; $In(v)$ and $Out(v)$ are respectively all ingoing and outgoing links of node v.

A player i determines the routing decisions for all the traffic that corresponds to the corresponding class i. The cost of player i is assumed to be additive over links

$$J^i(\mathbf{x}) = \sum_l J_l^i(\mathbf{x}_l) \tag{2}$$

We shall assume that

(i) $K_l^i := \frac{\partial J_l^i(\mathbf{x})}{\partial x_l^i}$ exist and are continuous in x_l^i (for all i and l),
(ii) J_l^i are convex in x_l^i (for all i and l),

We shall also make the following assumptions for each link l and player i:
A1: J_l^i depends on $\mathbf{x}_l$ only through the total flow x_l and the flow of x_l^i of player i over the link.
A2: J_l^i is increasing in both arguments.
A3: Whenever J_l^i is finite, $K_l^i(x_l, x_l^i)$ is strictly increasing in both arguments.

We further restrict the cost to satisfy the following:
B1: For each link l there is a nonnegative cost density $T_l(x_l)$. T_l is a function of the total flow through the link and $J_l^i = x_l^i T_l(x_l)$.
B2: T_l is positive, strictly increasing and convex, and is continuously differentiable.

The Lagrangian with respect to the constraints on the conservation of flow is

$$L_i(\mathbf{x}, \lambda) = \sum_{l \in \mathcal{L}} J_l^i(x_l, x) + \sum_{v \in \mathcal{N}} \lambda_v^i \left(r_v^i + \sum_{j \in In(v)} x_j^i - \sum_{j \in Out(v)} x_j^i \right), \quad (3)$$

for each player i. Thus a vector $\mathbf{x}$ with nonnegative components satisfying (1) for all i and v is an equilibrium if and only if the following Karush-Kuhn-Tucker (KKT) condition holds. Below we shall use uv to denote the link defined by node pair u, v. There exist Lagrange multipliers λ_u^i for all nodes u and all players, i, such that for each pair of nodes u, v connected by a directed link (u, v),

$$K_{uv}^i(x_{uv}^i, x_{uv}) \geq \lambda_u^i - \lambda_v^i, \quad (4)$$

with equality if $x_{uv} > 0$.

Assume cost structure B. Then, the Lagrangian is given by

$$\begin{aligned} L_i(\mathbf{x}, \lambda) = & \textstyle\sum_{l \in \mathcal{L}} \left[T_l(x_l) + x_l^i \frac{\partial T_l(x_l)}{\partial x_l} \right] \\ & + \textstyle\sum_{v \in \mathcal{N}} \lambda_v^i \left(r_v^i + \sum_{j \in In(v)} x_j^i - \sum_{j \in Out(v)} x_j^i \right), \end{aligned} \quad (5)$$

for each player i. Equation (4) can be written as

$$T_{uv}(x_{uv}) + x_{uv}^i \frac{\partial T_{uv}(x_{uv})}{\partial x_{uv}} \geq \lambda_u^i - \lambda_v^i. \quad (6)$$

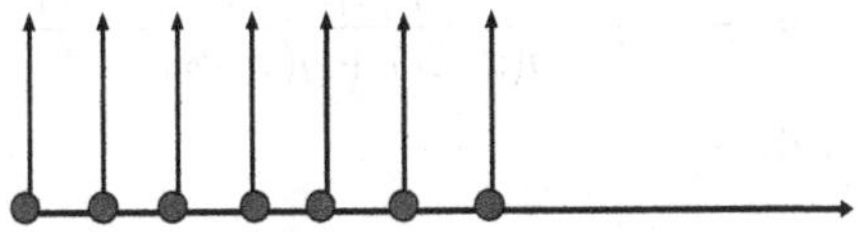

Fig. 1. Competitive routing on the line.

3 The Transient Equilibrium for Multi-user Sequential Game

Consider a sequential game: Assume at each day i, there are M new players that arrive. Player i comes with a demand of ϕ_i each competing for the link. This demand has to be shipped within 2 days. The decision of each player influences the cost of the others. This is a scheduling game: how much should player i send upon arrival and how much should it delay to the next day? If the game is already on for a long time, we can expect to have a symmetric solution (this will be made exact below). This means that at each day, the same amount will be sent. And since each day an amount of ϕ_i arrives, then the amount that will have to leave each day is also ϕ_i. An optimal solution will therefore be to send immediately all the arriving demand. We shall see however that at equilibrium, each player sends some of its traffic in the next day. We solve this problem by viewing it as an equivalent routing problem. The cost per unit of packet sent each day is $f(x)$. The cost for waiting another day is d.

Formally, let the demand of each player $k = 1, 2, \cdots, M$ arriving at day i be $\phi_{i,k} > 0$ that has to be shipped to destination within a period of 2 days. Let $x_j^{i,k}$ denotes the amount of flow sent by user k on day j knowing that user k arrived at day i. The total flow on day i is then denoted as $x_i = \sum_{k=1}^{M} x_i^{i,k} + x_i^{i-1,k}$. Let the vector $\mathbf{x}^{i,k} = (x_i^{i,k}, x_{i+1}^{i,k})$ denote the amount of flow sent by user k arriving at day i. The vector $\mathbf{x}^{i,k}$ is said to be feasible if $x_i^{i,k} + x_{i+1}^{i,k} = \phi_{i,k}$. For a given flow configuration of users $(\mathbf{x}^{i,1}, \mathbf{x}^{i,2}, \cdots, \mathbf{x}^{i,M})$, user k pays a congestion cost of $f(x_i)$ and delay cost of d per unit of its flow on day i. The objective of user l arriving at day i is to minimize his cost given by

$$J^{i,l} = x_i^{i,l} f(x_i) + x_{i+1}^{i,l}(f(x_{i+1}) + d) \tag{7}$$

By differentiating the cost function with respect to $x_i^{i,l}$ and setting the derivative equal to zero, we get:

$$x_i^{i,l} = \frac{d + f(x_{i+1}) - f(x_i) + \phi_{i,l} g(x_{i+1})}{g(x_i) + g(x_{i+1})} \tag{8}$$

so that

$$x_{i+1}^{i,l} = \phi_{i,l} - x_i^{i,l} = \frac{-d - f(x_{i+1}) + f(x_i) + \phi_{i,l} g(x_i)}{g(x_i) + g(x_{i+1})} \tag{9}$$

and also

$$x_{i+1}^{i+1,l} = \frac{d + f(x_{i+2}) - f(x_{i+1}) + \phi_{i,l} g(x_{i+2})}{g(x_{i+1}) + g(x_{i+2})} \tag{10}$$

Taking the sum, we obtain

$$\begin{aligned} x_{i+1} = \sum_{k=1}^{M} & \frac{d + f(x_{i+2}) - f(x_{i+1}) + \phi_{i,k} g(x_{i+2})}{g(x_{i+1}) + g(x_{i+2})} \\ & + \frac{-d - f(x_{i+1}) + f(x_i) + \phi_{i,k} g(x_i)}{g(x_i) + g(x_{i+1})} \end{aligned} \tag{11}$$

3.1 The Steady State

In the steady state, we have $x_i = \sum_{k=1}^{M} \phi_{i,k}, \forall i$. Hence, for every user l we have from Eq. (8)

$$x_i^{i,l} = \frac{\phi_{i,l}}{2} + \frac{d}{2g(\sum_{k=1}^{M} \phi_{i,k})} \tag{12}$$

3.2 The Case of Linear Cost

Similarly to the previous sections, let $f(x) = ax$. Then, Eq. (8) gives

$$-x_{i+2} + (\frac{2}{M} + 2)x_{i+1} - x_i = (\frac{2}{M})\sum_{k=1}^{M} \phi_k \tag{13}$$

The solution of this difference equation has the form

$$x_i = c_1(r_1)^i + c_2(r_2)^i + \sum_{k=1}^{M} \phi_k \tag{14}$$

where r_1 and r_2 are the solution of the characteristic equation

$$-r^2 + (\frac{2}{M} + 2)r - 1 = 0 \tag{15}$$

They are thus given by

$$r_{1,2} = 1 + \frac{1}{M}(1 \pm \sqrt{1 + 2M}) \tag{16}$$

Similarly, using the condition $x_0 = 0$ we conclude that

$$x_i = \sum_{k=1}^{M} \phi_k[1 - (1 + \frac{1}{M}(1 - \sqrt{1 + 2M}))^i] \tag{17}$$

4 The Global Optimum for a Semi Infinite Line

Let us now compute the global cost for the multi-user case at day i.

$$J^i(\mathbf{x}) = \sum_{i=1}^{M} J^{i,l}(\mathbf{x}) \tag{18}$$

Deriving the sum with respect to $x_i^{i,l}$, we have

$$\begin{aligned}\frac{\partial J^l(\mathbf{x})}{\partial x_i^{i,l}} &= f(x_i) + x_i^{i,l} g(x_i) - (\phi_{i,l} - x_i^{i,l})g(x_{i+1}) - f(x_{i+1}) - d \\ &+ (\phi_{i-1,l} - x_{i-1}^{i-1,l})g(x_i) - x_{i+1}^{i+1,l} g(x_{i+1})\end{aligned} \tag{19}$$

Equating the above equation to zero gives

$$x_i^{i,l} = \frac{d + f(x_{i+1}) - f(x_i) + \phi_{i,l}g(x_{i+1})}{g(x_i) + g(x_{i+1})} - \frac{\phi_{i-1,l}g(x_i) + x_{i+1}^{i+1,l}g(x_{i+1}) + x_{i-1}^{i-1,l}g(x_i)}{g(x_i) + g(x_{i+1})} \tag{20}$$

so that

$$\phi_i - x_i^{i,l} = \frac{-d - f(x_{i+1}) + f(x_i) + \phi_{i,l}g(x_i)}{g(x_i) + g(x_{i+1})} + \frac{\phi_{i-1,l}g(x_i) - x_{i+1}^{i+1,l}g(x_{i+1}) - x_{i-1}^{i-1,l}g(x_i)}{g(x_i) + g(x_{i+1})} \tag{21}$$

and also

$$x_{i+1}^{i+1} = \frac{d + f(x_{i+2}) - f(x_{i+1}) + \phi_{i+1,l}g(x_{i+2})}{g(x_{i+1}) + g(x_{i+2})} - \frac{\phi_{i,l}g(x_{i+1}) + x_{i+2}^{i+2,l}g(x_{i+2}) + x_i^{i,l}g(x_{i+1})}{g(x_{i+1}) + g(x_{i+2})} \tag{22}$$

Taking the sum, we obtain

$$\begin{aligned} x_{i+1} = & \sum_{k=1}^{M} \frac{-d - f(x_{i+1}) + f(x_i) + \phi_{i,l}g(x_i)}{g(x_i) + g(x_{i+1})} + \frac{\phi_{i-1,l}g(x_i) - x_{i+1}^{i+1,l}g(x_{i+1}) - x_{i-1}^{i-1,l}g(x_i)}{g(x_i) + g(x_{i+1})} \\ & + \sum_{k=1}^{M} \frac{d + f(x_{i+2}) - f(x_{i+1}) + \phi_{i+1,l}g(x_{i+2})}{g(x_{i+1}) + g(x_{i+2})} \\ & - \frac{\phi_{i,l}g(x_{i+1}) + x_{i+2}^{i+2,l}g(x_{i+2}) + x_i^{i,l}g(x_{i+1})}{g(x_{i+1}) + g(x_{i+2})} \end{aligned} \tag{23}$$

4.1 The Case of Linear Cost

Let $f(x) = ax$ and assume that $\phi_{i,k} = \phi_k, \forall i, k$ does not depend on i. Then

$$-\frac{M}{2}x_{i+2} + (M+1)x_{i+1} - \frac{M}{2}x_i = \sum_{k=1}^{M} \phi_k + \theta \tag{24}$$

where $\theta = \frac{1}{2}\sum_{k=1}^{M} x_{i+2}^{i+2,k} - x_{i+1}^{i+1,k} + x_i^{i,k} - x_{i-1}^{i-1,k}$. Noting $a_i = \sum_{k=1}^{M} x_i^{i,k}$, we have

$$x_{i+1} = \sum_{k=1}^{M} \phi_k - a_i + a_{i+1} \tag{25}$$

$$x_{i+2} = \sum_{k=1}^{M} \phi_k - a_{i+1} + a_{i+2} \tag{26}$$

From (25) and (26), we obtain

$$\begin{aligned} \theta &= \tfrac{1}{2}[a_{i+2} - a_{i+1} + -a_i - a_{i+1}] \\ &= \tfrac{1}{2}[x_{i+2} - x_{i+1}] \end{aligned} \tag{27}$$

We then have the following recursive function

$$-(M+1)x_{i+2} + (2M+3)x_{i+1} - Mx_i = 2\sum_{k=1}^{M} \phi_k \tag{28}$$

The solution of this difference equation has the form

$$x_i = c_1(r_1)^i + c_2(r_2)^i + \sum_{k=1}^{M} \phi_k \tag{29}$$

where r_1 and r_2 are the solution of the characteristic equation $-(M+1)r^2 + (2M+3)r - M = 0$. They are thus given by

$$r_{1,2} = 1 + \frac{1 \pm \sqrt{9+8M}}{2(M+1)} \tag{30}$$

Using the condition $x_0 = 0$, we conclude that, for every user l, we have

$$x_i = \sum_{k=1}^{M} \phi_k [1 - (1 + \frac{1-\sqrt{9+8M}}{2(M+1)})^i] \tag{31}$$

5 Performance Analysis

5.1 Price of Anarchy

At the steady state, the cost for player i is

$$\begin{aligned} J^{i,l}(d) &= x_i^i f(\textstyle\sum_{k=1}^{M} \phi_{i,k}) + x_{i+1}^i (f(\sum_{k=1}^{M} \phi_{i,k}) + d) \\ &= (x_i^i + x_{i+1}^i) f(\textstyle\sum_{k=1}^{M} \phi_{i,k}) + d x_{i+1}^i \\ &= \phi_{i,l} f(\textstyle\sum_{k=1}^{M} \phi_{i,k}) + d(\frac{\phi_{i,l}}{2} - \frac{d}{2g(\sum_{k=1}^{M} \phi_{i,k})}) \end{aligned} \tag{32}$$

Since $x_{i+1}^i \geq 0$, we have $d \leq \phi_{i,l} g(\sum_{k=1}^{M} \phi_{i,k})$. $J^{i,l}(d)$ is concave in d with a maximum at $d = \frac{\phi_{i,l} g(\sum_{k=1}^{M} \phi_{i,k})}{2}$. Interestingly, we observe that at $d = \phi_{i,l} g(\sum_{k=1}^{M} \phi_{i,k})$, the cost function $J^{i,l}(d)$ is minimized and equal to $\phi_{i,l} f(\sum_{k=1}^{M} \phi_k)$ which is equal to the cost at $d = 0$.

The price of anarchy (PoA) is then given by

$$\begin{aligned} PoA &= \frac{J^{i,l}(d)}{\phi_{i,l} f(\sum_{k=1}^{M} \phi_{i,k})} \\ &= 1 + \frac{d(\frac{\phi_{i,l}}{2} - \frac{d}{2g(\sum_{k=1}^{M} \phi_{i,k})})}{\phi_{i,l} f(\sum_{k=1}^{M} \phi_{i,k})} \end{aligned} \tag{33}$$

For the numerical results we set the value of $\phi_{i,l}$ to 1 and a =1.

Notice that the PoA is equal to 1 for $d = 0$ and $d = \phi_{i,l} g(\sum_{k=1}^{M} \phi_{i,k})$. We depict in Fig. 2 the price of anarchy as function of delay for different number of users. As already said, we notice that the PoA is equal to 1 for $d = 0$, and $d = 1$. We also remark that the PoA increases as the number of users increases which leads to the interaction of users and hence induces more cost to ship their demand over the line.

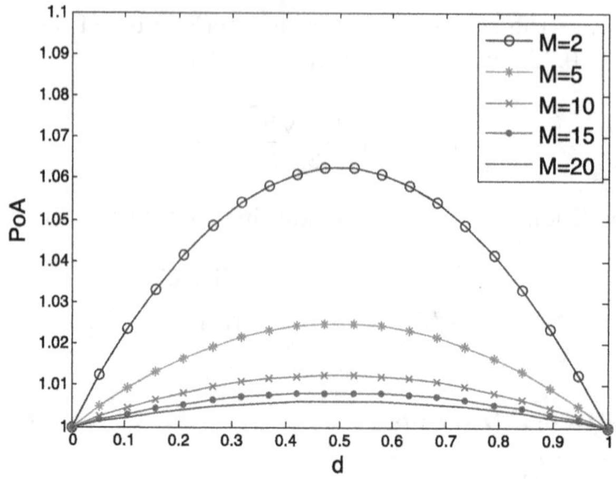

Fig. 2. Price of anarchy as function of cost

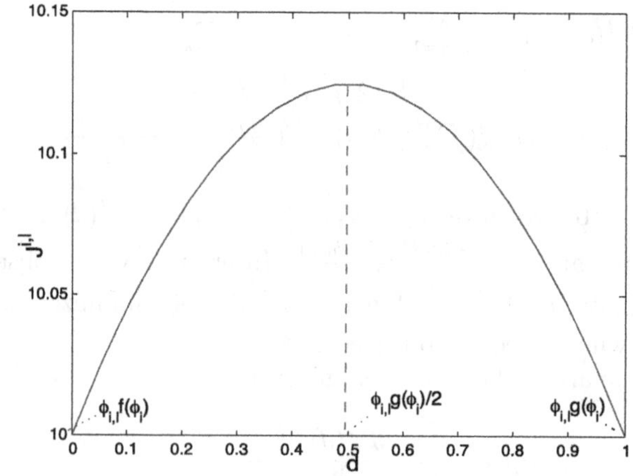

Fig. 3. The Braess-type paradox for the sequential game.

5.2 Braess-Type Paradox

At the steady state, the cost for player l at day i is:

$$\begin{aligned} J^{i,l}(d) &= x_i^i f(\textstyle\sum_{k=1}^M \phi_{i,k}) + x_{i+1}^i (f(\sum_{k=1}^M \phi_{i,k}) + d) \\ &= (x_i^i + x_{i+1}^i) f(\textstyle\sum_{k=1}^M \phi_{i,k}) + d x_{i+1}^i \\ &= \phi_{i,l} f(\textstyle\sum_{k=1}^M \phi_{i,k}) + d(\frac{\phi_{i,l}}{2} - \frac{d}{2g(\sum_{k=1}^M \phi_{i,k})}). \end{aligned} \tag{34}$$

It is clear that the cost for player i is non-negative for

$$d \in [\frac{\phi_{i,l} g(\sum_{k=1}^M \phi_{i,k}}{2}, \phi_{i,l} g(\sum_{k=1}^M \phi_{i,k})].$$

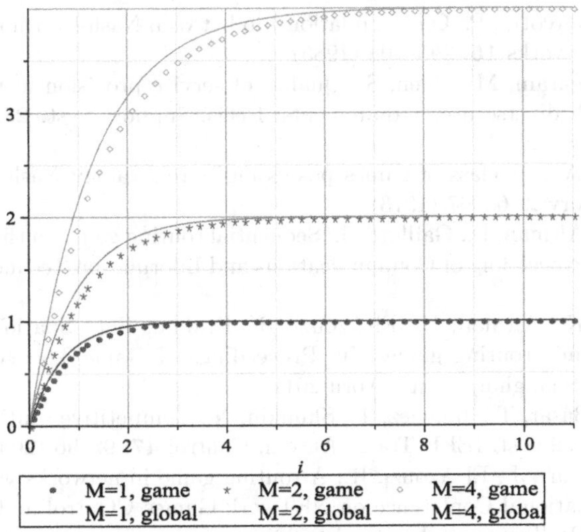

Fig. 4. Dynamics of the total flow sent over the horizon where $\phi_k = 1 \forall k = 1, \ldots, M$.

In this region, $J^{i,l}$ decreases as d increases, which is a Braess type paradox (see Fig. 3). This paradox was obtained in the context of a load balancing network in [11]. We depict in Fig. 4 the variation of the Nash equilibrium in Eq. (17) and the global optimum in Eq. (31) over the horizon for $\phi_k = 1; \forall k = 1, \ldots, M$. It is clearly illustrated that the Nash equilibrium over a semi infinite line converges to the global optimum from day $i = 4$.

6 Conclusion

We have considered a sequential routing game networks where several users coexist and competitively send their traffic to a destination on a line over a period of two days. Under some assumptions, we have obtained the explicit solutions for the Nash equilibrium and the global optimum and derive the price of anarchy. Finally, we have showed that under a semi infinite line, the Nash equilibrium converges to the global optimum and, have identified a Braess-type paradox behavior in the context of sequential games.

References

1. Wardrop, J.G.: Some theoretical aspects of road traffic research communication networks. Proc. Inst. Civ. Eng. Part 2 **1**, 325–378 (1952)
2. Patriksson, M.: The Traffic Assignment Problem: Models and Methods. VSP, Utrecht (1994)
3. Orda, A., Rom, R., Shimkin, N.: Competitive routing in multi-user environments. IEEE/ACM Trans. Netw. **1**, 510–521 (1993)

4. Haurie, A., Marcotte, P.: On the relationship between Nash-Cournot and Wardrop equilibria. Networks **15**, 295–308 (1985)
5. Park, K., Sitharam, M., Chen, S.: Quality of service provision in noncooperative networks with diverse user requirements. Decis. Support Syst. **28**(1–2), 101–122 (2000)
6. Rosenthal, R.W.: A class of games possessing pure strategy Nash equilibria. Int. J. Game Theory **2**, 65–67 (1973)
7. Haddad, M., Altman, E., Gaillard, J.: Sequential routing game on the line: transmit or relay? In: Proceeding of Communications and Information Technology (ICCIT), June 2012
8. Hanawal, M.K., Altman, E., El-Azouzi, R., Prabhu, B.J.: Spatio-temporal control for dynamic routing games. In: Proceedings of Game Theory for Networks (GameNets), Shanghai, China, April 2011
9. Altman, E., Basar, T., Jimenez, T., Shimkin, N.: Competitive routing in networks with polynomial cost. IEEE Trans. Autom. Control **47**, 92–96 (2002)
10. Altman, E., Kuri, J., El-Azouzi, R.: A routing game in networks with lossy links. In: 7th International Conference on NETwork Games COntrol and OPtimization (NETGCOOP), Trento, Italy, October 2014
11. Kameda, H., Pourtallier, O.: Paradoxes in distributed decisions on optimal load balancing for networks of homogeneous computers. J. ACM **49**(3), 407–433 (2002)
12. Wie, B.W., Friesz, T., Tobin, R.: Dynamic user optimal traffic assignment on congested multidestination networks. Transp. Res. **24B**(6), 431–442 (1990)

QoS-Aware Tactical Power Control for 5G Networks

Hajar El Hammouti[1(✉)], Essaid Sabir[2], and Hamidou Tembine[3]

[1] STRS Lab, INPT, Rabat, Morocco
elhammouti@inpt.ac.ma

[2] NEST Research Group, ENSEM, Hassan II University Casablanca, Casablanca, Morocco
e.sabir@ensem.ac.ma

[3] Learning and Game Theory Lab, New York University Abu Dhabi, Abu Dhabi, United Arab Emirates
tembine@nyu.edu

Abstract. Small-Cells are deployed in order to enhance the network performance by bringing the network closer to the user. However, as the number of low power nodes grows increasingly, the overall energy consumption of the Small-Cells base stations cannot be ignored. A relevant amount of energy could be saved through several techniques, especially power control mechanisms. In this paper, we are concerned with energy-aware self-organizing networks that guarantee a satisfactory performance. We consider satisfaction equilibria, mainly the efficient satisfaction equilibrium (ESE), to ensure a target quality of service (QoS) and save energy. First, we identify conditions of existence and uniqueness of ESE under a stationary channel assumption. We fully characterize the ESE and prove that, whenever it exists, it is a solution of a linear system. Moreover, we define satisfactory Pareto optimality and show that, at the ESE, no player can increase its QoS without degrading the overall performance. Finally, in order to reach the ESE and the maximum network capacity, we propose a fully distributed scheme based on the Banach-Picard algorithm and show, through simulation results, its qualitative properties.

1 Introduction

According to the Cisco visual network index (VNI) report [4], the monthly global mobile data traffic has reached 3.7 exabytes in 2015, and is expected to increase nearly eightfolds attaining 30.6 exabytes by 2020. In order to cope with this sheer volume of data traffic, a natural move to the next generation of wireless communication systems (5G) is needed. This is achieved by involving key technologies [2] including networks ultra-densification. The main driver behind ultra-densification is to substantially increase existing macro-cellular networks capacity [10]. Ultimately, forecasts predict that by the time 5G comes to fruition, there will be more base stations (BSs) than mobile handsets [1].

E. Sabir et al. (Eds.): UNet 2017, LNCS 10542, pp. 25–37, 2017.
https://doi.org/10.1007/978-3-319-68179-5_3

The growing number of BSs, typically low power nodes (micro, pico, and femto base stations), also called Small-Cells, gives rise to many new challenges. Especially, those related to heterogeneity, optimization, and scaling. Clearly, as the number of heterogeneous Small-Cells grows tremendously, the amount of interferences will increase significantly leading to the so-called *curse of dimensionality*. The amount of data, that is exchanged between BSs in order to handle interferences, raises exponentially with the number of interfering BSs (dimensionality) resulting in a heavily loaded network (mainly with signaling messages).

Self-organizing networks (SON) are by far the most important approach to rise above dimensionality issues related to Small-Cells deployments [7]. Not only do self-organizing networks enable to the network an automated resource management and improve BSs coordination, but SON can significantly reduce operators CAPEX (capital expenditures) and OPEX (operating expenses), especially by reducing human intervention and optimizing available resources.

However, as the number of low power nodes grows increasingly, the overall energy consumption of Small-Cells base stations cannot be ignored. A relevant amount of energy could be saved. Mechanisms for energy-aware nodes are more than desirable. SON should implement energy saving techniques in order to prolong the lifetime of the batteries and increase the energy efficiency.

In order to achieve energy efficiency, several techniques such as sleep mode optimizations [3], power control mechanisms [6], and learning algorithms can be used. In this work, we are interested in achieving energy efficiency through a satisfaction mechanism. Practically, instead of achieving the best network performance by maximizing QoS, which is generally energy costly, nodes can only target satisfactory QoS levels, and hence, work efficiently.

The main contribution of this paper is to present a novel approach while dealing with energy efficiency in SON. Our paper addresses the following questions: how to reach a target QoS while minimizing energy consumption? Given a realistic wireless framework, how to select the most efficient power allocation that meets with users expectations?

1.1 Literature Review

To answer these questions *efficiently* and *satisfactorily*, a game theoretical approach is adopted. Game theory provides powerful tools and gives clear insights on interacting nodes behaviors.

One of the well-known game theoretical solution concepts is the *Nash equilibrium* (NE). NE is a strategy profile where no player has the incentive to deviate unilaterally. It has been shown that the NE generally fails to model the network performance. Indeed, when each player acts selfishly by increasing its power, subsequent interferences increase driving the network to a suboptimal situation.

Alternatively, in order to support the users QoS requirements, the *constrained Nash equilibrium* (CNE, also called *generalized Nash equilibrium*) is introduced [5,13]. Particularly, constrained games are concerned with payoffs maximization (or minimization) subject to coupled and/or orthogonal constraints over the players strategies and/or payoffs. Hence, at a CNE, each player aims at achieving its optimal utility while satisfying QoS constraints. The CNE is designed to accommodate with QoS requirements that the NE fails to model. Nevertheless, from a practical point of view, the CNE can be a very restrictive solution that (i) reduces the set of players strategies, and (ii) requires costly efforts. More precisely, in order to reach the highest payoffs, greater efforts, such as higher powers, are generally needed. This may lead to a lower energy efficiency and cost effectiveness of the network.

Consequently, a less restrictive solution concept, namely *satisfaction equilibrium* (SE), has been introduced [8,15]. Mainly, in a less restrictive framework, players can only target satisfactory QoS levels without aiming at achieving the highest payoffs. At an SE, utilities optimization assumption is relaxed. The payoffs should only be above given thresholds based on users services requirements. Hence, (i) energy costs related to payoffs maximization are saved, and (ii) players constraints are satisfied. Note that the CNE can also be seen as an SE of a satisfaction game, since players constraints are always satisfied at a CNE [11]. Yet, the reverse is not necessarily true.

The energy efficiency function was introduced by Meshkati *et al.* in [9]. This function measures the performance of the network per Joule of consumed energy. For each node, the ratio: $\frac{\text{QoS}}{\text{Consumed energy}}$ is reduced. The work in [14] investigates energy efficiency in ultra-dense networks through joint power control and users scheduling. The problem of energy efficiency maximization is formulated as a dynamic stochastic game and cast as a mean-field game. The authors show that the mean-field equilibrium saves energy and reduces outage probability. In [14], the energy efficiency for multiple input multiple output antennas heterogeneous networks is studied using a non-cooperative and cooperative power control game. The authors propose a power allocation algorithm in order to reach Pareto optimal solutions.

1.2 Contribution

In this paper, while we refer to earlier works [11,12], the focus is different. Our emphasis is on the efficient satisfaction equilibrium, and our contribution is multifold.

- First, we study existence and uniqueness of ESE and prove that: if the ESE exists, it is necessarily a solution of a linear system.
- Second, we introduce "satisfactory Pareto optimality" property and show that the ESE is satisfactory Pareto optimal. Mainly, at the ESE, no user can increase its payoff without dissatisfying its opponents.
- Finally, we propose a distributed algorithm that reaches the efficient satisfaction equilibrium in only a few iterations, and present an adaptive version referred to as "the progressive Banach-Picard algorithm for capacity discovery" in order to reach the best QoS levels. We also study the qualitative properties of the proposed algorithms through simulation results.

1.3 Structure

The remainder of the paper is organized as follows. The next section presents the system model. Section 3 formulates the problem as a satisfaction game, and provides some satisfaction equilibria properties. In Sect. 4, we fully characterize the ESE, and study the conditions of its existence and uniqueness. In Sect. 5, we present a Picard-Banach based algorithm that reaches the ESE, and propose its adaptive version to reach the highest QoS levels. Section 6 presents numerical results to illustrate the performance of the studied algorithms. Finally, in the last section, we make a few concluding remarks and discuss various possible extensions of this work.

2 System Model

Consider a self-organizing network where N heterogeneous small-cells communicate with a common concentration point (e.g. a macro base station). We denote by $\mathcal{U}$ the set of small-cells. Small-cells operate over the same radio channel which is supposed stationary. We denote by h_i the channel gain between cell i and the concentration point. Each cell selects its transmit power within a bounded power space that we denote by $\mathcal{P}^i$. Each node i aims at guaranteeing a target throughput θ_i. We denote by r_i the bandwidth-normalized instantaneous throughput of node i.

$$r_i(\mathbf{P}) = \log(1 + \gamma_i(\mathbf{P})), \tag{1}$$

where γ_i denotes the instantaneous signal-to-interference-and-noise-ratio (SINR) of node i,

$$\gamma_i(\mathbf{P}) = \frac{h_i P_i}{\eta + \sum\limits_{j \in \mathcal{U} \setminus \{i\}} h_j P_j}, \tag{2}$$

with $\mathbf{P}$ the power vector composed of all nodes transmit powers. P_i is the power chosen by node i, and η is the variance of a Gaussian random variable that represents the additive Gaussian noise.

3 Game Formulation

Suppose the non-cooperative game $\mathcal{G} = \{\mathcal{U}, \{\mathcal{P}_i\}_{i \in \mathcal{U}}, \{r_i\}_{i \in \mathcal{U}}, \{\theta_i\}_{i \in \mathcal{U}}\}$ where $\mathcal{U}$ is the set of players, $\mathcal{P}_1, \ldots, \mathcal{P}_N$ are the sets of pure strategies of each user. The payoff of each user i, r_i, is given by its throughput. We will separate the strategy of a node i, P_i, and its opponents by using the following notation $(P_i, \mathbf{P}_{-i})$. Each user i aims at achieving a minimum throughput θ_i. Consequently, each user i is satisfied with its strategy P_i given the others strategies $\mathbf{P}_{-i}$, if

$$r_i(P_i, \mathbf{P}_{-i}) \geq \theta_i. \tag{3}$$

In order to achieve satisfactory solutions, only a set of strategies is allowed for each node given its opponents strategies. We refer to these strategies as "*feasible strategies*". Such a set can be characterized by a correspondence function $f_i : \mathcal{P}_{-i} \longrightarrow 2^{\mathcal{P}^i}$, where $\mathcal{P}_{-i} = \mathcal{P}^i \times \cdots \times \mathcal{P}^{i-1} \times \mathcal{P}^{i+1} \times \cdots \times \mathcal{P}^N$, and $2^{\mathcal{P}^i}$ is the set of all subsets of $\mathcal{P}^i$. For each $\mathbf{P}_{-i} \in \mathcal{P}_{-i}$, if $P_i \in f_i(\mathbf{P}_{-i})$, then $U_i(P_i, \mathbf{P}_{-i}) \geq \theta_i$. Accordingly, we define the set of satisfaction equilibria as in [8].

Definition 1 (Satisfaction equilibrium). *A strategy profile $\mathbf{P}^+$ is a satisfaction equilibrium of the game $\mathcal{G} = \{\mathcal{U}, \{\mathcal{P}^i\}_{i\in\mathcal{U}}, \{U_i\}_{i\in\mathcal{U}}, \{\theta\}_{i\in\mathcal{U}}\}$, if*

$$\forall i \in \mathcal{U},\ P_i^+ \in f_i(\mathbf{P}_{-i}^+),\ i.e.,\ U_i(P_i^+, \mathbf{P}_{-i}^+) \geq \theta_i. \tag{4}$$

It is important to note that an SE exists, if the constraints are feasible, mainly, if

$$\sum_{i\in\mathcal{U}} \theta_i \leq \mathcal{C}, \tag{5}$$

where $\mathcal{C}$ is the maximum network capacity (which is also solution to the rate-maximization problem as described in [17]). Hereafter, we assume that the constraints feasibility is satisfied.

Figure 1 illustrates the feasible powers allowed to device i given fixed transmit powers of its opponents. It can be seen from the figure that the satisfaction of device i can be achieved all along the interval between $P_i^{\min}$ and $P_i^{\max}$. Consequently, a continuum of transmit powers can meet with device i satisfaction.

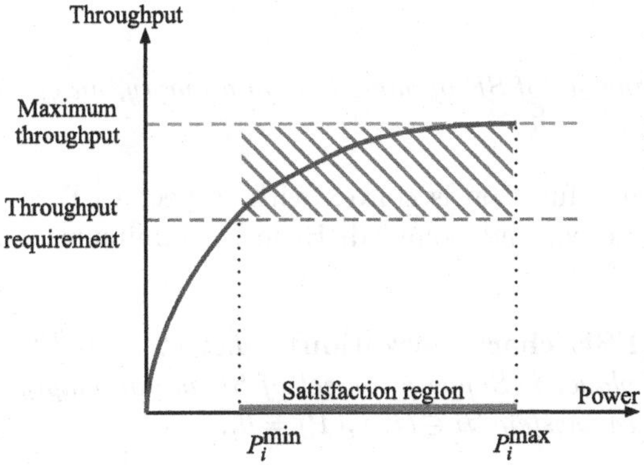

Fig. 1. A representation of the throughput of device i given fixed transmit powers of its opponents. This is an illustrative example where the QoS is measured in terms of throughput, other QoS metrics (delay, bit error rate, ...) could interchangeably be used.

Proposition 1. *For each $i \in \mathcal{U}$, let $P_i = [0, P_i^{max}]$ be the set of pure strategies of player i, P_i^{max} is the maximum transmit power value allowed to i.*

The set of SE of game $\mathcal{G}$ is convex, closed and bounded.

Proof.

- Convex: satisfaction equilibria are solution to linear inequalities system, each feasible region (inequality) is convex [16], and the intersection of convex sets is convex.
- Closed: the closeness of the SE set stems from the inequalities that are not strict. Each inequality is a union of two closed half planes, and the union and intersection of a finite number of closed sets is a closed set.
- Bounded: this holds true because the set of power states is supposed bounded.

□

4 Efficient Satisfaction Equilibrium

We denote by $\mathcal{S}$ the set of SE. Whenever $\mathcal{S}$ is non-empty, we define the *efficient satisfaction equilibrium* (ESE) concept as provided in [11].

Definition 2 (Efficient satisfaction equilibrium). *An SE $\boldsymbol{P}^+$ is said efficient SE if it minimizes the following efficiency function*

$$\forall \boldsymbol{P} \in \mathcal{S}, F(\boldsymbol{P}) = \sum_{i \in \mathcal{U}} P_i. \tag{6}$$

The next corollary prove the existence of an ESE when the set of SE is non-empty.

Corollary 1. *If the set of SE of game $\mathcal{G}$ is non empty, an efficient satisfaction equilibrium exists.*

Proof. The efficiency function is convex with respect to $\mathbf{P}$ over the set of SE which is convex, closed, and bounded. Hence, a minimum of F exists, which completes our proof. □

Proposition 2 (ESE characterization). *Let $P_i = [0, P_i^{max}]$ be the set of pure strategies of player i. Suppose the set of SE is non-empty. The ESE is the solution to the linear system $\forall i \in \mathcal{U}$, $r_i(\boldsymbol{P}) = \theta_i$.*

Proof. Let $\mathbf{P}^+$ be a solution to $\forall i \in \mathcal{U}, r_i(\mathbf{P}) = \theta_i$. We want to prove that $\mathbf{P}^+$ minimizes the efficiency function $F(\mathbf{P}) = \sum_{i \in \mathcal{U}} P_i$ with $\mathbf{P} \in \mathcal{S}$.

Suppose by absurd that there exists $\tilde{\mathbf{P}} \in \mathcal{S}$ such that

$$\sum_{i \in \mathcal{U}} \tilde{P}_i < \sum_{i \in \mathcal{U}} P_i^+. \tag{7}$$

We want to prove that under this assumption, there is at least one player whose target throughput is not satisfied. We suppose that for all the players apart from the Nth player, we have

$$r_i(\tilde{\mathbf{P}}) \geq \theta_i. \tag{8}$$

In order to show that the requirement of player N is, in this case, unsatisfied, meaning $r_N(\tilde{\mathbf{P}}) < \theta_N$, i.e. $r_N(\tilde{\mathbf{P}}) < r_N(\mathbf{P}^+)$ (since $\mathbf{P}^+$ is solution to the linear system), we only need to show that

$$\frac{\tilde{P}_N h_N}{\eta + \tilde{P}^t - \tilde{P}_N h_N} < \frac{P_N^+ h_N}{\eta + P^{t+} - P_N^+ h_N}, \tag{9}$$

with $P^t = \sum\limits_{i \in \mathcal{U} P_i h_i}$, and Eq. (9) becomes after a few algebras equivalent to

$$\eta(\tilde{P}_N - P_N^+) + \tilde{P}_N P^{t+} - P_N^+ \tilde{P}^t < 0. \tag{10}$$

Important to note that $\forall i \in \mathcal{U}, r_i(P^+) = \theta_i$. Hence, using the same previous reasoning, Eq. (8) becomes, $\forall 1 \leq i \leq N-1$

$$\eta(\tilde{P}_i - P_i^+) + \tilde{P}_i P^{t+} - P_i^+ \tilde{P}^t \geq 0. \tag{11}$$

By subsequent summation of inequalities described by Eq. (11) from $i = 1$ to $i = N - 1$, we obtain

$$\eta(\tilde{P}^t - \tilde{P}_N h_N - P^{t+} + P_N^+ h_N) + P^{t+}(\tilde{P}^t - \tilde{P}_N h_N) - \tilde{P}^t(P^{t+} - P_N^+ h_N) \geq 0. \tag{12}$$

After a few algebras, we obtain

$$\eta(\tilde{P}_N - P_N^+) + \tilde{P}_N P^{t+} - P_N^+ \tilde{P}^t < \frac{\eta}{h_k}(\tilde{P}^t - P^{t+}). \tag{13}$$

Since we supposed that $\sum\limits_{i \in \mathcal{U}} \tilde{P}_i < \sum\limits_{i \in \mathcal{U}} P_i^+$, then $\tilde{P}^t < P^{t+}$ (the total received power conserves the order as the channels gain are stationary and the same for both received powers). Thus,

$$\eta(\tilde{P}_N - P_N^+) + \tilde{P}_N P^{t+} - P_N^+ \tilde{P}^t < 0. \tag{14}$$

Hence, this is a contradiction since $\tilde{P}$ is an SE. Thus, $\sum\limits_{i \in \mathcal{U}} \tilde{P}_i > \sum\limits_{i \in \mathcal{U}} P_i^+$, and P^+ is the ESE. □

Proposition 2 states that, whenever it exists, the ESE is met when all players are exactly enough satisfied. The obtained result confirms intuitive expectations since only minimal efforts are needed to afford minimal satisfaction. Furthermore, the Pareto frontier is exactly defined by the efficient satisfaction equilibrium. The Next definition describes the Pareto efficiency in satisfaction games.

Definition 3 (Satisfactory Pareto optimality). *In a satisfaction game, a strategy profile is Pareto optimal if no player can increase its payoff without dissatisfying its opponents.*

The following corollary arises from the above definition.

Corollary 2 (Pareto optimality). *Suppose the set of SE is non-empty and the power spaces are non-empty, convex and compact sets. The ESE exists and is satisfactory Pareto optimal.*

Proof. At the ESE, given the other players strategies, if a player i decides to increase its payoff by increasing its transmit power, the interferences increase, and thus all the other players payoffs are deteriorated, mainly some nodes requirements are not satisfied. □

Next, we provide an analytical expression of ESE under existence conditions.

Proposition 3. *Let $P_i = [0, P_i^{max}]$ be the set of pure strategies of player i. The ESE of the game $\mathcal{G}$ exists if*

$$\begin{cases} \sum_{i=1}^{N-1} h_i(1-2^{\theta_i}) \prod_{j=1,j\neq i}^{N} 2^{\theta_j} h_j + h_N \prod_{j=1}^{N-1} 2^{\theta_j} h_j \neq 0, \\ 0 \leq P_N^+ \leq P_N^{max} \text{ and } P_i^+ \leq P_i^{max}, 1 \leq i \leq N-1, \end{cases} \tag{15}$$

such that

$$\begin{cases} P_N^+ = \dfrac{\eta(2^{\theta_N}-1)}{\sum_{i=1}^{N-1} h_i \frac{1-2^{\theta_N}}{2^{\theta_N} h_N} \frac{2^{\theta_i} h_i}{1-2^{\theta_i}} + \frac{h_N}{1-2^{\theta_N}}} \\ P_i^+ = \dfrac{1-2^{\theta_i}}{2^{\theta_i} h_i} \dfrac{2^{\theta_N} h_N}{1-2^{\theta_N}} P_N, 1 \leq i \leq N-1, \end{cases} \tag{16}$$

where P_N^+ and $P_i^+, 1 \leq i \leq N-1$, compose the ESE strategy profile.

Proof.

- The first equation in conditions (15) stems from the computation of the determinant of the linear system $\forall i \in \mathcal{U}, r_i(P) = \theta_i$. Particularly, an ESE exists if the determinant of the linear system is non zero.
- The second conditions in Eq. (15) ensure that solutions do not exceed minimum and maximum power bounds.
- Equation (16) gives the solution of the linear system. □

5 Distributed Learning: Banach-Picard Algorithm

5.1 Banach-Picard Algorithm for ESE

In order to reach an ESE, we propose a distributed learning scheme described by the Banach-Picard algorithm, also called "fixed point iterations". The Banach-Picard algorithm is known to be convergent with a geometrical rate to the solution of the equation $w(x) = x$ [18]. In order to converge to the unique fixed point of w, function w should be contractive. In our case, we suppose $w(x) = \frac{x}{\theta_i} r_i(x, \mathbf{P}_{-i})$, which is a contractive function. Notice that when the fixed point is reached, mainly $\frac{x}{\theta_i} r_i(x, \mathbf{P}_{-i}) = x$, we obtain, $r_i(x, \mathbf{P}_{-i}) = \theta_i$ (we suppose that the fixed point is different from zero otherwise nodes cannot target their satisfactory QoS levels).

The Banach-Picard algorithm is described in Algorithm 1.

Algorithm 1. Banach-Picard algorithm

Parameters initialization
Each node picks randomly a transmit power with initial probabilities p_i^0
repeat
  Learning pattern
  for Each node i **do**
Observes the value of its instantaneous throughput $r_i^t(p_i^t, \mathbf{P}_{-i})$
Updates its power as follows:
$p_i^{t+1} \leftarrow p_i^t \frac{\theta_i}{r_i^t}$
until The stopping criterion

p_i^t is the power of node i at instant t, and $r_i^t(p_i^t, \mathbf{P}_{-i})$ is the throughput of player i at instant t when its opponents choose $\mathbf{P}_{-i}$. The stopping criterion can be formulated as "all players have reached their target throughput".

5.2 Banach-Picard Algorithm for Capacity Discovery

In some use cases, achieving the best performance is more important than energy consumption. In such contexts, adapted version of Banach-Picard algorithm, referred to as the *progressive Banach-Picard algorithm for capacity discovery*, can be used. In the adaptive version, once a node's request is reached, the user increases its demand slightly, and adjusts its power accordingly in order to reach its new target. This process allows to the users to maximize their payoffs reaching a constrained Nash equilibrium (maximizing their payoffs subject to their initial requirements constraints) and avoiding any under-utilization of the network. The progressive Banach-Picard algorithm for capacity discovery is described in Algorithm 2.

Algorithm 2. Progressive Banach-Picard algorithm for capacity discovery

Parameters initialization
Each node picks randomly a transmit power with initial probabilities p_i^0
Each node has an initial requirement θ_i^0
repeat
  Learning pattern
  for Each node i **do**
Observes the value of its instantaneous throughput $r_i^t(p_i^t, \mathbf{P}_{-i})$
$p_i^{t+1} \leftarrow p_i^t \frac{\theta_i}{r_i^t}$
    if θ_i is reached and $\sum_i \theta_i < C$ **then**
Updates its power as follows:
$\theta_i \leftarrow \theta_i + \epsilon$
until The stopping criterion

where the parameter $\epsilon \in [0.1]$ is the throughput size step.

5.3 Fully Distributed Implementation

The Banach-Picard based algorithms we propose are fully distributed algorithms. They can be implemented on devices in an asynchronous way where each node updates its state depending on its own clock. The nodes do not need to know their opponents strategies or payoffs, they only observe their own throughput at each algorithm running iteration. Consequently, no signaling messages are needed between nodes. Only local (individual) information is required. The throughput is observed at each transmitter using the channel state information (CSI).

6 Simulation Results

In this section, we turn to present some representative simulations by which we validate our analysis and show the performance of the proposed algorithms.

6.1 QoS Requirement and Channel Gain Effects

First, we use Banach-Picard algorithm to reach the ESE. Consider Fig. 2 which depicts the transmit power evolution and subsequent throughput for each node. As the channel gain is supposed fixed ($h_i = 1$ for all i), final power decisions (Fig. 2(a)) follow the QoS requirements. For example, user 3, who is the most demanding among nodes, transmits with the highest power. It can also be seen from Fig. 2(b) that the final throughput of each node matches perfectly with its initial demand. Besides, the ESE is met in only a few ten iterations. Notice that the sum of transmit powers is set to the minimum at the end of the iterations which goes in the same direction with our prediction: the ESE minimizes the sum of transmit powers among all the satisfaction equilibria.

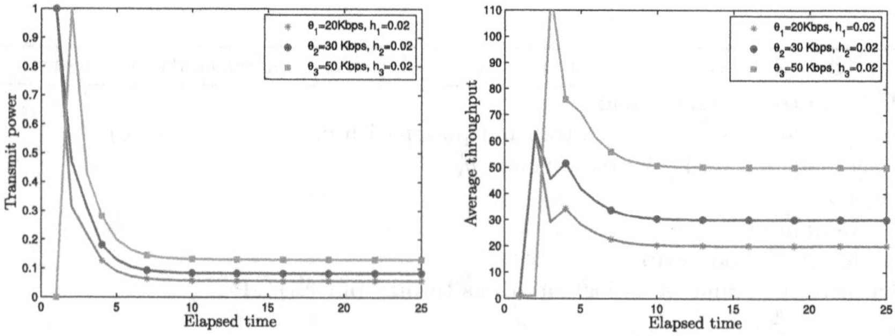

(a) (b)

Fig. 2. QoS requirement effect. Figure (a) represents the transmit powers decision evolution over time for 3 users. The resulting throughput is given by Figure (b). The starting power allocation is $(1, 1, 1)[mW]$, and the maximum network capacity $C = 120$.

6.2 Algorithm Recovery

Here, we turn to show the recovery property of Banach-Picard iterations. By the recovery property, we mean the algorithm's ability to adapt its results when the environment parameters change. Mainly, if a node changes its demand over time, a lower number of iterations should be needed in order to return back to the ESE allocation. Figure 3 shows that node 1 increases its demand at $t = 20$. This demand is quickly satisfied, and the algorithm converges rapidly to the new ESE.

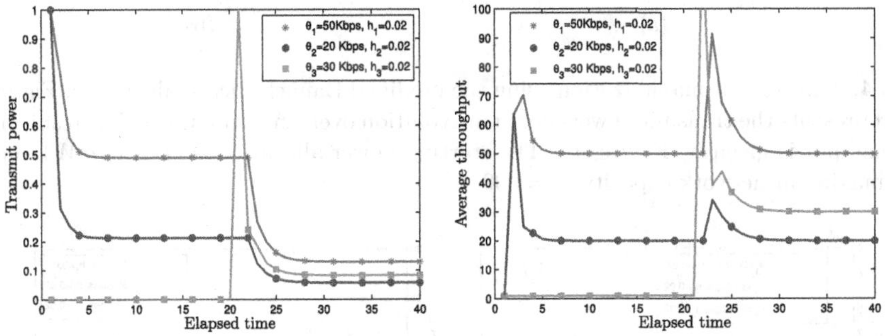

(a) (b)

Fig. 3. Algorithm recovery. Figure (a) represents the transmit powers decision evolution over time for 3 users. The resulting throughput is given by Figure (b). The first user increases its demand at $t = 20$. The starting power allocation is $(1, 1, 1)[mW]$, and the maximum network capacity $C = 120$.

6.3 Capacity Discovery

We are interested in maximizing the payoffs using the progressive Banach-Picard algorithm for capacity discovery. Figure 4 plots the transmit powers and payoffs evolution within time. It can be seen from the figure that users reach their optimal payoffs by the end of the iterations. It is worth noting that the sum of their final requirements corresponds to the maximum network capacity.

6.4 Constraints Feasibility

In this subsection, we suppose, that the sum of initial users requirements exceeds the network capacity. Figure 5 depicts the nodes behaviors when their requirements ($\sum_{i=1}^{3} \theta_i = 100$) go beyond the network capacity ($C = 20$). Hence, the nodes constraints are unfeasible (inequality (5) is not satisfied). It can be seen from Fig. 5(a) that nodes have to transmit with an infinite power in order to reach their satisfaction performance. Furthermore, even with the highest power levels, users are not able to achieve their request as it is depicted in Fig. 5(b) where the final throughput of each node is below its satisfaction. .

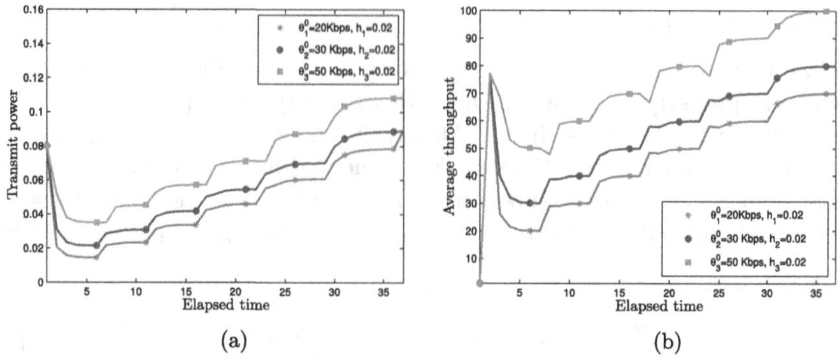

Fig. 4. Throughput maximization using the modified Banach-Picard algorithm. Figure (a) represents the transmit powers decision evolution over time for 3 users. The resulting throughput is given by Figure (b). The starting power allocation is $(1, 1, 1)[mW]$, and the maximum network capacity $C = 300$.

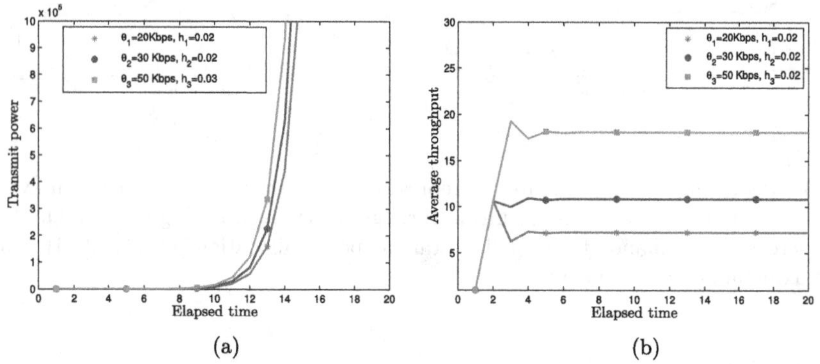

Fig. 5. Constraints feasibility. Figure (a) represents the transmit powers decision evolution over time for 3 users. The resulting throughput is given by Figure (b). The starting power allocation is $(1, 1, 1)[mW]$, and the maximum network capacity $C = 20$.

7 Conclusion

In this work, we have modeled the network performance as a satisfaction game where players aim at achieving a target QoS levels while taking into consideration their energy consumption. We have defined the efficient satisfaction equilibrium, and fully characterized the efficient satisfaction equilibrium. Finally, we have proposed distributed algorithms that converge to the efficient satisfaction equilibrium and the constrained Nash equilibrium respectively. In ongoing works, we will study the impact of the radio channel randomness on the existence and uniqueness of the efficient satisfaction equilibrium.

References

1. Andrews, J.G.: Seven ways that HetNets are a cellular paradigm shift. IEEE Commun. Mag. **51**(3), 136–144 (2013)
2. Andrews, J.G., Buzzi, S., Choi, W., Hanly, S.V., Lozano, A., Soong, A.C., Zhang, J.C.: What will 5G be? IEEE J. Sel. Areas Commun. **32**(6), 1065–1082 (2014)
3. Ashraf, I., Ho, L.T.W., Claussen, H.: Improving energy efficiency of femtocell base stations via user activity detection. In: Wireless Communications and Networking Conference (WCNC), Sydney, Australia, 18–21 April 2010
4. Cisco: Visual networking index: global mobile data traffic forecast update, 2015–2020. In: www.cisco.com, February 2016
5. Debreu, G.: Existence of an equilibrium for a competitive economy. Econom.: J. Econom. Soc. **22**(3), 265–290 (1954)
6. Holtkamp, H., Auer, G., Bazzi, S., Haas, H.: Minimizing base station power consumption. IEEE J. Sel. Areas Commun. **32**(2), 297–306 (2013)
7. Jorguseski, L., Pais, A., Gunnarsson, F., Centonza, A., Willcock, C.: Self-organizing networks in 3GPP: standardization and future trends. IEEE Commun. Mag. **52**(12), 28–34 (2014)
8. Mériaux, F., Perlaza, S., Lasaulce, S., Han, Z., Poor, V.: Achievability of efficient satisfaction equilibria in self-configuring networks. In: Krishnamurthy, V., Zhao, Q., Huang, M., Wen, Y. (eds.) GameNets 2012. LNICSSITE, vol. 105, pp. 1–15. Springer, Heidelberg (2012). doi:10.1007/978-3-642-35582-0_1
9. Meshkati, F., Poor, H.V., Schwartz, S.C., Mandayam, N.B.: An energy-efficient approach to power control and receiver design in wireless data networks. IEEE Trans. Commun. **53**(11), 1885–1894 (2005)
10. Osseiran, A., Boccardi, F., Braun, V., Kusume, K., Marsch, P., Maternia, M., Queseth, O., Schellmann, M., Schotten, H., Taoka, H., Tullberg, H., Uusitalo, M.A., Timus, B., Fallgren, M.: Scenarios for mobile and wireless communications: the vision of the METIS project. IEEE Commun. Mag. **52**(5), 26–35 (2015)
11. Perlaza, S., Tembine, H., Lasaulce, S., Debbah, M.: Quality-of-service provisioning in decentralized networks: a satisfaction equilibrium approach. IEEE J. Sel. Top. Signal Process. **6**(2), 104–116 (2012)
12. Perlaza, S.M., Poor, H., Han, Z.: Learning efficient satisfaction equilibria via trial and error. In: Proceedings of the Forty Sixth Asilomar Conference on Systems and Computers, Signals, Monterey, CA, 4–7 November 2012
13. Sabir, E., El-Azouzi, R., Kavitha, V., Hayel, Y., Bouyakhlefi, E.H.: Stochastic learning solution for constrained nash equilibrium throughput in non saturated wireless collision channels. In: Proceedings of the Fourth International ICST Conference on Performance Evaluation Methodologies and Tools, Pisa, Italy, 20–22 October 2009
14. Samarakoon, S., Bennis, M., Saad, W., Debbah, M., Latva-aho, M.: Ultra dense small cell networks: turning density into energy efficiency. IEEE J. Sel. Areas Commun. **PP**(99), 1–15 (2016)
15. Simon, H.A.: Rational choice and the structure of the environment. Psychol. Rev. **36**(2), 129–138 (1956)
16. Solodovnikov, A.S.: Systems of Linear Inequalities. Popular Lectures in Mathematics, University of Chicago Press (1980)
17. Tan, C.W., Chiang, M., Srikant, R.: Fast algorithms and performance bounds for sum rate maximization in wireless networks. IEEE/ACM Trans. Netw. **21**(3), 706–719 (2013)
18. Tembine, H.: Distributed Strategic Learning for Wireless Engineers. CRC Press, Boca Raton (2012)

A Game Theoretic Approach Against the Greedy Behavior in MAC IEEE 802.11

Mohammed-Alamine El Houssaini[1(✉)], Abdessadek Aaroud[1], Ali El Hore[1], and Jalel Ben-Othman[2]

[1] Department of Computer Science, Faculty of Sciences, Chouaib Doukkali University, El Jadida, Morocco
{elhoussaini.m, aaroud.a, elhore.a}@ucd.ac.ma
[2] Department of Computer Science, Galilee Institute, Paris 13 University, Paris, France
jalel.ben-othman@univ-paris13.fr

Abstract. In recent years, mobile ad hoc networks are invading more and more our daily lives. Indeed, several persons are linked daily to ad hoc networks, which aim to exchange data via smartphones, computers, or tablets. A mobile ad hoc network is a group of mobile stations equipped with wireless transmitters/receivers without fixed infrastructure use or centralized administration. In this sense, the network can be seen as a random graph due to the motion of nodes. The change of the network topology based on the time when nodes move or adjust their transmission and reception parameters. The design of these networks is characterized by its vulnerability to denial of service (DOS) attacks such as the greedy behavior (MAC layer misbehavior). In this paper, we formalized the reaction against this malicious behavior of the MAC layer by game theory. We have developed a model in the extensive form of our reaction scheme and a resolution of the game by Kühn's algorithm. A validation of results though the NS2 network simulator is then given to the end.

Keywords: Mobile ad hoc network · MAC IEEE 802.11 · Misbehavior reaction · NS2 simulation · Game theory

1 Introduction and State of the Art

In recent years, mobile ad hoc networks based on the IEEE 802.11 standard [1], are increasingly omnipresent in our lives. Indeed, several people are attached and connected daily to ad hoc networks, the purpose of which is to share data through smart phones, computers, or tablets.

One of the biggest advantages of the IEEE 802.11 standard [1] is the fair access to the transmission channel. However sharing this channel makes networks vulnerable to several DOS attacks such as jamming, and greedy behavior (MAC layer misbehavior) [2].

A greedy node intentionally modify the MAC layer of the IEEE 802.11 protocol for an additional network resources that honest nodes [3]. For this malicious behavior channel access, a greedy node can enjoy many benefits such as increasing its throughput and reduce its energy consumption.

E. Sabir et al. (Eds.): UNet 2017, LNCS 10542, pp. 38–47, 2017.
https://doi.org/10.1007/978-3-319-68179-5_4

Several studies have been proposed in literature to detect this type of attack:

In [4], authors present a new system for detecting malicious behavior of the MAC layer of the IEEE 802.11 standard, based on the statistical process control (SPC) borrowed from the industrial area in the quality management context. This system has the power to identify greedy nodes in real time using a graphical tool called (control chart) which measures the throughput and the inter-packet time for each node, and triggers an alarm if there are higher than a threshold defined.

Another work [5], proposed a new method for detecting malicious behavior of the MAC layer of the IEEE 802.11 standard using a multivariate control chart existing currently in industrial management with great success. This method is proposed to replace the Shewhart control chart that already exists in the literature for the detection of greedy nodes because it reduces the number of control chart. The proposed mechanism requires no modification to the 802.11 standard and it works in real time also it seems easy in implementation.

Because of the impact of this malicious behavior on the performance of communications, several works have been proposed in the state of the art to overcome this attack:

Authors in [6], propose a new reaction scheme against the MAC layer misbehavior of the IEEE 802.11 standard, with minimal changes to the IEEE 802.11 protocol. This reaction is in the form of an iterative and cooperative game played by all honest nodes, those who respect the protocol. Also authors offer a variant of their reaction system based on polynomial regression to reduce the response time. The proposed method tends to align honest nodes with the cheater node, while keeping the fair aspect of the IEEE 802.11 standard.

Other works have been proposed in the literature, which are based on the game theory against this greedy behavior:

Authors in [7] proposed a resilient MAC protocol though game theory to solve the problem of the MAC layer misbehaver. They modeled the Distributed Coordination Function (DCF) as a dynamic game and proposed an implementation and integration in the basic MAC layer, to the extent of forming the resilient MAC layer.

The work [8] modifies the MAC IEEE 802.11 standard by using a deterministic back-off. This modified back-off algorithm lead to supervision the network for the detection of greedy nodes. The base station in this mechanism updates a counter of the idle slots of the transmission channel, and then decides that a station is a cheater one if the value of the counter is greater than an expected time. The second contribution of this work is the correction scheme to penalize misbehaving nodes.

The rest of the paper is organized as follow. A presentation of the modeling of the game in an extensive form is given in the second section. The perfect equilibrium for our extensive game though the Kühn's algorithm is outlined in the third section. The fourth section is dedicated to present a validation with NS2 simulator. Finally, we conclude in the fifth section our contribution and we will give our perspectives in the future work.

2 The Modeling of the Game in an Extensive Form

Game theory is a theoretical discipline that formalizes situations where the players (decision makers) interact. A game is defined as a space in which each decision maker has a set of possible actions determined by the rules of the game. The game outcome then depends jointly on the actions taken by each decision maker. Game theory is a collection of models used to understand what is observed or experienced. They predict the evolution of a situation of concurrency or advise the players on the best strategy to follow [9].

This discipline has many applications especially for understanding economic phenomena, political or even biological. Among these phenomena, here are some situations where game theory can be applied [9]:

- Competition among politicians,
- Business competition,
- Participation in an auction,

We must focus on a major component in game theory (rationality), which stipulates that each player chooses the best action from those available, to the extent that it seeks to maximize his gain.

The extensive form modeling is one of the simplest ways to represent a game. This is a model where players choose their decisions sequentially until the game is finished [9].

To model our game, we need to specify the following main elements:

- The set of players or decision makers,
- Possible actions for each decision maker,
- The rules specifying the order in which the players play and when the game ends,
- The game outcome for each possible end in terms of gain or preference.

An extensive game can be represented by a tree (connected graph without cycle) as depicted in the Fig. 1 where [9]:

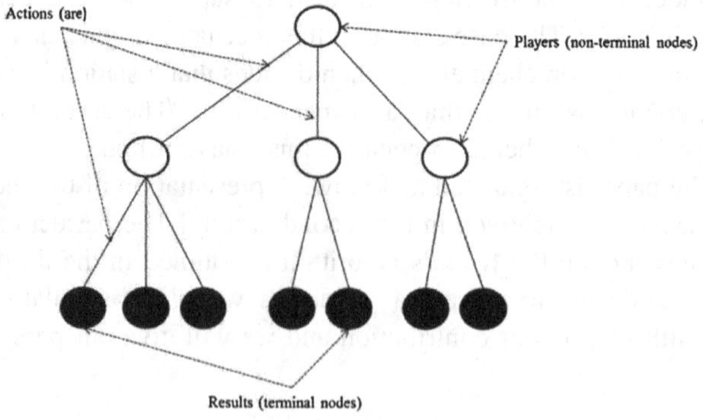

Fig. 1. Representation of an extensive game.

- To each terminal node is a result of the game,
- To each non-terminal node is associated a player: come to that point of the game is to his turn to play,
- Each arc represents each of the actions a player can take at this point of the game.

Now consider the reaction strategy against the greedy behavior of the MAC layer of the IEEE 802.11 protocol as described in Fig. 2 [6], and making the necessary mapping to the extensive form modeling. It is assumed that all players are rational and the game is in perfect information.

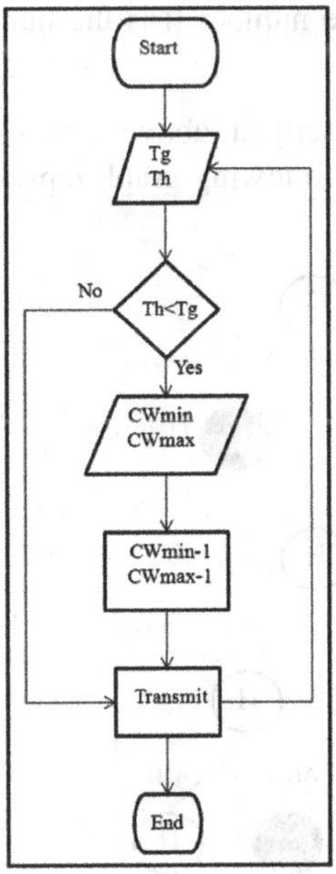

Fig. 2. Flowchart of the reaction scheme of the MAC layer misbehavior in IEEE 802.11.

In the presence of a greedy station which tends to maximize its throughput, honest stations in order to contest the MAC layer misbehavior, must cooperate at the same time, as much as they must reduce step by step their parameters of the contention window until their throughput exceed that of the cheating station. In fact, honest nodes always confront its throughput measured by the receiver with that of the cheater, if it's crossed, honest stations continues their communications without doing anything; otherwise they decrement the minimum and maximum of their contention window. The game played by all honest stations achieves its equilibrium in overcoming the greedy throughput [6].

Our game is defined by:

- The set of players i∊{H,G}, where H is the set of n honest nodes H = {H_1, H_2,..., H_n}, and G the greedy node,
- The set of actions for the player G is AG = {AG_1, AG_2}

where AG_1 is to cheat and AG_2 doesn't cheat.

- The set of actions for the player H is AH = {AH_1, AH_2}

where AH_1 is decrement parameters of the contention window (CWmin and CWmax of the IEEE 802.11 protocol) and AH_2 doesn't decrement these parameters.

- The rules of the game are: a greedy node decides whether to cheat, if so, the honest nodes if they govern, they begin to decrement the parameters of the contention window to the end of the game.
- The payment or the gain of players is their throughput (Th is the honest throughput and Tg is the greedy throughput), note that the index for the throughput of each player returns to the sequence number (i is the number of iterations to satisfy the condition Th >= Tg).

Summarizing all that is described above and using the representation in an extensive form, we arrive at the following graph represented in the Fig. 3.

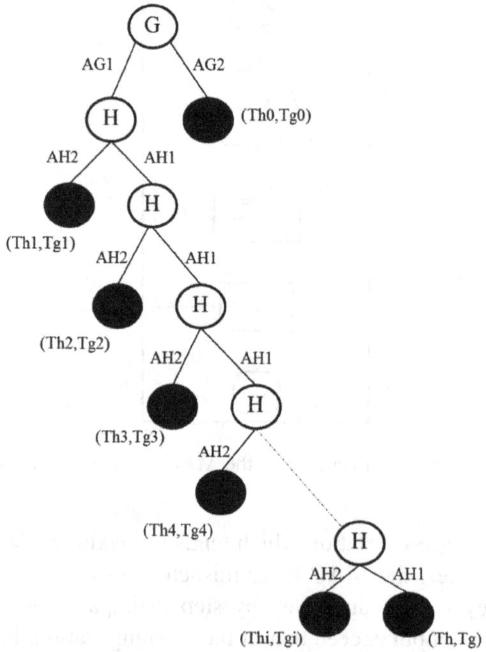

Fig. 3. Modeling in an extensive form of the reaction scheme against the MAC layer misbehavior in IEEE 802.11.

3 Perfect Equilibrium for Our Extensive Game Though the Kühn's Algorithm

Every finite game with complete and perfect information is solvable by Kühn's algorithm. This is one of the very first results in game theory [9].

Let us specify the terms:

- A game is finite, if it has a finite number of nodes.
- A game with complete and perfect information is a game in extensive form in which each node has a single set of information.

We place ourselves at the end of the game, in a predecessor node to a terminal node. Assume that the game outcome leads to this point. We can anticipate that the player at this node will play in rational manner and choose the action that maximizes its gain. We can delete the other actions from this node. The behavior is somehow totally predictable and one can replace the node in question by the terminal node (with the corresponding payments) associated with the optimal action. We start the analysis procedure for other nodes immediately preceding the terminal nodes. At each step of the algorithm, the game tree is strictly reduced. The game is reduced to a problem of a decision of the first player. The result of the Kühn's algorithm is called sub game perfect equilibrium [9].

The resolution of the game led to the perfect equilibrium (Th, Tg) as shown in Fig. 4 in red color. Indeed, the player H always chooses the AH1 strategy that maximizes its payoff, as the player G chooses to play the AG1 strategy insofar as it maximizes its gain.

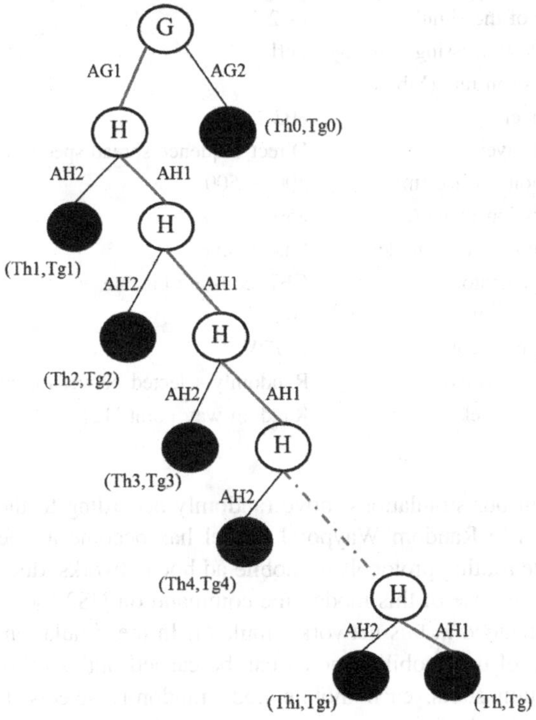

Fig. 4. Path to the perfect equilibrium of our extensive game. (Color figure online)

We can add that the successive elimination of dominated strategies also helps to find the same perfect equilibrium of our extensive game. In fact, the AG2 strategy is strictly dominated by AG1 [10]. Also AH2 strategy is strictly dominated by AH1 [10]. The strict dominance criterion means that one player's strategy strictly dominates another if, although doing the other players, that player has a strictly higher payment using this strategy. It is assumed that a dominated strategy is not played. In the case where one strategy dominates all the others, the latter being eliminated, it is therefore played with certainty. This is called a dominant strategy [9].

4 Validation of Our Extensive Game by NS2 Simulations

We simulate a network for different number of nodes with the NS2 simulator [11] with parameters shown in Table 1, with a receiving node and a greedy station. In these simulations, the cheating station selects a waiting time equivalent to half of the Minimum Contention Window (CWmin). Additionally, all the nodes of the network are deposited at the beginning, randomly on the surface of the simulation.

Table 1. Simulation parameters.

Parameters	Values
Version of the simulator	ns-2.34
Trace file processing language	Perl
Transmission rate (Mb/s)	2
MAC layer	802.11
Physical layer	Direct sequence spread spectrum
Simulation surface (m)	500 × 500
Transmission range (m)	250
Radio propagation model	Shadowing
Traffic generator	CBR constant bit rate
Packet size (byte)	1000
Routing protocol	AODV
Node speed (m/s)	Randomly selected between 0 and 15
Mobility model	Random way point [12]

All the nodes in our simulations move randomly according to the Random Waypoint model [12]. The Random Waypoint model has become a reference model of mobility to evaluate routing protocols in mobile ad hoc networks, due to its simplicity. To generate the node trace of this model, the command on NS2 "setdest" can be used which is already included in this network simulator. In the simulation scripts on NS2, the implementation of this mobility model can be carried out as follows [12]:

As the simulation starts, each mobile node randomly selects a location in the simulation field as the destination. It then moves to that destination with a constant speed. The speed and direction of a node are chosen independently of the other nodes. When it reaches the destination, the node stops for a predefined time. After this pause time, it again chooses another random destination in the simulation field and moves to it. The entire process is repeated again and again until the simulation ends.

The greedy node by playing the strategy AG1 increases its throughput at the expense of honest nodes. This proves the dominance of this strategy (Fig. 5).

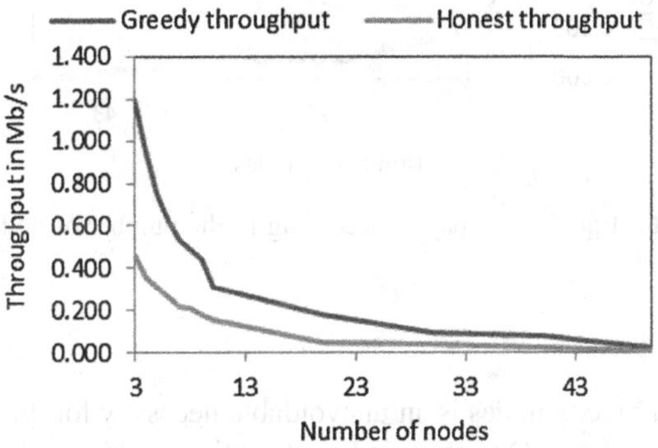

Fig. 5. Payoff according to the number of nodes in the case of playing AG1 by G.

In the second simulation scenario, we kept the same parameterization of the network but on the other hand we activated actions that lead to the game equilibrium. The Table 2 presents the game payoff for different number of nodes.

Table 2. Game payoff according to the number of nodes.

Number of nodes	Game payoff
3	(0.8388480, 0.8241600)
4	(0.5894240, 0.5448160)
5	(0.4148000, 0.4088160)
6	(0.3672000, 0.3609440)
7	(0.2864160, 0.2505120)
8	(0.2532320, 0.2292960)
9	(0.2197760, 0.2064480)
10	(0.1985600, 0.1770720)
20	(0.0878560, 0.0712640)
30	(0.0699040, 0.0623015)
40	(0.0361760, 0.0356320)
50	(0.0176800, 0.0141440)

By representing the data in the Table 2 with graphs (Fig. 6), we can conclude that our game attenuated the effect of the greedy station as depicted in the Fig. 6.

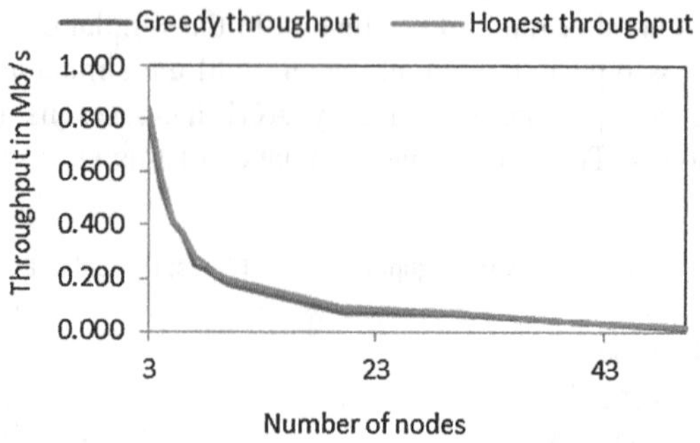

Fig. 6. Equilibrium payoff according to the number of nodes.

5 Conclusion

The reaction against greedy nodes is an unavoidable necessity for the normal operation of a mobile ad hoc network. Our proposed contribution in this work is borrowed from game theory and the suggested game demands a small and easy manipulation of the contention window parameters. In other words, we suggested a model of a reaction scheme against the MAC layer misbehavior in IEEE 802.11 protocol. Also we highlighted the resolution of the perfect equilibrium for our extensive game though the Kühn's algorithm, in order to reduce the impact of greedy stations. Simulation results have validated that our model is relevant to bypass the MAC layer misbehavior attack. We plan to propose other detection/reaction strategies for other types of attacks.

References

1. IEEE Standards Association, IEEE 802.11 Standard for Wireless LAN Medium Access Control (MAC) and Physical Layer (PHY) Specifications, IEEE Standards Association, pp. 818–840, March 2012
2. Giri, V.R., Jaggi, N.: MAC layer misbehavior effectiveness and collective aggressive reaction approach. In: Proceeding of 2010 IEEE Sarnoff Symposium, Princeton, USA (2010)
3. El Houssaini, M., Aaroud, A., Elhore, A., Ben-Othman, J.: Analysis and simulation of MAC layer misbehavior in mobile ad-hoc networks. In: Proceedings of the 5th International Workshop on Codes, Cryptography and Communication Systems, pp. 50–54 (2014)
4. El Houssaini, M., Aaroud, A., Elhore, A., Ben-Othman, J.: Real-time detection of MAC layer misbehavior in mobile ad hoc networks. Appl. Comput. Inform. (2015). doi:10.1016/j.aci.2015.11.001
5. El Houssaini, M., Aaroud, A., Elhore, A., Ben-Othman, J.: Multivariate control chart for the detection of MAC layer misbehavior in mobile ad hoc networks. Procedia Comput. Sci. **83**, 58–65 (2016)
6. El Houssaini, M., Aaroud, A., El Hore, A., Ben-Othman, J.: A novel reaction scheme against the MAC layer misbehavior in mobile ad hoc networks. Procedia Comput. Sci. **98**, 64–71 (2016)
7. Abegunde, J., Xiao, H., Spring, J.: A resilient MAC protocol for wireless networks. In: Presented at IMA Conference on Game Theory and its Applications, Oxford, UK (2014)

8. Kyasanur, P., Vaidya, N.H.: Handling MAC layer misbehavior in wireless networks. In: Proceedings of the Eighth Annual International Conference on Mobile Computing and Networking, Atlanta, USA (2002)
9. Osborne, M.J.: An Introduction to Game Theory, 1st edn. Oxford University Press, England (2003)
10. El Houssaini, M., Aaroud, A., El Hore, A., Ben-Othman, J.: Performance analysis under MAC layer misbehavior attack in mobile Ad-Hoc networks. Comput. Technol. Appl. **6**, 37–44 (2015)
11. Information Sciences Institute, The Network Simulator –ns-2, Information Sciences Institute (1995). http://www.isi.edu/nsnam/ns/. Accessed 9 Nov 2016
12. Bai, F., Helmy, A.: A Survey of mobility modeling and analysis in wireless ad-hoc networks. In: Wireless Ad-Hoc and Sensor Networks (2004)

Leveraging User Intuition to Predict Item Popularity in Social Networks

Nada Sbihi[1(✉)], Ihsane Gryech[1], and Mounir Ghogho[1,2]

[1] FIL, TICLab, Université Internationale de Rabat, Rabat, Morocco
{nada.sbihi,ihsane.gryech,mounir.ghogho}@uir.ac.ma
[2] School of EEE, University of Leeds, Leeds, UK

Abstract. We investigate the problem of *early* prediction of item popularity in online social networks. Prior work claims that the time taken by each item to reach i adopters (i being a small number around 5) has a higher predictive power than other non-temporal features, such as those related to the characteristics of the adopters. Here, we challenge this claim by proposing a new feature, based on the users' intuitions, which is shown to provide significantly better predictive power for the most popular items than the above-mentioned temporal feature. A GoodReads dataset is used to illustrate the merits of the proposed method.

Keywords: Social networks · Web content · Popularity · Prediction · Classification · Intuition

1 Introduction

With the rapid development of online social networks, content production has been drawing a lot of attention and has become an increasingly important area of research. Indeed, since an online item can reach audiences in inconceivable numbers, it may have a great socio-economic impact. The question of what makes items become popular in these networks continues to capture the imagination of many researchers. Predicting the popularity of a web content has many applications including the design of better advertising placement strategies and the design of more efficient content delivery platforms. It can also be used to better comprehend the dynamics of consumption processes. Further, it may drive the design of better analytic tools, which is a major market segment nowadays.

Although predicting the popularity of a web content has been the subject of numerous studies, it is still in its incipient stage. Indeed, despite the tremendous efforts, it is still widely recognised that popularity prediction for an online item before its release is a challenging task, even though we know that some features tend to influence its popularity, like its quality, the characteristics of the user sharing it, the time of its release, its geographic relevance and of course the anticipated users' emotions about the content. After the item is released, peeking into its initial adoptions was shown to make the problem of predicting its final

E. Sabir et al. (Eds.): UNet 2017, LNCS 10542, pp. 48–55, 2017.
https://doi.org/10.1007/978-3-319-68179-5_5

popularity more tractable [3]. It was also used to predict which items are more likely to virally spread through social networks.

Many features have been identified to characterise the initial adoptions of an item. These can be categorised into temporal features, such as the time to reach a fixed but small number of adopters, and features related to the characteristics of the first few adopters, such as the number of friends or followers of the early adopters on the social network. Recent work has shown that temporal features have generally higher predictive powers than non-temporal features, see [5] and references therein. This was shown in [5] by formulating the prediction problem as a classification task where the goal was to predict whether the final number of adoptions (e.g. view counts in the case of videos) of an item on a social network will be above or below the median[1]; non-temporal features, such as those related to the users' social networks, were claimed to be at best weak predictors of popularity, whereas the time to reach the first five adopters was shown to be a good predictor across social networks. Here, we challenge this claim by proposing a new early adopter-related feature, namely the adopter's intuition, which is shown to provide a significantly better predictive power, for the most popular items (e.g. the 10% most popular items), than the above-mentioned temporal feature. An adopter or a user with a good intuition is defined as a user who is, more frequently than others, among the first adopters of items that will end up being most popular.

2 Users' Intuitions

We argue that a user with a good intuition will, more frequently than others, like or recommend content that will end up being most popular. Using historical activities of the social network's users, we propose to measure the intuition of each user by evaluating the percentage of times he or she was among the very first adopters of items that ended up being most popular. Towards the goal of measuring the user's intuitions, we first define the following non-normalised measure for every user u in the social network:

$$f_k(u) = \frac{1}{\left|\mathcal{B}_u^{(k)}\right|} \sum_{b \in \mathcal{B}_u^{(k)}} N_a(b) \tag{1}$$

where b denotes an item (book for our dataset to be described in the next section), $\mathcal{B}_u^{(k)}$ is the set of all items of which user u was one of the first k adopters (appreciators of the book for our dataset), $N_a(b)$ is the 'final'[2] number of adoptions for item b by all users, and $|\mathcal{B}_u^{(k)}|$ denotes the cardinality of $\mathcal{B}_u^{(k)}$. We consider only the first k adopters, with k being a small number (set to 10 in this paper), because a user who does not have a good intuition can follow the general trend if the content is becoming popular.

[1] This is a two-class classification problem.

[2] i.e. long after the item was released.

The intuition of user u is now defined as the normalised version of the above metric (in order to have values between 0 and 1):

$$\text{user\_intuition}_k(u) = \frac{f_k(u)}{\max_{u \in \mathcal{U}} f_k(u)} \tag{2}$$

where $\mathcal{U}$ is the set of all active users in the network.

To predict the popularity for a set of new items, we propose to use as a predictor the average of the intuitions of its first i adopters (i may or may not be equal to k), i.e. the intuition score for item b is defined as

$$\text{intuition}_{k,i}(b) = \frac{1}{i} \sum_{u \in \mathcal{U}_b^{(i)}} \text{user\_intuition}_k(u) \tag{3}$$

where $\mathcal{U}_b^{(i)}$ denotes the set of the first i adopters of b. If i is set to be equal to k, the intuition score for item b is denoted as intuition_$i(b)$.

It is worth pointing out that what makes a user have a good intuition is as unclear as what makes a content popular. This issue is out of the scope of this paper.

3 Dataset and Preprocessing

In this paper, we use a dataset from Goodreads, a social cataloging website created for people of all ages to review, recommend and rate books.

The dataset consists of $1.3M$ items, and $252K$ users with their ratings before August 2010 [6] (Table 1).

Table 1. Dataset

Dataset	GoodReads
Number of users	$252K$
Number of items	$1.3M$
Number of adoptions	$28M$
Mean adoptions	21.4
Median adoptions	1
Maximum adoptions	88027

The dataset already contains many features, but we have also added additional ones. The features included in the dataset are: "user_id", "item_id", with the item being the user-rated book, "Collect_Date", i.e. the date where the information was collected, "rating", i.e. the score in the range of 0 to 5 that the user gave to a certain book. A user can rate many books and a book can be rated by many users. In our prediction task, only ratings of 4 or above are considered as adoptions.

To the dataset, we also add a temporal feature, named "time_i", as follows. We collect all items and peek into the first i adoptions. Then for each item, time_i will correspond to the time between the first and ith adoption.

The pre-processing that we have performed on the dataset consists of removing duplicates and keeping only items with at least 5 adoptions.

4 Adoption Time Versus User Intuition

As in [5], in this section, we formulate the prediction problem as a two-class classification task. However, unlike [5] where the two classes were separated by the median, i.e. the goal was to predict whether an item will end up above or below the median, here we tackle the more general problem of predicting the top $c\%$ most popular items, with c equal to 5, 10, 20, 30 or 50. In Sect. 6, we address the four-class classification problem.

To evaluate the classification performance, we randomly divide the dataset into a training set and a testing set. The users' intuitions and the classifiers are estimated using the training set, while the test error is evaluated using the test set. We have tried several classification methods, including logistic regression, random forests, and support vector machines. Since there are only two classes, the logistic regression turns out to give the best performance.

Here, the prediction accuracy is defined as the ratio of popular books (i.e. those which end up in the top $c\%$) in the testing dataset that were correctly classified.

The accuracy of time_i-based prediction versus i, when $c = 50$, is depicted in Fig. 1. In [5], $i = 5$ was used. Here, we set i for both features, time_i and intuition_i, to 10.

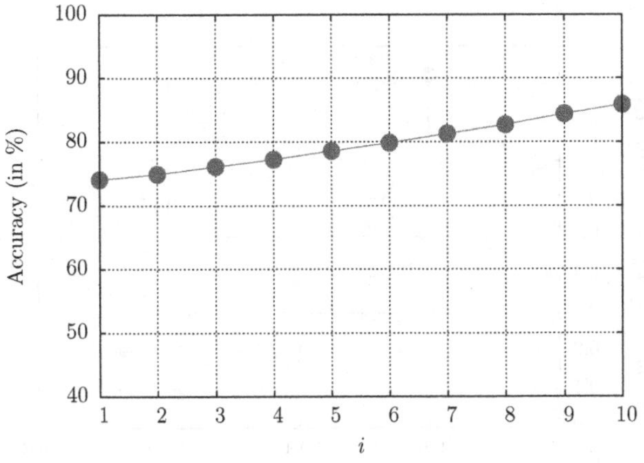

Fig. 1. Accuracy of time_i-based prediction versus i when the popularity size is 50%, i.e. $c = 50$.

Table 2 shows the prediction accuracy of three methods: the first one based solely on time_i, the second one based solely on intuition_i, and the third one based on both time_i and intuition_i. When the objective is to predict the top 10% most popular items, the time-based prediction method completely fails whereas the intuition-based method can accurately predict around 30% of those items. It is worth recalling that in many applications, one is most interested in predicting the top few percent of most popular items. Table 2 also shows that by using the two features, we obtain a slightly higher prediction accuracy for small popularity sizes, and an accuracy comparable to that of the time-based prediction for high popularity sizes.

Table 2. Prediction accuracy for different popularity sizes

Popularity size	Time_10	Intuition_10	Time_10 and Intuition_10
5%	**0%**	**29.5%**	**31.82%**
10%	**2.4%**	**29.65%**	**33.92%**
20%	43.93%	33.56%	48.48%
30%	66.26%	39.31%	64.36%
50%	85.88%	58.58%	84.49%

To further investigate the relationship between item popularity and the intuition score, we plot in Fig. 2 an estimate of the probability for an item to be in the top 5% most popular class conditioned on the intuition score, intuition_i, being larger than a certain value. The plot was generated using the testing data set. One can conclude that items with intuition scores higher than 0.05 will

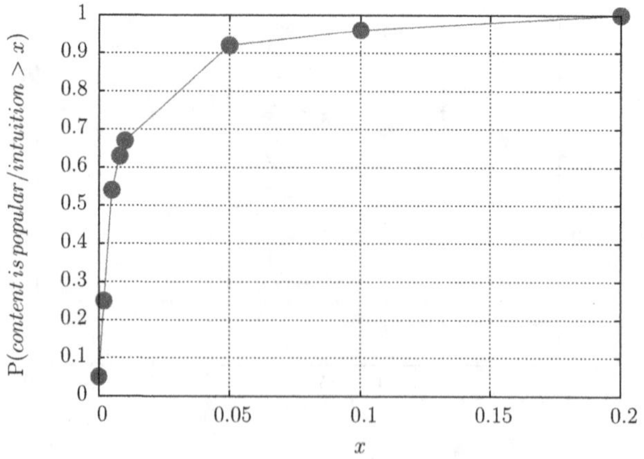

Fig. 2. Probability for an item to be in the top 5% most popular class conditioned on intuition_i.

end up in the top 5% most popular class with a probability higher than 0.9. Therefore, if an online social network has a good percentage of users who have good intuitions and are very active (in order to be frequently among the first adopters), popularity prediction may be highly accurate. The fact that the prediction accuracy for the intuition-based method in Table 2 was around 30% only may imply that, in GoodReads (at least in our dataset), the number of users with good intuition is not sufficiently high or that users with good intuitions are not sufficiently active; it may also be due to the fact that the top 5% most popular items have very different popularities; a better classification strategy is proposed in Sect. 6.

In Fig. 3, we plot the probability for an item to be in the top 5% most popular class conditioned on time_*i* (in hours). The figure shows that, unlike the user intuition-based feature, time_*i* is not a good predictor of item popularity. Indeed, the conditional probability does not exceed 0.5 even for very small values of time_*i*.

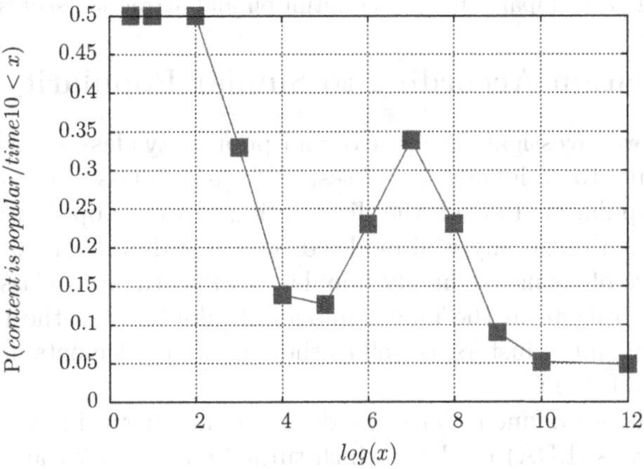

Fig. 3. Probability for an item to be in the top 5% most popular class conditioned on time_*i* (in hours).

5 Can the Relationships Between Users Influence Item Popularity?

In this section, we investigate whether the relationships between users can play a role in popularity prediction. Intuitively, one might think that a user who is 'connected' to a large number of users may have an influence of item popularity.

Using the GoodReads dataset, requests for friendships between users are recorded. The attraction parameter is then calculated for each user. Figure 4 depicts the side-by-side boxplots for the intuition and attraction scores when the popularity size is 30%. As pointed out in [5] and references therein, the attraction (or popularity) of a user is not a good predictor of item popularity, which may perhaps be explained by the fact that *online* friends are less likely than *real* friends to have similar interests and tastes.

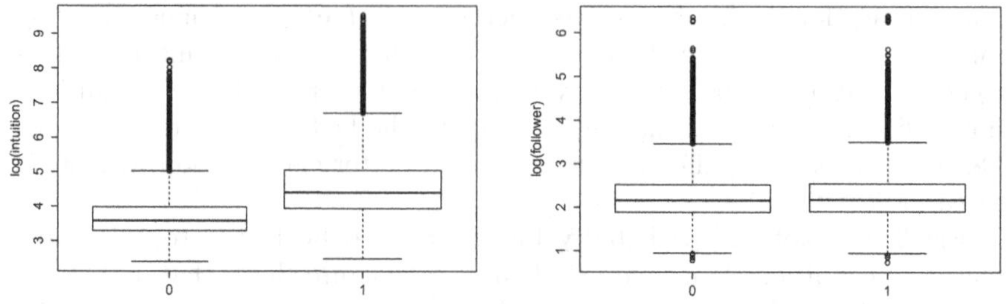

(a) A side by side boxplot using intuition score

(b) A side by side boxplot using attraction score

Fig. 4. Comparison between intuition and attraction scores

6 Classification According to Similar Popularity

In this section, we investigate the case of four popularity classes. Instead of using the three quartiles to designate the classes, we form the classes by grouping items with similar popularity. Indeed, the distribution of item popularity is far from being uniform; it is generally well modeled by a Zipf distribution, where only a small percentage of items are highly popular. To find the four classes, we apply the k-means algorithm on the final numbers of adoptions in the training data set. The resulting four clusters as well as the number of elements in each cluster are displayed in Table 3.

Using the classes defined above, we design a classifier using the Linear Discriminant Analysis (LDA) method, which turned out to offer the best results.

Table 3. Popularity groups interval using unsupervised learning

Item category	Number of adoptions	Number of items in each category
Very popular	$[28073 : +\infty[$	21
Popular	$[8586 : 28073[$	83
Unpopular	$[1620 : 8586[$	604
Very unpopular	$[0 : 1620[$	77587

Table 4 shows that the superiority of the intuition-based prediction method is even greater than in the two-class classification problem addressed in the previous sections. Indeed, using intuition_i, one can predict the very popular items with an accuracy of 63.16%, whereas none of these items could be predicted using time_i!

Table 4. Accuracy of popularity prediction

Accuracy	Time_10	Intuition_10
Very popular	0%	63.16%
Popular	0%	46.78%
Unpopular	0%	41.19%
Very unpopular	100%	99.42%

7 Conclusion and Future Work

In this paper, we challenged recent results which claim that temporal features, obtained by peeking into the early adoptions of items, have a higher predictive power than non-temporal features related to the characteristics of the early adopters. While we have confirmed that the network structure has little impact on popularity, we have shown that our proposed non-temporal feature, based on the users' intuitions, may have a much higher predictive power than temporal features for the most popular items. Our results were obtained using only one online social network, GoodReads. Future work will consist of exploring other social networks to investigate whether the intuition score is a *consistently* good predictor of item popularity, and also of exploring other temporal and non-temporal traits to further improve prediction accuracy.

References

1. Szabo, G., Huberman, B.A.: Predicting the popularity of online content. Commun. ACM **53**(8) (2010)
2. Pinto, H., Almeida, J.M., Gonalves, M.A.: Using early view patterns to predict the popularity of youtube videos. In: Proceedings of the Sixth ACM International Conference on Web Search and Data Mining, February 2013
3. Tatar, A., de Amorim, M.D., Fdida, S., Antoniadis, P.: A survey on predicting the popularity of web content. J. Internet Serv. Appl. **5**(1) (2014)
4. Figueiredo, F., Almeida, J.M., Gonalves, M.A., Benevenuto, F.: On the dynamics of social media popularity: a YouTube case study. ACM Trans. Internet Technol. (TOIT) **14**(4) (2014)
5. Shulman, B., Sharma, A., Cosley, D.: Predictability of popularity: gaps between prediction and understanding. In: Proceedings of the Tenth International AAAI Conference on Web and Social Media, March 2016
6. http://www.junminghuang.com
7. Huang, J., Cheng, X.Q., Shen, H.W., Zhou, T., Jin, X.: Exploring social influence via posterior effect of word-of-mouth recommendations. In: Proceedings of the Fifth ACM International Conference on Web Search and Data Mining, February 2012

Quality of Experience in HTTP Adaptive Video Streaming Systems

Zakaria Ye(✉), Rachid Elazouzi, and Tania Jiménez

LIA/CERI, University of Avignon, 84000 Avignon, France
zakaria.ye@univ-avignon.fr

Abstract. The main task of HTTP Adaptive Streaming (HAS) is to adapt video quality dynamically under variable network conditions. This is a key feature for multimedia delivery especially when quality of service cannot be granted network-wide and, e.g., throughput may suffer short term fluctuations. Hence, robust bitrate adaptation schemes become crucial in order to improve video quality of experience. The objective, in this context, is to control the filling level of the playback buffer and maximize the quality of the video, while avoiding unnecessary video quality variations. In this paper we study bitrate adaptation algorithms based on Backward-Shifted Coding (BSC), a scalable video coding scheme able to greatly improve video quality of experience. We design bitrate adaptation algorithms that balance video rate smoothness and high network capacity utilization, leveraging both on throughput-based and buffer-based adaptation mechanisms. Extensive simulations using an MPEG/DASH client server application on ns-3 show that the proposed scheme performs remarkably well even under challenging network conditions.

Keywords: Quality of experience · Adaptive streaming · Scalable video coding · Backward-Shifted Coding · Quality adaptation algorithms

1 Introduction

In the last years, smartphones and other mobile devices have emerged as one dominant technology for daily access to Internet services [6]. This, combined with the ever increasing broadband access supplied by operators has triggered pervasive demand on video streaming mobile services. In turn, this requires the exploration of novel approaches on video content delivery. To afford video streaming services at sustainable costs, the idea of adjusting the bit rate of video traffic depending on the (time-varying) available bandwidth has been actively investigated during the recent years. This technique is commonly referred to adaptive streaming technology. At the industrial level, many adaptive video streaming solutions exist. They are now undergoing a standardization process under the Dynamic Adaptive Streaming over HTTP (DASH) initiative. DASH will include existing solutions such as Microsoft's smooth streaming, Adobe's HTTP dynamic streaming and Apple's live streaming [7]. In order to fully exploit the potential of

E. Sabir et al. (Eds.): UNet 2017, LNCS 10542, pp. 56–69, 2017.
https://doi.org/10.1007/978-3-319-68179-5_6

DASH, though, new challenges arise for content providers, operators and device manufacturers. One of such challenges is the need to accurately assess users' Quality of Experience (QoE) in order to enhance service provisioning and optimize adaptation to network conditions.

Actually, the key concept in DASH is to dynamically adapt the video quality to the network bandwidth. This is done in order to cope with multiple playback interruptions. Those are likely to occur when the video quality is kept the same during the whole video session irrespective of possibly highly variable network conditions, e.g., those typical of mobile wireless connections. In DASH, a single video file is divided into smaller chunks of fixed playback duration called segments. Each segment is encoded at various bitrate levels (called representations). This is done using a specific compression algorithm or codec (e.g., H264/AVC). Then, given the available network bandwidth, a segment is selected with the appropriate bitrate. With the Scalable Video Coding (SVC) compression algorithm (extension of Advanced Video Coding), the video source is encoded in one base layer (BL) and one or more optional enhancement layers (ELs), as depicted in Fig. 1. The base layer is always provided. Then, given the available network bandwidth, the client adaptation engine adds the appropriate number of enhancement layers in order to improve the video quality/SNR, resolution and frame rate.

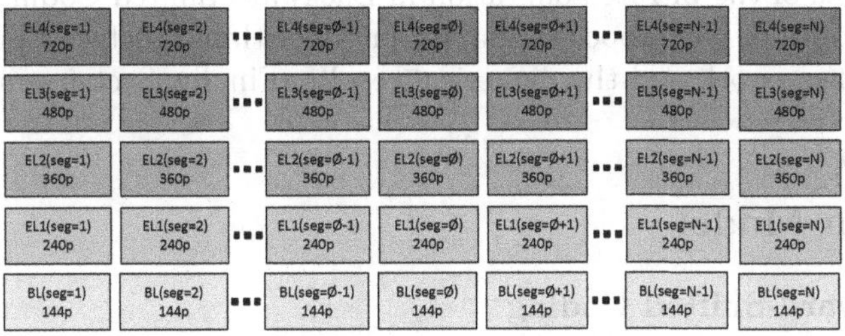

Fig. 1. Segments encoding with SVC

The design goal of DASH is to simultaneously obtain high performance over different key metrics including buffering delay, playback interruptions, average bitrate (video quality) and temporal variability of streaming quality. However, in an environment subject to highly variable throughput, attaining high performance across all these metrics is still considered a great challenge. In this paper, we propose a novel bitrate adaptation scheme which is based on our Backward Shifted Coding (BSC) introduced in [12]. This BSC system makes HTTP Adaptive Streaming (HAS) more robust to rapid fluctuations of the network capacity and provides more flexibility in increasing the quality of video without playback interruptions. The basic idea of BSC is to shift the base layer and its enhancement layers so that when an interruption of playback buffer occurs, the base layer can still be played.

In this paper, we incorporate a new version of BSC in HTTP adaptive streaming. Doing so we are able to strike the balance between responsiveness and smoothness in DASH. More in detail, this new version of BSC contains two layers: the *low layer segment*, which delivers only the base layer or the base layer with a minimal set of enhancement layers, and the *top layer segment* that contains only enhancement layers. During the video transmission, the two segments are shifted in time. Hence, our main focus in the following is the adaptation problem, i.e., how to jointly match the video quality of each layer (low layer and top layer) of the two shifted segments to the network conditions. Our proposed adaptation methods select the appropriate bitrates for both segments by adding the appropriate number of enhancement layers. Through extensive simulations we show that this BSC system performs remarkably well even under high throughput variability. This is due to the key property of this novel scheme. In fact, the DASH protocol can leverage on the time difference of the two BSC layers, which increases diversity. In turn, this mitigates the impact of inaccurate capacity estimation on HAS. In [13], we did simulations using generated throughput traces from Matlab and HSDPA throughput traces. In this paper, we use an MPEG/DASH client-server application on ns-3 simulator using LTE (Long Term Evolution) network.

The outline of the paper is as follows. In Sect. 2 we describe the Backward Shifted Coding system and its mapping to the DASH system. In Sect. 3, we give the details of the bitrate adaptation in Backward Shifted Coding including the pseudo-codes of our proposed adaptation algorithms. Section 4 presents the simulations framework and the numerical results. Finally, Sect. 5 concludes the paper.

2 System Model

2.1 Backward-Shifted Coding

We provide an overview of Backward-Shifted Coding system and briefly describe its integration in Dynamic Adaptive Streaming over HTTP standard. The BSC scheme is fully client driven. The main idea of the scheme is to send a complete segment (base layer and possibly some enhancement layers) together with the enhancement layers of another segment. We call the first one, *lower layer segment* and the second one is the *top layer segment*. During the video transmission, the two segments are shifted in time by a constant offset. We denote ϕ the offset between the two segments. Thus, each segment k has its enhancement layers in segment $k+\phi-1$ (Fig. 2). We call *block k* the combination of segment $k+\phi-1$ (lower layer) and of enhancement layers of segment k (top layer). Therefore, should the enhancement layer be missed, the player can still playout the lower layer segment which is sent in advance with low quality. The advantage of the BSC scheme is apparent if we consider the decoding operations at the user side, i.e., when incoming bits are reassembled into video frames by the decoder. The advantage compared to the basic SVC scheme in Fig. 1 is that in plain SVC, when lower layer segment k is transmitted, it is decoded to render the segment with a given quality. Later, if other enhancement layers of this segment are received, the segment is decoded again to increase its quality. BSC does not need to perform repeated decoding since each block is received only once, i.e., base layer and related enhancements layers.

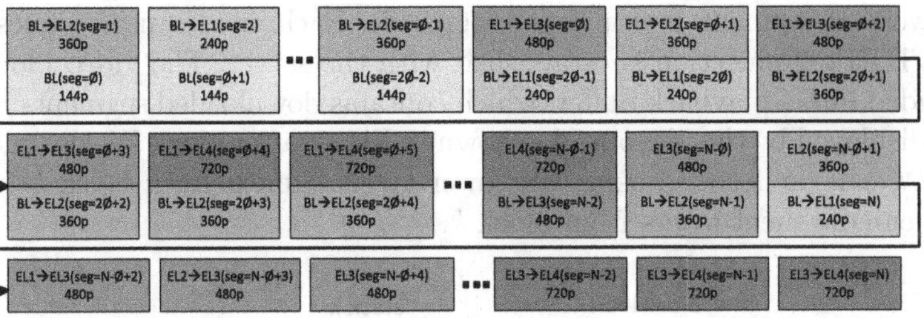

Fig. 2. Segments transmission with Backward-Shifted Coding: the lower layer segments contain the base layer (and possibly some enhanced layers) and are transmitted before the corresponding top layer segments, which follow after $\phi - 1$ blocks; the initial ϕ blocks carry only lower layer segments; the notation $BL \rightarrow EL_j$ indicates all segments $BL, EL_1, EL_2, \ldots, EL_j$ and $EL_i \rightarrow EL_j$ indicates $EL_i, EL_{i+1}, \ldots, EL_j$

The BSC scheme can be naturally adapted to DASH: under DASH/SVC, video servers store each tagged video into segments. For multi-layer codecs, such segments consists of a base layer and multiple enhancement layers. BSC requires to compound layers and to defer the transmission of top layer segments. Conversely, bitrate adaptation algorithms have not been standardized yet in DASH. The aim is to choose a bitrate ensuring good video quality and prevent video playback interruptions. They fall into two categories: the *throughput-based* approaches and the *buffer-based* approaches. Some schemes [10,14] may actually fall in both categories since they leverage on the estimation of the network throughput in combination with buffer-based mechanisms.

The main idea behind throughput-based schemes is that the MPEG-DASH client performs an estimation of the available bandwidth for the requested segments [1,9]. Then, based on the network throughput and the playout buffer occupancy level, an adaptation engine chooses the highest possible bitrate compatible with the available throughput in order to avoid possible playback interruptions. The simplest way to estimate the available throughput is to compute the segment throughput after it is completely downloaded. This is a standard throughput measure called *instant throughput* [10]. This method is simple and fast to react to the throughput variations but not accurate. Conversely, buffer-based methods leverage on the size of the buffer, with the aim of keeping it at a given nominal level. In comparison to the throughput-based schemes where the bitrate selection is based on the estimated throughput, buffer-based methods leverage on the size of the buffer, with the aim of keeping it at a given nominal level. In this context, the adaptation engine for BSC sets two segments at different bitrates, i.e., one bitrate for the low layer segment (base and enhancement layers) and one bitrate for the top layer segment which contains only enhancement layers.

2.2 Video Bitrate Adaptation

In this section, we develop a video rate adaptation algorithm suitable for the Backward-Shifted Coding scheme. In Backward-Shifted Coding, the media segments are encoded using H264/SVC (or equivalent multi-layers codec). As shown in Fig. 3, block k contains segment $k + \phi - 1$ (lower layer segment) and enhancement layers of segment k (top layer segment). Each time a user requests the video, a HTTP connection is established with the server. The video blocks are downloaded into a playback buffer, which contains downloaded segments but are not yet displayed by the playout. As shown in Fig. 3, after block k is downloaded, segment k can be decoded using the lower layer segment from block $k - \phi + 1$ and the enhancement layers from block k.

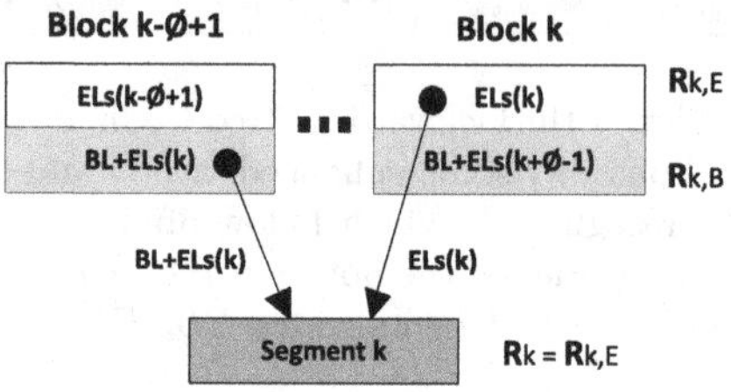

Fig. 3. Decoding of segment k: uses lower layer segment of block $k - \phi + 1$ (containing base layer and possibly some enhancement layers) and top layer segment of block k (containing enhancement layers only).

Let N be the number of segments contained in the video file. Each segment contains L seconds of video and it is encoded at different bitrates.

In standard SVC playout, a set of available bitrate levels per segment $\mathcal{R}$ corresponds to selecting the base layer and a certain number of enhancement layers. In the BSC system, the playout downloads the BSC block k with the bitrates $(R_{k,E}, R_{k,B}) \in \mathcal{R}^2$. In particular we denote:

- $R_{k,E}$ is the bitrate of segment k by *including the lower layer segment*, which is received through block $k - \phi + 1$
- $R_{k,B}$ is the bitrate of the lower layer segment $k + \phi - 1$ (which contains base layer and some enhancement layers).

Note that, with this notation, when we refer to the condition $R_{k,E} = R_{k-\phi+1,B}$, we mean that no enhancement layers are transmitted in block k.

3 Adaptation Methods in BSC

The goal of the bitrate adaptation is to maximize the quality of experience of the video streaming user depending on four key parameters: the startup delay, the playback interruption, the mean video bitrate and the bitrate switching.

We propose bitrate adaptation methods to choose the suitable bitrates for block k. We denote by R_{min} and R_{max} the smallest and the highest bitrate respectively in the set of available bitrates $\mathcal{R}$. We let $\mathcal{B}_k$ be the current playout buffer occupancy measured in seconds of video content.

In order to select bitrates $R_{k,B}$ and $R_{k,E}$, we are inspired from the two approaches described in Sect. 2, namely the buffer-based and the throughput-based approach in order to evaluate the performance of the BSC scheme. This results into two distinct algorithms: the throughput-based BSC algorithm (TB-BSC) and the buffer-based BSC algorithm (BB-BSC).

3.1 The Throughput Based Approach

We distinguish two cases based on the block index: $k < \phi$ and $k \geq \phi$.

Case $0 \leq k \leq \phi - 1$**.** For the $\phi - 1$ first blocks, each block contains (1) the whole (lower layer) segment k and (2) the lower layer segment $k + \phi - 1$ but at minimum bitrate $R_{k,B} = R_{min}$. Thus, for the first $\phi - 1$ blocks, the bitrate adaptation concerns only the whole segment k and must be operated such in a way that $R_k + R_{min} \leq \hat{A}_t$ where R_k is the bitrate of the whole segment k.

By assigning a minimum bitrate, R_{min}, to the lower layer segment $k + \phi - 1$, the startup delay is not greatly affected by the BSC scheme. Doing so, we immediately maximize the bitrate of the segments $1 \leq k \leq \phi - 1$ – for which no enhancement layers are expected later on – and we defer the bitrate enhancement of the lower layer segments $\phi \leq k \leq 2\phi - 2$ using the top layer segment carried by block $k + \phi - 1$.

Case $k \geq \phi$**.** It is interesting to observe that, in our TB-BSC scheme, we shall also leverage on information on the buffer level occupancy.

Let $\phi_t = \phi \cdot L$: it represents the offset in seconds between the lower layer segment and its enhancement layers. When the buffer size (in seconds) is not larger than ϕ_t, we no longer need to send the enhancement layers segments because their corresponding segments are already been played by the playout. In that case, the bitrate selection is equivalent to DASH/SVC. When $\mathcal{B}_k > \phi_t$ (Line 3), the adaptation is done on both the lower layer segments and the enhancement layers segments. The pseudo-code for this part of the TB-BSC adaptation algorithm is provided in Algorithm 1. We assume that it is invoked repeatedly each time t a block is downloaded; it starts immediately after the download of BSC block $k - 1$ is completed.

In the worst case, i.e. Line 4, when the estimated throughput is lower than R_{min}, the selected bitrate for the lower layer segment in block k is R_{min} and no enhancement layers are sent, i.e., $R_{k,E} = R_{k-\phi+1,B}$.

We denote by R_{t-}, the highest available bitrate compatible with the estimated throughput. In the same way, R_{t+} is the smallest available bitrate regarding the estimated throughput.

When the estimated throughput is lower than the bitrate of the lower layer segment in the previous block $k-1$, the bitrate of the lower layer segment in the next block k is set to R_{t-}. And the bitrate of the enhancement layers segment in the next block k is the maximum between R_{t+} and $R_{k-\phi+1,B}$ (Lines 8 and 9, respectively). It is worth remarking that in this case, the selected bitrate for the lower layer segment is not larger than the estimated throughput in order to prevent playback interruptions. But, we observe that the bitrate of the enhancement layers segment is larger than the estimated throughput. Indeed, we do not risk playback interruptions here: in fact the buffer level is large enough ($\mathcal{B}_k > \phi_t$).

Algorithm 1. TB-BSC Algorithm for $k \geq \phi$

Input: $\hat{A}_t$: Estimated throughput of block $k - 1$
$\mathcal{B}_k$: Buffer occupancy in seconds
Output: $R_{k,B}$: Bitrate of lower layer segment in block k
$R_{k,E}$: Bitrate of enhancement layer in block k

1: $R_{t-} \leftarrow \{max(R_i) : R_i \leq \hat{A}_t\}$
2: $R_{t+} \leftarrow \{min(R_i) : R_i \geq \hat{A}_t\}$
3: **if** $\mathcal{B}_k > \phi_t$ **then**
4: **if** $\hat{A}_t \leq R_{min}$ **then**
5: $R_{k,B} := R_{min}$
6: $R_{k,E} := R_{k-\phi+1,B}$
7: **else if** $\hat{A}_t < R_{k-1,B}$ **then**
8: $R_{k,B} := R_{t-}$
9: $R_{k,E} := max(R_{k-\phi+1,B}, R_{t+})$
10: **else if** $R_{k-1,B} < R_{max}$ **then**
11: $R_{k,B} := R^{\uparrow}_{k-1,B}$
12: $R_{k,E} := max(R_{k-\phi+1,B}, R^{\uparrow}_{k-1,E})$
13: **else**
14: $R_{k,B} := R_{max}$
15: $R_{k,E} := R_{max}$
16: **end if**
17: **end if**

When the available throughput increases compared the previous block (Line 10), we increase the bitrate in a smooth manner in order to avoid sudden video quality transitions [2]. In practice, when the estimated throughput is higher than the bitrate of the lower layer segment in the block $k - 1$, the selected bitrate of the lower layer segment in the block k is increased to a higher bitrate, i.e., $R_{k,B} = R^{\uparrow}_{k-1,B}$, (Line 11). The bitrate of the enhancement layers of block k is increased to a higher bitrate as well (Line 12).

3.2 The Buffer Based Approach

The use of buffer occupancy to select the segments' bitrate is a technique used by several schemes in the literature [8]. Typically, buffer thresholds are set (either two or three thesholds) and decisions on the bitrate are taken according to the level of current buffer occupancy with respect to such thresholds. Some of these methods use also the estimated throughput to smooth bitrate variations. Let us call BBA-0 this group of bitrate adaptation methods.

A second group of buffer-based algorithms employ an adjustment function in order to pick the appropriate bitrate [4,5]. Let us call them BBA-1: compared to BBA-0, they do not perform throughput estimation, thus avoiding the related estimation errors. This method for bitrate selection is the basis of our BB-BSC algorithm. We describe first the application to BSC of the template algorithm introduced in [5], shortly BBA-1. Then we specialize it to match the specific features of BSC and derive BB-BSC. BB-BSC will be finally composed of two procedures, one for the lower layer segments and one for the top layer segments. The lower layer segment algorithm is reported in Algorithm 2.

We have two buffer thresholds r and c where r is the reservoir and c is the cushion in seconds of video content. The bitrate selection is based on an adjustment function F [14] where $F(\mathcal{B}_k) = R_{min}$ for $\mathcal{B}_k \leq r$, $F(\mathcal{B}_k) = R_{max}$ for $\mathcal{B}_k \geq r + c$ and $F(\mathcal{B}_k) = R_{min} + \frac{\mathcal{B}_k - r}{c}(R_{max} - R_{min})$ otherwise. Then, given the current buffer occupancy $\mathcal{B}_k$, $F(\mathcal{B}_k)$ is computed to select the bitrate of the next segment. Our purpose is to increase the video quality and limit the number of quality variations. We do this in two steps. First, we remark that when using BBA-1 algorithm on the lower layer segments in BSC system with the adjustment function F, we still have a margin which can be used to add enhancement layers segments while avoiding playback interruptions. Therefore we define two adjustment functions F_1 and F_2. The two functions have the same formula as function F but differ in the value of c, i.e., F_1 uses c_1 and F_2 uses c_2 (Fig. 4). Given the values of c_1 and c_2, we can increase and decrease the margin between the two curves and then adjust the amount of enhancement layers segments we add to the lower layer ones. Then, we compute the bounds of the previous bitrate (R_+ and R_-) and the adjustment function F_1 regarding the buffer occupancy $\mathcal{B}_k$. The bitrate of the next lower layer segment is selected according to $F_1(\mathcal{B}_k)$ and the buffer occupancy.

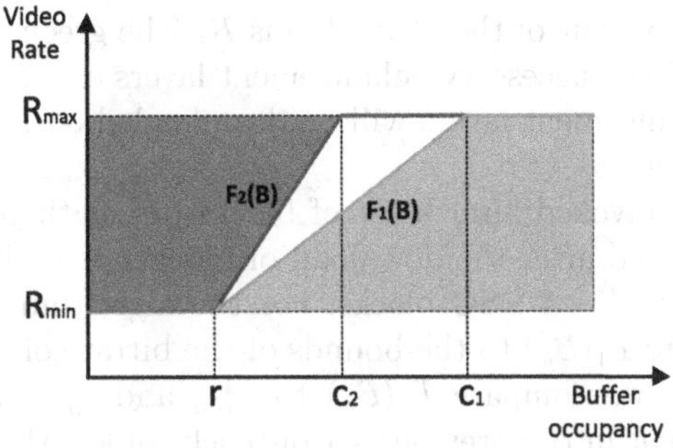

Fig. 4. The adjusment functions for the lower layer segments and the top layer segments: rates above the curve are risky for buffer depletion, rates below the curve are safer but correspond to lower quality.

Algorithm 2. Lower layer segment algorithm

Input: $\mathcal{B}_k$: Current buffer occupancy
r and c_1: Sizes of the reservoir and the cushion
Output: $R_{k,B}$: Bitrate of the segment in block k

$R_+ = min\{R_i : R_i > R_{k-1,B}\}$
$R_- = max\{R_i : R_i < R_{k-1,B}\}$
if $\mathcal{B}_k \leq r$ **then**
  $R_{k,B} = R_{min}$
else if $\mathcal{B}_k \geq r + c_1$ **then**
  $R_{k,B} = R_{max}$
else if $F_1(\mathcal{B}_k) \geq R_+$ **then**
  $R_{k,B} = max\{R_i : R_i < F_1(\mathcal{B}_k)\}$
else if $F_1(\mathcal{B}_k) \leq R_-$ **then**
  $R_{k,B} = min\{R_i : R_i > F_1(\mathcal{B}_k)\}$
else
  $R_{k,B} = R_{k-1,B}$
end if

Smoothing the bitrate variability. The main purpose of enhancement layers segments is to improve the quality of the video. They do not increase the video content in the buffer in terms of playout time. We use the adjustment function F_2 to select the bitrate of the enhancement layers segments as we did with the lower layer segments. Since $F_2 \geq F_1$, we will increase the video quality. But we also want to reduce the quality variations. For this purpose, we will apply the algorithm not on a single enhancement layer segment, but on a set of blocks of enhancement layers segments of length $\phi - 1$.

An example of this smoothing procedure is reported in Fig. 5 for $\phi = 4$. The algorithm is applied on blocks of 3 consecutive enhancement layers segments. The red part represents the lower layer segments. After the download of top layer segment 3, the output of the algorithm is R_i (the green bar). That means, we have to download the necessary enhancement layers of segment 4, 5 and 6 to reach R_i. These enhancement layers will be downloaded on lower layer segment 7, 8 and 9, respectively.

The algorithm is invoked after a set of blocks of length $\phi - 1$. Then, when the algorithm is invoked after the download of block $k-1$, the output remains the same for the next $\phi - 1$ BSC blocks. For the algorithm of the lower layer segments, we compare $F_1(\mathcal{B}_k)$ to the bounds of the bitrate of the previous lower layer segment. Here, we compare $F_2(\mathcal{B}_k)$ to r^+_{avg} and r^-_{avg}. r^+_{avg} (r^-_{avg}) is the bitrate of each segment in the previous set of blocks of length $\phi - 1$ to reach R_+ (R_-) where R_+ (R_-) is the top (lower) bound of the previous bitrate $R_{k-1,E}$. In other words, $r^+_{avg} = R_+$ and $r^-_{avg} = R_-$. Then, we compute the bounds of the previous bitrate and the adjustment function F_2 corresponding to buffer occupancy $\mathcal{B}_k$. The bitrate of the next enhancement layers segment is selected according to $F_2(\mathcal{B}_k)$ and the buffer occupancy.

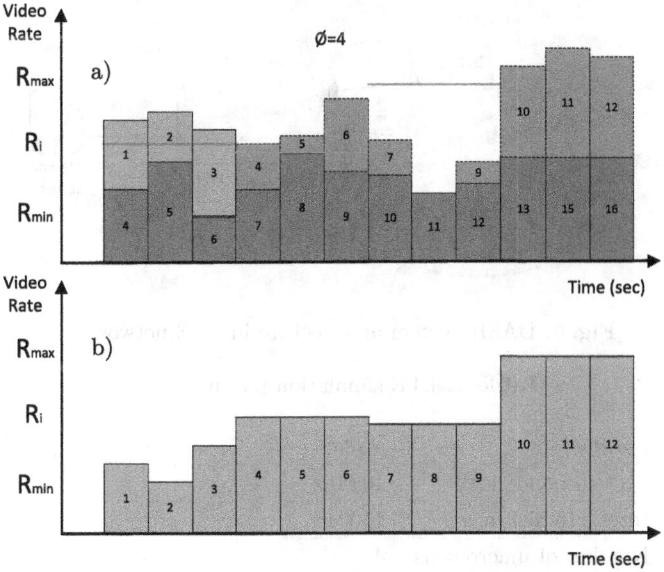

Fig. 5. (a) Example of application of the top layer algorithm: applied on several segments simultaneously it smooths the bitrate variability (b) Effect at the decoder side; $\phi = 4$. (Color figure online)

4 Simulations

We evaluate the bitrate adaptation in TB-BSC and BB-BSC using ns-3 and Matlab. We compare BSC bitrate adaptation algorithms with their equivalent DASH SVC algorithms. The network capacity is given by LTE (Long Term Evolution) simulations. The number of segments in the video file is N, the segment duration is L (seconds), BSC scheme offset is ϕ and the set of available bitrates $\mathcal{R}$.

4.1 Simulation Setup

We have performed LTE network simulations using ns-3 [3]. The network topology consists on four macro cells where the cell radius is $\rho = 1500$ m. The cells deployment is shown in Fig. 6. We consider multiple cells so as to account for cell interference. The eNodeB transmission power is 46 dBm. The signal propagation path loss model is COST231 with pedestrian fading model. The MAC scheduler is the well known Proportional Fair (PF) scheduler. The full simulation parameters are described in Table 1. The MPEG/DASH client-server application from [11] is installed on the UEs and the remote DASH video server.

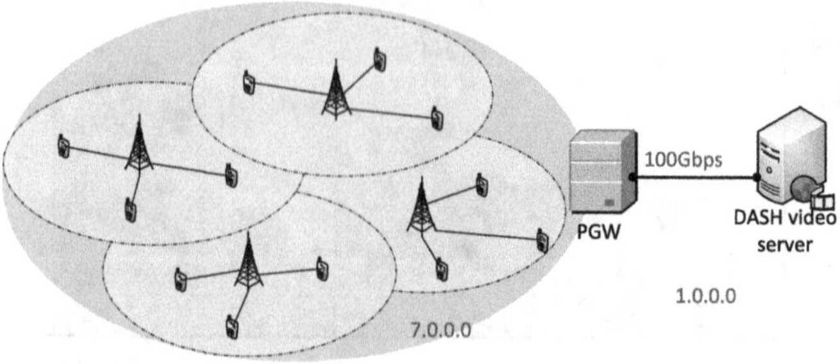

Fig. 6. DASH system architecture in LTE network

Table 1. LTE simulation parameters

Parameters	Value
System bandwidth	10 Mhz
Inter site distance	1500 m
Number of macro cells	4
Number of UEs per cell	50
eNodeB Tx power	46 dBm
UE Tx power	24 dBm
eNodeB noise figure	5 dB
UE noise figure	9 dB
Velocity of UEs	Uniform [5–16.67] m/s
Path loss model	COST 231
MAC scheduler	Proportional Fair
Fading model	Pedestrian
eNodeB antenna height	30 m
Transmission model	MIMO transmit diversity
Mobility model	RandomWaypointMobilityModel

4.2 Numerical Results

The set of experiments compares the requested bitrate with TB-BSC, BB-BSC, BBA-0 and BBA-1 algorithms. The file size in the experiments is up to 250 s of video while the playback frequency is 25 frames per second (fps). We consider the following set of available bitrates {140, 250, 420, 760, 1000, 1500, 2100, 2900} (Kbps). The video segment duration is set to 2 s.

In Fig. 7, we plot the requested bitrates for TB-BSC and TB-SVC, i.e., the throughput based algorithm, for $\phi = 4$. The throughput is estimated in a smooth manner to select the next bitrate. We observe that BSC outperforms a bit SVC in terms of video quality but with too much bitrate variations. We resort to the buffer based method to stabilize the bitrate variation. In Fig. 8, we plot the requested bitrates for BB-BSC and BBA-1 for $\phi = 10$ and the following buffer

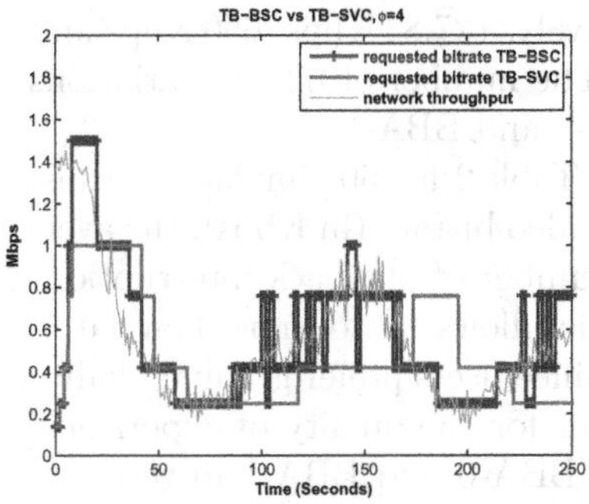

Fig. 7. Requested bitrates for TB-BSC and TB-SVC for smooth throughput estimation method

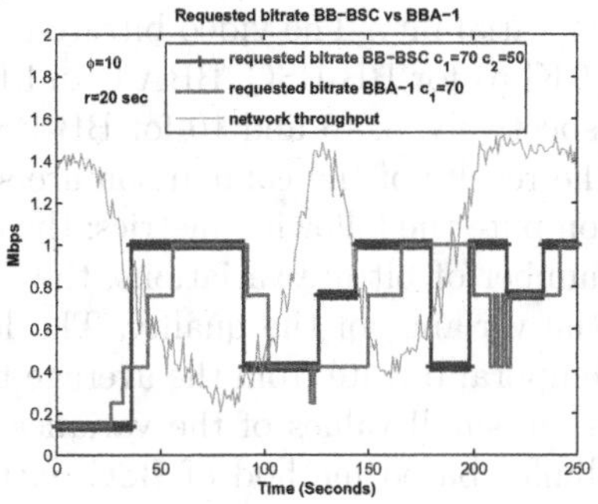

Fig. 8. Requested bitrates for BB-BSC and BBA-1, $\phi = 10$

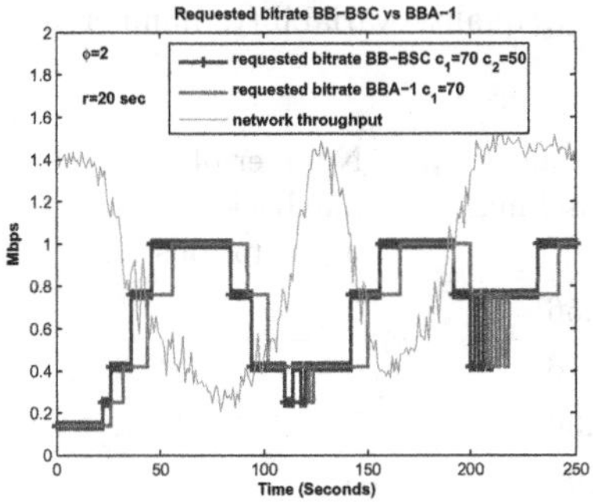

Fig. 9. Requested bitrates for BB-BSC and BBA-1, $\phi = 2$

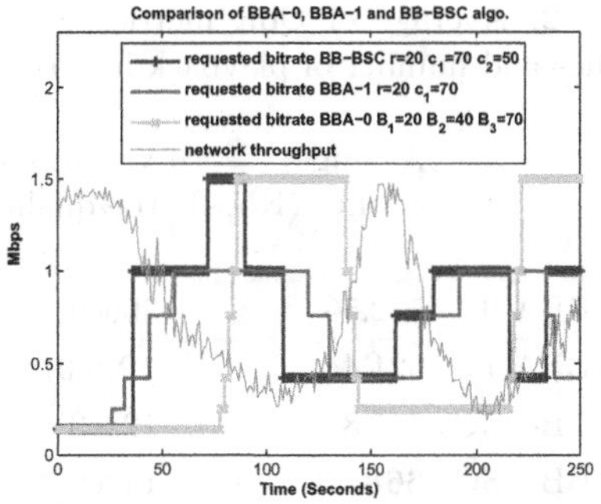

Fig. 10. Comparison of BBA-0, BBA-1 and BB-BSC algorithms

thresholds: $r = 20$, $c_1 = 70$ and $c_2 = 50$. The video bitrate is 716.32 Kbps for BB-BSC and 667.04 Kbps for BBA-1. Further, BB-BSC shows more robustness in terms of bitrate variability: the number of bitrate variations is 8 for BB-BSC against 18 for BBA-1. The same experiment for $\phi = 2$ is shown in Fig. 9. We observe that the number of bitrate variations increases untill 20. This shows the importance of the offset ϕ in BSC system.

The first observation is that it is difficult to have a value of ϕ which optimizes all the metrics of the quality of experience. So, we must find a tradeoff. The risk of the video playback interruption is really high for ϕ between 25 and 55. That corresponds to an offset of 50 s and 110 s duration, respectively. We must also avoid the values of ϕ such as $\phi \geq \frac{K}{2}$ (62 in this example). Indeed, for these values of ϕ, the video quality decreases and the number of quality switching increases. In this experiment, a good tradeoff is achieved for $\phi \in \{10, \ldots, 25\}$. This range corresponds to $\{10, \ldots, 50\}$ s of video duration. The bounds of the range are exactly the buffer thresholds: the reservoir $r = 10$ s and the cushion for the top layer segment $c_2 = 50$ s. Therefore the offset ϕ depends on the buffer thresholds. In Fig. 10, we compare BB-BSC, BBA-0 and BBA-1. The results show that BB-BSC outperforms BBA-0 and BBA-1 in terms of video bitrate and bitrate variability. The video bitrate is, respectively, 727.84 Kbps, 650 Kbps and 692.56 Kbps for BB-BSC, BBA-0 and BBA-1. The number of bitrate variations is, respectively, 8, 13 and 10 for BB-BSC, BBA-0 and BBA-1.

The results of the comparison are shown in Table 2 for 50 simulations runs. We compute the following metrics: the average video bitrate (in Kbps), the average number of bitrate variations, the average number of playback interruptions and the variance of the quality. The last metric allows us to know how far is the temporal bitrate from the average bitrate. Since users prefer gradual quality variation, small values of the variance are better for the quality of experience. The buffer based method of BSC outperforms BBA-0 and BBA-1 in terms of video bitrate and bitrate variability with a little risk of video playback interruption, those metrics considered as most important metrics in video quality of experience.

Table 2. Average of QoE metrics: average quality, quality variability, number of switches and number of playback interruption.

	Average quality (Kbps)	Variance of the quality	Number of switchings	Number of playback interruptions
BBA-0	572.56	306e9	11.56	0
BBA-1	621.44	**109e9**	18.76	0
TB-BSC	645.8	122e9	24.36	0
BB-BSC	**668.11**	142e9	**7.98**	0.2

The Backward-Shifted Coding system (for both throughput and buffer based methods) outperforms classic DASH algorithms in terms of video quality. But in order to reduce the number of quality variations, we need to adopt a buffer based approach.

5 Conclusion

In this paper, we studied the bitrate adaptation in the Backward-Shifted Coding (BSC) scheme and compared it with DASH based SVC solutions. Since BSC splits the segments into low layer segments and top layers segments and send them independently in two distinct blocks, the main challenge is how to choose the bitrates of those segments given the network capacity which tend to highly fluctuate. Furthermore, with this time redundancy property of BSC, we are able to transmit segments and improve later their quality by sending only the appropriate number of enhancement layers.

We have proposed two bitrate adaptation algorithms, namely TB-BSC and BB-BSC, which have been designed on top of BSC. They are based on network throughput measurements and playback buffer occupancy level, respectively. We show that BSC system (HTTP adaptive video streaming system in general) may suffer from throughput estimation errors, thus, impacting the resulting QoE since we have a high number of quality variations. The limitations of the throughput based methods are overcome with the buffer based methods which set a good tradeoff between the video quality and the quality variations.

We further performed simulations compare the efficiency of BSC adaptation methods to existing DASH based SVC solutions. The results show that BSC adaptation methods achieve better video quality under same network conditions, providing a DASH-compliant solution rendering high quality video in HTTP adaptive streaming.

References

1. 23009-1, I.I.: Dynamic adaptive streaming over HTTP (DASH) - part 1: media presentation description and segment formats (2012)
2. Akhshabi, S., Begen, A.C., Dovrolis, C.: An experimental evaluation of rate-adaptation algorithms in adaptive streaming over HTTP. In: Proceedings of the Second Annual ACM Conference on Multimedia Systems, pp. 157–168. ACM (2011)
3. Baldo, N., Miozzo, M., Requena-Esteso, M., Nin-Guerrero, J.: An open source product-oriented LTE network simulator based on ns-3. In: Proceedings of the 14th ACM International Conference on Modeling, Analysis and Simulation of Wireless and Mobile Systems, pp. 293–298. ACM (2011)
4. Huang, T.Y.: A buffer-based approach to video rate adaptation. Ph.D. thesis, Stanford University (2014)
5. Huang, T.Y., Johari, R., McKeown, N., Trunnell, M., Watson, M.: A buffer-based approach to rate adaptation: evidence from a large video streaming service. In: Proceedings of the 2014 ACM Conference on SIGCOMM, pp. 187–198. ACM (2014)
6. Cisco Visual Networking Index. Global mobile data traffic forecast update, 2015–2020. Cisco Systems (2015)
7. (ISO/IEC). Coding of audio-visual objects-part 10: advanced video coding (2012)
8. Miller, K., Quacchio, E., Gennari, G., Wolisz, A.: Adaptation algorithm for adaptive streaming over HTTP. In: 2012 19th International Packet Video Workshop (PV), pp. 173–178. IEEE (2012)
9. Stockhammer, T.: Dynamic adaptive streaming over HTTP-: standards and design principles. In: Proceedings of the Second Annual ACM Conference on Multimedia Systems, pp. 133–144. ACM (2011)
10. Thang, T.C., Le, H.T., Pham, A.T., Ro, Y.M.: An evaluation of bitrate adaptation methods for HTTP live streaming. IEEE J. Sel. Areas Commun. **32**(4), 693–705 (2014)
11. Vergados, D.J., Michalas, A., Sgora, A., Vergados, D.D., Chatzimisios, P.: Fdash: a fuzzy-based MPEG/DASH adaptation algorithm. IEEE Syst. J. **10**(2), 859–868 (2016)
12. Ye, Z., El-Azouzi, R., Jimenez, T., Altman, E., Valentin, S.: Backward-shifted strategies based on SVC for HTTP adaptive video streaming. In: Proceedings of the 15th International IFIP Networking Conference. IFIP (2016)
13. Ye, Z., Elazouzi, R., Jimenez, T., De Pellegrini, F., Valentin, S.: Bitrate adaptation in backward-shifted coding for HTTP adaptive video streaming. In: 2017 IEEE International Conference on Communications (ICC). IEEE (2017)
14. Yin, X., Sekar, V., Sinopoli, B.: Toward a principled framework to design dynamic adaptive streaming algorithms over HTTP. In: Proceedings of the 13th ACM Workshop on Hot Topics in Networks, p. 9. ACM (2014)

Community Detection Through Topic Modeling in Social Networks

Imane Tamimi[1(✉)], El Khadir Lamrani[2], and Mohamed El Kamili[3]

[1] LIMS, FSDM, Sidi Mohammed Ben Abdellah University, Fes, Morocco
imane.tamimi1@usmba.ac.ma

[2] LTIM, FSBM, Hassan II University, Fes, Morocco
khadir.lamrani@gmail.com

[3] LIMS, FSDM, Sidi Mohammed Ben Abdellah University, Fes, Morocco
mohamed.elkamili@usmba.ac.ma

Abstract. The research on communities in social networks takes many paths in the literature, among which: the problematic of accurately detecting communities; modeling the evolution of those communities within the evolving network; and then finding the patterns that characterize this evolution over time. In our work, we focused on the problematic of detecting communities in social networks based on the information disseminated among users of the social network and the type of content shared by these users. The work at hand consists of a brief introduction to the subject and the problem definition, then we move to state the main contribution of our work which consists of a multi-layer model to detect communities of users based on the content shared by users, the lowest layer would detect topics of interest of each user while the upper layer would form communities from generated topics. We conclude the paper stating our perspectives and future works.

Keywords: Community detection · Topic modeling · Social networks

1 Introduction

With the emergence of social networks, an increasing amount of data emerges as well, making social networks one of the main providers of data and knowledge about human interactions in modern times. it is now possible for a user not only to connect and interact with another user but to share content too, thus, analyzing these content-sharing platforms is a prominent research area in social network analysis, and one fundamental theme in social network analysis focuses on the detection of communities.

Communities represent a constant source of insight and information to the scientific community and a pillar supplier of data to analysts in quite a multitude of domains, such as computer science, physics, neuroscience, telecommunications, finance, marketing, microbiology, and many others. Some of the motivations behind assessing communities within social networks are their concrete

E. Sabir et al. (Eds.): UNet 2017, LNCS 10542, pp. 70–80, 2017.
https://doi.org/10.1007/978-3-319-68179-5_7

real life applications either in sentiment analysis, or in recommender systems, or in link prediction, or in geo-localization or even fraud and terrorism detection. The list goes on.

Since the last decade, a huge amount of work has been done on detecting communities and tracking their evolution over time. The major works so far include the elaboration of algorithms that study network topologies and the structures of networks, other algorithms aim at identifying the core elements of a network and study their attributes for a better understanding of the underlying network. One main difference between algorithms then and now is that, when clustering real life networks containing millions of nodes, current algorithms are supposed to be faster with a lower complexity unlike the slower ones that are more accurate and precise.

Recent work targets both the topology of the network and the content shared to better detect communities. In fact, communities represent a great means for information diffusion. On the other hand, the type of content social network users share among them plays a key role in determining their memberships to communities. Social networks are not just graphs with nodes and edges linking the nodes, they consist of content (information) diffused, spread and shared by users.

We are interested in the issue of content shared or information disseminated in social networks and its close impact on communities formation and evolution. The issue can be defined as follows: in a social network of nodes and edges, each node interacts with the remainder of the nodes through its content or the information it diffuses. Since each node shares a different type of content, the idea is to come up with an approach that combines the type of content users have, and the information they share or adopt among themselves, from which we extract the topics to define communities in a way that is likely the most accurate.

2 Related Work

In the last decade or so, communities detection has been extensively researched and explored, there exist numerous surveys [5,10,11,23], on the subject which review various works in terms of algorithms, methods, quality measures, evaluation, benchmarks, scalability and many other aspects of communities detection over the years.

Since the problematic of community detection is a wide area in research, this section presents without going into much detail, the recent prominent work on community detection by the means of topic modeling in social networks.

The authors in [4] addressed the issue of detecting communities using topological based approaches and using topic based approaches. The authors conducted a study on the two kinds of approaches and found that the merger of the two gives the best possible outcome in terms of accuracy and semantics.

[22] introduced a type of Deep Boltzmann Machine (DBM) that is trained as a standard Restricted Boltzmann Machine (RBM), to extract distributed

semantic representations from large unstructured collections of documents. By experiments, the authors claimed their model outperformed LDA and other models on document retrieval and document classification.

[13] compared two approaches to solve the digital publishing recommender problem: latent Dirichlet allocation (LDA) and Deep Belief Nets (DBN) that represent conceptual meanings of documents and find dimensional latent representations for documents. Results have proved that Deep Belief Nets is superior in comparison to the LDA model. It manages to find better representation of documents in an output space of low dimensionality, which in turn results in fast retrieval of similar documents.

In the work of [12], the main contribution involves integrating topics into basic word embedding representation and allowing the resulting topical word embeddings to model different meanings of a word under different contexts.

[21] presented an undirected topic model used to model and automatically extract distributed semantic representations from large collections of text documents. The model is though of as different sized Restricted Boltzman Machines RBM that share parameters. The learning process of the model is easy, stable and supports documents of different lenghts. Authors demonstrated that the proposed model is able to generalize much better than LDA in terms of both the log probability on held-out documents and the retrieval accuracy.

[18] introduced a model for community extraction which incorporates both the link and content information present in the social network. The model assumes that nodes in a community communicate on topics of mutual interest, and the topics of communication, in turn, determine the communities.

[2] surveyed Topic Modeling in Text Mining under two sections. The first one presented the state of the art methods in topic modeling among which Latent semantic analysis (LSA), Probabilistic latent semantic analysis (PLSA), Latent Dirichlet Allocation (LDA), and Correlated Topic Model (CTM). The authors stated the main differences between those methods in term of characteristics, limitations and the theoretical backgrounds. The second part of the survey discussed the topic evolution models where time is taken into account. Multiple attempts to model topic evolution were listed either by discretizing time, or by using continuous time models, and some of them employ citation relationship as well as time discretization to model topic evolution.

The work of [1] presented a community detection approach which captures the content shared within the social network. The approach uses generative Restricted Boltzmann Machines model to discover communities based on the assumption that users in a community share mutual topics, the model allows users to belong to more than a community. The resulting communities were topically meaningful.

Another work [19] evaluates the impact of topic modeling in detecting communities in social networks. The authors of the paper partitioned the network into topical clusters on which a community detection algorithm was applied. The authors compared results of their method and of classic community detection. The topic oriented community detection will give better results once combined with topic analysis.

In their paper, [6] presented a model to analyze dynamic text networks. This model links network dynamics to topic dynamics through a block structure that informs both the topic assignment of a document and the linkage pattern of the network. The goal is to discover latent communities of nodes using information from both the text generated by at the nodes and the links between nodes.

[20] studied the efficiency of considering topics in detecting more meaningful communities in social networks where users express their opinions about different objects. They partitioned the network into clusters with the same topics, then they used a community detection algorithm to assess communities, compared the results with those of traditional community detection where no content has been analyzed.

[24] presented a model for community detection named RW-HDP based on Random Walk and Hierarchical Dirichlet Process topic model. They conducted at first random walks on the network and then fitted the nonparametrical topic model Hierarchical Dirichlet Process to detect community structure in order to fetch automatically the number of communities. Yet the model does not allow for the detection of overlapping communities.

3 Contributions

We propose an approach to detect communities of users by combining the information contained in the nodes and the information shared by the nodes. We develop a deep learning model to resolve the community detection problem based on topic modeling, but first we would extract shared content and then prepare and significantly represent the data (content) to fit our model; the hidden layer would detect topics of interest of each user from shared content while the upper layer would form classes of topics from generated topics using a deep learning technique. Second, we would directly extract user information and combine it with the resulted communities (defined by user memberships) so we would obtain more refined communities. Note that our model allows for a user to be part of more than a community at once. Hence the notion of overlapping communities. The following figure sums up our approach for communities detection based on content in social networks:

3.1 Data Preparation

This phase is dedicated to the preparation and analysis of the shared content structure and syntax in order represent all types of data as textual data, cleaned and grouped by nodes. our model makes usage of a series of methods used in the text mining domain.

Data Transformation. This process has a goal to represent non textual data; such as images, videos, likes, shares and so on; by the means of textual descriptions and expressions (Fig. 1).

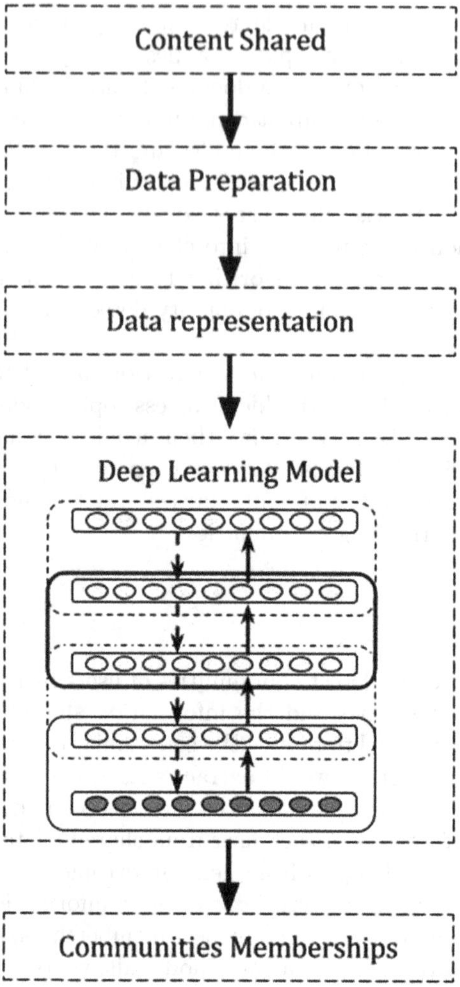

Fig. 1. Our deep learning model architecture

Preprocessing. This process has a goal to prepare the content shared by eliminating any character that does not share a useful special meaning to research information. Example: punctuation, stop words,... relating to the language used, etc.

Stemming and lemmatization. This is a preliminary operation for the recognition of words in a sentence. Indeed, It is interesting to turn all the words of the sentence in their canonical forms. We distinguish between the transformation to the root or stemme and transformation to the lemma. Lemmatisation is the name of natural language processing in the process of transforming the curls in their lemma. This process allows linguistic processing to see a lemma and its inflections semantically equivalent of fairly trivial way.

Unlike the lemma, corresponding to a real word of the language, the root or stemme is not usually a real word. The Stemming is the name given to the process that aims at transforming the flexions into their radical or stemme. Unlike lemmatisation which is therefore based on a knowledge base of inflected forms of the language to which the possible lemma is associated (called glossary), the stemmatisation only works with a basic knowledge of syntactic and grammatical rules of the language.

In the proposed system we used the lemmatisation not the stemmatisation to avoid that the words with different meaning are reduced to the same radical. For, such a transformation could distort the processing.

Group content by users: at this stage we have grouped all content shared by users, so we generate for each user, a vector that represents a set of information disseminated. each line is composed of a sequence of lemmas.

3.2 Data Representation

Most of the commonly used methods represent words in a corpus using values, thus ignore the context a word is used in. This motivates our choice for the use of Word2Vec.

Word2Vec [16,17] is a set of algorithms used for learning vector representations of words, known as word embeddings. Word2vec contains two distinct models (CBOW and skip-gram)can use either of two model architectures to produce a distributed representation of words: continuous bag of words (CBOW) or continuous skip-gram.

Word2vec has as an input a text corpus and as an output a set of vectors; feature vectors for words in that corpus. While Word2vec is not classified as a deep neural network, it turns text into a numerical form that deep networks interpret. The vectors are positioned such that those related to similar words are close in space. To achieve this, Word2vec assumes that one can determine the meaning of a word by examining its context. That said, the words appearing in the same contexts are likely similar. An extension of Word2Vec is Doc2Vec also called Paragraph2Vec, as in [15], which modifies the Word2Vec model into unsupervised learning of continuous representations for larger blocks of text, such as sentences, paragraphs or entire documents.

To implement the model, we used a training data set from "1-billion-word-language-modeling-benchmark" [3] which represents a standard training and test setup for language modeling experiments. The vectoral space of a Word2vec representation is set to a dimension equal to 300. The matrices representing the content of each user are thus of size $X_i \times 100$, X_i being the number of words shared by user i as a content.

3.3 Community Detection Using Deep Belief Nets for Topic Modeling

In this step, we present the part of the model that discovers topics using Deep Belief Nets, based on the work of [14].

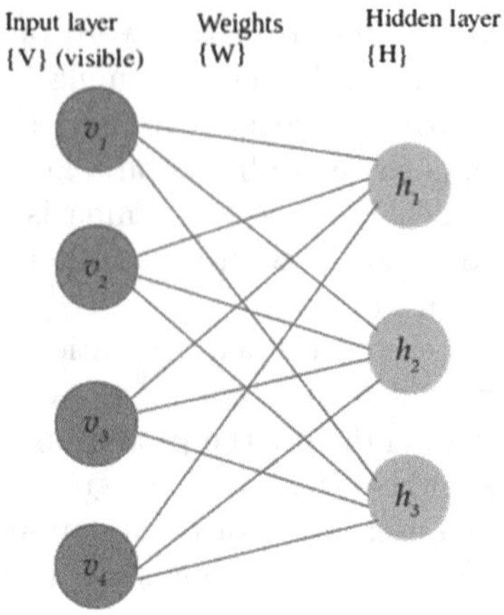

Fig. 2. Restricted Boltzman

The advantage of the DBN is that it has the ability of a highly nonlinear dimensionality reduction, due to its deep architecture. A very low-dimensional representation in output space results in a fast retrieval of similar documents to a query document. The output layer of the model groups the set of resulted topics into classes of semantically similar topics, based on the cosine distance.

A deep-belief network can be defined as a stack of Restricted Boltzman Machines [7], in which each RBM layer communicates with both the previous and subsequent layers. No lateral communication between the nodes of any single layer. To build a DBN model, Restricted Boltzmann Machine (RBM) model needs to be introduced first, which constitute the foundations of the deep learning model constructed in this article. RBMs are shallow, two-layer neural nets that represent the building blocks of deep-belief networks. The first layer of the RBM is called the visible, or input layer, the second is named the hidden layer.

Each circle in the graph below (Fig. 2) represents a node. The nodes are connected to each other through the layers, yet no node communicates nor connects with another node of the same layer. In other words, there is no intra layer communication in RBMs. Each node is a computing place that processes the input and starts by making stochastic decisions about whether or not to transmit this input. Each visible node takes a low level feature of an element of the dataset to be learned.

The visible layer reprensents the observed data and its size corresponds to the size of the data. The hidden layer represents unknown elements associated with the data and its size is randomly fixed. Depending on its size, a Restricted Boltzman Machine will be able to model more or less complex distributions.

The joint configuration (v, h) of the two layers has an energy [9] defined by:

$$E(v,h) = -\sum_{i \in visible} a_i v_i - \sum_{i \in hidden} b_j h_j - \sum_{i,j} v_i h_j w_{ij} \qquad (1)$$

where v_i and h_j are the states of the visible cells i and hidden cells j, a_i, b_j are respectively their bias and w_{ij} the weights between the cells.

A probability is associated to each joint configuration through this function:

$$p(v, h) = \frac{1}{z(\theta)} e^{-E(v,h)} \quad (2)$$

z is a partition function. It represents the sum of all possible joined configurations.

$$z(\theta) = \sum_{v,h} e^{-E(v,h)} \quad (3)$$

By marginalizing on h, we obtain the probability of a visible vector v:

$$p(v) = \frac{1}{z(\theta)} \sum_{h} e^{-E(v,h)} \quad (4)$$

Based on the configuration of a layer, it is possible to know the activation probability of another cell of the second layer:

$$p(h_j = 1 \mid v) = \sigma(b_j + \sum_i v_i w_{ij}) \quad (5)$$

where σ is a logistic function (sigmoid) defined by: $1/(1 + exp(-x))$. And reciprocally:

$$p(v_i = 1 \mid h) = \sigma(a_i + \sum_j h_j w_{ij} \quad (6)$$

In [8], Hinton developed the Contrast Divergence algorithm (CD) to train the RBM network. Unlike the general sampling method, Hinton mentioned that one only needs a small sampling frequency to obtain an approximate representation when using training samples to initialize visible nodes. It quickly increases the computation speed yet keeps the precision as is.

Using the Kullback-Leibler distance to measure the difference of two probability distributions, the following formula is used to calculate:

$$CD_m = KL(p_0 \parallel p_\infty) - KL(p_m \parallel p_\infty) \quad (7)$$

By constantly updating parameters θ, CD_m converges to θ, and its precision will not change. This paper uses Contrast Divergence algorithm in RBM training, setting the value of m to 1.

The DBN consist of a visible layer, output layer and a number of hidden layers. The training process of the DBN is defined by two steps: pre-training and fine-tuning. In pretraining the layers of the DBN are separated pairwise to form restricted Boltzmann machines (RBM). Each RBM is trained independently, such that the output of the lower RBM is provided as input to the next higher level RBM and so forth. This way the layers of the DBN are trained as partly independent systems. The goal of the pretraining process is to achieve

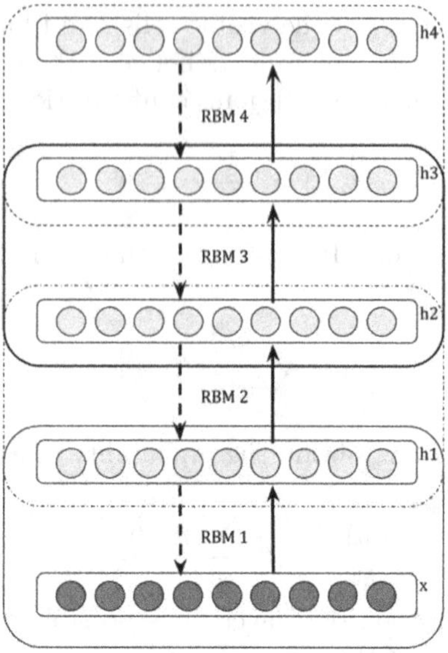

Fig. 3. The structure of DBN used in this paper

approximations of the model parameters. The model parameters from pretraining is passed on to the fine-tuning by replicating and mirroring the input and hidden layers and attaching them to the output of the DBN [14].

The structure of DBN network which is used in this paper is shown in the (Fig. 3). These networks are "limited" to a visible and a 4 hidden layers, and there are connections between the layers, but no links between the units in one layer. The hidden layer captures high data level correlation of the visible layer.

The Training Process of DBN

At the beginning of the time, by a non supervised greedy layer by layer method, the weights of the generated model are pre-trained and obtained, and Hinton has proved that unsupervised greedy layer by layer method is effective, and it is called Contrast Divergence.

The process is as follows:

1. Train the first layer as an RBM that models the raw input $x = h0$ as its visible layer. X represent vectors for users published content
2. Use that first layer to obtain a representation of the input that will be used as data for the second layer. This representation can be chosen as being the mean activations $p(h1 = 1|h0)$
3. Train the second layer as an RBM, taking the transformed data (mean activations) as training examples (for the visible layer of that RBM).
4. Iterate (2 and 3) for two layers, each time propagating upward either mean values.

The main idea of deep belief nets community detection model is to first generate a vector v among terms using word2vec distribution then passing the value to the hidden layer. In turn, the input of visual layer will be randomly selected to try to reconstruct the original input signal. Finally, these new visual neuron activation units will be transferred to reconstruct hidden layer activation unit in order to get $h1$, These back and forward steps are the familiar Gibbs sampling, and the correlation between the hidden activation unit and visual input will be the main basis for updating the weights. Next the hidden layer $h1$ is considered as an iput layer for another RBM for topic discovery phase and produce binary hidden units for topic discovery phase, and iterate for producing binary hidden units for detected community.

4 Conclusion and Perspectives

Currently, we are at the phase of elaborating the proposed model which would detect communities, based on content sharing (type of information diffused and the topics extracted from this content). We believe that the resulted communities are of high accuracy since the model allows for a user to be part of multiple communities at the same time, further future work will target the evaluation of our model with the state of the art methods of community detection and a comparison based on ground truth communities. Another possible direction of research is to study both the communities logically and topologically for more accurate results. Finally, and since this paper is a work in progress, we hope that the results we would obtain fit our theoretical hypothesis.

References

1. Abdelbary, H.A.: Semantic topics modeling approach for community detection **81**(6), 50–58 (2013)
2. Alghamdi, R., Alfalqi, K.: A survey of topic modeling in text mining. IJACSA Int. J. Adv. Comput. Sci. Appl. **6**(1), 147–153 (2015)
3. Chelba, C., Mikolov, T., Schuster, M., Ge, Q., Brants, T., Koehn, P., Robinson, T.: One billion word benchmark for measuring progress in statistical language modeling. Technical report, Google (2013)
4. Das, R., Zaheer, M., Dyer, C.: Gaussian LDA for topic models with word embeddings. Proc. ACL **2015**, 795–804 (2015)
5. Fortunato, S., Castellano, C.: Community structure in graphs. In: Computational Complexity. Theory, Techniques, and Applications 9781461418, pp. 490–512 (2012)
6. Henry, T., Banks, D., Chai, C., Owens-Oas, D.: Modeling community structure and topics in dynamic text networks. arXiv Preprint https://arxiv.org/abs/1610.05756 (2016)
7. Hinton, G.E.: A practical guide to training restricted boltzmann machines a practical guide to training restricted Boltzmann machines. Comput. (Long. Beach. Calif.) **9**(3), 1 (2010)
8. Hinton, G.E.: Training products of experts by minimizing contrastive divergence. Neural Comput. **14**(8), 1771–1800 (2002)

9. Larochelle, H.: Classification using discriminative restricted Boltzmann machines (2008)
10. Leskovec, J., Lang, K.J., Mahoney, M.: Empirical comparison of algorithms for network community detection. In: Conference on World Wide Web WWW, pp. 631–640 (2010)
11. Liu, G.: Community structure and detection in complex networks: a survey. Cs.Gsu.Edu (2012)
12. Liu, Y., Liu, Z., Chua, T.S., Sun, M.: Topical word embeddings, pp. 2418–2424 (2015)
13. Maaloe, L., Arngren, M., Imm, O.W.I., Dk, D.T.U.: Deep belief nets for topic modeling workshop on knowledge-powered deep learning for text mining arXiv: 1501. 04325v1 [cs. CL] 18 32 (2014)., January 2015
14. Maaloe, L., Arngren, M., Winther, O.: Deep belief nets for topic modeling, 32 (2015)
15. Campr, M., Ježek, K.: Comparing semantic models for evaluating automatic document summarization. In: Král, P., Matoušek, V. (eds.) TSD 2015. LNCS, vol. 9302, pp. 252–260. Springer, Cham (2015). doi:10.1007/978-3-319-24033-6_29
16. Mikolov, T., Chen, K., Corrado, G., Dean, J.: Distributed representations of words and phrases and their compositionality. In: NIPS, pp. 1–9 (2013)
17. Mikolov, T., Corrado, G., Chen, K., Dean, J.: Efficient estimation of word representations in vector space. In: Proceedings of International Conference on Learning Representations (ICLR 2013), pp. 1–12 (2013)
18. Pathak, N., DeLong, C., Erickson, K., Banerjee, A.: Social topic models for community extraction. In: 2nd SNA-KDD Workshop 2008 (2008)
19. Reihanian, A., Minaei-Bidgoli, B., Alizadeh, H.: Topic-oriented community detection of rating-based social networks. J. King Saud Univ. - Comput. Inf. Sci. pp. 1–8 (2015)
20. Reihanian, A., Minaei-Bidgoli, B., Alizadeh, H.: Topic-oriented community detection of rating-based social networks. J. King Saud Univ. - Comput. Inf. Sci. **28**(3), 303–310 (2016)
21. Salakhutdinov, R., Hinton, G.: Replicated softmax: an undirected topic model, pp. 1–8
22. Srivastava, N., Hinton, G.: Modeling documents with a deep Boltzmann machine
23. Xie, J., Kelley, S., Szymanski, B.K.: Overlapping community detection in networks: the state-of-the-art and comparative study. ACM Comput. Surv. **45**(4), 43:1–43:35 (2013)
24. Zhu, R., Jiang, W.: Combing random walks and nonparametric bayesian topic model for community detection, pp. 1–13 (2016)

A Formal Framework for Adaptation

Anne Marie Amja[1(✉)], Abdel Obaid[1], Hafedh Mili[1], and Zahi Jarir[2]

[1] University of Quebec at Montreal, Montreal, Canada
anne.amja@gmail.com, obaid.abdel@gmail.com, mili.hafedh@uqam.ca

[2] Cadi Ayyad University, Marrakesh, Morocco
jarir@uca.ma

Abstract. Context comprises everything in the environment that affects a system's structure and behavior. Self-adaptive systems aim to evaluate and to adjust itself in response to context changes. Developing self-adaptive systems is a challenging problem in component-based software engineering. This paper presents a formal model and framework for component-based adaptation founded on process algebra. With respect to this semantic model, we propose an adaptation method that consists of imposing constraints to restrain the behavior of components and transforming operators to modify a system's architecture. We also integrate our approach on the use of a control loop. We simulate the model using a simple application from the medical field.

Keywords: Self-adaptation · Component · Semantic model · Control loop

1 Introduction

Interest in self-adaptation system has grown dramatically in the past few years and significant efforts have been made by the research community to find new approaches of elucidating the challenges and principles of self-adaptivity theory and practice. Context-aware systems, as a type of self-adaptive systems, are able to react and adjust in response to context changes.

The process, which spans from acquiring contextual information to examine for relevant changes and enact adaptations, is known as the control loop model in the literature and is often related to control theory, autonomic computing or artificial intelligence.

A feedback loop is the generic mechanism for self-adaptation. IBM introduced the MAPE-K reference model [1], which is the first architecture for self-adaptive systems that explicitly exposes the feedback loop. MAPE-K consists of a monitor, an analyzer, a planner and an executor, which share a knowledge base.

Software component adaptation is a widely recognized problem in component-based software engineering. Existing work focuses on adapting component behavior (i.e. the change in the behavior of a program) and/or structure (i.e. the change in the composition of components). In most cases, these systems are described informally using graph notations that illustrate interconnections among components or models that describe the behavior of systems regardless of their structures.

E. Sabir et al. (Eds.): UNet 2017, LNCS 10542, pp. 81–94, 2017.
https://doi.org/10.1007/978-3-319-68179-5_8

In this paper, we propose a model for component-based adaptation inspired by Milner's process algebra [2]. Our model specifies a system's behavior in terms of its components' behaviour. This composition describes an architecture expressed with operators.

Based on this model, we propose a structural adaptation by the imposition of constraints and by the transformation of interconnection operators. We also integrate our approach based on the MAPE-K control model. We simulate our model and this control loop with Prolog [3].

The rest of this paper is organized as follows: Sect. 2 summarizes related work. Section 3 presents a proposed semantic model for adaptation. Section 4 details the imposition of constraints. Section 5 explains the labeled transition system. Section 6 presents the substitution of operators. Section 7 details the implantation of the model. In Sect. 8, we discuss the use of the MAPE-K control loop. Finally, Sect. 9 concludes this paper and provides a summary of future work.

2 Related Work

Arbab [4] suggested an integrated structural and behavioral channel-based coordination language (Reo), which has an application area in component and service composition. They exploit algebraic graph transformations for the reconfiguration of distributed connectors. Canal et al. [5] proposed a framework that unifies behavioral adaptation and structural reconfiguration of components used for statically detecting whether it is possible to reconfigure a system. They also present and formalize different notions of reconfigurations and their properties. Adaptors are used to synchronize components using the same name of actions. Bastide et al. [6] presented an approach aiming at dynamically adapting a component structure while preserving its behavior and its services. Their method consists of transforming the component by generating an adaptable component structure and adapting this component by the reconfiguration of its internal structure. Castaneda and Tamura [7] proposed a component-based architecture to implement the basic elements required for self-adaptation, which consists of monitoring, analyzing, planning and executing, independently from the system that is being adapted. Their architecture provides separation of concerns and extensible implementation capabilities.

3 Model for Adaptation

3.1 Architecture Description

A component is described as an entity that contains an internal behavior and two sets of ports: input ports *inP* and output ports *outP*. System components are interconnected by their set of input and output ports. Each port is described by a label and type of data (t) that pass through the ports. An action λ on a component corresponds to a data exchange activity that takes place on its ports. It consists of a port label p and accompanied by variables or values (v) that transit through this port. Synchronizing two actions λ_1 and λ_2 is dented sync (λ_1, λ_2) if type (v) = t and Cond is true. Cond is the condition applied to the values.

3.2 Semantic of a Component Behavior

To express the fact that a component performs an action λ and transforms into C′, we use the following notation: $C \xrightarrow{\lambda} C'$. In other words, if the context of the component C ensures that the action λ occurs, then the component transforms into C′. Components may be interconnected between them in various ways to express diverse configurations as explained below.

Invocation (Call()): Describes the activation of its input and output ports. This starts on operations on the input ports and ends with operations on the output ports:

$$\text{Call}(\text{C}(\text{inP},\ \text{outP})) \xrightarrow{\lambda} \text{C}(\text{inP}\backslash\lambda,\ \text{outP})\ \text{ if }\ \lambda \in \text{inP} \tag{1}$$

$$\text{Call}(\text{C}(\emptyset, \text{outP})) \xrightarrow{\lambda} \text{C}(\emptyset,\ \text{outP}\backslash\lambda)\ \text{ if }\ \lambda \in \text{outP} \tag{2}$$

Alternative (+): Only one of the components can be invoked:

$$\text{C1} + \text{C2} \xrightarrow{\lambda} \text{C1}' \text{ if } \text{C1} \xrightarrow{\lambda} \text{C1}' \tag{3}$$

$$\text{C1} + \text{C2} \xrightarrow{\lambda} \text{C2}' \text{ if } \text{C2} \xrightarrow{\lambda} \text{C2}' \tag{4}$$

Parallel (||): Components may be invoked in parallel and may synchronous. An action may be taken by one of the components. It is possible that actions synchronize, in which case each component progresses to its next state:

$$\text{C1} \parallel \text{C2} \xrightarrow{\lambda} \text{C1}' \parallel \text{C2} \text{ if } \text{C1} \xrightarrow{\lambda} \text{C1}' \tag{5}$$

$$\text{C1} \parallel \text{C2} \xrightarrow{\lambda} \text{C1} \parallel \text{C2}' \text{ if } \text{C2} \xrightarrow{\lambda} \text{C2}' \tag{6}$$

$$\text{C1} \parallel \text{C2} \xrightarrow{\lambda} \text{C1}' \parallel \text{C2}'\ \text{ if }\ \text{C1} \xrightarrow{\lambda_1} \text{C1}' \text{and } \text{C2} \xrightarrow{\lambda_2} \text{C2}'\ \text{ and }\ \text{sync}(\lambda_1, \lambda_2) \tag{7}$$

A version of this operator, noted |||, only uses the first two rules.

Pipeline (*): Acomponent can start the invocation on one of its input ports if the first one has already reached the invocation on one of its output ports:

$$\text{C1} * \text{C2} \xrightarrow{\lambda} \text{C1}' * \text{C2}\ \text{ if C1 } \xrightarrow{\lambda} \text{C1}' \text{ and } \lambda \in \text{inP(C1)} \tag{8}$$

$$\text{C1} * \text{C2} \xrightarrow{\lambda} \text{C2}' \text{ if C1 } \xrightarrow{\lambda} \text{C1}' \text{ and C2} \xrightarrow{\lambda} \text{C2}' \text{ and } \lambda \in \text{outP(C1)} \cap \text{inP(C2)} \tag{9}$$

As an example, let's consider *P1({a,b},{c,d}) * P2({c,d},{g})*. *{a,b}* and *{c,d}* are input ports of P1 and P2 respectively. *{c,d}* and *{g}* are their output ports. The pipeline composition yields:

$$P1(\{a,b\},\{c,d\}) * P2(\{c,d\},\{g\}) \xrightarrow{a} P1(\{b\},\{c,d\}) * P2(\{c,d\},\{g\})$$

$$\xrightarrow{b} P1(\{\},c,d\}) * P2(\{c,d\},\{g\})$$

4 Constraints

A constraint is a component whose role is to restrain the behavior of other components. This construct will allow us to impose constraints on a system in order to adapt it to a current situation of the current context. We use an operator noted as < and defined as follows:

$$C1 < C2 \xrightarrow{\lambda} C1' < C2' \text{ if } C1 \xrightarrow{\lambda} C1' \text{ and } C2 \xrightarrow{\lambda} C2' \tag{10}$$

Any expression as described above can be used to express a constraint. However, we may need to express constraints that are constructed with the help of a sequence of actions expressed as $\lambda; P \xrightarrow{\lambda} P$ where P is any expression or *null* component. This allows us to express constraints such as `a;(b;null+c;d;call(p,{e,f},{g})`.

5 Transition System

A system's behavior can be expressed as a graph representing a transition system ST defined as a tuple: ST = (N, Λ, s_0, tr). N is a set of nodes, L is a set of actions, s_0 is a root node (initial state) and tr is a transition function expressed as follows:

$$\text{tr}: \ N \times \Lambda \rightarrow N \text{ such that } \text{tr}(n_1, \lambda) = n_2 \text{ if } \text{expr}(n_1) \xrightarrow{\lambda} \text{expr}(n_2) \tag{11}$$

Given a node n_1, we define expr(n_1) as being the expression that describes its behaviour. We build a transition from n_1 by using the rules expressed in Sect. 3. For example, for three nodes n_1, n_2 and n_3 and their expressions:

- $expr(n1) = call(P1(\{a\},\{b\})) \,||\, call(P2(\{b\},\{d\}))$
- $expr(n2) = call(P1(\{\},\{b\})) \,||\, call(P2(\{b\},\{d\})))$
- $expr(n3) = call(P1(\{a\},\{b\})) \,||\, call(P2(\{\},\{d\}))$

We have tr(n_1, a) = n_2 and tr(n_1, b) = n_3.

From a given node n_0, we can execute a sequence of actions s and reach node n_m. If s = $\lambda_1, \lambda_2, \ldots, \lambda_m$, we define such execution from node n_0, as follows: $n_0 \xrightarrow{\{s\}} n_m$ if there are intermediary nodes $n_1, n_2, \ldots n_{m-1}$ such that tr(n_i, λ_i) = n_{i+1}.

6 Operator Substitution

Given an expression P, we define operator substitution [[/]]as follows: P [[op1/op2]] is obtained by replacing in P every occurrence of operators op1 by op2. The semantic of this transformation is given by the following rules:

$$(\mathrm{C1\ op1\ C2})[\mathrm{op1/op2}] = \mathrm{C1}[\mathrm{op1/op2}]\ \mathrm{op2}\ \mathrm{C2}[\mathrm{op1/op2}] \tag{12}$$

$$\mathrm{Call(inP,\ outP)}[\mathrm{op1/op2}] = \mathrm{Call(inP,\ outP)} \tag{13}$$

We can specify the level *n* at which to start a transformation as follows:

$$(\mathrm{C1\ op1\ C2})[\mathrm{op1/op2}]_{\mathrm{n}} = \mathrm{C1}[\mathrm{op1/op2}]_{\mathrm{n-1}}\mathrm{op2}\ \mathrm{C2}[\mathrm{op1/op2}]_{\mathrm{n-1}},\ \mathrm{n} > 1 \tag{14}$$

$$(\mathrm{C1\ op1\ C2})\ [\mathrm{op1/op2}]_1 = (\mathrm{C1\ op2\ C2}) \tag{15}$$

We can also specify the level *n* at which to finish a transformation as follows:

$$(\mathrm{C1\ op1\ C2})[\mathrm{op1/op2}]^{\mathrm{n}} = \mathrm{C1}[\mathrm{op1/op2}]^{\mathrm{n-1}}\mathrm{op1}\ \mathrm{C2}[\mathrm{op1/op2}]^{\mathrm{n-1}},\ \mathrm{n} > 1 \tag{16}$$

$$(\mathrm{C1\ op1\ C2})\ [\mathrm{op1/op2}]^1 = (\mathrm{C1\ op1\ C2})\ [\mathrm{op1/op2}] \tag{17}$$

If n = 0, then every occurrence of op1 is replaced by op2. With these transformations, we can modify the architecture and the system's behavior dynamically. For instance,

- $(P1\,||\,P2)\left[[||/+]^1\right] = P1 + P2$: transforms a parallel composition into alternative.
- $(P1\,||\,(P2\,||\,P3))\ [[||/+]_2] = P1\,||\,(P2 + P3)$: transforms the second component from parallel into alternative.
- $(P1\,||\,P2\,||\,P3)\ [[||/+]*] = P1 + P2 + P3$: transforms parallel compositions into alternatives.

Given a sequence of actions s = $\lambda_1, \lambda_2,\ldots, \lambda_m$, with $<n_0$, s, $[\mathrm{op1/op2}]^q>$ we apply a *transform* after the execution of s. q represents either the level of depth at which to start a transformation (subscript) or the depth at which we want to complete a transformation (superscript).

$$<\mathrm{n_0},\ \mathrm{s},\ [\mathrm{op1/op2}]^{\mathrm{q}}> \ = \mathrm{n_0} \overset{\{\lambda_1,\lambda_2,\ldots,\lambda_m\}}{\longrightarrow} \mathrm{n_{m+1}}[\mathrm{op1/op2}]^{\mathrm{q}} \tag{18}$$

$$<\mathrm{n_0},\ \mathrm{s},\ [\mathrm{op1/op2}]_{\mathrm{q}}> \ = \mathrm{n_0} \overset{\{\lambda_1,\lambda_2,\ldots,\lambda_m\}}{\longrightarrow} \mathrm{n_{m+1}}[\mathrm{op1/op2}]_{\mathrm{q}} \tag{19}$$

Given a system P and its constraint C, then if C executes a sequence s = $a_1,\ldots,a_n$, we must execute the same sequence on P i.e. if $C \overset{a_1,\ldots,a_n}{\longrightarrow} C'$, then P' exists such that $P \overset{a_1,a_2\ldots,a_n}{\longrightarrow} P'$. Hence, $P < C \overset{a_1,a_2\ldots,a_n}{\longrightarrow} P' < C'$.

7 Implementation of the Model

7.1 Operators' Implementation

We implement the inference rules presented in Sect. 3 in Prolog using the *infer/3* clause, which has three arguments: the current expression, the action to execute and the expression resulting from performing this action. Operators are represented by a fixed post notation as op(X1, X2). We use the *inPorts/2* and *outPorts/2* clauses to determines the input and output ports of components. With these notations, we provide the rules implementing these operators in Table 1.

Table 1. Operators in Prolog

Operator	Implementation
Sequence	infer(seq(A, P1, P1).
Alternative	infer(alt(P1, P2), A, P11):- infer(P1, A, P11). infer(alt(P1, P2), A, P21):- infer(P2, A, P21).
Parallel	infer(par(P1, P2), A, par(P11, P2)):- infer(P1, A, P11). infer(par(P1, P2), A, par(P1, P21)):- infer(P2, A, P21). infer(par(P1, P2), A, par(P11, P21)):- infer(P1, A1, P11), infer(P2, A2, P21), synch(A1, A2, A).
Pipeline	infer(pipe(P1, P2), A, pipe(P11, P2)):- infer(P1, A, P11), inPorts(P2, IP), not(member(A, IP)). infer(pipe(P1, P2), A, P22):-infer(P1, A, P11), infer(P2, A, P21), outPorts(P1, IP1), member(A, IP1), inPorts(P2, IP2), member(A, IP2).

The invocation operator requires special treatment because it uses the universal operator ∀ that does not exist in Prolog. To implement it, we used an *expansion mechanism*. We transform the expressions of type call(P, InP, OutP) by defining simpler inference rules to manipulate. We define this expansion as follows:

$$\mathrm{call}(\mathrm{P}, \mathrm{InP}, \mathrm{OutP}) = \sum\nolimits_{x \in InP} x.call(P, InP \backslash x, OutP) \tag{20}$$

$$\mathrm{call}(\mathrm{P}, [], \mathrm{OutP}) = \sum\nolimits_{y \in OutP} y.call(P, [], OutP \backslash y) \tag{21}$$

We do not define any rule for the expression of type call(P,[],[]), which provides terminal elements. We implement the expansion rules using the clause *bagof(C,P,X)* which produces all elements X that satisfy predicate P. The result is stored in C.

7.2 Executing Actions

To execute actions using the semantic rules above, we defined the clauses for the execution of the behavior of a component. They also give the result of running this execution as shown in the example below.

```
comp(p,par(call(p1,[a,b],[c,d]),call(p2,[c,e],[g,h]))).
execute(P):-
comp(P,Process),infer(Process,Action,Next),
write(Action), write('->'), write(Next).
?-execute(p2).
a-> par(call(p1,[b],[c,d]),call(p2,[c,e],[g,h]))
b-> par(call(p1,[a],[c,d]),call(p2,[c,e],[g,h]))
c-> par(call(p1,[a,b],[c,d]),call(p2,[e],[g,h]))
e-> par(call(p1,[a,b],[c,d]),call(p2,[c],[g,h]))
```

We also use the *trace/2* clause to determine if a sequence is accepted by a component:

```
?- comp(p, B), trace(B, [b,a]).
  Result: par(call(p1,[],[c,d]),call(p2,[c,e],[g,h]))
```

7.3 Implementing Constraints

To implement constraints, we have added the following rules:

```
infer(seq(A,P), A, P).
infer(const(P1,P2),A,const(P11,P21)):- infer(P1,A,P11),
infer(P2,A,P21).
```

In the example below, we impose constraint *c1* on process *p1* and show the execution of the overall system.

```
process(p11, call(pressure,[a,b,c],[])).
constraint(c1, alt(seq(a,seq(b,seq(c,null))),
                   seq(b,seq(a,seq(c,null))))).
applyConst(P,C):-process(P),constraint(C),
                 infer(const(P,C), A, Res),
write(A), write('->'),write(Res), fail.
?- applyConst(p11,c1).
a ->const(call(pressure,[b,c],[]),seq(b,null))
b ->const(call(pressure,[a,c],[]),seq(a,null))
```

7.4 Implementing Transforms

We have also implemented the transformation of operators. The *transf/4* clause takes an expression and two operators and produces an expression whose first operator is replaced by the second. It implements the operator [[op1/op2]]. To call the clause, we have defined the *go6/0* clause that gives the following result:

```
process(p11, par(call(p1,[a,b],[c,d]),
call(p2,[c,e],[g,h])).
transform(P,P1,P2):- process(P, Pr), transf(Pr,Op1,Op2,
Res), write('Initial expression : '), write(Pr),
write('Resulting expression : '), write(Res).

?- transform(p11par,pipe).
Initial expression:
par(call(p1,[a,b],[c,d]),call(p2,[c,e],[g,h]))
Resulting expression:
pipe(call(p1,[a,b],[c,d]),call(p2,[c,e],[g,h]))
```

We have also implemented the operator substitution (i.e. $[[op1/op2]^n]$ and $[[op1/op2]_n]$) after a specific sequence of actions.

8 Control Loop

To perform this adaptation using our formal model, we followed the MAPE-K control loop [2] model (Fig. 1). This loop contains at its core a knowledge database and a set of modules to perform tasks of monitoring, analyzing, planning, and executing.

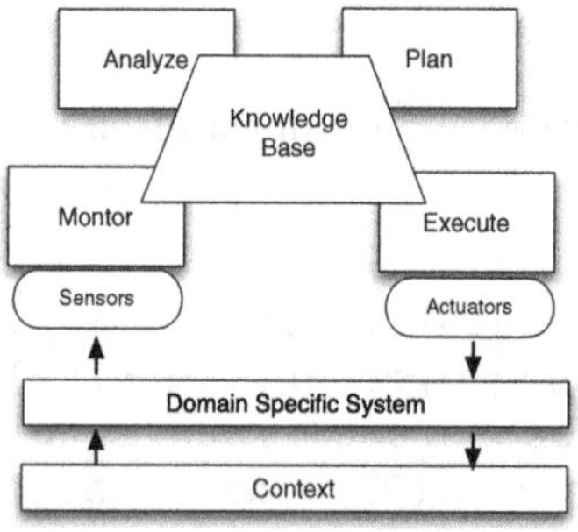

Fig. 1. MAPE-K control loop

The knowledge base provides a set of rules used for adaptation. It builds an adaptation template containing the following elements:

- *Name*: represents the name of the context.
- *Svalues*: category: $<e_1:i_1,e_2:i_2,\ldots,e_n:i_n>$: interval of possible values for a category.

- *Intervals*: {Category: <e_1:i_1, e_2:i_2, …, e_n:i_n> ,…}: a set of intervals of values for a context. At each interval is associated a state.
- *transforms*: transformations to apply after executing a sequence of actions.
- *transformApply*: states in which we must apply each transformation. It indicates the name of the transformation and the level in which it must be applied.
- *constraintApply*: indicates the list of states and the corresponding constraints
- *constraintAfter*: refers to the sequence after which we must apply the constraint. If this directive is not present, then the constraint is applied at the beginning.
- *constraints*: contains the list of constraints to apply.
- *sequences*: contains the list of sequences and their contents.

We give an example of a simplified system that consists of treating the symptoms of body temperature of a patient. We suppose that the patient feels a fever rise. If the increase is significant, then it should be treated by going to a nearby hospital. The simplified specification of such system, named *bodytemperature* is:

```
bodytemperature =
pipe(call(transport, [location], [hospital ,nohospital]),
      alt(par(call(treatement,[hospital],[normal,fever]),
              intl(call(feverState,[fever], [medication]),
                call(normalState,[normal],[nomedication])
         )),
  call(noTreatment, [nohospital],[nomedication])
    )
).
```

We present an excerpt of the execution of the system with no adaptation:

```
?- execute(bodytemperature)
1-location - Resulting behaviour: … Not shown
|: Choose an action: 1.
1-nohospital - Resulting behaviour: … Not shown
2-hospital - Resulting behaviour: … Not shown
|: Choose an action: 2.
1-normal - Resulting behaviour: … Not shown
…
```

8.1 Knowledge Base

The knowledge base contains the template generation rules, its transmission and the execution rules of the system (shared with the planner). After running the *context (bodytemperature)* clause, we build the set of rules to represent the adaptation template. The knowledge base also contains the rules that implement the logic of operators based on the *infer/3* clause. The knowledge base transmits the template to the monitor so that it can read context data. The template for *bodytemperature* context is:

```
Context values: {35, 41}.
States:
  Hypothermia={30, 35.5}
  Normal= {35.5, 37.5}
  Fever= {37.5, 42}
Transforms:
  T1: par to alt
    After: location.hospital.verification.diagnostics
    State: Normal
  T2: par to pipe
    After: location.hospital.verification.diagnostics
    State: Fever
Constraints:
  C1: location.hospital.fever.medication.null
    State:  fever
    After: location.hospital.verification.diagnostics
  C2: location.hospital.normal.nomedication.null.
State: normal
    After: location.hospital.verification.diagnostics
```

The knowledge base defines states and their associated intervals by dynamically creating proper rules. It also creates rules representing the constraints, the transformations, etc.:

```
state(hypothermia,[30,35.5]).
state(normal,[35.5,37.5]).
state(fever,[37.5,42]).
constraint(c1,seq(location,seq(hospital,
                 seq(fever,seq(medication ,null)))))).
constraint(c2,seq(location,seq(hospital,
                 seq(normal,seq(nomedication, null)))
applyConstraint(c1,fever).
applyConstraint(c2, normal).
transform(t1,seq1,par,alt).
transform(t2,seq2,par,pipe).
applyTransform(normal,t1,0,0).
applyTransform(fever,t2,0,0).
seq(seq1,[ location, hospital]).
seq(seq2,[ location, hospital]).
```

8.2 Monitor

The knowledge base communicates the content of the template to the monitor so that it can filter data. It reads data and determines its relevant state *(hypothermia, normal* or *fever).* An input data file containing temperature values is used instead of actual sensors. For each value read, it sets a time stamp. We show an excerpt of the monitor's execution:

```
Value: 35.5 - Time: 1464979388 ms, State: normal
Constraint: Constraint code, Transform: Transform de-
scription
Sequence: Actual sequence executed
...
```

8.3 Analyzer

The analyzer determines the current state and detects the state change if any. It determines *constraints* and *transforms* to apply in this new state. It informs the knowledge base about this change and it updates *constraints* and *transforms*. The analyzer also updates the knowledge base with rules to be used by the planner.

```
Value: 35.4 Time: 1485811766 ms, State: hypo - New State.
Constraint: none, Transform: none
Execution Sequence: [], Transform Sequence: none
...
```

8.4 Planner

The planner organizes the actions of the system by using the rules that are stored in the knowledge base. It performs several tasks. Given an action, the planner determines the behavior(s) of the system resulting from this action. For instance, the execution of action *location* to *bodytemperature* system results in:

```
pipe(
    call(transport,[],[nohospital,hospital]),
      alt(par(call(treatment,[hospital],[normal,fever]),
        intl(call(feverState,[fever],[medication]),
            call(normalState,[normal],[nomedication]))
          ),
    call(notreatment,[nohospital],[nomedication])))
```

The planner may submit a sequence of actions and verify if it is acceptable for a component and if so, obtains the results of its execution. The following example shows the execution of the sequence *[location, hospital]* on *bodytemperature*.

```
?-trace(System, [location,hospital], Result).
Sequence: [location,hospital]
Result:
par(call(treatment,[],[normal,fever]),intl(call(feverStat
e, [fever],[medication],
call(normalState,[normal],[nomedication])))
```

When the data indicates that the system must be in a new state, the planer determines the steps to get to that state by establishing: (a) the sequence to apply compared to the sequence to execute as indicated in the template and the sequence of actions executed so far by the system from the start, (b) the constraint to apply once this sequence is executed, and (c) the transformation to carry out and the sequences following which the transformations must be done.

8.5 Executer

Once the constraints are updated, the executor applies them to determine the current action to execute. In our example, it uses the constraints *c1* and *c2,* and the proper states:

```
const(c1,seq(location,seq(hospital,seq(fever,seq(s(fever)
,seq(medication,null))))))
const(c2,seq(location,seq(hospital,seq(normal,seq(nomedic
ation,null))))).
applyConstraint(fever,c1).
```

For instance, constraint *c1* imposes the execution of sequence *location.hospital.fever.medication* in a *fever* state and the transformation of operators of the current state:

```
transform(t1,seq1,par,alt).
transform(t2,seq2,par,pipe).
transformApply(normal,t1,0,0).
transformApply(fever,t2,0,0).
seq(seq1,[location,hospital]).
seq(seq2,[location,hospital]).
```

Transformation `t1` applies in a *normal* state and consists of transforming the parallelism into alternative. This transformation takes place after sequence *location.hospital*. By using the *constraints* and the *transforms*, the executor executes the system relative to its current state. If there is a state change, it determines the current constraints and the transformations. At each step, it calculates the sequence of actions that were executed so far and determines the updated constraint. If there is no state change, it continues the execution. We give an example below.

```
?- monitor.
Value:35.4 Time: 148539418, State: hypo - New State.
Constraint: none, Transform: none.
1-location-> - Resulting behaviour: …
|: Choose an action: 1.
Value:37.6. Time: 1485394190, State: fever - New State.
Constraint: seq(location,…), Transform: none.
1-location-> - Resulting behaviour: …
|: Choose an action: 1.
…
```

The template of the example indicates that `t1` and `t2` *transforms* must be applied in the specific states and after having executed specific sequences.

```
?-monitor.
Value:35.4. Time: 1485811766, State: hypo - New State.
Constraint: none, Transform: none.
Execution Sequence: [], Transform Sequence: none
1-location-> - Resulting behaviour: … Not shown
|: Choose an action: 1.
Value: 37.6. Time: 1485811770, State: fever - New State.
Constraint: seq(location,…))))), Transform: par/pipe
Execution Sequence: [location], Transform Sequence: [lo-
cation,hospital]
1-location-> - Resulting behaviour: … Not shown
|: Choose an action: 1.
…
```

9 Conclusion and Future Work

This paper presented a semantic model for component-based adaptation. This model is based on process algebra to describe a system's behavior. Our adaptation method consists of two aspects: imposing constraints to restrain a component's behavior and transforming operators to modify a system's architecture. We integrated our proposed approach based on the MAPE-K reference model. We simulated the model as well as the phases of the control loop.

As future work, we plan a feature-based adaptation method that consists of activating and deactivating features with respect to context. We express composition operators and sets of valid Software Product Line configurations. A context variation model validates these configurations. We first read the context data from input sources then the monitor and analyzer determine the current state of the system based on these context values. Various states are represented by context rules derived from the context variation model. The knowledge base decides what configuration is a target configuration. It then applies an algorithm that maps these state changes to a current set of features. Upon state changes, the system specifies the valid features that must be in the configuration. This change of feature is the core of our adaptation method.

References

1. IBM: An Architectural Blueprint for Autonomic Computing. Autonomic Computing White Paper (2003)
2. Milner, R. (ed.): A Calculus of Communicating Systems. LNCS, vol. 92. Springer, Heidelberg (1980). doi:10.1007/3-540-10235-3
3. SWI-Prolog Homepage. http://www.swi-prolog.org/. Accessed 06 Apr 2017
4. Arbab, F.: Reo: a channel-based coordination model for component composition. Math. Struct. Comput. Sci. **14**(3), 329–366 (2004)
5. Canal, C., Camara, J., Salaun, G.: Structural reconfiguration of systems under behavioral adaptation. Sci. Comput. Program. **78**(1), 46–64 (2012)
6. Batisde, G., Seriai, A., Oussalah, M.: Dynamic adaptation of software component structures. In: IEEE International Conference on Information Reuse and Integration, pp. 404–409 (2006)
7. Castaneda, L., Tamura, G.: A reference architecture for component-based self-adaptive software systems. Rev. Electronica En Construcción De Softw. **7**(1), 1–15 (2013)

A Comprehensive Study of Intelligent Transportation System Architectures for Road Congestion Avoidance

Sara El Hamdani(✉) and Nabil Benamar

University Moulay Ismail, Meknes, Morocco
saraelhamdani@gmail.com, benamar73@gmail.com

Abstract. Road congestion is considered as the bottleneck in Intelligent Transportation System (ITS). It has serious impact on human security, the environment and the economy. Thus, congestion avoidance is one of the main challenges facing ITS. In the aim of reducing the congestion problem, different ITS schemes were proposed. In this paper, we present a comprehensive study of the recent approaches dealing with the congestion issue. This study brings to the scientific community a new classification of the previous schemes based on their specific features. To this end, we introduce some new metrics to evaluate all the studied approaches. We found that the majority of the new congestion management approaches are cooperative and efficient in decreasing the travel delay. However, they are generally focusing on vehicles control and ignoring other elements, such as the use of the road in daily life. The current study presents a new direction of future researches on congestion management systems.

1 Introduction

The number of vehicles on the world's roads is growing rapidly. Nevertheless, capacities of roads cannot be developed in the same way to cope with the number of vehicles traveling on them, which cause road congestion. The latter decreases the traffic safety and efficiency. Consequently, it has a significant impact on both economy and human security.

Intelligent Transportation System (ITS) has a key role in diminishing traffic jams, CO2 emissions, travel delays and accident rates, while improving road safety, traffic flow and passenger comfort. The aim of congestion avoidance schemes is to increase the number of vehicles sharing the road in the same time, while decreasing the traveling delay. To achieve this objective, different architectures were developed to replace the inefficient traditional traffic control systems.

New ITS technologies inspired the researches to develop new approaches for congestion management. Self-driving vehicles; for instance; are capable to manage autonomously the road using their capacities and the Vehicle-to-Vehicle (V2V) communication. Moreover, the intelligent infrastructure are able as well to control the road circulation using sensors, computation capacities and Vehicle to Infrastructure (V2I) communication. Likewise, mobile phone software, centralized systems and vehicles applications could help as well in reducing the congestion problem.

E. Sabir et al. (Eds.): UNet 2017, LNCS 10542, pp. 95–106, 2017.
https://doi.org/10.1007/978-3-319-68179-5_9

In this paper, we study and classify different congestion management solutions based on different metrics such as communication type, vehicles priority, system behavior, road model, and stopping avoidance. Then, we evaluate them estimating the new ITS direction to be taken on congestion management area.

The reminder of this paper is as follows. Section 2 discusses the routing schemes. Section 3 investigates the intersection management systems. Section 4 analyzes the mentioned architectures. In Sect. 5, we conclude our analysis by introducing a new direction for congestion management researches.

2 Routing Mechanisms

Road collision can be avoided by routing vehicles from congested roads to alternative routes. Generally, routing vehicles architectures model the road network as a network flow, roads as edges and intersections as nodes (Fig. 1). Choosing the shortest path for vehicles could decrease the travel delay. However, affecting vehicles to the same alternative routes could lead to a new bottleneck. For example, the shortest path from a travel start "A" to a travel end "J" (Fig. 1) is A -> B -> F -> J. Nonetheless, if this path is congested, the vehicle traveling in it will waste a lot of time compared to choosing the less congested route A -> C -> G -> K -> J even if it is longer.

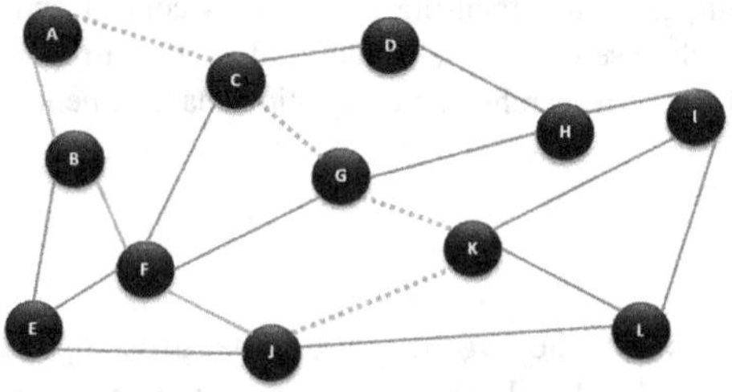

Fig. 1. An illustration of road network modeled as a network flow in routing vehicles architecture whereby edges represent the roads and nodes represent the intersections.

Proactive Vehicular Traffic Re-routing Entropy System [1] detects congestion signs and ranks the vehicles situated near to the congested road segments based on the urgency function. The system Compute alternative routes by using deferent rerouting strategies. For instance, Balanced k-Shortest Paths (EBkSP) strategy considers the impact that each selection has on the future density of the affected road segment.

Themis cooperative navigation system [2] estimates present traffic rhythm and the future traffic distribution based on information sent by Themis mobile application installed in the vehicles. Thus, the system manages the traffic alternative routes. Otherwise, the vehicles routing or re-routing could be done based on V2I communication in a multi-agent system. In MNRT architecture [3] the Traffic Management Center (TMC) detects an en route event (i.e. an accident) using the sensors of the infrastructure, and communicate the event to the traffic light located at the start junction of the affected road. The later suggests to vehicles in its segment the optimal turn using the V2I communication, respecting the global benefits.

A cooperative route allocation was proposed in CARAVAN system [4] that reduces the communication requirement. Virtual agents exchange their route information at the beginning of the route allocation process. Then, they execute virtual deals in their "mind" based on the individual utility, without any communication between them. As a final point, the agents exchange the resulting allocation.

Strengths and Weaknesses. Routing architectures aim to choose a less congested route for vehicles, thus to minimize the travel delay for them in a balanced way. Nonetheless, it is generally difficult to achieve a trade-off between the individual and global benefits. Thus routing vehicles, especially intersections management, cannot solve a big part of congestion problems.

3 Intersection Management

Congestion in road intersections is considered as the bottlenecks of urban transportation. The intersections are managed by the traditional stopping signs system like the traffic light controller system. These traditional systems are capable to deal with vehicles collision problem. Nevertheless, they are not efficient enough to cope with the large traffic flow aiming to cross the intersection simultaneously. Thus, improving the Traffic Light Controller (TLC) system is a challenging research area in Intelligent Transportation System.

3.1 Smart Traffic Light Controller Systems

Congestion in road intersections is caused essentially by stopping for red traffic lights. Based on V2I communication, Traffic Light Controller (TLC) broadcasts periodically its status data to vehicles in its road segment in the Belief-Desire-Intention (BDI) architecture [5]. Thus, the vehicles can make the right decisions to avoid stopping at the next traffic light. If the vehicle estimates that it is possible to arrive at the intersection while the traffic light is still green, it accelerates; if not, it decelerates and collaborates with other vehicles by changing lanes.

To minimize vehicles stopping, authors in [6] developed a PDDL+ Planning for controlling Traffic Light Green Phases. All traffic lights in this architecture are programmed with a PDDL+ formulation and collaborate between them to keep traffic lights as green as possible.

The smart TLC systems have the same objectives: maximizing the Green light phases and minimizing vehicles stopping. Authors in [7] proposed an adaptive traffic lights system based on Vehicle to Vehicle V2V Communication. When vehicles communicate with each other, the near TLC listens to exchanging information. Hence, it can realize how congested the intersection approaches are, and adapt its timing.

In the same way, the scheme proposed by the authors in [8] finds out the optimal green light phase based on the coming vehicles requests. The difference with this architecture is a control center that manages all the traffic lights in the city. Coming vehicles send their requests to the next traffic light in their routes. The traffic lights are responsible for sending those requests to the control center after receiving them. The communication technology used between vehicles and traffic lights is DSRC; consequently, only vehicles in the coverage zone (less than 1 km) can communicate directly with the lights. If the vehicle is not in radio coverage range, it must send its request by multi-hop communication to the front vehicle, which communicates it to the traffic light.

More than the bad management of traffic jams, traditional traffic light system control the intersections in a fixed mode all the time. By contrast, traffic conditions change completely from the early morning hours for example to the noontime. The framework developed by authors in [9] manage the flow dynamically based on traffic data collected using a simple sensor network.

The discussed intersection management works are focusing on smart intersection infrastructure and on how to improve it. Thus, they do not make a full use of autonomous/smart cars capacities. Unlike the autonomous driving architectures for non-signalized intersections that we will discuss later, authors in [10] tried to manage fully autonomous vehicles in intersections managed by traffic lights signals. A hierarchical planning architecture is proposed that processes the inputs in three levels: the route-planning layer chooses the driving direction; a task-planning layer develops the driving operation to a sequence of tasks concerning traffic signals, and the motion-planning layer yields paths for each task.

Batch-Light [11] is a greedy-based Conflict Matrix decision algorithm that manages vehicles reservations to cross the intersection using the traffic light system. This system outperforms the First Come First Served (FCFS) reservation system developed in AIM project [12] that we will discuss in Sect. 3.2.

Strengths and Weaknesses. Improving Traffic light system architectures attempt to reduce the red light phase duration in order to minimize vehicles stoppings in the intersection, while the existence of red light in this system means the inevitable presence of those stoppings. Moreover, this solution requires expensive infrastructure for intersection management and its faulty will block all the circulation.

3.2 Non-signalized Intersection Management

An intersection is a junction at-grade of two or more roads either meeting or crossing. We mean by non-signalized intersection an intersection that is not managed by traffic light system or any other stop signs.

3.2.1 Normal Intersection Management

In this paper, "Normal Intersection" means a road junction that does not contain a roundabout. The majority of normal intersection management schemes model the road junction as grid divided into numbered cells (Fig. 2). Each autonomous car crossing the intersection has known trajectory, which is represented as cells list [13]. If a vehicle is coming from the south; for example; and having the cell number 16 in its trajectory (Fig. 2), and another vehicle is coming from the west having the same cell number in its trajectory, this means that this cell is a conflicting point where a collision may happen. This conflicting zone must be managed by a collision avoidance mechanism to help vehicle cross the junction safely and without using any intersection stop signs.

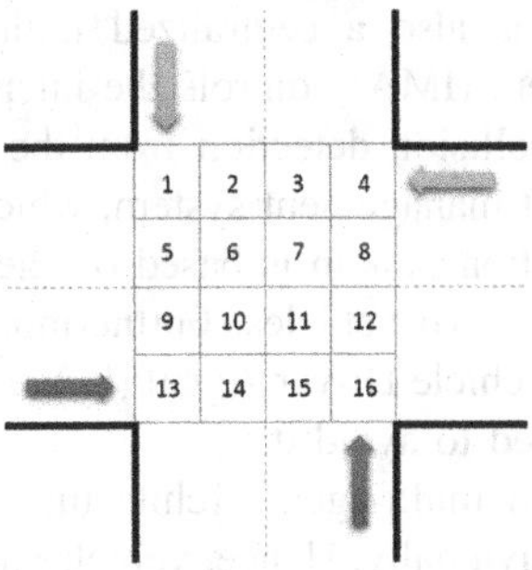

Fig. 2. An illustration of a non-signalized intersection modeled as a grid divided into numbered cells.

3.2.1.1 Multi-agent Schemes

A multi-agent system (M.A.S.) is a computerized system composed of multiple interacting intelligent agents within an environment. Multi-agent systems can be used to solve problems that are difficult or impossible for an individual agent to solve.

Dresner & Stone worked on the aforementioned AIM project known with its simplicity [12, 14–16]. In this multi-agent architecture, vehicles send a reservation request to Driver Agent while slowing down before arriving at the intersection. The later, receives the requests and accepts or refuses them based on a First In First out FIFO algorithm. If the vehicle receives the acceptance confirmation, it crosses the intersection immediately without sloping. In the case of a refused request, the vehicle must stop before entering the intersection and wait for the acceptance.

The limitation of AIM project is that when the traffic volume is too high, stopping is not guaranteed in case of non-accepted requests. In [17], a dynamic hierarchical reservation protocol was developed that categorized the requests into three classes. The first class includes the vehicles that cannot stop before getting into the intersection, thus it is the highest priority. The second class comprises vehicles that have been already stopping. The third class covers all other vehicles. Accordingly, reservation acceptance is given according to the vehicle class priority rather than the FIFO algorithm.

Look-ahead Intersection Control Policy (LICP) [18] also manages the intersection based on a reservation system that outperformed the famous FCFS system. LICP solves the non-guaranteed stopping problem of AIM project using a "passing permission" architecture. While a vehicle is crossing an intersection, it must apply a passing permission "PP" by sending its actual status information to the management agent (MA) of its next intersection among the vehicles to avoid any possible collision in the next coming intersection.

Another centralized system is proposed in [19] using vehicle reservation algorithm to manage the intersection. Nevertheless, this system varies from the other aforementioned centralized systems with its strength to manage all types of the intersection and to include a low percentage of vehicles not with V2V or V2I communication.

The architecture in [20] is also a centralized multi-agent system whereby an Intersection Management Agent (IMA) controls the intersection flow. Moreover, this architecture uses a different collision detection from the aforementioned system (the cells trajectory) and a different management system, which is not a reservation based. Therefore, this collision detection system is based on the Euclidian distance between the position vectors of a given two vehicles. Furthermore, instead of the reservation system, the IMA informs the vehicle Driver Agent (DA) about a possible collision and this last must maintain its speed to avoid it.

Unlike the other discussed multi-agent architectures, WIN-FIT system [21] the vehicles are not controlled individually. Hence, vehicles are dynamically gathered into groups and a designated winner group is permitted to drive as a batch through the intersection.

Strengths and Weaknesses. The Centralized intersection management architectures could replace as well the existing traffic light model and the other stop signs. Furthermore, they generally outperform the smart traffic light controller systems. Although, the communication between the intersection management agent and the vehicle driver agent requires some time which prevents the vehicles from executing the decided action in the real time and this could be very dangerous. Furthermore, this ITS applications type is highly costing and not scalable considering the powerful computation required to control the movement of hundreds of vehicles in real-time.

3.2.1.2 Decentralized Schemes

A decentralized system in systems theory is a system in which lower level components operate on local information to accomplish global goals. Thus, the completely autonomous vehicles can decide by themselves which vehicle should cross and which should wait applying different intersection management protocols. Approaching to the intersection area, vehicles exchange information between each other using Dedicated Short Range Communications (DSRC) and Wireless Access in a Vehicular Environment (WAVE) [22] and take the right decision before entering the intersection.

Earlier research [23–25] on the decentralized coordination of autonomous vehicles systems were inspired by the distributed control of the groups in nature, whereby individuals respond to their sensed environment but they are compelled by the comportment of their neighbors. Thus, traffic rules were encoded by means of "artificial potentials" that define interaction forces between neighboring vehicles.

Based on artificial potential functions, a control system [26] was proposed to coordinate agents whose intention is to cross an intersection while avoiding collisions. Consequently, vehicles are equipped with a decentralized navigation function where the goal and collision functions are decoupled.

A decentralized navigation functions were introduced in [27] and reviewed in [28], which are practical tools introduced in robotics to solve collision avoidance problem. This navigation functions could display local minimums leading vehicles to stop leading to deadlock situations. By the introduction of noise to the calculation of the location of other vehicles, this problem was solved by the scheme in [27]. Navigation function was reviewed in [29] by sharing additional information (information about their inertia and their intention at the intersection) of the vehicles rather than just the position to improve the performance of the system.

In [30], vehicles communicate also with others vehicles in the same lane. Vehicles send their information to the first one in the lane "the Head" before arriving at the intersection. Hence, this "Head" collaborate with other "Heads" in other approaches.

Another V2V communication-based scheme is proposed in [31], whereby each vehicle decides to preempt or yield coming vehicles according to the rules. This architecture proposes an algorithm to calculate the right deceleration value to ensure yielding.

Fully autonomous intersection management protocols were developed in [13, 32–35] based on the aforementioned grid model and the collision avoidance mechanism. The aim of those protocols is to avoid vehicles stopping at intersections using simple V2V-based algorithms.

Strengths and Weaknesses. The majority of V2V-based schemes minimize the intersection management total cost because they do not require any infrastructure. In addition, they employ the useful autonomous vehicles capacities to solve the congestion problem. Nevertheless, usually, this type of ITS applications require a specific road and vehicles conditions and do not accept the existence of a high percentage of normal vehicles.

3.2.2 Roundabout Intersection Management

A roundabout intersection is a road junction at which vehicles travels in one direction around a central island to get to one of the roads converging on it. The existence of this central island reduces the number of conflicting points at the simple intersection from 32 points to eight (Fig. 3).

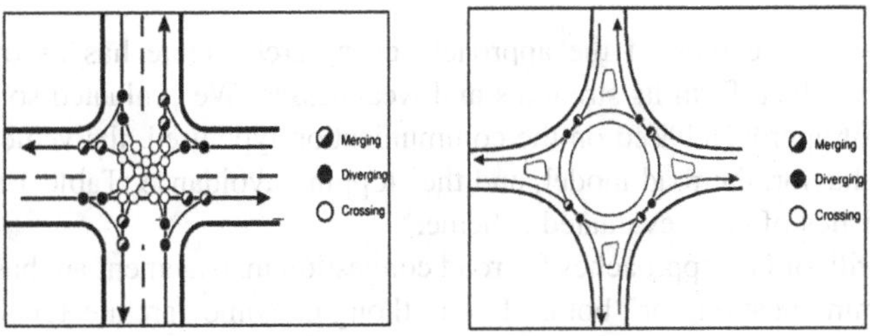

Fig. 3. The difference between a simple road intersection and a one-lane roundabout in the number of traffic conflicting points [36].

Previous works on the roundabout intersection interested on the method of traffic-signal control [37]. In [38], the researchers studied the impact of different traffic conditions and geometrical dimensions of the roundabout on the self-organized management system efficiency. Works in [39] treated the lateral control of self-driving vehicles in roundabouts. This scheme realized an automatic map generation considering the parametric equation of a circle, the radius, and the central coordinates.

Works in [40] study the appliance of previous suggested V2V-intersection protocols for autonomous vehicles at roundabout intersections and presented a new Collision Detection Algorithm for Roundabouts (CDAR).

The above-mentioned centralized scheme [19] and non-centralized scheme [34] are not dedicated just for normal intersection management, but they can also manage the roundabout intersection with the same systems. Thus, in STIP architecture [34] the roundabout is also divided into numbered cells and it is autonomously managed based only on V2V communication.

In [41], researchers proposed a cooperative intelligence for the roundabout intersection management combining between V2V and V2I communication, between cooperative and non-cooperative vehicles, also between the existence and the faulty of infrastructure controller and taking on the consideration that the real paths of vehicles are unknown.

Strengths and Weaknesses. As indicated previously the roundabout reduces the number of conflicting points, thus working on this type of road junction increase the ITS intersection management efficiency. Generally, simulated decentralized intersection management systems proved their effectiveness in avoiding congestion. Nonetheless, even if the autonomous vehicles is an existing technology, we cannot apply those applications in real life because they suppose that vehicles own the road.

4 Discussion

As highlighted in the previous sections, researchers have worked on different ITS application types and different road categories in the aim of reducing road congestion. In (Fig. 4) we present our new classification of ITS applications for road congestion avoidance.

Regardless of the type of the approach, every architecture has its own specific characteristics, which form its strengths and weaknesses. We evaluated some schemes of each type of approach based on the communication type used, the vehicles priority, the system behavior, the road model, and the stopping avoidance. Table 1 summarizes the characteristics of each evaluated scheme.

The majority of ITS approaches for road congestion management are based on V2V or V2I communication or both. Even though, some architectures used I2I (Infrastructure-to-Infrastructure) communication, Internet and cellular network. Virtual (indirect) communication was employed in [4] to minimize the communication cost. Moreover, the Architecture in [18] considered the case where no communication is possible.

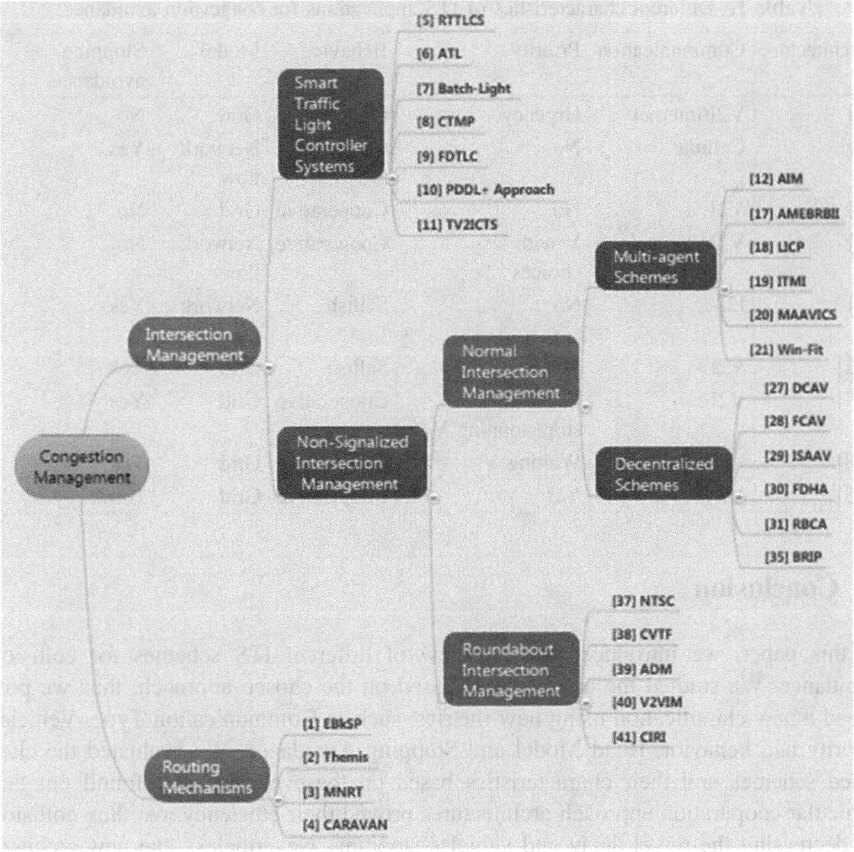

Fig. 4. A classification of existing ITS applications for congestion avoidance.

Excluding [2, 3, 6, 7], each approach use a different priority policy. Priority is given based on emergency or FCFS policy. Likewise, vehicles in critical areas or conditions are prioritized in other architectures. In the other hand, the new approaches are focusing on eliminating selfish behaviors between vehicles, thus encouraging the cooperation between them.

The studied architectures modeled the road network differently, where the common goal between them is to avoid vehicles stopping, which minimizes congestion. The architecture in [35] was able to eliminate vehicles stopping at intersection (100% without stopping).

We argue that new approaches use cooperation concepts to avoid stopping as much as possible. The problem is the more the schemes are cooperative and efficient the more they require communication consummation. Furthermore, most efficient architectures achieve their best result by eliminating the entire elements sharing the road in real (motorcycles, bicycles, pedestrians…) life and keeping vehicles only.

Table 1. Different characteristics of ITS applications for congestion avoidance.

Architecture	Communication	Priority	Behavior	Model	Stopping avoidance
[1]	V2I/Internet	Urgency	Cooperative	Grid	No
[2]	Cellular	No	Cooperative	Network flow	Yes
[3]	V2I	No	Cooperative	Grid	No
[4]	V2V/Virtual	V with less choices	Cooperative	Network flow	No
[6]	I2I	No	Selfish	Network flow	Yes
[12]	V2I	FCFS	Selfish	Grid	Yes
[17]	V2I	V can't stop/stopping V	Cooperative	Grid	Yes
[18]	V2I/V2 V	Waiting V	Cooperative	Grid	Yes
[35]	V2V	Yes	Cooperative	Grid	100%

5 Conclusion

In this paper, we introduced an overview of different ITS schemes for collision avoidance. We studied the architectures based on the chosen approach, thus we proposed a new classification using new metrics, such as Communication Type, Vehicles priority and behavior, Road Model and Stopping Avoidance. We evaluated the classified schemes and their characteristics based on these metrics. We found out that vehicular cooperation approach architectures proved their efficiency avoiding collision by decreasing the travel delay and vehicles stopping. Nevertheless, the new architectures focus generally on vehicles and ignore the presence of motorcycles, bicycles and pedestrian in real roads life.

Therefore, further work can focus on improving the efficient existing collision avoidance architectures by considering all the elements that use the road in real life and working on the cooperation between all of them.

References

1. Pan, J., Popa, I.S., Zeitouni, K., Borcea, C.: Proactive vehicular traffic rerouting for lower travel time. IEEE Trans. Veh. Technol. **62**(8), 3551–3568 (2013)
2. Liu, R., et al.: Balanced traffic routing: design, implementation, and evaluation. Ad Hoc Netw. **37**, 14–28 (2016)
3. Wang, S., Djahel, S., McManis, J.: A multi-agent based vehicles re-routing system for unexpected traffic congestion avoidance. In: 17th International IEEE Conference on Intelligent Transportation Systems (ITSC), pp. 2541–2548 (2014)
4. Desai, P., Loke, S.W., Desai, A., Singh, J.: CARAVAN: congestion avoidance and route allocation using virtual agent negotiation. IEEE Trans. Intell. Transp. Syst. **14**(3), 1197–1207 (2013)

5. Djahel, S., Jabeur, N., Barrett, R., Murphy, J.: Toward V2I communication technology-based solution for reducing road traffic congestion in smart cities. In: 2015 International Symposium on Networks, Computers and Communications (ISNCC), pp. 1–6 (2015)
6. Vallati, M., Magazzeni, D., De Schutter, B., Chrpa, L., McCluskey, T.L.: Efficient macroscopic urban traffic models for reducing congestion: a PDDL+ planning approach. In: Proceedings of the Thirtieth Conference on Artificial Intelligence (AAAI-16). AAAI Press (2016)
7. Gradinescu, V., Gorgorin, C., Diaconescu, R., Cristea, V., Iftode, L.: Adaptive traffic lights using car-to-car communication. In: 2007 IEEE 65th Vehicular Technology Conference-VTC2007-Spring, pp. 21–25 (2007)
8. Li, C., Shimamoto, S.: A real time traffic light control scheme for reducing vehicles CO_2 emissions. In: 2011 IEEE Consumer Communications and Networking Conference (CCNC), pp. 855–859 (2011)
9. Younis, O., Moayeri, N.: Cyber-physical systems: a framework for dynamic traffic light control at road intersections. In: Wireless Communications and Networking Conference (WCNC), pp. 1–6. IEEE (2016)
10. Chen, C., Rickert, M., Knoll, A.: Combining task and motion planning for intersection assistance systems
11. Wei, X., Tan, G., Ding, N.: Batch-light: an adaptive intelligent intersection control policy for autonomous vehicles. In: 2014 International Conference on Progress in Informatics and Computing (PIC), pp. 98–103 (2014)
12. Dresner, K., Stone, P.: A multiagent approach to autonomous intersection management. J. Artif. Intell. Res. **31**, 591–656 (2008)
13. Azimi, R., Bhatia, G., Rajkumar, R., Mudalige, P.: Intersection management using vehicular networks. SAE Technical paper (2012)
14. Van Middlesworth, M., Dresner, K., Stone, P.: Replacing the stop sign: unmanaged intersection control for autonomous vehicles. In: Proceedings of the 7th International Joint Conference on Autonomous Agents and Multiagent Systems-Volume 3. International Foundation for Autonomous Agents and Multiagent Systems (2008)
15. Dresner, K., Stone, P.: Multiagent traffic management: a reservation-based intersection control mechanism. In: Proceedings of the Third International Joint Conference on Autonomous Agents and Multiagent Systems, vol. 2, pp. 530–537 (2004)
16. Dresner, K., Stone, P.: Multiagent traffic management: an improved intersection control mechanism. In: Proceedings of the Fourth International Joint Conference on Autonomous Agents and Multiagent Systems, pp. 471–477 (2005)
17. Huang, S., Sadek, A.W., Zhao, Y.: Assessing the mobility and environmental benefits of reservation-based intelligent intersections using an integrated simulator. IEEE Trans. Intell. Transp. Syst. **13**(3), 1201–1214 (2012)
18. Zhu, M., Li, X., Huang, H., Kong, L., Li, M., Wu, M.-Y.: LICP: a look-ahead intersection control policy with intelligent vehicles. In: 2009 IEEE 6th International Conference on Mobile Adhoc and Sensor Systems, pp. 633–638 (2009)
19. Bento, L.C., Parafita, R., Santos, S., Nunes, U.: Intelligent traffic management at intersections: legacy mode for vehicles not equipped with V2V and V2I communications. In: 16th International IEEE Conference on Intelligent Transportation Systems (ITSC 2013), pp. 726–731 (2013)
20. Abdelhameed, M.M., Abdelaziz, M., Hammad, S., Shehata, O.M.: Development and evaluation of a multi-agent autonomous vehicles intersection control system. In: 2014 International Conference on Engineering and Technology (ICET), pp. 1–6 (2014)
21. Chen, G., Kang, K.-D.: Win-fit: efficient intersection management via dynamic vehicle batching and scheduling. In: 2015 International Conference on Connected Vehicles and Expo (ICCVE), pp. 263–270 (2015)

22. Draft sae j2735-200911 dedicated short range (DSRC) message set dictionary
23. Leonard, N.E., Edward, F.: Virtual leaders, artificial potentials and coordinated control of groups. In: Proceedings of the 40th IEEE Conference on Decision and Control, vol. 3. IEEE (2001)
24. Olfati-Saber, R., Murray, R.M.: Distributed cooperative control of multiple vehicle formations using structural potential functions. In: IFAC World Congress, vol. 15, pp. 242–248 (2002)
25. Baras, J.S., Tan, X., Hovareshti, P.: Decentralized control of autonomous vehicles. In: Proceedings of 42nd IEEE Conference on Decision and Control vol. 2. IEEE (2003)
26. Roozbehani, H., Rudaz, S., Gillet, D.: On decentralized navigation schemes for coordination of multi-agent dynamical systems. In: IEEE International Conference on Systems, Man and Cybernetics, SMC 2009, pp. 4807–4812 (2009)
27. Makarem, L., Gillet, D.: Decentralized coordination of autonomous vehicles at intersections. In: IFAC Proceedings, vol. 44.1, pp. 13046-13051 (2011)
28. Makarem, L., Gillet, D.: Fluent coordination of autonomous vehicles at intersections. In: 2012 IEEE International Conference on Systems, Man, and Cybernetics (SMC), pp. 2557–2562 (2012)
29. Makarem, L., Gillet, D.: Information sharing among autonomous vehicles crossing an intersection. In: 2012 IEEE International Conference on Systems, Man, and Cybernetics (SMC), pp. 2563–2567 (2012)
30. Hassan, A., Rakha, H.: A fully-distributed heuristic algorithm for control of autonomous vehicle movements at isolated intersections. Int. J. Transp. Sci. Technol. **3**(4), 297–310 (2014)
31. Lu, G., Li, L., Wang, Y., Zhang, R., Bao, Z., Chen, H.: A rule based control algorithm of connected vehicles in uncontrolled intersection. In: 17th International IEEE Conference on Intelligent Transportation Systems (ITSC), pp. 115–120 (2014)
32. Azimi, S.R., Bhatia, G., Rajkumar, R.R., Mudalige, P.: Vehicular networks for collision avoidance at intersections. SAE Int. J. Passeng. Cars-Mech. Syst. **4**(2011-01–0573), 406–416 (2011)
33. Azimi, S., Bhatia, G., Rajkumar, R., Mudalige, P.: Reliable intersection protocols using vehicular networks. In: 2013 ACM/IEEE International Conference on Cyber-Physical Systems (ICCPS), pp. 1–10 (2013)
34. Azimi, R., Bhatia, G., Rajkumar, R.R., Mudalige, P.: STIP: spatio-temporal intersection protocols for autonomous vehicles. In: ICCPS 2014: ACM/IEEE 5th International Conference on Cyber-Physical Systems (with CPS Week 2014), pp. 1–12 (2014)
35. Azimi, R., Bhatia, G., Rajkumar, R., Mudalige, P.: Ballroom intersection protocol: synchronous autonomous driving at intersections, pp. 167–175 (2015)
36. Hummer, J.E.: Intersection and interchange design. In: Handbook of Transportation Engineer, pp. 14.1–14.27 (2004)
37. Yang, X., Li, X., Xue, K.: A new traffic-signal control for modern roundabouts: method and application. IEEE Trans. Intell. Transp. Syst. **5**(4), 282 (2004)
38. Fouladvand, M.E., Sadjadi, Z., Shaebani, M.R.: Characteristics of vehicular traffic flow at a roundabout. Phys. Rev. E **70**(4), 46132 (2004)
39. Rastelli, J.P., Milanés, V., De Pedro, T., Vlacic, L.: Autonomous driving manoeuvres in urban road traffic environment: a study on roundabouts. In: Proceedings of the 18th World Congress The International Federation of Automatic Control (2011)
40. Azimi, R., Bhatia, G., Rajkumar, R., Mudalige, P.: V2V-Intersection management at roundabouts. SAE Int. J. Passeng. Cars-Mech. Syst. **6**(2013-01–0722), 681–690 (2013)
41. Bosankić, I., Mehmedović, L.B.: Cooperative intelligence in roundabout intersections using hierarchical fuzzy behavior calculation of vehicle speed profile (2016)

Enhancing Security in Optimized Link State Routing Protocol for Mobile Ad Hoc Networks

Houda Moudni[1(✉)], Mohamed Er-rouidi[1], Hassan Faouzi[1], Hicham Mouncif[2], and Benachir El Hadadi[2]

[1] Faculty of Sciences and Technology, Sultan Moulay Slimane University, Beni Mellal, Morocco
{h.moudni,m.errouidi,h.faouzi}@usms.ma

[2] Faculty Polydisciplinary, Sultan Moulay Slimane University, Beni Mellal, Morocco
hmouncif@yahoo.fr, benachirelhadadi@yahoo.fr

Abstract. Routing protocols in Mobile Ad hoc NETworks (MANETs) have received a lot of attention due to the challenges posed by the self-organized nature of the network, the dynamic topology and openness of wireless links. One of the most critical issues for MANETs is the security requirements. Hence, many researchers have focused their works on enhancing security in these networks. However, the security enhancements in routing protocols have been mostly proposed for reactive MANET protocols. In this paper, we propose a solution to secure a proactive topology discovery using a pre-existing routing protocol Optimized Link State Routing (OLSR), which is robust against wormhole attack and with the help of digital signatures the solution provides a security service such as authentication, data integrity, privacy and confidentiality. Also, the hash-chain is used to protect the mutable fields in the routing packets. Moreover, our proposal uses a timestamp to prevent the replay attack.

Keywords: Manets · Routing protocols · Attack · Security · OLSR

1 Introduction

Mobile Ad-hoc Networks are composed of autonomous nodes that are self-managed without having any fixed infrastructure or centralized access point such as a base station. Therefore, each wireless node operates not only as an end system, but also as a router to forward packets for other nodes. For these reasons, the network has a dynamic topology, so nodes can easily join or leave the network at any time. Due to these characteristics, MANETs are used in many critical applications, such as disaster relief, emergency operations, military service, vehicle networks, conferences and many more. Nevertheless, those mobile nodes severely lack essential resources such as processing power, memory, bandwidth, energy and others. For these constrained resources and the fact of the lack of centralized monitoring and the dynamic nature, the security mechanisms employed in traditional networks are not suitable. As a result of these vulnerabilities the network faces a variety of attacks such as eavesdropping, physical tampering, and impersonation attack and so on [1, 2].

E. Sabir et al. (Eds.): UNet 2017, LNCS 10542, pp. 107–116, 2017.
https://doi.org/10.1007/978-3-319-68179-5_10

To secure a mobile ad hoc network of these attacks, we consider the following security requirements: confidentiality, integrity, availability, authentication and non-repudiation [3]. This has motivated researchers to propose various security mechanisms [4–6]. Moreover, we find secure routing protocols among these mechanisms, which focus on establishing a secure route.

In this paper, our focus is to provide security in Optimized Link State Routing protocol [7]. For achieving this goal our approach is based on digital signatures and hash chains to authenticate and verify the integrity of the information in the control message with the inclusion of the timestamps and the geographical position, obtained by a Global Positioning System (GPS) device, for preventing replay and wormhole attacks.

The rest of the paper is organized as; Sect. 2 discusses the possible attacks occurring in routing protocols. Some existing solutions for secure Optimized Link State Routing protocol are described in Sect. 3. Section 4 gives an overview of the protocol OLSR. Section 5 presents our proposed extensions to secure Optimized Link State Routing Protocol. Finally, conclusions and future work are given in Sect. 6.

2 Attacks Against Routing Protocols in Mobile Ad Hoc Networks

MANETs are more vulnerable to be attacked than the wired network, due to their characteristics. We can distinguish two principal categories of attacks: passive and active attacks. A passive attack does not disrupt the normal operations of the network, but attempts to listen to valuable information in the traffic. Instead, an active attack disrupts the performance of the network, in order to degrade the network performance, gain unauthorized access, and restrict availability. A brief overview of several well-known routing attacks [1, 2, 8, 9] is presented below.

Routing Data Manipulation Attack: A manipulation attack occurs when an attacker alters the data it receives before forwarding it to the next node. Without any integrity measures the next receiving node will be unable to see any evidence of tampering, and hence, will process the incorrect information.

Replay Attack: A replay attack, also known as playback attack, occurs when an attacker stores routing information or a valid data transmission and then later retransmits the stored information.

Sybil attack: In a Sybil attack, a single node illegally appears in the network with multiple identities by either forging new identities, or stealing legal identities. This attack poses a significant threat to geographic routing protocol.

Denial of Service: A Denial of Service (DoS) attack is an attempt to make a resource unavailable for the purpose it was designed. There are many ways to make a service unavailable for legitimate users by flooding an amount of data in order to consume network bandwidth or to consume the resources of a particular node. Also, by sending excessive request packets to the nodes to authenticate with an invalid return addresses.

Black Hole Attack: In this attack, a malicious node falsely advertises a shortest path to a destination node during the route discovery process in order to the communicating packets passing through it. Consequently, instead of normal forwarding of the packets that it receives, the attacker drops all the packets. This attack becomes more serious when a group of attackers cooperate each other.

Tunnelling/Wormhole Attack: A Wormhole attack occurs when a malicious node receives packets at one location in the network, then "tunnels" them to another point in the network. The colluding nodes can communicate directly over long distances.

Passive Eavesdropping Attack: In this attack, the malicious nodes detect the information by listening to the secret or confidential routing information that should be kept hidden during the communication. From the information that have captured, it is able to discover sensitive topology information about the entire network. Generally, the eavesdropping attack is easy to accomplish in mobile ad-hoc network, due to the open nature of the broadcasting wireless medium.

3 Existing Solutions for Secure Optimized Link State Routing Protocol

Many researchers have been proposed several secured routing protocols for mobile ad hoc networks, in order to offer protection against the attacks mentioned in the previous section. However, security improvements in routing protocols have been proposed mainly for reactive protocols. Here we give an overview of some of proposed solutions which incorporate security mechanisms into a proactive routing protocol named Optimized Link State Routing Protocol.

In [10], the authors propose a new energy conversant and secured protocol by modifying standard OLSR which provide optimal MPR set and also protect network from node isolation attack. A secured OLSR framework is proposed in [11], to provide security with minimum overhead. The overhead is reduced by minimizing the number of Multipoint Relay nodes in the network and providing security for those selected nodes. The authors use a threshold cryptography to provide security measures by distributing the secret key shares and performing encryption with those shares of secrets. The authors in [12] proposed a solution to achieve anonymity and security in OLSR routing protocol by implementing four-way handshaking between two nodes using Host Identity Protocol. Their technique has a less message overhead compared to classical flooding mechanisms. A new approach to enhance quality, reliability and security of mobile communications based on a multipath routing protocol inspired on the RAID5 (Redundant Array of Independent Disks) technology was proposed in [13]. The proposed approach provides better security and ensures greater reliability of the information exchanged in a mobile network. The authors tested their proposition on the OLSR protocol, which offers better reliability and security than the standard OLSR protocol. In [14], the authors designed a specification based intrusion detection system to detect and prevent a modified version of wormhole attack called camouflaging wormhole attack in Optimized Link State Routing. They used Network Simulator (NS2) to measure the performance of their proposed algorithm.

4 Optimized Link State Routing Protocol (OLSR)

The Optimized Link State Routing protocol (OLSR) [7] is a proactive link state algorithm for mobile Ad Hoc networks. OLSR also called as a table-driven protocol in which, each node permanently stores and updates routes to any destination in its routing table. Hence, the major advantage of proactive nature is to have all the routes immediately available when required.

The control traffic in OLSR is exchanged through two kinds of messages: HELLO and Topology Control (TC) messages. Hello messages are used for neighbor sensing and Multipoint Relays (MPRs) calculation, and for the topology declarations, the protocol is based on TC messages. There is also Multiple Interface Declaration (MID) message which is used to inform other nodes that the announcing node may have multiple OLSR interface addresses. Another kind of messages in OLSR is Host and Network Association (HNA) which are used to declare host and associated network information. Through HNA messages, OLSR gives the possibility for routing to the external addresses.

The core optimization in OLSR is the use of Multipoint Relays (MPRs) to diffuse its messages in the network. Only MPRs of a node retransmit its broadcast messages (TC, MID, HNA) throughout the entire network, instead of allowing every node to broadcast them which happened in the classic flooding process, as shown in Fig. 1(a). For this reason, the routing overhead for OLSR is minimized. Figure 1(b) shows a node S with its neighbors and two hop neighbors. As illustrated in the figure, node S need to choose only four nodes among its neighbors to communicate with all neighboring nodes in two hops.

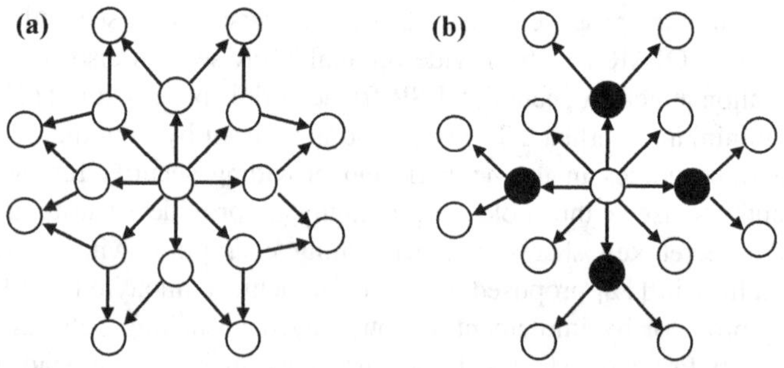

Fig. 1. (a) Classic Flooding (b) MPR flooding

5 Proposed Extensions to Secure Optimized Link State Routing Protocol

5.1 Assumptions

The physical layer and data link layer are vulnerable to some attacks such as jamming, interceptions, eavesdropping, traffic analysis and disruption of Medium Access Control protocols. There are security mechanisms that remedy these vulnerabilities. However, in this paper, we ignore attacks on these two layers.

Besides, links are assumed to be bi-directional, for instance, when node A is able to transmit to node B, similarly B is able to transmit to A.

We assume that key distribution and key management issues are resolved. Therefore, only legitimate node could get a public/private key pair, named KA− and KA+ for node A. This assumed key management allows to any legitimate node to know the public key of the all the other nodes.

In this work, we also assume that all nodes equipped with GPS devices are able of providing location information of each node.

Finally, we assume that the network may duplicate, reorder, or corrupt packets in transmission.

5.2 Secure Routing Packets

Due to OLSR is a proactive routing protocol, the exchange of control messages is periodically among nodes in order to manage the routing of data packets. Therefore, the control messages must be authenticated to prevent the creation of false routes to any desired destination. Additionally, all these data packets are transmitted in a unified packet format called "OLSR packets", as shown in Fig. 2.

```
 0                   1                   2                   3
 0 1 2 3 4 5 6 7 8 9 0 1 2 3 4 5 6 7 8 9 0 1 2 3 4 5 6 7 8 9
+-+-+-+-+-+-+-+-+-+-+-+-+-+-+-+-+-+-+-+-+-+-+-+-+-+-+-+-+-+-+-+
|      Packet Length            |  Packet Sequence Number    |
+-+-+-+-+-+-+-+-+-+-+-+-+-+-+-+-+-+-+-+-+-+-+-+-+-+-+-+-+-+-+-+
| Message Type |    Vtime     |          Message Size         |
+-+-+-+-+-+-+-+-+-+-+-+-+-+-+-+-+-+-+-+-+-+-+-+-+-+-+-+-+-+-+-+
|                     Originator Address                      |
+-+-+-+-+-+-+-+-+-+-+-+-+-+-+-+-+-+-+-+-+-+-+-+-+-+-+-+-+-+-+-+
|Time to Live | Hop Count |  Message Sequence Number |
+-+-+-+-+-+-+-+-+-+-+-+-+-+-+-+-+-+-+-+-+-+-+-+-+-+-+-+-+-+-+-+
|                           Message                           |
+-+-+-+-+-+-+-+-+-+-+-+-+-+-+-+-+-+-+-+-+-+-+-+-+-+-+-+-+-+-+-+
```

Fig. 2. OLSR packet format.

The fields of the OLSR control packets can be divided into two categories: ones are non-mutable during a transmission; another is mutable, such as Time To Live (TTL) and Hop Count (HC). For instance, we have used two mechanisms to secure the OLSR messages: digital signatures to ensure the non-mutable fields unaltered before received, and hash chains to secure the mutable information in the messages. The HELLO messages are used for the detection and reporting of one-hop neighbors. Therefore, the TTL of HELLO message is set to 1, since the neighbors don't forward them. For this reason, we consider the information of TTL and HC in the HELLO packet as non-mutable fields. So, in our plan, the signature extension assigned to HELLO message will not use the hash chains, opposite to other control messages which are TC, MID and HNA packets. The signature extensions are as follows (see Figs. 3 and 4).

```
0                   1                   2                   3
0 1 2 3 4 5 6 7 8 9 0 1 2 3 4 5 6 7 8 9 0 1 2 3 4 5 6 7 8 9
+-+-+-+-+-+-+-+-+-+-+-+-+-+-+-+-+-+-+-+-+-+-+-+-+-+-+-+-+-+-+
|        Timestamps             |         Localization        |
+-+-+-+-+-+-+-+-+-+-+-+-+-+-+-+-+-+-+-+-+-+-+-+-+-+-+-+-+-+-+
|                                                             |
|                          Signature                          |
|                                                             |
+-+-+-+-+-+-+-+-+-+-+-+-+-+-+-+-+-+-+-+-+-+-+-+-+-+-+-+-+-+-+
```

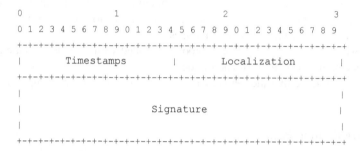

Fig. 3. Hello packet's security extensions format.

```
0                   1                   2                   3
0 1 2 3 4 5 6 7 8 9 0 1 2 3 4 5 6 7 8 9 0 1 2 3 4 5 6 7 8 9
+-+-+-+-+-+-+-+-+-+-+-+-+-+-+-+-+-+-+-+-+-+-+-+-+-+-+-+-+-+-+
|        Timestamps             |         Localization        |
+-+-+-+-+-+-+-+-+-+-+-+-+-+-+-+-+-+-+-+-+-+-+-+-+-+-+-+-+-+-+
|                            TopHash                          |
+-+-+-+-+-+-+-+-+-+-+-+-+-+-+-+-+-+-+-+-+-+-+-+-+-+-+-+-+-+-+
|                            HopHash                          |
+-+-+-+-+-+-+-+-+-+-+-+-+-+-+-+-+-+-+-+-+-+-+-+-+-+-+-+-+-+-+
|                                                             |
|                          Signature                          |
|                                                             |
+-+-+-+-+-+-+-+-+-+-+-+-+-+-+-+-+-+-+-+-+-+-+-+-+-+-+-+-+-+-+
```

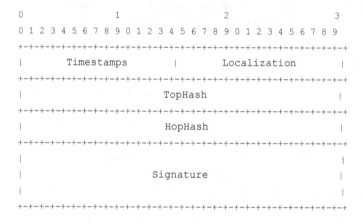

Fig. 4. TC, MID, HNA packet's security extensions format.

The Security Enhanced OLSR (SE-OLSR) signature extensions illustrated in Figs. 3 and 4 are generated by the originator of each OLSR control message and transmitted with the control message. These signatures must be the last message in the packet, in a way that each control message will be followed by his own signature extension. Finally, the OLSR packet header is adjusted to include the size of the signature extension in the size field. As shown in the Fig. 5.

Data authentication and integrity

SE-OLSR digital signatures

Digital signatures are used to authenticate and verify the integrity of the non-mutable data in the control message. Therefore, the use of asymmetric digital signatures is

```
 0                   1                   2                   3
 0 1 2 3 4 5 6 7 8 9 0 1 2 3 4 5 6 7 8 9 0 1 2 3 4 5 6 7 8 9
+-+-+-+-+-+-+-+-+-+-+-+-+-+-+-+-+-+-+-+-+-+-+-+-+-+-+-+-+-+-+-+
|                         Packet Header                       |
+-+-+-+-+-+-+-+-+-+-+-+-+-+-+-+-+-+-+-+-+-+-+-+-+-+-+-+-+-+-+-+
|                            Message 1                        |
+-+-+-+-+-+-+-+-+-+-+-+-+-+-+-+-+-+-+-+-+-+-+-+-+-+-+-+-+-+-+-+
|                     Signature of Message 1                  |
+-+-+-+-+-+-+-+-+-+-+-+-+-+-+-+-+-+-+-+-+-+-+-+-+-+-+-+-+-+-+-+
|                            Message 2                        |
+-+-+-+-+-+-+-+-+-+-+-+-+-+-+-+-+-+-+-+-+-+-+-+-+-+-+-+-+-+-+-+
|                     Signature of Message 2                  |
+-+-+-+-+-+-+-+-+-+-+-+-+-+-+-+-+-+-+-+-+-+-+-+-+-+-+-+-+-+-+-+
|                                                             |
|                               ...                           |
|                                                             |
+-+-+-+-+-+-+-+-+-+-+-+-+-+-+-+-+-+-+-+-+-+-+-+-+-+-+-+-+-+-+-+
```

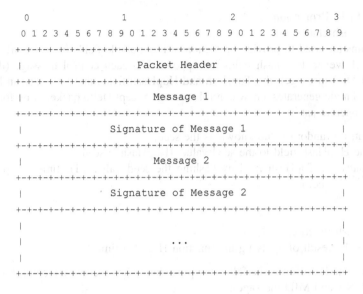

Fig. 5. OLSR packet format with the signatures

required. Hence, asymmetric digital signatures use two specially correlated keys. Unlike symmetric signatures that require the same key in the creation and verification process of a signature. However, OLSR message traversing several hops, so, the use of asymmetric key signature would protect the packets from compromised nodes.

Signature creation

A node generates a control message and signs the non-mutable fields with its private key. Moreover, the creation of the signature extensions follows the steps below:

- The hello packet will not forward, therefore, all fields of the packet will be signed. Because we consider the mutable fields in Hello packet unchangeable. Thus, the signature is: signature = sign(Hello packet).
- The other control messages (TC, HNA and MID) are transmitted around the network. Then, each hops the TTL field decremented by 1 and the Hop Count incremented by 1. As a result, the non-mutable fields are signed in the same manner, but we use hash chains for TTL and Hop Count which are a mutable field. So, the signature is: signature = sign(The unchanged contents).

Signature verification

At the reception, a receiving node verifies the digital signature with the originator's public key. However, if any modification noticed by a node the signature extension and his corresponding control message will be discarded.

Furthermore, every hop the following node verifies the signature extension of TC, MID and HNA, until the TTL field became 0. However, the neighbors only verify the signature extension assigned to Hello packet.

Mutable Field Protection

SE-OLSR hash chains

Hash Chains are used to provide protection of the mutable fields of an OLSR routing message. However, two hash fields are appended to each control message (the TC, HNA and MID message): the TopHash and HopHash fields that presented in Fig. 4.

When a node generates a new control message except Hello packet, it performs the following operations:

- Generates a random value known as the seed.
- Sets the HopHash field to the seed value. (HopHash = seed).
- Calculates the TopHash field by hashing the seed value TTL times. TopHash = $H^{TimeToLive}$ (seed)

where:

- H is a hash function;
- $H^i(x)$ is the result of applying the function H to x, i times.

The next node performs the following procedure when receiving a control message (the TC, HNA and MID message):

- Applies the hash function $H^{TimeToLive - HopCount}$ to the value in the HopHash field. $H^{TimeToLive - HopCount}$(HopHash).
- Compare the resulting value to TopHash field value.

- If the two values are equal, the message will be forwarded and the node alters the HopHash field by hashing it once in the signature extension to account for the new hop. (HopHash = H(HopHash))
- The message will be discarded when the two values are not equal.

Due to the one-way property of a hash function, the integrity of the messages is protected and the receiver can be sure that the messages have not been modified during their transmission.

Replay Attack Protection

To prevent replay attacks, a timestamp mechanism is required for each routing message. A timestamp is basically a piece of information at the time of generation of the sender's message. In order to allow a receiver to know if a message is new or being replayed. Furthermore, OLSR can determine which information is more recent by examining the MSN (Message Sequence Number) and ANSN (Advertised Neighbor Sequence Number). This mechanism is sufficient for the basic routing protocol functioning but not to provide complete security. For instance, the two fields are only 16-bit values which imply that wraparound will occur rather frequently. The method of employing a timestamp mechanism in a protocol differs greatly according to the clocks of the communicating entities if they are synchronized or not. In the following, we will explain the two approaches:

Synchronized Clocks

For each message being emitted by a node, a unique timestamp is associated with it. Hence, upon receiving a message the receiving node could compare the timestamp of the message with its current time (the value of its clock). The message is accepted when the difference of the two times is not greater than some predefined threshold. Consequently, the replay attack would be difficult.

Unsynchronized Clocks

If the clocks of the communicating entities are not synchronized, the difference of the timestamp of the message and the receiver's current time becomes meaningless. Thus, before a recipient node can verify a timestamp, it needs to have some form of knowledge regarding the sender's time.

Thus, we adopt a clock synchronization of nodes. In fact, for any control message generated or transmitted by a node, a timestamp is included. Then a receiving node checks the validity of the timestamp, by comparing the timestamp with its current time; the difference should not exceed a predefined threshold. In addition, securing timestamps for being altered requires an authentication.

Wormhole Attack Protection

To protect the network against a wormhole attack in the OLSR routing protocol, we use the solution presented in [15]. This approach is based on geographical position and requires the deployment of a public key infrastructure and timestamp synchronization between all nodes. In this solution, a sender of the control message embedded its current position and its current time in the packet. When receiving a message from a neighbor, the nodes compare their geographical data to the received geographical data. If the distance is bigger than the maximum transmission range, the node judges that the message might be tunneled by a wormhole attack. Then the false routing message is detected and discarded.

6 Conclusion and Future Work

In our security proposal of OLSR routing protocol, we used digital signatures to authenticate and verify the integrity of the non-mutable data in the control message. For the mutable fields, we have used hash chains mechanism. Also, our proposal offers protection against a wormhole attack with the help of geographical position which can be obtained by using Global Positioning System (GPS) devices embedded into the hardware of each node. Compared to existing securing routing protocols, our solution is lightweight. Due to the Hello packets that are the most frequent in the network don't use the hash chains, since we consider all the information in the HELLO packet as non-mutable fields. In later work, we will extend our security scheme to cover key management and we will present a detailed performance evaluation of SE-OLSR for various network instances and node processing capabilities.

References

1. Moudni, H., Er-rouidi, M., Mouncif, H., El Hadadi, B.: Performance analysis of AODV routing protocol in MANET under the influence of routing attacks. In: 2016 International Conference on Electrical and Information Technologies (ICEIT), Tangiers, pp. 536–542 (2016)

2. Moudni, H., Er-Rouidi, M., Mouncif, H., El Hadadi, B.: Attacks against AODV routing protocol in Mobile ad-hoc networks. In: 2016 13th International Conference on Computer Graphics, Imaging and Visualization (CGiV), Beni Mellal, pp. 385–389 (2016)
3. Akbani, R., Korkmaz, T., Raju, G.V.S.: Mobile ad-hoc networks security. In: Qian, Z., Cao, L., Su, W., Wang, T., Yang, H. (eds.) Recent Advances in Computer Science and Information Engineering. LNEE, vol. 127, pp. 659–666. Springer, Heidelberg (2012). doi:10.1007/978-3-642-25769-8_92
4. Moudni, H., Er-rouidi, M., Mouncif, H., Hadadi, B.E.: Modified AODV routing protocol to improve security and performance against black hole attack. In: 2016 International Conference on Information Technology for Organizations Development (IT4OD), Fez, pp. 1–7 (2016)
5. Moudni, H., Er-rouidi, M., Mouncif, H., El Hadadi, B.: Secure routing protocols for Mobile ad hoc networks. In: 2016 International Conference on Information Technology for Organizations Development (IT4OD), pp. 1–7. IEEE, March 2016
6. Nishani, L., Biba, M.: Machine learning for intrusion detection in MANET: a state-of-the-art survey. J. Intell. Inf. Syst. **46**(2), 391–407 (2016)
7. Jacquet, P., Muhlethaler, P., Clausen, T., Laouiti, A., Qayyum, A., Viennot, L.: Optimized Link State Routing protocol for ad hoc networks. In: Proceedings of IEEE International Multi Topic Conference, IEEE INMIC 2001, Technology for the 21st Century, pp. 62–68. IEEE (2001)
8. Balasubramani, S., Rani, S.K., Rajeswari, K.S.: Review on Security attacks and mechanism in VANET and MANET. In: Dash, S.S., Arun Bhaskar, M., Panigrahi, B.K., Das, S. (eds.) Artificial Intelligence and Evolutionary Computations in Engineering Systems. AISC, vol. 394, pp. 655–666. Springer, New Delhi (2016). doi:10.1007/978-81-322-2656-7_60
9. Paliwal, G., Mudgal, A.P., Taterh, S.: A study on various attacks of TCP/IP and security challenges in MANET layer architecture. In: Das, K.N., Deep, K., Pant, M., Bansal, J.C., Nagar, A. (eds.) Proceedings of Fourth International Conference on Soft Computing for Problem Solving. AISC, vol. 336, pp. 195–207. Springer, New Delhi (2015). doi:10.1007/978-81-322-2220-0_16
10. Malik, D., Mahajan, K., Rizvi, M.A.: Security for node isolation attack on OLSR by modifying MPR selection process. In: 2014 First International Conference onNetworks and Soft Computing (ICNSC), pp. 102–106. IEEE, August 2014
11. Selvi, K.T., Kuppuswami, S.: Enhancing security in Optimized Link State Routing protocol for MANET using threshold cryptography technique. In: 2014 International Conference on Recent Trends in Information Technology (ICRTIT), pp. 1–6. IEEE, April 2014
12. Azeez, A.A., Isaac, E., Thampi, S.M.: Anonymous and secured communication using OLSR in MANET. In: Abraham, A., Mauri, J.L., Buford, J.F., Suzuki, J., Thampi, S.M. (eds.) ACC 2011. CCIS, vol. 193, pp. 145–154. Springer, Heidelberg (2011). doi:10.1007/978-3-642-22726-4_16
13. Echchaachoui, A., Elmahdi, F., Elkoutbi, M.: OLSR-RAIP5: optimized link state routing with redundant array of independent paths 5. In: El Oualkadi, A., Choubani, F., El Moussati, A. (eds.) Information and Communication Technologies. LNEE, vol. 381, pp. 201–210. Springer, Cham (2016). doi:10.1007/978-3-319-30298-0_21
14. Dutta, C.B., Biswas, U.: Specification based IDS for camouflaging wormhole attack in OLSR. In: 2015 23th Mediterranean Conference on Control and Automation (MED), pp. 960–966. IEEE, June 2015
15. Raffo, D., Adjih, C., Clausen, T., Mühlethaler, P.: Securing OLSR using node locations. In: 11th European Wireless Conference 2005-Next Generation Wireless and Mobile Communications and Services (European Wireless), pp. 1–7. VDE, April 2005

A New Data Forwarding Scheme for DTNs Based on Coalition Game

Youness Larabi[1], Khalil Ibrahimi[1(✉)], and Nabil Benamar[2]

[1] MISC Laboratory, Faculty of Sciences, Ibn Tofail University, Kenitra, Morocco
larabiyounes.mc@gmail.com, khalil.ibrahimi@gmail.com
[2] High School of Technology, Moulay Ismail University, Meknes, Morocco
n.benamar@est.umi.ac.ma

Abstract. In this paper, we propose a new data forwarding scheme in this network DTN where all relay nodes take the decision of sending all bundles from the source to the destination. The nodes here cooperate to build groups called coalition, each constructed coalition counts both nodes that are infected (*relay that meets at least once the destination*) and nodes that are uninfected (*never met the destination*). Each relay that participates in the expedition of the message/data receive a reward under certain condition (if this relayed message is received with success). Finally, a distributed formation coalition algorithm is proposed and we search to find a state of stability of all relays such that no group of players have the incentive to leave structure a coalition (Nash-stable equilibrium). Numerical results show an acceptable performance of the proposed mechanism.

Keywords: Delay tolerant network · Forwarding · Coalition formation game

1 Introduction

The delay tolerant networks (DTNs) are networks with frequent partitions, long propagation delay, and intermittent connection. These networks require the existence of the relay to convey traffic based on opportunistic routing where bundles are stored in each relay before being sent opportunistically to any available node ("store and forward") [1]. Moreover, there are additional issues that routing strategies should be aware, such as: battery capacity limitations in some mobile nodes in the network or the connectivity disruptions, buffer space caused the long disconnections, messages must be stored for a long time in the buffers of intermediate relays, which implies that the routers require a space proportional to the storage request [2,3].

In [4], the authors propose a privacy-preserving social assisted mobile content dissemination scheme in DTNs. The mobile devices in DTNs (e.g., laptops, smartphonens, ...) are used by the users to opportunistically exchange and disseminate information. The authors in [5] focus on the DTN application and

E. Sabir et al. (Eds.): UNet 2017, LNCS 10542, pp. 117–126, 2017.
https://doi.org/10.1007/978-3-319-68179-5_11

protocols implementations. They propose several series of experiments, demonstrated the practicality of using their testbed for assessing the performance characteristics of DTN2 and IBR-DTN implementations.

In [6], the authors use the cooperative approach for a dynamic popular content over a VANET Networks. The results show that the proposed approach provides a significant improvement in performance compared to non-cooperative approach. In [7], the authors use the coalition formation models, adapting coordination and interaction mechanisms as they are known in multi-agent systems to the specific context of ad hoc networks that are evolving stochastic tasks. In the context of game theory, the concept of cooperation means acting together for a common interest. However, if two or more players work together for a common interest, it is therefore necessary to separate the individual utility to define a sort of common utility that will determine their common behavior. In general, game theory [8], can be classified into two classes: non-cooperative class that provides an analytical tool to study the interactions among competing players. Each player chooses its strategy independently so that its own utility improves. In non-cooperative games, players cannot make binding commitments. The main branch of cooperative games is focused on the formation of cooperating groups of players, referred to as coalitions.

In this paper, we propose a new data forwarding scheme in DTNs where all relays devices take the decision of sending all messages/data from the source to the destination. These relays cooperate with each other to form a coalition group composed by both infected relays [8] (*relay that meets at least once the destination*) and uninfected relay (*never met the destination*). Each relay participates in the expedition of the message/data can receive a reward, from the source under certain conditions. The proposed algorithm is evaluated for 4 relays and also in the case the 6 relays, because the running consume more times before getting the results. The different coalitions in each case are generated according to this algorithm at the Nash equilibrium and are discussed with comments.

The reminder of the paper is organized as follows: Sect. 2 presents the system model and Sect. 3 gives our algorithm for formation of coalitions. Section 4 presents the system performance and the Sect. 5 ends the paper.

2 System Model

2.1 System Description

We consider one area containing the N relays, one source (s) and one destination (d). In this paper, we use the Epidemic protocol where all nodes become senders. The messages sent must be assured with a wide range of probability. In this case, all resources are well consumed. The source generates a message which must be delivered to destination. Assuming that the message is not delivered directly, yet it must be sent to the relay that surrounds it which, in return, sends it before the expiration of a limited timing denoted by τ. The source has a packet generated at time 0 that wishes to send to the destination d. Let $X_e(t)$ denotes the number of relays randomly infected at time t (excluding the destination and source) where each relay at least can have a copy or not of the message. So the number of uninfected nodes at time t is denoted by $X_n(t)$ will $N - X_e(t)$. Let $X_c(t)$ the number of relays (infected or uninfected) that have a copy of the packet. The time of a contact between a pair of relays follows an exponential distribution with rate λ. The number of infected relays at t can be estimated by using the approximation of fluid model [9,10]:

$$X_e'(t) = \lambda(N - X_e(t)). \tag{1}$$

And the number of relays that have a copy of the packet is denoted by $X_c(t)$ and given by: $X_c'(t) = \lambda(N - X_c(t))$. Denote by $P_{succ}(\tau)$ the probability of a successful delivery of the packet in the time t. Then, given the process X_i (for which a fluid approximation will be used), we have the probability of successful delivery of packet as: $p_{succ}(\tau) = 1 - e^{-\lambda \int_0^{\tau}(X_n(t)+X_e(t))dt}$. The key hypothesis in our model is that the mobile relays situated near each others can form coalitions to get all the data to an out-of-reach destination. Here we are merely interested in a cooperative game in which all players/relays engage in playing to define an individual strategy so as to create another common strategy. This coalition is also defined as the reforming of players to cooperate with each others. This coalition formed by all players named the big coalition in which characterizes the super additive games in contrast to the non-super additive games in which the kernel can be constituted by several disjointed coalitions. In this framework, our proposition is focused on a non-super additive game in which all the relays are members in a coalition. We also suppose that each coalition composes both infected and non-infected relays.

2.2 Utility of Relay in a Coalition

Each coalition contains randomly nodes at each time t and it can be defined as follows: $S : \{X_e^c, X_e^{-c}, X_n^c, X_n^{-c}\}$, where X_e^c is the number of infected relays have a copy of the packet. X_e^{-c} is the number of infected relays that did not have a copy of the packet. X_n^c is the number of non infected relays and have a copy of the packet. X_n^{-c} is the number of uninfected relays that did not have a copy of the packet. In the coalition theory, we were able to distinguish between two entities: the value of coalition and the payoff got by each player. The value of a coalition represents the sum of use of the coalition. The payoff of the player represents the sum the player can get. Each adopted strategy by the relay follows certain use it gets. More than that, we can consider if a message is received successfully to its destination, all nodes participating in its sending share as a result, a reward r as indicated in the relay when the infected relay is superior to the value of a reward of non-infected relay. Each coalition is denoted by S. Let $X_e^S(t)$ (resp. $X_n^S(t)$) be the number of infected relays in each coalition (resp. uninfected relays). The time of a contact between a pair of relays follows an exponential distribution, the results will be marked by λ. The number of infected relays at time t in a coalition S is estimated as follows: $X_e^{S'}(t) = \lambda(||S|| - X_e(t))$. And the number of relays have a copy of the packet in time t at the same coalition. We focus here on the uninfected relays $X_n(t)$ and only the relays that have a copy of the packet, can be estimated as follows $X_n^c(t)$: $X_n^{c'}(t) = \lambda(||X_n^S|| - X_c(t))$. Where $||X_n^S|| = ||S|| - ||X_e^S(t)||$ is the number of the uninfected relays in the same coalition (or ||S|| is the shape of the coalition). And $||X_n^S|| = X_n^c + X_n^{-c}$.

The resolution of these equations if we use the initial condition $X(0) = 0$ is given by $X_e^S(t) = ||S||(1-e^{-\lambda t})$ and $X_n^c(t) = ||X_n^S||(1-e^{-\lambda t})$. Then, we need to find the probability that a packet is delivered successfully to the destination d. We assume that the packet is delivered with great probability if the relays in the coalition are infected (X_e^S) (because infected relay at time t in its road randomly achieve a desired destination and these relays at least have a copy of the packet [11,13]) and relays of the type uninfected that contain a copy of the packet. So the probability that a packet is delivered successfully to the destination d is given by:

$$p_{succ}(X_e^S, X_n^c, \tau) = 1 - e^{-\lambda_d \int_0^\tau X_e^S(t) + X_n^c(t) dt}. \tag{2}$$

Let r the reward is shared among the mobiles in the area, in each coalition S there are two types of relays infected and uninfected relays, so when the coalition contain only the infected (resp. uninfected) mobiles the reward is shared equalized among X_e^S (resp. X_n^c), while the coalition S contains both infected and uninfected mobiles the reward r is shared among the X_e^S differently X_n^c using p_1 and p_2 the reward percentages where $p_1 \gg p_2$ (i.e. the percentage of the reward r for the infected relays is greater than the uninfected relays). The utility of a relay in a coalition S is given as follows:

$$U_i^S(X_e^S, X_n^S, \tau) = h(p1, p2) p_{succ}(X_e^S, X_n^c, \tau) - g, \tag{3}$$

where $h(p1,p2) = \frac{rp_1}{||X_e^S||} + \frac{rp_2}{||X_n^S||}$, $||X_n^c||$ is the number of uninfected relays and have a copy of the packet in the same coalition and $g = \sum_{j \in S, i \neq j \neq s} C_{i,j} = \sum \beta \delta_{i,j}$. The average cost of mobile node i for delivering a packet to any mobile node j in the same coalition such as β is the wasted energy, and δ_{ij} is given by

$$\delta_{ij} = \begin{cases} 1 \; \textit{if the relay } i \textit{ meeting } j, \\ 0 \; \textit{otherwise.} \end{cases}$$

2.3 Structures of Coalitions and Preference Relation

Definition 1. *A coalitional structure is a set of coalitions spanning all the users in N which is defined as* $\psi = \{S_1.., S_l.., S_s\}$, *where* $S_l \cap S_{l'}$ *for* $l \neq l'$ *and S is the total number of coalitions for* $1 \leq S \leq N$, *and* $\bigcup_{l=1}^{s} \{S_l\} = N$. *The coalition consisting of all the mobile nodes is referred to as a grand coalition. There can be* $2^N - 1$ *distinct nonempty coalitions. Bell numbers can help us to find the different possible structures of coalitions from a finite number of relays* $\{1, 2, \ldots, N\}$. *It is computed step by step by the next recurrence relation, sometimes called relationship Aitken [12]:*

$$d(N) = \sum_{k=0}^{N-1} \binom{N-1}{k} d(k), \tag{4}$$

where $d(0) = 1$. *Then, the set of possible structures is given by:* $\Phi = \{\psi_1, \ldots, \psi_{d(N)}\}$, *where* ψ_x *is a coalition structure and* $d(N)$ *is the* N*th number of Bell. In each structure, we have a set of coalitions as follows:* $\psi_x = \{S_1^x, \ldots, S_y^x\}$. *When the state, such as the initial structure of the coalition follows changes based on the individual preferences of nodes until there is a stable final structure.*

Definition 2. *The preference of any mobile node* i *is denoted by* $(\succeq_i)$. $S_l^i \succeq_i S_{l'}^i$ *denotes that mobile node* i *strictly prefers to be a member of* S_l^i *over* $S_{l'}^i$. $S_l^i \succeq_i S_{l'}^i$ *is valid if two following conditions are true. First, all the other mobile nodes* j *in* S_l^i *believe that they are not worse off when mobile node* i *is a member of* S_l^i *(i.e.* $U_j(S_l^i) > U_j(S_l^i \backslash \{i\})$*),* $\forall j \in S_l^i \backslash \{i\}$*). Second, mobile node* i *believes that its payoff, when this node is a member of* S_l^i *is greater than that when this node is a member of* $S_{l'}^i$ *(i.e.* $U_i(S_l^i) > U_i(S_{l'}^i \backslash \{i\})$*).*

We define the following preference relation: each player i calculates the gain at the beginning in its initial coalition and compares it with the expected gain in other coalitions. If this gain is higher than in other coalitions, we go to calculate the number of infected nodes in these coalitions. If the player gain in a coalition is the same where we find many infected nodes. So this node will join this coalition, else it seeks the ideal state, which is the coalition composed of a significant number of infected nodes where the number of nodes in the first coalition is greater than that in the second coalition and their gain in this coalition, which does not fall.

Proposition 1 ***(Preference relation).*** *For any mobile node* $i \in N$, *we define the following preference relation* $S_1 \succeq_i S_2 \Leftrightarrow U_i(S_1) \succeq U_i(S_2)$. *It's can be written as follows:*

$$|X_e^{S_1}| \succeq |X_e^{S_2}| \ \&\& \ |U_i(S_2) - U_i(S_1)| \prec th\_gain, \tag{5}$$

where th_gain *is threshold to tack a decision.* $U_i(S_1)$ *(resp.* $U_i(S_2)$*) is the utility of a relay* i *in a coalition* S_1 *(resp.* S_2*).* $|X_e^{S_1}|$ *(resp.* $|X_e^{S_2}|$*) the number of infected relays in a coalition* S_1 *(resp.* S_2*).*

3 Join or Leave a Coalition

3.1 Proposed Algorithm

One key approach in coalition formation is to enable the players to join or leave a coalition based on well-defined preferences according to utility function. A set of autonomous nodes form a coalition to work together to deliver the packet to the desired destination. Using the next proposed coalition formation algorithm each node can leave its coalition to join another one in order to improve their gain until a balance of Nash Equilibrium, where no player can benefit from moving from its coalition to another coalition. At each iteration is chosen a random node that belongs to a coalition in the structure defined and another coalition in the structure to join. This operation is repeated for all nodes randomly. Then the initial weighted gain is calculated for the node that belongs to a coalition in the structure of the initial coalition, then we traverse all the coalitions comparing the expected gain of the node i in each coalition with the departure gain until we find a coalition with the best gain, but for that the node i join the new coalition, we make a test on the gains of the nodes in its latest, so that the gain of an random node in that coalition not fall. After we go to the second criterion that is based on the number of the infected nodes each coalition. We calculate the number of infected nodes in each coalition and then we select both coalitions that contain the best gain and those that contain a significant number of infected nodes. If we find it is the same coalition, then the node joins this coalition, else we calculate the difference of the gains between the new high gain with the gain of the coalition that contains a significant number of infected nodes, if the result does not pass a certain threshold. Finally the node i joins the coalition that presents the ideal state (the coalition which contains an average gain with an important number of infected nodes that guarantees the message delivery). Therefore, the initial structure of the coalition becomes a new structure of coalition after that the mobile node i joins a new coalition where we can have $2^N - 1$ non-empty distinct coalitions and $d(N)$ different structures of coalition as shown in (4). With the number of possible coalitions and the number of structures defined by the number of Bell which is finite, the algorithm converges to a coalition of structure Nash-stable.

Algorithm 1. Coalition formation algorithm

1: we choose an initial structure of coalitions for all the nodes at $t = 0$, among the set of structures (Φ) using bel. For example, $\psi_x = \{S_1^x, ..., S_y^x\}$,
2: we choose a random node i that belongs to a coalition S_l^x and an other coalition S_k^x $(l \neq k)$ in the same structure ψ_x to join it.
3: for each node i we calculate the expected gain $U_i(S_l^x)$ in the coalition S_l^x.
4: we traverse all the coalitions in the set ψ_x after the adding of the node i in S_k^x and we calculate the new gain $U_i(S_k^x)$.
5: if $U_i(S_l^x) < U_i(S_k^x)$, then

- for each iteration we choose randomly a node $j \in S_k^x$ and we calculate the gain $U_j(S_k^x \cup \{i\})$.
- if $U_j(S_k^x) < U_j(S_k^x \cup \{i\})$.
- we traverse all the coalitions in ψ_x and we calculate X_e^S, then we select the coalition that contains a many number of X_e^S. For example, S_m^x.
- if we find that coalition S_m^x is the same with the coalition of the best gain. The node i joins the coalition S_k^x.
- Else the node i joins the coalition S_m^x which verify $(U_i(S_k^x) - U_i(S_m^x) \leq th\_gain)$.

6: – Until a final structure Nash-stable contains all the relays.

3.2 Nash-Stability

Proposition 2 ***(Nash-stability).*** *For any coalition $S_x^y \subseteq N$, if the condition $\forall i \in S_x^y, S_x^y \succeq_i \{i\}$ is hold, then there exists at least a stable coalition structure ψ_x^* and also individual Nash stable according to [12] as all the coalitions in ψ_x^* are not singleton coalitions.*

In this observation, the mobile node chooses be coalition member and not acte alone ($S_x^y \succeq_i \{i\}$) since each mobile node achieve a better benefit by being a member of a coalition. This means that $U_i(\{i\}) < U_i(\{S_x^y\})$. According to the algorithm we can get in the end a Nash-stable structure.

Theorem 1 ***(Algorithm convergence).*** *The algorithm will converge to a structure of coalition Nash-Stable ψ_x^*.*

Proof 1. *Any mobile node among a coalition will be able to exchange a current coalition to another if one of the mobile node has a worse gain. (Each node can leave its coalition to join another one in order to improve their gain). If the mobile node $i \in S_l^i$ prefers to join a new coalition based on Definition 2 when (i.e., $S_k \cup \{i\} \succeq_i S_l^i, \ \forall\ S_k \in \psi \backslash S_l^i \cup \{0\}$). Then, the structure of coalition is not Nash stable. So there will be a change of current coalition structure to a new structure of coalition after mobile node i joins a new coalition (i.e., step 5 of Algorithm 1). Since there can be $2^N - 1$ distinct nonempty coalitions and d(N) different coalitional structures as given in (4), in non-super additive games [6] the kernel can be constituted by several disjointed coalitions and the worst case is that if mobile node i forms its singleton coalition based Proposition 2. Finally the algorithm converge to a Nash-stable structure.*

4 Numerical Results

In this section, we try to discuss via the numerical results performed using mathematical "MATLAB" the proposed mechanism. One goal of the paper is to find the Nash equilibrium preferences evaluating for each relay to join a coalition from the possible coalitions. In this case, the initial structure composed of the $N = 4$ relays are considered in order to evaluate our algorithm like $\psi_x = \{[1], [2], [3], [4]\}$. The possible coalitions are presented in the Table 1.

We consider in this simulation the next threshold $th\_gain = \frac{|U_i(S_j)+U_i(S_k)|}{2}$. By using the Bell number defined in the above section, we get the number of possible structures (total number of structures). This number is $d(4) = 15$ (structures) and the all possible structures are summarized in the below Table 2.

The results presented in this table show that the relay joins the new coalitions according to the algorithm and the final structure Nash stable is obtained. The next Fig. 1 present the structures evolution. We show that from the iteration $ts = 19$ the stable structure in which the iteration $\{19, 12\}$ correspond to the structure is $\#ID = 12$ and from the below Table 2 we find exactly the name of the stable structure like $\psi_x^* = \{[1, 2], [3, 4]\}$. The same thing here in this Fig. 2 for a number of relays equal to $N = 6$ and the number of bell in this case give 203 total of structures. The final structure of Nash stable is $\psi_x^* = \{[1, 4], [5, 3], [6, 2]\}$. Note that if we increase the number of relays the problem the complexity computational is meeting (i.e. the rate of finding a stable structure is very long because of repetition of the same structures in the times). We could try to optimize our algorithm in the future work.

Table 1. The possible coalitions.

Coalition #ID	Coalition members (S_x^y)
1	4
2	3
3	[3, 4]
4	2
5	[2, 4]
6	[2, 3]
7	[2, 3, 4]
8	1
9	[1, 4]
10	[1, 3]
11	[1, 3, 4]
12	[1, 2]
13	[1, 2, 4]
14	[1, 2, 3]
15	[1, 2, 3, 4]

Table 2. Possible structures identified by the proposed algorithm.

Structure #ID	Structure members (ψ_x)
tss{1}	{[1], [2], [3], [4]}
tss{2}	{[1, 2], [3], [4]}
tss{3}	{[1], [2], [3, 4]}
tss{4}	{[1, 3], [2], [4]}
tss{5}	{[1], [3], [2, 4]}
tss{6}	{[1, 4], [2], [3]}
tss{7}	{[1], [4], [2, 3]}
tss{8}	{[1, 3, 4], [2]}
tss{9}	{[1, 2, 3], [4]}
tss{10}	{[1, 2, 4], [3]}
tss{11}	{[1], [2, 3, 4]}
tss{12}	{[1, 2], [3, 4]}
tss{13}	{[1, 3], [2, 4]}
tss{14}	{[1, 4], [2, 3]}
tss{15}	{[1, 2, 3, 4]}

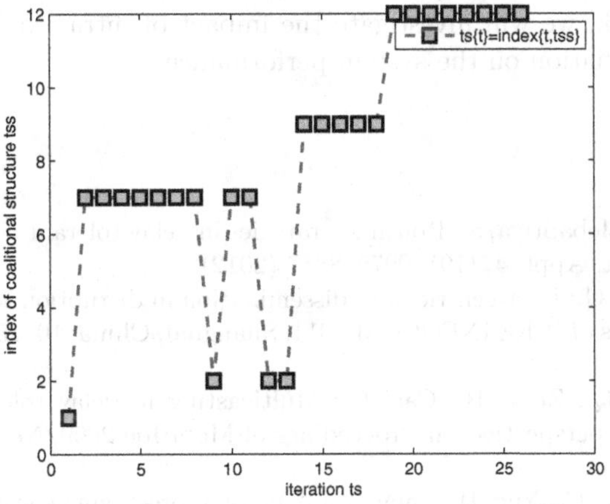

Fig. 1. Nash stable coalitions structure according to the coalition formation algorithm for 4 relays.

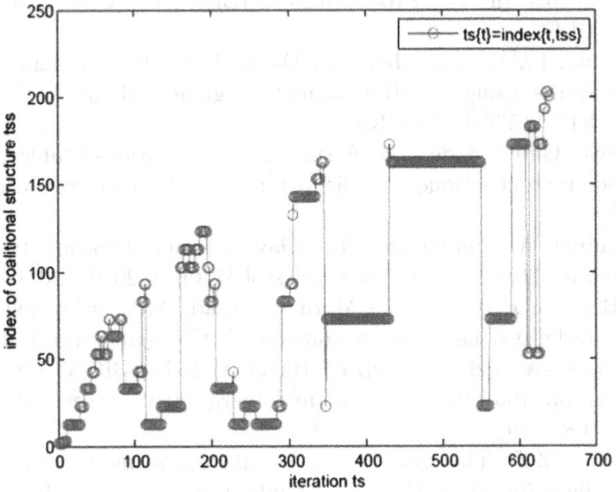

Fig. 2. Nash stable coalitions structure according to the coalition formation algorithm for 6 relays.

5 Conclusion

In this work, we have proposed a new data forwarding scheme in DTNs in which all relay nodes take the decision of sending all messages/data from the source to the destination. These relays cooperate with each other to form coalition composed by both infected (relay that meets at least once the destination) and non infected relay (never met the destination). Numerical results of this mechanism show the existing of Nash Stable Equilibrium.

In future work, we will investigate the impact of intra- coalition and inter-coalition differentiation on the system performance.

References

1. Abraham, A., Jebapriya, S.: Routing strategies in delay tolerant networks: a survey. Int. J. Comput. Appl. **42**(19), 0975–8887 (2012)
2. Gao, W., Cao, G.: User-centric data dissemination in disruption tolerant networks. In: Proceedings of IEEE INFOCOM 2011, Shanghai, China, 10–15 April, pp. 3119–3127 (2011)
3. Gao, W., Li, Q., Zhao, B., Cao, G.: Multicasting in delay tolerant networks: a social network perspective. In Proceedings of MobiHoc 2009, New York, USA, pp. 299–308 (2009)
4. Guo, L., Zhang, C., Yue, H., Fang, Y.: A privacy-preserving social-assisted mobile content dissemination scheme in DTNs. In: The Proceedings of IEEE INFOCOM 2013, Turin, Italy, 14–19 April 2013
5. Beuran, R., Miwa, S., Shinoda, Y.: Network emulation: testbed for DTN applications and protocols. In: The Proceedings of IEEE INFOCOM 2013, Turin, Italy, 14–19 April 2013
6. Wang, T., Song, L., Han, Z., Jiao, B.: Dynamic popular content distribution in vehicular networks using coalition formation games. IEEE J. Sel. Areas Commun./Suppl. **31**(9), 538–547 (2013)
7. Frana, P., Faye, C.M.: Modeles de Formation de Coalitions Stables Dans un Contexte Ad-hoc et Stochastique. Intelligence artificielle. Universit Claude Bernard, Lyon (2015)
8. Singh, C., Kumar, A., Sundaresan, R.: Delay and energy optimal two-hop relaying in delay tolerant networks. In: Proceedings of WiOPT 2010, India (2010)
9. El-Azouzi, R., Sidi, H.B.A., Rojas-Mora, J., Azad, A.P.: Delay tolerant networks in partially overlapped networks: a non-cooperative game approach. In: Altman, E., Carrera, I., El-Azouzi, R., Hart, E., Hayel, Y. (eds.) BIONETICS 2009. LNICSSITE, vol. 39, pp. 195–202. Springer, Heidelberg (2010). https://doi.org/10.1007/978-3-642-12808-0_19
10. Small, T., Haas, Z.J.: The shared wireless infostation model: a new ad hoc networking paradigm (or where there is a whale, there is a way). In: MobiHoc 2003, Maryland, USA, 13 June 2003
11. Singh, C., Kumar, A., Sundaresan, R., Altman, E.: Optimal forwarding in delay tolerant networks with multiple destinations. In: The Proceedings of WiOPT 2011, 9–13 May 2011
12. Akkarajitsakul, K., Hossain, E.: Coalition-based cooperative packet delivery under uncertainty: a dynamic Bayesian coalitional game. IEEE Trans. Mobile Comput. **12**(2), 371–385 (2013)
13. Altman, E., Basar, T., De Pellegrini, F.: Optimal monotone forwarding policies in delay tolerant mobile ad-hoc networks. In: ValueTools 2008, Athens, Greece, 20–24 October 2008

Impact of Link Lifetime on QoS in Mobile Ad-Hoc Networks

Nabil Mesbahi(✉) and Hamza Dahmouni

INPT, 2, Avenue Allal Al Fassi, Madinat Al Irfane, Rabat, Morocco
n.mesbahi@anrt.ma, dahmouni@inpt.ac.ma

Abstract. The provision of quality of service (QoS) in mobile ad hoc networks is a challenging task. Several factors such as node mobility, propagation environment, interference and access medium impact the link characteristics and may cause radio links to break frequently. Contributing to the understanding of the link properties is a key element to achieve efficiency and network performance in ad-hoc networks. In this paper, we present an analytical framework which determines the link lifetime and path lifetime by taking into consideration both node mobility and interference. This result is used in order to investigate the network connectivity properties by analyzing the link availability of a given node. Furthermore, to further understand the implication of link properties, analytical results are used to investigate network metrics that can be used in the ad-hoc routing design and the analysis of associated performance.

Keywords: Ad-hoc networks · Link lifetime · Link properties · Node mobility · Interference · Connectivity · QoS provisioning

1 Introduction

Mobile Ad-hoc network (MANET) is a set of mobile nodes, which are dynamically communicating through wireless links without the need for any static infrastructure. Among the limiting factors that impact the network performance and the quality of service is the mobility of nodes. In fact, nodes in MANET are free to move randomly and can enter and leave the network dynamically. The random mobility makes the topology of MANET dynamic and unpredictable. In this case, link breakage can occur when nodes move out of range of each other. Aside from node mobility, interference is an inherent characteristic of mobile ad-hoc networks. It is a major impact factor on the network performance because of the broadcast nature of the wireless medium and random propagation conditions. Communication between nodes are achieved through a single channel protocol and therefore potentially interfere with each other. In fact, mobile nodes in ad-hoc networks do not have a separate interface for each operation of data transmission and all stations must switch the channel regulatory. These are achieved by defining time slots which are switched periodically.

E. Sabir et al. (Eds.): UNet 2017, LNCS 10542, pp. 127–138, 2017.
https://doi.org/10.1007/978-3-319-68179-5_12

Many issues related to the link behavior are largely explored in the literature. However, existing works on link properties are based only on node mobility and do not take into account interference. Several studies analyze the impact of node mobility on the network performance [1,2]. Other simulation-based studies provide empirical distribution of link and multi-hop path lifetime [5,10] by considering mobility models such as Random Waypoint and Random Walk [3].

The properties of wireless links can be determined by link availability [21], link lifetime and link residual time [9,20]. In this context, authors of [25] provide an approximation of the distribution of the link lifetime due to linked nodes mobility. In this study, time is divided into equal length time steps Δt and a distance transition probability matrix is used in order to model the distance after every discrete time step based on a smooth mobility model [24]. The main result is an approximation of the link lifetime due to linked nodes mobility by an exponential distribution with parameter $\frac{\bar{V}}{R}$, where $\bar{V}$ is the mean of speed and R the transmission range. Understanding radio interferences is also important for the design and analysis of wireless network performance. Aside from node mobility, radio channel is subject to interferences in which the signal received is impacted by transmission from other nodes. Several studies have been focused on the prediction of interference in ad-hoc networks with general mobility models [13,22]. In this context, paper [6] investigates interference prediction using a general-order linear model for node mobility in order to give an estimation of the time-varying interference at a given time. Moreover, Authors of [23] model the interference field as a Poisson Point Process in order to derive the lower and upper bounds of the signal-to-interference ratio.

Other studies derived methods for evaluation outage probability given fading and shadowing [14] in order to add interference-awareness to the control function so that to enhance the overall network performance [11,19]. In a recent work [18], we have showed that the link lifetime due to interference can be approximated by an exponential distribution with parameter $\lambda = \frac{\bar{V}}{R}.\frac{N}{\alpha}.\frac{\beta}{\beta+1}$ where $\bar{V}$ is the average speed, R is the transmission range of the mobile node, β is an $SINR$ threshold corresponding to an acceptable BER, α is the path loss exponent and N is the maximum number of interfering nodes.

The goal in this paper is to provide understanding of the link lifetime characteristics and to study various aspects related to the QoS and the network connectivity. The problem of connectivity in mobile ad-hoc networks has been widely investigated through several analytical and simulation studies [7,8]. The main contributions concern usually the mobility as the main factor which causes link breakage and its impact on the network connectivity [4,5]. From a connectivity point-of-view, the impact of interference on the network connectivity needs further discussion.

Furthermore, providing guaranteed QoS in ad-hoc networks is a complex task to achieve. In fact, the link quality in mobile ad-hoc networks does not depend only on the bandwidth of that link, but also on many factors including the dynamic topology due to mobility and the unreliability of wireless medium which cause frequent link breakage. These limitations make the QoS provisioning difficult and we believe that understanding link properties, including link lifetime and link residual lifetime, is the key element to achieve efficiency and network performance in ad-hoc networks. Such understanding is helpful to gain insights through which the link properties can be used as link quality indicators for the network design and performance evaluation.

The rest of the paper is organized as follows. We present in Sect. 2 our approach used for modeling the lifetime of wireless links and multi-hop paths by taking into consideration interference and node mobility. In this section, the distribution of link lifetime due to interference is derived based on a transition probability matrix which models the link state after every discrete time step. Section 3, provides understanding of how link properties can be used as link quality metrics for the network design and performance evaluation. Finally, Sect. 4 concludes the paper.

2 Link Lifetime Modeling in the Presence of Interference

2.1 Assumptions

The link lifetime is the period of time between the establishment of the link until its breakage due to a failure. In this subsection, we consider the interference as the only factor that causes link breakage.

We denote by $d_{u,v}$ the distance between the node-pair (u, v), where u is the sender and v the receiver. The corresponding relative distance after k time steps is denoted by $d^{(k)}_{u,v}$. And let $SINR^{(k)}_{u,v}$ be the Signal-to-Interference Noise-Ratio at the kth time steps (the duration of the time step is denoted by Δt). Figure 1, shows that the link failure occurs in the presence of interference when the relative distance between the interferer and the receiver nodes is bellow the transmission range.

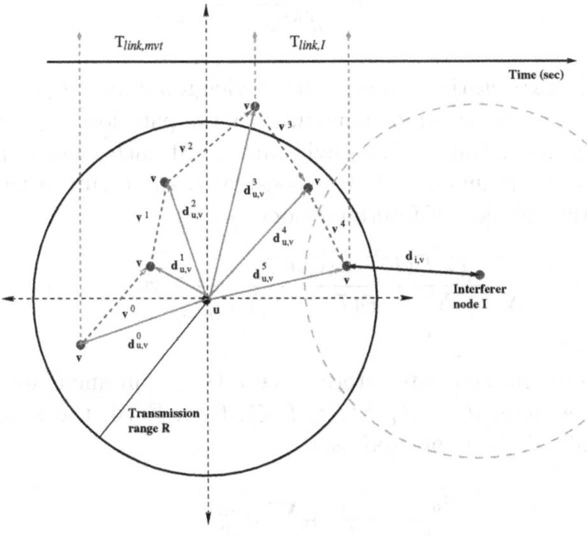

Fig. 1. Link breakage due to linked nodes mobility and interference

Definition 1. *The link lifetime due to interference, denoted by $T_{link,I}$, is the period of time between the establishment of the link until its breakage due to interference coming from other nodes. In this case, the Signal-to-Interference Noise-Ratio (SINR) is less than an SINR threshold β corresponding to an acceptable BER.*

$$T_{link,I} \triangleq \sup_{k}\{k.\Delta t \mid SINR_{u,v}^{(k)} \geq \beta\} \tag{1}$$

Consider a mobile ad-hoc network consisting of N nodes which choose a common power level P_e for all their transmissions. We focus on a particular link, called the tagged link whose receiver node is considered as the reference. Let L represents the subset of interferer nodes. The reference physical model that determines whether a transmission is successfully received or not is the Signal-to-Interference Noise-Ratio ($SINR$). In our analysis, we adopt the interference model introduced in [12].

$$SINR_{u,v}^{(k)}(m) = \frac{P_e.\gamma_{u,v}^{(k)}}{N_T + \sum\limits_{\substack{i\in L, i\neq u \\ |L|=m}} P_e.\gamma_{i,v}^{(k)}} \tag{2}$$

where $SINR_{u,v}^{(k)}(m)$ is the Signal-to-Interference Noise-Ratio after k time steps and in presence of m interferer nodes, P_e is the transmit power of nodes, N_T is the noise power supposed constant and $\gamma_{i,j}^{(k)}$ is the channel gain from node i to node j after k time steps, such that the received power at node j is $P_e.\gamma_{i,j}$. In this paper, the channel gain between a node pair (i, j) is given by:

$$\gamma_{i,j}^{(k)} = \frac{P_e.E(R^2).E(\zeta)}{(d_{i,j}^{(k)})^{\alpha}} \tag{3}$$

where, $E(R^2)$ is the expectation value of the Rayleigh fading, $E(\zeta)$ is the expectation value of the log-normal shadowing and α is the path loss exponent, which ranges from 2 to 5 depending on the environment. At each time step, a transmission from u to the intended node v is considered successful in the presence of simultaneous transmission of interferer nodes if:

$$\frac{P_e.E(R^2).E(\zeta).d_{u,v}^{-\alpha}}{N_T + \sum\limits_{i\neq u} P_e.E(R^2).E(\zeta).d_{i,v}^{-\alpha}} \geq \beta \tag{4}$$

where β is the minimum signal-to-interference ratio requirement for successful transmission. By defining $J_e = P_e.E(R^2).E(\zeta)$, from Eq. 4, the availability of communication link can be expressed as:

$$\frac{d_{u,v}^{-\alpha}}{\beta} \geq \frac{N_T}{J_e} + \sum_{i\neq u} d_{i,v}^{-\alpha} \tag{5}$$

Definition 2. *Let $f_{u,v}(m)$ be the probability that the transmission between the node pair (u,v) in the presence of m interfering nodes is successful:*

$$\begin{aligned} f_{u,v}(m) &\triangleq \Pr[SINR_{u,v}(m) \geq \beta \mid d_{u,v} \leq R] \\ &= \Pr[\frac{d_{u,v}^{-\alpha}}{\beta} \geq \frac{N_T}{J_e} + \sum_{\substack{i \in L, i \neq u \\ |L|=m}} d_{i,v}^{-\alpha} \mid d_{u,v} \leq R] \end{aligned} \quad (6)$$

2.2 Distribution of Link Lifetime

A transmission between a node pair is successfully received by the intended node in the presence of interference, if the $SINR$ is greater than its minimum requirement. The loss of connectivity after k time steps means that the $SINR$ has become greater than its threshold β.

We denote by X the random process which undergoes transitions from a state to another in discrete time. X is a stochastic process which describes the link availability in presence of a given number of interfering nodes. This behavior is captured by comparing the $SINR$ with its minimum requirement. Furthermore, link availability can be interpreted as sequential state transitions, in which the $SINR$ is greater than β in presence of a number of interfering nodes which vary from a state to another until the link fails (absorbing state).

We denote by $P = (p_{(i,j)})_{i,j}$ the probability transition matrix which model, at each time step, the quality of the communication link in the existence or the absence of interfering nodes. $p_{(i,j)}$ is the transition probability from a state S_i to a state S_j after one time step. The link between the node pair (u,v) fails due to interference when the system reaches the absorbing state S_{N+1}. In other words, the link duration expire after k time steps if the event $(SINR_{u,v}(l) < \beta; \forall l \in [0,N])$ first occurs. The transition probability $p_{(i,j)}$ is defined as follow:

$$p_{(i,j)} = \Pr[X \in S_j \mid X \in S_i] \quad (7)$$

We denote by $\pi^{(0)}$, the probability of the initial state and $\pi^{(0)} = (\pi_0^{(0)}, \ldots, \pi_{N+1}^{(0)})$. Furthermore, we denote, by $\pi_i^{(k)}$ the probability that the system lies in the state S_i after k time steps and $\pi^{(k)} = (\pi_0^{(k)}, \ldots, \pi_{N+1}^{(k)})$ the row vector whose k^{th} element is $\pi_i^{(k)}$.

The probability that the link fails due to interference after k time steps is $(\pi^{(0)}.P^k)_{N+1}$. Consequently, the complementary density function of the link lifetime due to interference is:

$$\Pr[T_{link,I} \leq k] = [\pi^{(0)}.P^k]_{N+1} = \pi_{N+1}^{(k)} \quad (8)$$

The corresponding PDF is presented as follow:

$$\begin{aligned} f_{T_{link,I}}(k) &= \Pr[T_{link,I} \leq k] - \Pr[T_{link,I} \leq k-1] \\ &= (\pi^{(0)}.P^k)_{N+1} - (\pi^{(0)}.P^{k-1})_{N+1} \end{aligned} \quad (9)$$

Proposition 2 [18]. *The link lifetime due to only interference, denoted by $T_{link,I}$, can be approximated by an exponential distribution with parameter $\lambda = \frac{\bar{V}}{R}.\frac{N}{\alpha}.\frac{\beta}{\beta+1}$:*

$$f_{T_{link,I}}(t) \approx \frac{\bar{V}}{R}.\frac{N}{\alpha}.\frac{\beta}{\beta+1}.exp(-\frac{\bar{V}}{R}.\frac{N}{\alpha}.\frac{\beta}{\beta+1}.t) \tag{10}$$

Proposition 3 [18]. *The overall link lifetime due to both mobility and interference, denoted by T_{link}, can be approximated by a Rayleigh distribution with parameter $\rho = \frac{R}{\bar{V}}.\sqrt{\frac{\alpha.(\beta+1)}{2.\beta.N}}$:*

$$f_{T_{link}}(t) \approx \frac{t}{\rho^2}.exp(-\frac{t^2}{2.\rho^2}) \tag{11}$$

This result is in harmony with previous simulation based-studies which concern the examination of the performance of routing protocols in multi-hop wireless networks and the identification of stable link based on the analysis of link durations under different mobility scenarios. In this context, authors of [9,15] show by simulation that there is a peak in the distribution of the link lifetime. Results of these simulations are obtained by considering several parameters including mobility and radio propagation. Moreover, paper [16] investigates how well an analytical model fits the link lifetime measurements obtained from simulation. They showed, by observation, that the Weibull distribution is a best approximation of the link lifetime. This approximation is argued by the fact that Weibull is among the distributions which are widely used in reliability theory to model the lifetime of objects.

3 QoS Provisioning in Mobile Ad-Hoc Networks

3.1 Bandwidth Reservation

Wired networks provide the possibility to make bandwidth reservation in order to guarantee the quality of service required by applications. The reservation of a certain amount of bandwidth requires that the node has the possibility to control the bandwidth. In this case, the source is responsible for determining the required bandwidth based on the residual capacity of links defining the path to the destination. MLPS is an example of networks which make bandwidth reservation. It is considered as a suitable architecture to support traffic engineering and which provide guaranteed bandwidth for flows. In this area, there has been much work which develop models to determine the amount of bandwidth required to transmit the data. Our previous work [17] is an example of such proposals which formulates several nonlinear objective functions according to the sensitivity of the application and which aims to determine bandwidth allocation as well as traffic flow routing through the network based on the optimization of the network link utilization. Approaches for bandwidth reservation used in wired networks are not directly applicable for wireless networks especially for Manets because many wired QoS characteristics do not hold in wireless networks. In fact, the available bandwidth of a given link do not depend only on the activity of this link, but also on many factors including the dynamic topology that changes over time, less battery power of the nodes, less bandwidth and transmission quality enhancement. These limitations make the reservation of bandwidth difficult in ad hoc networks.

Various factors must be taken into account in order to provide quality-of service (QoS) guaranteed in ad hoc networks. These factors include in particular the node mobility and interference which impact directly the characteristics of the link. In this case, it is important to understand the link properties, including link lifetime and link residual lifetime, in order to achieve efficiency and network performance in mobile ad hoc networks.

In this section, we intend to provide understanding of link properties by considering linked nodes mobility and interference as factors that cause link breakage and which can be used as link quality indicators for the network design and performance evaluation.

3.2 Link Lifetime and Route Selection

Achieving efficiency and network performance requires a deep comprehension of link properties. Factors such as node mobility and interference generally come into play in the determination of the link availability. The link lifetime is the period of time between the establishment of the link until its breakage due to a failure. The link lifetime can be classified into two main classes. Link duration in which the failure is caused by movement of the linked nodes and link lifetime in which the failure is due to interference. Results of [25] show that the link lifetime due to mobility of the linked nodes, denoted by $T_{link,Mvt}$, follows an exponential distribution with parameter $\varphi = \frac{\bar{V}}{R}$, where $\bar{V}$ is the mean speed and R the transmission range. Note that this study considers the mobility of the linked nodes as the only factor which causes link failures. In this regards, we had shown that the link lifetime due to interference follows an exponential distribution with parameter $\lambda = \frac{\bar{V}}{R}.\frac{N}{\alpha}.\frac{\beta}{\beta+1}$ and the overall link lifetime due both mobility and interference can be approximated by a Rayleigh distribution with parameter $\rho = \frac{R}{\bar{V}}.\sqrt{\frac{\alpha.(\beta+1)}{2.\beta.N}}$, where β is the $SINR$ threshold, N is the maximum number of nodes which can interfere with the receiver node and α the path loss exponent. The mean value of $T_{link,I}$, $T_{link,Mvt}$ and T_{link} are given by:

$$E[T_{link,I}] = \frac{1}{\lambda} = \frac{R.\alpha.(\beta+1)}{\bar{V}.\beta.N} \tag{12}$$

$$E[T_{link,Mvt}] = \frac{1}{\varphi} = \frac{R}{\bar{V}} \tag{13}$$

$$E[T_{link}] = \rho\sqrt{\frac{\pi}{2}} = \frac{R}{\bar{V}}.\sqrt{\frac{\alpha.(\beta+1)}{2.\beta.N}}\sqrt{\frac{\pi}{2}} \tag{14}$$

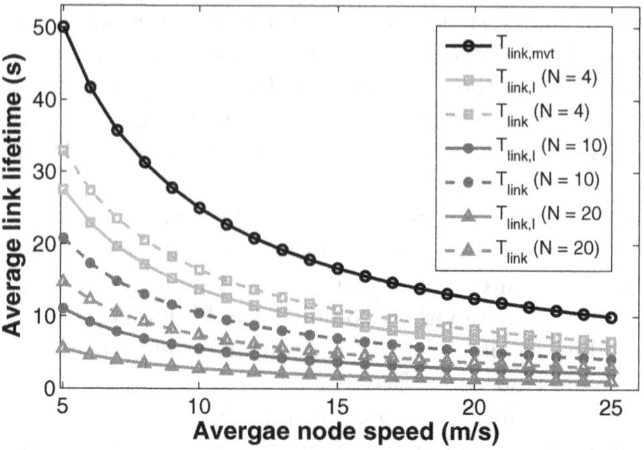

Fig. 2. Average link lifetime in function of speed

In order to investigate the impact of node mobility and interference on the link lifetime, we have plotted $T_{link,I}$, $T_{link,Mvt}$ and T_{link} by considering low mobility. Also, we have assumed that $\beta = 10$ and $\alpha = 2$. Results of Fig. 2 are obtained by considering a transmission range of 250 m and varying the average speed from 5 m/s to 25 m/s. We find that link breakage can be caused by node mobility when the number of interferer node is small. In this case, the link lifetime is simply the time a sender or receiver node take to move across the radius of the transmission zone of each other at their average speed $\bar{V}$. However, in the case of a high node density network, the link breakage can occur first due to interference and this becomes more important when the number of interferer nodes increases.

Moreover, Fig. 3 shows the effect of the transmission range on the average link lifetime due to interference and linked nodes mobility, and by considering $\bar{V} = 5$ m/s. The main result is that when the transmission range is small, the impact of interference and nodes mobility are nearly the same but the probability of link breakage due to interference remains high at high node density network. We can conclude that the link lifetime is an important link property which can be considered as a link quality to use in the design of routing protocols in order to improve the network performance.

Routing Protocols are used to discover and maintain routes between the source and destination nodes. These protocols are designed to provide a multi-hop wireless link between the sender and the receiver nodes. Generally, the sender node initiates the route discovery by broadcasting a route request packet, RREQ, through the network. Several copies of RREQ packet can be received by the receiver node coming through several routes. The receiver sends a route reply packet, RREP, back to the source node following the same path. The source node chooses the route in which the corresponding RREP packet was received first (Figs. 2 and 3).

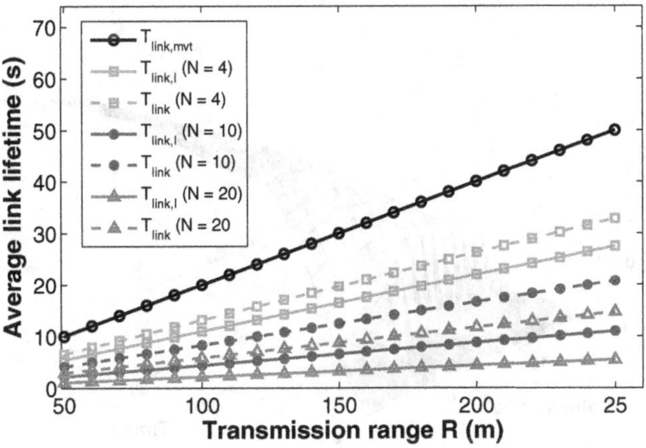

Fig. 3. Average link lifetime in function of transmission range

The route selection is generally based on the number of hops or path delay as metrics and do not take into account the path lifetime which is a deterministic element to avoid failures. In fact, the path lifetime, denoted by T_{Path}, is directly associated with the failures of links defining that path and which are caused by interferences or linked nodes mobility. If M is the number of links forming a path, then

$$T_{path} = min\{T^i_{link} \mid 1 \leq i \leq M\} \tag{15}$$

where

$$T^i_{link} = \min\{T^i_{link,Mvt}; T^i_{link,I}\} \tag{16}$$

Note that $T^i_{link,Mvt}$ and $T^i_{link,I}$ flow an exponential distribution with parameters, respectively, $\varphi = \frac{\bar{V}}{R}$ and $\lambda_i = \frac{\bar{V}.\beta.N_i}{R.\alpha.(\beta+1)}$ and T^i_{link} is Rayleigh distributed with parameter $\rho_i = \frac{R}{\bar{V}}\sqrt{\frac{\alpha.(\beta+1)}{2\beta N_i}}$. N_i is the number of interfere nodes detected by the intermediate node i. The detection of possible interfere nodes can be performed by broadcasting, periodically, a Hello message through the network. The period of broadcasting this type of message should be defined as small enough in order to ensure efficiency through the dynamics topology of mobile ad-hoc networks.

3.3 Impact of Residual Link Lifetime

The residual link lifetime given in Eq. 17 describes the time interval between a given instant a, after the establishment of the link, until its breakage due to interference or linked nodes mobility. In fact, communication between a node pair can start at an arbitrary moment after connection was already established. In this case, the residual link lifetime can be greatly useful in searching, by the

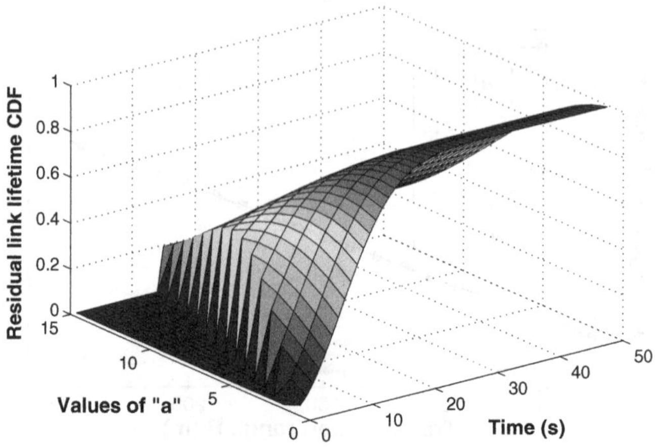

Fig. 4. Residual link lifetime

sender node, for a long-living links defining the path through which the data will be transmitted.

$$\begin{aligned}\Pr[T_{link,Res,a} \leq t] &= \frac{\Pr[T_{link} \leq t + a]}{1 - \Pr[T_{link,Mvt} \leq a]} \\ &= \frac{1 - exp(-\frac{(t+a)^2}{2.\rho^2})}{exp(-\frac{a^2}{2.\rho^2})}\end{aligned} \tag{17}$$

We plot in Fig. 4 the overall residual link lifetime CDF in which the failures can be caused by mobility and interference. Results show that a link has less change to be maintained if the period of time, between its establishment and the beginning of the communication between the linked nodes, is high. In fact, links and paths may exist before a sender establishes a path to the destination for end-to-end communication. In this case, a long living route is the one whose constituent links are recently established.

The use of multi-path routing schemes improve the performance in mobile ad-hoc networks as compared to single path routing protocols. In the context of MANETs, a lot of multi-path routing protocols have been proposed which define multiple disjoint paths, improve resilience to network failures and provide higher aggregate bandwidth especially in networks with high node density. The route selection, in the case of multi-path routing, aims to select a set of paths according to a determined metric such as hop count, path reliability, path disjoints, bandwidth availability and degree of route coupling. The traffic is forwarded using one path which has the best metric and the other paths are kept as backup. The source can send data using an alternate route when the primary route fails. In this context, the selection of an alternate route when the primary route fails should be based on a metric such as residual lifetime instead of an arbitrary choice. In fact, we can talk about the residual path lifetime only after completion of route discovery. A M-hop path may exist before a sender node initiates the route discovery operation. Consequently, the predictive path residual lifetime is an important measure when a sender node need a path to immediately send data packets or caches it as an alternative path to use it if the primary path fails.

4 Conclusion

In this paper, we have given a short summary of the link lifetime model developed in our previous work. This model provides an approximation of the link lifetime PDF by considering interference and node mobility as factors which cause link breakage. We have investigated challenges related to the provision of QoS in mobile ad hoc networks. Most of these challenges are due to the physical characteristics and topological nature of Manets. We have showed that it is important to understand the link properties, including link lifetime and link residual lifetime, and their implication as link quality metrics in order to achieve efficiency and network performance. Several insights are gained which can be helpful for routing optimization, network efficiency and the evaluation of the connectivity of paths, their lengths and their stability.

References

1. Bai, F., Sadagopan, N., Krishnamachari, B., Helmy, A.: Important: a framework to systematically analyze the impact of mobility on performance of routing protocols for ad hoc networks. In: Proceedings of IEEE INFOCOM, pp. 825–835 (2003)
2. Behrmann, G., Clausen, T., Hansen, G., Christensen, L.: The optimized link state routing protocol evaluation through experiments and simulation. In: Proceedings of IEEE Symposium on Wireless Personal Mobile Communications (2001)
3. Bettstetter, C.: Smooth is better than sharp: a random mobility model for simulation of wireless networks. In: Proceedings of the 4th ACM International Conference on Modeling, Analysis, and Simulation of Wireless and Mobile Systems (MSWiM), pp. 19–27 (2001)
4. Bettstetter, C.: On the minimum node degree and connectivity of a wireless multihop network. In: Proceedings of the 3rd ACM International Symposium on Mobile Ad Hoc Networking and Computing (2002)
5. Bettstetter, C.: On the connectivity of ad hoc networks. Comput. J. Spec. Issue Mob. Pervasive Comput. **47**(4), 432–447 (2004)
6. Cong, Y., Zhou, X., Kennedy, R.A.: Interference prediction in mobile ad hoc networks with a general mobility model. IEEE Trans. Wirel. Commun. (2015)
7. Coon, J., Dettmann, C., Georgiou, O.: Full connectivity: corners, edges and faces. J. Stat. Phys. 1–21 (2012)
8. Georgiou, O., Dettmann, C.P., Coon, J.P.: Connectivity of confined 3D networks with anisotropically radiating nodes. IEEE Trans. Wirel. Commun. **13**(8), 4534–4546 (2014)
9. Gerharz, M., Waal, C., Frank, M., Martini, P.: Link stability in mobile wireless ad hoc networks. In: IEEE Conference on Local Computer Networks, pp. 230–239 (2002)

10. Grossglauser, M., Tse, D.: Mobility increases the capacity of ad-hoc wireless networks. In: IEEE/ACM Transactions on Networking, pp. 477–486 (2002)
11. Guo, J., Durrani, S., Zhou, X.: Outage probability in arbitrarily shaped finite wireless networks. IEEE Trans. Commun. **62**(2), 699–712 (2014)
12. Gupta, P., Kumar, P.: The capacity of wireless networks. IEEE Trans. Inf. Theory **46**(2), 388–404 (2000)
13. Haenggi, M.: Diversity loss due to interference correlation. IEEE Commun. Lett. **16**(10), 1600–1603 (2012)
14. Karagiannidis, G.K.: Moments-based approach to the performance analysis of equal gain diversity in Nakagami-m fading. IEEE Trans. Commun. **52**(5), 685–690 (2004)
15. Korsnes, R., Ovsthus, K., Li, F.Y., Landmark, L., Kure, O.: Link lifetime prediction for optimal routing in mobile ad hoc networks. In: MILCOM, IEEE Military Communications Conference (2005)
16. Lenders, V., Wagner, J., May, M.: Analyzing the impact of mobility in ad hoc networks. In: Proceeding of International Workshop on Multi-hop Ad hoc Networks (2006)
17. Mesbahi, N., Dahmouni, H.: An efficient algorithm for traffic flow optimization in MPLS networks. In: International Conference on Protocol Engineering (ICPE) and International Conference on New Technologies of Distributed Systems (NTDS) (2015)
18. Mesbahi, N., Dahmouni, H.: Analytical framework for the characterization of the link properties in multi-hop mobile wireless networks. Ad-Hoc Netw. J. (2016). Elsevier
19. Parissidis, G., Karaliopoulos, M., May, M., Spyropoulos, T., Plattner, B.: Interference in wireless multihop networks: a model and its experimental evaluation. In: IEEE WoWMoM: World of Wireless, Mobile and Multimedia Networks, pp. 23–27 (2008)
20. Sadagopan, N., Bai, F., Krishnamachari, B., Helmy, A.: PATHS: analysis of PATH duration statistics and their impact on reactive MANET routing protocols. In: ACM International Symposium on Mobile Ad Hoc Networking and Computing (2003)
21. Samar, P., Wicker, S.B.: On the behavior of communication links of node in a multi-hop mobile environment. In: Proceedings ACM MobiHoc, pp. 145–156 (2004)
22. Schilcher, U., Bettstetter, C., Brandner, G.: Temporal correlation of interference in wireless networks with Rayleigh block fading. IEEE Trans. Mob. Comput. **11**(12), 2109–2120 (2012)
23. Tanbourgi, R., Dhillon, H., Andrews, J., Jondral, F.: Effect of spatial interference correlation on the performance of maximum ratio combining. IEEE Trans. Wirel. Commun. **13**(6), 43307–3316 (2014)
24. Zhao, M., Wang, W.: A unified mobility model for analysis and simulation of mobile wireless networks. Wirel. Netw. **15**(3), 365–389 (2009). ACM-Springer
25. Zhao, M., Wang, W.: Modeling and analytical study of link properties in multihop wireless networks. IEEE Trans. Commun. **60**(2), 445–455 (2012)

Mobile Edge Networking and Virtualization

A Multi-broker Cloud Architecture for the Purpose of Large Scale Sensing Applications Development

Soumaya Bel Hadj Youssef, Slim Rekhis(✉), and Noureddine Boudriga

Communication Networks and Security Research Laboratory,
University of Carthage, Tunis, Tunisia
youssef.soumaya@gmail.com, slim.rekhis@gmail.com,
noure.boudriga2@gmail.com

Abstract. In this paper, we propose a multi-broker cloud architecture for the purpose of large scale sensing applications development. A set of heterogeneous Sensor cloudlets are deployed everywhere to collect data and disseminate them to a set of known sink nodes. An Unmanned Aerial Vehicle (UAV) cloud is used for the purpose of data muling from sink nodes to data centers. In this work, we address the problem of optimal deployment of UAVs over the sky to serve the maximal possible number of incoming requests, maximize the connectivity between busy UAVs, and minimize the consumed UAV energy. A set of algorithms are provided for the re-deployment of idle UAVs, and the reallocation of data collection tasks of UAVs. A simulation is conducted to evaluate the proposal.

1 Introduction

Wireless Sensor Networks (WSNs) are intensively used for numerous environmental, healthcare, military and public safety applications [8] since they greatly enhance the capability of monitoring and controlling the physical environment. However, due to the severe shadowing caused by urban or mountainous terrain or the occurrence of accidents and natural disasters, many zones would suffer from lack of communication infrastructures. Moreover, mobile sensors carried by people or vehicles may be used to monitor the area. However, due to mobility, some groups could find themselves temporary unable to forward their data.

Depending on the requirements of the monitoring applications under execution, data collection requests (such as measures related to air quality in an area) may be generated toward sensor nodes for the purpose of data delivery. These sensors could belong to different WSNs which are located under different zones. In this context, it is very interesting to use sensor clouds [1] by forming cloudlets of sensors (static and mobile) managed by different brokers of WSNs. Through the use of sensor clouds, an application will have the opportunity to obtain various offers from many WSN brokers, and it becomes possible to dissociate such a monitoring application from the physical nodes in charge of data collection.

E. Sabir et al. (Eds.): UNet 2017, LNCS 10542, pp. 141–153, 2017.
https://doi.org/10.1007/978-3-319-68179-5_13

The integration of UAVs in WSNs and the use of UAVs as data mules has attracted a lot of interest, increasing the efficiency and scope of many monitoring applications [5]. Using UAV clouds for data collection is a promising solution for infrastructure-less areas where the deployment of sinks is very costly. The UAV cloud, managed by a broker [7], will be composed of a network of UAVs in charge of gathering data from the sensor cloud and cooperating together to relay them to one of the ground base stations. However, using UAVs for providing service of data collection from sensor clouds rises various challenges that need to be addressed, including loss of connectivity between UAVs which has potential negative consequences on the network performance. In fact, the movement of an UAV toward the request location may partition the UAV network into disjoint sub-networks and consequently prevent the connectivity between the UAVs. Thus, the efficient choice of the UAVs that will serve the requests and the appropriate scheduling of their movement are very crucial to minimize data delivery delay and energy consumption of UAVs.

In the literature, a variety of approaches have been produced for the restoration of connectivity under link or node failure or in case of movement of a node to respond to an occurring event. To overcome the connectivity, many research works exploited the mobility of nodes and chose an iterative process for nodes displacement. Least Distance Movement Recovery (LDMR) [2] exploited the existence of non cut-vertex nodes in the recovery process. When a node fails, its direct neighbors move toward its position while they get replaced by their nearest non cut-vertex nodes. It is very interesting that this approach exploited non critical nodes. However, it did not deal with the case of absence of non critical nodes in the neighborhood and also it required every node to maintain 2-hop neighbour information. On the other hand, some approaches such as Recovery through Inward Motion (RIM) [12], Volunteer-instigated Connectivity Restoration (VCR) [6], and Coverage Conscious Connectivity Restoration (C3R) [9] required each node to be only aware of its 1-hop neighbors. The main idea of RIM was that the neighbors of the failed node move towards it until they become connected. This procedure of relocation was recursively applied to handle any node that becomes disconnected. However, moving nodes inward may cause significant loss of coverage. Unlike RIM, the neighbors in VCR move towards the failed node while increasing their partially utilized transmission power until the failed node becomes connected. VCR applied a diffusion force among the volunteer nodes based on their transmission range. However, this diffusion is quite costly in terms of movement overhead. C3R cared for both connectivity and coverage without reconfiguring the network topology. The direct neighbors move back and forth to replace the failed node in order to provide intermittent rather than permanent restoration of connectivity. It is clearly that this solution leads to frequent topology changes, incurring a lot of overhead. All the aforementioned approaches are distributed and localized algorithms for recovery connectivity. However, this will be costly in terms of message overhead, especially in large-scale networks. To address this issue, we propose a centralized approach where an UAV broker takes all the decisions needed for the execution of the incoming requests, by selecting the suitable UAVs, optimally reorganizing the network to serve all the requests at the same time, and continuously supervising all the UAVs' state.

In this paper, we propose a multi-broker cloud architecture for the purpose of large scale sensing applications development. The architecture offers data collection services from heterogeneous cloudlets of WSNs that are scattered over an infrastructure-less area. Multiple brokers of WSNs and one broker of quadcopters responsible for muling and routing the requests, are used. Moreover, we provide techniques allowing to: (a) maximize the connectivity between busy UAVs; (b) optimize the movement of candidate idle UAVs to reduce their energy consumption; and (c) maximize the satisfaction rate of the incoming requests.

The paper contribution is three-fold. First, we propose an architecture composed of multi-brokers of sensor cloudlets allowing to develop a wide range of sensing applications, while calling for the use of a cooperative network of UAVs for the collection of data from heterogeneous sensor cloudlets that are deployed anywhere and do not provide the same types of sensing information. Second, we provide techniques for the selection of candidate UAVs that will participate in serving a new data collection request, by taking into account their positions, criticality, state engagement, and remaining energy. The system minimizes the displacements made by the candidates while ensuring the connectivity between the busy UAVs and the base stations. Third, we propose algorithms for the reconfiguration of the network topology of idle UAVs, while guaranteeing that all busy UAVs can still forward their data to one of the available base stations.

The remaining part of this paper is organized as follows. Section 2 describes the architecture of the designed system. Section 3 gives the formulation of our problem and Sect. 4 provides the solution. We present in Sect. 5 the results of the simulation. The last section concludes the work.

2 System Architecture

The proposed system architecture, described in Fig. 1, is composed of four layers. The first layer represents a sensor cloud composed of a set of scattered cloudlets of WSNs. Each cloudlet is composed of a network of sensors with limited resources, and a fixed collection point (sink) which has more computational and communication resources. The cloudlets can be (a) mobile, such as Wireless Body Area Networks (WBANs) carried by people, or (b) static, such as fixed WSNs deployed over the monitored area. Each WBAN is composed of a set of sensors (e.g., physiological and environmental sensors, a GPS receiver), and a hand-held device. All the data generated by the sensor cloudlet are transmitted to a fixed collection point. The cloudlets do not communicate with each other due to the large operation area. Each cloudlet is managed by a WSN broker which allows to dynamically control and configure the sensors depending on the user's demand. Moreover, the broker can virtualize the physical resources through the creation and management of virtual sensors.

The second layer consists of an UAV cloud which is composed of a network of UAVs, a set of base stations, and a set of maintenance centers. The UAVs form an ad hoc network enabling a wide coverage and deployment. Their main mission is to provide data collection service to the requests arriving from the end users. These users are using applications that require collecting data from the cloudlets of WSNs and relaying them to a base station, so that they can be transmitted to the applications over the network backbone. This cloud is managed by a broker of quadcopters which acts as an intermediary between the users and the UAV network. Its main function is to receive the requests from the users and determine the best UAVs that will participate in serving the requests.

The third layer represents the services which will be executed. They require a periodic data collection from the ground sensors which may belong to different brokers of WSNs. All the gathered data are firstly transmitted to the collection points, then collected by the UAVs, and finally sent to the users.

The last layer represents the end users, which use one of the offered service periodically induce it to generate data collection requests.

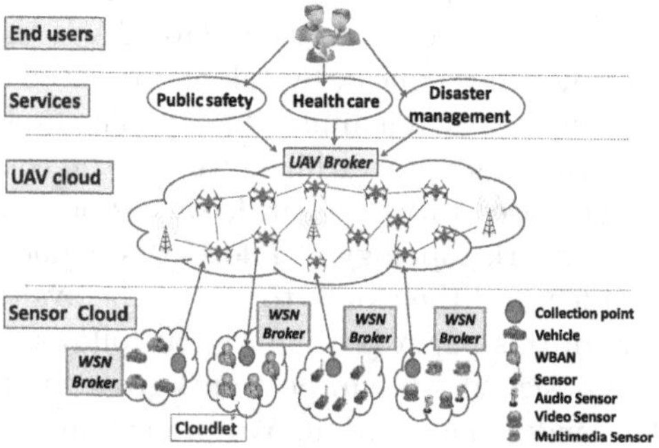

Fig. 1. System architecture

To exemplify our architecture, we consider an air pollution monitoring application. In fact, the public concern on air pollution is significantly increasing due the serious threat to public health, global environment, and worldwide economy. There are hundreds of hazardous pollutants which can be emitted by human activities and natural sources [11]. A sensor cloudlet may be (i) a set of static sensors usually mounted on the streetlight or traffic light poles, or deployed on carefully selected locations; (ii) a set of WBANs (composed of a set of low-cost ambient sensors and smart phones) carried by public or professional users, usually by volunteers who are enthusiastic for preserving air quality; (iii) a set of mobile sensors which are typically carried by the public transportation or specially equipped cars. In each cloudlet, a fixed collection point will be available to receive and buffer all the sensed data until an UAV visits it and gathers them. In fact, following a request by the user, an UAV will be chosen by the UAV broker.

3 Problem Formulation

In our work, we address a dynamic problem where we consider a set of requests generated at any time, and a self-organized network of n UAVs moving over the sky and cooperating together to serve these requests and relay the data. Let $r = (D, CP_1, \ldots, CP_K)$ be a data collection request, where D is its duration and $CP = \{CP_1, CP_2, \ldots CP_K\}$ is the possible set of collection points.

The inter-UAV topology can be modeled as a graph $G = (U, E)$, where U is the set of UAVs, and E is the set of edges. Each UAV has a unique static identity ID and knows its position within the network topology. At each instant, an UAV has two possible engagement states: busy or idle. An UAV is busy when it is collecting data from a collection point, so that it is not able to move. However, an idle UAV can move even if it is relaying data. We also assume that each UAV is able to compute its residual energy. To resume, we can say that each UAV $u \in U$ has the following characteristics at each instant: *position*, *engagement state*, and *remaining energy*. These characteristics vary with time. All the UAVs are assumed to have the same communication range R. Two UAVs u_i and u_j are considered as neighbors of each other if $(u_i, u_j) \in E$ and $dist(u_i, u_j) \leq R$. The set $N_i = \{u_j \mid (u_i, u_j) \in E\}$ is the set of u_i's neighbors, and $|N_i|$ is defined as the connectivity degree of node u_i. For simplicity, we assume that all the UAVs fly at the same height and with the same speed. Let $P = \{p_i = (x_i, y_i)\}$, $i = 1, 2, \ldots n$, be the set of coordinate positions of UAVs. We denote by p_i the coordinates of an UAV before changing its position, and by $\tilde{p}_i = (\tilde{x}_i, \tilde{y}_i)$ be its coordinates after moving the position required to serve the new received request.

In our proposed work, the busy UAVs cannot participate in serving the incoming requests and only idle UAVs are engaged to handle these requests. Also, we assume that the broker of quadcopters holds the information about all the UAVs (e.g., position, state engagement, remaining energy), the location of the base stations and the collection points. Thus, our problem will be solved in a centralized way. In other words, the broker will be responsible of finding the optimal solution. Firstly, it selects the UAVs candidates. Secondly, it computes the new positions of the candidates. Then, it orders them to move toward these new positions. In fact, the first candidate is the UAV which will move toward the location of the request to collect data from a possible collection point, and the other candidates will act as relay nodes in order to forward data to the base station. The main issue to be taken into consideration is how to serve and relay the request while maintaining the connectivity of all the busy UAVs.

Our problem consists in determining the set of UAVs that should participate in serving a request r, while maintaining the connectivity between the busy UAVs and the base station. Serving a request should minimize the total distance traveled by the UAVs, and should reduce to the maximum possible the execution time of the request. Such an execution time is the sum of: (1) *reconfiguration time*, which is the time needed for the reconfiguration of the network (i.e., UAV displacement); (2) *collection time*, which is the time needed for collecting data from the collection point; and (3) *data forwarding time*, which is the time required to forward data from the collection point to the base station.

Finding a solution S_r to a request r can be described as follows. Firstly, for each possible collection point $CP_i, i \in [1 \dots K]$, we aim to find the solution that minimizes the number of candidate UAVs to move among the set U of available UAVs, and the total distance traversed by each one of them, so that the execution delay of the request will not exceed a threshold delay $\mathcal{D}$, and the total connectivity between the busy UAVs and the base stations remains possible. Then, we try to find the absolute minimum of the solutions computed for each collection point. A solution S_r to the request r can be mathematically formulated as follows: $S_{r,CP_i} = min\left(\underset{u_x \in U}{\cup}\{u_x,\, m_x\}\right)$ $such\, that:\ D_{S_{r,CP_i}} \leq \mathcal{D}$, where m_x is the displacement made by the UAV x from an initial position $p_{x,\,s}$ (before relocation) to a final position $p_{x,\,f}$ (after relocation). The solution will be considered only if the UAVs that will serve the request have enough remaining energy (i.e., the UAVs can move to the new positions, collect and relay data).

4 Problem Solving

In this section, we describe the techniques used to solve the described problem.

4.1 Non-cut-vertex Idle UAVs Movement

We classify the UAVs into two types: cut-vertex and non cut-vertex. An UAV is considered as a cut-vertex, if it is moved toward the location of the request, the UAV network will be partitioned into isolated islands. In the opposite, an UAV is considered as a non cut-vertex (leaf or intermediate), if moving it from the current to the new position will not affect the UAV network connectivity (i.e., each connected can still forward its data to a base station). Only idle and non cut-vertex nodes are assigned to handle a given request (one UAV for collecting data and some other UAVs for relaying) since their movement does not impact the inter-UAV connectivity. In the sequel, these nodes will be called participating nodes or candidate nodes. The first candidate to be ordered to move toward the location of the request (i.e., the location of one possible collection point) is the UAV which has the shortest distance from the request. This allows to better save the energy of idle nodes. Then, from the new position of the first candidate, we search the nearest node from it having a link to the connected UAV network, and we construct the direct segment separating these two nodes. Finally, we compute the length of this segment (L) in order to determine the required number of idle node relays (L/R). After the phase of selection, the broker will firstly compute the new positions of the candidates and then order them to move toward these new positions. The selection of only non cut-vertex idle nodes as candidates is very beneficial in terms of connectivity and energy. However, it is applied only in case of availability of the required number of candidates, say $(1 + L/R)$.

4.2 Topology Reconfiguration of Idle UAVs

In this sub-section, we propose our second solution which is applied in case of unavailability of required number of non-cut-vertex idle nodes. It consists in reconfiguring the topology of idle UAVs, in order to maximize the availability of idle nodes that will serve the arrived requests. The idea is to: (a) remove all the idle nodes with their edges from the network, so that the busy UAVs will become isolated and will form separated islands, where each island will be composed of a set of busy UAVs; (b) compute the needed number of idle nodes in order to connect the isolated islands of busy nodes; and (c) add the required number of idle UAVs to the network of busy UAVs in the new computed positions, while minimizing the total movement of nodes. Our problem can be solved by determining the solution to the following three sub-problems.

(1) Number of isolated islands and their compositions: when the broker of quadcopters removes the idle nodes, the busy UAVs become disconnected and form separated sub-networks. Each island will represent a sub-graph (i.e., connected component) composed of a set of busy connected UAVs. We use the Breadth-First Search (BFS) traversal algorithm to find the connected components in our undirected graph G. Starting from an arbitrary vertex v, all the vertices reached from v will be visited, and the other connected components will still be non-visited vertices after the graph traversal is complete. Then, another traversal is started from one of those non-visited vertices in order to find other connected components. The process continues until all the vertices will be visited. The details are given in Algorithm 1.

Algorithm 1. Number of islands and their compositions

Input: graph G after removing idle nodes
Output : number of connected components and the list of nodes that form each connected component

```
For i = 1 to NbBusy
  Visited [i] = false // Mark all the busy UAV nodes as non-visited
  NbComp = 0 //for counting connected components
  For v = 1 to NbBusy
   //if v is not yet visited, it's the start of a newly discovered connected component containing v
    If (Visited [v] == false) // Process the component that contains v
     NbComp = NbComp + 1
     Display NbComp
     Create empty queue Q // For implimenting a breadth-first traversal
     Enqueue (Q, v) //Start the traversal from vertex v
     Visited [v] = true
     While (Q is not empty)
      w = dequeue (Q) // w is a node in this component
      Display w
      For each edge from w to some vertex k
       If (Visited [k] == false) // Finding another node in this component
        Visited [k] = true
        Enqueue(Q, k)
       EndIf
      EndFor
     EndWhile
    EnIf
  EndFor
EndFor
```

(2) Convex Hull linking all the islands: in the literature, numerous algorithms were proposed to compute the convex hull of a finite set of points. We choose the Quick Hull algorithm [3], which adopts a divide and conquer approach similar to that of the QuickSort sorting procedure [4]. In our solution, we are interested in determining the convex hull that links the islands, by minimizing the obtained polygon area. To achieve this, first, we construct the barycenter of all the busy nodes. Second, for each connected component, we compute the distances between each node belonging to the component and the barycenter. Third, we choose the node having the closest distance. This node contributes to obtain a minimum area of the convex hull and will be called hereafter the head node of the connected component. Let $HNs = \{h_1, h_2, \ldots, h_k\}$ be the set of head nodes. The Quick Hull algorithm will determine the polygon $Poly_1$ that links these head nodes, and determines the set of vertices forming the polygon. Let $S = \{v_1, v_2, \ldots, v_s\} = QuickHull\ (HNs)$ be the set of vertices that forms the polygon.

(3) Cover tree: determining the cover tree consists in finding the required set of idle nodes that will be inserted inside the polygon to cover all the islands with the shortest path. Starting with an arbitrary vertex $v_i \in S$, we check if there are other nodes (busy or idle) in the neighborhood of v_i. If it is the case, we remove the current vertex from the list and we construct the new polygon. If it is not the case, we first construct the angle bisector of the angle $\angle v_{i-1}v_iv_{i+1}$. Second, we construct the new point p in this bisector having a length R from v_i, and it will be added to the required list. The segment $[v_i, p]$ represents the new constructed edge. Then, we construct the new convex hull after adding the new constructed node and removing the current vertex v_i. This process is repeated to all the vertices of the polygon $Poly_1$ and at each time a new convex hull will be constructed. After visiting all the vertices, the same approach will be repeated to the new vertices, until we obtain a polygon having two vertices of distance $\leq R$. Our approach is illustrated in Fig. 2, and is detailed in Algorithm 2.

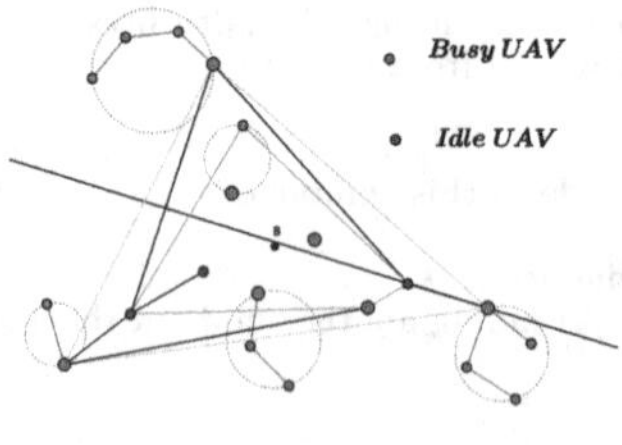

Fig. 2. Cover tree

Algorithm 2. Cover tree

```
Input : G, P = S ∪ nodes of connected components inside poly1
Output : minimum list L of idle nodes covering the separated islands
i = 1
count = 0 //count the required number of idle nodes
poly [1] = poly1
While (length (V_poly [i]) > 2)
 V_poly [i]= QuickHull (P) //set of vertices of poly [i]
 For each vertex v_i in V_poly [i]
  If v_i has neighbor nodes whether idle or busy
   P = P \ {v_i} //remove v_i from P
   V_poly [i]= QuickHull (P) //construct a new convex hull
  Else
   construct the bisector of the angle ∠v_{i-1}v_iv_{i+1} //v_{i-1}, v_i, and v_{i+1} are 3 consecutive vertices
   construct a point p in the bisector distant R from v_i
   If p is out of poly [i]
    remove p
    P = P \ {v_i} //remove v_i from P
    V_poly [i]= QuickHull (P) //construct a new convex hull
   Else
    newvertex = p
    P = P ∪ {newvertex} \ {v_i}//add p to P and remove v_i from P
    V_poly [i]= QuickHull (P) //construct a new convex hull
    add newvertex to L
    count = count + 1
    E = E ∪ new edge//add a new edge to E
    U = U ∪ newvertex
   EndIf
  EndIf
 EndFor
 i = i + 1
EndWhile
```

5 Simulation and Results

In this section, we aim to analyze the performance of our proposed models. The simulation environment is developed using Matlab. The deployment area is a square of length 120 m where two base stations are placed diagonally at the corners. We divide the whole area into a grid of 25 equal square sub-areas, and a collection point is deployed in the center of each sub-area. The duration of the request is between 30 and 180 s. We assume that a collection point can not be occupied by more than one UAV during the collection of data.

To evaluate the performance of our models, we use the following metrics: (a) Request rejection rate, which is the ratio between the number of rejected requests and the number of incoming requests. A request is rejected when the number of idle UAVs required to link the islands of the busy UAVs is not available; and (b) Average UAV energy consumption, which is the sum of energy consumed by all the UAVs per hour, divided by the number of quadcopters. The energy consumed by an UAV is the total travel energy consumed during its movement in addition to the communication energy [10] consumed during data reception and transmission. Thus, we can write: $E_{UAV} = E_{travel} + E_{Tx} + E_{Rx}$, where:

- $E_{travel} = E_d \times \sum_{i=1}^{nb_{relays}} \| \tilde{p_i} - p_i \|^2$, where p_i and $\tilde{p_i}$ are the positions before and after movement. E_d is the amount of battery energy consumed per distance unit.

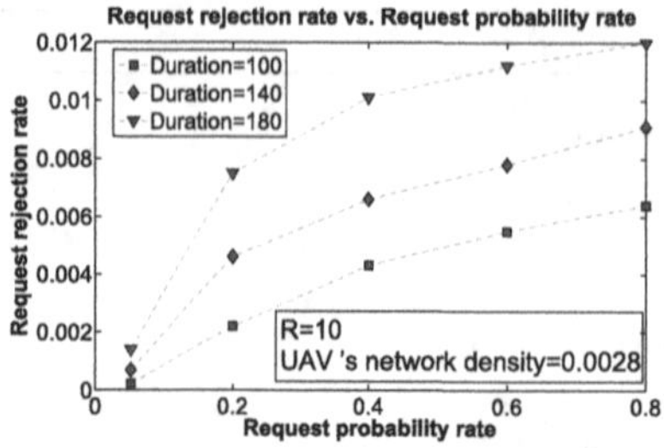

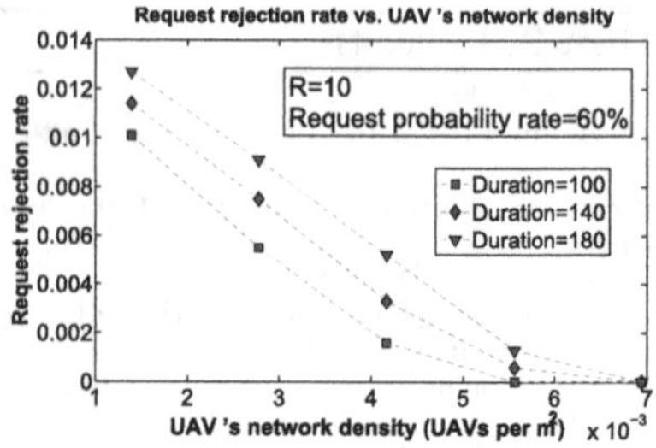

(a) Request rejection rate vs. probability rate (b) Rejection rate vs. UAV 's network density

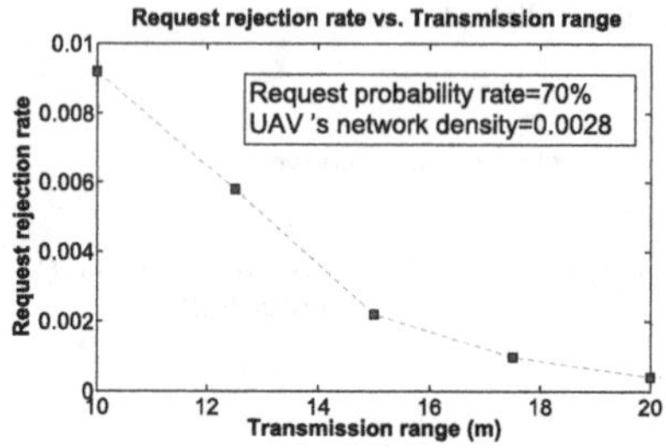

(c) Rejection rate vs. Transmission range

Fig. 3. Request rejection rate

- $E_{Rx} = (nb_{relays} - 1) \times Q \times E_{elec}$, where $Q = D \times Rate_{Tx}$ is the quantity of data to be collected and D is the request duration. E_{elec} is the electronics energy.
- $E_{Tx} = (nb_{relays} - 1) \times Q \times \left(E_{elec} + \epsilon_{fs} d_{BS}^2\right)$, where d_{BS} is the distance between the base station and the last UAV of the path connected to the base station. ϵ_{fs} is the amplifier coefficient.

Therefore, the energy E_{UAV} consumed by an UAV will be given by:

$$E_{UAV} = E_d \times \sum_{i=1}^{nb_{relays}} \parallel \tilde{p_i} - p_i \parallel^2 + (nb_{relays} - 1) \times D \times Rate_{Tx} \times \left(2E_{elec} + \epsilon_{fs} d_{BS}^2\right)$$

The values of the rate and energy model parameters are extracted from [10] by choosing the Aerosonde unmanned aerial vehicle. In the following, we describe the results of our simulation. In the first simulation, as shown in Fig. 3, we simulated the request rejection rate with respect to: (a) the request probability rate; (b) the UAV network density; and (c) the transmission range. As depicted in Fig. 3a, the request rejection rate increases with the increase of the request probability rate. In this simulation, we are interested in assessing the effect of increasing the request duration, on the variation of the request rejection rate. Three values of duration were considered. We observe that the more we increase the duration of the request, the higher will be the rejection rate of incoming requests. For the three considered values of duration, the request rejection rate increases fastly at first and then starts to increase slowly. In fact, when the

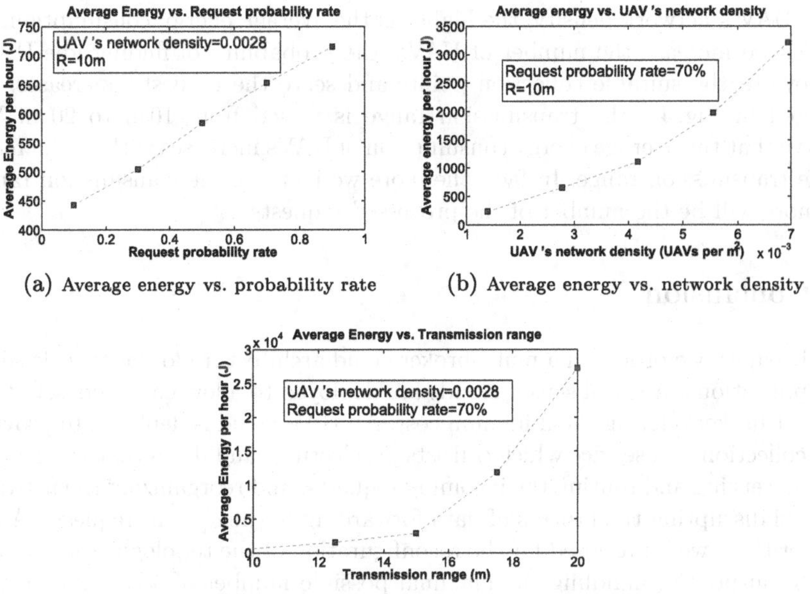

(a) Average energy vs. probability rate

(b) Average energy vs. network density

(c) Average energy vs. Transmission range

Fig. 4. Average UAV energy consumption

probability rate of incoming requests is low, the number of busy UAVs will be low and hence the chance that a request becomes rejected will be low. As shown in Fig. 3b, we evaluated the request rejection rate with respect to the UAV's network density, for different values of request duration. The UAV's network density is varied from 0.0014 to 0.0069 UAVs per m^2. The request rejection rate decreases with the increase of the density of the UAV network, until it reaches zero. In fact, the higher is the number of UAVs, the higher will be the probability of being able to serve the request. Moreover, we observe that the more we decrease the duration of the request, the less will be the rejection rate of the incoming requests. As shown in Fig. 3c, we simulated the request rejection rate with respect to the transmission range, which is varied from 10 m to 20 m. We observe that the higher is the transmission range of UAVs the lower is the request rejection rate. In fact, when we increase the transmission range, we will require less relay UAVs.

In the second simulation, as shown in Fig. 4, we evaluated the average UAV energy consumption per hour with respect to: (a) the request probability rate; (b) the UAV's network density; and (c) the UAV transmission range. As depicted in Fig. 4a, the request probability rate is varied from 10% to 90%. We observe that the higher is the probability rate of the incoming requests, the higher is the energy consumption. Indeed, when the rate of probability is high, the number of requests to be served will be high. As shown in Fig. 4b, the UAV's network density is varied from 0.0014 to 0.0069 UAVs per m^2. We observe that the higher is the UAV's network density, the higher is the average energy consumption. In fact, as we increase the number of UAVs, the probability of finding idle UAVs to move to the suitable collection points and serve the requests, increases. As depicted in Fig. 4c, the transmission range is varied from 10 m to 20 m. We observe that the average energy consumption of UAVs increases with the increase of the transmission range. In fact, the more we increase the transmission range the more will be the number of the processed requests.

6 Conclusion

In this paper, we proposed a multi-broker cloud architecture for large scale sensing applications. A set of sensor clouds are deployed to allow end-users selecting the best broker offering the minimum cost. An UAV cloud is deployed to provide data collection as a service which consists in selecting candidates that will participate in serving and routing the incoming requests, and reorganizing the network to avoid disrupting the process of data forwarding of the current requests. A set of algorithms were proposed for the reconfiguration of the topology of idle UAVs for the purpose of handling the maximal possible number of arriving requests. We evaluated the performance of our proposed models, by assessing the request rejection rate and the average UAV energy consumption. The simulation results showed that our proposed work generates a low request rejection rate.

References

1. Alamri, A., Ansari, W.S., Hassan, M.M., Hossain, M.S., Alelaiwi, A., Hossain, M.A.: A survey on sensor-cloud: architecture, applications, and approaches. Int. J. Distrib. Sens. Netw. **9**(2) (2013)
2. Alfadhly, A., Baroudi, U., Younis, M.: Least distance movement recovery approach for large scale wireless sensor and actor networks. In: 7th International Wireless Communications and Mobile Computing Conference (IWCMC), pp. 2058–2063, July 2011
3. Barber, C.B., Dobkin, D.P., Huhdanpaa, H.: The quickhull algorithm for convex hulls. ACM Trans. Math. Softw. **22**(4), 469–483 (1996)
4. Dean, B.C.: A simple expected running time analysis for randomized "divide and conquer" algorithms. Discret. Appl. Math. **154**, 1–5 (2006)
5. Hayat, S., Yanmaz, E., Muzaffar, R.: Survey on unmanned aerial vehicle networks for civil applications: a communications viewpoint. IEEE Commun. Surv. Tutor. **18**(4), 2624–2661 (2016)
6. Imran, M., Younis, M., Said, A.M., Hasbullah, H.: Volunteer-instigated connectivity restoration algorithm for wireless sensor and actor networks. In: IEEE International Conference on Wireless Communications, Networking and Information Security (WCNIS), pp. 679–683, June 2010
7. Mahmoud, S., Mohamed, N.: Broker architecture for collaborative UAVs cloud computing. In: International Conference on Collaboration Technologies and Systems (CTS), pp. 212–219, June 2015

8. Stankovic, J.A., Wood, A.D., He, T.: Realistic applications for wireless sensor networks. In: Nikoletseas, S., Rolim, J. (eds.) Theoretical Aspects of Distributed Computing in Sensor Networks. Monographs in Theoretical Computer Science. An EATCS Series, pp. 835–863. Springer, Heidelberg (2010). doi:10.1007/978-3-642-14849-1_25
9. Tamboli, N., Younis, M.: Coverage-aware connectivity restoration in mobile sensor networks. Netw. Comput. Appl. **33**(4), 363–374 (2010)
10. Tirta, Y., Lau, B., Malhotra, N., Bagchi, S., Li, Z., Lu, Y.-H.: Controlled mobility for efficient data gathering in sensor networks with passively mobile nodes. In: Sensor Network Operations, Wiley-IEEE Press (2006)
11. Yi, W.Y., Lo, K.M., Mak, T., Leung, K.S., Leung, Y., Meng, M.L.: A survey of wireless sensor network based air pollution monitoring systems. Sensors **12**, 31392–31427 (2015)
12. Younis, M.F., Lee, S., Abbasi, A.A.: A localized algorithm for restoring internode connectivity in networks of moveable sensors. Localized Algorithm Restoring Internode Connect. Netw. Moveable Sens. **59**(12), 1669–1682 (2010)

A Simulation Framework for IT Governance in the Context of Corporate Relocation

Rabii El Ghorfi[1(✉)], Mohamed El Aroussi[2], Mohamed Ouadou[1], and Driss Aboutajdine[1]

[1] Mohammed V-Rabat University, FSR, LRIT Associated Unit to the CNRST, Rabat, Morocco
rabii.elghorfi@outlook.com
[2] EHTP Engineering School, Casablanca, Morocco

Abstract. This research develops a varied set of techniques for making the right IT investment decisions in the context of an effective IT (Information Technology) governance. The progress of strategic governance objectives is managed with the help of the notions of gap and adjustment levers. A real-time decisional framework based on ROA (Real Options Analysis) is proposed to generate investment decisions in different configurations. This modeling approach stands out by simulating governance strategies in the conditions of the relocation. Thus, various scenarios are generated in both the current and new (post-relocation) environments via a Monte Carlo simulation.

Keywords: Information technology · Governance · Organization relocation · Modeling · Information systems · Real options theory · Monte Carlo

1 Introduction

IT governance is the combination of monitoring i.e. ensuring that today's decisions prepare tomorrow properly, and control i.e. measuring the gap in comparison to what was expected [12]. IT governance suggests the construction of a proper board based on control elements that can be measured in terms of their implementation so as to anticipate changes and rising issues. Measurement and accountabilities are critical to any good governance design [12]. The elaboration of IT strategies generates IT goals and IT projects. The study of the behaviors of IT projects is crucial in the decision making process, and more generally to reach effective IT governance.

A project which embeds real options offers managers the opportunity but not the obligation to adjust the future direction of the project in response to internal or external risks. ROA (Real Options Analysis) presents an attractive alternative because it explicitly accounts for the value of future flexibility in management decision making [9]. In the ROA literature, IT investments are valuated through option pricing models allowing the most profitable option to be identified [8–10, 17]. Within the framework of ROA, the cash flow of a project is continuously monitored and adjusted regarding the expected real option value. ROA thus allows an organization to assess uncertain IT investments and more importantly, it offers a framework that assumes that decision makers take a proactive stance to manage risk on IT projects [17].

E. Sabir et al. (Eds.): UNet 2017, LNCS 10542, pp. 154–165, 2017.
https://doi.org/10.1007/978-3-319-68179-5_14

This paper focuses on two main issues. The first one is the design and the implementation of a real options simulation model for IT governance decisions aiming for a known strategic objective. The second issue is the application of this model to appreciate the impact of the relocation of an organization on the IT. Relocation is a major event in the course of live of an organization. It determines the future operating environment which can have a significant impact on productivity, efficiency, workforce satisfaction, and the overall business objectives [19]. Choosing a new site and relocating thereto depends on the type and the size of the organization and possibly also the age [7]. This study emphasizes that analyzing IT governance strategies and their derived IT goals could highlight possible advantages and disadvantages of the relocation.

The contribution of this paper is to provide decision makers with the tools they need to predict the exact benefits of moving all IT resources to a new location or otherwise. The purpose is to implement a simulation platform that can replicate IT investment decisions in the new environment to compare both environments thus assessing the outcome of the relocation. For such needs, the traditional ROA framework is extended in a way that it will be capable of valuating simultaneously intangible value drivers and nonfinancial resources. IT resources are studied in a strategic level based on the related managerial literature [13, 14]. IT governance strategies are split into successive IT goals and monitored with the help of the notions of gap and adjustment levers [1, 3, 12, 16]. The proposed framework aims at elaborating the best investment strategy through consecutive investment decisions. These decisions are generated in two environments which are the old locations of an organization and its new one.

This article is organized as follows: Sect. 2 aims at defining the study area and data as well as IT governance notions, whereas Sect. 3 introduces the framework and discusses its potential to simulate investment decisions in the relocation conditions. Section 4 reports the experimental outcome of the framework, while a conclusion is drawn in Sect. 5.

2 Study Area and Data

2.1 Organization Resources Distribution

The case study is about an organization which its current information system is dispatched in several sites in the same city. This organization conducts research and other academic activities and intends to relocate from its existing sites to a new modern and larger facility. IT resources of this organization are scattered over five different locations L_i (i = 1 to 5) and mainly based in two sites: L_3 and L_5. As suggested in [13, 14, 20], IT resources can fall into four main categories R_i (i = 1 to 4): informational, human, technical and financial resources. These resources are related to the handling and the management of current IT projects. The simultaneous availability of each of the previous resources may be necessary for the proper completion of a project.

In the following, note that R_1 stands for: the informational resources, R_2 the human resources, R_3 the technical resources and R_4 the financial resources. Informational resources constitute all the resources related to the delivery of the information, whereas technical resources encompass the processes, the materials and the technologies which support the organization day-to-day running. Officers and company personnel - researchers, professors, engineers, administrative employees and other staff members-move regularly between sites in order to perform their tasks. This thus engenders several daily journeys leading to waste of time, effort and money. Financial resources are related to the site operating budget which often includes rental charges. The two studied configurations -the old one and the new one- are displayed in the following figure.

In the current configuration, IT projects depend on resources spread over several sites, while in the second configuration there is only one site Fig. 1. We consider that an IT project is the combination of the resources it uses and the objectives it meets The evolution of its portfolios is carried out through managing resources -software and human- and risks [13]. The objective is to study the gain from pooling resources.

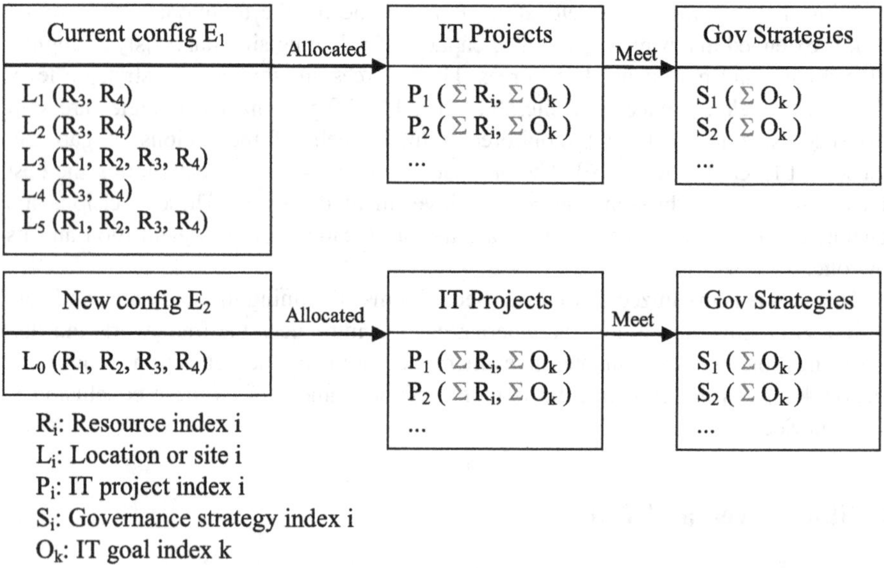

Fig. 1. IT resources distribution among the two configurations.

2.2 IT Governance Notions

In order to study the two preset configurations, we propose to model IT governance strategies S_i among the STOPE approach (Strategy, Technology, Organization, People and Environment) which is considered a basic generic IT governance requirement as seen in Table 1. Strategies are unbundled into consecutive short term objectives O_i which will be named IT goals. We support the idea of a scoreboard containing a set of control elements enabling to control the formulation and implementation of IT strategies [3]. To this end, the degree of importance and implementation of each control element determines the achievement of its related IT goal.

Table 1. IT governance strategies among the STOPE approach

IT Strategies		IT control elements (metrics)		IT goals	
S_1	The policy emphasizes human resources satisfaction and knowledge sharing	m_1	Correctly assigning responsibility for decision making	O_1	A partial implementation of m_1, m_2, m_3
		m_2	Correctly assigning responsibility and job description of IT personnel		
		m_3	Establishing "knowledge sharing" among all the people	O_2	A complete implementation of m_1, m_2, m_3
S_2	The policy considers effectiveness: cost: budgeting versus benefits: deliverables	m_4	Awareness level of IT benefits among decision makers	O_3	A partial implementation of m_4, m_5, m_6
		m_5	Awareness level of IT benefits among non-IT staff: users		
		m_6	IT governance responds to problems enabling business continuity	O_4	A complete implementation of m_4, m_5, m_6
S_3	The organization has a documented & communicated IT governance policy	m_7	Documentation is available of IT and IT related components, operation, projects, and cost	O_5	A partial implementation of m_7, m_8
		m_8	Documentation is available of the impact of IT use on business requirements	O_6	A complete implementation of m_7, m_8
S_4	The policy sets-up technology standards for required services	m_9	IT governance ensures secure environment for IT activities	O_7	A partial implementation of m_9, m_{10}, m_{11}, m_{12}
		m_{10}	Integration of services is available: internal level and external level		
		m_{11}	Standards are used for required services: acquiring and operating technology		
		m_{12}	IT infrastructure is suitable for servicing business requirements	O_8	A complete implementation of m_9, m_{10}, m_{11}, m_{12}

We caution that Table 1 is not an exhaustive list of all possible control elements. Strategies are considered as a mainstay of IT governance. So far as the target is moving, and depending on the situation of the overall resources, the decision maker is responsible for the corrective action levers. The notion of gap is used to model the achievement of an IT strategy in comparison to what was expected. As suggested in [12], the gap is computed by determining the difference between an IT goal (expected value) and its related IT control element (current state). The gap of a metric m_i related to an IT goal O_k can be expressed as such:

$$Gap(t) = O_k - m_i(t) \quad (1)$$

The adjustment levers reside in the ability to reduce the gap and regulate the investments. In compliance with effective IT governance precepts, decision makers have the ability to change the strategic objectives while they are monitoring their achievement. This concept can be modeled by the reduction or otherwise the increase in the initial values of O_k through successive additions. It thus enables strategic objectives to be reappraised at any time by the decision maker.

2.3 Data Collection

All the data was collected from the organization through audit related documents or direct interviews with officials in charge of the IT matter. In order to obtain an effective assessment of the IT, communication, collaboration and serene relationships between all parties are required [1]. The evaluation method requires collecting the maximum data possible so as to obtain the most accurate estimate of the valuation of IT resources as a whole. The assessment of resources follows a simple evaluation chart in which each assessment task is weighted with an importance coefficient and valuated through the number of times the assessment is conducted. Table 2 shows an example of the assessment of a resource R_i with the proposed method.

Table 2. Example of an assessment of a resource R_i

Assessment tasks	Number of times	Weight	Financial value
The interviews with IT staff	3	3	150 k
The interviews with external	2	1	200 k
Internal audit documents	3	2	120 K
External audit documents	2	2	100 K

Data gathered will be used in different scenarios aiming at illustrating different situations in which IT projects respond to strategic objectives in several sites. At the end, IT projects will be simulated in both the old and new configurations.

3 Proposed Investment Framework

3.1 Real Options

ROA starts with the idea that options on financial assets can be transferred to real investments on project assets [5]. It offers the possibility to study risk management of IT projects from an economic and financial perspective by linking risk, flexibility and economic value [17]. A real option itself is the right but not the obligation to undertake certain business initiatives, such as deferring, abandoning, expanding, staging, or contracting a capital investment of a project. The right timing for making the investments is particularly crucial to achieve higher returns. Trigeorgis [15] highlights the main real options that could be implemented in project management. Examples of these different types of real options include the option to invest, withhold, abort and the 'wait and see' option to be used in this paper.

The investment in IT projects should rather be modeled as an American call option [6] which allows to invest before the option expires unlike the European option. The valuation of the underlying options thus defined in ROA traditionally relies on the standard BSM (Black Scholes Model), described in [4]. A quantity called NPV (Net Present Value) is computed as a stochastic optimization problem aiming to maximize it. The BSM is based on continuous time and assumes that the benefit follows a Wiener process in which options evolve according to continuous stochastic processes, more precisely GBM (Geometric Brownian Motions) processes. Further information on Brownian motions within finance can be found in [2]. As mentioned in [8], the value of a call option is defined by its discounted excepted terminal value E[St]. In the case of continuous time with the assumption of the complete market, the NPV can be expressed as such:

$$NPV = E_Q\left[\int S_t(\mu, \sigma)e^{-r_f t}dt\right] \tag{2}$$

S_t: Share value where
μ: Drift parameter
σ: Diffusion coefficient
r_f: Risk free interest rate.
E_Q: Risk neutrality expectation

As shown in Eq. 2, the NPV depends on the three parameters: μ, σ and r_f. To solve this equation, ITO formulas are often used [2] and new expressions of volatility and drift parameter are thus retrieved.

3.2 Proposed Decision Algorithm

The purpose of this research is to predict the evolution of IT projects with the help of a simulation environment that can replicate investment decisions in different configurations, in this instance the configurations E_1 and E_2. The proposed algorithm generates, in a given time interval, a set of decisions meeting preset IT goals aiming at achieving preset IT strategies. The impact of these decisions on IT resources can be observed in terms of availability and present value at each site. Finally, this approach will allow decision makers to assess both configurations of IT resources and conclude whether the relocation is beneficial or not.

The algorithm developed for the simulation is implemented in a C#. NET application which provides a series of statistical and financial tools through the windows sharp control framework. The principle of the simulation is to create a variety of scenarios associated with different evolutions of NPVs of IT projects. This process embodies the very core of the Monte Carlo method as mentioned in [18]. At the end of each scenario, a set of decisions aiming at reducing the gap and maximizing the NPVs are generated. Figure 2 highlights the proposed modeling approach. It encompasses three main stages: before, during and after the simulation.

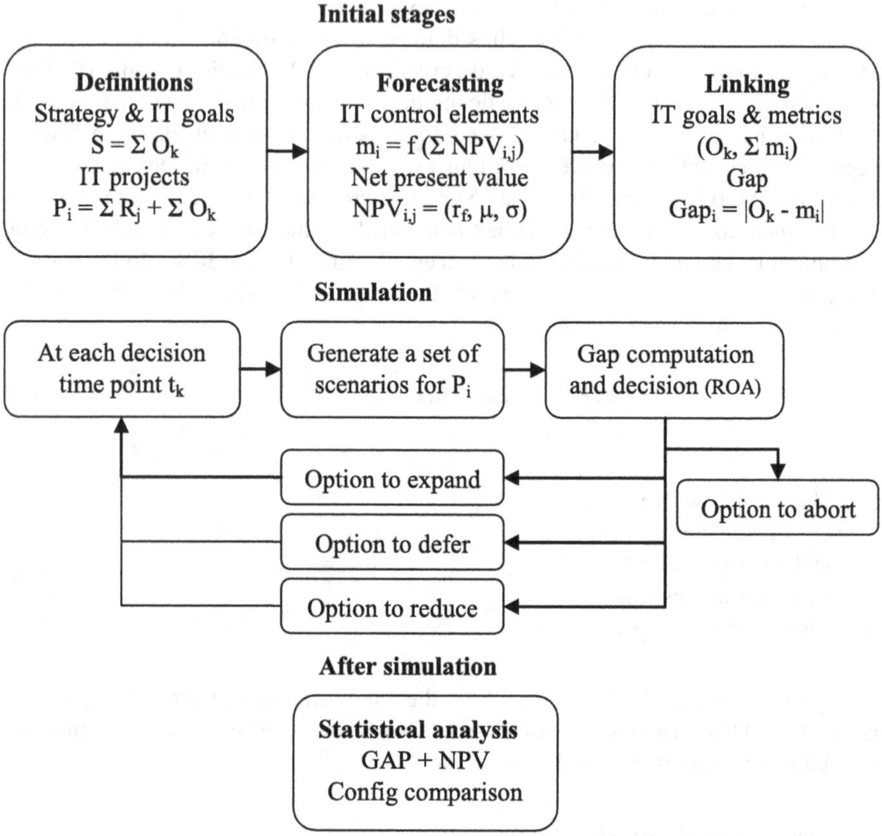

Fig. 2. Design of the decision problem.

Initial stages: The first step in the initial stages is to define the studied IT governance strategy from a set of IT goals over a period of time. This period is split into consecutive decision points (t_k). IT projects are also defined from the resources they use and the objectives they pursue. The second step consists of forecasting the metrics of strategic objectives based on the state of resources, in particular the NPV of each resource of each site. The notation $NPV_{i,j}$ refers to the net present value of a resource R_i of a site L_j. The second step also aims at retrieving NPV parameters via estimation methods. In the last step, desired values of the implementation of each IT goal O_k at each time point t_k are proposed with the collaboration of the IT staff. These reference values measure whether the objectives that have been assigned to an IT project or its portfolio are met. The notion of gap is proposed in order to compute the progress of strategic objectives.

Simulation: At this point, the studied IT strategy and its related IT projects and IT goals are well defined. The control elements and net present values are ready to be estimated at each time point t_k. The simulation starts with the generation of a set of random values of projects NPVs from Eq. (2). A single scenario related to a specific evolution of IT projects is hereby launched. Then, the gap between the current state $m_i(t_k)$ and what was expected O_k is calculated. Hence, a decision within the proposed framework is generated. The value of the option is one of four possible choices: expand, reduce, defer, or abort current investments. As long as projects exploit resources R_i, the NPV of each resource of each site is computed. Financial and non-financial resources are monetarily valuated.

After simulation: At last, simulation data is retrieved and a comparison between the two configurations is elaborated. In the following section, the proposed modeling approach is put into practice.

4 Experimental Results and Analysis

4.1 Metrics Variation and NPV Parameters Estimation

This subsection introduces the tools used for forecasting metrics. It consists in linking the metrics with the resources they depend on. The idea is to incorporate financial, human, technical and informational resources NPVs of each site on $m_i(t)$ function. This function measures the progress of a given IT goal. In order to retrieve the parameters that link these variables, regression analysis is performed on the collected data. Assuming that m_i depends on resources $R_{1,j}$, $R_{2,j}$, $R_{3,j}$ and $R_{4,j}$ of site L_j with their respective net present values $NPV_{1,j}$, $NPV_{2,j}$, $NPV_{3,j}$, $NPV_{4,j}$, the model could be expressed as such:

$$m_i = \alpha_0 + \alpha_1 NPV_{1,j}^k + \alpha_2 NPV_{2,j}^k + \alpha_3 NPV_{3,j}^k + \alpha_4 NPV_{4,j}^k + u_i(t) \quad (3)$$

α_i: Regression coefficients
u_i: Error term
k: Degree of the polynomial regression

The error term u_i captures all other factors which influence $m_i(t)$. The algorithm proceeds with the computation of linear regression (k = 1). Then, it moves on to a quadratic regression (k = 2). If it is still non-matching, the same process is repeated with cubic NPVs and so on. We hence talk about polynomial regressions.

Once regression coefficients α_i are retrieved, all that remains is to estimate net present values $NPV_{i,j}$. We do not assume that NPVs curves follow GBM processes with constant parameters, because the stochastic parameters of a NPV curve change with time without following the exact cash flow pattern. In order to estimate these parameters (r_f, μ, σ), a piecewise estimation [11] combined with MLE (Maximum-Likelihood Estimation) is used. MLE is well defined in case of Brownian motions because they are based on normal distributions and the method can thus be considered a nonlinear unconstrained optimization problem as shown in the following equation:

$$maxLL(\theta) = \sum_{i=1}^{n} lnf(x_i \mid \theta) \tag{4}$$

x_i: Observed data
θ: Vector of parameters
maxLL: Maximum of the log-likelihood function

The estimation of NPV curves associated to a given metric is carried out in a 6-month period. Then, the metric forecasting is done with a regression order ranging from 1 to 10. Figure 3 shows an example of a metric forecasting using the proposed analytical method.

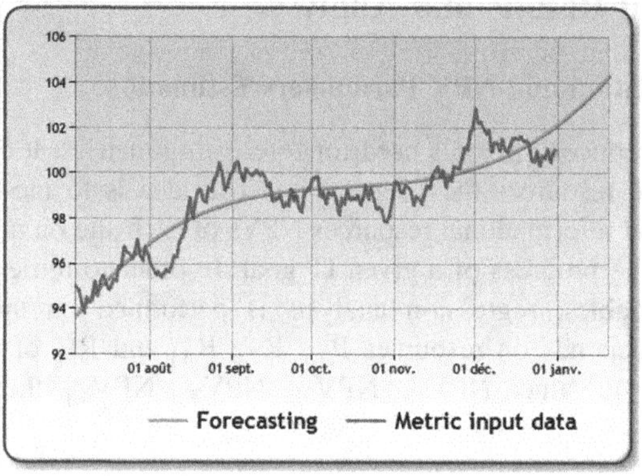

Fig. 3. Example of a metric forecasting.

The same process is repeated for all metrics in both environments. Once metric functions m_i are estimated, the simulation can be launched and five consecutive decisions can thus be generated (one decision at each month-end).

4.2 Simulation in the Two Environments

At this point, we will be proceeding with the main steps of the deterministic model described in Fig. 2. 1000 scenarios of the resources evolution of IT projects are launched by generating random values of their stochastic parameters. These scenarios are simulated in the two environments E_1 and E_2. Thereafter, the gap between what was expected (IT goals) and the state of IT projects is computed according to Eq. 1. For each scenario, five consecutive investment decisions of decision makers are thus obtained. Lastly, strategic objectives of IT governance are compared.

In the proposed framework, the possible investment decision in a resource related to a given site is calculated according to Eq. 2 and is one of the four real options: option to expand, reduce, abort and defer. A Monte Carlo simulation is performed at each decision time point t_k in order to estimate the probabilities of the four real options. Now, using this version of the algorithm on the very data which was obtained as an outcome to the assessment defined in Sect. 2.3, the probabilities of the four investment alternatives are graphically depicted in the following figure (Fig. 4).

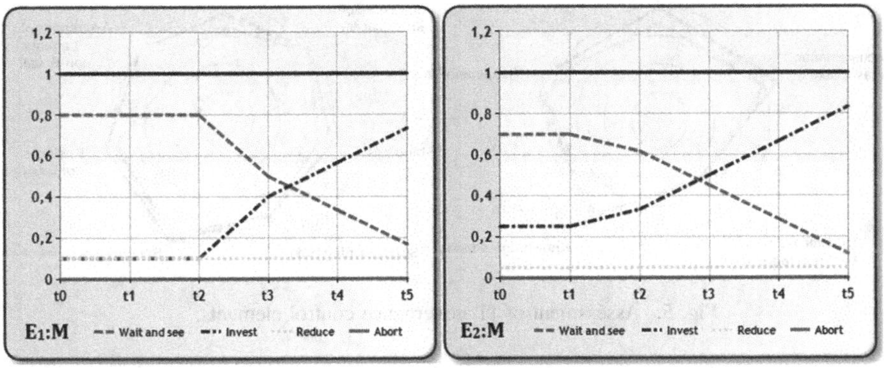

Fig. 4. Graphical depiction of the alternative probabilities (MC simulation). (Color figure online)

The probability distribution of each alternative is depicted in Fig. 4. If the expected market environment is totally unfavorable throughout the life of the real option, the abort option could occur. The abort option is marked in red (solid line). When the progress of a strategic objective is better than what has been expected, decision maker could decide to expand investments in more resources. The probability to expand is marked in blue (dash dot line). The manager could also delay an action to some future time when investment conditions look stable. The option to defer is marked in green (dash line). Lastly, the reduce option lies in the reduction of expected future investments. The option to reduce is marked in yellow (dot line). Lastly, the visual check corresponding to the sum of the four probabilities is marked in black.

The right timing for making the investments is particularly crucial to achieve higher returns. Since investments in E_2 come earlier than those of E_1, E_2 gives an interesting outcome in terms of defining the optimal time to invest. The gain from resources pooling gives decision makers the opportunity to expand existing investments and valuate IT projects and their related resources, thus increasing their profitability. Note that the probability of the option to reduce is lower in E_2 due to the fact of the balancing of the three other real options. We also notice that the abort option probability is null in both environments.

NPVs of IT projects and gaps related to IT goals are continuously updated during each scenario of the simulation, but the final values of the achievement of governance strategic objectives can be considered the result of a single scenario of the simulation. Strategic objectives of IT governance are thus assessed in terms of their final gap values (governance perspective) and their final net present values (financial perspective). A mark is given to IT control elements, ranging from 0 to 5 which happens to be the average of the adopted '0 through 5' grading system. The following figure (Fig. 5) displays the assessment of IT control elements in the two environments E_1 and E_2.

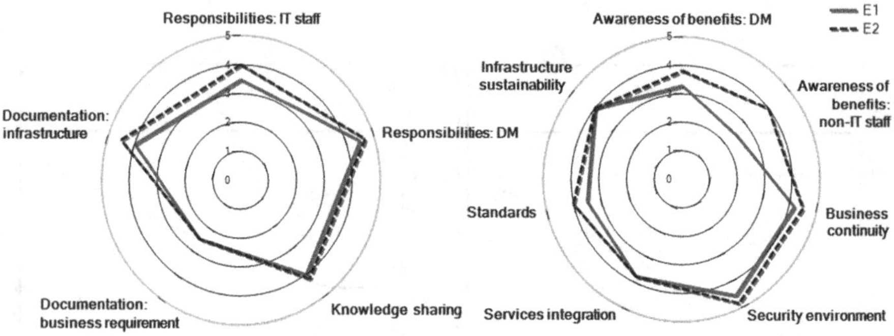

Fig. 5. Assessment of IT governance control elements.

In both configurations, the average mark of all control elements ranges from 2.5 to 4.8 out of 5. Control elements of IT governance associated with informational resources seems to have been neglected. Documentation of business requirement m_8 has the lower score 2.5 out of 5, while documentation of infrastructure m_7 is better managed in E_2. As regards technical resources, control element associated with security environment m_9 has the highest score. This shows that decision maker preoccupations in IT governance remain unchanged whatever the environment configuration. The best matches of control elements in the two environments are: services integration m_{10} and infrastructure sustainability m_{12}. Control elements associated with both human and informational resources such as knowledge sharing, responsibilities and awareness of benefits among IT and non-IT staff (m_1, m_2, m_3, m_4 and m_5) are in favor of the site pooling. Consequently, the simulation is in favor of configuration E_2.

5 Conclusion

In this paper, we have presented a model which aims at simulating investment decisions in two different configurations. A real options approach as a decision making tool combined with effective notions of IT governance is proposed. The simulation framework takes into account both financial and non financial resources in its pricing model and generates investment decisions in order to achieve the highest payoff. The best time to execute an option is computed through the analysis of the net present values of related resources. Lastly, through a Monte Carlo simulation, different scenarios are generated and a statistical and financial analysis is performed in order to compare both configurations, thus assessing the outcome of the relocation.

References

1. Niemann, K.: From Enterprise Architecture to IT Governance. Elements of Effective IT Management. Springer, Heidelberg (2004). ISBN 103-8348-0198-4
2. Shreve, S., Chalasani, P., Jha, S.: Stochastic Calculus and Finance. Carnegie Mellon University, Pittsburgh (1997)
3. Information Technology Governance Institute: COBIT 4: control objectives, management guidelines and maturity models, Rolling Meadows, Illinois, USA (2005)
4. Black, F., Scholes, M.: The pricing of options and corporate liabilities. J. Polit. Econ. **81**(3), 637–654 (1973)
5. Myers, S.C.: Interactions of corporate finance and investment decisions - implications for capital budgeting. J. Finan. **29**(1), 1–25 (1974)
6. Taudes, A.: Software growth options. J. Manag. Inf. Syst. **15**(1), 165–185 (1998)
7. Brouwer, A.E., Mariotti, I., Ommeren, J.N.: The firm relocation decision: an empirical investigation. Ann. Reg. Sci. **38**(2), 335–347 (2004)
8. Benaroch, M., Kauffman, R.J.: A case for using real options pricing analysis to evaluate information technology project investments. Inf. Syst. Res. **10**(1), 70–86 (1999)
9. Bardhan, I., Bagchi, S., Sougstad, R.: Prioritizing a portfolio of information technology investment projects. J. Manag. Inf. Syst. **21**(2), 33–60 (2004)
10. Angelou, G.N., Economides, A.A.: A decision analysis framework for prioritizing a portfolio of ICT infrastructure projects. IEEE Trans. Eng. Manag. **55**(3), 479–495 (2008)
11. Muñoz, J.I., Contreras, J., Caamaño, J., Correia, P.F.: A decision-making tool for project investments based on real options: the case of wind power generation. Ann. Oper. Res. **186**, 465–490 (2011)
12. Weill, P., Ross, J.: IT Governance: How Top Performers Manage IT Decision Rights for Superior Results. Harvard Business School Press, Boston (2004)
13. Georgel, F.: IT Gouvernance - Management stratégique d'un système d'information, 3ème édn. Ed. Dunod (2009). ISBN 978-2-10-052574-4
14. Reix, R.: SI et Management des Organisations, 5th edn., Paris (2005)
15. Trigeorgis, L.: Real Options: Management Flexibility and Strategy in Resource Allocation. MIT Press, Cambridge (1996)
16. Asundi, J., Kazman, R.: A foundation for the economic analysis of software architectures. In: Proceedings of the 3rd Workshop EDSER-3 (2001)
17. Hilhorst, C., Heck, E., Ribbers, P., Smits, M.: Combining real options and multiattribute decision analysis to define the favorable IT infrastructure implementation strategy: a case study. In: Proceedings of the European Conference on Information Systems (2006)
18. Raychaudhuri, S.: Introduction to Monte Carlo simulation. In: Proceedings of the Winter Simulation Conference (2008)
19. Rothe, P., Christersson, M., Heywood, C., Sarasoja, A.: Relocation management - challenges and service opportunities. In: Proceedings of the 20th Annual PRRES Conference (2014)
20. El Ghorfi, R., Ouadou, M., Aboutajdine, D., El Aroussi, M.: A modeling approach for IT governance basics application on IT projects and IT goals. In: Proceedings of 2nd International Conference on AIMS, pp. 211–216 (2014)

NGN Management with NGOSS Framework-Based IMS Use Case

B. Raouyane[1(✉)], S. Khairi[2], I. Haddar[2], and M. Bellafkih[2]

[1] N&DP Team, IT&NT Laboratory, Faculty of Sciences, Department of Mathematics and Informatics, Faculty of Sciences Ain Chock, Casablanca, Morocco
raouyane_brahim@yahoo.fr

[2] Department Telecommunications Systems, Networks and Services, National Institute of Posts and Telecommunications, Rabat, Morocco

Abstract. The success of a telecom operator depends on several criteria such as the ability to offer an improved architecture management. The IP Multimedia Subsystem (IMS) has emerged to allow to telecom operator to unify all access technologies namely wireless, wire line, and extended to agnostic access. However, the services provided by the IMS require Quality of Service (QoS) management with Service Level Agreement (SLA) negotiation which can be achieved by several solutions. Among these solutions, we propose the use of the New Generation Operations Systems and Software (NGOSS) Framework which is a functional framework used to model and analyze networks and services activities. To better understand the relationship and the projection of NGOSS Framework and IMS platform, the article proposes a new architecture of monitoring IMS services with correction of the Quality of Service (QoS) degradation. The performance of the proposed architecture is evaluated by experiments.

Keywords: IP Multimedia System (IMS) · Quality of Services (QoS) · enhanced Telecom Operations Map (eTOM) · Service Level Agreement (SLA) · Service Oriented Architecture (SOA) · Web Service (WS) · Business Process Execution Language (BPEL) · Software Defined Network (SDN)

1 Introduction

THE QoS management mechanisms as defined by 3GPP can be viewed as a network-centric approach to QoS, providing a signaling chain able to automatically configure the network to provision determined QoS to services on demand and in real time, for instance on top of a DiffServ-enabled network [1]. However, to envision a deployment of such technology in a carrier-grade context would mean significant further effort. In particular, premium paid-for services with Service Level Agreement (SLA) contracts such as targeted by IP Multimedia Subsystem (IMS) networks would require additional mechanisms able to provide some degree of monitoring in order to assert the SLAs. Although the IMS does not provide these mechanisms as it is, it is necessary to look for new solutions to cover this lack.

E. Sabir et al. (Eds.): UNet 2017, LNCS 10542, pp. 166–178, 2017.
https://doi.org/10.1007/978-3-319-68179-5_15

Furthermore, the enhanced Telecom Operations Map (eTOM) [3] framework proposes a complete set of hierarchically layered processes describing all operator activities in a standard way. In addition, it is sustained by a parallel specification of a standard information model named Shared Information Data (SID) [4]. From an eTOM point of view, the IMS can cover the fulfillment part of service management, but lacks any means to carry out service assurance. This can be dealt with by merging eTOM and IMS as depicted in our proposed architecture. Another problem that we have to deal with is that the eTOM has been designed at times when Services were viewed as centrally controlled and managed, whereas the IMS is a distributed layer network. The contribution presented in this work is a solution to achieve assurance functionality for enhancing QoS of IMS services following strictly the eTOM specifications. Thus to fill the functional gap as mentioned earlier, we proposed two distributed architectures for QoS monitoring and QoS management in IMS.

2 IMS and NGOSS Architectures

2.1 IMS Architecture and Service Supply

The service provisioning in the IMS (Fig. 1) follows a set of signalization steps. First, the operation begins with discovering application servers in relation and the evaluating criteria filter. After a successful contact between servers, the both extremities become reliable and ready for parameters negotiation namely: codec, ports, bandwidth, and type of service (i.e. audio and/or video). This procedure is done by the mean of the Session initiation Protocol (SIP) within Session Description Protocol (SDP) [5] protocol. The overall signaling for supply service chain, and resource reservation for a Video on Demand (VoD) service respect Rel-7 [6] specification.

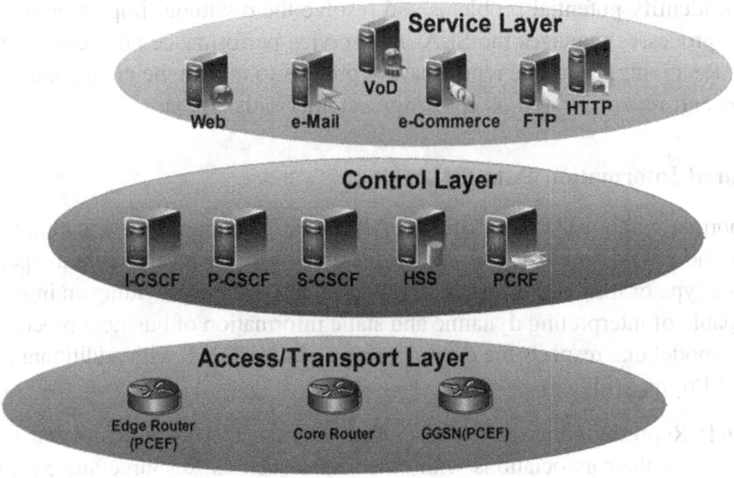

Fig. 1. IMS architecture layers

In the IMS network, the mechanism of QoS management can differentiate IMS services from the traditional architecture such as Internet; the QoS management scenario is based on the reservation, activation, and release of resources for services or applications. The mechanism is independent of QoS management model in the access/transport layer, and can apply any available management model at the appropriate network architecture; it shows its efficiency in QoS management for IMS networks. However, the mechanism has some disadvantages including services monitoring after delivery, which requires a reservation conflict for current and future services.

2.2 eTOM (enhanced Telecom Operations Map) Architecture

The eTOM [3] as a Framework provides a map within an organization of Business process modelling; overall processes are required for different features of an operator, including service integration and supply. The decomposition layer and areas (Customer, Service, Resource, and Enterprise) offers an opportunity to analyze operations and develop solutions in accordance with operation importance and processes related.

The eTOM outlines three main operations Fulfillment, Assurance and Billing. In this section, we present only those relating to Assurance especially execution scenarios of Service Level Agreement (SLA).

The principal processes in Assurance related to SLA management, and eTOM decomposing in Level 1 and Level 2.

The group of assurance vertical E2E processes is responsible for implementing the activities of proactive and reactive maintenance to ensure that services provided to clients are always available and satisfactory, and interpret the views or SLA performance levels and QoS.

The overall process continuously (Fig. 2) monitors resources status and performance in a proactive way to detect possible defects. It collects performance data and analysis to identify potential problems and resolve them without impact on the client. The set of processes manages the SLAs and service performance and sends reports to the client. Receiving of trouble reports active process to inform the client, and provides restoration and repair, as well as ensuring customer satisfaction.

2.3 Shared Information Data (SID)

Most important within eTOM operation (FAB) is the exchange of information between processes; the eTOM can just describe the features of each process without specifying information type or format. For that reason, the SID [4] role is providing an information model capable of interpreting dynamic and static information of business processes and provides a model that respects the decomposition of the eTOM, with additional areas as Policy and Product (Fig. 3).

- **Product:** Represents the main classes that describe the components and types of products and their associations with other areas such as Resource and Service.
- **Service:** The service domain consists of a set of layers that are used to manage the definition, development and operational aspects of services provided by an NGOSS.

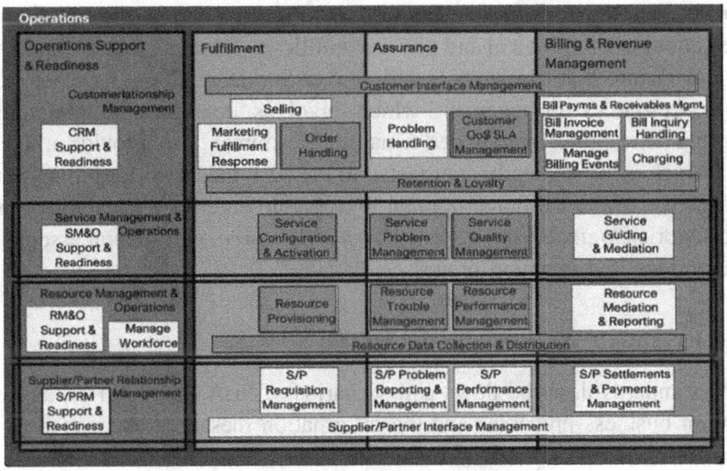

Fig. 2. eTOM processes map

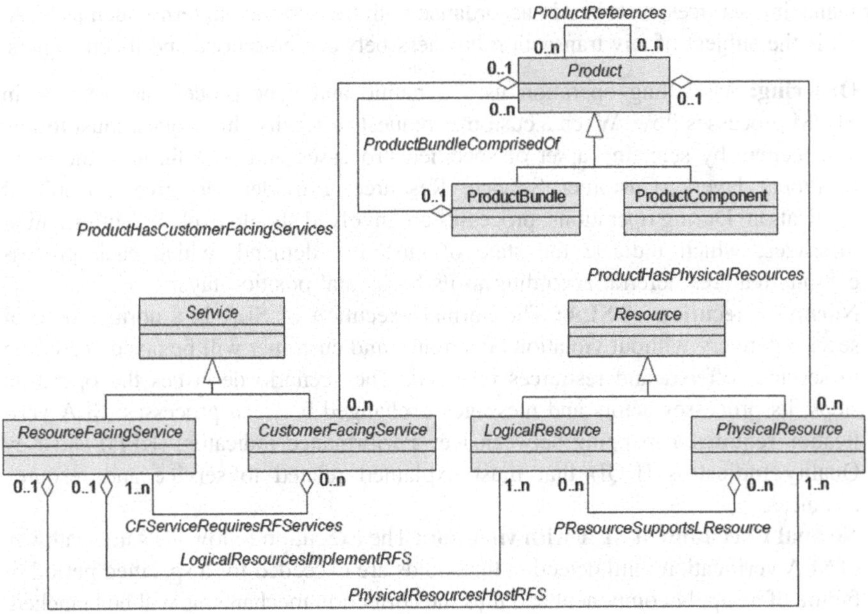

Fig. 3. Products are realized as services and resources (GB922 Addendum 4S-QoS v1.0)

The entities in this area support various eTOM processes. This includes an agreement on service levels to be offered, deployment and configuration services, problems management, performance estimation, quality analysis, and service classification. This area includes two major entities: *ResourceFacingservice* which represents the different QoS management techniques and service conditioning; and *CustomerFacingService* that exposes classes of services and clients.

- **Resource:** The domain associate Resources to Products and Services, and provide a detailed enough set of logical and physical entities to facilitate this relationship. The Resources ensure that can support and deliver Services offered by a set of operations as: resources management which involves configuration, planning, and monitoring to capture overall performance, Resources also provide usage information which is subsequently aggregated to the customer level for billing purposes. The objective of the Resource domain is to divide enterprise capabilities into two main categories *logicalResource* and *PhysicalResource* with several associations to enable strategy and planning processes.

2.4 SLA Execution Workflow in the ETOM

The eTOM standards describe flows and scenarios of SLA execution of, and interactions between business processes and the information messages exchanged to handle both cases normal execution and violation.

The scenarios of service management and monitoring processes are in a business context. In eTOM framework, the operations of service delivery and monitoring include Fulfillment and Assurance processes [3], these E2E processes are responsible for managing services customer in accordance with the contractual terms such as SLA, which is the subject of any transaction business between enterprise and its customers.

- **Ordering:** Modelling operation uses dynamic and sync process as describe in eTOM processes flow. When a customer requests a service, his request must follow a sequence, by selecting a set of specified processes and pass through the compositional layers (Customer Service, Resource, Provider), to give a result of application. During operations, processes are involved should exchange information messages, which indicate the state of customer demand, which each process exhibits features deferral according to its horizontal position layer.
- **Normal Execution of SLA:** The normal execution of SLA is a normal state of service delivery without violation occurrence and customer will be taxed according to services offered and resources reserved. The scenario describes the operation steps, its processes actors and messages exchanged between processes; SLA verification requires a mapping between Key Performance Indicators (KPIs) and Key Quality Indicators (KQI) that must explained related to service and resource instances.
- **Normal Execution of SLA with violation:** The execution follow the same pathway of SLA verification until detection thresholds are exceeded for a specified period or failure of a supply component and thus the correction mechanisms will be launched. Troubles take many forms and related solutions depend more on circumstances (type of Troubles, incidents and consequences). To solve problems, Resources processes try to offer solutions to address. Resources processes attempt to offer low-level solutions to correct troubles, otherwise if the problem persists; the Service layer therefore is responsible for offers a version of high-level solutions that are effective.

3 Issues and Related Work

3GPP specifications provide a basic architecture for IMS network with a mechanism for QoS management, which ensures an adequate level of service compared to service supply in traditional Internet [7].

However, the IMS services [8] need to be monitored and managed by a set of mechanisms and methods of high level and that take into considerations the constraints of the business enterprise. During the development of a Management Platform offers management, all versions are oriented IP management [9, 10], without taking into consideration the business or SLA part. The technical aspect is still dominant in the management, or the BSS part should be included. The NGOSS the proposal is still abstract and valid for any type of network. This set is explicitly represented by eTOM process that allows the management and integration of an operator with E2E processes Fulfillment, Assurance, and Billing (FAB). The eTOM describes its operations and processes in ways that are generic and applicable to any transaction, and the question arises how to project eTOM processes in monitoring and management operations for IMS network?

4 Functional Architecture

The architecture presents a functional interaction between the eTOM Framework and the IMS Platform (Fig. 4), this interaction is a link between business processes and network entities. The architecture of management and monitoring (SLM&M) [11] uses scenarios eTOM (Ordering, SLA Execution) in an IMS service.

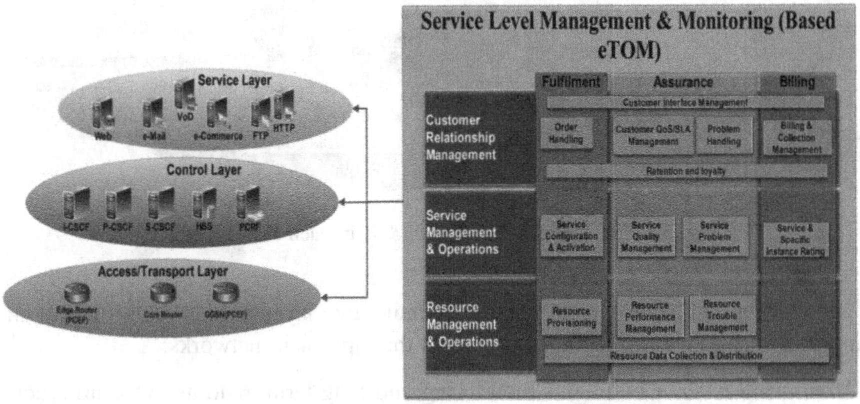

Fig. 4. Processes operating in the SLA verification

The Service Level Monitoring and Management (SLM&M) architecture contain the various entities:

- Translation Business Processes: Enterprise Java Bean (EJB).
- Presentation of WSs: Web Service Description Language (WSDL).
- Processes Communication: Simple Object Access Protocol (XML/SOAP).
- Operations Orchestration: Business Process Execution Language (BPEL).
- Communication between SLM&M and the IMS network entities: TCP/IP, XML.

Distributed architecture enables monitoring continues with verification of the SLA on demand, the paragraph outlines the various changes made in SLM&M architecture (Fig. 5).

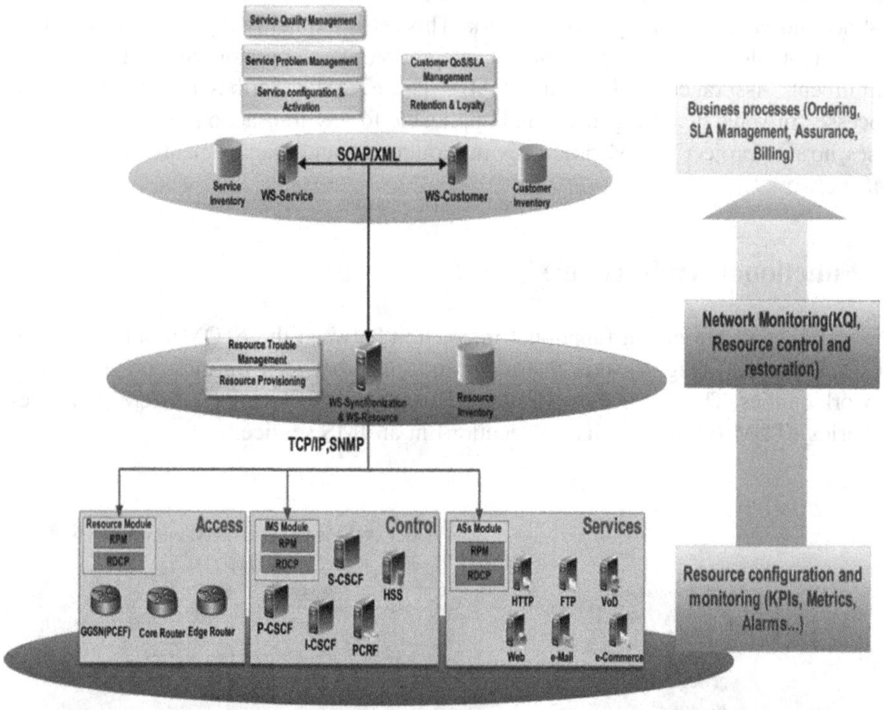

Fig. 5. Global functions of SLM&M in each IMS layer's

Monitoring and Management System contains two layers which allows the monitoring, treatment, and correction of problems that appear in networks:

- *Monitoring layer:* Continuous monitoring and long-term trend analysis are crucial for efficiently managing application service delivery. This diagnostic tool lets efficiently drill down to the causes of application performance problems and failures, and service degradation in IMS network. The Layer monitors the IMS network in real or near real time by:
  - **Store:** Automated collection, centralization and secure storage of log data for user, resource and service running.

- **Analyst:** Event examination, data filtering correlation and comprehensive reporting for audit and compliance.
- **Alarm:** Monitoring, alerting and notification on key defined events.

- *Assurance layer:* The layer capable ensure service delivery and provides intelligent processing of information collected by the monitoring layer, over the proposal of appropriate solutions that address several constraints snuff into account several and business technology constraints and may trigger the corrective action SLA-based. The Assurance layer will efficiently active by proposing of alternatives solution in the case of a persistent problem at the level of resources, the solutions proposed by the layer will be more experienced and offers a possibility to open a direct communication channel with the provider one hand and with the customer on the other.

5 Implementation and Results

The implementation architecture comprises two sub-architectures for the service provisioning and the other for service management and correction services (Fig. 6):

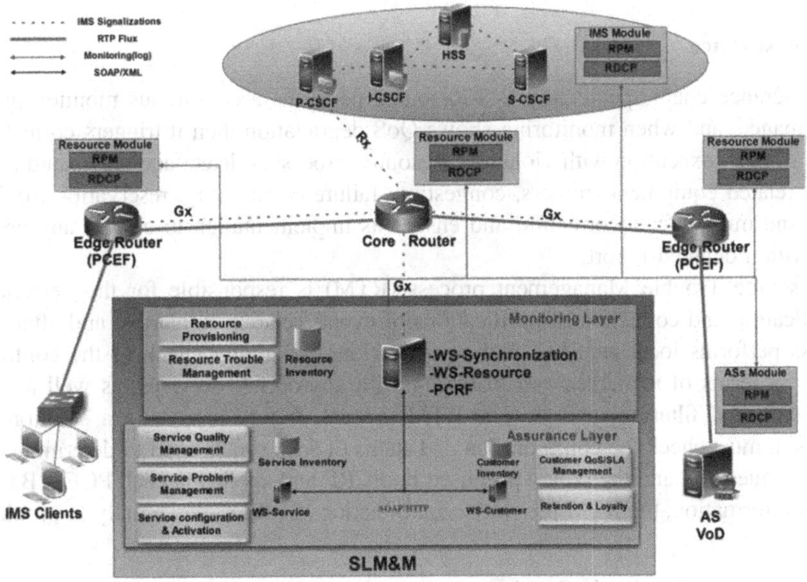

Fig. 6. Implementation architecture, test bed: IMS network, SLM&M

- **Supply Architecture:** which contains an IMS network for services providing that included both signaling and media plan. The architecture includes three routers to transmit the media stream; a central router contains the IMS control network. The Policy and Charging Rule Function (PCRF) is becoming an autonomous entity and includes other features as policy management, and both edge routers include the Policy and Charging Enforcement Function (PCEF) functionality to receive and execute policies or PCC rules.

- **Monitoring and management architecture:** SLM&M is divided into two layers
  - *Monitoring Layer:* contain the two WSs Resource and Synchronization, with the integration of RP and RTM processes and Resource Inventory, so the layer includes the functionality of PCRF for QoS management and control.
  - *Assurance Layer:* contain both servers and WS-Customer and WS-Service, and integrate process and Fulfilement and Assurance, that will be activated in SLA correction and violation.

The supply architecture provides a set of IMS services, when a client requests a VoD streaming service, the provisioning chain stimulates the IMS entities to provide a resource reservation and QoS management. The SLM&M in the supply, after the ordering operation, start the collection of configuration data for a normal SLA execution. Anomaly detection or exceeding threshold causes the activation of a scenario of a SLA violation to restore service to normal level.

The SLM&M must be a reactive by rapid detection of QoS degradation or anomalies, followed by an attempt to resolve troubles, that activates Assurance process and if necessary the Fulfilment process.

5.1 Assurance

The assurance chain specifically WS-Resource performs a continuous monitoring of performance, and when monitoring shows QoS degradation then it triggers corrective action or SLA execution with violation. Resource processes detect anomalies and their nature-related equipment (routers, congestion, failure of an entity, reservation trouble etc.). And must offer a correction and ensure its implementation to correct any problems with a detailed report.

Resource Trouble Management process (RTM) is responsible for the detection, identification and collection of notifications of events relating to alarms, and after the process performs local analysis of the notifications, a validity check of the configurations in terms of resources and matching with appropriate services, as well as the correlation and filtering records. The RTM process, before proposing a solution or actions, it must check the configuration and status of each router apart to determine the router in question, and the policy proposed by PCRF and applied at each PCEF. Based on this information, the RTM provides a set of actions that run sequentially to problem solving:

- Routers reconfiguring in the absence of configurations.
- Application of low-level rules in routers for the selection of traffic allowed, and the cancellation or reduction of non-interactive traffic.
- Change of queuing algorithms in the edge routers.
- Change the path or routing in failure case of component.

If the actions leading to resolution of trouble and restoring a normal operating condition, then the correction operation may be followed by a normal verification and continuous monitoring of SLA. If the problem persists, the Resource Trouble Management process is responsible for sending the results and actions made to Service processes to achieve a new concept of service that considers all the actions made and constraints.

5.2 Fulfillment

However, if WS-Resources and processes are insufficient to meet all SLAs violated, or the proposed solutions by WS-Resources are unable to resolve a trouble for a client, the solution should also include planning and system change by the WS-Service intervention. The process SPM begins with a study of service and composition, and also checks the configuration and service design with actual implementation.

Solutions must first activate the service request and offers solutions in the form of policies and operations-based system infrastructure. In the case of congestion, the solutions take the following forms:

- Changes in QoS management model in routers from DiffServ to RSVP or the inclusion of MPLS or other suitable model.
- Changing service settings in streaming video case: codec, resolution, rate audio or video, or other parameters.
- Proposal of new services by the application servers that comply with the proposed conditions and verification of services provided at the server level.
- Provide the services available and simple with the intent to keep a relationship with the customer satisfaction with the opening of a channel of communication with the customer and his needs.

The proposed solutions by Fulfillment process provide a definitive resolution of conflicts and troubles; at the end of operation processes can generate trouble tickets for customers, and reports of actions done for the system to keep the problem experience.

5.3 Results

Alice has registered in the IMS system with QoS classed Gold. The goal is to perform SLA Assurance tests in three representative cases and to compare the results for SLA correction with Assurance and Fulfillment.

The MOS-V [12] is a quality indicator for detecting the quality of a service requiring a video flow as Video on Demand (VoD) or IP Television (IPTV). It is a quantitative indicator taking values between 0 and 5. The MOS-V reflects the user satisfaction and Sla violation. In our case the value 2.5 represents a QoS degradation and SLA violation (Fig. 7).

The MOS-V indicator reflects customer satisfaction, when the thresholds are exceeded the values present a critical MOS-V.

To evaluate our proposed architecture, we have first launched the SLA violation. The experiment shows that our solution has successfully restored normal levels of service after 7 s for the first violation. The second violation requires the intervention of Assurance and Fulfillment. For this purpose, our solution takes 17 s to restore service.

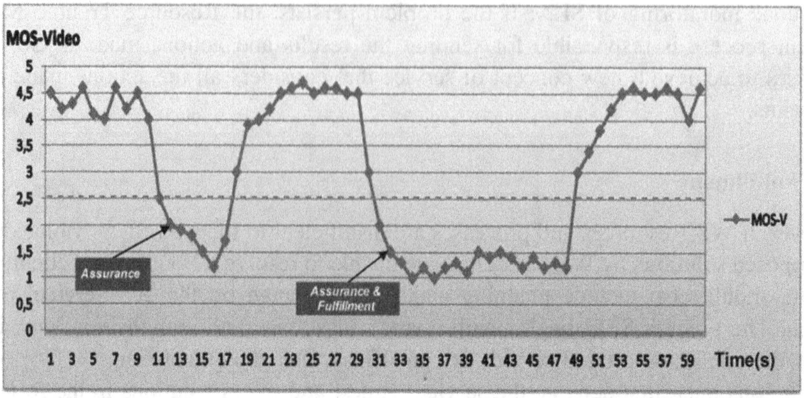

Fig. 7. Customer satisfaction during a time interval and the correction made

The architecture results are justified by using WSOA, and interactions between different Web Services (WS).

5.4 Discussion and Proposition

The behavior of our eco-system SLM&M in verification of SLA and violation demonstrate its feasibility. Recently, with the apparition of the Software Defined Network (SDN) [13] which facilitates QoS management at each switch, it's motivating to explore the projection of our SLM&M platform on SDN. This requires well placed SDN Controller in our SLM&M platform. After a thorough study and several proposals, we decided first to integrate an SDN Controller to manage the QoS in the IMS network. In future work, we will position the controller in our SLM&M. The result of the integration is shown in Fig. 8.

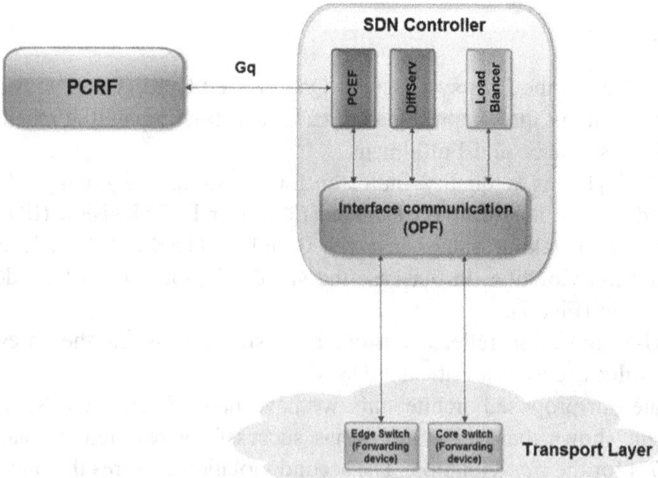

Fig. 8. QoS management for IMS architecture in SDN network

Our proposal will be evaluated in future work in terms of reliability and scalability. The QoS management architecture contains three main entities:

- PCRF as a standalone entity that communicates with the IMS network.
- SDN controller: contains a set of APIs based applications mainly PCEF, DiffServ and Load balancer. Other required modules to QoS management can be added (i.e. MultiProtocol Label Switching (MPLS), QoS-Routing …). Two communication modules are required namely: Gq (Diameter protocol) interface to communicate with the PCRF, and OpenFlow [14] to configure switches.
- SDN Switches: we defined two types, Edge and Core switches.

The architecture will be detailed with measurements and tests in future works.

6 Conclusion

The automatic Management of the SLA/QoS demands the mapping of the SLA requirements and SLS parameters to be translated into technical configuration of network equipment and the specification of tools in order to generate QoS parameters from SLA.

The SLA monitoring must be improved in order to determine service performance measurements relevant for efficient SLA to manage the network (i.e. to maintain the equipment reconfiguration) and to optimize the network performance and usage.

The ultimate role of QoS management is to help matching the expected quality with the perceived quality. This is accomplished by assuring that the achieved performance of service is in line with specifications and contracts.

The both operations "Fulfillment" and "Assurance" according to the descriptions of the eTOM are necessary and sufficient to guarantee a sucked telecom service. However, the occurrence of SDN favors the management by centralized configuration in a single entity named controller, for that our SLM&M platform will benefit from SDN advantages. The architecture will provide a direct communication with the controller without having to configure all network equipment.

In our next work, we have two main aims, the first is to integrate SDN controller in the QoS management architecture for the IMS network, and the second is the integration of SDN controller in SLM&M.

References

1. Raouyane, B., Bellafkih, M., Ranc, D.: QoS management in IMS: DiffServ model. Paper Presented at the Third International Conference on Next Generation Mobile Applications, Services and Technologies, Cardiff, Wales, UK, 15–18 September 2009
2. Creaner, M.J., Reilly, J.P.: NGOSS Distilled: The Essential Guide to Next Generation Telecoms Management. The Lean Corporation (2005)
3. Enhanced Telecom Operations Map (eTOM). The Business Process Framework for the Information and Communications Services Industry, Addendum D: Process Decompositions and Descriptions Release 6.0 GB921 D; TMF

4. Shared Information/Data (SID) Model System View Concepts and Principles, GB926 Version 1.0, Release 4.0, January 2004
5. Handley, M., et al.: SDP: Session Description Protocol, Request for Comments: 4566, July 2006
6. Raouyane, B., Bellafkih, M., Errais, M., Ranc, D.: WS-composite for management & monitoring IMS network. Int. J. Next-Gener. Comput. (IJNGC). ISSN 2229-4678, eISSN 0976-5034
7. 3rd Generation Partnership Project; Evolution of policy control and charging (Release 7), 3GPP TR 23.803 V7.0.0, September 2005
8. Tranoris, C., Denazis, S., Mouratidis, N., Dowling, P., Tynan, J.: Integrating OpenFlow in IMS networks and enabling for future internet research and experimentation. In: Galis, A., Gavras, A. (eds.) FIA 2013. LNCS, vol. 7858, pp. 77–88. Springer, Heidelberg (2013). doi:10.1007/978-3-642-38082-2_7
9. Schreiner, F., Blum, N., Jacak, P., Weik, P.: Towards standardized NGN OSS mechanisms for automated service provisioning and fault management for OSIMS-based NGNs. J. Netw. Syst. Manag. (2008). ISSN 1064-7570, Springer Netherlands
10. Mirchev, A., et al.: Survey of concepts for QoS improvements via SDN. In: Seminars FI/IITM SS 15, Network Architectures and Services (2015)
11. Raouyane, B., Bellafkih, M., Errais, M., Ramdani, M.: IMS management and monitoring with eTOM framework and composite web service. Int. J. Multimedia Intell. Secur. **2**(2), 172–185 (2011). Inderscience Publishers
12. Raouyane, B., Bellafkih, M., Errais, M., Ramdani, M.: MOS evaluation for VoD service in an IMS network. In: 5th International Symposium on I/V Communications and Mobile Networks, 30 September–1–2 October 2010. ISBN:978-1-4244-5996-4
13. Goransson, P., Black, C.: Software Defined Networks A Comprehensive Approach. Elsevier/Morgan Kaufmann, Burlington (2014)
14. McKeown, N., Anderson, T., Balakrishnan, H., Parulkar, G., Peterson, L., Rexford, J., Shenker, S., et al.: OpenFlow: enabling innovation in campus networks. SIGCOMM Comput. Commun. Rev. **38**(2), 69–74 (2008)

Migration from Web Services to Cloud Services

Hassina Nacer[1(✉)], Kada Beghdad Bey[2], and Nabil Djebari[3]

[1] MOVEP Laboratory, Computer Science Department, University of Science and Technology, USTHB, Algiers, Algeria
sino_nacer@yahoo.fr

[2] Informatics Systems Laboratory, Ecole Militaire Polytechnique, Algiers, Algeria
k.beghdadbey@gmail.com

[3] LIMED Laboratory, Computer Science Department, University of Bejaia, Bejaia, Algeria
djebari.n@gmail.com

Abstract. Nowadays, Cloud Computing has emerged as a new model for hosting, managing and delivering services over Internet on demand. It is rapidly changing the landscape of information technology. It has three services models namely, Software as a Service (SaaS). Platform as a Service (PaaS). Infrastructure as a Service (IaaS) and four deployment models (Private Cloud, Community Cloud, Public Cloud, Hybrid Cloud). In this paper, we have presented a comparison study about two types of services namely, Web services and Cloud services with their environments (definitions, concepts, languages, discovery, etc.). The obtained results, from this comparison study, provide useful guidelines for the design of services and development. They also accelerate Cloud Computing from early prototypes to production systems.

1 Introduction

Nowadays, the emergence of Cloud Computing (CC) continues the natural evolution of distributed systems, it represents a profound change in the way that resources are delivered to companies. By applying CC solutions, companies increase their business model capabilities and their ability to meet computing resource demands. In addition, they avoid investments in infrastructure, software, and training. The resources (Hardware, Platforms, Software, Data) are saved as services on physical servers or virtual maintained and controlled by a CC provider.

Cloud services are developed to be hosted by Infrastructure as a Service (IaaS), by Platform as a Service (PaaS) and Software as a Service (SaaS) which are CC services delivery models.

So what are Cloud services? what are Web services?

To reply to these questions, this paper explores concepts and features of the two kind of services and focuses on the migration from Web services to Cloud services.

The remainder of this article is organized as follows. Section 2 introduces some definitions, theoretical basis and standards for Services Oriented Architecture (SOA) and Web services technology. Section 3 presents the keys concepts

E. Sabir et al. (Eds.): UNet 2017, LNCS 10542, pp. 179–192, 2017.
https://doi.org/10.1007/978-3-319-68179-5_16

of CC. In Sect. 4, a comparison study between SOA and Cloud infrastructure is presented. Section 5 illustrates the motivation of the migration from Web services to Cloud services. In Sect. 6, we give an overview of the contemporary service description languages of resources. Section 7 gives a brief background and a related work in Cloud services discovery followed by a conclusion in Sect. 8.

2 SOA Architecture

SOA is an architectural style to re-use and integrate sub systems in existing systems in order to create new applications [1–3]. SOA enables flexible integration of applications and resources by: *(i)* representing each application or resource as a service with a standardized interface, *(ii)* enabling a service to exchange structured information (Messages, Documents, Business objects), and *(iii)* coordinating and mediating between services. SOA is based on the "service" concept. The major goal of SOA is to reverse the tendency which generally shows that the operational processes inside entreprises is adapt to the imposed constraints by data processing.

In SOA architecture, the constituent components of the software systems are reusable services. Services interact with each other through standard interfaces and communication protocols. XML Web services architecture is based on SOA and they take the same actors. The provider of services publishes a contract of interface and defines the functionality and the execution of a Web service. The client consumes the service and uses an universal registry to discover available services. Once a service is located, the client extracts the interface contract in order to execute a service. The registry of services is a virtual database of available services. Each provider publishes a contract of a XML Web service interface in the registry with required information (Localization, Access Control, etc.) The XML Web services technology was concretized around the specification of the W3C. It is divided into three areas: *(1)* Communication Protocols (SOAP) which is a protocol that exchanges structured information in a decentralized and distributed environment, *(2)* Service Description (WSDL) which provides a syntactic model and a XML format for describing Web services., and *(3)* Service Discovery (UDDI) which is a virtual registry that exposes information about Web services. These current standards revolve around XML[1] to achieve platform independence features.

SOA architecture is illustrated by Fig. 1.

2.1 Web Service Definitions

Several definitions of Web services have advanced in literature as follows:

According to Nacer and Aissani [4], a Web service is a software component of distributed applications which provides services to other applications by using

[1] XML is a markup language to describe different data types and it is the basis of interoperability between heterogeneous systems.

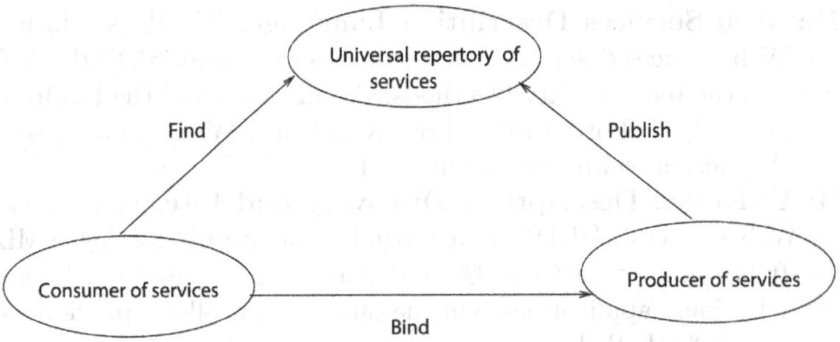

Fig. 1. SOA Architecture.

standard Internet technology[2]. It respects some properties such as autonomous object components, loosely coupled, self-described, self-contained, reusable, modular, synchronous and asynchronous, that can be published, located, and invoked over the Web.

According to Benatallah [5], a Web service is an accessible application that others applications and humans can discover and invoke. The author cited the following properties to a XML Web service: independent from specific platforms and computing paradigms, and easily composed.

The W3C group defined a Web service as a software application identified by an URI, whose interfaces and bindings can be defined, described, and discovered as XML artifacts. Thus, Web services can tackle the challenge of heterogeneous sources and interoperability.

According to Chappell and Jewell [6], a Web service is a piece of business[3] logic, located somewhere over the Internet, that is accessible through standard-based Internet protocols.

2.2 Standards of Web Services Technology

- **XML: eXtensible Murkup Language** is an universal model of data representation and exchange. It is a simple format text, flexible and also independent of any manufacturer. Adding to this, it gives structure to documents and data [7].
- **SOAP: Simple Object Access Protocol** is an exchange messages process in heterogeneous environments for application-to-application communication based on XML and on the standard protocol HTTP. It ensures interoperability between components independently from transport mechanisms, operating systems, and programming languages.

[2] by using the standard Internet technology such as Internet protocols: SMTP (Simple Mail Transfer Protocol), HTTP (Hypertext Transfer Protocol), FTP (File Transfer Protocol).

[3] It means that UDDI provide an universal registry for business to provide service listings (Web services description, etc.).

- **WSDL: Web Services Description Language.** WSDL is a formal language of Web services description according to the standard XML. A WSDL file describes the functionality (Methods, Parameters) and the localisation of a Web service (URI, Port, Protocol of invocation). WSDL can be seen as a traditional function, subroutine or method.
- **UDDI: Universal Description, Discovery and Integration.** The registry of Web services "UDDI" is a virtual database of existing XML Web services. It is similar to a CORBA trader and can be considered as a DNS service for business applications. On the one hand, it allows providers of services to record XML Web services under a standardized format and on the other hand, it concentrates on discovery process of XML Web services satisfying services' needs in SOA.

3 Cloud Computing

As a new model, CC is more than an online computing system, it provides the hardware, softwares, and data foundation for next generation companies. There is no standard or agreed definition about CC in the literature. Clouds consist of data centers which are owned by the same provider.

3.1 Definitions

According to NIST, CC Project, CC is a model for enabling convenient, on-demand network access to a shared pool of configurable computing resources (e.g. Networks, Servers, Storage, Applications, and Services) that can be rapidly provisioned and released with minimal management efforts or service provider interaction.

According to Buyya et al. [8], CC is the 5th utility after water, electricity, gas and telephony. The work argues that with cloud infrastructure, businesses and users are able to access to applications from anywhere in the world on demand.

According to Wang et al. [9], CC is a set of network, providing scalable, Quality of Service (QoS) guaranteed, normally personalized, inexpensive computing platforms on demand, which could be accessed in a simple and pervasive way.

According to Klems et al. [10], From an economic perspective, CC is defined as follows: Building on compute and storage virtualization technologies, and leveraging the modern Web, CC provides scalable and affordable compute utilities as on-demand services with variable pricing schemes and enabling a new consumer mass market.

We cite the features of CC as follows:

- **On-demande:** CC allows the client to use services on demand. The client uses the resources when he/she needs them;
- **Self-service:** The client can automatically provision its own computing resources as needed and without requiring an administrator, via an interactive portal that enables him/her to configure and manage these services themselves;

- **Elasticity:** The client can use any resource, he/she consumes these resources and he/she liberates theme after using;
- **Broad network access:** The client can access to these services from anywhere, via any computer and download them into any device;
- **Scalability:** In order to maximize scalability, applications and their data must be loosely coupled;
- **Reliability:** It means that applications do not fail and they do not lose data;
- **Speed, Capacity, and Flexibility:** CC stresses getting applications to market very quickly by using the most appropriate building blocks to get the task done rapidly;
- **Measured service with pay per use:** Access to services is monitored and measured constantly. The payment is calculated based on the duration and the quantity of services used;
- **Ability:** It means that an application is underlying infrastructure components can be updated or even replaced without disrupting its characteristics including availability and security.

3.2 Deployment Models

A Cloud can be available to public via Internet, can be restricted to a unique organisation or shared by several business. It can be categorized into four deployment models as listed below:

- **Public Cloud:** It allows services to be easily accessible to public;
- **Private Cloud:** It allows services to be accessible within an organization;
- **Community Cloud:** It allows services to be accessible by a group of several organizations;
- **Hybrid Cloud:** It is a combination of public, private, or community Cloud.

3.3 Services Models: Cloud Based Services

Cloud services made available to clients on demand over Internet. Tree models of services are defined: Software as a service (SaaS), Platform as a service (PaaS) and Infrastructure as a service (IaaS), and recently (DaaS) and (XaaS).

- **Saas: Software as a Service**
  SaaS can be summarized as the way that software is delivered and used. SaaS is a software distribution model in which applications are hosted by a service provider and made available to clients via Internet. SaaS is a Web application offered as a service on demand by using Cloud infrastructure. It aims at replacing the applications running on Personnel Computer (PC). There is no need to install and run the special software on your computer. Examples of SaaS implementations, the services provided by Google for office automation, such as Google Mail, Google Documents, and Google Calendar, which are delivered for free to the Internet users and charged for professional quality services. Examples of commercial solutions are SalesForce.com and Clarizen.com, which provide online CRM (Customer Relationship Management) and project management services, respectively [11].

- **PaaS: Platform as a Service**
  PaaS is a platform for the development of software delivered over the Web. It allows the creation of Web applications quickly and easily without the complexity of buying and maintaining the software and infrastructure underneath it [12].
- **IaaS: Infrastructure as a Service**
  IaaS providers offer physical or virtual machines that are able to fulfill customer needs to develop software solutions on it. It also provides various resources such as firewalls, load balancers, software solutions and many more. This type of service offers a great advantage to clients that need solid and flexible infrastructures [13].

4 Comparison Between SOA Architecture and Cloud Model

Both CC and SOA have an important overlapping concerns but they are not synonymous. The most important overlap occurs near the top of the CC stack, in the area of software services (SaaS), such as XML Web Services. However, they have a different goal. SOA focuses on integration systems and the objectif of CC is to leverage the Internet to outsource IT functions. Table 1 illustrates a comparative study between SOA Architecture and CC Model.

Table 1. Comparison between SOA and CC

Criterion	SOA	Cloud model
Year	2000	2010
Goal	Integration and components reuse	Offering services and commodities
Service	Software	Hard, platform, software, data
Standards	Mature	Specific to a particular provider of the cloud
Network dependence	Internet	Internet
Model	Producer/consumer	Provider/producer/consumer
Relationship	Contractual relationships and trust	Business
Implementation	Integration of software services	Virtualized IT resources
Engineering practices	- Abstraction - Loose coupling - Encapsulation	- Abstraction - Loose coupling - Encapsulation
Virtualization	No	Vital

5 Web Services vs. Cloud Services

What is the motivation of the migration from Web services to Cloud services?

Nowadays, more and more companies are moving their Web applications to a Cloud-based infrastructure to modernize their companies and to take immediate advantages such as: Cloud services provide access to a server infrastructure, Data storage, Security, Scalability, Configuration options, and Lower cost.

The Web services and Cloud services are not the same. Companies can have Web services without Cloud infrastructures. Web services refer to Web applications that allow clients to interact with softwares via Internet in a standardized way. However, Cloud services offer an environment to data, softwares, platforms, and infrastructure pieces. Furthermore, Cloud services are hosted on Clouds. This provides flexibility and on-demand services for several clients. In addition, a Cloud service through mode innovation of the hardware, software, and data delivery meets the companies information while reducing operating costs. By contrast, a Web service is hosted in a Web hosting server. The provider of the Web service focuses to serve an individual client.

However, to evolve a Web service into a Cloud service, it should exhibit some criteria such as.

- Support for virtualization technology;
- Support multi-tenancy (different clients requirements/needs): it means a single instance of software to serve multiple companies by accommodation their requirements through configuration at the same time [14];
- A rich infrastructure.

Table 2 illustrates a comparative study between Web services and Cloud services regarding to some criteria.

6 Description Language of Resources via Internet

6.1 Syntactic Description Languages

Various works about syntactic description have already been proposed like WSDL, Service Oriented Architecture Modeling Language (SoaML) [15], Unified Service Description Language (USDL) [16], BPSCloud [17], MapReduce [18], Drayad [19], Orleans [20], Blueprint [21], Cloud# [22], etc.

6.2 Semantic Description Languages

Languages which support semantic meta-data representation are required, so that any resource over the Web become accessible by any user. Various works about semantic description have already been proposed like: Resource Description Framework (RDF) [23], RDF Schema (RDFS) [24], Ontology Inference Layer(OIL), Darpa Agent Markup Language (DAML) [25], Web Ontology Language (OWL) [26], Ontology Web Language for Services (OWL-S) [27], Web

Table 2. Comparison between Web services and Cloud services

Criterion	Web service	Cloud service
Type	Software solutions (APIs)	Virtualization solutions (Environment) IaaS, PaaS, SaaS, DaaS, XaaS
Architecture	SOA	Cloud infrastructure
Standards	XML, SOAP, WSDL, UDDI	Lack of APIs
Language description	WSDL	No standard language
Functionality	Poor	Rich
Configuration	- Adaptable - Non configurable	- Adaptable - Configurable
Operating System	Any standard OS	A hypervisor (VM) on which multiple OSs run
Web hosting	Isolated tenancy	Multi-tenancy (Multi clients)
Interoperability	Yes	Lack of standards
Contract	Between clients and providers of web services	- Self-service - Subscription fee
Payment	A total payment	A partial payment for using time
Responsibility	Shared between clients and providers	Win-Win relationship between clients and providers
Management	- Distributed	- Centralized - Distributed
Access	Anywhere	Somewhere
Server localisation	Single data center	Replicated data centers
Run	Provider computing system	Client/provider computing system
Network	Internet or other	Internet or other

Service Modeling Language (WSML) [28], Web Service Modeling Ontology (WSMO) [29], Web Services Description Language Semantic (WSDL-S) [30] and Semantic Annotations for Web Services Description Language (SAWSDL) [31], and Cloud Service Description Model (CSDM) [32], etc.

Table 3 illustrates a comparative study between the above description languages regarding to the following criteria.

- **Resource:** It identifies the resource type over the Web (a Web page, a Web service (WS), SaaS, etc.). Each Web resource can be identified by an URI;
- **Concept:** It describes the basic property of the semantic model wether it exists or no (RDF, DL[4] [33], XML-S[5], etc.);

[4] Description logic.
[5] XML Schema.

Table 3. Comparison between description languages

Approach	Resource	Concept	SA	Research
RDF	Any URI	XML, triple	Yes	Knowledge engineering, WSem, ...
RDFS	Any URI	RDF, classes and sub	Yes	WSem, categorization
OIL	Any URI	Frame, DL	Yes	WSem, intelligence artificial, inter-ontology relations, ...
DAML+OIL	Any URI	XML-S, RDFS extended DL, relationship	Yes	Ontology sharing, ontology construction vocabulary, ...
OWL	Any URI	DAML+OIL	Yes	WSem, interoperability knowledge sharing, capabilities, ...
OWL-S	WS	OWL ontology	Yes	Discovery, composition, execution, monitoring, ...
	SaaS			
WSDL	WS	XML	No	Discovery, composition, invocation
	SaaS			
WSML	WS	Logical formalism	No	Interoperability
WSMO	WS	WSML ontology	Yes	Discovery, composition, ...
WSDL-S	WS	OWL ontology	Yes	Discovery, composition, ...
	SaaS			
SAWSDL	WS	Independent of any semantic model	Yes	Discovery, invocation
CSDM	SaaS	UML+OWL	Yes	Integration, discovery, selection composition
USDL	WS	MOF model	No	Matching, discovery
	SaaS			
SoaML	WS	UML	No	Design, discovery
	SaaS			
Blueprint	SaaS	Blueprint template	No	Selection, composition
Cloud#	SaaS	Model specification	No	Trust

- **Semantic annotations (SA):** It indicates wether semantic annotations are used or no;
- **Research:** It specifies the research area.

7 Cloud Services Discovery: SaaS

Such as the SaaS service is a new emerging business model in the software industry and due to the large number and diversity of available SaaS services using Cloud infrastructure, finding the service(s) that are relevant to a specific request remains a challenge. Thus, the clients will be able to access to SaaS services according to their requirements, without regard to where the services are hosted or how they are delivered. In the literature, it has been stated that current SaaS discovery does not have a reference model. We limit ourselves to some existing techniques and we present a comparative study in Table 4 according to the following criteria:

- **Architecture (AR):** It specifies the used architecture (P2P,Specific,etc.).
- **Representation (R):** It illustrates the used formalism to model Saas (Graph,Vector,etc.).
- **Language(L):** It defines the used description language (WADL,OWL,etc.).
- **Properties (P):** It includes Functional (Yes) or non-functional properties (No (QoS, Profile,etc.)).
- **Type (T):** It defines the Cloud type (Public, Private,etc.).

Table 4. Synthesis of SaaS discovery approaches

Ref.	AR	R	L	P	T
Khan et al. [34]	/	T vector	/	Yes	Community
Elgazzar et al. [35]	Mobile agent (DaaS)	/	WADL	Yes	Public
			WSDL	No (profile)	
Li et al. [36]	/	Ontology	OWL-S	Yes	Public
				No	
Talal et al. [37]	Specific (CSCE)	/	WADL	Yes	Public
			WSDL		
Mukhopadhyay et al. [38]	Specific	/	OWL	No(Qos)	Community
Hamza et al. [39]	Mobile Agent	/	/	Yes	Public
Xiangbing et al. [40]	/	Bayesian nets and graph	WSDL-S	Yes	Public
Chien et al. [41]	P2P	/	WADL	No	Public
			WSDL		
Ranjan et al. [42]	P2P	/	/	Yes	Public
					Private

Figure 2 shows our proposed classification of the most known approaches of SaaS discovery. Two big classes are defined in SaaS discovery: Models based approaches and architecture based approaches. A tremendous number of research papers had been published, focusing on different aspects of the SaaS discovery. The research tends to focus on issues related to the non-functional properties and functional properties. We divided them into two groups: First, approaches which consider a syntactic description and second, approaches which consider a semantic description. These usually deal with a specific model of interaction such as Graph theory, Vector, Matching, and Bayezian Nets. The approaches based on non-functional properties concern the quality of the execution process affected by the QoS(Quality of Service) attributes which are non- functional properties of services. Thus, we propose to classify the discovery approches as follow.

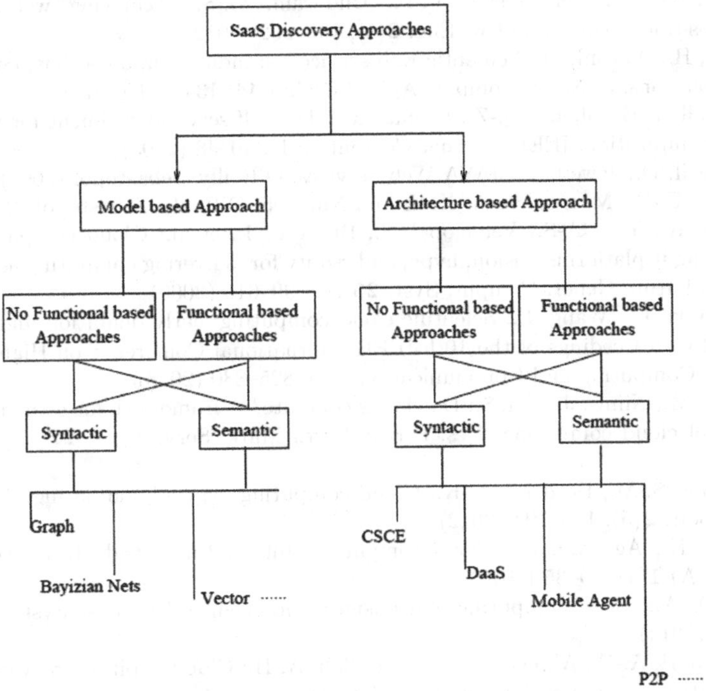

Fig. 2. Classification of discovery approches of SaaS services cloud.

8 Conclusion

In this paper, we have presented a comparison study between on two types of services, Web services and Cloud services. The obtained results, from a comparison study, provide useful guidelines for the design of services and accelerate CC from early prototypes to production systems. Web services and SOA have been offering many advantages by solving the communication problem: The Web services technology can let different platforms cooperate smoothly. Web services technology ensures the interoperabilty. However, with the virtualization, CC paradigm, viewed as a distributed online model, may be a promising solution in the future. Combined with Web services technology, it can be another alternative of distributed computing infrastructure: Cloud services with Web services technology can be the best solution for implementing commercial or open source software.

References

1. W3C. The world wide web consortium. http://www.w3.org/
2. Willy, C.: Technology SOA and web services. The performance paradox. http://www.ca.com/us/whitepapers/collateral.aspx?cid=147947
3. Portchelvi, V., Venkatesan, V.-P., Undaram, G.-S.: Achieving web services composition–a survey. Softw. Eng. **2**(5), 195–202 (2012)
4. Nacer, H., Aissani, D.: Semantic web services: standards, applications, challenges and solutions. J. Netw. Comput. Appl. (JNCA) **44**, 134–151 (2014)
5. Benatallah, B., Sheng, Q.-Z., Dumas, M.: The self-serv environment for web services composition. IEEE Internet Comput. **7**(1), 40–48 (2003)
6. Chappell, D., Jewell, T.: JAVA Web Services. O'Reilly, Sebastopol (2002)
7. Harold, E.-R., Means, W.-S.: XML in a Nutshell. O'Reilly, Sebastopol (2004)
8. Buyya, R., Yeo, C.-S., Venugopal, S., Broberg, J., et al.: Cloud computing and emerging it platforms: vision, hype, and reality for delivering computing as the 5th utility. Future Gener. Comput. Syst. **25**(6), 599–616 (2009)
9. Laszewski, G., Wang, L.: Scientific cloud computing: early definition and experience. In: Proceedings of the 10th IEEE International Conference on High Performance Computing and Communications, pp. 825–830 (2008)
10. Klems, M., Nimis, J., Tai, S.: Do clouds compute? A framework for estimating the value of cloud computing. Des. E-Bus. Syst.: Mark. Serv. Netw. **22**(4), 110–123 (2009)
11. Hashemi, S.-M., Bardsiri, A.-K.: Cloud computing vs. grid computing. ARPN J. Syst. Soft. **2**(5), 188–194 (2012)
12. Axena, K., Agarwal, K.: Cloud computing. Int. J. Eng. Stud. Tech. Approach (IJESTA) **1**(4), 29–35 (2012)
13. Tole, A.-A.: Cloud computing and business intelligence. Database Syst. J. **V**(4), 49–57 (2014)
14. Elsanhouri, A.-E., Ahmed, M.-A., Abdullah, A.-H.: Cloud applications versus web application: a differential study. In: 1st International Conference on Communications, Computation, Networks and Technologies, Venice, Italy, 21–26 October 2012
15. Elvesater, B., Jargen, B.-A., Sadovykh, A.: Specifying services using the service oriented architecture modeling language (SoaML): a baseline for specification of cloud-based services. In: Proceedings of the 1st International Conference on Cloud Computing and Services Science (Closer), Netherlands, pp. 276–285 (2011)
16. Cardoso, J., Barros, A., May, N., Kylau, U.: Towards a unified service description language for the internet of services: requirements and first developments. In: Proceedings of the 10th IEEE International Conference on Services Computing (SCC), Washington, USA, pp. 602–609 (2010)

17. Liu, X., Tong, W., ZhiRen, F., et al.: BSPCloud: a hybrid distributed-memory and shared-memory programming model. Int. J. Grid Distrib. Comput. **6**(1), 87–97 (2013)
18. Dean, J., Ghemawat, S.: MapReduce: simplified data processing on large clusters. Commun. ACM **51**(1), 107–113 (2008)
19. Isard, M., Budiu, M., Yuan Dryad, Y., et al.: Distributed data-parallel programs from sequential building blocks. In: Proceedings of the 2nd ACM SIGOPS/EuroSys European Conference on Computer Systems, Lisbon, Portugal, pp. 59–72 (2007)
20. WSM. Web service modelling language. http://www.wsmo.org/wsml/
21. Nguyen, D.K., Lelli, F.-L., Papazoglou, P., Van, W.-J., et al.: Blueprinting approach in support of cloud computing. Future Internet **4**(1), 322–346 (2012)
22. Liu, D., Zic, J.: Cloud#: a specification language for modeling cloud. In: Proceedings of 4th International Conference IEEE on Cloud Computing, pp. 533–540 (2011)
23. Baget, J.F., Canaud, E., Euzenat, J., et al.: Les langages du web semantique (in french). Technical report, INRIA Rhone-Alpes and LIRIS FRE 2672 CNRS University of Claude Bernard Lyon 1 (2003)
24. Charlet, J., Laublet, P., Reynaud, C.: Action web semantique specifique (in french). Technical report, V3, 32 CNRS/STIC (2003)
25. Lacot, X.: Introduction à owl, un langage xml d'ontologies web, enjeux, objectifs et mise en oeuvre. http://www.lacot.org/public/owl
26. Web-Site. DAML ontology library. http://www.daml.org/ontologies/
27. Web-Site. The owl services coalition, owl-s: semantic murkup for web services. http://www.w3.org/submission/owl-s/
28. Domingue, J., Cabral, L., Hakimpour, H., Sell, D., el al.: IRS-III: a platform and infrastructure for creating WSMO-based semantic web services. In: Proceedings of the Workshop on WSMO Implementations (WIW), vol. 113, pp. 29–30 (2004)
29. Web-Site. Web services modelling ontology. http://www.wsmo.org/
30. Akkiraju, R., Farell, J., Miller, J.-A., et al.: Web service semantics-WSDL-S. UGA-IBM Technical Note (2005). http://www.w3.org/2005/04/FSWS/Submissions/17/WSDL-S.htm
31. W3C. Semantic annotations for WSDL and XML schema. http://www.w3.org/tr/2007/rec-sawsdl-20070828
32. Sun, L., Jiangan, M., Wang, H., Yanchun, Z.: Cloud service description model: an extension of USDL for cloud services. IEEE Trans. Serv. Comput. 1 (2015). doi:10.1109/TSC.2015.2474386
33. Web-Site. Description logic. http://dl.kr.org/
34. Khan, G., Sengupta, S., Sarkar, A., Debnath, N.-C.: Web service discovery in enterprise cloud bus framework: T vector based model. In: Proceeding of 13th IEEE International Conference on Industrial Informatics (INDIN), pp. 1672–1677 (2015)
35. Elgazzar, K., Hassanein, H.-S., Martin, P.: DaaS: Cloud-based mobile web service discovery. Pervasive Mob. Comput. **13**, 67–84 (2014)
36. Li, H., Zhang, L., Jiang, R.: Study of manufacturing cloud service matching algorithm based on OWL-S. In: Proceeding of The 26th Chinese Conference n Control and Decision (CCDC), pp. 4155–4160 (2014)
37. Talal, H., Quan, Z., Anne, H., Schahram, D.: Analysis of web-scale cloud services. IEEE Internet Comput. **18**(4), 55–61 (2014)
38. Mukhopadhyay, D., Chathly, F.-J., Jadhav, N.: QoS based framework for effective web services in cloud computing. J. Softw. Eng. Appl. **5**(11), 952–960 (2012)

39. Hamza, S., Okba, K., Youssef, A., et al.: A cloud computing approach based on mobile agents for web services discovery. In: Proceeding of the 2nd International Conference on Innovative Computing Technology (INTECH), pp. 297–304 (2012)
40. Xiangbing, Z., Fang, M.: A semantics web service composition approach based on cloud computing. In: Proceeding of the 4th International Conference on Computational and Information Sciences (ICCIS), pp. 807–810 (2012)
41. Chien, H., Chang, J.-M., Liu, H.-T., Chao, H.-C.: Design a novel scheme for dual-stack cloud file service discovery based on distributed hash table. In: Proceeding of the 5th International Conference on Future Information Technology (FutureTech), pp. 1–6 (2010)
42. Buyya, R., Ranjan, R., Calheiros, R.N.: InterCloud: utility-oriented federation of cloud computing environments for scaling of application services. In: Hsu, C.-H., Yang, L.T., Park, J.H., Yeo, S.-S. (eds.) ICA3PP 2010. LNCS, vol. 6081, pp. 13–31. Springer, Heidelberg (2010). doi:10.1007/978-3-642-13119-6_2

Improving Attack Graph Scalability for the Cloud Through SDN-Based Decomposition and Parallel Processing

Oussama Mjihil[1(✉)], Dijiang Huang[2], and Abdelkrim Haqiq[1,3]

[1] Computer, Networks, Mobility and Modeling Laboratory, FST, Hassan 1st University, Settat, Morocco
o.mjihil@uhp.ac.ma, ahaqiq@gmail.com

[2] School of Computing, Informatics and Decision Systems Engineering, Arizona State University, Tempe, AZ, USA
Dijiang@asu.edu

[3] e-NGN Research Group, Africa and Middle East, Settat, Morocco

Abstract. Due to its fast growth, Cloud computing is a quick evolving research area. Security, which is among the most required Cloud features, is a very hard and challenging task when it's addressed for large networked systems. To automate security assessment, one should use an Attack Representation Model (ARM), such as Attack Graph (AG) or Attack Tree, to represent and analyze multi-host multi-stage attacks. In order to improve AG analysis for large-scale networked systems, our framework uses Software-defined Networking (SDN) to build a detailed and dynamic knowledge about the network configuration and the host access control list. Altogether with machine configuration information, our framework will be able to construct loosely connected sub-groups of virtual machines and perform a parallel security analysis. We have performed experimental validation using a real networked system to show the performance improvement in comparison with MULVAL network security analyzer.

Keywords: Attack Representation Models · Scalability · Graph theory

1 Introduction

Cloud computing allows tenants, individuals or organizations, to externalize totally or partially their networked systems, which might contain a large number of Virtual Machines (VMs) and virtual networking components. In this sense, we can easily observe that for a large number of tenants, the Cloud network topology becomes complex. Consequently, security assessment and mitigation becomes a very challenging task.

The main idea of this work is to address the scalability issue encountered during a graph-based security assessment of a large virtual network. We will

E. Sabir et al. (Eds.): UNet 2017, LNCS 10542, pp. 193–205, 2017.
https://doi.org/10.1007/978-3-319-68179-5_17

show in this paper how we reduce the security assessment time and improve the scalability of our graph-based security framework using decomposition and parallel computation altogether with Software-defined Networking [18] (SDN) features. Our framework is a model-based (here, we use Attack Graph [23,27] (AG)) distributed tool designed for scalable Cloud infrastructures.

For large and sparse networked systems, our security tool will break down the network, which will be a directed graph, into smaller sub-graphs using a well known and proven graph theory technique called Strongly Connected Components(SCC) decomposition (here, we use an adapted version of Kosaraju's algorithm [26]). After that, we perform a parallel security analysis for each component and also for the matching between them.

The current solution improves significantly AG visualization and evaluation for scalable Cloud platforms compared to the traditional model-based security analysis systems. It takes advantages of SDN features, graph partitioning, parallel and distributed systems to provide efficient and more scalable security analysis tool. The contributions of this work are presented as follows:

- This work addresses the security analysis scalability issue in the Cloud using graph partitioning.
- This framework will reduce the security analysis time in all its phases (reprocessing, construction, evaluation, countermeasure selection and application) in comparison with the current suggested model-based security tools, thanks to its distributed nature.
- This framework will be able to adapt to any reconfiguration that can occur in the cloud architecture using Software-Defined Networking.

This paper presents the design and implementation details and also a real application scenario of our framework. The rest of this paper is organized as follows. After presenting the related work in Sect. 2, we show the main security challenges in Cloud computing in Sect. 3, we present the framework design and implementation in Sect. 4 followed by the performance evaluation in Sect. 5, and finally, we conclude our paper in Sect. 6.

2 Related Work

In this section, we present previous researches related to Cloud computing security assessment, graph partitioning, and distributed security frameworks. For small networked systems containing a limited number of vulnerabilities, security evaluation can be performed manually by security experts. But the complexity of this task increases dramatically when the number of vulnerable hosts increases.

Many Attack Representation Models (ARMs) have been suggested to provide a pertinent representation of the system's vulnerabilities and their relationships. The well known ARMs are either graph-based [23,27] or tree-based [25]. The graph-based ARMs provide a complete picture about all attack paths that can be used by an attacker to compromise VMs, but these models suffer from a severe scalability problem when the number of vulnerabilities and their reachability are important.

Many distinguished research works have suggested frameworks, tools, and models to automate security assessment processes. As an example, MULVAL [24], which is a network security analyzer, use Datalog as a modeling language to represent vulnerabilities, network configuration, security rules and other security related information. This tool has been improved in a related work [23] to be able to generate a logical attack graph in quadratic time, and space polynomial in the network size. A performance comparison has proved that Mulval is more scalable than Sheyner's AG generation tool [27]. Sheyner's tool uses model-checking technique and suffers from an exponential explosion problem. The previous comparison is not enough to say that MULVAL is a scalable security analysis tool for the simple reason that AG generation is just one step among others in security assessment process. It has been confirmed that at the representation phase or attack scenarios generation from a logical attack graph, Mulval may encounter an exponential explosion problem [23]. Our work is focused on the exploitation of AG rather than its generation, so we improved the visualization and attack scenarios extraction using the previously mentioned techniques. Some recent works dealt with the state space explosion in AG processing using distributed systems. In our previous work [21], we presented a distributed model-based security assessment to attenuate the scalability problem in multi-tenant cloud platforms. Accordingly, a distributed AG generation using hypergraph partitioning, at the application level, has been suggested in [13].

Software-Defined Networking (SDN) [15,16,22] has been presented as a new computer networking paradigm which makes the virtual networks highly scalable and dynamically adjustable. In our work, we use OpenDayLight [1] SDN controller and OpenFlow protocol [19] to control and administrate dynamically the network configuration and security policies. From the SDN side, our framework is a northbound application which can manage the flow rules and update them as a form of countermeasures application technique.

Graph theory has been applied in a large number of domains, including security [13]. The graph partitioning problem is NP-complete. However, partitioning has been widely addressed either for directed or undirected graphs. For undirected graphs, many greedy and heuristic decomposition techniques have been introduced. Karypis *et al.* [10,11] presented multilevel partitioning and developed a widely used Parallel Graph Partitioning and Sparse Matrix Ordering Library, called ParMetis [12]. A heuristic decomposition approach called fill-reducing ordering have been introduced by Bui and Jones [5]. We mention also *Kernighan_Lin* algorithm, which is a heuristic procedure for partitioning graphs [14]. For directed graphs (e.g., VM reachability graph at the application level), Tarjan [29] introduced an efficient linear-time algorithm for finding strongly connected components using Depth-first Search (DFS). Accordingly, Kosaraju-Sharir [26] provided an algorithm using two Depth-first search to simplify the previous algorithm. Gabow [9] also developed an algorithm for strongly connected components that is based on cycles contraction and using two stacks to make it run in linear time.

3 Motivation

The objective of this paper is to address security challenges related to scalability and dynamic adjustment in Cloud computing. According to its standard definition, Cloud computing enables an agile and dynamic management of large scale computing resources, such as networks, servers, storage and so on [20].

3.1 Cloud Computing Agility

Cloud computing networking agility has a significant impact on security assessment in spite of its importance for the CSPs. Software Defined Networking (SDN) [8] concept has been introduced to extend the Cloud agility by separating the control plane which is practically represented by a set of applications, called SDN controllers, and the data plane which handles the network packets following the decisions made by the control plane. Although, it is difficult to keep track of the system's security status when the network topology or some of its parts are changing frequently. From another point of view, this automation can be used as a Moving Target Defence (MTD) technique. Thus, after any modification one should make sure that the security status remains intact, elsewhere security assessment process shall be performed at least for the updated parts of the network topology. We will show in this current work how a network decomposition will reduce the impact of the occurred configuration updates on the Cloud security status.

3.2 Cloud Computing Multi-tenancy

Cloud computing is generally designed to support multi-tenancy. In other words, CSPs ensure that virtual machines of one tenant are isolated from the rest of virtual machines in the Cloud. Moreover, tenant organizations are allowed not only to host their VMs in the Cloud, but they are able to build their own networked systems according to their own specifications. Some CSPs enable a network level isolation using VLANs or Private VLANs and, recently, others are suggesting a complete isolation of the tenant VMs and virtual networking components using nested virtualization [4,7]. At any time, tenants can assess the current security status of their virtual networked systems, which can be done either by a proprietary tool or relying on the CSP's security platform.

3.3 Cloud Computing Scalability

Scalability is one of the most critical challenges in Cloud computing. Many individuals and organizations are joining increasingly and unceasingly the Cloud, which drives the CSPs to scale up their IT infrastructures to be able to handle the increasing demand. Accordingly, security assessment frameworks are negatively impacted by this growth. For example, Model-based tools cannot yet be used for real Cloud Platforms since all models (e.g., Attack Graph, Attack Tree) are suffering from scalability problems. It has been proven that a few number of hosts and vulnerabilities can produce a nonhuman-readable graph in an exponential time. As we presented before, there have been many suggestions to deal with the scalability issue and the challenge still remains. In this work we use decomposition and parallel processing to deal with this issue.

4 Security Framework Design and Implementation

4.1 Capturing the Network Topology and Machine Configuration

The main concern of security assessment is to evaluate the network weakness and how it is vulnerable to possible attacks. Such measurement cannot be obtained without a high level of details and information about the network topology and the software level vulnerabilities altogether. In this work, we mean by network topology the combination of layer two, three and four connection between virtual machines, and we mean by machine configuration the set of security policies applied on each virtual machine and the list of their services and applications. For security reasons, a layer two and three connectivity information, referring to the OSI model, will not be sufficient. Layer four connection determined by source and destination addresses and a port number can provide additional information about the open ports, and hence the currently allowed/blocked protocols or services between two communicating hosts. Security analysis process, in previously suggested frameworks, generally requires two complementary information:

- Reachability information: The network topology.
- Vulnerability information: The result of the complete analysis of all virtual machines and hosts of the target network.

To provide more precision, our framework has a centralized vision about the networked system using an SDN controller. This information is stored in the network controller in form of flow rules which are sent and kept in accordance with the open-flow enabled switches of our network. The flow rules can go to an advanced level of granularity and target a specific port with an appropriate action. Additional information is supported by Open-flow protocol like the source and destination of the traffic, the priority of flow rules and whether a flow rule is permanent or temporary and so on. In our context, flow rules will be the key elements for the network topology construction.

Reachability graph is a directed graph which requires precise information about the network connectivity, applications, and services running on each host and in which direction the traffic is allowed to flow. We notice that when the flow rules mention that the traffic is allowed between a source and destination hosts, in both direction, using a given port, it will not be possible to determine where the service is installed. Moreover, any presentation based on only this information will give us the impression that the service (e.g., the web service) is installed in both the communicating machines. For the previous reasons, our framework use machine configuration information and security policies to be able to construct the reachability graph with more accuracy, so it will be aware also of the applications currently installed in each VM, and then it will use this knowledge for reachability graph construction, intrusion prevention, or countermeasure application. Figure 1 illustrates the most important components of our framework.

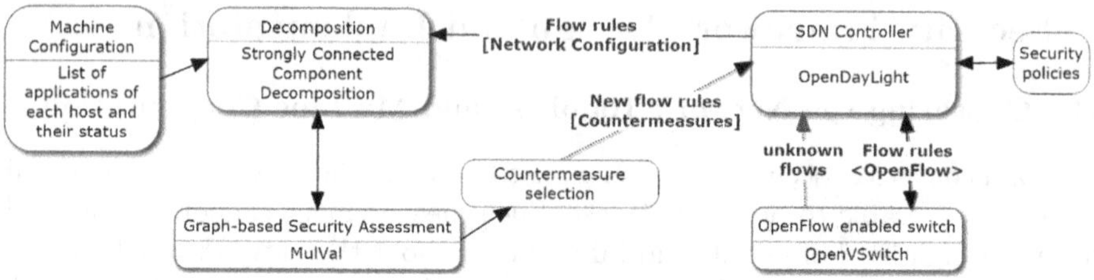

Fig. 1. SDN-based security framework modules

Security assessment is a sequence of consecutive phases. Each phase requires some input information and produces a result, which in turn will be used as input for the next phase. Figure 2 illustrates the sequence of operations performed in order to perform security assessment.

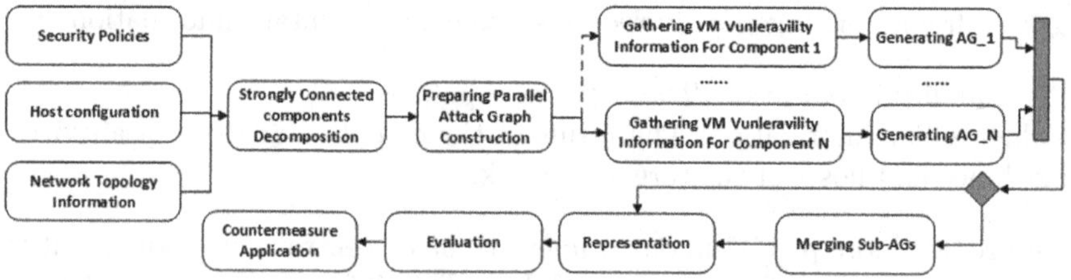

Fig. 2. Software architecture

4.2 Strongly Connected Components Decomposition

The Cloud is designed to host large networking infrastructures, so tenants can deploy an important number of connected VMs. We should mention that the sparsity of the reachability graph is required, because a high connectivity links between VMs is not desirable from the network design perspective (see Sect. 6), and the decomposition of complete graphs is an NP-Complete problem [6].

In networked systems, VMs and their connectivity information are forming a directed graph G = (V,E) where V (or V(G)) is a set of Vertexes and E (or E(G)) is a set of directed edges. Our goal is to break down the main directed graph into a set of sub-graphs without breaking down the links between the strongly connected vertexes (VMs). In graph theory, strongly connected components [26,29] of a directed graph are sub-graphs $C \subseteq V$ containing mutually reachable vertexes. From a security perspective, for each two adjacent components, the connectivity will be in one direction, which means that the influence and reachability between the adjacent AGs are unidirectional. After this decomposition, components will be processed in parallel in all security assessment phases. The matching process will rely on the number of edges connecting two adjacent SCCs and the reachable vulnerabilities in the direction of these edges.

The algorithm presented in [26] detects and returns the graph's strongly connected components, where each vertex of the graph appears in exactly one of the strongly connected components, in a linear time $\mathcal{O}(|V|+|E|)$. This algorithm accepts, as an input parameter, a linked list representing the vertexes' adjacency, which requires $\mathcal{O}(|V|+|E|)$ of memory. The algorithm we used in this work is derived from Kasaraju-Sharir's algorithm [26], which performs two Depth-First Searches (DFSs). The goal of the first DFS is to get the topological order of the vertexes, while the second DFS is applied on the transposed graph to discover the strongly connected components.

Figure 3 shows an example of a reachability graph and Fig. 4 shows the components obtained using Algorithm 1.

Algorithm 1. Strongly Connected Components

```
function FINDSCCs(Directed Graph G(V,E))
Step 1: Depth-First Search applied to G :
    S, Visited = ϕ
    for All vertexes do
        v ← The current vertex
        if v ∉ V then                              ▷ Select a non visited node
            topologicalSort(v,S)
        end if
    end for
Step 2: Depth-First Search applied to G^T :
    SCCs, Visited = ϕ; G^T = getTranspose(G)
    for each v in S do
        if v in visited: continue                  ▷ Ignore visited nodes
        SCC = graphTraversal(G^T,v,Visited)
        Visited.update(SCC)                        ▷ Mark C as visited
        SCCs.append(SCC)                           ▷ Add SCC to SCCs
    end for
    return SCCs
end function
```

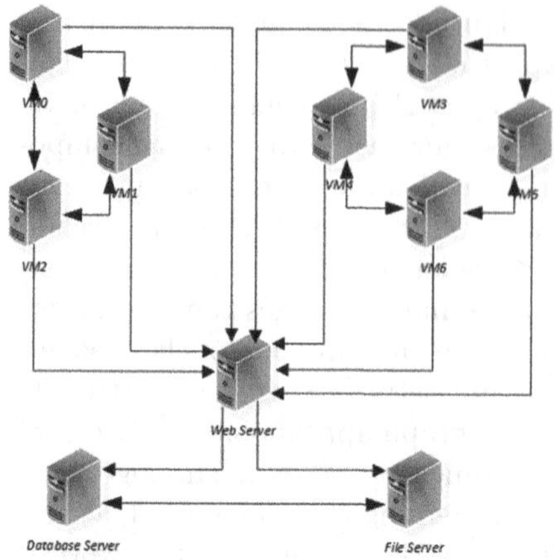

Fig. 3. Tenant's virtual networked system

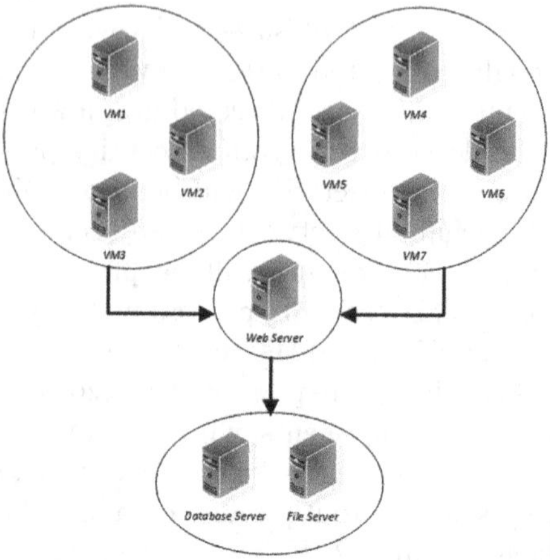

Fig. 4. Strongly connected components

4.3 Matching AGs

To guarantee that no information will be lost after decomposition, we generate two types of Attack Graph:

- An AG for each SCC, denoted as `Sub_AG`. This AG will represent only the internal interaction between SCC's vulnerabilities.
- AGs representing the external edges connecting the adjacent SCCs. We denote these graphs as `Match_AG`.

Once `Sub_AGs` are generated for each SCC, they can be used for security assessment purposes, such as |Sub_AG| visualization, local attack paths generation, and countermeasure selection. However, to build a complete knowledge (e.g., AG) about the entire network security, `Sub_AGs` and `Match_AGs` will be provided as input to the merging algorithm. This algorithm consists of two consecutive steps. The objective of the first step is to find the adjacent SCCs. Two SCCs are adjacent if, at least, one host in one SCC is connected to a host belonging to another SCC. We mention that, according to Algorithm 1, all edges connecting two SCCs have the same direction. In the second step, the algorithm will visit each two adjacent SCCs and match their `Sub_AGs` using information from the corresponding `Match_AG`. The list of edges of `Sub_AGs` vulnerabilities will be extended according to `Match_AG` vulnerability information.

Since each host can belong only to one SCC, the computational cost is giving by the number of hosts added to the number of edges. Thus, The complexity is directly proportional to the number of edges in the adjacency list. The complexity, of the first and the second steps, is $\mathcal{O}(|V| + |E|)$.

5 Performance Evaluation

5.1 System Setup

Our experimental environment was built using a 6th generation Core i7 Processor, 16 GB DDR4 2133 MHz and 1TB 5400 RPM+256GB SSD. We have built the networked system shown in Fig. 3 using OpenVSwitch, OpenDayLight controller, and OpenFlow protocol to manage the network configuration automatically. To interact with the SDN controller and use it for security purposes, we are using a RESTful northbound application. This application gets the active flow rules from the controller to build the reachability graph and sends new flow rules to the controller (e.g., blocking an IP address) as countermeasure application.

Building an ARM starts with gathering the system's vulnerability information using a vulnerability scanner, such as Nessus [3], Nmap [17], OpenVAS [2] and so on. Our system uses actually Nessus vulnerability scanner to discover the existent vulnerabilities in our VMs. As a scanning output, we get, for each host, the list of vulnerabilities and some additional information about them. This information is describing vulnerabilities in isolation, so we cannot easily deduce the potential exploits in case of multi-host multi-stage attacks. In this work, we are addressing the scalability issue encountered by graph-based security tools, such as MULVAL.

After decomposition and vulnerability scanning, we send the `Sub_AGs` and their `Match_AGs` to be executed in parallel using the 8 virtual cores of our system. We used GNU parallel [28] to execute these parallel tasks.

In our experiment, have considered four different types of virtual machines:

Web Server: For experimental reasons we have installed, on this host, vulnerable versions of Tomcat, Apache HTTP Server, Sun Java System Application Server, and other related services.

File Server: A virtual machine hosting Wing and other FTP Servers. We have installed ImageMagick as an example of applications that can impact the file servers' security. For example, ImageMagick could allow remote attackers to perform server-side request forgery using crafted image files.

Database Server: This host contains an Oracle MySQL server and a vulnerable version of Pluggable Authentication Modules (PAM), which are used to authenticate users.

Other VMs are hosting client applications for browsing, programming tools, and other services. We have installed, on these VMs, a vulnerable version of Safari, SSH Tectia Client Server Connector, and GNU C Library.

5.2 Experimental Results

The effectiveness of decomposition and parallel processing in AG generation and analysis have been verified using two complementary experiments, in which we measured the performance of AG generation and visualization before and after decomposition and also when the number of vulnerabilities increases. Our framework is using MULVAL, so the AG generated is a Logical Attack Graph. The improvement will concern the visualization phase, where MULVAL is facing a severe scalability issue.

After a general scan of our experimental networked system, Nessus vulnerability scanner reported the vulnerabilities shown in Table 1. In this experiment, we measured the required time to construct and visualize an AG using MULVAL for the entire network and we compare it with the time required to generate and visualize AG after decomposition. In this case, we are considering the same network architecture as illustrated in Fig. 3. The variation will concern the number of hosts and consequently the number of SCCs. During this evaluation, we took into account the external edges connecting adjacent SCCs using the matching technique we exposed previously.

Table 1. Vulnerability analysis report

Hosts	CVE ID	Service	Exportability	Consequence	CVSS v3
Web Server	CVE-2012-0053	http_server	Remote	privEscalation	Medium
Web Server	CVE-2009-3548	tomcat	Remote	privEscalation	Low
Web Server	CVE-2010-0386	java_server	Remote	privEscalation	Medium
Web Server	CVE-2016-0800	openssl	Remote	privEscalation	Medium
Web Server	CVE-2015-8874	php	Remote	service disruption	Low
File Server	CVE-2016-3718	image_magic	Remote	privEscalation	Medium
File Server	CVE-2015-4107	ftp	Remote	privEscalation	Medium
File Server	CVE-2015-4108	ftp	Remote	privEscalation	Medium
Database	CVE-2013-7041	pam_userdb	Remote	privEscalation	Medium
Database	CVE-2016-6662	pam_userdb	Remote	privEscalation	Medium
VMs	CVE-2015-2808	safari	Remote	privEscalation	Medium
VMs	CVE-2013-2207	glibc	Local	privEscalation	High
VMs	CVE-2008-5161	openssh	Remote	privEscalation	High

The evaluation result, shown in Fig. 5, confirmed the following information:

- Decomposition and parallel processing are improving the execution time of AG generation and exploitation.
- The more the network is sparse and balanced the more security assessment is less time consuming.

Figure 6 shows that decomposition will reduce the impact of the increasing number of vulnerabilities on AG generation and visualization. In this case, We kept the same number of hosts and SCCs and we changed only the number of vulnerabilities. The time difference started to increase when we injected vulnerabilities in different hosts located in different SCCs.

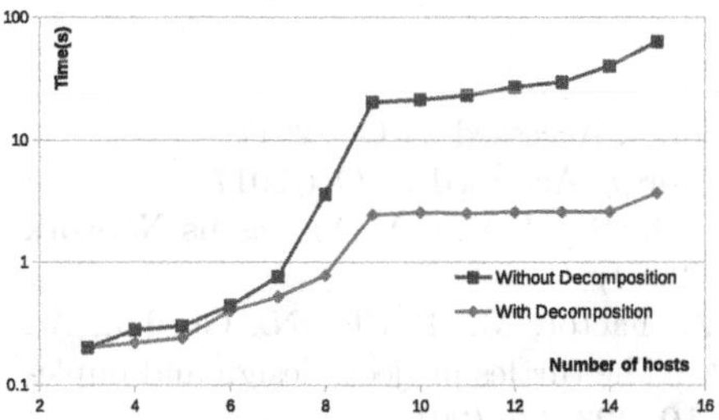

Fig. 5. The impact of the number of hosts and SCCs.

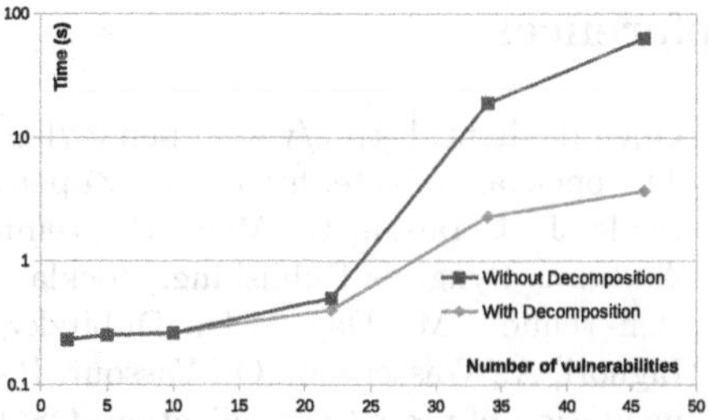

Fig. 6. The impact of the number of vulnerabilities.

5.3 Discussion

The Cloud Network Sparsity. In some extreme scenarios, the number of strongly connected nodes (VMs) can be important, due to a special network design allowing all VMs to communicate to each other, a poor network design, or the absence of security policies. It is well known that decomposition of complete graphs falls under the category of NP-hard problems, and It is not practically helpful to break down strongly connected components into sub-components. Accordingly, practical solutions for this kind of problems are based on heuristics and approximations.

Network Topology Updates. With SCC decomposition we obtain sub-groups, which are not mutually impacting each other. Thus, we distinguish two kinds of network topology updates:

- Internal update: When the update is concerning SCC hosts. Only the security status of the SCC will require an update and not the entire system.
- External update: When the update is concerning external edges connecting hosts located in different SCCs, The direction of the link will determine whether only the `Match_AG` shall be updated or both SCCs shall be merged.

6 Conclusion

We have proposed a security framework to improve Graph-based security assessment scalability using SDN-based techniques, decomposition, and parallel computation. Our framework has significantly improved AG generation and representation time in comparison with MULVAL's current AG generation and visualization techniques. We have presented how SDN features are used in the pre-processing phase as well as for countermeasure application. We discussed the level of granularity that the framework should have to be able to construct reachability graph and perform a meaningful decomposition. The experimental results have shown that our security framework can be very efficient for Cloud computing security assessment.

References

1. Open daylight. http://www.opendaylight.org/. Accessed 24 Oct 2017
2. The openvas website. http://www.openvas.org/. Accessed 24 Oct 2017
3. Beale, J., Deraison, R., Meer, H., Temmingh, R., Walt, C.V.D.: Nessus Network Auditing. Syngress Publishing, Rockland (2004)
4. Ben-Yehuda, M., Day, M.D., Dubitzky, Z., Factor, M., Har'El, N., Gordon, A., Liguori, A., Wasserman, O., Yassour, B.-A.: The turtles project: design and implementation of nested virtualization. OSDI **10**, 423–436 (2010)
5. Bui, T.N., Jones, C.: A heuristic for reducing fill-in in sparse matrix factorization. Technical report, Society for Industrial and Applied Mathematics (SIAM), Philadelphia, PA (United States) (1993)
6. Dor, D., Tarsi, M.: Graph decomposition is NP-complete: a complete proof of Holyer's conjecture. SIAM J. Comput. **26**(4), 1166–1187 (1997)
7. Fishman, A., Rapoport, M., Budilovsky, E., Eidus, I., et al.: HVX: virtualizing the cloud. In: HotCloud. Citeseer (2013)
8. Open Networking Foundation: Software-defined networking: the new norm for networks. ONF White Paper (2012)
9. Gabow, H.N.: Path-based depth-first search for strong and biconnected components. Inf. Process. Lett. **74**(3), 107–114 (2000)
10. Karypis, G., Kumar, V.: Analysis of multilevel graph partitioning. In: Proceedings of the 1995 ACM/IEEE Conference on Supercomputing, p. 29. ACM (1995)
11. Karypis, G., Kumar, V.: Multilevel k-way partitioning scheme for irregular graphs. J. Parallel Distrib. comput. **48**(1), 96–129 (1998)
12. Karypis, G., Schloegel, K., Kumar, V.: Parmetis: parallel graph partitioning and sparse matrix ordering library. Version 1.0, Department of Computer Science, University of Minnesota (1997)
13. Kaynar, K., Sivrikaya, F.: Distributed attack graph generation. IEEE Trans. Dependable Secure Comput. **13**(5), 519–532 (2016)
14. Kernighan, B.W., Lin, S.: An efficient heuristic procedure for partitioning graphs. Bell Syst. Tech. J. **49**(2), 291–307 (1970)
15. Kim, H., Feamster, N.: Improving network management with software defined networking. IEEE Commun. Mag. **51**(2), 114–119 (2013)
16. Lantz, B., Heller, B., McKeown, N.: A network in a laptop: rapid prototyping for software-defined networks. In: Proceedings of the 9th ACM SIGCOMM Workshop on Hot Topics in Networks, p. 19. ACM (2010)
17. Lyon, G.F.: Nmap Network Scanning: The Official Nmap Project Guide to Network Discovery and Security Scanning. Insecure, Cheers (2009)
18. McKeown, N.: Software-defined networking. INFOCOM Keynote Talk **17**(2), 30–32 (2009)
19. McKeown, N., Anderson, T., Balakrishnan, H., Parulkar, G., Peterson, L., Rexford, J., Shenker, S., Turner, J.: Openflow: enabling innovation in campus networks. ACM SIGCOMM Comput. Commun. Rev. **38**(2), 69–74 (2008)
20. Mell, P., Grance, T.: The NIST definition of cloud computing (2011)
21. Mjihil, O., Kim, D.S., Haqiq, A.: Security assessment framework for multi-tenant cloud with nested virtualization. J. Inf. Assur. Secur. **11**(2), 283–292 (2016)
22. Nunes, B.A.A., Mendonca, M., Nguyen, X.-N., Obraczka, K., Turletti, T.: A survey of software-defined networking: past, present, and future of programmable networks. IEEE Commun. Surv. Tutorials **16**(3), 1617–1634 (2014)

23. Ou, X., Boyer, W.F., McQueen, M.A.: A scalable approach to attack graph generation. In: Proceedings of the 13th ACM Conference on Computer and Communications Security, pp. 336–345. ACM (2006)
24. Ou, X., Govindavajhala, S., Appel, A.W.: MulVAL: a logic-based network security analyzer. In: USENIX Security (2005)
25. Schneier, B.: Attack trees. Dr. Dobbs J. **24**(12), 21–29 (1999)
26. Sharir, M.: A strong-connectivity algorithm and its applications in data flow analysis. Comput. Math. Appl. **7**(1), 67–72 (1981)
27. Sheyner, O., Haines, J., Jha, S., Lippmann, R., Wing, J.M.: Automated generation and analysis of attack graphs. In: Proceedings of 2002 IEEE Symposium on Security and privacy, pp. 273–284. IEEE (2002)
28. Tange, O., et al.: GNU parallel-the command-line power tool. USENIX Mag. **36**(1), 42–47 (2011)
29. Tarjan, R.: Depth-first search and linear graph algorithms. SIAM J. Comput. **1**(2), 146–160 (1972)

Performance Analysis of Intrusion Detection Systems in Cloud-Based Systems

Rachid Cherkaoui[1,2](✉), Mostapha Zbakh[1], An Braeken[2], and Abdellah Touhafi[2]

[1] ISeRT, ENSIAS College, Mohammed V University in Rabat, Rabat, Morocco
{rachid_cherkaoui,mostapha.zbakh}@um5.ac.ma
[2] INDI - Industrial Engineering Sciences Department, Vrije Universiteit Brussel - VUB, Brussels, Belgium
{rachid.cherkaoui,an.braeken,abdellah.touhafi}@vub.ac.be

Abstract. Cloud computing services are widely used nowadays and need to be more secured for an effective exploitation by the users. One of the most challenging issues in these environments is the security of the hosted data. Many cloud computing providers offer web applications for their clients, this is why the most handling attacks in cloud computing are Distributed Denial of Service (DDoS). In this paper, we provide a comparative performance analysis of intrusion detection systems (IDSs) in a real world lab. The aim is to provide an up to date study for researchers and practitioners to understand the issues related to intrusion detection and to deal with DDoS attacks. This analysis includes intrusion detection rates, time running, etc. In the experiments, we configured a cloud platform using OpenStack and an IDS monitoring the whole network traffic of the web server configured. The results show that Suricata drops fewer packets than Bro and Snort successively when a DDoS attack is happening and detect more malicious packets.

Keywords: Cloud computing · Anomaly detection · Intrusion detection · Performance analysis · IDS

1 Introduction

Nowadays, most of the companies working in the area of information and communication technologies offer their services through cloud computing applications. The latter could be web applications, mobile applications and/or software. The National Institute of Standards and Technology (NIST) [2] defines cloud computing as a model for enabling ubiquitous, convenient, on-demand network access to a shared pool of configurable computing resources (e.g., networks, servers, storage, applications, and services) that can be rapidly provisioned and released with minimal management effort or service provider interaction. The data hosted by cloud applications are in most cases sensitive, especially in the bank industry. The residing issues affecting the applications of cloud environments are network attacks, more specifically DDoS attacks [1]. The DDoS attack is a distributed

E. Sabir et al. (Eds.): UNet 2017, LNCS 10542, pp. 206–213, 2017.
https://doi.org/10.1007/978-3-319-68179-5_18

attack managed by a group of activists, hackers or other individuals that make the online cloud service unavailable for clients. Besides firewalls, IDSs are very useful for mitigating the risks of attacks in cloud environments. Intrusion detection and prevention are areas of interest for many researchers during the last years. An IDS in a computer network is an important element to the overall security of information systems. Intrusion prevention is even more important for critical systems. The ability to handle large volumes of data, to store it and to process it, is one of the features of the cloud technologies. The latter features help the IDS to process the data very fast and to detect more efficiently the attacks and intrusions. In this paper, we analyze the performance of three open source, well known IDSs: Snort [14], Suricata [15] and Bro [16]. These tools were deployed in a real environment called Cloudlab [3]. The paper is organized as follows: in Sect. 2 we provide related work, in Sect. 3 the test environment is described, in Sects. 4 and 5 respectively, we analyze the DDoS attacks scenarios and the results on the detection of attacks. Finally, we conclude our paper and discuss future work in Sect. 6.

2 Related Works

A number of comparative studies of IDSs in terms of performance, characteristics and environment (Linux or Windows) have been done by different authors. Eugene and Neil [6] compared both Snort and Suricata in real world environment, being the network of the US Naval Postgraduate School. The authors analyzed in three different experiments the speed, memory requirements and exactness of detection engines. The first experiment was using the network of the school, the second experiment was using a supercomputer with recorded IP packets from the backbone of the network and the third experiment was testing the detection level of known attacks by Snort and Suricata tools. The attacks were sent to a tool, called Pytbull. Irwin and van Riel [5] investigated network scans and the detection algorithms of the scans using Snort [14] and Bro [16] IDSs. The authors showed a better detection using a 3-D scatter plot visualization of network events (InetVis), than the detection of Bro and Snort. Without InetVis, the authors were not able to detect many scans and could not understand all the problems related to scanning using Bro and Suricata. Park and Ahn [10] compared Snort and Suricata performance for the detection of attacks. They concluded that Snort is efficient in an environment using single threading with single CPU core but Suricata performs better in a multi-threading CPU environment and much better if the GPU (graphics processing unit) is activated. Salah and Kahtani [11] evaluate the performance of Snort in network mode under different operating systems Windows and Linux. The authors measured the packet loss at the kernel level of the used operating system. They considered normal and malicious traffic during the experiments. As they concluded, Snort performs well under moderate normal traffic but better in Linux with some NAPI budgets (The Linux Foundation defines NAPI as "an extension to the device driver packet processing framework, which is designed to improve the performance of high-speed networking"). White et al. [12] qualitatively compared

Snort and Suricata. Their results indicate that a single instance of Suricata performs better than a single instance of Snort. The authors conclude that Suricata is better than Snort in terms of scalability both when using single and multiple cores. According to them, Suricata achieves lower average RAM and CPU usage. Alqahtani and John [7] analyzed the performance of Snort and Suricata IDSs within a cloud network created locally using MyCloud Server, vCenter Server, etc. The authors also used a Fuzzy-Logic classifier integrated with Snort and Suricata. The results performed showed that the fuzzy logic based IDS performs better that normal IDS in terms of many capabilities including detection rate. Table 1 summarize the main differences in the related work studies.

Table 1. Characteristics of the related work studies (multi-threading support, usage of a dataset, a test or simulation environment, single or multiple core and cloud environment)

Studies	Multi-threading	Dataset	Environment	Core	Cloud
[6]	Yes	No	Test	Multiple	No
[5]	No	Yes	Simulation	Single	No
[10]	Yes	No	Test	Multiple	No
[11]	No	No	Test	Multiple	No
[12]	Yes	Yes	Test	Multiple	No
[7]	No	Yes	Test	Single	Yes
Our study	Yes	No	Test	Multiple	Yes

For our study, we used a real-world cloud computing environment with multiple cores and multi-threading intrusion detection systems.

3 Experimental Setup

We configured a cloud computing environment using Cloudlab testbed [3] provided by a consortium of universities and companies (University of Utah, Clemson University, Cisco, Dell, etc.) for the computer science research community. The cloud platform used was OpenStack due to its popularity and because it is resilient [18], easy to use and well integrated into Cloudlab.

3.1 Hardware

The servers used during experiments had the configuration described in Table 2.

Table 2. Hardware used during the experiments

Server configuration	
Server	Cisco UCS C220 M4
Core	16 cores
Cloud platform	OpenStack
Operating system	Ubuntu 14.04
Hypervisor	Kernel-based Virtual Machine (KVM)
RAM	128 GB ECC memory
Graphics card	AST2300
Storage	2 TB
CPU	Intel E5-2630 v3 8-core CPUs (2.40 GHz)
Architecture	AMD64
Network controller	2 x Intel 10 GB + Intel 1 GB

3.2 Architecture

To build our cloud lab, we used nine servers described in Table 2. One server as a controller (and a network controller node at the same time) as required by OpenStack for this type of installation. Eight Servers for compute nodes which will contain the virtual machines. The Fig. 1 shows the servers used for installing the OpenStack Mitaka cloud platform. After installation and configuration of OpenStack using Cloudlab services. We created ten virtual machines behaving as normal tenants with the possibility of being compromised and then act as attackers. We created also another virtual machine which is a web server and at the same time running an intrusion detection system (Snort, Suricata, Bro) to analyze the traffic coming in and out from/to the web server.

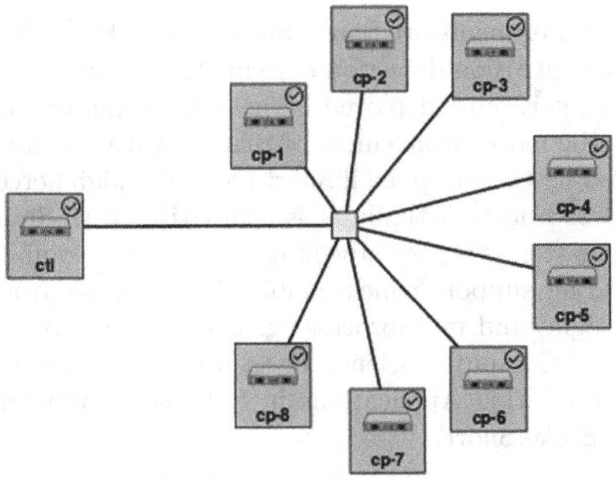

Fig. 1. Controller node and compute nodes used to install OpenStack Mitaka

Figure 2 shows the architecture of virtual machines, web server and intrusion detection systems we built. We created a flat network in OpenStack linking virtual machines and a router with an external network accessible from the Internet using floating IPs (public IPs) and SSH protocol.

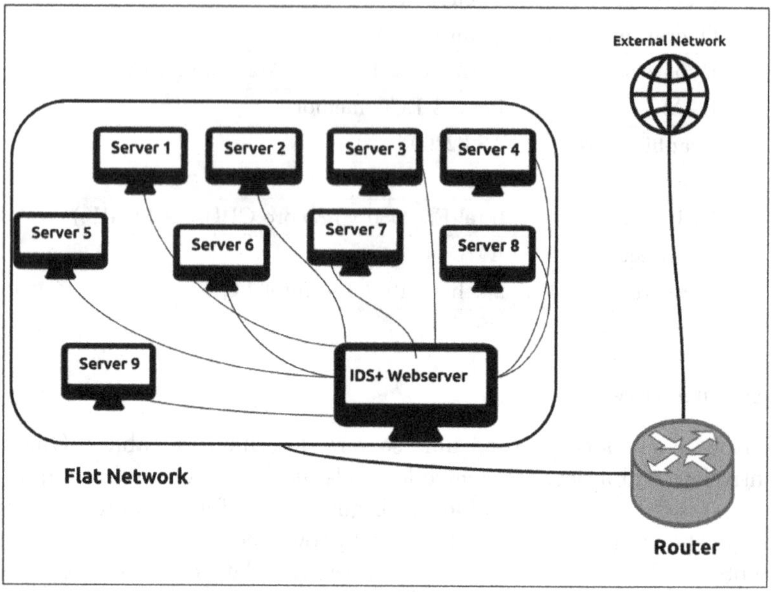

Fig. 2. Technical architecture

3.3 Tools

The tools used for experiments are Snort, Suricata and Bro. All of them are categorized as network intrusion detection systems (IDS). Snort [14] is well known in the industry and it is most deployed by network administrators. It is single-threaded which is the most inconvenient of this software because it causes many issues and many packets are dropped if Snort receives a high percentage of traffic. Suricata is similar to Snort. Actually, it is compatible with Snort and can read the log files of the latter. Another advantage of Suricata comparing it to Snort is the multi-threading support which enables it to benefit from the advanced multi-core technologies and multiprocessing. Bro is currently jointly developed by the International Computer Science Institute in Berkeley and the National Center for Supercomputing Applications in Urbana-Champaign [16]. Bro is a single-threaded IDS like Snort.

4 Attacks Scenario

For this study, our main focus was on detecting DDoS attacks efficiently. To test our IDSs performance. We configured 10 servers or tenants in our OpenStack cloud platform with a python script which launches a denial of service attacking a web server created for this purpose. The architecture used for this scenario of the attack is described in Fig. 3. All servers are running Ubuntu 14.04 OS with four virtual CPU, 2Go of RAM and 4Go of the hard drive. The web server which has also an IDS installed on it have 4Go of RAM, 4 VCPU and 8Go of the hard drive.

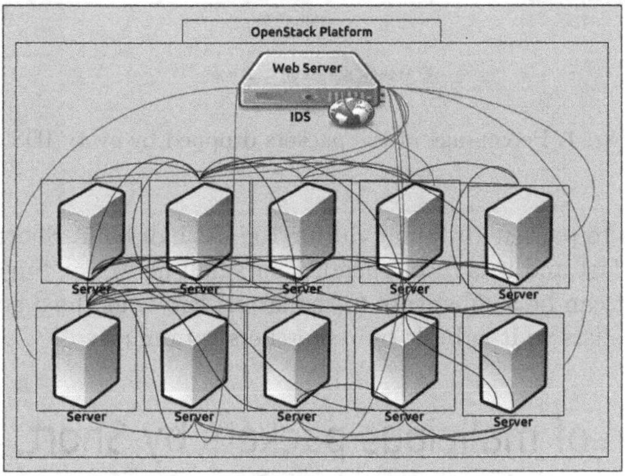

Fig. 3. Scenario of the attacks launched during experiments

5 Results and Discussion

After one hour of DDoS Attack, 9000 HTTP packets were sent to the web server (We send only 150 packets per minute as we want our traffic to look like normal one). This attack was tested three times and each time we use a different intrusion detection system to analyze its performance. Every IDS used was using the default setting with the default rules. We got the results shown in Figs. 4, and 5. Snort dropped 10% of the traffic sent to the web server (900 network packets). Bro dropped 8% of the packets (720) and Suricata performs better with only 5% of the traffic dropped (450 packets). Snort is efficient in the first quarter of the hour as it detects around 1970 of malicious packets at the fifteenth minute but start dropping a lot of packets in the second half hour and the efficiency reduces extensively due to its single threading characteristic.

Bro detected 2000 malicious packets at the fifteenth minute. The latter resisted the first half hour and start dropping packets in the second half hour. The performance of Suricata is somehow similar to the performance of Snort but

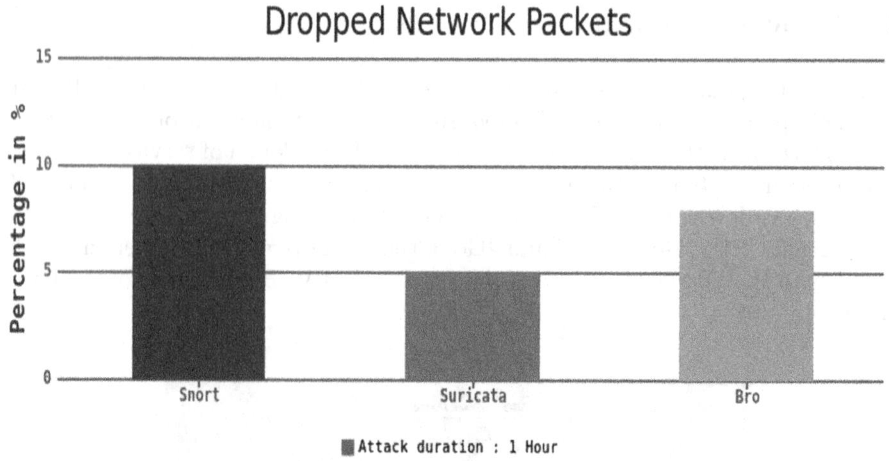

Fig. 4. Percentage of the packets dropped by every IDS

Suricata resists to packets dropping during the fist half hour. Snort detect malicious behavior fast and it is recommended for small networks. Suricata which is similar to Snort can be a substitute to the latter. Bro could be a good choice for academic specialists as it is built by researchers community.

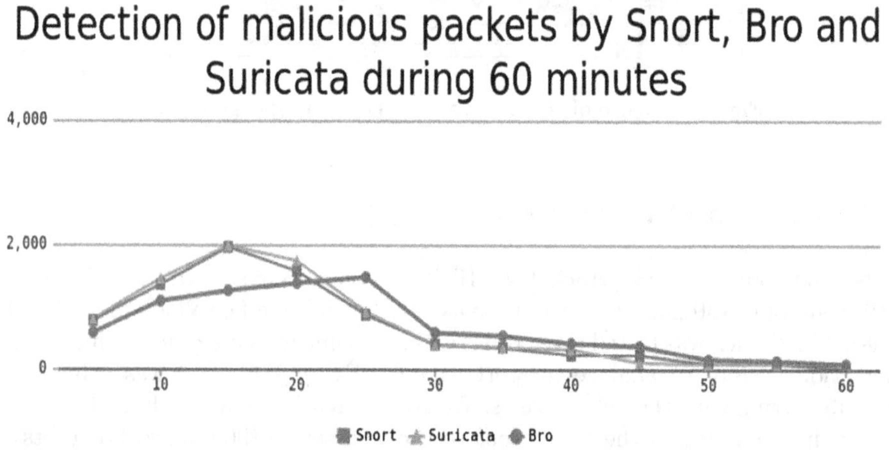

Fig. 5. Malicious packets detected by Snort, Bro and Suricata during 60 min

6 Conclusion and Future Work

After finishing the experiments of this study. we concluded that multi-threading supported by some of the studied IDSs can help resisting to packets dropping which will lead to more processing of the malicious traffic happening in the network. Suricata with its support of multi-threading and multi-cores showed a better performance in cloud computing environment. The DDoS attack launched was detected by the three IDSs in the first five minutes of the attack. As a future work, we will test other attacks with these three IDSs during a long time period. we will use also different configurations of every IDS with different rules. We expect also to deploy and test some IDS in IoT environments.

References

1. Yu, S., Tian, Y., Guo, S., Wu, D.O.: Can we beat DDoS attacks in clouds? IEEE Trans. Parallel Distrib. Syst. **25**, 2245–2254 (2014)
2. Mell, P.M., Grance, T.: The NIST definition of cloud computing, Gaithersburg, MD (2011)
3. Ricci, R., Eide, E.: The CloudLab Team: Introducing CloudLab: Scientific Infrastructure for Advancing Cloud Architectures and Applications. login, vol. 39. USENIX (2014)
4. Albin, E.: A comparative analysis of the Snort and Suricata intrusion-detection systems (2011)
5. Irwin, B., van Riel, J.-P.: Using InetVis to evaluate Snort and Bro scan detection on a network telescope. In: Goodall, J.R., Conti, G., Ma, K.L. (eds.) Mathematics and Visualization, pp. 255–273. Springer, Heidelberg (2008)
6. Albin, E., Rowe, N.C.: A realistic experimental comparison of the Suricata and Snort intrusion-detection systems. In: 2012 26th International Conference on Advanced Information Networking and Applications Workshops, pp. 122–127. IEEE (2012)
7. Alqahtani, S.M., John, R.: A comparative study of different fuzzy classifiers for cloud intrusion detection systems alerts. In: 2016 IEEE Symposium Series on Computational Intelligence (SSCI), p. 19. IEEE (2016)
8. Biermann, E., Cloete, E., Venter, L.: A comparison of intrusion detection systems. Comput. Secur. **20**, 676–683 (2001)
9. Moya, M.A.C.: Analysis and evaluation of the Snort and Bro network intrusion detection (2008)
10. Park, W., Ahn, S.: Performance comparison and detection analysis in Snort and Suricata environment. Wirel. Pers. Commun. **112**, 241–252 (2016)
11. Salah, K., Kahtani, A.: Performance evaluation comparison of Snort NIDS under Linux and Windows server. J. Netw. Comput. Appl. **33**, 6–15 (2010)
12. White, J.S., Fitzsimmons, T., Matthews, J.N.: Quantitative analysis of intrusion detection systems: Snort and Suricata. In: Ternovskiy, I.V., Chin, P. (eds.) Proceedings of SPIE, p. 875704 (2013)
13. National Center for Biotechnology Information. http://www.ncbi.nlm.nih.gov
14. Snort Project. https://www.snort.org/
15. Suricata. https://suricata-ids.org/
16. The Bro Network Security Monitor. https://www.bro.org/
17. OpenStack. https://www.openstack.org/
18. Vogel, A., Griebler, D., Maron, C.A.F., Schepke, C., Fernandes, L.G.: Private IaaS clouds: a comparative analysis of OpenNebula, CloudStack and OpenStack. In: 2016 24th Euromicro International Conference on Parallel, Distributed, and Network-Based Processing (PDP), pp. 672–679. IEEE (2016)

Towards Optimizing the Usability of Homomorphic Encryption in Cloud-Based Medical Image Processing

Mbarek Marwan(✉), Ali Kartit, and Hassan Ouahmane

Laboratory LTI, Department TRI, ENSAJ, University Chouaïb Doukkali, Avenue Jabran Khalil Jabran, BP 299, El Jadida, Morocco
marwan.mbarek@gmail.com, alikartit@gmail.com, hassan.ouahmane@yahoo.fr

Abstract. Undoubtedly, digital imaging continues to play a crucial role in the diagnosis and treatment of disease. In recent years, there has been growing interest in using Cloud services in the healthcare domain. Even though Cloud Computing offers many advantages, the shift to this new paradigm still poses many problems relating to privacy and data protection. Therefore, it is significantly important to revisit the issue of medical image processing adopting a new method namely Cloud services. We place heavy emphasis on homomorphic encryption schemes, which play a useful role in dealing with privacy and security challenges. In reality, running time is one of the major disadvantages of these types of algorithms. In this context, the present contribution can be conceived of as a novel approach to improve both performance and security. This is achieved by using Multi-Agent System (MAS) and encrypting only the content of a Region-of-Interest (RoI). This would dramatically minimize the size of the needed data. Consequently, it improves the response time of the proposed framework. Furthermore, the generated RoI is divided into certain number of shares, and hence, processed by different agents implemented in several nodes. Following this, this approach is meant to enhance both confidentiality and performance. The experimental results prove that this method is an efficient solution for data encryption in encrypted domain. In fact, the proposal is meant to reduce the running time required to process images that are encrypted using the homomorphic algorithms.

Keywords: Cloud Computing · Security · Homomorphic encryption · Image processing

1 Introduction

The primary objective of imaging tools is to improve the quality of medical services. In fact, healthcare professionals rely heavily upon these applications to extract meaningful information. In doing so, doctors can diagnose diseases at their earliest stages. For these reasons, unlimited amount of medical records are daily produced by healthcare industry to meet increasing demands. Even though Electronic Health Record (EHR) systems are useful tools, processing and analyzing a medical image necessitate powerful software and platforms. Cloud Computing system, therefore, has become a competitive solution

E. Sabir et al. (Eds.): UNet 2017, LNCS 10542, pp. 214–224, 2017.
https://doi.org/10.1007/978-3-319-68179-5_19

that has drawn the attention of healthcare institutions. This alternative is intended to handle on-site infrastructure concerns. In this regard, this model refers to a distributed system that offers on-demand services to the clients. It incorporates various technologies from different areas of computer science, including Service-Oriented Architecture (SOA), Parallel Distributed Systems (PDS), virtualization and data deduplication [1, 2]. As defined by the National Institute of Standards and Technology (NIST) [3], this new paradigm is meant to deliver needed resources to clients via the Internet. Moreover, Cloud services can be delivered and released with minimal management efforts according to clients' demand. This allows ubiquitous access to the vast majority of remote Cloud services anywhere and anytime. In this paradigm, users are charged based on a pay-per-use business model to cut costs. To summarize, Cloud Computing is an appropriate solution to analyze medical images by using cost-efficient cloud services. Within this framework, doctors or radiology centers send medical images to a Cloud provider in order to analyze them via specific image processing operations. Then, the result is returned to the consumers in a secure manner, as illustrated in Fig. 1.

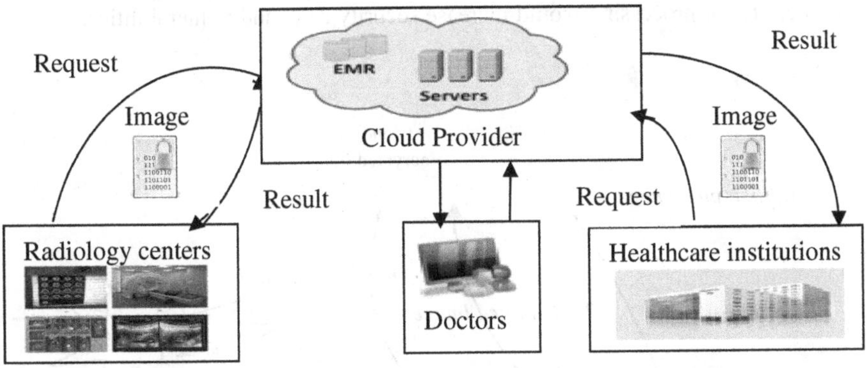

Fig. 1. Basic idea of Cloud-based medical image processing

However, the adoption of the Cloud-based medical image processing model in the healthcare field faces many obstacles, particularly security problems [4]. Generally speaking, these issues are mainly caused by vulnerabilities and threats related to cloud technologies, especially virtual resources management [5, 6]. Given the fact that medical images are crucial data, they require robust security measures to prevent unauthorized access, use and disclosure. In other words, protecting medical information when using cloud services needs more safety measures to comply with security requirements [7, 8]: confidentiality, integrity, availability, data ownership, authentication, access control, anonymization, unlinkability, auditing capability. To this end, we opt for a novel approach based on Multi-Agent System and homomorphic encryption to mitigate security risks.

The subsequent discussion is organized as follows. Section 2 presents the fundamentals of homomorphic encryption and its utilization in Cloud-based medical image processing. In Sects. 3 and 4, we discuss common implementations. Section 5 provides the proposed framework and techniques involved in the data security. In Sect. 6, we present the experimental results. Concluding remarks and recommendations for future research are addressed in Sect. 7.

2 Homomorphic Encryption in Cloud-Based Image Processing

2.1 Homomorphic Encryption Approach for Data Processing

Despite the fact that Cloud Computing has gained great economic benefit, much concern should be placed on the security and confidentiality of data processing. Hence, to outsource image processing to an external entity needs to guarantee data privacy during this operation. So far, conventional cryptography techniques such as RSA, DES and AES are used to maintain the confidentiality of digital records. However, all operations involved in image processing require decryption of the stored image to the plaintext image. Consequently, any algorithm used in image processing application is applied only after decryption procedure, as illustrated in Fig. 2. Although this approach protects data, it is not suitable for medical image processing. Moreover, sending a plaintext image to an external entity for processing would increase security risks and vulnerabilities.

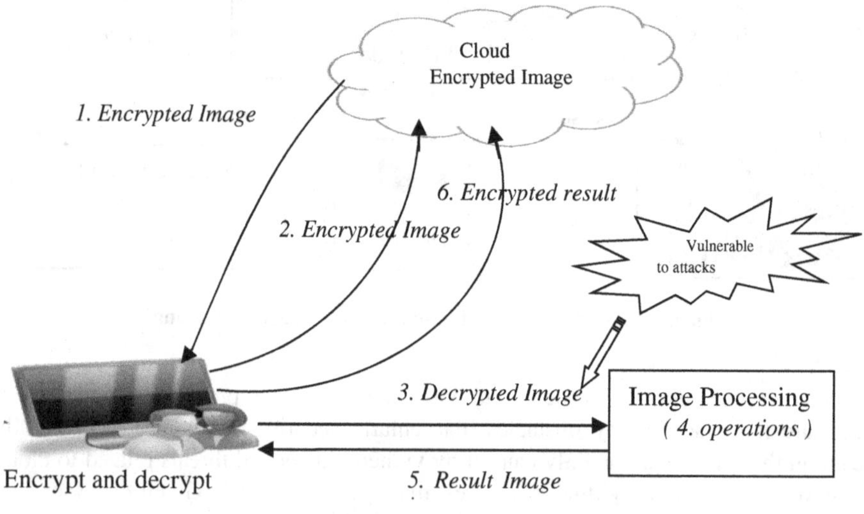

Fig. 2. Classical approach for image processing over the Cloud

To overcome this challenge, we propose the homomorphic encryption to secure image processing over Cloud Computing. In this scheme, computation operations are directly carried out on the encrypted images. Therefore, Cloud providers can perform basic algebraic operations without knowing the secret key. This would protect medical data against untrusted Cloud providers. In fact, homomorphic algorithms are designed so that the decryption of any operation performed on the encrypted data is equivalent to the result of the desired operations on the plaintext image. In this scheme, a user encrypts an image x to get E(x). Subsequently, Cloud provider applies a specific operation h on encrypted data $F_2(E(x), h)$. Thanks to the homomorphic properties of this scheme, authorized users use their private key to get the final result y, as illustrated in Fig. 3.

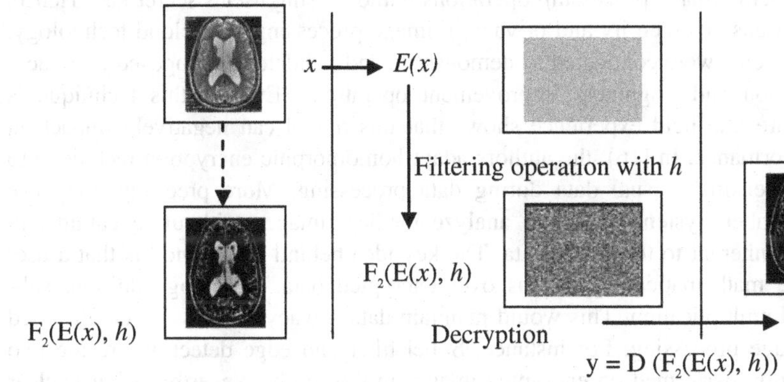

Fig. 3. Homomorphic encryption approach for image processing using the Cloud

2.2 Homomorphic Encryption Schemes

In general, an encryption system is homomorphic if it is possible to evaluate a function f Enc (f (x, y)) using two encrypted values Enc (x) and Enc (y), where f can be a basic operation like +, ×, ⊕. In other words, homomorphic encryption is a technique in which arithmetic operations are carried out on encrypted data [9–14]. In such an approach, organizations encrypt their medical images using homomorphic algorithms before uploading them into the Cloud Computing. Next, they perform computations over stored data. In general, these algorithms are classified into two categories according to their homomorphic properties: Fully Homomorphic Encryption (FHE) and Partially Homomorphic Encryption (PHE). Table 1 provides some well-known encryption schemes.

Table 1. Homomorphic encryption schemes

Algorithms	Year	Type	Property
RSA	1978	PHE	Multiplication
El Gamal	1985	PHE	Multiplication
Paillier	1999	PHE	Addition
Iterative	2009	PHE	Addition
Gentry	2009	FHE	Multiplication and addition
EHES	2013	FHE	Multiplication and addition

3 Related Work

In [15], Challa et al. use homomorphic encryption approach to protect digital records. This is achieved by using learning with error (LWE) scheme to secure data processing over cloud computing. In doing so, the authors are able to perform both addition and multiplication operations on encrypted data without ever decrypting them. In such a concept, clients encrypt their medical records before transferring them to the Cloud service providers (CSPs). Then, a third party relies on the proposed method for applying specific image processing operations without using user's secret key. Hence, this solution ensures security and privacy in image processing over cloud technology. Two experiments were conducted to demonstrate and validate the proposed approach: image addition and brightness improvement operations. Even if this technique is proven secure, the field experience shows that this model can negatively impact on system performance. In [16], the authors adapt homomorphic encryption technique to protect the sensitive visual data during data processing. More precisely, they use Residue Number System (RNS) to analyze medical images without revealing any information inherent to the secret data. The key idea behind the method is that a user can execute mathematical operations over encrypted data, including addition, subtraction and multiplication. This would maintain data privacy when using cloud-based medical image processing. For instance, Sobel filter and edge detection are the two main operation performed on encrypted images in this study. Nevertheless, it is clear that the computation time is one of the major disadvantages of this concept. Kanithi and Latha [17] suggest a solution based on homomorphic encryption to secure the discrete wavelet transform (DWT). In this framework, the Paillier cryptosystem is used to perform image processing operations in a secure manner. Typically, the proposal consists of executing algebraic operations on encrypted data, especially addition. In this regard, 2-D Haar wavelet transform is applied to the secret image. Accordingly, the Paillier algorithm is used to encrypt approximation coefficients. Finally, the secret image is recovered by using Paillier along with IDWT. In [18], Habeed and Dayal Raj present a new procedure to secure signal processing in the encrypted domain. Basically, this solution relies on homomorphic algorithms to meet security requirements. More precisely, multi-level DWT/IDWT is applied in the last step for data expansion issue. In this scheme, it uses multiplicative inverse method (MIM) to reduce the quantization factor. Technically, the authors rely on Paillier cryptosystem to protect medical images against insider attacks.

4 Discussion

In general, homomorphic encryption techniques are meant to enable Cloud providers to process medical images in its encrypted state. This has led to increased interest in applying homomorphic encryption in Cloud-based image processing services. Consequently, many frameworks have been recently developed on the basis of different schemes. Nevertheless, this approach still faces serious limitations, which makes the adoption of this concept questionable. On the one hand, Partial Homomorphic Encryption (P.H.E.) schemes are proven to be secure against common attacks and threats. But, most of them support only one type of algebraic operation. Hence, using these algorithms in practical applications that require more than one operation is a challenge. To mitigate this issue, a hybrid solution based on different schemes is suggested to meet application needs. In addition, Fully Homomorphic Encryption (FHE) scheme is introduced to enable a user to perform arithmetic different operations.

Thus, one scheme can perform both addition and multiplication. On the other hand, applying homomorphic cryptosystems has a negative effect on system performance, particularly the running time. This can cause serious reputational problems for Cloud providers. In reality, fully homomorphic encryption schemes improve the performance better than the partial ones. However, both schemes are still far from being practically suitable to medical image processing applications. Indeed, these cryptosystems are too slow and time-consuming, as illustrated in Fig. 4.

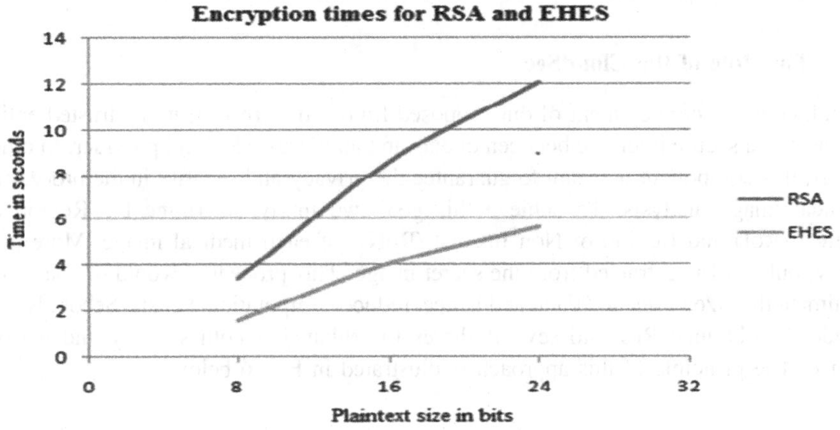

Fig. 4. Performance of two Homomorphic encryption schemes, i.e. RSA and EHES [19]

5 The Proposed Architecture to Improve Performance

The major drawback of applying homomorphic encryption schemes is that they have a negative temporal effect. In addition, the processing of a medical image often requires complex algorithms. To address this issue, we propose a framework that improves both the performance and security of Cloud services. To this end, the proposed solution is composed of two main components: CloudSec and CloudServ, as shown in Fig. 5.

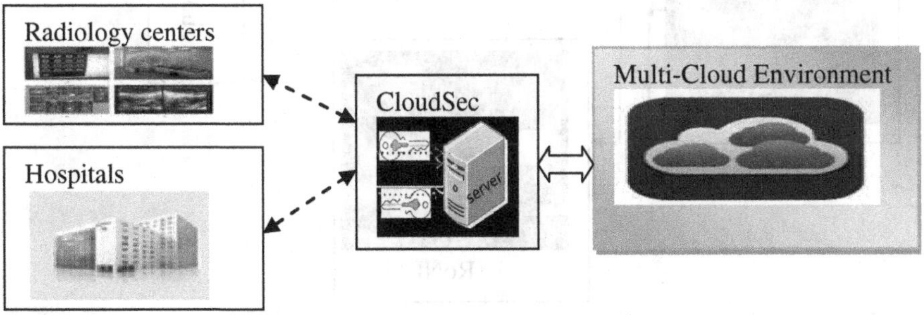

Fig. 5. An overview of the proposed architecture

Firstly, healthcare professionals send the secret medical image to the CloudSec using VPN for securing data exchange. Secondly, CloudSec save all information regarding the data owner in a local database and take all measures to secure image processing over Cloud Computing. Lastly, CloudServ delivers required computational resources and powerful imaging tools to meet application requirements.

The main idea behind this architecture is to introduce CloudSec for delegating all security measures. This module is a trusted external party that acts as a proxy. Unlike the traditional architecture, the proposed one avoids direct access to public Cloud services. This will reduce the risk of data breach and threats exposure.

5.1 The Role of the CloudSec

CloudSec is the core element of our proposed framework. In fact, it is a trusted entity that acts as a secure interface between clients and an untrusted Cloud provider. In other words, this component is meant to guarantee the privacy and security in the process of medical image analysis. To achieve this goal, we firstly determine the Region of Interest (RoI) and Region of Non Interest (RoNI) of each medical image. More precisely, only RoI is extracted from the secret image. This procedure would dramatically minimize the size of needed data, and hence, reduce computational costs. Secondly, we divide the obtained RoI into several shares for enhancing both security and performance. The principle of this approach is illustrated in Fig. 6 below.

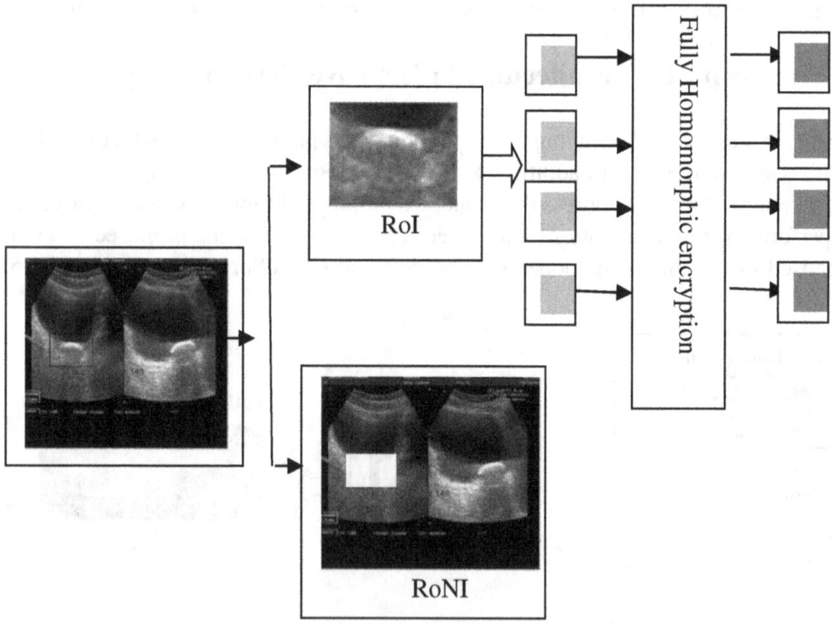

Fig. 6. The principle of the proposed method

Following this, the created shares are encrypted using Enhanced Homomorphic Encryption Scheme (EHES) before transferring them to the CloudServ. Hence, this solution provides a double security mechanism to protect the secret image.

5.2 The Role of the CloudServ

It is a public Cloud Computing that offers needed computational resource to perform complex medical image processing. In other words, this entity delivers on-demand imaging tools to the clients as a service. Hence, healthcare professionals use these advanced software to analyze their digital records. Technically, CloudServ relies on intelligent Multi-Agent Systems (MAS) for distributing tasks across available nodes. Thus, it enhances system capacity and response time. In this concept, each agent analyzes only one distinct share. Moreover, Agents Manger (AM) is used to enhance coordination and collaboration between agents involved in the image processing tasks. More precisely, the AM module is responsible for creating or removing agents in order to evaluate overload, and then, balance the loads, as illustrated in Fig. 7.

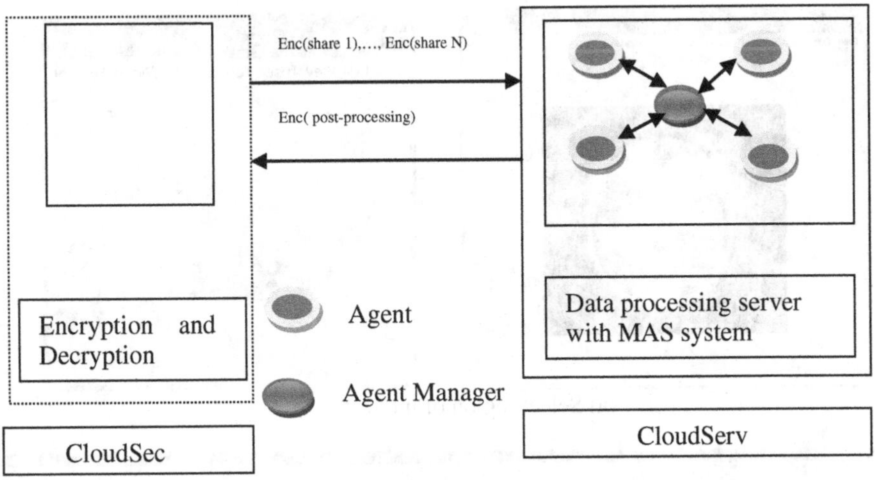

Fig. 7. The fundamentals of Multi-Agent System

In summary, this architecture is designed to allow parallel processing of medical images in a secure manner by using Multi-Agent Systems. Therefore, it is designed to improve both the security and performance of the proposed framework.

6 Experimental Validation

The proposed method is composed of two main procedures. First, we split the ROI into several regions to enhance both security and performance. In this case, the generated ROI is divided into four sub-regions. So, the steps of the proposed technique are presented in Algorithm 1 below:

Algorithm 1: Generating encrypted shares

Inputs: Host Image I (x × y),
Outputs: Secret Shares < R1, R2, R3, R4>
1: Select the region of interest
2: Extract the selected region from the input image
3: Divide the region RoI into four sub-regions
Return < R1, R2, R3, R4>

To prove the benefits of our proposed concept, we will present, in this section, an illustrative example. Thus, a simulation experiment was carried on using MATLAB. In this study, we use a medical image MRI with 256 × 256. So, client selects the RoI from the original image (a) to get the image (b). Next, this selected part is split into four pieces as in the image (c). The implementation results are shown in Fig. 8.

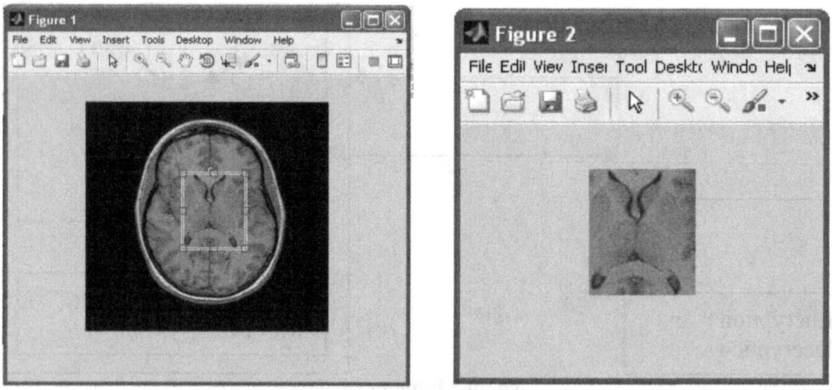

(a) Select region of interest

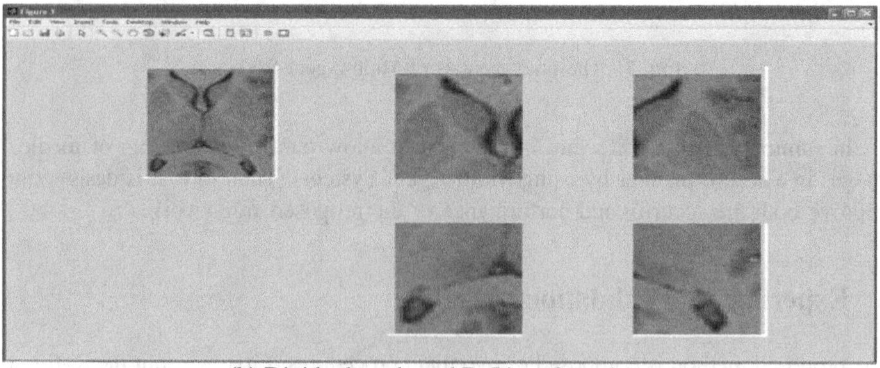

(b) Divide the selected RoI into four shares

Fig. 8. The implementation results

Afterwards, we encrypt each sub-region using EHES before send them to the CloudServ. The latter is a Multi-Agent System in which each sub-region is processed by a distinct intelligent agent.

7 Conclusion

Cloud-based medical image processing is a novel concept by virtue of which remote imaging tools are offered to healthcare professionals through the Internet. Unlike traditional models, these sophisticated software and applications are used only when needed and charged based on their utilization. Consequently, both academia and healthcare industry are attracted by this promising technology. Despite the advantages that this technology offers, it is still not fully protected against both external and internal threats. In this regard, security and privacy need more improvements to meet the healthcare professionals' demands. To this aim, various methods are proposed to promote medical image processing using Cloud services instead of on-site applications. In this study, we focus on homomorphic encryption approaches, which are used mainly to secure this new model. As outlined above, homomorphic algorithms allow users to perform arithmetic operations on encrypted data. However, the use of this proposed approach has limitations in terms of performance. In general, most of existing schemes are not sufficiently mature yet as they are time-consuming. Hence, these algorithms are not suitable for complex image processing operations because they are too slow. To overcome this challenge, we suggest an approach to promote the use of homomorphic encryption in data processing. In this model, CloudSec is a trusted Cloud, which is designed to reduce the security risks associated the Cloud technologies. To this objective, patients' identifying information like the name, address, social security number are stored in a secure local database to achieve anonymity and unlinkability. In addition, we divide the secret image into two main regions: Region of Interest (RoI) and Region of Non Interest (RoNI). In the same line, only RoI is processed to enhance system performance. Next, the generated RoI is split into many shares to ensure data confidentiality. Then, all shares are encrypted before sending them to the Cloud provider. The proposed framework also uses Multi-Agent Systems to reduce computational costs, which is the major drawback of homomorphic encryption. In our future work, we intend to encrypt the created sub-regions using EHES. Also, we will compare our framework with existing related work in terms of performance. As perspectives, we intend to apply some common image processing techniques demonstrate the correctness of the proposed solution, including contrast and edge enhancement.

References

1. Marwan, M., Kartit, A., Ouahmane, H.: Cloud-based medical image issues. Int. J. Appl. Eng. Res. **11**, 3713–3719 (2016)
2. Zhang, H., Jiang, C., Cheng, J., Leung, V.C.M.: Cooperative interference mitigation and handover management for heterogeneous cloud small cell networks. IEEE Wirel. Commun. **22**(3), 92–99 (2015)

3. Mell, P., Grance, T.: The NIST definition of cloud computing. Technical report, National Institute of Standards and Technology, vol. 15, pp. 1–3 (2009)
4. Mazhar, A., Samee, U.K., Athanasios, V.: Security in cloud computing: opportunities and challenges. Inf. Sci. **305**, 357–383 (2015). Elsevier
5. Zhang, H., Du, J., Cheng, J. Leung, V.C.M.: Resource allocation in SWIPT enabled heterogeneous cloud small cell networks with incomplete CSI. In: Proceedings of the IEEE Globecom, Washington, DC (2016)
6. Zhang, H., Dong, Y., Cheng, J., Hossain, M.J., Leung, V.C.M.: Fronthauling for 5G LTE-U ultra dense cloud small cell networks. IEEE Wirel. Commun. **23**(6), 48–53 (2016)
7. Abbas, A., Khan, S.U.: e-Health cloud: privacy concerns and mitigation strategies. In: Gkoulalas-Divanis, A., Loukides, G. (eds.) Medical Data Privacy Handbook, pp. 389–421. Springer, Cham (2015). doi:10.1007/978-3-319-23633-9_15
8. Al Nuaimi, N., AlShamsi, A., Mohamed., N., Al-Jaroodi. J.: e-health cloud implementation issues and efforts. In: Proceedings of the International Conference on industrial Engineering and Operations Management (IEOM), pp. 1–10 (2015)
9. Gomathikrishnan, M., Tyagi, A.: HORNS-A homomorphic encryption scheme for cloud computing using residue number system. IEEE Trans. Parallel Distrib. Syst. **23**(6), 995–1003 (2011)
10. Paillier, P.: Public-key cryptosystems based on composite degree residuosity classes. In: Stern, J. (ed.) EUROCRYPT 1999. LNCS, vol. 1592, pp. 223–238. Springer, Heidelberg (1999). doi:10.1007/3-540-48910-X_16
11. Bhabendu, K.M., Debasis, G.: Fully homomorphic encryption equating to cloud security: an approach. J. Comput. Eng. (IOSRJCE) **9**, 46–50 (2013)
12. Yi, X., Paulet, R., Bertino, E.: Homomorphic encryption and applications. SCS. Springer, Cham (2014). doi:10.1007/978-3-319-12229-8
13. Rao, G.V.S., Khan, M.S., Reddy, A.Y., Narayana, K.: Data security in bioinformatics. Int. J. Adv. Res. Comput. Sci. Softw. Eng. **3**(11), 590–598 (2013)
14. Gorti, V.S., Garimella, U.: An efficient secure message transmission in mobile ad hoc networks using enhanced homomorphic encryption scheme. Global J. Comput. Sci. Technol. Netw. Web Secur. **3**, 20–33 (2013). version 1.0
15. Challa, R.K., Kakinada, J., Vijaya Kumari, G., Sunny, B.: Secure image processing using LWE based homomorphic encryption. In: Proceedings of the IEEE International Conference on Electrical, Computer and Communication Technologies (ICECCT), pp. 1–6 (2015)
16. Gomathisankaran, M., Yuan, X., Kamongi, P.: Ensure privacy and security in the process of medical image analysis. In: Proceedings of the IEEE International Conference on Granular Computing (GrC), pp. 120–125 (2013)
17. Kanithi, S.R., Latha, A.G.: Secure image processing using discrete wavelet transform and paillier cryptosystem. Int. J. Mag. Eng. Technol. Manag. Res. **2**(10), 1270–1276 (2015)
18. Habeep, N., Dayal Raj, R.: Homomorphic encrypted domain with DWT methods. Int. J. Invent. Comput. Sci. Eng. **1**(3), 2348–3431 (2014)
19. El makkaoui, K., Beni Hassane, A.: Challenges of using homomorphic encryption to secure cloud computing. In: Proceedings of the International Conference on Cloud Technologies and Applications (CloudTech) (2015)

A Verifiable Secret Sharing Approach for Secure MultiCloud Storage

Kamal Benzekki(✉), Abdeslam El Fergougui, and Abdelbaki Elbelrhiti Elalaoui

Laboratory of Computer Networks and Systems, Faculty of Sciences,
Moulay Ismail University, Meknes, Morocco
benzekki@gmail.com, a.elfergougui@gmail.com, a.elbelrhiti@fs-umi.ac.ma

Abstract. Cloud computing is a model to access shared pool of configurable computing resources which comprise servers, applications, services and network components. The fact that this model can provide both computation and storage at low tax makes it popular among corporations. This also makes it a very captivating proposition for the future. But in spite of its promise and potential, security in the cloud proves to be a cause for concerns to the business sector. This is due to the outsourcing of data onto third party managed cloud platform. These security concerns also make the use of cloud services not so much flexible. The main issues associated with data storage management are confidentiality and integrity. However, a novel approach of "multi-cloud" or "cloud of clouds" has emerged currently using Shamir's Secret Sharing algorithm to address both confidentiality and integrity concerns. The implementation of Shamir's Secret Sharing algorithm is performed to authenticate a unique user and to access a particular file from the Cloud storage. There are many different Secret Sharing algorithms and each of them has its pros and cons. In this paper, data is protected using a secure Shamir's Secret Sharing scheme and our novel approach for Verifiable Secret Sharing to identify the honest dealer and the shareholders.

Keywords: Cloud computing · Shamir's secret sharing · Verifiable secret sharing · Hash · Outsourcing · Authentication

1 Introduction

Cloud computing offers many benefits in terms of low cost and accessibility of data. However, security is major aspect which needs to be considered in he way cloud computing environment is exploited. A user often uses cloud facility to store sensitive information with Cloud storage providers, but these providers may not be authenticate. Single Cloud providers are predicted to become less popular with customers due to the risks of service availability failure and the possibility of malicious insiders in the single Cloud. These issues lead to movement towards Multi-Clouds with different advantages but with some problems which need to be solved. The problems include Data Integrity, Data Availability and Data

E. Sabir et al. (Eds.): UNet 2017, LNCS 10542, pp. 225–234, 2017.
https://doi.org/10.1007/978-3-319-68179-5_20

Confidentiality. Cloud providers should address these issues as a matter of high and urgent priority.

In addition, doing business with single Cloud providers is becoming less popular due to potential problems that can affect our data, such as service availability failure (e.g. some catastrophe befalling the Cloud service provider and disruption of services) and the possibility that there are malicious insiders in the single Cloud (e.g. stolen data by an attacker who found a vulnerability). To this end the use of Multi-Clouds instead of single Cloud service provider to protect data is an optimal solution [1].

In order to protect data from attackers, we can encrypt it. But in order to protect the encryption key, we need a different method which increases the complexity of the intended solution. Another drawback of this approach is that the entire process of encryption and decryption which is time consuming.

The secret sharing schemes are a perfect fit in the Multi-Cloud environment to provide data security in Cloud without the drawbacks of encrypting data and service availability failure due to single Cloud providers.

Shamir's threshold secret sharing scheme [2] has been extensively studied in the literature to solve the problem of secret sharing. The Shamir's threshold secret sharing scheme is information theoretically secure but it does not provide any security against cheating as it assumes that the dealer and shareholders are honest but it is not always possible. A misbehaving dealer can distribute inconsistent shares to the participants or misbehaving shareholders can submit fake shares during reconstruction. To prevent such malicious behavior of cheaters, we need a Verifiable Secret Sharing scheme, first introduced in [3], through which the validity of shares distributed by the dealer are verified by shareholders without having any information about the secret. Initially, interactive Verifiable Secret Sharing schemes were introduced but it requires interaction between the dealer and shareholders to verify the validity of shares and it imposes the enormous amount of extra overhead on the dealer, as it has to deal with a large number of shareholders. Later non-interactive Verifiable Secret Sharing schemes were introduced to remove the extra overhead on the dealer, in which a share proves its own validity.

Existing approaches for Verifiable Secret Sharing either verify the shares, distributed by a dealer or submitted by shareholders for secret reconstruction, or verify the reconstructed secret but not both. In order to verify shares, a dealer either transfers some additional information like check vectors or certificate vectors or it uses different encryption mechanisms. If existing Verifiable Secret Sharing schemes are not using the check vectors or certificate vectors, security of such schemes depend on the intractability of computing hard to solve number theoretic problems in one way or another. If the scheme uses check vector or certificate vector then it increases an extra overhead on a dealer to compute and distribute that extra information among a large number of participants.

In this paper, we use and extend the Verifiable Secret Sharing approach to not only verify the validity of shares distributed by a dealer but to verify the shares submitted by shareholders for secret reconstruction, and to verify the reconstructed secret.

The reminder of this paper is organized as follows. Section 2 presents the related works. Section 3 details our proposed approach for secure multi-cloud storage using Shamir's Secret Sharing scheme in addition to our verification method. In Sect. 4, a security analysis of our proposed scheme is presented. Finally a conclusion is given in Sect. 5.

2 Related Works

The term Verifiable Secret Sharing was first introduced in [3] to provide ability to an individual shareholder to verify his/her share distributed by a dealer. The authors have proposed a constant round interactive Verifiable Secret Sharing scheme and suggested a cryptographic solution, which is based on the intractability of factorization.

An interactive Verifiable Secret Sharing scheme [4] has been proposed by using a homomorphism property and probabilistic encryption function. The scheme is only used to verify the shares distributed by the dealer, but it does not verify the shares submitted by shareholders for secret reconstruction and the reconstructed secret. Therefore, the scheme is only applicable in a situation where the shareholders are honest and the chance of accidentally submitting an erroneous share is zero. During the reconstruction, it assumes that the dealer is honest and reconstructs the secret correctly. In addition, the large number of encrypted shares of different polynomials increases the enormous amount of extra overhead on the dealer. As there are so much assumption about the honesty of a dealer and shareholders and the interactive nature of the scheme makes it infeasible to be used in a real world applications of secret sharing.

The first non-interactive Verifiable Secret Sharing scheme has been suggested in [5], in which a share proves its own validity. The homomorphic relations exist between the values and their encryptions are utilized by the scheme but like other schemes, it has its own limitations. The scheme broadcasts an encrypted secret and so the security of the scheme depends on the hardness of inverting an encryption function. In addition, it does not verify the shares submitted by shareholders for secret reconstruction and it does not verify the reconstructed secret.

Recently published paper in Verifiable Secret Sharing, proposed in [6], utilizes the redundant shares to detect and identify the cheaters. In their scheme, the authors assume that a dealer is honest. In their approach, shareholders only try to verify the reconstructed secret by using the majority of secret mechanism. The scheme only detects and identifies the cheaters when more than the threshold number of shares are available and majority of them and more than the threshold number of shares are from the honest shareholders. When there are only threshold number of shares are present, the scheme works exactly same as Shamir's [2] scheme and does not detect the cheating.

In [7], a scheme has been proposed which uses a hash function to verify the validity of the reconstructed secret. The authors have revisited the approach of

[8] and gave a more efficient solution to the problem of Verifiable Secret Sharing. In their scheme, they can only verify the reconstructed secret. They assume that the dealer is honest and does not distribute any fake shares.

Also, the scheme assumes that the shareholders receive the correct shares of the secret without any exception. At the end, the scheme is able to verify the reconstructed secret but if it is not correct then it cannot identify the faked shares and cheaters. In a real world, after the reconstruction of a secret, the secret is used to trigger some event or to perform some action and if it is not correct then it fails to do so. Therefore, we can verify the correctness of a secret at that time also, as we reconstruct the secret only when we need it. The scheme fails when the dealer or shareholders are not honest and intentionally or accidentally use fake shares during the secret sharing.

3 Our Verifiable Secret Sharing Scheme

3.1 Shamir's Secret Sharing Scheme

In a Shamir's Secret Sharing scheme [2], a dealer D divides a secret x into n number of shares $x_1, x_2, \ldots, x_n$ and distributes the shares among a set of n participants in such a way that for any threshold t or more shares are able to reconstruct an original secret back, but less then that leaves x completely undetermined. Shamir's solution is information theoretically secure and does not rely on any unproven cryptographic assumption, but it is not secure against cheating as it assumes that a dealer and shareholders are honest but it is not always possible. The two properties we need to guarantee in a Shamir's Secret Sharing scheme are:

1. *Recoverability*: Given any t shares, we can recover x.
2. *Secrecy*: Given any $< t$ share, absolutely nothing is learned about x. In other words, the conditional x should be the a priori distribution for x, so $Pr(x|shares) = Pr(x)$. Secrecy will be highlighted in Sect. 4.

Let F be a field (typically finite). Then $d+1$ pairs (a_i, b_i) uniquely determine a polynomial $f(z)$ of degree $\leq d$ such that $f(a_i) = b_i$. We are assuming $d < |F|$, so that the a_i's can be distinct.

In the fact above, $f(z)$ has degree $\leq d$ and not $= d$ because of degeneracy issues. So here is Shamir's Secret Sharing scheme, for *t–out–of–n* secret sharing: First, choose a large prime p, and let $F = Z/pZ$. To share secret x as $x \Rightarrow (x_1, x_2, \ldots, x_n)$.

Then:

1. Choose coefficients $f_1, \ldots, f_{t-1} \in Z = p/Z$, which are to be the coefficients of degree $t-1$ polynomial f.
2. Let $f(z) = f_0 + f_1 z + \ldots + f_{t-1} z^{t-1}$, *where* $f_0 = x$.
3. Give $f(i)$ to party i, $i = 1 \ldots n$.

Now we need a recovery procedure and we need to prove the secrecy condition to show that this is a secret sharing scheme.

Recovery is straightforward. When t parties have a secret, then we have t points on the curve of a degree $\leq (t-1)$ polynomial, so by the fact above, we get unique coefficient to a degree $\leq (t-1)$ polynomial. The secret is coefficient f_0. Formalizing, we use Lagrange Interpolation over a finite field. Given (i, x_i) for $i \in G$,

$$f(z) = \sum_{i \in G} x_i \prod_{j \in G, j \neq i} \frac{z-j}{i-j}$$

This is a linear system in t unknowns, the coefficients f_k, with t equations. The existence of a unique solution is guaranteed by the fact stated above. So Gaussian elimination can be used to solve. Then:

$$x = f_0 = f(0) = \sum_{i \in G} x_i \prod_{j \in G, j \neq i} \frac{-j}{i-j}$$

Letting $\prod_{j \in G, j \neq i} \frac{-j}{i-j} = c_i$, we have that $x = \sum_{i \in G} x_i c_i$. Note that c_i is a constant independent of the x_i's. Thus we can compute c_i, $i \in G$ ahead of time without knowing the x_i's, and then in linear time can find x, the secret, once we have the x_i's. So recoverability is quite efficient in this case.

As long as Secrecy is concerned, if the participants cheat in the recovery phase, the secret cannot be recovered. The other participants don't even have a way of knowing if someone cheated. There is no way to recognize for the Shamir's scheme whether an alleged share is valid.

There is total trust in the dealer, and thus in any single point of failure. If the application is ring the nuke, or voting, Shamir's scheme is obviously useless, as there is no single party all parties will agree to trust.

The dealer might hand out bogus or inconsistent shares with the Shamir scheme, and the other parties don't even know what went wrong, that the problem lies with the dealer and not with not enough participants wanting to share their secret.

3.2 Hash Based-Signature Verification

In our Verifiable Secret Sharing scheme we can group the operations and computations into two major actions (See Figs. 1 and 2):

Upload: A User can upload a file by sending it to the client Desktop (such as by drag-and-drop, or specifying the path). The client Desktop then breaks the file into multiple fragments to be encrypted using an AES–256 key. The secret key is also split into n shares and a SHA–512 hash is calculated for the key and for each share. Next, the client stores these hashes into his connected mobile device through a moblie application as a list with their corresponding IDs. The IDs maps the hashes to the order number of shareholders. Afterwards, the client distributes the shares across the Clouds, and then uploads the encrypted fragments equally, using the credentials (Username and Password) stored in the profile. The encrypted fragments should be uploaded to all available Cloud providers.

Download: In order to download a file a User has first to recover the secret key from the shareholders with respect to the Shamir's Secret Sharing scheme. Once the shares are retreived a SHA-512 hash is created for each one them to be compared with those stored in the device databases so as to verify the correctness of the shares and the honesty of each shareholders as well as the Dealer. If there is a match, then, the Dealer is informed to reconstruct and to generate a hash of the Key. A second verification is made against the mobile device's application database to check the correctness of the hash. If a match is found, decryption of the downloaded file fragments can be started in the client Desktop to recover the original file. During the exchanges, a secure communication channel should be established using certificates/secure protocols such as TLS to prevent attacks such as data tampering, Man in the middle, Brute force, Spoofing and Denial of Service attacks.

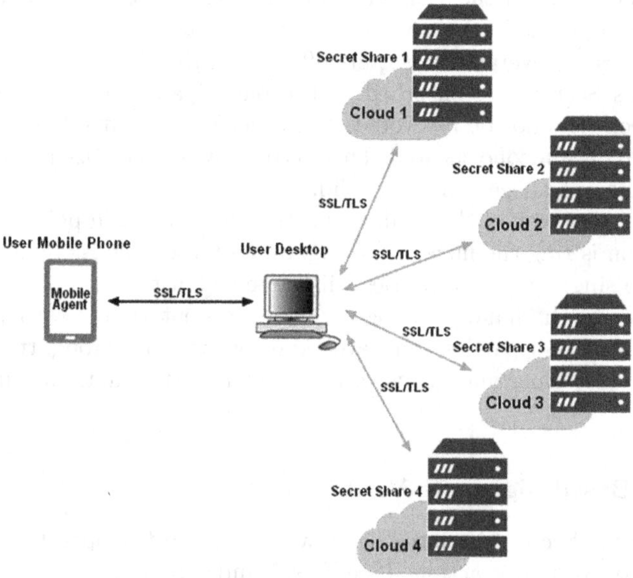

Fig. 1. Our proposed protected architecture

4 Security Analysis

Our Scheme is secure against brute force and guessing attacks. Suppose that an adversary gains a lot of information about the secret Key x with every x_i and

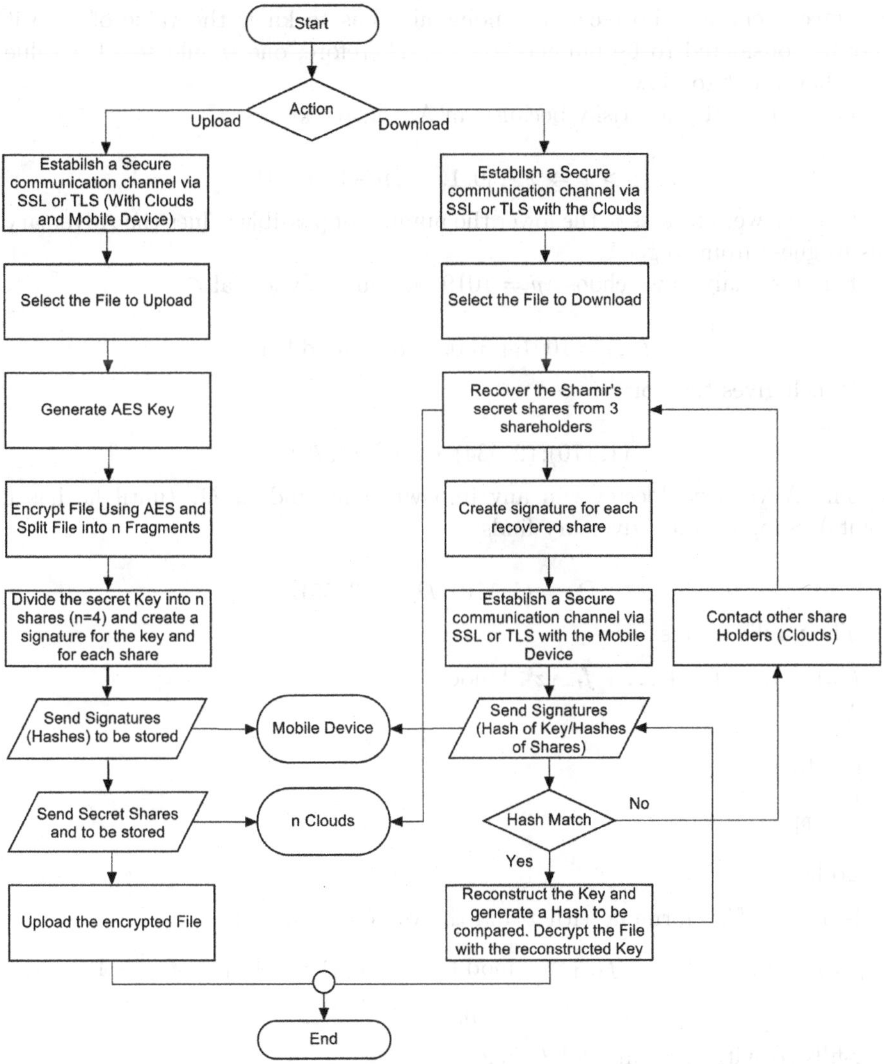

Fig. 2. Flowchart of our scheme

finds the 2 points D_0 and D_2, he still doesn't have $t = 3$ points, so in theory he shouldn't have gained any more info about the secret key x. But he combines the info from the 2 points with the public info.

For this case study we choose a finite field arithmetic in a field of size:

$$p \in \mathrm{P} : p > x, n.$$

We should choose a prime p that is bigger than the number of participants and every f_i including the secret $f_0 = x$.

Since everyone who receives a point also has to know the value of p so it may be considered to be publicly known. Therefore, one should select a value for $p$that is not too low.

Low values of p are risky because an Adversary knows:

$$p > x \Rightarrow x \in [0, 1, \ldots, p-2, p-1]$$

So the lower one sets p, the lower the number of possible values the Adversary has to guess from to get x.

For this analysis we choose $p = 1019$ and our polynomial:

$$f(z) = 1001 + 100z + 88z^2 \bmod 1019$$

Which gives the points:

$$(1, 170); (2, 534); (3, 55); (4, 771).$$

The Adversary doesn't win any info when he finds a D_x (until he has t points). Suppose the Adversary finds:

$$D_0 = (1, 170), D_2 = (3, 55)$$

The public info is:

$f(z) = f_0 + f_1 z + \ldots + f_{t-1} z^{t-1} \bmod p$
$n = 4$
$t = 3$
$p = 1019$
$f_0 = x$
$f_i \in \mathbb{N}$

So he:

1-fills the $f(x)$ formula with x and the value of t and p:

$$f(z) = x + f_1 z + \ldots + f_{3-1} z^{3-1} \bmod 1019 \Rightarrow f(z) = x + f_1 z + f_2 z^2 - 1019 m_x : m_x \in \mathbb{N}$$

2-fills (i) with the values of D_0's x and

$$f(z) : 170 = x + f_1 1 + f_2 1^2 - 1019 m_1 \Rightarrow 170 = x + f_1 + f_2 - 1019 m_1$$

3-fills (i) with the values of D_2's x and

$$f(z) : 55 = x + f_1 2 + f_2 2^2 - 1019 m_2 \Rightarrow 55 = x + 2f_1 + 4f_2 - 1019 m_2$$

4-does (ii)–(iii):

$$(170 - 55) = (x - x) + (2f_1 - f_1) + (4f_2 - f_2) + (1019 m_1 - 1019 m_2) \Rightarrow 115 = f_1 + 3f_2 + 1019(m_1 - m_2)$$

And rewrites this as:

$$f_1 = 115 - 3f_2 - 1019(m_1 - m_2)$$

5-knows that $f_2 \in \mathbb{N}$ so he starts replacing f_2 in (iv) with $0, 1, 2, \ldots$ to find all possible values for f_1:

$$*f_2 = 0 \rightarrow f_1 = 115 - 3 \times 0 - 1019(m_1 - m_2) = 115 - 1019(m_1 - m_2)$$
$$*f_2 = 1 \rightarrow f_1 = 115 - 3 \times 1 - 1019(m_1 - m_2) = 112 - 1019(m_1 - m_2)$$
$$*f_2 = 2 \rightarrow f_1 = 115 - 3 \times 2 - 1019(m_1 - m_2) = 109 - 1019(m_1 - m_2)$$
$$*\ldots\ldots$$

The Adversary can't stop because $(m_1 - m_2)$ could be any integer (even negative if $m_2 > m_1$) so there are an infinite amount of possible values for f_1. He knows that [115, 112, 109, ...] always decreases by 3 so if 1019 was divisible by 3 he could conclude $f_1 \in [1, 4, 7, \ldots]$ but because it's prime he can't even conclude that and so he didn't win any information.

Furthermore, the scheme is secure against cheating attempts. The scheme employs a second verification means to ensure the integrity of the shared secret key by using a hash signature of the secret shares which are generated in the client Desktop and stored in the user mobile device. In this fashion, we also achieve a strong authentication to verify that the Shareholders have correctly submitted their secret shares during the recovery process, and the Dealer is not handing out inconsistent shares. Typically, if one of the participants cheats about his secret share another shareholder will be prompted to submit his secret. Moreover, the hashes will help find out if the Dealer is not bogus and has done computations correctly on the shares in a first place with respect to the Shamir's Secret Sharing scheme.

The signature are resistant to cracking attacks as SHA-512 is a strong hashing algorithm. Furthermore, the hash storage is decentralized which makes other types of attacks such as malware-based attacks hard to achieve. The proposed infrastructure employs secure communication based on secure protocols which allow encrypting data and information to provide confidentiality.

5 Conclusion

We have proposed a Verifiable Secret Sharing sheme that addresses the issues of Shamir's Secret Sharing Scheme. In our suggestion, we have presented a novel approach to verify the secret shares of each participant by generating a hash based-signature for each share. Additionally, we have proven that the Shamir's scheme is more secure when using finite field arithmetic as compared to the classical scheme which uses integer arithmetic.

References

1. Benzekki, K., Elfergougui, A., Elbelrhiti, E.A.: A secure cloud computing architecture using homomorphic encryption. Int. J. Adv. Comput. Sci. Appl. (IJACSA) **7**(2), 293–298 (2016)
2. Shamir, A.: How to share a secret. Commun. ACM **22**(11), 612–613 (1979)

3. Chor, B., Goldwasser, S., Micali, S., Awerbuch, B.: Verifiable secret sharing and achieving simultaneity in the presence of faults. In: SFCS 1985 Proceedings of the 26th Annual Symposium on Foundations of Computer Science, pp. 383–395 (1985)
4. Benaloh, J.C.: Secret sharing homomorphisms: keeping shares of a secret secret (extended abstract). In: Odlyzko, A.M. (ed.) CRYPTO 1986. LNCS, vol. 263, pp. 251–260. Springer, Heidelberg (1987). doi:10.1007/3-540-47721-7_19
5. Feldman, P.: A practical scheme for non-interactive verifiable secret sharing. In: SFCS 1987 Proceedings of the 28th Annual Symposium on Foundations of Computer Science, pp. 427–438 (1987)
6. Harn, L., Lin, C.: Detection and identification of cheaters in (t, n) secret sharing scheme. Des. Codes Crypt. **52**(1), 15–24 (2009)
7. Cao, Z., Markowitch, O.: Two optimum secret sharing schemes revisited. In: FITME 2008 Proceedings of the 2008 International Seminar on Future Information Technology and Management Engineering, pp. 157–160 (2008)
8. Obana, S., Araki, T.: Almost optimum secret sharing schemes secure against cheating for arbitrary secret distribution. In: Lai, X., Chen, K. (eds.) ASIACRYPT 2006. LNCS, vol. 4284, pp. 364–379. Springer, Heidelberg (2006). doi:10.1007/11935230_24

A Priority Based Task Scheduling in Cloud Computing Using a Hybrid MCDM Model

Hicham Ben Alla(✉), Said Ben Alla, and Abdellah Ezzati

LAVETE Laboratory, Mathematics and Computer Science Department, Science and Technical Faculty, Hassan 1 University, 26000 Settat, Morocco
hich.benalla@gmail.com, abdezzati@gmail.com, saidb_05@hotmail.com

Abstract. Task scheduling is an interesting topic in cloud computing nowadays. The mapping of the cloud resources to process the customer requests is very challenging and a well-known NP-Complete problem. In this paper, we address this problem with the consideration of the priority as one of the critical issues in the task scheduling process. The priority is computed according to the most important parameters that can meet user's requirements and improve the resource utilization. We propose a new Dynamic Priority-Queue (DPQ) approach based on a hybrid multi-criteria decision making (MCDM) namely ELECTRE III and Differential Evolution (DE). Furthermore, to schedule the tasks, we introduce a hybrid meta-heuristic algorithm based on Particle Swarm Optimization (PSO) and Simulated Annealing (SA). The proposed DEELDPQ-SAPSO approach has been validated through the CloudSim simulator. The experimental results show that the proposed approach can achieve good performance, user priority, load balancing and improve the resource utilization.

Keywords: Cloud computing · Task scheduling · Dynamic queues · Priority

1 Introduction

Cloud computing has recently emerged as a new paradigm for hosting and delivering services over the Internet. The cloud computing environment offers many advantages to the users to manage all computing resources such as servers, software, storage, and networking. The cloud users pay only for the computing resources and services they have used. The cloud allows users to access to the services anytime from anywhere. These advantages make cloud computing a compelling paradigm for servicing computing needs for users [1]. Scheduling users' requests in the cloud computing environment is an NP-Complete problem. This problem is usually solved by using heuristic methods in order to reduce to polynomial complexity [2]. Scheduling tasks with the consideration of the priority as one of the most challenging issues in this environment can ensure a better satisfaction of cloud users as well as the provider, and achieve an efficient utilization of resource with maximum profit and a high-performance computing. In order to address this challenge, a new task scheduling approach is proposed. All the tasks are ranked using a new hybrid multi-criteria decision-making (MCDM)

E. Sabir et al. (Eds.): UNet 2017, LNCS 10542, pp. 235–246, 2017.
https://doi.org/10.1007/978-3-319-68179-5_21

method based on ELECTRE III and Differential Evolution. Then dispatch the prioritized tasks among dynamic queues [3]. We also tackle the priority of the dynamic queues created as well as the available resources to process the tasks. For mapping the tasks to the most suitable cloud resources, we use a hybrid meta-heuristic algorithm based on particle swarm optimization and simulated annealing algorithms. The remainder of the paper is organized as follows: Sect. 2 presents related works. In Sect. 3, the proposed work is described. Section 4 discusses the experimental setup and simulation results of the proposed work. Finally, the paper gives a conclusion in Sect. 5.

2 Related Work

Task scheduling in cloud computing is an important complex part in cloud computing. Many studies discuss this concept with consideration of the priority issue and some other parameters which can influence the scheduling of tasks and utilization of resources.

In the paper [4], the authors proposed a Simulation of Priority Based Earliest Deadline First Scheduling for Cloud Computing System. This paper discusses a task allocation algorithm, which use the priority and the earliest deadline first scheduling algorithm. The tasks are allocated on the basis of their priority and the task having higher priority get scheduled first. The proposed work achieves higher performance and also improves memory utilization. The authors in the paper [5] propose a priority-based task scheduling approach that prioritizes the workflow tasks based on the length of the instructions. This paper prioritized various independent tasks of a workflow using six sigma control charts. The tasks have been divided into various levels and further, the resources have been allocated according to the resource requirements of the various task levels. The experimental results validate that the proposed approach can considerably reduce makespan and execution time. In the paper [6], the key role of the algorithm proposed is the QOS-driven based on the priority of task which in turn is computed using many task attributes such as user privilege, expectation, and the length of task. Next, this task scheduled onto the service which has a minimum completion time. The results show that the proposed algorithm achieves better performance and load balancing by the priority and the completion time. In the paper [7], the authors propose a model for task-oriented resource allocation in a cloud computing environment. The pairwise comparison matrix technique is used to rank the resource allocation task and the Analytic Hierarchy Process (AHP) gives the available resources and user preferences. The tasks are pairwise compared according to network bandwidth, complete time, task expenses, and reliability of task. The weights of tasks are then calculated using the AHP method and the corresponding computing resources are allocated in terms of the weights of tasks. Authors in the paper [8] propose an algorithm based on multi-criteria decision-making method namely the Analytical Hierarchy Process. It consisted of three levels of priorities, including scheduling level, resources level and job level. Each job requests a resource with a determined priority. The priority of each job is compared with other jobs separately using comparison matrixes of jobs which are created according to the priority of resource accessibilities. In the paper [9], the authors propose an improvement in priority based job scheduling algorithm in cloud computing which is based on multiple criteria and multiple attribute decision-making model. This algorithm uses an iterative method to find priority of jobs and resources and also finds priority of jobs to achieve better performance. The results experiments show that this algorithm has preferable performance in term of makespan and consistency.

3 Proposed Work

3.1 Problem Description and Objectives

In cloud computing, a variety of attributes should be considered while scheduling. Therefore, an efficient scheduling algorithm in cloud environment must consider the multi-criteria of tasks, in order to achieve user and provider satisfaction which can be attained by assuring a good QoS and maximum profit for the user and cloud provider respectively [10]. However, there are some criteria to be taken into consideration such as the priority of tasks, which is an important issue to be solved in the scheduling process because some tasks need to be serviced earlier than other remaining tasks that can stay for a long time. The makespan is another important criterion which represents the time spent in executing all tasks. In fact, the makespan has a direct effect on utilization of resources. Therefore, an optimal tasks scheduling algorithm based on these parameters should be implemented in the cloud broker. On the basis of the issues mentioned above, the main objectives of the proposed work are:

- Compute the priority of tasks based on a hybrid multiple criteria decision-making model using Differential Evolution (DE) and ELECTRE III, and then divide the tasks in different level priority.
- Compute the prioritization of resources, and grouping them by availability and priority level.
- Dispatch the tasks among dynamic priority-queues based on decision distribution and priority level.
- Scheduling the tasks stored in the dynamic queues using a meta-heuristic algorithm. The Particle Swarm Optimization (PSO) has been proved to be a good optimization algorithm with outstanding global performance. Therefore, we use a hybrid algorithm based on modified PSO and simulated annealing.

3.2 Differential Evolution (DE)

The Differential Evolution method is an Evolutionary Algorithm (EA) proposed by Storn and Price in 1995 [11] for solving function optimization problems. This algorithm is a new floating point encoded evolutionary algorithm for global optimization, and it was named DE to describe the special kind of differential operator which they invoked when creating new offspring from parent chromosomes instead of classical crossover or mutation. DE algorithm uses NP solution vectors of D dimensions created randomly as the population. Then the mutation, crossover and selection operators are applied to improve this population successfully. The steps of DE method are as follows:

- Initialization: The initial population should ideally cover the entire search space, where each parameter of the initial vector is generated from the following equation:

$$x_{j,i}(0) = x_{j,L} + rand(0,1) \cdot \left(x_{j,U} - x_{j,L}\right) \quad (1)$$

  where $rand(0,\ 1)$ is a uniformly distributed random number between 0 and 1, and $x_{j,L}$, $x_{j,U}$ are respectively the lower and upper bounds of the search space.
- Mutation: For each target vector $x_{i,G}$ at generation G, an associated mutated (a mutant vector) vector $v_{i,G}$ can be generated using:

$$v_{i,G+1} = x_{r1,G} + F\left(x_{r2,G} - x_{r3,G}\right) \quad (2)$$

  where $r1$, $r2$ and $r3 \in (1,\ 2,\ \ldots,\ NP)$ are randomly chosen integers, different from each other and also different from the current index i. F is a real and constant factor $\in [0,\ 2]$ and controls the multiplication of differential variation $(x_{r2,G} - x_{r3,G})$.
- Crossover: This step is applied to each pair of the generated mutant vector $v_{i,G}$, and each element of the trial vector $u_{i,G+1}$ is generated as follows:

$$u_{j,i,G+1} = \begin{cases} v_{j,i,G+1} & \text{if } rand_j(0,1) \leq CR \text{ or } (j = k_{rand}) \\ x_{j,i,G} & \text{if } rand_j(0,1) > CR \text{ and } (j \neq k_{rand}) \end{cases} \quad (3)$$

  where j = (1,2, …., D), $rand_j(0,\ 1)$ is a randomly chosen integer in the range [0, 1] and CR is the crossover constant in the range [0, 1]. For ensure that the trial vector $u_{i,G+1}$ receives at least one parameter from the mutant vector, we choose a random index $k_{rand} \in (1, 2, \ldots, D)$.
- Selection: this step aim to choose the vector between the target vector and the trial vector with the aim of creating an individual for the next generation, and f(x) representing the objective function.

$$x_{i,G+1} = \begin{cases} u_{i,G} & \text{if } f\left(u_{i,G}\right) \leq f\left(x_{i,G}\right) \\ x_{i,G} & \text{if } f\left(u_{i,G}\right) > f\left(x_{i,G}\right) \end{cases} \quad (4)$$

3.3 Electre III

ELECTRE III is an MCDM method that provides an effective framework for comparison based on the evaluation of multiple conflict criteria [12, 13]. The ELECTRE III method consists of two steps: In the first step, a valued outranking relation is constructed for each pair of items a and b, by determining the degree of credibility of the statement that “a is at least as good as b” or although “a outperforms b”. In the second step, these valued outranking relations are used to generate a ranking of all items.

The credibility degree of the statement “a outranks b” denoted by $\sigma(a,\ b)$ can be measured using the four steps as follow:

- First step: Calculate the partial concordance index for each pair of items a and b:

$$C_j(a,b) = \begin{cases} 0 & \text{if } g_j(b) - g_j(a) \geq p_j \\ 1 & \text{if } g_j(b) - g_j(a) \leq q_j \\ \frac{p_j + g_j(a) - g_j(b)}{p_j - q_j} & \text{otherwise} \end{cases} \quad (5)$$

where $g_j(a)$ and $g_j(b)$ represent the evaluation of the items a and b respectively according to the criterion j. q_j is the indifference threshold and p_j represents the preference threshold.
- Second step: Calculate the global concordance index $C(a,\ b)$ for each pair of items a and b:

$$C(a,\ b) = \frac{\sum_{j=1}^{n} w_j \times C_j(a,\ b)}{\sum_{j=1}^{n} w_j} \quad (6)$$

where w_j is the weight of criterion j. The global concordance index $C(a,b)$ is a measure of the strength of arguments which agree with the statement "a outranks b".
- Third step: Calculate the partial discordance index D(a,b) for each pair of items a and b:

$$D_j(a,\ b) = \begin{cases} 0 & \text{if } g_j(b) - g_j(a) \geq p_j \\ 1 & \text{if } g_j(b) - g_j(a) \leq v_j \\ \frac{g_j(b) - g_j(a) - p_j}{v_j - p_j} & \text{otherwise} \end{cases} \quad (7)$$

where v_j is the veto threshold which represents the tolerance limit that decision - makers are willing to accept for any compensation. The partial discordance index D (a, b) represent the measure of the strength of arguments that disagree with the statement "a outranks b" according to the criterion j.
- Fourth step: Calculate the credibility index of the statement "a outranks b":

$$\sigma(a,b) = \begin{cases} C(a,b) & \text{if } D_j(a,b) \leq C(a,b) \quad \forall j \\ C(a,b) \times & \prod\limits_{D_j(a,b) \succ C(a,b)} \frac{1 - D_j(a,b)}{1 - C(a,b)} \end{cases} \quad (8)$$

The next step in the ELECTRE III method is to exploit the model and produce a ranking of alternatives from the credibility matrix. The general approach for exploitation is to construct two preorders using a descending and ascending distillation process (respectively) and then combine these to produce a partial preorder [14].

3.4 Particle Swarm Optimization (PSO)

Particle swarm optimization (PSO) is a population-based stochastic optimization technique was first introduced in 1995 [15]. Each particle represents a candidate solution to the optimization problem. The advantages of PSO over many other optimization algorithms are its simplicity in implementation and its ability to converge to a reasonably good solution quickly. We consider that the search space is d-dimensional. In every iteration, each particle is updated by following two position values, Pi called personal best (Pbest), is the best position achieved so long by particle *i* and Pg called global best (Gbest), is the best position found by the neighbors of the particle *i*. After finding the two best values, the particle updates its velocity and positions with following Eqs. (9) and (10):

$$v_i^{t+1} = \omega \cdot v_{id}^t + c_1 \cdot r_1 \cdot \left(p_i^t - x_i^t\right) + c_2 \cdot r_2 \cdot \left(p_g^t - x_i^t\right) \tag{9}$$

$$x_i^{t+1} = x_i^t + v_i^{t+1} \tag{10}$$

where v_i^t and x_i^t are the component in dimension d of the ith particle velocity and position in iteration t respectively. c_1, c_2 are constant weight factors, r_1, r_2 are random factors in the [0, 1] interval and ω is the Inertia weight. The parameters ω, c_1 and c_2 must be selected properly for increasing the capabilities of PSO algorithm [16]. In this paper, we use the strategy called Random Inertia Weight (RIW) [17] combined with simulated annealing method as it can achieve best convergence velocity and precision, and can help to keep swarm variety. However, the original PSO version is designed for continuous function optimization problems, not for discrete function optimization problems. So, a binary version of PSO (BPSO) algorithm was developed to solve discrete function optimization problems [18]. The logistic sigmoid function shown in (11) can be used for the needs that the probability stays in the range of [0, 1], in another word, it used to limit the speed of the particle:

$$S\left(v_i^{t+1}\right) = \frac{1}{1 + e^{-v_i^{t+1}}} \tag{11}$$

The equation that updates the particle position becomes the following:

$$x_i^{t+1} = \begin{cases} 1 & if \quad r_3 < S\left(v_i^{t+1}\right) \\ 0 & otherwise \end{cases} \tag{12}$$

where r_3 is a random factor in the [0, 1] interval.

3.5 Proposed Approach

Our contribution is centered on a novel technique for tasks scheduling taking into consideration the priority issue, and aiming for better performance by optimizing execution time, makespan, resource utilization, and load balancing. Our approach aims in one hand to prioritize dynamically the tasks using DE algorithm and ELECTRE III namely DEEL, and in the other hand, to schedule these tasks to the best suitable resource selected using a hybrid meta-heuristic algorithm namely SAPSO based on simulated annealing and particle swarm optimization algorithms. Therefore, the task's priority can be defined with different parameters and different levels. The parameters considered in this paper are the task length (size), waiting time, burst time and deadline. These metrics are arguably the most important parameters that can meet user's requirements and improve the resource utilization. In our model, we consider three levels of priorities (High, Medium and Low) to address the task priority, the queue priority and the Virtual Machine (VM) priority. In the first step, the DEEL model uses the DE method as a generator of solutions that respect the constraints imposed by the MCDM method. The learning process of the proposed model is provided by DE method. Therefore, each generated solution by the DE method represents the criteria weights vector. Then the ELECTRE III method uses each time a solution generated by the DE method as an input parameter. The ELECTRE III method aims to generate a priority score for each task. After calculating all the scores, the tasks ranking is made, and the tasks are sorted based on the score values in descending order.

In the system shown in the Fig. 1, the tasks are stored in the global queue according to their arrival time. Then, DEEL model is used in order to prioritize the tasks among the global priority-queue. Next, we apply a Dynamic Priority-Queues algorithm (DPQ). This algorithm, in general, manages the global priority queues automatically by classifying tasks into three level priorities (Low, Medium, and High). Then dispatch the tasks among dynamic priority-queues. The task having a higher priority is considered as a most urgent task to be scheduled. The classification is obtained based on the quartile method.

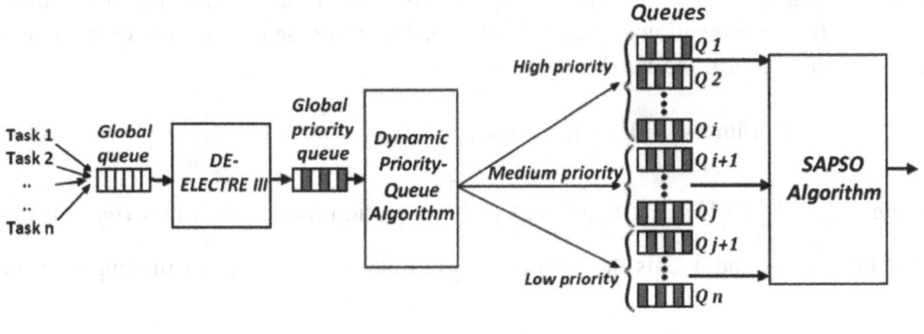

Fig. 1. DEELDPQ-SAPSO model

The lower quartile is the value of the middle of the first set, where 25% of the values are smaller than Q_L and 75% are larger. This first quartile takes the notation Q_L. Calculated by the following formula:

$$Q_L = \frac{1}{4}(n+1)th\ value \tag{13}$$

where n is the number of tasks.

The upper quartile is the value of the middle of the second set, where 75% of the values are smaller than Q_H and 25% are larger. This third quartile takes the notation Q_H. The Q_H formula is:

$$Q_H = \frac{3}{4}(n+1)th\ value \quad (14)$$

To prioritize the tasks, we divide all the tasks arranged in ascending order of ranking score into three priority levels using the Eqs. (13), (14) as follow:

- Low priority level task (Lpt) = all the tasks = < Q_L
- Medium priority level task (Mpt) = all the tasks between Q_L and Q_H
- High priority level task (Hpt) = all the tasks > = Q_H

Next, to prioritize the queues, we consider three different queue priority levels, described as follow:

- Low priority level queue (Lpq): each queue contains the tasks with Lpt.
- Medium priority level queue (Mpq): = each queue contains the tasks with Mpt.
- High priority level of queue (Hpq): = each queue contains the tasks with Hpt.

Then, for the prioritization of the virtual machines, the VMs are sorted in ascending order based on their processing power. The same method as the prioritization of tasks is used to divide all VMs into three priority levels: Low priority level VM (Lpv), Medium priority level VM (Mpv) and High priority level VM (Hpv).

When DPQ algorithm dispatches all tasks among dynamic priority-queue, then the SAPSO algorithm is applied to selects each queue and perform the best appropriate allocation map of tasks on resources [19]. Therefore, the fitness function in (15) is used to calculate the executions times of all possible tasks sequences on every cloud resource, then, return the maximum value.

$$\text{Fitness} = \text{Max}\{\alpha_{\text{vm}_1}, \alpha_{\text{vm}_2}, \ldots, \alpha_{\text{vm}_\text{j}}, \ldots\ldots\ldots, \alpha_{\text{vm}_\text{m}}\} \quad (15)$$

where $\alpha_{vm_j} = \sum_{i=0}^{n} Ex_j(Task_i)$, $Ex_j(Task_i)$ is the execution time of task i on vm_j, n is the number of tasks and α_{vm_j} is the total execution time of a set of tasks running on vm_j.

4 Results and Discussions

4.1 Simulation Environment and Configuration

To evaluate the proposed algorithm, the simulation is implemented using CloudSim simulator [20]. This simulator supports both modeling and simulation for single and inter-networked clouds. CloudSim enables seamless modeling, experiments and simulation of the cloud computing systems and application provisioning environments. The simulation is done using 10 Datacenter, [2–6] hosts, 30 virtual machines where processor MIPS in [1000–30000], Ram memory in [256–2048] and the Bandwidth in [500–1000]. For the tasks source, we get tasks from workload data. We use workload traces from real systems available from the Parallel Workload Archive (PWA). The workload data used is called The Los Alamos National Lab (LANL) CM-5 log [21]. We modified this trace by adding generated deadlines for all tasks, using the method presented in [22].

4.2 Experiments and Results Analysis

In the simulation experiments, we compare the proposed algorithm DEELDPQ-SAPSO with First-Come First-Served FCFS and PSO. Several experiments with different parameter setting were performed to evaluate the efficiency of proposed approach. The evaluation is done using independent tasks from workload data. The performance evaluation is compared in term of the average makespan and Degree of Imbalance (DI) with a different number of tasks.

Figure 2 illustrate the average makespan of both the algorithms. It has been found that DEELDPQ-SAPSO scheduling algorithm has shown the best performance while producing the shortest average makespan as compared to other scheduling algorithms PSO and FCFS. The makespan of DEELDPQ-SAPSO is better when compared with the other two algorithms and it can be seen that important makespan gains were obtained as well when the number of tasks is increased, because there are some criteria taken into consideration such as the priority of tasks, the dynamic queues using a meta-heuristic algorithm and the prioritization of resources. The proposed algorithm can effectively perform the most appropriate allocation map of tasks on resources.

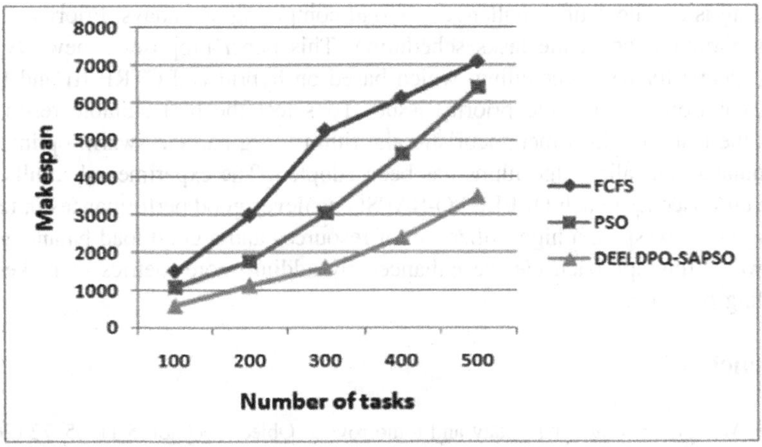

Fig. 2. Average makespan

The Degree of Imbalance measure the imbalance among VMs. The minimum value of DI signified that the system is more balanced [23, 24]. The Fig. 3 shows the average DI computed for each scheduling algorithm. The results illustrate that the proposed algorithm DEELDPQ-SAPSO minimizes the degree of imbalance and can achieve good system load balance with a different number of tasks. A good load balancing means that a good utilization of resource has achieved.

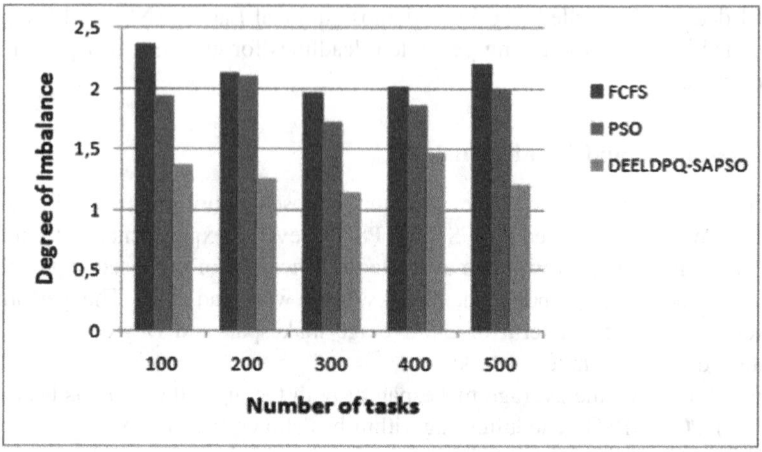

Fig. 3. Average Degree of Imbalance (DI)

These results demonstrated the effectiveness of the proposed algorithm and the average performance is better than other algorithms FCFS and PSO.

5 Conclusion

Scheduling is an interesting challenge in cloud computing nowadays. Priority of tasks is an important issue in the tasks scheduling. This paper proposes a new Dynamic Priority-Queue for task scheduling, which based on hybrid ELECTRE III and Differential Evolution to solve the priority issue. To select the best suitable resource to process the task, a hybrid meta-heuristic algorithm using particle swarm optimization and simulated annealing algorithms has been adopted. The experimental results show that the proposed approach DEELDPQ-SAPSO achieves good performances in term of reducing the makespan, a high utilization of resources and a good load balancing. For future work, this approach can be enhanced by adding more metrics to make good scheduling decisions.

References

1. Kim, W.: Cloud computing: today and tomorrow. J. Object Technol. **8**(1), 65–72 (2009)
2. Hoang, H.N., Le Van, S., Maue, H.N., Bien, C.P.N.: Admission control and scheduling algorithms based on ACO and PSO heuristic for optimizing cost in cloud computing. In: Król, D., Madeyski, L., Nguyen, N.T. (eds.) Recent Developments in Intelligent Information and Database Systems. SCI, vol. 642, pp. 15–28. Springer, Cham (2016). doi:10.1007/978-3-319-31277-4_2
3. Ben Alla, H., Ben Alla, S., Ezzati, A., Mouhsen, A.: A novel architecture with dynamic queues based on fuzzy logic and particle swarm optimization algorithm for task scheduling in cloud computing. In: El-Azouzi, R., Menasché, D.S., Sabir, E., Pellegrini, F.D., Benjillali, M. (eds.) Advances in Ubiquitous Networking 2. LNEE, vol. 397, pp. 205–217. Springer, Singapore (2017). doi:10.1007/978-981-10-1627-1_16

4. Gupta, G., Kumawat, V., Laxmi, P., Singh, D., Jain, V., Singh, R.: A simulation of priority based earliest deadline first scheduling for cloud computing system. In: 2014 First International Conference on Networks & Soft Computing (ICNSC2014) (2014)
5. Bala, A., Chana, I.: Multilevel priority-based task scheduling algorithm for workflows in cloud computing environment. In: Satapathy, S.C., Joshi, A., Modi, N., Pathak, N. (eds.) Proceedings of International Conference on ICT for Sustainable Development. AISC, vol. 408, pp. 685–693. Springer, Singapore (2016). doi:10.1007/978-981-10-0129-1_71
6. Wu, X., Deng, M., Zhang, R., Zeng, B., Zhou, S.: A task scheduling algorithm based on QoS-driven in cloud computing. Procedia Comput. Sci. **17**, 1162–1169 (2013)
7. Ergu, D., Kou, G., Peng, Y., Shi, Y., Shi, Y.: The analytic hierarchy process: task scheduling and resource allocation in cloud computing environment. J. Supercomput. **64**, 835–848 (2011)
8. Ghanbari, S., Othman, M.: A priority based job scheduling algorithm in cloud computing. Procedia Eng. **50**, 778–785 (2012)
9. Patel, S., Bhoi, U.: Improved priority based job scheduling algorithm in cloud computing using iterative method. In: International Conference on Advances in Computing and Communications (2014)
10. Karthick, A., Ramaraj, E., Subramanian, R.: An efficient multi queue job scheduling for cloud computing. In: World Congress on Computing and Communication Technologies (2014)
11. Storn, R., Price, K.: Differential evolution–a simple and efficient heuristic for global optimization over continuous spaces. J. Global Optim. **11**(4), 341–359 (1997)
12. Figueira, J., Greco, S., Roy, B., Słowiński, R.: An overview of ELECTRE methods and their recent extensions. J. Multi-Criteria Decis. Anal. **20**, 61–85 (2012)
13. Roy, B.: The outranking approach and the foundations of ELECTRE methods. Theory Decis. **31**, 49–73 (1991)
14. Hwang, C., Yoon, K.: Multiple Attribute Decision Making. Springer, Heidelberg (1981)
15. Kennedy, J., Eberhart, R.: Particle swarm optimization. In: International Conference on Neural Networks, vol. 4, pp. 1942–1948. IEEE (1995)
16. Clerc, M., Kennedy, J.: The particle swarm - explosion, stability, and convergence in a multidimensional complex space. IEEE Trans. Evol. Comput. **6**(1), 58–73 (2002)
17. Yue-lin, G., Yu-hong, D.: A new particle swarm optimization algorithm with random inertia weight and evolution strategy. In: International Conference on Computational Intelligence and Security (CISW 2007), pp. 199–203. IEEE (2007)
18. Kennedy, J., Eberhart, R.: A discrete binary version of the particle swarm algorithm. In: International Conference on Systems, Man, and Cybernetics. Computational Cybernetics and Simulation, pp. 4104–4108. IEEE (1997)
19. Ben Alla, H., Ben Alla, S., Ezzati, A., Touhafi, A.: An Efficient dynamic priority-queue algorithm based on AHP and PSO for task scheduling in cloud computing. In: Abraham, A., Haqiq, A., Alimi, Adel M., Mezzour, G., Rokbani, N., Muda, A.K. (eds.) HIS 2016. AISC, vol. 552, pp. 134–143. Springer, Cham (2017). doi:10.1007/978-3-319-52941-7_14
20. Calheiros, R., Ranjan, R., Beloglazov, A., De Rose, C., Buyya, R.: CloudSim: a toolkit for modeling and simulation of cloud computing environments and evaluation of resource provisioning algorithms. J. Softw. Pract. Experience **41**(1), 23–50 (2011). ACM
21. Parallel Workloads Archive: LANL CM-5
22. Venugopal, S., Chu, X., Buyya, R.: A negotiation mechanism for advance resource reservation using the alternate offers protocol. In: Proceedings of the 16th International Workshop on Quality of Service (IWQoS 2008), Twente, The Netherlands, June 2008

23. Ben Alla, H., Ben Alla, S., Ezzati, A.: A novel architecture for task scheduling based on dynamic queues and particle swarm optimization in cloud computing. In: 2016 2nd International Conference on Cloud Computing Technologies and Applications (CloudTech) (2016)
24. Li, K., Xu, G., Zhao, G., Dong, Y., Wang, D.: Cloud task scheduling based on load balancing ant colony optimization. In: 2011 Sixth Annual Chinagrid Conference (2011)

A Novel Approach for Security in Cloud-Based Medical Image Storage Using Segmentation

Mbarek Marwan(✉), Ali Kartit, and Hassan Ouahmane

Laboratory LTI, Department TRI, ENSAJ, University Chouaïb Doukkali–El Jadida, Avenue Jabran Khalil Jabran, BP 299 El Jadida, Morocco
marwan.mbarek@gmail.com, alikartit@gmail.com, hassan.ouahmane@yahoo.fr

Abstract. Over the past decade, imaging technology has played a vital role in modern medicine. In fact, it is mainly used to improve diagnosis and facilitate collaboration among healthcare professionals. Nevertheless, in order to build and deploy Electronic Medical Records (EMR), systems require powerful platform, including software and hardware. To address these issues, Cloud Computing has been recently introduced to reduce operating costs. In this respect, only needed resources are provided to the clients and billed according to services utilization. Accordingly, Storage-as-a-Service (SaaS) model aims at outsourcing the storage of medical data to a third party. In spite of its economic benefits, Cloud adoption still faces security challenges. Alternatively, various implementations based on traditional encryption algorithms have been suggested. However, most of them do not take into consideration image features, and hence, they are not suitable for medical images. They are also computationally expensive, and distort the medical image quality by using lossy methods. In this study, we rely on a segmentation approach to protect health information without affecting its quality. In this regard, the secret image is split into several portions by means of a K-means algorithm. Furthermore, each party is stored in a distinct Cloud to enhance data privacy. That is why we use DepSky as a Multi-Cloud environment for safeguarding patient's digital records. The implementation results show that our proposal guarantees both security and quality of medical images.

Keywords: Cloud computing · Security · Storage · K-means

1 Introduction

Due to the increase of medical services demand, healthcare organizations are under pressure to improve efficiency and reduce costs. For this reason, Electronic Medical Records (EMR) system is implemented in the healthcare sector, for it allows the automation of patient care workflow, enables collaborative work, facilitates access to medical information, etc. However, the IT services integration involves investing in a sophisticated in-house data center and hiring technical staff. This has led to a great interest in Cloud adoption for reducing operating expenses. In fact, clients rent Cloud services to satisfy a growing demand for computational resources. In addition, customers are billed according to resources utilization. With the continuous increase of

E. Sabir et al. (Eds.): UNet 2017, LNCS 10542, pp. 247–258, 2017.
https://doi.org/10.1007/978-3-319-68179-5_22

Cloud services demand, various delivery models have been proposed to fulfill client's needs: Software-as-a-Service (SaaS), Platform-as-a-Service (PaaS) and Infrastructure-as-a-Service (IaaS). Most importantly, Cloud-based storage has emerged as an important concept that aims at providing efficient access to remote storage systems. In spite of numerous financial benefits, storing medical imaging data on Cloud Computing actually faces security challenges [1]. In fact, Cloud technology evolved out of diverse other technologies, such as web 2.0, virtualization, SOA and High Performance Computing (HPC) [2]. Hence, this paradigm inherits threats and vulnerabilities associated with these techniques. In this regard, various framework based on cryptographic techniques are suggested to mitigate these problems. Unfortunately, these proposed algorithms are either of high computational complexity and inefficient or unsuitable for medical images. Therefore, we resort to a segmentation approach to enhance security in Cloud storage. In this paper, a K-means algorithm is used to split a medical image into various portions. At the same time, each region is stored in a different Cloud within a Multi-Cloud architecture. Our solution is not meant to replace existing techniques. It is rather an attempt that seeks to complement them by providing an efficient and simple method for securing medical data over Cloud Computing. The primary goal of this study is to provide an effective contribution to tackle the issue of security in Cloud storage.

The paper is organized as follows. In Sect. 2, we present previous related work and techniques involved to meet security requirements. Section 3 illustrates our proposed solution to ensure data confidentiality. In Sects. 4 and 5, we present and discuss the implementation results. Conclusions and future work are then drawn in Sect. 6.

2 Current Approaches

This section is devoted to the previous contributions akin to the issue of security of data processing over cloud. We classify them according to techniques involved in the encryption procedure. Luis et al. [3] present a secure architecture for building an off-site medical image archive. The proposal uses PACS (Picture Archiving and Communication System) and supports more than one Cloud providers. In this solution, two key components of a common PACS are deployed in the public Cloud system. The first module is DICOM object and the second module is a data storage system. The latter is composed mainly of repository and relational database (RDBMS). For this reason, it uses blobstore and database to save digital records. Technically, this framework relies on three components to maintain data privacy, namely Gateway, MasterIndex and Cloud Slaves. In this regard, MasterIndex is aimed at storing confidential patient information, such as user name and referring physician. This is meant to ensure anonymity. Meanwhile, it stores and manages key session encryption and provides access control mechanisms. The Cloud Gateway is designed to ensure interoperability between different public Cloud providers. This module consists of two main DICOM services, particularly storage (DICOM C-STORE) and query/retrieve (DICOM C-FIND and C-MOVE). For security purposes, the Cloud Gateway entity divides an image into chunks and encrypts them via AES (Advanced Encryption Standard) before storing them in the Cloud Slave. The Cloud Slave relies on local database to store metadata related to the patient. Additionally, it stores encrypted images in the blobstore.

Arkaa and Chellappana [4] develop a secure collaborative working platform over cloud computing. This cloud repository is meant to share medical imaging between healthcare professionals by using a mobile device. To this aim, the proposed architecture has four blocks, including the picture creation device, the image viewer, the web image database and the storage server. To meet security requirements, the proposal resort to a hybrid approach based on cryptographic techniques along with lossless compression algorithms. This mechanism is installed at the main Cloud storage server. More precisely, it uses compression and decompression algorithms to remove the statistical redundancy in order to achieve high compression ratio. Meanwhile, the secret image is encrypted using a secret key to maintain data confidentiality. In this framework, the user's email address is used to perform both authentication and access control.

Yang et al. [5] proposed a cloud solution to securely share medical data among healthcare organizations. To ensure privacy, the authors use a hybrid method based on cryptography and statistical analysis techniques. Technically, medical data are classified into many categories with various security levels. This is meant to guarantee multi-level privacy. To this objective, patient's identifying information is encrypted using the symmetric encryption for data anonymization. In contrast, the other medical data are saved in plaintext. Additionally, a medical record is vertically partitioned to enhance data protection. In doing so, legitimate clients are able to merge the partitioned data to recover the secret medical data. Consequently, this approach ensures integrity checking and unlinkability.

Pan et al. [6] designed a secure platform to promote data exchange between healthcare organizations. The proposal relies on cloud technologies to achieve this goal. To address security problems, the authors rely on the use case method to evaluate risks and security objectives for medical digital data. More precisely, this solution uses reversible watermarking techniques for integrity and authentication purpose. In addition, it guarantees the data confidentiality of medical records using Advanced Encryption Standard (AES). Simultaneously, the Organization Based Access Control (OrBAC) model is adopted for preventing unauthorized access to cloud resources and ensuring traceability of users' actions. Practically, this solution was implemented with java and SQLite.

Fabian et al. [7] introduced the Multi-Cloud environment to address security challenges and boost collaboration across healthcare organizations. In this regard, Ciphertext Policy Attribute Based Encryption (CP-ABE) is implemented to restrict access to the cloud services. This being the case, only authorized users can have access to specific medical records. For security reasons, a medical image is signed using DSA signature, which is based on the SHA1 function so as to protect the ownership of medical data. Besides, the Multi-Cloud Proxy (MCP) module divides an image into many portions by using Shamir's secret sharing scheme. Next, each part is stored at different Cloud providers. Hence, this approach has a dual purpose; it avoids unauthorized disclosure of sensitive data and also achieves unlinkability and anonymity. The proposed framework uses cryptographic hash functions to determine and locate a medical record in the Multi-Cloud system.

In Brindha and Jeyanthi [8], the researchers use visual cryptography technique to secure the cloud storage. This is achieved by dividing client's data into many parts. Hence, this technique guarantees both confidentiality and integrity and ensures a robust storage and retrieval of the user's files over cloud computing. Basically, it uses apache POI applications to convert a document file into text format. To enhance data security, it makes use of visual cryptography method to encrypt data. The authors compare this new approach with conventional techniques that are based on AES or DES. Accordingly, the proposal offers a significantly better performance compared to its predecessors.

In this respect, Kaur and Khemchandani [9] propose a secure solution for accessing clients' data. It consists in introducing a hybrid cryptosystem to protect digital images. The proposal uses visual cryptography techniques along with the RSA algorithm. The first one is designed to split the secret image into various pieces to ensure security. The second one encrypts the created sub-images to prevent the disclosure of confidential information.

Nelmiawati and Ibrahim [10] develop a framework to improve the quality and safety of Picture Archiving and Communication (PACS) systems. In this regard, the proposal uses Pixel-based dispersal scheme (PBDS) approach to meet security requirements. More precisely, it relies on Rabin's Information Dispersal Algorithm (IDA) along with Shamir's Secret Sharing Scheme (SSS) to protect patient's data. Besides, the authors suggest Salt factor to enhance the security of medical records. In this scheme, the IDA algorithm encrypts the pixels of original images. In parallel, the SSS technique facilitates the management of cryptographic keys in the proposed cryptosystem.

3 The Proposed Approach

The data security of digital medical images during its storage over Cloud Computing has become an important issue. This is due to the fact that Cloud technology still faces many security problems as outlined above. Moreover, personal health information is private, and hence, must be protected from unauthorized disclosure. Accordingly, a variety of cryptosystems are suggested to maintain data privacy. The majority of them use encryption approach to ensure data confidentiality. Nevertheless, these techniques are originally designed for encrypting textual data. Hence, they have been shown to be poorly suited to medical images. In fact, in traditional cryptosystems, each pixel or block of pixels of the original image is converted into a ciphered value. Because of this, previous approaches do not take into consideration some intrinsic features of digital records such as high pixel correlation and redundancy.

3.1 An Overview of the Proposed Solution

To address the challenges discussed above, we propose a novel approach based on segmentation to secure Cloud storage. Unlike the traditional approaches, the proposed technique does not encrypt the secret image. In this line of reasoning, a plain image is split into many regions based on similarity measures in order to achieve a high modification effect of a pixel value. In this study, we use K-means algorithm to carry out the region-based segmentation. That is, each pixel is affected to a specific region that satisfies a criterion of homogeneity and similarity. As a result, we create several scrambled regions from the original image. Meanwhile, each region is stored in a distinct Cloud to improve the security and privacy of digital records. For this reason, we use a Multi-Cloud environment to save medical images. At the same time, we use SSL (Secure Socket Layer) connection to transfer data securely between clients and cloud providers. Hence, healthcare organizations can safely rely on this protocol for transmitting medical images via the Internet in a secure manner. The schematic of the proposed method is shown in Fig. 1.

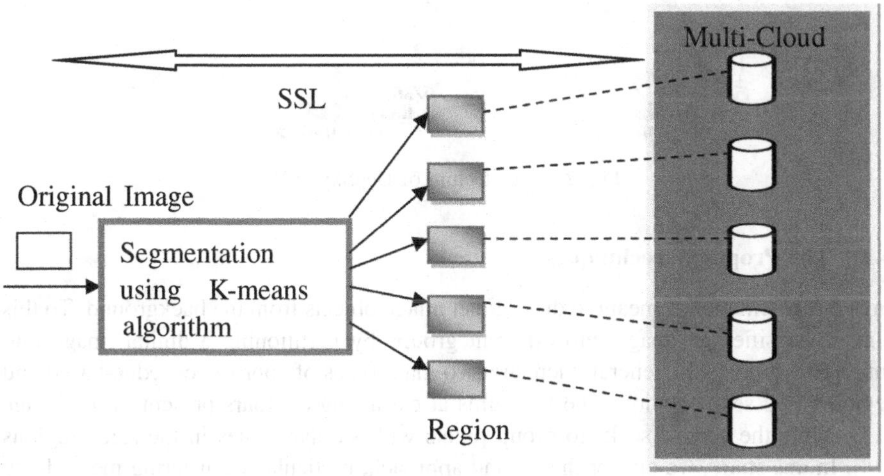

Fig. 1. Architecture of the image cryptosystem under study

According to this structure, a single Cloud provider is not able to reconstruct the original image from one region. In addition, most of existing cryptographic techniques require high computation time due to the large size of a medical image. In contrast, the proposed approach classifies the pixels of an image into different regions without need of a complex encryption and decryption procedure. Consequently, the proposal significantly improves response time. Thus, deploying our proposal in a Multi-Cloud environment seems to be of utmost importance to improve Quality-of-Service (QoS). The Multi-Cloud system is meant not only to enhance performance but also to reduce security challenges faced in a single Cloud. The Multi-Cloud architecture enables parallel and distributed computing across several Clouds. Currently, various Multi-Cloud solutions are available: Byzantine Fault tolerance, DepSky, Redundant Array of Cloud Storage (RACS), High Availability and Integrity Layer (HAIL) and InterCloud Storage (IC Store). In this respect, the DepSky model is the most popular and reliable scheme [11]. Typically, this infrastructure protects the confidentiality, integrity and availability of clients' data. For this task, this storage solution uses basically two protocols: DEPSKY-A, DEPSKY-CA. The former guarantees availability and integrity by duplicating data using quorum techniques. The latter maintains data confidentiality and availability by means of encryption algorithms and secret sharing scheme. That is, DepSky system uses four distinct Clouds in order to provide virtual resources to the consumers, as depicted in Fig. 2.

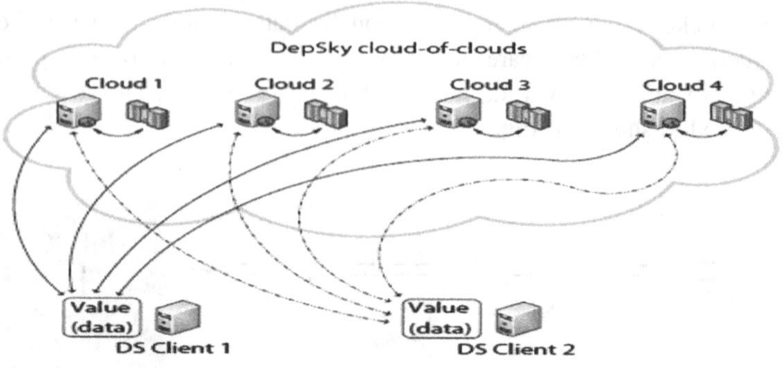

Fig. 2. Architecture of DepSky [12]

3.2 The Proposed Techniques

Image segmentation is meant to distinguish image objects from the background. To this aim, it classifies an image into different groups by partitioning a digital image into multiple segments. In general, there are two main types of approaches: edge-based and region-based segmentation. The first aims at extracting contours present in the image [13], while the second seeks to group pixels with similar values in the same regions [14]. In this study, we opt for the second approach, particularly clustering methods, to generate many regions. Recently, various techniques have been suggested for grouping of similar objects, including K-means clustering, Fuzzy C-means clustering, subtractive clustering method, etc. In this regard, we propose the most widely used method in clustering approaches, i.e. K–means algorithm. The latter is basically simple and computationally faster than other clustering methods [15]. In this scheme, the number of clusters K is assumed to be set in advance. Following this, the remaining data is allocated to the nearest clusters. This process is repeated until the error function reaches a finite steady-state. More formally, let a data set $X = \{x_1, x_2,\ldots, x_N\} \in \mathbb{R}^D$, this algorithm seeks to divide X into clusters $S = \{S_1, S_2,\ldots, S_K\}$, where $S_i \cap S_j = \phi$ for $1 \le i = j \le K$. This is achieved by minimizing the Sum of Squared Error (SSE), as in (1)

$$SSE = \sum_{k=1}^{K} \sum_{x_i \in S_k} \|x_i - c_k\| \tag{1}$$

where $\|.\|$ is the Euclidean norm and c_k is the center of cluster S_k calculated as the mean of the points that belong to this cluster. In this regard, the algorithm 1 presents the pseudocode of the conventional K-means clustering algorithm [16], where m[*i*] denotes the membership of point x_i.

Algorithm 1: K-means

Input: $X = \{x_1, x_2, \ldots, x_N\} \in \mathbb{R}^D$ (N×D input data set)
Output: $C=\{c_1, c_2, \ldots, c_k\} \in \mathbb{R}^D$ (K cluster centers)
we randomly choose a subset C of X as the initial set of cluster centers
While termination criterion is not satisfied do
  For (for (i = 1; i ≤N; i = i +1) do
    Each element xi is assigned to the nearest cluster;
      $m[i] = \underset{k \in \{1,2,\ldots,K\}}{\operatorname{argmin}} \| x_i - c_k \|^2$
  End
  Compute the cluster centers;
  For (k = 1; k ≤K; k = k + 1) do
    Cluster S_k contains the set of points x_i, which are basically nearest to the center c_k;
    $S_k = \{x_i \mid m[i] = k\}$;
    Determine the new center c_k as the mean of the points that belong to S_k;
    $c_k = \frac{1}{|S_k|} \sum_{x_i \in S_i}$
  End
End
Return $< c_1, c_2, \ldots, c_k >$

Practically speaking, clustering algorithms are designed principally to extract the area of interest from the background. In order to do so, numerous steps are required. First, a partial stretching enhancement is performed on the image under study to improve quality. Next, the subtractive clustering technique is done to create the centroids. To this end, we rely on the density of surrounding data points. The process of multi-region segmentation relies on these centers, which are considered to be the keystone of the K-means algorithm. In fact, each pixel connected with a specific region using K-means algorithm. Finally, a median filter is used to delete any unwanted regions from the final image to enhance the quality of the suggested method.

4 Implementation Results

First, we present, in this section, background information regarding algorithms used to meet privacy-preserving requirements. This is meant to ensure the data security of medical image during storage. Second, we apply the proposed method on medical images to demonstrate the correctness of this approach. On that account, we implement K-means algorithm using MATLAB to illustrate our suggested solution. In such a model, a medical image is divided into four distinct regions. That is, each region is stored in a separate Cloud to protect patients' medical information against untrusted Cloud providers and unauthorized access. To achieve this goal, the proposed technique consists of five main stages, as explained in the Algorithm 2 below [17, 18]:

Algorithm 2: Generating regions

Input: Host Image I ($x \times y$), Number of region k
Output: Secret Shares $< R_1, R_2, \ldots, R_k >$

Do until no object move group

Step 1: Determine the coordinate centroid (Random assignment).

Step 2: Determine the Euclidean distance d of each Object pixel to the centroids.

$$d = \|p(x, y) - c_k\| \quad //c_k \text{ the cluster centers}$$

Step 3: We group the object based on the minimum distance with the centroid.

$$c_k = \frac{1}{k} \sum_{y \epsilon c_k} \sum_{x \epsilon c_k} p(x,$$

Step 4: For each region $Reg_i \sqsubset I$, an image *Ri* is created by the bijective function Fpos

/*Fpos is the function that link each pixel of a region in the image I with image consisting Ri.

$$\text{Fpos}: \begin{array}{c} Regi \rightarrow Ri \\ (x, y) \rightarrow (z, t) \end{array}$$

Where (x, y) is the position pixel of the region Reg_i in the original image I, and (z, t) is the position pixel in the image Ri.

End do

Step 5: Reshape the cluster pixel into image

Return $< R_1, R_2, \ldots, R_k >$

Similarly, we reconstruct the secret image by using generated regions. To this end, we follow the steps listed in the Algorithm 3 below:

Algorithm 3: Reconstruction of original image

Input: Secret Shares $< R_1, R_2, \ldots, R_k >$
Outputs: processed image M ($n \times m$)

Step 1: receive processed *Ri*

Step 2:Find the reciprocal function of $Fpos^{-1}$

$$\text{Fpos}^{-1}: \begin{array}{c} Regi \rightarrow Ri \\ (z, t) \rightarrow (x, y) \end{array}$$

Where (z, t) is the position pixel of *Ri*, and (z, t) is the position pixel in the outputs image M.

Step 3: Apply $Fpos^{-1}$ for each Ri processed

Return < M>

We have conducted, in this study, some experiments to check the encryption quality of our proposed approach. In this context, we have undertaken our tests using color medical images. In the encryption process, we split the secret image into four regions to get an intermediate image called the segmented image. Next, we apply median filter to enhance image quality. Then, we extract each region to create the final image. To recover the original image, we use the four generated shares. The implementation result is illustrated in Figs. 3 and 4.

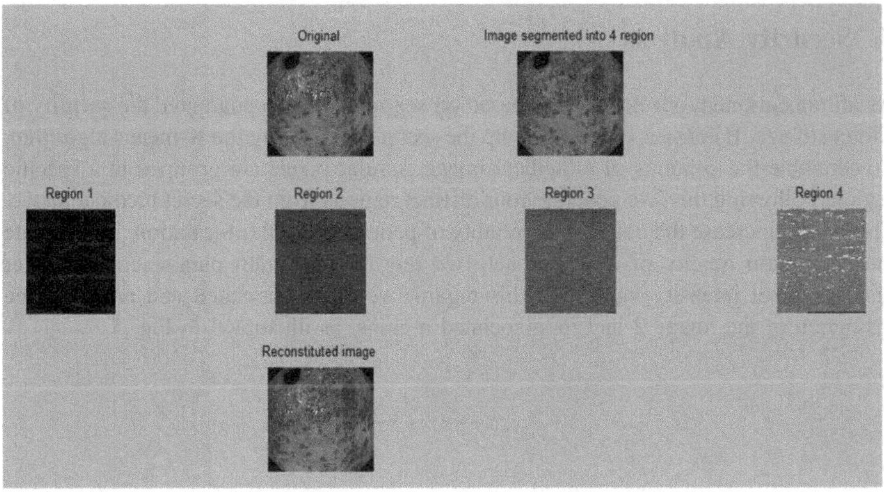

Fig. 3. The experimental results for image 1

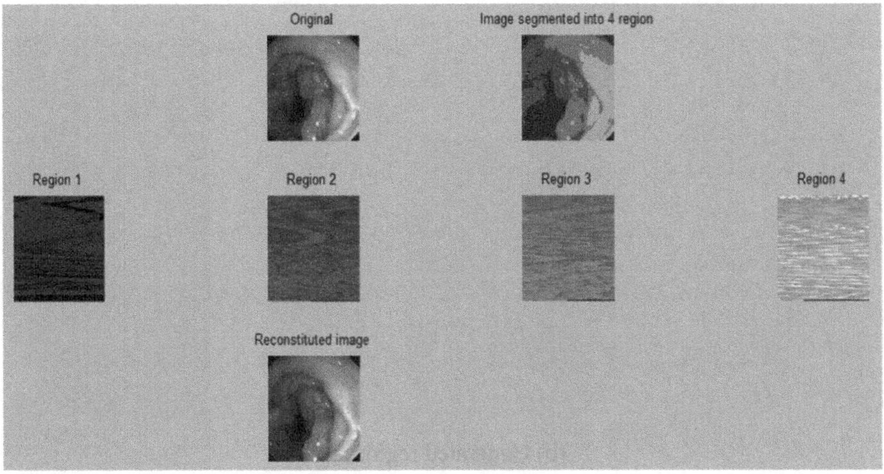

Fig. 4. The experimental results for image 2

Based on the implementation results, it is obvious that our proposed approach hides visual information in the encrypted image. Hence, using segmentation approach avoids disclosure of private medical information. To enhance data confidentiality, we suggest DepSky as a storage system. It is composed of four different Clouds. That is, each generated region is stored in a distinct Cloud. Consequently, any Cloud provider is able to reconstruct the secret image using a single share.

5 Security Analysis

As aforementioned, our proposal is based on segmentation to guarantee the security of Cloud storage. It consists of breaking up the secret image using the K-means algorithm. To scramble the contents of a medical image, similar pixels are grouped in a specific region. Following this, we generate four distinct regions from the secret medical image. This would increase the data confidentiality of patient medical information. To evaluate the encryption quality of our approach, we rely on histogram parameter. The latter displays pixel intensity values. In this regard, we have calculated and analyzed the histogram of the image 2 and its associated regions, as illustrated in Fig. 5.

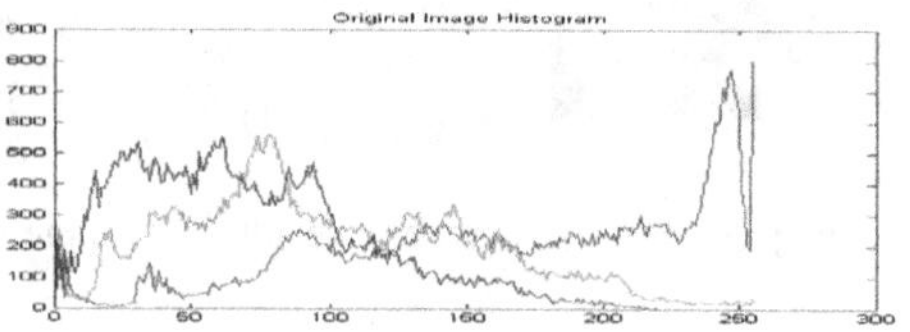

(a) Original image

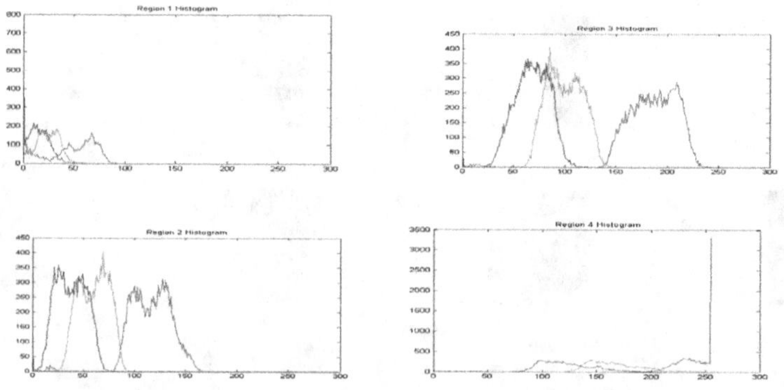

(b) Generated regions

Fig. 5. Histogram of different images. (a) Original image. (b) Generated regions

According to the graphs, we observe that the histogram of generated regions is totally different from the histogram of the original image. So, the proposed approach guarantees that a Cloud provider cannot get any information from a single share. Consequently, segmentation approach is an appropriate solution to secure Cloud-based medical image storage.

6 Conclusion

Cloud storage is an emerging concept to safeguard medical images. In such a model, clients are billed for space utilization. Besides, Cloud providers ensure the maintenance and availability of provided services. These advantages are the main reasons for the growth in demand for Cloud Computing. In this context, healthcare organizations are also starting to use Cloud storage for saving patients' digital records. Despite its great benefits, this model faces security challenges. To this objective, several cryptographic techniques are suggested: RSA, AES, homomorphic encryption, etc. Nevertheless, these techniques are time-consuming and do not take into account the image structure and its features. Having this concern in mind, we propose a novel approach to secure Cloud-based medical images storage. Our solution is based on segmentation techniques, particularly K-means. The basic idea behind this method is to split an image into different regions based on the similarity in pixel base. The implementation results show that this technique guarantees data confidentiality. To enhance privacy, each region is stored in a distinct Cloud. That is why we use a Multi-Cloud environment to improve data security. In this regard, DepSky system is used as a storage system. In sum, we suggested, in this article, a novel approach to meet privacy requirements in Cloud storage. In future work, we intend to study the quality of reconstructed images using different parameters, particularly PSNR and MSE. In fact, a medical image should be intact during encryption and decryption process. Besides, we will compare our solution with other existing techniques in terms of performance and security.

References

1. Ali, M., Khan, S.U., Vasilakos, A.V.: Security in Cloud Computing: opportunities and challenges. Inf. Sci. **305**, 357–383 (2015). Elsevier
2. Marwan, M., Kartit, A., Ouahmane, H.: Cloud-based medical image issues. Int. J. Appl. Eng. Res. **11**, 3713–3719 (2016)
3. Luis, A., Bastiao, S., Carlos, C., Oliveira, J.L.: A PACS archive architecture supported on Cloud services. Int. J. CARS **7**(3), 349–358 (2012). Springer
4. Arkaa, I.H., Chellappana, K.: Collaborative compressed I-Cloud medical image storage with decompress viewer. In: Proceedings of the International Conference on Robot PRIDE, Procedia Computer Science, Elsevier, pp. 114–121 (2014)
5. Yang, C.T., Chen, L.T., Chou, W.L., Wang, K.C., Implementation of a medical image file accessing system on Cloud computing. In: Proceedings of the International Conference in Computational Science and Engineering (CSE), IEEE, pp. 321–326 (2010)
6. Pan, W., Coatrieux, G., Bouslimi, D., Prigent, N.: Secure public Cloud platform for medical images sharing. Stud. Health Technol. Inf. **210**, 251–255 (2015)

7. Fabian, B., Ermakova, T., Junghanns, P.: Collaborative and secure sharing of healthcare data in multi-Clouds. Inf. Syst. **48**, 132–150 (2015). Elsevier
8. Brindha, K., Jeyanthi, N.: Secured document sharing using visual cryptography in Cloud data storage. Cybern. Inf. Technol. **15**(4), 111–123 (2015)
9. Kaur, K., Khemchandani, V.: Securing visual cryptographic shares using public key encryption. In: Proceedings of the International Conference on Advance Computing Conference, IACC, pp. 1108–1113 (2013)
10. Nelmiawati, N., Salleh, M., Ibrahim, S.: Medical image dispersal using enhanced secret sharing threshold scheme. In: Proceedings of the International Conference on Health Informatics and Medical Systems, HIMS 2015, pp. 132–138 (2015)
11. Marwan, M, Kartit, A. Ouahmane, H.: A Secure framework for medical image storage based on multi-Cloud. In: Proceedings of the International Conference on Cloud Computing Technologies and Applications, CloudTech 2016 (2016)
12. Bessani, A., Correia, M., Quaresma, B., Andre, F., Sousa, P.: DEPSKY: dependable and secure storage in a Cloud-of-Clouds. ACM Trans. Storage **9**(4), 12–33 (2013)
13. Jamil, N., Soh, H.C., Tengku Sembok, T.M., Bakar, Z.A.: A modified edge-based region growing segmentation of geometric objects. In: Badioze Zaman, H., Robinson, P., Petrou, M., Olivier, P., Shih, Timothy K., Velastin, S., Nyström, I. (eds.) IVIC 2011. LNCS, vol. 7066, pp. 99–112. Springer, Heidelberg (2011). doi:10.1007/978-3-642-25191-7_11
14. Haralick, R.M., Shapiro, L.G.: Image segmentation techniques. Compu. Vis. Graph. Image Process. **29**, 100–132 (1985)
15. Dhanachandra, N., Manglem, Kh., Jina Chanu, Y.: Image segmentation using K-means clustering algorithm and subtractive clustering algorithm. Procedia Comput. Sci. **54**, 764–771 (2015). Elsevier
16. Gan, G., Ma, C., Wu, J.: Data Clustering: Theory, Algorithms, and Applications. SIAM, Philadelphia (2007)
17. Abdul-Nasir, A.S., Mashor, M.Y, Mohamed, Z.: Colour image segmentation approach for detection of malaria parasiter using various colour models and K-means clustering. WSEAS Trans. Biol. Biomed., vol. 10, pp. 41–55 (2013)
18. Gulhane, A., Paikrao, P., Chaudhari, D.S.: A review of image data clustering techniques. Int. J. Soft Comput. Eng. **2**(1), 212–215 (2012)

Ubiquitous Internet of Things: Emerging Technologies and Breakthroughs

Toward Reliable Maritime Communication for a Safe Operation of Autonomous Ship

Abdelmoula Ait Allal(✉), Khalifa Mansouri, Mohamed Youssfi, and Mohammed Qbadou

Laboratory: Signals, Distributed Systems and Artificial Intelligence (SSDIA), ENSET Mohammedia, University Hassan II Casablanca, Casablanca, Morocco
aitallal.abdelmoula67@gmail.com, khmansouri@hotmail.com, med@youssfi.net, qbmedn7@gmail.com

Abstract. Among the main challenges for a safe operation of autonomous ship (AS) is to ensure a reliable ship to ship and ship to shore communication services in order to receive and transmit data and also to control remotely the ship in case of "Fail to safe". The approach presented in this paper aims to show how the existing communication systems on board of conventional ship and the nowadays available technologies can be embodied to ensure a reliable and uninterruptable connectivity of the autonomous ships. So, this paper presents a model of communication for each scenario of navigation considering the availability, reliability, security and cost effectiveness of the communication service carrier.

Keywords: Maritime communication · Inmarsat · Iridium · WiMAX

1 Introduction

There is a growing need for maritime industry connectivity to ensure its sustainability through the transfer of real time information, improvement of operation efficiency, on board security and surveillance and employee/passenger infotainment. The emerging technologies such as maritime mobile satellite communication and mobile communication systems are envisaged to facilitate a myriad of attractive applications for the safe operation of conventional ship and autonomous ship such remote control and real time monitoring [1]. A large capacity data such as HD videos, telemetry, collected from bridge, engine room (ER) and other critical regions of a ship can be efficiently exchanged via such a system, which is crucial to the shore control center (SCC), between ships in proximity and maritime administrative authority on shore [2] and the use of electronic chart display and information system (ECDIS) as navigation support. Moreover, the internet connection becomes vital in our daily life. The communication from ship to ship or ship to shore is ensured either with line of sight (LOS) type communication (e.g. AIS; Digital VHF (DSC); 3G/4G; WIFI; WiMAX) or maritime mobile satellite communication (e.g. Inmarsat; VSAT; Iridium). The sea areas and maritime communication requirements are defined in the international convention for the safety of life at sea [3].

E. Sabir et al. (Eds.): UNet 2017, LNCS 10542, pp. 261–274, 2017.
https://doi.org/10.1007/978-3-319-68179-5_23

The paper is organized as follow: in Sect. 2 we present the sea areas as defined by SOLAS and then we expose the possible scenarios of navigation. Then we expose the maritime mobile satellite communication, we limit our studies to Inmarsat, VSAT and Iridium communication systems. Thus, we develop the line of sight communication (LOS) and we propose AIS, digital VHF, 3G/4G, WiFi, WiMAX. As the communication for an autonomous ship is of high priority to keep it continuously either under autonomous or remote control to avoid maritime accident, the challenge is to ensure a secure, reliable and uninterruptible communication system. In Sect. 4 we propose a model of communication which meets this requirement for different scenarios of navigation. We found an optimum way to combine the relevant communication carriers reliably and cost effectively with an optimal security against hostile attacks and finally we present an example of application of our communication model in Sect. 5 before concluding.

2 Background

2.1 Sea Areas

In SOLAS, Sect. 4, the international maritime organization (IMO) has developed the communication requirements that a ship must comply with to ensure a safe navigation. The navigation sea areas were defined as A1, A2, A3 and A4. In Table 1, were defined the communication scenarios in respect of the sea areas, where the ship might operate, i.e. In port/shore, coastal, high sea, arctic and ship to ship.

Table 1. Sea area definition and navigation classes [3]

SOLAS sea areas	SOLAS definition	Classes	
A1	Means an area within the radiotelephone coverage of at least one VHF coast station in which continuous DSC alerting is available, as may be defined by a Contracting Government	In port/shore	Ship to Ship
A2	Means an area, excluding sea area A1, within the radiotelephone coverage of at least one MF coast station in which continuous DSC alerting is available, as may be defined by a Contracting Government	Coastal	
A3	Means an area, excluding sea areas A1 and A2, within the coverage of an Inmarsat geostationary satellite in which continuous alerting is available	High sea	
A4	Means an area outside sea areas A1, A2 and A3	Arctic	

2.2 Maritime Mobile Satellite Communication

The maritime mobile satellite communication (MMSC) system came after the conventional maritime radio communications system, which was successful for almost a century on the commercial and supporting distress scene at sea. The biggest mobile satellite service (MSS) operator for MMSC is Inmarsat, while others providers of MMSC are either global or regional or local geostationary earth orbit (GEO) or non-GEO systems such as Iridium, global star, Optus, Emsat, Thuraya, MSAT, AMSC, N-Star, Orbcomm, Leo One and others who have introduced their own MMSS [4].

The expected growing in global maritime satellite communication market is from USD 2.01 Billion in 2015 to USD 3.10 Billion by 2020 [5], at a CAGR of 9.0%. At the beginning of the decades, the communication industry estimates that approximately 112,500 ships with satellite services (68,000 merchant ships, 23,000 fishing vessels, 6,500passenger ships, 6,000 large yachts, 9,000 government vessels), and also there were 8,500 oil and gas platforms [5]. Furthermore, the market leading players are launching less expensive technology to seduce the end-users which had the potential to use satellite communication earlier. In this section, we develop Inmarsat, VSAT and Iridium satellite communication service and we will see how far can be relevant for each navigation scenario. The Fig. 1 shows the growing in network capacity from 2011 to 2016 and reflects the high demand in satellite communication service in maritime industry. The advanced satellite fleet broadband (FBB) enables to establish wideband transmission with data rate, up to 432 kbps. Nonetheless, the high capital expenditure to launch satellites results in high service cost by satellite system (e.g., voice service costs 13.75 U. S. dollars per minute). Consequently, the cost of conveying large capacity videos could be prohibitive. It is an imperious demand to develop a novel and cost-effective wide-band maritime communication network by innovative communication technologies [6].

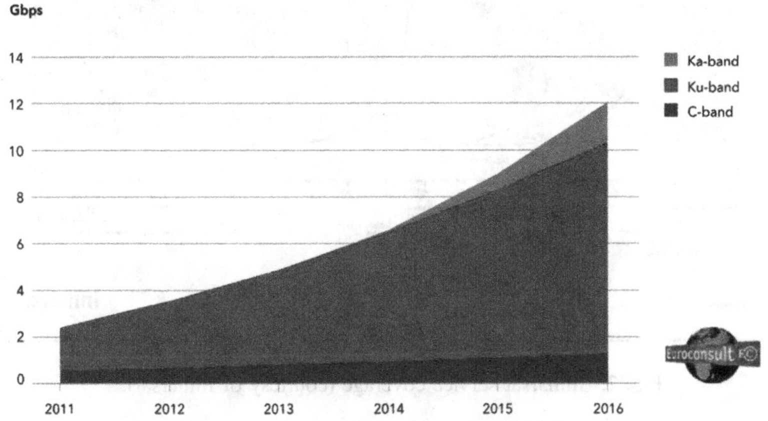

Fig. 1. Network capacity - Euroconsult [7]

2.2.1 Inmarsat

The Inmarsat system evolved from an entrepreneurial start by COMSAT in the late 1970s to an international maritime satellite service (MSS) private company called Inmarsat, joint venture of governments and telecommunication operators [8]. Inmarsat C uses a unidirectional antenna on the ship. It provides two-way packet data service, approved for use under the global maritime distress and safety system (GMDSS) and it meets the requirements for ship security alert systems (SSAS) as well as for long range identification and tracking (LRIT). Inmarsat is a store and forward system that cannot be used for voice or direct internet connections. It operates on L-band and assure a global coverage with the exception of the arctic. Since the GMDSS was introduced in the early 1990s, Inmarsat has kept its monopoly over marine satellite distress and safety communications. Through a combination of both GX (Ka-band) and fleet broadband service, Inmarsat offers worldwide coverage at high performant service with a downlink up to 50 Mbps and an uplink to 5 Mbps. Inmarsat GX will enable a continue, real-time operations between ships and shore offices, in addition to enhanced communications and crew infotainment [9]. The Fig. 2 shows the Inmarsat global and spot beam coverage.

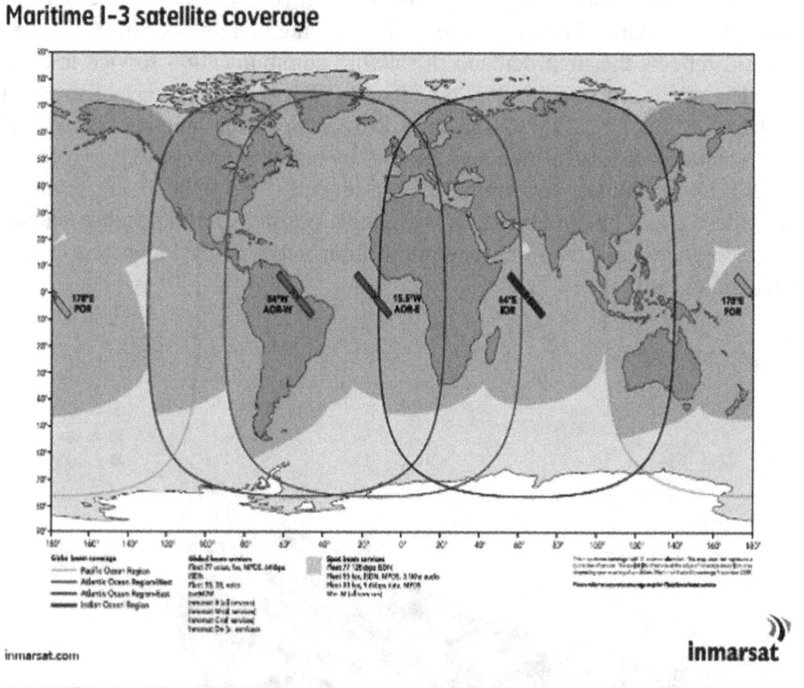

Fig. 2. Inmarsat service coverage (courtesy of Inmarsat).

Regarding the security issue, the Inmarsat communication seems easy to intercept, fake or jam, allowing hostiles parties disturb the communication with relatively simple means.

2.2.2 Iridium

The low earth orbit (LEO) at 700–1500 km in altitude approach, adopted by Motorola, locates the satellites in closest proximity to earth, with an orbit period of about 90 min.

This provides a time delay of less than 10 ms due to propagation but increases the number of satellites needed for continuous service. Importantly, Iridium represents the first system to offer ubiquitous service from space to handheld phones. The Iridium system is based on 66 satellites that are grouped in 6 orbital planes (60° apart), each containing 11 active satellites and one spare satellite. The orbits are circular at the height of 783 km at an inclination angle of 86 [10, 11]. As illustrated in Fig. 3, The benefit of this architecture is that it assures 100% coverage of the globe, including the poles [8].

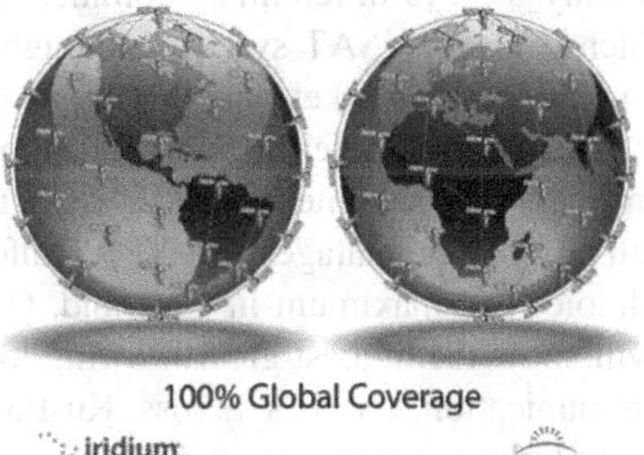

Fig. 3. Iridium service coverage. (Courtesy of Iridium)

Iridium Communications Inc. is a publicly traded company headquartered in USA. Iridium's mobile voice and data communications solutions, for a wide variety of industries (Fig. 4), are supported by a global communications network, including also the Polar Regions. An excellent advantage over other satellite service that have limited service regions. Iridium Open Port offers voice and digital communication services at a rate up to 128 kbps at L-band frequencies and permits users to communicate anywhere in the world, without passing through ground facilities. The use of these systems will be based on a cost/benefit trade-off.

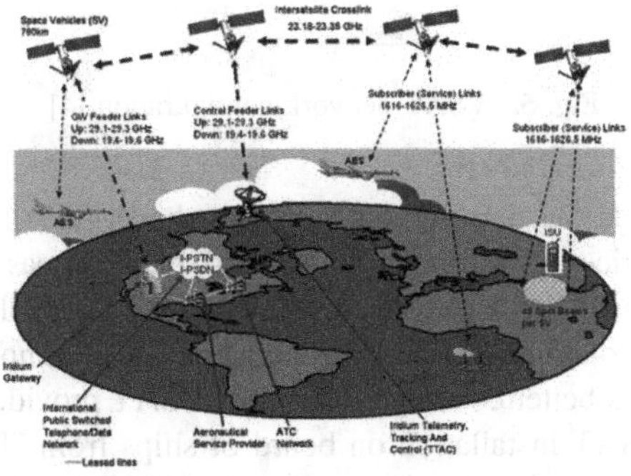

Fig. 4. Iridium satellite network [14]

Due to the complexity of the system, i.e. complex signaling mechanism, encryption and ground station authentication [12], the iridium system turns out to be difficult to manipulate and risk for hostile attacks is minim [13].

2.2.3 VSAT

Very small aperture terminal (VSAT) – is a term commonly describing a satellite system operating in the C-band or Ku-band with a shipboard antenna size with a diameter of 0.6 to 2 m. Systems operating in the Ka-band is also available, but currently not for bidirectional maritime traffic. Thus, VSAT is not a satellite system in itself, but is a term commonly used to differentiate commercial satellite services providers from Inmarsat (which is also a VSAT system, although on L-band). Currently, VSAT technology is dominating the market and this trend is expected to continue during the forecast period. The maritime satellite communication market has reflected a rapid technology shift from mobile satellite service (MSS) to VSAT. This shift is attributed to the bandwidth and cost advantages that VSAT offers to marine users. The penetration of VSAT technology is maximum in Ka-Band. On the other hand, penetration across Ku-Band will show the highest growth owing to increasing deployment of maritime satellite communication services across Ku-Band during the forecast period. the inbound satellite links are typically at 56 Kbps and the outbound link is typically at 256 Kbps (Fig. 5). The outbound carrier is different from the inbound link in two fundamental ways: it is at higher rate, allowing for multiple VSATs to receive a common outbound channel, and the outbound carrier uses continuous modulation enabling the VSAT terminals to use a low-cost demodulator [10].

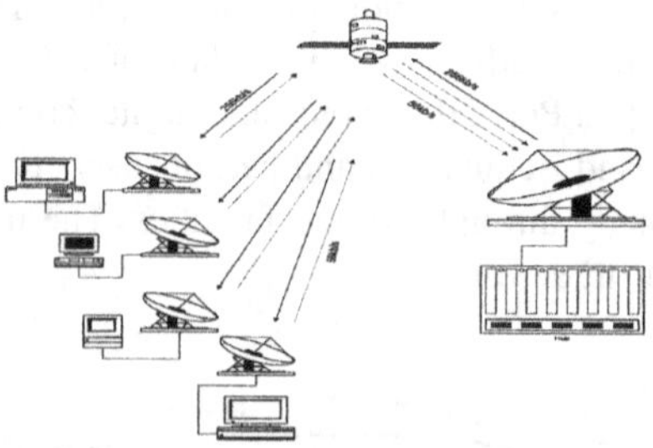

Fig. 5. VSAT network configuration [4]

Another drawback is that few service providers have global coverage. Good coverage at reasonable prices is normally only available in areas with relatively high density of users. However, VSAT seems to be a fast-growing solution for commercial messaging and crew infotainment. Bandwidth cost of VSAT is normally lower than for Inmarsat. Inmarsat has a better coverage than most VSAT providers. The Fig. 6 shows the fast growing of VSAT installation on board of ships from 2008 to 2016.

Regarding protection against hostile attacks, the VSAT has the same security issue as for Inmarsat [13].

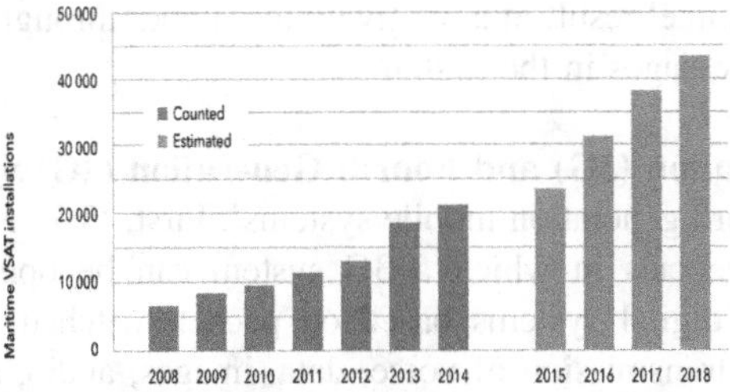

Fig. 6. VSAT fast growing of VSAT installation on board of ships from 2008 to 2016 [15]

2.3 Line of Sight Communication Systems

The line of sight communication system (LOS) is necessary for ship to ship, ship to shore, during port approach, and in port communication. It may give a high bandwidth at low cost with much lower latency than satellite systems. The LOS may use digital VHF, MF/HF, AIS, 3G/4G, WiFi, and WiMAX as communication carriers.

2.3.1 AIS – Automatic Identification System

The international maritime organization (IMO) have adopted regulations requiring all SOLAS crafts to be fitted with a universal automatic identification system transponder by 2008 at the latest. This device is known as the automatic identification system (AIS). The AIS system uses a TDMA (time Division Multiple Access) scheme to allow up to several thousand ships to exchange important information on position, heading, speed, identity etc. This information can then be integrated with electronic charts and radar plotting systems to give a very good overview of the traffic situation. Each message on the AIS's network can have up to about 160 bits of payload. This is transmitted in a 256 bit long packet at 9600 bits per second. 23 different message types are defined and some of these allow the ship or shore station to send more or less arbitrary data, e.g., as "safety messages". However, the capacity is very limited, particularly when bandwidth has to be shared with several ships. The range of the AIS transmission is as for normal VHF, 25 to 40 nautical miles.

Currently, only AIS can be called real time digital exchange of information. There are few AIS stations in the arctic and cannot be considered as available communication structures in that area [16]. As is implemented currently, the AIS is easily exposed to all types of hostile attacks, and due to its omnidirectional antenna, there is possibility to be jammed [13].

2.3.2 Digital VHF (Very High Frequency)

Telenor in Norway has recently started the deployment of digital VHF service in Norway. This is the continuation of a pilot project that has been running for some years. The specification for the transmissions is already being discussed in ITU and it is assumed that frequencies and transmission principle will be a new ITU specification in a reasonably short time. The system is using direct digital encoding of data on the radio signal and requires special receivers. The digital VHF is open to hostile attacks at the same level as AIS. The shared bandwidth, limited number of channels and low bandwidth in each channel result in a relatively low upper throughput on total number on total number of messages in the system.

2.3.3 Third Generation (3G) and Fourth Generation (4G) Systems

'3G' is a short for 'third generation mobile systems'. First, '3G' as in its spectrum: the particular radio frequencies in which a 3G system can be operated [17]. The 3G wireless systems are digital systems based on packet-switched network technology intended for wireless transmission of voice, data, images, audio, and video [18]. The benefits of 3G to consumers focus primarily on two dimensions: convenience and cost. 3G systems are being designed to get the most efficient use of the spectrum, and the tight competition created in the 3G services providers' field will most likely result in lower costs and prices. The bandwidth used is up to 2–4 Mbps.

The influence of the Internet will have a significant bearing on 4G capabilities, as operators move towards an all IP environment. While 3G can rightly claim to have brought forward the convergence of mobile and Internet technologies, 4G will herald the convergence of fixed, broadcast and mobile technologies. As technology continues to develop and evolve, the ability to deliver faster, broadband services at a premium QoS will be implicit requirements of next-generation technologies [11].

GSM: Mobile telephone is a good alternative for ships that trade close to the coast and with a limited number of ports to call in. Otherwise, the roaming costs associated with GSM and particularly high prices for digital transfers are serious obstacles. Coverage may also be a problem in some coastal areas and can be a problem for the implementation of our communication model. It is difficult to eavesdrop or insert message in the GSM networks. But still there is a risk of hostile attacks of the infrastructure [13].

2.3.4 WiFi Communication System

Wi-Fi, which stands for "wireless fidelity," is a radio technology that networks computers so they connect to each other and to the Internet without wires. The Wi-Fi Alliance is the global Wi-Fi organization that created the Wi-Fi brand. Users can share documents and projects, as well as an internet connection, among various computer stations and easily connect to a broadband internet connection while traveling. By using a WiFi network, individuals can network desktop computers, laptops, and PDAs and share networked peripherals such as servers and printers. A Wi-Fi network operates just like a wired network, but without the restrictions imposed by wires. Wi-Fi networks operate in the unlicensed 2.4-GHz range of the wireless spectrum, and 5-GHz radio bands with an 11-Mbps (802.11b) or 54-Mbps (802.11a) data rate, or with products that contain both bands (dual band). It has been developed as a WLAN technology; as such, the reach of its wireless signals extends outward to a range of 40 to 100 m. Data rate is a function of distance for all wireless and wireline technologies: the shorter the distance, the higher the data rate; the longer the distance, the lower the data rate [18].

2.3.5 WiMax – IEEE 802.16 Communication System

Worldwide interoperability for microwave access (WiMAX) spectrum owners alliance (WiSOA) is the first global organization composed exclusively of owners of WiMAX spectrum. WiSOA is focused on the regulation, commercialization, and deployment of WiMAX spectrum in the 2.3 to 2.5-GHz and the 3.4 to 3.5-GHz ranges. WiSOA is dedicated to educating and informing its members, industry representatives, and government regulators of the importance of WiMAX spectrum, its use, and the potential for WiMAX to revolutionize broadband [18].

Another way forward for 4G is encapsulated in the WiMAX. It supports LOS at a range of at least 50 km non line-of-sight (NLOS) typically up to 6–10 km for fixed customer premises equipment (CPE), which makes it suitable for metropolitan area networks (MANs). The data rates for the fixed standard will support up to 75 Mbps per subscriber, peak, in 20 MHz of spectrum, but typical data rates will be more like 20–30 Mbps. The mobile applications will likely support 30 Mbps per subscriber, peak, in 10 MHz of spectrum, with 3–5 Mbps, typical. The base station will support up to 280 Mbps to meet the needs of many simultaneous users [WiMax]. 802.16e certainly appears to offer an attractive prospect for areas currently either not covered at all, or poorly covered, by other types of network. However, this speed reflects the optimum channel size, power and best-case modulation, and takes no account of the network overheads [19]. Given that WiMAX is a point-to-multipoint network, the result of sharing the available spectrum among all those logged on at any one time means that a realistic downstream speed in mid-2010 was 3–5 Mbps combined with 1 Mbps upstream. WiMAX is merging as a promising broadband wireless access (BWA) technology to provide high speed, high bandwidth efficiency and high capacity multimedia service [10].

WiMax has been deployed in several places, e.g., on the coast of Norway and in the port of Singapore. However, deployments are currently for non-mobile services as roaming is not supported. WiMax currently operates on licensed frequencies which mostly have been bought by private operators. There are plans to deploy WiMax also in new frequencies of which some may be license exempt [WiMax]. WiMax is perhaps the most obvious choice for a shore based e-Navigation system. However, frequencies and areas are owned by different operators in different countries and it may be a challenge to standardize the services provided as different agreements are needed with the different operators. This can easily become a similar problem to the one that currently exists with GSM. Also, it may be difficult to provide public services on the frequencies already controlled by different private operators. WiFi is currently being supplemented with WiMax, typically with much longer range and capacity and which may be more suitable for ship use [16].

Due to its fairly advanced protocol with high security levels [13], we can assume that the communication via WiMAX is secure against the hostile attacks however, common use of internet as backhaul exposes the system to hostile attacks WiFi/WiMax: wireless internet networks are available in some ports. Drawbacks are very localized and limited availability. WiFi is currently being supplemented with WiMax, typically with much longer range and capacity and which may be more suitable for ship use. WiMax frequencies are, however, mainly owned by private companies which may make it difficult to apply in e-Navigation [16]. WiMAX will support line-of-sight (LOS) at a range up to 50 km and non line-of-sight (NLOS) typically up to 6–10 km for fixed customer premises equipment (CPE). The data rates for the fixed standard will support up to 75 Mbps per subscriber, peak, in 20 MHz of spectrum, but typical data rates will be more like 20–30 Mbps. The mobile applications will likely support 30 Mbps per subscriber, peak, in 10 MHz of spectrum, with 3–5 Mbps, typical. The base station will support up to 280 Mbps to meet the needs of many simultaneous users [WiMax].

2.3.6 UHF (Ultra High Frequency) Communication

UHF has been used for voice and data radio communications since the middle of last century. Frequency range 0.3 to 3 GHz (marine 457 to 467 MHz). The maritime communication and land communication use the same UHF channels; thus, it may be source of problem when the ship is close to shore. The benefit resides in that the frequencies are allocated and that can be used as far as it complies with the ITU requirements regarding cross talk and power.

2.3.7 MF/HF (Medium Frequency/High Frequency) Marine Radio Telephone

It produces and receives digital selective calls for quick and efficient establishment of distress, urgency, safety and routine communications with others ships and coast stations that install any MF/HF facilities. The HF may be used within a distance less than 3000 km during day and worldwide communication during night. The MF may be used within the area A1.

3 Relevant Communication Systems for Reliable Autonomous Ship Connectivity

The communication system to be used is depending on the area of navigation, data type to be exchanged, availability of communication carriers, capacity, and cost effectiveness. Based on the available communication carriers in the ship trading environment, a suitable model of communication in term of reliability, capacity, and cost was suggested. The Table 2 presents the characteristics of the communication carriers in term of bandwidth and range.

3.1 Port Approach and in Port Communication

When and autonomous ship approach the port a special team embarks on board to control and facilitate the port entry and berthing (rendezvous operation). In that scenario the ship needs to exchange information and data with the port authority, with shore control center, with vessel traffic services (VTS), with owner, pilot, with other ships and with port state control (PSC). As she is normally within the coverage of one or more land based short range wireless network, solutions with a high capacity (e.g. 3G/4G, WiFi, WiMAX) may be used to enhance the communication reliability. The WiFi has limited range (40–100 m) with a capacity up to 50 Mbps can be a good candidate for a communication within the port. The relatively low cost, high capacity, high quality of service (QoS) of shore based services make possible the real time exchange of information such as voice, HD video (3 Mbps), telemetry (32 Kbps), remote control (2 Kbps). With relatively sparse ship traffic will probably not be able to

Table 2. Communication carrier's characteristics

Communication service	Bandwidth	Range
Inmarsat	Voice: 2.4 Kbps Data: up to 64 Kbps	Global, Within +70°, −70° Latitudes Fig.
VSAT	64 Kbps to 2 Mbps	Selected Areas
IRIDIUM	128 Kbps	Global coverage Fig.
AIS	12 Kbps	<130 km
Digital VHF	21.1 Kbps	<130 km
3G–4G	264 Mbps	Few km
Wifi	11–50 Mbps	40–100 m
WiMax/LTE	70 Mbps (short range)	<50 km
UHF	300 MHz to 3 GHz	Few km
MF	0.3–3 MHz	<130 km
HF	3–30 MHz	Worldwide

provide high capacity (e.g. 3G/4G GSM or WiMAX). For these cases one will have to rely on satellite or a lower capacity radio solution as e.g., digital VHF which may be a backup option for medium capacity communication, but the availability of digital VHF and MF/HF systems are currently an issue. UHF can be an alternative for rendezvous communication. AIS may be used as part of a rendezvous and can be the best option type communication link. Inmarsat, VSAT, and Iridium may not be used where cheap land based radio is available. But this is purely a cost/benefit trade-off and could be still used in case a critical situation rise or when the other means of communication are interrupted or not available.

3.2 Coastal Communication

When the ship is in the coastal area <130 km, it needs to exchange information and data with the coastal authorities, the VTS, shore control center (SCC) and with other ship in her vicinity. With a good developed WiMAX, 3G/4G network along the coast will permit to the ship to have reliable and less costly communication service. Digital VHF, MF/HF, AIS are reliable communication carriers and can be used as means of information exchange. The satellite communication still be used as backup when communication's interruption occurs or when the communication services are not available.

3.3 High Sea Communication

In this scenario, there are few ships in the vicinity of each other. The ship need to change data and information with the SCC. The satellite communication and MF/HF can fulfill this role. VSAT, Inmarsat, iridium can ensure the exchange of information (HD Video, Telemetry, remote control) with the SCC and can also play the role of backup of each other.

3.4 Arctic Communication

The only satellite who has good coverage in that area and can be reliably used is Iridium. The ship has also the possibility to communicate with MF/HF marine radio telephone.

3.5 Ship to Ship Communication

There is a need for exchanging information directly between ships in all sea areas and at all navigation scenarios within few nautical miles (nm). The means of communication is depending on the navigation area and scenario. At high sea, the ship can use satellite communication, MF/HF, VHF, UHF and AIS. In coast areas, the ship can use Satellite communication, VHF, MF/HF, AIS, UHF, 3G/4G and WiMAX. In rendezvous scenario and in port, the ship has the possibility to use all means of communication depending on availability and cost/effectiveness of the communication carriers. In arctic area, the ship can use Iridium and MF/HF, VHF, AIS and UHF.

4 Example of Application of Our Communication Model

We present trough Fig. 7 our vision for the next decades on Gibraltar strait traffic where the autonomous ships (AS) and conventional ships (CS) have to communicate with each other, and with the shore side to avoid collision and to exchange information.

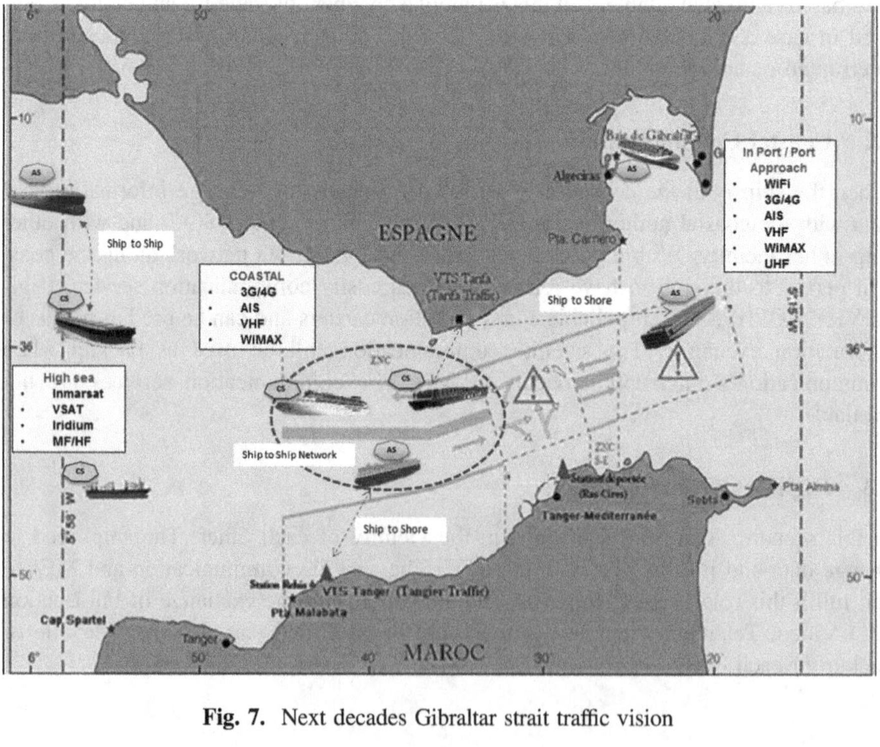

Fig. 7. Next decades Gibraltar strait traffic vision

To minimize communication costs the ship can use Moroccan telecommunication operators when it is close the Moroccan coast and when it is close to the Spanish coast, the ship can use the Spanish operators, as between ship within limited zone can build ship to ship network. The other communication carriers will play a role of backup in case of unavailability of a less costly communication means.

5 Conclusion

This paper focused on the maritime communication, such as mobile satellite communication and line sight communication. We went through the nowadays available communication technology, exploring the strong side of each communication carrier.

The main contribution of our paper was to propose a model of communication for each sea area depending on the navigation scenario to ensure a reliable and cost effective communication system. In the next decades, the autonomous ship will be a reality, and the connectivity of such type of ship will be a challenge. Our study aims to contribute to the implementation of unmanned ships.

Due to sensitive operation of autonomous ship and whatever means of communication used, the ship must be protected from hostile attacks. Different remedial actions can be implemented. Our future work will focus on security issue related to autonomous ship communication.

References

1. Låg, S.: Ship Connectivity - How Current Developments in Communication Technologies May Impact Shipping (2016)
2. Chen, H.-H., Zhang, Y.: Mobile WiMAX: Toward Broadband Wireless Metropolitan Area Networks (2008)
3. SOLAS: International Convention for the Safety of Life at Sea (1974)
4. Ilcev, S.D.: Global Mobile Satellite Communications for Maritime, Land and Aeronautic Applications (2005)
5. Global Market Analysis: Maritime satellite communication market global forecast to 2020 (2016)
6. Shen, X.S., Yang, T.: Maritime Wideband Communication Networks, Video Transmission Scheduling. Springer, Heidelberg (2014). doi:10.1007/978-3-319-07362-0
7. Euroconsult: Maritime Telecom Solutions by Satellite (2014)
8. Elbert, B.R.: The Satellite Communication Applications Handbook. Artech House, Norwood (2004)
9. Minoli, D.: Innovations in Satellite Communications and Satellite Technology (2015)
10. Zamir, S. (ed.): Handbook of Emerging Communications Technologies: The Next Decade. CRC Press LLC, Boca Raton (2000)
11. Hu, Y.F., Sheriff, R.E.: Mobile Satellite Communication Networks. Wiley, New York (2001)
12. ICAO Working Group M: SATCOM Availability Analysis (2006)
13. Ørnulf Jan Rødseth, B.K.M.: Evaluation of Ship to Shore Communication links (2012)
14. Steve Blank. https://steveblank.com/. Accessed 2016
15. COMSYS: The COMSYS Maritime VSAT Report, 4th edn. (2015)

16. Ørnulf Jan Rødseth, B.K.M.: Ship-Shore Communication Requirements (2009)
17. Eardley, P., Burness, L., Wisely, D., BTexact Technology: IP for 3G Networking Technologies for Mobile Communications (2002)
18. Radhamani, G., Radha Krishna Rao, G.S.V.: WIMAX a Wireless Technology Revolution. CRC Press, Boca Raton (2008)
19. Whalley, J., Curwen, P.: Fourth Generation Mobile Communication. The Path to Superfast Connectivity. Springer, Cham (2013). doi:10.1007/978-3-319-02210-9

A Secure Machine-to-Machine Wireless Communication Using DNP3 Protocol for Feeder Automation in Smart Grid

Anass Lekbich(✉), Abdelaziz Belfqih, Cherkaoui Nazha, Faissal Elmariami, Jamal Boukherouaa, Omar Sabri, and Mohamed Nouh Dazahra

Laboratory of Electric Systems and Energy, Team of Electrical Networks and Static Converters Superior National School of Electricity and Mechanics (ENSEM), University Hassan II of Casablanca, PO Box 8118 Oasis, Casablanca, Morocco
Anass.lekbich@gmail.com, nazha.cherkaoui@gmail.com, m.n.dazahra@gmail.com, a-belfqih@hotmail.com, sabo1805@hotmail.com, f_elmariami@yahoo.fr, j.boukherouaa@yahoo.fr

Abstract. Feeder automation in smart grid is continuously developing and it strongly depends on communication in order to coordinate all remote intelligent electronic devices. According to technical requirements of power grids related to security, the real-time and the coverage. A public IP-based secure communication networks allowing the machines to automatically exchange the data is the most effective solution. The Machine-to-Machine (M2M) communication as an application of the internet of the things (IoT) has the capacity to build a private environment of sharing data for smart grid equipment. This paper discusses the feeder automation communications requirements and suggests secure approaches for overcoming communication challenges using an encrypted end to end wireless communication and the DNP3 protocols for feeder automation in smart grid in order to increase the reliability of power system.

Keywords: M2M communication · Smart grid · Feeder automation · DNP3 protocol · SCADA · IoT

1 Introduction

With the current development of intelligent power grids, reliability and safety requirements have become very demanding. The current electrical grid has been emerged towards a reliable and flexible network, performing through the use of smart electrical devices equipped with a remote terminal unite (RTU) in order to receive data, to log the events and to share the valuable information with the control center. The control center is designed to allow human operator controlling, supervising, and collecting data from electrical networks.

The advanced in the area of embedded systems, computing and communication technologies are leading the current electrical networks to be more reliable and smart.

E. Sabir et al. (Eds.): UNet 2017, LNCS 10542, pp. 275–286, 2017.
https://doi.org/10.1007/978-3-319-68179-5_24

The collected data and the control orders can be transmitted via the internet to different locations in this case all remote devices in smart grid must be reachable in the internet. The internet of the things (IoT) is the result of the global interconnection of intelligent objects using Extended Internet Technologies [7]. In fact, IoT is an information sharing environment in which objects of everyday life are connected to wired and wireless networks [8].

Machine-to-Machine (M2M) communications as an application of IoT have been considered as a promising solution for the interconnectivity of machines that exchange information without any human interaction [1]. M2M aims at proving the means to transfer data from remote locations, and it combines telecommunication and information technology to automate processes to integrate a company's assets with its information technology system and to create value-added services [2].

A typical smart grid is designed to share information between heterogeneous devices. Therefore, various standard protocols such as IEC 60870-5, DNP3 and IEC 61850 are used to simplify data sharing, exchange the orders and standardize the coordination between these devices. A consistent part of this data need to be transmitted safely to the Control center level and must be protected against cyber-attacks.

This paper investigates the evolution of feeder automation in smart grids using a wireless M2M communication in order to build a secure data sharing environment between field devices for reliability enhancement in electrical networks.

2 Feeder Automation in Smart Grid

2.1 Feeder Automation

The implementation of Smart Grid provides complete solutions which will help improve the reliability of supply, operational performance and productivity for utilities [19]. The most important part of smart grid is the distribution automation system.

Referring to IEEE committee, distribution automation system is defined as "a set of technologies that enable an electric utility to remotely monitor, coordinate, and operate distribution components in a real-time from remote locations" [4].

Feeder automation has been recognized by utilities as effective tools to decrease the outage time and enhance service reliability in the electric power distribution systems. It consists of a remote terminal devices (intelligent electronics devices), communication networks and control center that include servers, gateways, supervisory control and data acquisition system (SCADA), fault location, isolation and service restoration system (FLISR) tools, voltage management tools, load management tools.

The core of FLISR is to obtain a self-heling grid, improving the reliability of the distribution system, increasing the availability of the electrical power, gaining economic benefits and accomplishing customer satisfactions by reducing the outage time from several hours to few minutes [5].

The SCADA system provides screen displays for the networks status, system topology, recloser and switch status, fault location, fault conditions, metering, alarms, and operator-initiated control actions within the system. The Fig. 1 show the architecture of feeder automation in smart cites.

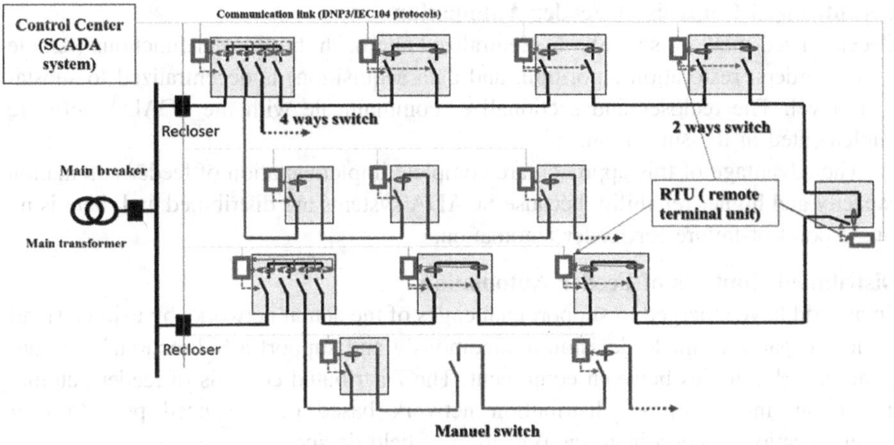

Fig. 1. Feeder automation in urban area

2.2 Feeder Automation Strategies in Smart Grid

Until now, many kinds of feeder automation schemes have been developed for automating of the distribution feeders. They can be categorized into three main approaches: Centralized, Decentralized and Distributed [17].

Centralized Controls of Feeder Automation

Centralized automation is the simple forms of feeder automation achieved by deploying combinations of switching devices such as circuit breakers, reclosers, sectionalizers and fault indicators in radial feeders [3] that are equipped with feeder terminal units installed through a utility network and connected to a centralized control. The FTU installed on every switch, implements the functions of acquiring remote data of distribution, controlling the equipment, catching and processing the fault event. All these information are shared in real time with the master station. This device can detect fault and operate automatically to accomplish a local control to isolate the faulted area of the feeder and to restore the unaffected sections.

The control center includes all the tools used to perform the feeder automation function, distribution application system function and geographic information system function etc. The feeder automation system can collect the field FTU data into master station and vice versa, send control commands from master station to the field FTU through a communication network. In this case the operation sequences of feeder equipment (recloser, sectionalizer and voltage regulator) are remotely managed by the SCADA system. This is allow to perform an accurate monitoring and fast reconfiguration of the distribution voltage network and reducing the outage time and the energy losses.

However, in this method response time of SCADA system is increased due to the high volume of required decisions; as a result, instantaneous control of the equipment is difficult.

Decentralized Controls of Feeder Automation
Decentralized method is similar to Centralized approach, but Master functions (remote control orders, restoration algorithm, and data acquisition) is decentralized to substations level. The recloser and sectionalizer communicate with the SCADA software implemented in the substation.

The advantage of this approach are complete implementation of feeder automation capacity and higher reliability because SCADA systems are distributed and there is no single-point-of-failure for feeder automation.

Distributed Controls of Feeder Automation
Smart grid have emerged to support challenges of the actual networks by using a smart devices capable to made decision autonomously and support a bidirectional communication technologies between equipment. The Distributed controls of feeder automation is an innovation of distribution network based on advanced peer to peer communication to coordinate the operation of field devices.

Cooperation and coordination between the fields devices (controllers and remote terminals unites) simplifies the tasks of controlling multiple constraints (current faults, voltages stabilities, power losses), improves the reliability of the networks by a rapid locating of faults and smart reconfiguration of the network. This strategies is a great development of actual electrical networks and need an efficient peer to peer communication system.

This control strategies can be implemented by applying IEC 61850 GOOSE messages exchanging between recloser controllers and disconnector controllers [6]. On one hand, The advantages of this approach are high scalability, autonomy and robustness because failure of one element does not influence the entire distribution network. However the drawback include high cost due to the use of smart algorithm in the controller to perform a smart decision on collaboration with other devices, and the implementation requires high performance peer to peer communication network.

3 Communication Architecture Requirements for Feeder Automation

Communication architectures that can meet the needs of feeder automation are not homely, and the choice of suitable communication technologies is subject to many technical and economic constraints. The intelligent electronic devices in feeder networks are distributed in a wide distance and require particular communication networks characterized by high reliability and availability, high coverage and security. The remote terminal unit in feeder automation should be accessible quickly as possible under all circumstances and in distributed control this devices must have access to a peer to peer communication.

All the components of feeder automation are connected through several communication technologies running from wired to wireless network. We divide the architecture on three networks extracted from the Smart Grid literature [12], namely, HAN (Home Area Networks), NANs (Neighborhood Area Networks) and WANs (Wide Area Networks).

The HAN connects the in-home smart appliances to a common network. Neighborhood Area Network or NAN is a collection of multiple HANs to collect sensed data for aggregation. It enables data collection from customers in a neighborhood for transmission to an electric utility company. NAN can also be called Field Area Network (FAN) when it connects with field devices such as intelligent electronic devices (IEDs) [13].

Wide Area Network or WAN connects various electric utilities, SCADA center and Home gateway. The WAN uses mainly wired communications such as fiber optical technologies or wireless communication such as WiMax and 3G/4G technologies, which are characterized by high speed data, high coverage and bulk delivery across domains [14].

The 3G/4G technologies for feeder automation presents several benefits like the latency the high coverage and the access to the internet but the cyber-security becomes a challenge. Securing this communication indirectly improves electrical service availability by ensuring performant feeder automation operation.

Figure 2 represents the structure of an end-to-end communication used in smart grid for monitoring and remote control of feeder automation.

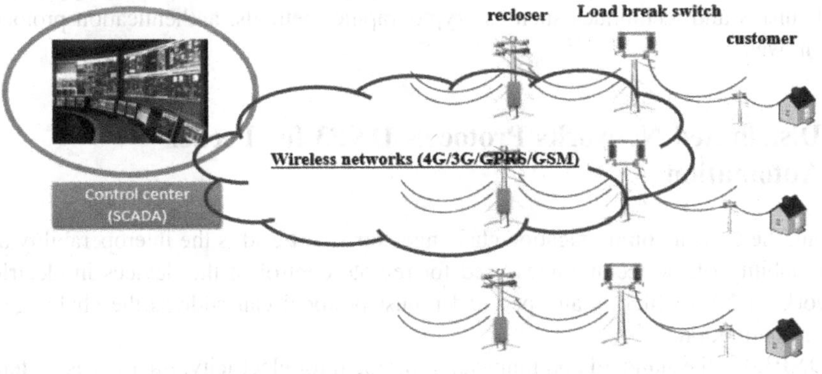

Fig. 2. End-to-End communication for SCADA

In addition of communication networks and gateways used to establish communication between the field devices and the control center, the smart grid used some specified protocols to transmit packets that include the command and data in a reliable manner. In this paper, we focus on the DNP3 protocols due to their capacities to remote control equipment in feeder automation.

4 Security Requirement for Feeder Automation in Smart Grids

Cyber-security in feeder automation is a real challenge and it is considered as one of the main requirements for its quality and reliability.

The data related to energy distribution are considered critical, in particular, when they are relevant for billing purposes or grid control; therefore, secure communication is important [10]. According to IEC62351, there are five basic security requirements for electric power system:

- Confidentiality: is to keep the privatization of data and messages exchanged between the equipment to prevent possible leakage of data. To do this, messages should be encrypted with a secret key which only intended receivers have.
- Integrity: preventing the information against unauthorized modification, manipulation during the transmission. Receivers need to make sure that the received message are not changed or modified by the attackers.
- Availability: preventing the denial of the service. Service in the feeder automation network should be always available to all nodes.
- Authentication: is the capability to ensure that the source of information is known and it is authorized. In the feeder automation all equipment must be sure that the remote end is authenticate.
- Nonrepudiation: preventing a user involved in a data exchange from denying his participation in the exchange.

To achieve a secure Smart Grid, it is necessary to use several security approaches, mechanisms and techniques such as cryptographic methods, authentication protocols and firewalls.

5 Distributed Networks Protocols DNP3 for Feeder Automation

Among the typical communication challenges for smart grid is the interoperability and the reliability of the technologies used for remote control of the devices in electrical networks. DNP3 which is an open and robust protocol can address the challenge of feeder automation.

DNP3.0 is the standard communication protocol for electricity, oil and gas systems. It collects and stores status information, analog and digital signals from remote devices in smart grids. The IEEE adopted DNP3.0 as an IEEE Std 1815 standard in July 2010. The purpose of DNP3 is to transmit relatively small packets of data in a reliable manner with the messages involved arriving in a deterministic sequence [9].

DNP3 is a SCADA protocol originally designed for serial communication with use of Ethernet and wireless communication in smart grid the DNP3 has been extended to allow using the TCP/IP to transport the DNP3 messages. The TCP/IP extension encapsulates the entire DNP3 frame with TCP/IP headers. This encapsulation preserves the original other DNP3 layers.

The DNP3 pseudo-transport layer and the link layer are part of the communication stack for serial connections. A DNP3/TCP packet has an Ethernet header, an IP header, and a TCP header, as shown in Fig. 3. Furthermore, in the TCP layer, a message has a link header, a transport header, and an application header followed by a number of DNP3 objects and header [16].

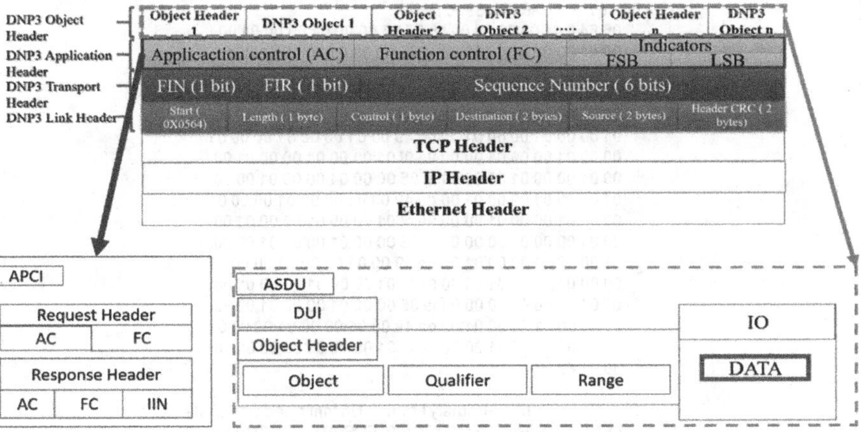

Fig. 3. DNP3 frame

The first field of the DNP3 is a 2 bit with the value 0x0564 that indicate the start of the frame and designate to identify the DNP3 protocol. Other field of the DNP3 are the following:

- Length - The Length field gives the length of the entire frame without CRC.
- Control - A byte control field that contains the direction of the message flow, data link function codes, and other indicators this fields defines the control action needed to be taken at the receiver end.
- Destination - A two-byte field that identifies the recipient of the message.
- Source - A two-byte field that identifies the sender of the message.
- FIN - A bit that indicates the last fragment.
- FIR - A bit that indicates the first fragment.
- Sequence number - Six-bit sequence number used for fragmentation and reassembly.
- Application control - a one-byte field used for fragmentation in the application layer. Also, is used to determine whether a given fragment has been received in the correct order.
- Function code - A one-byte field specifies the action of the request or response sent.
- Indicators - Two byte internal indicators indicate certain states and error conditions within outstations.
- DNP3 object header - Two byte header for each DNP3 object in the message
- DNP3 objects - DNP3 objects contain values (input reads and output updates) to and from external stations [9].

The Fig. 4 show an example of serial DNP3 frame exchanged with master scada and load break switch based on GSM communication. The master scada has the address 3 and the equipment has the address 45. This frame is captured by a frame simulator tool used in the controller of the load break switch.

```
12:53:06.801:  << UART Tx Send Data
        05 64 ff 44 03 00 2d 00 bb 57 07 00 00 01 00 00 01 00
        00 01 00 00 01 00 00 01 af 65 00 00 01 00 00 01 00 00
        01 00 00 01 00 00 01 00 db 49 00 01 00 00 01 00 00 01
        00 00 01 00 00 01 00 00 9e 0f 01 00 00 01 00 00 01 00
        00 01 00 00 01 00 00 01 fe 85 00 00 01 00 00 01 00 00
        01 00 00 01 00 00 01 00 db 49 00 01 00 00 01 00 00 01
        00 00 01 00 00 01 00 00 9e 0f 01 00 00 01 00 00 01 00
        00 01 00 00 01 00 00 01 fe 85 00 00 01 00 00 01 00 00
        01 00 00 01 00 00 01 00 db 49 00 01 00 00 01 00 00 01
        00 00 01 00 00 01 00 00 9e 0f 01 00 00 01 00 00 01 00
        00 01 00 00 01 00 00 01 fe 85 00 00 01 00 00 01 00 00
        01 00 00 01 00 00 01 00 db 49 00 01 00 00 01 00 00 01
        00 00 01 00 00 01 00 00 9e 0f 01 00 00 01 00 00 01 00
        00 01 00 00 01 00 00 01 fe 85 00 00 01 00 00 01 00 00
        01 00 00 01 00 00 01 00 db 49 00 01 00 00 01 00 00 01
        00 00 01 00 00 01 00 00 9e 0f 01 00 00 01 00 00 01 00
        00 01 49 97

12:53:06.816: <--- Serial     Primary Frame - Unconfirmed User Data
        LEN(255) DIR(0) PRM(1) FCV(0) FCB(0) DEST(3) SRC(45)
        05 64 ff 44 03 00 2d 00 bb 57
        08 00 00 01 00 00 01 00 00 01 00 00 01 00 00 01 e0 3e
        00 00 01 00 00 01 00 00 01 00 00 01 00 00 01 00 db 49
        00 01 00 00 01 00 00 01 00 00 01 00 00 01 00 00 9e 0f
        01 00 00 01 00 00 01 00 00 01 00 00 01 00 00 01 fe 85
        00 00 01 00 00 01 00 00 01 00 00 01 00 00 01 00 db 49
        00 01 00 00 01 00 00 01 00 00 01 2b 00 01 ef 51 33 5b
```

Fig. 4. DNP3 frame in GSM control order for a switch

The DNP3.0 application layer structure is shown in Fig. 3. The Application Protocol Data Unit (APDU) is the application layer data frame which is composed of an Application Protocol Control Information (APCI) and an Application Service Data Unit (ASDU). The APCI includes the Application Control (AC) which controls request/response messages, the Function Code (FC), which defines message types, and Internal Indications (IIN) which represent status and error conditions within the outstation. The Data Unit Identifier (DUI) and Input-Output (IO) constitute the ASDU. DNP3.0 can present information that users want in the DUI. The DUI includes the Object Group, Object Variation, Qualifier, and Range. The IO includes data that users want [12].

DNP3.0 uses objects to communicate values and information between devices. The DNP3.0 object library contains a description and encoding for each DNP3.0 object. It provides descriptions of various types of points and tips for choosing objects. The DNP3.0 group numbers can be categorized as follows: Device Attributes, Binary Inputs/Outputs, Counters, Analog Inputs/Outputs, Time, Classes, Data Sets, and Others. Object variation refers to state values or times tamps added to the data. The contents of the range depend on the value of the Qualifier byte. The range contains the index size of the DNP3.0 object.

In order to control the field devices, the master station and slave equipment must use the same mapping for Inputs/Outputs, Counters, Analog Inputs/Outputs.

6 A Secure M2M Solutions for Feeder Automation

6.1 A Secure M2M Architecture for Feeder Automation

There are various security solutions for the security requirements of feeder automation. Security solutions should be selected based on the devices capabilities, communication networks, data traffic and finally the cost. The most common idea is to isolate the SCADA network from internet connections as much as possible. This method consists of using private access points without internet access. But with increasing of the number of remote devices as well as wireless internet coverage is generalized everywhere. It is better to direct all remote monitoring and control system to use Internet with an accepted level of security. A virtual private network or VPN is a highly effective solution for transmitting data securely over the Internet or a wide area network. The objective of VPN is to create a secure tunnel in the communication network through which sensitive data can be transmitted. The tunnel is performed by encapsulating and encrypting the data.

The M2M machine-to-machine communication as a part of the internet of the things that use the virtual tunneling to send and receipt data is proposed in this article, the M2M communications in feeder automation must be efficient, private and secure because most functions running over them might be processed in autonomic manners [11], characterized by a real-time secure updating of data, cost effective and independent to the internet provider. The Fig. 5 show the structure of the M2M communication for feeder automation, this structure include a M2M gateway as a VPN concentrator, firewall to restrict unauthorized access, server to run the human machine interface and to store all networks data.

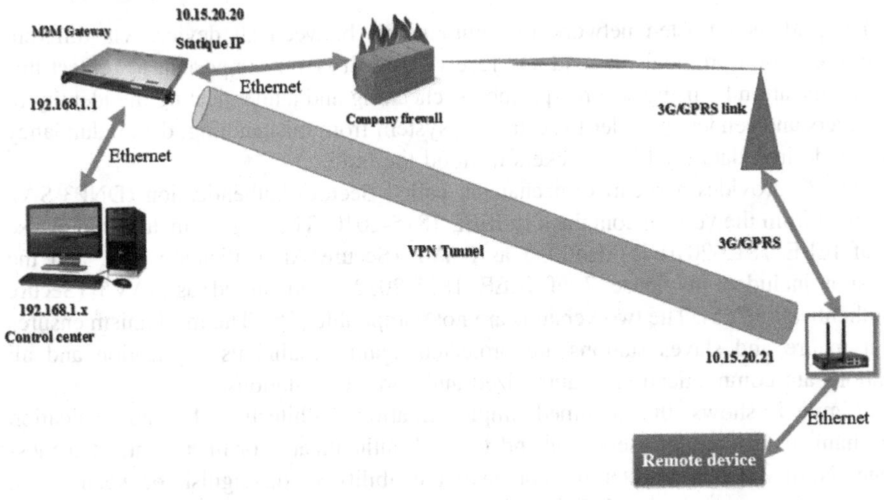

Fig. 5. Secure M2M communication for feeder automation architecture

The machine to machine gateway requires a fixed line Internet connection with a public and static IP address. A public static IP address is intended because the communication is initialized by the remote devices gateway and routed using the public internet. In this solution all remote field devices can be connected to the VPN concentrator with a high level secure end-to-end communication. The Fig. 6 present the 4 step to establish the M2M communication for feeder automation.

The APN is access point name

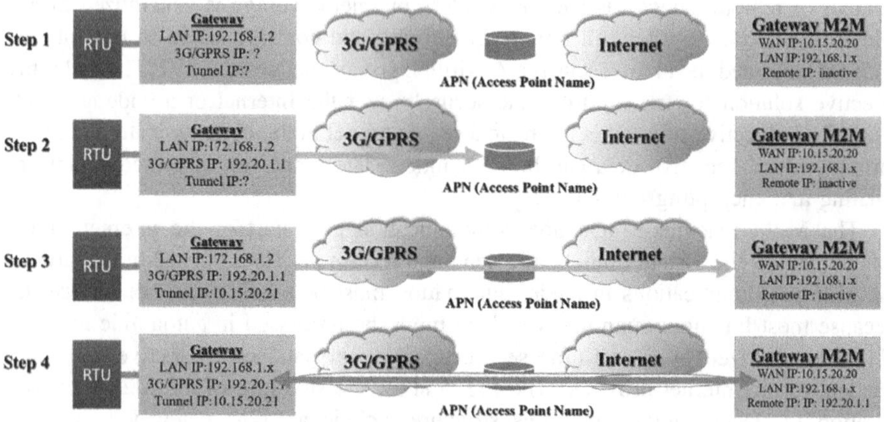

Fig. 6. Establishment of M2M communication

6.2 Secure DNP3 Protocol in Feeder Automation

Smart grid uses trusted network to communicate between all devices via different communication protocols to send and receive data. It is very important to protect this communication by using secured protocols, checking and authenticating the identity of receivers and senders in order to secure the system from mishandling, data redundancy and undesired data used by attackers to flood the buffer.

DNP3 provides a security mechanism called Secure Authentication (DNP3-SA), updated from the version contained in IEEE 1815-2010. The version included in clause 7 of IEEE 1815-2010 is identified as SAV2 (Secure Authentication V2), and the version included in clause 7 of IEEE 1815-2012 is identified as SAV5 (Secure Authentication V5). The two versions are not compatible [15]. The mechanism ensures that maître and slaves stations are protected against malicious application and all stations are communication to authorized and correct outstations.

Figure 7 shows the assumed implementation architecture for authentication mechanism. It is under users freehand to send authenticated or unauthenticated message. Normal DNP3 master do not have the ability to distinguish between users. Indeed, there are additional DNP3 function codes and object variations to ensure formal authentication manage.

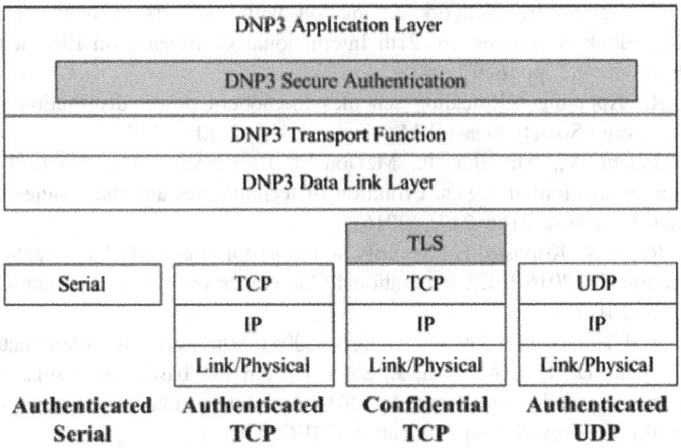

Fig. 7. DNP3 implementation architecture for authentication mechanism

Combining the secure DNP3 protocol with the M2M communication based on internet and using a DNP3 firewalls for filtering untrusted devices can ensure that all smart grid devices will be connected to the SCADA server in high level of security. Which will allowing new electrical networks to meet the requirement of the IEC62351 standard and accelerate the use of IoT technologies in the smart grid the future challenge is to and adapt the DNP3 and IEC61850 with IoT protocols like Coap and MQTT.

7 Conclusion

This paper discussed secure remote control of feeder automation based on VPN communication between the field remote devices and the control center. This communication is accomplished in two main steps. First step performed by using the advantages of the virtual protocol. In the second step, the DNP3 secure authentication is used to improve the security of the communication.

Integrating last advanced technologies of wireless communication and encryption technique enable to create a virtual private environment in which all devices use the Internet to exchange data and orders. This opportunity make the development of smart grid very easy and open the door for many industrial application. The challenge is to build a secure cloud to cluster all remote devices and adapting the industrial protocols such as DNP3 to the Iot standards.

References

1. Cheng, M.Y., Lin, G.Y., Wei, H.Y., Hsu, A.C.: Overload control for machine-type-communications in LTE-advanced system. IEEE Commun. Mag. **50**(6), 38–45 (2012)
2. Alam, M., Nielsen, R.H., Prasad, N.R.: The evolution of M2M into IoT. In: 2013 First International Black Sea Conference on Communications and Networking (2013)

3. Heinrich, C., Taylor, E.: Network automation with reclosers as new components for European distribution systems. In: 21th International Conference on Electricity Distribution CIRED, vol. 482, pp. 6–9 (2011)
4. Aguero, J.R.: Applying self-healing schemes to modern power distribution systems. In: Power and Energy Society General Meeting, pp. 1–4. IEEE (2012)
5. Das, R., Madani, V., Aminifar, F., McDonald, J., Venkata, S.S., Novosel, D., et al.: Distribution automation strategies: evolution of technologies and the business case. IEEE Trans. Smart Grid **6**(4), 2166–2175 (2015)
6. Jafary, P., Repo, S., Koivisto, H.: Security solutions for smart grid feeder automation data communication. In: 2016 IEEE International Conference on Industrial Technology (ICIT), pp. 551–557 (2016)
7. The Internet of Things. ITU Internet Reports (2005). http://www.itu.int/internetofthings
8. Adhya, S., Saha, D., Das, A., Jana, J., Saha, H.: An IoT based smart solar photovoltaic remote monitoring and control unit. In: 2016 2nd International Conference on Control, Instrumentation, Energy & Communication (CIEC) (2016)
9. IEEE 1815: IEEE Standard for Electric Power Systems Communications–Distributed Network Protocol (DNP3) (2010)
10. Sauter, T.: End-to-end communication architecture for smart grids. IEEE Trans. Ind. Electron. **58**(4), 1218–1228 (2011)
11. Doh, I., Lim, J., Chae, K.: Secure authentication for structured smart grid system. In: 2015 9th International Conference on Innovative Mobile and Internet Services in Ubiquitous Computing (2015)
12. Kuzlu, M., Pipattanasomporn, M., Rahman, S.: Communication network requirements for major smart grid applications in HAN, NAN and WAN. Comput. Netw. **67**, 74–88 (2014)
13. Zahid, S., Bah, S., En-Nouaary, A.: A synthesis of communication architectures and services of smart grid systems. In: 2016 Third International Conference on Systems of Collaboration (SysCo) (2016)
14. Dari, E.Y., Essaaidi, M.: An overview of smart grid cyber-security state of the art study. In: 2015 3rd International on Renewable and Sustainable Energy Conference (IRSEC) (2015)
15. IEEE 1815-2012: IEEE Standard for Electric Power Systems Communications-Distributed Network Protocol (DNP3)5 (2012)
16. Nivethan, J., Papa, M.: A Linux-based firewall for the DNP3 protocol. In: 2016 IEEE Symposium on Technologies for Homeland Security (HST) (2016)
17. Fan, J., Zhang, X.: Feeder automation within the scope of substation automation. In: Power Systems Conference and Exposition, IEEE PES, pp. 607–612 (2006)
18. Dazahra, M.N., Elmariami, F., Belfqih, A., Boukhrouaa, J., Anass, L., Nazha, C.: Decentralized control of substations in smart cities. In: El-Azouzi, R., Menasche, D., Sabir, E., De Pellegrini, F., Benjillali, M. (eds.) Advances in Ubiquitous Networking 2. LNEE, vol. 397, pp. 299–308. Springer, Singapore (2017). doi:10.1007/978-981-10-1627-1_23

L-CAHASH: A Novel Lightweight Hash Function Based on Cellular Automata for RFID

Charifa Hanin[1,2](✉), Bouchra Echandouri[1], Fouzia Omary[1], and Souad El Bernoussi[2]

[1] Laboratory of Computer Science Research(LRI), Faculty of Sciences, Mohammed V University in Rabat, BP1014 RP, Rabat, Morocco
charifa.hanin@gmail.com, bouchra.echandouri@gmail.com, omary@fsr.ac.ma

[2] Laboratory of Mathematics, Computing and Applications(LabMia), Faculty of Sciences, Mohammed V University in Rabat, BP1014 RP, Rabat, Morocco
s.elbernoussi@fsr.ac.ma

Abstract. Considered as the main element for building Internet of Things, Radio Frequency IDentification (RFID) is a non-contact automatic identification technology that identifies the tag signal, in order to collect instructions that should be transmitted to the controller. However, it suffers from some threats (i.e. physical attacks, eavesdropping, cloning, tracking, etc.). Thus, ensuring data privacy becomes one of the paramount security interests. Hash functions are an essential mechanism in achieving data integrity. Nevertheless, the heavy duty classical existent hash functions are unsuitable for these RFID tags, since they require small amount of computation. Accordingly, in this paper, a new lightweight hash function based on cellular automata (L-CAHASH) is proposed. This approach gives a high randomness quality and fast software hashing comparing to well-known lightweight hash functions. The robustness and the efficiency of our new proposed hash function is analyzed and the obtained results show that this new hash function meets the RFID tags' security requirement.

Keywords: Information security · Lightweight hash function · Cellular automata · Radio Frequency Identification (RFID) · Data integrity

1 Introduction

In the last decades of this century, new technology has witnessed big changes and developments. Further, according to Cisco, by 2020, the evolution of internet would help connect 50 billion devices. Soon every thing will be linked to the Internet. These things could represent a personal device like: smart phones, digital cameras, as it could be an object from our surroundings like: home, vehicle, or objects with tags like Radio-Frequency Identification (RFID) tags [1].

Especially, RFID tags are the most basic element in the Internet of Things' architecture. This latter have been universally applied in many fields in our

E. Sabir et al. (Eds.): UNet 2017, LNCS 10542, pp. 287–298, 2017.
https://doi.org/10.1007/978-3-319-68179-5_25

daily life and in the near future, the common known optical barcodes would be replaced by these Tags. They help identify the target tag signal automatically without any contact, collect and control the essential information, to thereafter send instructions to the controller [2].

Nevertheless, on one hand, being one of the most ubiquitous technologies, these RFID system's most principal security menaces are related to the communication of sensitive data between the reader and the tag such as eavesdropping, man-in-the-middle attack, tracking, data forging, Denial of Service (DoS), physical attacks, etc. For example, in the Data forging the unauthorized entity could modify the stored information existing on tags [3]. Thus, the need for security and efficient implementable cryptographic mechanism is seriously increasing. On the other hand, these tags suffer from the limited computational power capabilities and tiny memory size.

Hence, considered as a robust securing mechanism, cryptography is the science that helps ensure privacy protection of transmitted information, by coding and decoding data. Therefore, protecting integrity, of RFID tags, requires conceiving powerful securing mechanisms with the suitable balance between the needed security level and the less computation power. In that sense, the lightweight cryptography field concentrates on cryptographic mechanisms for devices with extremely constrained computation power. Further, a numerous lightweight cryptographic algorithms have been suggested namely block ciphers, hash function, authentication protocols, etc. It is worth noting that from implementation's point of view, the lightweight hash functions are one of the most suitable choices for ensuring RFID tags security and almost all the suggested algorithm are based on its use. Inherently, a hash function is the transformation of any input to a fixed size length output, called digest [4].

Additionally, RFID tags have limited processing capabilities namely a tiny memory size and restricted data storage. Thus, in order to strengthen the protection of data integrity in these latter's context, our proposed mechanism in this paper is the use of a lightweight hash function that is based on Cellular automata. Firstly introduced by Neuman [5], in 1966, Cellular automata are considered as a dynamical deterministic system that is composed of a set of cells, such that every cell changes its own state, according to a defined set of rules, in function of time. Moreover, besides providing robust cryptographic algorithms, this latter gives a high randomness quality, a fast operation and hardware implementation facilities [6]. The use of this latter in our proposed construction provides a highly robustness and efficiency. In addition, the experimental analysis and the obtained results proves that it meets the security requirement for RFID system. Our work is organized as follows: In Sect. 2, the cellular automata concept is introduced and some related works are presented in Sect. 3. Afterwords, in Sect. 4, our suggested design of a new lightweight hash function that is based on cellular automata for RFID tags context is described. Further, the obtained results from the experimental tests are presented in Sect. 5. Finally, the paper is concluded providing some future works.

2 Cellular Automata Preliminaries

Cellular automata (CA) were firstly introduced by Neuman (1966) [5].

One-dimensional CA is a dynamical system composed by a finite linearly connected array of cells whereby each cell takes a state from a set of states possibility. The value of one state is updated using a local transition rule taking into account the neighbor cells. Exactly, for each cell i at a time step t denoted by x_i^t, the neighbor cell is computed using a parameter r termed radius that is denoted by:

$$N_i^t = \{x_{i-r}^t, x_{i-r+1}^t, x_i^t, \ldots, x_{i+r-1}^t, x_{i+1}^t\}$$

A local transition rule f is a function that computes the next states of cell using the defined neighbors, and it is expressed by:

$$x_i^{t+1} = f(N_i^t)$$

The local transition rule depends only on the possible state values and the radius r that defines the set of neighbors.

A global transition function is defined as an application of $\sigma : \{0,1\}^* \rightarrow \{0,1\}^*$, that returns all cells' state at the next time step through the evolution of the CA as $x^{t+1} = \sigma(x^t)$. The boundary conditions can be null or periodic, etc. Where the extreme cells are connected to logic 0, and the extreme cells are adjacent respectively. In a CA, if the same rule is applied to all cells, it is called uniform CA; otherwise, it is called hybrid CA.

In this paper, let us take a uniform binary cellular automaton (states in$\{0, 1\}$) with periodic boundary conditions, defined as a Boolean function with $n = 2r+1$ variables that maps n binary inputs to single binary output. For CA with n = 3, the evolution of the ith cell in each time step t can be represented as a function of neighbors' state $N_i^t = \{x_{i-1}^t, x_i^t, x_{i+1}^t\}$ as:

$$x_i^{t+1} = f(x_{i-1}^t, x_i^t, x_{i+1}^t)$$

i.e. the new state of the ith cell depends on the actual state of its left, right and its one cells' state. A CA rule value can be expressed by a truth table representing a list with size 2^n of all possible outputs (see Table 2). The Table 1 presents an example of rule 30 proposed by Wolfram [7]. This rule can also be expressed by a combinatorial logic function, denoted by x_i^{t+1}. It associates each cell to the next state:

$$x_i^{t+1} = x_{i-1}^t \oplus (x_i^t \odot x_{i+1}^t)$$

where $\oplus$ denotes bit by bit mod n addition and $\odot$ denotes bit by bit mod n multiplication.

Accordingly, Cellular automata have numerous characteristics that are very suitable to the design of good hash functions, such as complex, chaotic and unpredictable behavior [5]. Also, it facilitates the hardware implementation and provides a high randomness quality.

In what follows, some related notions to our proposed Lightweight hash function based on cellular automata scheme are described.

Table 1. Representation of rule 30 with r = 1

Neighborhood number	7	6	5	4	3	2	1	0
N_i^t	111	110	101	100	011	010	001	000
$f(N_i^t)$	0	0	0	1	1	1	1	0

3 Related Works

The restricted hardware capabilities issue in RFID has raised a set of cryptographic tools' improvement attempts for efficiency. Even if hash functions are one of the most suitable choices for ensuring RFID tags security, recent implementation advances in hash function field have been done.

Especially, in [9], the author describes some hash functions based on the ultra-lightweight block cipher [10], whereby both hardware and security efficiency had the same importance during the design of the cipher. Further, the described (DM-PRESENT-80) and (DM-PRESENT-128) are both a 64-bit hash functions constructed from a 64-bit block cipher, using the Davies-Meyer construction where one 64-bit chaining variable H_i is refreshed using an extracted message M_i conforming to the computation: $H_i' = E(H_i, M) \oplus H_i$.

In addition, some other ones of these Lightweight hash functions are based on sponge construction [11], like KECCAK [12], PHOTON [13], SPONGENT [14], QUARK [15], GLUON [16] and Hash-one [17]. Unlike the existing hash functions based on the Merkle-Damgard mode, this construction has a fixed length permutation f, which is performed on a state with a fixed size of bits. It is used in order to produce from an arbitrary length input a fixed length output. It provides a good balance between security requirement and efficiency.

In KECCAK [12] the authors present reduced versions of the keccak hash function, the finalist in the SHA-3 Competition, which are lightweight. Beside its low-power and low-area, it is a decent throughput. Further, it was the first lightweight implementation utilizing the sponge function. Moreover, also the paper of the most known lightweight hash function family: PHOTON [13]. In a way to obtain a balance between speed and pre-image security, they used the sponge construction and the AES primitive as an internal un-keyed permutation. This permits to have the most compact and close hash function to the theoretical optimum. In addition, they presented a new method that helps generate a column mixing layer by extending a sponge framework that fits perfectly for tiny area.

Furthermore, in SPONGENT [14] they describe a family of lightweight hash functions based on a sponge construction with the present-type permutation [10], that produce the smallest digest among all known hash functions, providing more flexibility in terms of speediness and a high security against most crucial attacks though hardware requirements. Further, also based on the sponge construction, this contribution QUARK [15] was involving the stream cipher Grain and the block cipher KATAN, in a way to fit memory size requirements. This latter can be used for the construction of stream encryption, message authentication or authenticated encryption. Additionally, as the aforementioned PHOTON [13], and QUARK [15], the paper GLUON [16] is also based on the sponge construction, using specific Feedback with Carry Shift Register (FCSR), namely the stream ciphers F-FCSR-v3 and X-FCSR-v2, as the internal permutation.

In the following contribution hash-one [17], the authors present a lightweight hash function with a lower complexity considering hardware implementation while achieving security requirements. They proposed the design of a lightweight hash function with minimum permutation's building blocks, using sponge construction with the two updated non-linear feedback shift registers as permutation function.

Also, in another paper [18] the authors showed their proposed CASH a new hash function, that is secure against the most known attacks compared with the best top 5 SHA-3 candidates, since it provides excellent throughput and efficiency. This latter is also based on the sponge construction, employing the linear cellular automata for permutation. Especially, to construct a round dependent linear function providing a high diffusion, a round constant addition is combined with a linear element.

Thus, the attacks on these aforesaid hash functions are important in evaluating their strength that calls for enhancement. This have inspired us to propose the design of a new lightweight cryptographic hash function, based on Cellular Automata, that helps match RFID tags' constraints and security requirements.

4 Our Proposed Lightweight Cellular Automata Based Hash Function(L-CAHASH)

Given a message M, to be hashed, as an input of arbitrary finite length L, our proposed function H(M)(See Algorithm 1)process begins with a split operation into a fixed-length of $(128|256-bit)$ blocks M_i involving a padding operation, if needed. In particular, it is supposed that the form of message M after padding is $M_{pad} = \{M_1, \ldots, M_n\}$ where M_i is a $(128|256-bit)$ block. Then, the algorithm requires the use of a first randomly generated initial vector $IV_1 \in \{0,1\}^{(128|256)}$. The operator 'xor' is applied to this vector IV_1 with M_{index} the selected M_i chosen from M.

Thereafter, each M_i' modulo a selected number is calculated. The resulting M', that is the concatenation of all residues, is split into a fixed-length of $(128|256-bit)$ blocks M_i', that is padded if needed. Then, a 'xor' operation is applied to all M_i' with the second randomly generated initial vector $IV_2 \in \{0,1\}^{(128|256)}$. Otherwise, if the length of the overall M' is lower than $(128|256-bit)$, M' is concatenated with a part of the second randomly generated initial vector $IV_2 \in \{0,1\}^{(128|256)-M'bit\_length}$. Termed M_{rule}, the obtained bits of these operations will be the global transition function rule for evolving Cellular Automata: Evol(M_{rule}). The final result is our proposed hash function's output termed digest.

The Fig. 1 represents our proposed construction scheme.

In the following section the efficiency of our proposed lightweight hash function based on cellular automata is studied.

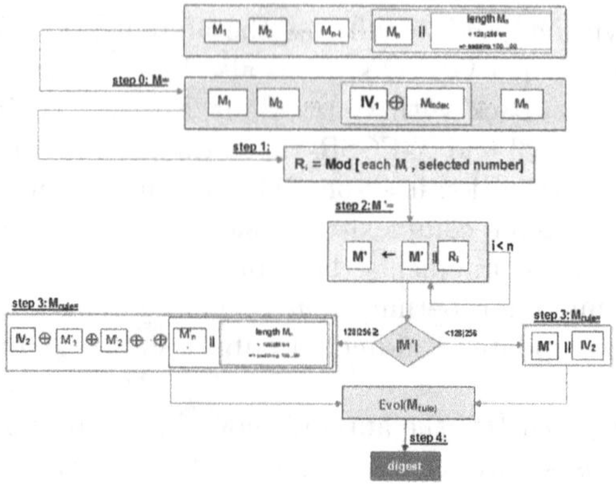

Fig. 1. Our proposed lightweight hash function based on cellular automata (L-CAHASH)

Algorithm 1. Our proposed L-CAHASH Algorithm

Input: Message M,IV_1,IV_2, index, selected number
Output: Digest

Split M into n blocks of 128|256;
if $M \neq$ *multiple of* 128|256 **then**
    Pad M ;
end
$M_{\oplus} \longleftarrow M_{index} \oplus IV_1$;
for *each i in n* **do**
    $R_i \longleftarrow mod[M_i, selectednumber]$;
end
$M' \leftarrow R_1 \| R_2 \| \ldots \| R_n$;
if $|M'| <$ 128|256 **then**
    $M_{rule} \longleftarrow M' \| IV_2$;
    else
        for *i=1 to n* **do**
            $M_{rule} \longleftarrow \oplus M'_i$;
        end
    end
end
Digest $\longleftarrow$ *Evol*(M_{rule})

---

5 Experiments and Security Analysis

Various hash algorithms was designed, since the hash-value (or digest) serves to verify data integrity. These hash function process begins with a split of data into blocks into fixed length followed by an iteratively computation using a transformation functions. Furthermore, for a one-way hash function with inputs m, m' and outputs h, h'. It follows these properties [8]:

- Pre-image resistance: it is computationally infeasible to find any input m from any fixed output h.
- 2nd-preimage resistance: it is computationally infeasible to find any second input m' which has the same output h=h' as any fixed m.
- collision resistance: It is computationally infeasible to find two distinct inputs m and m' that hash to the same output h=h'.

It is worth noting that 2nd-preimage resistance induces pre-image resistance, also, the collision resistance induces both 2nd-preimage resistance and pre-image resistance.

In this section our proposed scheme's security analysis and statistical tests are detailed.

5.1 Security Analysis

Complexity. As known, a hash function should be easy to compute and implement. Therefore, the complexity of our proposed L-CAHASH (see Algorithm 1), with the purpose to hash a message M, is as follow:

At the initialization step, in the worst case, $n - (L/n)$ is required (where L: the message length, n: the block size of $(128|256)bit$), to make the M's length a multiple of n-bit blocks. Thereafter, in the step of L-CAHASH processing, no more than (n + 2) mod 2 additions is employed, also (n + 1) mod 2 divisions is needed to calculate the modulo of each n-bits block. Finally, at the last step, it is noticed that the function Evol(M) is efficiently addressed by the truth tables in ROM. Thus, the overall complexity is O(n).

Pre-Image and Collision. Generally, given a one-way hash function, with an arbitrary bit length input and a fixed n-bit output, to verify that a hash function resists against the pre-image and 2nd-preimage attacks, the complexity of generic attack needs (2^n) operations, and finding collision for H requires about $O(2^{n/2})$ operations [19]. Therefore, the security of our proposed lightweight hash function depends especially on the selected number and the used global transition rule. Then, in order to verify these properties, it is supposed the appropriate used IV values is known. Therefore, $2^{(128|256)}$ operations it is needed to find the appropriate used rule. Thus our proposed scheme is pre-image and second pre-image resistant.

Further, to prove that our proposed scheme is collision resitant is by showing that to find: m, m' such that $m' \neq m$ and L-CAHASH(m) = L-CAHASH(m') is computationally unfeasible.

Cellular automata have chaotic behavior that evolves any state into a new state providing a sequence of $2^n - 1$ different possibilities. If a message $m' \neq m$ can be found such that L-CAHASH(m') = L-CAHASH(m), the expected hamming distance between x_i^t and x_i^{t+1} is $n/2$ which gives Hamming $(L - CAHASH(m), L - CAHASH(m')) = 2^{n/2}$. Thus, the complexity to find a collision is $O(2^{n/2})$.

Avalanche Criterion. This notion is defined as the capability of the function to spread a little change in the input through the output. Particularly, if a random one bit is modified in the message input M,($\forall x, y \in \{0,1\}^m$) : $Hamming(x, y) = 1$),this affects the output. Especially, The Hamming distance of the resulting obtained output should be a half of the output size average($Hamming(H(x), H(y)) = n/2$ [19].

A message input m of length 1MB is taken and its L-CAHASH(M) is computed. Figure 2 shows the average number of output bits changed in the message M, given a random one bit difference in the input, using a set of 10000 pairs of messages.

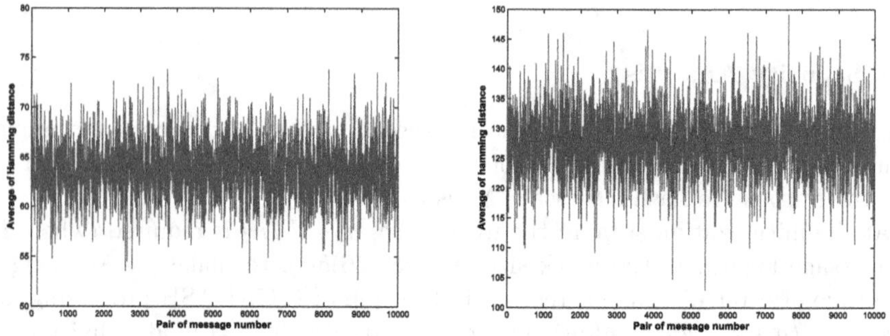

(a) The average number of output bits changed for L-CAHASH(128)

(b) The average number of output bits changed for L-CAHASH(256)

Fig. 2. The obtained Hamming distance between digest of random messages and digest of their one bit changed

The Table 2 shows the maximum, the average and the minimum value of hamming distances.

Table 2. Representation of Hamming distances

Changes	L-CAHASH 128	L-CAHASH 256
Max	77	149.4000
Mean	63.6904	127.7250
Min	51.2000	103

Further, the one bit change in the input of the range of 1 MB files affects $\simeq$ 50% the change in the output digest. Then, as shown in these figures and tables, our suggested scheme is a good hash function, since for different inputs with a small change, the obtained output is completely different.

5.2 Statistical Tests

In this following subsection, our proposed hash function's randomness quality is studied and its results are showed, in order to bypass statistical attacks. Therefore, as convenient, a secure hash function's output should be statistically indistinguishable from a random function's output. For this manner, There exist a several tests batteries serving to evaluate the randomness of such algorithm, like DIEHARD test [20]. DIEHARD test contains a package of various statistical tests, where, each test has its own verifying tools. These tests are considered strong at checking the randomness up to an extreme level. Further, this latter tests data in specified format. Especially, the random bit sequence obtained from a generator should be firstly converted to the suitable binary format to the DIEHARD test batteries and also with a size that is higher than 10 MB. To achieve good results it checks the random numbers' p-value that is in the range $0.025 \prec p \prec 0.975$. Hence, for our approach experiments, our hash function has been generating many digests in a way to obtain more than 10Mb data stream. This stream is created using a counter mode scheme employing our proposed lightweight hash function on an initial random seed S to compute a suc-

Table 3. Diehard battery results

Test name	Number of P-value (L-CAHSH-128)	Number of P-value (L-CAHSH-256)	Interpretation
Diehard birthdays	0.99382527	0.77406832	Passed
Diehard operm5	0.20283047	0.52739809	Passed
Diehard rank 32 × 32	0.23375371	0.17826534	Passed
Diehard rank 6 × 8	0.74949096	0.12930466	Passed
Diehard bitstream	0.95263853	0.84140473	Passed
Diehard opso	0.81691189	0.02067294	Passed
Diehard oqso	0.25326072	0.42563854	Passed
Diehard dna	0.21382142	0.49945611	Passed
Diehard count 1s str	0.73899357	0.75133654	Passed
Diehard count1s byt	0.77171583	0.71192291	Passed
Diehard parking lot	0.31899023	0.66754904	Passed
Diehard 2d sphere	0.20588755	0.52336168	Passed
Diehard 3d sphere	0.98001779	0.50229101	Passed
Diehard squeeze	0.16315019	0.25205728	Passed
Diehard sums	0.03424488	0.94046284	Passed
Diehard runs	0.24986756	0.80808597	Passed
Diehard craps	0.88191265	0.92017252	Passed
Marsaglia tsang gcd	0.18635514	0.55037610	Passed
Sts monobit	0.98521085	0.83124060	Passed

cessive values L-CAHASH(S), L-CAHASH(S + 1),..., L-CAHASH(S + 163840) that are (128|256 − *bit*) length. The obtained outputs are concatenated to create the data stream. Thereafter, this produced stream is statistically analyzed using Diehard [20]. Afterwards, these final results are averaged and then reported in the Table 3. Hence, from the showed results, it is worth noting that the binary stream obtained using our proposed design has successfully passed all DIEHARD tests. Furthermore, our proposed function has a good randomness behavior and could be statistically indistinguishable from random function.

5.3 Our Proposed L-CAHASH Software Performance

The Table 4 shows our proposed L-CAHASH(128|256) software implementation performances comparing to the other known lightweight hash functions, namely PHOTON [13], QUARK [15] and GLUON [16]. L-CAHASH was turned on an Intel Core i5-34227, OS 64-bit, 1.8 Ghz processor with 4 GB RAM.

Our presented results shows that our proposed hash algorithm achieves a good cycle per byte. Further, it has satisfying performances using simple software implementations.

Table 4. Comparison between our hash function and others lightweight hash functions

Hash function	Hash output size (bit)	Cycle per byte (cpb)	Clock (GHz)
L-CAHASH	128	7031	1.80
L-CAHASH	256	10547	1.80
GLUON [16]	112	1951	2.66
U-QUARK [16]	128	43373	2.66
D-QUARK [16]	160	35103	2.66
S-QUARK [16]	224	25142	2.66
PHOTON [16]	80	1243	2.66

6 Conclusion

In the near future, the optical barcodes would be replaced by the RFID tags. Then, one of the principal concerns is to achieve security and privacy for these contexts. Accordingly, in this paper, a high randomness quality and easy hardware implementation new lightweight hash function based on cellular automata (L-CAHASH) has been proposed to provide security. The obtained results show that this new hash function meets the RFID tags' security requirement, in addition, the robustness and the efficiency of our suggested hash function were analyzed. In terms of future work, an extension of this suggested scheme is intended by providing authentication.

References

1. Coetzee, L., Eksteen, J.: The internet of things-promise for the future? an introduction. In: IST-Africa Conference Proceedings. IEEE (2011)
2. Jing, Q., Vasilakos, A.V., Wan, J., Lu, J., Qiu, D.: QiuSecurity of the internet of things: perspectives and challenges. Wireless Netw. **20**(8), 2481–2501 (2014)
3. Khedr, W.I.: SRFID: a hash-based security scheme for low cost RFID systems. Egypt. Inf. J. **14**(1), 89–98 (2013)
4. Kitsos, P. (ed.): Security in RFID and Sensor Networks. CRC Press, Boca Raton (2016)
5. Wolfram, S.: A New Kind of Science, vol. 5. Champaign, Wolfram media (2002)
6. Shin, S.-H., Kim, D.-H., Yoo, K.-Y.: A lightweight multi-user authentication scheme based on cellular automata in cloud environment. In: 1st International Conference on Cloud Networking (CLOUDNET), pp. 176–178. IEEE (2012)
7. Wolfram, S.: Cryptography with cellular automata. In: Williams, H.C. (ed.) CRYPTO 1985. LNCS, vol. 218, pp. 429–432. Springer, Heidelberg (1986). doi:10.1007/3-540-39799-X_32
8. Küçük, Ö.: Design and analysis of cryptographic hash functions. Leuven: Katholieke Universiteit Leuven (2012)
9. Poschmann, A.Y.: Lightweight Cryptography: Cryptographic Engineering for a Pervasive World (2009)
10. Bogdanov, A., Knudsen, L.R., Leander, G., Paar, C., Poschmann, A., Robshaw, M.J.B., Seurin, Y., Vikkelsoe, C.: PRESENT: an ultra-lightweight block cipher. In: Paillier, P., Verbauwhede, I. (eds.) CHES 2007. LNCS, vol. 4727, pp. 450–466. Springer, Heidelberg (2007). doi:10.1007/978-3-540-74735-2_31
11. Bertoni, G., Daemen, J., Peeters, M., Van Assche, G.: On the indifferentiability of the sponge construction. In: Smart, N. (ed.) EUROCRYPT 2008. LNCS, vol. 4965, pp. 181–197. Springer, Heidelberg (2008). doi:10.1007/978-3-540-78967-3_11
12. Kavun, E.B., Yalcin, T.: A lightweight implementation of Keccak hash function for radio-frequency identification applications. In: Ors Yalcin, S.B. (ed.) RFIDSec 2010. LNCS, vol. 6370, pp. 258–269. Springer, Heidelberg (2010). doi:10.1007/978-3-642-16822-2_20
13. Guo, J., Peyrin, T., Poschmann, A.: The PHOTON family of lightweight hash functions. In: Rogaway, P. (ed.) CRYPTO 2011. LNCS, vol. 6841, pp. 222–239. Springer, Heidelberg (2011). doi:10.1007/978-3-642-22792-9_13
14. Bogdanov, A., Knežević, M., Leander, G., Toz, D., Varıcı, K., Verbauwhede, I.: SPONGENT: a lightweight hash function. In: Preneel, B., Takagi, T. (eds.) CHES 2011. LNCS, vol. 6917, pp. 312–325. Springer, Heidelberg (2011). doi:10.1007/978-3-642-23951-9_21
15. Aumasson, J.P., Henzen, L., Meier, W., Naya-Plasencia, M.: Quark: a lightweight hash. J. Cryptol. **26**, 313–339 (2013)
16. Berger, T.P., D'Hayer, J., Marquet, K., Minier, M., Thomas, G.: The GLUON family: a lightweight hash function family based on FCSRs. In: Mitrokotsa, A., Vaudenay, S. (eds.) AFRICACRYPT 2012. LNCS, vol. 7374, pp. 306–323. Springer, Heidelberg (2012). doi:10.1007/978-3-642-31410-0_19
17. Mukundan, P.M., Manayankath, S., Srinivasan, C., Sethumadhavan, M.: Hash-One: a lightweight cryptographic hash function. In: IET Information Security (2016)

18. Kuila, S., Saha, D., Pal, M., Chowdhury, D.R.: CASH: cellular automata based parameterized hash. In: Chakraborty, R.S., Matyas, V., Schaumont, P. (eds.) SPACE 2014. LNCS, vol. 8804, pp. 59–75. Springer, Cham (2014). doi:10.1007/978-3-319-12060-7_5
19. Castroa, J.C.H., Sierrab, J.M., Sezneca, A., Izquierdoa, A., Ribagordaa, A.: The strict avalanche criterion randomness test. Math. Comput. Simul. **68**, 1–7 (2005)
20. Marsaglia, G.: Computer code DIEHARD http://stat.fsu.edu/pub/diehard/. Accessed 31 Jan 2017

Group Authentication with Fault Tolerance for Internet of Things

Otmane Elmouaatamid[1,2](✉), Mohamed Lahmer[1,2], and Mostafa Belkasmi[1,2]

[1] SIME Lab, ENSIAS, Mohamed V University, Rabat, Morocco
otmane.elmouaatamid@gmail.com, mohammed.lahmer@gmail.com,
m.belkasmi@um5s.net.ma

[2] My Ismail University, Meknes, Morocco

Abstract. With proliferation of the Internet of Things (IoT) applications, it is expected that 50 billion connected devices will be operating amongst us by 2020, so the normal authentication mechanism will be a big issue to handle to avoid causing a serious burden to server. As it is known, some devices could share the same characteristics such as the same geographical area, the same features. In this case, these devices could be in the same group and the group will be identify by an identity. Taking advantages from this mechanism, all devices can be authenticated at the same time using the group identity. Among group authentication issues are if a member device of the group cannot authenticate with the distributor of the group intentionally or unintentionally, the group loses its identity. This loss of identity causes the authentication failure of the other group devices. To solve this issue in IoT a fault tolerance scheme introduced for the group authentication architecture. Our algorithm of fault tolerance allows reconstructing the group authentication identity despite the lack of broken devices of the group. Indeed, reconstructing the group identity can be performed by using multi-secret sharing scheme based on an error correcting codes if a sufficient number of the group devices are available.

1 Introduction

Emerging technologies are turning the Internet of Things (IoT), into the Internet of Everything. The IoT brings to life a vision of the future where the more manual aspects of life can be automated so we can enjoy more meaningful living. Through widespread advancements in smart technologies, the time to a fully connected world is rapidly advancing. Internet of things becomes of utmost importance as it is almost involved in all our daily tasks. The development of IoT requires the use of new technologies which mean new challenges can arise. Security of exchanged data is one of these challenges that needs to be addressed. In order to ensure security of information in IoT, some security requirements such as authentication, confidentiality, and integrity have to be satisfied. Security threats to Internet of Things are not theoretical, they are already happening. Recent attacks like *the smart light bulb password leaks*, *hacks of Foscam baby*

E. Sabir et al. (Eds.): UNet 2017, LNCS 10542, pp. 299–307, 2017.
https://doi.org/10.1007/978-3-319-68179-5_26

monitors, *Belkin home automation systems*, and *hacks of smart cars systems*, are just the beginning. As the number of intelligent devices rises, the potential damage that could be caused by lack of security will continue to increase. Devices authentication is one of the most important security services in IoT application. But the unicast authentication communication from big amount devices will merge together in the network, and will cause serious burden to the server in particular at the level of energy consumption availability. Some devices have the same characteristics, such as having same features, being in the same place, working at the same time, etc. With group authentication mechanism [9], all devices can be authenticated with little signaling and calculation at the same time which reduce the network burden and save time. The group authentication is no longer a one-to-one type of authentication as most conventional devices' authentication schemes that have one prover and one verifier, but it is a many-to-many type of authentication that has multiple provers and multiple verifiers. During the process of group authentication, one or several devices of the group can be interrupted during the life cycle of the network. There are many causes of these failures ones that are intentionally or unintentionally like lacking in energy resources, damage to property, environmental interference, compromise of devices, etc. These failures will affect the overall operation of the authentication of the group. The fault tolerance [7,10] is then defined as the ability of group members to continue to function normally without interruption even after the malfunction of one or more of its devices. In this paper, we describe the security of group authentication. Then, we provide a group authentication procedures for the IoT and we explain the different steps to integrate fault tolerance into a group authentication architecture which is based on the aspect of multi-secret sharing scheme based on an error correcting codes [11]. The remainder of this paper is organized as follows. In Sect. 2, we provide an overview of the related work. Section 3 gives the procedures and a background on group authentication. Section 4 presents a detailed description of fault tolerance scheme based bounded distance decoding of linear codes. Finally, we give a brief conclusion and present some perspectives.

2 Related Work

Harn [1] introduces a new type of authentication called group authentication, which authenticates all users belonging to the same group. But they include polynomial operations so it becomes more complicated. As well as reuse of token is done so it becomes more risky for alteration of data. In [2], Mahalle and Jadhav proposed a group authentication using paillier threshold cryptography in which RSA algorithm is used to generate keys. As well as Shamir's secret sharing is used to distribute a secret to all members [5]. In this scheme, Group Manager (GM) plays a vital role in communication. GM has to stay active all the time between communication. Shamir's secret sharing [3] proposes to break data D into n parts in such a way that D is easily constructible from k pieces. There are two main requirements for this scheme: the first is when we have information of any t or more than t parts can recreate the master secret s; The second is with information of less than t parts can't reveal any information about the master secret s. This is called as $(t, n) - threshold$ scheme. In this reference paper [4], key management is considered. When we want to keep data secure, we encrypt it. But when we want to keep key secure, we keep it at a secure location. But this not optimal: an unusual situation can make the information inaccessible.

3 Group Authentication in IoT

Group authentication is a sort of authentication technologies [1] with which a group of users or devices can be authenticated together at the same time. Instead of authenticating a number of terminals of a group one by one, group authentication mechanism treats these devices in the group as a whole, and authenticates them together. Each group has a unique identifier, and a distributor, which can be called as group distributor, cluster distributor, etc.

Group authentication scenario description: Group authentication consists of three steps as follows:

The first step: Devices should be authenticated whether it belong to a specific group. This can be implemented through the proprietary authentication technology in a group, such as IEEE 802.15.4, ZigBee, Bluetooth or any other protocol of Communication/Transport layer.

The second step: A mutual authentication should be made between a specific network entity, and a group distributor who is eligible to delegate all devices in the group.

The third step: An authentication between network server and IoT cloud services will establish [8].

After the success of the authentication, devices and network entity can generate separated session keys individually if there is some demand to make individual communication between network entity and each device.

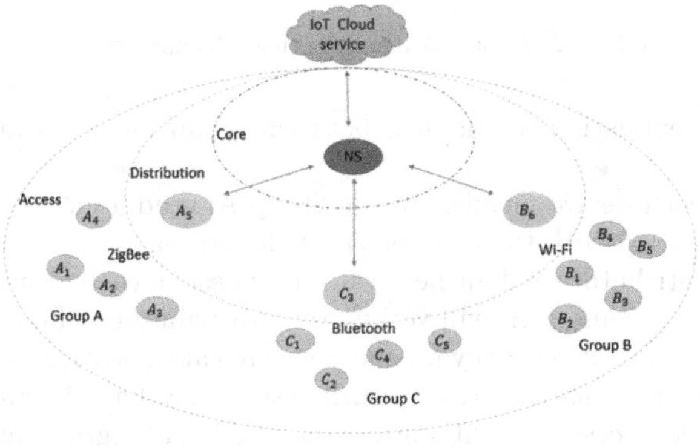

Fig. 1. Group authentication in hierarchical network for IoT

The Fig. 1 present a Group Authentication Architecture for IoT, there is detailed architecture description as following in Fig. 1. There are three Communication/Transport layer protocols IEEE 802.15.4, ZigBee, and Bluetooth. In each area of this protocols there are devices inside a given group. for example, in the group A devices communicate via Zigbee protocol: Where A_1, A_2, A_3, A_4 represent the network access and A_5 represent the group distributor. All devices in the group A can communicate with each other. Furthermore, the distributor A_5 of group A is able to communicate with others Groups distributors and with network entity directly via other protocols e.g. WiMax, LTE, GPR. etc. Network entity will stock the group information, such as identifiers, root keys used for all devices inside the group. Network entity is also in charge of for generating group authentication vector. The scenario is illustrated above.

Group Authentication procedures: As mentioned in the beginning of this section the group authentication procedure can be divided into three steps as shown in Fig. 2.

In the first step authentication between group members and the distributor of the group, the second step authentication will be performed between the group distributor and network server and the finally step is the authentication between network server and IoT cloud services.

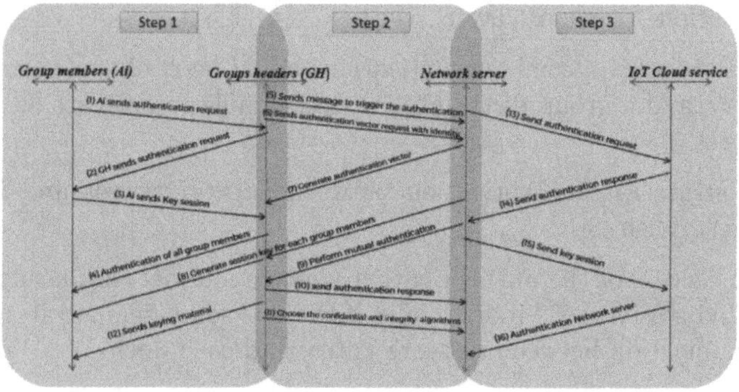

Fig. 2. Group Authentication Mechanism

- Step 1: Authentication mechanism between group members and the group distributor.
    1. At first each device member of the group Ai send a message to establish authentication with the distributor of the group.
    2. Group distributor send authentication request to each group member Ai.
    3. Each group member Ai will verify group distributor at first. If successful, Ai will generate session key for the communication with group distributor, and sends response mentioned such session key back to group distributor. If not success, the authentication is failed and group authentication procedure will be abort.

4. Group Header authenticate each group member Ai through the response message and record the authentication result in a mapping table.

   If all member of the group success to authenticate by the group distributor the group authentication will past to second step.

- Step 2: Authentication mechanism between each group distributor and the network server.

5. Group distributor sends message to network server to establish the authentication outside the group.
6. For now, the distributor of the group sends authentication vector request to network server with identity.
7. Network Server will generate authentication vector according to group distributor identity.
8. What is more, network server should be able to recognize that a group authentication is being performing based on group distributor identity and will generate session key for each group members. Network Server will send such authentication vector and session keys together back to group distributor.
9. Network server will perform mutual authentication with group distributor.
10. Group distributor authenticate group members and send authentication response back to network server.
11. Network server authenticates group distributor. If successful, it can be considered that group distributor and all group devices is authenticated successfully.
12. Group distributor will communicate with network server to choose the confidential and integrity protection algorithms. After that, group distributor will send keying material, selected algorithms to each group member.

   After these two steps, each device of the group is authenticated with network server.

- Step 3: authentication mechanism between the network server and IoT cloud service.

13. Network server sends a message to trigger authentication with the IoT cloud service at first.
14. Cloud service sends authentication request to the network server.
15. Network server verifies cloud server at first. If success, network server will generate session key for the communication with IoT cloud service.
16. IoT cloud service authenticates the network server.

4 Fault Tolerance Scheme Based Error Correcting Codes

In the third section, we presented the procedures and steps of Group Authentication. If every device is functioning then the authentication will be successful. Otherwise, if device member of the group breakdown, the other group members become unable to authenticate. Because a part of the identity of the group is missing, so we have proposed a fault tolerance scheme based on bounded distance decoding of linear codes [5,6]. In this section, we present how to reconstruct the identity of the group despite the absence of a number (threshold) of the members of the group which they have a breakdown. We proposed an algorithm based on multisecret sharing schemes [12,13]. The principe of this algorithm is as follows: It allows a secret known from a member call the group distributor to be distributed to n members of the group. The secret is unknown to each member but some special subsets of the network called the coalition of group members, can distribute the secret throughout the network. Because of this secret, we can construct the identity of the group. If the coalition of the group authentication did not happened we can reconstruct the group identity by the reconstruction of the secret based a $(m, n) - threshold$ system such that $m > 1$ member of the group can reconstruct the secret but $m - 1$ cannot.

4.1 Sharing Secret Key Scheme Based on an Error Correcting Code

In this section we present a group authentication sharing secret key scheme based on an error correcting code where secret key reconstruction is made by using bounded distance decoding of the code.

Error correcting code. Let $C(n, k)$ be a linear code over the finite filed of order q denote by F_q is a subspace in $(F_q)^n$ with q a prime power.

Where k is the dimension of the code and n is length of C and the dual code of C is defined to be the set of those vectors $(F_q)^n$ which are orthogonal to every codeword of C. It is denoted by $C^\perp$. The code $C^\perp(n, n-k)$ is a linear code. A generator matrix G for a linear code C is a $k * n$ matrix for which the rows are a basis of C. A parity-check matrix for a linear code C is a generator matrix for its dual code $C^\perp$. It is denoted by H.

The code C contains q^k codewords and can be used to communicate any one of q^k distinct messages.

We encode the message vector $x = x_1, x_2, \ldots, x_k$ as $(x_1, x_2, \ldots, x_k)G$; hence $C = \{uG | u \in (Fq)^k\}$. The map $u \to uG$ sends the vector space q^k onto a k-dimensional subspace of $(F_q)^n$.

Suppose that C is an $[n, k]$-linear code over F_q and a is any vector in $(F_q)^n$. Then the set $a + C$ defined by $a + C = \{a + x | x \in C\}$ is called a coset of C [6]. Suppose that a codeword x is sent, and that a vector y is received. Then $e = y - x (x, y \in (F_q)^n)$, $e = e_1, e_2, \ldots, e_n$, is an error vector.

Theorem. Suppose $C(n, k)$ is a linear code over F_q.

1. *Every vector of $(F_q)^n$ is in some coset of C,*
2. *Every coset contains exactly q^k vectors,*
3. *Two cosets either are disjoint or coincide,*
4. *C contains exactly q^{n-k} cosets.*

Proof: In this scheme, the key secret is recovered due to the minimal access sets. The minimal access sets consist of the vectors as $c + h$ with the support of h contained in the support of c and h of weight t.

There are n members participants in every set, as many as coordinates of C. The set of participants that is recovering the secret is also the support of these minimal access sets.

The number of the participants in each of minimal access set is equal to the weight of $c + h$.

This scheme satisfied the hypothesis of theorem above is also a $(d - t, n)$-threshold secret sharing scheme, where d is the minimum distance and t the error-correcting capacity of C.

4.2 Fault Tolerance Scheme Description

This scheme permit to reconstruct the secret key based on linear codes with a known bounded distance [14].

We consider a code $C(n, k)$ over F_q which is a t-error correcting code.

We construct now this scheme based on code C.

Let $(F_q)^k$ be the key space and $(F_q)^n$ be the share space. The distributor uses a share function $f : (F_q)^k \to (F_q)^n$ to compute the shares among the n members of the group. The sharing function is chosen as $f(s) = sG + h$, where $s = (s_1, \ldots, s_k) \in (F_q)^k$ is the secret and G is a $k * n$ generator matrix over $(Fq)^n$ with rank k. Suppose for convenience $s \neq 0$. Thus $c = sG$ is a nonzero codeword of the code C.

The translation vector h is chosen by the leader to satisfy the following requirements:

- the weight of h is t.
- the support of h is included in the support of c.

Then the n members recover the key secret by combining their shares as follows:

- get $c + h$ by collecting its n coordinates (shares)
- get c from $c + h$ by decoding
- get the secret s from c by solving the linear system $sG = c$ of rank k.

This scheme satisfied the hypothesis of the theorem is also a $(m = d - t, n)$-threshold secret key sharing scheme, where d is the minimum distance and t the error-correcting capacity of C.

Application Example

In our architecture we consider the group A consist of $n = 5$ members participants of group authentication, the distributor of the group and other four members.

Let $C(5, 2)$ be a binary linear code with generator matrix

$$G = \begin{pmatrix} 1\,0\,1\,0\,1 \\ 0\,1\,0\,1\,1 \end{pmatrix} \tag{1}$$

With a minimum distance $d = 3$ and the code C corrects a single error $t = 1$. Now we can construct a $(2, 5)$ threshold scheme based on C by using bounded distance decoding and examine some properties of this scheme.

$$C = 00000, 10101, 01011, 11110$$

and the cosets of C are:

$$\begin{aligned}
00000 + C &= 00000, 10101, 01011, 11110 \\
10000 + C &= 10000, 00101, 11011, 01110 \\
01000 + C &= 01000, 11101, 00011, 10110 \\
00100 + C &= 00100, 10001, 01111, 11010 \\
00010 + C &= 00010, 10111, 01001, 11100 \\
00001 + C &= 00001, 10100, 01010, 11111 \\
11000 + C &= 11000, 01101, 10011, 00110 \\
10010 + C &= 10010, 00111, 11001, 01100
\end{aligned}$$

Let the message vector 10 be the key secret s. So, the sharing function will be as:

$$\begin{aligned}
f(s) &= sG + h \\
&= (10) * \begin{pmatrix} 1\,0\,1\,0\,1 \\ 0\,1\,0\,1\,1 \end{pmatrix} + (10000) \\
&= (10101) + (10000) \\
&= (00101)
\end{aligned} \tag{2}$$

We get $c = sG = (10101)$ from (00101) by decoding. Then we get the key secret s from c by solving the linear system $sG = c$ of rank $k = 2$: $(s1, s2)$.

$$\begin{pmatrix} 1\,0\,1\,0\,1 \\ 0\,1\,0\,1\,1 \end{pmatrix} = (10101) \tag{3}$$

Therefore we recover the key secret as $s = (10)$.

5 Conclusion and Perspective

In this paper, we proposed a new solution to secure group authentication in IoT with fault tolerance. Our solution is based on the fact that some users can share some similarities such as they can belong to the same area or launch a task at the same time. Taking advantage of these similarities users can form a group and get authenticated at the same time. Our scheme does not only establish a simultaneous authentication of all the members belonging to the same group, but also allows them to be authenticated even if one member or more encounter a problem this can be achieved by using a fault tolerance scheme based on an error correcting codes.

As future work we intend to integrated a key pre-distribution technique which is based on Balanced Incomplete Block Design (BIBD) to ensure the fault tolerance of group authentication in IoT environment.

References

1. Harn, L.: Group authentication. IEEE Trans. Comput. **62**(9), 1893–1898 (2013)
2. Mahalle, P., Jadhav, P.: Group authentication using Pailliar threshold cryptography. IEEE ISBN 978-1-4673-5999-3
3. Harari, S.: Application des codes correcteurs au partage du secret. Traitement du Sig. **4**(4), 353–356 (1987)
4. Liu, Y., Cheng, C.: An improved authenticated group key transfer protocol based on secret sharing. IEEE Trans. Comput. **62**(11), 2335–2336 (2013)
5. Csirmaz, L.: Gruppen secret sharing or how to share several secrets if you must? Mathematica Slovaca **63**(6), 1391–1402 (2013)
6. Hill, R.: A First Course in Coding Theory. Oxford University, Oxford (1986)
7. Geeta, D.D., Nalini, N., Biradar, R.C.: Fault tolerance in wireless sensor network using hand-off and dynamic power adjustment approach. J. Netw. Comput. Appl. **36**(4), 1174–1185 (2013)
8. Kalra, S., Sood, S.K.: Secure authentication scheme for IoT and cloud servers. Pervasive Mob. Comput. **24**, 210–223 (2015)
9. Sakarindr, P., Ansari, N.: Survey of security services on group communications. IET Inf. Secur. **4**(4), 258–272 (2010)
10. Anurag, D., Bandyopadhyay, S.: Achieving fault tolerance and network depth in hierarchical wireless sensor networks. In: International Conference on Communications Systems and Telecommunications (2008)
11. MacWilliams, F.J., Sloane, N.J.A.: The Theory of Error-Correcting Codes. North Holland, Amsterdam (1977)
12. Massey, J.L.: Minimal codewords and secret sharing. In: Proceedings of the 6th Joint Swedish-Russian International Workshop on Information Theory, pp. 276–279 (1993)
13. Ding, C., Kohel, D.R., Ling, S.: Secret-sharing with a class of ternary codes. Theor. Comput. Sci. **246**(1–2), 285–298 (2000)
14. Bulygin, S., Pellikaan, R.: Bounded distance decoding of linear error-correcting codes with Grbner bases. J. Symbolic Comput. **44**(12), 1626–1643 (2009)

Fully Distributed Indexing over a Distributed Hash Table

Simon Désaulniers[2(✉)], Adrien Béraud[1], Alexandre Blondin Massé[2], and Nicolas Reynaud[1,2]

[1] Savoir-Faire-Linux, 7275, rue Saint-Urbain, Bureau 200, Montréal, QC H2R 2Y5, Canada
[2] Département d'informatique, Université du Québec à Montréal, Case postale 8888, succursale Centre-Ville, Montréal, QC H3C 3P8, Canada
desaulniers.simon@courrier.uqam.ca

GPG Key Fingerprint: 70B9 F71B 74C9 553D 01A1 A0EF 824A 8B97 F97E 4B08

Abstract. Real-time communication, as well as simple data and file sharing motivates relevant research in network design nowadays. While centralized structures are generally favored over distributed ones for sake of simplicity, a considerable amount of literature has been devoted to the latter. In particular, the problem of distributed indexing is not trivial, and has been addressed by extending classical data structures such as tries, kd-trees. However, all proposed solutions seem to assume that there is a central and unique entity handling the indexing. In this paper, we propose a fully distributed indexing strategy by extending a data structure called prefix hash tree (PHT). More precisely, in this strategy, each node is part of the distributed network and participates in maintaining the distributed index. Our ideas have been implemented in a freely available framework called OpenDHT.

1 Introduction

Since the Internet has become the main foundation of large scale communications, various logical network designs lying on top of this huge network have reached a state of standard. As such, there are networks which rely on a central point of authority providing lower concern complexity when designing client end-user applications. However, those systems lack the ability to scale, they are more vulnerable to straightforward denial of service attacks and have power over the client nodes communication capability. All of these concerns can be avoided or mitigated by using a distributed network design. Indeed, distributed networks have no central authority over a subset of nodes and no central point of failure, and in general, these systems can also easily recover from node failures.

Distributed Hash Tables (DHT) [1,7] are scalable peer-to-peer storage systems providing a simple interface based on the two canonical get/put operations. DHTs are used in a number of applications today where load distribution is an important factor. Those systems are scalable in the sense that they can sustain

E. Sabir et al. (Eds.): UNet 2017, LNCS 10542, pp. 308–318, 2017.
https://doi.org/10.1007/978-3-319-68179-5_27

growing participant load by automatically accommodating for that growth. More precisely, the requests resolution grows logarithmically in the number of nodes [1]. This quality is what makes this type of system of great interest today considering the growing number of participating devices in many networks. Applications include file sharing [2], VoIP [9], large scale website load distribution [12] and many others.

When the only supported operations are `get` and `put`, the implementation of DHTs is straightforward. However, it becomes more involved when other more complex operations have to be supported.

In [4], the authors describe a data structure called *range search tree*, which allows efficient range queries in a fully distributed manner. An alternative data structure called *distributed segment tree* was also considered in [11] to support range queries as well as cover queries. Similarly, partial queries, *i.e.* queries for which the information is incomplete, can be efficiently supported by organizing the data hierarchically [5]. The authors also showed that their strategy is viable in realistic contexts by illustrating it on a bibliographic database.

All kind of queries mentioned in the previous paragraph arise in natural contexts and in most storage access applications, which can potentially include:

- *A distributed media storage* in which access for a subset of media entries based on the name of the author is needed and may be partial (non-exact). Obviously, this use case extends to file searching in general;
- *Distributed scientific computing system* where discovery of resources is based on a parameter being within a certain range;
- *A distributed profile directory* where you obviously search for profiles by first name, last name, city, etc.;

The authors of [8] propose a data structure, called a *prefix hash tree* (PHT), for building an index over a distributed hash table. Their model provides a simple interface for performing "insert" and "lookup" operations on the distributed index. Similarly in [13], the authors use the ideas of the PHT and focus on multidimensional keys aspect by extending the well-known kd-tree data structure. They linearize the keys using traditional projections, following a *space filling curve* like the Z-curve. However, in both cases, very few details are given about the actual implementation and suggest that the indexing data structure is a *centralized* entity sitting on a distributed hash table, *i.e.* that the index itself is not maintained asynchronously by multiple nodes.

Our main contribution consists in proposing an augmented model of the PHT [8] in a fully distributed manner, *i.e* in which the index lies on the DHT and is maintained by the participants performing operations on it. Our construction is inspired from the Kademlia [7] protocol and is freely available as a framework called OpenDHT [10]. We also discuss strategies that were designed to improve significantly the overall efficiency of the basic operations.

2 Motivations

Very few end-user communication applications guarantee complete privacy to their users. In practice, all data about users and their interaction within their personal network is stored in some central database and can be retrieved by anyone with access. In most cases, even the files and messages exchanged between users are not encrypted. Some applications like Signal, a messaging solution, makes a step in addressing these matters, by offering end-to-end and perfect secure encryption of the *content* exchanged. However, it is not possible to hide the *metadata* (who talked with whom, when, how frequently, etc.) [3].

With these concerns in mind, a software called Ring [9] is being under heavy development and aims to offer a completely secured exchange environment. One of the main concerns of the developers is their users' privacy. In particular, while it is virtually impossible to hide all metadata about communications between two users in a given public network, there is a concern about letting the users know exactly what information they share is public or private. More precisely, Ring is a distributed peer-to-peer communication software for chat and VoIP. It uses standard and secure protocols such as TLS (Transport Layer Security) and SRTP (Secure Real-time Transport Protocol). Ring is distributed since all users are part of a DHT network and can establish communication between each other after completing negotiations for NAT traversal using the ICE [6] (Interactive Connectivity Establishment) protocol. This software stands out from the other applications in the sense that no central server is needed and, therefore significantly mitigating privacy concerns associated with threats coming from central authorities.

A diagram illustrating the logical components of Ring is depicted in Fig. 1. The main component we are interested in here is called OpenDHT [10]. This

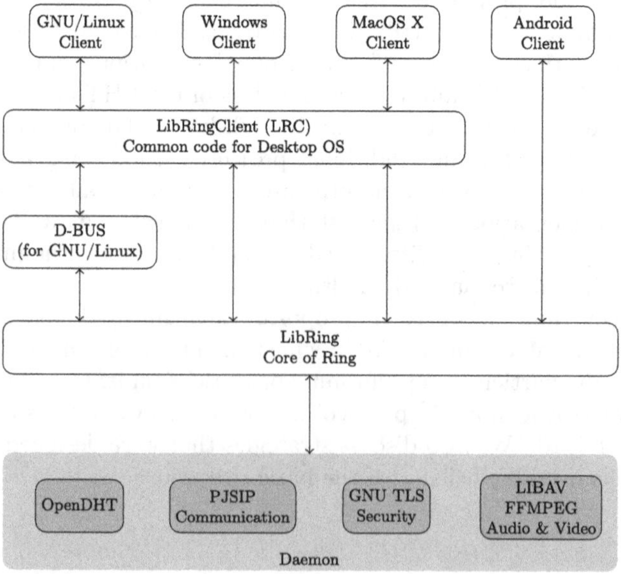

Fig. 1. Architecture of the Ring project.

distributed hash table is a `C++11` implementation of the Kademlia [7] protocol with some novel features such as a `listen(key)` operation for on-going updates about a certain key, a subset of SQL syntax queries capability and a complete cryptographic layer available on its API.

One subproblem encountered during the development of Ring has been the conception of a solution for username directory which is being achieved using a blockchain system called Ethereum [14]. Moreover, a distributed directory for user profiles and a distributed index for DHT nodes proxy discovery is being resolved with the help of the PHT enrichment discussed in the following sections.

3 Prefix Hash Tree

We now recall from [8] the main ideas around a prefix hash tree data structure (PHT). A PHT is a binary tree, more specifically a *trie*. Every leaf is associated with a unique path down the trie which yields a unique *label*. A label is a prefix of a key $k \in \{0,1\}^D$ for some $D \in \mathbb{N}$. Data is stored only in leaf nodes in such a way that the label of the leaf is a prefix of the key to the stored data. The following constraints must also be satisfied [8]:

1. (*Universal prefix*) Each node has either 0 or 2 children;
2. (*Key storage*) A key K is stored at a leaf node whose label is a prefix of K;
3. (*Split*) Each leaf node stores atmost B keys;
4. (*Merge*) Each internal node contains at least $B+1$ keys in each of its sub-tree.

For sake of simplicity, we assume that the values stored in the data structure are equal to their corresponding key even though in practice, stored elements can be arbitrary complex data.

Example 1. Figure 2 shows potential content of an instance of a PHT. The key `000110` is stored in the leaf labelled `000` and so are all other keys having `000` as a prefix. In particular, the two longest labels of length 3 are `000` and `001` with one of the associated leaves empty (no stored data).

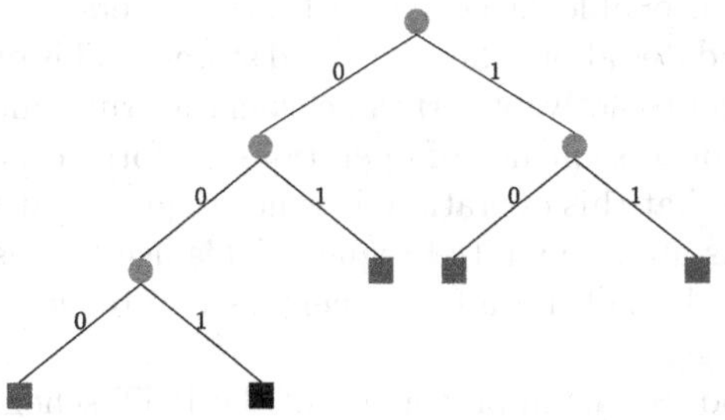

Leaf label	Key
000*	000000 000001 000011 000110 000111
001*	
01*	010000 010110
10*	100011 101011 101010
11*	111011 111110

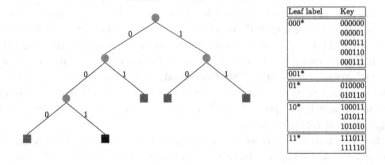

Fig. 2. A PHT storing 12 pairs key-value.

From the picture, we must have $B \geq 5$. Moreover, the labels 000, 01 and 001 all have 0 as prefix. Therefore, the total amount of keys indexed under prefix 0 can explain the expansion of the left part of the tree. As a consequence, depending on the distribution of the keys, the data structure may become unbalanced, which might have a critical impact on performances.

In its most basic form, the PHT data structure support at least two simple operations, called `lookup(key)` and `insert(key, value)`, which respectively return a view on the data stored in a given node and insert some value with given key. In order not to overload access to higher nodes in the PHT, a binary search scheme is used to find the correct node each time a "lookup" operation is performed. See [8] for the original algorithms and performance analysis.

4 Distributed Indexing

The PHT layer sits on three layers: cryptographic algorithms, the distributed hash table and the transport layer. OpenDHT uses UDP as transport layer. The cryptographic layer will mostly expose asymmetric encryption algorithms which is appropriate to compensate for the untrusted public space in the DHT network.

Indeed, it is worth mentioning OpenDHT is designed for public use. Therefore, significant trade-offs are implied in its design in order to keep a viable and consistent overall behavior. One important design choice that was made consists in preventing anyone to be able to remove values. Instead, a time expiration mechanism was introduced, which implies that all values are stored on the DHT for a limited amount of time. The value lifetime is a key feature used in the PHT layer: When a value has been stored on the DHT, it can only be removed when it expires, according to its time duration specification.

As mentioned before, OpenDHT is an implementation of the Kademlia protocol [7]. Therefore, it uses the XOR metric to perform searches on the key space. In OpenDHT the eight closest nodes to a hash target will be used to perform fundamental operations. At any given time, when some nodes in the eight closest nodes leave, others will take their place as implied by the XOR metric. OpenDHT also features data maintenance to ensure that any content is always available, even when the network topology is significantly modified.

The `listen(key)` operation enables a peer to ask other peers closest to a given hash to yield on-going updates about the associated storage. This operation is used in the PHT layer in order to actively perform elementary rules mentioned in Sect. 3. Figure 3 shows a typical sequence of operations performed according to a "listen" operation. Notice that this operation does not require that the peer A instantiates any further calls after the initial request. This usually last thirty seconds, upon which the *peer A* shall initiate another "listen" request to keep being updated on further changes.

We are now ready to introduce our improvement of the PHT scheme introduced in [8]. Let D be the length of the PHT keys. A *canary* is a value stored in the DHT for the purpose of identifying a node as part of the indexing structure.

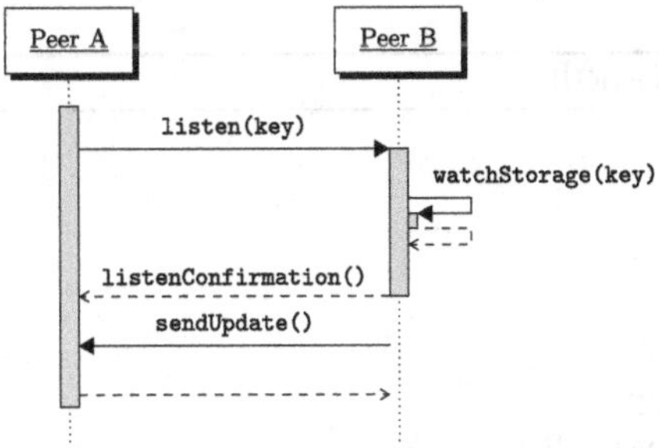

Fig. 3. Listen operation chronological sequence.

Also, let $\ell \in \{0,1\}^m$ be a label with $m \leq D$. If DHT_LOOKUP(ℓ) succeeds and yields a set of values containing at least one canary, then the node labeled ℓ is called a *PHT node*. In particular, it is called a *leaf node* if there is no PHT node either labelled $\ell \cdot 0$ or $\ell \cdot 1$, where $\cdot$ denotes the concatenation, and it is called an *internal node* otherwise.

Based on the definitions introduced in the previous paragraph, algorithms for performing "lookup" and "insert" operations differ from the original algorithms from [8]. Algorithm 1 describes the steps performed for the "lookup" operation. Note that $\text{Pref}_\alpha(k)$ denotes the prefix of length α of a key k. First, two DHT lookups have to be performed to identify the type of the node, which is consistent with how leaf nodes have been defined. Also, it is worth mentioning that the formal definition of a leaf node suggests to perform a third DHT lookup on the other child of the target node. However, this third lookup is not necessary as the algorithm for performing insertion will assure that either both nodes yield a canary or none of them does.

Next, Algorithm 2 describes in details the "insert" operation, where B is the maximal number of values per leaf. Also, it is important to notice that the resulting "leaf" from the call to PHT-LOOKUP is not final. Indeed, by Rule 4, the definition of a leaf node and inherited properties from OpenDHT, merging and splitting PHT nodes is an on-going process which consists in selecting the appropriate node to consider as a leaf based on the number of values yielded by the underlying DHT-LOOKUP operation. We use the canonical "listen" operation from OpenDHT to execute the algorithm again (Line 19) when new PHT node are created below. In addition to inserting the value in the index, the algorithm has to complete the task of maintaining canary values on the network as they are simple DHT values which also expire.

Such strategy for performing concurrently those operations can raise questions about data consistency. The first scenario one can consider when thinking of data inconsistency is data query failure during split and merge operations. The "listen" operation provided by OpenDHT assures high reliability since it is designed to provide quick and light updates. Therefore, when split (or merge) occurs, other indexing participant will quickly react and sync data in new leaves. The time for completing such operation for one index entry is less than a second. Optimizations leading to even lower response time are discussed in Sect. 5.

Algorithm 1. PHT-LOOKUP

```
Input: A key K
Output: leaf(K)
lo ← 0
hi ← D
while lo ≤ hi do
    mid ← (lo + hi)/2
    node ← DHT-LOOKUP(Pref_mid(K))
    if mid < D then
        node_child ← DHT-LOOKUP(Pref_mid+1(K))
    end if
                                ▷ The type is deduced from the presence of a canary
    node_type ← NODE-TYPE(node.values(), node_child.values())
    if node_type = "leaf" then
        return node
    else
        if node_type = "internal" then
            lo ← mid + 1
        else
            hi ← mid − 1
        end if
    end if
end while
```

Algorithm 2. PHT-INSERT

```
Input: A key K and a value v
leaf ← PHT-LOOKUP(K)                          ▷ Might not be a leaf at the end
β ← LENGTH(leaf.prefix())
if COUNT(leaf.values()) < B then
    parent ← DHT-LOOKUP(Pref_β−1(K))
    sibling ← DHT-LOOKUP(Pref_β(K) ⊕ 0x00...1)
    count ← COUNT(leaf.values() + parent.values() + sibling.values())
    if count < B then                                           ▷ Merge
        ℓ ← β − 1
    else                                                        ▷ Straight insert
        ℓ ← β
    end if
else                                                            ▷ Split and insert
    ℓ ← β + 1
end if
DHT-INSERT(Pref_ℓ(K), v)
UPDATE-CANARY(Pref_ℓ(K))
DHT-LISTEN(Pref_ℓ+1(K), PHT-INSERT, K, v)     ▷ Listen for new canaries below
```

Algorithm 3. UPDATE-CANARY

function UPDATE-CANARY(p: word)
    DHT-INSERT(p, $canary$) ▷ Update canary in leaf
    DHT-INSERT($p \oplus 0 \times 00\ldots1, canary$) ▷ Update canary in sibling
    $x \leftarrow$ RAND(0, 1)
    if $x \leq P(p)$ **then** ▷ Probability of updating the parent
        UPDATE-CANARY(SHIFTRIGHT(p, 1)) ▷ Bit shift yields the parent's prefix
    end if
end function

To conclude this section, we describe in details the strategy used to maintain canary values in Algorithm 3. If the data was stored in a centralized database, this step would be straightforward. However, in the distributed case, since different nodes maintain the PHT structure, and since data can expire—in particular canaries—additional care must be taken. We propose a strategy that is very simple to implement and which provides a reasonable guarantee that all canaries are present at all time, at least in the case where the PHT structure is not too unbalanced.

Assume that a call to UPDATE-CANARY() is done for some prefix p. Then we let $P(p)$ be the probability of updating the parent of p. There are two unwanted scenarios that can occur when recursively updating the parent this way:

(i) The root of the PHT, or some internal nodes are not up-to-date;
(ii) The root of the PHT, and some internal nodes, are updated too often.

For instance, if we set $P(p) = 1$, then Scenario (i) never occurs, but the root would be updated as many times as half the number of nodes (a binary tree of n nodes might contain up to $(n+1)/2$ leaves), which could easily overload it. Obviously, setting $P(p) = 0$ would be worst: Scenario (ii) would never occur, but the PHT would completely disappear. Therefore, it is quite intuitive to set $P(p)$ close to 1. We explore two strategies for handling the updates. For this purpose, let R be the number of times the root is updated.

A first interesting candidate is $P(p) = 1/2$ or a value slightly larger than $1/2$. If the PHT data structure is a perfectly balanced tree, then the probability of not updating the root is

$$P(R = 0) = (1 - P(p)^d)^{2^d} \to 0,$$

where d is the current depth of the PHT. Similarly, the probability of updating the root too often is also small in the perfectly balanced case since $R \sim$ BINOMIAL$(2^d, P(p)^d)$, so that

$$E[R] = 2^d \times P(p)^d = 2^d \cdot \frac{1}{2^d} = 1.$$

Another interesting strategy consists in setting a probability dependent on the actual depth (or prefix length), such as $P(p) = 1 - 1/2^{|p|+a}$, where $|p|$ is the length of the prefix p and $a \geq 0$ is some integer parameter. Let K be the set of prefixes that trigger an initial call to UPDATE-CANARY. Then

$$P(\text{not updating the root with prefix } p) = 1 - \prod_{i=1}^{|p|} P(\text{Pref}_i(p))$$

and

$$\begin{aligned} P(R=0) &= \prod_{p \in K} P(\text{not updating the root with prefix } p) \\ &= \prod_{p \in K} \left(1 - \prod_{i=1}^{|p|} P(\text{Pref}_i(p))\right) \\ &\leq 1 - \prod_{i=1}^{D} \left(1 - \frac{1}{2^{i+a}}\right), \end{aligned}$$

the worst case being when there is a single key at depth D. The values of this upper bound can be found in Table 1, with respect to the value of the parameter a and by setting $D = 160$.

Table 1. Upper bound for the probability $P(R = 0)$.

a	0	1	2	3	4	5	6	7
$P(R=0) \leq$	0.7113	0.4225	0.2299	0.1199	0.0613	0.0310	0.0156	0.0078

However, if a is too large, then the nodes close to the root (including the root itself) are updated too often, so that this second scenario can also be problematic. In the future, we intend to study further what would be best to handle the canaries updating and, in particular, what information about the network should be known or estimated in order to control both situations.

5 Optimizations

Our algorithm performing insertion is autonomous in that when a new leaf appears below the node on which a value was first inserted, the old values are automatically "moved" on the new leaf. However, as mentioned by [8], naive implementation of Rule 3 can produce unwanted behavior such as splitting nodes continuously down to the end of the trie. Such scenario can occur if, for instance, B values share a same long prefix of their respective keys. In order to avoid such complications we propose two optimizations. First, double values counting should be avoided when identifying the type of the node based on the number of values yielded by a DHT "lookup". Secondly, splitting should imply the computation of the longest common prefix between all values already present on the leaf. This prefix indicates the number of PHT nodes to mark with a canary. The participant performing the split shall be the one creating this branch of PHT nodes from bottom to top so that other listening participants shall perform a single PHT-INSERT on the appropriate node. Figure 4 illustrates this process. Note that in this figure, canary update of each siblings of the respective leafs labelled $p_\ell, p_{\ell-1}, \ldots, p_{\ell-i}, \ldots, p_{\ell_0+1}$ is implied. This is needed as per Rule 1.

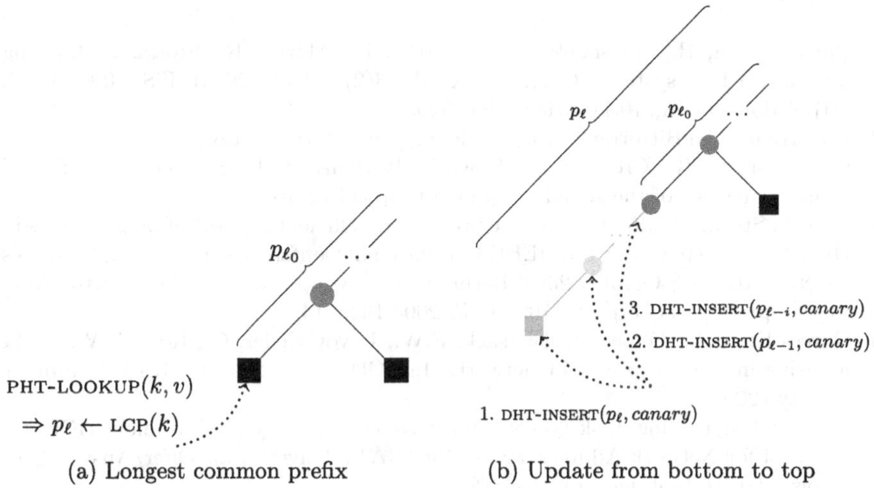

Fig. 4. Optimization: split down the trie

In order to provide further enhancements, we propose using a local cache for each instance of indexing participant. Then, subsequent operations in a same region in the tree will benefit from information gathered from previous operations. Algorithms 1 and 2 will use and maintain this cache such that a "lookup" will adjust initial values for *lo* and *hi* variables before commencing.

6 Conclusion

We have proposed a way of maintaining the trie data structure in a distributed manner and according to specific rules inspired by the initial authors of a data structure called PHT. The indexation is assumed to be performed by multiple nodes simultaneously and assures good efficiency and consistency in case that data set is balanced.

Our implementation of our solution is currently still under development. In particular, we are finalizing writing on range query concerns.

In the future, we will provide a more advanced analysis of this strategy in extreme cases such as strongly unbalanced data set. Another angle to address this problem is to remap the data according to a relevant distribution (like Zipfian as suggested by [8]) such that resulting insertions and lookups occur in a mostly balanced space. Our future work to provide public Ring profiles indexation could require such a strategy. Finally, we plan on providing test and benchmark results in order to support our argumentation on efficiency and data consistency. We hope that our contribution generates more interest and development in the field of distributed systems.

References

1. Balakrishnan, H., Kaashoek, M.F., Karger, D., Morris, R., Stoica, I.: Looking up data in P2P systems. Commun. ACM **46**(2), 43–48 (2003). ISSN 0001–0782. http://doi.acm.org/10.1145/606272.606299
2. Bittorrent: The Bittorrent Protocol. http://www.bittorrent.org/
3. Cohn-Gordon, K., Cremers, C., Dowling, B., Garratt, L., Stebila, D.: A formal security analysis of the signal messaging protocol (2016)
4. Gao, J., Steenkiste, P.: An adaptive protocol for efficient support of range queries in DHT-based systems. In: 12th IEEE International Conference on Network Protocols (ICNP 2004), 5–8 October 2004, Berlin, Germany, pp. 239–250 (2004). http://doi.ieeecomputersociety.org/10.1109/ICNP.2004.1348114
5. Garcés-Erice, L., Felber, P., Biersack, E.W., Urvoy-Keller, G., Ross, K.W.: Data indexing in peer-to-peer DHT networks. In: ICDCS, pp. 200–208. IEEE Computer Society (2004)
6. Internet Engineering Task Force: Interactive connectivity establishment (ICE): A Protocol for Network Address Translator (NAT) Traversal for Offer/Answer Protocols. https://tools.ietf.org/html/rfc5245
7. Maymounkov P., Mazieres, D.: Kademlia: A Peer-to-peer Information System Based on the XOR Metric (2002). http://pdos.csail.mit.edu/~petar/papers/maymounkov-kademlia-lncs.pdf
8. Ramabhadran, S., Ratnasamy, S., Hellerstein, J.M., Shenker, S.: Prefix hash tree: an indexing data structure over distributed hash tables (2004)
9. Savoir-faire Linux: Ring/ring gives you a full control over your communications and an unmatched level of privacy. https://ring.cx/
10. Savoir-faire Linux: A C++11 distributed hash table implementation (2016). http://opendht.net
11. Shen, G., Zheng, C., Wei, P., Li, S.: Distributed segment tree: a unified architecture to support range query and cover query. Technical report MSR-TR-2007-30, Microsoft Research, March 2007. http://research.microsoft.com/apps/pubs/default.aspx?id=70419
12. Sumbaly, R., Kreps, J., Gao, L., Feinberg, A., Soman, C., Shah, S.: Serving large-scale batch computed data with project Voldemort. In: Proceedings of the 10th USENIX Conference on File and Storage Technologies, FAST 2012, p. 18, Berkeley, CA, USA. USENIX Association (2012). http://dl.acm.org/citation.cfm?id=2208461.2208479
13. Tang, Y., Xu, J., Zhou, S., Lee, W.-C.: m-LIGHT: indexing multi-dimensional data over DHTs. In: 29th IEEE International Conference on Distributed Computing Systems (ICDCS 2009), 22–26 June 2009, Montreal, Québec, Canada, pp. 191–198. IEEE Computer Society (2009). ISBN 978-0-7695-3659-0. http://dx.doi.org/10.1109/ICDCS.2009.30
14. Wood, G.: Ethereum: A Secure Decentralised Generalised Transaction Ledger (2014)

IoT-Empowered Smart Agriculture: A Real-Time Light-Weight Embedded Segmentation System

Saad Abouzahir(✉), Mohamed Sadik, and Essaid Sabir

LRI Laboratory, NEST Research Group, ENSEM,
Hassan II University of Casablanca, Casablanca, Morocco
{saad.abouzahir,m.sadik,e.sabir}@ensem.ac.ma

Abstract. Internet of Things (IoT) is an emerging technology where standalone equipments and autonomous devices are connected to each other and users via Internet. When IoT concept meets agriculture, the future of farming is pushed to the next level, giving birth to what is called "Smart Agriculture" or "Precision Agriculture". The most important benefit from IoT is that a user can daily monitor his crop online in a seamless fashion. High quality data gathered from various sensors and transferred wirelessly to farm database will increase farmers understanding to their landuse leading to increasing income and product quality. One of the monitoring process is weeds detection and crop yield estimation using camera sensors. The acquired images help farmers to build map of weeds distribution or yield quantity all over the field, these maps can be used either for real-time processing or to predetermine weeds regions based on field maps history of the previous seasons. This process is referred to as segmentation problem. Several algorithms have been proposed for that purpose, however, these algorithms were run only on high performance computers. In this paper, we evaluate performance and the robustness of the most used legacy algorithms under local conditions. We focused on implementing these schemes within real-time application constraint. For instance, these algorithms were implemented and run in a low-cost embedded system.

Keywords: Internet of Things · Precision agriculture · Smart agriculture · Segmentation · Back Propagation Neural Network · Vegetation color index · Fuzzy C means

1 Introduction

Within-field variabilities were known over decades as a problem affecting crop production. These variabilities were visually detected and manually treated by the growers, but, with the enlargement of fields, lack of knowledge and experience among farmers, field surveying becomes difficult. Efficient and low-cost mapping tools of landuse variabilities are required for early intervention and precise treatment. Recently The IoT concept becomes an important part in

E. Sabir et al. (Eds.): UNet 2017, LNCS 10542, pp. 319–332, 2017.
https://doi.org/10.1007/978-3-319-68179-5_28

agricultural applications. Many farmers start to connect their tractors or drones to the internet for field surveying and site-specific treatment. In addition, various Websites and Mobile applications were developed to provide online access to field data and monitoring ability of agricultural activities (e.g., ONFARM SYSTEMS, CROPX and FARMOBILE).

One of the main issues in agriculture is weeds infestation. The latter compete with crop plants for nutrients and water, leading to a loss in yield production and quality. For several years, a great effort has been devoted to the study of the effect of weeds on crop yields [17]. It has been found that the effect increase as much as when weeds are near crop plants. Several approaches were proposed to deal with weed infestation. Namely, herbicides, in-row hand hoeing, hot water... etc. However, these approaches are costly and harmful. Therefore, the focus of recent research has been on the adoption of artificial intelligence, machine vision and remote sensing techniques to build autonomous tractors with precise application systems [17]. Such an innovation will decrease the expenses of manual labour, the cost and the impact of herbicides products by site-specific treatments and will increase the profits. Moreover, with the availability of such intelligent tractors, farmers can remotely launch any agricultural activities from an on-line platforms which denote the power of IoT utilities.

As reported by [17], autonomous robots for weed control has four core technologies: Guidance System able to estimate both heading and offset of row structure at sufficient fast rate (real-time GPS, machine vision), Weed detection and identification with fast and robust algorithms (machine vision, remote sensing), Precision In-Row weed control (micro-spray, cutting, thermal... etc.), and Mapping (GPS and machine vision). In this context, accurate and efficient segmentation technique to identify crop (region of interest) is crucial for both Guidance and weed detection system, allowing real-time precise spraying of herbicides or automatic hoeing [8]. Furthermore, the generated maps and the rate of herbicide applications are sent to the farm's database in a daily manner to help farmers to track weeds condition and herbicides efficacy as it's shown in Fig. 1. Moreover, years accumulated maps will help farmers to understand weeds behavior.

Several publications have appeared in recent years discussing the robustness of segmentation for plant recognition and crop row identification. However, All these works are limited to the case of a real-time test in high performance and expensive computers.

In this paper, we provide a comparative study of one of the most popular segmentation techniques used in agriculture as reported by [8]. The comparison was conducted in term of segmentation quality and embeddability for light-weight real-time applications in agriculture. Our primary consideration for choosing these algorithms was to ensure that they cover a wide application range. Therefore, the algorithms were chosen such that: They are independent to plant species, and robust to outdoor illumination.

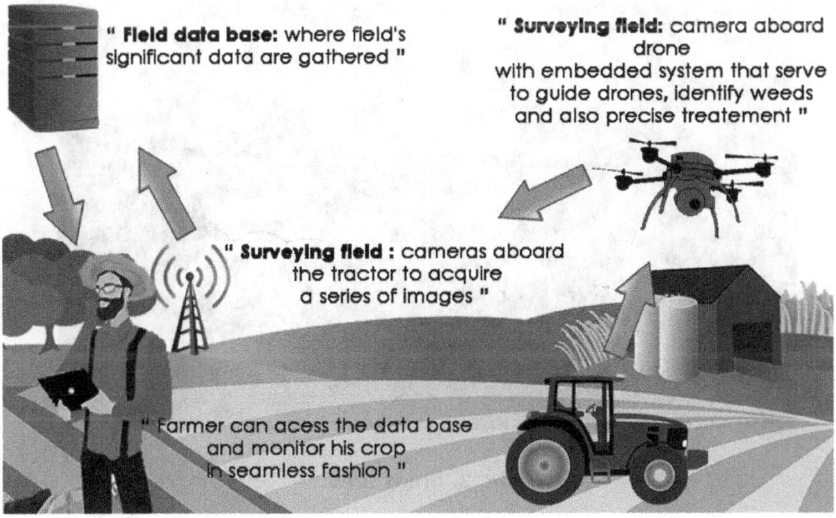

Fig. 1. Illustration of IoT technologies for smart agriculture

2 Methods and Materials

2.1 Study Area and Image Acquisition

In our study, the target crop was wheat in the tillering stage, the field is located at el Haouz Marrakech Morocco Fig. 2.

For the image acquisition, a mobile phone digital camera (Camera Xperia Z2 21mpx) was used to acquire a top-view image of the wheat patch. Two RGB images (1280 × 720) were acquired per day at a different time (12:00 and 16:00) and for different patches; from 30 December 2017 to 7 January 2017. A total of 20 images were taken under various light and background conditions.

2.2 OMAP4430 Platform

Our segmentation system is targeted at processors from the desktop machine down to low power arenas. Therefore, all our experiments were made using an embedded platform to ensure real time performance on a low-cost architecture. Precisely, we have used the OMAP4430 embedded processor with Dual-core ARM Cortex A9 at 1, 2 GHz which is widely used in many smart phones, tablets and drone applications [1]. Such embedded device is gaining in popularity and acquiring more capable cameras and mobile processors. We carefully select this platform to be representative of the actual devices used by consumers and industry, mobile and embedded categories. For the sake of a comparative study, our system was also implemented on a high-end laptop machine. The developments were made using Python 2.7 and OpenCV3.0 libraries.

Fig. 2. Study area

2.3 Color-Index

Due to the inability of grayscale images to distinguish between crop and background, alternative monochrome images were created to enhance image segmentation [8]. Based on the vegetation color indexes, each RGB image is transformed into a new single channel image with pixels value ranged from $[a, b]$ where $a, b \in \Re$. In the generated monochrome images, details of the plants are accentuated, while soil's details are attenuated and vice versa depending on the type of the index. Later the new interval is scaled to $[0, 255]$ and then binarized using a proper threshold.

In this section, we focused on the evaluation of four widespread color vegetation indexes: Normalized Difference Index (NDI), Excess Green minus Excess Red Index (ExGR), Color Index for Vegetation Extraction (CIVE) and Combined Index 1 (COM1). Due to their performance, these indexes were used as reference to evaluate new algorithms, however, indexes performance depends on thresholding technique, environment conditions, and background complexity [8]. To our knowledge, these indexes weren't evaluated in term of computation time in low-cost systems.

Normalized Difference Index (NDI): In [18] the author proposed this index to separate green plants (crop/weed) from background and discriminate between crop species and weeds. As Red and Green bands found to be less sensitive to soil and residues, [18] substracted these two bands, assuming that dense vegetation regions will have higher Green value. The normalization was conducted for the consistency under variable illumination condition.

$$NDI = \frac{G - R}{G + R} \tag{1}$$

Excess Green Minus Excess Red Index (ExGR): As the success of Excess Red Index (ExR) [12] to accentuate soil regions from green plants, and the good performance of Excess Green Index (ExG) [19] to enhance green plants regions. [13] combined the advantages of both indexes to efficiently separate plants from background regions. ExR and ExG are calculated using the following equations,

$$ExG = 2g - r - b \tag{2}$$

where $r = \frac{R^*}{R^*+G^*+B^*}$ $g = \frac{G^*}{R^*+G^*+B^*}$ $b = \frac{G^*}{R^*+G^*+B^*}$, R^* G^* B^* are the normalization of pixel bands by its maximum value in the image.

$$ExR = 1.3R - G \tag{3}$$

Thus, ExGR is obtained,

$$ExGR = ExG - ExR \tag{4}$$

Color Index for Vegetation Extraction (CIVE): [9] Proposed this index in order to estimate crop growth level for precision agriculture. The weighted sum of three visible channels is used to generate CIVE; each channel is weighted based on their contribution in the green plants color.

$$CIVE = 0.441R + 0.811G + 0.385B + 18.78745 \tag{5}$$

Combined Index 1 (COM1): As the fact that each index present advantages and weaknesses. [6] arranged the four indexes (ExG, ExGR, CIVE, and VEG) in order to overcome their limits. This method was applied on barley and corn crops. ExG, CIVE, ExGR are calculated using Eqs. 2, 4 and 5 respectively, while VEG is the Vegetative Index proposed by [7] for plant weed discrimination and was tested on the cereal crops. The index is obtained by,

$$VEG = \frac{G}{R^a * B^{(1-a)}} \tag{6}$$

where a is a constant equal to 0.667 according to [7].

Thus, COM1 is obtained,

$$COM1 = ExG + CIVE + ExGR + VEG \tag{7}$$

In order to generate a binary image, a proper thresholding method is required. Due to the unstable outdoor conditions, a dynamic thresholding technique is recommended for accurate segmentation. Otsu thresholding [11] were widely used in agriculture, for weed plant discrimination [10] and crop rows identification for machines guidance [4]. Because of its good results, Otsu thresholding was the most suited for our application.

2.4 Back Propagation Neural Network (BPNN)

Back Propagation Neural Network is a learning algorithm that simulates the learning process of human's brain. Neural Network proved its utility in solving various segmentation problems for precision agriculture and crop monitoring. For instance, weed identification [5], and plant type identification [2].

The architecture contains neurons distributed in layers, each neuron is connected to all neurons in the next layer. Rosenblat was the first to modelize the neuron as weighted sum of inputs with an activation function as illustrated in Fig. 3.

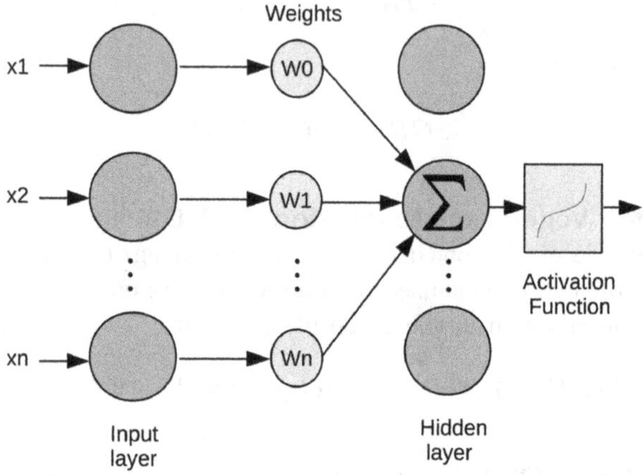

Fig. 3. Model of Neural Network

There are two main architecture of BPNN, Simple Perceptron (SP) which contains only one layer, and Multi-layer Perceptron (MLP) which constitutes multiple layers. In our work, we used a MLP architecture with three layers, which is adequate to the majority of problems. However, in the case of non-linear complex problems, an additional hidden layer is required. Neurons in the input layer is equal to the feature vector size, hidden layer neuron's number is determined by trial-and-error, and the neuron in the output layer is equal to the number of classes.

Basic Back Propagation algorithm [15] was employed to train the Neural Network. In each iteration, weights are adjusted by an amount proportional to the error between ANN output and the desired output, the process is repeated until the generalization, where the weights are no longer changing or the maximum iteration number is achieved.

2.5 Fuzzy C-Means (FCM)

Fuzzy C-means was improved by [3] as a fuzzy generalization of K-means clustering algorithm. FCM is an unsupervised algorithm that consists of grouping similar pixels into homogenous regions called "Clusters". Similarity between pixels is determined by the measurement of the euclidean distance of each pixel from the prototype (class center) and their degree of membership to each class using [3] equations,

$$J_m(U,Y) = \sum_{k=1}^{n}\sum_{j=1}^{c} u_{jk}^{m} E_j(x_k) \tag{8}$$

where J_m is the criteria to minimize with respect to the centers set $Y = \{y_j | j = 1, 2, \ldots c\}$, c is the number of classes. $X = \{x_k | k = 1, 2, \ldots n\}$ image pixels and n is the total number of pixels. U is matrix contain degrees of membership u_{jk} of each pixel to each class. $E_j(x_k)$ is the euclidean distance between k_{th} pixel and center of j_{th} class. $m > 1$ is a parameter of fuzziness which changes with the type of the problem, its default value is 2 [3].

u_{jk} is computed by the following equation,

$$u_{jk} = \left(\sum_{l=1}^{c} \left(\frac{E_j(x_k)}{E_l(x_k)} \right)^{2/m-1} \right)^{-1} \tag{9}$$

where $\sum_{j=1}^{c}(u_{jk}) = 1$.

Centers are updated using the equation below,

$$y_j = \frac{\sum_{k=1}^{n}(u_{jk})^m x_k}{\sum_{k=1}^{n}(u_{jk})^m} \tag{10}$$

FCM have been used in various applications of precision agriculture such as insect infestation [21], crop disease [16]. Its utility motivated us to test its embeddability for a real-time application for a plant segmentation.

3 Experiment and Results

3.1 Vegetation Color Indices Computation

Without a prior preprocessing, RGB bands of each pixel were extracted to compute indexes. Results were then stored in matrix for thresholding to generate the binary image as described below,

PseudoCode:

```
image <- read image
For y From 0 to width
  For x From 0 to height
     [R,G,B] <- extract pixel elements
     index <- calculate index using one of the Eqs. (1), (4), (5) or (7)
scale the matrix to \cite{bib0,bib255}
apply Otsu threshold
save image
```

3.2 Features Vector and Neural Network Architecture

Features vector used in this study is the one proposed in [20]. Each pixel was represented with four features, $G-R$, $G-B$, H and S. A total of 14 images were chosen randomly as training data, 4 for the test and the rest 2 images with two different lighting conditions (sunny, cloudy) remains for the evaluation. From each training and test data set, three squares of 7×7 size were extracted from different plant and background regions as illustrated in Fig. 4. For both classes, a total of 2058 training data, and 588 test data were extracted. Final architecture of BPNN was 4-6-2. BPNN were trained for 20 iterations, and an accuracy of 64.2% for green plants and 56.4% for the background was achieved.

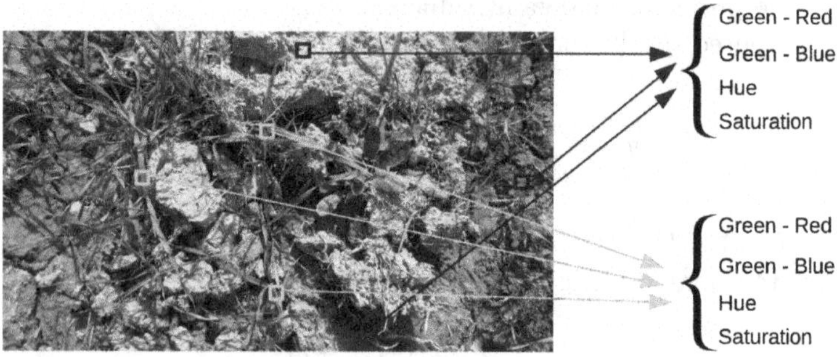

Fig. 4. Example of the training data acquisition by setting ROIs of 7×7 pixels on the training images (Color figure online)

3.3 Fuzzy C-Means Implementation

As the Hue of the image found to be efficient for distinguishing plants from background [14], evaluation images were transformed to HSI using equations cited in [14]. Later, the hue channel was extracted for the clustering process as described below,

PseudoCode FCM:

```
class <- 2 (green plants/background)
m <- 2
e <- 0.0000001 center variations
iteration_max <- 100
initialize centers using random labeling
while (d < e)&(t<iteration_max)):
  U <- Calculate membership function using Eq. (9)
  Y <- update centers using Eq. (10)
  d <- check center variation
save image
```

3.4 Results of Segmentation

Evaluation images were chosen carefully, for different illumination and background complexity in order to test the robustness of the algorithms as it's shown in Fig. 5. The results of color indices, BPNN and FCM are shown respectively in Figs. 6, 7 and 8.

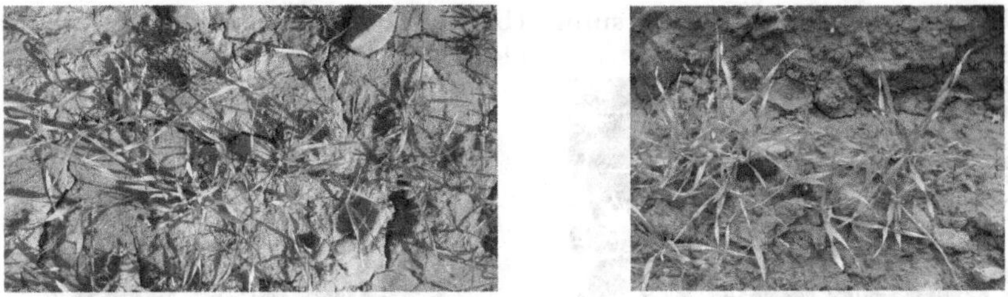

(a) Wheat in sunny condition **(b) Wheat in cloudy condition**

Fig. 5. Example of evaluation images taken under different light conditions (Color figure online)

The segmentation quality of each method was evaluated using the approach reported by [8]. A manually extracted image using Adobe Photoshop CS5 was considered as a gold standard, and the quality of the segmentation is determined based on the similarity degree to the gold standard image. The similarity degree was computed using the Structural Similarity Index (SSIM). The overall measurement results are summarized in Table 1.

Table 1. Results of the segmentation quality for both the cloudy and the sunny day

Algorithm	SSIM for sunny condition (%)	SSIM for cloudy condition (%)
CIVE	76.30	70.71
ExGR	32.26	40.98
NDI	65.82	63.39
COM1	19.03	16.03
FCM	72.47	69.86
RNA	31.32	56.57

In the segmentation results, CIVE showed the highest segmentation quality degree in both conditions. For NDI, a little consistency is observed in the quality of the segmentation for both illumination conditions, Which indicate its robustness against variable illumination. Unlike the case of greenhouse plants under

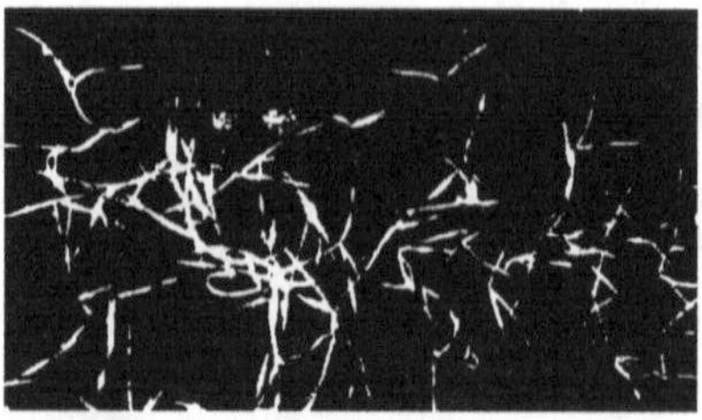

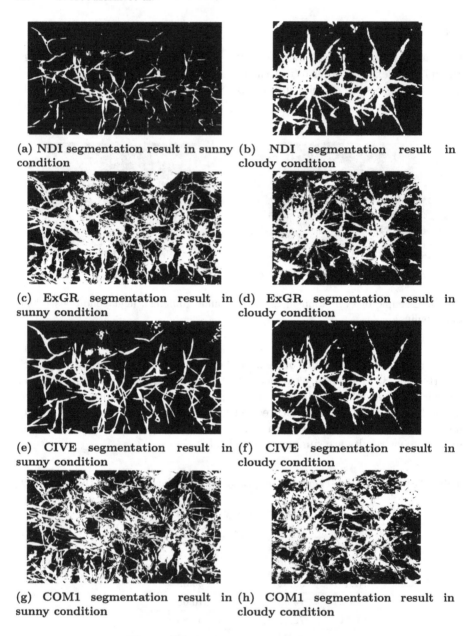

(a) NDI segmentation result in sunny condition

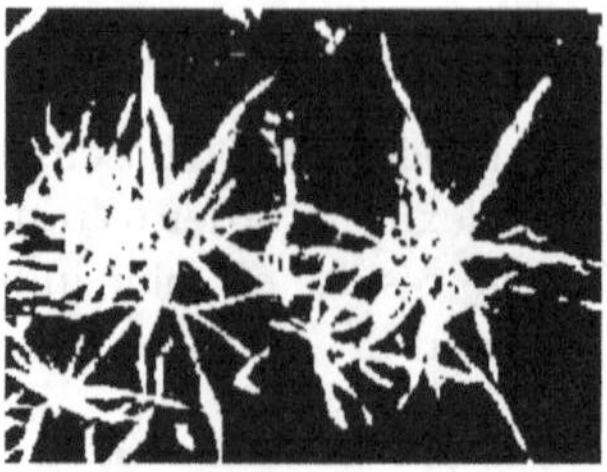

(b) NDI segmentation result in cloudy condition

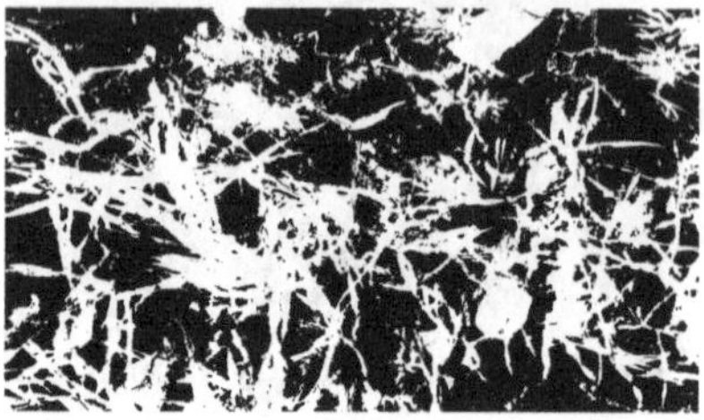

(c) ExGR segmentation result in sunny condition

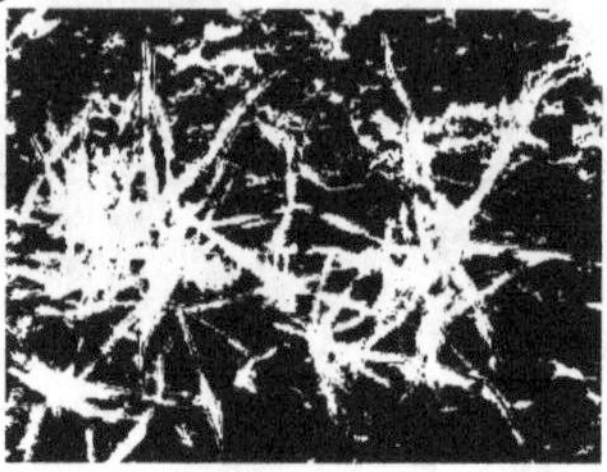

(d) ExGR segmentation result in cloudy condition

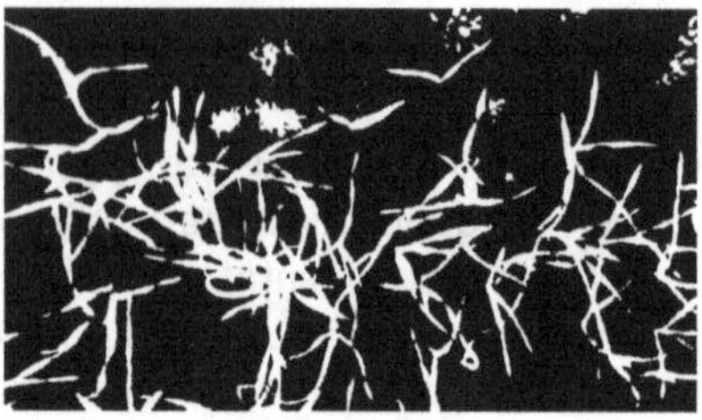

(e) CIVE segmentation result in sunny condition

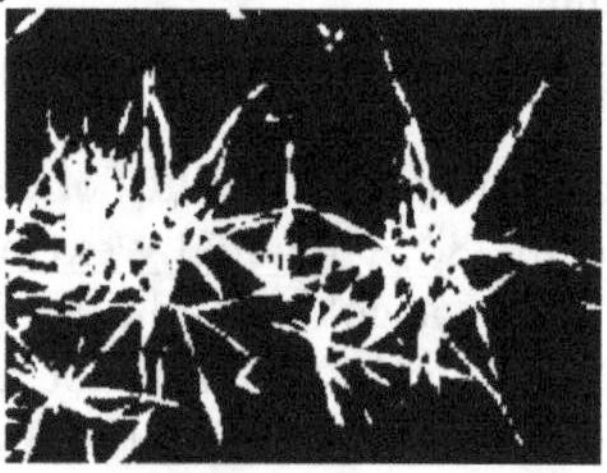

(f) CIVE segmentation result in cloudy condition

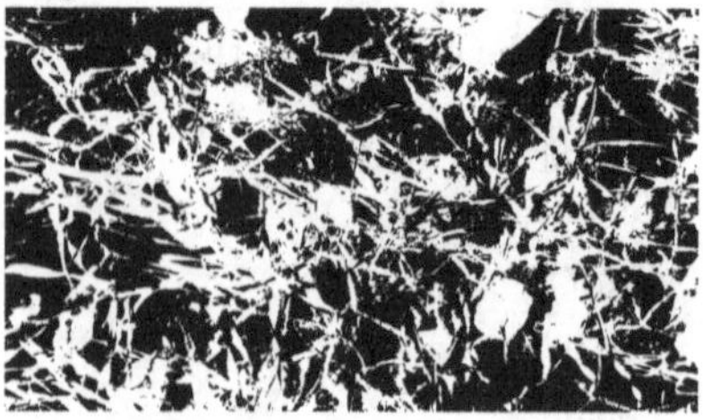

(g) COM1 segmentation result in sunny condition

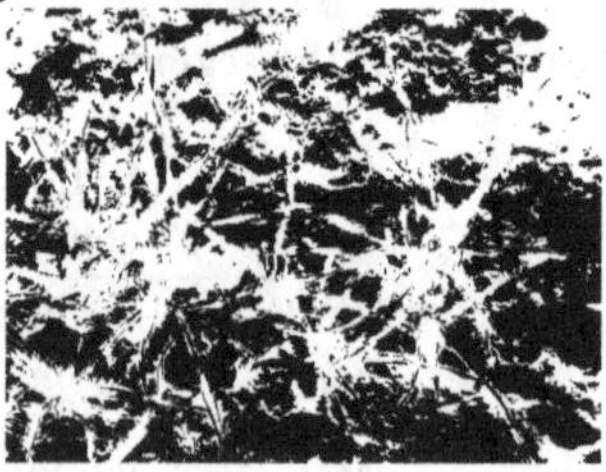

(h) COM1 segmentation result in cloudy condition

Fig. 6. Color index segmentation results

controlled illumination [8], a moderate results was generated by ExGR demonstrating its inability to perform well under outdoor illumination. The lowest results among the applied methods were obtained by COM1 for the both conditions. In the case of BPNN, a moderate segmentation quality was obtained in

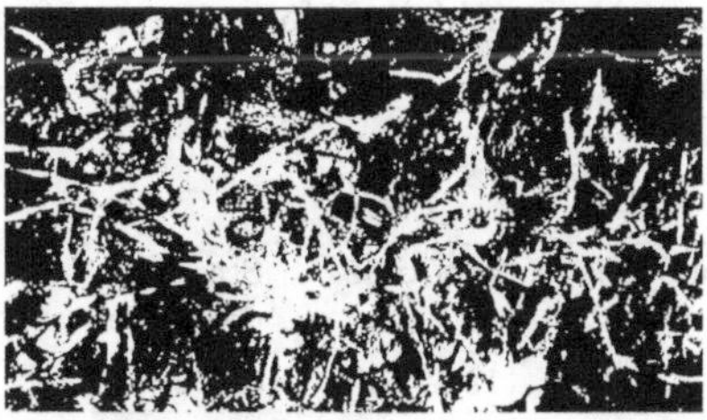

(a) ANN segmentation results under sunny condition

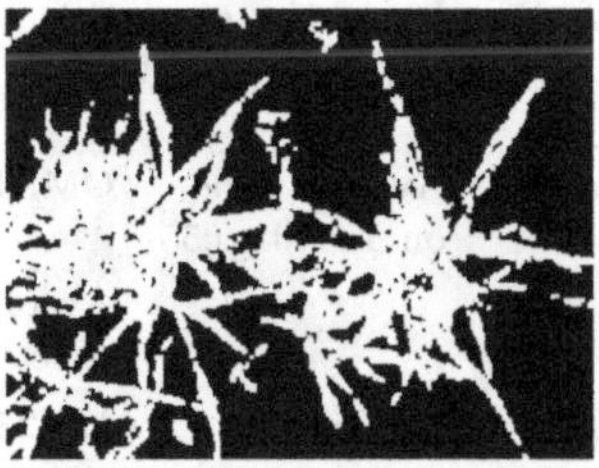

(b) ANN segmentation result under cloudy condition

Fig. 7. Artificial neural network segmentation result

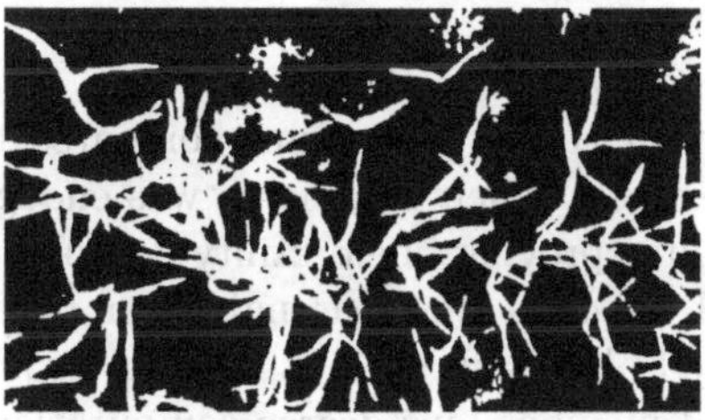

(a) FCM clustering result under sunny condition

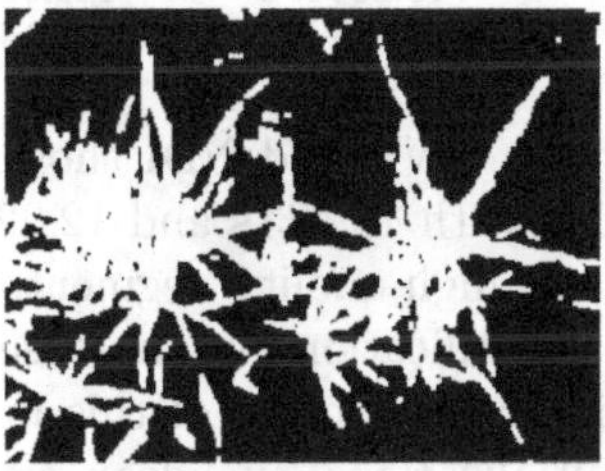

(b) FCM clustering result for cloudy condition

Fig. 8. Fuzzy C-means segmentation results

the cloudy condition, whereas, in the sunny day, the poor segmentation quality was due to the shadows and sun reflections. However, segmentation rate can be improved either by selecting a proper features that present more distinguishing ability between plant and background, or by improving the quality of the training data. Finally, In spite of the good results of FCM, performance depends strongly on the color space and The number of classes. Furthermore, clusters generated by FCM are unlabeled, which require a supervision to determine which class represent plants.

3.5 Processing Time Evaluation

For real-time tasks, fast algorithms is required. In addition, algorithms must be embeddable in low-cost architectures to encourage the adoption of such intelligent technologies among farmers. For this purpose, algorithms were implemented in open multimedia applications processor OMAP4430 described above. A series of 50 measurements of the execution time were taken for each algorithm. Then, the average time, maximum time, minimum time and the standard deviation were computed. At Table 2, execution time of each algorithm is given for both personal computer (Toshiba i3 2.5 GHz) and OMAP4430.

As it can be seen from Table 2 metrics, run-time in OMAP4430 is approximately 10 times superior than the personal computer in all the cases. For the

Table 2. Results of the execution time of algorithms on high-performance platform and low-cost architecture

Algorithms	Average time on Toshiba c55	OMAP4430			
		Average time	Max time	Min time	Standard deviation
CIVE	1.313 s	12.42339 s	12.43448 s	12.42575 s	0.00295 s
ExGR	12.44754 s	136.4493 s	136.59011 s	135.79077 s	0.20526 s
NDI	1.25954 s	12.22128 s	12.23352 s	12.17349 s	0.01702 s
COM1	21.62031 s	211.75667 s	216.54647 s	208.80413 s	3.55244 s
FCM	3.33385 s	28.40563 s	43.84362 s	19.8287 s	3.92116 s
RNA	13.80016 s	149.32789 s	149.35809 s	149.29733 s	0.01960 s

algorithms, CIVE and NDI showed the lowest computation time compared to the others with 12.423 s and 12.221 s respectively. Their simplicity, was enough to provide high-quality segmentation results, proving their utility for plants regions identification. In the case of FCM, 28.405 s was reasonable compared to the intensive process of this unsupervised algorithm such as random prototypes initializations, euclidean distance and memberships degree computations for each single data point. ExGR, COM1 and BPNN scored the highest run-time among the algorithms with 136.449 s, 211.756 s and 149.327 s respectively. This was due to the intensive computation steps for ExGR and COM1. However, BPNN execution time was due to the classification of each data point separately. Therefore, processing image by grouping neighbouring pixels with proper kernel can strongly reduce BPNN run-time.

4 Conclusion

This paper provided a comparative study of segmentation algorithms in terms of robustness under complex environment, and execution time on a low-cost architecture. The objective of this work is exploring the possibility of creating light-weight and intelligent systems that can serve for real-time applications in agriculture. First, we started our work by describing the utilities of IoT in solving agricultural issues. We provided a clear and well-summarised overview on the studied algorithms and their recent applications. The segmentation quality and computation time were parametrically assessed to elucidate the performances. The results of the study demonstrate that CIVE and NDI can be used to identify plants regions in a complex environment with small computation time. However, for weed identification, indices alone is insufficient and a classification algorithm is required to distinguish between weeds patches and crop plants, which can dramatically increase the computation time. In The case of FCM and BPNN, both algorithms can discriminate between plants regions and background with reasonable computation time that can be reduced. In addition, they can discriminate also between crop plants and weeds, but, only if more interpreting and consistent color features are provided.

References

1. Abouzahir, M., Elouardi, A., Bouaziz, S., Latif, R., Abdelouahed, T.: An improved Rao-Blackwellized particle filter based-SLAM running on an OMAP embedded architecture. In: 2014 Second World Conference on Complex Systems (WCCS), pp. 716–721, November 2014
2. Al-Hiary, H., Bani-Ahmad, S., Reyalat, M., Braik, M., ALRahamneh, Z.: Fast and accurate detection and classification of plant diseases. Mach. Learn. **14**(5) (2011)
3. Bezdek, J.C., Ehrlich, R., Full, W.: FCM: the Fuzzy C-means clustering algorithm. Comput. Geosci. **10**(2–3), 191–203 (1984)
4. Cui, Y., Qiao, Z., Zou, X., Wang, B.: Study on the method of visual navigation baseline identification and extraction of agricultural machinery. In: 2015 6th IEEE International Conference on Software Engineering and Service Science (ICSESS), pp. 766–769. IEEE (2015)
5. De Rainville, F.M., Durand, A., Fortin, F.A., Tanguy, K., Maldague, X., Panneton, B., Simard, M.J.: Bayesian classification and unsupervised learning for isolating weeds in row crops. Pattern Anal. Appl. **17**(2), 401–414 (2014)
6. Guijarro, M., Pajares, G., Riomoros, I., Herrera, P., Burgos-Artizzu, X., Ribeiro, A.: Automatic segmentation of relevant textures in agricultural images. Comput. Electron. Agric. **75**(1), 75–83 (2011)
7. Hague, T., Tillett, N., Wheeler, H.: Automated crop and weed monitoring in widely spaced cereals. Precis. Agric. **7**(1), 21–32 (2006)
8. Hamuda, E., Glavin, M., Jones, E.: A survey of image processing techniques for plant extraction and segmentation in the field. Comput. Electron. Agric. **125**, 184–199 (2016)
9. Kataoka, T., Kaneko, T., Okamoto, H., Hata, S.: Crop growth estimation system using machine vision. In: 2003 IEEE/ASME International Conference on Advanced Intelligent Mechatronics, AIM 2003, Proceedings, vol. 2, pp. b1079–b1083. IEEE (2003)
10. Lavania, S., Matey, P.S.: Novel method for weed classification in maize field using Otsu and PCA implementation. In: 2015 IEEE International Conference on Computational Intelligence & Communication Technology (CICT), pp. 534–537. IEEE (2015)
11. Otsu, N.: A threshold selection method from gray-level histogram. IEEE Trans. Syst. Man Cybern. **9**(1), 62–66 (1979)
12. Meyer, G.E., Hindman, T.W., Laksmi, K.: Machine vision detection parameters for plant species identification. In: Photonics East (ISAM, VVDC, IEMB), pp. 327–335. International Society for Optics and Photonics (1999)
13. Meyer, G.E., Neto, J.C., Jones, D.D., Hindman, T.W.: Intensified Fuzzy clusters for classifying plant, soil, and residue regions of interest from color images. Comput. Electron. Agric. **42**(3), 161–180 (2004)
14. Ruiz-Ruiz, G., Gómez-Gil, J., Navas-Gracia, L.: Testing different color spaces based on hue for the environmentally adaptive segmentation algorithm (EASA). Comput. Electron. Agric. **68**(1), 88–96 (2009)
15. Rumelhart, D.E., Hinton, G.E., Williams, R.J.: Learning internal representations by error propagation. Technical report, DTIC Document (1985)
16. Sekulska-Nalewajko, J., Goclawski, J.: A semi-automatic method for the discrimination of diseased regions in detached leaf images using Fuzzy C-means clustering. In: 2011 Proceedings of VIIth International Conference on Perspective Technologies and Methods in MEMS Design (MEMSTECH), pp. 172–175. IEEE (2011)

17. Slaughter, D., Giles, D., Downey, D.: Autonomous robotic weed control systems: a review. Comput. Electron. Agric. **61**(1), 63–78 (2008)
18. Woebbecke, D.M., Meyer, G.E., Von Bargen, K., Mortensen, D.A.: Plant species identification, size, and enumeration using machine vision techniques on near-binary images. In: Applications in Optical Science and Engineering, pp. 208–219. International Society for Optics and Photonics (1993)
19. Woebbecke, D., Meyer, G., Von Bargen, K., Mortensen, D., et al.: Color indices for weed identification under various soil, residue, and lighting conditions. Trans. ASAE-Am. Soc. Agric. Eng. **38**(1), 259–270 (1995)
20. Zheng, L., Zhang, J., Wang, Q.: Mean-shift-based color segmentation of images containing green vegetation. Comput. Electron. Agric. **65**(1), 93–98 (2009)
21. Zhou, Z., Zang, Y., Li, Y., Zhang, Y., Wang, P., Luo, X.: Rice plant-hopper infestation detection and classification algorithms based on fractal dimension values and Fuzzy C-means. Math. Comput. Modell. **58**(3), 701–709 (2013)

Random Access Procedure Based on an Adaptive Prioritization Method for Integration of MTC in Mobile Networks

Alejandro Borrajo Romero(✉), Raquel Pérez Leal, and Ana García Armada

Signal Theory and Communications Department, Universidad Carlos III de Madrid, Av. de la Universidad, 30, 28911 Leganés, Spain
{aborrajo,rpleal,agarcia}@tsc.uc3m.es

Abstract. This document addresses the issue of organizing the random access for IoT and MTC in advanced mobile networks. We define a simple and efficient model of the early-stage random access procedure, based on LTE-A. Based on this model and to avoid the signalling saturation, we propose one step solution which manages MTC device priorities based on multiple ACB factors trough the definition of adaptive thresholds related to the traffic characteristics. The simulations results that we provide for different scenarios show that the option of using different categories of MTC based on multiple ACB factors for prioritization can provide good results in a real environment. Furthermore, the proposed method could be easily adapted to the new NB-IoT standard requirements and procedures, which would bring additional capabilities.

Keywords: NB-IoT · LTE-A · MTC · M2M · RA procedure · PRACH · Overload control · MAC · Prioritizations · Multiple ACB factors

1 Introduction

The present concept of Internet of Things (IoT) and the trend towards the massive use of sensor-based networks bring up the question of how to transport the information from these networks in a feasible and efficient way. A promising choice is using the mobile cellular network (LTE/LTE-A and beyond) to support machine type communications (MTC) and to transport machine to machine (M2M) traffic.

Sensor networks with a large number of nodes and low data traffic can interfere with the users traditional voice/data communication due to saturation of the control channels causing a general delay in all the terminals of the network and increasing the power consumption. Indeed, in the existing mobile networks, the introduction of MTC produces more a saturation problem of the signalling channels than a limitation of the network capacity [1]. There is currently very active research and it is one of the standardization activities of 3rd Generation Partnership Project (3GPP) for both adapting the next versions of the current technologies (Releases 13 and 14) and defining the next generation of mobile systems, 5G, in which this problem is foreseen to be a key factor.

E. Sabir et al. (Eds.): UNet 2017, LNCS 10542, pp. 333–344, 2017.
https://doi.org/10.1007/978-3-319-68179-5_29

The issue of the medium access control and resource allocation, both in LTE-A and in the future networks, is being addressed from different perspectives: signalling is reorganized into access and shared physical channels to avoid saturation; new signalling mechanisms are arbitrated; or, even more, some of the previous control signals or channels are suppressed to avoid the problem. On the other hand, the recently defined NB-IoT standard (R13 LTE-Advanced Pro) [2] proposes to handle separately human type (H2H) and machine type communications (MTC) incorporating new access procedures [3].

The goal of this paper is to provide a promising solution to the uplink access control channels overload caused by the massive access of MTC devices and, simultaneously, to solve the problem of access of different categories of devices to the network. The proposed solution is a one-step solution based on a modified LTE-A random access (RA) procedure applied only to machine devices. It is in line with the new procedures defined in the NB-IoT standard [2], with additional functionality such as handling MTC devices priorities. The paper proposes an adaptive prioritization procedure based on [4,5] and designed for MTC nodes with different priorities. The proposed procedure allows MTC nodes with different priorities to access to the network depending on how urgently the data needs to be sent, giving higher priority to the nodes that need to convey their information in real time and lower priority to those ones that do not handle urgent data.

The remainder of the paper is organized as follows. In Sect. 2, we present the background and the related work. The detail of the system model is pointed out in Sect. 3. Section 4 describes the proposed procedure. Simulation scenarios and results are given in Sect. 5. Finally, the conclusions of the study are provided in Sect. 6.

2 Background and Related Work

2.1 Random Access Procedure in LTE Networks

When a node requests a connection setup to any cellular system it initiates a random access procedure (RAP). The RAP can either be contention-free or contention-based. The former one is used for regular nodes that select a preamble so that two nodes may select the same preamble bringing about a collision. This type of RAP may be used not only for initial access, but also after periods of uplink inactivity, to move from idle to active state, or as a result of an incoming call or an incoming packet data flow. Regarding the contention-free RAP, the preambles are assigned by the eNodeB avoiding a possible collision; this mechanism is commonly used to perform a handover. In this paper, we focus on the contention-based RAP, which consists of the following steps [6] (Fig. 1):

1. **Random Access (RA) preamble transmission (Msg 1):** The node selects one preamble to convey on the Physical Random Access Channel (PRACH), so that the eNodeB with this preamble information can estimate the transmission timing of the node.

2. **Random Access Response (RAR) (Msg 2):** This RAR is sent by the eNodeB on the Physical Downlink Shared Channel (PDSCH) and includes information such as the identity of the detected preamble, a time alignment instruction, and an initial uplink resource grant to be used in the third step. It should be noted that in case multiple nodes collide by conveying the same preamble, they would receive the same RAR.
3. **Radio Resource Control (RRC) Connection Request (Msg 3):** This message, denoted as Msg 3, is transmitted in the first scheduled uplink resource on the Physical Uplink Shared Channel (PUSCH). It contains information related to the node including its ID (identification). In case of collision in the preamble at the first step, the colliding users receive the same RAR, and thus, their Msg 3 will also collide.
4. **RRC Connection Setup (Msg 4):** The eNodeB sends a contention-resolution message as an answer to Msg 3, thus, when the node does not receive Msg 4 indicates a rejection in the collision resolution process.

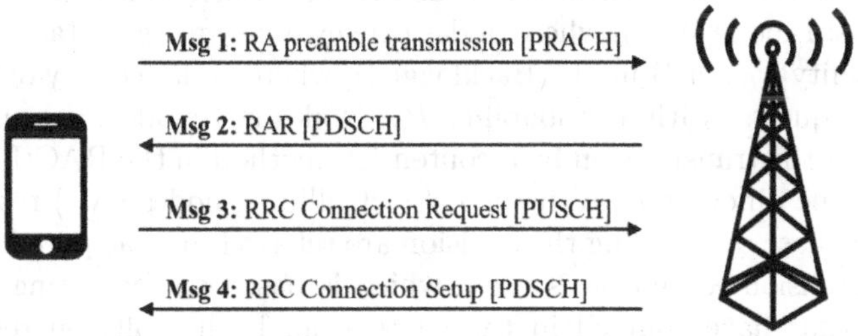

Fig. 1. Scheme of the contention-based RAP

2.2 Related Work

Some previous works [4,7,8] are focused on dealing with PUCCH (Physical Uplink Control Channel) and PRACH together, so that, to avoid the problem of the PUCCH saturation they propose to set up sensors to use the PRACH instead of the PUCCH for transmission requests, i.e., the PUCCH is suppressed. Thus it prevents the increasing delay from starting the transmission of the other devices.

Other solutions are based on both the access class restriction (ACB) and the information of timing advance for stationary devices to avoid overloading. In the ACB mechanism the eNodeB sends a barring probability $p \in [0 - 1]$ to all MTC nodes waiting for accessing the network, then, MTC nodes begin the RAP by choosing a random number $q \in [0 - 1]$, so that, when q is less than the barring factor p can access to the network else the MTC node is rejected over a barring time duration [9]. Reference [10] proposes an extended random access scheme to increase access success probability of sensor UEs by allocating the available radio resources to the accessing UEs in two stages. Authors in [11] introduce a congestion control scheme for the bursty traffic scenario of MTC in LTE networks. They allocate dynamically to the MTC devices the number of preambles during each time slot based on the number of backlogged users and they propose an iterative algorithm to adaptively update the ACB factor. Reference [5] points out a solution to prioritize the access of MTC devices to the network based on an algorithm to define multiple adaptive ACB factors, according to the M2M service delay and drop rate category.

Among the miscellaneous solutions, we focus on the proposals based on using the PRACH instead of the PUCCH and the work based on MTC nodes with different priorities, by using multiple ACB factors that are dynamically adapted according to the number of nodes and the overload present in the network.

3 Model Description

The model used is shown in Fig. 2. It is a simple RAP model, based on [4,7], which takes into account the key access parameters. We consider a total number of N MTC nodes (sensors) involved in the network. Each node can be configured in two modes: I-mode (Idle), where nodes convey a new message (access request) with probability P_N, or B-mode (Backlogged), where nodes convey old messages (old access requests) with a probability P_R. Nodes in I-mode (N_I) and B-mode (N_B) perform the transmission by a contention method in the RACH choosing a preamble of the different K available (N_T). Colliding nodes (N_P) return to the B-mode and those overcoming the collision are referred to as acquired (N_A). The concept of collision resolution is used, which is based on recovering a message from those that have collided in the contention. If the collision resolution is enabled on the evolved NodeB (eNB), whenever there is a collision in a preamble, one of the transmissions will be recovered and that node will be taken as acquired.

Of those nodes that manage to overcome the contention, only a number of L can be dispatched by the eNB in a RACH opportunity due to time and hardware constraints. This concept has been implemented by a number of L servers without queue that decode the messages of the acquired nodes. Those nodes that overcome this selection are considered as successful (N_S) and are planned to transmit in the uplink. These nodes return to the I-mode, while those nodes rejected in the servers (N_F) return to B-mode. N_N and N_R represent the number of nodes performing a new transmission and a retransmission, whilst, N_Q is defined as the total number of failed nodes.

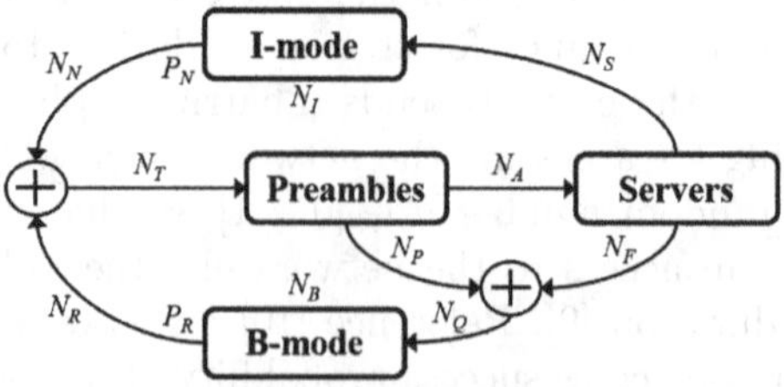

Fig. 2. RAP model [5,7]

4 Proposed Procedure

The proposed approach is based on ACB service differentiation and MTC nodes with priorities [5]. It is working with three different categories of nodes, each one of them with a different priority in the network. These priorities depend on the delay tolerance of the nodes and there are three different types: high priority (HP) nodes, medium priority (MP) nodes, and low priority (LP) nodes. In summary, the key points of this solution are:

- Using multiple ACB factors.
- Dynamic adjustment of congestion level.
- MTC nodes with different priorities.

This selected option is in line with the highlighted features in the NB-IoT standard [2]. The next flowchart (see Fig. 3) describes the general steps that are followed in the proposed model, where N is the number of nodes and M is the RACH cycle number.

Therefore, during the simulation the following phases can be distinguished:

1. **Access request generation:** The requests for network access are generated at nodes in I-mode with a P_N probability according to a Beta distribution as proposed by 3GPP in [12].

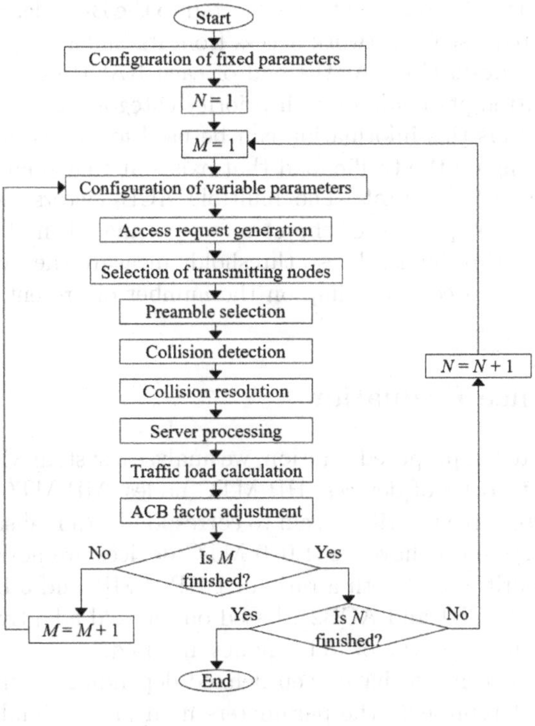

Fig. 3. General flowchart of the model

2. **Selection of transmitting nodes:** Nodes in I-mode in which a request for network access is generated attempt to transmit. The nodes in B-mode attempt to transmit with a probability P_R. The retransmission counter of those nodes that convey their information is incremented by one. In our simulations we will assume P_R is always equal to 1, i.e., nodes in B-mode always try to transmit every RACH cycle. We have chosen this value assuming that we have optimal conditions in the system. We want to optimize this value in future work.
3. **Preamble selection:** Transmitting nodes select a preamble $\in \{1, \ldots, K\}$.
4. **Collision preamble detection:** The nodes are ordered based on their preambles. Nodes with the same preamble are reordered based on their transmission counters. Moreover, for each preamble is counted the number of times that it has been chosen by a device to access the network, and if the sum is not 1, a collision has occurred.
5. **Collision preamble resolution:** If the collision resolution is not enabled, the nodes that have collided turn to B-mode. The nodes whose preamble is unique are marked as acquired. If the collision resolution is enabled, the first node of the list is chosen for each preamble, as they are sorted secondarily by their transmission counter. This node is marked as acquired along with the nodes whose preamble is unique. The remaining nodes turn to B-mode.
6. **Server processing:** Only a number of L nodes can be successful. So that those in which the number of retransmissions is greater are chosen. Successful nodes return to the I-mode and those rejected to the B-mode. Successful nodes removed that request for network access from its buffer.
7. **Traffic load calculation:** At the end of each RACH cycle, the number of transmission attempts made in each priority category are stored in different counters, and thus this information can be used for adjusting the two ACB factors depending on the traffic load that exists at that point in the system.
8. **ACB factors adjustment:** The multiple ACB factors (MACB) can be reconfigured by comparison of the counters calculated in the previous step with predefined thresholds. These thresholds measure the overload in MTC nodes and are updated depending on the number of present devices at that time in the system.

5 Performance Evaluation

In order to evaluate the proposed solution, we analyse a system with the following three different categories of devices: HP MTC nodes, MP MTC nodes and LP MTC nodes. These three priorities seem to correspond to a realistic scenario. We analyse how the system behaves as 1.000 MTC devices are added randomly of three different priorities and with a ratio of 1 HP, 4 MP, and 5 LP MTC nodes. Two ACB factors (ACB1 and ACB2), based on [5], and adaptive thresholds to measure overload in each type of MTC nodes are used.

Two simulation scenarios have been defined depending on the type of ACB considered. Table 1 represents the parameters used in the simulations for both scenarios:

- **Scenario 1:** The threshold values are updated taking into account the default values chosen in Table 2 and depending on the number of MTC nodes present at that time on the network. Only the MACB procedure is used.
- **Scenario 2:** In this scenario, the system performance is compared for different methods of selecting nodes to transmit: with ACB, with MACB and neither ACB nor MACB (i.e., ACB = 1, there is no constraint).

Table 1. Simulation parameters

Parameter	Value
Number of HP MTC nodes	100
Number of MP MTC nodes	400
Number of LP MTC nodes	500
Number of total MTC nodes	1000
Number of preambles	48
Number of servers	48
P_N of HP MTC nodes	Beta distribution
P_N of MP MTC nodes	Beta distribution
P_N of LP MTC nodes	Beta distribution
Threshold 1 for HP MTC nodes	Adaptive
Threshold 2 for MP MTC nodes	Adaptive
Threshold 3 for LP MTC nodes	Adaptive
ACB1 factor for MP MTC nodes	Variable
ACB2 factor for LP MTC nodes	Variable
Fixed ACB1 factor for MP MTC nodes	–/0.8
Fixed ACB2 factor for LP MTC nodes	–/0.6
Number of RACH cycles	1–1000

The number of preambles has been chosen in line with [2], and the number of servers has been set equal to the number of preambles so that in this case the capacity of the servers will never be a limitation. With respect to the probability value of generating an access request (P_N) a Beta distribution has been set up.

Regarding the thresholds (Th_i), being $i \in \{1, 2, 3\}$, the adaptive calculation (1) takes into account the number of devices in the system ($n \in \{1, \ldots, N\}$), the average of the probability of generating access requests ($\bar{P}_{N,j}$) where $j \in$ {HP, MP, LP}, a multiplicative factor depending on the type of priority (m_j) and an offset to avoid a bad performance at the beginning of the procedure (o_j). The multiplicative factor is chosen to ensure the access to the network to any type of device, even LP ones. ACB factors are adapted according to the thresholds [5]. The related algorithm is implemented in phases 7 and 8, explained above in

Sect. 3. The fixed ACB factors have been used only for scenario 2. The expression used to update the thresholds is shown below:

$$Th_i(n) = (n\bar{P}_{N,j}(n)m_j) + o_j \quad (1)$$

In both scenarios we evaluate two options, so that, the difference between each of the options are ACB1 and ACB2 values which are updated with each threshold. In Option A more restrictive ACB values are chosen, whilst, in option B they are chosen less restrictively in order to see how they affect the system performance, as shown in Table 2.

Table 2. MACB factor values (option A and option B)

	Option A		Option B	
	ACB1	ACB2	ACB1	ACB2
Threshold 1	0	0	0.3	0.3
Threshold 2	0.8	0.4	0.9	0.7
Threshold 3	0.8	0.8	0.9	0.9

It should be noted that the main improvement introduced with respect to [5] is that the thresholds are not fixed values but they are being updated based on the number of users and the overload in the system. In this way the performance of the algorithm has no restrictions with respect to the number of users, since, when fixed thresholds are used, the system does not take into account the dynamic character of the algorithm. This is summarized as follows:

- When low thresholds are configured, the algorithm works efficiently until a minimum number of users is exceeded in which the highest threshold will always be chosen due to the high number of devices present in the network.
- If higher thresholds are configured, the same problem happens, with the difference that for the first analysis with few nodes in the system, the algorithm does not work efficiently, since the defined thresholds are not reached, i.e., there will be no dynamic adaptation.

Before moving on to analyse the results we would like to clarify the meaning of the parameters used for graphics:

- The normalized throughput (T) is equal to the number of end nodes that have successfully accessed to the network (N_S) divided by the minimum available value of preambles or servers:

$$T = \frac{N_S}{min(K, L)} \quad (2)$$

- The number of transmission attempts corresponds to all transmissions needed for a device till it has successfully accessed to the system.
- The number of RACH cycles corresponds to all RACH cycles elapsed since the first transmission attempt is made until it is successfully granted access to the system.

5.1 Scenario 1

This scenario shows how the system behaves for the ACB factors defined - ACB1 and ACB2 - in options A and B (see Table 2).

In Fig. 4 the graph on the left shows a better throughput in the option B, which is the option with less restrictive ACB values. In both scenarios, Option A presents a drop in the throughput with approximately 180 nodes working in the network. It is related to the threshold values, since the more MTC nodes there are in the system, the more congestion there is and the more restrictive the access for the nodes with lower priority becomes, so this is the reason for the decrease in the overall performance.

Figure 5 presents the number of average transmissions used by MTC nodes and the number of average RACH cycles needed by MTC nodes for Scenario 1 respectively. It can be seen that the option that best categorizes traffic and therefore offers better performance to nodes with high priority traffic is option A, because it uses more restrictive ACB factors and manages to separate in a better way the resources meant for the nodes with higher priority with respect to the nodes with lower priority.

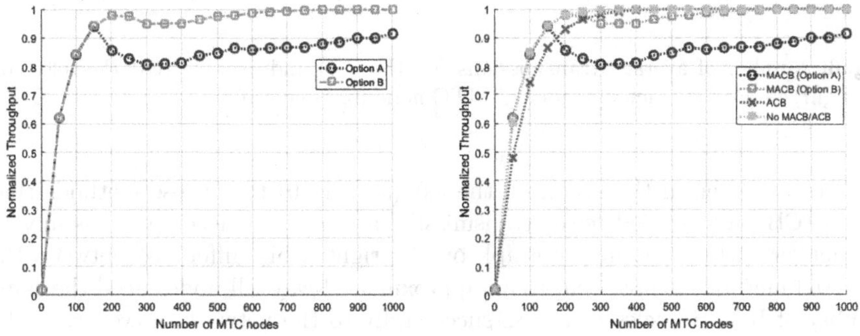

Fig. 4. Normalized throughput of MTC nodes for Scenario 1 (on the left) and Scenario 2 (on the right)

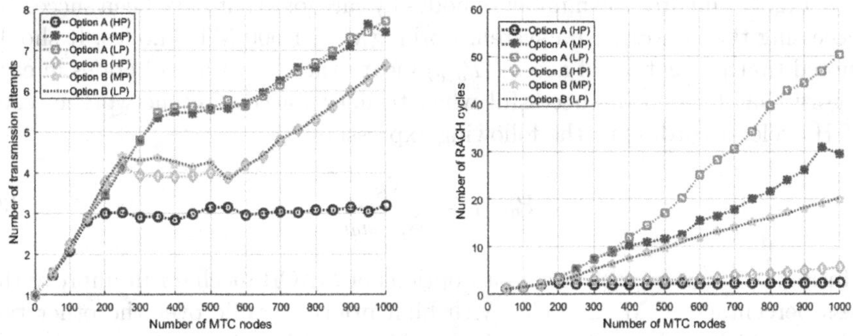

Fig. 5. Number of average transmissions (on the left) and average RACH cycles (on the right) needed by each category of MTC node for Scenario 1

5.2 Scenario 2

This scenario analyses the system behaviour for different methods: with multiple ACB factors (MACB), with only one ACB factor, and neither MACB nor ACB.

In Fig. 4, the graph on the right shows a better throughput in the option without MACB or ACB mechanism because there are no constraints for MTC nodes to access the network. This measure can be misleading since it may be gaining throughput in return for a higher overload in the system.

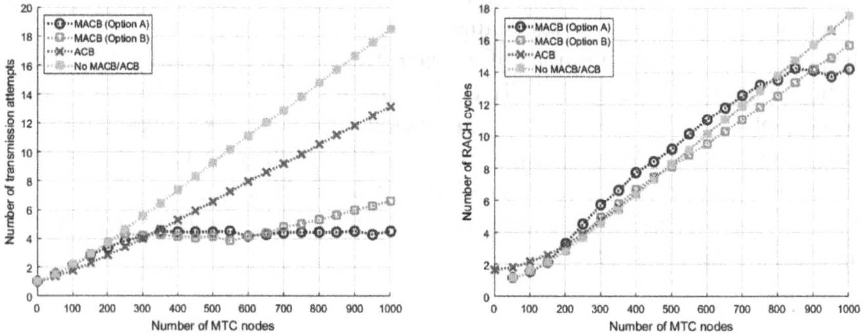

Fig. 6. Number of average transmissions (on the left) and average RACH cycles (on the right) needed by each category of MTC node for Scenario 2

It can be seen in the graph on the left (see Fig. 6) that those methods that use MACB factors need fewer transmission attempts to access successfully to the network. However, in the graph on the right a big difference between the analysed methods is not seen. In an approximated way, all nodes need the same number of RACH cycles to access successfully to the network, however, at the end of the curves it can be appreciated a better performance for the MACB mechanism with more restrictive values.

To analyse the behaviour of different methods using nodes with traffic categories, Fig. 7 compares the number of nodes by category that have been successful in accessing the network, in a system working with 1.000 MTC nodes. It should be noted that percentage of access (P_{acc}) means the percentage of nodes in each category that have been successful when trying to access the network in each RACH cycle, according to the following expression:

$$P_{acc,j} = \frac{N_{S,j}}{N_{S,total}} \tag{3}$$

In Fig. 6, it can be seen that both options of MACB mechanism improve the access percentage of MTC nodes with high priority traffic over the other two methods, which is the main objective of this algorithm. It can be also checked that option A for MACB (graph on the left) has a more aggressive performance and greatly improves the percentage of access of MTC nodes with high priority traffic but lowering the access percentage for both MTC nodes with medium and low priority. While option B (graph on the right) has a more moderate performance, improving the behaviour for high priority traffic without harming much to devices with medium and low priority traffic.

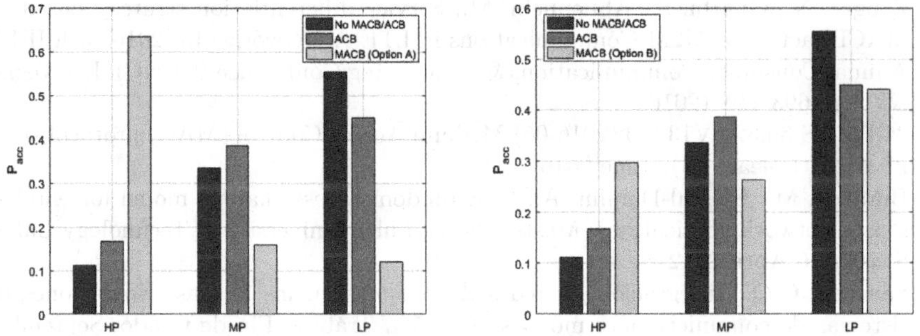

Fig. 7. Comparison of different algorithms for option A (on the left) and option B (on the right)

6 Conclusions

We have proposed and evaluated the performance of a promising random access prioritization procedure for integration of MTC in mobile networks. This adaptive prioritization procedure manages MTC nodes with different transmission priorities by using multiple ACB factors that are dynamically adapted according to the number of nodes and the overload present in the network. The simulation results show that the scenario including adaptive thresholds and MACB provides better performances related to ACB or no ACB/MACB options. Moreover, it is possible to improve access to the network of those MTC nodes that need higher priority. Furthermore, this mechanism could be adapted to the new 3GPP NB-IoT standard [2] requirements and procedures.

The simulation results show some key factors, such as ACB values and thresholds used, to be studied and optimized as a future work.

Acknowledgments. This work has been partly funded by projects MACHINE (TSI-100102-2015-17) and ELISA (TEC2014-59255-C3-3-R).

References

1. Mehmood, Y., Görg, C., Muehleisen, M., Timm-Giel, A.: Mobile M2M communication architectures, upcoming challenges, applications, and future directions. EURASIP J. Wirel. Commun. Netw. **2015**, 250 (2015)
2. 3GPP Standardization of Narrow-Band IoT (NB-IoT). Release 13 (LTE Advanced Pro), 22 June 2016

3. 3GPP TR 37.869 V12.0.0 (2013-09). Study on Enhancements to Machine-Type Communications (MTC) and other Mobile Data Applications. Radio Access Network (RAN) aspects (Release 12)
4. Osipov, E., Riliskis, L., Eldstal-Damlin, A., Burakov, M., Nordberg, M., Wang, M.: An improved model of LTE random access channel. In: 2013 IEEE 77th Vehicular Technology Conference (VTC Spring), Dresden, pp. 1–5 (2013)
5. Zangar, N., Gharbi, S., Abdennebi, M.: Service differentiation strategy based on MACB factor for M2M Communications in LTE-A Networks. In: 2016 13th IEEE Annual Consumer Communications & Networking Conference (CCNC), Las Vegas, NV, pp. 693–698 (2016)
6. 3GPP TS 36.321 V13.2.0 (2016-06) Medium Access Control (MAC) protocol specification (Release 13), June 2016
7. Burakov, M., Eldstal-Damlin, A.: LTE random access channel model for wireless sensor network applications. Master thesis, Lulea University of Technology Lulea, Sweden, 6 April 2012
8. Sánchez, G.Q.: Integración de redes de sensores en las nuevas generaciones de sistemas de comunicaciones móviles 4G y 5G. Trabajo Fin de Grado, September 2015
9. Leyva-Mayorga, I., Tello-Oquendo, L., Pla, V., Martinez-Bauset, J., Casares-Giner, V.: Performance analysis of access class barring for handling massive M2M traffic in LTE-A networks. In: 2016 IEEE International Conference on Communications (ICC), Kuala Lumpur, pp. 1–6 (2016)
10. Morvari, F., Ghasemi, A.: Two-stage resource allocation for random access M2M communications in LTE network. IEEE Commun. Lett. **20**(5), 982–985 (2016)
11. Duan, S., Shah-Mansouri, V., Wang, Z., Wong, V.: D-ACB: adaptive congestion control algorithm for bursty M2M traffic in LTE networks. IEEE Trans. Veh. Technol. **PP**(99), 1 (2016)
12. 3GPP, TSG RAN WG2 #71 R2–104663, [70bis#11]-LTE: MTC LTE simulations. 3rd Generation Partnership Project (3GPP), August 2010

Adopting Fuzzy Technique to Save Energy in Smart Home Control System

Sergio Henrique Monte Santo Andrade[1(✉)], Edvar da Luz Oliveira[1], Rodrigo Dias Alfaia[1], Anderson Vinicius de Freitas Souto[1], Nandamudi Lankalapalli Vijaykumar[2], and Carlos Renato Lisboa Francês[1]

[1] High Performance Network Planning Laboratory (LPRAD), Federal University of Pará, Rua Augusto Corrêa. 01, Belém 66050-000, Brazil
sergioautomacao@gmail.com,
{edvaroliveira, andersonvfs, rfrances}@ufpa.br,
rodrigo.alfaia@itec.ufpa.br

[2] Laboratory of Computing and Applied Mathematics (LAC), National Institute for Space Research (INPE), São José dos Campos, São Paulo 12245-970, Brazil
vijay@lac.inpe.br

Abstract. With the advances in welfare information technology, Smart Home-based solutions have been gaining importance and becoming accepted as an alternative means of energy-saving based on HEMS – Home Energy Management Systems. This paper defines a decision-making fuzzy technique to be used in a novel architecture (SmartCoM). A fuzzy system has been implemented to provide an efficient energy control method based on power consumption and its respective management. The SmartCoM end-to-end architecture is set out in detail by means of consumer optimization strategies for both the end customer and the utility. The main advantages of using the SmartCoM is shown by the numerical results obtained from the proposed architecture. The aim of this article is to show the current state-of-the-art of SmartCoM decision-making, as well as the next stages of related research.

Keywords: Smart home · Consumer electronics · Middleware · Device software platforms · Fuzzy systems

1 Introduction

In recent years, the panorama of the power system has been subject to change owing to the introduction of new business models, for example, electric power distribution. These new models enable consumers to actively participate on the basis of Smart Grid experiences. This participation makes the scenario more complex with regard to services since it raises challenges when integrating, for example, software and hardware elements. This is because there is a significant heterogeneity of power systems and power companies within their operational environments. This leads to an indispensable factor, which is a strategy that can operate at a certain level of safety (an inherent

E. Sabir et al. (Eds.): UNet 2017, LNCS 10542, pp. 345–356, 2017.
https://doi.org/10.1007/978-3-319-68179-5_30

feature of the electricity sector). There is also a need to include services that outrank the traditional distribution of electricity.

In general, Smart Grid can be regarded as a network that can manage electrical devices in several domains, and provide efficiency, reliability, safety and quality of services [1–4]. It has a set of seven interconnected domains [5]. The first four (large-scale generation, transmission, distribution and end consumers or customers) are responsible for generation, transmission and distribution. These domains must ensure a bi-directional communication between the customer and Advanced Metering Infrastructure (AMI) to provide a full controller (e.g. data exchange) for all the system domains. The last three (market, operations and service providers) refer to the power management market, power distribution and provision of services.

In particular, in the case of the end-user domain [6], it specifically refers to power management on the side of the customer, together with control and management of electrical appliances to balance and optimize residential power consumption. This is one of the nine requirements for Smart Grid applications (Demand response and consumer energy efficiency), when employed for the Smart Home scenario, and is the focal point of this paper.

From the established scenario for developing a new level of applications for Smart Home, a new proposal arises to combine information technology solutions, advanced communications and sensor systems to create a variety of new Smart Home applications allied to decision-making techniques. Based on this proposal, it is possible to create ambient-intelligent to inform or make a decision to reduce a residential consumption of energy.

In light of this, this paper sets out an innovative architecture for HEMS (Home Energy Management Systems). This is known as Smart Consumption Management Architecture (SmartCoM), and is based on the rules established in [4] for the interoperability and applicability of Smart Grids within the context of Smart Home.

In addition, the proposal seeks to develop a proactive fuzzy aware home-control system combined with a statistic treatment based on user comfort to achieve electric savings and maintain.

2 Related Literature

Within the general scenario of Smart Home, several HEMS have been proposed to reduce power consumption costs. This reduction is basically made possible by exclusive monitoring and controlling or even by adopting computational intelligence solutions to help optimize the consumption.

With regard to computational intelligence in the Smart Home domain: fuzzy logic was employed to adjust the room temperature by means of thermal sensors and patterns from rules recommended by residents to automatically optimize temperature and thus save energy [7]; similarly [8] uses fuzzy logic to decide how to schedule the use of appliances on the basis of estimated costs and comfort. In [9] fuzzy is used to reduce the residential demand based on different parameters such as occupancy, outdoor temperature, any kind of pricing, thermal comfort, and different schedule a preference.

Applying fuzzy inference machine brought more intelligence to existing simulation, wireless sensors and smart grids initiatives.

Fuzzy logic is also used to a responsive context awareness. In [10], fuzzy intelligence shows a 95.14% accuracy and 6.98 *ms* faster when compared to other techniques.

In [11], the fuzzy logic is used for implementing the pricing scheme for the consumer's consumption from the grid as well as for the consumption of grid from the consumer. Load on the grid acts as the parameter which alerts the fuzzy logic controller of the period being a peak period or not. The system is based on the consumer peak period aware and scheduling the appliance manually by user, intending to maintain the energy consumption levels.

However, these solutions have some limitations: (i) no flexibility as there is no integration with different management platforms; (ii) no flexibility to adopt computational intelligence methods, among other factors; (iii) no appliance ranking according to user comforts sets. In this paper, the decision-making fuzzy technique with consumer comforts analysis, is able to overcome these limitations and will provide to the consumer a smart method to manage energy consumption.

3 Background

Decision-making techniques have been in use for some time to produce results in natural language based on the analysis and modeling of complex scenarios. The results are obtained from computational intelligence heuristics, for example, decision trees, neural networks, fuzzy logic, etc. These methods can deal with complex variables, by classifying and/or predicting results to assist decision-making.

In this paper, the focus is on fuzzy logic to inform residents of homes about increases in energy consumption and, apply the one of three strategies of optimization of the energy consumption, from the parameterization at the moment of the SmartCoM configuration.

Fuzzy logic offers the means to interact with processes that are inherently analogous to digital computers [12]. It involves dividing continuous numerical values into a range of states. These states are overlapping or distorted and defined by using Membership Functions-MF. During the overlapping procedure, a state of a variable does not change all of a sudden. Instead, it gradually loses its value in a MF while renewing it in the next.

The control process starts with fuzzification. At any moment, the system uses the MF of a crisp input variable to be converted into a fuzzy input in which each MF receives a degree of accession. For example, one can convert input value of "Consumption Index" (Fig. 1) to a diffuse set in which values of "Consumption on Average" (C.O.A.), "Consumption Above Average" (C.A.A.), "C.A.A. 20%", "C.A.A 40%", "C. A.A 60%", "C.A.A 80%" and "C.A.A 100%" receive membership degree 1 for C.O.A, and > 1, for consumption within the C.A.A. range.

As a result, a system can then use all the fuzzy sets of the input variables in fuzzy logic. This inference process is based on a set of pre-determined Fuzzy rules that are viewed from the perspective of a specialist, as shown in Fig. 1.

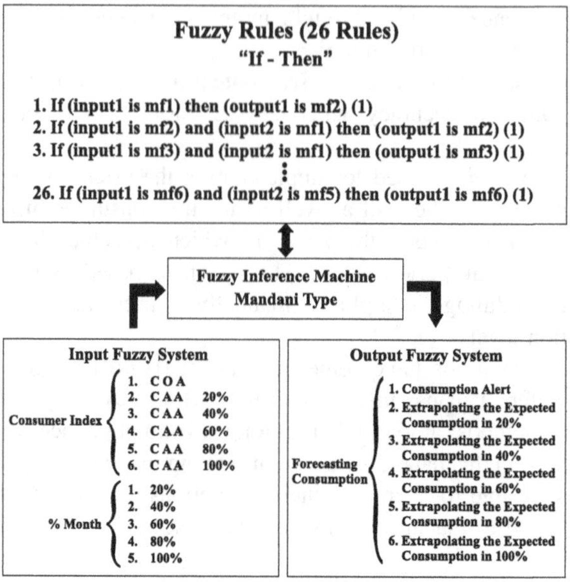

Fig. 1. Fuzzy inference machine

A context is defined by combining all the input values. The system adopted here applies appropriate rules to a particular context. For example, if the "Consumer Index" has a Degree of Membership 1 for "C.O.A." or 1 for "C.A.A 20%", the system checks all the rules containing "C.O.A." or those resulting from "CAA 20%". All these rules produce fuzzy output values that are combined to create a fuzzy set for each output variable. A variation in the value of the rules is applied so that some rules can be more effective than others. This weight factor is usually between 0 (no effect) and 1 (maximum effect). Finally, the defuzzification phase calculates the final results for the output variables using the fuzzy sets that are obtained.

In order to set the strategies of optimization of the energy consumption, the Comfort Index (CI) can be calculated from the output of the fuzzy logic.

In establishing criteria for a zone of comfort in the relationship between household electric appliances and human comfort levels, the Comfort Index(CI) formula was conceived as:

$$CI = (HEU / HAH) * DW \tag{1}$$

From (1), in which HEU (Hours of Equipment Use), HAH (Hours at Home) and DW (Days of the Week).

After this, the user is requested to choose one of the 3 strategies (profiles) of Smart Energy Control (SEC), that will be based on average power consumption and the user's comfort. The SEC system will stop reducing energy from each appliance when the new consumption reaches a level that is equal to the consumer standards (175. 25 Kwh). These strategies (profiles) are as follows:

(a) Energy Consumption Reduction as a Priority Order (Profile 01): The value of excess consumption is subtracted from the amount used by the appliance on which the consumer has least dependence;
(b) Reduction of Energy Consumption Based on a Percentage of the Excess Consumption (Profile 02): The strategy is designed to reduce energy consumption without the need for any household appliances to be turned off, in order to maintain the users comfort zones. The excessive electricity consumption will be shared between the appliances, since there is a need to maintain a Smart Energy Control system. The SEC will be calculated for each household appliance, and provide its occupants with a new system for controlling electricity consumption.
(c) Consumers Energy Reduction Rate based on Consumer Choice (Profile 03): The user reduces the excess energy power, manually, from selected electrical appliances.

All the strategies described above take into account the degree of comfort that each household appliance provides for the user. When seeking to maintain user comforts and ensure there is less impact on the use of equipment, 3 profiles can be established to help the consumer when his/her daily average energy consumption is exceeded. If one of these three profiles is chosen, the user's electrical requirements can be adjusted to energy consumption standards.

4 Proposed Architecture

The proposed architecture offers an innovative model of interoperability for Smart Home. It defines the methodology of a REST-based middleware and integrates the supervision system of the power utility (company) with the metering elements available to the consumer. It is also responsible for controlling alternative energy sources (distributed generation) as well as enabling the automation of domestic appliances by means of intelligent devices, message control of consumption (for example, rules to schedule routine activities, real-time consumption, effective management of appliances, etc.

The purpose of the SmartCoM architecture is to guide and assist in the development of applications of interoperability for Smart Home in a transparent, modular, flexible, scalable and reliable way, while respecting the rules established [13] in and [4], which are the most widely used interoperability solutions in the Smart Home domain. This architecture must be generic so that more efficient solutions can be developed.

Since it is not just concerned with solving the problem of how the consumers should carry out the residential management, the architecture also designs a weakly-coupled middleware with publish/subscribe features. This enables different interoperability solutions to be used to support interoperability between different middleware not only for purposes of utility but also for the client, so that communication is possible between systems by exchanging messages, and hence the scalability of the system can be increased without being restricted to a single solution.

The proposed architecture also allows functionalities of intelligent management to be adopted, in which heuristics based on computational intelligence can be employed.

Fuzzy system analyzes variables obtained from metering equipment and extract patterns to characterize consumption for each consumer so that an optimized model can be eventually applied in Smart Metering.

Figure 2 shows the block diagram, which gives a general picture of the proposed architecture.

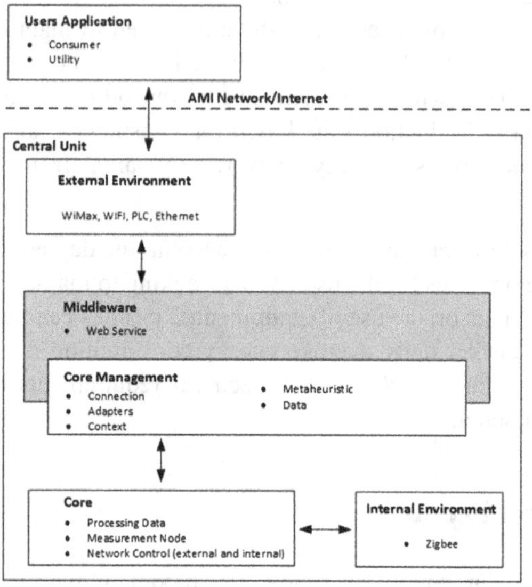

Fig. 2. SmartCoM block diagram

Figure 2 represents the conceptual model that underpins the proposed architecture. Each block plays a well-defined role that considers the functioning and characteristics of the architecture. It is possible to adapt it to scalability and flexibility.

The core specifies the physical and logical parts that are needed to acquire and manage the meter nodes. The central node acquires data, supplied by the meter nodes, and it internally handles the data and passes it on to the visualization layer.

Two communication interfaces are provided to satisfy the communication features specified in the architecture. Integrity is maintained by establishing a dedicated communication channel for the metering elements and thus avoid the loss of information. For example, if there is a network bottleneck, a communication interface IEEE 802.15/Zigbee is employed (Internal Environment). This is a wireless network protocol for sensors and low-rate networks, which is widely used to build automation networks such as home security, industrial control and military applications [14].

The presence of data communication interfaces for the external environment (internet), using standards such as Wi-Fi, Ethernet, WiMAX, PLC, etc., can help users handle the data. This is described in the architecture as External Environment.

Some management levels are defined in core management such as: connection, adapter, context, meta-heuristics and data, among other areas, and require the use of the architecture.

Connection management controls the communication between the supervisor (central node) and multiple connections of metering devices installed at the consumer side (metering node). This brings the adapter management into the picture to communicate between middleware as the proposal requires a communication interface to be established by means of Web Service (WS). Moreover, connection management can preempt traffic to prioritize supervisor messages, when necessary, when they are urgently required by the supervision system of the utility.

Context management plays a role in managing the environment variables of the architecture, such as: communication ports, message priority classes for control and supervision, rules of cryptography, etc.

The meta-heuristics management is responsible to implement computational intelligence techniques, like Fuzzy, that is responsible for extracting consumption patterns or creating a set of optimization rules to be applied in smart devices.

Data management stores and manipulates the data that emerges from metering devices and environment variables.

The middleware layer, based on REST services, generally provides a view of all its components and can be used, for example, to produce control messages such as: remotely turn off, consumption adjustment, alternating between energy sources, storing variables of the internal and external environment of each user and others.

The user applications monitor and manage the elements in accordance with SmartCoM. These applications must be developed and platform-independent and must be compatible with REST.

5 Fuzzy Implementation

With respect to implementing a meta-heuristic for validation, a solution has been found that is based on fuzzy systems. From the input variables (consumption index and rates), the system can inform the user about the need to reduce consumption, and, after that, a data treatment is going to be done to ensure energy savings, by choosing between 3 profiles.

The Consumption Index (IND), shown in Fig. 1, is calculated from the data supplied by the automatic residential system. These data include: Consumption up to the day (C), Date (DM), Historical average (A) and Number of Days in the month (DR). On the basis of this information, the index is calculated by:

$$\mathrm{IND} = \mathrm{C}/(\mathrm{DM}(\mathrm{A}/\mathrm{DR})) \tag{2}$$

After the inference from the Fuzzy machine, the output variable "Exceeded Consumption" (Fig. 3), can assume six possible states starting from the initial point of the diagram, which means that consumption is within the average range. If it is within the ranges of 20% to 100%, then the Consumption level has been exceeded.

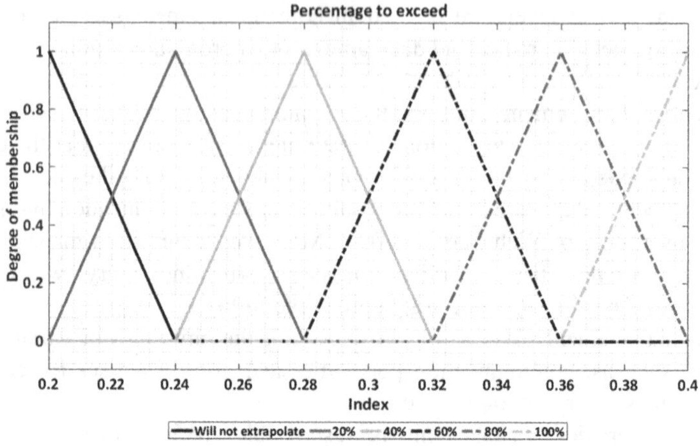

Fig. 3. Output of exceeded consumption

Besides, once the Fuzzy system outputs the result, the resident will be notified by an alert in the mobile application. The notification will also list any appliances that exceeded the expected rate of consumption. As a result, the user can take action to ensure a better and more efficient use.

The output of the fuzzy system's output intrinsically depends on its input variables "Index" and "% month". When the input values are changed, the output is also affected.

On the basis of the output, the configuration management system can enable decision-making to be carried out with greater precision by checking the intelligent consumption of the electronic devices so that the user can be notified of the present status of energy consumption.

In addition, the factors that lead to a greater use of energy can be listed from the monitored data of each appliance, in the face of excessive consumption shown by the fuzzy system. This means that the user can decide which elements should be turned off or reduce its use, based on the strategies defined, and thus ensure an optimization of energy consumption.

6 Demonstration and Results with a Case Study

6.1 Demonstration Module for Intelligent, Operating Systems

Surveys and measurements were first carried out for testing the intelligent systems. These involved collecting the input data required for the validation of the outputs, which represent the potential for optimizing energy consumption.

On the basis of the collected data (Fig. 4), the intelligent system was employed to evaluate its potential outputs for optimizing energy consumption.

As a result of the choice of Profile 01 (Fig. 5), it was possible to reduce the energy consumption of the last item in the priority list until its excessive rate of energy consumption had been reduced. This was the case with the microwave that previously

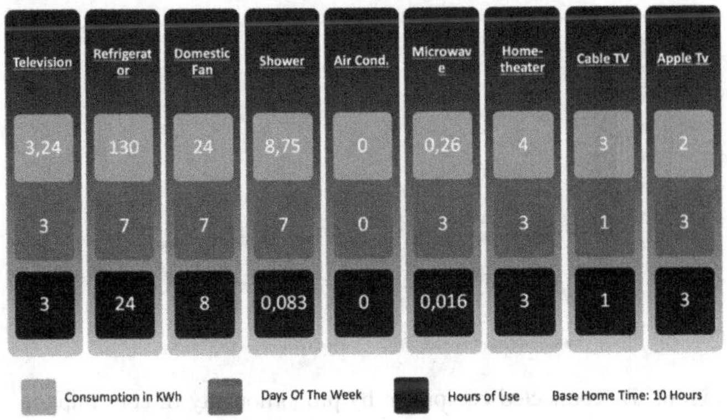

Fig. 4. Usage and consumption average.

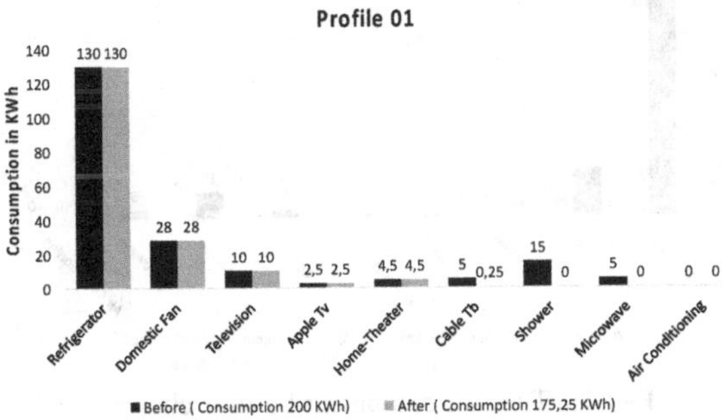

Fig. 5. Equipment turned off by priority order

had a rate of consumption of 5 KWh, after the consumption control devices, began to be turned off. The shower previously had a consumption rate of 15 KWh but after the regulatory measures for consumption had been implemented, this was reduced to zero. The rate of consumption for Air Conditioning was already at 0 KWh, so the system withdrew consumption from the next item on the priority list, in this case the microwave.

Figure 6 shows that there was no need for the appliance to be turned off, which meant that the user's comfort was not affected. The surplus of energy consumption was redistributed proportionally between the other electrical appliances.

In Fig. 7, as suggested in Profile 03, the user preferred to remove the KWh excess from the shower, Home-Theater, Television, Domestic Fan and Microwave manually, and thus was able to keep all the appliances connected.

6.2 User Interface System

A mobile system was designed for the architecture. The purpose of these system is to demonstrate the feasibility of the proposed architecture and its validation.

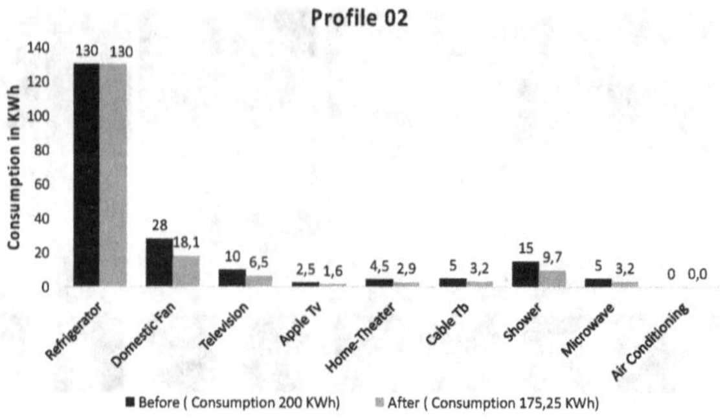

Fig. 6. Disconnected equipment by proportionality of consumption

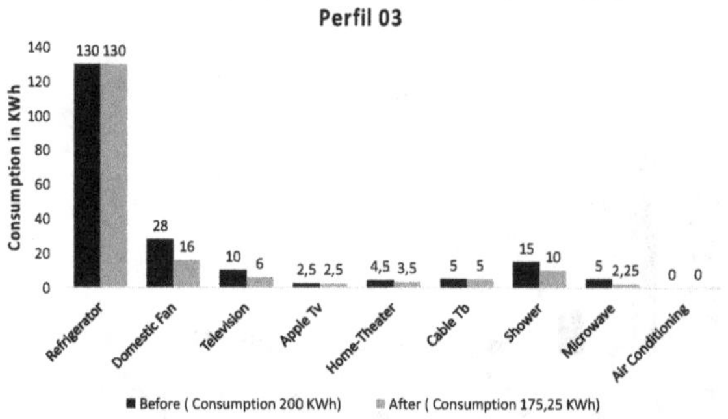

Fig. 7. Turn off equipment by user choice.

The Figs. 8 (a), (b) and (c) shows energy and time results after profile technic.

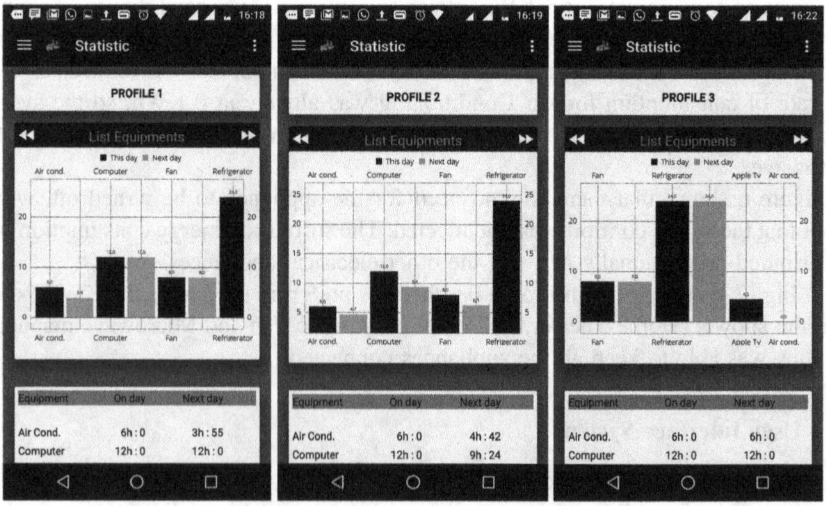

Fig. 8. Profile technic results.

7 Conclusion

The main objective of SmartCoM is to find a complete end-to-end solution for Smart Home, on the basis of concepts from device development, metering, interoperability, computational intelligence, and user-friendly applications. By implementing the SmartCoM architecture, the following have been developed: a hardware solution for monitoring and a middleware to provide an interoperable service bus for developing user-friendly applications aimed at the management module. The architecture also takes into account particular technological features, such as: availability of information, service transparency, modularity, high level of flexibility and reusability.

The SmartCoM architecture was the focal point of the essential aspects of the Smart Home domain. Its characteristics and particular features are not only appropriate for the context of monitoring and managing but also are able to provide an interface for the management by means of legacy systems of monitoring derived from the utility. However, this does not mean that one cannot develop one's own solutions to monitor and manage the residences. The paper also showed a decision-making method by applying Fuzzy Systems to alert the user about excessive power consumption.

It is worth mentioning that, the generated data obtained from SmartCoM, will make it possible to devise efficient mechanisms that represent an effective means of implementing public policies for reducing power consumption. As can be noted, by employing SmartCoM, it is possible to trace the consumption pattern of each connected residential customer. The system can also enhance the environment by applying effective computational intelligence techniques to produce indicators that can assist in reducing the waste of electric power.

References

1. Rohjans, S., Uslar, M., Bleiker, R., Gonzalez, J., Specht, M., Suding, T., Weidelt, T.: Survey of smart grid standardization studies and recommendations. In: 2010 First IEEE International Conference on Smart Grid Communications, pp. 583–588. IEEE (2010)
2. Shahid, B., Ahmed, Z., Faroqi, A., Navid-ur-Rehman, R.M.: Implementation of smart system based on smart grid smart meter and smart appliances. In: 2012 2nd Iranian Conference on Smart Grids (ICSG 2012), pp. 1–4 (2012)
3. Sooriyabandara, M., Ekanayake, J.: Smart grid - technologies for its realisation. In: 2010 IEEE International Conference on Sustainable Energy Technologies, pp. 1–4 (2010)
4. IEEE Std 2030–2011: IEEE Guide for Smart Grid Interoperability of Energy Technology and Information Technology Operation with the Electric Power System (EPS), End-Use Applications, and Loads (2011)
5. Greer, C., Wollman, D.A., Prochaska, D.E., Boynton, P.A., Mazer, J.A., Nguyen, C.T., FitzPatrick, G.J., Nelson, T.L., Koepke, G.H., Hefner Jr., A.R., Pillitteri, V.Y., Brewer, T.L., Golmie, N.T., Su, D.H., Eustis, A.C., Holmberg, D.G., Bushby, S.T.: NIST framework and roadmap for smart grid interoperability standards, release 3.0., Gaithersburg, MD (2014)
6. Nelson, T.L., FitzPatrick, G.J.: NIST role in the interoperable smart grid. In: 2011 IEEE Power and Energy Society General Meeting, pp. 1–3. IEEE (2011)

7. Walek, B., Zacek, J., Janosek, M., Farana, R.: Adaptive fuzzy control of thermal comfort in smart houses. In: Proceedings of the 2014 15th International Carpathian Control Conference (ICCC), pp. 675–678. IEEE (2014)
8. Mohsenzadeh, A., Shariatkhah, M.H., Haghifam, M.-R.: Applying fuzzy techniques to model customer comfort in a smart home control system. In: 22nd International Conference and Exhibition on Electricity Distribution (CIRED 2013), pp. 10–13. IET Conference Publications (2013)
9. Keshtkar, A., Arzanpour, S., Keshtkar, F., Ahmadi, P.: Smart residential load reduction via fuzzy logic, wireless sensors, and smart grid incentives. Energy Build. **104**, 165–180 (2015)
10. Patel, A.: Fuzzy logic based algorithm for context awareness in IoT for smart home environment. In: IEEE Region 10 Conference, pp. 1057–1060 (2016)
11. Seema, P.N., Deepa, V., Nair, M.G.: Implementation of consumer level intelligence in a smart micro-grid along with HEMS based price prediction scheme. In: 2016 IEEE 1st International Conference on Power Electronics, Intelligent Control and Energy Systems (ICPEICES), pp. 1–5. IEEE (2016)
12. Keshtkar, A., Arzanpour, S.: An adaptive fuzzy logic system for residential energy management in smart grid environments. Appl. Energy **186**, 68–81 (2016)
13. Council, G.A.: GridWise interoperability context-setting framework. In: Smart Grids Interoperability, pp. 1–52 (2008)
14. Han, J., Choi, C., Park, W.: Smart home energy management system including renewable energy based on ZigBee and PLC. In: IEEE International Conference on Consumer Electronics, pp. 544–545 (2014)

Multi-hop Clustering Solution Based on Beacon Delay for Vehicular Ad-Hoc Networks

Soufiane Ouahou[1(✉)], Slimane Bah[1], Zohra Bakkoury[1], and Abdelhakim Hafid[2]

[1] AMIPS Research Group, Mohammadia School of Engineers, Mohammed V University, Rabat, Morocco
soufiane.ouahou@research.emi.ac.ma, {Bah, Bakkoury}@emi.ac.ma

[2] Department of Computer Science and Operation Research, University of Montreal, Montreal, QC, Canada
ahafid@iro.umontreal.ca

Abstract. Vehicular ad hoc networks (VANET) are a specific type of networks, wherein nodes are vehicles equipped with wireless receivers. The vehicles can exchange data by using wireless communication either in ad-hoc mode or infrastructure mode through equipments installed on the road side. In vehicular networks, clustering is one of the main dissemination methods, as it enhances the communication reliability and performance. However, a good clustering solution for VANETs has to address the highly dynamic and complex aspects (e.g. real time) of such environments. Of this fact, we propose a novel multi-hop clustering model including: cluster construction/destruction mechanism, multi-hop links establishment and cluster head election algorithm based on a new metric. Indeed, the proposed metric captures real environment parameters. The simulation results show that our clustering solution performs better than existing solutions especially when the obstacle shadowing model is used which is the most likely scenario in real situations.

Keywords: Vehicular ad hoc networks · Clustering · Multi-hop communication

1 Introduction

Vehicular Ad-Hoc Network or VANET is becoming increasingly important and essential for human development, thanks to socio-economic and environmental services offered by: reducing risks, congestion management, air pollution control and also increasing safety and reliability. In VANET nodes are vehicles equipped with a specific device called on-board unit (OBU), which allows them to communicate via V2V communication; Nodes can be also a particular equipment set on the road side called Road Side Unit (RSU), which is able of exchange data with the surrounding vehicles through V2I communication. The V2V communication is made on ad-hoc mode since

E. Sabir et al. (Eds.): UNet 2017, LNCS 10542, pp. 357–367, 2017.
https://doi.org/10.1007/978-3-319-68179-5_31

we do not need a prior infrastructure to ensure the data exchange. The V2I communication is made on infrastructure mode by different kind of technologies such as IEEE 802.11 [3], WiMax [4], and 3G etc.

However, Due to major challenges in VANET including highly dynamic topology and small transmission coverage etc.; a multi-hop clustering solution will improve the vehicular communication by extending the coverage transmission range of clusters and getting more advantages comparing to 1-hop solutions.

In this paper, we propose a dynamic multi-hop clustering solution for VANETs. Our solution is an improvement of a previous solution published on SITA 2016 conference. In the new approach, we have made our existing solution a multi-hop solution, with a new cluster head election/selection algorithm and cluster maintenance algorithm for the same metric.

2 Related Work

In VANET, clustering consists of partitioning the whole network into subsets called clusters, based on one or more identical criteria. Each cluster is managed by a specific vehicle called cluster-head, which manages communication of cluster members in the cluster and with other clusters through getaways as shown in Fig. 1.

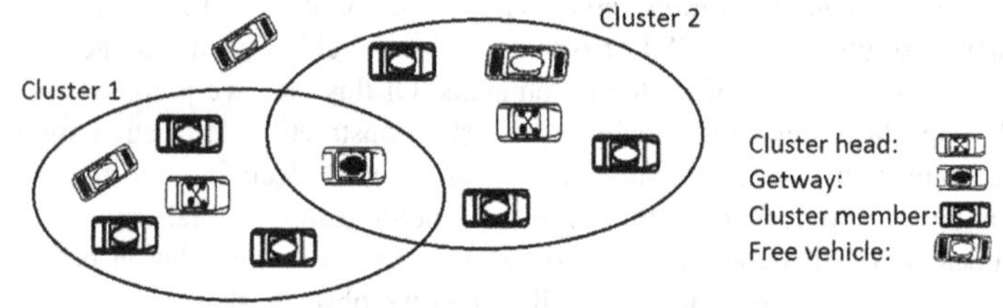

Fig. 1. Clustering architecture in VANET

In the last few years, many clustering schemes have been developed [5] for VANET. However, most of these schemes are developed for MANET and subsequently just adapted to VANET. Therefore, they are not completely suitable for VANETs.

In One-hop solutions, each vehicle can exchange data with others using direct links; without the intervention of any stationary infrastructure or other member of the network. The benefit of a one-hop approach is its ease of data dissemination, and the short transmission delay. Despite of these benefits, one-hop solution isn't effective for VANET because of the small coverage range and many clusters are constructed which decreases the efficiency of solution.

Dynamic Clustering Algorithm (DCA) [15] is a one-hop cluster solution of VANET. In this solution, the cluster head is selected by combining several metrics that are the average linear velocity, acceleration and the distance between vehicles to get spatial dependencies (SD) of neighboring vehicles. The vehicle with the highest cluster relation (CR); which is the average of the total spatial dependencies (SD) of neighboring vehicles; is selected as CH.

In [16], we proposed a dynamic clustering algorithm based on beacon delay for VANET. The main idea of this approach is to construct more stable clusters with long life for real scenario by applying obstacle shadowing model [1, 2] that is the most likely scenario to real scenarios. In this work, the cluster head is elected based on a Fitness value as a metric. The vehicle with the least Fitness in its one-hop surrounding is selected as CH.

Ahizoune and Hafid [17] proposed a one-hop stability-based clustering algorithm (SBCA) for VANET networks. The main idea of this solution is to make cluster maintenance as fast as possible by the election of a secondary cluster head (SCH) that plays the role of primary cluster head (PCH) once it leaves the cluster. This solution takes mobility, number of neighbors, and leadership duration into consideration to construct more stable clusters with long life.

Azizian et al. [18] proposed a clustering solution for an efficient data exchange in VANET. The clusters are constructed based on mathematical optimization solutions to maximize throughput and minimize delay in data delivery as well as make the transmission more robust and scalable. The proposed system implements a medium access control based channel conditions.

The lowest ID clustering algorithm [6] consists of assigning random and unique IDs to all the nodes. After broadcasting the IDs in the beacons, the node with the lowest ID is selected as cluster-head in its surrounding; the other nodes become cluster members. This solution is very simple and limited, since it just allows cluster head selection and clusters construction without any common criterion or metric calculation.

In multi-hop solutions, the inter-vehicles exchange is made through intermediate vehicles whose function is to disseminate data from one vehicle to another and /or from one cluster to another. In spite of the good benefits of the multi-hop solution including: the fast deployment with lower-cost, large coverage ranges; they are hard to manage because of the routing path complexity and the high delay of multi-hop links.

In order to elect the suitable cluster head, MOBIC [7] introduced the mobility of one-hop nodes in the cluster head election. The concept is that the nodes broadcast two successive beacons in order to calculate relative mobility. The node with the least relative mobility is elected as a cluster head. The weakness of MOBIC is the frequent disconnection of cluster members, since the cluster head is elected differently from the other nodes in the surrounding, and it may be that cluster members are fast enough the cluster head.

In [8] Zhang propose a new multi-hop clustering scheme for vehicular ad-hoc networks. In this solution, the vehicle with the least aggregate mobility value becomes a cluster head. This last is elected based on the relative mobility between multi-hop vehicles as a metric. This metric is calculated from beacon (radio propagation) delay on each vehicle. Since the weakness of this solution is the environment influence on the signal, it is the closest solution to our; of this fact we were compared with it.

The Distributed D-hop clustering algorithm [9] consists of organizing vehicles in D-hop clusters of variable size non-overlapping according to mobility and distribution of vehicles on the road. The cluster head is elected based on speed and location differences as metrics.

VMaSC [10] is multi-hop algorithm, which consists on constructing stable clustering by choosing the vehicle with the least mobility as metric. The metric calculation is made by the difference in speed among neighboring vehicles in multi-hop. The weakness of VMaSC Is that it requires a location services to obtain mobility data.

Most of the above mentioned algorithms are based on proportional metrics, which doesn't give good results in real scenarios. Accordingly, many clusters are constructed and frequent links are disconnected, which reduces cluster stability.

3 The Proposed Approach

In this section, we describe our multi-hop clustering solution for vehicular ad-hoc networks. The main concept of the solution is to make it more suitable for real scenarios, by introducing measurable parameters into the metric including beacon delay in our case, in addition to speed and the number of neighboring vehicles, to calculate a combined metric called Fitness (F). The reason we chose beacon delay is that it results from several parameters such as links quality, the inter-distance between vehicles, and the environment influence on the signal; and these parameters completely differ between the simulations and the real world. Fortunately, veins framework has developed the obstacle shadowing model [1, 2], which was developed with measures from the real world.

According to the best of our knowledge, most of clustering solutions do not incorporate the real environment in the solution; therefore, they do not achieve good results once they are implemented in the real scenario.

For the rest of the paper, we define the following terms (Table 1):

Table 1. Notations.

Notation	Description
F	Fitness: the combined metric of our approach
F_O	Own fitness: the fitness of the current vehicle
F_R	Received fitness: the received fitness from the neighbors
F_B	The best fitness that the vehicle has received
V_C	The current speed of vehicle
V_A	The average speed of all the neighboring vehicles in one hop
N	The number of all the neighboring vehicles in one hop
T	The sum of beacons delay with all the neighboring vehicles in one hop
CH	Cluster head
CM	Cluster member
FV	Free vehicle

We admit, in the network a given vehicle is either a:

- Cluster head (CH).
- Cluster member (CM).
- Gateway, which can link clusters between them.
- Free vehicle.

3.1 The Proposed Metrics

The main challenge of clustering in VANET is the cluster head election, as it the central unit of cluster and a long cluster head life grows the cluster stability. For that, it's mandatory to choose this unit carefully.

In VANET, cluster head can be elected based on a single parameter or a combination of many parameters to calculate the metric. On the one hand, these parameters can be local including location, speed, and direction; on the other hand, they may be measurable parameters, such as radio propagation, connectivity, vehicles density, etc.

Studies have shown that a combination of local parameters and measurable parameters gives a good election of a cluster head [11].

In this paper, we propose a new metric based on several parameters including: beacon delay, speed and the number of neighboring vehicles in one-hop. Our metric called fitness (F) is calculated by the following function:

$$F = |V_C - V_A| * \frac{\sum_{i=1}^{N} T_i}{N}$$

where:

- V_C: current speed of vehicle.
- V_A: average speed of vehicles in reach.
- N: the number of vehicles in reach.
- T: The sum of beacons delay of vehicles in reach.
- $|V_C - V_A|$: This value means that the cluster head speed should be close as much as possible to average speeds of vehicles in reach to construct suitable clusters.
- $\frac{\sum_{i=1}^{N} T_i}{N}$: This report means that more the vehicle has many neighbours and quick exchange of beacons delay more it deserves to be a cluster head.
- The beacon delay is a combination of several environmental parameters including: quality of links established between vehicles, distance between vehicles and the environment influence on the signal etc. The main reason to choose beacon delay as a part of metric is to make the scenario more dynamic and adaptive to reality. The latter is the time between the transmission of a beacon and the receipt of a reply.

3.2 Election and Construction Phase

Once a vehicle joins the network, it starts to send beacons to discover the surroundings, and in this case there will be two possible situations:

- If the vehicle doesn't find already constructed clusters in the surroundings, then it begins the construction phase.
- Else, the free vehicle chooses the suitable cluster based on the number of hops and the cluster head fitness F.

In the Initial state of the network, all the vehicles are free. Once they aim to construct cluster; each vehicle computes its own fitness F_O and broadcast it with the neighbors in one-hop; at this state the best Fitness is the same own fitness of vehicle. If the received fitness F_R is less than the stored best fitness F_B, then the vehicle updates the stored best fitness F_B and it rebroadcast it. Once a vehicle receives its fitness from the neighbors, it elects itself as a cluster head (Fig. 2).

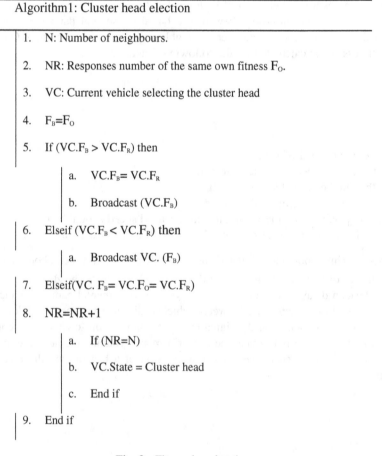

Algorithm1: Cluster head election

---

1. N: Number of neighbours.
2. NR: Responses number of the same own fitness F_O.
3. VC: Current vehicle selecting the cluster head
4. $F_B = F_O$
5. If ($VC.F_B > VC.F_R$) then
    a. $VC.F_B = VC.F_R$
    b. Broadcast ($VC.F_B$)
6. Elseif ($VC.F_B < VC.F_R$) then
    a. Broadcast VC. (F_B)
7. Elseif($VC.\ F_B = VC.F_O = VC.F_R$)
8. NR=NR+1
    a. If (NR=N)
    b. VC.State = Cluster head
    c. End if
9. End if

Fig. 2. Fitness broadcasting

Once the cluster head is elected, the construction phase begins. In the first step, the service is offered by the cluster head itself to direct neighbors. Once the links are established with the previous direct neighbors which have become cluster members, these are responsible for the cluster extension by offering the service of free vehicles including: cluster head ID, cluster head fitness as well as the number of hops between it and the cluster head. There may be a free vehicle receives several offers at the same time; in this case the free vehicle chooses the cluster with fewer hops to achieve the cluster head, if there are several proposals with the same number of hops the vehicle chooses the cluster head with the best fitness (F).

Algorithm2: Cluster head selection

1. N: Number of neighbours.
2. NC: Number of cluster heads offers.
3. VC: Current vehicle selecting the cluster head
4. For (i = 0 to N)
   a. If (V(i).stat = cluster head) then
      i. j=i
      ii. NC=NC+1
   b. End if
5. End for
6. If(NC=1) then
   a. VC.cluster head = V(j).id
   b. VC.state = cluster member
7. Elseif(NC>1) then
   a. VC.cluster head = V(j).id // where V(j) is the cluster head with the less hops number.
   b. VC.state = cluster member
   c. If (NC>1) then
      i. VC.cluster head = V(j).id // where V(j) is the cluster head with the best fitness.
      ii. VC.state = cluster member
   d. End if
8. End if

3.3 Maintenance Phase

After electing the cluster head and selecting the cluster, the maintenance phase aims to improve the stability and increase the clusters life by fighting against frequent election of cluster head. In our solution, once a cluster head is elected, it's the only one which can change is state to a free vehicle. For that a cluster head which loses all its cluster members should change its state to a free vehicle as shown in this algorithm.

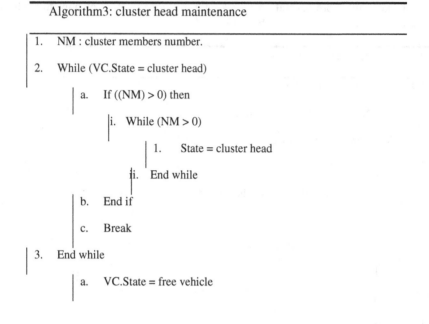

Algorithm3: cluster head maintenance

```
1. NM : cluster members number.
2. While (VC.State = cluster head)
   a. If ((NM) > 0) then
      i. While (NM > 0)
         1. State = cluster head
      ii. End while
   b. End if
   c. Break
3. End while
   a. VC.State = free vehicle
```

4 Simulation and Results

In this section, we present and analyze our solution results before compared the performances with Zhang solution [8]. Our solution and Zhang solution have been developed using OMNET ++ simulator [12], enhanced by the framework VEINS (vehicles in network simulation) [13] and finally SUMO [14] as a road traffic mobility regenerator and emulator. The real scenario is made by the implementation of Obstacle Shadowing model proposed by veins framework. This model was developed with measures from the real world [1, 2]. The mobility model used in the simulation is the freeway mobility model. We consider a network of 1000 m^2 and 100 vehicles. All the parameters are shown in Table 2.

The Fig. 3 shows the average cluster heads lifetime according to transmission range. In this simulation, the transmission range is fixed and the vehicles speed varied randomly between 10 m/s and 20 m/s.

As can be seen; In the graph of our multi-hop clustering solution (MH BD); the average cluster head lifetime increases when the transmission range of vehicles

Table 2. Simulation parameters.

Parameters	Value
Network size	1000 m^2
Number of vehicles	100
Simulation time	300 s
Speed of vehicles	10 m/s < and < 20 m/s
Transmission range	50 m > and < 250 m
Broadcast interval	2 s
Speed interval	1 s

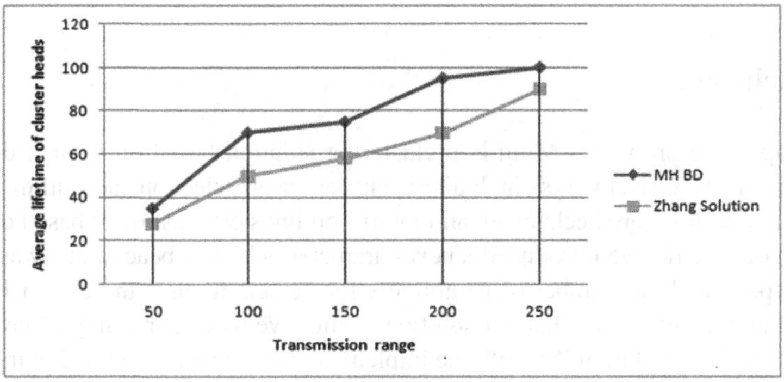

Fig. 3. Average cluster heads lifetime according to transmission range

increases; and that refers to large links between vehicles, which enhance the reach of cluster head; so the cluster head has enough cluster members which allows it to survive as a cluster head.

Compared to zhang solution [8], our solution is stronger in term of cluster stability, and that amounts to the cluster head election, because in our solution we take into account the surrounding by electing the cluster head with maximum number of neighbors with small beacon delay; unlike Zhang solution which takes into account just the relative mobility, adding to this the re-election of cluster head once a new vehicle with smallest aggregate mobility joins the network.

The Fig. 4 shows the relationship between the transmission range and cluster members lifetime. The experience shows that cluster members lifetime increases by the transmission range increase, and it is logical since with a large transmission range, the communication between the cluster head and its cluster members is near enough to reduce the possibility of disconnection.

Compared to zhang solution [8], our solution is stronger with a large gap especially in transmission range under 200 m where our solution is the best since the influence of real scenario (Obstacle Shadowing model [1, 2]) manifests more on the small coverage.

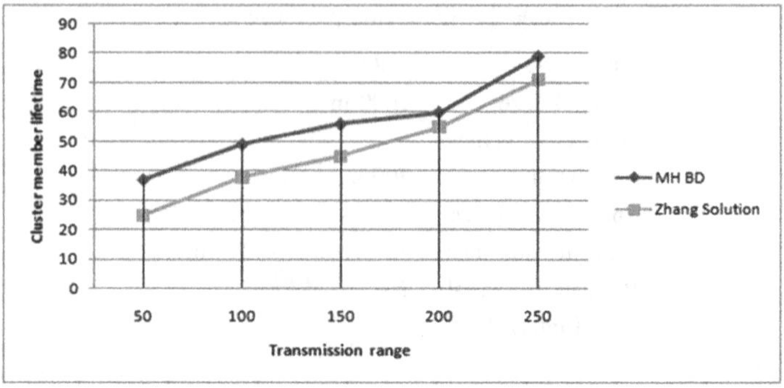

Fig. 4. Average cluster members lifetime according to transmission range

5 Conclusion

In this paper, we propose a Multi-hop clustering solution based on beacon delay for Vehicular Ad-Hoc Networks including: cluster head election algorithm, cluster construction/destruction mechanism, and multi-hop links establishment based on a new metric. In our metric, we introduced a new parameter, which is beacon delay as well as vehicles speed and the number of neighbours for vehicle to elect the cluster head.

Simulation results show that our solution is effective by constructing stable clusters compared to zhang solution [8], with the implementation of Obstacle Shadowing model [1, 2] proposed by Veins framework.

In our future work, we intend to improve this solution by adding some mathematical aspects and manage the data exchange to enhance the QoS.

References

1. Sommer, C., Eckhoff, D., German, R., Dressler, F.: A computationally inexpensive empirical model of IEEE 802.11p radio shadowing in urban environments. In: Proceedings of 8th IEEE/IFIP Conference on Wireless On demand Network Systems and Services (WONS 2011), Bardonecchia, Italy, pp. 84–90, January 2011
2. Sommer, C., Eckhoff, D., Dressler, F.: IVC in cities: signal attenuation by buildings and how parked cars can improve the situation. IEEE Trans. Mob. Comput. **13**(8), 1733–1745 (2014)
3. IEEE standard for information technology-telecommunications and information exchange between systems-local and metropolitan area networks-specific requirements - part 11: wireless lan medium access control (MAC) and physical layer (PHY) specifications (2007). http://standards.ieee.org/getieee802/802.11.html
4. IEEE standard for local and metropolitan area networks part 16: air interface for fixed and mobile broadband wireless access systems amendment for physical and medium access control layers for combined fixed and mobile operation in licensed bands (2005). http://standards.ieee.org/getieee802/802.16.html
5. Yu, J., Chong, P.: A survey of clustering schemes for mobile ad hoc networks. IEEE Commun. Surv. Tutor. **7**(1), 32–48 (2005)

6. Gerla, M., Tsai, J.T.C.: Multicluster, mobile, multimedia radio network. Wirel. Netw. **1**, 255–265 (1995). doi:10.1007/BF01200845
7. Basu, P., Khan, N., Little, T.D.: A mobility based metric for clustering in mobile ad hoc networks. In: International Workshop on Wireless Networks and Mobile Computing (WNMC2001), pp. 413–418, April 2001
8. Zhang, Z.: A novel multi-hop clustering scheme for vehicular ad-hoc networks. In: Proceedings of the 9th ACM International Symposium on Mobility Management and Wireless Access (2011)
9. Azizian, M., Cherkaoui, S., Hafid, A.: A distributed D-hop cluster formation for VANET. In: IEEE Wireless Communications and Networking Conference (WCNC 2016), Doha, Qatar (2016)
10. Ucar, S., Ergen, S., Ozkasap, O.: VMaSC: vehicular multi-hop algorithm for stable clustering in vehicular ad hoc networks. In: Wireless Communications and Networking Conference (WCNC), Shanghai (2013)
11. Vodopivec, S., Bester, J., Kos, A.: A survey on clustering algorithms for vehicular ad-hoc networks. In: 35th International Conference on Telecommunications and Signal Processing, Prague (2012)
12. Varga, A.: OMNET ++ discrete event simulation system user manual, version 4.2.2 (2011)
13. Sommer, C., German, R., Dressler, F.: Bidirectionally coupled network and road traffic simulation for improved IVC analysis. IEEE Trans. Mob. Comput. **10**(1), 3–15 (2011)
14. Behrisch, M., Erdmann, J., Krajzewicz, D., Bieker, L.: SUMO—simulation of urban mobility: an overview. In: The Third International Conference on Advances in System Simulation, SIMUL, pp. 63– 68 (2011)
15. Fan, W., Shi, Y., Chen, S., Zou, L.: A mobility metrics based dynamic clustering algorithm for VANETs. In: ICCTA, Beijing (2011)
16. Ouahou, S., Bah, S., Bakkoury, Z., Hafid, A.: Dynamic clustering algorithm based on beacon delay. In: The 11th International Conference on Intelligent Systems: Theories and Applications SITA (2016)
17. Ahizoune, A., Hafid, A.: A new stability based clustering algorithm (SBCA) for VANETs. In: IEEE 37th Conference on Local Computer Networks Workshops (LCN Workshops), Clearwater, FL (2012)
18. Azizian, M., Cherkaoui, S., Hafid, A.S.: A distributed cluster based transmission scheduling in VANET. In: 2016 IEEE International Conference on Communications (ICC). IEEE (2016)

F2CDM: Internet of Things for Healthcare Network Based Fog-to-Cloud and Data-in-Motion Using MQTT Protocol

Istabraq M. Al-Joboury(✉) and Emad H. Al-Hemiary(✉)

Department of Networks Engineering, College of Information Engineering, Al-Nahrain University, Baghdad, Iraq
{estabriq_94, emad}@coie-nahrain.edu.iq

Abstract. Internet of Things (IoT) evolves very rapidly over time, since everything such as sensors/actuators linked together from around the world with use of evolution of ubiquitous computing through the Internet. These devices have a unique IP address in order to communicate with each other and transmit data with features of wireless technologies. Fog computing or so called edge computing brings all Cloud features to embedded devices at edge network and adds more features to servers like pre-store data of Cloud, fast response, and generate overhasty users reporting. Fog mediates between Cloud and IoT devices and thus enables new types of computing and services. The future applications take the advantage of combing the two concepts Fog and Cloud in order to provide low delay Fog-based and high capacity of storage Cloud-based. This paper proposes an IoT architecture for healthcare network based on Fog to Cloud and Data in Motion (F2CDM). The proposed architecture is designed and implemented over three sites: Site 1 contains the embedded devices layer, Site 2 consists of the Fog network layer, while Site 3 consists of the Cloud network. The Fog layer is represented by a middleware server in Al-Nahrain University with temporary storage such that the data lives inside for 30 min. During this time, the selection of up-normality in behavior is send to the Cloud while the rest of the data is wiped out. On the other hand, the Cloud stores all the incoming data from Fog permanently. The F2CDM works using Message Queue Telemetry Transport (MQTT) for fast response. The results show that all data can be monitored from the Fog in real time while the critical data can be monitored from Cloud. In addition, the response time is evaluated using traffic generator called Tsung. It has been found that the proposed architecture reduces traffic on Cloud network and provides better data analysis.

Keywords: Internet of Things · Web of Things · Fog computing · Cloud Computing · Edge computing · Fog to cloud computing · MQTT · Data in Motion

1 Introduction

IoT is a new concept of future wireless telecommunication that integrates real world of devices with digital world via smart things. There are a lot of factors and concepts that must investigate more broadly for the advancement of IoT because it is the emerging

E. Sabir et al. (Eds.): UNet 2017, LNCS 10542, pp. 368–379, 2017.
https://doi.org/10.1007/978-3-319-68179-5_32

field of information interest. The most advantage of IoT is that objects; such as sensors and actuators, are linked together to improve all fields of everyday human lives without their intervention and enable everything to anyone. These objects (sometimes called ubiquitous computing devices) which is expected to generate huge amount of data need to employ unique IP addressing using IPv6 [1]. IoT available in all areas of life, especially in the medical field, where it has emerged to improve community life and health using the latest technologies and services. IoT-based applications for health and fitness are expected to remodel in order to enhance cost, societies, and governments. In addition, ambulance, patients, medicine and equipment for healthcare network can be monitored in real time by doctors and patient`s family. Thus, electronic and mobile health (eHealth - mHealth) and Ambient Assisted Living (AAL) are enabled for monitoring the patient at home or in smart hospital for fast reporting [2].

A huge number of IoT devices for real-time applications are handled by a new concept that is introduced by Cisco called *"Fog Computing"* in 2012 to bring Cloud Computing features as close as possible to the network edge [3]. Servers, routers, switches and Access Points (APs) can be Fog devices to enable storage, computing and networking services given that these features exist in the Cloud devices. The only difference is that they are closer to users resulting in low latency [4]. This concept is specialized for sensitive applications with a massive amount of data so that IoT societies are enabled to bring benefit Information to governments and communities. Data from these applications are sent to Cloud to be permanently stored and monitored. Cloud Computing has three types of services for users: Software as a Service (SaaS), Infrastructure as a Service (IaaS), and Platform as a Service (PaaS). Applications that depend on centralized storage are suitable for Cloud Computing, whilst application such as smart hospitals that rely on distributed servers are more applicable for Fog Computing [5].

The number of embedded devices such as low power, low bandwidth and low cost sensors grow exponentially with time and the world becomes more interconnected. Thus, a huge amount of data is produced by these devices. Currently, IoT is considered as a major factor and directly proportional to Big Data [6]. Big Data is defined as it mixes the features of 6 V's of data: (volume - the amount of data created by different devices and now days' database cannot handle it), (variety -the kind of data such as voice, video and text), (velocity – the speed of process and analysis of data), (variability – the conflict of disturbed data), (value – which data is chosen to be analyzed) and (veracity - the quality of data) [7]. In other words, Big Data represents a huge number of data that is difficult to be handled by databases [8]. It consists of two types: Data in Motion and Data at Rest. The first one is defined as a method of analyzing and providing actions on data in real time and storage is not required in this type. The latter one is a method of storing, providing actions and analyzing of data after making decisions [9]. This paper proposes an IoT architecture based on F2CDM for healthcare network. Also, it provides an overview of MQTT protocol and discusses the operation of the proposed architecture. In addition, performance analysis like response time is provided for MQTT protocol based on Fog or Cloud with and without quality of services (QoS). The contribution of this paper proposes a new procedure based on Data in Motion. Then, it provides a Fog to Cloud extension using MQTT.

The rest of this paper is organized as follows: Sect. 2 provides an overview of MQTT protocol and its operation. Section 3, proposes IoT architecture based on F2CDM. Section 4, discuss the operation of the proposed IoT architecture. Section 5, demonstrates practical implementation for the proposed architecture and shows results. Finally, Sect. 6 concludes this paper.

2 MQTT Protocol

The MQTT is a messaging-oriented protocol, the first version was developed by Stanford-Clark and Nipper from IBM [10] in 1999. Then, the latest version v3.1.1 was standardized by Advancing Open Standards for the Information Society (OASIS) [11] in Nov 2014. It becomes standard as ISO/IEC 20922 [12] in Jun, 2016. MQTT is an application layer protocol, publish/subscribe model, similar to the client/server model and runs over Transmission Control Protocol (TCP)/Internet Protocol (IP). It is designed for IoT and Machine to Machine (M2M) applications. In addition, it is optimized for resource constrained devices like low power, low bandwidth, and low latency. MQTT is an open source code protocol, simple and not difficult to implement [13].

There are three types of MQTT topic-based elements: the clients that produce messages called Publisher, the clients consume these messages called Subscriber, and the final type is a single server called Broker. The subscribers do not need to know the IP address of the publisher and this is the main advantage of the protocol, while broker must be identified by IP address and port of MQTT protocol in each client [14]. The client can register itself as publisher or subscriber in the broker so that it can recognize messages by publishers. For instance, if publisher sends message M and this message is identified by topic T, then subscribers for T topic receive that message M [15]. The broker acts as hub/spoke model and mediates the clients in order to establish connection and forward data between them. Thousands of clients can be connected to one broker and can subscribe to several topics at the same time. Also, the broker must filter all subscribed clients with a specific topic. Topics are structured in the same way as the structure of the folder such as “hospital/heartbeat/75” where the “/75” represents the value of heartbeat rate. For security reasons, the broker uses Secure Sockets Layer (SSL)/Transport Layer Security (TLS) encryption methods between itself and clients. This method is the same as Secure Hyper Text Transfer Protocol (HTTPS) encryption methods. Also, it requires username and password for each client. Facebook and most critical applications like smart hospitals uses MQTT protocol to communicate and enable reports between doctors, nurses, patients and people around the world [16, 17].

MQTT features include a synchronous communication, a lower overhead and has three levels of QoS for a delivery assurance between clients and broker (see Fig. 1) [17]:

- QoS level 0: at most once, the publisher sends data to subscribers via broker. Publisher does not know if data is arrived to subscribers or not. Subscribers do not send an acknowledgement to publisher that they receive data from and publisher in turn do not re-send data. At this level, lost data may happen depends on network

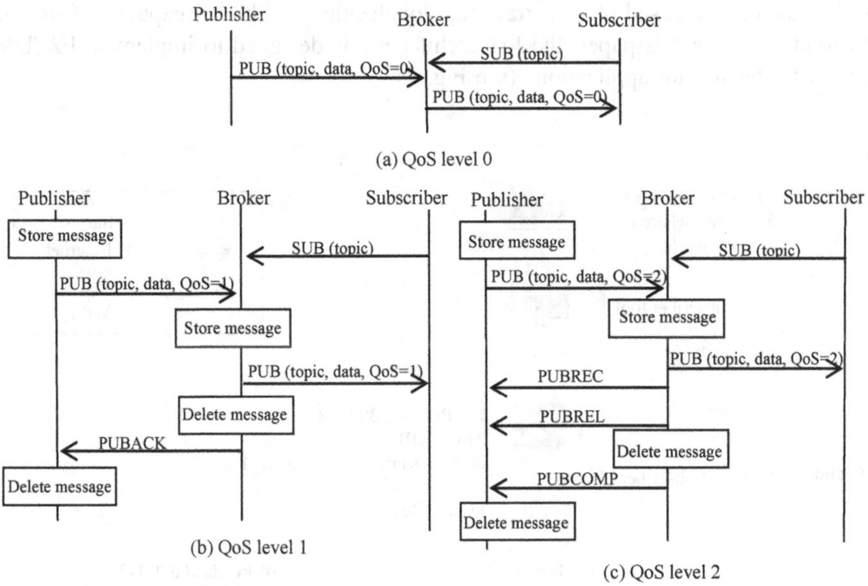

Fig. 1. The operation of MQTT: (a) with QoS level 0 (b) with QoS level 1 (c) with QoS level 2.

issues. This level is also known as "fire and forget". Publisher sends PUNLISH (it contains data with QoS level 0 and topic) message (see Fig. 1(a)).

- QoS level 1: at least once, the publisher sends data to subscribers through broker. The broker sends PUBACK to publisher in order to acknowledge the publisher that broker subscribers receive data. In this level, if data gets lost the broker re-send PUBACK to publisher (see Fig. 1(b)).
- QoS level 2: at exactly once, publisher sends messages to subscribers, by using four-way handshake. Thus, this level leads to increase in the overhead (see Fig. 1(c)).

3 IoT Based F2CDM Architecture

Smart applications include thousands of devices, each one of them sends data in every second and this leads to the emergence of Big Data. Thus, it will lead to high traffic on network and higher delays. All these data are transferred to Cloud for processing and monitoring. However, Big Data must be handled instantly for analysis. Cloud computing cannot handle this huge number of data, since Cloud could be anywhere and away from application. In addition, transferred data from embedded layer to Cloud layer becomes an inefficient method for storing data. The emerging of Fog computing may lead to lower delays by moving the Cloud features to the network edge. To combine the good features of both concepts for enabling critical applications; Fog can be integrated with Cloud in order to benefit from low delay, distributed storage and localization of Fog-based plus centralized, globalization and higher capacity of storage of Cloud-based. In this paper, the IoT architecture is designed to implement F2CDM method for healthcare applications (see Fig. 2).

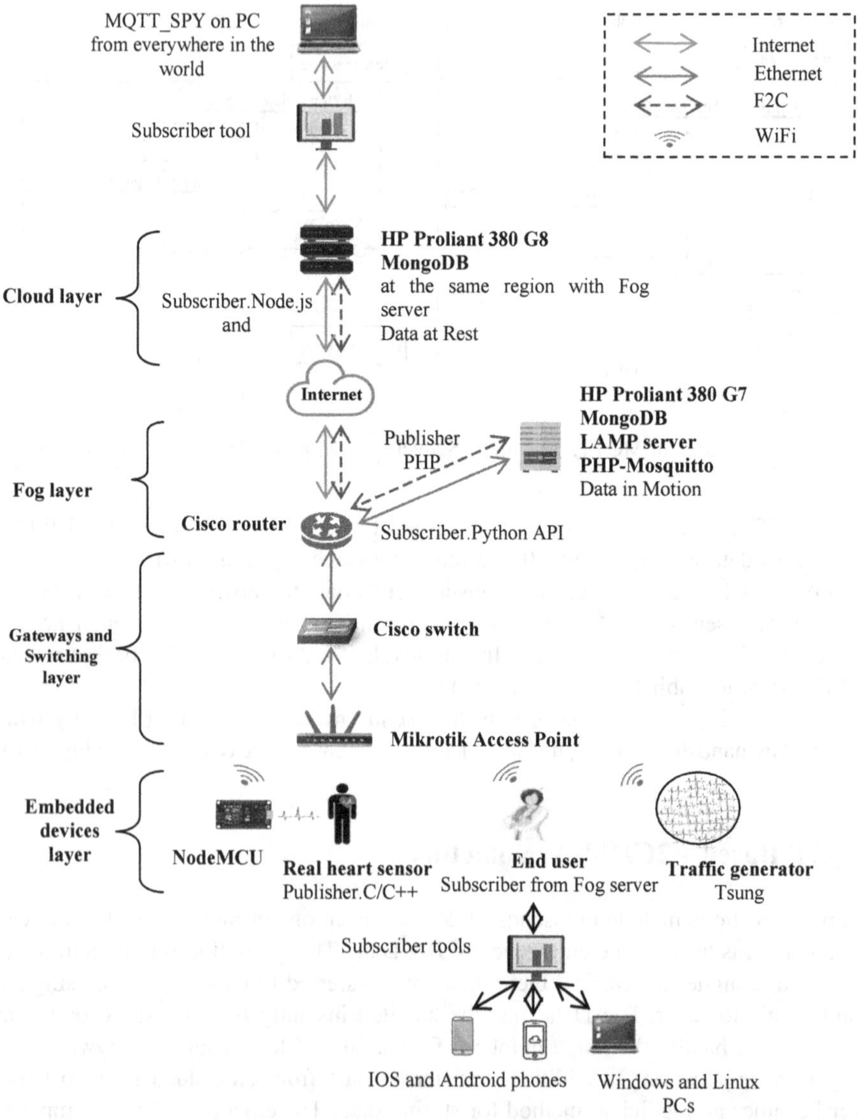

Fig. 2. The proposed IoT architecture for healthcare network based F2CDM.

3.1 Embedded Devices Layer

This layer is similar to the physical layer of Open Standard Interconnection the (OSI) model and consists of sensors, actuators, and microcontrollers. The aim of this layer is sensing data from different IoT devices connected to patients. Then, these data are collected and transmitted to Fog devices via communication methods such as WiFi or Bluetooth to enable users reporting. The features of these devices are limited with constrained resources like low power and storage. Also, the data can be monitored and managed in the same Local Area Network (LAN) by using smart phones and PCs. In this paper, pulse heartbeat sensor [18] is used for reading heartbeat rate values. To emulate the large number of sensors, Tsung [19] (also called Tsunami) is used as a traffic generator. With Tsung, the problem of having hundreds or even thousands of sensors in the experimental setup is solved. In addition, NodeMCU [20] is used for transmitting the data to gateway layer using WiFi. Regarding the protocol in this layer, MQTT v3.1.1 publisher is programmed using C/C++ programming language by Arduino IDE v1.6.12 software.

3.2 Gateway and Switching Layer

This layer consists of three sublayers: physical, switching, and network of the OSI model. The aim of this layer is to send information from embedded devices to Fog layer or receives responses from Fog layer to the organization level. In this paper, an IEEE802.11n AP is used to connect the heartbeat sensor to Fog layer via Cisco switch. In addition, routing mechanism is used in this layer for forwarding data to another network via the Internet.

3.3 Fog Layer

This layer is represented by a middleware server, its aim to receive values from heartbeat sensors and provide actions on these data that are determined by experts. Then, Fog server sends the abnormal data to Cloud layer. In this paper, Fog server acts as an interface between embedded devices and Cloud layer. Mosquitto broker is used for subscribing data from the sensors using python Application Program Interface (API) and then these data are temporally stored in MySQL database. Also, Fog server provides Data in Motion method and sends them - after this process - to Cloud using PHP5 and Mysqli programming language. The connection F2CDM procedure is discussed in details in the next section.

3.4 Cloud Layer

The aim of this layer is to store the critical data permanently. In this paper, MongoDB database is used for storing data. Mosquitto broker is configured to subscribe these data from Fog server using Node.js as an interface. The data is formatted in Java Script Object Notation (JSON) language and can be monitored from anywhere in order to provide user reporting of critical issues of the patients.

4 Operation of IoT Based F2CDM Architecture

In this section, the operation of the proposed architecture for healthcare network based on F2CDM is explained with the aid of Fig. 3. The operation is as follows:

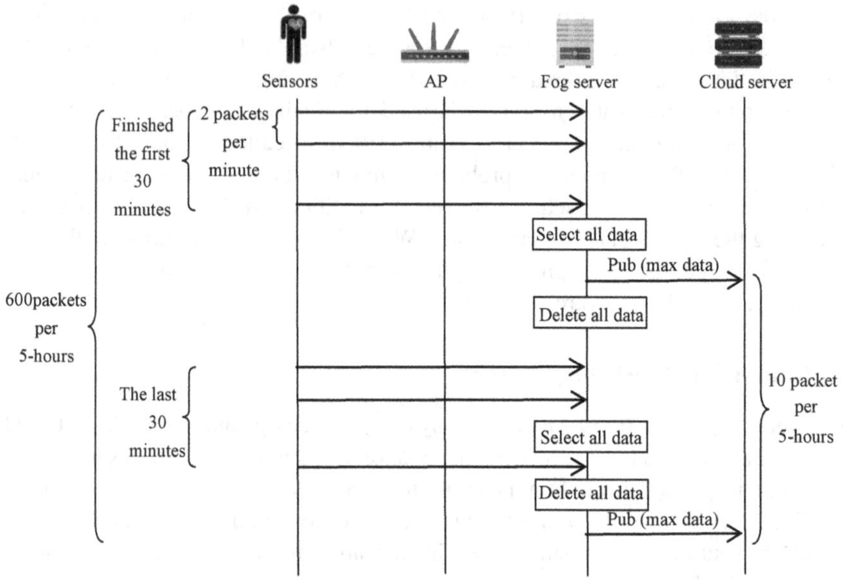

Fig. 3. The operation of proposed architecture from sensor, AP, Fog to Cloud with Data in Motion.

4.1 From Sensors to Fog Server

This step starts by generating real heartbeat rate measurements from sensors placed on the patient's body. In this paper, one real pulse sensor is used to sense heartbeat rate every 30 s (this time can be adjusted via programming), and all these values are aggregated by NodeMCU and temporally stored in the prepared MySQL database. Every 30 min, Data in Motion procedure is implemented to select the max value and send it to Cloud in real-time, while the rest of data are deleted. Then, the procedure moves to the next 30 min and so on. Cronjob tool is used in this step to run a PHP script to publish data to the Cloud every 30 min.

4.2 From Fog Server to Cloud Server

In this step, all the abnormality values of Fog server are received within every 30 min. Here, data is called Data at Rest, which can be permanently stored and monitored in MongoDB and Robomongo GUI for making decisions.

5 Need for F2CDM

To overcome the limitations of Cloud represented by the expected high delay for high traffic and to enable high performance of sensitive applications, Fog can be emerged in existing architectures. The upcoming revolution is expected to mix these two concepts (Fog and Cloud) into a new architecture Fog-to-Cloud (or simply: F2C) to combine all the powerful features of Fog and Cloud (see Fig. 4(c)). Moreover, to enable instant analysis and efficient data storage, Data in Motion (or simply: DM) is expected to increase performance when combined to F2C. Therefore, each of the three combined methods or aspects achieves part of the required enhancement needed in analysis, reporting, or storage.

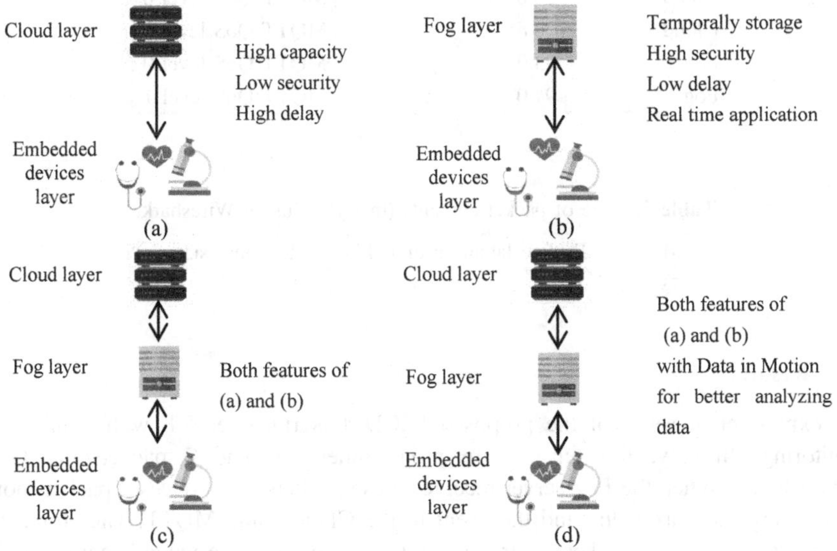

Fig. 4. The evolution of computing from Cloud, Fog, F2C to F2CDM.

6 Results and Discussions

6.1 Experimental Setup

The experimental setup of the proposed IoT architecture consists of the following: Mosquitto and MongoDB with PHP are installed on Fog (private server located in Al-Nahrain University, College of Information Engineering), Cloud (public server located in Ministry of Higher Education and Scientific Research). The Fog server is HP ProLiant 380 G7 16 Core 32 with 32 GB of dynamic memory and 500 GB of permanent storage. While the Cloud server is HP ProLiant 380 G8 16 Core with 32 GB of dynamic memory and 500 GB of permanent storage. Both servers run on Ubuntu server 14.04 LTS Operating system (OS). Mqtt_spy is configured in VMware workstation runs on

Ubuntu 14.04.5 LTS OS installed on Intel (R) Core (TM) i7-6700HQ CPU @ 2.60 GHz, with 8 GB of dynamic memory. In addition, Tsung is installed on a different machine with Ubuntu 14.04.5 LTS OS, 4 GB dynamic memory, processor: Intel(R) Core(TM) i3-380 CPU @ 2.53 GHz * 4, and 500 GB permanent storage.

To clarify the connection speed between different parts of the proposed architecture, IPerf tool [21] is used for this task as shown in Table 1. This tool is used with TCP and based on client/server model. The size of the MQTT protocol packet from sensors is captured using Wireshark [22] as shown in Table 2.

Table 1. Bandwidth between sensors and servers using IPerf tool.

Type of servers	Bandwidth (Mbits/sec)	Protocol
Cloud	26.8	MQTT QoS level 0
Cloud	26.8	MQTT QoS level 1
Fog	93.9	MQTT QoS level 0
Fog	94.0	MQTT QoS level 1

Table 2. Size of packet contents (in Bytes) using Wireshark.

Message	Packet datagram unit (PDU)	Response size
75	11	2

6.2 Results

The experimental setup of the proposed F2CDM is run over 5 h with continuous monitoring. Initially, the sensors are programmed to send 2 packets/min (120 packets/hour). When the Fog server receives these packets, it produces 2 packets/hour by selecting the max value and then sent to the Cloud using MQTT. Therefore, the Cloud packet rate is 2 packets/hour. As shown in Fig. 5(a), the value becomes (null) after 5 h because the rest of data is deleted in Fog server. Two types of monitoring are provided: One from Fog server in real time using IoT MQTT Dashboard v1.9.3 and the second using MQTTool v1.21 on Android and IOS smart devices. Physicians can follow-up patient's status in real-time as shown in Fig. 5(c). On the other hand, data is monitored from Cloud server using Mqtt_spy v0.5.4 which is used for monitoring the critical data of the patient in order to send fast feedback to observers. Also, it is helpful for debugging and fault troubleshooting on MQTT topics and payload. The graph of Mqtt_spy presents the value of the payload for specified time the data arrived to Cloud server. These tools used with MQTT protocol (see Fig. 5(d)). There are tools for monitoring data directly from the sensor like Processing Development Environments (PDE) v3.2.1 which is a simple environment to monitor a patient's heartbeat (BPM) and the time interval between beats (IBI) on PC, these values are taken from the port of Arduino IDE using Java programming language (see Fig. 5(e)).

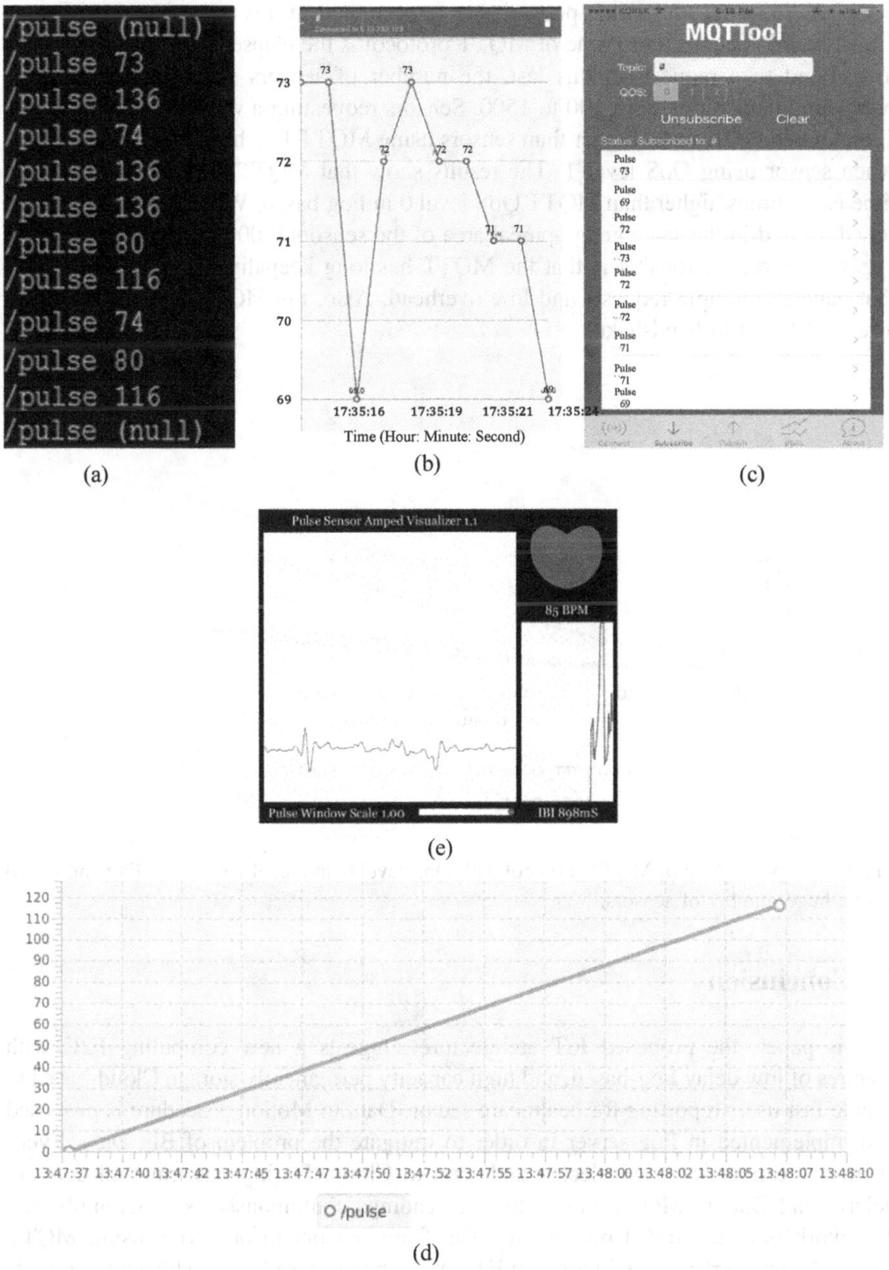

Fig. 5. Monitoring tools and results: (a) incoming data from Fog server to Cloud server based on F2CDM (b) IoT MQTT Dashboard for android (c) MQTTool for IOS (d) Mqtt_spy on Pc from anywhere in the world (e) processing development environments on PC gets data directly from sensor.

In addition, response time performance is presented in this paper based on Fog or Cloud based. The response time of MQTT protocol is the elapsed time taken by a web to respond to a request. In this test, the number of sensors set for requesting and publishing data varies from 100 to 1500. Sensors requesting a web page using MQTT Cloud based is 3.4 times higher than sensors using MQTT Fog based. The same results when sensor using QoS level 1. The results show that MQTT QoS level 1 response time is 1.1 times higher than MQTT QoS level 0 in Fog based. While, it is 1.4 in Cloud based located in the same geographical area of the sensors (1000 sensors) as shown in Fig. 6. The reason for that is that the MQTT has long keepalive time for connection that handles multiple requests and low overhead. Also, the MQTT has low overhead size of 2 Bytes in handshake.

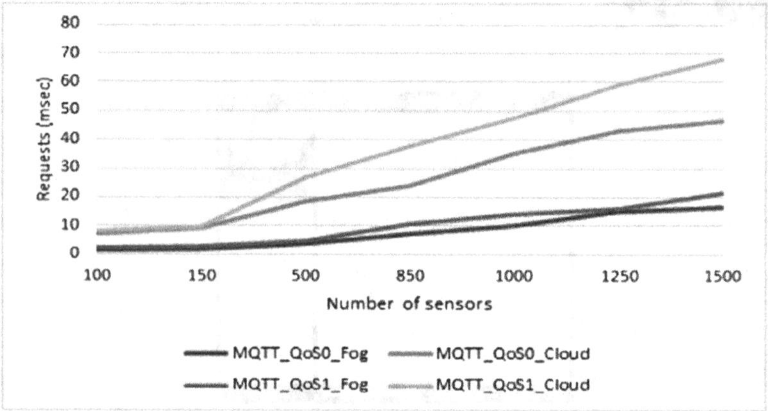

Fig. 6. Response time of MQTT protocol with QoS level 0 and level 1 based on Fog and Cloud over a huge number of sensors.

7 Conclusion

In this paper, the proposed IoT architecture suggests a new computing F2C with features of low delay Fog-based, and high capacity permanently storage Cloud-based to enable fast users reporting for healthcare sector. Data in Motion procedure is proposed and implemented in Fog server in order to mitigate the problem of Big Data. Every 30 min, the max value is selected and send to Cloud. During this time, all data are deleted and Data in Motion moves to next readings continuously using Cronjob tool. The work is concentrated on sending data from sensors to observers using MQTT protocol client/server model based on F2CDM. The proposed IoT architecture consists of: Cloud, Fog, gateways and switching, and embedded devices layers. A huge amount of data is generated from real heartbeat pulse sensor with low cost, power, and complexity in cooperation with traffic generation tool. The proposed architecture shows that F2CDM reduces load traffic on Cloud server. In addition, data can be monitored based on Fog/Cloud by using MQTT monitoring tools on smart devices and PCs.

References

1. Rahmani, A.M., Gia, T.N., Negash, B., Anzanpour, A., Azimi, I., Jiang, M., Liljeberg, P.: Exploiting smart e-Health gateways at the edge of healthcare internet-of-things: a fog computing approach. Future Gener. Comput. Syst. **78**, 641–658 (2017)
2. Silva, B.N., Khan, M., Han, K.: Internet of things: a comprehensive review of enabling technologies, architecture, and challenges. IETE Tech. Rev. 1–16 (2017). doi:10.1080/02564602.2016.1276416
3. Stojmenovic, I., Wen, S.: The fog computing paradigm: scenarios and security issues. In: Proceedings of the 2014 Federated Conference on Computer Science and Information Systems (2014)
4. Mahmud, R., Buyya, R.: Fog computing: a taxonomy, survey and future directions. arXiv preprint arXiv:1611.05539 (2016)
5. Dastjerdi, A.V., Gupta, H., Calheiros, R.N., Ghosh, S.K., Buyya, R.: Fog computing: principles, architectures, and applications. Distributed, Parallel, and Cluster Computing. arXiv:1601.02752 (2016)
6. Papadokostaki, K., Mastorakis, G., Panagiotakis, S., Mavromoustakis, C.X., Dobre, C., Batalla, J.M.: Handling big data in the era of internet of things (IoT). In: Mavromoustakis, C. X., Mastorakis, G., Dobre, C. (eds.) Advances in Mobile Cloud Computing and Big Data in the 5G Era. SBD, vol. 22, pp. 3–22. Springer, Cham (2017). doi:10.1007/978-3-319-45145-9_1
7. Leadbetter, A., Smyth, D., Fuller, R., O'grady, E., Shepherd, A.: Where big data meets linked data: applying standard data models to environmental data streams. In: 2016 IEEE International Conference on Big Data (Big Data) (2016)
8. Gilchrist, A.: The technical and business innovators of the industrial internet. Industry 4.0, pp. 33–64. Apress, Berkeley (2016). doi:10.1007/978-1-4842-2047-4_3
9. Ebbers, M.: 5 Things to Know About Big Data in Motion. IBM (2013)
10. MQTT (2014). http://mqtt.org/. Accessed 22 Mar 2017
11. Banks, A., Gupta, R.: MQTT Version 3.1. 1. OASIS standard (2014)
12. ISO - International Organization for Standardization. ISO/IEC 20922:2016 - Information technology – Message Queuing Telemetry Transport (MQTT) v3.1.1. http://www.iso.org/iso/catalogue_detail.htm?csnumber=69466/. Accessed 22 Mar 2017
13. Fysarakis, K., Askoxylakis, I., Soultatos, O., Papaefstathiou, I., Manifavas, C., Katos, V.: Which IoT protocol? Comparing standardized approaches over a common M2M application. In: 2016 IEEE Global Communications Conference (GLOBECOM) (2016)
14. Triawan, M.A., Hindersah, H., Yolanda, D., Hadiatna, F.: Internet of things using publish and subscribe method cloud-based application to NFT-based hydroponic system. In: 2016 6th International Conference on System Engineering and Technology (ICSET) (2016)
15. Thangavel, D., Ma, X., Valera, A., Tan, H.-X., Tan, C.K.-Y.: Performance evaluation of MQTT and CoAP via a common middleware. In: 2014 IEEE Ninth International Conference on Intelligent Sensors, Sensor Networks and Information Processing (ISSNIP) (2014)
16. Sethi, P., Sarangi, S.R.: Internet of things: architectures, protocols, and applications. J. Electr. Comput. Eng. (2017). Hindawi
17. Grgic, K., Speh, I., Hedi, I.: A web-based IoT solution for monitoring data using MQTT protocol. In: 2016 International Conference on Smart Systems and Technologies (SST) (2016)
18. Pulse sensor. https://pulsesensor.com/. Accessed 23 Mar 2017
19. Tsung. http://tsung.erlang-projects.org/. Accessed 23 Mar 2017
20. NodeMCU. http://nodemcu.com/index_en.html. Accessed 23 Mar 2017
21. IPerf. https://iperf.fr/. Accessed 23 Mar 2017
22. Wireshark. https://www.wireshark.org/. Accessed 23 Mar 2017

Compact Dual-Band CPW-Fed Patch Antenna for 2.45/5.80 GHz RFID Applications

Mohamed Tarbouch(✉), Abdelkebir El Amri, and Hanae Terchoune

RITM Laboratory, CED Engineering Sciences, Ecole Supérieure de Technologie, Hassan II University of Casablanca, Casablanca, Morocco
mtarbouch@gmail.com

Abstract. In this paper, a Coplanar Wave Guide (CPW)-Fed microstrip octagonal patch antenna for RFID Applications is proposed. The studied structure is suitable for 2.45/5.80 GHz applications. The octagonal shape is obtained by making a cut in the four angles of the rectangular microstrip patch antenna; in addition the using of CPW-Fed allows obtaining UWB characteristics in the higher band. The miniaturization in the antenna size for lower band is achieved by introducing an inverted E slot in the radiating element. The proposed antenna is designed on a single and a small substrate board of dimensions 29.5 × 29.5 × 1.6 mm^3. The simulated bandwidth of 5.73% (2.37 GHz to 2.51 GHz) and 34.36% (4.70 GHz to 6.65 GHz) is achieved for the lower band and the upper band, respectively. Moreover the miniaturized antenna has a good impedance matching and an enhanced gain. All the simulations were performed in CADFEKO, a Method of Moment (MoM) based solver.

Keywords: CADFEKO · CPW-Fed · Microstrip · Miniaturization · RFID

1 Introduction

Radio Frequency Identification (RFID) is the wireless use of electromagnetic field to identify tagged objects and is used in a variety of fields such as access control, transport, banks, health, and logistic. An RFID system is generally composed of a reader and tags. The communication between the reader and the tags is achieved by modulated backscattering of the reader's carrier wave signal [1].

In a typical RFID system [2], passive tags are attached to an object such as goods, vehicles, humans, animals, and shipments, while a vertical/circular polarization antenna is connected to the RFID reader. The RFID reader and tag can radio-communicate with each other using a number of different frequencies, and currently most RFID systems use unlicensed spectrum. The common frequencies used are low frequency (125 kHz), high frequency (13.56 MHz), ultra high frequency (860–960 MHz/2.45 GHz), and microwave frequency (3.6/3.9/5.8/5.9/8.2 GHz [3]). The typical RFID readers are able to read (or detect) the tags of only a single frequency but multimode readers are becoming cheaper and popular which are capable of reading the tags of different frequencies [4].

E. Sabir et al. (Eds.): UNet 2017, LNCS 10542, pp. 380–389, 2017.
https://doi.org/10.1007/978-3-319-68179-5_33

The miniaturization can affect radiation characteristics, bandwidth, gain, radiation efficiency and polarization purity. The miniaturization approaches are based on either geometric manipulation (the use of bend forms, meandered lines, PIFA shape, varying distance between feeder and short plate, using fractal geometries [5–8]) or material manipulation (Loading with a high-dielectric material, lumped elements, conductors, capacitors, short plate [9]), or the combination of two or more techniques [10]. Also several works [11–15] have appeared in the literature in which the size of the microstrip patch antenna has been reduced by introducing various types of slots in the radiating element.

In this paper, the authors propose a compact CPW-Fed microstrip octagonal patch antenna with inverted E slot loading in the radiating element. The proposed structure is particularly simple in manufacturing owing to its single dielectric and single metal layer. In this study, many series of optimization are investigated by simulation, and the characteristics of the final circuit are analyzed and discussed.

The proposed antenna is designed in two steps. In the first step, we describe the design procedure of the CPW-feed octagonal patch antenna. In the second step we introduce an inverted E slot in the radiating element which leads to generate a new resonance frequency and therefore allow covering the lower bandwidth [2.37–2.51].

2 Design Methodology

2.1 Step 1: Desing of CPW-Feed Octagonal Patch Antenna at 5.80 GHz

As demonstrated in several studies, the CPW-Feeding allows having a wide bandwidth comparing with the probe feeding [16–18]. The configuration of the proposed antenna is shown in Fig. 1. The antenna is constructed on a FR4 substrate with a dielectric constant of 4.4, thickness of 1.6 mm and size of 29.5 mm $\times$ 29.5 mm. The antenna has a coplanar configuration in which both the conductor and ground plane are on one side of the PCB.

In this step we make a cut of a small triangular shape in the four angles of the microstrip patch antenna as shown in Fig. 1. With this manner we obtain an octagonal patch antenna. To study the behavior of the obtained antenna regarding the dimension (Lcut and Wcut) of the triangular cut, a new parameter D is defined: Lcut = L/D and Wcut = W/D. we set Ws = 29.5 mm, Ls = 29.5 mm, W = 28 mm, L = 20.5 mm, S = 0.3 mm, G = 0.2 mm, Wf = 3.06 mm and Yg = 7.8 mm.

By varying the parameter D from 2.5 to 4, the S11 parameter of the octagonal patch antenna versus frequency is shown in Fig. 2. Table 1 summarizes the resonant frequency and the bandwidth obtained by varying the D parameter. Note that there is a close relation between the parameter D and the final size of the radiating element, as D decreases the total size of the octagonal patch decreases also.

From Table 1 we note that making a triangular cut in the four angles of the microstrip patch antenna we obtain easily an UWB antenna. Also we can consider that D = 3 is the most adapted value in term of bandwidth, compactness and also adaptation in the whole operating frequency band. This value allows the antenna covering the −10 dB operating bandwidth of 2.71 GHz (3.81 to 6.52 GHz).

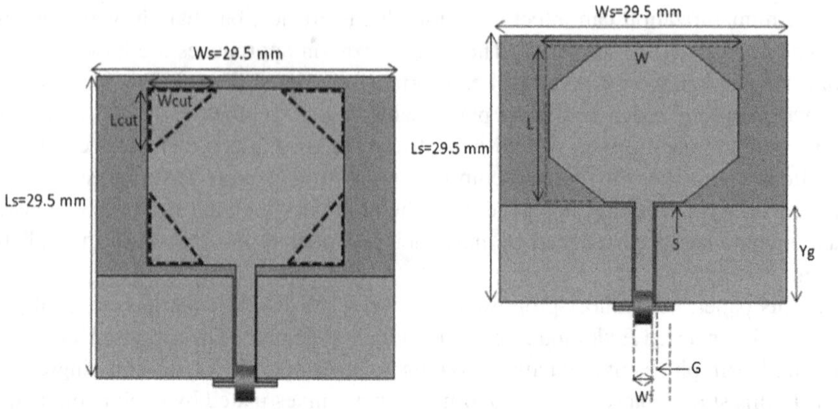

(a) Geometry of the triangular cut **(b)** Designed octagonal patch antenna

Fig. 1. The design of the octagonal patch antenna

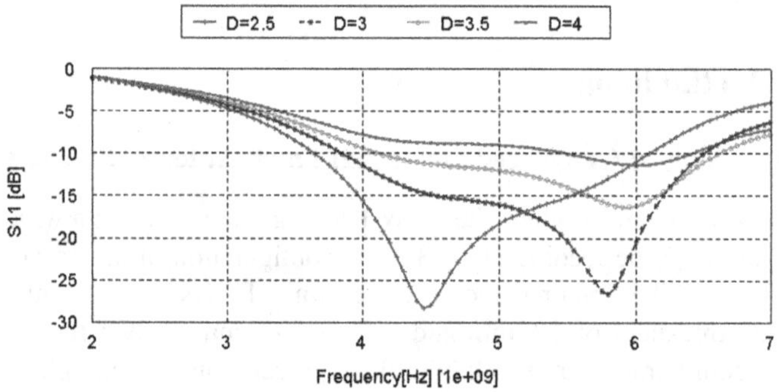

Fig. 2. Simulated S11 versus frequency by varying D

Table 1. Resonant frequency and bandwidth versus the parameter D

D	Resonant frequency (GHz)/S11 (dB)	Bandwidth (GHz)
2.5	4.45/−28.56	2.51: 3.61 to 6.12
3	5.80/−26.89	2.71: 3.81 to 6.52
3.5	5.94/−16.47	2.57: 4.07 to 6.64
4	6.01/−11.45	0.99: 5.44 to 6.43

The analysis of the S11 parameter (Fig. 2) for the D = 3 shows that, for the band of 2–7 GHz, the antenna have one resonant frequency fr = 5.8 GHz. Figure 3 shows the 3D Total gain for the resonant frequency 5.80 GHz. We observe that the 3D-Total gain is almost Omnidirectional for the frequencies around 5.80 GHz. Moreover the total gain of this antenna is about 3.7 dB in the resonant frequency 5.80 GHz.

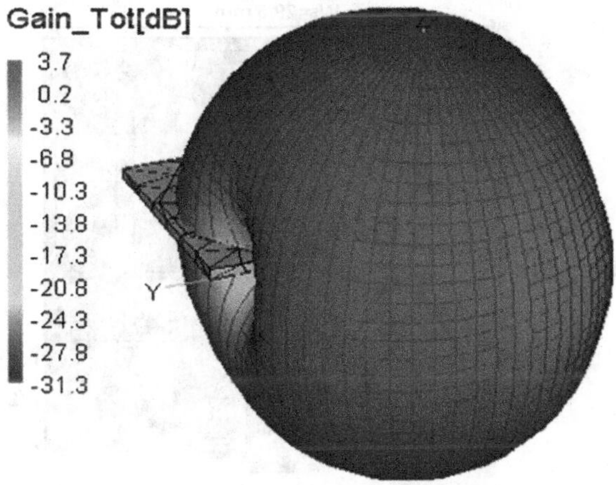

Fig. 3. Simulated 3D-Total gain for the resonant frequency 5.80 GHz

2.2 Step 2: The Setup of an Inverted E Slot Structure on the CPW-Fed Octagonal Patch Antenna

In this section we present the second step of Antenna design which consists of introducing an inverted E slot structure on the CPW-Fed octagonal patch antenna designed in Sect. 2.1. The final designed Antenna is shown in Fig. 4.

We set Ws = 29.5 mm, Ls = 29.5 mm, W = 28 mm, L = 20.5 mm, Yg = 7.8 mm, Wf = 3.06 mm, G = 0.2 mm, S = 1.1 mm, S1 = 0.3 mm, Eh = 19 mm and Ev = 11.3 mm, e = 2.1 mm, D = 3.55. Figure 5 shows the S11 parameter of the octagonal patch antenna with inverted E slot versus frequency. It's clear from Fig. 5 that the setup of the inverted E slot allows generating new resonant frequency: fr = 2.45 GHz, we note that this resonant frequency is lower than the first resonant frequency obtained with the simple octagonal patch antenna and it does not belong to the higher bandwidth. Also two −10 dB bandwidths are obtained, 140 MHz (2.37–2.51 GHz) and 1.95 GHz (4.70–6.65 GHz) witch the resonant frequencies/S11 are 2.45 GHz/−16.34 dB and 5.80 GHz/−38.32 dB respectively. Therefore the proposed antenna is suitable for 2.45/5.80 GHz RFID applications.

To study the effects of loading of the inverted E slot in the radiating element, the variation of its main geometrical parameters is investigated.

The inverted E slot parameters are Ev and Eh, by varying the parameter Ev from 9 mm to 13 mm the S11 parameter of the antenna versus frequency is shown in Fig. 6. From the simulation results, it's clear that the parameter Ev affects mainly the first resonant frequency and the higher frequency of the higher bandwidth, while the lower frequency of the higher bandwidth remains almost unchanged. In addition from the graph we note that as Ev is increased, the first resonant frequency of the structure is decreased.

Table 2 summarizes resonant frequencies and bandwidths obtained by varying the parameter Ev. From this table we note that Ev = 11.3 mm will allows the antenna to be centred in the two resonant frequencies 2.45 GHz and 5.80 GHz.

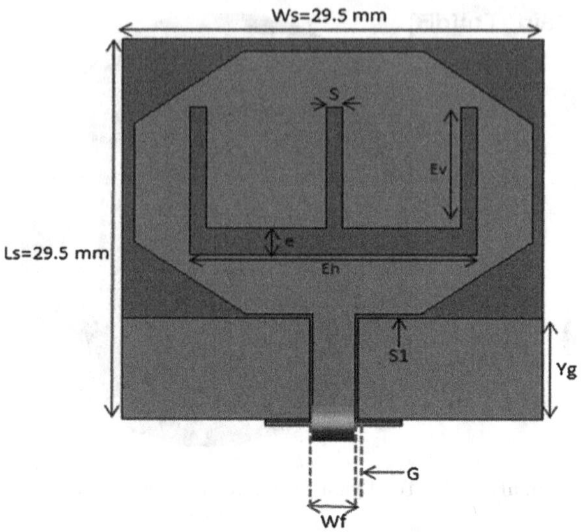

Fig. 4. The CPW-Fed Octagonal patch antenna with inverted E slot loading

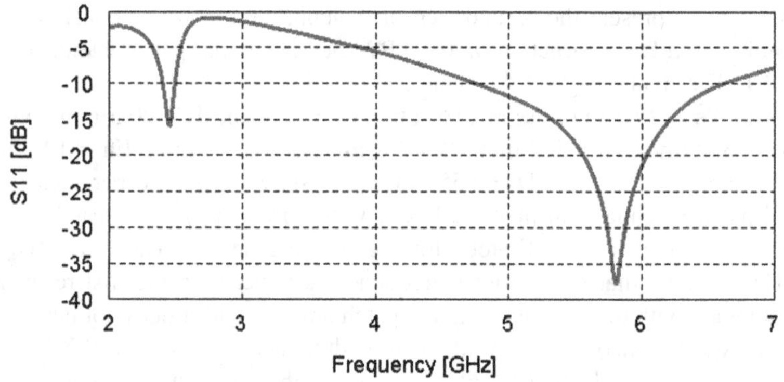

Fig. 5. The simulated S11 of the Octagonal patch antenna with inverted E slot

We set Ev = 11.3 mm, then we change Eh from 17 mm to 21 mm, by varying Eh the S11 parameter of the antenna versus frequency is shown in Fig. 7. From the simulation results, we note that the parameter Eh affects also mainly the first resonant frequency and the higher frequency of the higher bandwidth, while the lower frequency of the higher bandwidth remains almost unchanged. In addition from the graph we note that as Eh is increased, the first resonant frequency of the structure is decreased.

Table 3 summarizes the resonant frequencies and bandwidths obtained by varying the Eh parameter. From this table we note that Eh = 19 mm is the most adapted value in term of operating bandwidth, and will allows the antenna to be centred in the two resonant frequencies 2.45 GHz and 5.80 GHz.

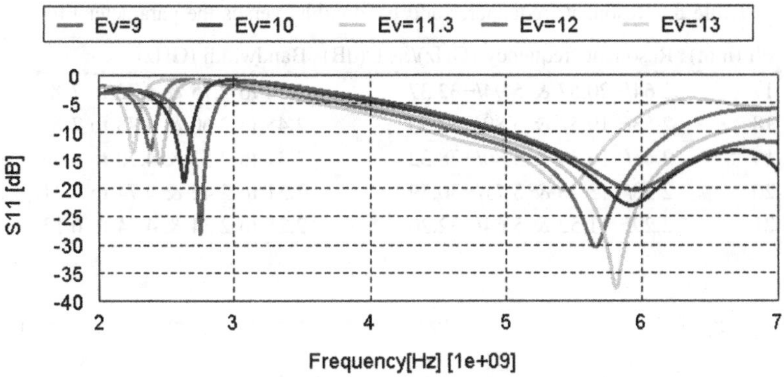

Fig. 6. Simulated S11 versus frequency by varying the parameter Ev

Table 2. Resonant frequencies and bandwidths versus the parameter Ev

Ev (mm)	Resonant frequency (GHz)/S11 (dB)	Bandwidth (GHz)
9	2.75/−28.46 & 5.95/−20.59	2.63 to 2.84 & 4.95 to 7.X
10	2.62/−19.18 & 5.91/−23.23	2.54 to 2.70 & 4.88 to 7.X
11.3	2.45/−16.34 & 5.80/−38.32	2.37 to 2.51 & 4.70 to 6.65
12	2.37/−13.54 & 5.66/−30.76	2.32 to 2.42 & 4.59 to 6.26
13	2.25/−14.09 & 5.43/−20.49	2.19 to 2.29 & 4.40 to 5.86

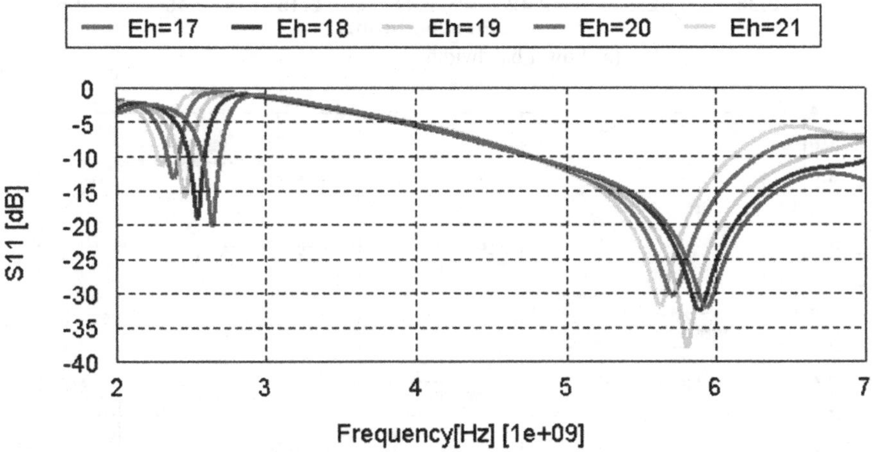

Fig. 7. Simulated S11 versus frequency by varying the parameter Eh

Figure 8 shows the behavior of the gain versus frequencies in the two operating bandwidths. The total gain of the proposed antennas varies between 1.9 dB and 2.1 dB in the −10 dB lower operating bandwidth and varies between 2.6 dB and 3.7 dB in the −10 dB higher operating bandwidth.

Table 3. Resonant frequencies and bandwidths versus the parameter Eh

Eh (mm)	Resonant frequency (GHz)/S11 (dB)	Bandwidth (GHz)
17	2.64/−20.57 & 5.94/−32.37	2.54 to 2.75 & 4.72 to 7.X
18	2.53/−19.52 & 5.89/−32.93	2.45 to 2.60 & 4.73 to 7.X
19	2.45/−16.34 & 5.80/−38.32	2.37 to 2.51 & 4.70 to 6.65
20	2.38/−13.46 & 5.71/−30.59	2.31 to 2.42 & 4.74 to 6.31
21	2.29/−11.52 & 5.64/−32.20	2.25 to 2.34 & 4.74 to 6.13

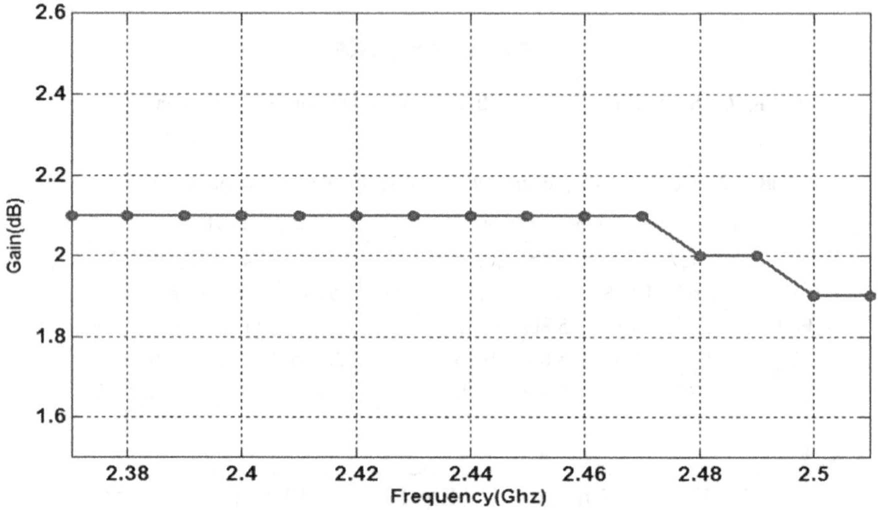

(a) Lower bandwidth

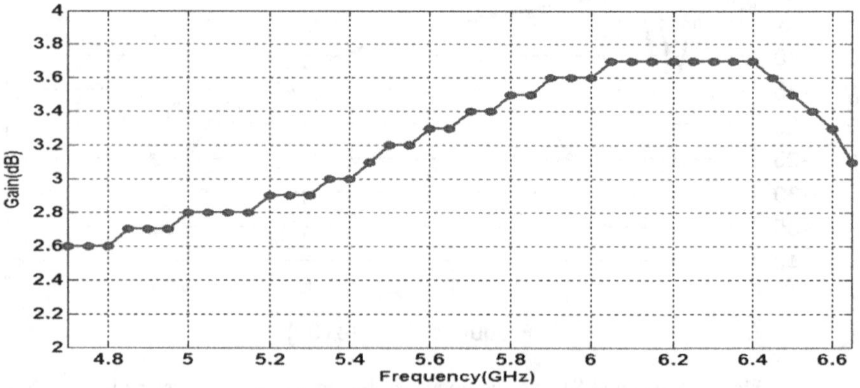

(b) Higher bandwidth

Fig. 8. The simulated Gain of the designed antenna in the two operating bandwidths

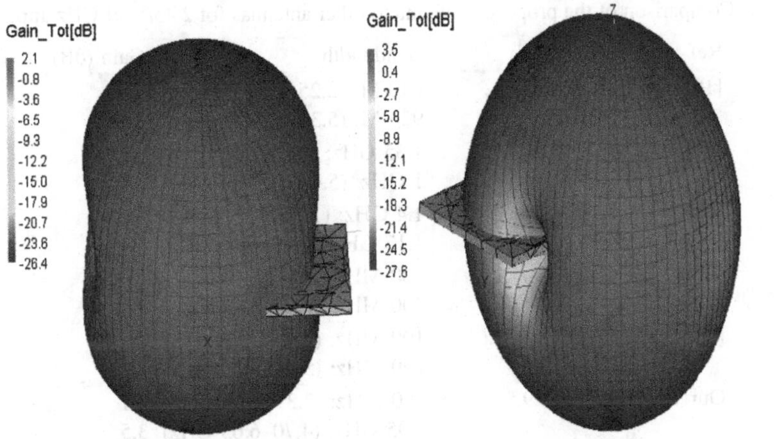

(a) the 3D-Gain for fl = 2.45GHz **(b)** the 3D-Gain for f2 = 5.8GHz

Fig. 9. The 3D-Gain of the CPW-Fed Octagonal patch antenna with inverted E slot loading

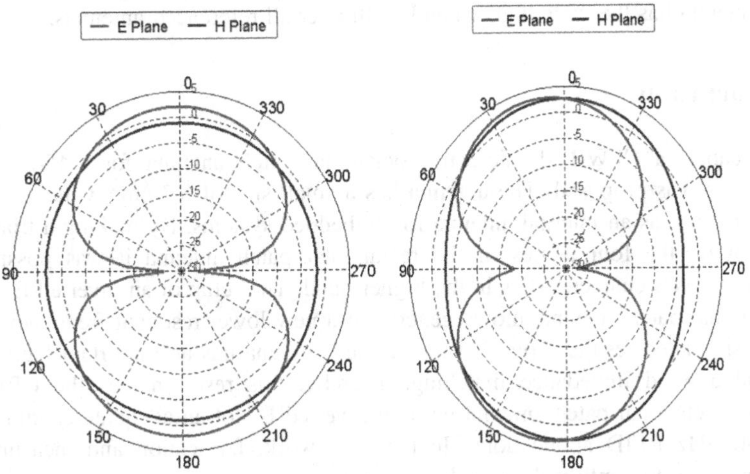

(a) fl = 2.45GHz **(b)** f2 = 5.80GHz

Fig. 10. The 2D radiation patterns of the proposed antenna at 2.45 GHz and 5.80 GHz

Figure 9 shows the 3D Total gain for the two resonant frequencies 2.45/5.80 GHz of the octagonal patch antenna with inverted E slot loading, the total gain of this antenna is about 2.1 dB and 3.5 dB for the two resonant frequencies 2.45 GHz and 5.80 GHz, respectively. We note that the 3D-Total gain is almost Omnidirectional for the two resonant frequencies 2.45 GHz and 5.80 GHz.

The 2-D radiation patterns of the proposed antenna simulated at 2.45 GHz and 5.80 GHz are shown in Fig. 10.

Table 4. Comparison of the proposed antenna to other antennas for 2.45/5.80 GHz applications

Ref	Size (mm^3)	Bandwidth	Gain (dB)
[19]	40*30*1.5	640 M: (2.25–2.89 GHz) 920 M: (5.30–6.22 GHz)	2.5 4
[20]	36*39*0.175	1.35 GHz: (1.6–2.95) 1 GHz: (5.4 GHz–6.4 GHz)	−3.25 −4.53
[21]	50*50*1.6	1.4 GHz: (1.83–3.23 GHz) 1.17 GHz: (4.99–6.16 GHz)	6.6 7.4
[22]	65 × 56 × 1.6	100 MHz (2.4–2.5 GHz) 200 MHz (5.6–5.8 GHz)	- -
[22]	44 × 41 × 1.6	100 MHz: (2.4–2.5 GHz) 200 MHz: (5.8–6.0 GHz)	- -
Our work	29.5 × 29.5 × 1.6	140 MHz: (2.37–2.51 GHz) 1.95 GHz: (4.70–6.65 GHz)	2.1 3.5

Also, comparison between several different antennas for 2.45/5.80 GHz applications is illustrated in Table 4. From this table it's clear that our structure has a miniaturized design with very important gain compared to most other antennas. Moreover the proposed antenna has the wide higher bandwidth over all referenced antennas.

3 Conclusion

In this paper, a CPW-Fed microstrip octagonal patch antenna for 2.45/5.80 GHz applications was proposed. The antenna has a small size of 8.7 cm^2, which makes it suitable for use as an internal antenna for embedded systems. By making a triangular shape cut on the four angles of the rectangular patch antenna it was possible to implement UWB characteristics in the higher band. The setup of an inverted E slot on the octagonal patch antenna allows generating a new lower resonant frequency.

The simulated results show that the studied antenna has an important bandwidth, gain and a good impedance matching. Thereby, this result makes the CPW-Fed microstrip octagonal patch antenna with an inverted E slot an adequate candidate for 2.45/5.80 GHz RFID applications. In the next work, fabrication and measurement should be done to confirm the simulated results.

References

1. Bhatt, H., Glover, B.: RFID Essentials, pp. 1–50. O'Reilly, Sebastopol (2006)
2. Miles, S.B., Sharma, S.E., Williams, J.R.: RFID Technology & Applications. Cambridge University Press, New York (2011)
3. Varadhan, C., Pakkathillam, J.K., Kanagasabai, M., Sivasamy, R., Natarajan, R., Palaniswamy, S.K.: Triband antenna structures for RFID systems deploying fractal geometry. IEEE Antennas Wirel. Propag. Lett. **12**, 437–440 (2013)
4. Vardadhan, C., Pakkathillam, J.K., Kanagasabai, M., Sivasamy, R., Natarajan, R., Palaniswamy, S.K.: Triband antenna structures for RFID systems deploying fractal geometry. IEEE Antenna Wirel. Propag. Lett. **12**, 437–440 (2013)

5. Chen, H.-T., Wong, K.-L., Chiou, T.-W.: Pifa with a meandered and folded patch for the dual-band mobile phone application. IEEE Trans. Antennas Propag. **51**(9), 2468–2471 (2003)
6. Reha, A., El Amri, A., Benhmammouch, O., Oulad Said, A.: Fractal antennas: a novel miniaturization technique for wireless networks. Trans. Netw. Commun. **2**(5), 165–193 (2014)
7. Sun, S., Zhu, L.: Miniaturised patch hybrid couplers using asymmetrically loaded cross slots. IET Microwaves Antennas Propag. **4**(9), 1427 (2010)
8. Chi, P.-L., Waterhouse, R., Itoh, T.: Antenna miniaturization using slow wave enhancement factor from loaded transmission line models. IEEE Trans. Antennas Propag. **59**(1), 48–57 (2011)
9. Skrivervik, A.K., Zürcher, J.-F., Staub, O., Mosig, J.R.: PCS antenna design: the challenge of miniaturization. IEEE Antennas Propag. Mag. **43**(4), 12–27 (2001)
10. Reha, A., El Amri, A., Saih, M., Benhmammouch, O., Oulad Said, A.: The behavior of a CPW-fed microstrip hexagonal patch antenna with H-Tree Fractal slots. Rev. Méditerranéenne Télécommunication **5**(2), 104–108 (2015)
11. Kakoyiannis, C.G., Constantinou, P.: A compact microstrip antenna with tapered peripheral slits for CubeSat RF payloads at 436 MHz: miniaturization techniques, design, and numerical results. In: IEEE International Workshop on Satellite and Space Communications (IWSSC08), pp. 255–259, October 2008
12. Anguera, J., Boada, L., Puente, C., Borja, C., Soler, J.: Stacked H-shaped microstrip patch antenna. IEEE Trans. Antennas Propag. **52**(4), 983–993 (2004)
13. Bokhari, S.A., Zurcher, J.-F., Mosig, J.R., Gardiol, F.E.: A small microstrip patch antenna with a convenient tuning option. IEEE Trans. Antennas Propag. **44**(11), 1521–1528 (1996)
14. Chatterjee, S., Ghosh, K., Paul, J., Chowdhury, S.K., Chanda, D., Sarkar, P.P.: Compact microstrip antenna for mobile communication. Microwave Opt. Technol. Lett. **55**(5), 954–957 (2013)
15. Chen, W.-S., Wu, C.-K., Wong, K.-l.: Square-ring microstrip antenna with a crossstrip for compact circular polarization operation'. IEEE Trans. Antennas Propag. **47**(10), 1566–1568 (1999)
16. Naser-Moghadasi, M., Sadeghzadeh, R.A., Sedghi, T., Aribi, T., Virdee, B.S.: UWB CPWFedFractal patch antenna with band-notched function employing folded T-shaped element. IEEE Antennas Wirel. Propag. Lett. **12**, 504–507 (2013)
17. Reha, A., El Amri, A., Benhmammouch, O., Oulad Said, A.: Compact dual-band monopole antenna for GPS/GALILEO/GLONASS and other wireless applications. In: IEEE Conferences-ICMCS 14, April 2014
18. Reha, A., El Amri, A., Benhmammouch, O., Oulad Said, A.: UWB compact monopole antenna for LTE, UMTS and WIMAX applications. CMT 2014 (2014)
19. Jianhui, G., Shunshi, Z., Linglong, X., Zhu, S.: Dual-band monopole antenna for 2.45/5.8 GHz RFID applications. In: Microwave Conference, 2008 China-Japan Joint, September 2008
20. Malek, M.A., Hakimi, S., Abdul Rahim, S.K., Evizal, A.K.: Dual-band CPW-fed transparent antenna for active RFID tags. IEEE Antennas Wireles. Propag. **14**, 919–922 (2014)
21. Weng, W.C., Sze, J.Y., Chen, C.F.: A dual-broadband circularly polarized slot antenna for WLAN applications. IEEE Trans. Antennas Propag. **62**(5), 2837–2841 (2014)
22. Hamad, E.K.I.: Design and implementation of dual-band microstrip antennas for RFID reader application. Ciência e Técnica Vitivinícola, vol. 29, no. 9, pp. 2–10, September 2014

MRA*: Parallel and Distributed Path in Large-Scale Graph Using MapReduce-A* Based Approach

Wilfried Yves Hamilton Adoni, Tarik Nahhal(✉), Brahim Aghezzaf, and Abdeltif Elbyed

Laboratoire Informatique, Modélisation des Systèmes et Aide à la Décision (LIMSAD), Faculty of Sciences of Casablanca, Hassan II University, Km 8 Route d'El Jadida, B.P 5366, 20100 Maarif, Casablanca, Morocco
adoniwilfried@gmail.com, {t.nahhal,b.aghezzaf,a.elbyed}@fsac.ac.ma
http://www.fsac.ac.ma

Abstract. In this paper, we present a contribution for the Single Source Shortest Path Problem (SSSPP) in large-scale graph with A* algorithm. A* is one of the most efficient graph traversal algorithm because it is driven by a heuristic which determines the optimal path. A* approach is not efficient when the graph is too large to be processed due to exponential time complexity. We propose a MapReduce-based approach called MRA*: MapReduce-A* which consists to combine the A* algorithm with MapReduce paradigm to compute the shortest path in parallel and distributed environment. We perform experiments in a Hadoop multi-node cluster and our results prove that the proposed approach outperforms A* algorithm and reduces significantly the computational time.

Keywords: A* algorithm · Large-scale graph · Shortest path problem · Hadoop · MapReduce · Parallel and distributed computing

1 Introduction

The graph search is one of the most populate problem in graph theory and artificial intelligence. One of the problems related is the SSSPP between two vertices. The graph traversal is done by the exploration of all reachable vertices until the goal vertex. In real-world it has several fields of application such as transportation, logistic, medical health, etc. SSSPP allows to find the shortest path in road network, this can be for: Vehicle Routing Problem (VPR), Traveling Salesman Problem (TSP) and the Pickup and Delivery Problem (PDP). SSSPP application in road network is widely used by embedded GPS systems in vehicles to compute road routing between two points [2]. The graph search algorithms present different complexities going from calculation time until finding the shortest path. The actual SSSPP algorithms [6,10–12,18] are traditional and not adapted for intensive computation when the graph is too large to be handle on single machine. For example in bioinformatic, the classical computing

E. Sabir et al. (Eds.): UNet 2017, LNCS 10542, pp. 390–401, 2017.
https://doi.org/10.1007/978-3-319-68179-5_34

techniques of graph search for DNA finding are not efficient because of genetic informations contained in the human body (between 10 and 100 trillion) [8]. Moreover, in transportation engineering application the shortest path computational time becomes very long when the road network size is to large to be explored. This constitutes the main problem of A* search algorithm. A* works well with little graph but the runtime increases significantly with the growth of graph size and consumes more ram memories. In this context, we propose an enhanced version of A* algorithm that runs in distributed and parallel computing with large amount of graph data and faces the challenge of volume and velocity. To perform this task, we opt for Hadoop with MapReduce framework because it gives advantage of reliability, scalability and fault tolerance.

The rest of this paper is organized as follows. Section 2 presents background. Section 3 reviews related work. In Sect. 4, we depict the MapReduce-A* based approach. Next, we expose our experiment results in Sect. 5 and conclude with further works in Sect. 6.

2 Background

2.1 A* Algorithm and Limitations

A* is an extension of Dijkstra's algorithm [11] by adding a heuristic function that guides the search [7]. It's the most populate graph search algorithm because of path optimality. Moreover, for too short distances where the heuristic evaluation returns near zero, A* simply runs Dijkstra's algorithm [11]. The completeness of this algorithm is driven by heuristic function f and the time complexity is $O(l^b)$ [14,20] where l is the path length and b is the average number of vertices successors per state.

A* works with two mains list: the 'open list' that contains all visited vertices and 'closed list' that contains all selected vertices. First of all, we add all successors of the starting vertex in the 'open list' and evaluate the heuristic cost: f of each vertex such as $f = g + h$ [15], where g is the cost from starting vertex to the current vertex and h is the heuristic estimated cost from the current vertex to the goal vertex. Next, we update the current vertex by the visited vertex that minimizes f, we remove it from the 'open list' to add it into the 'closed list'. We repeat recursively the same operation until the 'open list' is empty or the current vertex is equal to the goal vertex. The final step consists to generate the optimal path, from the ending vertex we point on it's predecessor and so on until the predecessor is the starting vertex.

A* works as DFS (Depth-First-Search) [21] and expands all explored vertices until finds the goal vertex or finds vertex without successors. This method of exploration makes it ineffective in large-scale graph because it wastes time to explore in depth non promising vertices and consumes exponential space memory. However, in term of hardware requirement, A* requires sophisticated computers equipped with good ram memory and multi-core processor for intensive calculation. The main objective of our work is to reduce the runtime into large-scale graph. This is made possible with MapReduce, but has an impact on result quality. In term of veracity, the time improvement can degrade the path optimality. The most appropriate way is to find a balance point that satisfies the criteria of optimality and computation time. This depends on the input/output parameters of the proposed framework.

2.2 Hadoop and MapReduce Framework

According to Hadoop documentation [3], Hadoop is a cornerstone of big data technology, it's scalable, reliable, fault tolerance and distributed computing of huge volume of data, it's inspired by Google File System (GFS) [13] and initiated by Yahoo. Hadoop is open-source and offers possibility to use commodity hardwares. Hadoop is designed to work in a cluster of multiple computers (nodes) connected under a master-slaves architecture [3]. Hadoop is based on two main technologies: MapReduce [9] and Hadoop Distributed File System (HDFS) [3,19].

HDFS is a distributed file system designed to run on commodity hardware [3,16]. It supports very large files of data, each file is split into chunk files and replicated across Hadoop nodes for fault tolerance.

MapReduce is a framework for easily develop java program to process large dataset in parallel and distributed environment [3,9]. The MapReduce program inputs and outputs are defined as <key, value> pairs [9]. MapReduce program works in two phases: Map phase and Reduce phase. The two different phases are controlled by the master node (JobTracker) which assigns map and reduce tasks to all slave nodes (TaskTracker) [3,9]. The mapper task splits the input files into little pieces. Next, it takes each input line by line and produces a set of intermediate <key, value> pairs based on the map function defined by the developer. Finally, all intermediate values with same keys are collected and grouped before passed to the reducer. When all tasks are completed, the reducer tasks take the intermediate results of each mapper and merge them with other mapper results to produce a set of smaller <key, value> pair. Moreover, one node is chosen to process a set values with same key. When all reduce tasks have been completed, the final output from each reducer is written into the HDFS.

3 Related Works

Recent works [1,4,17] has shown that MapReduce approach in graph search is very beneficial due to the fast computational time and its capability to handle huge volume of large-scale graph. Moreover, data-intensive or compute-intensive problems emanating from large graphs can be solved using parallelism approach [1]. However, developers face limitation when they need to implement existing programs to run as MapReduce jobs. Plimpton and Devine [1] created an open-source library for enabling existing graph search algorithms to be easily written in MapReduce paradigm. This means that the library provides utility functions for "map" and "reduce" tasks. Different tests performed with graph search algorithms showed that parallelism approach runs faster than traditional approach.

MapReduce can create an innovative strategies for solving others graph search problems such as graph mining [4]. The use of parallel and distributed approach for graph mining comes from impossibility to handle large graph with traditional algorithm [17]. In this scope, Aridhi et al. [4] proposed a parallel computing for large-scale graph mining via the technique of graph partitioning under specific graph size. The experiments demonstrated that their approach reduces significantly the execution time and works well with the increasing number of nodes.

In [5], the authors presented a MapReduce based approach for SSSPP in large-scale network. The proposed approach works in two phases: map phase and reduce phase. In the map phase, they partitioned the large graph under subgraph blocks and map them to each machines. Next, Dijkstra's algorithm [11] runs on each machine to generate a set of intermediate shortest paths. Finally in the reduce phase, all intermediate paths are aggregated to obtain the final shortest path. The numerical experiments showed that authors contribution enables to improve significantly the time calculation.

4 Proposed Framework: MapReduce-A*

The proposed MRA*: MapReduce-A* based approach allows to execute in parallel and distributed computing the shortest path with large-scale graph. As show in Fig. 1, the proposed framework is composed of four main phases: input phase, map phase, reduce phase and output phase. The MRA* program is submitted by the user on the master node and the master node pushes them to all the slave nodes to run simultaneous in the map and reduce phase. Thus the total

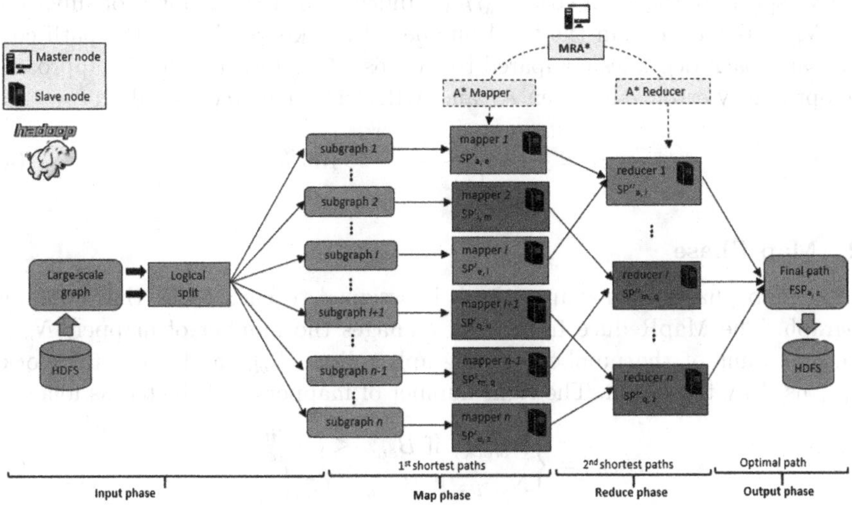

Fig. 1. MRA* framework in practice.

computation time: T_{MRA^*} to satisfy the MRA* job depends of the times: t_{map} and t_{red} passed respectively in map and reduce phase such as:

$$T_{MRA^*} = t_{map} + t_{red} \tag{1}$$

4.1 Input Phase

First of all, we need to upload the large graph with specific size: G_{size} into the HDFS. Hadoop splits physically the graph into chunk files according to the defined block size: B_{size} and replicates them across the Hadoop cluster. The total number of block file: N_{block} used by the graph is calculated as follow:

$$N_{block} = E\left[\frac{G_{size}}{B_{size}}\right] + \theta_1 \quad \text{where } \theta_1 = \begin{cases} 0, \text{if } \mathrm{G}_{size} \equiv B_{size} \\ 1, else \end{cases} \tag{2}$$

After, we need to specify logically the subgraph input splits. Unlike block file, the input split size: G_{size}^{split} is driven by the maximum number of vertices containing on each subgraph. From the starting vertex, we create the first split of subgraph, the intermediate vertices located on subgraph extremities serve as starting and ending vertex of each subgraph. The starting vertex of the ith subgraph is the ending vertex of the $(i-1)th$ subgraph so on until the last subgraph which contains the goal vertex. The total number of subgraph: N_{split} based on logical split is calculated as:

$$N_{split} = E\left[\frac{G_{size}}{G_{size}^{split}}\right] + \theta_2 \quad \text{where } \theta_2 = \begin{cases} 0, \ \text{if } \mathrm{G}_{size} \equiv G_{size}^{split} \\ 1, \ else \end{cases} \tag{3}$$

It's important to note that the input parameters can influence on the result quality especially the path cost: C_{MRA*}. Indeed when the number of subgraph split N_{split} is bigger than the total number of block size: N_{block}, the path cost of our approach degrades compared to the cost: C_{A*} returned by A* approach. The optimality error: ϵ between A* and MRA* is calculated as follow:

$$\epsilon = \frac{|C_{MRA*} - C_{A*}|}{C_{A*}} \times 100\% \tag{4}$$

4.2 Map Phase

During map phase, each mapper task is assigned to each block that contains subgraph. The MapReduce framework manages the number of mapper: N_{map} taking account of the number of subgraph splits: N_{split} and the total block: N_{block} used by the graph. The right number of mappers is deducted as follow:

$$N_{map} = \begin{cases} N_{block}, \text{ if } B_{size} \leq G_{size}^{split} \\ \mathrm{N}_{split}, \text{ if } B_{size} > G_{size}^{split} \end{cases} \tag{5}$$

Multiple mapper tasks can parallelize the shortest path computation by running the **A*_Mapper** procedure (see Algorithm 1) across the number of Hadoop nodes: N_{node}. Each mapper j assigned to each node i transforms line by line the input of subgraph data as a set of key-value pairs and produces others key-value pairs of intermediate shortest paths. Next, the result set of tasks running on each slave node will be grouped, sorted and stored locally. Moreover, the maximum map tasks archived simultaneously on each node depends of the number of core processor allocated: N_{core}^{map}. When one node finishes performing these mapper tasks, it waits until the last node completes these tasks. the time: t_{map} to complete the map tasks on all slave nodes is calculated as follow:

$$t_{map} = \max\{ \sum_{i=1}^{N_{node}} \sum_{j=1}^{N_{map}} m_i^j \} \mid m_i^j \in M \tag{6}$$

This time remains stationary when the size of the subgraph input split: G_{size}^{split} is bigger than the Hadoop physical block size: B_{size} (see Remark).

Remark. $\forall B_{size}$ and n $\in$ R, $\exists G_{size}^{split} = \text{n} \times B_{size}$ such as

$$\lim_{n \geq 1} t_{map} = K$$

Algorithm 1. A*_Mapper

```
{Assuming start and goal vertices are respectively: vi and vn};
 input : data from HDFS
  <key := vi , value := {vi,hi,gi} ... {vi+1,hi+1,gi+1} ... {vn,hn,gn} >
     ...                             ...                  ...
  <key := vn , value := {vi,hi,gi} ... {vi+1,hi+1,gi+1} ... {vn,hn,gn} >
 var
  openlist := ∅;
  closelist := ∅;
  tmp := null; % current vertex %
  sp'i,n := null; % intermediate path %
 begin
  tmp.key := vi;
  tmp.value := getValue(vi);
   while (openlist ≠ ∅ and tmp.key ≠ vn) do
     for v ∈ tmp.value do
       key =: v.token[0];
       g =: v.token[1];
       h =: v.token[2];
       openlist.addVertex(key,g,h);
     end
    tmp.key := openlist.GetVertexWithMinF(); % f = g + h %
    tmp.value := getValue(tmp.key);
    openlist.removeVertex(tmp);
    closelist.addVertex(tmp);
  end
 sp'i,n := closelist.generatePath(vi,vn);
 storeLocally(<key := vi->vn, value := sp'i,n>);
end
```

4.3 Reduce Phase

In reduce phase, each reducer aggregates and concatenates the set of intermediate paths which share same keys. This is archived by the procedure **A*_Reducer** (see Algorithm 2). The ending extremity of the $(i-1)th$ shortest path becomes the starting extremity of the ith shortest path so on until the last path. Moreover, the right number of reducers for good parallelism depends of the allocated number of core processor per node: N_{core}^{red} and it's calculated as follow [3]:

$$N_{red} = \begin{cases} 0.95 \times N_{node} \times N_{core}^{red} \\ 1.75 \times N_{node} \times N_{core}^{red} \end{cases} \tag{7}$$

With 0.95 we suppose that all slave nodes have the same configurations (ram and cpu) and run averagely the same number of tasks in the same gap of time. While with 1.75 the faster nodes will run more tasks and launch immediately another wave of reducers when they finish. If all tasks j are completed on slave nodes i, they wait until all reducer tasks completed on the last node before send the final result to the master node. The runtime of the reduce phase is then calculated as follow:

$$t_{red} = \max\{\sum_{i=1}^{N_{node}} \sum_{j=1}^{N_{red}} r_i^j\} \mid r_i^j \in R \tag{8}$$

Algorithm 2. A*_Reducer

```
{Assuming the reducers are able to access the mapper results};
input : set of intermediate path from local disk node
  <key := v_i->v_n , value := {sp'_{i,k}, sp'_{k,l}, ... ,sp'_{m,n}}>
var
  sp''_{i,n} := null;
begin
  for (sp ∈ value) do
    sp''_{i,n} := sp''_{i,n} ∪ sp;
  end
 sendToMasterNode(<key := v_i->v_n , value := sp''_{i,n}>);
end
```

4.4 Output Phase

In the final phase, the master node uploads the final path from each reducer into the HDFS. Each reducer output is written into separate files.

5 Experimental Results

All the experiments have been performed on a 6-node Hadoop cluster, which composed of 1 master node and 5 slave nodes. The set of nodes are connected through a local area network consisting of switch DES-1016D 100 Mbps and ethernet cables Cat-5 100 Mbps. Each node within the cluster is based on Intel Core i5-2410M running at 2.3 GHz CPUs with 2 GB RAM under Linux SUSE-3.0.101 32- bit. The number of core used on each node is set to 1 for all experiments. The experiments have been achieved on Hadoop 2.2.0. For the tests, we use Manhattan distance as heuristic [20] to guide the path search. The replication factor of graph data across the cluster is set to 1. The result analysis were performed with RStudio. Table 1 shows the set of parameters of our experiment.

Table 1. Experimental parameter set

Parameter type	Parameter value
N_{node}	6
G_{size}	[0.2, 7] Gb
B_{size}	$\{64, 128, 256\}$ Mb
G_{size}^{split}	[40, 256] Mb
N_{core}^{map}	1
N_{core}^{red}	1

5.1 Comparison of Computational Time: A* Versus MRA*

We run the proposed approach with different graphs on a single-node Hadoop. This means that all map and reduce tasks are not parallelized on other nodes. Table 2 shows the comparison of the computational time between A* and MRA*. For example with graph of 7 Gb containing 3.6 billion data, we compute the shortest path in 1600 s (≈26 min) with our MRA* versus 177948 s (≈49 h) with A*. This represents a improvement ratio of 111.2, about 2.3 million processed data per second with MRA* against 2000 data per second with A*.

Table 2. A* versus MRA* with 1 node

			Direct resolution approach: A*	Proposed resolution approach: MRA*			Ratio
Vertices	Data	G_{size} (Gb)	T_{A*} (s)	t_{map} (s)	t_{red} (s)	T_{MRA*} (s)	$\frac{T_{A*}}{T_{MRA*}}$
8000	64×10^6	0.25	15752	157	11	168	93.8
15000	22.5×10^7	0.5	35331	183	18	201	157.8
20000	40×10^7	0.8	51469	233	36	269	191.3
25000	62.5×10^7	1.2	77378	330	53	366	211.4
30000	90×10^7	2	101909	405	76	481	212
40000	16×10^8	3	129343	698	91	789	164
50000	25×10^8	5	152863	1035	103	1137	134.4
60000	36×10^8	7	177948	1397	203	1600	111.2

5.2 Influence of Number of Slave Nodes on Computational Time

Figure 2 presents the impact of the increasing number of Hadoop nodes on computational time. We remark an improvement of computational time when adding new nodes. For each additional node, the exponential time decreases until the linearity time is obtained. For example with graph size of 7 Gb, the time decreases from 1600 s to 764 s (+52% of time gain) with 2 nodes and from 764 s to 322 s (+80% of time gain) with 3 nodes. Beyond 3 nodes we obtain the time stationarity, thus the nodes 4, 5 and 6 do not influence the calculation time. This means that Hadoop needs just 3 nodes to satisfy the shortest path computation.

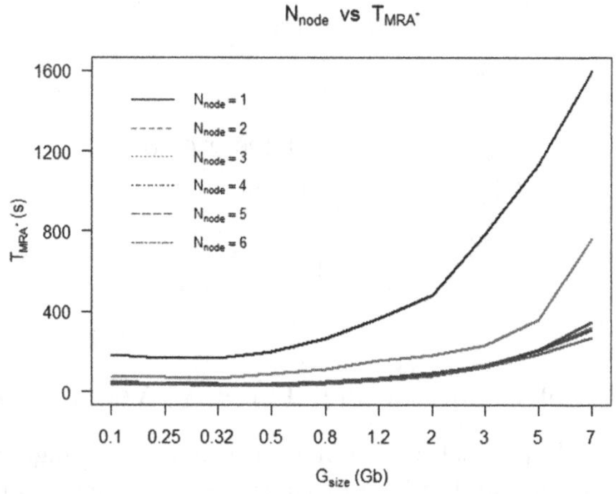

Fig. 2. Influence of increasing nodes on runtime.

5.3 Impact of Subgraphs Size on Result Quality

We fix the block size: B_{size} to 128 Mb and perform the experiment with graph of 1.2 Gb ($N_{block} = 9$). Figure 3 shows the result quality with different subgraph input splits: $N_{split} \in [1, 16]$. When $N_{split} \in [1, N_{block}]$, we remark that the optimality of the path cost is guaranteed. The best time: T^*_{MRA*} that guarantees the path optimality is obtained when $N_{split} = N_{block} = 9$. In case that $N_{split} \in]N_{block}, \infty[$, we obtain a gain in term of calculation time but to the detriment of the path optimality.

5.4 Influence of Block Size on Computational Time

Generally, the computing time is driven by the map time because it requires more time that the reduce phase. Figure 4 shows the impact of block size on map phase. We perform the experiment with different block size while varying G^{split}_{size} between 40 and 256 Mb. Firstly, we remark that MRA* runs faster with small block sizes. Secondly, the computing time is reduced when the graph is split

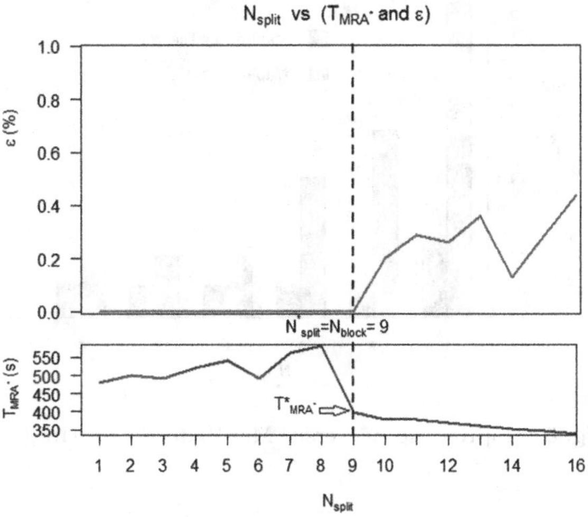

Fig. 3. Subgraph input split versus result quality.

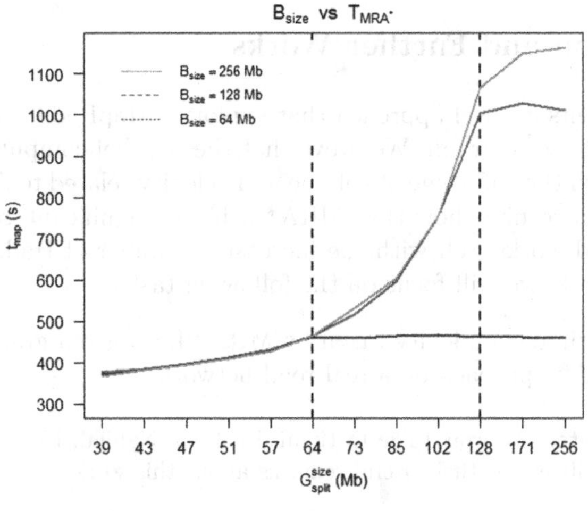

Fig. 4. Influence of block size on map runtime.

under small size. When $G_{size}^{split} > B_{size}$ the time remains stationary. For example, with $B_{size} = 64$ Mb, for $G_{size}^{split} \in]64, \infty[$ the computing time remains constant ($T_{MRA*} \approx 460$ s). This allows thereby to highlight the remark of stationarity.

5.5 Comparison with MapReduce Version of Dijkstra

Figure 5 presents an evaluation between MapReduce-A* and the MapReduce version of Dijkstra presented in [5]. At first glance, we remark that MapReduce-A* outperforms and runs faster that MapReduce-Dijkstra. Based on our results

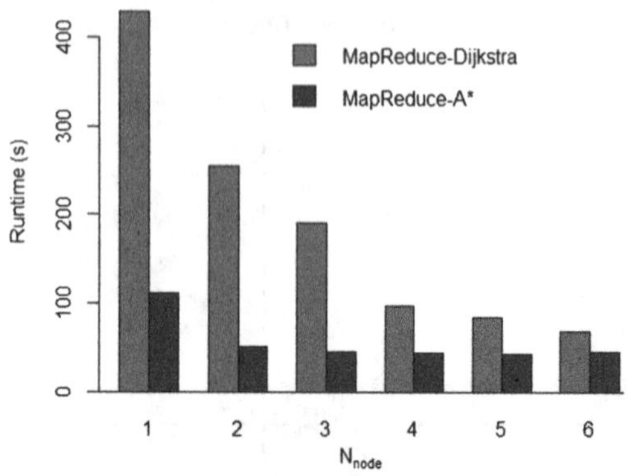

Fig. 5. MapReduce-A* versus MapReduce-Dijkstra [5].

and results in [5], we can conclude that our work presents a great impact because of improvement of the time complexity of shortest path computing.

6 Conclusion and Further Works

This paper presents a novel approach that exploit a MapReduce framework for A* search in large-scale graph. We prove that the parallel computing concept is suited to face with the challenge of volume and velocity related to A* limitations. The experimental results show that MRA* achieves significant gain of computational time and works well with the increasing number of Hadoop nodes. As part of future work, we will focus on the following tasks:

- Quantify the time complexity taken by MRA* for a given graph size.
- Apply of MRA* approach on a real road network.

Acknowledgments. We would like to thank Pr Tarik Nahhal, Pr Brahim Aghezzaf and Pr Abdeltif Elbyed for their useful remarks about this work.

References

1. Plimpton, S.J., Devine, K.D.: MapReduce in MPI for large-scale graph algorithms. Parallel Comput. **37**, 610–632 (2011). doi:10.1016/j.parco.2011.02.004
2. Chen, Y.-Z., Shen, S.-F., Chen, T., Yang, R.: Path optimization study for vehicles evacuation based on Dijkstra algorithm. Procedia Eng., 159–165 (2014). 2013 International Conference on Performance-Based Fire and Fire Protection Engineering (ICPFFPE 2013), Wuhan
3. Welcome to apache hadoop. http://hadoop.apache.org/
4. Aridhi, S., d'Orazio, L., Maddouri, M., Mephu Nguifo, E.: Density-based data partitioning strategy to approximate large-scale subgraph mining. Inf. Syst. **48**, 213–223 (2015)

5. Aridhi, S., Lacomme, P., Ren, L., Vincent, B.: A MapReduce-based approach for shortest path problem in large-scale networks. Eng. Appl. Artif. Intell. **41**, 151–165 (2015)
6. Bellman, R.: On a routing problem. Q. Appl. Math. **16**(1), 87–90 (1958)
7. Cherkassky, B.V., Goldberg, A.V., Radzik, T.: Shortest paths algorithms: theory and experimental evaluation. Math. Program. **73**, 129–174 (1993)
8. Chowdhury, L., Khan, M.I., Deb, K., Kamal, S.: MetaG: a graph-based metagenomic gene analysis for big DNA data. Netw. Model. Anal. Health Inform. Bioinform. **5**(1), 27 (2016)
9. Dean, J., Ghemawat, S.: MapReduce: simplified data processing on large clusters. Commun. ACM **51**(1), 107–113 (2008)
10. Dechter, R., Pearl, J.: Generalized best-first search strategies and the optimality of a*. J. ACM (JACM) **32**(3), 505–536 (1985)
11. Dijkstra, E.W.: A note on two problems in connexion with graphs. Numer. Math. **1**(1), 269–271 (1959)
12. Fredman, M.L., Tarjan, R.E.: Fibonacci heaps and their uses in improved network optimization algorithms. J. ACM (JACM) **34**(3), 596–615 (1987)
13. Ghemawat, S., Gobioff, H., Leung, S.T.: The Google file system. In: ACM SIGOPS Operating Systems Review, vol. 37, pp. 29–43. ACM
14. Goldberg, A.V., Kaplan, H., Werneck, R.F.: Reach for a*: efficient point-to-point shortest path algorithms. In: Proceedings of the Meeting on Algorithm Engineering and Experiments, pp. 129–143. Society for Industrial and Applied Mathematics (2006)
15. Hart, P.E., Nilsson, N.J., Raphael, B.: A formal basis for the heuristic determination of minimum cost paths. IEEE Trans. Syst. Sci. Cybern. **4**(2), 100–107 (1967)
16. Howard, J.H., Kazar, M.L., Menees, S.G., Nichols, D.A., Satyanarayanan, M., Sidebotham, R.N., West, M.J.: Scale and performance in a distributed file system. ACM Trans. Comput. Syst. **6**(1), 51–81 (1988)
17. Inokuchi, A., Washio, T., Motoda, H.: An apriori-based algorithm for mining frequent substructures from graph data. In: Zighed, D.A., Komorowski, J., Żytkow, J. (eds.) PKDD 2000. LNCS, vol. 1910, pp. 13–23. Springer, Heidelberg (2000). doi:10.1007/3-540-45372-5_2
18. Ira, P.: Bi-directional search. Mach. Intell. **6**(127–140), 13 (1971)
19. Kim, B.S., Kim, T.G., Song, H.S.: Parallel and distributed framework for standalone Monte Carlo simulation using MapReduce. Indian J. Sci. Technol. **8**(25), 1 (2015)
20. Pearl, J.: Heuristics: Intelligent Search Strategies for Computer Problem Solving. Addison-Wesley Longman Publishing Co., Inc., Boston (1984)
21. Tarjan, R.: Depth-first search and linear graph algorithms. SIAM J. Comput. **1**(2), 146–160 (1972)

Study of Energy Consumption in Wireless Sensor Networks Using S-Rhombus, S-Square and S-Circle Deployment

Saleh Bouarafa[1](✉), Rachid Saadane[2], Moulay Driss Rahmani[1], and Driss Aboutajdine[1]

[1] LRIT, Associated Unit to CNRST (URAC No 29), Faculty of Sciences, Mohammed V University in Rabat, B.P. 1014 RP, Rabat, Morocco
bouarafas@yahoo.fr, {mrahmani,aboutaj}@fsr.ac.ma
[2] SIR2C2S/LASI-EHTP, Hassania School of Public Labors, Km 7 EI Jadida Road, B.P. 8108 Casa-Oasis, Casablanca, Morocco
saadane@ehtp.ac.ma

Abstract. In this paper we have proposed three methods of static multi-hop routing, the nodes are scattered over the vertices of a $4 * 4$ array. The distance between vertices at the beginning is 10 m, after it takes the following values: 20 m, 30 m, 40 m, 50 m, 60 m, 70 m, 80 m. These methods are called: S-Square, S-Rhombus and S-Circle. The simulation results show that the S-Square is better than S-Rhombus and that one is better than S-Circle.

Keywords: Energy consumption · Deployment · Wireless sensor network · S-Rhombus method · S-Square method · S-Circle method

1 Introduction

In wireless sensor networks, nodes spend the most of their energy on data transmission. In many applications these nodes are small and have limited energy supplies. Research in the field of sensors undergoes today a serious change, which leads to root improvements, on their different applications (safety, health, environment, insurance food, manufacturing, telecommunications, robotics,...). Modern technologies admit to decrease the size, cost and power consumption and to increase the accuracy and performance of the sensors. Much work has been done to reduce the total required transmission power, to transmit a source node to a destination node by choosing a transmission system that requires only the amount minimum transmission power. A set of techniques is considered as the routing cooperative based on cooperation between neighbouring nodes of the source. In [2–4] the authors examined various cooperation routing algorithms using the wireless broadcast advantage and relays. These systems, however, tend to overlook the energy levels of nodes in the network whose overuse leads inevitably to a network partitioning. Different Algorithms have been developed to maximize the duration of life of the network. In [5] a globally optimal

E. Sabir et al. (Eds.): UNet 2017, LNCS 10542, pp. 402–410, 2017.
https://doi.org/10.1007/978-3-319-68179-5_35

solution problem of maximizing the lifetime of a network Static was examined through an approach based on graph theory. Studies have been made to increase the lifetime of the system, taking into account the energy remaining nodes in the network [1], when choosing of the transmission path. However, in several literatures minimize transmission power and increase the lifetime of the network has been studied separately. The organization of this paper is as follows: Sect. 2 describes the topology and the state of the art. Section 3 explains the proposed topology: S-Rhombus, S-Square and S-Circle. Section 4 give the simulation results and Sect. 5 is reserved for the conclusion.

2 Topology and WSN in the State of the Art

In the literature there are many topologies proposed to serve a WSN, in this section we will introduce the principal of them. We can divide the topology used in the WSN field into two classes: The first one is a geographic routing and sensor holes problems based, and the second one is on the sensor coverage sensor connectivity. The first topology family uses geographic and topological information of the network to attain best routing schemes with elevated routing effectiveness and minimum power utilization. Various sensor holes, such as Jamming holes, sink/black holes and worm holes, may form in a WSN and create network topology variations which trouble the upper layer applications. For examples, intense communication may cause jamming holes which will fail to deliver message to exterior nodes. Sink/Black holes and worm holes are caused by nodes exhausted around sink node or pretended sinks or by malicious nodes. If sensor holes issues are not treated carefully, they will create costly routing table and exhaust the intermediate nodes rapidly. The Topology Control Problems based can be further divided into two categories: Sensor Coverage Topology and Sensor Connectivity Topology. The coverage topology describes the topology of sensor coverage and is concerned about how to maximize a reliable sensing area while consuming less power. The connectivity topology on the other hand is more concern more about network connectivity and emphasizes the message retrieve and delivery in the network. Two kinds of mechanisms have been utilized to maintain an efficient sensor connectivity topology: Power Control Mechanisms and Power Management Mechanisms. The former controls the radio power level to achieve optimized connectivity topology and the later maintains a good wake/sleep schedule. To evaluate the effectiveness of a given topology the used parameters are: Range and coverage: Range and coverage are almost certainly the mainly noticeable necessities for a WSN preliminary from the node to node range at a given transmission power/antenna gain and data rate. The main factors affecting range of a wireless network are the quality of physical layer and the efficiency of data transmission through the network. The coverage requirements are elimination of dead spots in the network and the extent of coverage area in range, both of which are closely related to range. Scalability: Scalability is the property of being able to cope up with network cells as small as a few nodes to cells of thousands or even tens of thousands of nodes as well as increasing the size of existing network by order of magnitude without employing expensive cellular communication or other long range solutions. Expected Transmission Count ($E_{T(x)}$: It accounts for data loss due to medium access contention and environmental hazards and considers the number of transmissions needed to successfully transmit a packet over a link. Hop Count: Hop count is the most commonly used metric in wireless multi-hop networks. The path having the minimum number of links between a given source and the destination node is selected. Power consumption/Network Longevity: In most of the published communication protocols for WSNs, network lifetime extension has been mentioned as an important optimization objective. The position of nodes can affect the network lifetime significantly. For example, a no uniform node distribution in a given area may lead to bottlenecks and unbalanced traffic. On the other hand, uniform distribution of nodes in a network may result in depletion of energy of nodes that are close to the base station at a rate higher than the other nodes, which in turn will shorten the network lifetime.

3 Proposed Topology

In this section we will treat three methods of topology used to optimize transmission efficiency between nodes and sink, at different routing, and then we compare them for number of nodes include sink = 25 and each d_{cel} = 10, 20,..., 80. Or d_{cel} is the distance between two heads of table cell.

3.1 Method S-Rhombus

In Fig. 1a below, the same color nodes form a rhombus, the communication between them follows this form: the node sends the data to its next neighbour in the same rhombus and so on for the others. When it comes to the end the last node sends to its nearest neighbour in another rhombus, this mechanism is repeated until the sink, that is located in the middle.

3.2 Method S-Square

In Fig. 1b below, the same color nodes form a square, the communication between them follows this form: the node sends the data to its next neighbour in the same square and so on for the others. When it comes to the end, the last node sends to its nearest neighbour in another square, this mechanism is repeated until the sink, that is located in the middle.

3.3 Method S-Circle

In Fig. 1c below, the same color nodes form a circle, the communication between them follows this form: the node sends the data to its next neighbour in the same circle and so on for the others. When it comes to the end, the last node send to its nearest neighbour in another circle, this mechanism is repeated until the sink, that is located in the middle.

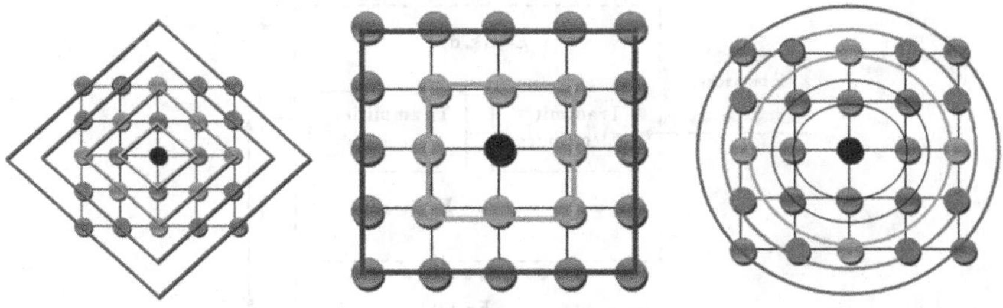

(a) Nodes Around The Base Station Formed a rhombus (b) Nodes Around The Base Station Formed a Square (c) Nodes Around The Base Station Formed a circle

Fig. 1. Three proposed methods of routing in WSN (Color figure online)

The WSN nodes send out their position in a small message to the Base Station. In our work, we employ the energy mode and analysis that are presented in [4,5]. The radio energy dissipation model is illustrated in Fig. 3. In this figure, $E_{T(x)}$ (k, d) presents the energy spent to transmit k-bits over a distance d, and E_{Rx} is the energy spent to process a k-bit message. The parameter E_{elec} denotes the energy per bit dissipated to run both the transmitter and the receiver circuits. This parameter depends on many factors such as digital coding, modulation, filtering, and the spreading of the signal [5]. The energy spent by the radio transmitter is given by Eq. 1 and by receiver is given by Eq. 2 (Fig. 2).

$$E_{t(x)}(k,d) = \begin{cases} k.E_{elec} + k.E_{fs}.d^2 \text{ if } d < d_0; \\ k.E_{elec} + k.E_{mp}.d^4 \text{ if } d \geq d_0. \end{cases} \tag{1}$$

$$E_{Rx} = k.E_{elec} \tag{2}$$

$$E_{agr} = k.E_{DA} \tag{3}$$

where and present the amplifier energy respectively in a free space model (with d^2 power loss) and in a multipath fading (with d^4 power loss) channel models. They depend on d, where d is the distance between the transmitter and the receiver. If the distance d is less than a threshold d_o, then the free space model is used; otherwise, the multipath model is used. The value of the threshold d_o has been given by Heinzelman et al. in [6]. It is defined as follows:

$$d_0 = \sqrt{\frac{E_{fs}}{E_{mp}}} \tag{4}$$

In this paper the sensor which will send this data at first time takes the value 1, the second takes the value 2, and so on until reaching the base station these numbers is given by the path followed for each static routing of three proposed methods: The 1 is the first node that transmits its data, the number 2 receives the data of 1 and aggregates with its data and sends it all to nodes 3, the sensors receive the data of their predecessors and aggregate with their own data and send the whole to their successors this is repeated until the base station. The routing

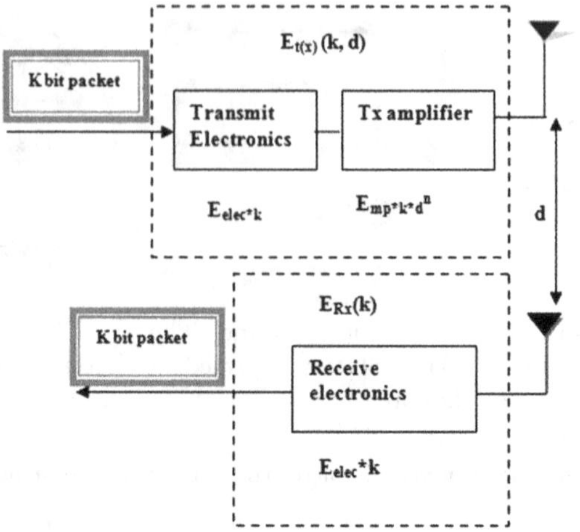

Fig. 2. Radio energy dissipation model [6]

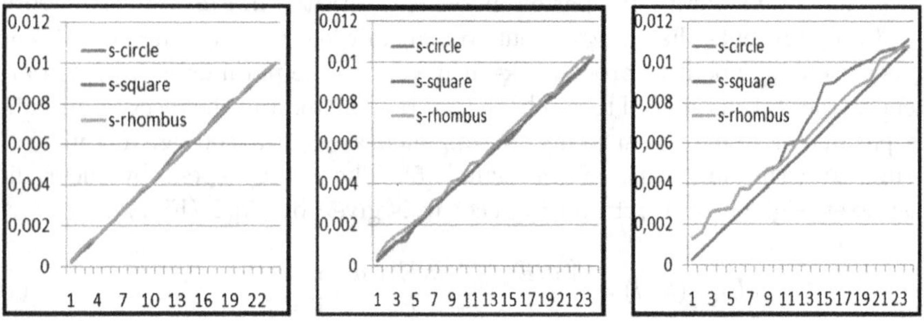

(a) d_{cel}=10m (b) d_{cel}=20m (c) d_{cel}=30m

Fig. 3. Consumption of energy for each node according to d_{cel}: 10 m, 20 m and 30 m.

Table 1. Distance between sensor and its next neighbour: method S-Rhombus

Sensor number	Distance between sensor and its next neighbour
1, 2 and 3	$4.d_{cel}$
4, 12, 20 and 24	$1.d_{cel}$
5, 7, 9 and 11	$2.d_{cel}$
6, 8, 10, 13, 14, 15, 16, 17, 18, 19, 21, 22 and 23	$\sqrt{2}.d_{cel}$

follows a form as already reported. Using Eqs. 1, 2, 3 and 4, it is possible to adjust for each sensor since in 1 to 24 its total energy consumption:

$$E_{total(i)}(k,d) = \begin{cases} k.(i-1).(E_{elec} + E_{DA}) + k.i.(E_{elec} + E_{fs}.d^2) \text{ if } d < d_0; \\ k.(i-1).(E_{elec} + E_{DA}) + k.i.(E_{elec} + E_{fs}.d^4) \text{ if } d \geq d_0. \end{cases} \quad (5)$$

with: i is the sensor number, d is the distance between sensor and its next neighbour we can show that in Tables 1, 2 and 3.

Table 2. Distance between sensor and its next neighbour: method S-Square

Sensor number	Distance between sensor and its next neighbour
1, 2, 3, 4, 5, 6, 7, 8, 9, 10, 11, 12, 13 14, 15, 16, 17, 18, 19, 20, 21, 22, 23 and 24	$1.d_{cel}$

Table 3. Distance between sensor and its next neighbour: method S-Circle

Sensor number	Distance between sensor and its next neighbour
1, 2 and 3	$4.d_{cel}$
4, 20 and 24	$1.d_{cel}$
5, 7, 9, 11, 17, 18 and 19	$2.d_{cel}$
6, 8, 10, 16, 21, 22 and 23	$\sqrt{2}.d_{cel}$
12	$\sqrt{5}.d_{cel}$
13, 14 and 15	$\sqrt{8}.d_{cel}$

4 Simulation Results

We sorted the energy consumption obtained by each sensor then we plot the results, and we get these figures, each sensor sends data to its neighbour already known according to said topology, the sensor do the aggregation of data from its predecessor and sends all the data to its successor. This procedure is repeated until the aggregated data reaches the base station. All simulations are based on the following protocol. We consider many wireless sensor networks with N = 25 nodes dispersed on the heads of the table cells $4 * 4$, over a $320\,\text{m} * 320\,\text{m}$ area. The Base Station is located at the middle. Moreover, we ignore the effect caused by the signal collision and the interference in the wireless channel. Since the nodes have limited energy, they consume their energies during the course of simulations. Once a node runs out of energy, it is considered dead and cannot transmit or receive data. For these simulations, energy decreases whenever a node

Table 4. Radio characteristics used in our simulations

Parameter	Value
E_{elec}	50 nJ/bit
E_{fs}	10 pJ/bit/m^2
E_{mp}	0.0013 pJ/bit/m^4
E_0	0.5 J
k	4000 bits
E_{DA}	50 nJ/bit/message
d_0	88 m

transmits or receives data and whenever it performs data aggregation using the radio parameters shown in Table 4. We sorted the energy consumption obtained by each sensor then we plot the results, and we get these figures, each sensor sends data to its neighbour already known according to said topology, the sensor do the aggregation of data from its predecessor and sends all the data to its successor. This procedure is repeated until the aggregated data reaches the base station. The simulation stops when the last byte arrives to the sink.

In this simulation we have proposed and evaluated the three types of routing called: S-Rhombus, S-Square, S-Circle, in these three networks, which are homogeneous and multi-hup networks. Each sensor sends to its neighbour indicated in its list of the neighbours. In this case the list of neighbours contains only one neighbour. We suppose that the networks is synchronized, and all sensors have data to transmit it, our goal here is to calculate the energy consumption of each sensor, then the calculate of energy consumption of all network.

In Fig. 3a the curves are almost the same: the curve of S-Rhombus is identical to that of S-Circle in 17 point and is identical to that of S-Square in 4 point, and the curve of S-Circle with S-Square are the same in 3 point, in other points the S-Square is better than S-Rhombus and this one is better than S-Circle.

In Fig. 3b S-Square consumes more than one S-circle on average 3.81E−05 and consume less than one S-Rhombus on average 2.6E−04. S-Circle consumes less than one S-Rhombus on average 3E−04 then S-Circle is better than S-Square and this one is better than S-Rhombus.

The curve of S-Rhombus is identical to that of S-Circle in:

- 10 point in Fig. 3c
- 7 point in Fig. 4a
- 5 point in Fig. 4b
- 3 point in Fig. 4c
- 2 point in Fig. 5a
- 1 point in Fig. 5b.

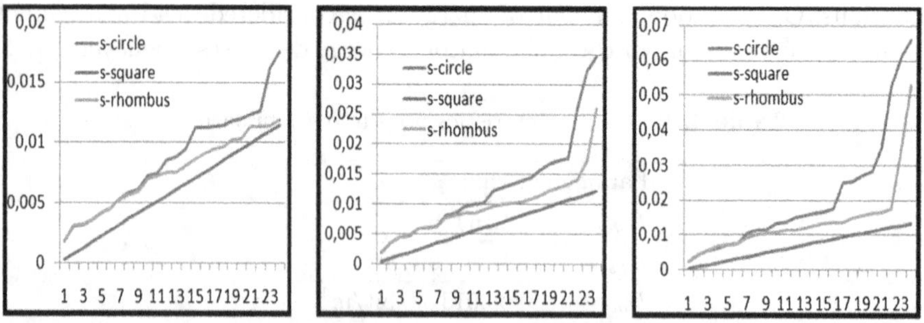

(a) d_{cel}=40m (b) d_{cel}=50m (c) d_{cel}=60m

Fig. 4. Consumption of energy for each node according to d_{cel}: 40 m, 50 m and 60 m.

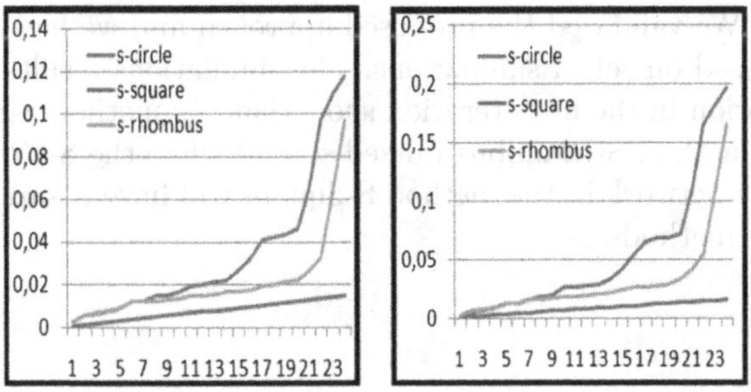

(a) d_{cel}=70m (b) d_{cel}=80m

Fig. 5. Consumption of energy for each node according to d_{cel}: 70 m and 80 m.

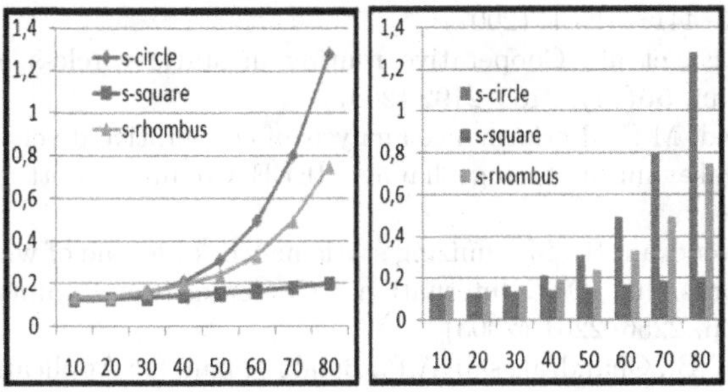

(a) (b)

Fig. 6. Total energy consumption according to d_{cel} = 10 m,..., 80 m for S-Rhombus, S-Square and S-Circle.

Except for points which are identical, S-Circle consumes more than S-Rhombus in all the figures cited, S-Square is better than S-Rhombus and this one is better than S-Circle in energy consumption.

In Fig. 6b and a S-Square outperforms S-Rhombus and this one outperforms S-Circle in total energy consumption according to d_{cel} =10...80: in S-Square the sensors consume less than one S-Rhombus and less than one S-Circle.

5 Conclusion

In this paper we have proposed and evaluated three methods of transmission called: S-Rhombus, S-Square, S-Circle to establish a realistic routing based on a specific topology of homogeneous wireless sensor networks. In first time we have reviewed the main classes of topologies and presented some universally used parameters to evaluate the effectiveness of a given topology. We distributed sensors on the heads of each table cell 4 $*$ 4, and the sink in the middle. We observed that the distribution of sensors around the sink can be in form of a square, a rhombus or a circle, that why we chose to make static routes as these forms obtained. We validated the proposed approach and we have evaluated its performances based on set of simulations. The simulations results based on the energy consumption in the first iteration show that the method S-Square is best followed by the method S-Rhombus ranked second while the S-Circle method is ranked third: the network in the method S-Square will have a long lifetime than in the two other methods.

References

1. Chang, J.-H., Tassiulas, L.: Maximum lifetime routing in wireless sensor networks. IEEE/ACM Trans. Netw. **12**(4), 609–619 (2004)
2. Ibrahim, A.S., Han, Z., Liu, K.J.R.: Distributed energy-efficient cooperative routing in wireless networks. In: Global Telecommunications Conference, Globecom 2007, pp. 4413–4418. IEEE (2007)
3. Khandani, A.E., et al.: Cooperative routing in static wireless networks. IEEE Trans. Commun. **55**(11), 2185–2192 (2007)
4. Ikki, S., Ahmed, M.H.: Performance analysis of cooperative diversity wireless networks over Nakagami-m fading channel. IEEE Commun. Lett. **11**(4), 334–336 (2007)
5. Kang, I., Poovendran, R.: Maximizing static network lifetime of wireless broadcast ad hoc networks. In: IEEE International Conference on Communications, ICC 2003, vol. 3, pp. 2256–2261 (2003)
6. Heinzelman, W.B., Chandrakasan, A.P., Balakrishnan, H.: Application specific protocol architecture for wireless microsensor networks. In: IEEE Transactions on Wireless Networking (2002)
7. Beigy, H., Meybodi, M.R.: A self-organizing channel assignment algorithm: a cellular learning automata approach. In: Liu, J., Cheung, Y., Yin, H. (eds.) IDEAL 2003. LNCS, vol. 2690, pp. 119–126. Springer, Heidelberg (2003). doi:10.1007/978-3-540-45080-1_18
8. Ganguly, N., Sikdar, B.K., Deutsch, A., Canright, G., Chaudhuri, P.P.: A survey on cellular automata, Technical report, Centre for High Performance Computing, Dresden University of Technology, Dresden (2003)
9. Boondirek, A., Triampo, W., Nuttavut, N.: A review of cellular automata models of tumor growth. In: International Mathematical Forum, vol. 5, no. 61, pp. 3023–3029 (2010)
10. Tome, T., De Felicio, J.R.D.: Probabilistic cellular automata D. Phys. Rev. E **53**(4), 3976–3981 (1996)
11. Sloot, P., Chen, F., Boucher, C.: Cellular automata model of drug therapy for HIV infection. In: Bandini, S., Chopard, B., Tomassini, M. (eds.) ACRI 2002. LNCS, vol. 2493, pp. 282–293. Springer, Heidelberg (2002). doi:10.1007/3-540-45830-1_27
12. Kacimi, R.: Techniques de conservation d'nergie pour les rseaux de capteurs sans fil, Institut National Polytechnique de Toulouse (2009)

Toward a New Extension of IPv6 Addressing to Connect Non IP Objects

Ali El Ksimi(✉), Cherkaoui Leghris, and Faddoul Khoukhi

L@M Lab, RTM Team, Faculty of Science and Technology of Mohammedia, Mohammedia, Morocco
ali.elksimi-etu@etude.univcasa.ma, cleghris@yahoo.fr

Abstract. Nowadays, we use many small objects that are transforming our habits, our behaviors, and more generally our societies. We are surrounded by these objects which can communicate with their environment and exchange data, which offer us more and more services, facilitating our activities, and with which we interact frequently. But how these objects can communicate via the Internet knowing that they do not have their own IP address? To answer this question, several solutions are proposed in the literature. In this paper, we propose an approach based on modulo-2 addition between the network prefix and the tag ID of non-IP object to derive an IPv6 address of the tag from its ID. In this way, the NonIP-IPv6 mapping provides a better solution for objects because it minimizes the chances of address conflicts in the network given the large number of IP addresses to identify given objects in an IoT context and accelerates the program execution time.

Keywords: IPv6 · IoT · NFC · RFID · Small objects · EPC

1 Introduction

SmObnet6 (Small Objects Network with IPv6) is a generic term that we use to define all networks, from small such as PANs (Personal Area Network) to larger, interconnecting small objects. The common point between these networks is that they will use the IPv6 protocol for communication between objects to collect and exchange data within the existing internet infrastructure.

Nowadays, the Internet becomes the main vector for disseminating all types of information. It has established itself in many areas as an essential infrastructure for individuals, businesses and institutions. However, its extensive capabilities, beyond computers and mobile terminals, are still considerable because it should allow the interaction of an increasing number of objects between themselves or with ourselves. The Internet is gradually transforming itself into an extensive network, called the Internet of Things, linking billions of human beings but also tens of billions of objects. These objects connecting to require, among other things, a tag or an identification code that makes it possible to identify each object in a unique way. It already exists in the market for physical labeling mechanisms of these objects, such as bar code, RFID (Radio Frequency Identification) and NFC (Near Field Communication). However, to ensure unique network addressing and easy, global, secure and mobile connectivity, research

E. Sabir et al. (Eds.): UNet 2017, LNCS 10542, pp. 411–421, 2017.
https://doi.org/10.1007/978-3-319-68179-5_36

has come to the conclusion that the natural candidate will be IPv6, as addressing mechanism, connectivity and transmission to all networks and platforms. The huge IPv6 address space can identify these billions of objects in a uniform, hierarchical way, whether connected to the Wi-Fi, Ethernet, Bluetooth, 802.15.1, ZigBee or LTE-A network, and Regardless of the physical labeling used. All these objects will have an IPv6 address, normal or compressed, to connect to multiple networks and communicate. In this article, we propose an algorithm to derive the tag IPv6 address of RFID, NFC, and EPC from their identifier using the reader as a router generates the network prefix.

2 Related Work

Many objects used in our life don't have microprocessors and therefore, cannot join a computer network. Using non-IP technology and tag integration in objects, this communication will be possible.

In [1], the authors have proposed strategy for forming IPv6 addresses from legacy protocol information using a hashing function (CRC32) and mapping function. The use of hashing techniques to construct an IPv6 address from an EPC (Electronic Product Code), as opposed by using a compressed EPC format [2], eases practical implementations and al lows the use of the same mapping scheme for all EPC types.

Other approach proposes to provide the tags themselves with the IPv6 protocol stack, making them able to use IPv6 communication over the Internet whenever close to a reader [3]. However, it is proved that this proposition represent a great challenge because several changes are required to the design of existing tags more specifically providing tags with an alimentation source. However, these changes make tags too expensive for integration into the Internet of Things since the price of the tags could easily exceed the value of the "things" themselves.

In [4], the authors use objects EPCs to create their current IPv6 addresses. Replacement of the network prefix of an IPv6 address by the EPC was suggested, which only works for 64-bit EPCs. The reader calls the tag to generate IP address from the EPC and transmits it to the corresponding EPCIS (xxx) server. The reader stores the created IPv6 address as well. The EPCIS server holds information about the current IP address of particular tags. If someone wants to retrieve data from the tag, the EPCIS server is asked for the IPv6 address and the tag can be contacted.

In [5], RFID networking mechanism using Address management agent is proposed. In this paper, idea of generating unique 48 bits virtual MAC address based on RFID tag was proposed which can be further used by the DHCP server to allocate IP address to RFID tag dynamically. As DHCP server assigns IP address dynamically, after the lease time is finished, the client has to reclaim for new IP address which may not be same as given previously by DHCP on other network.

In [6], Jara has considered the need to make legacy technologies accessible via the Internet to an end-to-end addressing mechanism based on IPv6. Thereby, end devices can be identified via the IPv6 address, and emerging protocols, such as CoAP (Constrained Application Protocol), could be accessed by the native functionality. The proposed addressing proxies carry out this double task: on the one hand, the addressing mapping and, on the other hand, the functionality mapping from web services, such as

RESTful, and the already mentioned CoAP to native protocols. For this purpose, Jara [6] presents a set of mapping techniques between legacy technologies from home automation, industrial and logistic areas to IPv6. The mapping offers a homogeneous addressing and identification framework for the IoT.

However, we can conclude from the different studied works that the translation of address requires either extra nodes in the network to construct network addresses or additional functionalities to RFID readers residing at the network edge.

In our paper, we used another different method that could generate easily the IPv6 address which minimize conflicts and accelerate the program execution time.

3 Non IP Protocol Objects

Among the wireless communication technologies for the Internet of Objects, we can distinguish two main types of radio communication networks: short-range networks and medium and long-range networks. The first type concerns technologies - well known to the general public - that emit from a few centimeters to a few hundred meters maximum: WiFi, Bluetooth, RFID, NFC, ZigBee, etc.

The second concerns technologies that have larger ranges, from a few hundred meters to several tens of kilometers. It is the traditional cellular networks (GSM, GPRS, LTE, etc.) that we also use for our mobile communications.

In this paper, we study the first type: non-IP protocols.

3.1 Object

An object is, above all, a physical entity; for example, a book, a car, an electric coffee machine or a mobile phone. In the precise context of the Internet of things, regardless of the vision, this object has at least one unique identifier attached to an identity [7] expressing its immutable properties (type, color, weight, etc.) and its state, i.e. all its characteristics can change over time (position, battery level, etc.).

A communicating object can be defined as a device that can interact with its environment by responding to stimuli, and exchanging with peers using communication.

3.2 RFID

RFID or Radio Frequency Identification technology is a method generally used to facilitate the identification data and the identification of remote objects, using one or more RFID chips integrated into objects or even, in some cases, implanted in living organisms. RFID chips can contain an identifier or a number of information and/or additional data. This system consists of transponders or RFID tags with one or more readers. Become more and more sophisticated, the technology is now contributing to the development of the IoT (Internet of Things).

3.3 Basic Principle of RFID Communication

The RFID system consists of a transponder and a radio receiver, more often known as a tag and reader. Information related to a given object is stored on an affixed tag and transmitted to a reader over a radio frequency (RF) connection. The reader in turn connects via wired or wireless networks to servers hosting RFID applications that make use of transmitted RFID data, and, in the case of supply chain applications, middleware manages the flow of RFID data between readers and enterprise applications. Figure 1 shows the basic principle of RFID system.

Fig. 1. Basic principle RFID communication

3.4 EPC

Each RFID object is identified by its Electronic Product Code (EPC) whose length may vary from 96 to 256 bits, and its namespace that is segmented into four hierarchically encapsulated partitions as follows:

Table 1. EPC partitions

Header	EPC manager	Object class	Serial number
36	28	24	36

Table 1 shows the structure of the EPC numbering scheme. An EPC number consists of four parts. The first part is the header which defines the version of the EPC number used. The second is the identifier of the EPC-Manager that assigns the EPC number to the object. The third part is the object class identifier that essentially defines the object product type. The last part is reserved for the unique serial number that identifies the product from other products among the same object class.

To compare EPC identification with IPv6 addressing, we provide some comparison features on Table 2.

Table 2. IPv6 vs. EPC comparison

	IPv6	EPC
Objects to identify	Network interfaces	Physical objects
Primary application	Routing address	Pointer to information
Address located by	Network manager	Item manufacturer
Unique identifier	Yes	yes
Identifier length	128 bits	64, 96 others
Can identifier change	Yes	no
Area of difficulty	Mobility	No location information

3.5 RFID Message Format

The objects with RFID technology could exchange messages with readers. The Table 3 shows the EPC message header.

Table 3. RFID header

RFID type	Message type	Reserved
RFID code		
Message data		

3.6 NFC

NFC is a near-field, near-field communication technology for real-time and contactless data exchange. This exchange of information takes place between two peripherals (mobile terminals, readers, etc.) by radio Frequency (frequency range: 13.56 MHz), less than 10 cm. Generally, the NFC is integrated into most of our mobile phones as a chip, as well as in some transport or payment cards.

RFID and NFC are devices that rely on the same technology - contactless communication - to make a difference: RFID allows data transmission over a greater distance than the NFC whose main feature is proximity to distance - a few centimeters between the reader and the NFC tag.

3.7 IPv6 Basics

The specification of IPv6 can be found in RFC 2640 [8]. The most important change is the augmentation of the address space from 32 bits (IPv4) to 128 bits (IPv6). Based on the most pessimistic estimates of address assignment efficiency, with this address space is predicted to provide over 1500 addresses per square foot of the earth's surface, which certainly seems like it can serve as basis for an Internet of Things.

An IPv6 packet consists of a fixed-size header followed by multiple optional extensions headers and the data portion. The basic IPv6 header has a fixed size of 40 bytes (including version, traffic class, flow label, payload length, next header, hop limit, and source and destination address).

The Table 4 shows the structure of an IPv6 packet [8].

Table 4. IPv6 header

Version	Traffic class	Flow label
Payload length	Next header	Hop limit
Source address (128 bits)		
Destination address (128 bits)		

3.8 IPv6-RFID Mapping

The Fig. 2 shows the mapping of IPv6 and RFID:

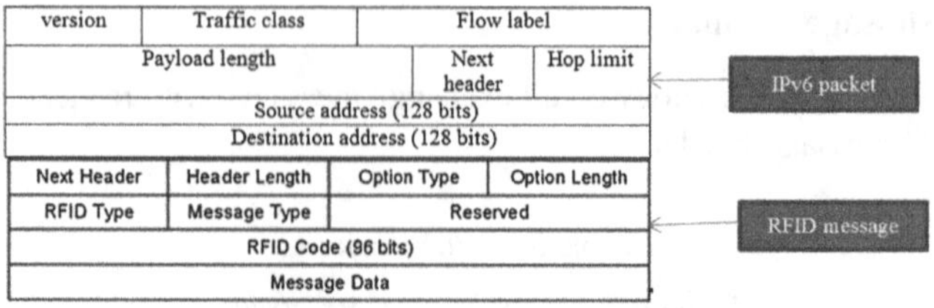

Fig. 2. The mapping IPv6-RFID

4 Proposed Method

The principle of our approach consists in the use of logical function modulo-2 addition between the network prefix which is the same as reader prefix and the tag ID to construct IPv6 address of the tag (i.e. of the object).

4.1 The Addition-2 Modulo

The logical operator (+) can be defined by the following sentence:

"The output is TRUE if and only if both inputs are different".

A logical function translates the relationship between the logical states of the input and output variables.

The practical realization of logical functions implementing binary operators or logical operators.

In a binary operator, the input and output variables; variables are binary variables interconnected by defined functions which characterize the function of the binary operator.

In our case, we use the function addition-2 modulo.

Call A and B both operands considered. Agree to represent their value as well: 1 = TRUE and 0 = FALSE.

The operator (+) is defined by its truth table (Table 5), indicating, for all possible values of A and B, the value of the result S:

Table 5. Table of truth of addition-2 modulo

A	B	S = A + B
0	0	0
0	1	1
1	0	1
1	1	0

4.2 Classical Modular Addition Method

Following is the algorithm of a classical modular addition method (Fig. 3):

Algorithm: classical modular addition method

Input: p, A= $(a_{n-1}...a_1, a_0) < p$, B= $(b_{n-1}, ...b_1, b_0) < p$

Output: S =A +B (mod p)

1. S←A +B
2. S′←S−p
3. If S′ <0 then
4. Return S
5. Else
6. Return S′
7. Endif

Fig. 3. Algorithm of classical modular addition method

4.3 Our Approach

In this section, we propose a mechanism to generate an IPv6 for Non-IP Objects from Tag ID. For that, we will use the modulo-2 addition operator with the two operands that are the network prefix and the tag ID.

In our case, the reader of the technologies non-IP plays the role of a router. In other word: reader prefix = network prefix.

Based on the length of the tag ID, three scenarios are present:

1. The length of the tag ID is less than or more than 64 bits;
2. The length of the tag ID is equal to 64 bits.

With this:

- For the first case, in order to get the 64 bits, we apply the hash function CRC-32. Then, we add to the tag ID left zero-padding;
- In the second case, we use directly the 64 bits of the tag ID.

– **IPv6 address construction phase**

After obtaining the ID with 64 bits, we use the modulo-2 addition with the network prefix to generate the IPv6 address of the tag.

The Fig. 4 shows an example of IPv6 network address construction using our proposed approach:

Let assume that the prefix of the network is 2001::

ID of non-IP object	127 0 58 207 19
Binary format	0000 0000 0000 0000 0000 0000 0111 1111 0000 0000 0011 1010 1100 0001 0011
Hexadecimal format	0000 007f 003a cf13
Prefix + ID	2001:007f:003a:cf13
IPv6 address of the non-IP object	2001::007f:003a:cf13

Fig. 4. Example of our approach

The process of address mapping is shown in the scheme in Fig. 5.

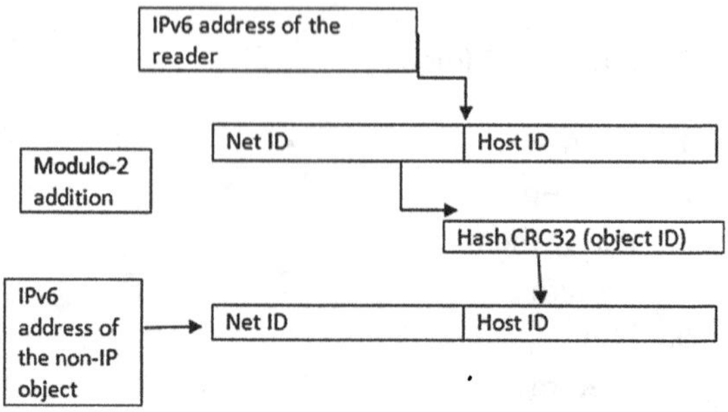

Fig. 5. A scheme of the proposed mapping method using modulo-2 addition function.

The following chart shows the algorithm of our approach (Fig. 6):

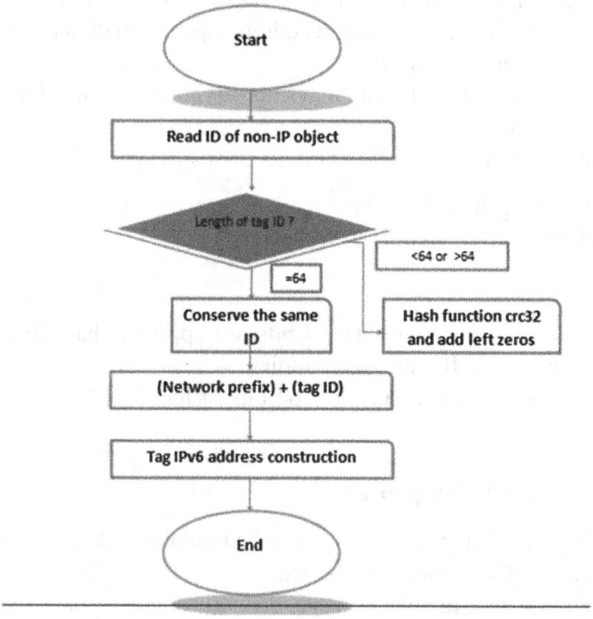

Fig. 6. The flow chart of the proposed approach using addition-2 modulo function

We suppose that:

- F is a function defined by: F: (x, y) ➔ x + y;
- Example:

Given x = 1011 and y = 0110 then

F(x, y) = x + y = 1011 + 0110

Following the Truth table of (+), F(x, y) = 1101

- F is reversible; it means that the ID of tag is easily recovered from its IPv6 address;
- According to this property "C = A + B => B = A + C".

4.4 IPv6 Autoconfiguration

IPv6 Auto-configuration means that an object gets all the necessary information to connect to a local network IP without human intervention. The whole process is called stateless address (auto) configuration and specified in RFC 4862 [9] and 4861 [10].

In our approach, we used this process to generate the IPv6 address of the tag.

a. **Creation of the Link-Local Address**

IPv6 link-local addresses are a special scope of address which can be used only within the context of a single layer two domain. Packets sourced from or destined to a link-local address are not forwarded out of the layer 2 domain by routers.

Link-local addresses are defined in Sect. 2.5.6 [11] as having a ten-bit prefix of 0xfe80 followed by 54 zero bits and a 64-bit interface ID.

In our case the link local address of a tag will be written in the following form: FE80::[interface ID], knowing that interface ID is the suffix of the IPv6 address, it is constructed in Sect. 4.3.

b. **Creation of a Global Unicast Address**

A global unicast address is simply what we call a public IP address in IPv4—that is, an IP address that is routed across the whole Internet.

5 Performance Evaluation

In this section, we will present the efficiency of our algorithm as a function of program execution time.

5.1 Network Topology

The configuration of the network of Fig. 7 is composed of a tag and an RFID reader, the latter is attached to an arduino card which is also connected to the PC via a serial cable. The RFID Reader performs the role of the router.

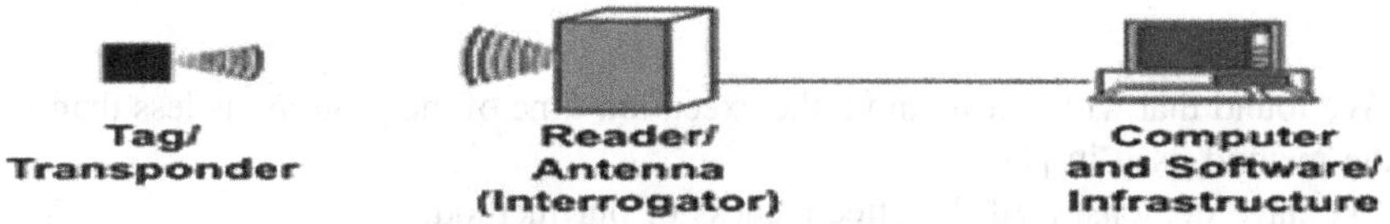

Fig. 7. Network configuration

5.2 Measurement Technique

Many different methods exist to measure execution time, but there is no single best technique. In our paper, we evaluated the execution time of our method with a pre-defined function in language C. this function is called clock ().

The C library function clock_t clock (void) returns the number of clock ticks elapsed since the program was launched. To get the number of seconds used by the CPU, you will need to divide by CLOCKS_PER_SEC.

The following example shows the usage of clock () function (Fig. 8):

```
#include<time.h>
#include<stdio.h>
Int main ()
{
//start_t: start time of the program
//end_t: end time of the program
//total_t: time execution of the program (in seconds)
  clock_t start_t, end_t, total_t;
  start_t= clock ();
//Here we write the instructions of our method
 end_t = clock ();
  total_t = (double) (end_t - start_t) / CLOCKS_PER_SEC;
  Printf ("Total execution time taken by CPU: %f\n", total_t);
  Return (0);
}
```

Fig. 8. The use of clock () function

5.3 Methods Evaluation

Our study is based on a single tag. The Fig. 9 shows the execution time of the programs according to number of bits of tag identifier.

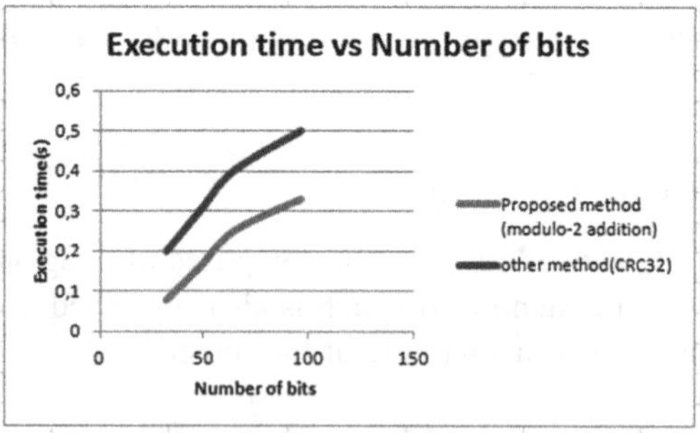

Fig. 9. Execution time according to number of bits

We found that with our method, the execution time of the program is less than that of the method used in [1].

We have demonstrated the effectiveness of our method.

6 Conclusion and Future Work

In this paper, we have proposed an approach to derive address IPv6 from non-IP technology's tag ID. We have used the modulo-2 addition and hash function. This method ensures its effectiveness compared to other methods because it allows minimization of IPv6 address conflicts in the network and accelerates the execution time of the program. In the future work, we will study other performances.

References

1. Rizzo, G., Jara, A.J., Olivieri, A., Bocchi, Y., Palattella, M.R.: IPv6 mapping to non-IP protocols, 11 February 2014
2. Dominikus, S., Aigner, M., Kraxberger, S.: Passive RFID technology for the internet of things. In: 2010 International Conference for Internet Technology and Secured Transactions (ICITST), pp. 1–8, November 2010
3. Barisch, M., Matos, A.: Integrating user identity management systems with the host identity protocol. In: IEEE Symposium on Computers and Communications, ISCC, pp. 830–836 (2009)
4. Piispanen, M.: EPC and IPv6 -based discovery services, 1 December 2011
5. Yoon, D.G., Lee, D.H., Seo, C.H., Choi, S.G.: RFID networking mechanism using address management agent. In: 4th Networked Computing and Advanced Information Management (NCM 2008), vol. 1, pp. 617–622, September 2008
6. Jara, A.J., Moreno-Sanchez, P., Skarmeta, A.F., Varakliotis, S., Kirstein, P.: IPv6 addressing proxy: mapping native addressing from legacy technologies and devices to the internet of things (IPv6) **13**(5), 6687–6712 (2013). doi:10.3390/s130506687
7. Atzori, L., Iera, A., Morabito, G.: The internet of things : a survey. Comput. Netw. **54**(15), 2787–2805 (2010)
8. Request for Comments: 2460, RFC 2460. Internet Protocol, Version 6 (IPv6) Specification (1998)
9. Buenaventura, F.J., Gonzales, J.P., Lu, M.E., Ong, A.V.: IPv6 Stateless Address Autoconfiguration (SLAAC) Attacks and Detection, 2 March 2015
10. Shelby, Z., Chakrabarti, S., Nordmark, E., Bormann, C.: Neighbor Discovery Optimization for IPv6 over Low-Power Wireless Personal Area Networks (6LoWPANs), RFC 4944, November 2012
11. Hinden, R., Deering, S.: IP version 6 Addressing Architecture, 21 January 2016

Enablers, Challenges and Applications

Channel Coherence Classification with Frame-Shifting in Massive MIMO Systems

Ahmad Abboud[1], Oussama Habachi[1(✉)], Ali Jaber[2], Jean-Pierre Cances[1], and Vahid Meghdadi[1]

[1] XLIM, University of Limoges, Limoges, France
ahm.abboud@gmail.com, {oussama.habachi, jeanpierre.cances,vahid.meghdadi}@xlim.fr
[2] Department of Statistics, Lebanese University, Nabatieh, Lebanon

Abstract. This paper considers the uplink pilot overhead in a time division duplexing (TDD) massive Multiple Input Multiple Output (MIMO) mobile systems. A common scenario of conventional massive MIMO systems is a Base Station (BS) serving all user terminals (UTs) in the cell with the same TDD frame format that fits the coherence interval of the worst-case scenario of user mobility (e.g. a moving train with velocity 300 km/s). Furthermore, the BS have to estimate all the channels each time-slot for all users even for those with long coherence intervals. In fact, within the same cell, sensors or pedestrian with low mobility UTs (e.g. moving 1.38 m/s) share the same short TDD frame and thus are obliged to upload their pilots each time-slot. The channel coherence interval of the pedestrian UTs with a carrier frequency of 1.9 GHz can be as long as 60 times that of the train passenger users. In other words, conventional techniques waste 59-uploaded pilot sequences for channel estimation. In this paper, we are aware of the resources waste due to various coherence intervals among different user mobility. We classify users based on their coherence interval length, and we propose to skip uploading pilots of UTs with large coherence intervals. Then, we shift frames with the same pilot reused sequence toward an empty pilot time-slot. Simulation results had proved that the proposed technique overcome the performance of conventional massive MIMO systems in both energy and spectral efficiency.

Keywords: Massive MIMO · Uplink pilot contamination · Time-shifted frames · TDD channel estimation · Pilot allocation

1 Introduction

MASSIVE Multiple Input Multiple Output (MIMO) systems is a promising technology to meet future demands of 5G wireless networks. Indeed, this interesting technology boosts both the spectral efficiency and the energy efficiency [1, 2]. In this regard, a large number of antennas at the base station (BS) are utilized to communicate with a significantly smaller number of single-antenna user terminals (UTs) over the same frequency and time domain [3]. However, several challenging problems for massive

E. Sabir et al. (Eds.): UNet 2017, LNCS 10542, pp. 425–437, 2017.
https://doi.org/10.1007/978-3-319-68179-5_37

MIMO with a large number of antennas at the BS persist such as the uplink pilot contamination in Time Division Duplexing (TDD) [1]. It is worth noting that channel state information (CSI) are required at the BSs for multi-user MIMO in order to separate the received uplink signals and to direct each downlink signal towards its desired receiver. Pilot sequences sent by the UTs are used to obtain CSI by estimating the channel responses from the received signals. In fact, during a limited coherence interval and under a TDD reciprocity scheme, UTs in each cell must upload orthogonal pilot sequence to their BS for channel estimation lagged with the uplink data. Then, the BS precede the downlink data based on the estimated channel matrix using uploaded pilots. Indeed, the BS require a very low interference in the pilot transmission phase in order to be able to estimate CSI accurately, which make pilot sequences precious resources for massive MIMO systems. Nowadays, the number of the orthogonal pilots is not problematic since the number of orthogonal pilots is much higher than the number of active UTs per cell. However, in massive MIMO systems, the number of active UTs is expected to increase as possible in order to achieve a high sum spectral efficiency. Therefore, this scenario is fundamentally limited by the number of orthogonal uplink pilot sequences that can be generated, which will lead to pilot reuse in adjacent cells and inter-cell interference, i.e. pilot contamination [4]. In view of this, many research efforts have been made to mitigate uplink pilot contamination in massive MIMO systems [5–11]. Most efforts in this field can be categorized into two groups, pilot-based estimation approach and subspace-based estimation approach [12]. Selective uplink training based on channel temporal correlation had been recently proposed in [13] to reduce training overhead. The authors exploit the temporal correlation of UT channels to classify them into two groups. In each channel block, the BS select part of the UTs for training, while the other UT CSIs are determined by prediction. This approach adds channel prediction complexity to the training channel block, where our proposed technique makes benefit from pilot sparsity to shift frames into empty pilot spectral space.

Note also that 5G will be vital for the continued development of Internet of Thing (IoT) letting devices to communicate over vast distances while reducing latency issues. In fact, IoT represents an umbrella keyword that extends the Internet and the Web into the physical world thanks to the widespread deployment of embedded devices having sensing and communication capabilities. It is obvious that the effects of the IoT will be visible in the next few years in both working and domestic fields. Indeed, a big leap forward is coming, related to the use of the 5G network to connect machines and smart communicating objects. The central issues are how to achieve full interoperability between high mobility UTs and low mobility or static sensors, and how to provide them access with a high degree of smartness. Another crucial problem in enabling large numbers of low-cost sensors is energy efficiency. Indeed, the energy efficiency has received a considerable attention when designing communication protocols. In fact, ecological concerns increasingly attract attention in communication systems. Therefore, novel solutions that maintain a limited energy consumption are always welcomed in both system and device levels. This paper proposes to use heterogeneous TDD frame structure by skipping pilots upload in some frames, for UTs with low mobility such as sensors, to reduce pilot contamination and increase energy efficiency (EE) on the uplink of massive MIMO systems. We introduce a sparse pilot model with time-shifted

TDD frames to increase system spectral efficiency (SE) and reuse the same pilot sequence while preserving pilot orthogonality. We classify users into different classes according to their coherence intervals and assign to each class a pool of sparse shifted pilot sequences that best matches their coherence intervals length, taking into consideration the overall system performance. We then prove the effect of our proposed technique through simulation results. Our work is different from [5, 6, 13–15] in the sense that these works present time-shifted pilots in an inter-cell manner. In the aforementioned works, each group of cells uses a time-shift frame, while in our work we group users according to their coherence interval length and we use time shift of unit length equal to an entire time-slot. Furthermore, we skip pilot upload in some time-slots for classes that encountered longer coherence intervals. This skipping makes it possible to reuse the same pilot in the same cell several times without encountering pilot contamination. To the best of our knowledge, UTs classification based on their coherence interval length coped with time-shifted TDD frame structure was not proposed in the literature.

The main contributions of this paper are threefold:

- UTs classification based on their coherence interval length,
- UTs with large coherence intervals will skip uploading pilots for some time slots depending on their assigned classes,
- We shift frames with the same reused pilot sequence toward an empty pilot time-slot to take profit from pilot skipping of other users,
- Skipping sending pilot for some time-slots not only enhances the energy efficiency of the UT since it remains idle during the pilot duration but also increase the number of users that can be served by the BS without any pilot contamination.

The remainder of the paper is organized as follows. The next section describes the system model. In Sect. 3, we discuss the proposed time-shifted pilots and sparse pilot. Section 4 is devoted to introduce the classification criteria and UTs classification algorithm. In Sect. 5, we discuss the spectral and energy efficiency. Before concluding the paper in Sect. 7, we introduce, Sect. 6, some numerical results to illustrate the performance of our proposed technique.

Notations: In this article, transpose and Hermitian transpose are denoted by $(.)^{T}$, $(.)^{H}$, respectively. $(.)^{*}$ denote the conjugate, det(A) denote the determinant of A, $\odot$ denote element-wise multiplication and denote by $\|A\|$ the Frobenius norm.

2 System Model

We consider a hexagonal cellular system with L cells, assigned with an index in the set $\mathcal{L} = \{1, \ldots, L\}$, each served by one BS holding M-antennas and communicating with K single-antenna UTs that share the same bandwidth. Note that the frame structure should be matched to the coherence interval of the UTs so that the channel between them and the BS can be described by a constant channel response within a frame. Specifically, τ symbols of the frame are allocated for pilot signaling and the remaining T- τ symbols are used for uplink transmission. According to the conventional massive MIMO system, in order to avoid pilot contamination, τ pilot symbols can generate τ

orthogonal pilot sequences, and then at most τ UTs can transmit pilots. We assume the use of Orthogonal Frequency Division Multiplexing (OFDM) flat fading channel for each subcarrier. We denote by $g_{jmk} \triangleq [G_j]_{m,k}$ the channel coefficient between the m-th antenna of the j-th BS and the k-th user of the l-th cell.

$$g_{jmk} = h_{lmk}\sqrt{\beta_{lk}}$$

$m = 1, 2,\ldots, M;\ k = 1, 2, \ldots, K\ and\ l = 1, 2,\ldots, L.$

$h_{lmk}$and β_{lk} represent the small-scale fading and large-scale fading coefficients respectively, where $h_{lmk} \sim \mathbb{C}N(0,1)$ is statistically independent across UTs and $\sqrt{\beta_{lk}}$ models the geometric attenuation and shadow fading. In addition, β_{lk} is assumed to be independent over m and to be constant over many coherence time intervals and known prior.

In general form, we can represent the channel matrix:

$$\boldsymbol{G} = \boldsymbol{H}\boldsymbol{D}^{1/2} \tag{1}$$

where $\boldsymbol{H}$ is the M × K matrix of fast fading coefficients between the K users and the M antennas of the BS, i.e. $h_{mk} \triangleq [\boldsymbol{H}]_{m,k}$ and D is the K × K diagonal matrix, where: $[\boldsymbol{D}]_{k,k} = \beta_k$ represents the large-scale fading between the BS and the K UTs.

At the reverse-link, the received signal vector of dimension M × 1 at the j-th BS during uplink session can be represented as follows:

$$\mathbf{Y}_j^{up} = \sqrt{P_u}\sum_{l=1}^{L}\boldsymbol{H}_l\mathbf{D}_l^{1/2}\boldsymbol{X}_l^{up} + \mathbf{W}_j^{up} \tag{2}$$

$$\mathbf{Y}_j^{up} = \underbrace{\sqrt{P_u}\boldsymbol{H}_j\mathbf{D}_j^{1/2}\boldsymbol{X}_j^{up}}_{prefered\ signal} + \underbrace{\sqrt{P_u}\sum_{l=1,l\neq j}^{L}\boldsymbol{H}_l\mathbf{D}_l^{1/2}\boldsymbol{X}_l^{up}}_{contaminated\ siganl} + \underbrace{\mathbf{W}_j^{up}}_{noise\ vector} \tag{3}$$

$\boldsymbol{X}_l^{up}$ denotes the K × 1 symbol vector uploaded from users in the l-th cell and $\mathbf{W}_j^{up}$ denotes the additive AWGN i.i.d noise vector with zero-mean, unit-variance $\mathbb{C}N(0,1)$ received at BS antennas as a vector of dimension M × 1. P_u denotes the uplink transmission power of each UT.

We follow the system model represented by [16], and we denote by K′ the number of UTs that uploads their pilots in the current time-slot and by K″ the number of UTs that does not upload their pilots during the current time-slot, i.e. K = K′ +K″. Considering the uplink pilot session of length τ×1, then the received signal at the j-th BS is expressed as follows:

$$\mathbf{Y}_j^{p} = \sqrt{\tau P_u}\sum_{l=1}^{L}\boldsymbol{G}_l\left[\boldsymbol{X}_l^{p}\odot\boldsymbol{S}_l\right] + \mathbf{W}_j^{up} \tag{4}$$

where S_l is a $K \times 1$ binary matrix with elements $s_k \in \{0, 1\}$. $s_k = 0$ for UT that uploads a TDD format without pilots and $s_k = 1$ if UT uploads TDD format using pilots. X_l^p is the $K \times 1$ matrix with elements x_{lk}^p, where each represents an orthogonal pilot sequence uploaded from the k-th UT of the l-th cell.

Assuming that the same pilot sequences are reused once in the same time-slot in all cells, then the probability to encounter pilot contamination in any cell will be $\alpha = \frac{K'}{OP}$, where OP denotes the number of orthogonal pilot sequences in the system. Following this assumption, $L' = r(L \times \alpha)$ represents the number of cells that upload the same pilot sequence, where $r(\cdot)$ is a function that rounds to the nearest integer. Note that $L \times \alpha$ denotes the number of users per pilot, but since we assumed that every pilot is used once per cell, L' represents the number of contaminated cell.

The Least Squares Estimation of the channel matrix at the j-th BS can be written as:

$$\widehat{G}_j = \arg\min_{G_l} \left\| \frac{1}{\sqrt{\tau P_u}} \mathbf{Y}_j^p - G_l X_j^{pH} \right\|^2 \tag{5}$$

The solution of (5) can be expressed as (6):

$$\widehat{G}_j = \sqrt{\tau P_u} G_j + \sqrt{\tau P_u} \sum_{l=1, l \neq j}^{L'} G_l + \widehat{\mathbf{W}}_j^{up} \tag{6}$$

where $\widehat{\mathbf{W}}_j^{up}$ AWGN still has i.i.d distribution with zero-mean, unit-variance and CN (0, 1).

At the forward-link, the j-th BS transmits a precoded vector to the K′ UTs based on the estimated version of (6) and uses the "last estimated channel state information (CSI)" to precode the downlink vector to the K″ UTs. The use of the last estimated CSI by the BS do not deteriorate the UTs' performances since the coherence interval of those K″ UTs is long enough to preserve channel characteristics during several time slots. Considering the use of Eigen-beamforming linear precoder, the K × 1 received vector at the K UT of the l-th cell can be represented as (7):

$$\mathbf{Y}_j^d = \sqrt{P_d} \sum_{l=1}^{L} G_j^T \left[\widehat{G}_j + \overline{\widehat{G}_j} \right]^* X_j^d + \mathbf{W}_j^d \tag{7}$$

$\overline{\widehat{G}_j}$ is a matrix of dimension M × K that denotes the sparse complement matrix of $\widehat{G}_j$, where $\overline{g_{jmk}} \triangleq \left[\overline{\widehat{G}_j} \right]_{m,k}$

$$\overline{\widehat{g}_{jmk}} = \begin{cases} 0 & if\; k \in SK' \\ \widehat{g}_{jmk}(t-n) & if\; k \in SK'' \end{cases}$$

SK' and SK" are the set of UTs that upload their pilots and the set of UTs that skip uploading their pilots respectively during the current time-slot.

In the same manner, $\widehat{\boldsymbol{G}}_j$ of dimension M × K denotes the sparse complement matrix of $\overline{\widehat{\boldsymbol{G}}_j}$ and

$$\widehat{g}_{jmk} = \begin{cases} \widehat{g}_{jmk}(t) & if\ k \in SK' \\ 0 & if\ k \in SK'' \end{cases}$$

where $t \in \mathbb{N}$ represent the current time-slot and $n \in \mathbb{N}$ represent the time-slot that contains the last estimated version of the channel. $\boldsymbol{X}_j^d$ is the K × 1 symbols vector received by the K users in the l-th cell, P_d is the normalized received SNR at each UT and the K × 1 matrix $\mathbf{W}_j^d$ represents additive AWGN i.i.d noise vector with zero-mean and unit-variance.

Following the analysis in [17], as $M \gg K$ the following relation holds:

$$\left(\frac{\boldsymbol{G}_l^H \boldsymbol{G}_l}{M}\right)_{M \gg K} = \boldsymbol{D}_j^{1/2} \left(\frac{\mathbf{H}_l^H \mathbf{H}_l}{M}\right)_{M \gg K} \boldsymbol{D}_j^{1/2} \approx \boldsymbol{D}_j^{1/2} \tag{8}$$

and $\frac{1}{M} \boldsymbol{H}_l^T \boldsymbol{H}_l^* = \boldsymbol{I}_K \delta_l$, where $\boldsymbol{I}_K$ is an Identity matrix with dimension $K \times K$ and δ_l corresponds to the covariance factor of $\mathbf{H}_l$.

The received signal at the k-th UT in the j-th cell can be deduced from (7) and (8):

$$\frac{1}{M\sqrt{\tau P_u P_d}} y_{jk}^d = \beta_{jk} x_{jk}^d + \sum_{l=1, l \neq j}^{L'} \beta_{lk} x_{jk}^d \tag{9}$$

where β_{lk} corresponds to the large-scale fading between the k-th UT in the l-th cell and the j-th BS, and x_{jk} is the k-th element of symbol vector $\boldsymbol{X}_j^d$. The signal to interference noise ratio of each UT can be written as:

$$SINR = \frac{\beta_{jk}^2}{\sum_{l=1, l \neq j}^{L'} \beta_{lk}^2} \tag{10}$$

3 Time-Shifted Pilots

The diversity among UT coherence intervals depends on the propagation environment, user mobility, and the carrier frequency [3]. Since not all UTs encounter the same mobility within the cell, we can classify them according to their coherence interval length. Therefore, users belonging to Class 1 encounter the shortest coherence interval of length T, which is also considered as the TDD frame size. Indeed, users of Class 1 should upload their pilots each TDD frame. Furthermore, users of Class n with a coherence interval of length T' > nT should upload their pilots once each n TDD frames. Within one channel estimation during the coherence interval, BS can be pre-code all downlink data belong to this coherence interval based on the last estimated

CSI. In Fig. 1, we introduce an example of a sequence of TDD frames related to 3 UTs belonging to Class 3 using the same pilot sequence (represented by P). The 3 UTs exchange different data streams with the BS (represented by D). By shifting the frame toward a pilot free time-slot, users of Class n can reuse the same pilot n times subjected to T (n-1) $\leq$ Q. We denote by Q the maximum acceptable coherence interval which can be assigned by the network designers according to performance demands.

By following the definition of the sample duration of the slots, expressed in [18] as the number of OFDM symbols times, the tone duration of the Nyquist sampling interval $T = \frac{T_{slot}T_u}{T_s T_g}$. For typical OFDM parameters, symbol interval is $T_s = 1/14\,\text{ms}$, usable interval is $T_u = 1/15\,\text{ms}$, guard interval is $T_g = 1/220\,\text{ms}$. Assuming delay-spread equals T_g, Nyquist interval is equivalent to $\frac{T_u}{T_g} = 14$ tones.

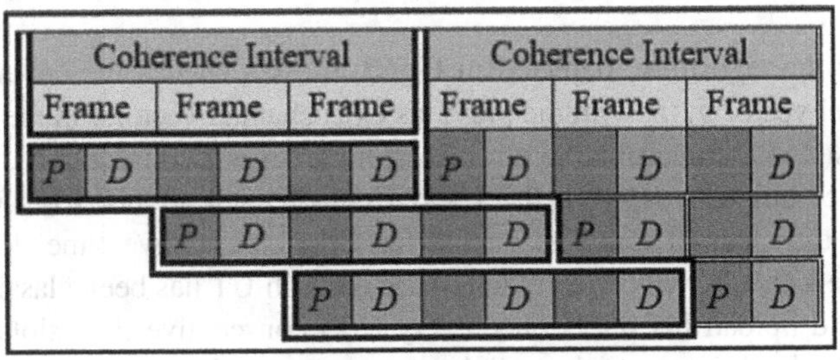

Fig. 1. Time-Shifted frames of class 3 UTs

Consider Class 1 corresponding to UTs moving in a train of speed 300 km/h, thus it took 473.7 μs to pass ¼ wavelength at frequency 1.9 GHz which has an equivalent sample duration of T = 99. Assuming that a pedestrian uses moves with an average speed of 1.38 m/s their sample duration will be Tp = 5606 which will lead to n = 60 and hence, UTs related to this class can reuse the same pilot 60 times (ignoring the maximum shift delay limit).

4 User Terminal Classification

In this section, we propose a UTs classification algorithm that will allow us to take benefit from the proposed pilot shifting technique. One way to classify UTs is to monitor their consecutive CSI covariance matrices and classify them according to their speed of change among several time-slots. Indeed, UTs with high mobility profiles will be assigned to lower classes and low mobility UTs will be assigned to higher classes. Assume that the BS had a prior assigned Class C(k) corresponding to the coherence interval T of UT k. The BS can run the following algorithm (Fig. 2) periodically or on SNR failure, to update the assigned class C(k) of the k-th UT.

```
1-  i=1, C(k)=c
2-  while ( i ≤ C(k)+1 )
3-  if ( |ĝ_k(t)(ĝ_k(t − i))^H| ≥ (1 − |ε|)
4-  if( i > C(k) & C(k) < C(Q))
5-  C(k)++
6-  i++ , GoTo 2
7-  else
8-  C(k)= i − 1
9-  end if
10- end while
```

Fig. 2. User classification algorithm

Following the algorithm, depicted in Fig. 2, the BS checks the covariance of the current channel vector $\widehat{g}_k(t)$ with the previous C(k) channel vectors. In the case that the channel persists with an acceptable error of $|\varepsilon|$ for C(k) + 1 consecutive time-slots and still below the limit Class C(Q), the Class C(k) of the k-th UT C(k) is promoted. Otherwise, if the channel failed to persist for C(k) consecutive time-slots, the class assigned to the k-th UT will be degraded. After the k-th UT has been classified to Class C(k), he should upload his pilots once every C(k) consecutive time-slots, which will lead not only to the decrease of the uplink pilot contamination, but also to the reduction in the transmitted power at the UT and the increase of the density of UTs/cell.

Recent advances in massive MIMO systems recommend coordinating the pilot allocation between interfering cells by ensuring no pilot reuse between adjacent cells to avoid pilot contamination from the first tier of interfering cells. These techniques solve radically the pilot contamination problem for practical numbers of antennas. However, the number of UTs per cell decreases drastically since only a fraction of the pilot sequences are used in each cell. Interestingly, the proposed sparse pilot assignment allows pilot reuse within the same interference domain by shifting pilots toward a pilot free time-slot, which increases the UTs density per cell while mitigating inter and intra cell interference.

5 Spectral and Energy Efficiency

We follow the definition of spectral efficiency given by [2] to evaluate the spectral efficiency of our proposed model. Considering channel estimation processed using maximum ratio combination (MRC) receiver, the general uplink spectral efficiency SE, is given by:

$$SE = \frac{T-\tau}{T} K log_2(1 + SINR) \tag{11}$$

The signal to interference noise ratio (SINR) represented as follows:

$$SINR = \frac{\tau(M-1)P_u^2}{\tau\left(K\overline{L'} - 1 + \gamma\left(\overline{L'} - 1\right)(M-2)\right)P_u^2 + \overline{L'}(K+\tau)P_u + 1} \tag{12}$$

where $\gamma \in [0, 1]$ represents the inter-cell interference factor and $\overline{L'} \triangleq (L'-1)\gamma + 1$. The Energy Efficiency EEn for Class n is expressed as:

$$EE_n = \frac{1}{P_u}\left(\frac{n(T-\tau)}{nT-(n-1)\tau}\right)K_n log_2(1 + SINR) \tag{13}$$

where K_n is the number of users of Class n.

6 Numerical Results

In this section, we illustrate the performances of the proposed technique through Matlab simulations. We simulate a scenario with L = 7 hexagonal cells. We assume pilot reuse once at the same time-slot in each cell, and that each cell owns τ = 30 pilot sequences. The system uses a carrier frequency of 1.9 GHz and we consider UTs with several channel coherence profiles. We also assume that the transmit power P_u is upper bounded by 100 mdB. Inter-cell interference factor is γ = 0.3 and K = 30. We consider Class 1 time-slot of sample duration T = 99 OFDM symbols and C(Q) = 30.

In the first scenario, we simulate a conventional massive MIMO system (with only Class 1 users, i.e. all UTs send pilot every time slot) and a system with Class 3 users (every UTs uploads pilot once every 3-time slots). We recall that the time slot corresponds to the smaller coherence interval of all the UTs. Figures 3 and 4 illustrate respectively the energy efficiency and the spectral efficiency of Class 1 and Class 3 UTs. We can clearly observe that Class 3 overcome the classical massive MIMO in both SE and EE, and the gap between Class 1 and 3 still increase with the number of antennas. Specifically, for 100 antennas, we can see that the EE of Class 3 UTs is almost 4 times better than conventional massive MIMO system. Note that, in conventional massive MIMO system, if there is only one UT having a coherence interval of Ts (Class 1) and all the other UTs have a coherence interval higher than 3*Ts (Class 3), all the UTs have to upload pilot to the BS every Ts.

To illustrate the performance of different classes of UTs, we further simulate the EE depending on the class index. In Fig. 5, we consider M = 300 antennas and vary the class index from 1 to 30, wherein Fig. 6 we vary M and we illustrate the EE of the set of classes from 1 to 30. Both figures demonstrate the significant advantage of using our proposed technique in terms of both: energy efficiency and spectral efficiency.

Indeed, there is a gap between the EE performance of the set of classes with indices greater than 1 and the EE performance of Class 1 (the curve at the bottom, Conventional massive MIMO). This result supports our claim about the utility of frame-shifting and sparse frame pilot for massive MIMO. Note also that frame-shifting and sparse frame pilot reduce the computational estimation costs at the BS due to sparse received channel matrix. Moreover, by pilot skipping, pilot reuse will lead to the increase of the

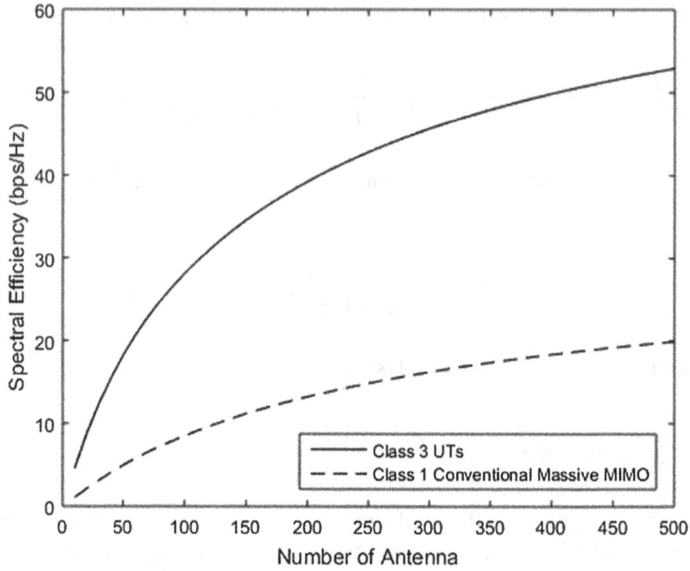

Fig. 3. Spectral efficiency vs M

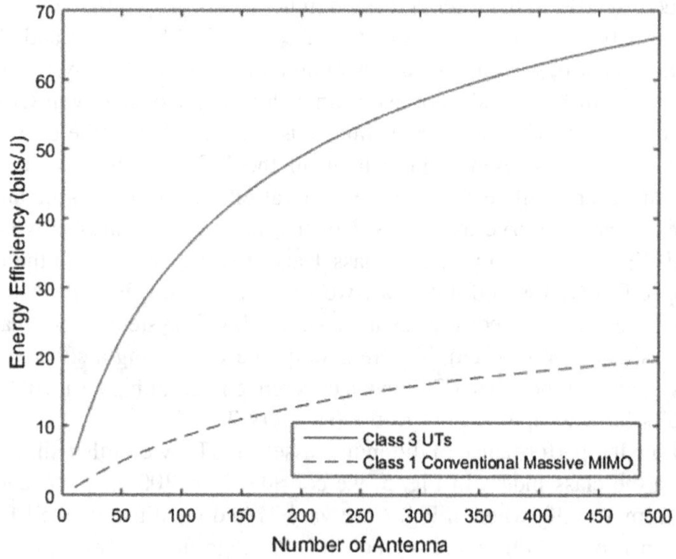

Fig. 4. Energy efficiency vs M

number of UTs/cell without any pilot contamination. Furthermore, the transmitted power of each UT can be reduced due to the reduction of inter and intra cell interference.

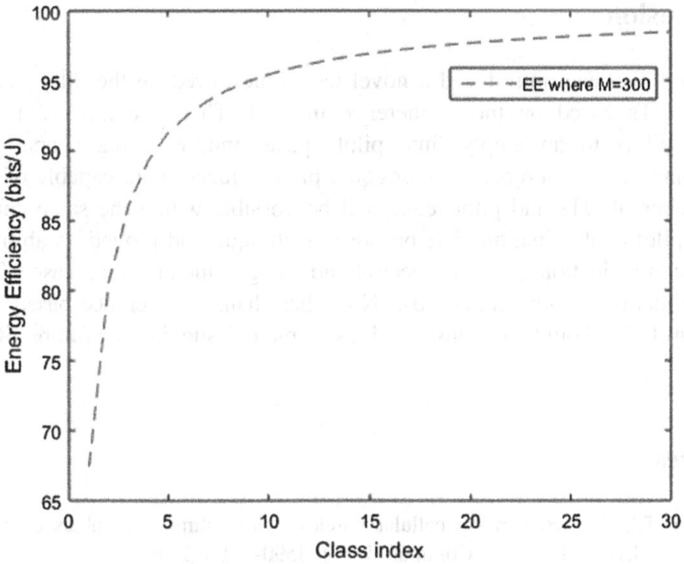

Fig. 5. Energy efficiency vs class index

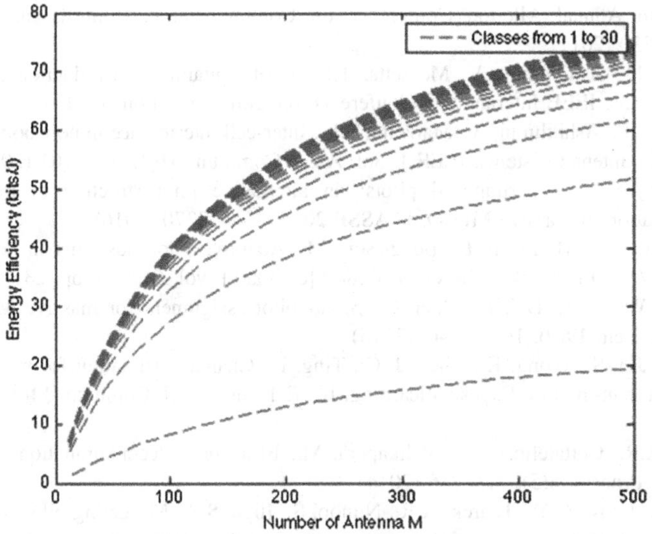

Fig. 6. Classes indices from 1 to 30 vs EE

7 Conclusion

In this paper, we have introduced a novel technique to reduce the pilot overhead by classifying UTs based on their coherence interval. Then, we have shifted frames containing pilots to an empty time pilot space. Indeed, using sparse pilot and frame-shifting, a little number of orthogonal pilot sequences are capable of serving a higher number of UTs and pilot reuse will be possible within the same cell without leading to pilot contamination. The proposed technique had proved its ability to mitigate pilot contamination, increase spectral and energy efficiency, increase UT/cell and reduces estimation computational cost. Note that channel coherence based classification among UTs should be considered as a main issue in the future 5G mobile networks.

References

1. Marzetta, T.L.: Noncooperative cellular wireless with unlimited numbers of base station antennas. IEEE Trans. Wirel. Commun. **9**(11), 3590–3600 (2010)
2. Ngo, H.Q., Larsson, E.G., Marzetta, T.L.: Energy and spectral efficiency of very large multiuser MIMO systems. IEEE Trans. Commun. **61**(4), 1436–1449 (2013)
3. Björnson, E., Larsson, E.G., Marzetta, T.L.: Massive MIMO: ten myths and one critical question, pp. 1–10 (2015)
4. Hoydis, J., ten Brink, S., Debbah, M.: Massive MIMO: how many antennas do we need? In: 2011 49th Annual Allerton Conference on Communication, Control, and Computing, pp. 545–550 (2011)
5. Appaiah, K., Ashikhmin, A., Marzetta, T.L.: Pilot contamination reduction in multi-user TDD systems. IEEE International Conference on Communications (2010)
6. Fernandes, F., Ashikhmin, A., Marzetta, T.L.: Inter-cell interference in noncooperative TDD large scale antenna systems. IEEE J. Sel. Areas Commun. **31**(2), 192–201 (2013)
7. Vorobyov, S.A.: Superimposed pilots: an alternative pilot structure to mitigate pilot contamination in massive MIMO. ICASSP **2016**, 3366–3370 (2016)
8. Mochaourab, R., Björnson, E., Bengtsson, M.: Adaptive pilot clustering in heterogeneous massive MIMO networks. arXiv1507.04869 [cs, math], vol. 619086, pp. 231–235 (2015)
9. Zhu, X., Wang, Z., Dai, L., Qian, C.: Smart pilot assignment for massive MIMO. IEEE Commun. Lett. **19**(9), 1644–1647 (2015)
10. Wen, C., Jin, S., Wong, K., Chen, J.-C., Ting, P.: Channel estimation for massive MIMO using gaussian-mixture Bayesian learning. IEEE Trans. Wirel. Commun. **14**(3), 1356–1368 (2015)
11. Müller, R.R., Cottatellucci, L., Vehkaperä, M.: Blind pilot decontamination. IEEE J. Sel. Top. Sig. Process. **8**(5), 773–786 (2014)
12. Elijah, O., Leow, C.Y., Tharek, A.R., Nunoo, S., Iliya, S.Z.: Mitigating pilot contamination in massive MIMO system - 5G: an overview. In: 2015 10th Asian Control Conference: Emerging Control Techniques for a Sustainable World, ASCC 2015, no. c (2015)
13. Li, C., Zhang, J., Song, S., Letaief, K.B.: Selective uplink training for massive MIMO systems, no. 16211815 (2016)
14. Fan, D., Zhongt, Z., Wangt, G., Gao, F.: Channel estimation for wireless cellular systems with massive linear receiving antennas. In: 10th International Conference on Communications and Networking in China (ChinaCom), pp. 95–99. IEEE (2015)

15. Yao, T., Li, Y.: Pilot contamination reduction by shifted frame structure in massive MIMO TDD wireless system. Wuhan Univ. J. Nat. Sci. **20**(3), 221–228 (2015)
16. Abboud, A., Jaber, A.H., Cances, J.-P., Meghdadi, V.: Indoor massive MIMO: uplink pilot mitigation using channel state information map. In: 2016 IEEE International Conference on Computational Science and Engineering (CSE) and IEEE International Conference on Embedded and Ubiquitous Computing (EUC) and 15th International Symposium on Distributed Computing and Applications for Business Engineering (DCABES). IEEE (2016)
17. Rusek, F., Persson, D., Lau, B.K., Larsson, E.G., Marzetta, T.L., Edfors, O., Tufvesson, F.: Scaling up MIMO: opportunities and challenges with very large arrays. IEEE Sig. Process. Mag. **30**(1), 40–60 (2013)
18. Marzetta, T.L.: Massive MIMO: an introduction. Bell Labs Tech. J. **20**, 11–22 (2015)

Spectral Efficiency Analysis of Two-Way Massive MIMO Full-Duplex Relay Systems with Direct Link

Houda Chafnaji(✉)

Institut National des Postes Et Telecommunications (INPT), Rabat, Morocco
chafnaji@inpt.ac.ma

Abstract. In this paper, we consider a one-pair two-way full-duplex relaying system where two source nodes exchange information with the aid of an amplify-and-forward relay with massive antennas. In this work, we assume the direct link between source nodes is non-negligible and propose a combining scheme, at the destination side, that captures the joint benefit of relay and direct links. First, we drive the communication model and the sum spectral efficiency (SE) of the proposed combining scheme. Then, we quantify the asymptotic expression of SE when the number of antennas at the relay goes to infinity. Asymptotic results show that the transmit power of the source nodes and the relay node have different effect on the asymptotic SE, which is confirmed by numerical results. Using simulations, we also show that, for long packet transmissions, the proposed combining scheme outperforms the classical scheme, where the direct signal is considered as interference at the destination. However, it is not the obvious choice for the short packet transmissions and the transmission where the processing delay at the relay is greater than the packet length.

Keywords: Full-Duplex · Massive MIMO · Two-way relaying · Amplify-and-forward · Cooperative diversity

1 Introduction

To meet the 5G requirements, in term of higher data rates, higher spectral efficiency and higher energy efficiency, many new techniques have been proposed, such as, massive multiple-input multiple-output (MIMO), full-duplex (FD), and cooperative communications [1]. In fact, very large antenna arrays is a technique that has recently attracted a lot of attention due to its capability to mitigate small scale fading and inter-user interference, and reduce the total transmit power, yielding the huge improvement in both the spectral efficiency (SE) and energy efficiency (EE) [2,3]. The new physical paradigm of simultaneously transmit and receive at the same time slot and on the same frequency band, i.e., FD technique, allows to double the SE of the traditional half-duplex (HD) system [4,5]. Cooperative communications have also been widely investigated due to

E. Sabir et al. (Eds.): UNet 2017, LNCS 10542, pp. 438–449, 2017.
https://doi.org/10.1007/978-3-319-68179-5_38

their various advantages such as capacity improvement, coverage extension and diversity gain [6–8].

In the field of cooperative communications, two-way relaying, where two source nodes exchange their information with the assistance of a relay node, has been widely investigated for high SE [9–16]. In [9–12], the authors have proposed and studied different two-way schemes based traditional HD relaying. In order to further enhance the SE, authors, in [13–16], have integrated FD mode into two-way relay system. In fact, in FD two-way relaying, all nodes transmit and receive at the same time and within the same frequency band, which improves both the attainable SE and the resource utilization. Despite of aforementioned FD communications benefits, the key challenge in realizing such a system lies in the self-loop interference (SI) cancellation. Traditionally, SI cancellation techniques were designed in the antenna domain, which may require sophisticated electronic implementation [17]. Recently, massive MIMO has been considered together with FD relaying to suppress the SI in spatial domain [18]. In [19,20], Zhang et al. have studied one-pair and multi-pair FD relay system with massive MIMO and shown that, with a large-scale antenna array at the relay, the self-interference can be mitigated via low complexity zero-forcing (ZF) or maximum-ratio combining/maximum-ratio transmission (MRC/MRT) strategy. However, the study presented in both papers assumed that the source nodes are set far a part that there is no direct link between them, which may not be suitable for certain practical scenarios.

In this paper, we consider a one-pair two-way FD massive MIMO AF relaying with direct link and propose a combining scheme, at the destination side, that captures the joint benefit of relay and direct links. In [20,22], it has been shown that, for large-scale antenna array at the relay, the transmission powers of the source and/or the relay can be scaled down, i.e. inversely proportional to the number of relay antenna, without compromising the performance. In this work, we consider the case II, studied in [22], where the massive MIMO relay is equipped with low transmit power antennas. First, we drive the communication model and the sum SE of the studied system with the proposed combining scheme. Then, we quantify the asymptotic SE of the system when the number of relay antennas approaches the infinity. Monte-Carlo simulations are used to confirm the asymptotic results. Both simulations and asymptotic results show that the transmit power of the source nodes and the relay have different effect on the SE. Finally, using simulations, we compare three transmission modes: the proposed combining transmission mode, the classical transmission mode, where the direct link is considered as interference, and the direct transmission mode without relaying. We show that the three transmission modes outperform each other depending on the relay processing delay, packet length, and the direct link gain.

The remainder of the paper is organized as follows: In Sect. 2, we introduce the communication model and the sum SE of the studied system with the proposed combining scheme. Section 3 drives and analyzes the asymptotic SE of the proposed scheme when the number of relay antennas goes to infinity. Simulation results are presented in Sect. 4. Finally, the paper is concluded in Sect. 5.

Notations

- x, $\mathbf{x}$, and $\mathbf{X}$ denote, respectively, a scalar quantity, a column vector, and a matrix.
- $(.)^{\star}$,$(.)^{\top}$, and $(.)^{\mathrm{H}}$ are conjugate, the transpose, and the Hermitian transpose, respectively.
- $\mathbb{C}$ is set of complex number.
- $\mathcal{CN}(\mu, \sigma)$ represents a circularly symmetric complex Gaussian distribution with mean μ and variance σ.
- $\mathrm{Tr}(.)$ is the trace of a square matrix.
- $\mathrm{diag}\{\mathbf{X}_1, \cdots, \mathbf{X}_m\}$ denote the diagonal matrix constructed from $\mathbf{X}_1, \cdots, \mathbf{X}_m \in \mathbb{C}^{n_1 \times n_2}$.
- $\otimes$ denotes the Kronecker product.
- For $\mathbf{x} \in \mathbb{C}^{TN}$, $\mathbf{x}_f$ denotes the discrete Fourier transform (DFT) of $\mathbf{x}$, i.e. $\mathbf{x}_f = \mathbf{U}_{T,N}\mathbf{x}$, with $\mathbf{U}_{T,N} = \mathbf{U}_T \otimes \mathbf{I}_N$, where $\mathbf{I}_N$ is the $N \times N$ identity matrix, $\mathbf{U}_T$ is a unitary $T \times T$ matrix whose (m, n)th element is $(\mathbf{U}_T)_{m,n} = \frac{1}{\sqrt{T}} e^{-j(2\pi mn/T)}$, $j = \sqrt{-1}$.
- $\|.\|_2$ denotes the euclidean norm.
- $\mathbb{E}\{.\}$ is used to denote the statistical expectation.

2 Communication Model

We consider a one-pair two-way full duplex relay system where an AF massive MIMO relay (R) assists the communication between two source nodes (S_1 and S_2). In this paper, we assume the direct link between the source nodes is non negligible. Both the AF relay and the source nodes work on FD mode. Each source node is equipped with one antenna for transmission and another for reception, while the relay node is equipped with N transmitting and N receiving antennas. At time instance n, each source node broadcasts its signal to both the relay and the other source node. At the same time instance, the relay broadcasts the received and amplified signal back to both source nodes. The source-relay ($\mathrm{S}_k \rightarrow \mathrm{R}$), source-destination ($\mathrm{S}_k \rightarrow \mathrm{S}_{k'}$), and relay-destination ($\mathrm{R} \rightarrow \mathrm{S}_{k'}$) links are assumed to be flat fading. The channel vectors corresponding to the $\mathrm{S}_k \rightarrow \mathrm{R}$, $\mathrm{S}_k \rightarrow \mathrm{S}_{k'}$, and $\mathrm{R} \rightarrow \mathrm{S}_{k'}$ links are denoted $\mathbf{h}_{\mathrm{u}_k} \in \mathbb{C}^{N \times 1}$, $h_{kk'} \in \mathbb{C}^{1 \times 1}$, and $\mathbf{h}_{\mathrm{d}_{k'}} \in \mathbb{C}^{1 \times N}$, respectively. Their entries are independent identically distributed (i.i.d) zero-mean circularly symmetric complex Gaussian random variables $\sim \mathcal{CN}(0, \beta_i)$, i.e. $i \in \{\mathrm{u}_k, kk', \mathrm{d}_k\}$. In this work, we assume a limitted channel state information (CSI) at the source node transmitter, i.e., the transmitter is only aware of the processing delay at the relay, and suppose perfect CSI at the relays and the source node receiver (Fig. 1).

The received signal at the relay and the destination node S_k can be expressed as,

$$\begin{aligned} \mathbf{y}_{\mathrm{R}}(n) &= \sqrt{P_{\mathrm{S}_1}}\mathbf{h}_{\mathrm{u}_1}x_1(n) + \sqrt{P_{\mathrm{S}_2}}\mathbf{h}_{\mathrm{u}_2}x_2(n) \\ &\quad + \mathbf{H}_{\mathrm{RR}}\tilde{\mathbf{x}}_{\mathrm{RR}}(n) + \boldsymbol{\eta}_{\mathrm{R}}(n), \end{aligned} \tag{1}$$

$$y_k(n) = \sqrt{P_{\mathrm{S}_{k'}}} h_{k'k}x_{k'}(n) + \mathbf{h}_{\mathrm{d}_k}\mathbf{x}_{\mathrm{R}}(n) + h_{kk}\tilde{x}_k(n) + \eta_k(n), \tag{2}$$

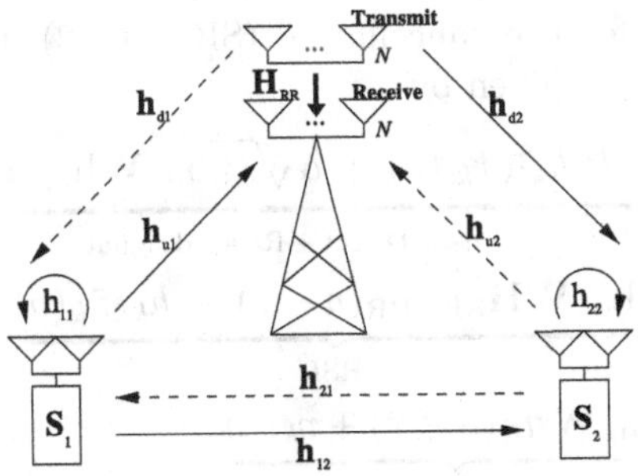

Fig. 1. Two-way full-duplex relay system.

where $\sqrt{P_{S_k}}x_k$ is the source node S_k transmitted signal. For simplicity, we assume that the transmitted signals for both source nodes are independent $\mathbb{E}\left[x_k(n)x_{k'}^{\star}(n')\right] = \delta_{k-k',n-n'}$ and have equal transmit power $P_{S_1} = P_{S_2} = P_S$. The residual self-loop interference (RSI) after undergoing all known cancellation techniques and practical isolation at the relay and the source node S_k are, respectively, denoted $\mathbf{H}_{RR}\tilde{\mathbf{x}}_{RR}(n)$ and $h_{kk}\tilde{x}_k(n)$. In this paper, we assume the elements of $\mathbf{H}_{RR}$ and h_{kk} to be i.i.d random variables $\sim \mathcal{CN}\left(0, \sigma_{\text{LIr}}^2\right)$ and $\sim \mathcal{CN}\left(0, \sigma_{k,k}^2\right)$, respectively, and $\tilde{x}_k(n)$ and $\tilde{\mathbf{x}}_{RR}(n)$ are, respectively, Gaussian noise $\sim \mathcal{CN}(0, P_S)$ and $\sim \mathcal{CN}(\mathbf{0}_{N\times 1}, \frac{P_R}{N}\mathbf{I}_N)$, where P_R is the relay transmitted power. $\boldsymbol{\eta}_R(n) \in \mathbb{C}^{N\times 1}$ is additive white Gaussian noise (AWGN) vector at the relay $\sim \mathcal{CN}(\mathbf{0}_{N\times 1}, \sigma_r^2\mathbf{I}_N)$ and $\eta_k(n) \in \mathbb{C}^{1\times 1}$ is AWGN at S_k $\sim \mathcal{CN}(0, \sigma^2)$. The relay transmitted signal $\mathbf{x}_R(n)$, at time instant n, is given by,

$$\mathbf{x}_R(n) = \alpha \mathbf{W}\mathbf{y}_R(n-\tau), \tag{3}$$

where τ is the relay processing delay and α is the amplification constant factor chosen to satisfy the total power constraint at the relay and can be writing as,

$$\alpha = \sqrt{\frac{P_R}{P_S.\Delta_1 + \sigma_r^2.\Delta_2 + P_R\Delta_3}}, \tag{4}$$

with

$$\Delta_1 = \text{Tr}\left(\mathbf{W}\mathbf{H}_u\mathbf{H}_u^H\mathbf{W}^H\right), \tag{5}$$

$$\Delta_2 = \text{Tr}\left(\mathbf{W}\mathbf{W}^H\right), \tag{6}$$

$$\Delta_3 = \frac{1}{N}\text{Tr}\left(\mathbf{W}\mathbf{H}_{RR}\mathbf{H}_{RR}^H\mathbf{W}^H\right), \tag{7}$$

where $\mathbf{W} \in \mathbb{C}^{N\times N}$ is the relay processing matrix. In this paper, we consider the MRC/MRT processing where the relay applies MRC technique to process the received signals, then takes MRT technique to broadcast the processed signals. According to [22], the MRC/MRT matrix is given by

$$\mathbf{W} = \mathbf{H}_d^*\mathbf{P}\mathbf{H}_u^H, \tag{8}$$

where $\mathbf{H}_d = [\mathbf{h}_{d_1}, \mathbf{h}_{d_2}]$, $\mathbf{H}_u = [\mathbf{h}_{u_1}, \mathbf{h}_{u_2}]$, and $\mathbf{P} = [0\,1; 1\,0]$ is the permutation matrix.

Using the self-interference cancellation (SIC) in (2), the received signal at the destination node S_k is given by,

$$
\begin{aligned}
y_k(n) =& \underbrace{\sqrt{P_{\mathrm{S}}}h_{k'k}x_{k'}(n) + \alpha\sqrt{P_{\mathrm{S}}}\mathbf{h}_{\mathrm{d}_k}\mathbf{W}\mathbf{h}_{\mathrm{u}_{k'}}x_{k'}(n-\tau)}_{\text{Direct + Relayed signal}} \\
&+ \underbrace{\alpha\mathbf{h}_{\mathrm{d}_k}\mathbf{W}\mathbf{H}_{\mathrm{RR}}\tilde{\mathbf{x}}_{\mathrm{RR}}(n-\tau) + h_{kk}\tilde{x}_k(n)}_{\text{RSI}} \\
&+ \underbrace{\alpha\mathbf{h}_{\mathrm{d}_k}\mathbf{W}\boldsymbol{\eta}_{\mathrm{R}}(n-\tau) + \eta_k(n)}_{\text{Noise}}.
\end{aligned} \tag{9}
$$

From (9), we can see that the destination node S_k will receive the source node $\mathrm{S}_{k'}$ transmitted signal $x_{k'}$ at different time due to the processing delay τ at the relay. In order to alleviate the inter-symbol interference (ISI) caused by the delayed signal, equalization is needed at the destination side. For that purpose, we propose a cyclic-prefix (CP) transmission at the source side in order to perform frequency-domain equalization (FDE) at the destination node. Therefore, before transmission, the source node $\mathrm{S}_{k'}$ appends a CP of length τ_{CP} $(=\tau)$ to the transmitted signal $x_{k'}$. At the destination side S_k, after the CP removal and SIC application, the received signal at time instance n can be expressed as,

$$
\begin{aligned}
y_k(n) =& \underbrace{\sqrt{P_{\mathrm{S}}}h_{k'k}x_{k'}(n) + \alpha\sqrt{P_{\mathrm{S}}}\mathbf{h}_{\mathrm{d}_k}\mathbf{W}\mathbf{h}_{\mathrm{u}_{k'}}x_{k'}\left[(n-\tau) \bmod L\right]}_{\textit{Direct + Relayed signal}} \\
&+ \underbrace{\alpha\mathbf{h}_{\mathrm{d}_k}\mathbf{W}\mathbf{H}_{\mathrm{RR}}\tilde{\mathbf{x}}_{\mathrm{RR}}(n-\tau) + h_{kk}\tilde{x}_k(n)}_{\text{RSI}} \\
&+ \underbrace{\alpha\mathbf{h}_{\mathrm{d}_k}\mathbf{W}\boldsymbol{\eta}_{\mathrm{R}}(n-\tau) + \eta_k(n)}_{\text{Noise}}.
\end{aligned} \tag{10}
$$

We assume all channel gains remain constant over a block duration of $L+\tau_{\mathrm{CP}}$ time instance corresponding to L code-words transmitted from the source and the CP length τ_{CP}. Hence, we can rewrite (10) in vector form as:

$$
\mathbf{y}_k = \boldsymbol{\mathcal{H}}^k\mathbf{x}_{k'} + \underbrace{\mathbf{G}_{\mathrm{RR}}\tilde{\mathbf{x}}_{\mathrm{R}} + H_{k,k}\tilde{\mathbf{x}}_k}_{\text{RSI}} + \underbrace{\boldsymbol{\eta}}_{\text{Noise}}, \tag{11}
$$

where $\mathbf{y}_k \triangleq [y_k(0), \cdots, y_k(L-1)]^\top \in \mathbb{C}^{L\times 1}$, $\mathbf{x}_k = [x_k(0), \cdots, x_k(L-1)]^\top \in \mathbb{C}^{L\times 1}$, $\tilde{\mathbf{x}}_{\mathrm{RR}} = [\tilde{\mathbf{x}}_{\mathrm{RR}}(0), \cdots, \tilde{\mathbf{x}}_{\mathrm{RR}}(L-1)]^\top \in \mathbb{C}^{LN\times 1}$, $\tilde{\mathbf{x}}_k = [\tilde{\mathbf{x}}_k(0), \cdots, \tilde{\mathbf{x}}_k(L-1)]^\top \in \mathbb{C}^{LN\times 1}$, $\boldsymbol{\eta} = [\eta(0), \cdots, \eta(L-1)]^\top \in \mathbb{C}^{L\times 1}$ with $\eta(n) = \alpha\mathbf{h}_{\mathrm{d}_k}\mathbf{W}\boldsymbol{\eta}_{\mathrm{R}}(n-\tau) + \eta_k(n)$, $H_{k,k} = h_{k,k}\mathbf{I}_L$, $\mathbf{G}_{\mathrm{RR}} = \mathbf{I}_L \otimes \alpha\mathbf{h}_{\mathrm{d}_k}\mathbf{W}\mathbf{H}_{\mathrm{RR}} \in \mathbb{C}^{L\times LN}$ is block diagonal matrix, and $\boldsymbol{\mathcal{H}}^k \in \mathbb{C}^{L\times L}$ is a circulant matrix whose first $L\times 1$ column matrix is

$$
\left[a_0^k, \mathbf{0}_{1\times(\tau-2)}, a_\tau^k, \mathbf{0}_{1\times(L-\tau)}\right]^\top, \tag{12}
$$

where $a_0^k = \sqrt{P_{\mathrm{S}}}h_{k'k}$ and $a_\tau^k = \alpha\sqrt{P_{\mathrm{S}}}\mathbf{h}_{\mathrm{d}_k}\mathbf{W}\mathbf{h}_{\mathrm{u}_{k'}}$. Note that the circulant matrix $\boldsymbol{\mathcal{H}}^k$ can be block diagonalized in a Fourier basis as

$$
\boldsymbol{\mathcal{H}}^k = \mathbf{U}_{L,1}^{\mathrm{H}}\boldsymbol{\Lambda}^k\mathbf{U}_{L,1}. \tag{13}
$$

where

$$\begin{cases} \mathbf{\Lambda}^k \triangleq \operatorname{diag}\left\{\lambda_0^k, \cdots, \lambda_{L-1}^k\right\}, \\ \lambda_n^k \triangleq a_0^k + a_\tau^k e^{-j(2\pi n\tau/L)}. \end{cases} \tag{14}$$

Therefore, applying the discrete Fourier transform (DFT) to the block signal vector (11) yields the following frequency domain block communication model,

$$\mathbf{y}_f^k = \mathbf{\Lambda}^k \mathbf{x}_f^{k'} + \mathbf{G}_{\mathrm{RR}} \tilde{\mathbf{x}}_f^{\mathrm{R}} + H_{k,k} \tilde{\mathbf{x}}_f^k + \boldsymbol{\eta}_f^k. \tag{15}$$

Using (15), the node S_k received signal-to-interference-plus-noise ration (SINR), at frequency bin n, can be expressed as,

$$\begin{aligned} \gamma_{f_n}^k &= \frac{\lambda_n^k {\lambda_n^k}^H}{\alpha^2 \frac{P_{\mathrm{R}}}{N} \left\|\mathbf{h}_{\mathrm{d}_k} \mathbf{W} \mathbf{H}_{\mathrm{RR}}\right\|_2^2 + P_{\mathrm{S}} \left|h_{kk}\right|^2 + \alpha^2 \sigma_r^2 \left\|\mathbf{h}_{\mathrm{d}_k} \mathbf{W}\right\|_2^2 + \sigma^2}, \\ &= \alpha_k + 2\left|\beta_k\right| \cos\left(\frac{2\Pi\tau n}{L} + \theta_k\right), \end{aligned} \tag{16}$$

where $\alpha_k = \frac{\left|a_0^k\right|^2 + \left|a_\tau^k\right|^2}{\alpha^2 \frac{P_{\mathrm{R}}}{N} \left\|\mathbf{h}_{\mathrm{d}_k} \mathbf{W} \mathbf{H}_{\mathrm{RR}}\right\|_2^2 + P_{\mathrm{S}} |h_{kk}|^2 + \alpha^2 \sigma_r^2 \left\|\mathbf{h}_{\mathrm{d}_k} \mathbf{W}\right\|_2^2 + \sigma^2}$, $\beta_k = \frac{a_0^k a_\tau^k}{\alpha^2 \frac{P_{\mathrm{R}}}{N} \left\|\mathbf{h}_{\mathrm{d}_k} \mathbf{W} \mathbf{H}_{\mathrm{RR}}\right\|_2^2 + P_{\mathrm{S}} |h_{kk}|^2 + \alpha^2 \sigma_r^2 \left\|\mathbf{h}_{\mathrm{d}_k} \mathbf{W}\right\|_2^2 + \sigma^2}$, and $\theta_k = \operatorname{angle}(\beta_k)$. The sum spectral efficiency of the system is given by

$$R = \mathbb{E}\left\{C(\gamma_f^1) + C(\gamma_f^2)\right\}, \tag{17}$$

where the function $C(x) = \frac{1}{L+\tau_{\mathrm{CP}}} \sum_{n=0}^{L-1} \log_2(1+x)$, and the factor $\frac{1}{L+\tau_{\mathrm{CP}}}$ means that the transmission of L useful code-words occupies $L + \tau_{\mathrm{CP}}$ time instances. In order to simplify (17), the function $C(\gamma_f^k)$ can be expressed as,

$$\begin{aligned} C(\gamma_f^k) &= \frac{1}{L + \tau_{\mathrm{CP}}} \sum_{n=0}^{L-1} \log_2 \left\{ (1+\alpha_k)\left(1 + \frac{2\left|\beta_k\right| \cos\left(\frac{2\Pi\tau n}{L} + \theta_k\right)}{1+\alpha_k}\right) \right\} \\ &= \frac{L}{L+\tau_{\mathrm{CP}}} \log_2(1+\alpha_k) + \frac{1}{L+\tau_{\mathrm{CP}}} \sum_{n=0}^{L-1} \log_2\left(1 + \frac{2\left|\beta_k\right| \cos\left(\frac{2\Pi\tau n}{L} + \theta_k\right)}{1+\alpha_k}\right). \end{aligned} \tag{18}$$

Using the arithmetic-geometric mean inequality, we have $\alpha_k \geq 2\left|\beta_k\right|$, and hence $1 + \alpha_k > 2\left|\beta_k\right| \cos(\frac{2\Pi\tau n}{L} + \theta_k)$. Thus, by using the first order Taylor expansion, we have $\ln(1 + \frac{2|\beta_k| \cos(\frac{2\Pi\tau n}{L} + \theta_k)}{1+\alpha_k}) \approx \frac{2|\beta_k| \cos(\frac{2\Pi\tau n}{L} + \theta_k)}{1+\alpha_k}$. Noting that $\sum_{n=0}^{L-1} \cos(\frac{2\Pi\tau n}{L} + \theta_k) = 0$, the function $C(\gamma_f^k)$ can be approximated as [21],

$$C(\gamma_f^k) \approx \frac{L}{L+\tau_{\mathrm{CP}}} \log_2(1+\alpha_k), \tag{19}$$

and the desired sum spectral efficiency (SE) of the system is obtained as,

$$R \approx \frac{L}{L+\tau_{\mathrm{CP}}}\mathbb{E}\left\{\log_2(1+\alpha_1)+\log_2(1+\alpha_2)\right\}. \quad (20)$$

3 Asymptotic SINR Analysis of Massive MIMO Relay

In this section, asymptotic SINR of one-pair two-way AF relaying with direct link is analyzed in the regime of infinite number of antennas, i.e. $N \to \infty$.

In this work, we consider the case II, studied in [22], where the massive MIMO relay is equipped with low transmit power antennas, i.e., $P_{\mathrm{S}} = E_{\mathrm{S}}$ and $P_{\mathrm{R}} = \frac{E_{\mathrm{R}}}{N}$ with E_{S} and E_{R} are fixed. Based on lemma 1 in [22], when $N \to \infty$, the block received signal in (11) is given by

$$\mathbf{y}_f^{k,\infty} = \mathbf{\Lambda}^{k,\infty}\mathbf{x}_f^{k'} + H_{k,k}\tilde{\mathbf{x}}_f^k + \mathbf{n}_f^k, \quad (21)$$

where

$$\begin{cases} \mathbf{\Lambda}^{k,\infty} \triangleq \mathrm{diag}\left\{\lambda_0^{k,\infty},\cdots,\lambda_{L-1}^{k,\infty}\right\}, \\ \lambda_n^{k,\infty} \triangleq a_0^k + a_\tau^{k,\infty}e^{-j(2\pi n\tau/L)}, \end{cases} \quad (22)$$

with $a_\tau^{k,\infty} = \sqrt{\frac{E_{\mathrm{R}}}{(\beta_{\mathrm{d}_1}\beta_{\mathrm{u}_2}^2+\beta_{\mathrm{d}_2}\beta_{\mathrm{u}_1}^2)}}\beta_{\mathrm{d}_k}\beta_{\mathrm{u}_{k'}}$.

Therefore, the asymptotic SINR at the node S_k is expressed as,

$$\begin{aligned} \gamma_n^{k,\infty} &= \frac{\lambda_n^{k,\infty}\lambda_n^{k,\infty H}}{\sigma^2+E_{\mathrm{S}}\left|h_{kk}\right|^2}, \\ &= \alpha_{k,\infty} + 2\left|\beta_{k,\infty}\right|\cos(\frac{2\Pi\tau n}{L}), \end{aligned} \quad (23)$$

where $\alpha_{k,\infty} = \frac{|a_0^k|^2+|a_{\tau,,\infty}^k|^2}{\sigma^2+E_{\mathrm{S}}|h_{kk}|^2}$ and $\beta_{k,,\infty} = \frac{a_0^k a_\tau^{k,,\infty}}{\sigma^2+E_{\mathrm{S}}|h_{kk}|^2}$. The sum spectral efficiency of the system is approximated as,

$$\begin{aligned} R_\infty &\approx \frac{L}{L+\tau_{\mathrm{CP}}}\mathbb{E}\left\{\log_2(1+\alpha_{1,,\infty})+\log_2(1+\alpha_{2,,\infty})\right\} \\ &= \frac{L}{L+\tau_{\mathrm{CP}}}\mathbb{E}\left\{\log_2(1+\frac{E_{\mathrm{S}}\gamma_{21}+\gamma_{2\mathrm{R}1}}{1+E_{\mathrm{S}}\gamma_{\mathrm{LI},1}})+\log_2(1+\frac{E_{\mathrm{S}}\gamma_{12}+\gamma_{1\mathrm{R}2}}{1+E_{\mathrm{S}}\gamma_{\mathrm{LI},2}})\right\}, \end{aligned} \quad (24)$$

where $E_{\mathrm{S}}\gamma_{k'k} = E_{\mathrm{S}}\frac{|h_{k'k}|^2}{\sigma^2}$, $\gamma_{k'\mathrm{R}k} = \frac{|a_\tau^{k,\infty}|^2}{\sigma^2}$, and $E_{\mathrm{S}}\gamma_{\mathrm{LI},k} = E_{\mathrm{S}}\frac{|h_{kk}|^2}{\sigma^2}$ denote the instantaneous SINRs for $\mathrm{S}_{k'} \to \mathrm{S}_k$, $\mathrm{S}_{k'} \to \mathrm{R} \to \mathrm{S}_k$, and the S_k loop interference channels, respectively.

Equations (21) and (22) show that, when $N \to \infty$, the small-scale fading from the relay links is averaged and both the RSI and the noise from the relay are reduced to zero. However, the source RSI and the noise at the source node still remain. Moreover, we note that the transmit power of source nodes and of the relay have different effect on the asymptotic SINR. In fact, we can see clearly from (24) that asymptotic SINR increases proportionally with the relay transmit power E_{R}, while the E_{S} effect on the asymptotic SINR is derived by the instantaneous SINRs $\gamma_{k'k}$, $\gamma_{k'\mathrm{R}k}$, and $\gamma_{\mathrm{LI},k}$ values. Actually, when $\gamma_{k'k} = \gamma_{k'\mathrm{R}k}\gamma_{\mathrm{LI},k}$, the source node transmit power effect disappears and the asymptotic SINR becomes equal to $\gamma_{k'\mathrm{R}k}$. In the case where the direct link has a low gain such as $\gamma_{k'k} < \gamma_{k'\mathrm{R}k}\gamma_{\mathrm{LI},k}$, the asymptotic SINR decreases when increasing E_{S}. In the case when $\gamma_{k'k} > \gamma_{k'\mathrm{R}k}\gamma_{\mathrm{LI},k}$, the asymptotic SINR increases with the source node transmit power E_{S}.

4 Simulation Results

In this section, we analyze the sum SE of the studied system. We use Monte Carlo simulations to evaluate sum SE of the system and the asymptotic results given by (20) and (24), respectively. For the sake of simplicity, we assume that the system structure is symmetric, i.e. $\beta_{\mathrm{d}_1} = \beta_{\mathrm{d}_2} = \beta_{\mathrm{u}_1} = \beta_{\mathrm{u}_2} = 10\,\mathrm{dB}$ and $\beta = \beta_{12} = \beta_{21}$, the noise variance $\sigma^2 = \sigma_r^2 = 1$, and the RSI variance $\sigma_{\mathrm{LIr}}^2 = \sigma_{k,k}^2 = 1$.

Figure 2 plots the sum SE of the system versus the number of relay antennas N. Here we assume that the direct link is as good as the relay link, i.e. $\beta = 10\,\mathrm{dB}$ and consider three system configurations, i.e. $E_{\mathrm{S}} = 0\,\mathrm{dB}$ and $E_{\mathrm{R}} = 10\,\mathrm{dB}$, $E_{\mathrm{S}} = 10\,\mathrm{dB}$ and $E_{\mathrm{R}} = 10\,\mathrm{dB}$, and $E_{\mathrm{S}} = 10\,\mathrm{dB}$ and $E_{\mathrm{R}} = 20\,\mathrm{dB}$. As expected, for all configurations, when N increases, the sum SE of the system increases. This is due to the fact that the relay link small-scale fading is averaged and the relay RSI diminish by deploying more antennas at the relay. When $N \to \infty$, we see clearly that the curves accurate with the asymptotic results obtained in (24). Moreover, the simulations show that the sum SE of the system increases proportionally

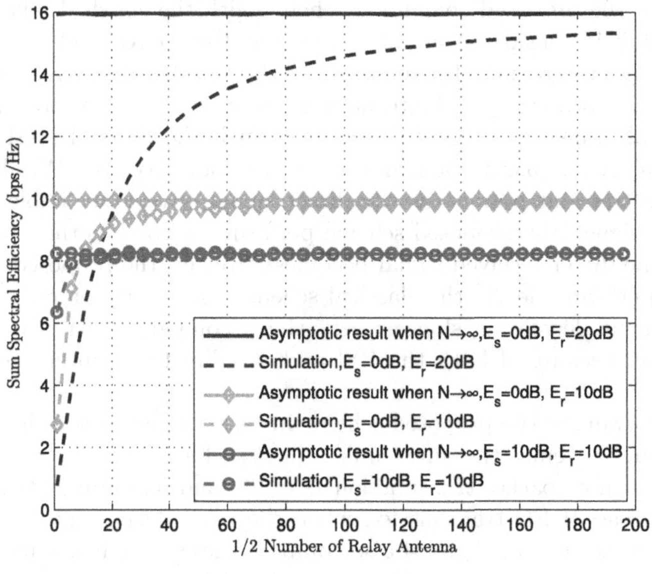

Fig. 2. The sum spectral efficiency versus the number of relay antennas N

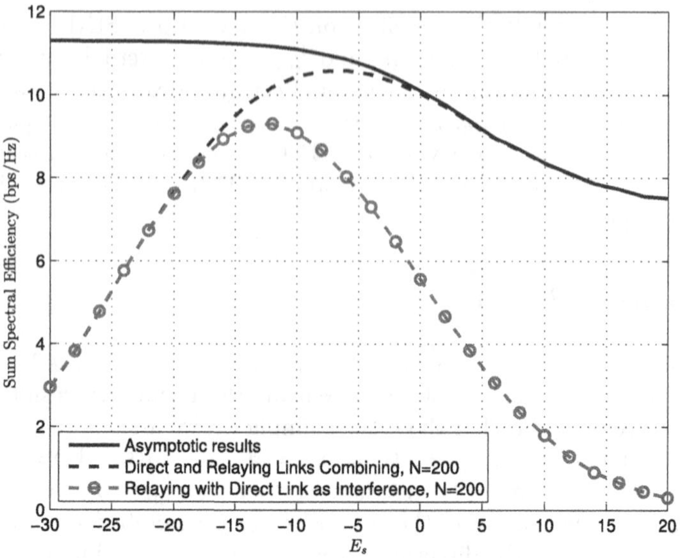

Fig. 3. The spectral efficiency versus the source node transmit power E_S

with E_R and therefore confirm the Sect. 3 analysis. The system configuration simulated in Fig. 2 presents the case where $\gamma_{k'k} < \gamma_{k'Rk}\gamma_{LI,k}$, which explains the fact that the sum SE of the system decreases with the increase of E_S.

In Fig. 3, we keep consider the direct link as good as the relay link, i.e. $\beta = 10\,$dB, we plot the sum SE versus the source node transmit power E_S, and compare the proposed combining scheme with the classical scheme, where the direct link is considered as interference at the source node receiver side. As noticed in the previous figure, when $N \to \infty$, the SE decreases with the increase of E_S. However, for finite number of antenna N, we note that there is an optimal transmit power E_S^{opt}, above which the SE will start to slowly decrease, mainly because of the RSI at the source node receiver. We also observe that for low transmit powers, as the direct signal is very negligible compared to the relay signal, the proposed scheme performs as good as the classical one. Still, once the direct received signal becomes stronger, the proposed combining scheme outperforms clearly the classical scheme. Moreover, for $E_S > E_S^{opt}$, the classical scheme decreasing slope is very sharp compared with the combining scheme slope, because of both the RSI and the direct link interference at the receiver.

Now, we evaluate the proposed scheme in term of packet length L. Figure 4 plots the sum SE versus the direct link gain $\beta_{kk'}$, for long packet transmission, i.e. $L = 500$, short packet transmission $L = 20$, and half-duplex transmission, deployed instead of FD transmission when the relay delay is greater than the packet length, i.e. $\tau \geq L$. Figure 4 also compare these three transmission modes with the classical mode, where the direct signal is considered as interference

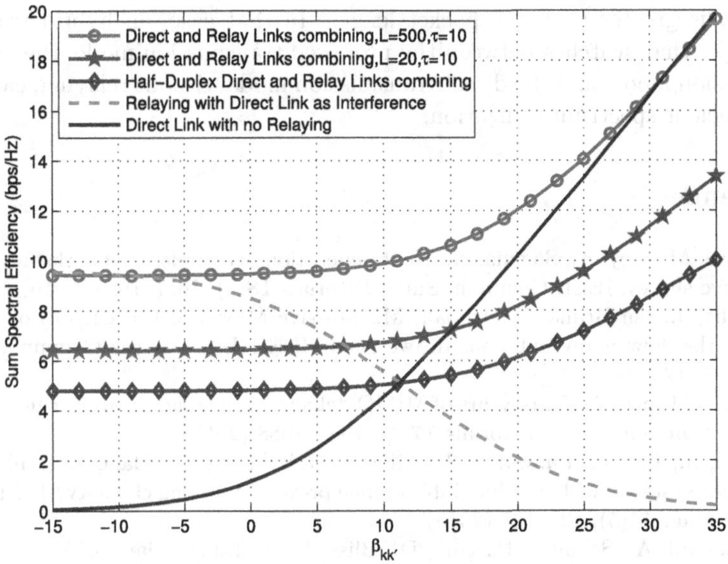

Fig. 4. The spectral efficiency versus the direct link gain $\beta_{kk'}$. Here, $E_S = 0\,\text{dB}$.

at the destination, and the direct transmission mode with no relaying. First, we notice that the proposed combining scheme offers the best performances for long packet applications, i.e. $L \gg \tau$. However, for short packet applications, i.e. $\tau = \frac{L}{2}$, or half-duplex transmissions, i.e. $L \leq \tau$, none of the plotted transmission modes is the obvious choice. In fact, when direct link gain is very weak, it is better to use the low complexity classical scheme at the destination. As $\beta_{kk'}$ increases, the direct signal becomes non-negligible at the destination and treating it as interference badly degrades the system performances. Therefore, using the proposed scheme becomes the best choice. Moreover, for transmission with $\tau \geq L$ and non-negligible direct link, we note that the direct transmission mode offers the best performance.

5 Conclusion

In this paper, we proposed a combining scheme for one-pair two-way FD massive MIMO AF relaying system where the direct link between source nodes is non-negligible. When the number of antennas at the relay goes to infinity, the SE asymptotic expression of the proposed scheme was derived, analyzed, and verified by numerical results. We showed that the transmit power of the source nodes and the relay have different effect on the asymptotic SE. Moreover, it has been demonstrated that, for long packet transmissions, the proposed combining scheme outperforms the classical scheme, where the direct signal is considered as interference at the destination. However, it is not the obvious choice for the short packet transmissions and the transmission where the processing delay at the relay is greater than the packet length. In that case, an hybrid transmission mode, that switches between the proposed transmission mode, the classical transmission mode, and the direct transmission mode without relaying, can leads to an efficient spectrum utilization.

References

1. Agiwal, M., Roy, A., Saxena, N.: Next generation 5G wireless networks: a comprehensive survey. IEEE Commun. Surv. Tutorials **18**(3), 1617–1655 (2016)
2. Hoydis, J., ten Brink, S., Debbah, M.: Massive MIMO in the UL/DL of cellular networks: how many antennas do we need? IEEE J. Sel. Areas Commun. **31**(2), 160–171 (2013)
3. Yang, S., Hanzo, L.: Fifty years of MIMO detection: the road to large-scale MIMOs. IEEE Commun. Surv. Tutorials **17**(4), 1941–1988 (2015)
4. Goyal, S., Liu, P., Panwar, S.S., DiFazio, R.A., Yang, R., Bala, E.: Full duplex cellular systems: will doubling interference prevent doubling capacity? IEEE Commun. Mag. **53**(5), 121–127 (2015)
5. Sabharwal, A., Schniter, P., Guo, D., Bliss, D.W., Rangarajan, S., Wichman, R.: In-band full-duplex wireless: challenges and opportunities. IEEE J. Sel. Area Commun. **32**(9), 1637–1652 (2014)
6. Laneman, J.N., Wornell, G.W., Tse, D.N.C.: An efficient protocol for realizing cooperative diversity in wireless networks. IEEE International Symposium Information Theory (ISIT), Washington, DC, June 2001
7. Sendonaris, A., Erkip, E., Aazhang, B.: User cooperation diversity Part I and Part II. IEEE Trans. Commun. **51**, 1927–1948 (2003)
8. Nosratinia, A., Hedayat, A.: Cooperative communication in wireless networks. IEEE Commun. Mag. **42**(10), 74–80 (2004)
9. Rankov, B., Wittneben, A.: Spectral efficient protocols for half-duplex fading relay channels. IEEE J. Sel. Areas Commun. **25**(2), 379–389 (2007)
10. Oechtering, T.J., Schnurr, C., Bjelakovic, I., Boche, H.: Broadcast capacity region of two-phase bidirectional relaying. IEEE Trans. Inf. Theor. **54**(1), 454–458 (2008)
11. Liu, P., Kim, I.-M.: Performance analysis of bidirectional communication protocols based on decode-and-forward relaying. IEEE Trans. Commun. **58**(9), 2683–2696 (2010)
12. Nam, W., Chung, S.-Y., Lee, Y.H.: Capacity of the Gaussian twoway relay channel to within $\frac{1}{2}$ bit. IEEE Trans. Inf. Theor. **56**(11), 5488–5494 (2010)
13. Ju, H., Oh, E., Hong, D.: Catching resource-devouring worms in next-generation wireless relay systems: two-way relay and full-duplex relay. IEEE Commun. Mag. **47**(9), 58–65 (2009)
14. Vaze, R., Heath, R.W.: On the capacity and diversity-multiplexing tradeoff of the two-way relay channel. IEEE Trans. Inf. Theor. **57**(7), 4219–4234 (2011)
15. Cheng, X., Yu, B., Cheng, X., Yang, L.: Two-way full-duplex amplify-and- forward relaying. In: Proceeding of IEEE Military Communications Conference (MILCOM), pp. 1–6 (2013)
16. Zhang, Z., Ma, Z., Ding, Z., Xiao, M., Karagiannidis, G.K.: Full-duplex two-way and one-way relaying: average rate, outage probability, and tradeoffs. IEEE Trans. Wirel. Commun. **15**(6), 3920–3933 (2016)
17. Riihonen, T., Werner, S., Wichman, R.: Mitigation of loopback selfinterference in full-duplex MIMO relays. IEEE Trans. Sign. Process. **59**, 5983–5993 (2011)

18. Ngo, H.Q., Suraweera, H., Matthaiou, M., Larsson, E.: Multipair full-duplex relaying with massive arrays and linear processing. IEEE J. Sel. Areas Commun. **32**(9), 1721–1737 (2014)
19. Zhang, Z., Chen, Z., Shen, M., Xia, B.: On capacity of two-way mas- sive MIMO full-duplex relay systems. In: Proceeding of International Conference on Communications (ICC), pp. 4327–4332 (2015)
20. Zhang, Z., Chen, Z., Shen, M., Xia, B.: Spectral and energy efciency of multipair two-way full-duplex relay systems with massive MIMO. IEEE J. Sel. Areas Commun. **34**(4), 848–863 (2016)
21. Khafagy, M.G., Ismail, A., Alouini, M.S., Assa, S.: On the outage performance of full-duplex selective decode-and-forward relaying. IEEE Commun. Lett. **17**(6), 1180–1183 (2013)
22. Cui, H., Song, L., Jiao, B.: Multi-pair two-way amplify-and- forward relaying with very large number of relay antennas. IEEE Trans. Wirel. Commun. **13**(5), 2636–2645 (2014)

Robust Trajectory Planning for Robotic Communications Under Fading Channels

Daniel Bonilla Licea[1], Vineeth S. Varma[2], Samson Lasaulce[3], Jamal Daafouz[2], Mounir Ghogho[1,4], and Des McLernon[1](✉)

[1] School of Electronic and Electrical Engineering, University of Leeds, Leeds, UK
dbonillalicea85@gmail.com, D.C.McLernon@leeds.ac.uk
[2] CNRS and Université de Lorraine, CRAN, UMR 7039, Vandœuvre-lès-Nancy, France
{vineeth.satheeskumar-varma,daafouz6}@univ-lorraine.fr
[3] L2S (CNRS-CentraleSupelec-Univ. Paris Sud), Gif-sur-yvette, France
samson.lasaulce@l2s.centralesupelec.fr
[4] International University of Rabat, Rabat, Morocco
mounir.ghogho@uir.ac.ma

Abstract. We consider a new problem of robust trajectory planning for robots that have a physical destination and a communication constraint. Specifically, the robot or automatic vehicle must move from a given starting point to a target point while uploading/downloading a given amount of data within a given time, while accounting for the energy cost and the time taken to download. However, this trajectory is assumed to be planned in advance (e.g., because online computation cannot be performed). Due to wireless channel fluctuations, it is essential for the planned trajectory to be robust to packet losses and meet the communication target with a sufficiently high probability. This optimization problem contrasts with the classical mobile communications paradigm in which communication aspects are assumed to be independent from the motion aspects. This setup is formalized here and leads us to determining non-trivial trajectories for the mobile, which are highlighted in the numerical result.

1 Introduction

Traditionally in wireless literature, the trajectory of the mobile node is assumed to be an exogenous variable and the communication resources are optimized based only on the wireless parameters. However, we have seen an emergence of new technology like unmanned aerial or ground vehicles, drones and mobile robots which have communication objectives in addition to their destination or motion based objectives [1]. Several works [2] have studied trajectory optimization problems when the communication constraint is that of having a target SNR.

D. McLernon—The present work is supported by the LIA project between CRAN, Lorea and the International University of Rabat.

E. Sabir et al. (Eds.): UNet 2017, LNCS 10542, pp. 450–460, 2017.
https://doi.org/10.1007/978-3-319-68179-5_39

However, we are interested in the case where the communication requirement is downloading a certain number of bits within a given time.

Previously, we have studied the problem where a mobile robot (MR) must download (or upload) a given amount of data from an access point and also reach a certain destination within a given time period in [1]. However, in [1], we did not account for wireless channel fading and in fact assumed that the wireless signal strength is determined purely based on the path loss. In this work, we want to relax this strong assumption and account for small-scale fading and shadowing effects. In this article we will show how to design offline a robust reference trajectory under limited amount of information and high uncertainty about the wireless channel. This trajectory will allow the MR to reach the goal point and completely transmit the content of its buffer to the access point (AP) with a sufficiently high probability.

In practice, this reference trajectory will be preloaded on the MR prior to the execution on the task and it will serve the MR as guide which may need to be slightly modified according to the wireless channel measurements collected by the MR while executing its task. This adaptation mechanism is outside the scope of this article and we will only focus on the design of the reference trajectory. Future works will address the online adaptation mechanism. The main contributions of this paper are as follows.

- Trajectory planning of a MR starting from an arbitrary point, which must reach a certain target point and download a certain number of bits from a nearby access point.
- Optimization of the trajectory to minimize a cost function which depends on the amount of data left in the buffer to be downloaded and the energy consumed.
- Considering a robust cost function which accounts for the random fluctuations of the wireless channel due to small-scale fading and shadowing effects.

Note that the first two contributions were also provided in [1] for the much more simpler case in which only path-loss is assumed to determine the wireless signal. The rest of the paper is structured in the following manner. We provide the model for the wireless communication system and the robot motion in Sect. 2. We then provide the problem statement in Sect. 3 and provide a solution concept in Sect. 4. Finally, we provide numerical simulations in Sect. 5.

2 System Model

The position of the MR is given by $\mathbf{p}(t) \in \mathbb{R}^2$, at any time $t \in \mathbb{R}_{\geq 0}$. We assume that the robot starts at position $\mathbf{s}$, i.e. $\mathbf{p}(0) = \mathbf{s}$. The MR and the AP communicate with a frame duration T during which the channel fading is assumed to be a constant, i.e. we assume a block fading model. The robot has a buffer with state $b(k) \in \mathbb{Z}_{\geq 0}$ denoting the number of bits it must transmit at the discretized time $k = \lfloor \frac{t}{T} \rfloor$. The initial buffer size is the total file size and is assume to be given by N, i.e., $b(0) = N$. The robot is equipped with a wireless system to communicate with an access point at $\mathbf{p}_{\mathrm{AP}}$ satisfying the following properties.

2.1 Communications System

The MR will move among dynamic scatterers and the bandwidth used for the communication will be lower than the coherence bandwidth. As a consequence the wireless channel between the MR and the access point (AP) will experience time-varying and flat multipath (small scale) fading as well as shadowing (large-scale fading). With loss of generality, we assume, from now on, that the communication problem consists in uploading data from the MR to the AP. The signal received by the AP at time t can be written as

$$y_{\mathrm{AP}}(t, \mathbf{p}(t)) = \left(\frac{h(\mathbf{p}(t), t)s(\mathbf{p}(t))}{\|\mathbf{p}(t) - \mathbf{p}_{\mathrm{AP}}\|_2^{\alpha/2}} \right) x(t) + n_{\mathrm{AP}}(t), \tag{1}$$

where $\mathbf{p}_{\mathrm{AP}}$ is the location of the AP, $h(\mathbf{p}(t), t)$ represents the time-varying small-scale fading which we assume to be Nakagami distributed and $s(\mathbf{p}(t))$ represents the shadowing term which we assume to be lognormal distributed [3]. Nakagami fading is well suited to model the behavior of the multipath fading in many practical scenarios [4]. Without loss of generality we assume $\mathbb{E}[|h(\mathbf{p}(t))|^2] = 1$ and so the p.d.f. of $|h(\mathbf{p}(t))|$ becomes

$$f_h(z, m) = \frac{2m^m}{\Gamma(m)} z^{2m-1} \exp\left(-mz^2\right), \tag{2}$$

where m is the shape factor of the Nakagami distribution. As mentioned before, the shadowing term $s(\mathbf{p}(t))$ is lognormal distributed and so we have $\log\left(s(\mathbf{p}(t))\right) \sim \mathcal{N}\left(0, \sigma_s^2\right)$ with σ_s^2 being the its variance. Also, the normalized spatial correlation of the shadowing is

$$r(\mathbf{p}, \mathbf{q}) = \exp\left(-\frac{\|\mathbf{p} - \mathbf{q}\|_2}{\beta} \right), \tag{3}$$

where β is the decorrelation distance which will be unknown to the MR prior to the execution of the trajectory. Now, the coefficient α in (1) is the power path loss coefficient which usually takes values between 2 and 6 depending on the environment; $x(t)$ is the signal transmitted by the robot with average power $\mathbb{E}[|x(t)|^2] = P$ and $n_{\mathrm{AP}}(t) \sim \mathcal{CN}(0, \sigma_n^2)$ is the zero mean additive white Gaussian (AWGN) noise at the AP's receiver. From (1) we have that the signal-to-noise ratio (SNR) at the AP (in dB) is:

$$\begin{aligned}\Gamma_{\mathrm{dB}}(\mathbf{p}(t)) = 10\log_{10}\left(\frac{P}{\sigma_n^2}\right) + 20\log_{10}\left(s(\mathbf{p}(t))\right) + 20\log_{10}\left(|h(\mathbf{p}(t), t)|\right) \\ - 10\alpha\log_{10}\left(\|\mathbf{p}(t) - \mathbf{p}_{\mathrm{AP}}\|_2\right).\end{aligned} \tag{4}$$

As a result, the number of bits in the MR's buffer is given by:

$$b(k) = \left[N - \sum_{j=0}^{k} R\left(\widehat{\Gamma}(\mathbf{p}(jT))\right) \right]^+ \tag{5}$$

where and $\lceil a \rceil^+ = a$ for $a > 0$ and $\lceil a \rceil^+ = 0$ for $a \leq 0$; $\widehat{\Gamma}(\mathbf{p}(jT))$ is the estimate of $\Gamma(\mathbf{p}(jT))$ which is $\Gamma_{dB}(\mathbf{p}(jT))$ in linear scale, N is the initial number of bits in the buffer and $R\left(\widehat{\Gamma}(\mathbf{p}(kT))\right)$ is the number of bits in the payload of the packet transmitted during the duplexing period k. As mentioned above, the number $R\left(\widehat{\Gamma}(\mathbf{p}(kT))\right)$ of bits transmitted in the payload is computed by the MR according to its most recent SNR estimate. So we have (for $b(k) \neq 0$):

$$R\left(\widehat{\Gamma}\right) = R_j, \quad \forall\, \widehat{\Gamma} \in [\eta_j, \eta_{j+1}), \quad j = 0, 1, \cdots, J \tag{6}$$

with $R_j < R_{j+1}$, $\eta_j < \eta_{j+1}$, $R_0 = 0$, $\eta_0 = 0$ and η_1 must be above the sensitivity of the AP's receiver.

2.2 Mobile Robot

We assume the MR to be omnidirectional and its velocity is assumed to be controlled directly. This results in its motion described by

$$\dot{\mathbf{p}}(t) = \mathbf{u}(t), \tag{7}$$

where $\mathbf{p}(t)$ is the MR position at time t and $\mathbf{u}(t)$ is the control input which is bounded by:

$$\|\mathbf{u}(t)\|_2 \leq u_{\max}, \tag{8}$$

Finally, the mechanical energy spent by the MR between t_0 and t_1 while using the control signal $\mathbf{u}(t)$ is:

$$E_{\text{mechanical}}(t_0, t_1, \mathbf{u}) = m \int_{t_0}^{t_1} \|\mathbf{u}(t)\|^2 \mathrm{d}t. \tag{9}$$

where m is the mass of the MR.

3 Problem Statement

The objective of the robot is to depart from a starting point $\mathbf{s}$ to a goal point $\mathbf{g}$ within a time t_f and transmit the all the content from its buffer to the AP. The desired trajectory is such that it consumes little mechanical energy from the robot and also allows the robot the transmit all the content of the buffer quickly. In addition we want that when the MR follows this trajectory it succeeds in emptying its buffer with a high probability.

We assume that the only knowledge available to the MR (and the designer) about the environment (prior to the execution of the trajectory) is the position of the starting and goal points (i.e., $\mathbf{s}$ and $\mathbf{g}$); an estimate of the path loss coefficient α, but we assume no knowledge about the severity of the small-scale fading (i.e., about the shaping factor m in (2)). Solving the general problem with no approximation is very hard due to the large amount of stochastic perturbations, the shadowing correlation and the large number of terms in the sum of (5). This results in a very complicated expression for the probability of the buffer to be empty at t_f. Therefore, we look at the *most likely* buffer state given by

$$\widetilde{b}(k) = \left[N - \sum_{j=0}^{k} \widetilde{R}\left(\Gamma(\mathbf{p}(jT))\right) \right]^{+} \tag{10}$$

where $\widetilde{R}\left(\Gamma(\mathbf{p}(jT))\right)$ is the statistical mode of $R\left(\Gamma(\mathbf{p}(jT))\right)$, i.e.,

$$\widetilde{R}\left(\Gamma(\mathbf{p}(kT))\right) = \max\left(\underset{R \in \{R_j\}_{j=0}^{J}}{\text{argmax}} \ \Pr\left(R\left(\Gamma(\mathbf{p}(kT))\right) = R\right) \right). \tag{11}$$

This results in the following optimization problem

$$\begin{aligned}
&\underset{\mathbf{u}}{\text{minimize}} \quad \theta_1 \int_0^{tf} \frac{\|\mathbf{u}(t)\|_2^2}{u_{\max}^2} \mathrm{d}t + \theta_2 \sum_{k=0}^{\lfloor \frac{t_f}{T} \rfloor} \frac{T\widetilde{b}(k)}{N} \\
&\text{s.t.} \\
&\dot{\mathbf{p}}(t) = \mathbf{u}(t) \\
&\|\mathbf{u}(t)\|_2 \leq u_{\max}, \\
&\mathbf{p}(0) = \mathbf{s}, \quad \mathbf{p}(t_f) = \mathbf{g}, \\
&\sum_{k=0}^{\lfloor \frac{t_f}{T} \rfloor} \widetilde{R}\left(\Gamma(\mathbf{p}(kT))\right) \geq r_R N.
\end{aligned} \tag{12}$$

The optimization target is a convex combination of the energy spent in motion by the robot (9) and of a second term which estimates how quickly the buffer is emptied. This second term is a sum over the most likely number of bits left in the buffer at time instant $t = kT$ (i.e., $\mathbb{E}\left[b(k)\right]$). The coefficients $\{\theta_k\}_{k=1}^{2}$ of the convex combination determine the relative importance of each optimization criterion.

Note that due to the stochastic nature of the channel we can not ensure that when the MR follows the reference trajectory it will always be able to empty its buffer but we can ensure that this happens with a certain probability. As calculating the actual probability of failing to meet the communication requirement constitutes a very hard task as explained above, we introduce $r_R \geq 1$ which is an overestimation parameter selected by the designer. The final constraint in (12) ensures that the sum of the statistical mode of the bits transmitted in the payload over all the trajectory is equal to an overestimation of the initial number of bits in the buffer, i.e., $r_R N$. So when the trajectory is actually executed, the probability that the buffer will be emptied will be high and by increasing the overestimation parameter r_R we can reduce the probability of the MR failing to empty its buffer when it reaches the goal point $\mathbf{g}$. The term $\widetilde{b}(t)$ is a discreet and deterministic function of the MR's position. This difference makes the problem much more feasible to solve.

4 Proposed Solution

Now, to solve the optimization problem (12) we first define the region $\mathcal{A}_j$ as:

$$\mathcal{A}_j = \{\mathbf{p} \mid \widetilde{R}(\Gamma(\mathbf{p})) = R_j\}. \tag{13}$$

Due to the wireless channel model the region $\mathcal{A}_J$ is circular while the shape of region $\mathcal{A}_j$, for $j = 1, 2, \cdots, J-1$, is a ring with inner and outer radii of r_{j+1} and r_j respectively. And r_j is given by:

$$r_j = \min\left(\left\{r \mid \widetilde{R}\left(\Gamma\left(r[\cos(\theta) \quad \sin(\theta)] - \mathbf{p}_{\mathrm{AP}}\right)\right) = R_j\right\}\right) \tag{14}$$

The radii r_j are computed from the channel statistics which can be estimated using the techniques presented in [5]. Nevertheless, for lack of space we do not provide here the details on how to compute it.

We also define $\mathbf{u}_j(t)$ as any control law that takes the vehicle through the regions $\{\mathcal{A}_k\}_{k=0}^{j}$. The set of all control laws $\mathbf{u}_j(t)$ will be denoted as $\mathcal{U}_j$ and $\mathcal{U} = \cup_{j=0}^{J}\mathcal{U}_j$ is the set of all control laws.

One simple way to solve (12) is to first solve it with the additional constraint $\mathbf{u} \in \mathcal{U}_j$, once for each different value of $j = 1, 2, \cdots, J$. We will denote as $\mathbf{u}_j^*(t)$ the optimum control law that solves (12) under the additional constraint $\mathbf{u} \in \mathcal{U}_j$ and $\mathbf{u}^*(t)$ as control law that solves (12) under the constraint $\mathbf{u} \in \{\mathbf{u}_j^*(t)\}_{j=1}^{J}$. Therefore to solve (12) we will calculate all the optimum control signals $\mathbf{u}_j^*$.

In order to minimize the mechanical energy term in the optimization target of (12) the optimum control law $\mathbf{u}_j^*(t)$ must make the robot enter and exit the convex hull of each region $\{\mathcal{A}_n\}_{n=0}^{j}$ at most once. These input and output points to the convex hull of the area $\mathcal{A}_j$ are denoted by $\mathbf{i}_j$ and $\mathbf{o}_j$ respectively. We regroup these points in the following set $\mathcal{C}^j = \{\mathbf{s}, \mathbf{i}_1, \mathbf{i}_2, \cdots, \mathbf{i}_j, \mathbf{o}_j, \mathbf{o}_{j-1}, \cdots, \mathbf{o}_1, \mathbf{g}\}$ and index them as follows:

$$\begin{aligned}
&\mathbf{c}_0^j = \mathbf{s}, \\
&\mathbf{c}_n^j = \mathbf{i}_n, \quad \text{for} \quad n = 1, 2, \cdots, j, \\
&\mathbf{c}_n^j = \mathbf{o}_{2j+1-n}, \quad \text{for} \quad n = j+1, j+2, \cdots, 2j, \\
&\mathbf{c}_{2j+1}^j = \mathbf{g}.
\end{aligned} \tag{15}$$

where $\mathbf{s}$ and $\mathbf{g}$ are the starting and goal points for the robot. In addition, t_n is the time instant in which the robot is at $\mathbf{p}_n^j$ and:

$$\tau_n t_f = (t_{n+1} - t_n), \quad n = 0, 1, \cdots, 2j \tag{16}$$

where:

$$\sum_{n=0}^{2j} \tau_n = 1, \quad \tau_n > 0, \tag{17}$$

Note that the coefficients $\{\tau_n\}_{n=0}^{2j}$ determine the portion of time t_f that the robot takes to go from $\mathbf{c}_{n-1}^j$ to $\mathbf{c}_n^j$. Let us also write the points belonging to $\mathcal{C}^j$ in polar coordinates as:

$$\mathbf{c}_n^j = r_n^j[\cos(\phi_n^j) \quad \sin(\phi_n^j)]^T. \tag{18}$$

From the definition of $\mathbf{i}_n$ and $\mathbf{o}_n$ we know that they lie in a circle of radius r_n which can be computed from the p.m.f. of $R(\Gamma(\mathbf{p}(kT)))$. Therefore we know $\{r_n^j\}_{n=1}^{2j}$ and as a consequence the only unknowns to uniquely determine $\mathcal{C}^j$ are the angles[1] $\{\phi_n^j\}_{n=1}^{2j}$, where the ϕ_n^j is the angle of $\mathbf{c}_n^j$ respect to the AP.

Now, the optimum control law $\mathbf{u}_j^*(t)$ takes the robot from $\mathbf{c}_0^j$ up to $\mathbf{c}_{2j+1}^j$ in ascending order through each point in $\mathcal{C}^j$. We can also see that the second term in the optimization target of (12) depends only the time spent in each region $\mathcal{A}_j$ (i.e., on the durations $\tau_k t_f$) and not on the shape of the particular path followed by the robot nor by its velocity profile. So, the velocity profile and the path must be selected to minimize the mechanical energy (i.e., the first term in the optimization target (12)). To do so the vehicle must go from $\mathbf{c}_{n-1}^j$ to $\mathbf{c}_n^j$ in a time $\tau_n t_f$ (to be determined) using minimum energy. Using calculus of variations [6] we can show that this is achieved by:

$$\mathbf{u}_j(t) = \frac{\mathbf{c}_n^j - \mathbf{c}_{n-1}^j}{\tau_{n-1} t_f} \quad \forall \quad t \in [t_{n-1}, t_n). \tag{19}$$

Therefore if we add the constraint $\mathbf{u} \in \mathcal{U}_j$ and then we optimize $\{\tau_n\}_{n=0}^{2j}$ and the angles $\{\phi_n^j\}_{n=1}^{2j}$ we obtain $\mathbf{u}_j^*(t)$. Now, if we use the constraint $\mathbf{u} \in \mathcal{U}_j$ and select $\mathbf{u}_j(t)$ to take the form (19) then the optimization target of problem (12) becomes:

$$\mathcal{J}\left(\{\tau_n\}_{n=0}^{2j}, \{\phi_n^j\}_{n=1}^{2j}\right) = \theta_1 \sum_{n=1}^{2j+1} \frac{\|\mathbf{c}_n^j - \mathbf{c}_{n-1}^j\|^2}{u_{max}^2 \tau_{n-1} t_f} + \theta_2 \sum_{k=0}^{\lfloor \frac{t_f}{T} \rfloor} \frac{T\widetilde{b}(k)}{N}. \tag{20}$$

And using (13), (19) and the constraint in (12) we have the following approximation:

$$\frac{\tau_j t_f}{T} R_j + \sum_{n=0}^{j-1} \left(\frac{(\tau_{2j-n} + \tau_n) t_f}{T} \right) R_n \geq r_R N \tag{21}$$

So, taking into account (19)–(21) the optimization problem (12) becomes:

$$\begin{aligned}
&\underset{\{\tau_n\}_{n=0}^{2j}, \{\phi_n^j\}_{n=1}^{2j}}{\text{minimize}} \quad \mathcal{J}\left(\{\tau_n\}_{n=0}^{2j}, \{\phi_n^j\}_{n=1}^{2j}\right) \\
&\text{s.t.} \\
&\sum_{n=1}^{2j+1} \tau_n = 1, \quad \tau_n > 0, \\
&\frac{r_n^2 + r_{n-1}^2 - 2 r_n r_{n-1} \cos(\phi_n^j - \phi_{n-1}^j)}{\tau_n^2 t_f^2} \leq u_{max}^2, \; n = 0, 1, \cdots, 2j \\
&\mathbf{c}_n^j = r_n^j [\cos(\phi_n^j) \;\; \sin(\phi_n^j)]^T, \\
&\mathbf{c}_0^j = \mathbf{s} \;\; \mathbf{c}_{2j+1}^j = \mathbf{g}, \\
&\frac{\tau_j t_f}{T} R_j + \sum_{n=0}^{j-1} \left(\frac{(\tau_{2j-n} + \tau_n) t_f}{T} \right) R_n \geq r_R N
\end{aligned} \tag{22}$$

[1] Since ϕ_0 and ϕ_{2j+1} are the angles of $\mathbf{s}$ and $\mathbf{g}$ they are also known.

where the first line of constraints ensures that the coefficients $\{\tau_k\}_{k=0}^{2j}$ determine the portion of the total time t_f taken to go from one point in $\mathcal{C}^j$ to the next one. The next line of constraints establishes the maximum velocity of the robot. The final constraint is the robust constraint which will allow the designer to obtain a high probability of the MR emptying completely its buffer.

To solve the optimization problem (22) we first express the angles $\{\phi_n^j\}_{n=1}^{2j}$ as function of the durations $\{\tau_n\}_{n=0}^{2j}$. This is achieved by deriving the optimization target of (22), see more details in [1]. Then we use simulated annealing algorithm (SAA) [7] to optimize the durations $\{\tau_n\}_{n=0}^{2j}$. This concludes the discussion about the optimization of the trajectory and in the next section we present some simulations to better understand its behaviour and observe its performance.

5 Simulations

In this section we present some simulations to gain some insight about the trajectories obtained by the method presented in this paper. We select $10\log_{10}\left(\frac{P}{\sigma_n^2}\right) = 33dB$. Now, the initial number of bits in the buffer $b(0) = 600N_s$ while the possible amount of bits transmitted in one packet can be $R_0 = 0$, $R_1 = 4N_s$, $R_2 = 16N_s$, $R_3 = 64N_s$ where N_s is the number of symbols transmitted in one packet. Note that such values for the number of bits transmitted in the payload can be obtained using a rectangular M-QAM modulation. Now, regarding the thresholds $\{\eta_j\}_{j=0}^{J}$ we fix them so that the bit error rate is at least 10^{-3}.

Now regarding the channel we select the path loss coefficient as $\alpha = 2$, shadowing variance $\sigma_s^2 = 2.5$ and then for the decorrelation distance we select $\beta = 10\lambda$, where λ is the wavelength of the RF carrier used for communications.

We select the starting and the goal points to be $\mathbf{s} = [8\lambda\ \ 0]$ and $\mathbf{g} = [9 - 6]\lambda$ while we locate the access point at the origin. Then the time to reach the goal point is $t_f = 20\,\text{s}$, the period between packets $T = 100\,\text{ms}$ and the maximum velocity of the MR is 10λ per second.

First of all we consider for references a trajectory that goes from $\mathbf{s}$ to $\mathbf{g}$ using minimum energy. This is achieved by a linear path between both points and a constant velocity profile. We will denote such trajectory as $\mathcal{T}_0$. Then we consider a trajectory $\mathcal{T}_1$ optimized according to (22) with $\theta_1 = 1$, $\theta_2 = 0$ and $r_R = 1$. This trajectory is optimized to use minimum energy while satisfying constraint (21). Then we also consider another trajectory $\mathcal{T}_1$ optimized according to (22) with $\theta_1 = 0$, $\theta_2 = 1$ and $r_R = 1$. This trajectory is optimized to empty the buffer as quick as possible.

In Fig. 1 we can observe the paths corresponding to the trajectories $\mathcal{T}_0$, $\mathcal{T}_1$ and $\mathcal{T}_2$. We first note that the path corresponding to $\mathcal{T}_1$ is shorter than the path corresponding to $\mathcal{T}_2$ which agrees with the fact that the trajectory $\mathcal{T}_1$ is optimized to minimize the energy consumed (while satisfying constraint (21)). Then regarding the shape of the paths we see that the path of $\mathcal{T}_2$ reaches $\mathcal{A}_2$ through the shortest path, this is done in order improve as quick as possible the transmission rate in order to empty the buffer as soon as possible. Now, regarding

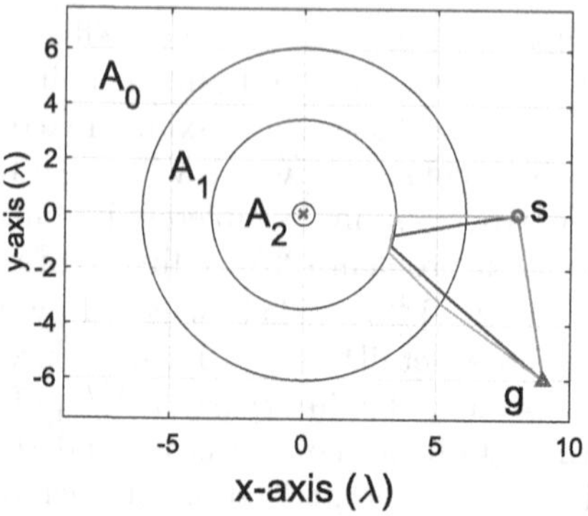

Fig. 1. Paths corresponding to trajectories $\mathcal{T}_0$ (green), $\mathcal{T}_1$ (blue) and $\mathcal{T}_2$ (magenta). Starting point $\mathbf{s}$ represented by a circle, goal point $\mathbf{s}$ represented by a triangle and AP location at the origin. We observe as well the delimitation of the areas $\{\mathcal{A}_j\}_{j=0}^{3}$ (Color figure online).

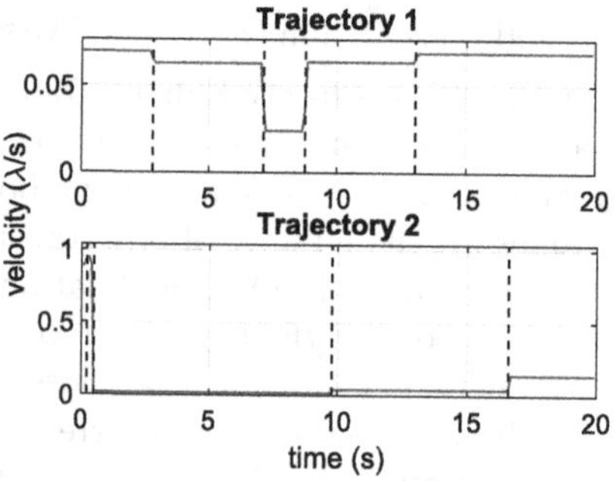

Fig. 2. Velocity profiles of trajectory $\mathcal{T}_1$ (top) and $\mathcal{T}_2$ (bottom). The vertical dashed lines separate the durations $\{\tau_n\}_{n=0}^{2j}$.

the path for $\mathcal{T}_1$ the robot reaches $\mathcal{A}_2$ by moving in an orthogonal direction with respect to the vector $\mathbf{g} - \mathbf{s}$, by doing so the robot minimizes the amount of deviation from $\mathbf{g}$ which reduces then the distance total distance travelled and consequently the energy spent.

When we observe the velocity profiles of both trajectories in Fig. 2 we first note that the period with highest velocity takes place from $t = 0$ until $t = \tau_1$ this is because the robot is rushing to get out from $\mathcal{A}_0$ to start transmitting as many bits as possible. Then we also observe that the minimum velocity occurs when the robot reaches the inner most area of the trajectory (in this case $\mathcal{A}_2$). This is in order to spend as much time as possible in that area with the best channel conditions in the trajectory.

Then, in Table 1 we observe the average time in which the buffer is emptied $\mathbb{E}[t_{empt}]$, the probability of success P_S (i.e., the probability of emptying the buffer when reaching $\mathbf{g}$) and the amount of mechanical energy used normalized by $m\lambda^2$.

Table 1. Performance of different trajectories

Trajectory	$\mathbb{E}[t_{empt}]$ (s)	P_S	$Energy/(m\lambda^2)$ (J)
$\mathcal{T}_0$	14.46	0.0868	0.1859
$\mathcal{T}_1$	10.41	0.7206	0.8139
$\mathcal{T}_2$	7.72	0.9347	4.8924
$\mathcal{T}_3$	7.68	0.8652	3.8928
$\mathcal{T}_4$	7.59	0.9262	4.7909

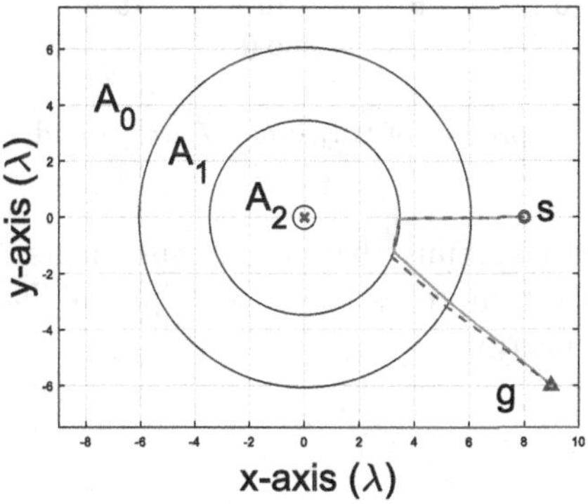

Fig. 3. Paths corresponding to trajectories $\mathcal{T}_3$ (green) and $\mathcal{T}_4$ (dashed red) (Color figure online).

As it is expected the trajectory $\mathcal{T}_0$ uses minimum energy but its probability of success is very low (0.0868). On the other hand the probability of success for the optimized trajectories $\mathcal{T}_1$ and $\mathcal{T}_2$ is much higher, 0.7206 and 0.9347 respectively, but due to the larger paths and velocities their energy consumption is higher.

Now, we observe the effect of the robustness parameter r_R, see (21). To do so we consider two more trajectories. The first one, denoted $\mathcal{T}_3$, is optimized according to (22) with $\theta_1 = 0.3$, $\theta_2 = 0.7$ and $r_R = 1$. While the second trajectory, denoted $\mathcal{T}_4$, is optimized according to (22) with $\theta_1 = 0.3$, $\theta_2 = 0.7$ and $r_R = 1.5$. We observe in Fig. 3 that their path is really similar (the path corresponding to $\mathcal{T}_4$ is slightly larger) but their velocity profiles are clearly different as we can observe in Fig. 4. The trajectory $\mathcal{T}_4$ spends a larger time in the area $\mathcal{A}_2$ in order to increase the average data rate and therefore increase the probability of success. But by doing so the robot has to move quicker when it gets out from $\mathcal{A}_2$ in order to reach $\mathbf{g}$ in time. By comparing the probabilities of success of $\mathcal{T}_4$ with $\mathcal{T}_3$ in Table 1 we observe that increasing the robustness parameter r_R indeed increases the probability of success although it also increases the energy consumption.

Note that all the optimized predefined trajectories were able to produce a relatively large probability of success in a fading channel without the use of any kind of diversity. This large probability of success was achieved by optimizing the trajectories using only first order statistics of the wireless channel. In the

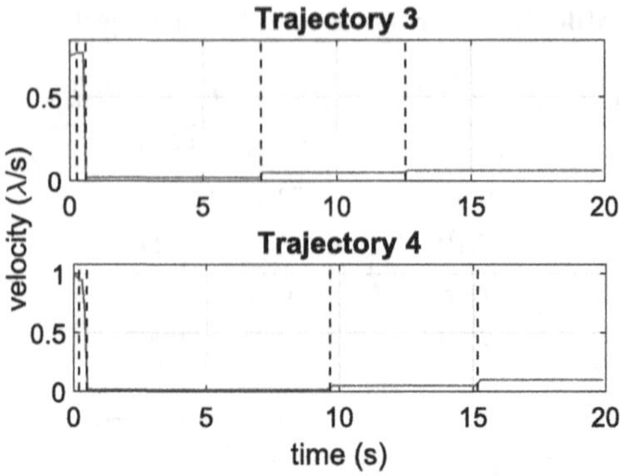

Fig. 4. Velocity profiles of trajectory $\mathcal{T}_3$ (top) and $\mathcal{T}_4$ (bottom).

future we will take into account channel measurements to develop an online mechanism which further improves the success probability while reducing the amount of mechanical energy.

6 Conclusions

We have formulated the problem of robust trajectory optimization for an MR with a target point to reach and a certain number of bits to transmit within a given time. Due to small scale fading and shadowing effects, obtaining a suitable reference trajectory offline is non-trivial. Therefore, we consider the most likely buffer state at each time determined based on the statistical mode and optimize the desired metric by introducing an overestimation parameter for robustness. This approach results in an optimization problem with a feasible solution.

References

1. Licea, D.B., Varma, V.S., Lasaulce, S., Daafouz, J., Ghogho, M.: Trajectory planning for energy-efficient vehicles with communications constraints. In: Proceedings of the 2016 International Conference on Wireless Networks and Mobile Communications (WINCOM), October 2016
2. Ooi, C.C., Schindelhauer, C.: Minimal energy path planning for wireless robots. Mob. Netw. Appl. **14**(3), 309–321 (2009)
3. Cai, X., Giannakis, G.B.: A two-dimensional channel simulation model for shadowing processes. IEEE Trans. Veh. Technol. **52**(6), 1558–1567 (2003)
4. Simon, M.K., Alouini, M.S.: Digital Communications over Fading Channels. Wiley, New york (2005)
5. Malmirchegini, M., Mostofi, Y.: On the spatial predictability of communication channels. IEEE Trans. Wirel. Commun. **11**(3), 964–978 (2012)
6. Kirk, D.E.: Optimal Control Theory: An Introduction. Dover Publications Inc. (2004)
7. Russell, S., Norving, P.: Artificial Intelligence: A Modern Approach. Prentice Hall (2003)

Performance of Enhanced LTE OTDOA Positioning Approach Through Nakagami-*m* Fading Channel

Ilham El Mourabit(✉), Abdelmajid Badri, Aicha Sahel, and Abdennaceur Baghdad

EEA&TI Laboratory Faculty of Science and Techniques (FSTM), Hassan II University of Casablanca, BP 146, Mohammedia, Morocco
Elmourabit.ilham@gmail.com

Abstract. Location Based Services (LBS) has known a huge progress with the 4G mobile networks (LTE, LTE-A). Since the LTE introduced a new signal dedicated to positioning purposes called Positioning Reference Signal (PRS), many studies were conducted to use this feature to improve the system performance. In this context, we have developed a new positioning approach called Adaptive Observed Time Difference of Arrival (A-OTDOA) which is compatible with both 3G and 4G user equipment and respond to the emergency calls accuracy criteria. In this paper, we will analyze the performance of the A-OTDOA technique in a propagation environment combining Nakagami-m fading channel, MIMO channel and additive white Gaussian noise.

Keywords: OTODA · LTE · Nakagami-m · Adaptive OTDOA · AWGN · Adaptive filters · Fading channels · Positioning

1 Introduction

Location Based services (LBS) refers to services that utilizes the position estimate of a mobile station. LBS are implemented in different areas such as commercial applications, the public safety and emergency services. The demand to locate a mobile phone in emergency calls is commonly accepted as the main driving force for LBS regarding the great benefit of such services in rescuing operations. The estimated position of the mobile equipment must meet the accuracy standards, generally within 50 to 300 m in more than 67% of calls, as mandated by the Federal Communications Commission (FCC) for E-911 emergency cases [1].

Long Term Evolution or LTE network was introduced as a new standard for mobile communication networks stepping toward the 4th generation. The majority of its functions were derived from those of the 3rd generation. Moreover, new features were introduced by the LTE as the Orthogonal Frequency Division Multiple Access (OFDMA), Multiple Input Multiple Output (MIMO) data transmission and the main special addition related to the positioning domain is the Positioning Reference Signal (PRS) [2]. This new signal is dedicated only for positioning services, which make its extraction and processing easier compared to other standards (UMTS, GSM). The aim

E. Sabir et al. (Eds.): UNet 2017, LNCS 10542, pp. 461–471, 2017.
https://doi.org/10.1007/978-3-319-68179-5_40

of cellular positioning approaches is to estimate the position of a user equipment (UE) in a noisy environment without external assistance. In this context, the positions of the base stations (eNodeB) are fixed and known while those of the UEs are unknown and need to be determined [3]. Positioning techniques in cellular networks can be sorted in three main categories: Handset based (position estimated by the UE), network based (position estimated by the network units then send to the UE) and hybrid techniques (collaborative work between the handset and the network units). Since we are interested in the PRS which is a downlink dedicated positioning signal the second category will serve our goal and especially the Observed Time Difference of Arrival (OTDOA) method.

In this work, we will introduce an enhanced version of the OTDOA method called Adaptive OTDOA. This enhanced version allows us to cancel the noise effect due to propagation environment, minimize the multipath effect and reach a higher accuracy. In addition, we will analyze the performance of our approach in a worst case scenario including a Nakagami-m channel, additive white Gaussian noise and MIMO channel. In the first section, the proposed approach is presented along with a brief explanation of the used features. The second section will be dedicated to the modeling of the Nakagami-m, white Gaussian noise and MIMO channels. In the third part, the simulation environment will be discussed along with the obtained results.

2 Enhanced OTDOA or Adaptive OTDOA

2.1 Observed Time Difference of Arrival Positioning Technique

Observed Time Difference of Arrival is a real time downlink locating technique that uses the multi-lateration method (hyperbolic positioning) based on timing difference between the received signals in order to estimate the UE position. It measures the time of arrival of the PRS signals received from multiple eNodeBs. To perform the measurements, one of the eNodeBs is chosen to be the reference of time, by default is the one serving the UE at the positioning time. Geometrically, Each TDOA measurement define a hyperbola and the unknown UE position lays in their intersection. A set of three eNodeBs, at least, is needed to determine the handset location in a 2-D plan. Since the time measurements has a certain uncertainty, in reality the intersection will be an area instead of a single point [4]. The TOA measurements performed by the UE are related to the geometric distance between the UE and the eNodeBs.

We denote (xi, yi) the known coordinates of the ith eNodeB (the reference eNodeB is denoted as the 1st one) and (x, y) the unknown coordinates of the UE.

$$RSTD_{i,1} = \frac{\sqrt{(x_i - x)^2 + (y_i - y)^2}}{c} - \frac{\sqrt{(x_1 - x)^2 + (y_1 - y)^2}}{c} + (T_i - T_1) + (n_i - n_1) \tag{1}$$

Where $(T_i - T_1)$ is the time offset between the two eNodeBs referred to as RTDs (Real Time Differences), ni and n1 represent the UE Time of Arrival measurement errors and c is the speed of light.

2.2 Adaptive OTDOA

In reality, the TOA measurements are obtained via performing a cross correlation between the different versions of the PRS signal issuing from the pairs of eNodeBs, one of them should be currently serving the mobile user. A peak detection corresponds to the unknown TOA value.

The received PRS signal at the ith eNodeB can be written as:

$$PRS_i[n] = A_i PRS[n - \tau_i] + n_i[n] \quad (2)$$

Where, A_i is signal amplitude, $PRS[n - \tau_i]$ is a delayed version of the positioning reference signal PRS, and $n_i[n]$ is the attached propagation noise.

Considering that the 1st eNodeB is the one actually serving the UE, eventually, it has the shortest time of arrival among all the other stations. Then, the received PRS signals equations can be written as:

$$PRS_1[n] = A_1 PRS[n] + n_1[n] \quad (3)$$

$$PRS_i[n] = A\,PRS[n - \tau_d] + n_d[n] \quad (4)$$

Where, $\tau_d = \tau_i - \tau_1$ is the time difference of arrival between the two base stations (i and 1), and A is the amplitude ratio.

The cross-correlation equation is given as:

$$R_{1,2}[k] = \sum\nolimits_{n=-\infty}^{+\infty} PRS_1[n] PRS_2[n - k] \quad (5)$$

where k is the estimation of TDOA which correspond to a peak detection.

As shown in the previous equations modeling the received PRS signal, an additional term corresponding to the propagation noise is attached denoted by n[n]. This term affects the time measurements precision if the cross correlation is performed directly on the received signal, then the positioning accuracy will be also affected. From here came the idea of pre-filtering the received PRS signal with adaptive filters before performing the cross correlation or any other signal processing function, so we can minimize the noise effect to have more accurate position.

Previous work that we carried out aimed to enhance the accuracy of TDOA using adaptive filters as a noise cancellation system before the TOA estimation via the cross correlation [5], and so the new method is called Adaptive OTDOA (A-OTDOA). This kind of filters is controlled by an adaptive algorithm to update the filter's coefficients in function of the received signal and the error signal.

We have studied the effect of using different kind of these algorithm in order to choose the more adequate one. As presented in [6] the Normalized Least Mean Square algorithm was chosen to be the suitable one as it has shown better performances and less complexity comparing to other type of controlling algorithms (LMS and RLS). In the following, a brief introduction of the NLMS algorithm is given.

2.3 Normalized Least Mean Square Algorithm

In the standard LMS algorithm the filter's coefficients are updated according to the following equation

$$w(n+1) = w(n) + \mu\, e(n)\, r(n) \tag{6}$$

μ is the convergence factor, r(n) is the received PRS signal, and e(n) is error signal defined as e(n) = r(n) − y(n). where y(n) = w(n) r(n − Δ).

The value of the convergence factor has a great importance in the noise cancellation process. The algorithm experiences a gradient noise amplification problem if the convergence parameter is too big, and a slow convergence rate if it is too small. In order to solve this difficulty, we can use the NLMS algorithm. The correction applied to the weight vector w(n) at iteration n + 1 is "normalized" with respect to the squared Euclidian norm of the input vector r(n) at iteration n. We may view the NLMS algorithm as a time-varying step size algorithm [7], defining the convergence factor μ as

$$\mu = \frac{\alpha}{c + \|r(n)\|^2} \tag{7}$$

Where α is the NLMS adaption constant, which optimizes the convergence rate of the algorithm and should satisfy the condition $0 < \alpha < 2$. c is the constant term for normalization and is always less than 1.

So for the NLMS algorithm, the filter weights are updated by the given equation:

$$w(n+1) = w(n) + \frac{\alpha}{c + \|r(n)\|^2} e(n)\, r(n) \tag{8}$$

In order to test the performance of our method we decided to try it in a worst case scenario with no direct line of sight between the UE and the eNodeBs and a multiple fading channels. The following section introduce the fading models used in our study.

3 Propagation Channels

3.1 Nakagami-m Fading Channel

In communications theory, channel fading was experienced as an unpredictable and stochastic phenomenon for both user and system planner. However, powerful models have been developed in order to predict average system behavior accurately. Therefore, Countermeasures can be planned to avoid system failure, even if the channel exhibits fade at particular frequencies of particular locations [8].

The developed models are based on probability distributions such as Nakagami distributions, Rician distributions, and Rayleigh distributions which are used to model scattered signals that reach a receiver by multiple paths. Depending on the density of the scatter, the signal will present different fading characteristics. Rayleigh and Nakagami distributions are used to model dense scatters with no line-of-sight between the transmitter and the receiver, while Rician distributions model fading with a stronger line-of-sight. Rayleigh distributions and Rician distributions are special cases of the Nakagami distributions that's why the Nakagami model gives more control over the extent of the fading.

The Nakagami-m probability density function is given as:

$$f(x) = \frac{2}{\Gamma(m)}\left(\frac{m}{\omega}\right)^{m} x^{2m-1} e^{-\frac{mx^2}{\omega}} \tag{9}$$

Where $\Gamma(.)$ is the Gamma function and $\omega = 2\sigma^2 = E\{x^2\}$.

With shape parameter m and scale parameter $\omega > 0$, for $x > 0$. If x has a Nakagami distribution with parameters μ and ω, then x^2 has a gamma distribution with shape parameter m and scale parameter ω/m [9].

3.2 MIMO Channel

Since we are interested in the effect of a Nakagami-m fading channel, we chosen a simple MIMO channel with additive white Gaussian noise (AWGN). The transmitted signal T_x reaches the receiver's antenna via an already set model of the propagation channel. The MIMO fading channel model emulates the effects of the multipath propagation while The AWGN represents the co-channel interference.

The delay profile chosen is an EPA 5 Hz corresponding to a maximum Doppler frequency of 5 Hz [10]. The antennas configuration between the eNodeB and the UE is a 2×2 scheme.

4 LTE Simulation Environment

In this section, we will present our LTE simulation environment based on Matlab software. This simulation environment (or simulator) was subject of a published paper [11]. This tool was designed and tested according to the 3GPP requirements in order to emulate the behavior of an LTE transmitter, receiver and a MIMO channel for positioning purposes (only the Positioning Reference Signal and the Cell Reference Signal were generated). Firstly, we will describe the cellular structure or topology then we will introduce the global structure of the LTE link simulator.

4.1 Network Topology

The network cells are designed as a regular hexagonal pattern. The eNodeBs are placed each in the center of a hexagon with a distance of 500 m. To avoid an eventual underestimation of the total interference in the system a 7-cell topology is chosen [12] as shown in the following Fig. 1.

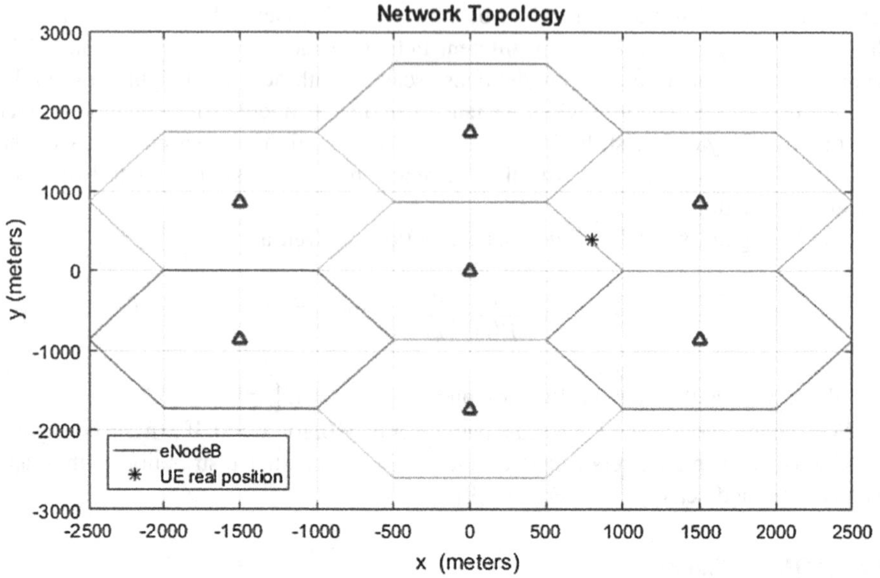

Fig. 1. Network topology

4.2 Designed LTE Link Simulator

The link allowing a wireless communication between the UE and the eNodeBs is modeled Based on the system-level radio network model presented in [11]. Time measurements obtained by this link will be processed in order to estimate the user position. The link-level simulator model includes an LTE transmitter, a MIMO communication and propagation channel and an LTE receiver.

LTE Transmitter Model

As shown in Fig. 2, we have two blocks within the transmitter model of our simulator: the transport channel processing block and the physical channel processing block according to the standards set by the 3GPP [13].

Transport Channel. In this block we perform data generation, Cyclic Redundancy Code (CRC) generation and attachment, turbo coding and rate matching.

Physical Channel. In the physical channel processing block the encoded data is coded and transmitted to the UE [14]. The main functions of this block are:

(a) Scrambling of coded bits
(b) Modulation of scrambled bits (here a 16QAM is used)
(c) Layer mapping (in our case spatial multiplexing with 2 antenna ports and 2 layers)
(d) Pre-coding
(e) Mapping to resource elements
(f) Generation of Cell Specific Reference Signal (CSR) and the Positioning Reference Signal (PRS)
(g) Generation of the OFDM signal for each antenna port.

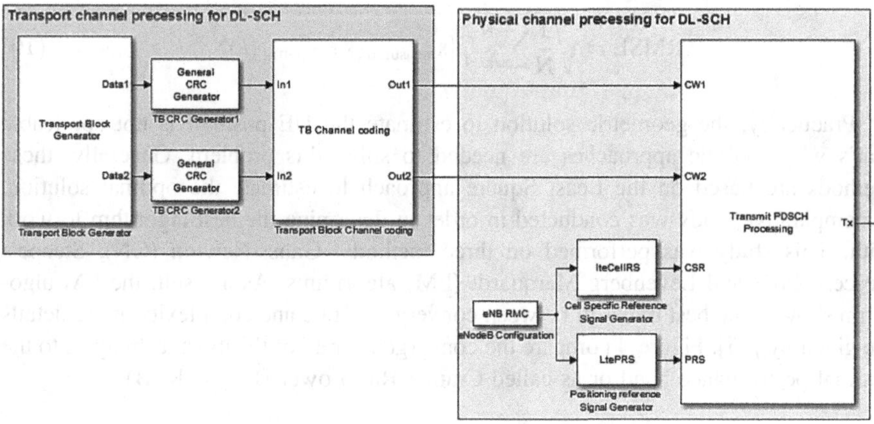

Fig. 2. LTE transmitter block diagram.

LTE receiver Model.
At the reception this block performs the inverse functions of these already done by the transmitter in order to extract the reference signals (PRS and CRS) and the original sent code words as shown in Fig. 3.

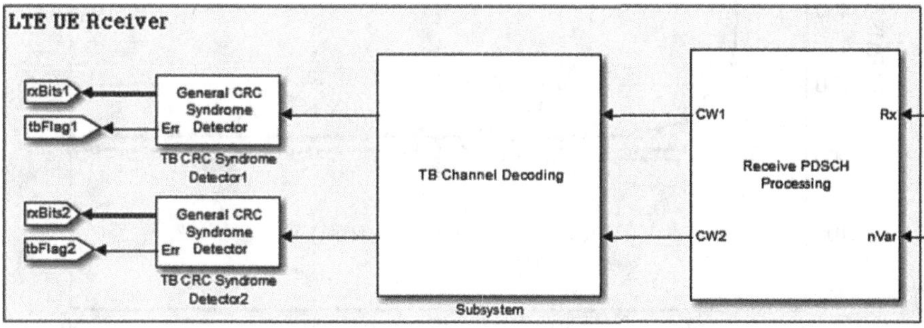

Fig. 3. LTE user equipment receiver

5 Results Discussion

Computer simulation was done by MATLAB software, using the designed LTE link simulator and communication toolbox in order to build the channel models.

To evaluate the accuracy parameter of the positioning methods, the Root Mean Square Error is used, which can be defined as the difference between the estimated and the true position of the UE as given by the following equation:

$$\text{RMSE} = \sqrt{\frac{1}{N}\sum\nolimits_{k=1}^{N}\left[x_{\text{measured}}(k) - x_{\text{true}}(k)\right]^2} \tag{10}$$

Practically, the geometric solution to estimate the UE position is not applicable that's why analytic approaches are needed to solve this problem. Generally, these methods are based on the Least Square approach to estimate the optimal solution. A comparative study was conducted in order to determine the best algorithm to work with. This study was performed on three methods: Gauss-Newton (GN), Steepest Descent (SD) and Levenberg Marquardt (LM) algorithms. As a result, the LM algorithm showed the best trade-off between convergence rate and complexity, more details are given by [15]. Figure 4 compare the convergence rate of the three techniques to the optimal performance band or as called Cramer Rao Lower Band (CRLB).

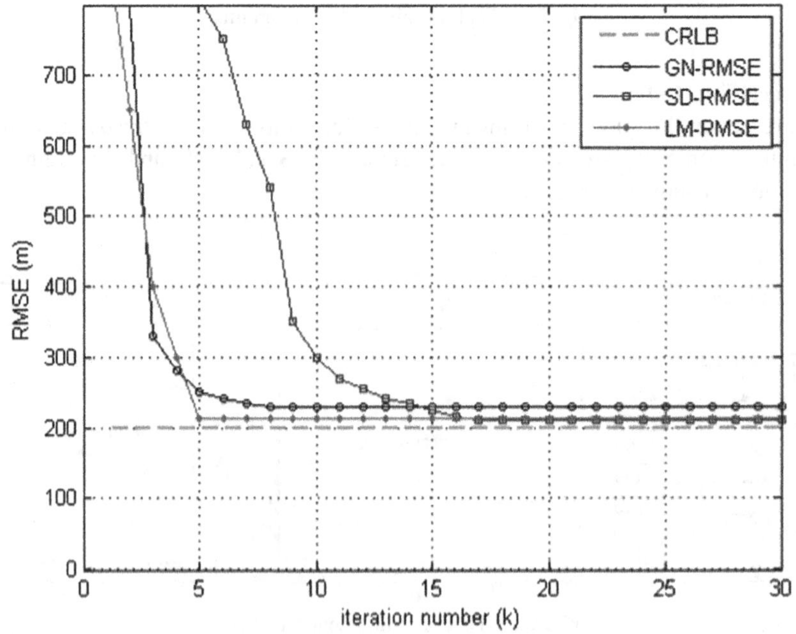

Fig. 4. RMSE vs iteration number k for σ^n = 200 m

In this part, we investigate the accuracy of our method compared with the standard OTDOA in different propagation conditions. At first, Fig. 5 shows the accuracy obtained by the OTDA technique when the propagation environment is an AWGN channel, a MIMO channel and a Nakagami channel. The RMSE (or accuracy error) should be between 50 m and 300 m for all the developed positioning methods in more than 67% of calls according to the FCC E-911 criteria.

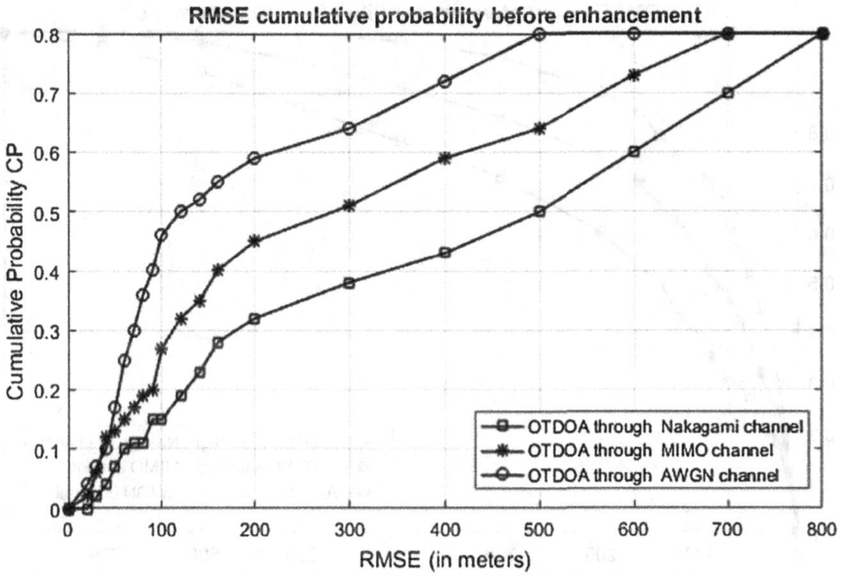

Fig. 5. OTDOA RMSE cumulative probability before enhancement.

Table 1 summarize the obtained results before enhancement for the acceptable error interval [50 m–300 m]. The RMSE value decreases with the change of channel from a simple model (AWGN) to a more complicated one (Nakagami-m). The desired 67% criteria cannot be obtained even with the higher marge of error (300 m) even for the simplest model.

Table 1. Accuracy values before enhancement

Propagation channels	RMSE (m)		
	50	100	300
AWGN	18%	47%	64%
MIMO	13%	28%	51%
Nakagami-m	8%	15%	48%

With the enhancement given to the OTDOA technique by adding the adaptive filtering process (A-OTDOA) method it is clearly shown by Fig. 6 and Table 2 that the accuracy has reached significantly high levels even for the worst case scenario with the Nakagami-m fading channel. It was enhanced by 22%, 25% and 22% for 50 m, 100 m and 300 m RMSE respectively.

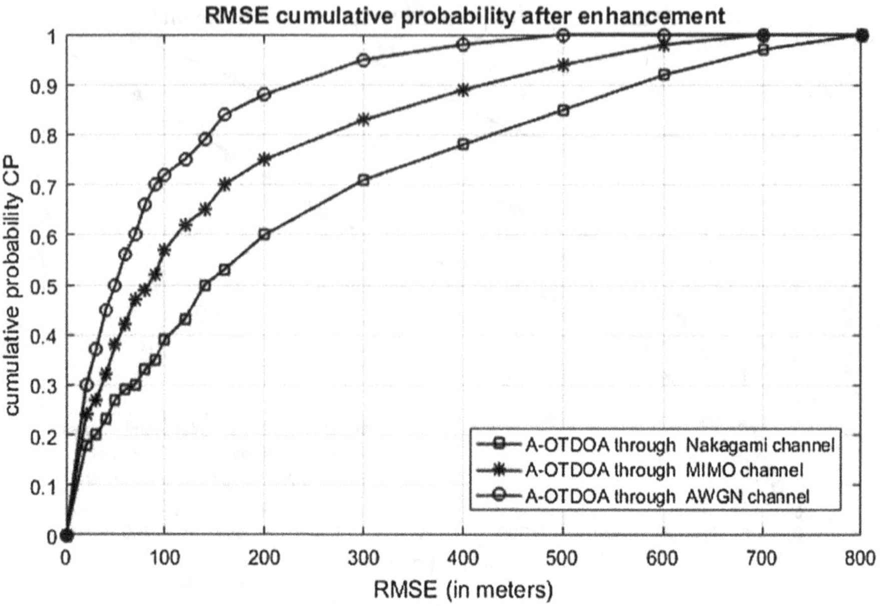

Fig. 6. OTDOA RMSE cumulative probability after enhancement.

Table 2. Accuracy values before enhancement

Propagation channels	RMSE (m)		
	50	100	300
AWGN	50%	72%	95%
MIMO	42%	68%	83%
Nakagami-m	30%	40%	70%

6 Conclusion

As shown in the study carried out through this paper, OTDOA enhancement based on adaptive filtering can increase enormously the accuracy of mobile positioning, and compensate the degradation caused by the propagation noise and multipath. The developed method for LTE users has shown high performance level through different kind of propagation channels even in a worst case scenario with no Line-Of-Sight (LOS) as for the Nakagami-m distributions fading channel. In this paper, the enhancement was investigated in a fixed and known mobile position in outdoor, ongoing works aim to improve this technique to take in charge the mobility of users and extend it to indoor areas.

Acknowledgment. This work falls within the scope of telecommunication projects. Our sincere thanks to the Faculty of Sciences and Technology, Hassan II University, Mohammedia, Morocco, for providing us an opportunity to carry out our work in a well-equipped laboratory (EEA & TI). We are also thankful to all our colleagues who helped us while working on this project.

References

1. FCC official website: 9-1-1 and E9-1-1 Services. https://www.fcc.gov/general/9-1-1-and-e9-1-1-services
2. Adusei, I.K., Kyamakya, K., Jobmann, K.: Mobile positioning technologies in cellular networks: an evaluation of their performance metrics
3. Damosso, E.: Digital Mobile Radio towards Future Generation Systems (1999). http://kom.aau.dk/antprop/pub/cost231.html
4. Fisher, S.: Observed Time Difference Of Arrival (OTDOA) Positioning in 3GPP LTE. Qualcomm technologies Inc
5. El Mourabit, I., Sahel, A., Badri, A., Baghdad, A.: Enhanced mobile positioning technique for UMTS users in both outdoor and indoor environments. In: IEEE Xplore Digital Library, January 2015
6. El Mourabit, I., Sahel, A., Badri, A., Baghdad, A.: Performance of multiple adaptive algorithms for uplink time difference of arrival positioning technique. Int. J. Emerg. Trends Eng. Dev. **1**(5), 143–155 (2015). ISSN 2249-6149
7. El Mourabit, I., Sahel, A., Badri, A., Baghdad, A.: Comparative study of the least mean square and normalized least mean square adaptive filters for positioning purposes. In: 14th Mediterranean Microwave Symposium (mms), Marrakech. IEEE, pp. 1–4 (2014)
8. Nakagami Distributions in Matlab: https://www.mathworks.com/help/stats/nakagami-distribution.html
9. Vaishnav, S., Dholariya, T.: Performance analysis of 8 × 8 MIMO system for LTE-A in Nakagami-m fading channel. In: International Conference on Communication and Signal Processing, 3–5 April 2014, India (2014)
10. Propagation Channel Model: https://www.mathworks.com/help/lte/propagation-channel-models.html?searchHighlight=epa&s_tid=doc_srchtitle
11. El Mourabit, I., Badri, A., Sahel, A., Baghdad, A.: LTE mobile positioning and tracking simulator using Kalman filter. In: The International Conference on Wireless Networks and Mobile Communications Wincom 2016, at fez – morocco (2016)
12. Technical Specification Group Radio Access Networks, Radio Frequency (RF) system scenarios (Release 9), 3GPP, Technical Specification 3G TS 25.942 v. 9.0.0, December 2009
13. 3rd Generation Partnership Project; Technical Specification Group Radio Access Network; Evolved Universal Terrestrial Radio Access (E-UTRA); Base Station (BS) radio transmission and reception
14. 3rd Generation Partnership Project; Technical Specification Group Radio Access Network; Evolved Universal Terrestrial Radio Access (E-UTRA); Physical Channels and Modulation (Release 9)
15. El Mourabit, I., Badri, A., Sahel, A., Baghdad, A.: Hyperbolic equation solving algorithms for LTE mobile positioning using TDOA measurements. In: International Conference on Information Technologies and Integrated Production Systems, Mai 2016, Oujda, Morocco (2016)

Chaotic ZKP Based Authentication and Key Distribution Scheme in Environmental Monitoring CPS

Wided Boubakri, Walid Abdallah(✉), and Noureddine Boudriga

Communication Networks and Security Research Lab, University of Carthage, Tunis, Tunisia
ab.walid@gmail.com

Abstract. The Cyber Physical System (CPS) is an open system that combines physical, computational, and communication capabilities and bridges between the physical world and the cyber world. Based on the feedback loops between the computation components and the physical process, the CPS could implement the function of real-time sensing and dynamic monitoring. In particular, CPS that is implemented for environment monitoring can use Machine-to-Machine (M2M) communication, where devices could be deployed in a hostile and time-varying environments and may be the target of many attacks. Therefore, providing security for the exchanged data is one of the main requirements to allow the accomplishment of the CPS's mission. This paper proposes a chaotic Zero Knowledge Proof (ZKP) authentication and key distribution scheme to ensure security in a CPS. In this scheme, the chaotic Chebyshev polynomial is investigated to generate private and public keys whilst the ZKP protocol is used to validate the identity and the device's public key. We demonstrate the efficiency of the proposed scheme and its resilience to man-in-the-middle attack. Also, we show that the achievement of key generation and distribution induces less energy consumption and reduces false rejection and acceptance rates.

Keywords: CPS · M2M · Security · Authentication · Chaotic · ZKP

1 Introduction

A cyber physical system (CPS) integrates computational and physical capabilities and ranges from relatively small systems, such as aircraft or automobile, to large-scale systems including national power grid, public safety, health monitoring, etc. Particularly, an environmental monitoring CPS can provide means to monitor water quality and leakages, evaluate air pollution level, gather radiation intensity, and detect forest fire. This complex systems is based on the interaction with the physical system to ensure a real time reporting and a dynamic actuation. The ability to interact with the physical process through communication capabilities makes security in environment monitoring CPS critical since in

E. Sabir et al. (Eds.): UNet 2017, LNCS 10542, pp. 472–483, 2017.
https://doi.org/10.1007/978-3-319-68179-5_41

such a large scale application, machines could be deployed in uncontrolled and even hostile environment and could be the target of many attacks. Consequently, implementing security services is very crucial to ensure an efficient and reliable operation. In particular, authentication and encryption services are required to provide both devices and data exchange security. In this context, some research works got interested in developing authentication protocols for CPSs [2,4,6].

In [6], authors proposed a certificateless signature scheme for mobile wireless CPSs based on the bilinear Diffie-Hellman assumption. In this technique, the user exploits its identity, a secret value, and the system's public parameters to compute its private and public keys. In contrast to traditional public key encryption techniques, this scheme does not require certificates management to verify the validity of the public key. Authors evaluated the efficiency of the proposed scheme under the black hole and the rushing attacks. However, due to the lack of public key authentication, this scheme is still vulnerable to the man-in-the middle attack.

In [7], authors designed a Polynomial-based Compromise-Resilient En-route Filtering scheme that can filter false injected data. In this work, the Message Authentication Codes (MAC) is replaced by a pool of authentication polynomial which is used to endorse sensor authentication and then mitigate node impersonating attacks against legitimate devices. This scheme seems to be efficient in terms of ensuring security but using a pool of authentication polynomial for sensor devices may requires extensive computational and storage resources which increases the deployment cost. In [4], authors proposed a dynamic-encryption mechanism to authenticate mobiles devices in the M2M communication network where a set of encryption algorithms defined by an index is provided. Moreover, in each authentication procedure, the mobile device and the M-to-M service provider (MSP) shall select the same encryption algorithm. The security functionality has been significantly improved by applying the proposed lightweight encryption algorithm. However, it still depends on the size of the pre-shared key space.

The main objective of this paper is to design an appropriate authentication and key distribution scheme for environmental monitoring applications based CPS. Therefore, Chaotic Zero Knowledge Proof (ZKP) authentication and key distribution scheme is proposed to provide authentication, integrity, and confidentiality services. The proposal exploits firstly the chaotic Chebyshev polynomial properties to generate the private key from the device identity and to derive the corresponding public key, and then the ZKP protocol is used to prove the authenticity of the generated public key. This will allow device identity verification before data exchange and prevent vulnerability to the man-in-the-middle attack. The designed ZKP protocol is less complex and requires reduced message exchanges than existing schemes whilst it improves the offered security level. The usage of the chaotic encryption using the Chebyshev polynomial map ensures a dynamic and independent key generation and derivation. In addition, the deployment of the probabilistic ZKP protocol to authenticate machines ensures not only the network security but also it takes into account the capacity and the resource constraint of each machine. Consequently, the main contributions of this work with respect to existing literature are as follows:

- The design of an environmental monitoring CPS architecture that involves the M2M communication to ensure an efficient and real time management;
- The establishment of a distributed chaotic Zero Knowledge Proof (ZKP) scheme to ensure authentication and security in the machine-to-machine network that support the CPS operation. This scheme consists on generating chaotic keys based on the machine identity and then using the ZKP to prove its authenticity;

The remaining parts of the paper are as follows: Sect. 2 presents the adopted environmental monitoring system architecture and assesses security requirements. Section 3, describes firstly the proposed chaotic ZKP based authentication and key distribution scheme then it analyzes the security level provided by the proposed scheme. Section 4 is devoted to present simulation work conducted to evaluate the effectiveness of the proposed scheme. Section 5, concludes the paper by summarizing the achieved work.

2 Environmental Monitoring CPS Architecture

In this section, we present the architecture of CPS used to monitor events in a physical area. We adopted an hierarchical network topology where different kinds of devices are deployed to perform diverse processing tasks. We begin by describing the different network elements as well as their deployment and then we analysis security requirements of the network topology.

2.1 Environmental Monitoring CPS Topology

A typical environmental monitoring CPS architecture consists of three major tiers: (i) sensing and acquisition tier which is composed of different types of machines including sensor nodes as well as smartphones, (ii) processing and control tier which can be implemented using cloud technology, and (iii) service and action tier that could be formed by the different types of actuators. The first tier is responsible of collecting information from physical system and sending gathered report to the second tier which is handled by the distributed controllers. After processing the information, the controllers communicate with the actuators to issue appropriate actuation and operations. Then, the actuators will act to impose the physical world through activating the related operations and generate feedback. An architectural map of the environmental monitoring CPS is shown in Fig. 1.

Sensing and acquisition tier: The major function of this tier in the environmental monitoring CPS is to collect and transmit the environmental information over the communication network. The fundamental feature of this tier is to sense, aggregate and transmit the information to the processing and control

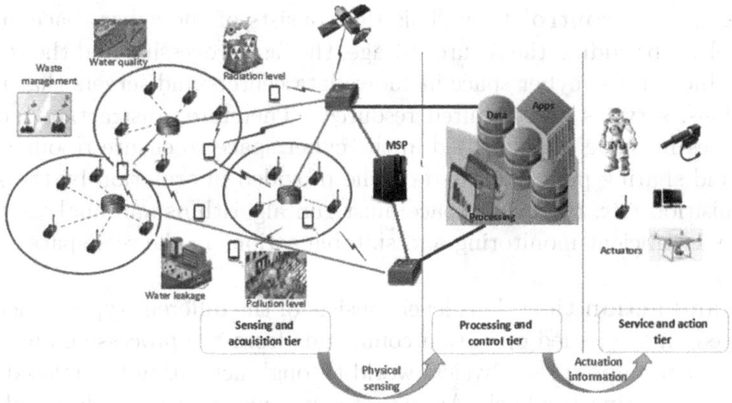

Fig. 1. Environmental monitoring CPS structure

tier without human intervention. This is based on an M2M communication or Machine-Type-Communication (MTC) paradigm where intelligent and programmable devices will communicate to each other end-to-end. The M2M communication encompasses three layers: (i) an M2M area domain including an M2M area network with server gateways, (ii) a communication network domain including wired/wireless networks such as xDSL, 4G and eventually 5G, and (iii) An application services domain consists of the M2M Service Provider (MSP) and the end users applications required in the CPS for environmental monitoring services The M2M area in the CPS for environmental monitoring application integrates structured and unstructured machines laid out over the monitoring area forming terrestrial, underwater, underground and mobile networks. The structured machines could be considered as the Wireless sensor networks that consist of numerous sensor nodes which are deployed in a pre-defined manner at strategic locations, to ensure an effective and periodic measures of different environmental parameters (water, air, waste, radiation, etc.).

Sensor nodes are grouped into clusters and each cluster is managed by a sub-gateway that is responsible of gathering data from nodes under its control and forward it to the serving gateway that must be equipped with a larger amount of resources, such as storage capacity and communication range. On the other hand, unstructured machines are presented by the set of the deployed smartphones that could be either equipped with specific sensors to take measures when they are near to a specific environmental parameter or they could gather data from closet sensors and transmit it to the processing and control tier. The deployment of smartphones may enhance the data acquisition and the real time sensing. The collected information from the environment will be delivered from the M2M area domain to the network domain via server gateways which decide about the used communication protocols and convert the received information into the formats required by the corresponding communication systems. The communication systems in the network domain can be of any type such as WLANs, satellite or cellular networks. The information must be transmitted to the processing and control tier to be at the end integrated into various environmental applications.

Processing and control tier: This tier consists of the cyber space and it is responsible of providing the secure storage, the fast processing and the real-time analytic. Indeed, the cyber space includes data centers and servers that provide applications, services and required resources. Therefore, abstraction tools and technologies must be implemented in the cyber space to ensure resource provisioning and sharing policies. Based on the provided information by the sensing and acquisition tier, the cyber space must run algorithms and analytic process to ensure an efficient monitoring and suitable actions in the real space.

Service and action tier: This level consists of the different types of actuators that, based on the issued operation commands from the processing and control tier, will act to impose the physical world through activating the related operations and generating feedback. An actuator is a mechanical or electrical device for moving or controlling a mechanism, thus enabling a system to perform a physical function by converting an electrical signal to a physical interaction on the environment. Actuators may be stand-alone (i.e. just an output device), or may be combined with a smart structure like an IoT input sensor in order to generate the appropriate response to a detected environmental variation.

2.2 Security Requirements

The environmental monitoring CPS is a distributed, complex and hybrid real-time dynamic system with many different types of critical applications operating at different time and space scales. Based on the input from the physical environment, the cyber space may analyze data, run algorithms and decide the suitable actions. Therefore, an attacker does not need to break into the cloud of processing to affect a such system, but could cause a coordinated series of physical actions that are sensed and which incite the system to respond in an unexpected manner. Indeed, an attacker could masquerade as a legal user to steal information or insert wrong information into the system. Hence, when a machine receives a message, it must verify that it is transmitted from an identified and authentic origin. Therefore, an authentication mechanism should be established between different machines. However, the sensing and acquisition tier could be composed by an important number of devices that are deployed through a specific environment. Thereby, the authentication scheme should be scalable to any network size by ensuring efficiency and security features for small-size as well as large size networks whilst taking into account the resource constraints of the deployed machines. On the other hand, an intruder can easily access to the wireless medium and may be able to capture transmitted data and even inject forgery messages. Consequently, sensing data and transmitted information must be encrypted to ensure confidentiality. Cryptographic primitives using symmetric keys must be established between machines before the data exchange. Consequently, specific key distribution scheme should be developed to securely share different secret keys between the different machines. The key distribution scheme must be flexible to cope with the dynamic topology of the CPS.

3 Authentication and Key Distribution Scheme

This section describes the proposed chaotic ZKP authentication and key distribution scheme. Our objective is to ensure authentication, confidentiality and integrity services by combining different protocols. Firstly, we use the chaotic Chebyshev polynomial to dynamically construct a private key from a given machine identity and its corresponding public key. We investigate then the ZKP protocol to prove the authenticity of the machine's identity and validate its chaotic public key.

3.1 Chaotic Based Key Generation

In our scheme, we assume that each deployed machine m in the sensing and acquisition tier can be identified by a sequence of numbers: $ID_m = k_1 k_2 k_3 \ldots k_v$ where v is the length of the identity. We suppose also that all identities are manged and stored in the MSP data base. Each machine must generate a pair of private and public keys using chaotic Chebyshev polynomial map. This chaotic map is characterized by its sensitivity to the initial conditions, random behavior, continuous broadband power spectrum and a polynomial complexity which ensure a high security cleveland fit the limited resources of the deployed machines. In our scheme we adopted the extended Chebyshev polynomial described in [1] and defined as: $T_n(x) : \mathbb{Z}p \rightarrow \mathbb{Z}p : T_n(x) = 2xT_{n-1}(x) - T_{n-2}(x)\, mod(p)$ where p is a large prime and n, $x \in Z_p^*$. The initial terms of this map are $T_0(x) = 1\, mod\,(p)$ and $T_1(x) = x\, mod\,(p)$. The Chebyshev polynomial is a useful tool to securely share the pairwise keys thanks to its semi-group property characterized by the following equality. Given two elements r and n belonging to Z_p^* we have: $T_n(T_r(x))\, mod(p) = T_r(T_n(x))\, mod(p) = T_{r.n}(x)\, mod(p)$.

Before deployment, each machine must be pre-configured with the numbers x, p, and a sequence of secret prime numbers that has the same length as its identity, $S = S_1 S_2 S_3 \ldots S_v$. At its bootstrap period the machine m calculates its private key $n = S_1^{k_1} * S_2^{k_2} * S_3^{k_3} * \ldots * S_v^{k_n}$ and its corresponding chaotic public key $B = T_n(x)\, mod\,(p)$. It then deletes the sequence S from its memory to prevent its disclose in case of machine capture and hence threaten the security of the key generation process.

3.2 Chaotic Based ZKP Authentication and Key Distribution Scheme

Before initiating any communication, each machine must be authenticated. We investigate, in this work, the employment of a Zero Knowledge Proof (ZKP) protocol to achieve machine authentication and public key validation procedures. This has the advantage of reducing the bandwidth, computational power, and memory requirements when compared to traditional public key based authentication protocols [3]. The ZKP is an interactive proof system that consists of a prover P, and verifier V, where the role of the prover P is to convince the verifier V that he possesses an authentic private key through a series of communications without ever revealing it. These proofs are based on a series of steps and some computed values related to the private key of the prover. In this work, we design a chaotic probabilistic ZKP protocol where the verification process takes the form of a questionnaire provided at each iteration and it is completely independent from the others given in previous iterations. The motivation of adopting a such approach is that the verifier could configure the authentication protocol executed by each machine according to its capacity and its relevant vulnerability level to be at the end convinced of its authenticity with a certain accuracy probability. Given the limited resources of most deployed machines, we adopted a distributed authentication that is performed between the machine and the serving sub-gateway. In our work, the sub-gateway is considered as the verifier that should flip at each iteration a coin and based on its outcome it may ask the machine (prover) to provide a specific value.

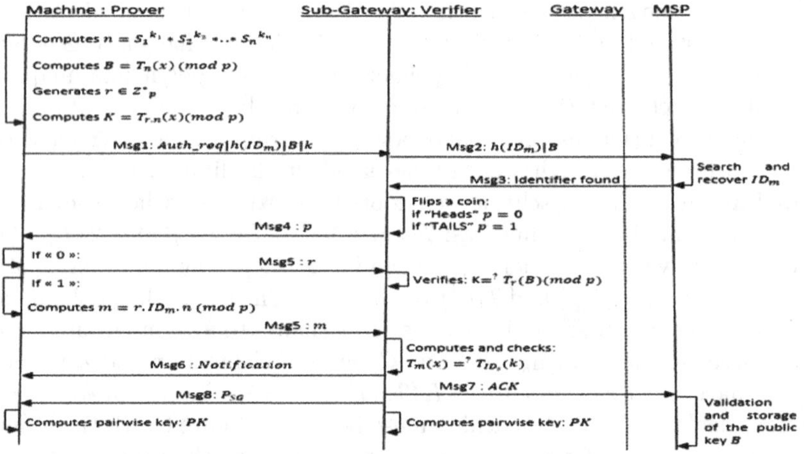

Fig. 2. The chaotic ZKP authentication scheme

The authentication scenario is summarized in the diagram depicted by Fig. 2 where we can distinguish the following steps:

1. After generating its pair of private and public keys, the machine chooses a large random value $r \in Z_p^*$ and computes a chaotic value $k = T_{r.n}(x)\ (mpd\, p)$ that involves its private key n. Then it sends an authentication request with its identity $h(ID_m)$, its public key B and the chaotic number k to the serving sub-gateway;
2. The serving gateway forwards this request to the MSP which will search in its data base the machine identity corresponding to the received hash value. Once the identity was found the MSP authorizes the sub-gateway to initiate the authentication procedure;
3. The sub-gateway flips a coin and informs the machine about the Boolean outcome denoted as p. If $p = 0$, the machine sends the value r to the sub-gateway that must in its turn use it as a Chebyshev polynomial degree and the machine

public key as an input and computes the corresponding chaotic value $T_r(B)$. The outcome of this polynomial will be compared to the already received k by verifying the equality: $T_r(B) = T_r(T_n(x)) = T_{r.n}(x) = k$. Otherwise, if $p = 1$, the machine computes the number $m = r.ID_m.n(mod\, p)$ and sends it to the serving sub-gateway which uses the received m as Chebyshev polynomial degree to compute the chaotic value $T_m(x)$ and compare it to the outcome of the chaotic value $T_{ID_m}(k)$ by using the machine identity as a Chebyshev polynomial degree and the value k as the polynomial input. We have $T_{ID_m}(k) = T_{D_m}(T_{r.n}(x))\,(mpd\,p) = T_{n.ID_m.r}(x)\,(mpd\,p) = T_m(x)\,(mpd\,p)$;

4. The sub-gateway sends to the relevant machine a notification which could be a negative acknowledgment (if the compared values are not equal) or a request to repeat the authentication process (if the compared values are equal but the sub-gateway is not yet convinced) or also a positive acknowledgment (if the sub-gateway is convinced that the machine knows the secret value n). In the last case, the machine is considered as authentic and the serving gateway sends a positive ACK to the MSP which validates the machine public key B and saves it in its data base;
5. Finally, the sub-gateway sends its public key $P_{SG} = T_u(x)\,(mod\,p)$ to the authenticated machine. Consequently, the machine and the sub-gateway could generate a shared pairwise key, P_k by applying the semi-group property: $P_k = T_n(T_u(x))\,(mod\,p) = T_u(T_n(x))\,(mod\,p) = T_{n.u}(x)\,(mod\,p)$.

   It is worthy to note that steps 1 and 3 are repeated k times until the sub-gateway is convinced with an accuracy probability equal to $1 - 2^{-k}$ that the machine knows the private key n. In addition, to enhance the security level of the authentication scheme, the machine credentials and the established pairwise keys must be updated periodically at the beginning of each re-keying period. At the end of the validity period of the current key, each machine must generate a new sequence of prime number and use it to establish the new private key n' as the trapdoor information, then it derives the corresponding chaotic public key B' that must also be validated and saved in the MSP data base. To this end, the relevant machine must send its identity, the previous and the new public keys B and B' respectively to the MSP that must remove B from its memory and replace it with B'. After that, the MSP communicates the new public key to the serving sub-gateway to update the pairwise shared key P'_k.

3.3 Security Analysis

The CPS is an heterogeneous and real-time system where machines are vulnerable to many security attacks including the Man-in-the-Middle. In this subsection, we evaluate the efficiency of the proposed authentication protocol and then the robustness of our approach in preventing a such security attacks.

Chebyshev polynomial based public key encryption security: The machine private key n is considered as a trapdoor information that can be written as: $n = S_1^{k1} \dots S_m^{km}$. This private key is used as a Chebyshev polynomial degree to derive the corresponding chaotic public key $B = T_n(x)$. We assume that an adversary can obtain the pair $(T_n(x), x)$, to find n, it must compute $T_r(x)$ for all $r = S_1^{k1} \dots S_l^{km}$, $l \in Z$ and compare one by one if $T_n(x) = T_r(x)$. This has been proved in [1] as infeasible in the case of large n.

ZKP with coin flip protocol security: To prove its authenticity, a given machine must use its private key n to firstly compute the chaotic value $k = T_{r.n}(x)$ and then the trapdoor information $m = n.r.ID_m$, where r is a random number. This is performed without revealing the private key n. The two values k and m are considered as challenges for the adversary which as long as it cannot access to the private key it could not guess them. This can ensure the robustness of the proposed authentication scheme.

Security against Man-in-the-Middle Attack: In this case an attacker will try to intercept the authentication procedure and impersonate the machine (prover) in order to make an independent connection with the sub-gateway (verifier) as a legitimate machine. In our proposal, the authentication is based on a possession proof of the private key that never gets transmitted and the intruder cannot guess it because it is a trapdoor information based on random numbers. Consequently, the intruder could never provide the two challenge values k and m that the authentication protocol is based on. In another scenario, the intruder tries to subvert the encryption and gain access to the clear-text. In our model, this could not be performed since the pairwise key establishment procedure is based on the semi group property where each entity has the half of the shared key and generates the full key independently using its own private key which cannot be transmitted on the network.

4 Performance Evaluation

In this section, we assess the communication and security efficiency of the proposed authentication method by evaluating its energy consumption, its resilience to nodes compromising and its false acceptance and rejection rates. To this end, we developed a simulation model using Matlab software where we consider an M2M network deployed on a smart city to monitor and control environmental related events. In this network machines are randomly deployed through the monitored area and are structured in a hierarchical topology where the number of the sub-gateways was taken as 2% of the total number of machines. In each simulation, we randomly generate a network topology, we execute the authentication procedure between machines and sub-gateways, and evaluate performance parameters consisting on the total amount of energy consumed to accomplish the authentication, the compromised link ratio, the False Acceptance Rate (FAR), and the False Rejection Rate (FRR). Each simulation is repeated 5 times and the final result is the average calculated on values obtained in all simulations. We firstly assess the variation of the energy consumption of the global authentication and key distribution procedure with the accuracy probability which depends on the number of iterations k executed to ensure the validity of the machine identity and the corresponding public key. This is performed for different number of re-keying procedures. Figure 3 depicts the simulation results where we can see that the energy consumption increases with the accuracy probability. This can be explained by the fact that our authentication scheme is based on the probabilistic ZKP protocol which require iterative repetition of the identity verification process until the Verifier be convinced about the authenticity of the machine according to the configured accuracy probability. This will generate more communication overhead and contribute in a higher energy consumption level. On the other hand, with a fixed verification probability, when the number of the re-keying procedures increases the total energy consumption increases because machines must consume more energy to update their credentials and validate the new public key. Finally, we can see that configuring the ZKP protocol with an accuracy probability equal to 0.95 can achieve a moderate energy consumption with an acceptable risk of accepting unauthorized machines.

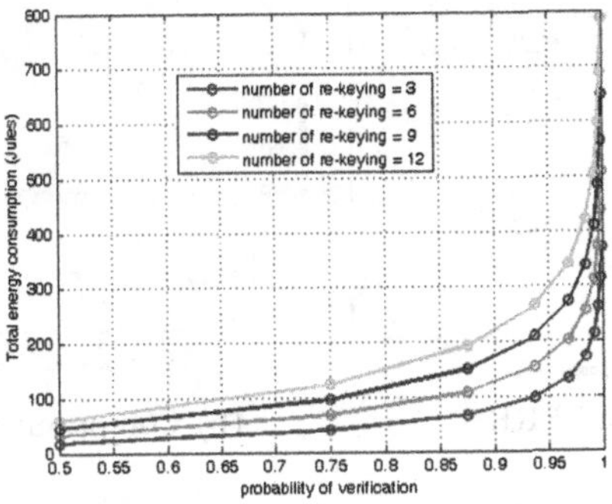

Fig. 3. Total energy vs verification probability and re-keying number

We evaluate now the efficiency of the proposed authentication scheme in terms of FAR and FRR. The FAR reflects the possibility that a non authentic machine is wrongly accepted by the authentication scheme while the FRR evaluates the probability that an authentic machine is faulty rejected. Recall, that in the proposed authentication scheme at each iteration, a given machine must be able to prove that it possesses secret chaotic value to be considered as authentic and which must be successfully verified by the sub-gateway. In this performance evaluation work, we adopted a random verification method, where at each iteration we randomly choose a Boolean number. When the chosen Boolean is equal to "0" this means that the chaotic values transmitted by the machine are not valid. However, when it is equal to "1" this means that they had been successfully validated by the sub-gateway. A machine is considered as authentic if and only if all Boolean values are equal to "1" otherwise it considered as impersonated machine. The two curves presented by Fig. 4a depict the variation of FAR and FRR in function of the accuracy probability. We can observe that the

FRR increases with the accuracy probability however the FAR decreases. The variation is more rapid when the accuracy probability is near 1. This is predictable, because when the accuracy probability increases the selectivity of the system increases and consequently the likelihood of rejecting authentic machines is higher while the probability of accepting false ones is lower. In another hand, as is depicted by Fig. 4a, the FAR and the FRR variation curves cross in a point corresponding to the an accuracy probability equal to 0.93 which is equivalent to an iteration number equal to 4. In this context, this value could considered as, the threshold that could be used by the ZKP based authentication protocol to efficiently separate the impostors from the authorized machines. Consequently, all machines that will reach a verification probability above this value will be considered as authentic otherwise they will be classified as originated from an impostor.

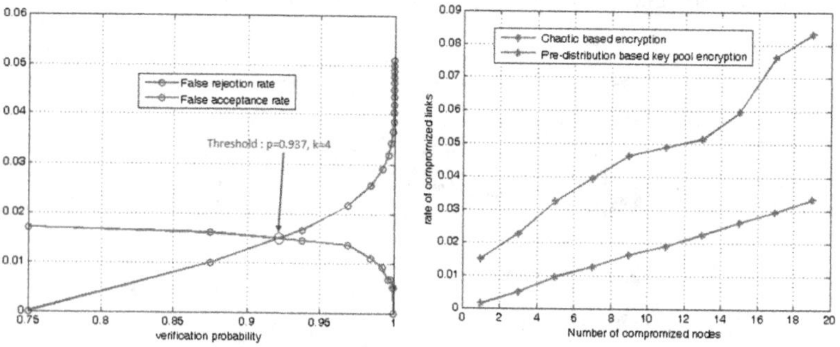

(a) FAR and FRR

(b) Compromised links ratio

Fig. 4. Security performances evaluation

A very important performance criteria to evaluate key distribution techniques in M2M networks is their resilience to node compromise. This is because in an M2M networks machines are generally unattended and therefore several ones of them could be captured by an adversary. Therefore, to assess the security efficiency of the designed authentication and key distribution scheme, we evaluate the ratio of the compromised links in the network when a given number of machines are captured by an attacker. We compare the performances of our scheme to the pre-distribution based key pool encryption scheme [5]. We vary the number of compromised nodes from 1 to 20 nodes. We can observe that the ratio of compromised links when using our scheme is less than the basic key pre-distribution technique. This can be argued by the fact that, in our work each machine generates a private key as a random trapdoor information and it derives the corresponding chaotic public key, hence it is infeasible that two machine will be able to generate the same public key. Consequently, when a node is captured only links that are secured using shared keys generated from its public key will be compromised. However, in the pre-distribution based key encryption scheme, each node is pre-loaded by a set of keys that are randomly selected from the same pool of keys. Hence, the same key can be used to secure communication of many links established between different nodes and especially when the size of the pool is reduced. Therefore, in the pre-distribution scheme, capturing several nodes can reveal keys used by non-captured ones.

5 Conclusion

In this paper, we addressed security issues in an M2M network implemented in an environment monitoring CPS by establishing a chaotic ZKP based authentication and key distribution scheme. The designed security scheme ensures a scalable authentication with a decreased error rate and can cope with the heterogeneity of the deployed machines. The authentication procedure uses the ZKP protocol to verify the identity of the machine and validate its public key by applying the chaotic Chebyshev polynomial map as a trapdoor function and its semi-group property. Performance evaluation using simulation work demonstrates that our scheme ensures an efficient security level while reducing false acceptance and rejection rates and optimizing the communication overhead needed to perform machine to machine authentication.

References

1. Algehawi, M.B., Samsudin, A.: A new identity based encryption IBE scheme using extended Chebyshev map over finite fields Zp. Phys. Lett. **42**(22), 4670–4674 (2010)
2. Boubakri, W., Abdallah, W., Boudriga, N.: A Chaos-based authentication and key management scheme for M2M. In: Proceedings of the 9th International Conference on Internet Technology and Secured Transactions (ICITST), pp. 366–371 (2014)
3. Chatzigiannakis, I., Pyrgelis, A., Spirakis, P.G., Stamatiou, Y.C.: Elliptic curve based zero knowledge proofs and their applicability on resource constrained devices. In: Proceedings of the IEEE 8th International Conference on Mobile Adhoc and Sensor Systems (MASS), pp. 715–720, October 2011
4. Chen, S., Ma, M.: A dynamic-encryption authentication scheme for M2M security in cyber-physical systems. In: Proceedings of the IEEE International Conference on Global Communications (GLOBECOM), pp. 2897–2901 (2013)
5. Nguyen, T.D., Al-Saffar, A., Huh, E.N.: A dynamic ID-based authentication scheme. In: Proceedings of the 6th International Conference on Networked Computing and Advanced Information Management (NCM), pp. 248–253, Seoul, August 2010
6. Xu, Z., Liu, X., Zhang, G., He, W.: A certificateless signature scheme for mobile wireless cyber-physical systems. In: Proceedings of the 28th International Conference on Distributed Computing Systems Workshops, pp. 489–494 (2008)
7. Yang, X., Lin, J., Yu, W., Moulema, P., Fu, X., Zhao, W.: A novel en-route filtering scheme against false data injection attacks in cyber-physical networked systems. In: Proceedings of the IEEE 32nd International Conference on Distributed Computing Systems (ICDCS), pp. 1–14 (2012)

Implementation and Performance Evaluation of Network Intrusion Detection Systems

Mohammed Saber(✉), Mohammed Ghaouth Belkasmi, Sara Chadli, and Mohamed Emharraf

Laboratory LSE2I, National School of Applied Sciences,
First Mohammed University, Oujda, Morocco
mosaber@gmail.com, ghaouth@gmail.com, chad.saraa@gmail.com,
m.emharraf@gmail.com
http://ensao.ump.ma

Abstract. Modern intrusion detection systems (IDS) are deployed in high-speed networks. Thus, they must be able to process a large amount of data in real time. This raises the issue of performance and required an evaluation of these IDS.

We present in this paper an evaluation approach, based on a series of tests. The aim is to measure the performance of the components of an IDS and their effects on the entire system, as well as to study the effect of the characteristics of the deployment environment on the operation of the IDS. So, we have implemented the IDS SNORT on machines with different technical characteristics and we have designed a network to generate a set of experiments to measure the performances obtained in the case of a deployment in high-speed networks. These experiments consist in injecting various traffic loads, characterized by different transmission times, packet numbers, packet sizes and bandwidths, and then analyzing, for each situation, the processing performed on the packets.

Our experiments have revealed the weaknesses of the IDS in a precise way. Mainly, the inability to process multiple packets and the propensity to deposit, without analysis, packets in high-speed networks with heavy traffic. Our work also determined the effect of a component on the entire system and the effect of hardware characteristics on the performance of an IDS.

Keywords: Intrusion detection system · SNORT · Performance evaluation · Traffic · Packet dropped · Packet analysed

1 Introduction

For many years attacks made on networks have risen dramatically. The major reason for this is the unlimited access to and use of software by inadequately trained people. Network disruptions may be caused intentionally by several types of directed attack. These attacks are made at various layers in the TCP/IP protocol suite, including the application layer. Besides the external body, attacks can be made on the network by the internal body as well. However, an IDS is

E. Sabir et al. (Eds.): UNet 2017, LNCS 10542, pp. 484–495, 2017.
https://doi.org/10.1007/978-3-319-68179-5_42

considered to be one of the best technologies to detect threats and attacks. IDSs have attracted the interest of many organisations and governments, and any Internet user can deploy them.

The evaluation of intrusion detection systems is a challenging task; it requires a thorough knowledge of techniques relating to different disciplines, especially intrusion detection, methods of attack, networks and systems, technical testing and evaluation [1,2]. What makes the evaluation more difficult is the fact that different intrusion detection systems have different operational environments and can use a variety of techniques for producing alerts corresponding to attacks.

In practice, most of IDSs suffer from several problems, taking into consideration the large number of false positives and false negatives, and the evolution of attacks. All these problems increase the need of implementing an IDSs evaluation system. In this context, many attempts took place [3–9].

We present in this paper an evaluation approach, based on a series of tests. The aim is to measure the performance of the components of an IDS and their effects on the entire system, as well as to study the effect of the characteristics of the deployment environment on the operation of the IDS. So, we have implemented the IDS SNORT on machines with different technical characteristics and we have designed a network to generate a set of experiments to measure the performances obtained in the case of a deployment in high-speed networks. These experiments consist in injecting various traffic loads, characterized by different transmission times, packet numbers, packet sizes and bandwidths, and then analyzing, for each situation, the processing performed on the packets.

In the remaining sections of this article, we quote related works in Sect. 2. We discuss the proposed evaluation approach for evaluating performances of IDS in Sect. 3. In Sect. 4, we present, we present the results and evaluation. Finally, we end up our paper with a conclusion and future works in the Sect. 5.

2 Related Works

2.1 IDS Overview

An IDS is a solution implemented by organizations to monitor networks and/or systems for malicious activities or security policy violations. Host-based and network-based IDS solutions are the most common form implemented [10]. For the detection of network and/or system security policy violations, most IDSs use one of two detection techniques: statistical anomaly based and/or signature based.

In practice, most of IDSs suffer from several problems, taking into consideration the large number of false positives and false negatives, the evolution of attacks, and performances of these components. All these problems increase the need of implementing an IDSs evaluation system. In this context, many attempts took place [3–9].

2.2 IDS Evaluation Overview

The evaluation of the intrusion detection systems is a difficult task, demanding a thorough knowledge of techniques relating to different disciplines, especially intrusion detection, methods of attack, networks and systems, technical testing and evaluation [1,2].

The evaluation of intrusion detection systems is problematical for three reasons. First, it is difficult to collect data representative of the threat. Since the threat is constantly changing as new attacks are developing, it is vital that an IDS copes with these changes and developments. It is well-known to be difficult to make predictions outside ones data, and this is precisely what is expected of IDS evaluations. Second, if real data are used to test the IDS, the evaluation team can never be sure that there are no subtle attacks hiding undiscovered in the data, which affects both the calculation of the probability of detection and false alarms and consequently affects the evaluation process. Third, the human factor that is involved in the operation of IDSs should be considered in the evaluation process since few IDSs are truly automated.

The evaluation team should treat the human analyst as part of the overall system and evaluate performance with the human in the loop, which adds another level of variability to the evaluation process.

3 The Proposed Approach for Evaluating Performances IDS

3.1 Performance Test

To measure the performance of the IDS components. We focus on the IDS SNORT [11,12] capability as a network intrusion detection system as we aim to see how many packets could be analysed by SNORT under varying conditions. It has been shown previously that in high speed and heavy load conditions, some packets are dropped (skipped or not processed) [5,8]. In the proposed experiments SNORT analyser is not set up to perform actions based on user defined rules. It simply analyses and identifies the packets.

3.2 Test Scenarios

These scenarios were designed to test the performance of SNORT on different station. IDS were subject to the same tests and under the exact same conditions. In order to get more accurate results, we consider the following scenarios:

- **Scenario 1: High speed traffic:** we have sent the packets (1 kB in size) at different transmission time frames (1, 4, 8 and 16 ms), to analyze the system response within high speed traffic.
- **Scenario 2: Heavy traffic:** we have sent the different sets of packets having different volumes (100, 1000, 5000 and 10000), to analyze the system response within heavy traffic.

- **Scenario 3: Large data traffic:** we have sent the different sizes (lengths) of packets (128, 256, 512 and 1024 bytes), to analyze the system response in case of large data traffic.
- **Scenario 4: Traffic bandwidth:** we have generated traffics with different bandwidth (250 Mbps, 500 Mbps, 1.0 Gbps and 2.0 Gbps), to analyze the system response according to traffic bandwidth.

3.3 Test Bench

To perform those tests, we selected the SNORT version 2.9.7.2. And we have created a network including a computer connected to our platform for supervising operations and gathering results. The network is composed of 14 computers (Table 1), depending on our need of generating (running both open source tools and commercial tools) smaller packet size on high traffic speeds. All these computers are connected via Cisco Catalyst Series 2960-G switch using 24 ports of 1 GB Ethernet desktop connectivity as shown in Fig. 1.

3.4 Evaluation Methodology

The evaluation methodology is based on the following specifications, according each scenario:

- **Scenario 1:** We generated a number of packets (TCP, and UDP) having 1 kB in size at different transmission time frames (1, 4, 8, and 16 ms).

Table 1. Network components specifications test scenarios

Machine	Hardware description	Operating system	Tools used
Generator	Dell T1650 μp i3, 4 GB RAM, 1Gbps network card	Windows 7/Debian 8	LAN Traffic generator (TCP and UDP)
SNORT1	DELL PowerEdge R910 4 x Intel Xeon E7-4820 8 core 2 Ghz, 64GB RAM, network card Broadcom 57711(2 × 10 GbE et 2 × 1 GbE)	Debian 8	SNORT
SNORT2	Station HP Z620 Intel Xeon E5-1607 4 core, 12GB RAM, Intel(R) 82579LM Gigabit network connection	Windows Server 2008 R2	SNORT
SNORT3	Station HP Z620 Intel Xeon E5-1607 4 core, 12GB RAM, Intel(R) 82579LM GB network connection	Debian 8	SNORT
SNORT4	Dell T1650 μp i3, 4GB RAM, 1Gbps network card	Debian 8	SNORT
SNORT5	HP Pro 3010 Intel Core 2 Duo E7500, 4GB RAM, 1Gbps network card	Debian 8	SNORT

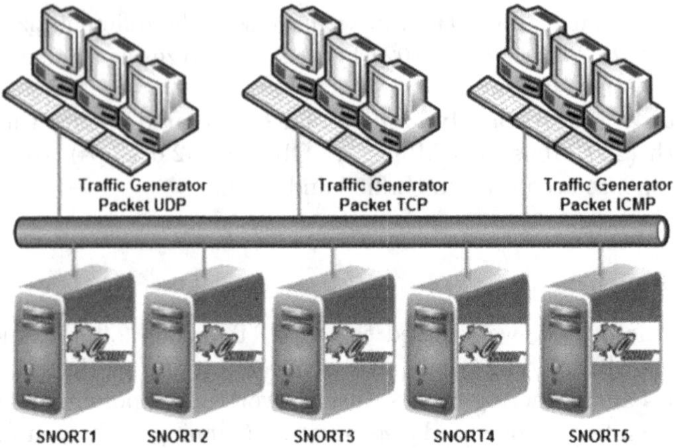

Fig. 1. Network test for scenario

- **Scenario 2:** Different number of packets (100, 1000, 5000 and 10000 packets) were generated.
- **Scenario 3:** Different packet sizes (128, 256, 512 and 1024 bytes) were generated.
- **Scenario 4:** Different bandwidth traffic (100 Mbps, 250 Mbps, 500 Mbps, 750 Mbps, 1.0 Gpbs, and 2.0 Gbps) were generated.

The IDS performance characteristics will be evaluated in terms of packets received, packets analysed and packets dropped.

3.5 Packet Generation

The performance of TCP, and UDP protocols was measured when running over the IPv4 header. The LAN traffic generator (WinPcap and Packets Generator tool) were used to vary the type of traffic in terms of IP header protocol (TCP, and UDP), speed, the number of packets and packet size. The traffic generator was used to send a packet of various sizes (128, 256, 512 and 1024 Bytes) that contain data and other attacks.

3.6 Performance Metrics

Performance metrics are used in the experiments to measure the ability of the SNORT to perform a particular task and to fit within the performance constraints. These metrics measure and evaluate the parameters that impact SNORT performance. The following aspects were measured in the experiments. The metrics are the percentages of the total packets processed by system SNORT. The specific metrics used are shown in Table 2.

Table 2. Description of performance metrics

Performance metrics	Description
Packets captured (PCA)	The number and percentage of packets received
Packets analysed (PAN)	The number and percentage of packets analysed from the total packets captured
Packets dropped (PDR)	The number and percentage of the packets dropped from the total packets captured

4 Scenarios Results and Evaluation

4.1 Scenario 1: SNORTs Response to High-Speed Network Traffic

For this scenario, we sent ≅60000 packets 1 kB in size (≅40000 TCP, and ≅20000 UDP) at different transmission time frames (1 ms, 4 ms, 8 ms, and 16 ms) for the five systems (SNORT1, SNORT2, SNORT3, SNORT4 and SNORT5). Figure 2 shows the SNORT output and results of experiments.

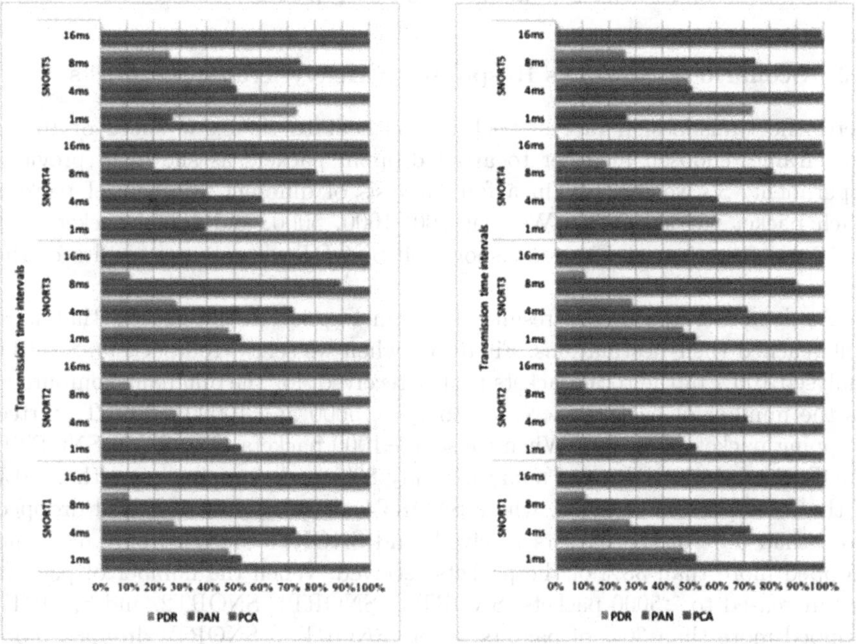

(a) TCP Traffic (b) UDP Traffic

Fig. 2. Results: packets (PCA, PAN, PDR (%))

As demonstrated in the results shown in Fig. 2, all the packets that were sent reached their destinations. SNORT has analysed almost all packets in incoming traffic when packets were transmitted in 16 ms time frame within all stations, but when the speed of transmission was increased to 8 ms, SNORT started dropping packets. SNORT in SNORT1, SNORT2, and SNORT3 analysed only 89% and dropped more than 11% of the total packets received. Meanwhile, SNORT in SNORT4 was analysing only 80% and dropping more than 20% of the total packets received, and SNORT in SNORT5 analysing only 74% and dropping more than 26% of the total packets received (Fig. 2). When the speed of transmission was increased to 4 ms time frame, SNORT in SNORT1, SNORT2, and SNORT3 dropped more than 28% of packets, where SNORT in SNORT4 dropped more than 40% of packets, and SNORT in SNORT5 dropped more than 49% of packets (Fig. 2). When the speed of transmission was increased to 1 ms, SNORT in SNORT1, SNORT2, and SNORT3 was analysing only 52% and dropping more than 48% of the total packets received, SNORT in SNORT4 analysing only 39% and dropping more than 41% of the total packets received, where SNORT in SNORT5 analysing only 27% and dropping more than 73% of the total packets received (Fig. 2).

In this experiment we notice that SNORT analysis performance decreased as the speed of transmission was increased. We deduce that the components ability of analysis becomes weaker as we increase the transmission speed.

4.2 Scenario 2: SNORTs Response to Heavy-Traffic Networks

Here, the transmission rate of packets was kept to the same speed of 16 ms time frame, choosen in order to avoid droppin packets as shown in previous experiment. So we will obtain a fair analysis of different numbers of packets (each packet carried 1024). We sent 100, 1000, 5000, and 10000 packets sets at 16 ms time frame. Figure 3a show the SNORT output and results of the experiment.

As demonstrated by the results shown in Fig. 3a, all the packets that were sent reached their destinations. Figure 3a, when we sent ≅100 packets, SNORT analysed 100% of the total packets that it received, for the differents computers. As the number of packets increased to 1000, 5000 and 10000, SNORT started dropping packets (Fig. 3a). When we sent ≅1000 packets, SNORT in SNORT1, SNORT2, and SNORT3 was analysing only 80% and dropping more than 20% of the total packets received, where SNORT4 analysed only 70% and dropped more than 30% of the packets received, and SNORT5 analysed only 62% and dropped more than 38% of the packets received. When the number of packets was increased to ≅5000 packets, SNORT in SNORT1, SNORT2, and SNORT3 dropped more than 30% of packets, where SNORT in SNORT4 dropped more than 43% of packets, and SNORT in SNORT5 dropped more than 49% of packets. As the number of packets increased to ≅10000, SNORT in SNORT1, SNORT2, and SNORT3 was analysing only 52% and was dropping more than 48% of the total packets received. Meanwhile, SNORT4 analysed only 39% and

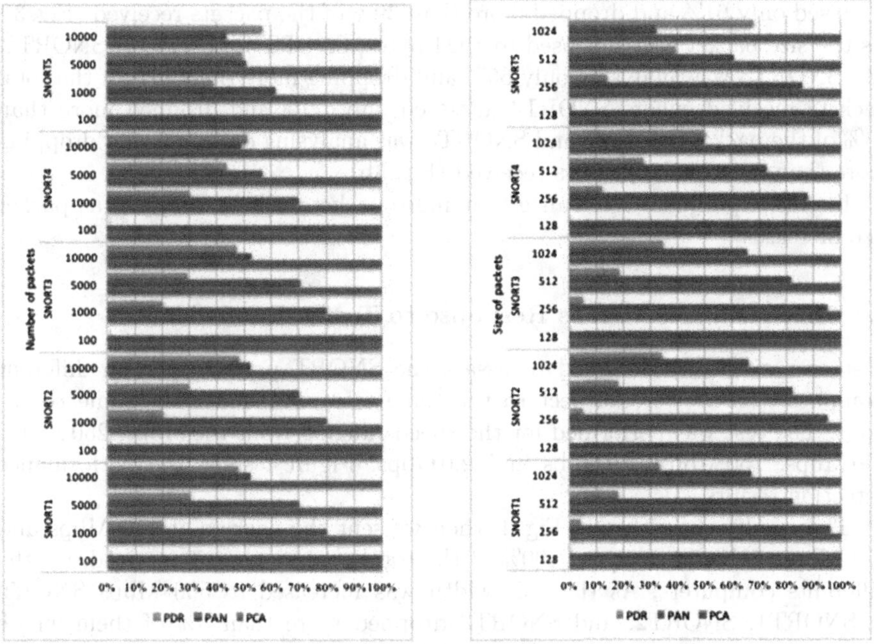

(a) Different Numbers of Packets (b) Different size of Packets

Fig. 3. Results: packets (PCA, PAN, PDR (%))

dropped more than 61% of the packets received, where SNORT5 analysed only 29% and dropped more than 71% of the packets received.

This experiment shows that as the number of packets increases, more packets are dropped (Fig. 3a).

4.3 Scenario 3: SNORTs Response to Large Packets

For this experiment, the number of packets was kept to the same value (≅30000) and the same speed (16 ms) to obtain a fair analysis of different sizes (lengths) of packets which are: 128, 256, 512 and 1024 bytes. Table 2 and Fig. 3 show the performance detection results.

As shown in Fig. 3b, when we sent ≅30000 packets at 16 ms time frame (each packet carries 128 bytes), SNORT analysed 100% of the total packets that it received, for the different computers. As the size of the packets was increased to 256 bytes SNORT in SNORT1, SNORT2, and SNORT3 dropped more than 5% of them where SNORT4 dropped more than 13% and SNORT5 dropped more than 15% (Fig. 3b). When the packet size was increased to 512 bytes, SNORT in SNORT1, SNORT2, and SNORT3 analysed only 83% and dropped more than 17% of the total packets received, where SNORT4 analysed only 73% and dropped more than 27% of the packets received and SNORT5 analysed only 61% and dropped more than 39% of the packets received (Fig. 3). As the size packet was increased to 1024 bytes, SNORT in SNORT1, SNORT2, and SNORT3 was analysing only 65% and dropping more than 35% of the total packets received, where SNORT4 analysed only 50% and dropped more than 50% of the packets received and SNORT5 was analysing only 32% and dropping more than 68% of the packets received (Fig. 3b).

In this experiment we realize that more packets will be dropped as packet size increases.

4.4 Scenario 4: SNORTs Response to Traffic Bandwidth

Test scenarios were designed to assass the SNORT performance on different Computers. IDSs were subject to the same tests and under the same conditions. The test was performed for the speed ranging from 100 Mbps, 250 Mbps, 500 Mbps, 750 Mbps, 1.0 Gpbs and 2.0 Gbps. Figure 4 show the performance detection results.

The results show that in Fig. 4 when we sent the packets at 100 Mbps and 250 Mbps, SNORT analysed 100% of the total packets that it received, for the differents computers. As the bandwidth was increased to 500 Mbps SNORT in SNORT1, SNORT2, and SNORT3 dropped more than 3% of them where SNORT4 dropped more than 10% and SNORT5 dropped more than 15% (Fig. 4). When the bandwidth was increased to 750 Mbps, SNORT in SNORT1, SNORT2, and SNORT3 was dropping more than 5% of the total packets received, where SNORT4 dropped more than 20% of the packets received and SNORT5 dropped more than 30% of the packets received (Fig. 4). As the bandwidth was increased

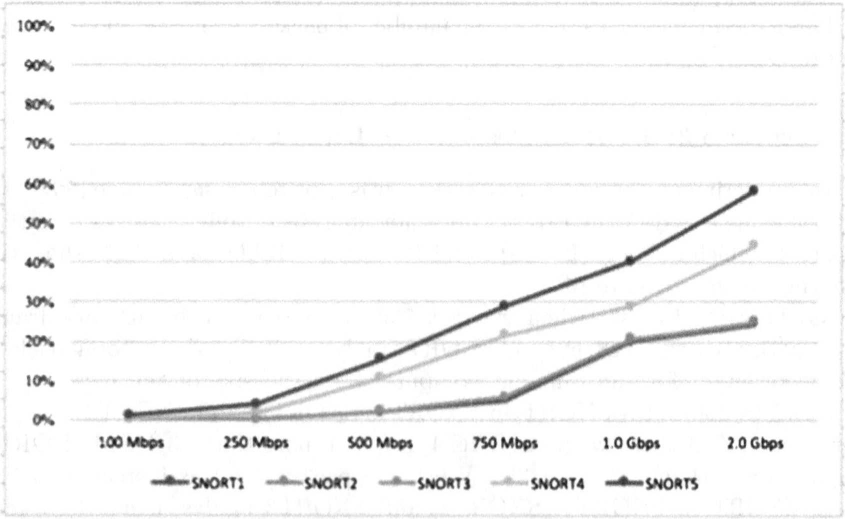

Fig. 4. Results: packets dropped (PDR (%)), different bandwidth traffic

to 1.0 Gbps, SNORT in SNORT1, SNORT2, and SNORT3 was dropping more than 19% of the total packets received, where SNORT4 dropped more than 28% of the packets received and SNORT5 dropped more than 40% of the packets received (Fig. 4). When the bandwidth was increased to 2.0 Gbps, SNORT in SNORT1, SNORT2, and SNORT3 was dropping more than 25% of the total packets received, where SNORT4 dropped more than 45% of the packets received and SNORT5 dropped more than 58% of the packets received (Fig. 4).

This experiment demonstrated that more packets will be dropped as bandwidth increases.

4.5 Discussion of Results

Test scenarios were designed to evaluate the SNORT performance on different computers. IDS were subject to the same tests and under the same conditions. In order to get more accurate results, all IDS in scenario 1, were tested with different transmission time frames (1 ms, 4 ms, 8 ms, and 16 ms). When, all systems were tested with number of packet (100, 1000, 5000, and 10000) in scenario 2. In scenario 3, all systems were tested with packet sizes (128, 256, 512 and 1024 bytes). Finally, all systems were tested for the speed ranging from 250 Mbps, 500 Mbps, 1.0 Gpbs, and 2.0 Gbps.

On the basis of the results obtained from the four experiments, we noticed an increase of rejected packets number for all five environments, either with a lessening of transmission time in Scenario 1, or with an increase of packets number in Scenario 2, or increased packet size in Scenario 3, or with the increase in bandwidth in Scenario 4.

Our experiments have revealed the weaknesses of the IDS in a precise way. Mainly, the inability to process multiple packets and the propensity to deposit, without analysis, packets in high-speed networks with heavy traffic. Our work also determined the effect of a component on the entire system and the effect of hardware characteristics on the performance of an IDS within the environment SNORT4 and SNORT5. Hence, the problem is not primarily related to the physical characteristics of the deployment environment, but rather to the limitations of the IDS itself, so we have to look for a solution which will combine the IDS with other network components to improve the efficiency of our system.

5 Conclusion

This research has focused on ways of determining the efficacy of the performances concept for IDS in high-speed network environments. The test scenarios employed involved the use of the widely deployed open-source IDS, namely SNORT. The results obtained have shown a number of significant limitations in the use of IDS, where both packet-handling and processing capabilities at different traffic loads were used as the primary criteria for defining system performance. We have further shown that performance is further degraded as the traffic is increased, irrespective of the host hardware used. Furthermore, we have demonstrated a number of significant differences in the performance characteristics of the five different environments in which SNORT was deployed.

This work has identified specific and replicable bottlenecks in commonly used implementations IDS in high-speed networks. The results obtained can be taken as a benchmark for improving the performance of these systems in future research work.

References

1. Khorkov, D.A.: Methods for testing network-intrusion detection systems. Sci. Tech. Inf. Process. **39**(2), 120–126 (2012). https://doi.org/10.3103/S0147688212020128
2. Berthier, R., Sanders, W.H., Khurana, H.: Intrusion detection for advanced metering infrastructures: requirements and architectural directions. In: 2010 First IEEE International Conference on Smart Grid Communications, Gaithersburg, MD, 2010, pp. 350–355. https://doi.org/10.1109/SMARTGRID.2010.5622068
3. Akhlaq, M., Alserhani, F., Awan, I., Mellor, J., Cullen, A.J., Al-Dhelaan, A.: Implementation and evaluation of network intrusion detection systems. In: Kouvatsos, D.D. (ed.) Network Performance Engineering. LNCS, vol. 5233, pp. 988–1016. Springer, Heidelberg (2011). https://doi.org/10.1007/978-3-642-02742-0_42
4. Saber, M., Chadli, S., Emharraf, M., El Farissi, I.: Modeling and implementation approach to evaluate the intrusion detection system. In: Bouajjani, A., Fauconnier, H. (eds.) NETYS 2015. LNCS, vol. 9466, pp. 513–517. Springer, Cham (2015). https://doi.org/10.1007/978-3-319-26850-7_41
5. Shiri, F.I., Shanmugam, B., Idris, N.B.: A parallel technique for improving the performance of signature-based network intrusion detection system. In: 2011 IEEE 3rd International Conference on Communication Software and Networks (ICCSN), pp. 692–696, 27–29 May 2011. https://doi.org/10.1109/ICCSN.2011.6014986
6. Jamshed, M.A., Lee, J., Moon, S., Yun, I., Kim, D., Lee, S., Yi, Y., Park, K.: Kargus: a highly-scalable software-based intrusion detection system. In: Proceedings of the 2012 ACM conference on Computer and communications security (CCS 2012), NY, USA, pp. 317–328 (2012). https://doi.org/10.1145/2382196.2382232
7. Saber, M., Chadli, S., Emharraf, M., El Farissi, I.: Performance evaluation of an intrusion detection system. In: El Oualkadi, A., Choubani, F., El Moussati, A. (eds.) Proceedings of the Mediterranean Conference on Information and Communication Technologies. LNEE, vol. 381, pp. 509–517. Springer, Cham (2016). https://doi.org/10.1007/978-3-319-30298-0_52
8. Albin, E., Rowe, N.C.: A realistic experimental comparison of the Suricata and SNORT intrusion-detection systems. In: 2012 26th International Conference on Advanced Information Networking and Applications Workshops (WAINA), pp. 122–127, 26–29 March 2012. https://doi.org/10.1109/WAINA.2012.29
9. Wang, X., Kordas, A., Hu, L., Gaedke, M., Smith, D.: Administrative evaluation of intrusion detection system. In: Proceedings of the 2nd Annual Conference on Research in Information Technology (RIIT 2013). ACM, New York, NY, USA, pp. 47–52 (2013). https://doi.org/10.1145/2512209.2512216
10. Mudzingwa, D., Agrawal, R.: A study of methodologies used in intrusion detection and prevention systems (IDPS). In: 2012 Proceedings of IEEE Southeastcon, Orlando, FL, pp. 1–6 (2012). https://doi.org/10.1109/SECon.2012.6197080

11. Chi, R.: Intrusion detection system based on SNORT. Proceedings of the 9th International Symposium on Linear Drives for Industry Applications, vol. 3, pp. 657–664. Springer, Heidelberg (2014). https://doi.org/10.1007/978-3-642-40633-182
12. Roesch, M.: SNORT - lightweight intrusion detection for networks. In: Proceedings of the 13th USENIX conference on System administration (LISA 1999). USENIX Association, Berkeley, CA, USA, pp. 229–238 (1999)

An Efficient Authentication Protocol for 5G Heterogeneous Networks

Younes El Hajjaji El Idrissi(✉), Noureddine Zahid, and Mohamed Jedra

Laboratory of Conception and System, Faculty of Science, Avenue Ibn Batouta, B.P. 1014, Rabat, Morocco
youneselhajjaji@gmail.com

Abstract. Network security is an important service in the evolution of mobile communication technologies. The user authentication and key agreement process in 2G, 3G and 4G generations have tried to cover all security requirements. However, the deployed Authentication and Key Agreement (AKA) protocol suffers from several security and performance weaknesses, such as, user identity disclosing, high authentication delay and bandwidth consumption. All these, impact negatively the handover process and the quality of service. The new 5G network technology will utilize a basic 5G access authentication similar to the current 4G/LTE platform. This new technology creates novel security challenges that the next generation of AKA must support. In addition, the authentication protocol must address the newly discovered security weaknesses that have been exposed in the present networks. In this paper we propose an enhancement of existed AKA protocol to improve authentication and authorization in 5G networks by using new key framework based on the Elliptic Curve Cryptosystem (ECC). Our key framework will improve the performance and will achieve fast re-authentication during the handover. The security properties of the proposed method are checked by using formal verification (AVISPA) which has proved a high talent in automatically finding potential attacks in security protocols.

Keywords: 5G · LTE · EAP · AKA · Authentication · Handover · ECDH

1 Introduction

With the rapid evolution of wireless networks, security authentication has become a mandatory service in the new generations. The explosive growth of data traffic requests novel development researches on the new technologies. The 5G networks face more aggressive performance and security challenges than 2G/3G/4G [1]. The security architectures and privacy features from earlier generations serve as a good starting point and a basis for 5G security [2]. However, due to the presence of new security requirements and architecture it is not sufficient just to provide the same security features as in the legacy systems. Therefore, by using the right design approach, 5G networks will be able to meet growing demands for security and privacy. This implies there will be a special emphasis on security and privacy requirements that will improve the quality of services [2].

E. Sabir et al. (Eds.): UNet 2017, LNCS 10542, pp. 496–508, 2017.
https://doi.org/10.1007/978-3-319-68179-5_43

The 5G networks lead to increased data rate and reduced handover delay. For this, 5G network will be based on heterogeneous architecture with small cell deployment [3]. This cannot be primarily driven by increased throughput, reduced latency and other quantitative aspects. The deployment of small cells in heterogeneous networks invokes new challenges in network resources management and security administration. The mobility of users between different cells introduces an additional latency during handover process. This constraint the user mobility, decreases the quality of service and exposes networks to impersonation/key-distinguishing and man-in-the-middle (MitM) attacks [2, 4]. As consequence, 5G network needs to have robust, fast and efficient handover authentication schemes which ensure security and protection of connected users.

Security is the most important feature in public network architecture. All other services depend on and no higher level services can be used without authentication of connected users. Authentication process is moved from 2G mono-authentication where the network authenticates the User Equipment (UE) to 3G/LTE mutual authentication. In addition the LTE/3G supports an interworking architecture between heterogeneous wireless networks [5]. LTE/3G can use WLAN/WiMAX as access network and benefit from the low cost and the high bandwidth of these networks. However, this inter-working presents a big security challenge for user authentication in both networks. The LTE/3G architecture uses AKA protocol [6] to authenticate UE attached to the visited network and to ensure secure heterogeneous network. The UE must be authenticated by the Home Subscriber Server (HSS), Home Location Registry (HLR) and Mobile Management Entity (MME) [5, 6].

In The Third Generation Partnership Project (3GPP) interworking architecture, all computation operation during authentication process is handled by UE and home network (HN). The role of the visited network is limited to forward the authentication packets between UE and LTE/3G home network [7]. AKA protocol is based on challenge-response mechanism and a pre-shared secret key K between UE and HSS. AKA provides a mutual authentication and generation of cipher and integrity keys. The authentication process can be divided in two types of authentication, full authentication invoked the first time User Equipment (UE) attached to a wireless network and a fast re-authentication mechanism invoked in the case of UE handover. Figure 1 presents a general overview of the full AKA authentication procedure. The UE authentication is done by MME based on the received Authentication Vector (AV) from HLR/HSS and on the number of re-authentication allowed time. Each AV is composed from Random Number (RAND), Authentication Token (AUTN), Expected Response (XRES), Cipher Key (CK), Integrity Key (IK) and Session key. After reception of AVs from HSS, MME sends an authentication request to UE with RAND and AUTN. If AUTN is accepted by UE, it produces a Response (RES) that is sent back to MME. UE also computes CK and IK. MME compares the received RES with expected XRES. If they match, MME considers the AKA authentication is successfully completed [6].

To enable handover between different wireless networks, 3GPP has provided a specific key hierarchy and handover message flows for different mobility scenarios. The target network needs to contact the connected customer network authentication server for UE identification and to retrieve UE authentication key. This handover process introduces high authentication delay, increases the exchanged messages and

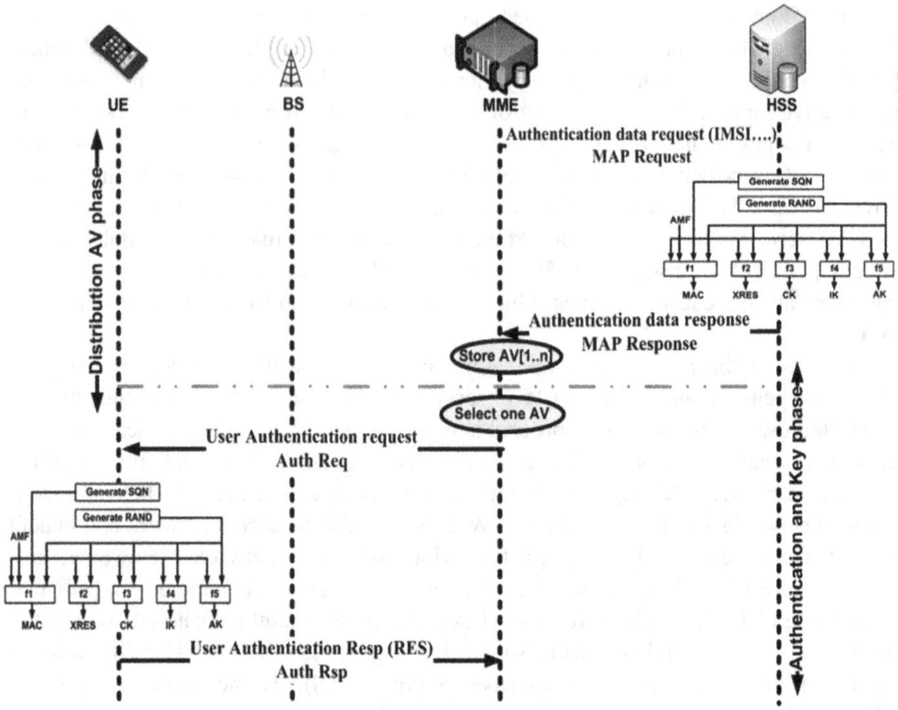

Fig. 1. Overview of LTE authentication protocol

the handover complexity. As consequence the actual handover authentication protocol is not suitable for next network generation 5G [8].

A seamless handover in 5G architecture is absolutely required. The authentication delay has an impact on handover performance. For this, a simplified authentication scheme will reduce the handover delay and will increase the network performance. In this paper, we propose an enhanced authentication method based on the existed standard AKA protocol with using hybrid key framework (Elliptic Curve with symmetric key). The visited network authenticates UE locally during the handover process. Our method simplifies the authentication schema, reduces the authentication delay and the number of authentication keys, achieves mutual authentication and protects the user identity. The rest of the paper is organized as follows. In Sect. 2 we detail our proposed method. In Sects. 3 and 4 we analyze and evaluate the performance of our method and we conclude in Sect. 5.

2 Enhanced EAP Authentication Method for 5G

5G network technology is going to face a large number of unknown pattern and new applications. This new technology needs to be able to handle user-mobility and to ensure connectivity anywhere and anytime. 5G network will be designed to be open, flexible, and able to grow more easily than the traditional networks [1]. In comparison with LTE, signaling efficiency, coverage and handover latency should be improved. Developing efficient handover procedures in 5G heterogeneous architecture is a challenging problem. The 5G authentication framework needs to support multiple access technologies and to merge authentication, confidentiality and privacy services of different networks. This model will reduce the complexity of security management by allowing devices to share the created security context when moving between different accesses technologies [3].

It is recommended that the 5G authentication framework be based on the Extensible Access Protocol (EAP) [9]. EAP protocol is designed to support multiple authentication methods, such as EAP Authentication and Key Agreement (EAP-AKA) and EAP Transport Layer Security (EAP-TLS) [9]. Several research papers are investigating new ways to facilitate interworking between wireless technologies in heterogeneous networks. The authors in [10] propose an enhancement method of AKA protocol called Enhancement Mobile Security and User Confidentiality (EMSUCU). The proposed method bypasses some standard AKA issues, such as user identity disclosure and secret key revelation by encryption of IMSI. EMSUCU enhances the handover performance by using hash function instead of encryption functions and by using new security function f11 to generate the key used to encrypt IMSI. In addition it eliminates the use of shared key and protects the exchanged message of AKA protocol that contains (RAND, RES, AUTN, CK, IK). In the same context, the research presented in [11] addresses some issues detected in EPS-AKA, such as, user identity disclosing and protection from malicious MME. The authors proposed a modified AKA protocol called hybrid scheme HSK-AKA based on the method proposed in [12]. HSK-AKA protocol minimizes the use of public key cryptography by using digital signature and symmetric key cryptography in USIM functions. In terms of computational overhead and authentication delay, this method achieves better performance compared to some protocols such as SEAKA [13].

Re-authentication methods can avoid full authentication in handover by reusing the information exchanged between UE and MME in the previous authentication. The authors in [14] propose a key caching mechanism to eliminate the non-necessary authentication cost. To speed the handover process, the old BS station re-uses the Master Session Key MSK when the UE revisits the BS station in the future. The old BS still keeps the UE key and profile until the end of the key lifetime. This approach can improve authentication performance, but constraints UE mobility to the old BS and consumes extra storage (512 bits for the MSK, 32 bits for the MSK lifetime and 1,024 bits for the UE authorization profiles) to keep UE key records at the old BS. In addition, this approach does not respect security requirements due to the absence of a fresh round of mutual authentication between UE and visited network. In [15], the authors propose an efficient EPS-AKA protocol by using a simple and strong mechanism based on SPEKE protocol. In this approach, the shared secret key is not exchanged, instead it is computed using a method in UE and HSS.

To simplify the handover process in 5G network and to address the high authentication delay and UE identity disclosing, we propose a fast local authentication method Fast EAP-AKA. The proposed method does not require any modification in the existing authentication infrastructures or the usage of public key operations. Our method offers mutual authentication mechanism and guaranties data confidentiality by using hybrid cipher cryptosystem. Our key framework permits to authenticate UE by visited network in reasonable authentication delay which will improve the handover performance and QoS.

There are five roles in our authentication method: UE, Base Station (BS), Visited network authentication server (AAA), MME and HLR/HSS. The following sections present the proposed authentication method Fast EAP-AKA. We assume the following assumptions:

- A secure channel between BS and AAA and between MME and HSS.
- The UE can identify the ID of BSS.
- Each operator service selects a finite field Fq over a large odd prime $q > 2^{160}$, defines an elliptic curve equation Eq(a, b): $y^2 = x^3 + ax + b \pmod q$ with the order n over Fq where a, b $\in$ Fq, $q > 3$, and $4a^3 + 27b^2 \neq 0 \bmod q$. And selects a public point Q with the order n over Eq(a, b).
- Each authentication server MME has a known public encryption key $U_H = d_H * Q$ (with d_H indicating the private key and "*" denoting the point multiplication over Eq(a, b).
- Each authentication server AAA has a known public encryption key $U_W = d_W * Q$ (with d_W indicating the private key of AAA server).
- Each UE has a pair of pre-shared secret keys with the HSS server, composed of (U_E, d_E) with $U_E = d_E * Q$.
- The UE ID is composed by two parts. The first part is a prefix which refers to the network operator ID_N and the second one is randomly generated for each authentication operation ID_{NTE}.

In our protocol the UE is locally authenticated by the visited authentication server AAA by using a novel key framework. For this some modifications to the standard AKA authentication protocol are necessary. The proposed modification will remove the problem of IMSI identity disclosing and allows fast re-authentication and fast vertical and horizontal handover in heterogeneous architecture. The Fig. 2 presents the proposed 5G Modified EA-AKA authentication protocol. UE generates a temporary identity to hide its identity (IMSI) during the first authentication. MME generates the next local user ID to be used in the next UE authentication process. HSS determines the life cycle of the main local authentication key. The proposed protocol consists of seven steps

Step 1: After UE detection, BS sends an EAP request identity to UE

Step 2: To protect user identity (IMSI), UE generates a temporary ID_{TE} that can be computed in this way:

- UE randomly selects an integer $r_U \in Z_q^*$ and calculates $R_U = r_U * U_E$, $R'_U = r_U * U_H$.
- The encryption key is $TK_U = d_E * R'_{UE}$ and the temporary user ID is $ID_{TE} = E_{TKu}(IMSI, TK_U)$
- UE sends to BS response message composed by ($ID_N \| ID_{TE} \| R_U$)

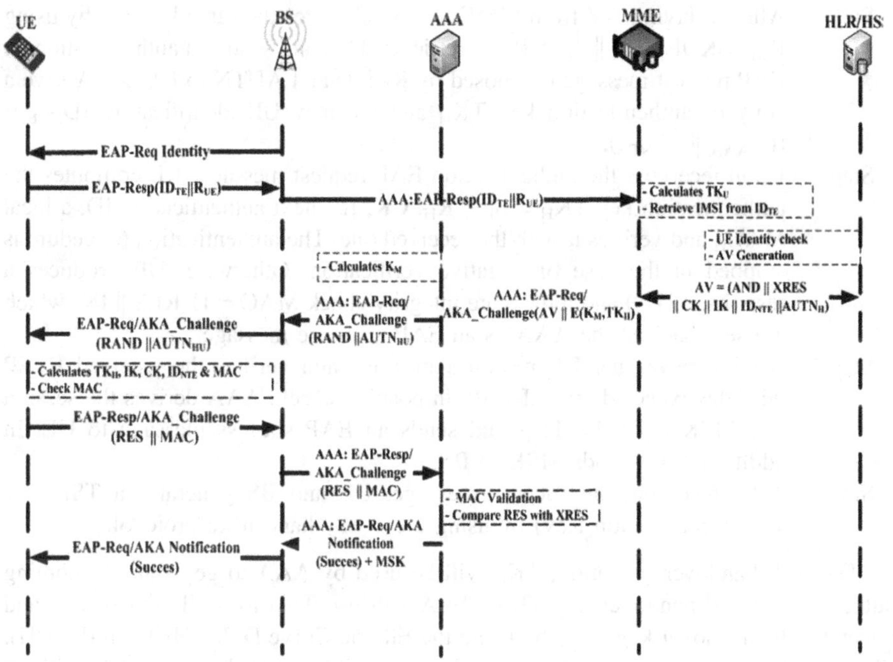

Fig. 2. Modified EAP- AKA authentication protocol for 5G network

Step 3: According to ID_N, AAA forwards the UE response to the correct MME. Upon reception of this message, MME calculates the local decryption key TK_U by: $TK_U = d_H * R_U$ and retrieves the user IMSI by decryption of the received ID_{TE} (D_{TKu} (ID_{TE}) = IMSI). Then, MME contacts the HSS server to obtain the authentication vector which is built in this way: The HSS generates a random number RAND, randomly selects an integer $r_H \in Z_q^*$, computes $R_H = r_H * U_H$, $R_H' = r_H * U_E$ and creates the authentication key $TK_H = d_H * R_H'$. The TK_H is used with the help of AKA functions (f0 − f9) to generate the authentication vector AV composed by:

- EAP authentication key $CK = f3(TK_H, RAND)$ and $IK = f4(TK_H, RAND)$.
- Next authentication ID, $ID_{NTE} = f_{TKH}$ (IMSI, TK_H), expected response $XRES = f2(TK_H, RAND)$, $MAC_H = f1(IK, RAND, ID_{NTE})$ and the authentication token $AUTN_{HU} = R_H \| RAND \| MAC_{HU}$.
- HSS sends AV and TK_H to MME which will be shared with AAA to authenticate UE locally by visited network. MME protects the exchanged traffic between MME and AAA with new generated key K_M by using Integrated Encryption Scheme (IES) in this way. MME randomly selects an integer $r_M \in Z_q^*$, computes $R_M = r_M * Q$, $R_M' = r_M * U_W$ and creates the cipher key $K_M = KDF(ID_N \| R_M')$. The MME sends AV, R_M and E_{KM} (TK_H, K_M) to AAA.

Step 4: After receiving AV from MME, AAA calculates the same key K_M by using K_M = KDF (ID_N || d_W * R_M'), retrieves TK_H and sends an authentication an EAP request message composed by RAND and AUTN to UE. AAA save a copy of authentication key TK_H and the new UE identification ID_{NTE} = (ID_{AAA} || ID_{NTE}).

Step 5: Upon receiving the authentication EAP request message, UE computes the authentication key TK_H = d_E * R_H, CK, IK, next authentication ID, a local MAC_H and verifies it with the received one. The authentication procedure is stopped in the case of negative verification. Otherwise, UE produces a response (RES) and a message integrity check MAC = f1(RES || IK) which are sent back to the AAA as an EAP response message.

Step 6: AAA receives the UE response message and verifies the received RESP with the expected one XRESP. In positive check, AAA derives the session key MSK from the TK_H and sends an EAP success message to UE. In addition AAA sends MSK to BS.

Step 7: After receiving the success message, UE and BS generates a TSK key (Transient Session Key) by using the 4-way handshake protocol.

For each handover operation, TK_H will be used by AAA to generate UE coming authentication and handover key TK_W. AAA will use TK_H as a UE shared key and generates the handover key TK_W by using the Elliptic Curve Diffie–Hellman (ECDH). This key hierarchy offers to the AAA the possibility to authenticate UE without intervention of MME and without knowing the pre-shared key of UE (d_E, U_E).

2.1 Handover Authentication Method in Heterogeneous 5G Networks

The UE is involved in handover when experiencing poor signal-strength from the associated BS. Re-authentication mechanism is invoked in the case of UE re-association with the same BS or association with a new BS in the same visited network domain. The re-authentication process is executed by the LTE/3G home network. The UE re-authentication is done by MME based on the previously received AV from the HLR/HSS and on the number of re-authentications allowed. All this introduces high authentication delay and increase the handover time. To achieve a fast re-authentication, we propose to authenticate UE locally by visited authentication network on behalf of MME. The Fig. 3 describes the proposed handover authentication protocol for 5G networks. Our proposed protocol proceeds as follows:

Step 1: After UE detection, Target BS (TBS) sends an EAP request identity to UE.

Step 2: UE sends to AAA the previous received temporary identity ID_{NTE}.

Step 3: After receiving UE identity ID_{NTE}. AAA checks the received ID_{NTE} and classifies the request as an intra-handover if it has the same ID_{AAA} as ID_{NTE} postfix. Then, AAA validates the life cycle of authentication key TK_H, generates a random number $RAND_W$, randomly selects an integer $r_W \in Z_q^*$, computes R_W = r_W * U_W, R_W' = r_W * TK_H and the handover key TK_W = U_W * R_W'. Also, AAA computes the next UE local ID (ID_{NTE} = (ID_{AAA} ||

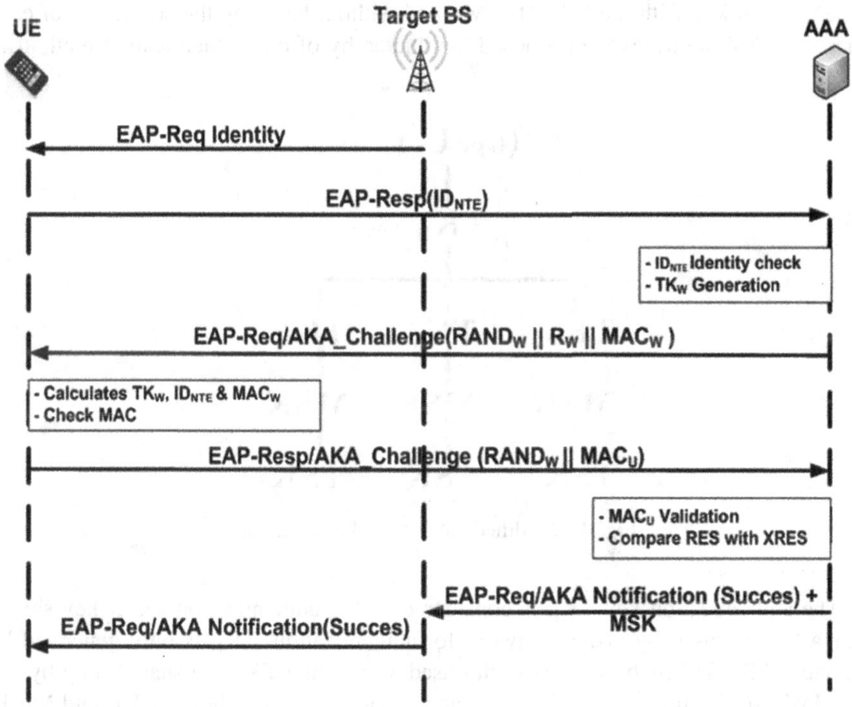

Fig. 3. Modified EAP-AKA authentication method during handover

fTK$_H$ (ID$_{NTE}$, ID$_{AAA}$, TK$_W$))), the message integrity token check MAC$_W$ = f1(RAND$_W$ || ID$_{NTE}$ || TK$_W$) and sends to UE an EAP request message with RAND$_W$, R$_W$, MAC$_W$ through TBS.

Step 4: After receiving EAP request message, UE computes authentication key $TK_W = d_E * R_W$, next authentication ID, a local MAC$_W$ and verifies it with the received one. The authentication procedure is stopped in the case of negative check, otherwise UE replies with an EAP response message with the RAND$_W$ and a message integrity check MAC$_U$ = PRF (RAND$_W$ || TK$_W$).

Step 5: AAA receives EAP response message from UE and verifies if the received RAND$_W$ is identical with the generated one. In positive check AAA derives the session key MSK from the TK$_W$ (MSK = SHA1 (TK$_W$, ID$_{NTE}$ || ID$_{TAP}$ || ID$_{AAA}$) and sends an EAP success message to UE and MSK to TBS.

Step 6: After receiving EAP success message, UE and TBS generate a TSK key (Transient Session Key) by using the 4-way handshake protocol.

3 Security Analysis

To avoid domino effect problem [17], unnecessary distribution of key must be avoided. For this, all generated keys must be used in a specific context. UE secret key is hold only by UE and MME in network operator. UE and AAA can share the same authentication key with the help of MME and without knowing the secret key of each other. Figure 4 describes the proposed key hierarchy of our authentication methods.

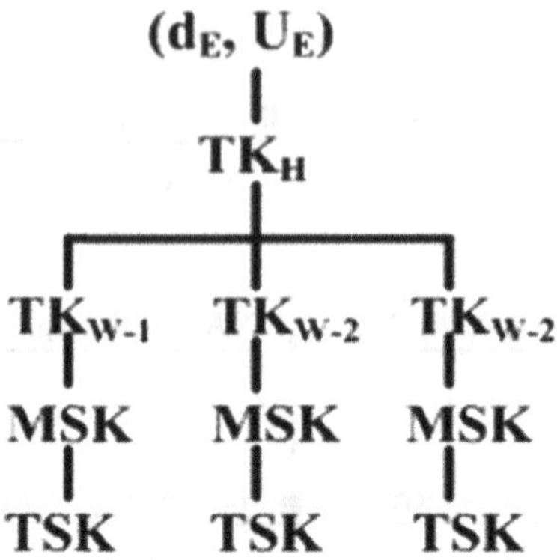

Fig. 4. Modified EAP-AKA key hierarchy

The authentication key TK_H is considered as UE authentication secret key shared with AAA and used by visited network for authentication. TK_H is only generated by UE and MME. This is because (U_E, d_E) used to generate TK_H are shared only by UE and MME. In addition, the used RAND and r_H values are only held by UE and MME. The key TK_H is only used by UE and AAA during a valid life cycle defined by MME. Also, it can be shared by different AAA servers residing in the same network domain. Note that TK_H is deleted from MME database after their delivery to AAA.

The handover key TK_W is only generated by UE and AAA because no other nodes have access to TK_H used in the generation process. Both TK_H and r_w are used in the generation of TK_W. These values aid in limiting the scope and uniqueness of this key. TK_W is only used by UE and its associated BS to drive new session key. It is never shared between different BSs in network domain and never re-used in future re-authentications. New handover key TK_W is generated for each re-authentication operation. To satisfy the principle of least privilege, TK_W must be deleted from AAA's database after delivery to BS. To avoid replay attacks, all authentication keys are used one time. This key framework gives UE more flexibility to move freely in the heterogeneous network without disclosing its identity IMSI and without sharing with visited network its pre-shared key (U_E, d_E).

The proposed protocols satisfy all network security requirements defined by 3GPP. The Table 1 shows security proprieties comparison between standard EAP-AKA and our proposed protocol Mod EAP-AKA. The comparison results demonstrate that our protocol can provide the most comprehensive security requirements compared to the standard protocol. Providing UE identity protection, heterogeneous network access and mutual authentication are the main advantages of our protocol. To verify this, our protocol is evaluated by using formal security verification platform AVISPA [16].

Table 1. Security comparison between our protocol and standard EAP-AKA.

	Modified EAP-AKA	Standard EAP-AKA
Type of cryptosystem	Hybrid (Symmetric with ECDH)	Symmetric
Computational overhead	Smaller	Smaller
Protection of user identity	Yes	No
Heterogeneous network access	Yes	Yes
Secure against man-in-the middle attack	Yes	No

The proposed protocol is defined in Peer (UE) and Server (AAA) model and is expressed in the formal language HLPSL. We use formal request and witness goal specification to check the mutual authentication between UE and AAA. The assertion (witness(S,P,at_rand,AT_RAND')) means that AAA should be authenticated by UE and agreeing on the value AT_RAND. The assertion (request (P,S,at_rand,AT_RAND')) indicates that UE authenticates AAA and agrees on the value AT_RAND. Figure 5 shows the message returned by AVISPA verification tool OFMC. Our protocol achieves mutual authentication, assures confidentiality of shared keys TK_H and TK_w between UE and AAAs and is safe to use by booth verification check tools.

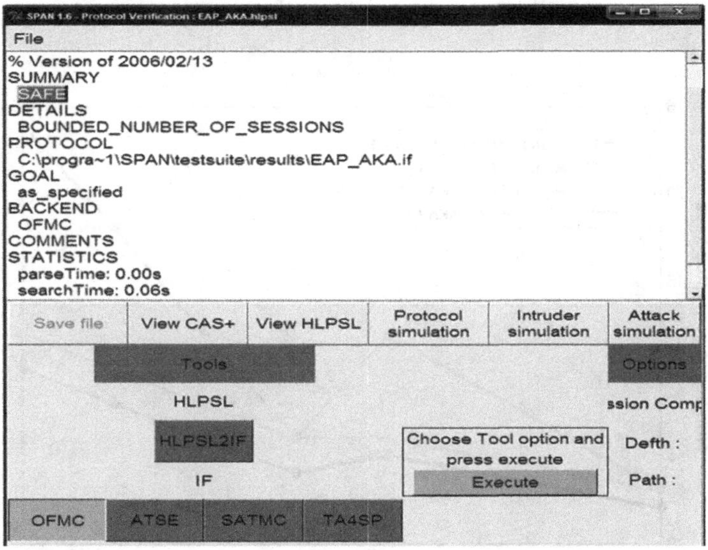

Fig. 5. Modified EAP-AKA analyze message returned by OFMC tool

4 Performance Analysis

Security enhancement of authentication protocol must not impact the handover performance. In order to evaluate the performance of the proposed protocol, we make a performance comparison between our authentication methods and the standard EAP-AKA. The performance comparison is based on the number of generated keys and Bandwidth consumption.

Number of generation Keys: We propose a new key hierarchy to achieve local UE authentication. In this section we compare the total number of generated keys by UE, AAA and MME in standard EAP-AKA with the number of keys in fast EAP-AKA. The total number of generated keys depends essentially on the number of full authentication and re-authentication times. The total number of keys generated by MME, UE and AAA in the standard protocol are calculated by 3a (1 + r), 3a (1 + r), 0 where "a" is the number of EAP-AKA full authentications and "r" is the number of EAP-AKA fast re-authentications. The total number of keys generated by MME, UE and AAA in fast EAP-AKA is 4a, a (3 + r) and a (2 + r).

Figure 6 presents the number of keys generated by MME, UE and AAA in the standard and the modified EAP-AKA. We can conclude that the number of keys generated by the MME and UE in the proposed method is less than those generated in the standard protocol. As there is no key generations by the AAA in the standard protocol, the number of keys generated by AAA in our protocol is more than the standard protocol due to the local re-authentication.

Bandwidth consumption: In the standard EAP-AKA re-authentication the user is authenticated by the MME. However in our authentication method the UE authentication is delegated to the visited authentication server AAA. This can reduce the

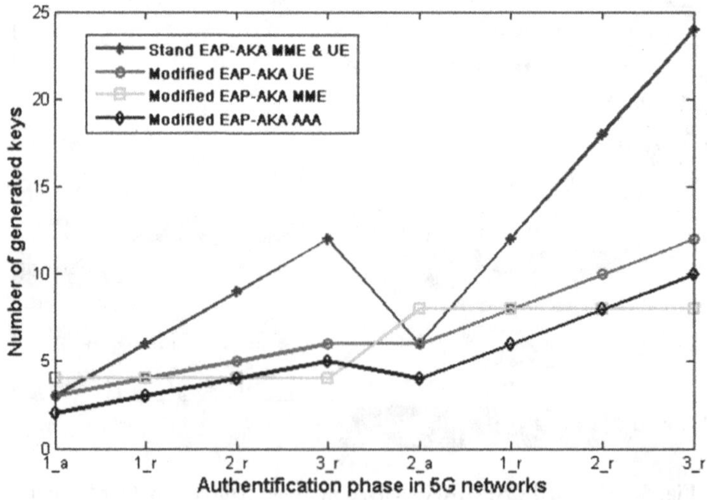

Fig. 6. Number of generated keys by MME, AAA and UE

bandwidth consumption between MME and AAA by 50% compared to EAP-AKA. Also our protocol does not require any SQN synchronization between the UE and the core network, which can reduce the bandwidth consumption.

5 Conclusion

In this paper we have proposed new authentication methods to reduce authentication delay for 5G heterogeneous networks. The modified EAP-AKA protocol resolves the user identity issue and drives the authentication key necessary to manage UE movement between heterogeneous networks. The proposed authentication methods aim to minimize authentication delay and cost of authentication signalling for stationary and roaming users by eliminating the need to contact the core network on every UE re-authentication. Proposed methods show superior performance results in comparison to existing standard EAP-AKA.

References

1. Third Generation Partnership Project (3GPP), 3GPP TR 22.861 V14.1.0, Feasibility Study on New Services and Markets Technology, September 2016
2. Third Generation Partnership Project (3GPP), 3GPP TR 33.899 V1.0.0, Study on the security aspects of the next generation system, March 2017
3. Duan, X., Wang, X.: Authentication handover and privacy protection in 5G hetnets using software-defined networking, security and privacy in emerging networks. IEEE Commun. Mag. **53**(4), 28–35 (2015)
4. Nunes, B.A.A., et al.: A survey of software-defined networking: past, present, and future of programmable networks. IEEE Commu. Surv. Tutorials **99**, 1–18 (2014)
5. 3rd Generation Partnership Project, 3GPP Technical Specifications. 3G Security; WLAN Interworking security (Release 7). 3GPP TS 33.234 v7.0.0, March 2006
6. Arkko, J., Haverinen, H.: Extensible Authentication Protocol Method for 3rd Generation Authentication and Key Agreement (EAP-AKA). In: IETF RFC 4187, January 2006
7. Kambourakis, G., Rouskas, A., Gritzalis, S.: Advanced SSL/TLS based authentication for secure WLAN-3G interworking. IEEE Commun. Proc. **151**(5), 501–506 (2004)
8. Idrissi, Y., Zahid, N., Jedra, M.: Security analysis of 3GPP (LTE)—WLAN interworking and a new local authentication method based on EAP-AKA. FGCT, pp. 137–142 (2012)
9. Norrman, K.: 5G security standardization Security, Master Researcher, Ericsson Research (2016)
10. Caragata, D., El Assad, S., Shoniregun, C., Akmayeva, G.: UMTS security: enhancement of identification, authentication and key agreement protocols. In: Internet Technology and Secured Transactions (ICITST), pp. 278–282 (2011)
11. Hamandi, K., Sarji, I., Chehab, A., Elhajj, I., Kayssi, A.: Privacy enhanced and computationally efficient HSK-AKA LTE scheme. In: Advanced Information Networking and Applications Workshops (WAINA), pp. 929–934 (2013)
12. Huan, C.K.: Security analysis and enhancements in LTE-advanced networks, doctoral dissertation. Department of Mobile Systems Engineering, Sungkyunkwan University, South Korea (2011)

13. Abdeljebbar, M., Elkouch, R.: Security analysis of LTE/SAE networks over E-UTRAN. In: 2016 International Conference on Information Technology for Organizations Development (IT4OD), pp. 1–5 (2016)
14. Song, M., Choi, J.-Y., Cho, J.-D., Jeong, J., Song, B.-H., Lee, H.: Reduction of authentication cost based on key caching for inter-MME handover support. In: High Performance Computing and Simulation (HPCS) (2014)
15. Alezabi, K.A., Hashim, F., Hashim, S.J., Ali, B.M.: An efficient authentication and key agreement protocol for 4G (LTE) networks. In: 2014 IEEE Region 10 Symposium, pp. 502–507 (2014)
16. Armando, A., et al.: The AVISPA tool for the automated validation of internet security protocols and applications. In: Etessami, K., Rajamani, S.K. (eds.) CAV 2005. LNCS, vol. 3576, pp. 281–285. Springer, Heidelberg (2005). doi:10.1007/11513988_27
17. IEEE Standard for local and metropolitan area networks: Mobility Sensitive Master Key Derivation and Fast Re-authentication for 802.16m. C802.16m-07/029, February 2007

An Agreement Graph-Based-Authentication Scheme for 5G Networks

Maroua Gharam(✉) and Noureddine Boudriga

Communication Networks and Security Research Laboratory,
University of Carthage, Carthage, Tunisia
maroua.gharam@supcom.tn

Abstract. Recently, densified small cell deployment with overlay coverage through coexisting heterogeneous access networks has emerged as a viable solution for 5G mobile network architectures. While they provide useful features, these architectures bring new challenges to security provisioning due to the potential frequent mobility and authentication requirements in small cells and HetNets. This paper proposes a new authentication approach that copes with users mobility. It is based on a concept called agreement graph, allows 5G users to move freely, and improves machine access continuity and seamless authentication to registered users, while allowing local and temporary identification of non registered machines.

Keywords: Graph theory · 5G networks · Cellular mobility · Users authentication

1 Introduction

Over the last decade, anywhere and anytime wireless connectivity has become a reality and has resulted in increased mobile traffic. 5G networking and other emerging wireless communication technologies are expected to constitute a new generation of cooperative ubiquitous mobile information networks to meet the demand of mobile customers. The remarkable growth of the resulting data traffic is supposed to pose huge loads on the radio spectrum resources in future 5G cellular networks. Therefore, network densification using small cells is considered to be an essential solution in the emerging networks. Nonetheless, the massive deployment of small cells presents several challenges in network management and security, including interference alignment, extensive back hauling, and incompatibility of security mechanisms over heterogeneous networks (HetNets).

Network management and service provisioning are particularly challenging in 5G networks due to the increased number of heterogeneous base stations, the complexity of network architecture, and the repetitive change of cell attachments. In fact, 5G users may leave one cell and join another more frequently. As the cells have reduced sizes, excessive handovers could introduce unacceptable levels of latency. Coupled with access heterogeneity, this situation may generate

E. Sabir et al. (Eds.): UNet 2017, LNCS 10542, pp. 509–520, 2017.
https://doi.org/10.1007/978-3-319-68179-5_44

security vulnerabilities. Therefore, faster, efficient, robust, and cooperative handover authentication scheme need to be developed for complex 5G HetNets. In this context, many research works have been conducted to address such vulnerabilities in the presence of heterogeneous access networks [9,10].

To enable handover between different wireless networks, various authentication servers and protocols can be involved due to the closed nature and structure of each network composing the HetNet, providing frequent establishments of trust relationships and authentications during the mobility of the users [1]. For this, the Third Generation Partnership Project (3GPP) has proposed a specific key hierarchy and handover message flows for different mobility scenarios [5]. However, the specific key designed for handover and the different handover procedures tend to increase the handover operation complexity in 5G HetNets, if applied as they are. As the authentication server is often located remotely, the delay due to frequent inquiries between access points (APs) and the authentication server for user verification may be unacceptable (with up to hundreds of milliseconds [8]).

The authors of [2,3] have proposed simplified handover authentication schemes involving direct authentication between APs and users based on public cryptography method. These schemes realize mutual authentication and key agreements with the visited network through a three-way handshake without implicating any third party, as the authentication, authorization, and accounting (AAA) server. However, although the handover authentication procedure is simplified, the computation cost and delay are increased due to the overhead for exchanging more cryptographic messages through the wireless interface [8].

On the other hand, since roaming may be defined as the set of mechanisms that allows extending the connectivity service offered by a network to a location that is not covered by it, but is covered by a visited network (VN), the roaming process presents several similarities with the handover including the authentication, reservation, and connection reestablishment. Roaming support is accommodated through the implementation of mobility, authentication, authorization, and billing procedures. Therefore, the concept of agreement, generally used in roaming, may be the basis for a useful concept to define the relation between the home network and the customer, on one hand, and the relationship between the home network and the visited network, on the other hand. The new concept should be able to provide new features such as composition and delegation, if needed.

Motivated by all these issues, we propose in this paper an authentication schemes based on an agreement graph for 5G users/machines. In this scheme, the authentication process is always assigned to the home network by adding a communication layer between the home network and the foreign network. The communication layer is created according to the communication agreements established either through a direct link between the home network and the foreign network, or through an intermediate network, if agreement is allowed. The contributions are three fold. First, we define and analyze an agreement based graph (AbG) and show how it can support seamless handover in a 5G network.

Second, based on AbG, we build an authentication procedure for 5G networks distinguishing three types of communication agreements; they are: the roaming agreement, user2network agreement, and M2M agreement. Third, we provide a scheme capable of allowing local registration capabilities authorization a machine to identify and authenticate other machines.

The remaining of this paper is organized as follows. In Sect. 2, we extend the concept of roaming agreement so that it includes several forms of data structures supporting roaming and handover. In Sect. 3, the agreement-based graph (AbG) is detailed and some of its properties are highlighted. In Sect. 4, the description of the proposed schemes are developed for 5G HetNets. In Sect. 5, the simulation results are provided to evaluate the performance of the proposed authentication schemes. Finally, we conclude the paper in Sect. 6.

2 Communication Agreements: Role and Structure

The recent trend is to integrate more than one wireless interface into a single mobile device (MD). This allows users to benefit from the advantages of different technologies, depending on which one is available at their current location. In fact, the users should be able to access different technologies of different providers with only one subscription and only one bill. To this end, it is crucial to build communication agreements between communicating parties that unifies the traditional types of agreement; namely, the roaming agreement and user profile (or agreement); and allow the definition of a new type of agreement called M2M agreement. To this end, let us discuss the features that should ensured by the different agreements.

Roaming Agreement. The goal of roaming procedures is to provide network access to users in a wider coverage area than the one offered by a single provider, regardless of the network technology used. To make roaming available, network providers enter into roaming agreement procedures for the mobility of their users under the coverage of the other. The resulting agreement can be seen as a contract carried out between the providers. It enables users to roam across the networks with only one registration process and only one bill built by their home provider. Also it can be considered as a data structure that contains useful information for authentication, authorization, and accounting purposes.

The roaming agreement contains a set of contract terms that are negotiated to define the responsibility of the two network providers in natural and legal senses. According to GSM Association [7], the terms of the roaming agreement are based on technical and financial aspects. The technical aspect includes principally security and QoS information. In fact, it is critical that proper security procedures are adequately defined and continuously held throughout the entire security chain. On the other hand, it is essential to respect the QoS parameters declared in the roaming agreement during roaming [6]. Moreover, the financial aspect includes information about charging and billing. In particular, the concept of QoS-based charging is introduced, and there can be some additional charging parameters based on combinations of data, usage, and duration to be considered.

User Agreement. Mobile users are required to register with their home provider. In the registration process, users and their home providers must agree upon a set of information in a contract form that engages both of them. The information includes principally the access network technology to be used, the available services and coverage, the QoS profiles, the credentials to be used, the home provider liability, rights and duties of the user, and the pricing information.

In addition, a roaming profile may also be negotiated between users and their home providers in order to roam across different access networks. The roaming profile terms are based on the information of the user contract and the roaming agreement. It may include the set of foreign networks, the services the user will be able to access upon roaming.

M2M Agreement. Due to its wide coverage, a 5G cellular network is expected to support, besides traditional voice and data traffic, M2M communication. For this, the machine implementing M2M communication, should be able to register, identify, and authenticate machines in their vicinity. Indeed, the M2M is expected to play an important role as it is considered as an emerging technology to provide ubiquitous connectivity among devices without human intervention. Such type of communication requires the establishment of a special M2M agreement guaranteeing a reliable communication, while reducing security risks. The M2M agreement may include the set of services that one machine is able to offer to the other and their associated costs, the security procedures and related keys used to establish the communication channel between the two devices, and the payment method of service's consumption.

Based on the aforementioned types of agreements, we set up the following definition for the notion of communication agreement.

Definition 1. *A communication agreement is a data structure between a service provider and a service recipient of the form* $<A, B, C, D, F>$, *where:*

- *A defines the type of agreement and the information about its composability;*
- *B contains parameters for the identification of the service provider and recipient;*
- *C contains parameters related to the authentication process and the credentials to be used;*
- *D contains parameters describing the QoS that the recipient is allowed to get from the provider; and*
- *F, contains parameters describing the roaming profile of the recipient, if any.*

3 Agreement-based Graph (AbG)

The agreement-based graph (AbG) is a directed graph that represents a large amounts of network entities as well as the relationships between them in a clear and easy-to-understand format.

Definition 2. *An agreement-based graph AbG is a three tuple* $AbG = (V, E, \lambda)$, *where* V *is a set of vertices representing communication networks (or service providers);* E *is a set of edges* $(v, v') \in VxV$ *representing an agreement, where the provider is* v*, the recipient is* v'*, and* λ *is a label assigning to each vertice* v *a predicate* $\pi(v)$.

Examples of labels are multiple. A label can, for example, report on whether the labeled network is trustable (i.e., $\pi(v) = 1$ if, and only if v can be trusted). Other forms of labels can be used to support the authentication robustness, the quality of service provision, or the composability of the communication agreements.

A path in AbG is a sequence of agreements $(ag_1, \ldots, ag_n)$, where the recipient of ag_i is the provider of ag_{i+1}, for all i, and the pair (ag_i, ag_{i+1}) is composable. Therefore, a path of length 1 is nothing but an agreement between two networks, between a network and machine, or a machine and another machine. In the following, a path will be used to establish the authentication of a user. Figure 1 gives an example of AbG.

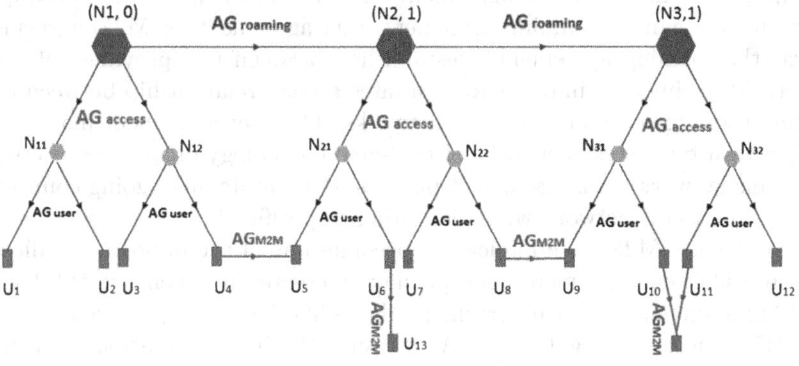

Fig. 1. Agreement-based Graph

Let us now show how AbG can be used to check several features. The following requirements are essential for a seamless mobility of users.

- *Service continuity:* The continuity states that the user can access a service anywhere any time in the area covered by the 5G network. To provide such a feature the AbG should comply with the following statement: For any user a that is the recipient of a communication agreement e provided by a network v, if a is under the coverage of a visited network v', then there is a path between v and v'; and all the recipients in that path are trustable.
- *Home network identification:* As the identity of the communicating parties is one of the important terms of a communication agreement, the foreign network should able to determine the identity of the user's home network. This is achieved by simple checking that there is a path between the home

network of the roaming user and the visited node, and the networks involved in that path are trustable.

- *User's authentication:* This requirement demands that the home network is already identified. User authentication can be achieved through a path linking the home network and the visited network involving trusted nodes. This path can help establishing a secure channel to allow the home network authenticating the user.

Many other feature can established using AbG, in particular those involving machine communication. For the sake of space, we choose to not discuss them.

Now, we notice that a 5G network is not only a single wireless technology, but also a fusion of existing wireless cooperating communication technologies. Each wireless communication technology comprises a set of specific network elements, protocols, and mechanisms. To simplify the manipulation of such complex architecture, we adjust the content of the communication agreement to those specified in 5G networks. As a result, a node in the AbG refers to an authentication center (AuC) of a cellular access network, an authentication module in a wireless access point (AP), or simply a 5G device in the M2M communication. In addition, a communication agreement refers to one of the standardized types of agreements; namely roaming agreement, user agreement, or M2M agreement. In fact, the roaming agreement is established between two providers of different network technology in order to guarantee a trust relationship between them enabling users to roam across these networks. The user agreement may be created between two access networks of the same technology or between users and their home network. This agreement permits to maintain an ongoing connection with a given access network while delivering a specific QoS.

Finally, since M2M communication becomes one of the important indices in 5G systems, a new agreement concept may be created between two 5G devices, called M2M agreement. Such agreement allows 5G devices to provide services to other 5G devices in a legal terms. As a result, the implementation of all these agreements ensures a trusted 5G architecture.

4 Authentication in 5G: An Approach Using AbG

An authentication scheme is developed in this section to prevent unauthorized access and protect against sensitive information disclosure. The authentication process requires verification of user's identities that are generated and recorded during the registration process.

4.1 Registration and Authentication Processes

The network registration or network attachment consists on making contact with the access network first, and next the mobile has to register to get access to and use the network. According to the 3GPP LTE [4], in order to make contact with the access network, the mobile uses a paging or control channel to send an "attach" message. Once this has been achieved, it is necessary for the mobile to be accepted onto the access network. For this purpose, it is crucial to have a register of the subscribed users, known as the Authentication Center (AuC), where the users credentials are stored.

However, when the users are not subscribed to a specific access network, the case of an M2M communication, they demand services from machines that are already attached to an access network. In this case, the machine that demands a service must be registered in the database of the M2M Service Provider (MSP), by sending its name and its geographic position.

Three methods can be distinguished to provide authentication:

- *Password-based authentication:* This method is the easiest authentication method, where a verification table is used to check the validity of the pair of "username-password" introduced during the authentication process by the user. The user name is the user identity and the entry of the password authenticates the user as the rightful owner.
- *Certificate-based authentication:* A certificate is an electronic document issued by a trusted third party named Certification Authority (CA). This document contains a particular public key, the user name, the CA name, expiration date, among other information. During authentication, the user sends its certificate and responds to a challenge showing that has the associated private key. The user authentication is based on the response that the user provides.
- *Challenge/response-based authentication:* In a challenge/response-based authentication, a user is identified by an authentication server with a shared security association (SA), which is a trust relationship with many parameters such as keys and algorithms for secure services. During authentication, the server sends a random number to the user for encryption, and verifies the returned value, after decryption. This authentication method is widely used with the cellular networks, [4].

4.2 The Authentication Scheme

This subsection describes the users' authentication procedure during their mobility under 5G HetNets basing on the AbG. As illustrated in Fig. 2, when a subscribed user requests a service from a visited network, it must be authenticated by sending its credentials as well as its home network identity. In this case, the visited network creates the path to reach the home network basing on the composable agreements through the trusted networks. Once the path is established, the visited network sends the user' credentials to its home network. This latter verifies the received credentials by applying the authentication method specified in the home network technology. After a successful authentication, the user is able to benefit from the requested service within the visited network.

However, for the M2M communication, when a machine is not subscribed to an access network, it requests a service from an other machine that is attached to a specific access network. In this case, the authentication procedure requires that the two machines must be neighbours. As depicted in Fig. 3, the machine

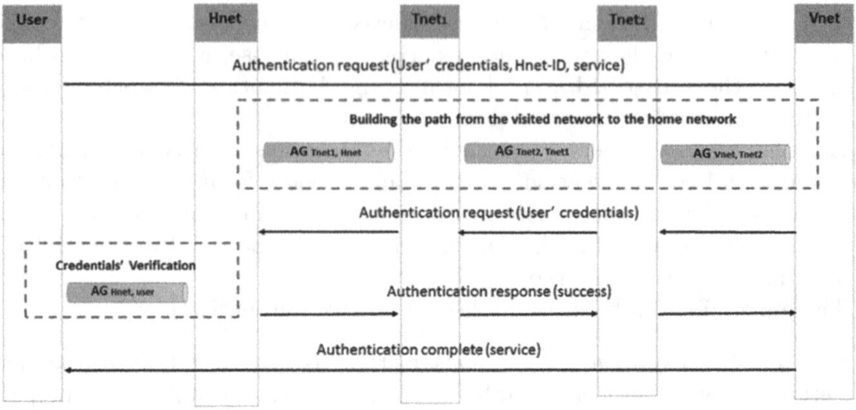

Fig. 2. Authentication within the visited network

sends a service request to its neighbour. If the neighbour machine accepts the request, it creates a temporary identity for the other machine and stores it in the MSP for future communications. In addition to the temporary identity, an M2M agreement is created between them, for a defined period of time, including the requested service, the provided QoS, the identification keys, and the associated costs. Once the M2M agreement lifetime is not expired, some other M2M communications may be established between these two machines.

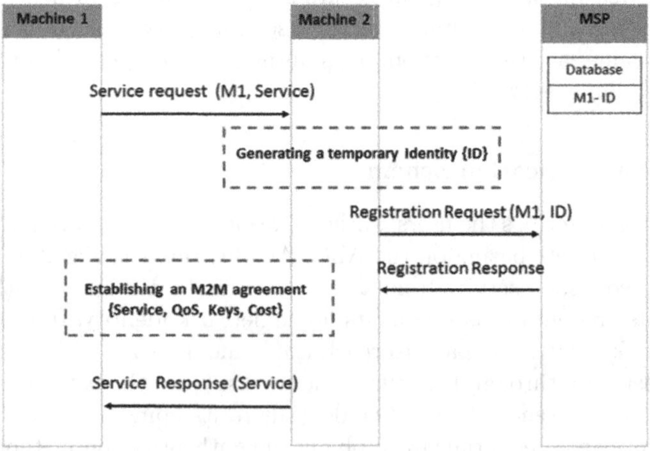

Fig. 3. Authentication in the M2M communication

5 Performance Evaluation

During simulation, we consider a network consisting of a small city equipped with four different access network technologies (e.g.WiFi, 2G, 3G, and 4G). We also consider three types of services, voice call, streaming video, and conversational video, with respectively maximal duration equal to 4 min, 15 min, and 30 min respectively. Initially, each user is subscribed in a single home network and able to move to the other network technologies. During mobility, the authentication process is based on the link created between the home and the foreign network according to the inter-technology agreement as specified in Table 1, where $AG_{i,j}$represents the agreement created between the foreign network i and the home network j, and (1, 0) indicates whenever the network$i$ accept to trust the users of network j toward an other network or not. In this simulation, we assume that the users are able to leave their home network with probability rate of 50% each minute during one hour. To evaluate the performance of our platform, we use Matlab simulator.

Table 1. Inter-technology agreements

F \ H	WiFi	2G	3G	4G
WiFi	**	$AG_{wifi,2G}$, 1	$AG_{wifi,3G}$, 0	$AG_{wifi,4G}$, 1
2G	—	**	—	$AG_{2G,4G}$, 1
3G	$AG_{3G,wifi}$, 0	—	**	—
4G	$AG_{4G,wifi}$, 1	$AG_{4G,2G}$, 1	—	**

First, we begin by studying the blockage of users during mobility (Fig. 4) while varying the number of users as well as the user's mobility rate. In fact, the blockage represents the number of times users are blocked while asking services from the foreign network per time slot. The mobility rate represents the portion of users who moves during their communication relatively to the total number of users in the network. Indeed, users are blocked during mobility when there is no inter-technology agreement between the home and the foreign network, in addition to the absence of an intermediate network that can trust these users.

We noticed that for a low mobility rate (lower than 50%), the blockage increases slightly, it also remains fairly constant, when the number of users increases. However, for a high mobility rate (higher than 50%) and a great number of users in the network, the blockage increases to reach the value of 16 for 250 users. This is mainly explained by the mobility effect, when users move frequently to foreign networks with the absence of a link to reach the user's home network.

Figure 5 shows that the blockage of users during mobility is also affected by the intermediate network decision. So when the other networks refuse to accept users, the blockage increases. Figure 6 shows the variation of the overhead referring to the number of the exchanged messages during mobility followed by

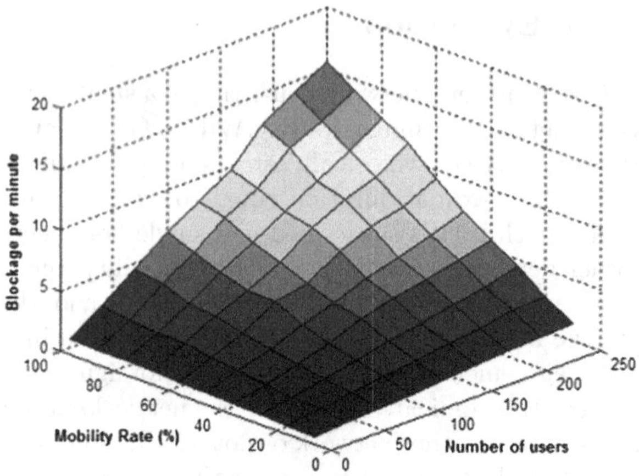

Fig. 4. Blockage in function of number of users and mobility rate

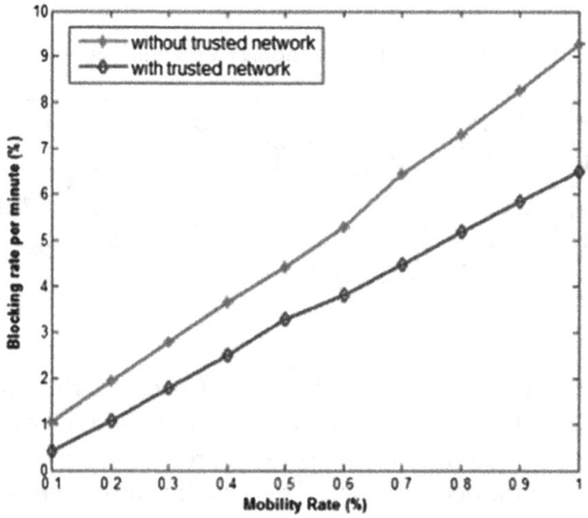

Fig. 5. Blocking rate in function of mobility rate

the authentication procedure in three-dimensional representation while varying the number of users as well as the user's mobility rate. We noticed that the overhead increases constantly while increasing the mobility rate and the number of users.

During mobility, the user can undergo one of the following possible states. Firstly, it can get the service in the foreign network while an inter-technology agreement is already established. This generates an the overhead of 14 messages. Secondly, it can get it through an intermediate trusted network, and the overhead is 16 messages in this case. Thirdly, it can be blocked within the foreign network, the overhead is 2 messages. However, when the user is authenticated by its home

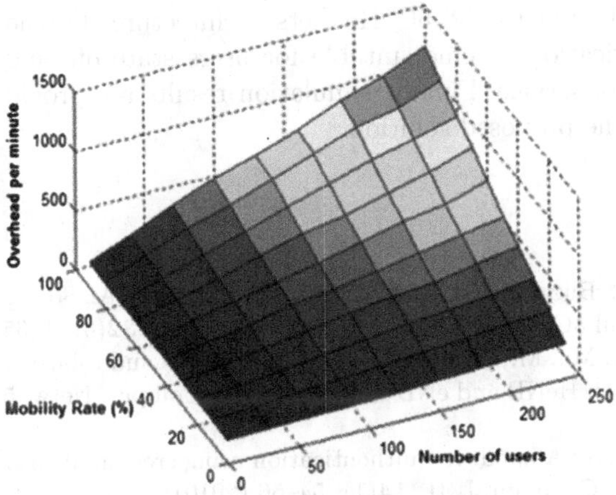

Fig. 6. Overhead in function of number of users and mobility rate

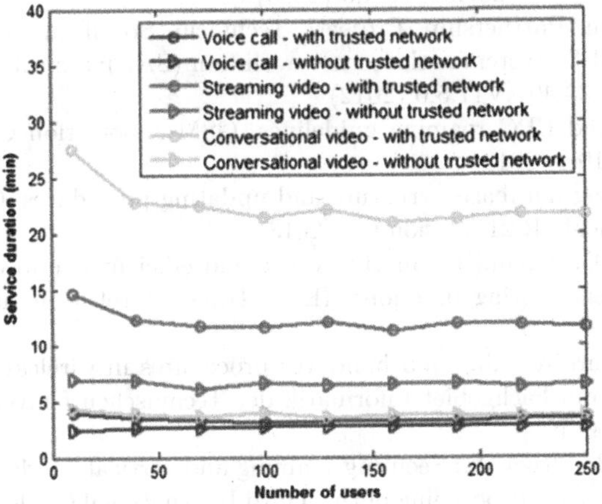

Fig. 7. Service duration in function of number of users

network, the overhead is 10 messages. So, we can conclude that, in each time slot, the overhead is in the range of $(2 * n)$ and $(16 * n)$ where n is the number of users. Figure 7 illustrates the effect of user's blockage on the service duration for voice call, streaming video, and conversational video. In fact, each service can end successfully when the blockage is null.

6 Conclusion

In this paper, we focused on the authentication of users during mobility in 5G HetNets. We first present the different agreement types enabling a flexible communication between network elements. Then, we propose an agreement-based graph (AbG) adapted to the 5G HetNets architecture. Furthermore, we propose an authentication scheme suitable for users state offering the continuity and the quality of service. Finally, simulation results are provided showing the performance of the proposed solution.

References

1. Andrews, J.G., Buzzi, S., Choi, W., Hanly, S.V., Lozano, A., Soong, A.C.K., Zhang, J.C.: What will 5G be? IEEE J. Sel. Areas Commun. **32**(6), 1065–1082 (2014)
2. Cao, J., Li, H., Ma, M., Zhang, Y., Lai, C.: A simple and robust handover authentication between HeNB and eNB in lte networks. Comput. Netw. **56**(8), 2119–2131 (2012)
3. Choi, J., Jung, S.: A handover authentication using credentials based on chameleon hashing. IEEE Commun. Lett. **14**(1), 54–56 (2010)
4. 3rd Generation Partnership Project: Technical Specification Group Services and System Aspects; 3GPP. System architecture evolution (SAE), security architecture (release 9). 3GPP. TS 33.401 V9.4.0 (2009)
5. 3rd Generation Partnership Project: Technical Specification Group Service, Aspects, S: 3GPP. System architecture evolution (SAE); security architecture (rel 11), 3GPP. TS 33.401 V11.5.0 (2012)
6. GSMA: LTE and EPC roaming guidelines. GSM Association Official Document IR.88 Version 10.0 (2013)
7. GSMA: Roaming database, structure and updating procedures. GSM Association Official Document IR.21 Version 9.1 (2013)
8. He, D., Chen, C., Chan, S., Bu, J.: Secure and efficient handover authentication based on bilinear pairing functions. IEEE Trans. Wirel. Commun. **11**(1), 48–53 (2012)
9. Meyer, U.: Secure roaming and handover procedures in wireless access networks. Ph.D. thesis, Vom Fachgebiet Informatik der Technischen Universitat Darmstadt genehmigte (2005)
10. Krichene, N., Boudriga, N.: Securing roaming and vertical handover in fourth generation networks. In: Proceeding of the Third International Conference on Network and System Security (NSS 2009), pp. 225–231 (2009)

Green Base Station Placement for Microwave Backhaul Links

Alonso Silva[1(✉)] and Antonia Maria Masucci[2]

[1] Nokia Bell Labs, Nokia Paris-Saclay, Route de Villejust, 91620 Nozay, France
alonso.silva@nokia-bell-labs.com
[2] Orange Labs, 44 Avenue de la République, 92320 Châtillon, France
antoniamaria.masucci@orange.com

Abstract. Wireless mobile backhaul networks have been proposed as a substitute in cases in which wired alternatives are not available due to economical or geographical reasons. In this work, we study the location problem of base stations in a given region where mobile terminals are distributed according to a certain probability density function and the base stations communicate through microwave backhaul links. Using results of optimal transport theory, we provide the optimal asymptotic distribution of base stations in the considered setting by minimizing the total power over the whole network.

1 Introduction

There are several scenarios in which wired alternatives are not the best solution to satisfy the traffic demand of users due to economical or geographical reasons. Wireless mobile backhaul networks have been proposed as a solution to these types of situations. Since these networks do not require costly cable constructions, they reduce total investment costs. However, achieving high speed and long range in wireless backhaul networks remains a significant technical challenge.

In this work, we consider a clique network of base stations and we assume that data is transmitted independently in different radio frequency channels. We use optimal transport theory, also known as theory of mass transportation, to determine in this simplified scenario the optimal asymptotic placement of base stations communicating through backhaul links.

Optimal transport theory has its origins in planning problems, where a central planner needs to find a transport plan between two non-negative probability measures which minimizes the average transport cost. Resource allocation problems and/or assignment problems coming from engineering or economics are common applications of this theory.

In the present work, we study the problem of minimizing the total power used by the network to achieve a certain throughput and we use recent results of optimal transport theory to find the optimal asymptotic base stations locations.

E. Sabir et al. (Eds.): UNet 2017, LNCS 10542, pp. 521–531, 2017.
https://doi.org/10.1007/978-3-319-68179-5_45

1.1 Related Works

Location games have been introduced by Hotelling [1], who modeled the spatial competition along a street between two firms for persuading the largest number of customers which are uniformly distributed. Problems similar to location games, as for example the maximum capture problem, have been analyzed by [2,3] and references therein.

Within the communication networks community, Altman et al. [4,5] studied the duopoly situation in the uplink scenario of a cellular network where users are placed on a line segment. Considering the particular cost structure that arises in the cellular context, the authors observe that complex cell shapes are obtained at equilibrium. Silva et al. [6–8] analyzed the problem of mobile terminals association to base stations using optimal transport theory and considering the data traffic congestion produced by this mobile terminals to base stations association.

1.2 Energy Efficiency

Our objective is to conceive wireless backhaul networks able to guarantee quality of service while minimizing the energy consumption of the system. We follow the free space path loss model in which the signal strength drops in proportion to the square of the distance between transmitter and receiver since it is a good approximation for outdoor scenarios.

The works on stochastic geometry are related to our study (see e.g. the books of Baccelli and Blaszczyszyn [9,10]) but we do not consider any particular deployment distribution function such as e.g. Poisson point processes.

The remaining of this work is organized as follows. In Sect. 2 we provide the model formulation of the considered problem where we redefine the probability density function of mobile terminals to incorporate their throughput requirements and determine the power cost function of inter-cell and intra-cell communications. In Sect. 3 we provide the main results of our work by considering the free-path loss approximation and asymptotic results from optimal transportation theory. In Sect. 4 we provide illustrative simulations for the asymptotic results obtained in the previous section, and in Sect. 5 we conclude our work.

2 Model Formulation

A summary of the notation used on this work can be found in Table 1.

We are interested on the analysis of a microwave backhaul network deployed over a bounded region, which we denote by $\mathcal{D}$, over the two-dimensional plane. Mobile terminals are distributed according to a given probability density function $f(x,y)$. The proportion of mobile terminals in a sub-region $\mathcal{A} \subseteq \mathcal{D}$ is

$$\iint_{\mathcal{A}} f(x,y)\,dx\,dy.$$

Table 1. Notation

N	Total number of mobile terminals in the network
K	Total number of base stations
f	Deployment distribution function of mobile terminals
(x_k, y_k)	Position of the k-th base station
C_i	Cell determined by the i-th base station
N_i	Number of mobile terminals associated to the i-th BS
h_i	Channel gain function in the i-th cell
h_{ij}	Channel gain between base station i and base station j
m_i	Traffic requirement satisfied by base station i
m	Total traffic requirement satisfied by the network

The number of mobile terminals in sub-region $\mathcal{A} \subseteq \mathcal{D}$, denoted by $N(\mathcal{A})$, can be approximated by

$$N(\mathcal{A}) = N \cdot \left(\iint_{\mathcal{A}} f(x,y)\, dx\, dy \right),$$

where N denotes the total number of mobile terminals in the network.

We consider K base stations in the network, denoted by $\mathrm{BS}_1, \mathrm{BS}_2, \ldots, \mathrm{BS}_K$, at positions $(x_1, y_1), (x_2, y_2), \ldots, (x_K, y_K)$ to be determined. Our objective is to minimize the energy consumption in the system.

We denote by C_i the set of mobile terminals associated to base station BS_i and by N_i the number of mobile terminals within that cell, i.e., the cardinality of the set C_i.

2.1 Modification of the Distribution Function

The probability density function and the throughput requirements of mobile terminals both depend on the location. To simplify the problem resolution, we consider the following modification of the probability density function to have the location dependency in only one function. The probability density function of mobile terminals considered in our work and denoted by $f(x,y)$ is general. Instead of considering a particular probability density function, denoted by $\tilde{f}(x,y)$, and an average throughput requirement, denoted by $\tilde{\theta}(x,y)$, in each location (x,y), we consider a constant throughput $\theta > 0$ to be determined and redefine the distribution of mobile terminals $f(x,y)$ as follows

$$f(x,y) := \frac{\tilde{f}(x,y)\tilde{\theta}(x,y)}{\theta} \quad \text{for all } (x,y) \in \mathcal{D}.$$

Since $f(x,y)$ must be a probability density function, we need to impose

$$\iint_{\mathcal{D}} f(x,y)\, dx\, dy = 1,$$

or equivalently,

$$\frac{1}{\theta}\iint_{\mathcal{D}} \tilde{f}(x,y)\tilde{\theta}(x,y)\,dx\,dy = 1.$$

For this equation to hold, we have to impose

$$\theta = \iint_{\mathcal{D}} \tilde{f}(x,y)\tilde{\theta}(x,y)\,dx\,dy.$$

We have that the following equation holds:

$$f(x,y)\theta = \tilde{f}(x,y)\tilde{\theta}(x,y).$$

The previous equation simply states that, e.g., a mobile terminal with double demand than another mobile terminal would be considered as two different mobile terminals both at the same location with the same demand as the other mobile terminal.

Since in a microwave backhaul network, we need to consider the energy from within base stations and from base stations to mobile terminals, we need to consider both the intra-cell costs and the inter-cell costs. This is the subject of the following two subsections.

2.2 Intra-cell Costs

The power transmitted, denoted by P^T, from base station BS_i to a mobile terminal located at position (x,y) is denoted by $P_i^T(x,y) = P_i(x,y)$. The received power, denoted by P^R, at the mobile terminal located at position (x,y) associated to base station BS_i is given by $P_i^R(x,y) = P_i(x,y)h_i(x,y)$, where $h_i(x,y)$ is the channel gain between base station BS_i and the mobile terminal located at position (x,y), for every $i \in \{1,\ldots,K\}$.

We assume that neighboring base stations transmit their signals in orthogonal frequency bands and that interference between base stations that are far from each other is negligible. Consequently, instead of considering the SINR (Signal to Interference plus Noise Ratio), we consider as performance measure the SNR (Signal to Noise Ratio).

The SNR received at mobile terminals at position (x,y) in cell C_i is given by

$$\text{SNR}_i(x,y) = \frac{P_i(x,y)h_i(x,y)}{\sigma^2},$$

where σ^2 is the expected noise power. We assume that the associated instantaneous mobile throughput is given by the following expression, which is based on Shannon's capacity theorem:

$$\theta_i(x,y) = \log(1 + \text{SNR}_i(x,y)).$$

The throughput requirement translates into

$$\theta_i(x,y) \geq \theta.$$

Thanks to our previous development, we can consider a constant throughput requirement through the modification of the probability density function.

Therefore, the throughput requirement becomes

$$\log\left(1+\frac{P_i(x,y)h_i(x,y)}{\sigma^2}\right)=\theta,$$

or equivalently,

$$P_i(x,y)=\frac{\sigma^2}{h_i(x,y)}(2^\theta-1). \tag{1}$$

Therefore the intra-cell power required by base station i is given by

$$P_i^{\text{intra}}=\iint_{C_i}P_i(x,y)f(x,y)\,dx\,dy. \tag{2}$$

The previous equation provide us an energy cost function for the intra-cell requirements of the network. In the following subsection, our analysis will be focused on the inter-cell requirements.

2.3 Inter-cell Costs

In order to take into account the routing cost, we consider the power transmitted P^T from base station BS_i to base station BS_j denoted by $P_{ij}^T=P_{ij}$. The received power P^R at the receiving base station BS_j from the transmitting base station BS_i is given by $P_{ij}^R=P_{ij}h_{ij}$, where h_{ij} is the channel gain between base station BS_i and base station BS_j. The SNR received at the receiving base station BS_j from the transmitting base station BS_i is given by

$$\text{SNR}_{ij}=\frac{P_{ij}h_{ij}}{\sigma^2},$$

where σ^2 is the expected noise power. We assume that the associated instantaneous base station throughput at the receiving base station BS_j from the transmitting base station BS_i is given by the following expression, which is based on Shannon's capacity theorem:

$$\theta_{ij}=\log(1+\text{SNR}_{ij}).$$

Let us define by m_i the traffic requirement concentrated at base station BS_i, i.e.

$$m_i=\theta\iint_{C_i}f(x,y)\,dxdy.$$

We assume that the traffic requirement m_i concentrated at base station BS_i is sent at the other base stations proportionally to the traffic requirement at the other base stations. Therefore, the traffic between the receiving base station BS_j and the transmitting base station BS_i is given by $m_i(m_j/m)$.

We make the simplifying assumption $\log(1 + \mathrm{SNR}_{ij}) \approx \mathrm{SNR}_{ij}$. Then the throughput requirement translates into

$$\frac{P_{ij} h_{ij}}{\sigma^2} = m_i \frac{m_j}{m},$$

or equivalently

$$P_{ij} = \frac{\sigma^2}{h_{ij}} \frac{m_i m_j}{m}. \tag{3}$$

The power cost to transmit the traffic m_i is thus given by

$$\sum_{j=1}^{K} \frac{\sigma^2}{h_{ij}} \frac{m_i m_j}{m}, \tag{4}$$

where

$$\begin{aligned} m &= \sum_{j=1}^{K} m_j \\ &= \theta \sum_{j=1}^{K} \iint_{C_j} f(x,y)\,dxdy \\ &= \theta \iint_{D} f(x,y)\,dxdy. \end{aligned}$$

Similar to Eq. (2) of the previous subsection, Eq. (4) provides us a power cost function for the inter-cell requirements of the network. In the next section, we consider both inter-cell and intra-cell cost functions to determine the total power cost and obtain the asymptotic location of base stations to minimize this total power cost.

3 Results

From the previous section, the total power of the network is equal to the sum of intra-cell power (the sum of the power used within each cell in the network) and the inter-cell power (the sum of the power used over the pairs of communicating base stations in the network), i.e.

$$P_{\mathrm{total}} = \sum_{i=1}^{K} P_i^{\mathrm{intra}} + \sum_{i=1}^{K} \sum_{\substack{j=1 \\ j \neq i}}^{K} P_{ij}^{\mathrm{inter}},$$

where

$$P_i^{\mathrm{intra}} = \iint_{C_i} P_i(x,y)\, f(x,y)\, dx\, dy,$$

is the intra-cell power consumption in cell C_i and from Eq. (1), we obtain

$$P_i^{\text{intra}} = \iint_{C_i} \frac{\sigma^2}{h_i(x,y)}(2^\theta - 1)f(x,y)\,dx\,dy,$$

and from Eq. (3) the inter-cell power consumption is

$$P_{ij}^{\text{inter}} = \frac{\sigma^2}{h_{ij}}\frac{m_i m_j}{m}.$$

In the following subsection, thanks to the free-space path loss approximation, we are able to find an expression for the channel gain and the total power cost.

3.1 Free-Space Path Loss Approximation

Let $d_i(x,y)$ denote the Euclidean distance between mobile terminal at position (x,y) and base station BS_i located at (x_i,y_i), i.e.

$$d_i(x,y) = \sqrt{(x_i - x)^2 + (y_i - y)^2}.$$

Similarly, let d_{ij} denote the Euclidean distance between base station BS_i located at (x_i,y_i) and base station BS_j located at (x_j,y_j), i.e.

$$d_{ij} = \sqrt{(x_i - x_j)^2 + (y_i - y_j)^2}.$$

The free-space path loss approximation gives us that the channel gain between base station BS_i and the mobile terminal located at position (x,y) is given by

$$h_i(x,y) = d_i(x,y)^{-2},$$

and analogously the free-space path loss approximation give us that the channel gain between base station BS_i and base station BS_j is given by

$$h_{ij} = d_{ij}^{-2}.$$

The total power cost is therefore given by

$$\sum_{i=1}^{K} \iint_{C_i} (2^\theta - 1)\sigma^2 d_i(x,y)^2 f(x,y)\,dx\,dy + \frac{\sigma^2}{m}\sum_{i=1}^{K}\sum_{\substack{j=1\\ j\neq i}}^{K} m_i m_j d_{ij}^2. \tag{5}$$

When the number of base stations K is very large, in our setting tends to infinity, instead of looking at the locations of base stations (x_i,y_i), we will look into the limit density ν of the locations (x_i,y_i). To do that, we identify each set of K points with the measure

$$\nu_K = \frac{1}{K}\sum_{i=1}^{K} \delta_{(x_i,y_i)},$$

where $\delta_{(x_i,y_i)}$ is the delta Dirac function at location (x_i,y_i).

The asymptotic analysis of these functions has been performed (see e.g. [11, 12]) within the context of optimal transport theory with the extensive use of Γ-convergence.

The inter-cell power cost in terms of the measure ν_K is given by

$$\frac{\sigma^2}{m}\int_{\mathcal{D}}\int_{\mathcal{D}}\|(x_i,y_i)-(x_j,y_j)\|^2\,d\nu_K\,d\nu_K,$$

which is equivalent to

$$\frac{\sigma^2}{m}\int_{\mathcal{D}\times\mathcal{D}}\|(x_i,y_i)-(x_j,y_j)\|^2\,d(\nu_K\otimes\nu_K).$$

We notice that the discrete sum of Eq. (5) becomes an integral by considering the limit of measures $\{\nu_K\}_{K\in\mathbb{N}}$.

The total cost taking into account both cost functions gives the problem

$$\begin{aligned}&\text{Min}\sum_{i=1}^{K}\iint_{C_i}(2^\theta-1)\sigma^2\|(x,y)-(x_i,y_i)\|^2 f(x,y)\,dxdy\\&+\frac{\sigma^2}{m}\int_{\mathcal{D}\times\mathcal{D}}\|(x_i,y_i)-(x_j,y_j)\|^2\,d(\nu_K\otimes\nu_K).\end{aligned}$$

We denote the function

$$V(x)=|x|^2.$$

The necessary conditions of optimality (see [13]) are

$$(2^\theta-1)\sigma^2\phi+\frac{2\sigma^2}{m}V*\nu=c\quad \nu-\text{a.e.} \tag{6}$$

where ϕ is the Kantorovich potential for the transport from f to ν and c is the Lagrange multiplier of the mass constraint on ν.

A connection between the Kantorovich potential ϕ and the transport map T from f to ν is given by the Monge-Ampère equation

$$f=\nu(T)\det(\nabla T).$$

From Eq. (6), we obtain

$$(2^\theta-1)\sigma^2\nabla\phi+\frac{2\sigma^2}{m}\nabla V*\nu=0.$$

Since

$$T(x)=x-\nabla\phi(x).$$

Therefore we have the system

$$\begin{cases}(2^\theta-1)\sigma^2(x-T(x))+\frac{2\sigma^2}{m}\nabla V*\nu=0\\ f=\nu(T)\text{det}(\nabla T).\end{cases} \tag{7}$$

We can proceed by an iterative scheme, fixing an initial ν_0 and obtaining T_0 from the first equation of the system (7) and obtaining ν_1 from the second equation and proceed iterating the scheme above.

The previous system of equations allows us to find the optimal asymptotic base stations placement ν as a function of the distribution of mobile terminals f when the solution exists.

4 Simulations

We follow the development done in [13]. We simulate the example for the one-dimensional case. If we suppose that the barycenter of ν is in the origin, we obtain:

$$V * \nu = mx^2 + \int y^2 \, d\nu(y),$$

so that

$$A\phi'(x) + 4Bx = 0,$$

which gives

$$\phi'(x) = -\frac{4}{(2^\theta - 1)} x \quad \text{and} \quad T(x) = \left(1 + \frac{4}{(2^\theta - 1)}\right).$$

Putting previous expressions in the one-dimensional Monge-Ampère equation and indicating by v the density of ν, we obtain

$$f(x) = \nu\left(\left(1 + \frac{4}{(2^\theta - 1)}\right) x\right) \left(1 + \frac{4}{(2^\theta - 1)}\right),$$

and changing variables

$$v(y) = \frac{1}{1 + \frac{4}{(2^\theta - 1)}} f\left(\frac{y}{1 + \frac{4}{(2^\theta - 1)}}\right). \tag{8}$$

We consider that mobile terminals are distributed over the line as a normal distribution function with zero mean and standard deviation equal to one, i.e. $\mathcal{N}(0, 1)$. We consider that the throughput requirement θ is constant and equal to 24 Kbps. We notice that as explained in Subsect. 2.1 we could have considered a non-constant throughput requirement and redefine the mobile terminal probability density function for the throughput requirement to be constant. From Eq. (8), we can compute the optimal base station distribution given by Fig. 1. We notice that the optimal base station distribution corresponds to a smoother normal probability distribution.

Motivated by the previous simulation, we consider a second scenario where mobile terminals are distributed as a truncated normal distribution function between $[-1, 1]$. From Eq. (8), we can compute the optimal base station distribution given by Fig. 2. From Fig. 2, we notice that surprisingly the optimal base

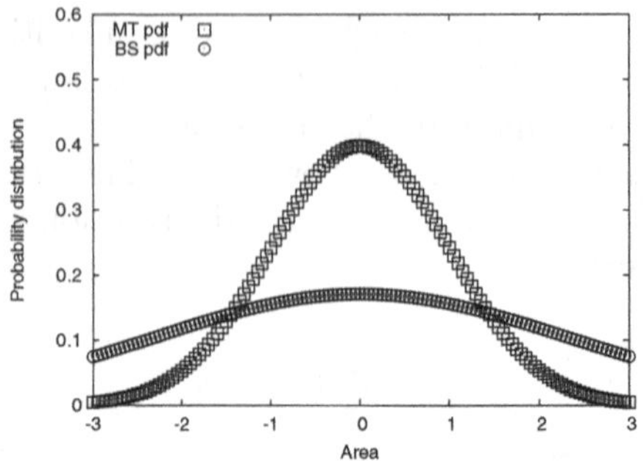

Fig. 1. Optimal probability distribution function of the base stations given the probability density function of the mobile terminals.

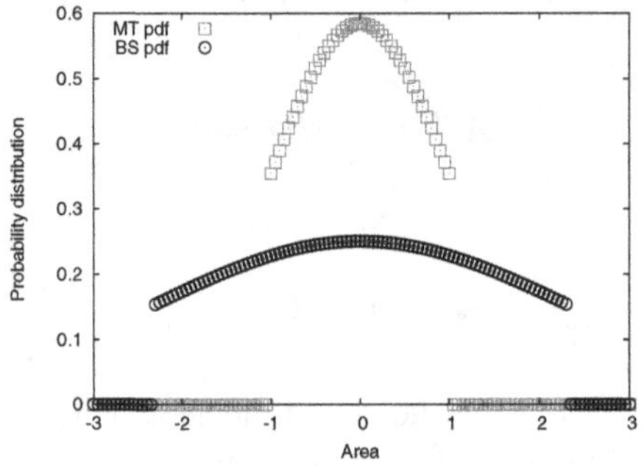

Fig. 2. Optimal probability distribution function of the base stations given the probability density function of the mobile terminals.

stations distribution has a support that does not coincide with the mobile terminals distribution. If we only consider the intra-cell cost we would have obtained the exact same probability distribution of mobile terminals (it is easy to see since in that case the cost would have been zero). We have thus verified that the optimal base station probability density function would have been modified by the intra-cell cost as given by Fig. 2. Similar to the first scenario, the optimal base station distribution corresponds to a smoother probability distribution.

5 Conclusions

In this work, we investigated the asymptotic optimal placement of base stations with microwave backhaul links. We considered the problem of minimizing the total power of the network while maintaining a required throughput. Using optimal transport theory, we provided the optimal asymptotic base station placement. Moreover, the case where routing cost is taken into account is also analyzed.

Acknowledgment. The work of A. Silva has been partially carried out at LINCS (http://www.lincs.fr).

References

1. Hotelling, H.: Stability in competition. Econ. J. **39**(153), 41–57 (1929)
2. Plastria, F.: Static competitive facility location: an overview of optimisation approaches. Eur. J. Oper. Res. **129**(3), 461–470 (2001)
3. Gabszewicz, J.J., Thisse, J.-F.: Location. In: Handbook of Game Theory with Economic Applications, vol. 1, pp. 281–304, Chapter. 9, Elsevier (1992)
4. Altman, E., Kumar, A., Singh, C.K., Sundaresan, R.: Spatial SINR games combining base station placement and mobile association. IEEE INFOCOM, 1629–1637 (2009)
5. Altman, E., Kumar, A., Singh, C.K., Sundaresan, R.: Spatial SINR games of base station placement and mobile association. IEEE/ACM Trans. Networking **20**(6), 1856–1869 (2012)
6. Silva, A., Tembine, H., Altman, E., Debbah, M.: Optimum and equilibrium in assignment problems with congestion: mobile terminals association to base stations. IEEE Trans. Autom. Control **58**, 2018–2031 (2013)
7. Silva, A., Tembine, H., Altman, E., Debbah, M.: Spatial games and global optimization for the mobile association problem: the downlink case. In: Proceedings of the 49th IEEE Conference on Decision and Control, CDC 2010, 15–17 December 2010, pp. 966–972, Atlanta, Georgia, USA (2010)
8. Silva, A., Tembine, H., Altman, E., Debbah, M.: Uplink spatial games on cellular networks. In: Proceedings of the 48th Annual Allerton Conference on Communication, Control, and Computing (Allerton), pp. 800–804. September 2010
9. Baccelli, F., Blaszczyszyn, B.: Stochastic geometry and wireless networks, volume 1: theory. Found. Trends Networking **3**(3–4), 249–449 (2009)
10. Baccelli, F., Blaszczyszyn, B.: Stochastic geometry and wireless networks, volume 2: applications. Found. Trends Networking **4**(1–2), 1–312 (2009)
11. Bouchitté, G., Jimenez, C., Rajesh, M.: Asymptotique d'un problème de positionnement optimal. C.R. Math. **335**(10), 853–858 (2002)
12. Buttazzo, G., Santambrogio, F.: A model for the optimal planning of an urban area. SIAM J. Math. Anal. **37**(2), 514–530 (2005)
13. Buttazzo, G., Bianco, S.G.L., Oliviero, F.: Optimal location problems with routing cost. arXiv preprint arXiv:1306.6070 (2013)

Joint Frame Detection and Channel Estimation for DCO-OFDM LiFi Systems

Yufei Jiang(✉), Majid Safari, and Harald Haas

LiFi Research and Development Centre, Institute for Digital Communications, The University of Edinburgh, Edinburgh EH9 3JL, UK
{Yufei.Jiang,majid.safari,h.haas}@ed.ac.uk

Abstract. Light Fidelity (LiFi) allows wireless data transmission via Light Emitting Diode (LED) using the visible light spectrum between 400 THz and 800 THz, with high transmission rate of 10 Gbps achieved. In order to guarantee reliable data transmission, we propose a joint frame detection and channel estimation approach for DC biased Optical Orthogonal Frequency Division Multiplexing (DCO-OFDM) LiFi systems, with a single DCO-OFDM training block used. By designing a training structure, frame detection and channel estimation can be performed simultaneously. The proposed frame detection method is powerful and suitable for high-speed LiFi systems, as it is robust against the effect of Inter-Symbol Interference (ISI) caused by the response speed of the LED. Simulation results show that the proposed frame detection approach significantly outperforms existing Radio Frequency (RF) based frame detection methods in terms of probability of false detection. Using the frame detection method, the channel estimation scheme can provide a Mean Square Error (MSE) performance, better than the Least-Square (LS) channel estimation with perfect frame detection.

Keywords: LiFi · DCO-OFDM · Frame detection · Channel estimation

1 Introduction

It is forecast that by 2020 a number of 80 billion Internet-of-Things (loT) devices will be used, generating a large number of 44 zettabytes of data [1]. Lots of data is expected to be transmitted via wireless communication links. However, the current Radio Frequency (RF) spectrum is very scarce, and cannot meet the trend of exponential increase in data volumes [1,2]. A potential solution to this spectral bottleneck is to use high carrier frequency for wireless communications where a large bandwidth can be utilized. Light Fidelity (LiFi), first coined in [4], is considered as a promising technology for future networks, using high brightness Light Emitting Diode (LED) for data transmission [3]. It is shown in [5] that a high data rate of 10 Gb/s achieved using LEDs.

Orthogonal Frequency Division Multiplexing (OFDM) [5] has been widely employed, since high spectral efficiency can be achieved. Also, it can be utilized to combat the Inter-Symbol Interference (ISI) caused by the response speed of

E. Sabir et al. (Eds.): UNet 2017, LNCS 10542, pp. 532–541, 2017.
https://doi.org/10.1007/978-3-319-68179-5_46

the LED [6,7]. By imposing Hermitian symmetry on the signals, OFDM can be employed for Intensity Modulation Direct Detection (IM/DD) LiFi systems, to allow the modulated signals to be real. Apart from being real, optical signals must be non-negative. This can be achieved by introducing a positive level of DC added into the OFDM signals, which is referred to as DC biased Optical OFDM (DCO-OFDM). By clipping the negative parts of DC biased signals, the resulting signals are non-negative and unipolar, and can be used for LiFi systems.

However, OFDM based systems are vulnerable to timing errors. In order to avoid the errors, the high accuracy of frame detection is required. That is to correctly detect the starting point of each frame before decoding the received signals. In [8], the correlation of repetition of codes is used for frame detection. However, the method suffers from shallow gradient peaks, and thus the frame detection is not accurate. An improved method is proposed in [9], where there is a sharp peak at the correct point of frame detection. However, the requirement of cancellation of positive and negative parts of signals is impossible for LiFi systems, where there are only non-negative and real signals. In [10], a number of training sequences are designed particularly for Asymmetrically Clipped Optical OFDM (ACO-OFDM), however, not for DCO-OFDM systems.

Channel estimation is still important to guarantee reliable communications for LiFi systems. Channel estimation errors lead to system performance degradation [11]. In [11], Least-Square (LS) channel estimation is used by the inversion of channel matrix at the receiver side. However, noise is amplified if the power of channel coefficients is low. In [12], the Minimum Mean Square Error (MMSE) scheme is applied. The channel estimation errors are used for the joint optimization of precoder and equalizer. However, a large number of iterations are required to achieve the convergence of Mean Square Error (MSE) minimization of imperfect channel estimation.

In this paper, we propose a joint frame detection and channel estimation approach for DCO-OFDM LiFi systems, using a single training block. The contributions of this work can be elaborated in the following. First, we propose a frame detection method, by formulating a cost function designed specifically for DCO-OFDM systems, where traditional RF based methods [8,9] are not suitable. By minimizing the cost function, the correct time index can be detected. Second, channel estimation is performed together with the frame detection. In order to provide good frame detection and channel estimation, a training structure is designed. Simulation results show that the proposed frame detection approach significantly outperforms Schmidl's method [8] in terms of probability of false detection. With the proposed frame detection, the proposed channel estimation scheme provides a MSE performance, better than LS channel estimation [11] with perfect frame detection.

The rest of the paper is organized as follows. The system model is presented in Sect. 2. The joint frame detection and channel estimation is presented in Sect. 3. Simulation results are presented in Sect. 4. Section 5 draws the conclusion.

2 System Model

We consider a downlink DCO-OFDM LiFi wireless communication system, with a strong Line-of-Sight (LoS) channel between transmitter and receiver. The LiFi channel can be described as the combination of a diffuse channel component and a LoS component. Define η_{LoS} as the LoS channel component, expressed as [13]

$$\eta_{\text{LoS}} = \begin{cases} \frac{(m_{\text{Lam}}+1)A_{\text{rx}}}{2\pi D^2}\cos^m(\phi)\cos(\phi)T(\phi)G(\varphi), & \varphi < \Psi \\ 0, & \varphi > \Psi \end{cases}, \tag{1}$$

where $T(\phi)$ and $G(\varphi)$ are the optical filter gain at the transmitter and the concentrator gain at the receiver, respectively, ϕ and φ are the light radiance angle from transmitter to receiver and the light incidence angle from receiver to transmitter, respectively, $m_{\text{Lam}} = -\ln(2)/\ln[\cos(\phi_{1/2})]$ represents the Lambertian emission order, with $\phi_{1/2}$ denoting the half-power semi-angle of LED, A_{rx} is the detection area of receiver. The channel frequency response at frequency f can be written as [14]

$$H_{\text{LiFi}}(f) = \eta_{\text{LoS}} + H_{\text{diffuse}}(f), \tag{2}$$

where $H_{\text{diffuse}}(f)$ is the diffuse frequency component, expressed as

$$H_{\text{diffuse}}(f) = \eta_{\text{diff}}\frac{e^{j2\pi f\Delta t}}{1+j\frac{f}{f_0}}, \tag{3}$$

where f_0 is the 3 dB cutoff frequency, Δt is the delay between the LoS signal and the first arriving diffuse signal, and η_{diff} is the diffuse signal gain, expressed as

$$\eta_{\text{diff}} = \frac{A_{\text{rx}}}{A_{\text{room}}}\frac{\rho}{1-\rho}, \tag{4}$$

where A_{room} is the surface area of a room, and ρ is the average reflectivity of walls. Transforming the channel frequency response by discrete Fourier transform (DFT), the time-domain channel response can be obtained [14]

$$h_{\text{LiFi}}(t) = \eta_{\text{LoS}}\delta(t) + h_{\text{diffuse}}(t-\Delta t). \tag{5}$$

where $\delta(t)$ is the Dirac delta function, and $h_{\text{diffuse}}(t-\Delta t)$ is the diffuse channel component in the time domain.

The response speed of the LED could cause ISI for DCO-OFDM LiFi systems, and the effect can be approximately modelled as [6, 7]:

$$h_{\text{LED}}(t) = e^{-j2\pi f_b t}, \tag{6}$$

where f_b is the cutoff bandwidth of the LED.

The equivalent channel can be written as [7]

$$h(t) = h_{\text{LiFi}}(t) \otimes h_{\text{LED}}(t), \tag{7}$$

where $\otimes$ denotes the convolution operation. The sample-spaced channel in (7) can be denoted as $\mathbf{h} = [h(0), h(1), \ldots, h(L-1)]^T$ with $h(l)$ being the l-th

$(l = 0, 1, \ldots, L-1)$ channel impulse response. The channel from transmitter to receiver is assumed to be constant with the channel length of L_g.

Assuming that the DCO-OFDM LiFi systems consist of N subcarriers. Let $s(n)$ denote the M-ary Quadrature Amplitude modulation (M-QAM) symbol on the n-th $(n = 0, 1, \ldots, N-1)$ subcarrier. Let $\mathbf{F}$ denote the $N \times N$ DFT matrix, with (u, v) entry $F(u, v) = 1/\sqrt{N}\exp(-j2\pi uv/N), (u, v = 0, 1, \ldots, N-1)$. The time-domain signal can be expressed as $\tilde{x}(n) = \frac{1}{\sqrt{N}} \sum_{m=0}^{N-1} s(m) e^{\frac{j2\pi mn}{N}}$. The DC bias is calculated from $\tilde{x}(n)$, defined as [15]

$$\sigma_{\text{DC}} = K\sqrt{\text{E}\{\tilde{x}^2(n)\}}, \tag{8}$$

where $\text{E}\{\cdot\}$ denotes the expectation, and K is the DC bias ratio.

After introducing a DC bias and clipping the negative parts, the resulting signal is $x(n) = \tilde{x}(n) + \sigma_{\text{DC}} + w_{\text{clip}}(n)$, with $w_{\text{clip}}(n)$ being the clipping noise as

$$w_{\text{clip}}(n) = \begin{cases} 0, & [\tilde{x}(n) + \sigma_{\text{DC}}] > 0 \\ -\tilde{x}(n) - \sigma_{\text{DC}}, & [\tilde{x}(n) + \sigma_{\text{DC}}] \leqslant 0 \end{cases}. \tag{9}$$

Let $\mathbf{F}(:, 0 : L-1)$ denote the submatrix of DFT matrix $\mathbf{F}$, with all N rows and columns from 0 to $L-1$. Define $\mathbf{s} \triangleq [s(0), s(1), \ldots, s(N-1)]^T$ as the transmit signal vector, with Hermitian symmetry. The source data stream is first modulated onto different subcarriers by left-multiplying the N-point inverse DFT matrix as

$$\tilde{\mathbf{X}}_L = \mathbf{F}^H \text{diag}\{\mathbf{s}\}\mathbf{F}(:, 0 : L-1), \tag{10}$$

with $\text{diag}\{\cdot\}$ denoting the diagonal matrix. After introducing a DC bias on $\tilde{\mathbf{X}}_L$ and clipping, the resulting signal can be written as

$$\mathbf{X}_L = \tilde{\mathbf{X}}_L + \sigma_{\text{DC}}\mathbf{1}_{N\times L} + \mathbf{W}_{\text{clip}}, \tag{11}$$

where $\mathbf{W}_{\text{clip}} \triangleq [\mathbf{w}_{\text{clip}}(0), \ldots, \mathbf{w}_{\text{clip}}(L-1)]$ with $\mathbf{w}_{\text{clip}}(l) \triangleq [w_{\text{clip}}(0, l), \ldots, w_{\text{clip}}(N-1, l)]^T$, and $\mathbf{1}_{N\times L}$ is the all-one matrix of size $N \times L$.

In order to avoid inter-block interference, each OFDM block is prepended with a cyclic prefix (CP) of length L_{cp} before transmission. The received signal vector is written as

$$\mathbf{y} = \mathbf{X}_L\mathbf{h} + \mathbf{w}, \tag{12}$$

where $\mathbf{w} \triangleq [w(0), w(1), \ldots, w(N-1)]^T$ is the noise vector, with $w(n)$ denoting the shot and thermal noise element, modelled as Additive White Gaussian Noise (AWGN) whose entries are independent identically distributed (i.i.d.) Gaussian random variables with zero mean and the summed variance σ^2 of short noise and thermal noise.

3 Joint Frame Detection and Channel Estimation

In this paper, we propose a joint frame detection and channel estimation structure for DCO-OFDM LiFi systems, using a single DCO-OFDM block. For frame detection, the proposed method is performed in the time domain using a window size on the received samples to move forward or backward. A cost function is formulated for frame detection. By minimizing the cost function, the correct time index can be detected. This is different from traditional RF based frame detection methods as in [8,9], where negative and positive parts of received signals are required for frame detection. These RF based approaches are not suitable for DCO-OFDM LiFi systems, as the optical signals are real and non-negative. Also, these methods are sensitive to the effect of the response speed of the LED.

We use a number of N received samples, and search for the time index by moving forward or backward on the received samples. Define $\tilde{\epsilon}$ as the trial time index. The Probability Density Function (PDF) of the received signal can be given as

$$\Lambda\big(\mathbf{y}^{(\tilde{\epsilon})};\tilde{\epsilon},\mathbf{h}^{(\tilde{\epsilon})}\big)=\frac{1}{(\pi\sigma^2)^N}\cdot\exp\Big\{-\frac{1}{\sigma^2}\Big[\mathbf{y}^{(\tilde{\epsilon})}-\mathbf{X}\mathbf{h}^{(\tilde{\epsilon})}\Big]^H\Big[\mathbf{y}^{(\tilde{\epsilon})}-\mathbf{X}\mathbf{h}^{(\tilde{\epsilon})}\Big]\Big\},\quad(13)$$

where $\mathbf{y}^{(\tilde{\epsilon})}$ is the received signal vector with the trial time index $\tilde{\epsilon}$, and $\mathbf{h}^{(\tilde{\epsilon})}$ is the estimate of channel with $\tilde{\epsilon}$. For RF systems, joint frame detection and channel estimation can be performed by maximizing (13). However, this is not the case for DCO-OFDM LiFi systems, as the received signals are real and not complex, unipolar and not bipolar. Thus, maximizing (13) does not correspond to the correct time index for DCO-OFDM LiFi systems. However, we can search for another solution which is to minimize the cost function as

$$\min\ \Big|\Big|\mathbf{y}^{(\tilde{\epsilon})}-\mathbf{X}\mathbf{h}\Big|\Big|_F^2,\quad(14)$$

where $||\cdot||_F^2$ is the Frobenius norm. Define P as the length of training. Using (10), the training can be formulated as $\tilde{\mathbf{X}}_P=\mathbf{F}^H\text{diag}\{\mathbf{s}\}\mathbf{F}(:,0:P-1)$. Using (11), the training can be further expressed as $\mathbf{X}_P=\tilde{\mathbf{X}}_P+\sigma_{\text{DC}}\mathbf{1}_{N\times P}+\mathbf{W}_{\text{clip}}$. Using the training $\mathbf{X}_P$ of size $N\times P$, the channel $\mathbf{h}^{(\tilde{\epsilon})}$ at the trial timing index is written as

$$\mathbf{h}^{(\tilde{\epsilon})}=\Big[\mathbf{X}_P^T\mathbf{X}_P\Big]^{-1}\mathbf{X}_P^T\mathbf{y}^{(\tilde{\epsilon})}.\quad(15)$$

The channel $\mathbf{h}^{(\tilde{\epsilon})}$ is used to reconstruct a received signal by substituting (15) into (14) as

$$\mathbf{y}_P^{(\tilde{\epsilon})}=\mathbf{X}_P\mathbf{h}^{(\tilde{\epsilon})}.\quad(16)$$

By minimizing the difference of powers between the reconstructed signal $\mathbf{y}_P^{(\tilde{\epsilon})}$ and the received signal $\mathbf{y}^{(\tilde{\epsilon})}$, the estimate of timing index $\hat{\epsilon}$ is obtained by

$$\hat{\epsilon}=\arg\min_{\tilde{\epsilon}}\Big|\Big|\mathbf{y}^{(\tilde{\epsilon})}-\mathbf{y}_P^{(\tilde{\epsilon})}\Big|\Big|_F^2.\quad(17)$$

By using the estimated timing index $\hat{\epsilon}$ and the training $\mathbf{X}_P$, the channel $\hat{\mathbf{h}}$ can be estimated as

$$\hat{\mathbf{h}}=\Big[\mathbf{X}_P^T\mathbf{X}_P\Big]^{-1}\mathbf{X}_P^T\mathbf{y}^{(\hat{\epsilon})}.\quad(18)$$

4 Performance Analysis

The proposed joint frame detection and channel estimation can only be available when the training $\mathbf{X}_P$ is singular, *i.e.*, $P < N$. If $P = N$, $\mathbf{X}_P$ is square, and (15–17) are independent of $\tilde{\epsilon}$. Thus, when $P \longrightarrow N$, $\mathbf{X}_P$ becomes close to square matrix, and the proposed method provides worse performance; when $P \longrightarrow 1$, there is good performance for frame detection. However, channel estimation performs worse. This is because there is a rank deficiency for channel estimation with $P < L$. This can be verified in the simulation results, and is consistent with Figs. 1 and 3. Therefore, in order to allow frame detection and channel estimation to be performed simultaneously, the minimum length of training could be $P = L$.

The computational complexity of the joint frame detection and channel estimation scheme is present for DCO-OFDM LiFi systems, in terms of the number of multiplications. As $\mathbf{X}_P^T\mathbf{X}_P$ can be calculated offline before frame detection, the computational complexity of $\mathbf{X}_P^T\mathbf{X}_P$ can be excluded for online calculation. The proposed frame detection method has a $N(P^4N^2+1)$ multiplication operations, while channel estimation has P^3N^2 operations. When $P = 1$, $\mathbf{X}_P^T\mathbf{X}_P$ becomes a scaler, and has no impact on the frame detection. There is no need to calculate $(\mathbf{X}_P^T\mathbf{X}_P)^{-1}$ with $P = 1$. Also, when $P = 1$, the frame detection demonstrates the best performance, as shown in Fig. 1. Thus, the lowest complexity of frame

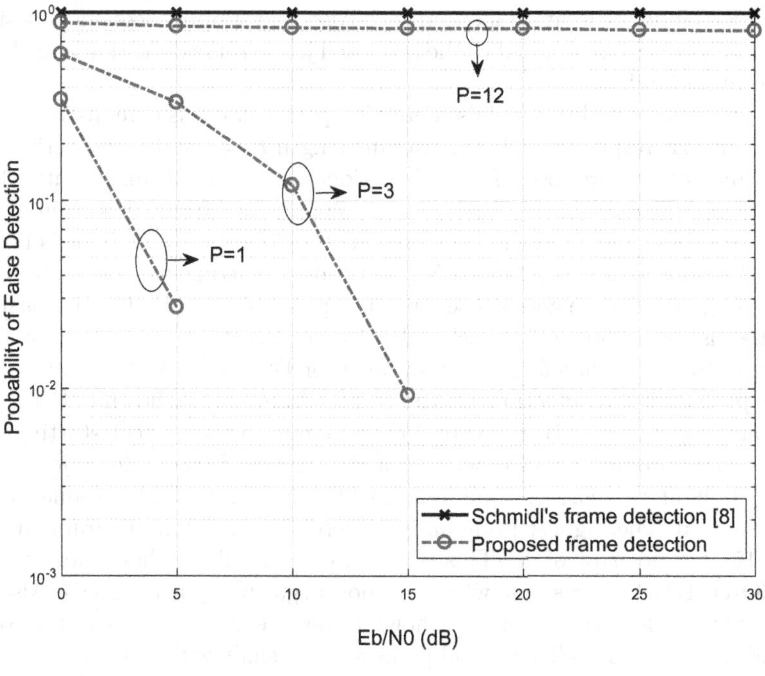

Fig. 1. Probability of false detection performance of the proposed frame detection method, with $P = 1$, 3 and 12 training

detection is $N(N+1)$ operations. As channel estimation can perform well only when $P \geq L$, the lowest complexity of channel estimation is N^2L operations. Overall, the proposed joint frame detection and channel estimation scheme has $N(NL+N+1)$ operations as the lowest complexity.

5 Simulation Results

We use Monte-Carlo simulations to demonstrate the performance of the proposed joint frame detection and channel estimation method for DCO-OFDM LiFi wireless communications systems. A number of of $N = 64$ subcarriers are used. The DC bias ratio is set $K = 1$ for training. The training sizes are $P = 1$, 3 and 12, respectively. The MSE of channel estimation is defined as $\text{MSE} = \text{E}\{(\mathbf{h} - \hat{\mathbf{h}})^2\}$. The CP of length $L_{\text{cp}} = 10$ is used. The room size is set as 3 m × 3 m × 3 m (length × width × height). The LED is located on the ceiling, with the coordinate (3 m, 3 m, 3 m). The receiver is on the desk of height 1 m, with the coordinate (1.5 m, 2.5 m, 1 m). The transmitter's radiance angle of $\phi = 40°$ is used, while the receiver's light incidence angle is $\varphi = 60°$. The receiver detection area of $A_{\text{rx}} = 1\ \text{cm}^2$ is used. The half-power semi-angle of LED is $\phi_{1/2} = 60°$. The average reflectivity of walls is set as $\rho = 0.8$. Optical filter gain of $T(\phi) = 1$ is used at the transmitter, while concentrator gain of $G(\varphi) = 1$ is used at the receiver.

For performance comparison, we consider Schmidl's frame detection method [8] and LS channel estimation method [11]. Also, the training sequences designed by Schmidl as in [8] are applied to the proposed joint frame detection and channel estimation method.

In Fig. 1, the probability of false detection performance is demonstrated, with $P = 1$, 3 and 12, respectively. Using training length $P = 1$ and 3, respectively, the performance of the proposed frame detection scheme significantly outperforms that of Schmidl's method [8]. With $P = 1$, the proposed frame detection method provides the best performance, compared to $P = 3$ and $P = 12$. This is because when P becomes large and close to N, the training matrix gets close to be square so that the performance gets worse with a large number of P. This is consistent with the discussion in Sect. 4. Schmidl's frame detection method [8] suffers a high error floor and therefore is not suitable for DCO-OFDM LiFi systems.

The probability of detection v.s. time errors (samples) is shown in Fig. 2, with $P = 1$ and $E_b/N_0 = 5$ dB. Error of 0 corresponds to the correct starting point of frame. The probability of detection of the proposed frame detection scheme is about 0.98 at the correct time index, while that of Schmidl's frame method [8] is near to 0. The highest probability of detection of Schmidl's frame method [8] is 0.15 at time error of 45. This is because Schmidl's method does not work for DCO-OFDM LiFi systems with only non-negative optical signals. Also, the proposed frame detection scheme is shown to be a very sharp peak at the correct time index, while Schmidl's method [8] provides a shallow flat area at the wrong time index.

In Fig. 3, the MSE performance of the proposed channel estimation scheme is demonstrated. Three training sizes, $P = 1$, 3 and 12 are used for comparison.

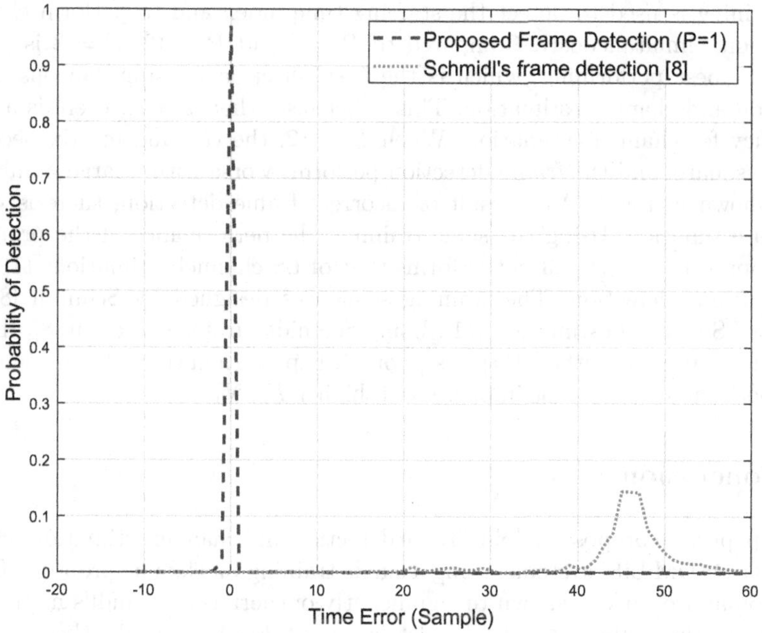

Fig. 2. Probability of detection performance of the proposed frame detection method, with $P = 1$ training and Eb/N0=5 dB

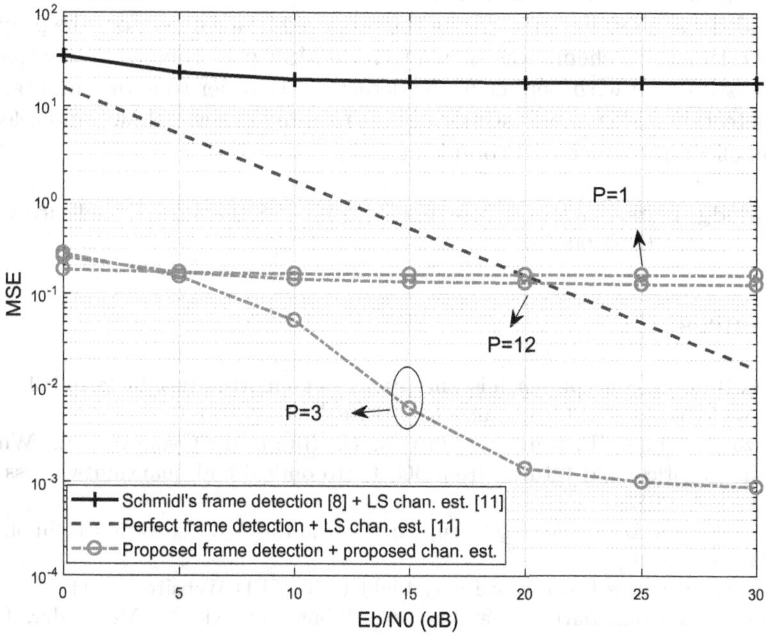

Fig. 3. MSE performance of the proposed channel estimation in comparison to LS channel estimation, with $P = 1, 3, 12$ training (chan.:channel, est.: estimation)

The training is used to detect the starting time index and to perform channel estimation, simultaneously. Compared to $P = 1$ and $P = 12$, $P = 3$ is shown to be the best performing, which is the best selection for simultaneous frame detection and channel estimation. This is because when $P = 1$, there is a rank deficiency for channel estimation. When $P = 12$, the training matrix becomes close to square, and the frame detection performs worse with a large number of P, as shown in Fig. 1. As a result of incorrect frame detection, there is worse channel estimation. Using the same training, the performance of the proposed joint approach with $P = 3$ outperforms that of LS channel estimation [11] with perfect frame detection. The training sequences designed by Schmidl [8] are used for LS channel estimation [11]. Using Schmidl's frame detection [8], the LS channel estimation method [11] has poor MSE performance at 2×10, and the MSE performance does not improve with higher E_b/N_0.

6 Conclusion

In this paper, we proposed a joint frame detection and channel estimation scheme for DCO-OFDM LiFi systems, using a single training block. The proposed frame detection approach was shown to significantly outperform Schmidl's method [8] in terms of the probability of false detection. At $E_b/N_0 = 5$ dB, the proposed frame detection scheme provides the probability of correct detection of 0.98, higher than Schmidl's frame method [8] with probability of almost 0. Also, the proposed frame detection scheme had a very sharp peak, while Schmidl's method [8] provided a shallow flat area. Using the proposed frame detection, the proposed channel estimation scheme was shown to have MSE performance better than LS channel estimation with perfect frame detection. In order to allow simultaneous frame detection and channel estimation, the training size was shown and selected, to trade off performance and complexity.

Acknowledgments. This work was supported by EPSRC under Established Career Fellowship Grant EP/K008757/1.

References

1. Haas, H.: LiFi: conceptions, misconceptions and opportunities. In: 2016 IEEE Photonics Conference (IPC), pp. 680–681. IEEE Press (2016)
2. Hanzo, L., Haas, H., Imre, S., O'Brien, D., Rupp, M., Gyongyosi, L.: Wireless myths, realities, and futures: from 3G/4G to optical and quantum wireless **100**, 1853–1888 (2012)
3. Haas, H., Yin, L., Wang, Y., Chen, C.: What is LiFi? J. Lightwave Technol. **147**, 1533–1544 (2016)
4. Haas, H.: Wireless Data from Every Light Bulb. TED Website (2011)
5. Chun, H., Rajbhandari, S., Faulkner, G., Tsonev, D., Xie, E., McKendry, J.J.D., Gu, E., Dawson, M.D., O'Brien, D.C., Haas, H.: LED based wavelength division multiplexed 10 Gb/s visible light communications. J. Lightwave Technol. **34**, 3047–3052 (2016)

6. Zeng, L., Obrien, D., Le-Minh, H., Lee, K., Jung, D., Oh, Y.: LiFi: improvement of date rate by using equalization in an indoor visible light communication system. In: 4th IEEE International Conference on Circuits and Systems for Communications, pp. 678–682. IEEE Press (2008)
7. Wu, L., Zhang, Z., Dang, J., Liu, H.: Adaptive modulation schemes for visible light communications. J. Lightwave Technol. **33**, 117–125 (2015)
8. Schmidl, T.M., Cox, D.C.: Robust frequency and timing synchronization for OFDM. IEEE Trans. Commun. **45**, 1613–1621 (1997)
9. Park, B., Cheon, H., Kang, C., Hong, D.: A novel timing estimation method for OFDM systems. IEEE Commun. Lett. **7**, 239–241 (2003)
10. Tian, S., Panta, K., Suraweera, H.A., Schmidt, B.J.C., McLaughlin, S., Armstrong, J.: A novel timing synchronization method for ACO-OFDM based optical wireless communications. IEEE Trans. Wireless Commun. **7**, 4958–4967 (2008)
11. Burton, A., Minh, H.L., Ghassemlooy, Z., Bentley, E., Botella, C.: Experimental demonstration of 50-Mb/s visible light communications using 4 × 4 MIMO. IEEE Photonics Technol. Lett. **26**, 945–948 (2014)
12. Ying, K., Qian, H., Baxley, J.R., Yao, S.: Joint optimization of precoder and equalizer in MIMO VLC systems. IEEE J. Sel. Areas Commun. **33**, 1949–1958 (2015)
13. Kahn, J.M., Barry, J.R.: Wireless infrared communications. Proc. IEEE **85**, 265–298 (1997)
14. Jungnickel, V., Pohl, V., Nonnig, S., Helmolt, C.V.: A physical model of the wireless infrared communication channel. IEEE J. Sel. Areas Commun. **20**, 631–640 (2002)
15. Tsonev, D., Videv, S., Haas, H.: Unlocking spectral efficiency in intensity modulation and direct detection systems. IEEE J. Sel. Areas Commun. **33**, 1758–1770 (2015)

SIR Based Performance Analysis of Dual-Branch SC Over Correlated $\kappa - \mu$ Fading Channels

Stefan Panic(✉), Caslav Stefanovic, and Hranislav Milosevic

1-Faculty of Natural Science and Mathematics, University of Pristina, Lole Ribara 29 Kosovska, 38220 Mitrovica, Serbia
stefanpnc@yahoo.com

Abstract. In this paper, we will analyze signal-to-interference ratio (SIR) based selection combining (SC) diversity system over dual correlated $\kappa - \mu$ fading channels, in the presence of mutually $\kappa - \mu$ correlated interferences. Infinite series expressions for probability density function (PDF), and cumulative distribution function (CDF) of the output SIR, for proposed system SC diversity model will be presented. Further, important wireless communication performance criterion of proposed system, Outage probability (OP), will be efficiently evaluated and analyzed in the function of system parameters.

Keywords: Bivariate $\kappa - \mu$ distribution · Correlation · Fading channels · Co-channel interference (CCI) · Selection combining (SC) · Outage probability (OP)

1 Introduction

Key tool for carrying out performance analysis of space diversity systems operating over correlated fading channel are multivariate distributions [1].

Space diversity reception is group of techniques based on using multiple antennas at the receiver, for combining multiple received copies of signal exposed to fading, in order to improve system's quality of service (QoS)[2]. Among space diversity techniques, less complicated for practical realization is selection combining (SC) diversity technique. SC chooses the branch with the highest signal-to-noise ratio (SNR), or specially in fading environments with sufficiently high level of the co-channel interference (CCI) comparing to the thermal noise, SC chooses the branch with the highest signal-to-interference ratio (SIR), that is the branch with the strongest signal [3,4].

Various models are used to describe fading in wireless environments in communications systems analysis [1]. In the case when a line of sight (LOS) component between the transmitter and the receiver is present, the most general fading model which describes the short-term signal variation is kappa-mu ($\kappa - \mu$) fading model [5], since it describes a scenario in which the channel exhibits arbitrary number clusters of multipath with a LOS component in each cluster. This general fading model, defined as the function of parameters: κ, related to the

E. Sabir et al. (Eds.): UNet 2017, LNCS 10542, pp. 542–549, 2017.
https://doi.org/10.1007/978-3-319-68179-5_47

dominant/scattered components powers quotient, and parameter μ, related to the number of propagating clusters, easily reduces to other fading models, by setting corresponding values for parameters κ and μ. How this model reduces to Ricean and Nakagami-m fading models and further to Rayleigh fading model is explained in [6]. Provided model and its performance has been extensively exploited in wireless communication research [7–9] since it has been shown to yield the best fit to data collected in field trials whenever dominant components were present, both for indoor as well as outdoor environments [6].

Recently in [10] a bivariate $\kappa - \mu$ model was presented, in terms of its corresponding parameters κ_i and μ_i, ($i = 1$, 2), and ρ parameter describing the correlation between $\kappa - \mu$ fading channels, expressed in terms of the related physical terms: Doppler shift, the separation distance between two reception points, frequency, and delay spread.

The effect of correlated fading on the performance metrics of wireless communication system, has been extensively analyzed, however no analytical study of dual-branch SC, involving assumed correlated $\kappa - \mu$ fading, in the presence of $\kappa - \mu$ CCI, is present in the literature.

In this paper, signal-to-interference ratio (SIR) based selection combining (SC) over dual correlated $\kappa - \mu$ fading channels, in the presence of mutually $\kappa - \mu$ correlated interferences will be considered. Infinite series expressions for probability density function (PDF), and cumulative distribution function (CDF) of the output SIR, for proposed system SC diversity will be derived. Capitalizing on derived expressions, standard wireless communication performance criterion, outage probability (OP), will be efficiently evaluated and analyzed in the function of system parameters.

2 System Model

Joint PDF, for desired signal $\kappa - \mu$ correlated envelopes, could be expressed by [10]:

$$
\begin{aligned}
p_{R_1,R_2}(R_1,R_2) &= \frac{4R_1R_2\Gamma(\mu_d-1)\mu_d^2(1+\kappa_{d1})(1+\kappa_{d2})(1-\rho_d^2)^{2\mu_d-3}}{\Omega_{d1}\Omega_{d2}\left(\rho_d\mu_d(\sqrt{\kappa_{d1}}-\rho_d\sqrt{\kappa_{d2}})(\sqrt{\kappa_{d2}}-\rho_d\sqrt{\kappa_{d1}})\right)^{\mu_d-1}}\\
&\times \exp\left(-\frac{\mu_d}{1-\rho_d^2}\left(\kappa_{d1}+\kappa_{d2}+2\rho_d\sqrt{\kappa_{d1}\kappa_{d2}}+\frac{(1+\kappa_{d1})R_1^2}{\Omega_{d1}}+\frac{(1+\kappa_{d2})R_2^2}{\Omega_{d2}}\right)\right)\\
&\times \sum_{p=0}^{\infty}\frac{(\mu_d+p-1)(2\mu_d-2)_p}{p!}I_{\mu_d+p-1}\left(\frac{2\rho_d\mu_dR_1R_2(1+\kappa_{d1})(1+\kappa_{d2})}{(1-\rho_d^2)\sqrt{\Omega_{d1}}\sqrt{\Omega_{d2}}}\right)\\
&\times I_{\mu_d+p-1}\left(\frac{2\mu_dR_1(1+\kappa_{d1})(\sqrt{\kappa_{d1}}-\rho_d\sqrt{\kappa_{d2}})}{(1-\rho_d^2)\sqrt{\Omega_{d1}}}\right)\\
&\times I_{\mu_d+p-1}\left(\frac{2\mu_dR_2(1+\kappa_{d2})(\sqrt{\kappa_{d2}}-\rho_d\sqrt{\kappa_{d1}})}{(1-\rho_d^2)\sqrt{\Omega_{d2}}}\right) \qquad (1)
\end{aligned}
$$

Here, $E(R_1^2) = \Omega_{d1}$ $E(R_2^2) = \Omega_{d2}$ denote average powers of amplitudes of desired signals, correlation coefficient of desired signals is denoted as ρ_d, κ_{d1} and

κ_{d2} are ratios between the total power of the dominant components and the total power of the scattered waves in each channel, while it has been assumed that $\mu_{d1} = \mu_{d1} = \mu_d$. $I_p(x)$ being the p-th order modified Bessel function of the first kind [11, Eq. 8.445], while $\Gamma(a)$ denotes Gamma function [9, Eq. 8.310.1], and $(a)_p$ stands for Pocchammer symbol.

In similar manner Joint PDF, for $\kappa - \mu$ correlated envelopes of interfering signal, could be expressed as [10]:

$$p_{r_1,r_2}(r_1,r_2) = \frac{4r_1r_2\Gamma(\mu_c-1)\mu_c^2(1+\kappa_{c1})(1+\kappa_{c2})(1-\rho_c^2)^{2\mu_c-3}}{\Omega_{c1}\Omega_{c2}\left(\rho_c\mu_c(\sqrt{\kappa_{c1}}-\rho_c\sqrt{\kappa_{c2}})(\sqrt{\kappa_{c2}}-\rho_c\sqrt{\kappa_{c1}})\right)^{\mu_c-1}}$$
$$\times \exp\left(-\frac{\mu_c}{1-\rho_c^2}\left(\kappa_{c1}+\kappa_{c2}+2\rho_c\sqrt{\kappa_{c1}\kappa_{c2}}+\frac{(1+\kappa_{c1})r_1^2}{\Omega_{c1}}+\frac{(1+\kappa_{c2})r_2^2}{\Omega_{c2}}\right)\right)$$
$$\times \sum_{q=0}^{\infty}\frac{(\mu_c+q-1)(2\mu_c-2)_q}{q!}I_{\mu_c+q-1}\left(\frac{2\rho_c\mu_c r_1r_2(1+\kappa_{c1})(1+\kappa_{c2})}{(1-\rho_c^2)\sqrt{\Omega_{c1}}\sqrt{\Omega_{c2}}}\right)$$
$$\times I_{\mu_c+q-1}\left(\frac{2\mu_c r_1(1+\kappa_{c1})(\sqrt{\kappa_{c1}}-\rho_c\sqrt{\kappa_{c2}})}{(1-\rho_c^2)\sqrt{\Omega_{c1}}}\right)$$
$$\times I_{\mu_c+q-1}\left(\frac{2\mu_c r_2(1+\kappa_{c2})(\sqrt{\kappa_{c2}}-\rho_c\sqrt{\kappa_{c1}})}{(1-\rho_c^2)\sqrt{\Omega_{c2}}}\right) \tag{2}$$

Here, $E(r_1^2) = \Omega_{c1}$ $E(r_2^2) = \Omega_{c2}$ denote average powers of amplitudes of interferers, correlation coefficient of interfering signals is denoted as ρ_c, κ_{c1} and κ_{c2} are ratios between the total power of the dominant components of interferers and the total power of the scattered interfering waves in each channel, while it has been assumed that $\mu_{c1} = \mu_{c1} = \mu_c$.

Let $\lambda_1 = R_1^2/r_1^2$ and $\lambda_2 = R_2^2/r_2^2$ represent the instantaneous SIR on the diversity branches, respectively [3]. Using specific real time SIR estimators in base and mobile stations, this magnitudes could be measured [11]. The joint PDF of λ_1 and λ_2 can be expressed by [3]:

$$p_{\lambda_1,\lambda_2}(\lambda_1,\lambda_2) = \frac{1}{4\sqrt{\lambda_1\lambda_2}}\int_0^\infty\int_0^\infty p_{R_1,R_2}(r_1\sqrt{\lambda_1}, r_2\sqrt{\lambda_2})p_{r_1,r_2}(r_1,r_2)r_1r_2dr_1dr_2 \tag{3}$$

After substituting (1) and (2) into (3), with respect to some mathematical transformations, $p_{\lambda_1,\lambda_2}(\lambda_1,\lambda_2)$, could be written in the form of multiple infinite sums as:

$$p_{\lambda_1,\lambda_2}(\lambda_1,\lambda_2) = \sum_{p,q,a,b,c,d,e,f=0}^{\infty}\exp\left(-\frac{\mu_c}{1-\rho_c^2}\left(\kappa_{c1}+\kappa_{c2}+2\rho_c\sqrt{\kappa_{c1}\kappa_{c2}}\right)\right)$$
$$\times \exp\left(-\frac{\mu_d}{1-\rho_d^2}\left(\kappa_{d1}+\kappa_{d2}+2\rho_d\sqrt{\kappa_{d1}\kappa_{d2}}\right)\right)\frac{(\mu_c+q-1)(2\mu_c-2)_q}{q!}$$
$$\times \frac{(\mu_d+p-1)(2\mu_d-2)_p}{p!}(\sqrt{\kappa_{c1}}-\rho_c\sqrt{\kappa_{c2}})^{2d+q}(\sqrt{\kappa_{c2}}-\rho_c\sqrt{\kappa_{c1}})^{2f+q}$$

$$\times(\sqrt{\kappa_{d1}}-\rho_d\sqrt{\kappa_{d2}})^{2a+p}(\sqrt{\kappa_{d2}}-\rho_d\sqrt{\kappa_{d1}})^{2c+p}S_1^{d+q+e+\mu_c}S_2^{f+q+e+\mu_c}$$
$$\times\frac{(1-\rho_d^2)^{2\mu_c+2q+d+2e+f-p-a-c}(1-\rho_c^2)^{2\mu_d+2p+a+2b+c-q-d-f}\rho_d^{2b+p}\rho_c^{2e+q}}{\Gamma(\mu_d+p+a)a!\Gamma(\mu_d+p+b)b!\Gamma(\mu_d+p+c)c!}$$
$$\times\frac{\mu_d^{2a+2b+2c+3p+2\mu_d}\mu_c^{2d+2e+2f+3q+2\mu_c}\Gamma(\mu_d-1)\Gamma(\mu_c-1)}{\Gamma(\mu_c+q+d)d!\Gamma(\mu_c+q+e)e!\Gamma(\mu_c+q+f)f!}$$
$$\times(1+\kappa_{d1})^{a+b+p+\mu_d}(1+\kappa_{c1})^{c+b+p+\mu_d}(1+\kappa_{d2})^{d+e+q+\mu_c}(1+\kappa_{c2})^{f+e+q+\mu_c}$$
$$\times\frac{\lambda_1^{a+b+p+\mu_d-1}\Gamma(\mu_d+\mu_c+p+q+a+b+d+e)}{((1-\rho_c^2)\mu_d(1+\kappa_{d1})\lambda_1+(1-\rho_d^2)\mu_d(1+\kappa_{c1})S_1)^{\mu_d+\mu_c+p+q+a+b+d+e}}$$
$$\times\frac{\lambda_1^{a+b+p+\mu_d-1}\Gamma(\mu_d+\mu_c+p+q+a+b+d+e)}{((1-\rho_c^2)\mu_d(1+\kappa_{d1})\lambda_1+(1-\rho_d^2)\mu_d(1+\kappa_{c1})S_1)^{\mu_d+\mu_c+p+q+a+b+d+e}} \quad (4)$$

where $S_1=\frac{\Omega_{d1}}{\Omega_{c1}}$ and $S_2=\frac{\Omega_{d2}}{\Omega_{c2}}$ denote the average SIRs at the input branch of the dual-branch SC.

As mentioned, SC chooses and outputs the branch with the largest SIR:

$$\lambda=\lambda_{out}=max(\lambda_1,\lambda_2), \quad (5)$$

therefore CDF of SIR at the output of SC could be determined according to [3,12] as:

$$F_\lambda(\lambda)=\int_0^\lambda\int_0^\lambda p_{\lambda_1,\lambda_2}(\lambda_1,\lambda_2)d\lambda_1 d\lambda_2 \quad (6)$$

After substituting (4) into (6), with respect to some mathematical transformations, $F_\lambda(\lambda)$, could be written in the form of multiple infinite sums as:

$$F_\lambda(\lambda)=\sum_{p,q,a,b,c,d,e,f=0}^{\infty}\exp\left(-\frac{\mu_c}{1-\rho_c^2}\left(\kappa_{c1}+\kappa_{c2}+2\rho_c\sqrt{\kappa_{c1}\kappa_{c2}}\right)\right)$$
$$\times\exp\left(-\frac{\mu_d}{1-\rho_d^2}\left(\kappa_{d1}+\kappa_{d2}+2\rho_d\sqrt{\kappa_{d1}\kappa_{d2}}\right)\right)\frac{(\mu_c+q-1)(2\mu_c-2)_q}{q!}$$
$$\times\frac{(\mu_d+p-1)(2\mu_d-2)_p(\sqrt{\kappa_{d1}}-\rho_d\sqrt{\kappa_{d2}})^{2a+p}(\sqrt{\kappa_{d2}}-\rho_d\sqrt{\kappa_{d1}})^{2c+p}\rho_d^{2b+p}\rho_c^{2e+q}}{(1-\rho_d^2)^{p+a+c}(1-\rho_c^2)^{q+d+f}\Gamma(\mu_d+p+a)a!\Gamma(\mu_d+p+b)b!\Gamma(\mu_d+p+c)c!p!}$$
$$\times\frac{\mu_d^{a+p+c}\mu_c^{d+q+f}\Gamma(\mu_d-1)\Gamma(\mu_c-1)(\sqrt{\kappa_{c1}}-\rho_c\sqrt{\kappa_{c2}})^{2d+q}(\sqrt{\kappa_{c2}}-\rho_c\sqrt{\kappa_{c1}})^{2f+q}}{\Gamma(\mu_c+q+d)d!\Gamma(\mu_c+q+e)e!\Gamma(\mu_c+q+f)f!}$$
$$\times B\left(\mu_d+p+a+b,\mu_c+q+d+e,\frac{(1-\rho_c^2)\mu_d(1+\kappa_{d1})\lambda}{(1-\rho_c^2)\mu_d(1+\kappa_{d1})\lambda+(1-\rho_d^2)\mu_d(1+\kappa_{c1})S_1}\right)$$
$$\times B\left(\mu_d+p+c+b,\mu_c+q+f+e,\frac{(1-\rho_c^2)\mu_d(1+\kappa_{d2})\lambda}{(1-\rho_c^2)\mu_d(1+\kappa_{d2})\lambda+(1-\rho_d^2)\mu_d(1+\kappa_{c2})S_2}\right) \quad (7)$$

with $B(z,a,b)$ denoting the incomplete Beta function [11, Eq. 8.39]. Convergence of multiple infinite sum in (7) is shown in Table 1. Equation (7) converge for any

Table 1. Terms need to be summed in each infinite sum of (7) to achieve accuracy at the 5th significant digit, $\kappa_{d1} = \kappa_{d2} = \kappa_d, \kappa_{c1} = \kappa_{c2} = \kappa_c$.

$S/t = 10\,\text{dB}$, $S_1 = S_2 = S$	$\mu_d = \mu_c = 1$	$\kappa_d = 1$, $\kappa_c = 1$	$\kappa_d = 1.5$, $\kappa_c = 1.2$
$\rho_d = 0.2$	$\rho_c = 0.2$	7	7
$\rho_d = 0.4$	$\rho_c = 0.4$	8	9

value of observed parameters, but as is shown in this table, the number of the terms needs to be summed in each sum to achieve accuracy at 5th significant digit, depends strongly on the correlation coefficients values ρ_d and ρ_c. As visible from Table 1, number of the terms increases as correlation coefficients increase.

The PDF of the SIR at the output of the SC can be obtained easily from previous expression as [3, 12]:

$$p_\lambda(\lambda) = \frac{d}{d\lambda} F_\lambda(\lambda) \tag{8}$$

After substituting (7) into (8) it obtains:

$$\begin{aligned}
p_\lambda(\lambda) = & \sum_{p,q,a,b,c,d,e,f=0}^{\infty} \exp\left(-\frac{\mu_c}{1-\rho_c^2}\left(\kappa_{c1}+\kappa_{c2}+2\rho_c\sqrt{\kappa_{c1}\kappa_{c2}}\right)\right) \\
& \times \exp\left(-\frac{\mu_d}{1-\rho_d^2}\left(\kappa_{d1}+\kappa_{d2}+2\rho_d\sqrt{\kappa_{d1}\kappa_{d2}}\right)\right)\frac{(\mu_c+q-1)(2\mu_c-2)_q}{q!} \\
& \times \frac{(\mu_d+p-1)(2\mu_d-2)_p\left(\sqrt{\kappa_{d1}}-\rho_d\sqrt{\kappa_{d2}}\right)^{2a+p}\left(\sqrt{\kappa_{d2}}-\rho_d\sqrt{\kappa_{d1}}\right)^{2c+p}\rho_d^{2b+p}\rho_c^{2e+q}}{(1-\rho_d^2)^{p+a+c}(1-\rho_c^2)^{q+d+f}\Gamma(\mu_d+p+a)a!\Gamma(\mu_d+p+b)b!\Gamma(\mu_d+p+c)c!p!} \\
& \times \frac{\mu_d^{a+p+c}\mu_c^{d+q+f}\Gamma(\mu_d-1)\Gamma(\mu_c-1)\left(\sqrt{\kappa_{c1}}-\rho_c\sqrt{\kappa_{c2}}\right)^{2d+q}\left(\sqrt{\kappa_{c2}}-\rho_c\sqrt{\kappa_{c1}}\right)^{2f+q}}{\Gamma(\mu_c+q+d)d!\Gamma(\mu_c+q+e)e!\Gamma(\mu_c+q+f)f!} \\
& \times \frac{1}{\lambda}\left\{\left(\frac{(1-\rho_c^2)\mu_d(1+\kappa_{d1})\lambda}{(1-\rho_c^2)\mu_d(1+\kappa_{d1})\lambda+(1-\rho_d^2)\mu_d(1+\kappa_{c1})S_1}\right)^{\mu_d+p+a+b}\right. \\
& \times \left(\frac{(1-\rho_d^2)\mu_d(1+\kappa_{c1})S_1}{(1-\rho_c^2)\mu_d(1+\kappa_{d1})\lambda+(1-\rho_d^2)\mu_d(1+\kappa_{c1})S_1}\right)^{\mu_c+q+d+e} \\
& \times B\left(\mu_d+p+c+b,\mu_c+q+f+e,\frac{(1-\rho_c^2)\mu_d(1+\kappa_{d2})\lambda}{(1-\rho_c^2)\mu_d(1+\kappa_{d2})\lambda+(1-\rho_d^2)\mu_d(1+\kappa_{c2})S_2}\right) \\
& + \left(\frac{(1-\rho_c^2)\mu_d(1+\kappa_{d2})\lambda}{(1-\rho_c^2)\mu_d(1+\kappa_{d2})\lambda+(1-\rho_d^2)\mu_d(1+\kappa_{c2})S_2}\right)^{\mu_d+p+c+b} \\
& \times \left(\frac{(1-\rho_d^2)\mu_d(1+\kappa_{c2})S_2}{(1-\rho_c^2)\mu_d(1+\kappa_{d2})\lambda+(1-\rho_d^2)\mu_d(1+\kappa_{c2})S_2}\right)^{\mu_c+q+f+e} \\
& \left.\times B\left(\mu_d+p+a+b,\mu_c+q+d+e,\frac{(1-\rho_c^2)\mu_d(1+\kappa_{d1})\lambda}{(1-\rho_c^2)\mu_d(1+\kappa_{d1})\lambda+(1-\rho_d^2)\mu_d(1+\kappa_{c1})S_1}\right)\right\}
\end{aligned} \tag{9}$$

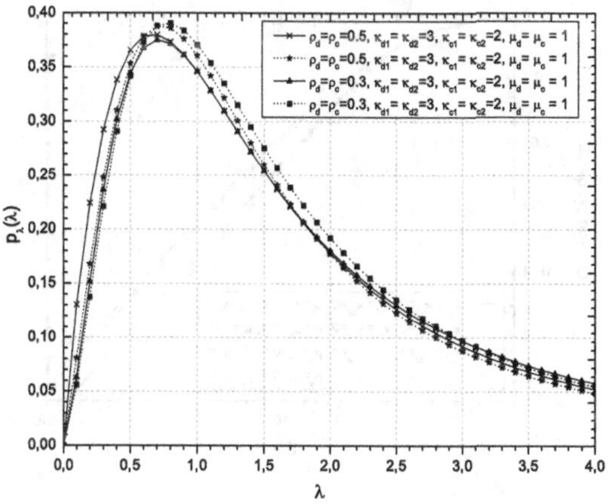

Fig. 1. Probability density functions of output SIR

Figure 1 shows the output SIR PDF of dual branch SC for some values of correlation coefficients and fading defining parameters.

3 Outage Probability

Outage probability (OP,P_{out}) is a performance criterion of wireless communication systems, and in the interference-limited environment is defined as the probability which combined-SIR falls below a given outage threshold, γ_{th}, called protection ratio, which depends on used modulation technique. Mathematically, P_{out} can be defined as [2]:

$$P_{out} = P_R\left(\lambda < \gamma_{th}\right) = \int\limits_0^{\gamma_{th}} p_\lambda(\lambda) d\lambda = F_\lambda(\gamma_{th}). \tag{10}$$

By taking into account properties of Eq. (7), OP can be efficiently evaluated.

OP versus normalized parameter S/γ_{th} for various values of parameters ρ_d, ρ_c,μ_d,μ_c, κ_{d1}, κ_{d2}, κ_{c1} and κ_{c2} is shown on Fig. 2. It is observed that $S_1 = S_1 = S$

Here we can observe that, OP values increase when the values κ_{c1} and κ_{c2} comparing to the values of κ_{d1}, κ_{d2} increase. Namely, OP values increase (better performances are reached) for case when $\kappa_{c1} = \kappa_{c2} = \kappa_{d1} = \kappa_{d2}$=1 comparing to the case when they are not equal with κ_{d1} and κ_{d2} having higher values, for example when $\kappa_{c1} = \kappa_{c2} = 2$, $\kappa_{d1} = \kappa_{d2} = 3$. Also we can see that for the same values of $\kappa_{c1} = \kappa_{c2}$ and $\kappa_{d1} = \kappa_{d2}$ OP increases when the values of correlation coefficients increase, i.e., when observing cases of $\rho_d = \rho_c = 0.4$ and $\rho_d = \rho_c$ =0.5.

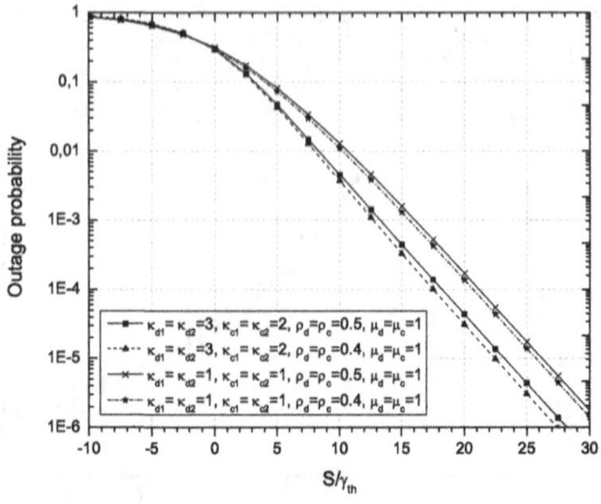

Fig. 2. Outage probability for observed system parameters

4 Conclusion

In this paper, for the first time are presented infinite-series expressions for PDF and CDF of dual branch output SIR, when transmission is carried out over the correlated $\kappa - \mu$ fading channels exposed to the influence of correlated $\kappa - \mu$ distributed interference. Based on presented expressions OP was efficiently evaluated and observed in the function of transmission parameters. This analysis has high level of generality since for corresponding values of system parameters, observed propagation model could be reduced to other well-known propagation models.

References

1. Panic, S., et al.: Fading and Interference Mitigation in Wireless Communications. CRC Press, Boca Raton (2013)
2. Simon, M.K., Alouini, M.S.: Digital Communication Over Fading Channels, 1st edn. Wiley, Hoboken (2000)
3. Karagiannidis, G.K.: Performance analysis of SIR-based dual selection diversity over correlated Nakagami-m channels. IEEE Trans. Veh. Technol. **52**(5), 1207–1216 (2003)
4. Neasmith, E.A., Beaulieu, N.C.: New results in selection diversity. IEEE Trans. Commun. **46**(1), 695–704 (1998)
5. Filho, J.C.S., Yacoub, M.D.: Highly accurate $\kappa - \mu$ approximation to sum of M independent non-identical Ricean variants. Electron. Lett. **41**(6), 338–339 (2005)
6. Yacoub, M.D.: The $\kappa - \mu$ distribuition and the $\eta - \mu$ distribution. IEEE Antennas Propag. Mag. **49**(1), 68–81 (2007)
7. Cotton, S., Scanlon, W.: Higher-order statistics for $\kappa - \mu$ distribution. Electron. Lett. **43**(22), 1215–1217 (2007)
8. Paris, J.: Statistical characterization of $\kappa - \mu$ shadowed fading. IEEE Trans. Veh. Technol. **63**(2), 518–526 (2014)

9. Panić, S.R., et al.: Second order statistics of selection macro-diversity system operating over Gamma shadowed $\kappa - \mu$ fading channels. EURASIP J. Wirel. Commun. Netw. **151**(1), 1–7 (2011)
10. Villavicencio, M., De Souza, R.A.A., de Souza, G., Yacoub, M.D.: A bivariate $\kappa - \mu$ distribution. IEEE Trans. Veh. Technol. **65**(7), 5737–5743 (2016)
11. Brandao, A.L., Lopez, L.B., McLernon, D.C.: Co-channel interference estimation for M-ary PSK modulated signals. IEEE. Wirel. Pers. Commun. **1**(1), 23–32 (1994)
12. Panic, S.R., Stefanovic, M.C., Mosic, A.V.: Performance analyses of selection combining diversity receiver over $\alpha - \mu$ fading channels in the presence of co-channel interference. IET Commun. **3**(11), 1769–1777 (2009)

Performance Analysis of Asynchronous and Non Linear FBMC Systems

Brahim Elmaroud[1(✉)], Ahmed Faqihi[1,2], and Driss Aboutajdine[1]

[1] LRIT, Associated Unit to CNRST (URAC29), FSR, Mohammed V University, Rabat, Morocco
b.elmaroud@gmail.com
[2] ENSIAS, Mohammed V University, Rabat, Morocco

Abstract. This paper provides a theoretical analysis of the joint effect of synchronization errors and High Power Amplifiers (HPA) non linear distortions on filter bank based multicarrier (FBMC) systems. A promising class of FBMC modulation called Cosine Modulated Multitone (CMT) will be considered. For the studied system, analytical expressions of the signal to interference ratio (SIR) and bit error rate (BER) will be derived in the presence of HPA distortions, timing errors and carrier frequency offset (CFO). To this end, we have developed a closed-form expression of interference and useful signal powers using some acceptable approximations. The proposed model is compared with existing models designed for the considered system or for other multicarrier systems like SMT (Staggered Modulated Multitone) or OFDM.

Keywords: Filter Bank Multicarrier · Cosine Modulated Multitone · HPA · Nonlinear distortion · Carrier frequency offset · SINR

1 Introduction

Orthogonal Frequency Division Multiplexing (OFDM) can be considered as the most widely used form of multicarrier modulations since it has been adopted by many major communication standards, e.g. DAB, DVB-T, IEEE802.11a/g (Wi-Fi), IEEE 802.16 (WiMAX) and LTE. However, despite their advantages which include robustness against frequency selective channels, enhanced immunity to Inter-Symbol Interference (ISI), simplified channel equalization task and efficient implementation using Fast Fourier Transform (FFT), OFDM systems still have some issues: The use of a Cyclic Prefix (CP) (which does not carry useful information) to avoid ISI induces a loss of the spectral efficiency, also the high side lobes of the rectangular pulse shape used in OFDM causes a large Inter-Carrier Interference (ICI) making the system very sensitive to frequency synchronization errors. Because of the aforementioned weaknesses, researchers are more and more interested by another class of multicarrier modulations called Filter Bank Multicarrier (FBMC). This technique employs a frequency well localized FIR filter with small side lobes instead of the rectangular pulse shape used

E. Sabir et al. (Eds.): UNet 2017, LNCS 10542, pp. 550–561, 2017.
https://doi.org/10.1007/978-3-319-68179-5_48

in OFDM, which makes FBMC systems less sensitive to frequency errors compared to OFDM [14]. Furthermore, FBMC provides higher bandwidth efficiency than OFDM since it does not require a guard interval or a cyclic prefix extension.

Unfortunately, FBMC systems, like any other multicarrier scheme, are very sensitive to timing errors and carrier frequency offset (CFO) which is introduced by frequency mismatch in the transmitter and the receiver oscillators and the Doppler effect if the transmitter/receiver is moving. This sensitivity has been illustrated in terms of signal to interference ratio (SIR) in [14,15], and in terms of signal to noise ratio (SNR) degradation in [10], by deriving accurate and approximate expressions of ICI and ISI. A simple closed form approximation of SIR over an additive white Gaussian noise (AWGN) channel was proposed in [14] and it is accurate over a relatively broad range of CFO and timing offset. Another serious issue with FBMC systems is the fact that the transmitted signal is a sum of a large number of independently modulated subcarriers. Thus, it suffers from high Peak-to-Average Power Ratio (PAPR) which makes the system very sensitive to nonlinear distortion (NLD) caused by nonlinear devices such as high power amplifiers (HPA). This problem has been largely studied for OFDM systems. The impact of NLD on OFDM signals was presented in [1,4] and some solutions to estimate and compensate this NLD were given by [5,16]. As for FBMC systems, the authors in [3] carried out a theoretical analysis of bit error rate (BER) performance for non-linearly amplified FBMC/OQAM signals under AWGN and Rayleigh fading channels.

In this paper, we aim to study the joint effect of synchronization errors and HPA nonlinear distortions on FBMC modulations. A theoretical expression of SIR will be derived for a non-synchronized and non-linearly distorted FBMC signal. The proposed SIR expression is obtained by following the same derivations as in [14] and taking into account the effects of the NLD distortion. A theoretical analysis of the BER performance will also be carried out, and the impact of HPA NLD and/or CFO will be highlighted in this paper. It is worth noting that there are limited studies that investigate the problem of joint effects of non-synchronization and HPA nonlinearities. An interesting one is [11], where the authors analyzed the interference caused by nonlinear power amplifiers together with timing errors for multicarrier OFDM/FBMC transmissions. Recently, we have proposed a theoretical analysis of asynchronous and non linear FBMC based multi-cellular networks by deriving an exact BER expression in the presence of a frequency-selective channel [6,7]. In this work, we will consider frequency errors instead of timing errors and we will plot the SIR and BER curves as functions of the normalized CFO and the SNR respectively. Regarding the FBMC modulation, a CMT system will be considered and the results can be easily extended to SMT systems since a CMT signal can be obtained from an SMT one through a simple modulation step [9].

The remainder of this paper is organized as follows: In Sect. 2, the CMT system considered in this work is introduced and the joint effect of HPA NLD and synchronization errors is described. In Sect. 3, we develop a theoretical analysis of the SIR and BER. Section 4 includes the evaluation of the obtained SIR and BER expressions through simulation results. Finally, Sect. 5 concludes this paper.

2 System Model: Asynchronous and Nonlinearly Distorted CMT Signal

2.1 Considered CMT System

The block diagram of a CMT transceiver is presented in Fig. 1. The input signal $s_k(t)$ at the kth subcarrier is the succession of PAM data symbols s_n^k at the transmission rate of 1/T. It is given by

$$s_k(t) = \sum_{n=-\infty}^{\infty} s_n^k \delta(t - nT) \tag{1}$$

According to VSB modulation, each input signal $s_k(t)$ should be passed through a shifted version of the prototype filter $h(t)$ centered at frequency $f = 1/4T$, i.e., $h(t)e^{j(\pi/2T)t}$. The obtained VSB modulated signals are then multiplied by the frequency shifted modulators $e^{jk((\pi/T)t+\pi/2)}$ (with $k = 0, \ldots, N-1$) and summed to form the transmitted CMT signal $x(t)$ given by

$$x(t) = \sum_{n=-\infty}^{\infty} \sum_{k=0}^{N-1} s_n^k h(t - nT) e^{j\frac{\pi}{2T}t} e^{jk(\frac{\pi}{T}t+\frac{\pi}{2})} = \sum_{n=-\infty}^{\infty} \sum_{k=0}^{N-1} s_n^k \gamma_{k,n}(t) \tag{2}$$

where $\gamma_{k,n}(t) = h(t - nT)e^{j\frac{\pi}{2T}t}e^{j\Phi^k(t)}$ and $\Phi^k(t) = k(\frac{\pi}{T}t + \frac{\pi}{2})$.

At the receiver side, if we consider an ideal transmission without any source of distortion, the estimated data symbol on the kth subcarrier in the mth time index is given by

$$\begin{aligned} \hat{s}_m^l &= Re\left\{\langle x(t), \gamma_{l,m}(t)\rangle\right\} = Re\left\{\int_{-\infty}^{\infty} x(t)\gamma_{l,m}^*(t)dt\right\} \\ &= \sum_n \sum_k s_n^k \int_{-\infty}^{\infty} h(t - nT)h(t - mT)\cos\Phi^{k-l}(t)dt \end{aligned} \tag{3}$$

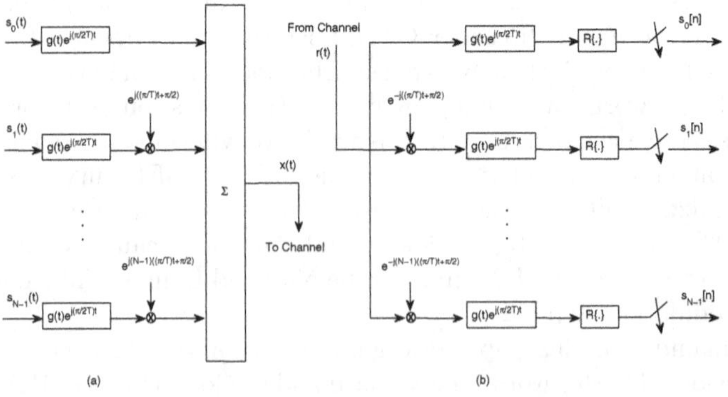

Fig. 1. Block diagram of a CMT transceiver: (a) transmitter; (b) receiver.

where

- $\gamma^*_{l,m}(t)$ is the complex conjugate of $\gamma_{l,m}(t)$,
- $\langle .,. \rangle$ stands for the inner product.

In these conditions, the estimated data symbol $\hat{s}^l_m$ is equal to the transmitted symbol s^l_m thanks to the special structure of the prototype filter h which leads to a natural cancellation of the interference signals [8].

2.2 Joint Effect of HPA NLD and Synchronization Errors

In this subsection we will show how HPA non linear distortions and synchronization errors affect jointly the transmitted CMT signal. Figure 2 presents the system description including HPA NLD and synchronization errors blocks.

According to this figure, the CMT signal is first affected by the HPA non linear distortion block. A HPA model can be described by its AM/AM and AM/PM conversions which measure the amount of undesired amplitude changes and phase deviations caused by envelope variations of the signal. In literature, it is customary to model the non linear distortions, caused by high power amplifiers, using the Bussgang theorem which states that the output signal of the HPA block of Fig. 2 can be written as follows [4]

$$y(t) = \alpha x(t) + d(t) \tag{4}$$

where $\alpha = |\alpha| e^{\phi_\alpha}$ is a complex factor and $d(t)$ is a zero mean additive noise, which is uncorrelated to $x(t)$.

After the non linearity block, the resulting signal $y(t)$ is then affected by a symbol timing offset (STO) τ, a carrier frequency offset (CFO) ϵ, a carrier phase offset ϕ and an AWGN noise $n(t)$. Hence, the received signal can be written as

$$\begin{aligned} r(t) &= y(t-\tau) e^{j(2\pi\epsilon t+\phi)} + n(t) \\ &= \alpha x(t-\tau) e^{j(2\pi\epsilon t+\phi)} + d(t) e^{j(2\pi\epsilon t+\phi)} + n(t) \end{aligned} \tag{5}$$

Recall that $x(t)$ is given by Eq. (2). At the receiver side, the demodulated signal at the lth subcarrier on the 0th time index (for simplicity's sake) is given by

$$\begin{aligned} \hat{s}^l_0 &= Re\left\{\langle r(t), \gamma_{l,0}(t)\rangle\right\} \\ &= Re\left\{\int_{-\infty}^{\infty} \alpha x(t-\tau) e^{j(2\pi\epsilon t+\phi)} h(t) e^{-j\frac{\pi}{2T}t} e^{j\Phi^{-l}(t)} dt\right\} + \hat{d}^l_0 + \hat{n}^l_0 \end{aligned} \tag{6}$$

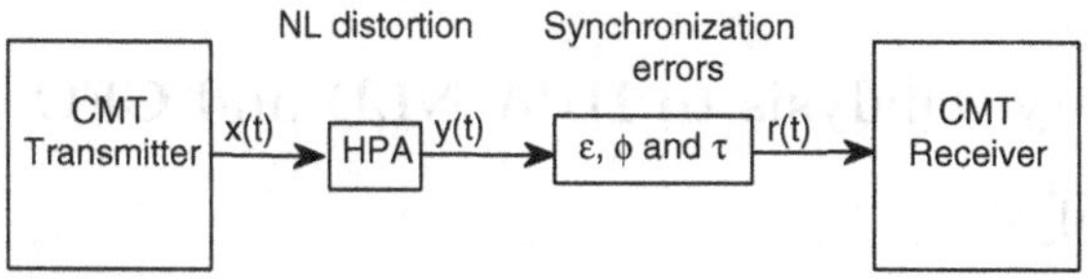

Fig. 2. System description with HPA NLD and synchronization errors.

where $\hat{d}_0^l$ and $\hat{n}_0^l$ are given by

$$\hat{d}_0^l = Re\left\{\int_{-\infty}^{\infty} d(t)e^{j(2\pi\epsilon t+\phi)}\gamma_{l,0}^*(t)dt\right\} \tag{7}$$

$$\hat{n}_0^l = Re\left\{\int_{-\infty}^{\infty} n(t)\gamma_{l,0}^*(t)dt\right\} \tag{8}$$

In the following, we assume that the coarse frequency and timing estimations and compensation have already been performed. Nevertheless, residual CFO ϵ and STO τ still affect the transmitted signal even if they are small enough to warrant some mathematical approximations which will be considered later in this paper. We will also assume that the phase offsets ϕ and ϕ_α are perfectly compensated within the channel equalization process. This can be done by using a single tap equalizer and setting the equalizer coefficients properly [14].

Taking into account the above observations and replacing $x(t-\tau)$ by its expression in Eq. (6), the estimated data symbol $\hat{s}_0^l$ can be rewritten as

$$\hat{s}_0^l = Re\left\{\sum_{n=-\infty}^{\infty}\sum_{k=0}^{N-1}\int_{-\infty}^{\infty}|\alpha|s_n^k h(t)h(t-nT-\tau)\right. \\ \left. \times\, e^{j(\Phi^{k-l}(t,\tau)+2\pi\epsilon t)}dt\right\} + \hat{d}_0^l + \hat{n}_0^l \tag{9}$$

where $\Phi^{k-l}(t,\tau) = \Phi^{k-l}(t) - k\frac{\pi}{T}\tau$.

Equation (9) reveals that, in addition to the AWGN noise, the received symbol suffers from a constant attenuation factor $|\alpha|$ and a non linear noise $\hat{d}_0^l$ due to the non linear power amplifier block. Furthermore, the CFO ϵ and the STO τ will, respectively, destroy orthogonality between subcarriers and the Nyquist property of the prototype filter which will result in ICI and ISI as shown by the following expression of $\hat{s}_0^l$

$$\hat{s}_0^l = |\alpha|s_0^l Re\left\{\int_{-\infty}^{\infty} h(t)h(t-\tau)e^{j(2\pi\epsilon t - l\frac{\pi}{T}\tau)}\right\} + \xi_{ici,isi}(\epsilon,\tau) + \hat{d}_0^l + \hat{n}_0^l \tag{10}$$

where

$$\xi_{ici,isi} = |\alpha| Re\left\{\sum_{n=-\infty}^{\infty}\sum_{\substack{k=0\\(n,k)\neq(m,l)}}^{N-1} s_n^k\int_{-\infty}^{\infty} h(t)h(t-nT-\tau)e^{j(\Phi^{k-l}(t,\tau)+2\pi\epsilon t)}dt\right\} \tag{11}$$

3 Sensitivity Analysis to HPA NLD and CFO

3.1 SIR Analysis

The first measure of performance that we will consider in this paper is the signal to interference ratio (SIR) which can be defined in the presence of HPA NLD and synchronization errors by

$$SIR(\epsilon,\tau) = \frac{P_s(\epsilon,\tau)}{P_i(\epsilon,\tau) + E\left[|\hat{d}_0^l|^2\right]} \tag{12}$$

where $P_s(\epsilon,\tau)$, $P_i(\epsilon,\tau)$ and $E\left[|\hat{d}_0^l|^2\right]$ are the useful signal power, the interference power and the expectation of the non linear noise $\hat{d}_0^l$, respectively.

From Eq. (10), we can write the power of the useful signal as follows

$$P_s(\epsilon,\tau) = |\alpha|^2\sigma_s^2 \left|\int_{-\infty}^{\infty} h(t)h(t-\tau)\cos\left(2\pi\epsilon t - l\frac{\pi}{T}\tau\right)dt\right|^2 \tag{13}$$

where σ_s^2 is the variance of the transmitted symbol.

Regarding the power of the interference, it is equal to

$$\begin{aligned} P_i(\epsilon,\tau) &= E\left[\left|\xi_{ici,isi}\right|^2\right] \\ &= |\alpha|^2\sigma_s^2 \sum_{n=-\infty}^{\infty} \sum_{\substack{k=0 \\ (n,k)\neq(m,l)}}^{N-1} \left|\int_{-\infty}^{\infty} h(t)h(t-nT-\tau)\right. \\ &\quad \left. \times \cos\left(\Phi^{k-l}(t,\tau) + 2\pi\epsilon t\right)dt\right|^2 \end{aligned} \tag{14}$$

This expression can be significantly simplified if we take into account some observations. First, we assume that only adjacent subchannels overlap significantly. Therefore, the ICI is caused only by adjacent subcarriers $k = l-1$ and $k = l+1$. The same assumption can be made for the time index n since the prototype filter $h(t)$ is designed to minimize the effects of ISI beyond adjacent time symbols. Furthermore, we consider for simplicity that the signal is received on the subcarrier $l = 0$ which means that the summations over n and k in Eq. (14) will be limited to the values -1, 0 and 1. Finally, we assume that the CFO ϵ is very small. Hence, we can write $\sin(2\pi\epsilon t) \approx 2\pi\epsilon t$ and $\cos(2\pi\epsilon t) \approx 1$.

Using the above assumptions and following the same derivations as in [14], the useful signal power and the interference power can be rewritten, respectively, as follows

$$P_s(\epsilon,\tau) \approx |\alpha|^2\sigma_s^2\beta(\tau) = |\alpha|^2\sigma_s^2 \left|\int_{-\infty}^{\infty} h(t)h(t-\tau)dt\right|^2 \tag{15}$$

and

$$\begin{aligned} P_i(\epsilon,\tau) &= 2|\alpha|^2\sigma_s^2 \sum_{n=-1}^{1} \left|\int_{-\infty}^{\infty} h(t)h(t-nT-\tau)\sin\left(\frac{\pi}{T}(t-\tau)\right)dt\right|^2 \\ &+ |\alpha|^2\sigma_s^2 \left|\int_{-\infty}^{\infty} h(t)h(t\pm T-\tau)dt\right|^2 \\ &+ 8\pi^2|\alpha|^2\sigma_s^2\epsilon^2 \sum_{n=-1}^{1} \left|\int_{-\infty}^{\infty} t\,h(t)h(t-nT-\tau)\cos\left(\frac{\pi}{T}(t-\tau)\right)dt\right|^2 \end{aligned} \tag{16}$$

Let us define the following coefficients

$$\lambda(\tau) = 8\pi^2 \sum_{n=-1}^{1} \left| \int_{-\infty}^{\infty} t\, h(t)h(t-nT-\tau)\cos\left(\frac{\pi}{T}(t-\tau)\right) dt \right|^2 \tag{17}$$

and

$$\eta(\tau) = 2\sum_{n=-1}^{1} \left| \int_{-\infty}^{\infty} h(t)h(t-nT-\tau)\sin\left(\frac{\pi}{T}(t-\tau)\right) dt \right|^2 + \left| \int_{-\infty}^{\infty} h(t)h(t \pm T-\tau)dt \right|^2 \tag{18}$$

Therefore, the interference power can be expressed as

$$P_i(\epsilon,\tau) = |\alpha|^2\sigma_s^2\left(\lambda(\tau)\epsilon^2 + \eta(\tau)\right) \tag{19}$$

And the SIR expression (12) becomes

$$SIR(\epsilon,\tau) = \frac{\beta(\tau)}{\lambda(\tau)\epsilon^2 + \eta(\tau) + \frac{\sigma_d^2}{|\alpha|^2\sigma_s^2}} \tag{20}$$

Where we assumed that

$$E\left[\left|\hat{d_0^0}\right|^2\right] = E\left[\left|Re\left\{\int_{-\infty}^{\infty} d(t)e^{j2\pi\epsilon t}\gamma_{0,0}^*(t)dt\right\}\right|^2\right] \approx \sigma_d^2 \tag{21}$$

With σ_d^2 is the variance of the non linear noise $d(t)$.
As in [14], for small values of τ, we will consider the following approximations

$$\begin{aligned} \beta(\tau) &\approx \beta(0) = \left| \int_{-\infty}^{\infty} h^2(t)dt \right|^2 = 1 \\ \lambda(\tau) &\approx \lambda(0) = 8\pi^2 \sum_{n=-1}^{1} \left| \int_{-\infty}^{\infty} t\, h(t)h(t-nT)\cos\frac{\pi}{T}t dt \right|^2 \\ \eta(\tau) &\approx \eta(0) = 0 \end{aligned} \tag{22}$$

Where the first and third equalities result from the orthogonality condition of CMT systems defined as [8]

$$\int_{-\infty}^{\infty} h(t-m)h(t-nT)\cos(\Phi^{k-l})dt = \delta_{kl}\delta_{mn} \tag{23}$$

This approximation leads to the following simplified expression of the SIR

$$SIR(\epsilon) = \frac{1}{\lambda(0)\epsilon^2 + \frac{\sigma_d^2}{|\alpha|^2\sigma_s^2}} \tag{24}$$

This expression can be compared with that obtained in [14] for a SMT system suffering from CFO and STO but in the absence of HPA NLD. The expression obtained by the authors of [14] is given by

$$SIR_{[1]}(\epsilon, \tau) = \frac{1}{\lambda_{[1]}(0)\epsilon^2 + \eta_{[1]}(0)\tau^2} \tag{25}$$

Equation (24) can also be compared with the expression obtained for an OFDM system [12]

$$SIR_{ofdm}(\epsilon) = \frac{1}{(\pi^2/3)\,\epsilon^2} \tag{26}$$

Always without considering HPA non linearities. These comparisons and others will be carried on in Sect. 4.

3.2 BER Analysis

In this subsection, we will develop a BER analysis of the considered CMT system. In particular, the focus will lie on the effect of CFO and HPA non linear distortions on the BER performance.

Considering the SIR expression given by Eq. (24), we can derive the expression of the signal to interference plus noise ratio (SINR) by taking into account the AWGN noise $n(t)$. Accordingly, the SINR can be expressed as

$$SINR(\epsilon) = \frac{|\alpha|^2}{|\alpha|^2\lambda(0)\epsilon^2 + \frac{\sigma_d^2}{\sigma_s^2} + \frac{1}{SNR}} \tag{27}$$

where $SNR = \sigma_s^2/\sigma_n^2$ is the SNR value in the absence of synchronization errors and HPA non linear distortions.

The BER of 4-PAM modulation in AWGN channels is given by the following expression [13]

$$BER = \frac{3}{4} erfc\left(\sqrt{\frac{1}{5}SNR}\right) \tag{28}$$

By substituting (27) in (28), we obtain the exact closed form of the BER in the presence of CFO ϵ and HPA non linearities for the studied CMT system

$$BER(SNR) = \frac{3}{4} erfc\left(\frac{1}{5}\frac{|\alpha|^2}{|\alpha|^2\lambda(0)\epsilon^2 + \frac{\sigma_d^2}{\sigma_s^2} + \frac{1}{SNR}}\right)^{1/2} \tag{29}$$

This expression shows clearly that the BER performance is affected by HPA non linearities and CFO. The amount the sensitivity of the CMT system in terms of BER and SIR will be quantified in the next section via computer simulations.

4 Results

In this section, we present numerical results for the analytical SIR and BER expressions that we have derived in the previous section for the considered CMT system. The proposed models will be compared with existing models designed for other multicarrier systems such as SMT and OFDM. In all our simulations, we have considered a CMT system with N = 64 subcarriers transmitting 4-PAM modulated symbols. Furthermore, PHYDYAS prototype filter is used with overlapping factor of 4 [2]. We recall that the fractional normalized CFO $\epsilon_N = 2T\epsilon$ is defined in the range $-0.5 \leq \epsilon_N \leq 0.5$, which means that the CFO ϵ takes values between -0.16 and 0.16. The SIR curves presented in the next subsection will be plotted as a function of ϵ_N instead of ϵ and only the range of values $[0, 0.5]$ will be considered since the SIR expressions are even functions of ϵ_N.

4.1 SIR Performance

Figure 3 shows the SIR curves corresponding to Eqs. (24), (25) and (26). We recall that these expressions are derived, respectively, for a CMT system suffering from HPA NLD and CFO, a SMT system suffering from CFO and STO and an OFDM system suffering from CFO. Moreover, we have plotted the SIR curves of the considered CMT system without NLD, a SMT system with CFO, STO and NLD and an OFDM system with CFO and NLD. The results illustrated by Fig. 3 show that in the absence of NLD, the CMT signal is less sensitive to CFO than the SMT and OFDM ones. This can be explained by the high side lobes of the rectangular pulse shape used in OFDM systems and the presence of additional source of SIR degradation induced by the mutual interference between real and imaginary parts of the transmitted SMT symbol. Figure 3 also shows that the SIR of the 3 systems is very sensitive to HPA non linear distortions.

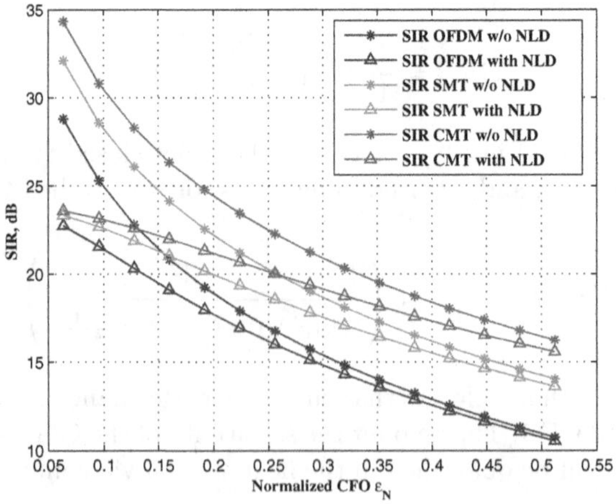

Fig. 3. SIR as a function of normalized CFO for the 3 multicarrier systems.

This sensitivity becomes less significant as the CFO increases. Such a result can be explained by the fact that for large values of CFO, this latter is the main source of distortions and the effect of HPA NLD becomes minimal. Moreover, one can observe that in the presence of HPA NLD, the CMT system still perform better than SMT and OFDM systems.

4.2 BER Performance

In this subsection we will show the joint effect of HPA NLD and CFO on the BER performance of the studied CMT system. As shown by Fig. 4, the proposed BER expression given by Eq. (29) is compared with the BER of a CMT system suffering only from CFO or HPA NLD. The perfect synchronized scenario without HPA non linearities is also considered for comparison purposes. As shown in Fig. 4, HPA non linearities and CFO cause a severe degradation in the BER performance. However, when the CMT signal is affected jointly by NLD and CFO as illustrated by the proposed model (Eq. (29)), the BER degradation is more significant. For example, to achieve a BER of 10^{-2}, the non linear CMT system with CFO requires a value of SNR equal to 15 dB while the CMT system suffering only from NLD (resp. CFO) requires only 14.3 dB (resp. 12.5 dB) of SNR, which means a loss of 0.7 dB (resp. 1.5 dB) in the transmitted signal power. Figure 4 also shows that, for relatively low SNR ($SNR < 5$ dB), the BER performance of the 3 systems is very close to the BER performance of the optimal scenario. This is due to the fact that the residual degradation of the BER, which is caused by the nonlinear HPA and CFO, is negligible compared to the AWGN noise. On the other hand, when the SNR level increases the BER degradation becomes important for the 3 models. This can be explained by the fact that the interference caused by CFO and/or HPA NLD are prominent compared to the noise level at high SNR values.

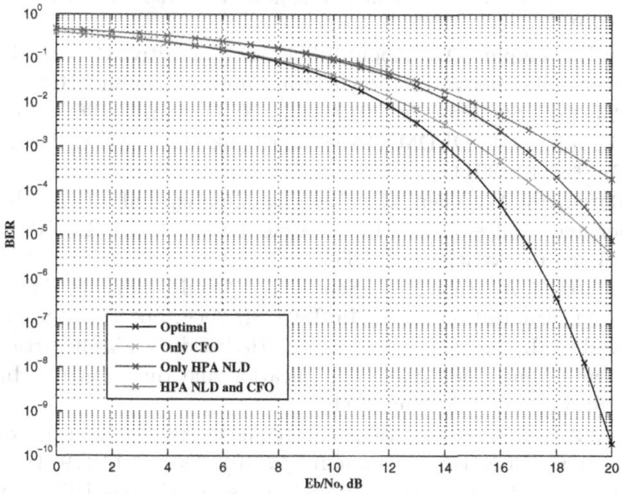

Fig. 4. BER vs. SNR for CMT with and without CFO and/or HPA NLD.

5 Conclusion

In this paper, we have studied jointly the impact of CFO and HPA non linear distortions on FBMC systems. A CMT transceiver was considered and analytical expressions of the SIR and BER was derived. The proposed SIR expression was compared with existing models designed for other multicarrier systems such as SMT and OFDM. We have shown that the SIR performance is highly sensitive to nonlinear distortions and therefore the effect of HPA can not be ignored for multicarrier systems. The same conclusion has been made for the BER performance which is severely affected by non linear distortions caused by non linear amplifiers.

References

1. Araujo, T., Dinis, R.: On the accuracy of the Gaussian approximation for the evaluation of nonlinear effects in OFDM signals. IEEE Trans. Commun. **60**(2), 346–351 (2012)
2. Bellanger, M.: Specification and design of a prototype filter for filter bank based multicarrier transmission. In: IEEE ICASSP 2001, vol. 4, pp. 2417–2420 (2001)
3. Bouhadda, H., et al.: Theoretical analysis of BER performance of nonlinearly amplified FBMC/OQAM and OFDM signals. EURASIP J. Adv. Sig. Proc. **2014**(1), 60 (2014)
4. Dardari, D., Tralli, V., Vaccari, A.: A theoretical characterization of nonlinear distortion effects in OFDM systems. IEEE Trans. Commun. **48**(10), 1755–1764 (2000)
5. Dohl, J., Fettweis, G.: Iterative blind estimation of nonlinear channels. In: IEEE ICASSP, pp. 3923–3927, May 2014
6. Elmaroud, B., Faqihi, M.A., Abbad, M., Aboutajdine, D.: BER analysis of FBMC based multi-cellular networks in the presence of synchronisation errors and HPA NLD. In: 2016 IEEE 84th Vehicular Technology Conference (VTC-Fall), pp. 1–6, September 2016
7. Elmaroud, B., Faqihi, A., Aboutajdine, D.: Sensitivity analysis of FBMC-based multi-cellular networks to synchronization errors and HPA nonlinearities. EURASIP J. Adv. Sig. Process. **2017**(1), 3 (2017). doi:10.1186/s13634-016-0441-0
8. Farhang-Boroujeny, B.: OFDM versus filter bank multicarrier. IEEE Sig. Process. Mag. **28**(3), 92–112 (2011)
9. Farhang-Boroujeny, B., Yuen, G.: Cosine modulated and offset QAM filter bank multicarrier techniques: a continuous-time prospect. EURASIP J. Appl. Sig. Process., 16 (2010). Article ID 165654
10. Fusco, T., Petrella, A., Tanda, M.: Sensitivity of multi-user filter-bank multicarrier systems to synchronization errors. In: ISCCSP 2008, pp. 393–398, March 2008
11. Khodjet-Kesba, M., Saber, C., Roviras, D., Medjahdi, Y.: Multicarrier interference evaluation with jointly non-linear amplification and timing errors. In: 2011 IEEE 73rd VTC Spring, pp. 1–5, May 2011
12. Moose, P.H.: A technique for orthogonal frequency division multiplexing frequency offset correction. IEEE Trans. Commun. **42**(10), 2908–2914 (1994)
13. Proakis, J.G.: Digital Communications, 4th edn. McGrawHill, New York City (2001)

14. Saeedi-Sourck, H., Wu, Y., Bergmans, J.W., Sadri, S., Farhang-Boroujeny, B.: Sensitivity analysis of offset QAM multicarrier systems to residual carrier frequency and timing offsets. Sig. Process. **91**(7), 1604–1612 (2011)
15. Sourck, H., Wu, Y., Bergmans, J., Sadri, S., Farhang-Boroujeny, B.: Effect of carrier frequency offset on offset QAM multicarrier filter bank systems over frequency-selective channels. In: 2010 IEEE Wireless Communications and Networking Conference (WCNC), pp. 1–6, April 2010
16. Tellado, J., Hoo, L., Cioffi, J.: Maximum-likelihood detection of nonlinearly distorted multicarrier symbols by iterative decoding. IEEE Trans. Commun. **51**(2), 218–228 (2003)

An Improved Bernoulli Sensing Matrix for Compressive Sensing

Hamid Nouasria(✉) and Mohamed Et-tolba

Department of Communication Systems, INPT, Rabat, Morocco
{nouasria,ettolba}@inpt.ac.ma

Abstract. Compressive Sensing (CS), also known as compressive sampling, is a new digital signal processing technique that aims at recovering the original signal from a very few number of measurements. Recently, several algorithms have been proposed to reconstruct the signal by exploiting its sparsity property. This signal reconstruction depends strongly on the sensing matrix, which key to CS. In this paper, we propose an improved Bernoulli sensing matrix based on full-orthogonal Hadamard codes. Simulations show that the use of the proposed sensing matrix in CS improves significantly the performance of signal reconstruction. In fact, it outperforms the Bernoulli and the Partial Hadamard matrices.

Keywords: Compressive sensing · Sensing matrix · A*OMP algorithm

1 Introduction

Conventional sampling methods can generate a very large number of samples when a high sampling frequency is used. Consequently, it is difficult to process high dimensional data such as biological, climate and financial data. To deal with this problem, Compressive Sensing (CS) has been introduced. It aims to reconstruct a sparse signal from a few number of measurements. CS takes benefits from the fact that a compressible signal can be approximated by a sparse signal. In order to reach CS goal, there are two principal challenges. First, one has to derive a suitable concise representation of the original signal which is compressible, this is highly dependent on the sensing matrix. Secondly, one has to be able to recover this latter from a significantly reduced number of measurements. For an accurate signal recovery, the sensing matrix has to be designed so as to satisfy some properties. The issues above have been subject of several works in recent years.

In CS, one of the most important tasks is to construct a sensing matrix that verifies some properties. Moreover, the sensing matrix is very important because it relates to the ratio of signal compression and the accuracy of signal reconstruction [1]. At present, several sensing matrices have been proposed in the literature. To the best of our knowledge, we can divide them into two categories, random and deterministic sensing matrices. Random matrices also can be taken

E. Sabir et al. (Eds.): UNet 2017, LNCS 10542, pp. 562–571, 2017.
https://doi.org/10.1007/978-3-319-68179-5_49

into two categories: (i) matrices whose entries are independent identically distributed (e.g. Gaussian and Bernoulli [2] matrices), (ii) matrices whose rows are randomly taken from an orthogonal transform matrix (e.g. Partial Hadamard [1] matrix, Partial Walsh [1] matrix).

In fact, the major problem of CS is the reconstruction of the original sparse signal from its compressed form (i.e. incomplete set of linear measurements), for that, CS proposes several reconstruction algorithms. For instance, we give here the most popular families of algorithms, such as convex optimization algorithms, greedy algorithms and combinatorial algorithms. Greedy algorithms are less complex than the convex optimization algorithms and requires a fewer number of measurements M than the combinatorial algorithms. For that, several versions of greedy algorithms have been proposed in the literature, such as (Matching Pursuit) MP [3], (Orthogonal MP) OMP [4] and A*OMP [5]. In general, this family of algorithms searches the original signal iteratively by identifying the indexes and values of the most significant coefficients in the signal.

In this paper, we propose an improved Bernoulli sensing matrix called hereafter Bernoulli-Hadamard matrix based on the full-orthogonal Hadamard codes. We construct our new sensing matrix by randomly changing some Bernoulli pseudo-orthogonal columns by full-orthogonal Hadamard codes. The fact that improves the orthogonality property of columns, and then improves the performance of such reconstruction algorithms that use this orthogonality property between columns. Simulations show that the use of the proposed sensing matrix in CS improves significantly the performance of signal reconstruction. In fact, it outperforms the Bernoulli and the Partial Hadamard matrix. The remainder of this paper is organized as follows: In Sect. 2 we give Compressive Sensing in a nutshell. In Sect. 3 we give a detailed description of the proposed sensing matrix. Simulation results are given in Sect. 4. We conclude in Sect. 5

2 Compressive Sensing in a Nutshell

Compressive Sensing (CS) is a new digital signal processing framework dealing with sparse signals (i.e. signals with few non-zero coefficients), it aims to acquire sparse signals into a compressed form called measurements vector for enable more efficient processing and storage. In CS framework, the measurements vector is obtained by simply correlating the sparse signal with a sensing matrix, and by utilizing a reconstruction algorithm we can invert the problem and reconstruct the original sparse signal from its measurements vector.

For more clarity, let's consider the process of acquiring a N-dimensional signal x into a M-dimensional measurements vector y:

$$y = \Phi x \tag{1}$$

where $\Phi_{M,N}$ is a sensing matrix, with $M \ll N$. The transformation from a N-dimensional signal x to a M-dimensional measurements vector y provoke a dimensionality reduction. So inverting the undetermined problem given in (1) is impossible (i.e. reconstruct x from y is impossible). But CS, by exploiting the sparsity property of signals (i.e. S-sparse signals, with $S < M \ll N$), demonstrates that with the use of special sensing matrices, the reconstruction becomes possible and the problem given in (1) has a unique solution.

Given that the problem (1) has a unique solution x, and this x is sparse. Then, the ultimate way to search x is by solving the optimization problem P_0:

$$(P_0)\ \hat{x} = argmin \parallel x \parallel_{l_0}\ \ subject\ to\ \ y = \Phi x \tag{2}$$

where $\parallel x \parallel_{l_0}$ is the pseudo-norm l_0 of x, which gives the number of non-zero coefficients in x. It is demonstrated that the problem P_0 is Non-deterministic Polynomial-time Hard (NP-Hard). For that, several algorithms have relaxed this problem by proposing a new problem P_1:

$$(P_1)\ \hat{x} = argmin \parallel x \parallel_{l_1}\ \ subject\ to\ \ y = \Phi x \tag{3}$$

where $\parallel x \parallel_{l_1}$ is the norm l_1 of x, that gives the sum of the absolute values of coefficients in x.

In noisy cases, the problem given in (1) is redefined as:

$$y = \Phi x + e \tag{4}$$

where e represents a noise term, with l_2 norm bounded by ϵ. Other optimization problems are defined in this case, the P_2 and the unconstrained problem P_3 defined below:

$$(P_2)\ \hat{x} = argmin \parallel x \parallel_{l_1}\ \ s.t\ \parallel \Phi x - y \parallel_{l_2} \leq \epsilon \tag{5}$$

$$(P_3)\ \hat{x} = argmin(\frac{1}{2} \parallel y - \Phi x \parallel_{l_2} + \lambda \parallel x \parallel_{l_1}) \tag{6}$$

with $\parallel x \parallel_{l_2}$ denotes the euclidean norm. The choice of λ can be based on how much weight we want to put on the fidelity to the sparsity of the signal.

The sensing matrix Φ must verify some properties. One of the most popular properties in the literature is the RIP property defined as:

For each S=1, 2, 3..., we define the constants (δ_S, δ_{2S}) for a given matrix Φ for all S-sparse signals x_1, x_2 as:

$$(1-\delta_S)\|x_1\|^2_{l_2} \leq \|\Phi x_1\|^2_{l_2} \leq (1+\delta_S)\|x_1\|^2_{l_2} \tag{7}$$

$$(1-\delta_{2S})\|z\|^2_{l_2} \leq \|\Phi z\|^2_{l_2} \leq (1+\delta_{2S})\|z\|^2_{l_2}, z = x_1 - x_2 \tag{8}$$

we say that Φ verifies the RIP of order S if:

$$0 < \delta_S, \delta_{2S} \ll 1 \tag{9}$$

Sensing matrices that satisfy the RIP property guarantee that it exists one sparse signal x that verifies (1) for a given y and Φ, the fact that guarantees an exact reconstruction of x from y. For more properties, the reader can refer to [6,7].

Hence, the sensing matrix construction is a very important step in CS framework. For that, several sensing matrices have been introduced in the literature. To the best of our knowledge, these matrices can be divided into two major categories, random and deterministic sensing matrices. In this paper, we focus on random sensing matrices.

Random matrices have more advantages compared to deterministic ones. For instance, random matrices are easy to construct and guarantee an exact reconstruction. One of the most prominent random sensing matrices that verifies the RIP with high probability is the uniformly distributed Bernoulli sensing matrix, whose elements are defined below:

$$\phi_{i,j} = \begin{cases} +\frac{1}{\sqrt{M}} & probability = 1/2 \\ -\frac{1}{\sqrt{M}} & probability = 1/2 \end{cases} ; 1 \leq i \leq M; 1 \leq j \leq N \tag{10}$$

In most cases, the original signal x is not sparse, but fortunately has a sparse representation α in a transform domain Ψ, however, we still refer to x as a sparse signal:

$$x = \Psi\alpha \tag{11}$$

In this case, we acquire the signal x into a measurements vector y by using the same formula (1). In contrast, in the reconstruction step, the reconstruction algorithm using the matrix $A = \Phi\Psi$, reconstructs the sparse representation α instead of the signal x. For that, the problems given in (2), (3), (5) and (6) are reformulated as:

$$(P_0) \quad \hat{\alpha} = argmin \parallel \alpha \parallel_{l_0} \ subject\ to \ \ y = \Phi\Psi\alpha \tag{12}$$

$$(P_1) \quad \hat{\alpha} = argmin \parallel \alpha \parallel_{l_1} \ subject\ to \ \ y = \Phi\Psi\alpha \tag{13}$$

$$(P_2) \quad \hat{\alpha} = argmin \parallel \alpha \parallel_{l_1} \ s.t \ \parallel \Phi\Psi\alpha - y \parallel_{l_2} \leq \epsilon \tag{14}$$

$$(P_3) \quad \hat{\alpha} = argmin(\frac{1}{2} \parallel y - \Phi\Psi\alpha \parallel_{l_2} + \lambda \parallel \alpha \parallel_{l_1}) \tag{15}$$

Finally, it is worth noting, provided that Ψ is an ortho-normed matrix, the matrix $A = \Phi\Psi$ keeps the same properties of Φ. In other words, if Φ verifies the RIP property, the matrix A also verifies the RIP.

3 Improved Bernoulli Sensing Matrix Based on Hadamard Codes

The Bernoulli sensing matrix is one of the most popular random sensing matrices in the literature, it is famous for its construction simplicity and reconstruction efficiency. It is demonstrated verifying the RIP property with high probability.

In this paper, we propose an improved sensing matrix which is constructed from the Bernoulli matrix $\Phi_{M,N}$, defined in (10), by randomly changing M pseudo-orthogonal columns by M full-orthogonal Hadamard codes.

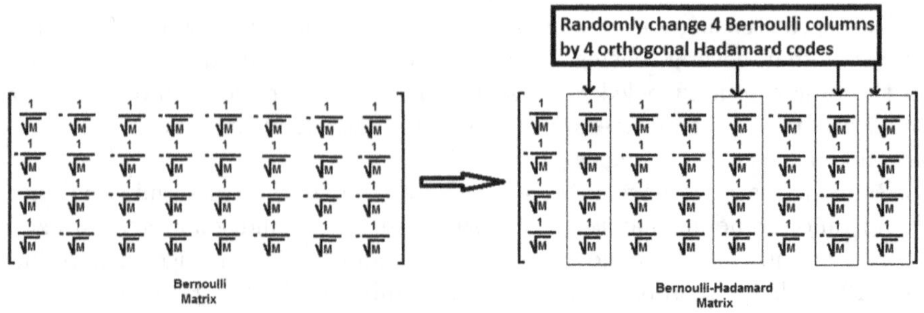

Fig. 1. Design schematic of the construction of a 4 × 8 Bernoulli-Hadamard sensing matrix from a Bernoulli sensing matrix

The Hadamard introduced codes are normalized by $\frac{1}{\sqrt{M}}$ to maintain the same structure of Bernoulli matrix. The new matrix is called Bernoulli-Hadamard matrix. Figure 1 illustrates all the construction process for $M = \frac{N}{2} = 4$.

In matrix-vector form, we construct our new sensing matrix Φ_{BH}, based on a $M \times N$ Bernoulli matrix Φ_B and a set Σ of M indexes taken randomly from $\{1, 2, 3, \ldots, N\}$:

$$\Phi_{BH} = \Phi_B - \Phi_{B\Sigma} + \Phi_{H\Sigma} \tag{16}$$

where, $\Phi_{B\Sigma}$ is constructed from Φ_B by setting all the columns to zero except those whose indexes are in Σ, also, $\Phi_{H\Sigma}$ is constructed from a full-zero matrix by changing the columns that have indexes in Σ by the M normalized full-orthogonal Hadamard codes.

Randomly changing M Bernoulli matrix pseudo-orthogonal columns by M full-orthogonal Hadamard codes improves the orthogonality property of columns with keeping a bit the same uniform distribution. In other words, the new matrix called Bernoulli-Hadamard matrix has columns more orthogonal than the Bernoulli matrix columns.

In general, the performance of a set of sequences (i.e. sensing matrix columns in our case) is usually evaluated as introduced in [8] by mean square aperiodic auto-correlation R_{AC} (MSAAC) and mean square aperiodic cross-correlation R_{CC} (MSACC) measures. For a set of N sequences c_i of length M, the discrete aperiodic correlation function $r_{i,j}$, R_{AC} and R_{CC} are defined as:

$$r_{i,j}(\tau) = \frac{1}{M} \sum_{n} c_i(n) c_j(n + \tau) \tag{17}$$

$$R_{AC} = \frac{1}{N} \sum_{i=1}^{N} \sum_{\tau=1-M, \tau \neq 0}^{M-1} \mid r_{i,i}(\tau) \mid^2 \tag{18}$$

$$R_{CC} = \frac{1}{N(N-1)} \sum_{i=1}^{N} \sum_{j=1, j \neq i}^{N} \sum_{\tau=1-M}^{M-1} \mid r_{i,j}(\tau) \mid^2 \tag{19}$$

In this paper, we fix τ to zero, because we are interested to measure just the orthogonality property (i.e. the inner-product between columns). For that, (17), (19) are redefined as:

$$r_{i,j}(\tau = 0) = \frac{1}{M} \sum_{n=1}^{M} c_i(n) c_j(n) \tag{20}$$

$$R_{CC}(\tau = 0) = \frac{1}{N(N-1)} \sum_{i=1}^{N} \sum_{j=1, j \neq i}^{N} | r_{i,j} |^2 \tag{21}$$

Figure 2 illustrates the $R_{CC}(\tau = 0)$ over the number of introduced Hadamard codes and demonstrates that the transformation from the Bernoulli matrix to the Bernoulli-Hadamard matrix improves the orthogonality property between columns.

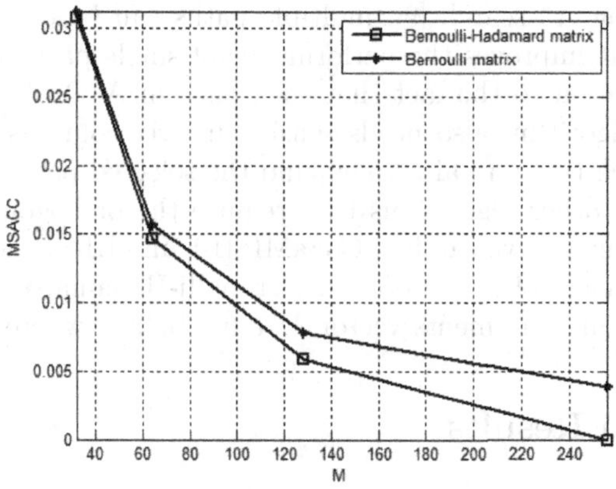

Fig. 2. MSACC between columns from a M × 256 sensing matrix

Our idea is inspired from the fact that several reconstruction algorithms use the orthogonality property of sensing matrix columns. We give below an example of Orthogonal Matching Pursuit (OMP) algorithm and his need for the columns orthogonality.

Algorithm 1. Orthogonal Matching Pursuit(OMP)
Input:
- the $M \times N$ sensing matrix Φ
- M-dimensional measurement vector y
- error threshold ϵ.

Output: approximate solution $\hat{x}$
1: Set $j = 0$
- Set the initial solution $x_0 = 0$
- Set the initial residual $\mathrm{r}_0 = y - \Phi \hat{x}_0 = y$
- Set the initial support $\Lambda_0 = \emptyset$

2: repeat
3: Set $j = j + 1$
4: Select index i so that $\max \| \Phi_i^T r_j \|_{l_2}$, where Φ_i is the ith column of Φ.
5: update $\Lambda_j = \Lambda_{j-1} \cup i$
6: update $\hat{x}_j = argmin \| y - \Phi x \|_{l_2}$, subject to Supp$(x) = \Lambda_j$
7: update $\mathrm{r}_j = y - \Phi \hat{x}_j$
8: until $\| \mathrm{r}_j \|_{l_2} \leq \epsilon$
9: $\hat{x} = \hat{x}_j$

In the algorithm above, we can clearly see the importance of columns orthogonality in steps 4 and 6. In step 4, we use the orthogonality property of sensing matrix columns to select the index of most significant coefficients in the sparse signal x. Also in step 6, we use the orthogonal projection to approximate the values of the most significant coefficients.

The A*OMP is a greedy algorithm that employs OMP algorithm in a tree search. By utilizing A* search [9], multiple paths can be evaluated simultaneously, the fact that improves the performance of single path structure of OMP algorithm. In addition to the fact that each path in A*OMP is an OMP algorithm, A*OMP algorithm also needs sensing matrix columns orthogonality to initialize the search tree and also to expand the selected path at each iteration.

There are also other algorithms that require the orthogonality property of sensing matrix columns, we can list, CoSaMP [10] and L1-magic [11] algorithms. Finally, one drawback of the proposed Bernoulli-Hadamard sensing matrix is that the length of measurements vector M must be 2^m, where m is an integer.

4 Simulation Results

In this section, we compare the performance of the proposed Bernoulli-Hadamard sensing matrix with the Bernoulli matrix, Partial Hadamard matrix and Gaussian matrix. It is worth noting that Partial Hadamard matrix is normalized by $\frac{1}{\sqrt{M}}$, and the Gaussian matrix has a zero mean and variance equal to $\frac{1}{M}$. For that, we run our simulations over three type of signals, Gaussian signals, uniform signals and binary signals using A*OMP algorithm.

A*OMP has four cost models, in this paper we employ adaptive-multiplicative (AdapMul) cost model with parameters $I = 3, B = 2, P = 200$, $\beta = 1.25$ and $\alpha = 0.8$. For all the simulations, we take $M = 32$ measurements from a S-sparse 64-dimensional signal. Comparison is given in terms of both the average normalized mean squared error (NMSE) and the exact reconstruction rate. The NMSE is defined as the ratio of the l_2 norm of the error to the l_2 norm of the signal. Also, the exact reconstruction rate is defined with assuming that the reconstruction is exact if the signal to noise ratio is greater than 50 dB.

First, we employ Gaussian sparse signals (e.i. whose non-zero coefficients are drawn from a standard Gaussian distribution, zero mean and variance equal to 1). Figure 3 illustrates that the proposed Bernoulli-Hadamard sensing matrix gives better results than the other sensing matrices all over the sparsity levels S. In that, it gives highest rate of exact reconstruction and lowest amount of error per failure. for $S > 16$, Bernoulli-Hadamard matrix and Partial Hadamard matrix give the same results in terms of the rate of exact reconstruction.

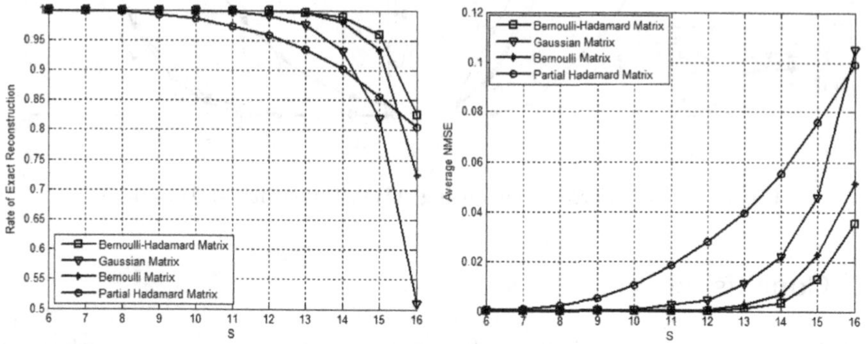

Fig. 3. Gaussian sparse signals using A*OMP algorithm: $M = 0.5N$

Second, we employ uniform sparse signals (e.i. whose non-zero coefficients take values +1 or −1 with equal probability ($p = \frac{1}{2}$)). As depicted in Fig. 4, the new sensing matrix gives better results than the Bernoulli, Gaussian and Partial Hadamard matrix except for $S = 16$ where the Bernoulli-Hadamard matrix gives higher amount of error than the Gaussian matrix.

Third, in this case, we employ binary sparse signals (e.i. whose non-zero coefficients are fixed to +1). Figure 5 shows that the results is similar to the case of uniform signals.

Finally, we note that, for ease of exposition, we have fixed the dimension of the sparse signal as $N = 2M = 64$. In fact, the proposed sensing matrix well performs even when high dimensional signals are used.

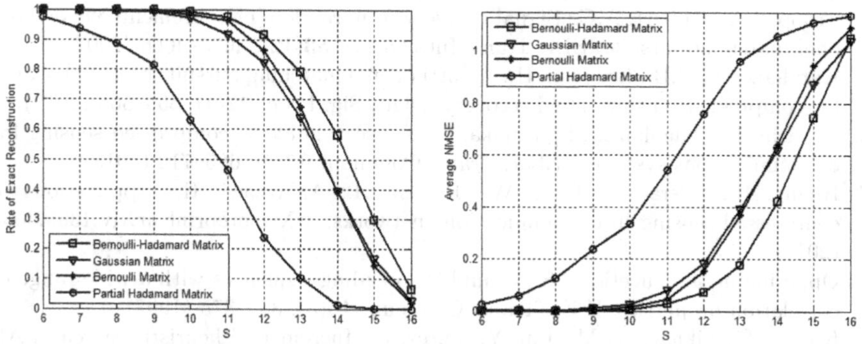

Fig. 4. Uniform sparse signals using A*OMP algorithm: $M = 0.5N$

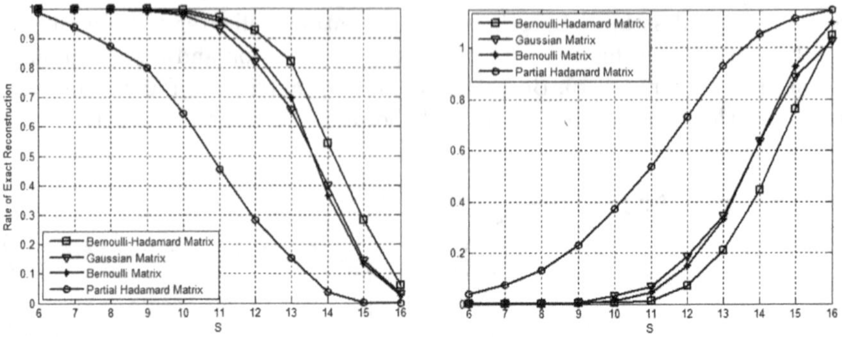

Fig. 5. Binary sparse signals using A*OMP algorithm: $M = 0.5N$

5 Conclusion

In this paper, an improved Bernoulli sensing matrix based on full-orthogonal Hadamard codes for compressive sensing is proposed. The simulation results show that this new sensing matrix outperforms the Bernoulli and Partial Hadamard matrices in terms of the normalized mean squared error (NMSE) and the rate of exact reconstruction.

References

1. Zhuoran, C., Honglin, Z., Min, J., Gang, W., Jingshi, S.: An improved Hadamard measurement matrix based on Walsh code for compressive sensing. In: 2013 9th International Conference on Information, Communications and Signal Processing (ICICS), pp. 1–4. IEEE, December 2013
2. Zhang, G., Jiao, S., Xu, X., Wang, L.: Compressed sensing and reconstruction with Bernoulli matrices. In: 2010 IEEE International Conference on Information and Automation (ICIA), pp. 455–460. IEEE, June 2010
3. Mallat, S.G., Zhang, Z.: Matching pursuits with time-frequency dictionaries. IEEE Trans. Sig. Process. **41**(12), 3397–3415 (1993)
4. Tropp, J.A., Gilbert, A.C.: Signal recovery from random measurements via orthogonal matching pursuit. IEEE Trans. Inf. Theory **53**(12), 4655–4666 (2007)
5. Karahanoglu, N.B., Erdogan, H.: A* orthogonal matching pursuit: best-first search for compressed sensing signal recovery. Digit. Sig. Proc. **22**(4), 555–568 (2012)
6. Hayashi, K., Nagahara, M., Tanaka, T.: A user's guide to compressed sensing for communications systems. IEICE Trans. Commun. **96**(3), 685–712 (2013)
7. Huang, H., Misra, S., Tang, W., Barani, H., Al-Azzawi, H.: Applications of compressed sensing in communications networks. arXiv preprint arXiv:1305.3002 (2013)
8. Oppermann, J., Vucetic, B.S.: Complex spreading sequences with a wide range of correlation properties. IEEE Trans. Commun. **45**(3), 365–375 (1997)
9. Koenig, S., Likhachev, M., Liu, Y., Furcy, D.: Incremental heuristic search in AI. AI Mag. **25**, 99–112 (2004)

10. Needell, D., Vershynin, R.: Uniform uncertainty principle and signal recovery via regularized orthogonal matching pursuit. Found. Comput. Math. **9**(3), 317–334 (2009)
11. Candes, E., Romberg, J.: l1-magic: recovery of sparse signals via convex programming, vol. 4, p. 14 (2005). www.acm.caltech.edu/l1magic/downloads/l1magic.pdf

Contribution to the Study of Beamforming at 2.4 GHz of a Smart Antenna Alimented by a 4 × 4 Butler Matrix for Wireless Applications

Mohamed Hanaoui[1(✉)] and Mounir Rifi[2]

[1] IEEE Student Member, CED Engineering Science, ENSEM, Laboratory RITM/ESTC, Hassan II University, Casablanca, Morocco
Hanaoui.mohamed@gmail.com
[2] CED Science Engineering, ENSEM, Laboratory RITM/ESTC, Hassan II University, Casablanca, Morocco
rifi@email.com

Abstract. Wireless communication has created a continuing demand for increased bandwidth and better quality of services. Smart antenna systems are one of the ways to accommodate this demand which can provide numerous benefits to service provider and the customer. Therefore, this paper present a planar design, simulation and implementation of a smart antenna system for wireless networks using microstrip antenna array with beamforming network. An 4 × 4 Butler matrix is designed as a feeding network to excite the patch antenna array. Owning to the linear phase distribution induced by the Butler matrix, the antenna array can generate different beams in desired direction.

1 Introduction

The smart antenna system has received great attention in recent years since it takes advantage of the diversity effects to improve data capacity and communication quality [1–3, 12, 13]. Multiple antennas in a smart antenna system can create various beam patterns, such as switched beam or continuous beam, based on the different beam-forming technologies.

The Butler matrix has been widely adopted in the switched-beam system due to its simplicity and easy realization [4, 5]. However, an N-way Butler matrix can only generate N sets of phase distribution, which corresponds to N beam directions. Although increasing N can improve the beam resolution, the size of Butler matrix will become impractically large [6].

Another beamforming approach is using the tunable phase shifters to generate the continuous beam steering. However, it requires a considerable amount of phase tuning for the same coverage, which implies a great design challenge.

In this work, we propose a passive beamforming network combining both the Butler matrix and phase shifters. The radiation beam can be switched to a certain direction through the Butler matrix, and then slightly adjusted by the phase shifters. By using this approach, the Butler matrix can remain small order, and the needed phase

E. Sabir et al. (Eds.): UNet 2017, LNCS 10542, pp. 572–583, 2017.
https://doi.org/10.1007/978-3-319-68179-5_50

tuning is also limited since the phase shifters are only responsible for a small steering range between two adjacent fixed beams.

In this paper, a smart antenna array based on Butler Matrix network at 2.4 GHz is demonstrated for wireless communication. In order to achieve beam switching, an 4 × 4 Butler matrix is designed as a feeding network to excite the patch antenna array. Owning to the linear phase distribution induced by the Butler matrix, the antenna array can generate different beams in desired direction. The sections below describe the circuit design and its simulation and measurement results.

The governing equations in the form of matrix for butler matrix shown in Fig. 1 are as follows:

$$\begin{bmatrix} 2R \\ 1R \\ 1L \\ 2L \end{bmatrix} = \begin{pmatrix} 0 & -135 & 90 & -45 \\ 0 & -45 & -90 & -135 \\ 0 & 45 & 90 & 135 \\ 0 & 135 & -90 & 45 \end{pmatrix} \cdot \begin{bmatrix} A1 \\ A2 \\ A3 \\ A4 \end{bmatrix} \quad (1)$$

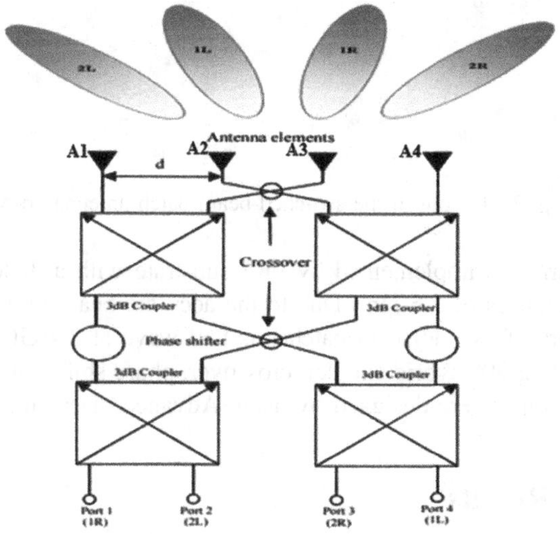

Fig. 1. Design of the switched-beam patch antenna array

2 Implementation of System and Design Procedure

Figure 1 shows the design of our switched-beam patch antenna array. The switched-beam patch antenna array is formed by antenna array, the Butler matrix works as the feeding network and switch network.

The Butler matrix mainly consists of the 90° hybrid coupler, crossover, phase shifter and phase-delay lines. In order to combine with the antenna array and the switch network, the Butler matrix networks is basically implemented by 50-Ω microstrip lines. To prevent the propagation of substrate and surface waves which affect the antenna characteristics, the FR4 substrate with a dielectric constant of $\varepsilon_r = 4.4$ and a thickness of 1.6-mm was chosen.

The layout of Butler matrix network at 2.4 GHz in Fig. 2. The 90° hybrid coupler that can generate signals 90° out of phase at its outputs consists of two pairs of Z_0 (50 Ω) and Z_1 (35.4 Ω) quarter-wavelength microstrip lines. Crossover that can cross two transmission lines without power lost is implemented by cascading two 90° hybrid couplers. The work of the phase shifter is using phase-delay lines to get the change of phase as 45° and 0°.

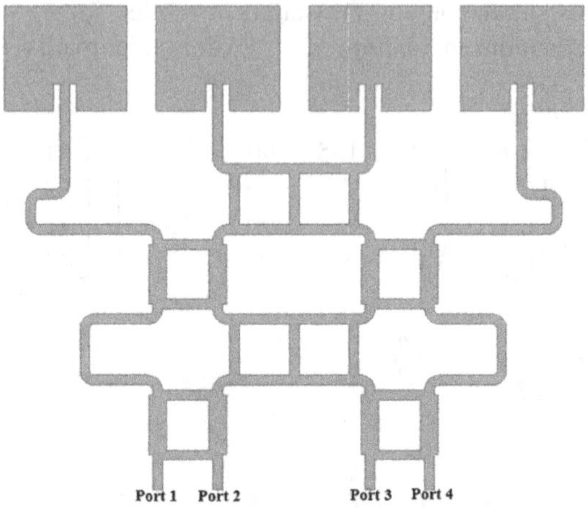

Fig. 2. Layout of the switched-beam patch antenna array

The antenna array is implemented by FR4 substrate with a dielectric constant of $\varepsilon_r = 4.4$ and a thickness of 1.6 mm. Due to the accurate beam pointing, the distance between the centers of two adjacent patches is half-wave at 2.4 GHz. The individual components including 90° hybrid coupler, crossover, phase shifter, as well as the entire Butler matrix structure, were designed by using Advanced Design System (ADS).

3 Simulation Results

3.1 Design of −3 dB Hybrid Coupler

The −3 dB hybrid coupler is the most significant part within the Butler matrix, since it is the most element exist in the structure. The theoretical part is shown in [8].

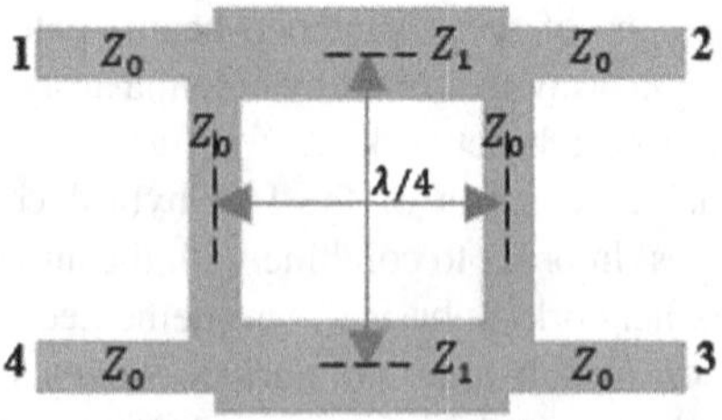

Fig. 3. Structure of hybrid coupler

Figure 3 shows the −3 dB hybrids. The return losses, coupling and isolation of the designed hybrid coupler are shown in Fig. 4(a). The return losses S11 and isolation S41 are about −31.8 dB and −34.7 dB, respectively, around the resonant frequency. Therefore, it can be concluded that we got a good matching and a very good isolation around the operating frequency 2.4 GHz. The coupling is about −3 dB throughout the operating frequency band, which shows that the power is halved on both output ports. In terms of phase, the output signals on ports 2 and 3 are almost in phase quadrature. The phase difference is shown in Fig. 4(b), which is around 90°.

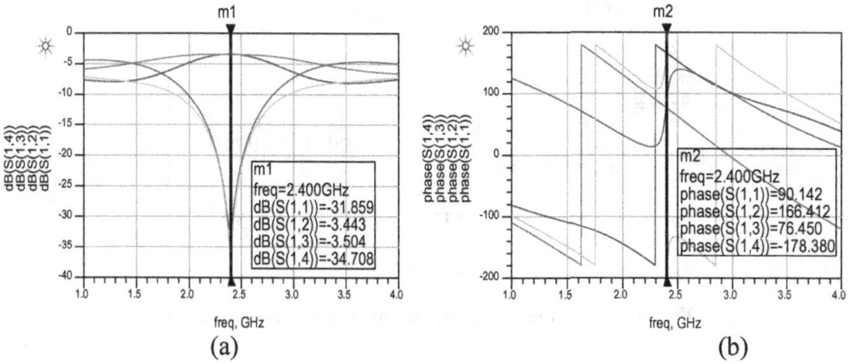

Fig. 4. (a) S parameters versus frequency for the hybrid coupler; (b) The phase difference for the hybrid coupler

The simulation results of the coupler are encouraging. They have an equiamplitude and quadrature phase in the output. Therefore, it has good impedance matching.

3.2 Design of Crossover (0 dB Coupler)

Crossover is the biggest hurdle in the realization of the Butler matrix [9]. The crossover can be built by cascading two −3 dB hybrid couplers network with 2 inputs and 2 outputs [7, 9, 10], see Fig. 5 This type of coupler is also called 0 dB coupler. The perfect design of crossover is accomplished if every adjacent ports are isolated.

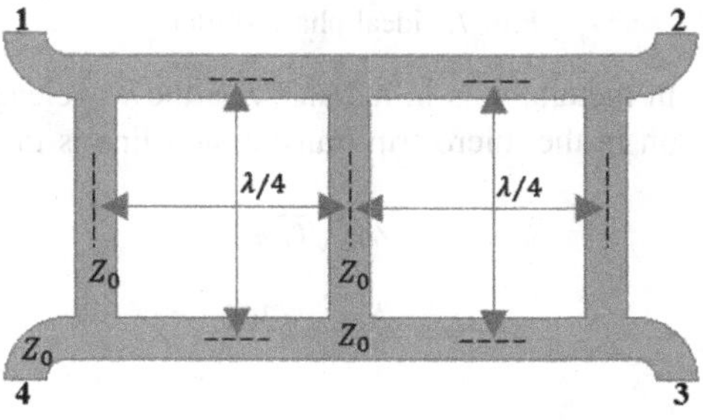

Fig. 5. Structure of crossover.

In the same way, the crossover has been designed using 50 Ω microstrip transmission lines as shown in Fig. 5. The insertion loss for the coupled port S13 is −0.74 dB while return loss S11 and the isolated ports S12 and S14 are about −30 dB respectively for the frequency of interest. These results are shows in Fig. 6 are satisfactory in terms of reflection and isolation parameters.

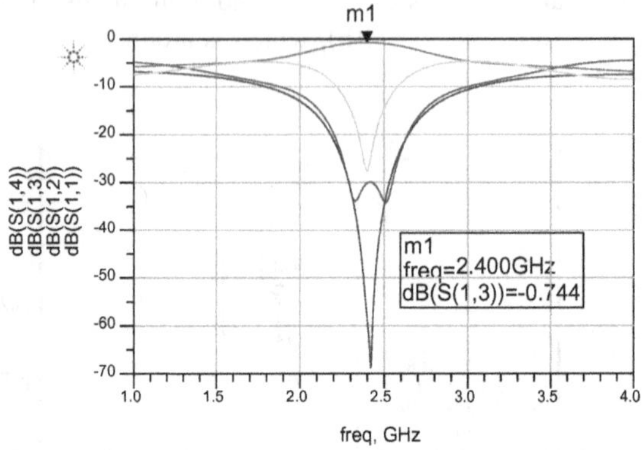

Fig. 6. S parameters versus frequency for the crossover

3.3 Design of Phase Shifter

The phase shifter is implemented using microstrip transmission line. As seen in Fig. 7. The length of the line corresponding to 45° phase shift and 0° phase shift is given by the formula [11]:

$$\phi = \frac{2\pi}{\lambda} L \tag{2}$$

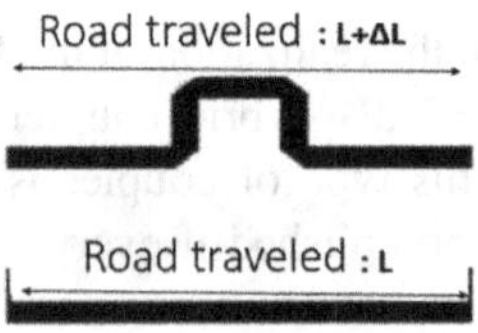

Fig. 7. Ideal phase shifter

where L is the length in meters, ϕ is in radians, λ is the wavelength in the microstrip line, and the wavelength in the microstrip transmission line is given by:

$$\lambda = \lambda_0 / \sqrt{\varepsilon_{reff}} \tag{3}$$

$$\Delta L = \Delta\varphi.\lambda_g / 360 \tag{4}$$

$$\lambda_g = \lambda_0 / \sqrt{\varepsilon_r} \tag{5}$$

where λ_0 is the free space wavelength, λ_g is the guided wavelength and ε_r is the dielectric constant of the microstrip line. Since the phase shift is implemented using simple transmission line, therefore it is linearly frequency dependent, Fig. 8 shown the structure of simulated 45° phase shifter and 0° phase shifter.

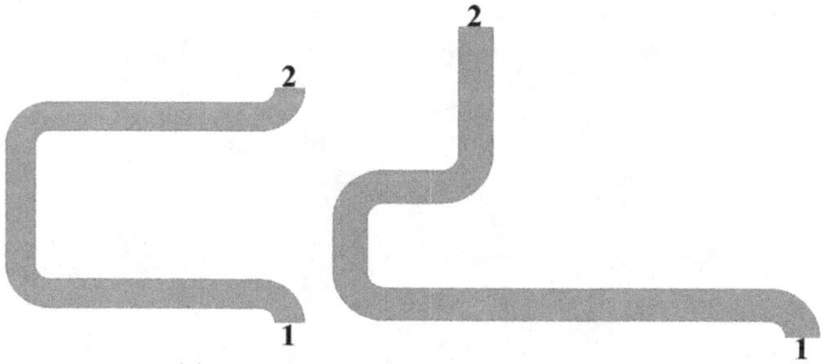

Fig. 8. (a) Structure of 45° phase shifter; (b) Structure of 0° phase shifter

For the phase shift, the simulation result is shown in Fig. 9(a). The phase difference between the ports 1 and 2 is 45° at the desired frequency. And in Fig. 9(b). The phase difference between the ports 1 and 2 is 0° at the desired frequency.

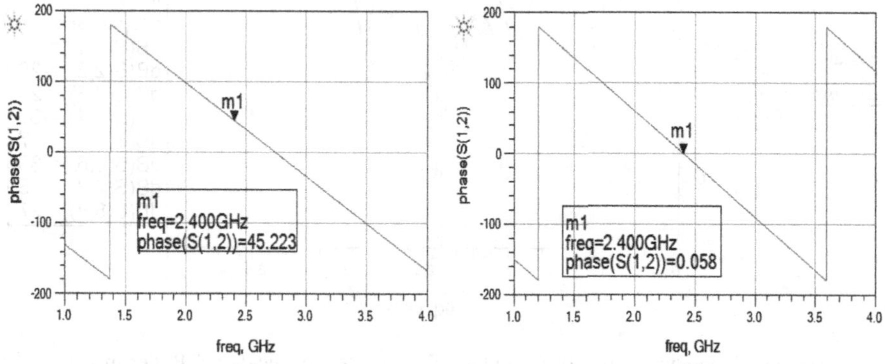

Fig. 9. (a) Simulated phase difference between the ports 1 and 2 in 45° phase shifter; (b) Simulated phase difference between the ports 1 and 2 in 0° phase shifter

3.4 4 × 4 Butler Matrix Design and Setup

The layout of the proposed 4 × 4 Butler matrix is presented in Fig. 10. Combining the components presented in Sects. 3.1, 3.2 and 3.3, the proposed Butler matrix was designed as a passive microstrip network on the same substrate FR4. When one of the input ports (port 1, port 2, port 3 or port 4) was excited by an RF signal, all the output ports (port 5, port 6, port 7 and port 8) were excited, though with equal amplitude and specified relative phase differences.

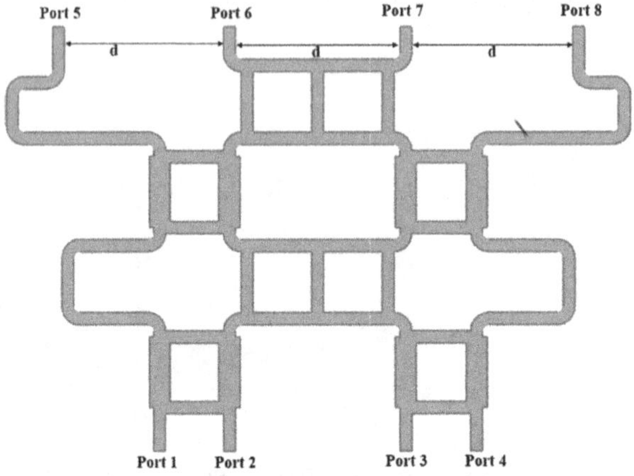

Fig. 10. Microstrip layout of the 4 × 4 Butler matrix network.

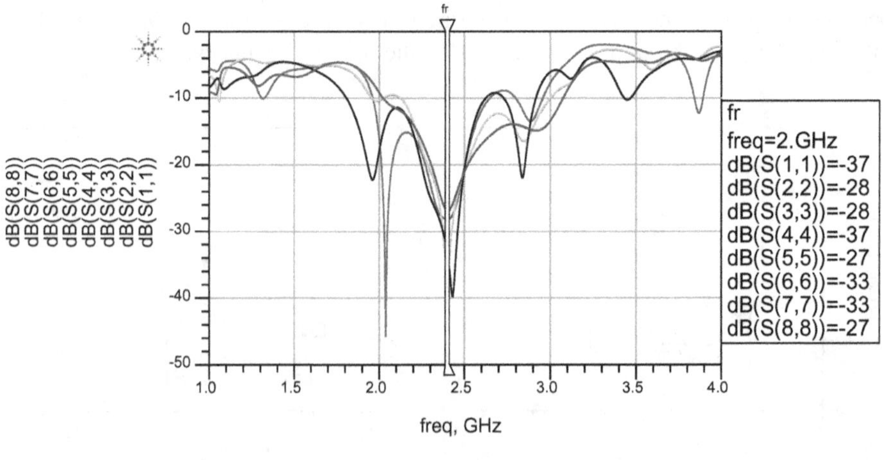

Fig. 11. Simulated results of magnitude S parameters of the 4 × 4 Butler matrix

Table 1. Optimized value of phase distribution of outputs ports.

	Port 5	Port 6	Port 7	Port 8	B
Port 1	62.71	16.93	−28.74	−72.85	45
Port 2	−28.47	107.76	−117.05	16.94	−135
Port 3	16.95	−117.04	107.76	−28.45	135
Port 4	−72.83	−28.73	16.92	62.71	−45

Table 1 illustrated the final optimized simulated butler matrix results without antennas, it can be seen that, the outputs phase shift was ±45°, ±135°with phase error of 6°. And the overall return loss was below −16 dB to −20 dB is illustrated in Fig. 11. The distance d between antennas was considered to be $\lambda/2$ in order to obtain a minimum mutual coupling between the elements and thus preserve the orthogonality condition between the various radiation beams.

4 Microstrip Smart Antenna System

4.1 Microstrip Patch Antenna

In this part, the microstrip patch antenna is used as radiating element. The antenna is fabricated on FR4 board and measured at our laboratory; the dielectric permittivity is 4.4 and thickness is 1.6 mm, Figs. 12 and 13 shows the layout and the computed input return loss S11 of the microstrip patch antenna. The simulation was performed using Advanced Design System (ADS) software. The simulated results show good return loss better than −20 dB at the resonant frequency 2.4 GHz.

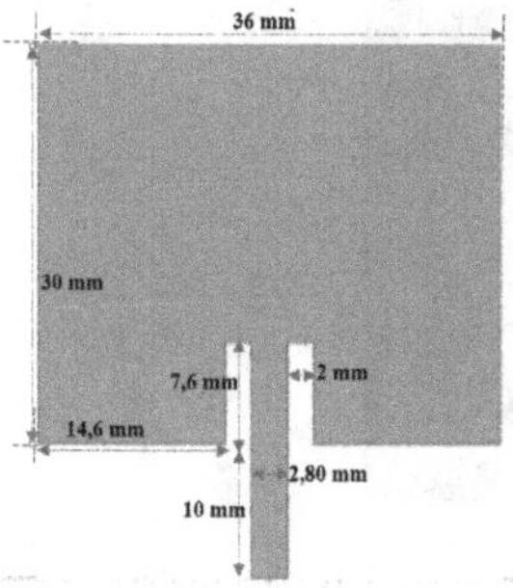

Fig. 12. Layout of microstrip patch antenna

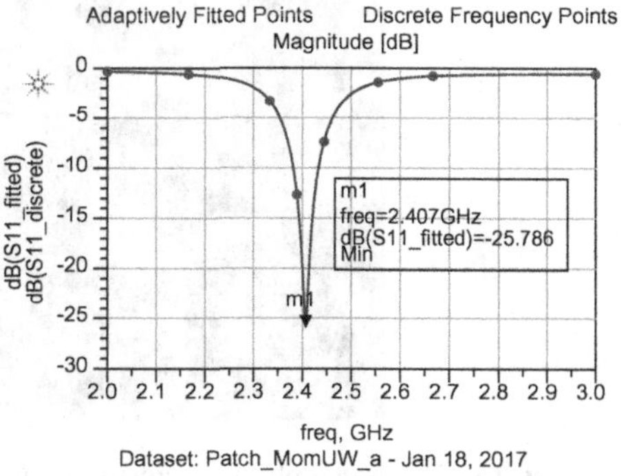

Fig. 13. Simulated input return loss of microstrip patch antenna.

4.2 Optimized Smart Antenna Design

Now after the Butler Matrix was designed, it was integrated with four inset fed microstrip patch antennas implemented on the same board, the layout of the planar microstrip smart antenna array with 4 × 4 Butler matrix as shown in Fig. 14 and the Fabricated planar microstrip smart antenna array with 4 × 4 Butler matrix The far field radiation patterns were simulated using Advanced Design System at the center frequency of 2.4 GHz. The generated beams were found to be at ±16° and ±45°; +16°, −45°, +45° and −16° when ports 1, 2, 3 and 4 are fed with signals, respectively with 5° error in both cases. This topology of multibeam antenna is suitable for beamforming applications; it can cover an area of 120°. Figure 18 shows the resulting beam directions.

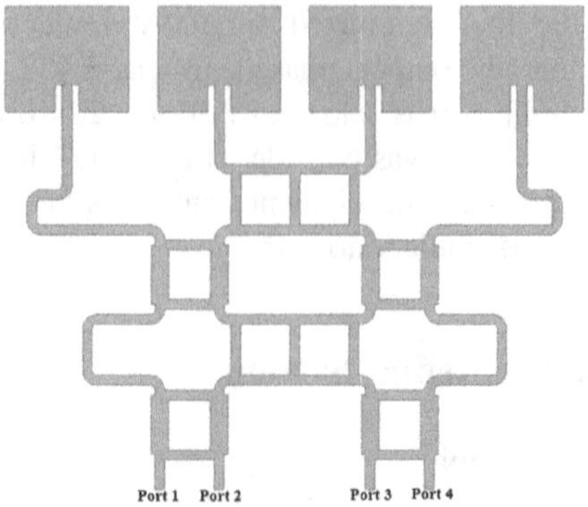

Fig. 14. ADS layout of the planar microstrip smart antenna array with 4 × 4 Butler matrix

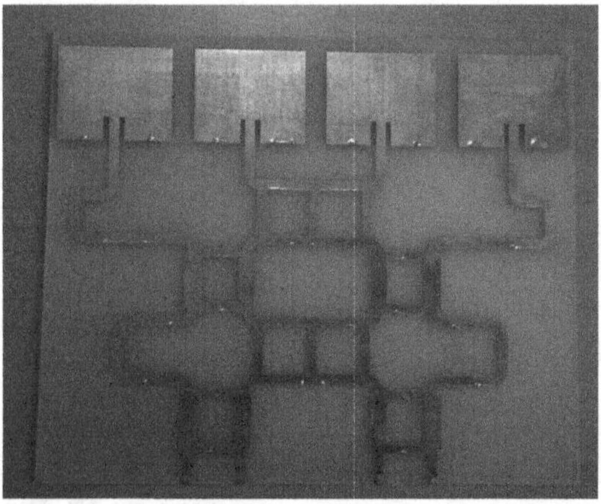

Fig. 15. Fabricated planar microstrip smart antenna array with 4 × 4 Butler matrix

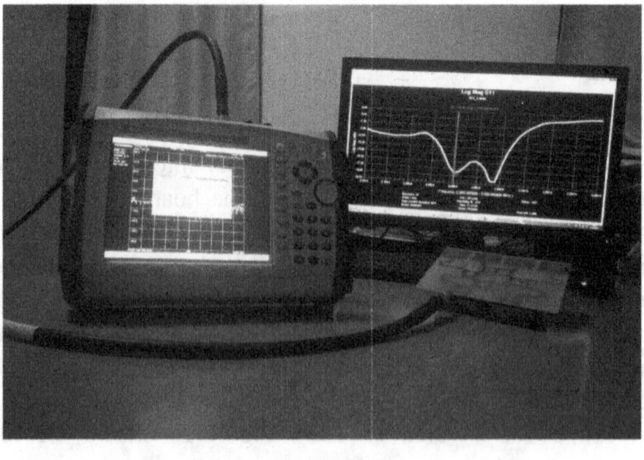

Fig. 16. Measurement setup

To verify the performance of the proposed smart antenna system, the design prototype was fabricated Fig. 15 shows the fabricated planar microstrip smart antenna array with 4 × 4 Butler matrix. The prototype was measured using a Vector Network Analyser (VNA) is illustrated in Fig. 16. The comparison between the simulated and measured reflection coefficients versus frequency band [2 GHz; 3 GHz] are illustrated in Fig. 17.

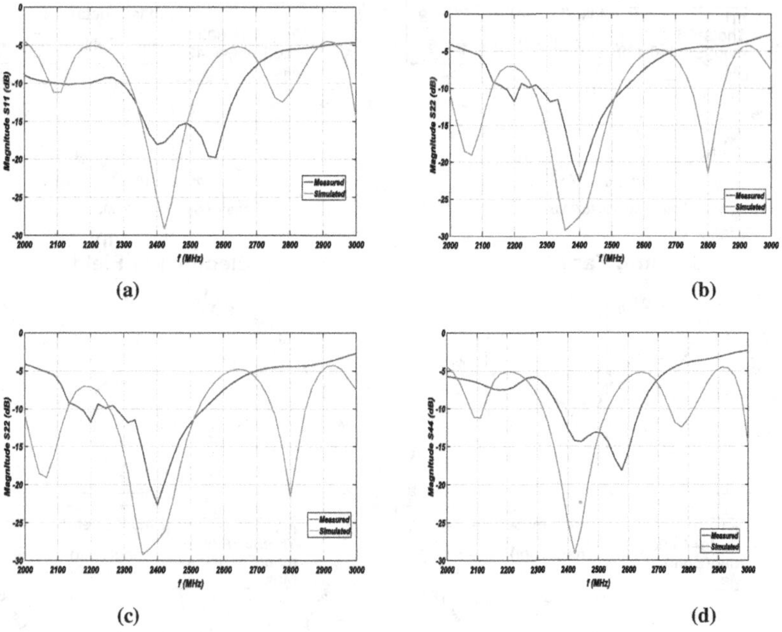

Fig. 17. Reflection coefficients versus frequency for the planar microstrip antenna array with 4 × 4 Butler matrix

All the overall Reflection coefficients values was below −15 at the resonant frequency (2.4 GHz). Whereas, we can see a little difference between simulation and measurement results but it has the same form. Hence, there is a satisfactory agreement. However, the differences due to the experimental conditions. Measurements were performed in an indoor environment. Therefore, there are a lot of multipath due to the presence of walls and others objects metallic devices. We can also see that a slight deviation of the graph relative to the simulation results, this gap explained by the uncertainty about the exact value of the frequency that we have chosen for our measures. All the mentioned elements above justify the differences observed between measurements and simulations. These measures can be improved, if they are done in an anechoic environment.

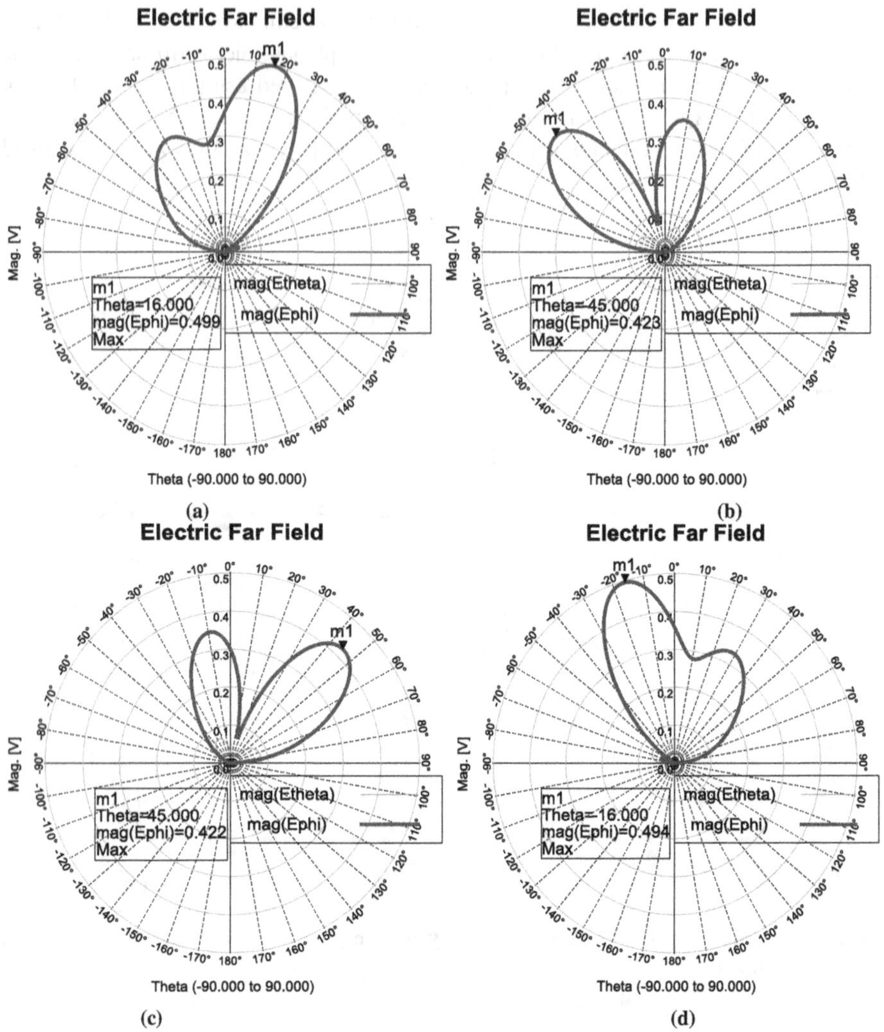

Fig. 18. Beam directions for microstrip smart antenna system

5 Conclusion

In this work, a Butler Matrix with patch antennas were designed as an application to work at 2.4 GHz for wireless applications. Our system consists of (four patch antennas, four 3 dB couplers, two-phase shifters, and two 0 dB couplers (crossover)). Our project can be developed to work in other frequencies for different applications. The number of input and output ports can be increased to get better beamforming coverage area, and several types of antenna can be used in our system depending on the application. To verify modeling and simulation procedures of our smart antenna, the main basic elements such as patch antenna, hybrid coupler, phase shifter and crossover are fabricated and measured. Very good agreement between measurements and simulations is obtained which validates the design. Finally, the microstrip smart antenna array is simulated and optimized to achieve the required parameters at the 2.4 GHz.

Acknowledgments. This work was made of the priority research program under contract: PPR/2015/28 financed by CNRST- Morocco.

References

1. Jeng, S.S., Okamoto, G.T., Xu, G., Lin, H.-P., Vogel, W.J.: Experimental evaluation of smart antenna system performance for wireless communications. IEEE Trans. Ant. Propag. **46**(6), 749–757 (1998)
2. Desmond, N.C.T.: Smart antennas for wireless applications and switched beamforming. Department of Information Technology and Electrical Engineering the University of Queensland (2001)
3. Corona, A., Lancaster, M.J.: A high-temperature superconducting Butler matrix. IEEE Trans. Appl. Supercond. **13**(4), 3867–3872 (2003)
4. Wang, F., Wang, H.: A broadband compact low-loss 4 × 4 Butler matrix in CMOS with stacked transformer based quadrature couplers. In: IEEE MTT-S International Microwave Symposium (IMS) (2016)
5. Huang, F., Chen, W., Rao, M.: Switched-beam antenna array based on Butler matrix for 5G wireless communication. In: IEEE International Workshop on Electromagnetics: Applications and Student Innovation Competition (iWEM) (2016)
6. Wincza, K., Rydosz, A., Slomian, I.: Reduced sidelobe multibeam antenna array with broadside beam fed by 4 × 8 Butler matrix. In: 2015 International Symposium on Antennas and Propagation (ISAP) (2015)
7. Pozar, D.M.: Microwave Engineering, 3rd edn. Wiley, Hoboken (2005). ISBN 0-471 44878-8
8. Fathelbab, W.M.: The synthesis of a class of branch-line directional couplers. IEEE Trans. Microwave Theor. Techn. **56**(8), 1985–1994 (2008)
9. Ahmad, S., Seman, F.: 4-port Butler matrix for switched multibeam antenna array. In: conference of Applied Electromagnetics (2005). ISBN 0-7803-9431-3
10. Fooks, E.H., Zakarevicius, R.: Microwave Engineering using Microstrip Circuits. Prentice Hall, New York (1990). ISBN-13 978-0136916505,1990
11. Zhang, Z., Jiao, Y.: Modified broadband Schiffman phase shifter using dentate microstrip and patterned ground plane. Prog. Electromag. Res. Lett. **24**, 9–16 (2011)
12. Gross, F.B.: Smart Antenna for Wireless Communication with Matlab. McGraw-Hill Companies, Inc., United States of America (2005)
13. Ballanis, C.A.: Antenna Theory Analysis and Design, 3rd edn. willey, New York (2005)

Adaptive Mapping for Multiple Applications on Parallel Architectures

Ismail Assayad[1(✉)] and Alain Girault[2]

[1] LIMSAD, Faculty of Sciences, ENSEM, University Hassan II Casablanca, Casablanca, Morocco
iassayad@gmail.com
[2] INRIA Rhône-Alpes and LIG, Grenoble, France
alain.girault@inria.fr

Abstract. We propose a novel adaptive approach capable of handling dynamism of a set of applications on network-on-chip. The applications are subject to throughput or energy consumption constraints. For each application, a set of non-dominated Pareto schedules are computed at design-time in the energy, period and processors space for different cores topologies. Then, upon the starting or ending of an application, a lightweight adaptive run-time scheduler reconfigures the mapping of the live applications according to the available resources, i.e., the available cores of the network-on-chip. This run-time scheduler selects the best topology for each application and maps them to the network-on-chip using the tetris algorithm. This novel scheduling approach is adaptive, it changes the mapping of applications during their execution, and thus delivers just enough power to achieve applications constraints.

Keywords: Adaptive mapping · Multi-objective optimization · Energy · Throughput · Iterative applications · Network-on-chip

1 Introduction

With an incessant technology improvement, we have witnessed a series of remarkable developments in systems on chip. One of them is the increasing processing capability of the system. The increase is not only achieved by the performance improvements between the generations of uniprocessors, but also comes from the advent of multi-core or many-core architectures where tens to hundreds of processors or cores can be integrated on a single chip. Examples of such architectures is presented in [1]. This introduces new big challenges.

The first challenge is the support for a variety of applications: mobile communications, networking, automotive and avionic applications, multimedia in the automobile and Internet interfaced with many embedded control systems. These applications may run concurrently, start and stop at any time. Each application may have multiple configurations, with different constraints imposed by the external world or the user (throughput constraints, deadlines and quality requirements, such as audio and video quality, output accuracy). The second challenge

E. Sabir et al. (Eds.): UNet 2017, LNCS 10542, pp. 584–595, 2017.
https://doi.org/10.1007/978-3-319-68179-5_51

is to alleviate the power cost especially for battery powered devices. For instance, the new generation of smart watches, led by Apple, have a recharging cycle measured in hours, some as low as eighteen [2]. It is clear that future wearables must deliver user functionality measured in days and weeks, not hours [3].

To address the previously mentioned challenges dynamic resource allocation and dynamic reconfiguration of applications must be supported. Also, resources must be scaled dynamically by operating frequency and voltage scaling (DVFS) in order to control the power consumption and to deliver just enough power. Power saving may be pushed even further by an adaptive scheduler strategy as performance constraints of applications and available resources to be used for each application may vary over time. This strategy is based on a careful evaluation of the power efficiency of combining DVFS with more application parallelism, as applications are launched or complete.

Since such a scheduler is intended for embedded platforms, only a lightweight implementation is acceptable at run-time. Therefore it is important to alleviate the run-time decision making on the one hand and to avoid the combinatorial complexity of the set of applications and over-approximations of fully pre-computed schedules on the other hand. For that we advocate an approach consisting of running applications in isolation, and computing off-line the set of optimal schedules for each application in isolation, before deciding on-line on the best combination of these schedules in function of the number of available processors and the performance constraints, whenever a change in the system configuration occurs. This approach is consistent because when aplications are run in isolation a strong pareto schedule of a combination of applications is necessarily a combination of weak or strong pareto schedules of individual applications.

The off-line part is performed by the tri-criteria optimization, to calculate 3D set of pareto schedules of individual applications. From a given software application graph, the optimization produces a static multiprocessor schedule that optimizes three criteria: its *schedule power*, its *period*, and its *processors number*. We target homogeneous mesh network-on-chip architectures. Our tricriteria scheduling uses DVFS to lower the power consumption. For a given number of processors all possible contiguous topologies are considered which results in a set of strong or weak pareto schedules.

The on-line part is performed by the run-time scheduler at each change to system configuration due to user requests. These changes include the start of a new application, the end of an application, a change of an application configuration, and a processor failure. The scheduler has then to adapt the schedules of the applicatiosn according to the new system configuration. For that it chooses, among the set of pre-computed 3D pareto solutions, one schedule per each application so that the set schedules is a optimal schedule for the current set of applications. To dot that, first the pareto schedules corresponding to the minimum number of processors and the maximum period are assigned to individual application. Then, if there are remaining processors, the on-line scheduler adapts the mapping by adding them to the applications that turn to achieve the most energy saving.

Selected solutions are then mapped on the NoC using a mapping technique based on an improved version of dellacherie algorithm (tetris) [4]. Since a set of schedules with given topologies may not be feasible due to topology constraint, tetris may fail to pack all topologies into the 2D mesh NoC. Hence, the run-time scheduler has also to explore the space of processor topologies when assigning processors to applications in decreasing order of energy saving. In that order when tetris fails it is possible for the run-time scheduler algorithm to backtrack to the last best set of schedules with no extra cost. This assignment problem is an instance of the multiple-choice knap-sack problem (MCKP), which is a variant of the 0–1 knapsack combinatorial optimization an NP-Hard problem [5]. Hence, we use a greedy linear heuristics which assigns one processor at a time to the set of applications in decreasing order of topology energy saving.

The main contribution of this paper is the adaptive scheduling method, the *first* adaptive scheduling heuristics able to produce, starting from applications algorithms graphs, NoC architecture graph, and throughput constraints, schedules with near-optimal energy savings based on pre-computed pareto schedules of individual applications.

The remainder of the paper is organized as follows. Section 2 introduces applications, architecture models, power and period definitions. Section 3 presents the scheduler part computed off-line while Sect. 4 formulates the schedules selection problem solved by our run-time scheduler heuristics. State-of-the-art on adaptive scheduling techniques for multiple applications on multi-core architectures is overviewed in Sect. 5. Finally, Sect. 6 reports the simulation results. Conclusions are drawn in Sect. 7.

2 Framework

In this section, we detail the application model, the platform model and the energy model. We end with the formal definition of the tri-criteria multiprocessor mapping problem.

2.1 Application Model

We consider stream-based real-time application. Our model is therefore that of an application algorithm graph $\mathcal{A}lg$ which is executed repeatedly in a pipelined manner to achieve a better throughput.

$\mathcal{A}lg$ is an *acyclic oriented graph* $(\mathcal{X}, \mathcal{D})$ (See Fig. 1(a)). Its nodes (the set $\mathcal{X}$) are software blocks called *operations*. Each arc of $\mathcal{A}lg$ (the set $\mathcal{D}$) is a *data-dependency* between two operations. If $X \rhd Y$ is a data-dependency, then X is a *predecessor* of Y, while Y is a *successor* of X. The set of predecessors of X is noted $pred(X)$ while its set of successors is noted $succ(X)$. X is also called the *source* of the data-dependency $X \rhd Y$, and Y is its *destination*. Operations with no predecessor (resp. successor) are called *input* operations (resp. *output*). Operations do not have any side effect, except for input/output operations: an input operation (resp. output) is a call to a sensor driver (resp. actuator).

Input and output operations read input data from the input drivers and write their output data to output drivers, respectively.

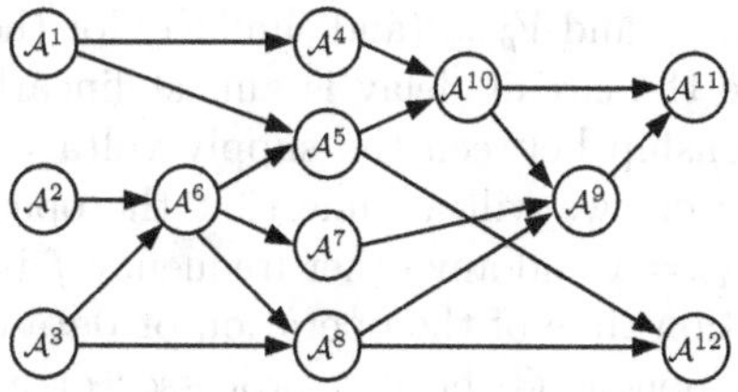

Fig. 1. An example of algorithm graph $\mathcal{A}lg$: I_1, I_2, and I_3 are input operations, O_1 and O_2 are output operations, A–G are regular operations.

2.2 Platform Model

The target plateform is a homogeneous 2-D mesh-based NoC using deterministic X-Y communication strategy and providing computation and communication resources to implement multiple applications (Fig. 2). A NoC is modeled as an architecture graph ($\mathcal{A}rc$). $\mathcal{A}rc = <\mathcal{P}, \mathcal{L}>$ is a graph where $\mathcal{P} = p_1, p_2, \ldots, p_q$ denotes the set of tiles on the NoC, corresponding to the set of $\mathcal{A}rc$ vertices, and $\mathcal{L} = \{(p_i, p_j, l_{ij})\}$ designates the set of communication links from nodes p_i to nodes p_j, corresponding to the edges of $\mathcal{A}rc$. l_{ij} represents the communication length from node p_i to node p_j. The number of nodes q in $\mathcal{A}rc$ is denoted as the size of the NoC.

The run-time scheduler schedules the given set of applications (e.g. $\mathcal{A}, \mathcal{B}, \mathcal{C}$ in Fig. 3) and manages the resources on the NoC. It runs on a dedicated processor and executes the proposed scheduling algorithms to map each application on a feasible region and loads all tasks on the tiles according to the mapping solution. This work deals with on-line scenarios, i.e., the scheduler does not know in advance when each application arrives or when it finishes. In this paper, we focus on the mapping algorithms of the scheduler.

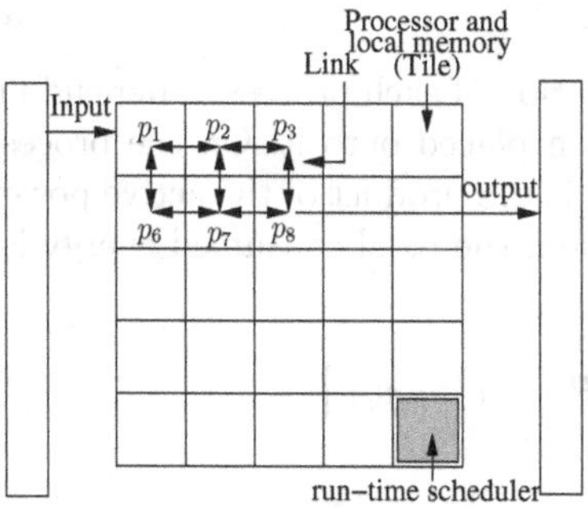

Fig. 2. NoC architecture.

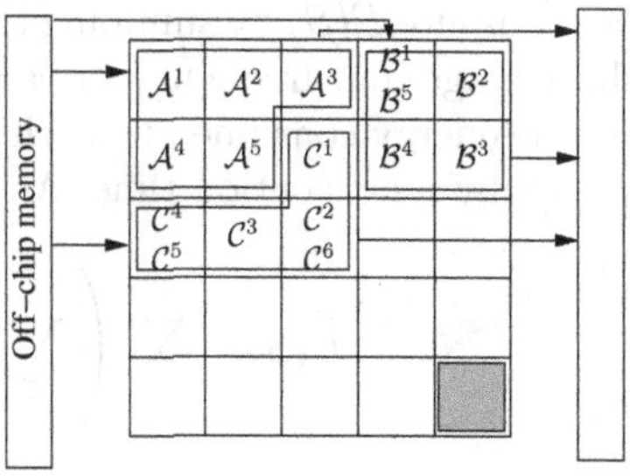

Fig. 3. Distributed mapping on NoC.

2.3 Voltage, Frequency, and Power Consumption

The maximum supply voltage is noted V_{max} and the corresponding highest operating frequency is noted f_{max}. For each operation, its WCET assumes that the processor operates at f_{max} and V_{max} (and similarly for the WCCT of the data-dependencies). Because the circuit delay is almost linearly related to $1/V$ [6], there is a linear relationship between the supply voltage V and the operating frequency f. From now on, we will assume that the operating frequencies are *normalized*, that is, $f_{max} = 1$ and any other frequency f is in the interval $(0, 1)$. Accordingly, the execution time of the operation or data-dependency X placed onto the hardware component C, be it a processor or a communication link, which is running at frequency f (taken as a scaling factor) is:

$$\mathcal{E}xe(X, C, f) = \mathcal{E}xe(X, C)/f \tag{1}$$

The power consumption P of a single operation placed on a single processor is computed according to the classical model of Zhu et al. [7]:

$$P = P_s + h(P_{ind} + P_d) \qquad\qquad P_d = C_{ef} V^2 f \tag{2}$$

where P_s is the static power (power to maintain basic circuits and to keep the clock running), h is equal to 1 when the circuit is active and 0 when it is inactive, P_{ind} is the frequency independent active power (the power portion that is independent of the voltage and the frequency; it becomes 0 when the system is put to sleep, but the cost of doing so is very expensive [8]), P_d is the frequency dependent active power (the processor dynamic power and any power that depends on the voltage or the frequency), C_{ef} is the switch capacitance, V is the supply voltage, and f is the operating frequency. C_{ef} is assumed to be constant for all operations, which is a simplifying assumption, since one would normally need to take into account the actual switching activity of each operation to compute accurately the consummed energy. However, such an accurate computation is infeasible for the application sizes we consider here.

For a multiprocessor schedule S, we cannot apply directly Eq. (2). Instead, we must compute the total energy $E(S)$ consumed by S, and then divide by the schedule length $L(S)$:

$$P(S) = E(S)/L(S) \tag{3}$$

We compute $E(S)$ by summing the contribution of each processor, depending on the voltage and frequency of each operation placed onto it. On the processor p_i, the energy consumed by each operation is the product of the active power $P^i_{ind} + P^i_d$ by its execution time. As a conclusion, the total consumed energy is:

$$E(S) = \sum_{i=1}^{|\mathcal{P}|} \left(\sum_{o_j \in p_i} (P^i_{ind} + P^i_d).\mathcal{E}xe(o_j, p_i) \right) \tag{4}$$

2.4 Period Computation of a Multiprocessor Schedule

Figures 4 and 5 show an example of an application graph with three tasks, X which is mapped on P_2 and Y, Z which are mapped on P_1. Data dependencies are communicated through link L_{12}. The period P of the schedule is the time duration between two outputs of the application. Since Z is the output task, P is depicted as the duration of the time interval between ends of two occurence of Z. As suggested in the Fig. 5 by the rising arrow indicating the application second iteration movement toward the first one, the period can also be defined as the maximal utilization, including slack times, over processors and communication links. For this example for instance, this definition can be written as in Eq. (5) where b and e denote the begin time and end time, respectively.

$$P = \max\left\{e(X,p_2)-b(X,p_2), e(Z,p_1)-b(Y,p_1), e(X\triangleright Z,l_{12})-b(X\triangleright Y,l_{12})\right\} \quad (5)$$

It is worth noticing that this definition is interesting as it allows to reduce the number of MILP variables.

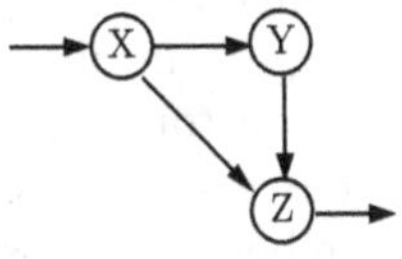

Fig. 4. Graph example.

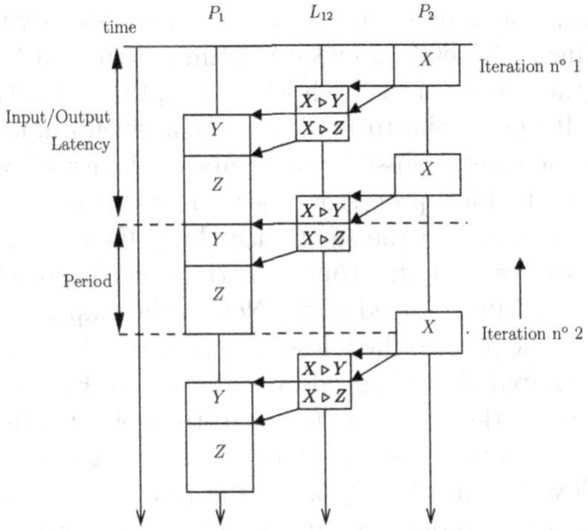

Fig. 5. A schedule and its period.

3 Off-line Tri-Criteria Optimization

For each application, optimal schedules are computed off-line using an MILP tricriteria scheduling program. Inputs of the program are the application model $\mathcal{A}lg$, the NoC model $\mathcal{A}rc$ and the worst case execution-times WCETs of tasks and data communication. Outputs of the program is the pareto set composed of the optimal schedules of $\mathcal{A}lg$ on $\mathcal{A}rc$ s.t. in terms of Energy $E(S)$, Number of processors $N(S)$ and Throughput P.

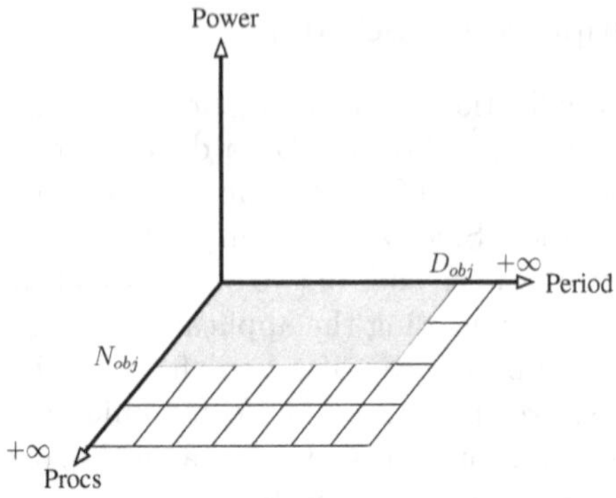

Fig. 6. Building a grid with the constraints.

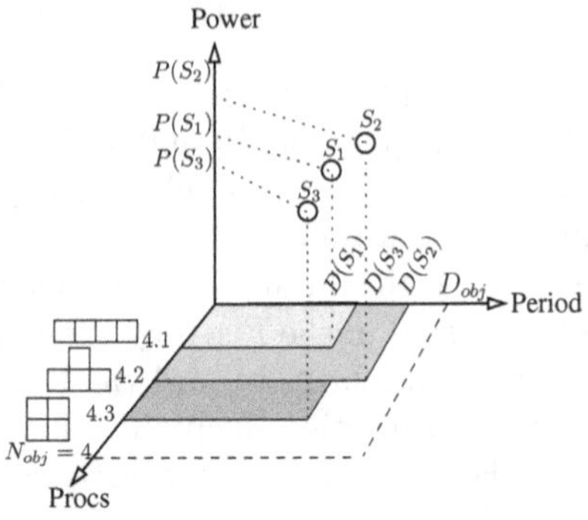

Fig. 7. Schedules for three tile topologies of $N_{obj} = 4$ processors under D_{obj} constraint.

DVFS is used to minimize the energy consumption of the architecture by exploiting the fact that a linear decrease of a processor frequency running a task, results in a cubic decrease in processor dynamic power at the price of only a linear decrease in execution-time of that task. DVFS can be done per island of tiles basis that is each island is optimized with its own supply voltage.

It is essential to note that for a given number of processors we might have one or several possible NoC sub-topologies whose pareto schedules may e. For example, for 4 processors there are 3 different topologies: the line topology, the T topology and the square topology. Except for the line topologies, we cannot guarantee at design-time that the other topologies will be feasible, i.e. may be successffully mapped on the NoC in the mapping phase of the run-time scheduler. Thus the pareto schedules for all NoC topologies alternatives with equal size must be computed and keeped by the program. For ease of presentation only we depict them on the same pareto set instead of separate ones by giving them different indexe values: the line topology, the T topology and the square topology are indexed with 4.1, 4.2, 4.3 in the processors axis. However, it is worth noticing that a total order is not defined on topologies with identical number of processors although it appears to be this way on the figure.

Figure 6 shows the grid with the constraints which is used to incrementally build the set of pareto schedules, and Fig. 7Â shows index values notation used for three sub-architectures of different topologies but same size, 4 processors.

4 Run-Time Scheduler

4.1 Working Principle

The role of the run-time scheduler is that, given the current system configuration and the new set of active applications, it computes the next system configuration such that throughput constraints are met and power consumption is minimized.

It should be noted, in passing, that although the throughput-case is adressed in this paper, the proposed approach is easily applicable to the power-mode case, i.e. satisfying all power constraints and minimizing period, on a simple condition that the pareto fronts are inverted.

After the off-line phase in which the static schedules are computed for each application individually comes the on-line phase. In this phase, at each change in the set of applications, the run-time scheduler has to choose the best schedule for each application so that the chosen schedules satisfy the following requirements:

- throughput constraints are still met for existing applications and the new one if any,
- power consumption of the architecture is minimized,
- schedules topologies best fit into the NoC architecture (a)
- applications reconfiguration cost will be amortized as the applications run repeatedly (b)

Requirement (a) means that the topologies should be mapped onto the NoC such that the number of Noc holes, i.e. unused tiles, is minimized. Requirement (b) means that the reconfiguration cost in term of energy consumption due to topologies re-mapping on the NoC should be compensated by the energy gain that would be achieved by the new configuration otherwise the re-mapping should be discarded to the extent possible.

Importance of these two requirements appears when many applications are competing for the NoC architecture. When the number of application increases and from a certain point, not all applications could benefit from the maximal number of processors as suggested by their respective pareto sets. This means that reconfigurations become inevitable and any unecessay hole may be prejudicial to the system in that it is a lost resource.

At run-time, to select the mapping of the next configuration we need to:

- select a schedule for each application,
- select NoC tiles for each schedule topology.

5 Related Work

There has been a quite lot of research in multiple application design space exploration. Some researchers focus on scenario-based approaches where multiple application mapping schenarios are explored at design time in order to handle dynamism in the number of active applications at runtime [9,10]. Others focus on one application with many configurations [11]. The scenario-based approaches, however, are not scalable even for small-sized applications as the number of scenarios increases exponentially with the number of applications and their configurations and become intractable; not to mention that these approaches forces the designer to recompute the whole schedules form scratch even after the addition of single new application or configuration.

In [12], authors proposed a mapping method whereby multiple applications can be simultaneously mapped on the many-core NoCs. However the proposed mapping is not adaptive and applications do not have constraints and are not reactive or iterative. In [13], authors include only a single mapping having minimum average power consumption. In [14] authors perform a mapping of tasks based on dynamically computed weighted sum of resources usage including processors, memories amd bandwidth utilization with the objective of optimizing resources utilization by minimizing the latter sum.

[15,16] presented an hybrid mapping technique where performance and energy schedules are computed at design-time and one schedule is selected at run-time to minimize energy consumption while satisfying performance constraints. in [15] constraint on end-to-end execution times of applications are considered rather than throughput of iterative applications. In [16] applications are iterative and throughput is optimized but the proposed technique is not adaptive. For instance it does not take advantage from system configuration change to minimize the energy consumption, neither by a combined re-parallelization and DVFS when additional ressources become available nor by some schedule sequentialization when throughput constraint is lowered. This can be explained by the fact that at design-time it generates a set of schedule by minimizing the throughput for each application for all possible number of processors rather than constraining the throughput. [17] work includes mappings having trade-offs between power consumption and performance but throughputs constraints are not included in the optimization. Moreover proposed approach adaptivity is limited as one schedule for each number of processors is retained for each application. In this case for instance the mapping of an application when a constraint is relaxed by the user can be changed only by assigning more processors and not by modifying current schedule.

Furthermore these works do not consider adaptivity regarding architecture topologies. They either over-approximate communication latencies using values computed assuming a (virtual) topology with max-hop links between every pair of processors like in [16], or use latencies computed by simulation for one fixed communication architecture (one schedule per a given number of processors) like in [15,17].

In our approach this level of adaptivity is also considered because NoC pareto schedules with less processors and better topologies may strongly dominate schedules with more processors but inefficient topologies.

6 Simulations

We have compared the performance of our approach called adaptive approach with the approach proposed in [16], called hybrid approach.

We have plotted in Fig. 8 (left), and (right), respectively the total energy consumption, and the total number of used processors of the schedules computed by adaptive and by hybrid. The values have been evaluated for a workload scenario starting from 1 up to 8 application graphs $\mathcal{A}lg$ of 8 operations each on a 4×4 $\mathcal{A}rc$ with throughput constraints equal to 100 units for all applications. Notice that in order to make comparisons under identical conditions, we use the

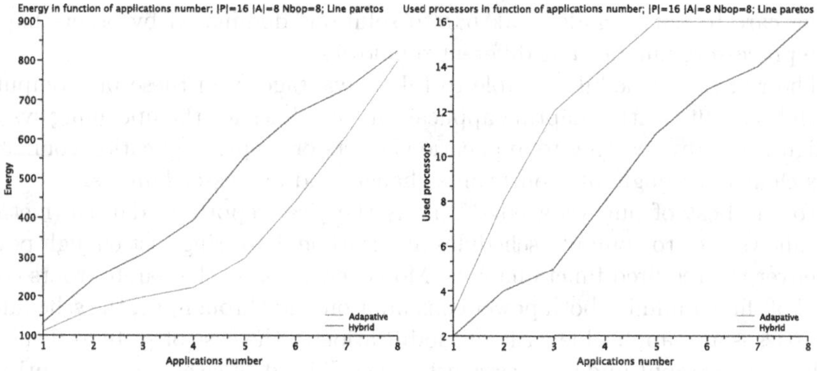

Fig. 8. Configurations computed by our approach and the ones computed by hybrid algorithm.

results obtained when using only line topologies for the adaptive approach, i.e. without exploiting topology-level adaptability.

Simulation results in Fig. 8 (left) show that adaptive approach performs systematically better than hybrid approach and that the energy saving reaches 36, 33% when 5 applications are running on the NoC. This is explained by the fact that the adaptive approach better exploits the available resources in the NoC thanks to the parallelism-level adaptability as shown in the results of Fig. 8 (right). For instance, when 3 applications are running on the NoC, adaptive approach is able to use twice as many processors as the hybrid approach. This can be explained by the fact that the schedule algorithmics used in the former approach combines parallelism with DVFS to achieve more energy saving while being below the throughput constraints, whereas the algorithmics of the later appraoch exploits parallelism to achieve the maximal throughput.

7 Conclusion

We have presented the adaptive energy throughput scheduling heuristics, called **adaptive**, to minimize the energy consumption and to satisfy throughput constraints for multiple applications on NoC. Our run-time scheduler goes beyond the traditional voltage scaling and power management level of adaptability of related scheduling approaches. It uses three levels of adaptability to achieve better energy savings: schedule-level adaptability, DVFS-level adaptability, and topology-level adaptability.

These advanced, and needed, levels of adaptability were possible for the run-time scheduler thanks to the multi-curve form of pareto sets derived off-line for each application individually. Both the throughput and the processors number are taken as *constraints*, so adaptive attempts to minimize the power while satisfying these constraints. By running the off-line part of adaptive with several values of these constraints, we are able to produce a set of pareto solutions taking care to not exclude weak pareto solutions dominated by others having same processors number but different topologies.

The run-time scheduler is able to take advantage from these pre-computed schedules by efficiently adapting applications schedules for the upcoming system configurations by reacting to applications starts or stops, application configurations change, throughputs constraints change, and processor failures.

To the best of our knowledge, this is the *first* reported adaptive method that allows user to compute schedules at run-time delivering just enough power to deliver the required functionalities. Moreover, because the pareto fronts computed off-line minimize both power consumption and throughput, the scheduling heuristics is also applicable without modification to the case of systems demanding high throughput under power constraints. This advance comes at the price of system re-configuration costs in transcient regimes which has to be minimized, a detailed analysis of this is beyond the scope of this paper and is a subject of future work.

References

1. Vangal, S.R., Howard, J., Ruhl, G., Dighe, S., Wilson, H., Tschanz, D.F.J., Singh, A., Jacob, T., Jain, S., Erraguntla, V., Roberts, C., Hoskote, Y., Borkar, N., Borkar, S.: An 80-tile sub-100-W Tera-FLOPS processor in 65-nm CMOS. IEEE J. Solid-State Circuits **43**(1), 29–41 (2008)
2. Apple watch battery life: how many hours does it last?. http://www.techradar.com/news/wearables/apple-watch-battery-life-how-many-hours-does-it-last-1291435. Accessed 09 Jan 2015
3. The battery is dead; long live power management. http://www.design-reuse.com/industryexpertblogs/38079/the-battery-is-dead-long-live-power-management.html. Accessed 09 Jan 2015
4. Thierry, C., Scherrer, B.: Building controllers for Tetris. Int. Comput. Games Assoc. J. **32**(1), 3–11 (2010). http://hal.archives-ouvertes.fr/docs/00/41/89/54/PDF/article.pdf
5. Karp, R.M.: Reducibility among combinatorial problems. In: Miller, R.E., Thatcher, J.W., Bohlinger, J.D. (eds.) Complexity of Computer Computations. The IBM Research Symposia, pp. 85–103. Springer, Boston (1972). doi:10.1007/978-1-4684-2001-2_9
6. Burd, T., Brodersen, R.: Energy efficient CMOS micro-processor design. In: Hawaii International Conference on System Sciences, HICSS 1995, Honolulu (HI), USA. IEEE, Los Alamitos (1995)
7. Zhu, D., Melhem, R., Mossé, D.: The effects of energy management on reliability in real-time embedded systems. In: International Conference on Computer Aided Design, ICCAD 2004, San Jose (CA), USA, pp. 35–40, November 2004
8. Elnozahy, E., Kistler, M., Rajamony, R.: Energy-efficient server clusters. In: Workshop on Power-Aware Computing Systems, WPACS 2002, Cambridge (MA), USA, pp. 179–196, February 2002
9. van Stralen, P., Pimentel, A.: Scenario-based design space exploration of MPSoCs. In: 2010 IEEE International Conference on Computer Design (ICCD), pp. 305–312, October 2010

10. Stuijk, S., Geilen, M., Basten, T.: A predictable multiprocessor design flow for streaming applications with dynamic behaviour. In: 2010 13th Euromicro Conference on Digital System Design: Architectures, Methods and Tools (DSD), pp. 548–555, September 2010
11. Murali, S., Coenen, M., Radulescu, A., Goossens, K., De Micheli, G.: A methodology for mapping multiple use-cases onto networks on chips. In: Proceedings of the Conference on Design, Automation and Test in Europe: Proceedings, SER. Date '06, 3001, pp. 118–123. European Design and Automation Association, Leuven (2006). http://dl.acm.org/citation.cfm?id=1131481.1131519
12. Yang, B., Guang, L., Xu, T., Yin, A., Santti, T., Plosila, J.: Multi-application multi-step mapping method for many-core network-on-chips. In: NORCHIP 2010, pp. 1–6, November 2010
13. Schranzhofer, A., Chen, J., Thiele, L.: Dynamic power-aware mapping of applications onto heterogeneous MPSoC platforms. IEEE Trans. Ind. Inform. **6**(4), 692–707 (2010). http://dx.doi.org/10.1109/TII.2010.2062192
14. Huang, J., Raabe, A., Buckl, C., Knoll, A.: A workflow for runtime adaptive task allocation on heterogeneous MPSoCs. In: Design, Automation Test in Europe Conference Exhibition (DATE), pp. 1–6, March 2011
15. Mariani, G., Avasare, P., Vanmeerbeeck, G., Ykman-Couvreur, C., Palermo, G., Silvano, C., Zaccaria, V.: An industrial design space exploration framework for supporting run-time resource management on multi-core systems. In: Design, Automation Test in Europe Conference Exhibition (DATE), pp. 196–201, March 2010
16. Singh, A.K., Kumar, A., Srikanthan, T.: Accelerating throughput-aware runtime mapping for heterogeneous MPSOcS. ACM Trans. Des. Autom. Electron. Syst. **18**(1), 1–29 (2013). http://doi.acm.org/10.1145/2390191.2390200
17. Ykman-Couvreur, C., Avasare, P., Mariani, G., Palermo, G., Silvano, C., Zaccaria, V.: Linking run-time resource management of embedded multi-core platforms with automated design-time exploration. IET Comput. Digital Techn. **5**(2), 123–135 (2011)

Verification of SystemC Components Using the Method of Deduction

Elbouanani Soumia(✉), Assayad Ismail, and Sadik Mohammed

NEST Research Group, LRI Lab ENSEM, LIMSAD Faculty of Sciences, University Hassan II of Casablanca, Casablanca, Morocco
Elbouanani.soumia@gmail.com , iassayad@gmail.com , m.sadik@ensem.ac.ma

Abstract. The verification of the embedded systems would play an important role in its scenario of manufacturing. The SystemC language of the embedded systems material description became the basic language of most of industrial productions companies. This allows several research works to focus on the verification methods of the SystemC designs. The formal verification that bases on mathematical proofs is a powerful method to describe the existence or the absence of the designs errors. It is a combination of two parallel and in collaboration operations; the first one is the specification of the generic and specific properties of the system under a formal language, the second is the description of its behavior under state-transition representations. In spite of its mathematical power, it knows limitations in terms of the systems length. It enters in the type of the state explosion problems that effect on the speed of the check. In this paper, we represent a new approach of verifying the SystemC designs using SPIN Model Checker, based on the deduction method that extract the executions of equivalence "scenarios of equivalence" through which we can deduct the satisfaction or the non-satisfaction of the systems specification.

Keywords: SystemC designs · Formal verification · Deduction method · SPIN Model checker

1 Introduction

The verification of the embedded systems would play an important role in the scenario of manufacturing of the embedded systems. The formal verification is a powerful method because it bases itself on mathematical proofs to describe the existence or the absence of the errors, most of them demonstrate by the counter-example method. The SystemC language of the embedded systems material description became the basic language of most of industrial productions companies. This allows several research works to focus on the methods of checking the SystemC models. However, some methods based on checking during the simulation (test) and others on the formal verification by presenting formally the behavior of the system (Model Checking...). The latter are been manifested in two parallel and in collaboration operations; the first one is the specification of the generic

E. Sabir et al. (Eds.): UNet 2017, LNCS 10542, pp. 596–606, 2017.
https://doi.org/10.1007/978-3-319-68179-5_52

and specific properties of the system under a formal language (LTL, CTL.), the second is the description of its behavior under state-transition representations. The formal verification, in spite of its mathematical power, knows limitations in terms of the systems length of the application. It enter in the type of state explosion problem that effect on the speed of the check. SPIN (Simple Promela INterpreter) is a tool designed for the check of the distributed systems; it has as inputs two data: the code under the language of modelling Promela describing the representative automaton of the SystemC model and the properties of specification with the linear temporal logic (LTL). The size of the automaton is a relevant factor which reacts on the checking speed of which the simulator SPIN has to cover all the paths submitting the properties. Several contributions are interested in avoiding the combinatorial explosion by exploiting the redundancy and by reducing the state space. Our contribution bases on this aspect to extract the delta-cycle of equivalence "scenarios of equivalence" through which we can deduct the satisfaction or the non-satisfaction of the systems specification.

This paper is organized as follows: it is started in Sect. 2 by discussing some related works to ours. Section 3 describes the method of deduction that represents our contribution. In practical aspect, we present an application to the FIFO component to illustrate our methodology in Sect. 4. Finally, Sect. 5 concludes the paper.

2 Related Work

Todays verification is growing into an irresistible task in the structure of the embedded systems design procedure, caused by the increasing complexity of embedded electronics, that demand high performance, high integration, and a long list of features (safety, liveness, concurrency) [1].

SystemC is becoming the de-facto-standard for industrial-scale problems [2], addresses to hardware modeling and the description of level-system behavior. To combat complexity and explore design space effectively, it is necessary to represent systems at multiple levels of abstraction, like Register Transfer Level (RTL) and Transaction Level Modeling (TLM) [3]. The model checking or formal verification is a set of algorithms and formal techniques which generate accessible state space and verify the satisfaction of a systems specification; amongst the model checker software more usable for hardware systems: SPIN [6,25], SMV [4], and UPPAAL [5]. SPIN is a model checker used for formal verification of embedded designs, whose input language is Promela (Process Meta Language), and the desired properties expressed in LTL (Linear Temporal Logic). For instance, the work [7], shows the efficiency and the flexibility of this tool, with which they verified and validated the design of the cardiac pacemaker system.

Within the scope of the formal verification, two different kinds of verification are distinguished here: (1) the dynamic verification is the simulation-based verification born out with the checking through programs scheduling, like testing and runtime verification [17]; (2) the static verification is a translating-based verification based on a static analysis of a system behavior using mathematic proofs. With formal methods, one translates the designs to a formal representation that can be verified along with the model checking software. This one has two ways of the verifications process as well: (a) the direct methods, which translate the SystemC programs to the verifier language, nevertheless, they have good results only for small examples (few hundred line of code) [11,12]. (b) The indirect methods, using intermediate processes either algebraic process [14] or automaton-based intermediate [9,13] representation, for describing the systems behavior. These methods suffer from the famous state space problem of model checking. Pinapa [8] and PinaVM [10] SystemC front-ends use the last process (2b) inwardly, but they do not ensure an optimized verification.

Our approach targets the method (2b) using automaton-based intermediate representation. There are several approaches for SystemC modeling using state-transition based representations: Labelled Kripke Structures (LKSs), Finite State Machines (FSMs), Petri-Nets, SystemC Waiting State Automata (WSA), etc. The LKSs [19] and state-event analysis keep all the intermediate states within a SystemC process model, and provide a syntactic way of partitioning the model into hardware and software parts. In [21], the authors propose two algorithms to generate FMSs from SystemC models, and in [20] authors give a formalization method to create a set of communicating state machines for the TLM modelling, as well as some rules for finite state representation of the scheduler, the timed, and untimed events. The Petri-Nets representation is used especially to represent SystemC parallel designs, it requires considering and representing all possible interactions and communications between concurrent components [24] The WSA model is based on an abstraction at the level of delta-cycles using the symbolic construction [22]. Harrath and Monsuez [23] extended the work in [22] to represent the time notion on SystemC waiting state automata. The model in [18] is the one on which we based our contribution in this article, it models delta-cycle and delta-step simulation notions. It is centered around the use of extended automata whose behavior is restricted by using priorities on interactions rather than transition cuts. This makes the approach compositional and thus suitable for system and component-based verification.

The complication of the formal verification process is mainly due to the problem of state space explosion; besides that it requires too much model construction. Some related works are close to the work presented in this paper since they concentrate on the optimization of the abstraction level by reducing the size of the state-transition representation [15,16,21,23,24]. In [21] authors contribution consists in the use of states grouping technique. The work presented in [23,24] use symbolic reduction to get the minimum step within the SystemC waiting state automata. In contrast, our approach gives better results because, beyond state reductions, is able to select execution scenarios by choosing representative states and scenarios with respect to equivalent classes. Furthermore, our modeling approach is based on a previous work by Assayad et al. presented in [18]. The latter uses compositional extended automata, with SystemC delta-step reduction, while preserving system execution semantics at processes-level and thus allowing both system and component-based verification.

3 Contribution

3.1 Description of the Contribution

The formal verification is a method known by the use of the formal techniques to prove the satisfaction of the properties of the considered system, such as state-transition representation for the behaviors description and the linear temporal logic for the properties specification. The aim of this is to detect modeling errors by giving counter-examples in the case of their presence. Far from the methods of reduction used to confront the combinatorial explosion, our contribution focus on the deductions aspect through representative situations by exploiting existing redundancies to limit the verification just at the level of the critical tracks.

To have a fast and reliable verification is to have a representation which includes all the possible combinations between the processes in any order with the minimum number of states, while keeping the equivalence with the initial behavior of the design.

Our contribution focus on the idea to verify just the paths of execution which represent other similar paths, and contain the critical tracks with respect to the specification under verification. We name those paths the scenarios of equivalence that contain the delta-cycles of equivalence. To cross these scenarios equate to cross all the scenarios of the system, and to verify that these scenarios satisfy the specification equate to verify that all the system satisfies the specification.

Our approach is a suite of data manipulation procedures whose purpose is the search for the scenarios of equivalence. It comprises two construction and three extraction algorithms, through which it is going to browse exhaustively all the transitions of the system: (a) Algorithm for the tracks generation, (b) Algorithm for the eligible tracks extraction, (c) Algorithm for the scenarios generation, (d) Algorithm for the eligible scenarios extraction and (e) Algorithm for the search of scenarios of equivalence. These procedures reflect the redundancy study and the restriction of the verification to the critical parts exclusively in our deduction method. As a consequence of this, the time of the design verification will be reduced.

3.2 Problem Modeling

In order to verify formally the embedded systems, both the model of the system and the property specification have to be formulated in some precise formal or mathematical language. In the following sections, before we state our method of deduction, we start by describing how to specify the properties of the system and some automata vocabulary.

Specification Properties. The formal verification is the act of proving or disproving the correctness properties of finite-state systems. These properties represent the system specification that describes the operational and performance requirements of a system. We categorize the verified properties into two groups -generic properties and specific properties. The generic properties are general requirements on the system behavior- liveness and security. The specific properties are derived from the component specification.

State-Transition Representation. A SystemC design is a C++ program using the SystemC library classes. This program consists of modules definitions plus a top-level function that starts the simulation. These modules $SC\_MODULE()$ contain processes (C++ methods) and instances of other modules. These processes called by the scheduler to perform the simulation, they connect themselves together and they run concurrently.

In the phase of the formal modelling of a SystemC design, we have to translate all the process and signals and entities of the simulation modules. Hereineafter, we present a set of notation and a vocabulary on the treatment of the system automata.

S	Embedded system
N	Number of process
M	Number of proprieties
A_k	Process automaton of index k
A_k^r	Reduced automaton of A_k
l_k	Number of states of A_k^r
$(l_k - 1)$	Number of interactions of A_k^r
l_{el}	Number of eligible tracks
$c_{i_k j}$	Track condition
$a_{i_k j}$	Track action

$tr_{i_k}^{A_k^r} = \sum_l [interaction]_l = \sum_l [c_{i_k 1}\|\ldots\|c_{i_k n}\|a_{i_k 1}\|\ldots\|a_{i_k n}]_l$ $l \leq l_k$	Track of the automaton A_k^r. It represent the i_k delta-step for the system simulation, always the final action is an action of suspension (wait (.), break...).
$TR_k = \bigcup_{i_k=0}^{i_k=l_{el}} tr_{i_k}^{A_k^r}$	Set of eligible track of the automaton A_k^r
C_r	Set of critical track. A critical path is the one that its end is a critical State where we can verify
$SC_j = \sum_{k=0}^{k=N-1} tr_{i_k}^{A_k^r}$	Eligible scenario A sum of delta-steps and it is the simulation of the system between two successive delta-cycles

$S_{(el)}$	Set of eligible scenarios A scenario j is eligible if at least one of the starting conditions of trace i+1 are the final state of the previous process i.
$S_{(eq)}$	Set of scenarios of equivalence A 'scenario of equivalence' is the shortest scenario that has the greatest number of critical traces.
PA_j	Atomic proposition represent the property j
$P = \bigcup_0^{M-1} PA_j$	Set of atomic propositions and their opposites

3.3 Deduction Method Algorithims

In this section we present the following algorithms using in the method of deduction:

The Generation Algorithm of the Eligible Tracks. Let P a process of l interactions T_i. We initialize the set of the eligible tracks of each automaton: $k[1, N], TR_k = \{\}$.

1- If there exists an action a = wait(.) or a=break then do $tr^{A_k^r} = tr^{A_k^r} + T_i, TR_k = TR_k \cup tr^{A_k^r}$ and suspend;

Else go to the stage 2;

2- If there exits a=notify(.) then do $tr^{A_k^r} = tr^{A_k^r} + T_i$, pass to T_j such that $T_j \neq T_i, j \in [1, n]$, and return to stage 1;

We denote the eligible tracks $l_(el)k$ of the process k by $TR_k[l_(el)k]$.

To generate the set of critical tracks C_r for each automaton A_k, we follow those conditions:

$$\exists PA_j \subseteq tr_{i_k}^{A_k^r} \Rightarrow C_r = C_r \cup tr_{i_k}^{A_k^r}$$
$$\text{unless } i_k + +$$

The Generation Algorithm of the Eligible Scenarios.

- **Generation of all scenarios,**

Let $l_{(el)k}$ the number of the eligible tracks of the automaton A_k^r. Therefore, the number of the possible combinations between all eligible tracks of all processes is $\prod_{k=0}^{k=N-1} l_{(el)k}$.

We denote by $SC_j[N]$ the multi-dimensional array of N lines and each line is a table of i_k columns, such that:

$$For(intk = 0; k < N; k + +)i_k, SC_j[k] = tr_{i_k}^{A_k^r}; j + +$$

Where:

$$\forall i_k \in [0, l_{(el)k}], \forall j \in [0, \textstyle\prod_{k=0}^{k=N-1} l_{(el)k}]$$

- **Extraction of eligible scenarios,**

We initialize the set of eligible scenarios by the set of all combinations of scenarios $S_{(el)} = S$.

In each scenario SC_j, we extract the eligible scenario as follows:

$$\forall k \in N / tr_{i_k}^{A_k^r} = C_e^{A_k^r} | C_s^{A_k^r} | A_e^{A_k^r} | A_s^{A_k^r};$$

$$\exists k, \exists c_e C_e^{A_{k+1}^r}, \exists c_s C_s^{A_k^r} / c_e = \neg c_s \Rightarrow S_{(el)} := S_{(el)} - SC_j;$$

The Generation Algorithm of the Scenarios of Equivalence. For each eligible scenario $S_{(el)d}$, let $A_d \subset C_r$ the set of critical tracks of eligible scenario $S_{(el)d}$.

Firstly, we collect the critical tracks for each eligible scenario.

We initialize the set of eligible tracks by an empty set $A_d = \{\}$ and the scenriaos of equivalence set by any eligible scenario $S_{(eq)} = S_{(el)0}$:

1-, For $d = 0$:

$$PA_i \subseteq tr_{i_k}^{A_k^r} \Rightarrow A_0 =: A_0 \cup tr_{i_k}^{A_k^r}$$
$$\text{unless } k + +$$

2-, For each $d \in [1, N]$, where $L \leqslant \prod_{k=0}^{k=N-1} l_{(el)k}$. Going over the set of eligible tracks:

$$PA_i \subseteq tr_{i_k}^{A_k^r} \Rightarrow A_d =: A_d \cup tr_{i_k}^{A_k^r}$$
$$\text{unless } k++$$

And, incrementing $d++$.

Secondly, we search the equivalences scenarios after the construction of the critical tracks set for each eligible scenario.

Let $S_{(eq)}$ the set of the equivalences scenarios:

$$[\forall o, A_d \subset A_o \text{ avec } S_{(el)o} \subset S_{(eq)}] \Rightarrow S_{(eq)} = S_{(eq)}$$
$$[\forall o, A_o \subset A_d \text{ avec } S_{(el)o} \subset S_{(eq)}] \Rightarrow S_{(eq)} = (S_{(eq)} \setminus S_{(el)o}) \cup S_{(el)d}$$
$$[\forall, A_o \cap A_d \neq (A_o, A_d) \text{ avec } S_{(el)o} \subset S_{(eq)}] \Rightarrow S_{(eq)} = S_{(eq)} \cup S_{(el)d}$$

After obtaining the cycles of equivalence, we search for the existence of the paths of execution from the combination of these scenarios. Afterwards we verify the specification at the level of these paths of execution builds.

4 Application

Let us start by a simple SystemC model an implementation of simple FIFO. The model contains a First-In-First-Out buffer and three modules cooperating through the buffer a producer module which continuously puts data into the buffer and two consumer modules which continuously retrieve data from the buffer.

In a formal verification technique using SPIN Model checker, we specify the specification properties of the components with formulae of LTL (Linear Temporal Logic) and code the automata that represent the systems behavior with Promela language (Fig. 1).

4.1 Specification Properties

The properties, which we want to verify at the level of the system FIFO, are generic properties:

P1: Always Eventually, the FIFO is full.

$$[] \diamond num_{elts} = size$$

P2: Always Eventually the FIFO is empty.

$$[] \diamond num_{elts} = 0$$

Following the proprieties of our modelling, the atomic proposals are:

$$P = (num_{elts} = size;\ num_{elts} = 0)$$

4.2 Reduced Automaton of FIFO System

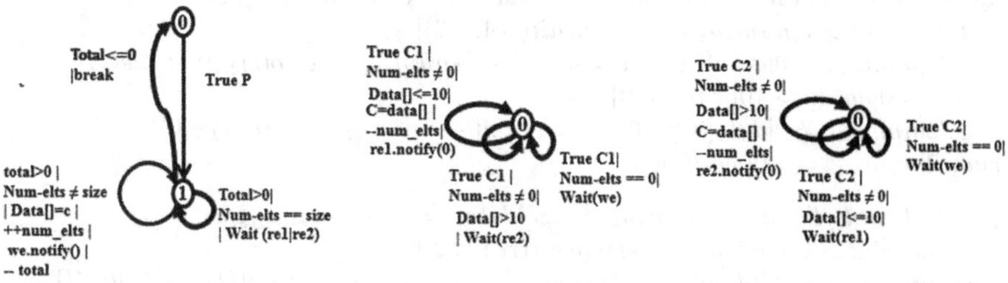

Fig. 1. Reduced Automaton of Producer, Consumer 1 and Consumer 2 Processes.

4.3 Application of Deduction Method

Producer automaton has five interactions:
$T0_1 = TrueP$;
$T0_2 = [Total > 0|num_{elts} \neq size|data[.] = c|{+}{+}num_{elts}|we.notify(.)|{-}{-}total]$,
$T0_3 = [Total > 0|num_{elts} == size|wait(re1 \mid re2)]$,
$T0_4 = [total \leqslant 0 \mid break]$.

Consumer 1 automaton has four interactions:
$T1_1 = [TrueC1|num_{elts} \neq 0|data[.] \leqslant 10c = data[.]| - -num_{elts}|re1.notify(0)]$,
$T1_2 = [TrueC1|num_{elts} \neq 0|data[.] > 10|wait(re2)]$,
$T1_3 = [TrueC1|num_{elts} == 0|wait(we)]$.

Consumer 2 automaton has four interaction:
$T2_1 = [TrueC2|num_{elts} \neq 0|data[.] > 10c = data[.]| - -num_{elts}|re2.notify(0)]$;
$T2_2 = [TrueC2|num_{elts} \neq 0|data[.] \leqslant 10|wait(re1)]$,
$T2_3 = [TrueC2|num_{elts}s == 0|wait(we)]$.

We considered that the simulation order is predefined as follows:
Producer (1) Consumer 1 (2) Consumer 2 (3)
The eligible tracks for each automaton (delta-steps):

$$tr_0^{A_1^r} = T0_1|T0_2|T0_3, tr_1^{A_1^r} = T0_1|T0_2|T0_4, tr_2^{A_1^r} = T0_1|T0_3, tr_3^{A_1^r} = T0_1|T0_4.$$
$$tr_0^{A_2^r} = T1_1|T1_2, tr_1^{A_2^r} = T1_1|T1_3, tr_2^{A_2^r} = T1_2, tr_3^{A_2^r} = T1_3.$$
$$tr_0^{A_3^r} = T2_1|T2_2, tr_1^{A_3^r} = T2_1|T2_3, tr_2^{A_3^r} = T2_2, tr_3^{A_3^r} = T2_3.$$

Critical tracks for each automaton are:

$$C_1 = tr_0^{A_1^r}, tr_2^{A_1^r}$$
$$C_2 = tr_1^{A_2^r}, tr_3^{A_2^r}$$
$$C_3 = tr_1^{A_3^r}, tr_3^{A_3^r}$$

Thus, from the set of critical tracks $Cr = C_1, C_2, C_3$, we are going to have 64 combinations 64 scenarios.

By applying the algorithm of the eligible scenarios, we had 21 eligible scenarios.

After the application of the algorithm of the scenarios of equivalence:

$s_{(eq)0} = TrueP|Total > 0|num_{elts} \neq size|data[.] = c| + +num_{elts}|we.notify(.)|$
$- - total|total > 0|num_{elts} == size|wait(re1|re2)|$
$TrueC1|num_{elts} \neq 0|data[] \leqslant 10|c = data[]| - -num_{elts}|re1.notify(0)|TrueC1|$
$num_{elts} \neq 0|data[] > 10|wait(re2)|$
$TrueC2|num_{elts} \neq 0|data[.] > 10 \mid c = data[.]| - -num_{elts}|re2.notify(0)|$
$TrueC2|num_{elts} == 0|wait(we)|$

$s_{(Eq)1} = TrueP|Total > 0|num_{elts} \neq size|data[.] = c| + +num_{elts}|we.notify(.)|$
$- - total|total > 0|num_{elts} == size|wait(re1|re2)|$
$TrueC1|num_{elts} \neq 0 \mid data[.] \leqslant 10c = data[.]| - -num_{elts}|re1.notify(0)|TrueC1|$
$num_{elts} == 0|wait(we)|$
$TrueC2|num_{elts} == 0|wait(we)$

$s_{(Eq)2} = TrueP|Total > 0|num_{elts} == size|wait(re1re2)|$
$TrueC1|num_{elts} \neq 0|data[] \leqslant 10|c = data[]| - -num_{elts}|re1.notify(0)|TrueC1|$
$num_{elts} \neq 0|data[] > 10|wait(re2)|$
$TruceC2|num_{elts} \neq 0|data[.] > 10c = data[.]| - -num_{elts}|re2.notify(0)|TrueC2|$
$num_{elts} == 0|wait(we)$

$s_{(Eq)3} = TrueP|Total > 0|num_{elts} == size|wait(re1re2)|$
$TrueC1|num_{elts} \neq 0|data[.] \leqslant 10|c = data[.]| - -num_{elts}|re1.notify(0)|TrueC1|$
$num_{elts} == 0|wait(we)|$
$TrueC2|num_{elts} == 0|wait(we)$

4.4 Preliminary Results

To assess the efficiency of the proposed approach, we have compared the results of the use of our contribution with those of related works which are based on the abstraction and preservation of the simulation semantics of SystemC. The table below shows preliminary results concerning the gain in terms of the verification time between the three methods: WSA [23], Reduction [18] and the method of deduction (Table 1).

Table 1. Verification time (in percentage) with different approaches. WSA time is taken as the reference time.

Simple FIFO : Producer//Consumer1// Consumer2	Building SystemC WSA	Method of Reduction with priorities	Method of Deduction
Gain in terms of verification (%)	-----	30%	40%

This result on the FIFO component is very encouraging since it shows that we can achieve a gain of 40% using our approach compared to WSA approach. We are currently conducting more extensive experiments to confirm the trend of this preliminary result.

5 Conclusion

We proposed in this article a new vision towards the verification of SystemC models. Our contribution focus on the idea to verify just the paths of execution which represent other similar paths, and contain the critical tracks with respect to the specification under verification. We named those paths the scenarios of equivalence that contain the delta-cycles of equivalence.

Our approach is a suite of data manipulation procedures whose purpose is the search for the scenarios of equivalence. It comprises two construction and three extraction algorithms: in the first place, we modeled every SystemC process, represented using state transition representation [18]. Then, the extraction of the eligible tracks in every automaton with the aim of combining them to create all the possible scenarios between two successive delta-cycles. After this stage, we look for the subsets of the combinations that contain redundant scenarios or which have common critical tracks. In every subset, we look for the scenarios of equivalence which represent the others and which contain the largest number of critical tracks. Finally, we translate these scenarios of equivalence to the Promela language to check the specification of the system under SPIN Model Checker.

We illustrated our approach on the FIFO component with three processes. The method of deduction showed its efficiency on the FIFO example by reducing the verification time through the stages of construction and extraction. In the future work, we are going to treat more complex systems to confirm these preliminary results.

References

1. Chen, X., Watanabe, Y.: Formal verification for embedded system designs. Des. Autom. Embed. Syst. **8**, 139–153 (2003)
2. Grotker, T., Lio, S., Martin, G., Swan, S.: System Design with SystemC^{TM}. Kluwer Academic Publishers, Hingham (2002)
3. Maillet-Contoz, L., Ghenassia, F.: Transaction level modeling. In: Ghenassia, F. (ed.) Transaction Level Modeling with SystemC. Springer, Boston (2005). doi:10.1007/0-387-26233-4_2
4. McMillan, K.L.: Symbolic Model Checking. Carnegie Mellon University, Pittsburgh (1993)
5. Behrmann, G., David, A., Larsen, K.G.: A Tutorial on Uppaal 4.0. (2006)
6. Holzmann, G.J.: The model checker spin. IEEE Trans. Softw. Eng. -Spec. Issue Formal Methods Softw. Pract. **23**(5), 279–295 (1997)
7. Sharma, A.: End to End Verification and Validation with SPIN (2013)
8. Moy, M., Maraninchi, F., Maillet-Contoz, L.: PINAPA: an extraction tool for SystemC descriptions of systems-on-a-chip. In: EMSOFT05. ACM (2005)
9. Moy, M., Maraninchi, F., Maillet-Contoz, L.: LusSy: an open tool for the analysis of systems-on-a-chip at the transaction level. Des. Autom. Embed. Syst. **10**, 73–104 (2006). Springer Science+Business Media, LLC
10. Marquet, K., Moy, M.: PinaVM: a SystemC Front-End Based on an Executable Intermediate Representation (2010)

11. Marquet, K., Jeannet, B., Moy, M.: Efficient encoding of SystemC/TLM in Promela. In: The International MultiConference of Engineers and Computer Scientists, vol II (2011)
12. Traulsen, C., Cornet, J., Moy, M., Maraninchi, F.: A SystemC/TLM semantics in PROMELA and its possible applications. In: Bošnački, D., Edelkamp, S. (eds.) SPIN 2007. LNCS, vol. 4595, pp. 204–222. Springer, Heidelberg (2007). doi:10.1007/978-3-540-73370-6_14
13. Herber, P., Fellmuth, J., Glesner, S.: Model checking SystemC designs using timed automata. In: International Conference on Hardware/Software Codesign and System Synthesis, pp. 131–136 (2008)
14. Garavel, H., Helmstetter, C., Ponsini, O., Serwe, W.: Verification of an industrial SystemC/TLM model using LOTOS ans CADP. In: 7th ACM-IEEE International Conference on Formal Methods and Models for Codesign MEMOCODE2009, Cambridge, MA, USA (2009)
15. Helmstetter, C., Maraninchi, F., Maillet-Contoz, L., Moy, M.: Automatic generation of schedulings for improving the test coverage of systems-on-a-chip. In: FMCAD, pp. 171–178 (2006)
16. Pelanek, R.: Reduction and abstraction techniques for model checking. Masaryk University Faculty of Informatics (2006)
17. Chupilko, M., Kamkin, A.: Runtime verification based on executable models: on-the-fly matching of timed traces. In: Petrenko, A., Schlingloff, H. (eds.) Eighth Workshop on Model-Based Testing (MBT), pp. 67–68 (2013)
18. Essayad, I., Zakari, A., Sadik, M., Nahhal, T.: Modelling and and analysis of heterogenous architectures and application to SystemC. In: FSKKP Anjur Persidangan ICSECS 2013 (2013)
19. Kroening, D., Sharygina, N.: Formal verification of SystemC by automatic hardware/software partitioning. In: The Third ACM and IEEE International Conference on Formal Methods and Models for Co-Design. pp. 101–110 (2005)
20. Niemann, B., Haubelt, Ch.: Formalizing TLM with communicating state machines. In: Forum of Specification and Design languages (2006)
21. Moinudeen, H., Habibi, A., Tahar, S.: Generating finite state machines from SystemC. In: Gielen, G.G.E. (ed.), DATE DesignerForum, pp. 76–81 (2006)
22. Védrine, F., Zhang, Y., Monsuez, B.: SystemC waiting-state automata. In: First International Workshop on Verification and Evaluation of Computer and Communication Systems, pp. 5–6 (2007)
23. Harrath, N., Monsuez, B.: Timed SystemC waiting-state automata. In: Third International Workshop on Verification and Evaluation of Computer and Communication Systems (2009)
24. Karlsson, P., Eles, D., Peng, Z.: Formal verification of SystemC designs using a petri-net based representation. In: Proceedings of the Conference on Design, Automation and Test in Europe, pp. 1128–1233 (2006)
25. Ruys, T.C.: SPIN tutorial: how to become a SPIN doctor. In: Bošnački, D., Leue, S. (eds.) SPIN 2002. LNCS, vol. 2318, pp. 6–13. Springer, Heidelberg (2002). doi:10.1007/3-540-46017-9_3

Image Segmentation by Deep Community Detection Approach

Youssef Mourchid[1(✉)], Mohammed El Hassouni[2], and Hocine Cherifi[3]

[1] LRIT, Associated Unit to CNRST (URAC No 29)- Faculty of Sciences, Mohammed V University in Rabat, B.P. 1014 RP, Rabat, Morocco
youssefmour@gmail.com

[2] DESTEC, FLSHR, Mohammed V University in Rabat, Rabat, Morocco
mohamed.elhassouni@gmail.com

[3] LE2I, UMR 6306 CNRS, University of Burgundy, Dijon, France
hocine.cherifi@gmail.com

Abstract. To address the problem of segmenting an image into homogeneous communities this paper proposes an efficient algorithm to detect deep communities in the image by maximizing at each stage a new centrality measure, called the local Fiedler vector centrality (LFVC). This measure is associated with the sensitivity of algebraic connectivity to node removals. We show that a greedy node removal strategy, based on iterative maximization of LFVC, has bounded performance loss relative to the optimal, but intractable, combinatorial batch removal strategy. A remarkable feature of this method is the ability to segments the image automatically into homogeneous regions by maximizing the LFVC value in the constructed network from the image. The performance of the proposed algorithm is evaluated on Berkeley Segmentation Database and compared with some well-known methods. Experiments show that the greedy LFVC strategy can efficiently extract deep communities from the image and can achieve much better segmentation results compared to the other known algorithms in terms of qualitative and quantitative accuracy.

Keywords: Image segmentation · Complex networks · Deep community detection · Local Fiedler vector centrality · Removal strategy

1 Introduction

Image segmentation is an essential tool for most image processing tasks which consists of partitioning the image into spatially coherent regions with similar attributes that represent similar features and constitutes an essential issue. It's a pre-processing process to group image pixels into some sizable homogeneous regions so that the complexity of further analysis can be substantially reduced. Image segmentation has received an important attention since the problem was proposed, a number of segmentation techniques have been proposed and studied in the last decades to solve this problem. Some of them are based on graph partitioning, image threshold methods [1] and others on region growing methods [2].

E. Sabir et al. (Eds.): UNet 2017, LNCS 10542, pp. 607–618, 2017.
https://doi.org/10.1007/978-3-319-68179-5_53

Image segmentation algorithms are classified into three major approaches: spatial segmentation, feature-space based clustering, and graph-based approaches. In these approaches, grouping is based on factors such as similarity and continuation, the common idea is the formation of a weighted graph, where each image pixel or region corresponds to a vertex in the graph, and the weight of each edge connecting two vertices represents the similarity that they belong to the same segment.

With the development of complex networks theory, the study and research on networks have become one of the most interesting topics nowadays. Community structure, which is an important property of complex networks, can be described as the gathering of vertices into groups such that there is a higher density of edges within groups than between them. In social, biological and technological image analysis [4], community detection aims to extract tightly connected sub-graphs or regions from the generated graph of the image. This problem has attracted a great deal of interest in network science because identifying this community structure is one of the most important problems in the understanding of functions and structures of real-world complex systems, which is still a challenging task. A number of methods have been proposed so far to extract the community structure in networks by detecting nodes with high centrality. The centrality of the node is a quantitative measure that is used to evaluate the level of importance and/or influence of a node in the image graph. There are different combinatorial measures which centrality can be based such as the graph diffusion distances between every node pair or the shortest paths. These measures can also be based on spectral properties of the adjacency graph and graph Laplacian matrices. Several measures need a global topological information and thus, may not be computationally feasible for very large networks. Non-parametric community detection methods can be viewed as edge removal strategies, such as the edge betweenness method [4] and the modularity method [5], its aim is the maximization of the centrality measure, e.g., the betweenness or modularity measures. It is worth mentioning that these methods consider that each node in the graph is affiliated with a community. It often occurs in some community detection applications that graphs has spurious edges which are connected to irrelevant "noisy" nodes that are not members of any community. Noisy nodes in such cases hide the true communities in the graph. The detection of these hidden or masked communities is a difficult problem which we call "deep community detection". A deep community in image graph is a connected component or regions that can only be seen after the removal of nodes from the rest of the graph. A new partitioning strategy of the image is applied to detect deep communities. Its goal is using a new local measure of centrality which can specifically unhide or unmask image communities in the presence of spurious edges. This partitioning strategy is based on local Fiedler vector centrality (LFVC) which is a new spectral measure [6] of centrality. This measure is associated with the sensitivity of algebraic connectivity, when a subset of nodes are removed from a graph. The proposed approach in this paper uses LFVC to iteratively remove nodes in the image graph to reveal deep communities [16].

If a removed node connects multiple deep communities is assigned mixed membership: it is shared among these communities. As compared with other image segmentation methods, we show that the proposed greedy LFVC approach has superior deep community detection performance for image segmentation task.

Compared with another state of the art methods, the proposed algorithm can automatically detect the number of communities into an image and achieve better segmentation result. The results are compared with two state of the art methods JSEG [3] and EDISON [8], all of them are well known and usually used for image segmentation tasks.

The rest of the paper is organized as follows. In Sect. 2, we show how an image can be represented as a complex network. Section 3 summarizes the centrality measures, the definitions of community, and the Fiedler Vector. In Sect. 4 we give the definition of deep communities. Section 5 gives the definition of the proposed local Fiedler vector centrality (LFVC). In Sect. 6, experiments are shown to illustrate the performance of the LFVC on the publicly Berkeley Segmentation Data Set (BSDS300). Finally in Sect. 7, we present our conclusions.

2 Image Representation as a Complex Network

Images can be considered as graphs where each node and weight in the graph represents a pixel in the image, they are computed according to a similarity or a weight function. Different weight functions are used, some of them are based on Euclidian distance, others on Manhattan, Gaussian, others. Firstly, nodes are linked to each other with a function based on the intensity, given by the formula below:

$$A = A_{i,j} = \begin{cases} 1 \text{ if } |I_i - I_j| > t \\ 0 \text{ sinon} \end{cases} \tag{1}$$

where A denotes the image adjacency matrix, $A_{i,j}$ (i = 1,..., n; j = 1,..., m) represents the edge weight between the pixels i and j, I_j and I_i represent respectively the intensity of pixel j and i. If the weight $A_{i,j}$ is greater than threshold t, in this case, we can consider that the two pixels are connected. The value of t varies according to pixel intensity similarity. In addition, connections are defined only inside a circular pixel neighborhood of radius R, which varies between 4 and 8. The idea behind this graph generation approach is that human vision tends to focus on high-contrast places.

3 Centrality Measures, Community Detection, and Fiedler Vector

3.1 The Graph Laplacian Matrix and Algebraic Connectivity

Consider the image adjacency matrix A defined in the previous section. We denote by n the number of nodes and m the number of edges. let $d_i = \Sigma_{j=1}^{n} A_{i,j}$ denote the degree of node i. The degree matrix $D = diag(d)$ is a diagonal matrix where the degree vector $d = [d_1, d_2, \ldots, d_n]$ on it's diagonal. The graph Laplacian matrix of the image graph is defined as $L = D - A$. Let λ_i denote the ith smallest eigenvalue of the Laplacian matrix and let $1 = [1, \ldots, 1]^T$ be the vector of ones. We have the formula below

$$x^T Lx = \frac{1}{2}\sum_{i\in V}\sum_{j\in V} A_{i,j}(x_i - x_j)^2 \tag{2}$$

which is non-negative, and $L_1 = (D - A)1 = 0$ denote the vector of all zeros. Thus $\lambda_1(L) = 0$ and L is a positive semi-definite (PSD) matrix.

We define the algebraic connectivity of the image graph G as the second smallest eigenvalue of L, i.e. $\lambda_2(L)$. the image graph G is connected if and only if $\lambda_2(L) > 0$. Moreover, it is a well-known property [7] that for any non-complete graph,

$$\lambda_2(L) \leqslant \text{ node connectivity} \leqslant \text{ edge connectivity} \tag{3}$$

where node/edge connectivity is the least number of node/edge removals that disconnects the graph. The formula (2) is the main motivation for the proposed node pruning approach. A graph with high algebraic connectivity value is more resilient to node removals. Furthermore, let d_{min} be the minimum degree of the image graph, it is also well-known [6] that $\lambda_2(L) \leqslant 1$ if and only if $d_{min} = 1$. A graph with a leaf node cannot have algebraic connectivity larger than 1. We can represent the algebraic connectivity of any connected graph as

$$\lambda_2(L) = \min_{\|x\|_2=1, x\perp 1} x^T Lx \tag{4}$$

using the Courant-Fischer theorem [9] and the fact that the constant vector is the eigenvector associated with $\lambda_1(L) = 0$.

3.2 Centrality Measures

Centrality measures are classified into two categories, local and global measures. Local centrality measures only need local topological information from neighboring nodes, whereas global centrality measures require the complete topological information for their computation. A quick review of some node centralities is shown below.

Closeness [10]: is a global measure of the geodesic distance of a node to all other nodes. We can say that node has high closeness if the sum of its shortest path distances to other nodes is small. Let $\rho(i, j)$ be the shortest path distance between nodes i and j in a connected graph. Then we define $closeness(i) = 1/\Sigma_{j\in V, j\neq i}\rho(i, j)$.

Degree (d_i): is the simplest local centrality measure which accounts for the number of neighboring nodes.

Betweenness: it is equal to the number of shortest paths from all vertices to all others that pass through that node. A node with high betweenness centrality has a large influence on the transfer of items through the network, under the assumption that item transfer follows the shortest paths. Specifically, betweenness centrality is a global measure defined as $betweenness(i) = \Sigma_{k \neq i} \Sigma_{j \neq i, j > k} \frac{\phi_{kj}(i)}{\phi_{kj}}$, where $\phi_{kj}(i)$ is the number of each shortest paths passing through i and ϕ_{kj} is the total number of shortest paths from k to j.

3.3 Community Detection

Community structure is one of the most relevant features of graphs representing real systems. The representation of vertices in communities, with many edges joining vertices of the same community and comparatively few edges joining vertices of different communities. Besides, rather than focusing on how communities can be detected, the classification is based on the community definition used by the algorithms. The community detection has a fundamental problem, it's how to find the best division of the network into their constituent communities. Newman proposed a measure called modularity Q to solve this problem, which indicates the quality of a partition of the network. The formula of Q is defined as follows $Q = \Sigma_i(e_{ii} - a_i^2)$ where e_{ii} is the fraction of network edges that are inserted into a community i, and a_i^2 is the fraction considering that edges are inserted randomly, the value of Q range from 0 to 1, if values are close to 1, the existence of communities is not by chance. For dividing a network into more than two communities, Newman proposes a recursive approach of partitioning. There is no performance difference between the modularity method, the statistical inference method and the normalized cut method [1]. Nevertheless, the modularity method may fail to detect the small communities even when community structures are apparent. A node removal strategy in [11] based on targeting high degree nodes is presented to improve the performance of the modularity method.

3.4 The Fiedler Vector

In a graph, the Fiedler vector is the eigenvector associated with the second smallest eigenvalue $\lambda_2(L)$ of the graph Laplacian matrix [12]. It has been widely used in image segmentation, graph partitioning, and data clustering [1,13]. Analogously for modularity partitioning, the Fiedler vector detects communities by separating the nodes in the graph according to the signs of the corresponding Fiedler vector elements. Similarly, the hierarchical structure detection of a community can be done by recursive partitioning with the Fiedler vector. In this paper, the Fiedler vector is used to define a new centrality measure. The advantage of using it over other global centrality measures is that it can be computed in a distributed manner via local information exchange over the graph.

4 Deep Community

Let $A_1, \ldots, A_g$ denote the $n \times n$ mutually orthogonal binary adjacency matrices of the image, associated with g non-singleton connected components in a noiseless graph G_0 over n nodes. The nodes of the image graph have been permuted so that $A_1, \ldots, A_g$ represent the block diagonal with non-overlapping block indices $I_1, \ldots, I_g$. Specifically, let A_{nse} be the random adjacency matrix for the image where $A_{nse}(i,j) = 0, (i, j \in I_k)$, for $k = 1, \ldots, g$ and the rest of the elements of A_{nse} are Bernoulli. Then the image adjacency matrix A of the graph G satisfies the signal plus noise model

$$A = \sum_{k=1}^{g} A_k + A_{nse} \tag{5}$$

The problem of deep community detection is how to recover connected components $A_1, \ldots, A_g$ from the noise corrupted observations A. The A_k's are called deep communities, they are embedded in an image graph with random interconnections between connected components. Deep community detection is equivalent to the planted clique problem [14] in the case that g = 1 and the non-zero block of A_1 corresponds to a complete image graph, i.e., all off-diagonal elements of this block are equal to one.

In this paper, we present an iterative denoising algorithm to recover deep communities that are based on node removals. This algorithm uses a spectral centrality measure (see Sect. 5) to determine the nodes which can be pruned from the observed graph with the image adjacency matrix.

Let $\widetilde{L}$ denote the resulting graph Laplacian matrix when we remove a subset of nodes from the image graph. The Theorem 1 in [16] gives an upper bound on the number of deep communities in the remaining image graph.

$$\epsilon \leqslant n - r \leqslant n - \frac{\|\widetilde{L}\|*}{\lambda_n(\widetilde{L})} = n - \frac{2\widetilde{m}}{\lambda_n(\widetilde{L})} \text{ [16]} \tag{6}$$

where R denote the node removal set of G with $\|R\| = q$, $\|\widetilde{L}\|* = \Sigma_i \lambda_i(\widetilde{L})$ denote its nuclear norm, r is the rank of the resulting graph Laplacian matrix $\widetilde{L}$. ϵ is the number of remaining non-singleton connected components in $\widetilde{G}$ and $\widetilde{m}$ denote the number of edges in $\widetilde{G}$.

The Theorem 2 in [16] shows that the size of the largest non-singleton connected component can be represented as a matrix one norm of a matrix whose column vectors are orthogonal and sparsest among all binary vectors that form a basis of the null space of $\widetilde{L}$. Let $\psi(\widetilde{G})$ be the largest non-singleton connected component size of $\widetilde{G}$, we have the this formula:

$$\psi(\widetilde{G}) = \|X\|_1 = max_i \|x_i\|_1 \text{ [16]} \tag{7}$$

where $null(\widetilde{L})$ denote the null space of $\widetilde{L}$ and X denote the matrix whose columns are orthogonal and they form the sparsest basis of $null(\widetilde{L})$ among binary vectors.

Theorems 1 and 2 are the keys of our motivation and theoretically they justify the proposed local Fiedler vector centrality measure introduced below. Theorem 1 establishes that the number of deep communities is closely related to the number of node removals that are required to reveal them. Theorem 2 establishes that norm of the sparsest basis for the null space of the graph Laplacian matrix can be used to estimate the size of the largest deep community in the network.

5 The Node Centrality: Local Fielder Vector Centrality

The deep community detection algorithm proposed in this paper is based on removing nodes from image graph according to how the removals affect the measure of algebraic connectivity which is called the local Fiedler vector centrality (LFVC). This measure is computed from the graph Laplacian matrix of the image graph. The LFVC, in particular, is motivated by the fact that node removals result in low-rank perturbations to the graph Laplacian matrix when $n \geqslant d_{max}$, where d_{max} is the maximum degree. The node LFVC are then defined to correspond to an upper bound on algebraic connectivity.

5.1 Node-LFVC

When we remove a node $i \in V$ from the graph G, all the edges attached to i will also be removed and the resulting graph Laplacian matrix $\widetilde{L}(i)$ can be considered as a rank d_i matrix perturbation of L. We obtain an upper bound since $L - \widetilde{L}(i) = \Sigma_{j \in N_i}(e_i - e_j)(e_i - e_j)^T$, where N_i is the set of neighboring nodes of node i

$$\begin{aligned} \lambda_2(\widetilde{L}) &\leqslant y^T \widetilde{L}(i) y \\ &= y^T (L + \widetilde{L}(i) - L) y \\ &= \lambda_n(L) - \sum_{j \in N_i} (y_i - y_j)^2 \end{aligned} \tag{8}$$

For any connected graph, there exists at least one node removal that leads to a decrease in algebraic connectivity. If a subset of nodes $R \subset V$ are removed from G, where $\|R\| = q$ then

$$\begin{aligned} L - \widetilde{L}(R) = &\sum_{i \in R} \sum_{j \in N_i} (e_i - e_j)(e_i - e_j)^T \\ &- \frac{1}{2} \sum_{i \in R} \sum_{j \in R} A_{ij} (e_i - e_j)(e_i - e_j)^T, \end{aligned} \tag{9}$$

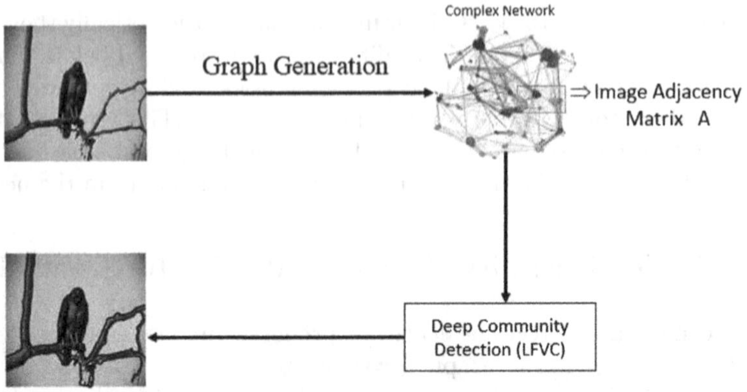

Fig. 1. Image segmentation process by deep community detection.

where the last term accounts for the edges that are attached to the removed nodes at both ends. Consequently, we obtain an upper bound for multiple node removals

$$\lambda_2(\widetilde{L}(R)) \leqslant \lambda_2(L) - \sum_{i \in R} \sum_{j \in N_i} (y_i - y_j)^2 + \frac{1}{2} \sum_{i \in R} \sum_{j \in R} A_{ij} (y_i - y_j)^2. \tag{10}$$

Finally, The local Fiedler vector node centrality is defined as

$$\text{node-LFVC(i)} = \sum_{j \in N_i} (y_i - y_j)^2 \tag{11}$$

which is the sum of the square terms of the Fiedler vector elementwise differences between node i and its neighboring nodes. From (8) and (10), node-LFVC is associated with the upper bound on the resulting algebraic connectivity for node removal when $\|R\| = 1$. A node with a high centrality means that it plays a more important role in the network connectivity structure.

We describe the methodology used in this work by the diagram of Fig. 1. First, we give an image which is represented as pixel matrix, from this matrix a complex network is created which represented by an image adjacency matrix, Then we use the deep community detection based on the maximization of the local Fiedler vector centrality, finally, we show the segmented image result by this measure.

6 Anisotropic Diffusion Filter for Merging Small Communities

The proposed segmentation algorithm described in the previous section may it's segmentation of the image into communities is not good enough, in the situations

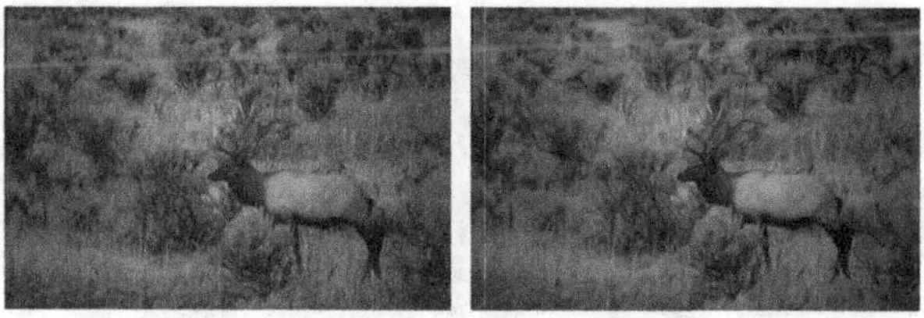

Fig. 2. (a) Original image, (b) Image after applying the Anisotropic diffusion filter.

in which the algorithm detects regions with a very small area as a community. Hence the anisotropic diffusion, also called Perona and Malik diffusion method is used before detecting deep communities, to merge the small regions in the image and to obtain a minimal number of the detected communities. This technique is based on reducing image noise without removing important information of the image content, as edges, lines or other details that are meaningful for interpreting the image. Each image result is a combination of a filter and the original image that depends on the image local content as shown in Fig. 2.

7 Experiments and Results

In this section, we provide experiments to show the performance of the local Fiedler vector centrality in image segmentation task. To demonstrate the effectiveness of LFVC for deep community detection in the image, we compare its detection performance to that of another state of the art methods. In the implementations of the proposed deep community detection algorithm, the number of removed nodes or edges is a user-specified free parameter. For LFVC (Algorithm 1) this parameter can be selected based on the bounds established in Theorem 1. The proposed algorithm is carried out on a 2.60 GHz; i5 processor with 4 GB RAM on Windows 8 platform. MATLAB 7.13 and image processing toolbox are used. Our experiments were tested on a subset of the Berkeley Segmentation Data Set (BSDS300) which contains 100 validation images of size 321×481 pixels that are randomly chosen from the Corel database. Images in (BSDS300) are manually segmented by humans in a natural way.

We have performed comparisons of the proposed algorithm with some existing segmentation techniques. As shown in the Fig. 3 the proposed algorithm result is compared to the two segmentation methods mentioned in Sect. 1. We can notice that the proposed algorithm can achieve much better results and can separate correctly the main object of the image. We can also see that the proposed algorithm can produce sizeable homogeneous segments for all selected images.

We have also evaluated quantitatively the segmentation performance of our proposed algorithm. The results of the image segmentation are compared with the two segmentation methods, we investigate for the quantitative evaluation the Probabilistic Rand Index [15] which is described as below:

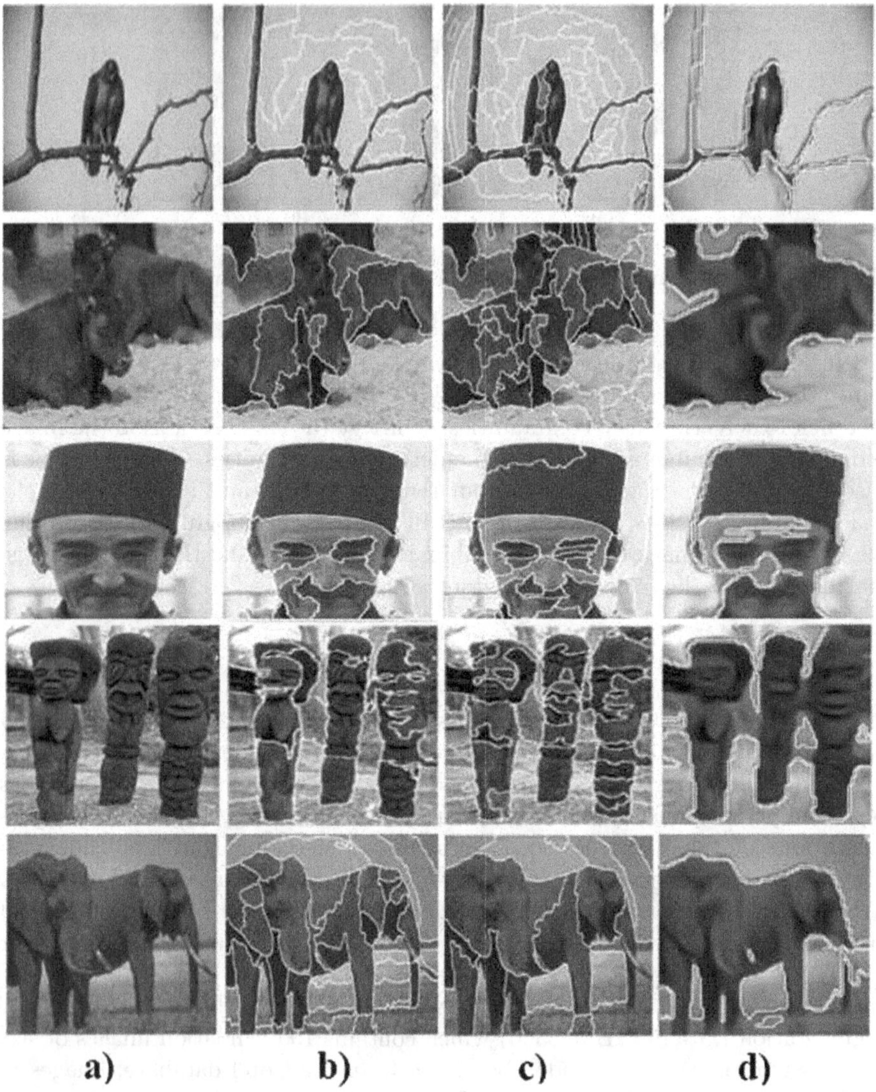

Fig. 3. (a) Input images; (b) EDISON; (c) JSEG; (d) Proposed Algorithm.

The PRI is a classical clustering evaluation criteria which measure the consistency of labelings between the segmented image and its ground truth by the ratio of pairs of pixels having the same labels, averaging across multiple ground truth segmentation to account for variation in human perception. The range of PRI is [0, 1]; a large value indicates a great similarity between the two segmentation. Table 1 presents the average values of the PRI, which are calculated, when the EDISON, JSEG and the proposed Algorithm (LFVC), were applied to all of the 100 images in the Berkeley segmentation dataset.

Results in the Table 1 show the superiority of the proposed algorithm compared to the two popular methods, also our algorithm achieves the best performance among all the popular segmentation algorithms. In terms of PRI, LFVC has a close performance to human and outperform the rest of other algorithms.

Table 1. Quantitative comparison of different algorithms on Berkeley dataset by Probabilistic Rand Index (PRI)

Algorithms	PRI
Humain	0.87
The proposed algorithm (LFVC)	**0.802**
EDISON	0.782
JSEG	0.760

8 Conclusion

Image segmentation technique is the most important step to cluster an image into salient image regions, i.e., regions which correspond to individual surfaces, objects, or natural parts of objects. This paper proposes a centrality measure called local Fiedler vector centrality (LFVC) for deep community detection task based on bounds on the sensitivity of algebraic connectivity to node removals. Our preliminary results of the Fiedler vector show that LFVC can achieve better community detection performance in correctly identifying the embedded deep communities in the image, which means that can be a useful component of image segmentation tasks. In comparison with JSEG and EDISON the proposed method provides better resolution for discovering important communities in the image, also it is reported that the proposed algorithms achieve the best performance among all of the other experimented popular methods in terms of PRI value on the Berkeley dataset. The qualitative results established that the proposed method have the ability to segment the input image into an optimal number of segments and homogeneous regions.

References

1. Shi, J., Malik, J.: Normalized cuts and image segmentation. IEEE Trans. Pattern Anal. Mach. Intell. **22**(8), 888–905 (2000)
2. Haralick, R.M., Shapiro, L.G.: Image segmentation techniques. Comput. Vis. Graph. Image Process. **29**(1), 100–132 (1985)
3. Deng, Y., Kenney, C., Moore, M.S., et al.: Peer group filtering and perceptual color image quantization. In: Proceedings of the 1999 IEEE International Symposium on Circuits and Systems, ISCAS 1999, pp. 21–24. IEEE (1999)
4. Girvan, M., Newman, M.E.J.: Community structure in social and biological networks. Proc. Nat. Acad. Sci. **99**(12), 7821–7826 (2002)

5. Newman, M.E.J.: Modularity and community structure in networks. Proc. Nat. Acad. Sci. **103**(23), 8577–8582 (2006)
6. Chung, F.R.K.: Spectral Graph Theory. American Mathematical Soc., Providence (1997)
7. Fiedler, M.: Algebraic connectivity of graphs. Czech. Math. J. **23**(2), 298–305 (1973)
8. Christoudias, C.M., Georgescu, B., Meer, P.: Synergism in low level vision. In: Proceedings of the 16th International Conference on Pattern Recognition, pp. 150–155. IEEE (2002)
9. Horn, R.A., Johnson, C.R.: Matrix Analysis. Cambridge University Press, Cambridge (2012)
10. Sabidussi, G.: The centrality index of a graph. Psychometrika **31**(4), 581–603 (1966)
11. Wen, H., Leicht, E.A., D'Souza, R.M.: Improving community detection in networks by targeted node removal. Phys. Rev. E **83**(1), 016114 (2011)
12. Pothen, A., Simon, H.D., Liou, K.-P.: Partitioning sparse matrices with eigenvectors of graphs. SIAM J. Matrix Anal. Appl. **11**(3), 430–452 (1990)
13. von Luxburg, U.: A tutorial on spectral clustering. Stat. Comput. **17**(4), 395–416 (2007)
14. Alon, N., Krivelevich, M., Sudakov, B.: Finding a large hidden clique in a random graph. Random Struct. Algorithms **13**(3–4), 457–466 (1998)
15. Unnikrishnan, R., Pantofaru, C., Hebert, M.: Toward objective evaluation of image segmentation algorithms. IEEE Trans. Pattern Anal. Mach. Intell. **29**(6), 929–944 (2007)
16. Chen, P.-Y., Hero, A.O.: Deep community detection. IEEE Trans. Signal Process. **63**(21), 5706–5719 (2015). MLA

Data Mining Approaches for Alzheimer's Disease Diagnosis

El Mehdi Benyoussef[1(✉)], Abdeltif Elbyed[1], and Hind El Hadiri[2]

[1] LIMSAD, Faculty of Science, Hassan II University, Casablanca, Morocco
elmehdibenyoussef@gmail.com, a.elbyed@fsac.ac.ma
[2] Geriatric Service, Emile Roux hospital, Paris, France
hind.elhadiri@aphp.fr

Abstract. Alzheimer's disease (AD) is known for its diagnosis difficulty, we can say that if someone is suffering from Alzheimer, he could have been affected years before the diagnosis. Geriatricians are mostly confronted with a large number of patients to treat without being able to reduce their number or classify them automatically. Related to the Moroccan context, and due to magnetic resonance imaging (MRI) scan costs and MRI scanners absence in most of Moroccan regions, we choose to use clinical data to understand the disease and help classifying its subjects to increase the quality of Alzheimer's diagnosis in Morocco. This work is about the treatment of Alzheimer's clinical data, using Data Mining. We propose a model composed by three classification and prediction algorithms which are "Decision trees", "Discriminant analysis" and "Logistic regression". Our model will firstly be able to classify and categorize suffering patients (AD) from those with mild cognitive impairment (MCI) and healthy subjects (HS), secondly it will offer some affectation rules for new subjects so we can place them in the right category.

Keywords: Alzheimer's diagnosis · Data Mining · Disease prediction · Data classification

1 Introduction

Alzheimer's disease (AD), known as a progressive neurodegenerative disease that particularly causes neuronal loss and brain's volume reduction, especially to aged population. The diagnosis of that disease is non representative, which is why the focus on recent researches has been set on defining a pertinent diagnosis.

Estimatedly, more than 36 million people worldwide have AD [3], 5.3 million Americans, aged 65 years, 200000 are aged less than 65 year [3]. According to The National Institute for Statistics and Economic Studies (INSEE), over 1 million French people are suffering from AD and this number is still growing faster. It also shows to be the case in Morocco, more than 20 000 Moroccan are affected. According to those numbers, Moroccan health institutes require a stronger automated system for AD diagnosis contribution.

E. Sabir et al. (Eds.): UNet 2017, LNCS 10542, pp. 619–631, 2017.
https://doi.org/10.1007/978-3-319-68179-5_54

For instance, a doctor's decision about a patient suffering from Alzheimer's disease could be years late. In Morocco, Alzheimer's disease seems to be a big burden because of Health facilities and specialist's lack. Geriatric medicine is almost absent in Morocco that it is usually neurologists that are faced with both diagnosing subjects and treating the recorded cases representing AD's symptoms, a process that is heavy when they have to deal with the large number of subjects manually. In order to help doctors diagnose subjects, we think of a configured automatic solution.

Trying to associate clinical data and MRI data and combine results to improve the decision aid for Alzheimer's disease, we chose to start with a classification using Data Mining approaches on clinical data such as logistic regression (LR), discriminant analysis (DA) and decision trees (DT) to generate some affectation rules based on the results of those algorithms to associate a new subject to the appropriate class. In fact, subjects information will be inserted by an administrator, treated, normalized, and then passed to comparison and classification algorithms to assign a diagnosis result which will be later confirmed by a doctor or a specialist.

The main idea is to combine results from Data Mining classification algorithms to increase the affectation rules quality. The aim is to create later on a solution that can superimpose the results from the algorithms to help the specialists making decisions.

The paper's content is explained next. Section 2 provides a review of the literature. In Sect. 3 we provide a description of the methodology used for the classification and the experimental subjects used in the paper. In Sect. 4 we describe and show the results of our classification work followed by the discussion of the given results. Conclusion is provided in Sect. 5.

2 State of Art

In recent years, most of the researches are focused on segmenting MRI images to identify patients and accelerate the diagnosis of AD, using some well-known machine learning algorithms with adaptations for image processing. Support vector machines (SVM), K-nearest neighbor (KNN), artificial neural networks (ANN) [12], and convolutional neural network (CNN) [11], are notable algorithms used for classification and regression analysis in medical settings [12].

Structural magnetic resonance imaging approaches have also been well developed in recent years [8], using segmentation to detect and analyze cerebral atrophy especially hippocampal atrophy which turns out to be a number one detection rule for patients suffering from AD [4]. Knowing that cerebral and hippocampal atrophy leads us to a better diagnosis of Alzheimer's disease [4], understanding its progression becomes important to carry out the early detection.

Some other researches were based on the information histogram encapsulated in the images [2], which contains different contrast areas that corresponds to brain's different tissues, that can be used for image segmentation.

A literature survey showed that there have been studies on medical prediction problems using Data Mining approaches [7], however there is some studies related to medical diagnosis that uses Data Mining approaches like decision trees [9]. Data Mining is becoming increasingly popular in medical domain [9].

A prediction model was proposed for the prediction of Alzheimer Disease using decision tree approach [5]. Authors considered five risk factors related to Alzheimers disease. In their work, the decision tree induction used Information Gain as a measure for predicting Alzheimers disease.

Table 1 summarizes some research efforts, some of which have been described above, and states the data they use, the classification method used and their objectives.

Table 1. A summary of related works

Author	Title	Year	Data source	Classification techniques used	Objectives
Sofia Matoug et al. [10]	Clustering-Based Detection of Alzheimer's Disease Using Brain MR Images	2016	ADNI	K-Nearest Neighbors	To propose a general framework for segmenting and classifying brain ventricles from MRI
Dana Al-Dlaeen et al. [5]	Using Decision Tree Classification to Assist in the Prediction of Alzheimer's Disease	2014	Clinical Data	Decision Trees	To develop an effective model for the prediction of Alzheimer's disease
B. Al-Naami et al. [1]	Automated Detection of Alzheimer's Disease Using Region Growing Technique and Artificial Neural Network	2013	Jordanian Hospitals	Artificial Neural Network	To develop a statistical-automated brain MRI diagnostic system to classify Alzheimer's patients
Ahsan Bin Tufail et al. [12]	Automatic Classification of Initial Categories of Alzheimer's Disease from Structural MRI Phase Images: A Comparison of PSVM, KNN, ANN Methods	2012	OASIS	PSVM, KNN and ANN	To compare the performance of PSVM, KNN and ANN classifiers for the classification of AD patients from 3D structural MRI

According to what was said before about related works, Data Mining was used in medical diagnosis since years. There also was some Machine Learning models used to segmentate MRIs. The problem is to combine results from multiple data treatment models to enhance AD diagnosis, which will lead us to first try classification techniques.

3 Context and Methodology

To diagnose a particular disease, a patient has to undergo a number of tests in the hospital. In developing countries such as Morocco, this process is more of a high cost and time-consuming manual process. As there is a lack of proper medical care and limited access to medical facilities in most of Moroccan regions, disease control should be prioritized among people. So, there is an essential need to solve this problem and to design a novel Data Mining technique that is self-automated and self-configured all while having least complexity and better knowledge understanding and accuracy.

As it's shown in Fig. 1, our solution's framework will contain data sets from multiple databases, normalized and uploaded by an administrator. We use a clinical data set from Open Access Series of Imaging Studies (OASIS), this clinical data will be split into two segments. The first is the estimate sample which will be treated using Data Mining algorithms, while the second is the validation sample which will be processed using the models built previously, to provide a number of classification probabilities, which will be confirmed or rejected by a specialist.

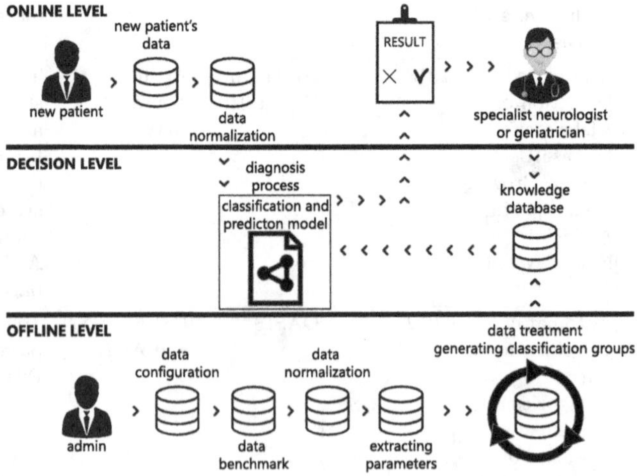

Fig. 1. The solution's architecture

Medical diagnosis is regarded as an important yet complicated task that needs to be executed accurately and efficiently, that is what drives us to try improve Alzheimer's disease diagnosis. We tried to classify clinical data related to AD using some Data Mining techniques, as a first step of trying to standardize heterogeneous Alzheimer's data sets.

3.1 Data Subjects

Alzheimer's disease includes several types of data to be treated which are MRI and clinical data. Because of the lack of MRI scanners in Morocco and the high costs of MRI scans, we choose to increase AD diagnosis using at first clinical data.

The used data comes from Open Access Series of Imaging Studies (OASIS) database, which freely provides data sets for research and data analysis. The data consists of an ensemble of information about 416 subjects with a known diagnosis result.

The data set used consists of a cross-sectional collection of right handed subjects aged between 18 and 96, having demographic variables like gender, education (Educ) and SocioEconomic Status (SES), clinical examination variable called Mini Mental State Examination (MMSE), derived anatomic volumes variables like estimated Total Intracranial Volume (eTIV), Atlas Scaling Factor (ASF) and normalized Whole Brain Volume (nWBV), including the Clinical Dementia Rating (CDR) scale, the table below show a sample of the used data set. This data have proven useful in studying diseased aging [8]. Note that the ASF has not been used because of being just a transformation equal to 1755 divided by eTIV variable [10].

The CDR is a dementia-staging factor that categorize subjects for impairment in each of the six domains: memory, orientation, judgment and problem solving, function in community affairs, home and hobbies, and personal care [12]. Absence of dementia is indicated by a CDR of 0, very mild, mild, moderate, and severe dementia are respectively represented by CDRs of 0.5, 1, 2, and 3 [11].

The chosen data set counts 214 subjects out of the 416 initial ones. We eliminated those with null values so we can understand all of OASIS data set variables to have classification rules with more information gain. We have chosen to work with 184 patients as an estimation sample and the other 30 patients as a validation sample. An example of the data set structure is shown in the Table 2.

3.2 Methodology

The amount of data stored in databases continues to grow fast. Intuitively, this large amount of data contains valuable knowledge, which could be used to improve the decision-making process of a whole domain. For instance, data about diseases might contain interesting knowledge. The discovery of such relationships can be very useful to increase the diagnosis of a disease.

Data Mining consists of mathematical methods that are differentiated by their utility, it's used where large volumes of data have to be analyzed, sometimes with the aim of decision making. The use of Data Mining for classification and

Table 2. A clinical dataset sample from OASIS

P.ID	Age	Educ	SES	MMSE	eTIV	nWBV	CDR
1	74	2	3	29	1344	0.743	0
2	55	4	1	29	1147	0.81	0
3	73	4	3	27	1454	0.708	0.5
9	74	5	2	30	1636	0.689	0
10	52	3	2	30	1321	0.827	0
12	81	5	2	30	1664	0.679	0
15	82	2	4	27	1477	0.739	0.5
26	86	2	4	27	1449	0.738	1
29	88	1	4	26	1419	0.674	1

prediction has received large attention from researchers, especially to assist in medical diagnosis and improve health conditions. We will choose those with classification and prediction goals.

Decision Trees. The decision tree technique is one of the most intuitive and popular Data Mining methods [13]. Decision trees are the result of algorithms that works by identifying the ways to split data set into segments, analyzing the correlations between target and explicative variables over their multiple modalities. A decision tree is a collection of affectation rules which are used to put a new subject to his correspondent class or segment.

Logistic Regression. Logistic regression is a predictive technique. It aims to construct a model to predict and explain the values taken by a qualitative target variable from a set of quantitative or qualitative explanatory variables [13]. Logistic regression is becoming universal, because it can handle dependent variables with more than 3 ordered values and the independent variables can be quantitative or qualitative [13]. Finally, logistic regression is one of the most reliable classification methods, and this reliability is easy to monitor using a large number of statistical indicators [13].

Discriminant Analysis. Discriminant factor analysis is a statistical technique that aims to describe, explain and predict the belonging of a set of observations to predefined groups from a series of predictor variables using least squares methods to separate data into groups. Data points are characterized by several variables; the optimal discriminant function is assumed to be a linear function of the variables which is determined by maximizing the between group sum of squares [6].

In the model learning stage, the knowledge database consists of the results of the classification algorithms on the data set estimate sample, decision tree starts by choosing which variable to use to split subjects into segments to and makes classification rules, while logistic regression and discriminant analysis aim to produce a linear combination of dependent variables. Based on the results of each one of those three algorithms on the used data set, we can build three classification models which will be used for prediction.

Prediction stage is about applying the three models produced by the Data Mining algorithms on the data set validation sample, each model will be based on its understood knowledge from the first learning stage, in order to predict subjects and to assign them into a class which is meant to be their right class.

The three algorithms are supposed to be the best Data Mining classifiers, but in a context where the data is human and where the human is supposed to be unique, affectation to a class may appear to be mathematically correct, whereas it may be false from a medical point of view. This is where correcting false learning can be the best solution, and it is the reason why we include the result of the diagnosis made by a specialist doctor in our knowledge database.

4 Results and Discussion

After describing the data set and the methodology, we will produce confusion matrices for the classification and prediction results of the three algorithms, to assess their behaviors towards the data.

For a classification model, performance can result in a confusion matrix, that allows evaluation of the performance of an algorithm, each column of the matrix represents the subjects in a predicted class while each row represents them in their right class. It helps with measuring the classification error also known as bad ranking.

4.1 Algorithms Results

Decision Trees. Decision tree algorithm seems to be the most powerful Data Mining technique for knowledge understanding of the data sets as it can be shown in Table 3, but sometimes its understanding of the data can't help to solve complex queries effectively, because of its way to make rules based on a group of people, little groups can drive it to weak decision rules.

Logistic Regression. Regression analysis is robust when it comes to study the relationship between several variables in the presence of random errors. The result can lead us to a medium data understanding on estimate sample as shown in the Table 4, but can keep that medium score at the validation stage which can be seen on the right side of Table 4.

Table 3. Confusion matrix for decision tree model

	Estimate sample			Validation sample		
	0	0.5	1	0	0.5	1
0	116	2	0	14	0	1
0.5	5	40	1	5	3	3
1	0	5	15	0	3	1

Table 4. Confusion matrix for logistic regression model

	Estimate sample			Validation sample		
	0	0.5	1	0	0.5	1
0	110	8 0		15	0	0
0.5	18	23	5	4	3	4
1	2	6	12	0	2	2

Discriminant Analysis. The discriminant analysis result is a linear function describing independent variable using the other independent variables of the dataset, it turns up a good data understanding. We can also see in Table 5 that discriminant analysis have more correct predictions for validation sample and this is due to the way it understands the data.

Table 5. Confusion matrix for discriminant analysis model

	Estimate sample			Validation sample		
	0	0.5	1	0	0.5	1
0	114	4	0	15	0	0
0.5	22	15	9	5	2	4
1	2	3	15	0	1	3

4.2 Results Comparison

To compare the performances of the three techniques, accuracy has been measured as the percentage of cases (subjects) that the algorithm classifies correctly. We applied the three algorithms on OASIS data set, each one gave us a classification accuracy for estimate sample and validation sample that we show in the tables below.

The accuracy (ACC), which is the probability of correct healthy subjects HS(0), Mild Cognitive Impairment MCI(0,5) and suffering patients AD(1) predictions have been calculated using the formula below and shown in the Table 6.

The "T" means true, which is used to identify the subjects figuring in the diagonal of the matrices, and it corresponds to those who were correctly predicted. The "F" means false and is used for the badly predicted subjects.

$$ACC = \frac{T(0) + T(0,5) + T(1)}{(T(0) + F(0) + T(0,5) + F(0,5) + T(1) + F(1))} * 100 \ . \quad (1)$$

Table 6. Accuracies representation

	Decision tree	Logistic regression	Discriminant analysis
Estimate sample accuracy	92%	67%	78%
Validation sample accuracy	60%	59%	66%

Each classification and prediction model has its strengths and weaknesses, and as shown in Table 6, each of the used algorithms have made prediction errors. For instance decision tree's estimate accuracy was 92% which can be explained by its adequacy to understand every little piece of data knowledge, but can still make decision based on some weakly understood rules, which proves its 60% of validation accuracy. On the other hand, logistic regression and discriminant analysis have medium estimate accuracy, but can still prove to be a good data understanding which can be noticed in validation accuracy, none of them lost as much accuracy as decision tree between estimate and validation accuracies.

Decision trees, logistic regression and discriminant analysis are the mostly used to help decision making over Alzheimer's disease diagnosis based on multiple data sets.

According to the results of the three models shown on the right side of Tables 3, 4 and 5, the decision tree model had an accuracy of 60%, 70% for the logistic regression model and 66% for the discriminant analysis model. These results are based on OASIS data set using its specific variables, which can lead us to say that comparison with other works can just be made using the same data sets.

Related to these results, OASIS data set was used as a first training data set to validate the classification models. Trying to homogenize AD data sets from multiple databases will surely be important to move forward to the next AD diagnosis researches stages. Discussion will show more about results and its combinations.

4.3 Discussion

Now that the three classification models have been constructed as a result of Data Mining algorithms, we can use them to predict to which class goes a new

Table 7. Results of the prediction models applied on the validation sample

P.ID	DT PRED	LR PRED	DA PRED	CDR	GROUP
234	0	0	0	0	T1
236	0	0	0	0	T1
240	0	0	0	0	T1
244	0	0	0	0	T1
245	0	0	0	0	T1
248	0	0	0	0	T1
252	0	0	0	0	T1
253	0	0	0	0	T1
257	0	0	0	0	T1
262	0	0	0	0	T1
265	0	0	0	0	T1
271	0	0	0	0	T1
275	0	0	0	0	T1
242	1	0.5	1	1	T2
243	0.5	0.5	1	1	T2
246	0.5	0.5	0	0.5	T2
247	0.5	0.5	1	0.5	T2
259	1	0.5	1	0.5	T2
260	1	0.5	1	0.5	T2
261	0.5	0.5	1	0.5	T2
263	0	0.5	0.5	0.5	T2
264	0.5	0.5	1	1	T2
266	0	0.5	0	0	T2
270	1	0.5	0.5	0.5	T2
273	1	0	0	0	T2
237	0	0	0	0.5	F
241	0	0	0	0.5	F
251	0.5	0.5	0.5	1	F
272	0	0	0	0.5	F
276	0	0	0	0.5	F

patient based on his clinical data. In order to discuss the models performance and powerfulness, Table 7 shows the 30 validation subjects whose CDR rate have been predicted using decision tree, logistic regression and discriminant analysis models applied on their clinical information.

After showing prediction results made by the three Data Mining algorithms, Fig. 2 will describe those results using percentages of the correctly and the badly predicted subjects of the validation sample.

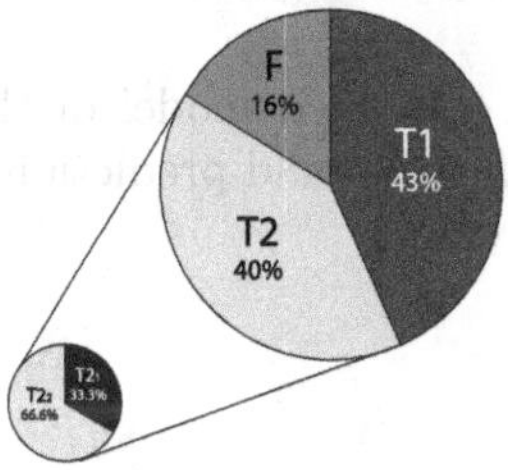

Fig. 2. Comparison of prediction groups

By analyzing the fault column in Table 7, we can notice first some subjects with a "T1" were correctly predicted by all of the three algorithms, also shown in Fig. 2 as a percentage of 43%, but we can see that all of them were diagnosed healthy subjects, which can lead us to conclude that healthy subjects can be easy to predict.

The other group of patients with a "T2" were predicted by one or two algorithms out of the three, we can say that those patients have shown some prediction difficulties. As shown in Fig. 2, "$T2_1$" and "$T2_2$" are respectively the subgroups of "T2" having correctly predicted subjects with one and two algorithms.

Patients with an "F" in the group column were not correctly predicted by any algorithm, that is what leads us to say that in humans data analysis, there can always be wrong understanding related to unique properties of a particular patient.

However, it can be difficult to assess the predictions of an algorithm compared to the others, so in order to correct a wrong data understanding, we need to combine the knowledge acquired by all of the three algorithms to create an homogenous model which can in some cases correct bad predictions, and in other cases report them to the administrator of the solution, so they can be treated by a specialist doctor and then they can be included in the learning base of the model. Since AD can be diagnosed using other data types like MRI data, which have a good correlation with AD diagnosis, we will try to treat them using Machine Learning algorithms and combine their results with those of the three Data Mining algorithms.

5 Conclusion

In this paper, we presented a new approach for Alzheimer's disease classification using some Data Mining algorithms. To our knowledge, Data Mining algorithms have not been used in the past to classify Alzheimer's patients. We construct three models based respectively on decision tree, logistic regression and discriminant analysis algorithms, which gave us some representative accuracies.

Finally, after the models were constructed, we applied them to the validation sample which gave us some prediction groups between those correctly predicted and those badly predicted.

We think that creating a combined model of the three used algorithms is the best way to gain on classification and prediction accuracy, and to guarantee good results for most patient cases.

References

1. Al-Naami, B., Gharaibeh, N., Kheshman, A.A.: Automated detection of Alzheimer disease using region growing technique and artificial neural network. In: Proceedings of World Academy of Science, Engineering and Technology. World Academy of Science, Engineering and Technology (WASET), p. 12 (2013)
2. Atkins, M.S., Mackiewich, B.T.: Fully automatic segmentation of the brain in MRI. IEEE Trans. Med. Imaging **17**(1), 98–107 (1998)
3. Boada, M., Trraga, L., Hernandez, I., Valero, S., Alegret, M., Ruiz, A., Lopez, O.L., Becker, J.T., Fundació ACE Alzheimer Research Center, Memory Clinic: Design of a comprehensive Alzheimers disease clinic and research center in Spain to meet critical patient and family needs. Alzheimer's Dementia **10**(3), 409–415 (2014)
4. Colliot, O., Chtelat, G., Chupin, M., Desgranges, B., Magnin, B., Benali, H., Dubois, B., Garnero, L., Eustache, F., Lehricy, S.: Discrimination between Alzheimer disease, mild cognitive impairment, and normal aging by using automated segmentation of the hippocampus 1. Radiology **248**(1), 194–201 (2008)
5. Dana, A.D., Alashqur, A.: Using decision tree classification to assist in the prediction of Alzheimer's disease. In: 2014 6th International Conference on Computer Science and Information Technology (CSIT), pp. 122–126. IEEE (2014)
6. Harper, P.R.: A review and comparison of classification algorithms for medical decision making. Health Policy **71**(3), 315–331 (2005)
7. Jain, D., Singh, V.: Utilization of data mining classification approach for disease prediction: a survey (2016)
8. Marcus, D.S., Wang, T.H., Parker, J., Csernansky, J.G., Morris, J.C., Buckner, R.L.: Open access series of imaging studies (OASIS): cross-sectional MRI data in young, middle aged, nondemented, and demented older adults. J. Cogn. Neurosci. **19**(9), 1498–1507 (2007)
9. Maroco, J., Silva, D., Rodrigues, A., Guerreiro, M., Santana, I., de Mendona, A.: Data mining methods in the prediction of dementia: a real-data comparison of the accuracy, sensitivity and specificity of linear discriminant analysis, logistic regression, neural networks, support vector machines, classification trees and random forests. BMC Res. Notes **4**(1), 299 (2011)
10. Matoug, S., Abdel-Dayem, A.: Clustering-based detection of Alzheimer's disease using brain MR images. World Acad. Sci. Eng. Technol. Int. J. Comput. Electr. Autom. Control Inf. Eng. **10**(5), 875–880 (2016)
11. Payan, A., Montana, G.: Predicting Alzheimer's disease: a neuroimaging study with 3D convolutional neural networks (2015). arxiv preprint arXiv:1502.02506

12. Tufail, A.B., Abidi, A., Siddiqui, A.M., Younis, M.S.: Automatic classification of initial categories of Alzheimer's disease from structural MRI phase images: a comparison of PSVM, KNN and ANN methods. In: Proceedings of World Academy of Science, Engineering and Technology, World Academy of Science, Engineering and Technology (WASET), p. 1731 (2012)
13. Tuffery, S., Riesco, R.: Data Mining and Statistics for Decision Making. Wiley, Hoboken (2011)

Image Search Engine Based on Color Histogram and Zernike Moment

Nawal Chifa[1(✉)], Abdelmajid Badri[1], Yassine Ruichek[2], and Aicha Sahel[1]

[1] EEA&TI Laboratory, Faculty of Sciences and Techniques (FSTM) Mohammedia, Hassan II University of Casablanca, Casablanca, Morocco
NAWAL.CHIFA-ETU@etude.univcasa.ma
[2] IRIES-SET-UTBM, 90010 Belfort Cedex, France

Abstract. Though numerous approaches were proposed for image recognition, in this paper we proposed implementation of CBIR, using color descriptor combined to the shape features (Zernike moments). A practical and efficient system has been implemented based on image division and extraction color histogram of color from each block, and combined the result vector to the global shape one. We experimented our system on several image bases, and it gave satisfactory results.

Keywords: CBIR · HSV histogram · Zernike moments · Image block

1 Introduction

The world we live in is becoming inherently inter-connected and digital. In addition, the use of digital cameras increased dramatically and thereby the amount of digital images. Private image collections, or images on the Internet might be the most obvious example, but the use of digital imaging has spread too many application areas.

The wealth of visual information available on the web or in professional field induced a major problem for the end users: how to find the visual information needed.

Traditional search engines were built with the assumption that the media in general and in the web was mainly composed of text or its content can be described by a set of keywords associated to it. The framework of keyword-based image retrieval is no longer appropriate to handle such rich media because it suffers from the no fixed set of words that describe the content of images, To overcome these difficulties, query by visual content been proposed as an alternative to text-based retrieval [1].

The visual image search systems called CBIR are based on extracting features using the content of digital images to produce descriptor vectors, which represent important details of an image. The feature vectors of the images in database will be compared with the query one using similarity measurements. A great similarity between these vectors corresponds to a high probability of resemblance.

The performance of image retrieval systems depends to a much of the choice of descriptors and technical employees to extract them. In the literature, there are several types of descriptors. We distinguish two kinds, the global [2], such as color histogram [3, 4],

E. Sabir et al. (Eds.): UNet 2017, LNCS 10542, pp. 632–640, 2017.
https://doi.org/10.1007/978-3-319-68179-5_55

Hu Moments [5], Zernike Moment [6], texture co-occurrence [7], the local binary pattern (LBP) [8] and so on.

However, these features tend to lose the spatial correlation among pixels. To overcome the problem, many researchers proposed the local features who focus mainly on key points [6], the most popular ones: SIFT [9], SURF [10], HOG [11].

Color, texture and shape information have been the substantial features of an image in content based image retrieval, these global descriptors describe the whole image. They are generally not very robust as a change in part of the image may cause it to fail, as it will affect the resulting descriptor. In our work, we have used general bases of image, and we looking for the similarity of the whole image and note only for objects, for that we have opted for the global features, histogram color, because we have colored image, and the shape descriptor.

The color histogram does not take into account the local distribution of the colors at the level of the image. To overcome this problem, we propose our method, that divide the image into block and extracting the histogram color from each block, and then concatenate all the vectors to one descriptor.

Moreover, for more precision, we add to the result vector, the feature of Zernike moment who give is a stable feature and it can easily distinguish the objects, which are in the same category.

We introduce a method to divide image to block, in the next section, we expose our method of extraction, in the Sect. 3, we present our simulation in different bases and in Sect. 4, and we compare our result.

2 Techniques and Methods Used

In the presented method, the images were taken from the database one after another for extracting the features of the images to form feature vectors and stored these feature vectors in the feature database.

As described before, we use the color histogram because is the most basic aspect of an image to describe, and arguably the most computationally simple and because is relatively invariant to changes in image size and orientation. However, the color histogram do not consider any spatial distribution of the colors in an image [12].

To overcome this problem we proposed dividing image into block and extraction histogram color from each blocks and concatenate them. The result vector give us local distribution of color in every image.

And for shape information, we extract the Zernike moment and concatenate it to the color vector (Fig. 2).

Suitable distance measurement was used for similarity matching between the query image and database images on the bases of the computed feature vectors. In this paper, we have considered the Euclidean distance as similarity measurements [13].

2.1 Extraction of Histogram Color

In our system, the database images are color images. Algorithms calculate histograms colors are easy to implement with a very short turnaround time, introducing invariance to rotation and translation. However, these histograms have no spatial information on the colors of the positions [14]. To overcome this problem we used an image division method for extracting aggregate information partially and collect them later in the same order [2] (left to right ant top to down) Fig. 1 to have local feature color for the whole image. And we have use the HSV space who can be clearly defined by human perception, which is not always the case with RGB or CMYK.

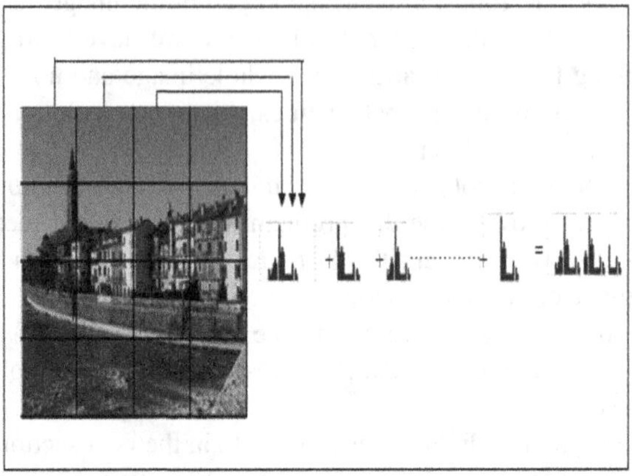

Fig. 1. Division image to block and extract HSV histogram from each block, and concatenate all of them.

$$V = \max(R, G, B)$$

$$S = \begin{cases} \frac{V - m(R,G,B)}{V} & \text{if } V \# 0 \\ 0 & \text{otherwise} \end{cases}$$

$$H = \begin{cases} 60(G - B)/(V - \min(R, G, B)) & \text{if } V = R \\ 120 + 60(B - R)/(V - \min(R, G, B)) & \text{if } V = G \\ 240 + 60(R - G)/(V - \min(R, G, B)) & \text{if } V = B \end{cases}$$

2.2 Zernike Moments

Zernike moments were frequently used to capture the overall characteristics of an image in recognition and image analysis. Introduced for the first time in computer vision by Teague [15], this shape descriptor proved its superiority over the others Functions of moments due to its capacity of description and its robustness to noise and deformations. Very recently, many researchers have studied these moments, mainly to optimize their calculation time and improve their accuracy [16].

The magnitudes of the Zernike moments are independent of the rotation of the object, which is an extremely nice property when working with shape descriptors [17].

The Zernike moments were based on orthogonal functions defined on the unit disc: the polynomials of Zernike.

Mathematically, the moments of Zernike defined with an Order p and a repetition q on $D = \{(p, q) \mid 0 \leq p \leq \infty, |q| \leq p, |p - q| \text{ peer}\}$:

$$Z_{pq} = \frac{p+1}{\pi} \iint_{2+y^2} V * p(x,y) f(x,y) d \tag{1}$$

And V^*_{pq} Denotes the complex conjugate of V_{pq}:

$$V_{pq}(\rho, \theta) = R \quad (\rho) * e^{i} \tag{2}$$

From Eqs. (1) and (2), we can express The Zernike moments of an image turned from an angle α around its origin in polar coordinates:

$$Z_{\alpha pq} = Z_{pq} e_{iq\alpha} \tag{3}$$

3 Our System Implementation

As indicated above, we will prepare our database of descriptor, we divide our image in block, and then we extract from each block our color histogram. We obtain our local histogram color, which we combine to the Zernike moents. The same procedure is applied to extract the descriptor vector from the query image, and the query vector will be compared to those of the base using Euclidean distance, Fig. 2 illustrates our approach.

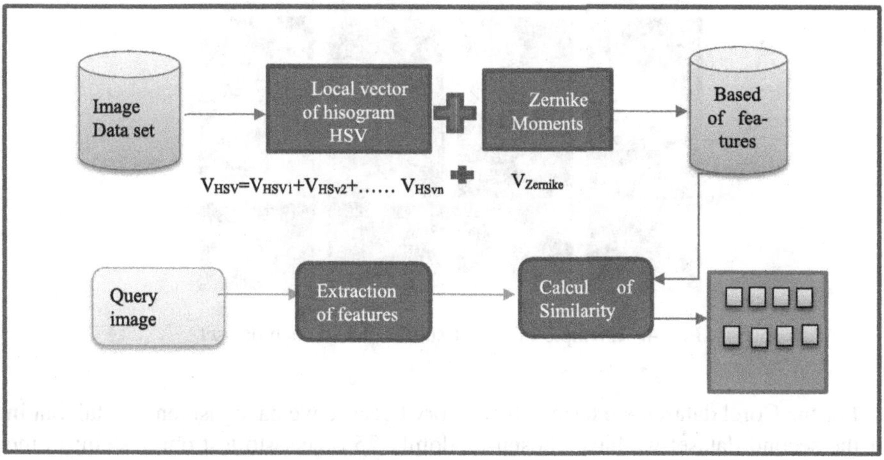

Fig. 2. Architecture of our image search system.

In our study, we used Corel image databases; of nature scenes classified according to several themes, the sample images are displayed in Fig. 3: The Simplicity dataset is a subset of COREL image dataset. It contains 1000 images, which are equally divided into 10 different categories, the image are with the size of 256 * 384 or 384 * 256.

Fig. 3. The simplicity dataset is a subset of COREL

And for more experimentation we tested our algorithm to another image base, the Ukbench dataset (Fig. 4), the set consists of 10200 groups of 2550 objects, each object has 4 images of different viewpoints, and all the image are 640 × 480.

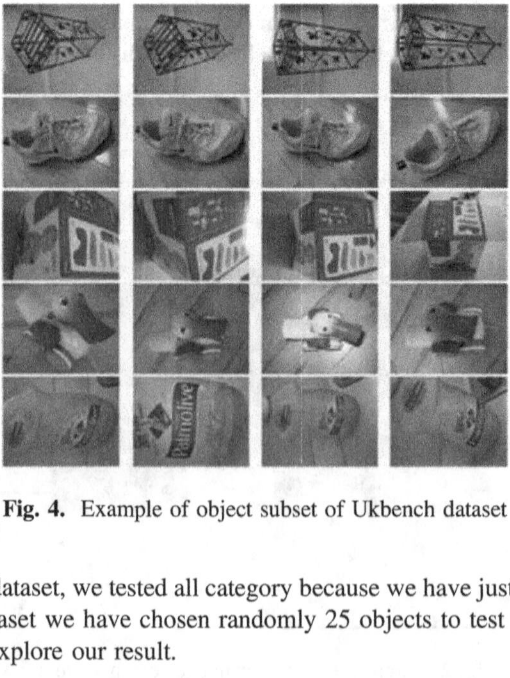

Fig. 4. Example of object subset of Ukbench dataset

For the Corel dataset, we tested all category because we have just ten in total, but in for the second dataset we have chosen randomly 25 objects to test our system; in the next section, we explore our result.

4 The Experimental Result

To evaluate our methods described above, we have set up an image search system that extracts the visual signatures of each image of the database as a vector of digital values and stores it in a data file. The signature of the query image will be compared later to those stored in the file according to the Euclidean distance, and return images with zero minimum distance to see the query image. To measure the quality of our system search, parameters precision and recall are conventionally used [18]. We define Ai as set of all relevant image results for a given query and Bi represents all the images result returned by the system. The precision is define as percentage of retrieved images belonging to the same category as the query image [19]:

$$\text{Pi} = \frac{A \cap B}{B}$$

Our system is designed to return 16 pictures following a query image; for each query we calculate the average retrieval precision (ARP):

$$\text{ARP} = \frac{1}{N} \sum\nolimits_{i=1}^{N} P$$

where N is the size of testing category in dataset.

In this experiment, our proposed method is compare with other image retrieval approaches reported in the literature [18, 20, 21] on the Corel-1000 dataset. To evaluate the performance of our method, we chose randomly ten images from every class (100 image in global) and very image is turned as query and then the precision rate is computed among all the query images under the number of retrieved image is 16. The average precision of each category using our method and the other approaches are shown in Table 1.

Table 1. Comparison of different image retrieval approach on Corel-1000

Class	Subrm [18]	Irtaza [19]	Elalami [18]	Chifa [17]	Our method
Africa	69.57	65.00	72.60	77.77	92
Beaches	54.25	60.00	59.30	63.50	65.2
Building	63.95	62.00	58.7	58.12	65.4
Bus	89.65	85.00	89.10	70.62	84
Dinosaur	98.7	93.00	99.30	100	100
Elephant	48.8	65.00	70.2	74.30	66.66
Flower	92.3	94.00	92.8	98.32	97.6
Horses	89.45	77.00	85.6	100	100
Mountain	4.30	73.00	56.20	53.75	60.2
Food	70.90	81.00	77.20	82.95	71.1
Total ARP	72.51	75.00	76.10	77.93	80.2

As we can say, our method gives better results compared to those already found, may not be on all categories but in overall value ca remains very satisfactory as result. Figure 5 give same example.

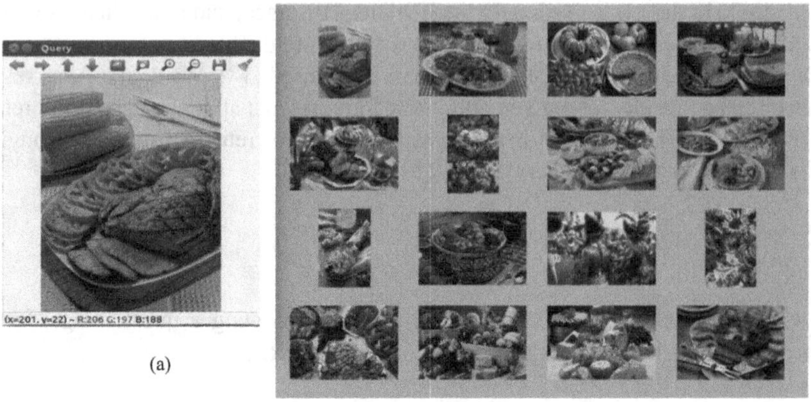

(a)

(b)

Fig. 5. Preview of some similar results of same query image (a) food, (b) bus

We have tested our research system to the Ukbench dataset. Then we quantified the results by choosing the random objects of the database, and we calculate the precision for the 25 tested objects. The total average obtained was 73.6%. Figure 6 give same example of simulation: at first (a), we have used just the descriptor color, and the second (b) after adding the Zernike features.

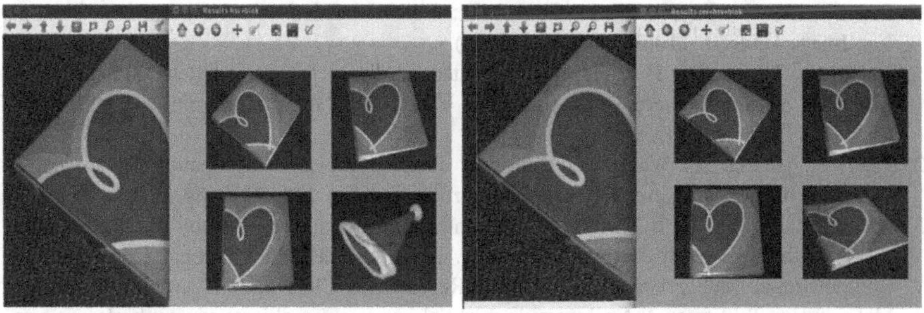

Fig. 6. Different result for the same request, the (a) with block color, and (b) with combined block color and Zernike moment

5 Conclusion and Perspectives

We have proposed a novel method for image retrieval using combination of color, and shape features. Division the image of block has allowed us to overcome the problem of semantic distribution of colors in the image, and the combination of the Zernike moments provided us with more precision.

The effectiveness of a descriptor depends largely on the type of data and their heterogeneity, and in our two dataset of image we obtained successful result that we can improve by adding another type of descriptor like the texture one.

References

1. Kabbai, L., Abdellaoui, M.: Content based image retrieval using local and global features descriptor. In: 2nd International Conference on Advanced Technologies for Signal and Image Processing - Tunisia ATSIP'2016, 21–24 March 2016 (2016)
2. Chifa, N., Badri, A., Ruichek, Y.: Powerful combination of color descriptor and LBP descriptor for image retrieval. Int. J. Comput. Appl. Technol. Res. **5**(4), 210–214 (2016)
3. Swain, M.J., Ballard, D.H.: Color indexing. Int. J. Comput. Vis. **7**(1), 11–32 (1991)
4. Stricker, M.A., Orengo, M.: Similarity of color image. In: Proceedings of Storage and Retrieval for Image and Video Databases, pp. 381–392 (1995)
5. Hu, M.K.: Visual pattern recognition by moment's invariants. IRE Trans. Inf. Theory **8**, 179–187 (1962)
6. Khotanzad, A., Hong, Y.H.: Invariant image recognition by Zernike moments. IEEE Trans. Pattern Anal. Mach. Intell. **12**, 489–497 (1990)
7. Ojala, T., Pietikainen, M., Harwood, D.: A comparative study of texture measures with classification based on feature distribution. Pattern Recogn. **29**, 51–59 (1996)
8. Lowe, D.G.: Distinctive image features from scale-invariant keypoints. Int. J. Comput. Vis. **60**(2), 91–110 (2004)
9. Ke, Y., Sukthankar, R.: PCA-SIFT: a more distinctive representation for local image descriptors. In: Proceedings of IEEE Conference on Computer Vision and Pattern Recognition, vol. 2, pp. 506–513 (2004)

10. Bay, H., Ess, A., Tuytelaars, T., Gool, L.V.: SURF: speeded up robust features. Comput. Vis. Image Underst. **110**(3), 346–359 (2008)
11. Dalal, N., Triggs, B.: Histograms of oriented gradients for human detection. In: IEEE Computer Society Conference on Computer Vision and Pattern Recognition, CVPR 2005, pp. 886–893. IEEE (2005)
12. Zeng, S., Huang, R., Wang, H., Kang, Z.: Image retrieval using spatiograms of colors quantized by Gaussian mixture models. Neurocomputiong **171**, 673–684 (2016)
13. Shrivastava, S., Gupta, B., Gupta, M.: Optimization of image retrieval by using HSV color space, Zernike moment & DWT technique. In: 2015 IEEE International Conference on Computational Intelligence and Computing Research (ICCIC), pp. 1–5, Madurai (2015)
14. Malisiewicz, T., Efros, A.A.: Improving spatial support for objects via multiple segmentations. In: BMVC (2007)
15. Teague, M.R.: Image analysis via the general theory of moments. J. Opt. Soc. Am. **70**(8), 920–930 (1980)
16. Amayeh, G., Erol, A., Bebis, G., Nicolescu, M.: Accurate and efficient computation of high order Zernike moments. In: Bebis, G., Boyle, R., Koracin, D., Parvin, B. (eds.) ISVC 2005. LNCS, vol. 3804, pp. 462–469. Springer, Heidelberg (2005). doi:10.1007/11595755_56
17. Revaud, J., Lavoué, G., Baskurt, A.: Une nouvelle mesure de distance entre descripteurs de moments de Zernike pour une similarité optimale et un angle de rotation entre les images. In: CORESA, March 2009
18. Subrahmanyam, M., Wu, Q.M.J., Maheshwari, R.P., Balasubramanian, R.: Modified color motif co-occurrence matrix for image indexing and retrieval. Comput. Electr. Eng. **39**, 762–774 (2013)
19. Chifa, N., Badri, A., Ruichek, Y., Sahel, A., Safi, K.: Efficient combination of color, texture and shape descriptor, using SLIC segmentation for image retrieval. In: Lu, H., Li, Y. (eds.) Artificial Intelligence and Computer Vision. SCI, vol. 672, pp. 69–80. Springer, Cham (2017). doi:10.1007/978-3-319-46245-5_5
20. Irtaza, A., Jaffar, M.A., Aleisa, E., Choi, T.S.: Embedding neural networks for semantic association in content based image retrieval. Multimed. Tool Appl. **72**(2), 1911–1931 (2014)
21. ElAlami, M.E.: A new matching strategy for content based image retrieval system. Appl. Soft Comput. **14**, 407–418 (2014)

Risk Assessment and Alert Prioritization for Intrusion Detection Systems

El Mostapha Chakir[1(✉)], Mohamed Moughit[1,2,3], and Youness Idrissi Khamlichi[1,4]

[1] IR2M Laboratory, FST, University Hassan 1, Settat, Morocco
{e.chakir,mohamed.moughit}@uhp.ac.ma
[2] IR2M Laboratory, ENSA, University Hassan 1, Khouribga, Morocco
[3] EEA&TI Laboratory, FST, University Hassan 2, Mohammedia, Morocco
[4] LERS Laboratory, ENSA, University Sidi Mohamed Ben Abdellah, Fes, Morocco
youness.khamlichi@usmba.ac.ma

Abstract. The main objective of an Intrusion Detection System is to analyze system and network activity to detect unauthorized entry and/or malicious activity. IDSs protect a system or network from attack, misuse and compromise. They can also monitor network activity, analyze system and network configurations against vulnerability and more. Having detected abnormal activities, IDSs trigger alerts to report them, these alerts are presented to the security analyst. In practice, IDSs generate a large number of alerts per day, especially false alerts (i.e., false positives). This makes it very difficult for the analyst to correctly identify alerts related to attack. In this paper, we review the existing approaches for Intrusion Risk Assessment and Alert Prioritization and we propose a new model, the objective is to determine the criticality of certain events on the security status of a network. Most existing approaches are limited to manual Risk Assessment, that are not suitable for Real-time use. In this approach, we evaluate the risk of an alert as a composition of certain parameters of each alert, also in this work we evaluate the Risk of Cluster of Alerts (i.e., Meta-Alerts), then we integrate the Risk Assessment model with our last work, thus, we apply the results to prioritize alerts produced by the IDS and generate alarms if Risk is high.

Keywords: Intrusion detection · Risk assessment · Pattern matching · False positive · Priority · Severity · Events · Alerts · Reliability · KDD cup 99

1 Introduction

The main aim of Intrusion Detection Systems is to gather and analyze events from networks and hosts to detect abnormal activity before and after a security breach [1]. They have been around for many years and formed the backbone of any good security practice. But in recent years, it has become apparent that traditional IDSs are not sufficient to deliver a complete security solution. They need to be improved with other security capabilities to achieve effective threat detection and response. Researchers are over stressed trying to stay ahead of the evolving threat landscape, and often do not

E. Sabir et al. (Eds.): UNet 2017, LNCS 10542, pp. 641–655, 2017.
https://doi.org/10.1007/978-3-319-68179-5_56

have the time to analyze thousands of alerts one by one. Organizations need an IDS solution that can prioritize alerts and provide a level of context to each alert. In addition, the Risk Assessment of each alert is another crucial component to augment the effectiveness of the IDS solution. Risk Assessment (RA) is the process of evaluating and characterizing risks of events. Risk assessment helps Security analyst to determine the probability that a detected anomaly is a valid attack that requires attention [4].

In this paper, we classify existing **Risk Assessment** and **Alert Prioritization** approaches, and we propose our own **RA** model based on our latest work using Pattern Matching [29]. The goal is to improve our model with a Real-Time Risk Assessment.

This paper is organized as follows: Sect. 2, introduces key concepts of Intrusion Detection Systems; Sect. 3 presents related works in Intrusion Risk Assessment and Alerts Prioritization; Sect. 4 describe our proposed model to assesses the Risk of alerts and the different layers of processing; Sect. 5 presents the experiments used to test our approach and the corresponding results; Finally, in Sect. 6, we summarize the conclusions derived from this work and indicates possible future works.

2 Intrusion Detection System (IDS)

An intrusion detection system (IDS) is a hardware or a software, typically a designated system, which monitors activities to identify malicious or suspicious events from network and hosts. It is placed inside an organization to monitor what happens within the network of the organization [5]. The goal of an intrusion detection system is to detect security incidents, and generate alerts, then notify network administrators.

IDSs can monitor network traffic **NIDS** or local hosts **HIDS** [7, 8]. An NIDS performs an analysis of all traffic passing through the network and matches the traffic to the library of known attacks, while HIDS monitors individual hosts on the network for malicious activity [10, 11]. The Host-based IDS takes a snapshot of the existing system key files and applications and matches it to the previous snapshot. If the system files are modified, an alert is sent to the administrator to analyze it.

IDSs are divided into two Detection techniques categories: **Signature-Based** and **Anomaly-Based** [12, 13]. Signature-Based detection generates an alert whenever traffic matches a known attack pattern while anomaly detection compares current traffic against normal traffic and generates an alert on the network [14]. An alert does not necessarily mean the IDS find a problem, but just they detect traffic that match a signature or pattern. These alerts are called False positives; by false positives we mean normal events being classified as attacks. An attack may in fact be happening, and the network administrator needs to be able to properly identify it. They need to analyze each IDS alert manually, whether it is a false or a true alert. So, it is a quiet time-consuming process. The optimal way to deal with this problem is to use an IDS solution that has the ability to calculate the Risk of each event, correlate and prioritize alerts. Thereby it can help the network administrator focus the efforts on detecting actual threats. In this paper, we propose a Real-Time Intrusion Risk Assessment to improve our model in [29].

3 Related Work

3.1 Risk Assessment

The results of **Risk Assessment** are very important, in terms of saving time and effort of the network security administrator. Researchers have proposed many approaches [15–17, 25, 30] that use an offline Risk Assessment, which is calculated by evaluating all the resources in advance. An Online Risk Assessment model can help measure intrusion damage. Researchers have suggested many Real-Time Risk Assessment models during the last decade. These approaches can be divided into three main categories: Attack Graph-Based, Service Dependency Graph-Based and Non-Graph-Based:

- **Attack Graph-Based:** This approach helps to identify attacks and analyze their severity on the critical services in the network, based on the attacker's behavior and vulnerabilities that can be exploited [6, 8, 9]. The main aim of attack graph is to show the attack paths in a network based on service vulnerabilities [18, 19] and correlate the events generated by the IDS [20, 21].
- **Service Dependency Graph-Based:** In this approach Three properties are defined for each service: the confidentiality C(S), integrity I(S), and availability A(S) of service (S). The impact of the attack on a service is based on the type of dependency with other services. In this approach, the attack graph is not used to evaluate attack cost [22].
- **Non-graph-Based:** Risk assessment is evaluated independently of the attack detected by the IDS [5]. This means that the IDS detect an attack and sends an alert to the risk assessment model, which performs a risk analysis based on alert statistics and other useful information provided in the alert(s).

In [3], Kanoun et al. presented a Risk Assessment model based on attack graphs to evaluate the severity of the Risk of the supervised system. They use the LAMBDA [23] language to model attack graphs when an attack is detected. The RA model calculates the risk as a combination of two major parameters: Potentiality and Impact, the most interesting point with this model is that the impact parameters are calculated dynamically using the importance of the target assets, and the impact of the level of reduction measures deployed on the system when the attack is successful.

In [17], Wang et al. presented a middleware approach that uses attack graphs and Hidden Markov Models HMM together for evaluating the relation between system observations and states. A set of security metrics cost and defense cost factors was specified in this work for calculating attack and defense cost. Attack impact was measured by denial of service, public embarrassment, confidentiality loss, privilege escalation and integrity loss, while defense cost factors was calculated by installation cost, system downtime, operation cost, training cost, and incompatibility cost.

In [2], Jahnke et al. proposed a graph-based approach for modeling the effects of attacks against the effects of the response measures taken in action to those attacks. The proposed approach extends the work initiated by Toth and Kregel in [21] by showing dependencies between resources, using directed graphs, and by deriving quantitative differences between system states from these graphs.

In [4], Mu et al. proposed a non-graph-based Real-Time Risk Assessment model. Their model is based on D-S evidence theory. This method is used for solving a complex problem where the evidence is uncertain. The proposed model consists of two steps, which are: Risk Index and Risk Distribution. The former consists in calculating the risk index. Five factors are used to calculate this parameter: Number of alerts, Alert Type, Alert Confidence, Alert Severity, and Alert Relevance Score. It has two inputs: the risk index, and the value of the target host. Risk distribution is the real evaluation of risk, and can be low, medium, or high.

Eventually, the most used approaches for online mode are the quantitative approaches based on hard numbers, complex calculations, probability theory and statistics to evaluate the risk and may be difficult for non-technical people to understand [31].

3.2 Alerts Prioritization

IDSs present attacks to a security administrator through alerts. It is common that an IDS generates a large number of alerts. With a large number of alerts, it becomes difficult for security administrator to manually distinguish between the real attacks and the false attacks. Reducing the number of alerts, prioritizing the most critical attacks, and discarding the false alerts are the main objectives of IDS alert management approaches.

Proposed approaches in prioritizing alerts include **Static prioritization**, **Attacks pre-prioritization** and **Post-incident prioritization**. The static prioritization approach tags and tunes signatures and prioritizes known Attacks based on the current characteristics of the Attacks [35]. The Attack pre-prioritization offers a similar approach to the static prioritization but uses additional systematic methods like risk assessments on analyzing potential incidents. In the Attack pre-prioritization, a potential risk for potential Attacks is estimated before any real incidents are detected [36].

In [37] Dondo et al. applied a fuzzy system approach in accessing relative potential risks by associating potential Attacks with computer network assets. Post-Alert prioritization extends the usage of risk assessment and cost-sensitive analysis.

In [32] Porras et al. developed a system called M-Correaltor, which ranked alerts based on the likelihood of success, the importance of target, and attack type interest. Alerts are prioritized based on the degree to which they targeted critical assets, and the amount of interest the user has towards the attack type. Each incident will be ranked using an adoption of Bayesian network. The Bayesian tree is made of three main branches: outcome, relevance, and priority. The outcome branch represents the information provided by the security devices. The priority sub-tree represents both the incident class importance and the severity of the attack. The last branch concerns the compression between the target environment and the vulnerability requirement of the corresponding attack.

In [33], Yu et al. evaluates alerts based on two aspects: alerts that do not correspond to any attack in the vulnerability knowledge base are prioritized for further investigation. The applicability of the attack against the protected network is examined.

In [34] Qin and Lee compute the alert priority based on the severity of the attack and the relevance of the alert to the networks and hosts.

All aforementioned approaches have the ability to prioritize alerts, but they also have limitations, particularly in the technical aspects of the methods adopted in these approaches. For example, existing approaches consider multiple decision factors, but they do not use different weightings based upon the importance of different decision factors Anuar et al. [36].

4 Proposed Model

Processing and correlating alerts generated by IDS is key to an effective security management solution, unfortunately, they generate a high number of alerts and many false positives [24]. Therefore, managing all the alerts generated by these devices overwhelms the security staff of most organizations. To tackle the excess of false positives, we propose a Real-Time Risk Assessment solution based upon three major concepts: (1) **Alert fusion into meta-alerts**: collecting, normalizing and fusing together alerts that are likely to be part of the same attack; (2) **classification of meta-alerts**, (3) **calculate the Risk and prioritize alerts according to the level of Risk**.

Based upon our last work [29], we propose an improvement of handling alerts generated by IDS, we will add other sub-layers in the post-processing unit. The implementation of our model was tested against the KDD Cup 99 Intrusion Detection Evaluation, Snort IDS to analyze binary traffic of KDD Cup 99 [26, 27] and generate alerts, and a stateful pattern matching algorithm using PERL language to design the model. The results indicated that this approach can classify alerts according to several classes [29].

The contribution of this paper is proposing an approach to improve our last work, we propose a Real-Time Risk Assessment System for Intrusion Detection System, we evaluate the risk as a combination of certain parameters of alerts and target hosts, and we apply the results of the Risk Assessment to prioritize and filter alerts produced by the IDS as High Risk, Medium Risk or Low Risk.

4.1 System Description

Our approach encompasses three units for processing stages: Pre-processing unit, Aggregation and Normalization unit and Post-processing unit. Each unit provides a level of abstraction to the following one. Figure 1 shows the three unit.

Preprocessing Unit: In this unit Snort analyze **KDD cup 99** binary Traffic and generate alert files. These alert files are entered in our proposed model as Inputs.

Aggregation and Normalization Unit. In this unit, all information sent and received at one location. Aggregation aimed at unifying alerts in a single format on just one location. Normalization requires a parser familiar with the types and formats of generated alert from Snort after processing them. Then we will need to organize them to labeled alerts. A labeled alert is an alert with its own attack type and where they come from and where they go. The parser used in our approach is Perl using regular expression.

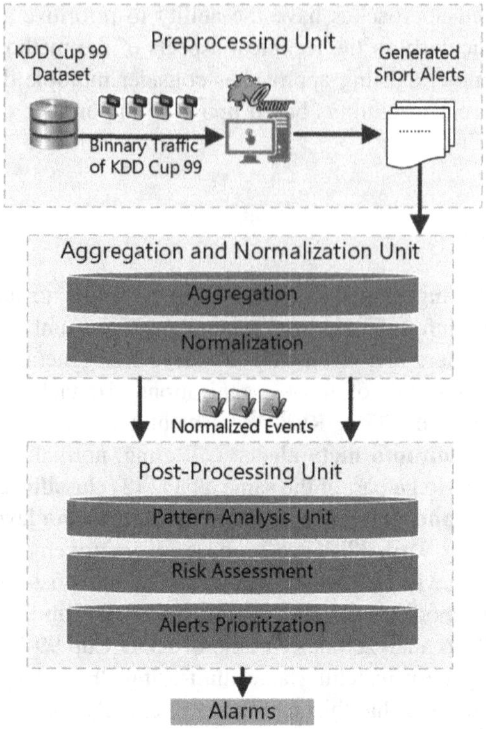

Fig. 1. Architecture of the proposed module

Post-processing Unit: In this unit, once we have all the information in one place, we can implement mechanisms that will improve detection sensitivity and reliability. In our model, we use three Post-Processing methods:

- **Pattern analysis:** In this unit we extract the desired date like: Date, IP source, IP Destination, Attack name … and we store theme into a database. This data extracted by parsing the alert file using Perl and regular expression as we will see in Sect. 5.
- **Risk assessment:** Each alert is evaluated in relation to its attack type, and the target host.
- **Prioritization:** We prioritize alerts received automatically after calculating the Risk.

4.2 Risk Assessment

Several parameters make it possible to qualify the level of dangerousness (Risk) of an alert, these parameters are: Alert Priority, Target device value, Alert Reliability and Alert Severity. It is important to understand their significance in order to be able to manage correctly the alerts according to their level of importance (Table 1). But First, we must differentiate between event, alert and alarm [24]:

Table 1. Description of parameters used to assess the risk of alerts

Parameters	Description
Priority	Priority defines the order in which we should take an action. A classification type rule assigns a default priority that may be overridden with a priority rule [28]. In our model, we categorized priority into three types: **Low = 1; Medium = 2; High = 3** This value is associated with each classification type of snort IDS, and is stored into a MySQL Database
The value of the target Device associated with the alert (V)	This is a value to define the importance of a machine on the network. A DNS or Web server is more valuable resources for an organization than a network printer. As we will see later, these specifications will be taken into account when calculating the risk of each alert. This value must be between *1 and 5* (**1 = machine Less important, 5 = very important machine**). This value is stored into a MySQL Database for each device of the organization
The likelihood that the event will occur (R)	In terms of risk, this parameter could be called "Reliability". This is defined for each independent event; an event may be a set of many alerts. The term reliability can be translated by the reliability that an event is not a *false positive*. The value of this parameter is between **1 and 10 (equivalent to 1% = this is a false positive and 100% = it is not a false positive**). This value is stored into a MySQL Database and it associated with an independent type of event (Alert Classification [28])
The severity level of Alert	Severity level is defined as the degree of impact of an attack, it is associated with each generated alert (Classification Type) to help us to know the threat represented by the event, Severity are categorized into four types: **Critical = 4; Major = 3; Moderate = 2; Minor = 1**

- An **event** presents a low-level entity that is analyzed by the Snort IDS.
- An **alert** is generated by the IDS after analyzing event to notify security administrator. A single event can cause many alerts especially in a networked IDS environment, and a single alert can describe a set or sequence of events.
- An **alarm** is the user interface mechanism by which a user can manages an alert.

As described in Table 1, several parameters used to calculate the Risk, each parameter has a value, for the Alert Priority, Alert Reliability and Alert Severity, these values are stored in a MySQL database. For Target Device Value, the security administrator must add all the organization's devices, including Servers, Firewalls, Switches, Access Points, Network Printers …, and must assign to each equipment a value between 1 and 5 according to the value and the criticality of the device. On the other hand, the other parameters are related to each type or classification of attack by SNORT [28], we store these values in a MySQL database to using them later.

We calculate The Risk using the previous parameters by the following formula (4.8):

$$\textbf{Alert Priority (P)} = [\mathbf{1-3}] \quad (4.1)$$

$$\textbf{Device Value (V)} = [\mathbf{1-5}] \quad (4.2)$$

$$\textbf{Alert Reliability (R)} = [\mathbf{1-10}] \quad (4.3)$$

$$\textbf{Alert Severity (R)} = [\mathbf{1-4}] \quad (4.4)$$

$$\textbf{Risk Assessment(RA)} = \frac{\mathbf{(P)*(V)*(R)*}(S)}{\mathbf{X}} * \mathbf{10} \quad (4.5)$$

The Risk Assessment RA must not exceed 100%, so to calculate X, we use the maximum value for each parameter, the result of RA should be a 100%.

MAX (P) = 3; MAX (V) = 5; MAX (R) = 10; MAX (S) = 4; MAX (RA) = 100

$$\mathbf{RA} = \frac{\mathbf{MAX(P)*MAX(V)*MAX(R)*MAX(S)}}{\mathbf{X}} * \mathbf{10} = \mathbf{100} \quad (4.6)$$

$$\mathbf{X} = \frac{\mathbf{3*5*10*4}}{\mathbf{100}} * \mathbf{10} = \mathbf{60} \quad (4.7)$$

$$\textbf{Risk Assessment(RA)} = \frac{\mathbf{(P)*(V)*(R)*(S)}}{\mathbf{60}} * \mathbf{10} \quad (4.8)$$

Using the Risk Assessment, the Overall Risk of an attack can be calculated according to the alert rate, the Alert Rate is calculated using formula (4.9) [29], the **Overall Risk Assessment ORA** is used to evaluate the Risk of an attack in a Meta-Alerts. Meta-Alerts can be generated for the clusters that contain all the relevant information whereas the amount of data (i.e., alerts) can be reduced substantially, for example all alerts to a specific host with the same attack type, or all alerts from the same source to the same destination and with the same attack type…; thus, the ORA is calculated using formula (4.10).

$$\mathbf{AR} = \frac{\textbf{Number of Alerts by Attack}}{\textbf{Tolal Alerts}} * \mathbf{100\%} \quad (4.9)$$

$$\mathbf{ORA} = \frac{\mathbf{Risk\ Assessment\ (RA) * Alert\ Rate\ (AR)}}{\mathbf{100}} \tag{4.10}$$

The resulting value can be mapped to the following Risk Categories, Table 2:

Table 2. Risk Assessment Categories

Risk value	Signification
[0%–30%]	Low
[40%–60%]	Medium
[70%–100%]	High

Alerts will be automatically prioritized according to their Risk level, if the Risk level is High, the alert will be displayed first, also an alarm is generated to notify the security administrator that there is an attack that aims to compromise the network security, otherwise if the risk is medium, the alert will be displayed below, the rest of the alerts with low risk level will be overlooked as they present false positives, and present no problem to the network security. Thus, the security administrator will see just the alerts that presents a real threat with high Risk, and with this we can reduce the number of false positives.

4.3 Proposed Algorithm

The Algorithm can be explained as follows:

Input: Snort Log File, a sequence of alerts
Output: The complete set of the classified alerts
Step 1: Initializes the program
Step 2: Processes the configuration and data files
Step 3: Begins the main loop and reads the first alert data file
Step 4: Extracts and records details of each alert, these details are: Signature ID, At tack Name, Attack classification, Priority, Source IP, Destination IP, Source Port, Destination Port, and Protocol.
Step 5: Correlate and classify alerts into many types.
Step 6: Calculate the Risk using of each single alert (4.8)
Step 7: Calculate the Overall Risk Assessment ORA of Meta-Alerts using (4.10)
Step 8: Prioritize Alerts according to the Risk Assessment
Step 9: Generate alarms if the Risk ≥ 70 %

A basic flowchart diagram for the proposed algorithm is shown below (Fig. 2):

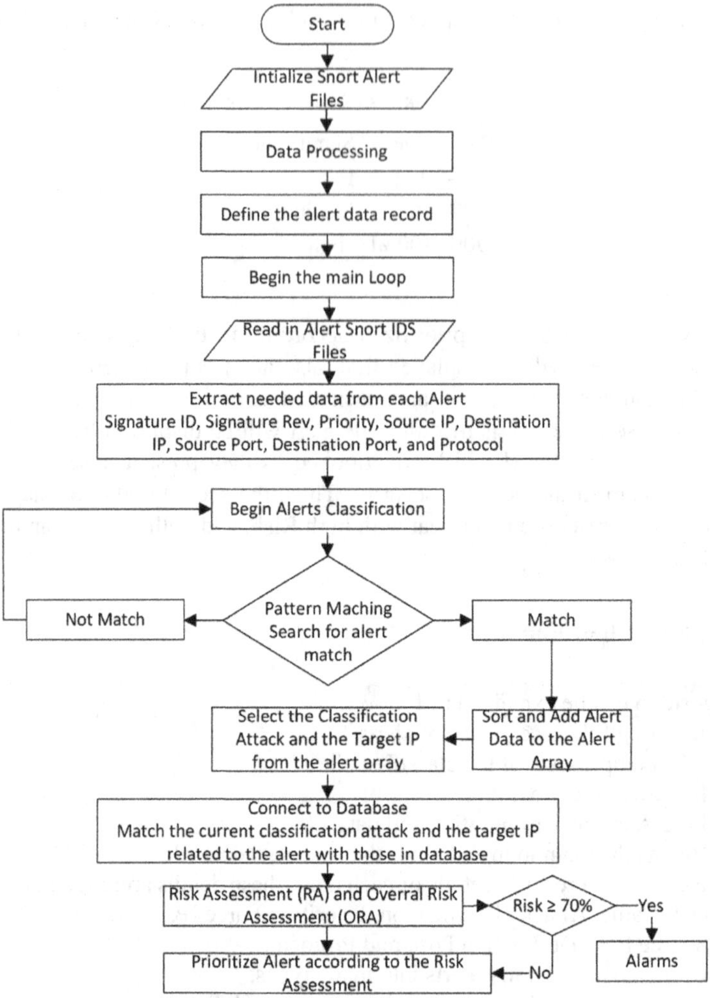

Fig. 2. Flowchart of the proposed approach

5 Experimental Results

This section evaluates the effectiveness of our proposed model. We have used the KDD 99 dataset as well as the Snort to scan the binary traffic of the dataset. Alerts generated by Snort were analyzed by our model based Pattern Matching proposed in [29] and stored into multiple files. To examine each alert, we wrote a Perl program that parse the alert files and extracts specific parameters. We have chosen Perl Language because it's a very speedy one for the text processing using regular expression. Finally, we use the formula (4.8) to assess the Risk of each alert and (4.10) to evaluate the Overall Risk.

An example of alert to deal:

```
[**] [1:2008581:3] ET P2P BitTorrent DHT ping request [**]
[Classification: Potential Corporate Privacy Violation] [Priority: 3] 03/04-
14:41:19.314918 213.159.36.182:17613 -> 172.16.114.50:161 UDP TTL:128 TOS:0x0
ID:15417 IpLen:20 DgmLen:131 Len: 103 [Xref => http://doc.emerg-
ingthreats.net/bin/view/Main/2008581]
```

The Associated Pattern Matching rule:

```
^(?P<delimeter1>\[\*\*\])\s(?P<SigID_Rev>\[[0-9:]+\])\s(?P<At-
tack_Name>[^\"]+)\s+(?P<delimeter2>\[\*\*\])\s\[Classification\:(?P<At-
tack_Class>[^\]]*)\]\s\[Priority\:(?P<Attack_Prior-
ity>[^\]]*)\]\s+(?P<Date>\d+\/\d+\-
\d+\:\d+\:\d+)\.\d+\s(?P<SrcIP>\d{1,3}\.\d{1,3}\.\d{1,3}\.\d{1,3})\:(?P<SrcPORT>\d
+)\s\->\s(?P<DstIP>\d{1,3}\.\d{1,3}\.\d{1,3}\.\d{1,3})\:(?P<DstPORT>\d+)\s(?P<Pro-
tocol>\w+)\s+[^\]]*.*$
```

Extracting Data to variables:

```
Attack_Name={$Attack_Name}
Attack_Class={$Attack_Class}
Attack_Priority={$Attack_Priority}
SrcIP={$SrcIP}
DstIP={$DstIP}
DstPORT ={$DstPORT}
Protocol={$Protocol}
```

In our example the extracted values are:

```
Attack Name = ET P2P BitTorrent DHT ping request
Attack Class = Potential Corporate Privacy Violation
Attack Priority = 3
SrcIP = 213.159.36.182
DstIP = 172.16.114.50
DstPORT=161
Protocol= UDP
```

We store these variables into a MySQL Database, thereby we can calculate the Risk for each generated Alert using these parameters and the formula (4.8), after that, using (4.10) we estimate the ORA. The example bellow shows how our approach works (Fig. 3):

Table 3 presents our experiment results using the output of Snort IDS and KDD cup 99 Dataset (with 52920 Alerts) that contains different 19 attempted attacks, 533 Source IP, 389 Destination IP. Knowing that our platform for the experiment are described as follows:

- Processor: Intel (R) Core (TM) i7-6500U CPU @ 2.50GHZ 2.59 GHZ,
- Memory: 4 GB
- System (OS): Linux Ubuntu Server 16.04 64-bit

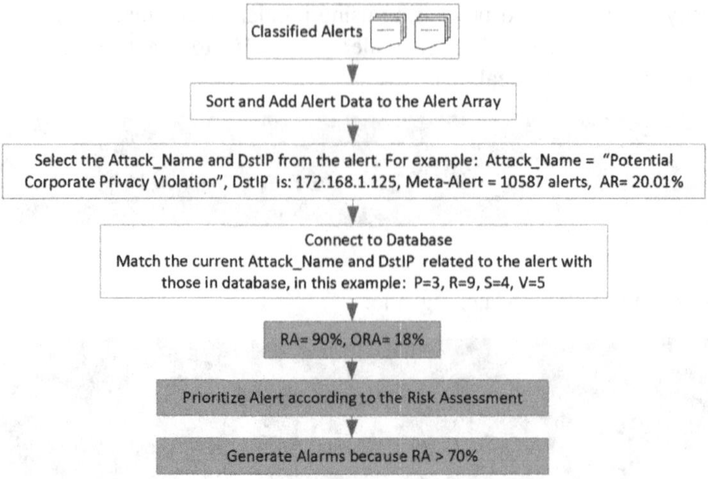

Fig. 3. An example how our approach works

Table 3. Risk Assessment according to the alert and target host parameters

N° events (meta-alert)	To target	Attack name	Class-type	AR %	RA %	ORA %	Ranking
23753	172.16.114.50	(spp_ssh) Protocol mismatch (128:4:1)	Detection of a non-standard protocol or event	44.8	80	35.91	High
10587	172.16.112.50	(spp_ssh) Protocol mismatch (128:4:1)		20.1	64	12.80	Medium
3663	192.168.177.69	(spp_ssh) Protocol mismatch (128:4:1)		6.92	80	5.54	High
332	172.16.117.103	(http_inspect) NO CONTENT-LENGTH OR TRANSFER-ENCODING IN HTTP RESPONSE (120:3:1)	Unknown traffic	0.63	0.33	0.00	Low
322	172.16.112.207	(http_inspect) NO CONTENT-LENGTH OR TRANSFER-ENCODING IN HTTP RESPONSE (120:3:1)		0.61	0.66	0.00	Low
109	192.168.43.182	Consecutive TCP small segments exceeding threshold (129:12:1)	Type potentially bad traffic	0.21	24	0.05	Low

In this table, we take just 6 examples from all results. The results show that the most attacked hosts that present a real threat to the organization with a high-level Risk are 172.16.114.50, 192.168.177.69 and 192.168.112.50.

6 Conclusion and Future Work

In this paper, we reviewed the existing approaches used for Intrusion Risk Assessment and alert prioritization, and we presented a method that evaluates IDS alerts and Meta-alerts using a new Risk Assessment model based on several parameters extracted from alerts to calculate the Risk and qualify the level of dangerousness of each attack, thereby prioritizing alerts generated by IDS and save time and effort for the network security administrator.

This model is presented to improve our last work. We used a Pattern Matching algorithm in order to classify, calculate the Risk and prioritize alerts, we applied our approach to the alerts generated by scanning the binary traffic of KDD Cup 99 dataset using Snort NIDS, and we successfully prioritized the most critical alerts. The experimental results have shown that the proposed model is effective to assess and quantify the risk of attacks and prioritize alerts by their criticality. The next step of this work is to improve this model by using alerts from different IDS. The objective is to adapt our Perl parsers to extract data from several other IDS products not just Snort.

References

1. Zhou, C.V., Leckie, C., Karunasekera, S.: A survey of coordinated attacks and collaborative intrusion detection. Comput. Secur. **29**(1), 124–140 (2010)
2. Jahnke, M., Thul, C., Martini, P.: Graph-based metrics for intrusion response measures in computer networks. In: Proceedings of the 3rd LCN Workshop on Network Security. Held in conjunction with the 32nd IEEE Conference on Local Computer Networks (LCN), Dublin, Ireland, pp. 1035–1042 (2007)
3. Kanoun, W., Cuppens-Boulahia, N., Cuppens, F., Araujo, J.: Automated reaction based on risk analysis and attacker's skills in intrusion detection systems. In: Third International Conference on Risks and Security of Internet and Systems, pp. 117–124 (2008)
4. Mu, C.P., Li, X.J., Huang, H.K., Tian, S.F.: Online risk assessment of intrusion scenarios using D-S evidence theory. In: Proceedings of the 13th European Symposium on Research in Computer Security, Malaga, Spain, pp. 35–48 (2008)
5. Gehani, A., Kedem, G.: Rheostat: real-time risk management. In: 7th International Symposium on Recent Advances in Intrusion Detection, (RAID 2004), France, pp. 296–314 (2004)
6. Scarfone, K., Mell, P.: Guide to intrusion detection and prevention systems. Technical report, NIST: National Institute of Standards and Technology, U.S. Department of Commerce (2007)
7. Lee, S., Chung, B., Kim, H., Lee, Y., Park, C., Yoon, H.: Real-time analysis of intrusion detection alerts via correlation. Comput. Secur. **25**(3), 169–183 (2006)
8. Anuar, N.B., Sallehudin, H., Gani, A., Zakaria, O.: Identifying false alarm for network intrusion detection system using hybrid data mining and decision tree. Malays. J. Comput. Sci., 110–115 (2008). ISSN 0127-9084
9. Lazarevic, A., Ertz, L., Kumar, V., Ozgur, A., Srivastava, J.: A comparative study of anomaly detection schemes in network intrusion detection. In: Proceedings of the Third SIAM International Conference on Data Mining (2003)
10. Xiao, F., Jin, S., Li, X.: A novel data mining-based method for alert reduction and analysis. J. Netw. **5**(1), 88–97 (2010)

11. Adetunmbi, A.O., Falaki, S.O., Adewale, O.S., Alese, B.K.: Network intrusion detection based on rough set and k-nearest neighbour. Int. J. Comput. ICT Res. **2**(1), 60–66 (2008)
12. Han, J., Kamber, M.: Data Mining: Concepts and Techniques, 2nd edn. Elsevier, San Francisco (2006)
13. Stakhanova, N., Basu, S., Wong, J.: A cost-sensitive model for preemptive intrusion response systems. In: Proceedings of the 21st International Conference on Advanced Networking and Applications, pp. 428–435. IEEE Computer Society, Washington, DC (2007)
14. Foo, B., Wu, Y.S., Mao, Y.C., Bagchi, S., Spafford, E.: ADEPTS: adaptive intrusion response using attack graphs in an e-commerce environment. In: International Conference on Dependable Systems and Networks, pp. 508–517 (2005)
15. Wang, L., Islam, T., Long, T., Singhal, A., Jajodia, S.: An attack graph-based probabilistic security metric. In: Proceedings of the 22nd Annual IFIP WG 11.3 Working Conference on Data and Applications Security (DBSEC08) (2008)
16. Noel, S., Jajodia, S.: Understanding complex network attack graphs through clustered adjacency matrices. In: Proceedings of the 21st Annual Computer Security Conference (ACSAC), pp. 160–169 (2005)
17. Wang, L., Liu, A., Jajodia, S.: Using attack graph for correlating, hypothesizing, and predicting intrusion alerts. Comput. Commun. **29**(15), 2917–2933 (2006)
18. Kheir, N., Cuppens-Boulahia, N., Cuppens, F., Debar, H.: A service dependency model for cost sensitive intrusion response. In: Proceedings of the 15th European Conference on Research in Computer Security, pp. 626–642 (2010)
19. Cuppens, F., Ortalo, R.: Lambda: a language to model a database for detection of attacks. In: Proceedings of the Third International Workshop on Recent Advances in Intrusion Detection (RAID 2000), pp. 197–216, Toulouse, France (2000)
20. Wang, S., Zhang, Z., Kadobayashi, Y.: Exploring attack graph for cost-benefit security hardening: a probabilistic approach. Comput. Secur. **32**, 158–169 (2013)
21. Toth,T., Kregel, C.: Evaluating the impact of automated intrusion response mechanisms. In: Proceedings of the 18th Annual Computer Security Applications Conference, Los Alamitos, USA (2002)
22. Årnes, A., Sallhammar, K., Haslum, K., Brekne, T., Moe, M.E.G., Knapskog, S.J.: Real-time risk assessment with network sensors and intrusion detection systems. In: Hao, Y., Liu, J., Wang, Y.-P., Cheung, Y.-m., Yin, H., Jiao, L., Ma, J., Jiao, Y.-C. (eds.) CIS 2005. LNCS, vol. 3802, pp. 388–397. Springer, Heidelberg (2005). doi:10.1007/11596981_57
23. Haslum, K., Abraham, A., Knapskog, S.: Fuzzy online risk assessment for distributed intrusion prediction and prevention systems. In: Tenth International Conference on Computer Modeling and Simulation, pp. 216–223. IEEE Computer Society Press, Cambridge (2008)
24. Chakir, E., Youness, I.K., Moughit, M.: False positives reduction in intrusion detection systems using alert correlation and datamining techniques. In: IJARCSSE, vol. 5, Issue 4 (2015). ISSN 2277 128X
25. Lo, C.C., Chen, W.J.: A hybrid information security risk assessment procedure considering interdependences between controls. Expert Syst. Appl. **29**(1), 247–257 (2012)
26. Clifton, C., Gengo, G.: Developing custom intrusion detection filters using data mining. In: 21st Century Military Communications Conference Proceedings, MILCOM 2000 (2000)
27. Engen, V., Vincent, J., Phalp, K.: Exploring discrepancies in findings obtained with the KDD Cup 99 data set. Intell. Data Anal. **15**, 251–276 (2011)
28. The Snort Project, Snort user's manual 3 (2016)

29. Chakir, E., Khamlichi, Y.I., Moughit, M.: Handling alert for intrusion detection system using stateful pattern matching. In: Proceedings of the 4th IEEE International Colloquium on Information Science and Technology (CiSt 2016), pp. 139–144 (2016)
30. Shameli-Sendi, A., et al.: Taxonomy of Intrusion Risk Assessment and Response System, vol. 45, pp. 1–16. Elsevier, September 2014
31. Debar, H., Curry, D., Feinstein, B.: The Intrusion Detection Message Exchange Format (IDMEF). http://www.ietf.org/rfc/rfc4765.txt
32. Porras, P.A., Fong, M.W., Valdes, A.: A mission-impact-based approach to INFOSEC alarm correlation. In: Proceedings of the 5th International Symposium on Recent Advances in Intrusion Detection (RAID 2002), pp. 95–114 (2002)
33. Yu, J., et al.: TRINETR: an intrusion detection alert management system. In: WETICE 2004 (Washington, DC, USA) (2004)
34. Qin, X., Lee, W.: Statistical causality analysis of infosec alert data. In: RAID, pp. 73–93 (2003)
35. Alsubhi, K., et al.: Alert prioritization in Intrusion detection systems. In: IEEE Xplore Conference: Network Operations and Management Symposium (2008)
36. Anuar, N.B., Furnell, S., Papadaki, M., Clarke, N.: A risk index model for security incident prioritization. In: Originally published in the Proceedings of the 9th Australian Information Security Management Conference, Edith Cowan University, Perth, Western Australia, 5th–7th December 2011
37. Dondo, M.G.: A vulnerability prioritization system using a fuzzy risk analysis approach. In: Proceedings of the 23rd International Information Security Conference, Milano, Italy, pp. 525–539 (2008)

Author Index

Aaroud, Abdessadek 38
Abboud, Ahmad 425
Abdallah, Walid 472
Aboutajdine, Driss 154, 402, 550
Abouzahir, Saad 319
Adoni, Wilfried Yves Hamilton 390
Aghezzaf, Brahim 390
Ait Allal, Abdelmoula 261
Alfaia, Rodrigo Dias 345
Al-Hemiary, Emad H. 368
Al-Joboury, Istabraq M. 368
Altman, Eitan 14
Amja, Anne Marie 81
Andrade, Sergio Henrique Monte Santo 345
Armada, Ana García 333
Assayad, Ismail 584

Badri, Abdelmajid 461, 632
Baghdad, Abdennaceur 461
Bah, Slimane 357
Bakkoury, Zohra 357
Beghdad Bey, Kada 179
Bel Hadj Youssef, Soumaya 141
Belfqih, Abdelaziz 275
Belkasmi, Mohammed Ghaouth 484
Belkasmi, Mostafa 299
Bellafkih, M. 166
Ben Alla, Hicham 235
Ben Alla, Said 235
Benamar, Nabil 95, 117
Ben-Othman, Jalel 38
Benyoussef, El Mehdi 619
Benzekki, Kamal 225
Béraud, Adrien 308
Berri, Sara 3
Blondin Massé, Alexandre 308
Bouarafa, Saleh 402
Boubakri, Wided 472
Boudriga, Noureddine 141, 472, 509
Boukherouaa, Jamal 275
Braeken, An 206

Cances, Jean-Pierre 425
Chadli, Sara 484
Chafnaji, Houda 438
Chakir, El Mostapha 641
Cherifi, Hocine 607
Cherkaoui, Rachid 206
Chifa, Nawal 632

da Luz Oliveira, Edvar 345
Daafouz, Jamal 3, 450
Dahmouni, Hamza 127
Dazahra, Mohamed Nouh 275
de Freitas Souto, Anderson Vinicius 345
Désaulniers, Simon 308
Djebari, Nabil 179

Echandouri, Bouchra 287
El Amri, Abdelkebir 380
El Aroussi, Mohamed 154
El Bernoussi, Souad 287
El Fergougui, Abdeslam 225
El Ghorfi, Rabii 154
El Hadadi, Benachir 107
El Hadiri, Hind 619
El Hamdani, Sara 95
El Hammouti, Hajar 25
El Hassouni, Mohammed 607
El Houssaini, Mohammed-Alamine 38
El Idrissi, Younes El Hajjaji 496
El Ksimi, Ali 411
El Mourabit, Ilham 461
Elalaoui, Abdelbaki Elbelrhiti 225
Elazouzi, Rachid 56
Elbyed, Abdeltif 390, 619
Elmariami, Faissal 275
Elmaroud, Brahim 550
Elmouaatamid, Otmane 299
Emharraf, Mohamed 484
Er-rouidi, Mohamed 107
Et-tolba, Mohamed 562
Ezzati, Abdellah 235

Faouzi, Hassan 107
Faqihi, Ahmed 550
Francês, Carlos Renato Lisboa 345

Gharam, Maroua 509
Ghogho, Mounir 48, 450
Girault, Alain 584
Gryech, Ihsane 48

Haas, Harald 532
Habachi, Oussama 425
Haddad, Majed 14
Haddar, I. 166
Hafid, Abdelhakim 357
Hanaoui, Mohamed 572
Hanin, Charifa 287
Haqiq, Abdelkrim 193
Hore, Ali El 38
Huang, Dijiang 193

Ibrahimi, Khalil 117
Ismail, Assayad 596

Jaber, Ali 425
Jarir, Zahi 81
Jedra, Mohamed 496
Jiang, Yufei 532
Jiménez, Tania 56

Kamili, Mohamed El 70
Karouit, Abdelillah 14
Kartit, Ali 214, 247
Khairi, S. 166
Khamlichi, Youness Idrissi 641
Khoukhi, Faddoul 411

Lahmer, Mohamed 299
Lamrani, El Khadir 70
Larabi, Youness 117
Lasaulce, Samson 3, 450
Leal, Raquel Pérez 333
Leghris, Cherkaoui 411
Lekbich, Anass 275
Licea, Daniel Bonilla 450
Lmater, Moulay Abdellatif 14

Mansouri, Khalifa 261
Marwan, Mbarek 214, 247
Masucci, Antonia Maria 521
McLernon, Des 450
Meghdadi, Vahid 425
Mesbahi, Nabil 127
Mili, Hafedh 81
Milosevic, Hranislav 542
Mjihil, Oussama 193
Mohammed, Sadik 596
Moudni, Houda 107
Moughit, Mohamed 641
Mouncif, Hicham 107
Mourchid, Youssef 607

Nacer, Hassina 179
Nahhal, Tarik 390
Nazha, Cherkaoui 275
Nouasria, Hamid 562

Obaid, Abdel 81
Omary, Fouzia 287
Ouadou, Mohamed 154
Ouahmane, Hassan 214, 247
Ouahou, Soufiane 357

Panic, Stefan 542

Qbadou, Mohammed 261

Radjef, Mohammed Said 3
Rahmani, Moulay Driss 402
Raouyane, B. 166
Rekhis, Slim 141
Reynaud, Nicolas 308
Rifi, Mounir 572
Romero, Alejandro Borrajo 333
Ruichek, Yassine 632

Saadane, Rachid 402
Saber, Mohammed 484
Sabir, Essaid 25, 319
Sabri, Omar 275
Sadik, Mohamed 319
Safari, Majid 532
Sahel, Aicha 461, 632
Sbihi, Nada 48

Silva, Alonso 521
Soumia, Elbouanani 596
Stefanovic, Caslav 542

Tamimi, Imane 70
Tarbouch, Mohamed 380
Tembine, Hamidou 25
Terchoune, Hanae 380
Touhafi, Abdellah 206

Varma, Vineeth S. 3, 450
Vijaykumar, Nandamudi Lankalapalli 345

Ye, Zakaria 56
Youssfi, Mohamed 261

Zahid, Noureddine 496
Zbakh, Mostapha 206

Printed in the United States
By Bookmasters

Printed in the United States
By Bookmasters